Elements of
Argument

Elements of Argument

A Text and Reader

Eighth Edition

Annette T. Rottenberg

Donna Haisty Winchell
CLEMSON UNIVERSITY

Bedford/St. Martin's
Boston ◆ New York

For Bedford/St. Martin's

Senior Developmental Editor: John E. Sullivan III
Production Editor: Deborah Baker
Production Supervisors: Yexenia Markland and Jennifer Wetzel
Senior Marketing Manager: Rachel Falk
Editorial Assistants: Christina Gerogiannis and Kaitlin Hannon
Copyeditor: Lisa Peachey Flanagan
Text Design: Gretchen Toles
Cover Design: Donna Lee Dennison
Cover Art: Victor Pesce, *Pile of Boxes 2002,* oil on canvas. Elizabeth Harris
  Gallery.
Composition: Pine Tree Composition
Printing and Binding: Haddon Craftsmen, Inc., an R.R. Donnelley & Sons
  Company

President: Joan E. Feinberg
Editorial Director: Denise B. Wydra
Editor in Chief: Karen S. Henry
Director of Marketing: Karen Melton Soeltz
Director of Editing, Design, and Production: Marcia Cohen
Managing Editor: Elizabeth M. Schaaf

Library of Congress Control Number: 2004118167

0   9   8   7   6   5
f   e   d   c   b

For information, write: Bedford/St. Martin's, 75 Arlington Street, Boston, MA
02116 (617-399-4000)

ISBN: 0–312–45380–9
EAN: 978–0–312–45380–0

Acknowledgments

Charles Adams. "Lincoln's Logic." From *When In the Course of Human Events* by Charles Adams.
  Copyright © 2000 by Rowman & Littlefield Publishing. Reprinted by permission of the publisher.
Gordon Allport. "The Nature of Prejudice." From the 17th Claremont Reading Conference Yearbook, 1952. Reprinted by permission of Robert B. Allport.
Julia Álvarez. "A White Woman of Color." From *Half and Half: Writers on Growing Up Biracial and Bicultural,* edited by Claudine Chiawei O'Hearn. Copyright © 1998 by Julia Álvarez. Used by permission of Pantheon Books, a division of Random House, Inc.

PREFACE FOR INSTRUCTORS

PURPOSE

Argumentation as the basis of a composition course should need no defense, especially at a time of renewed pedagogical interest in critical thinking. A course in argumentation encourages practice in close analysis, use of supporting materials, and logical organization. It encompasses all the modes of development around which composition courses are often built. It teaches students to read and to listen with more than ordinary care. Not least, argument can engage the interest of students who have been indifferent or even hostile to required writing courses. Because the subject matter of argument can be found in every human activity—from the most trivial to the most elevated—both students and teachers can choose the materials that appeal to them.

Composition courses using the materials of argument are, of course, not new. But the traditional methods of teaching argument through mastery of the formal processes of reasoning cannot account for the complexity of arguments in practice. Even more relevant to our purposes as teachers of composition is the tenuous relationship between learning about induction and deduction, however helpful in analysis, and the actual process of student composition. The challenge has been to find a method of teaching argument that assists students in defending their claims as directly and efficiently as possible, a method that reflects the way people actually go about organizing and developing claims outside the classroom.

One such method, first adapted to classroom instruction by teachers of rhetoric and speech, uses a model of argument advanced by Stephen

Toulmin in *The Uses of Argument*. Toulmin was interested in producing a description of the real process of argument. His model was the law. "Arguments," he said, "can be compared with lawsuits, and the claims we make and argue for in extra-legal contexts with claims made in the courts."[1] Toulmin's model of argument was based on three principal elements: claim, evidence, and warrant. These elements answered the questions, "What are you trying to prove?" "What have you got to go on?" "How did you get from evidence to claim?" Needless to say, Toulmin's model of argument does not guarantee a classroom of skilled arguers, but his questions about the parts of an argument and their relationship are precisely the ones that students must ask and answer in writing their own essays and analyzing those of others. They lead students naturally into the formulation and development of their claims.

In this text we have adapted—and greatly simplified—some of Toulmin's concepts and terminology for first-year students. We have also introduced two elements of argument with which Toulmin is not directly concerned. Most rhetoricians consider them indispensable, however, to discussion of what actually happens in the defense or rejection of a claim. One is motivational appeals—warrants based on appeals to the needs and values of an audience, designed to evoke emotional responses. A distinction between logic and emotion may be useful as an analytical tool, but in producing or attacking arguments human beings find it difficult, if not impossible, to make such a separation. In this text, therefore, persuasion through appeals to needs and values is treated as a legitimate element in the argumentative process.

We have also stressed the significance of audience as a practical matter. In the rhetorical or audience-centered approach to argument, to which we subscribe in this text, success is defined as acceptance of the claim by an audience. Arguers in the real world recognize intuitively that their primary goal is not to demonstrate the purity of their logic but to win the adherence of their audiences. To gain this adherence, students need to be reminded of the necessity for establishing themselves as credible sources for their readers.

We hope *Elements of Argument* will lead students to discover not only the practical and intellectual rewards of learning how to argue but the real excitement of engaging in civilized debate.

ORGANIZATION

In Part One, after two introductory chapters, a chapter each is devoted to the chief elements of argument—the definitions that lay a foundation for shared understanding, the claims that students make in their arguments, the support they must supply for their claims, and the warrants that underlie their arguments. Popular fallacies as well as induction and deduction are

---

[1] Stephen Toulmin, *The Uses of Argument* (Cambridge: Cambridge UP, 1958), p. 7.

treated in Chapter 7; because fallacies represent errors of reasoning, a knowledge of induction and deduction can make clear how and why fallacies occur. Chapter 8 deals with the power of word choice in arguing effectively.

We have provided examples, readings, discussion questions, and writing suggestions that are, we hope, both practical and stimulating. The examples include essays, articles, speeches, news reports, editorial opinions, letters to the editor, excerpts from online sources, cartoons, and advertisements. They reflect the liveliness and complexity of argumentation that exercises with no realistic context often suppress.

The fifty-four selections and seven advertisements in Part One support in several ways the discussions of argumentation. First, they illustrate the elements of argument; in each chapter, one or more essays have been analyzed to emphasize the principles of argument explained in the chapter. Second, they are drawn from current publications and cover as many different subjects as possible to convince students that argument is a pervasive force in the world they read about and live in. Third, some of the essays are obviously flawed and thus enable students to identify the kinds of weaknesses they should avoid in their own essays.

Part Two takes up the process of writing, researching, and presenting arguments. Chapter 9 explains how to find a topic, define the issues that it embraces, organize the information, and draft and revise an argument. Chapter 10 introduces students to the business of finding sources and using and documenting those sources effectively in research papers. The chapter concludes with two annotated student research papers: one that employs the Modern Language Association (MLA) documentation system; the other that represents research in the social and natural sciences and uses a modified American Psychological Association (APA) documentation style. Chapter 11 provides guidelines for presenting arguments orally.

Part Three, Multiple Viewpoints, exhibits arguers in action, using informal and formal language, often debating head-on. The topics of its fifty-nine selections and nine cartoons capture headlines everyday, and despite their immediacy, they are likely to arouse passions and remain controversial for a long time. Whether as matters of national policy or personal choice, these topics call for decisions based on familiarity with competing views.

Part Four, Classic Arguments, reprints eight selections that have stood the tests of both time and the classroom. They are among the arguments that teachers find invaluable in any composition course.

NEW TO THIS EDITION

This revision presented, as have earlier revisions of this text, both challenges and opportunities. Previous users will notice that this is the first time that two authors have collaborated on *Elements of Argument.* Our hope is that the union of two perspectives and our combined experience using the earlier editions in first-year classes will enrich the quality of the text that you use with your students. Donna Haisty Winchell, the new member of the team, comes to this revision having taught extensively with *Elements of Argument* and having served as the composition director for several years at Clemson University. She learned from the experiences of others in her program and understood the challenges of revising a text used by instructors with diverse teaching styles and interests. By building on that knowledge of what works in the classroom, we have been able to gather many recent high-interest readings that will appeal to students.

Although the principles and concerns of the book have not changed, the new material in this edition should enhance the versatility of the text, deepen students' awareness of how pervasive argument is, and increase their ability to think critically and communicate persuasively. In short, we've added more help for students researching and writing argumentative papers, including new advice on finding, working with, and documenting sources. The new material first helps students understand *why* they should use sources and then helps students use them more effectively. There are also many new selections on current topics; 66 of the 124 readings are new.

In addition, we have revised some of the Writer's Guides and have added eight others to offer students more writing instruction, and we have elaborated on how to smoothly incorporate quoted material into an essay. We have included two additional student essays and three additional professional models that illustrate correct documentation of sources. This edition incorporates a suggestion from past users that the definition chapter precede the chapters on claims, support, and warrant rather than breaking up that sequence.

For the short debates, we have retained one popular topic from the seventh edition—animal research—and have added five other timely ones: gay marriage, college costs, fast foods and obesity, stem-cell research, and gun control. Updated annotated Web links accompany these debates, encouraging students to conduct further research online.

Part Three, Multiple Viewpoints, retains four popular topics from the seventh edition, with updated titles and some updated readings that reflect recent events and recent changes in perspective: What Is the Future of the Family? Are Limits on Freedom of Speech Ever Justified? What Threats to Privacy Exist in the Information Age? What Is the Role of Sex and Violence in Popular Culture? There are four new topics: How Far Will We Go to Change Our Body Image? How Has Terrorism Affected the American Idea of Justice? What Does the Future Hold for Sports? Have We Become Too Reliant on Standardized Testing? Each of the selections is preceded by a prereading question that provides direction for students and will stimulate class discussion. Each chapter ends with suggestions for thinking and writing about the issue, a list of possible topics for research, and suggested online sources that will help students investigate the topic in more depth.

Part Four now includes a provocative essay by Carrie Chapman Catt that investigates women as "assets" during World War I.

ANCILLARIES

The instructor's manual, *Resources for Teaching* ELEMENTS OF ARGUMENT, provides additional suggestions for using the book as well as for finding and using the enormous variety of materials available in a course on argument.

A companion Web site at <bedfordstmartins.com/rottenberg> includes annotated links for students and instructors looking for further information on controversial topics, online debates, and rhetorical theory. It also includes a sample syllabus and exercises for students on fallacies and warrants.

Mixed media and everyday arguments can be both more accessible and more challenging for students to examine. The i•claim CD-ROM offers a new way to visualize argument. It features six tutorials and an illustrated glossary. The i•claim CD-ROM can be packaged for free with *Elements of Argument*. To see a sample tutorial, visit <bedfordstmartins .com/iclaim>. For ordering information, contact your local sales representative or e-mail us at sales_support@bfwpub.com.

Also available is *Teaching Argument in the Composition Course*, by Timothy Barnett. It offers a range of perspectives, from Aristotle to the present day, on argument and on teaching argument. The twenty-eight readings—many of them classic works in the field—present essential insights and practical information. For ordering information, contact your local sales representative or e-mail us at sales_support@bfwpub.com.

ALSO AVAILABLE

A briefer edition, *The Structure of Argument*, Fifth Edition, is available for instructors who prefer a shorter text with fewer readings. It presents only Parts One and Two, an appendix of four Classic Arguments, and the appendix, Arguing about Literature, from the longer edition.

ACKNOWLEDGMENTS

This book has profited by the critiques and suggestions of reviewers and instructors who responded to a questionnaire. We appreciate the thoughtful consideration given to previous editions by Nancy E. Adams,

Timothy C. Alderman, Yvonne Alexander, John V. Andersen, Lucile G. Appert, William Arfin, Alison K. Armstrong, Karen Arnold, Angel M. Arzán, Mark Edward Askren, Michael Austin, David B. Axelrod, Jacquelyn A. Babush, Peter Banland, Carol A. Barnes, Tim Barnett, Marilyn Barry, Marci Bartolotta, Bonnie C. Bedford, Frank Beesley, Don Beggs, Martine Bellen, Bruce Bennett, Maureen Dehler Bennett, Chester Benson, Robert II. Bentley, Scott Bentley, Arthur E. Bervin, Patricia Bizzell, Don Black, Kathleen Black, Stanley S. Blair, Laurel Boyd, Mary Virginia Brackett, Robert J. Branda, Dianne Brehmer, Alan Brown, Megan Brown, Paul L. Brown, Bill Buck, W. K. Buckley, Alison A. Bulsterbaum, Clarence Bussinger, Deborah N. Byrd, Gary T. Cage, Ruth A. Cameron, Rita Carey, Barbara R. Carlson, Eric W. Cash, Donna R. Chaney, Gail Chapman, Linda D. Chinn, Roland Christian, Gina Claywell, John O. Clemonts, Paul D. Cockeram, Tammy S. Cole, John Conway, Thomas S. Costello, Martha J. Craig, David J. Cranmer, Edward Crothers, Jennifer Cunningham, Sara Cutting, Jo Ann Dadisman, Sandra Dahlberg, Mimi Dane, Judy Davidson, Cynthia C. Davis, Philip E. Davis, Stephanie Demma, Loretta Denner, Cecile de Rocher, Julia Dietrich, Marcia B. Dinnech, Felicia A. Dixon, Jane T. Dodge, Ellen Donovan, L. Leon Duke, P. Dunsmore, Bernard Earley, Carolyn Embree, Carolyn L. Engdahl, Gwyn Enright, Stephen Ersinghaus, David Estes, Kristina Faber, Lester Faigley, Faridoun Farroth, B. R. Fein, Delia Fisher, Philip L. Fishman, Catherine Fitzgerald, Evelyn Flores, David D. Fong, Donald Forand, Mary A. Fortner, Alice R. France, Leslye Friedberg, Sondra Frisch, Richard Fulkerson, Maureen Furniss, Diane Gabbard, Donald J. Gadow, Eric Gardner, Frieda Gardner, Gail Garloch, Darcey Garretson, Victoria Gaydosik, E. R. Gelber-Beechler, Scott Giantralley, Michael Patrick Gillespie, Paula Gillespie, Wallace Gober, Sara Gogol, Stuart Goodman, Joseph Gredler, Lucie Greenberg, Mildred Buza Gronek, Marilyn Hagans, Linda L. Hagge, Lee T. Hamilton, Carolyn Han, Phillip J. Hanse, Pat Hardré, Susan Harland, A. Leslie Harris, Carolyn G. Hartz, Theresia A. Hartz, Fredrik Hausmann, Michael Havens, William Hayes, Ursula K. Heise, Anne Helms, Tena Lea Helton, Peter C. Herman, Diane Price Herndl, Heidi Hobbs, William S. Hochman, Sharon E. Hockensmith, Andrew J. Hoffman, Joyce Hooker, Richard S. Hootman, Laura Hope-Aleman, Clarence Hundley, Patrick Hunter, Richard Ice, Mary Griffith Jackson, Ann S. Jagoe, Katherine James, Missy James, Ruth Jeffries, Owen Jenkins, Ruth Y. Jenkins, Iris Jennings, Linda Johnson, Richard M. Johnson, Janet Jubnke, E. C. Juckett, Catherine Kaikowska, George T. Karnezis, Richard Katula, Mary Jane Kearny, Joanne Keel, Patricia Kellogg-Dennis, N. Kesinger, Susan Kincaid, Joanne Kirkland, Judith Kirscht, Nancy Klug, John H. Knight, Paul D. Knoke, Frances Kritzer, George W. Kuntzman, Barbara Ladd, Jocelyn Ladner, M. Beardsley Land, Marlene J. Lang, Lisa Lebduska, Sara R. Lee, William Levine, Mary Levitt, Diana M. Liddle, Jack Longmate, Cynthia Lowenthal, Marjorie Lynn, Marcia MacLennan, Chantelle MacPhee, Nancy McGee, Patrick McGuire, Ray McKerrow, Michael McKoski, Pamela J. McLagen, Suzanne McLaughlin,

Dennis McMillan, Donald McQuade, Christina M. McVay, D'Ann Madewell, Beth Madison, Susan Maloney, Dan M. Manolescu, Barbara A. Manrigue, Joyce Marks, Quentin E. Martin, Michael Matzinger, Charles May, Alan Merickel, Jean-Pierre Meterean, Ekra Miezan, Carolyn R. Miller, Lisa K. Miller, Logan D. Moon, Dennis D. Moore, Dan Morgan, Karen L. Morris, Curt Mortenson, Philip A. Mottola, Thomas Mullen, Charlotte A. Myers, Joan Naake, Michael B. Naas, Joseph Nassar, Byron Nelson, Elizabeth A. Nist, Jody Noerdlinger, Paralee F. Norman, Dr. Mary Jean Northcutt, Thomas O'Brien, James F. O'Neil, Mary O'Riordan, Arlene Okerland, Renee Olander, Elizabeth Oldfield, Amy Olsen, Richard D. Olson, Steven Olson, Lori Jo Oswald, Sushil K. Oswald, Roy Kenneth Pace II, Gary Pak, Linda J. Palumbo, Edna Parker, Jo Patterson, Laurine Paule, Leland S. Person, Betty Peters, Kelly S. Petersen, Nancy L. Peterson, Susan T. Peterson, Steve Phelan, Gail W. Pieper, Gloria Platzner, Mildred Postar, Ralph David Powell, Jr., Rossana Pronesti, Teresa Marie Purvis, Mark Razor, Barbara E. Rees, Karen L. Regal, Pat Regel, Charles Reinhart, Thomas C. Renzi, Janice M. Reynolds, Douglas F. Rice, G. A. Richardson, Beverly A. Ricks, James M. Ritter, Katherine M. Rogers, Marilyn Mathias Root, Judith Klinger Rose, Cathy Rosenfeld, Robert A. Rubin, Norma L. Rudinsky, Lori Ruediger, Cheryl W. Ruggiero, Richard Ruppel, Victoria Anne Sager, Joseph L. Sanders, Irene Schiller, Suzette Schlapkohl, Sybil Schlesinger, Richard Schneider, Eileen Schwartz, Esther L. Schwartz, Eugene Senff, Jeffrey Seyall, Ron Severson, Lucy Sheehey, William E. Sheidley, Sallye J. Sheppeard, Sally Bishop Shigley, John Shout, Craig L. Shurtleff, Dr. Barbara L. Siek, Thomas Simmons, Michael Simms, Jacqueline Simon, Richard Singletary, Roger L. Slakey, Thomas S. Sloane, Beth Slusser, Denzell Smith, Rebecca Smith, Margaret Smolik, James R. Sodon, Katherine Sotol, Donald L. Soucy, Minoo Southgate, Linda Spain, Richard Spilman, Sarah J. Stafford, Jim Stegman, Martha L. Stephens, Arlo Stoltenberg, Elissa L. Stuchlik, Judy Szaho, Andrew Tadie, Fernanda G. Tate-Owens, R. Terhorst, Marguerite B. Thompson, Arline R. Thorn, Mary Ann Trevathan, Sandia Tuttle, Whitney G. Vanderwerff, Jennie VerSteeg, Les Wade, David L. Wagner, Jeanne Walker, James Wallace, Linda D. Warwick, Carol Adams Watson, Roger D. Watson, Karen Webb, Raymond E. Whelan, Betty E. White, Julia Whitsitt, Toby Widdicombe, Mary Louise Willey, Heywood Williams, Matthew C. Wolfe, Alfred Wong, Bonnie B. Zitz, and Laura Zlogar.

In addition, we would like to thank those instructors who completed a questionnaire for the eighth edition: Effrossini Piliouni Albrecht, Kathleen Allison, Jim Bonnett, Nick Boone, Eleanor Bunting, Karen Craig, Harry Costigan, David Hulm, Jennifer Kirchoff, Beth Madison, Jim Matthews, Kathryn McCormick, John McKinnis, Patrick McMahon, Amy Minervini, Dana Nkana, Nancy Raftery, Marlisa Santos, Martha Smith, James Sodon, Deborah Steward, Andrea Van Vorhis, and Joseph Walker.

We are also grateful to Kate Kiefer and Meg Morgan for their in-depth reviews.

We appreciate the contributions that Gail Stygall of the University of Washington made to the previous edition of the instructor's manual, which have been retained in this edition. We also thank once again Fred Kemp of Texas Tech University, who drafted the section on responding online in Chapter 2; Barbara Fister of Gustavus Adolphus College, who revised Chapter 10's discussion of information technologies; and Tim Barnett of Northeastern Illinois University, who enlarged and updated the sections on critical reading, evaluating electronic sources, note taking, and summarizing, and for drafting the sample analysis of a Web site. All of their contributions have been retained in this edition.

We are grateful to those at Bedford/St. Martin's who have smoothed the process of bringing a new author on board and have helped in numerous ways large and small: Joan Feinberg, Elizabeth Schaaf, Denise Wydra, Karen Henry, Steve Scipione, Sandy Schechter, Coleen O'Hanley, Warren Drabek, Christina Gerogiannis, Gillian Speeth, Deborah Baker, and, most especially, John Sullivan.

BRIEF CONTENTS

CONTENTS

2. Responding to Argument *25*

3. Definition   *62*

4.   Claims   *104*

5. Support *157*

6.   Warrants   *220*

SAMPLE ESSAY: AN INDUCTIVE ARGUMENT

True or False: Schools Fail Immigrants   *271*

RICHARD ROTHSTEIN

The national education columnist for the *New York Times* looks at the complex issues behind the question of whether public schooling has failed immigrants.

Deduction   *274*

SAMPLE ANNOTATED ESSAY: A DEDUCTIVE ARGUMENT

Divorce and Our National Values   *279*

PETER D. KRAMER

A clinical professor of psychiatry at Brown University affirms that our epidemic of divorce reflects the increased emphasis on the characteristic American virtue of autonomy, which has been a goal of our psychotherapy for the past fifty years.

A Note on the Syllogism and the Toulmin Model   *283*
Common Fallacies   *285*

Writer's Guide: Avoiding Logical Fallacies   *295*

READINGS FOR ANALYSIS

On Nation and Race   *296*

ADOLF HITLER

This excerpt from *Mein Kampf* expounds the principles of Nazi racist ideology.

Cheryl Silas had a highway collision . . . [advertisement]   *301*

Show Biz Encourages Looser Teen Sex Habits   *302*

SHERYL McCARTHY

An adult evaluates the current sex habits of teenagers and laments how things have changed since she herself was a teen.

Food for Thought (and for Credit)   *304*

JENNIFER GROSSMAN

The director of the Dole Nutrition Institute advocates returning to a modernized version of the old home economics course to teach young people to be more responsible consumers and better guardians of their health and that of their own children.

DEBATE: SHOULD THE FEDERAL GOVERNMENT FUND EMBRYONIC STEM-CELL RESEARCH?

Use the Body's "Repair Kit": We Must Pursue Research on Embryonic Stem Cells   *306*

CHRISTOPHER REEVE

An actor, director, and quadriplegic advocates support of the stem-cell research that might make those like him walk again.

The Misleading Debate on Stem-Cell Research   *308*

MONA CHAREN

A syndicated columnist and mother of a child with juvenile diabetes weighs the hope of help for her child against the morality of stem-cell research.

Part Two
Writing, Researching, and Presenting Arguments 371

9. Writing an Argumentative Paper 373

10. Researching an Argumentative Paper   *394*

A writer for *Psychology Today* argues that plastic surgery "promises the ultimate validation: a chance for the world to see us as we see ourselves."

A television reviewer points out the harmful messages sent by shows that glorify the use of plastic surgery to remake one's body image.

14. What Is the Future of the Family?   557

16. What Threats to Privacy Exist in the Information Age? *599*

18. Have We Become Too Reliant on Standardized Testing?   *658*

19. What Is the Role of Sex and Violence in Popular Culture? *692*

Part Four
Classic Arguments   733

Elements of
Argument

Part One

The Structure
of Argument

CHAPTER 1

Understanding Argument

THE NATURE OF ARGUMENT

A conversation overheard in the school cafeteria:

> *"Hey, how come you didn't order the meat loaf special? It's pretty good today."*
> *"Well, I read this book about vegetarianism, and I've decided to give up meat. The book says meat's unhealthy and vegetarians live longer."*
> *"Don't be silly. Americans eat lots of meat, and we're living longer and longer."*
> *"Listen, this book tells how much healthier the Danes were during World War II because they couldn't get meat."*
> *"I don't believe it. A lot of these health books are written by quacks. It's pretty dumb to change your diet after reading one book."*

These people are having what most of us would call an argument, one that sounds dangerously close to a quarrel. There are, however, significant differences between the colloquial meaning of argument as a quarrel and its definition as a process of reasoning and advancing proof, although even the exchange reported above exhibits some of the characteristics of formal argument. The kinds of arguments we deal with in this text are not

quarrels. They often resemble ordinary discourse about controversial issues. You may, for example, overhear a conversation like this one:

> *"This morning while I was trying to eat breakfast I heard an announcer de-
> scribing the execution of that guy in Texas who raped and murdered a
> teenaged couple. They gave him an injection, and it took him ten minutes
> to die. I almost lost my breakfast listening to it."*
>
> *"Well, he deserved it. He didn't show much pity for his victims, did he?"*
>
> *"Okay, but no matter what he did, capital punishment is really awful, bar-
> baric. It's murder, even if the state does it."*
>
> *"No, I'd call it justice. I don't know what else we can do to show how we feel
> about a cruel, pointless murder of innocent people. The punishment ought
> to be as terrible as we can make it."*

Each speaker is defending a value judgment about an issue that tests ideas
of good and evil, right and wrong, and that cannot be decided by facts.

In another kind of argument the speaker or writer proposes a solution
for a specific problem. Two men, both under twenty, are engaged in a
conversation.

> *"I'm going to be broke this week after I pay my car insurance. I don't think
> it's fair for males under twenty to pay such high rates. I'm a good driver,
> much better than my older sister. Why not consider driving experience in-
> stead of age or sex?"*
>
> *"But I always thought that guys our age had the most accidents. How do you
> know that driving experience is the right standard to apply?"*
>
> *"Well, I read a report by the Highway Commission that said it's really driving
> experience that counts. So I think it's unfair for us to be discriminated
> against. The law's behind the times. They ought to change the insurance
> laws."*

In this case someone advocates a policy that appears to fulfill a desirable
goal—making it impossible to discriminate against drivers just because
they are young and male. Objections arise that the arguer must attempt
to answer.

In these three dialogues, as well as in all the other arguments you will
read in this book, human beings are engaged in explaining and defending their own actions and beliefs and opposing those of others. They do
this for at least two reasons: to justify what they do and think both to
themselves and to their opponents and, in the process, to solve problems
and make decisions, especially those dependent on a consensus among
conflicting views.

Unlike the examples cited so far, the arguments you will read and
write will not usually take the form of dialogues, but arguments are implicit dialogues. Even when our audience is unknown, we write to persuade the unconvinced, to acquaint them with good reasons for changing
their minds. As one definition has it, "Argumentation is the art of influencing others, through the medium of reasoned discourse, to believe or

act as we wish them to believe or act."[1] This process is inherently dramatic; a good argument can create the kinds of tensions generated at sporting events. Who will win? What are the factors that enable a winner to emerge? One of the most popular and enduring situations on television is the courtroom debate, in which two lawyers (one, the defense attorney, the hero, unusually knowledgeable and persuasive; the other, the prosecuting attorney, bumbling and corrupt) confront each other before an audience of judge and jury that must render a heart-stopping verdict. Tensions are high because a life is in the balance. In the classroom the stakes are neither so intimidating nor so melodramatic, but even here a well-conducted argument can throw off sparks.

Of course, not all arguments end in clear victories for one side or another. Nor should they. In a democratic society of competing interests and values, a compromise between two or more extreme points of view may be the only viable solution to a vexing problem. Although formal debates under the auspices of a debating society, such as take place on many college campuses, usually end in winners and losers, real-life problems, both public and private, are often resolved through negotiation. Courtroom battles may result in compromise, and the law itself allows for exemptions and extenuating circumstances. Elsewhere in this book we speak of the importance of tradeoffs in social and political transactions, giving up one thing in return for another.

Keep in mind, however, that some compromises will not be morally defensible. In searching for a middle ground, the thoughtful arguer must determine that the consequences of a negotiated solution will contribute to the common good, not merely advance personal interests. (In Chapter 9 you will find a detailed guide for writing arguments in which you look for common ground.)

Most of the arguments in this book will deal with matters of public controversy, an area traditionally associated with the study of argument. As the word *public* suggests, these matters concern us as members of a community. "They are," according to one rhetorician, "the problems of war and peace, race and creed, poverty, wealth, and population, of democracy and communism. . . . Specific issues arise on which we must take decision from time to time. One day it is Suez, another Cuba. One week it is the Congo, another it is the plight of the American farmer or the railroads. . . . On these subjects the experts as well as the many take sides."[2] Today the issues are different from the issues that writers confronted more than twenty years ago. Today we are concerned about terrorism, the environment, privacy, and medical ethics, to name only a few.

[1] J. M. O'Neill, C. Laycock, and R. L. Scale, *Argumentation and Debate* (New York: Macmillan, 1925), p. 1.
[2] Karl R. Wallace, "Toward a Rationale for Teachers of Writing and Speaking," *English Journal*, September 1961, p. 386.

Clearly, if all of us agreed about everything, if harmony prevailed everywhere, the need for argument would disappear. But given what we know about the restless, seeking, contentious nature of human beings and their conflicting interests, we should not be surprised that many controversial questions, some of them as old as human civilization itself, will not be settled nor will they vanish despite the energy we devote to settling them. Unresolved, they are submerged for a while and then reappear, sometimes in another form, sometimes virtually unchanged. Capital punishment is one such stubborn problem; abortion is another. Nevertheless, we value the argumentative process because it is indispensable to the preservation of a free society. In *Areopagitica,* his great defense of free speech, John Milton, the seventeenth-century poet, wrote, "I cannot praise a fugitive and cloistered virtue, unexercised and unbreathed, that never sallies out and sees her adversary." How can we know the truth, he asked, unless there is a "free and open encounter" between all ideas? "Give me liberty to know, to utter, and to argue freely according to conscience, above all liberties."

WHY STUDY ARGUMENT?

Perhaps the question has already occurred to you: Why *study* argument? Since you've engaged in some form of the argumentative process all your life, is there anything to be learned that experience hasn't taught you? We think there is. If you've ever felt frustration in trying to decide what is wrong with an argument, either your own or someone else's, you might have wondered if there were rules to help in the analysis. If you've ever been dissatisfied with your attempt to prove a case, you might have wondered how good arguers, the ones who succeed in persuading people, construct their cases. Good arguers do, in fact, know and follow rules. Studying and practicing these rules can provide you with some of the same skills.

You will find yourself using these skills in a variety of situations, not only in arguing important public issues. You will use them, for example, in your academic career. Whatever your major field of study—the humanities, the social sciences, the physical sciences, business—you will be required to defend views about materials you have read and studied.

HUMANITIES Why have some of the greatest novels resisted translation into great films?

SOCIAL SCIENCE What is the evidence that upward social mobility continues to be a positive force in American life?

PHYSICAL SCIENCE What will happen to the world climate as the amount of carbon dioxide in the atmosphere increases?

BUSINESS Are the new tax laws beneficial or disadvantageous to the real estate investor?

For all these assignments, different as they may be, you would use the same kinds of analysis, research techniques, and evaluation. The conventions or rules for reporting results might differ from one field of study to another, but for the most part the rules for defining terms, evaluating evidence, and arriving at conclusions cross disciplinary lines. Many employers, not surprisingly, are aware of this. One sheriff in Arizona advertised for an assistant with a degree in philosophy. He had discovered, he said, that the methods used by philosophers to solve problems were remarkably similar to the methods used in law enforcement.

Whether or not you are interested in serving as a sheriff's assistant, you will encounter situations in the workplace that call for the same analytical and argumentative skills employed by philosophers and law enforcement personnel. Almost everywhere—in the smallest businesses as well as the largest corporations—a worker who can articulate his or her views clearly and forcefully has an important advantage in gaining access to positions of greater interest and challenge. Even when they are primarily informative, the memorandums, reports, instructions, questions, and explanations that issue from offices and factories obey the rules of argumentative discourse.

You may not anticipate doing the kind of writing or speaking at your job that you will practice in your academic work. It is probably true that in some careers, writing constitutes a negligible part of a person's duties. But outside the office, the studio, and the salesroom, you will be called on to exhibit argumentative skills as a citizen, as a member of a community, and as a consumer of leisure. In these capacities you can contribute to decision making if you are knowledgeable and prepared. By writing or speaking to the appropriate authorities, you can argue for a change in the meal ticket plan at your school or the release of pornographic films at the neighborhood theater or against a change in automobile insurance rates. Most of us are painfully aware of opportunities we lost because we were uncertain of how to proceed, even in matters that affected us deeply.

A course in argumentation offers another invaluable dividend: It can help you to cope with the bewildering confusion of voices in the world around you. It can give you tools for distinguishing between what is true and what is false, what is valid and what is invalid, in the claims of politicians, promoters of causes, newscasters, advertisers, salespeople, teachers, parents and siblings, employers and employees, neighbors, friends, and lovers, any of whom may be engaged at some time in attempting to persuade you to accept a belief or adopt a course of action. It can even offer strategies for arguing with yourself about a personal dilemma.

So far we have treated argument as an essentially pragmatic activity that benefits the individual. But choosing argument over force or evasion has clear moral benefits for society as well. We can, in fact, defend the study of argumentation for the same reasons that we defend universal education despite its high cost and sometimes controversial results. In a democracy, widespread literacy ultimately benefits all members of society, not only those who are the immediate beneficiaries of education, because only an informed citizenry can make responsible choices. One distinguished writer explains that "democracy depends on a citizenry that can reason for themselves, on men who know whether a case has been proved, or at least made probable."[3]

It is not too much to say that argument is a civilizing influence, the very basis of democratic order. In repressive regimes, coercion, which may express itself in a number of reprehensible forms—censorship, imprisonment, exile, torture, or execution—is a favored means of removing opposition to establishment "truth." In free societies, argument and debate remain the preeminent means of arriving at consensus.

Of course, rational discourse in a democracy can and does break down. Confrontations with police at abortion clinics, shouting and heckling at a meeting to prevent a speaker from being heard, student protests against university policies—such actions have become common in recent years. The demands of the demonstrators are often passionately and sincerely held, and the protesters sometimes succeed through force or intimidation in influencing policy changes. When this happens, however, we cannot be sure that the changes are justified. History and experience teach us that reason, to a far greater degree than other methods of persuasion, ultimately determines the rightness or wrongness of our actions.

A piece of folk wisdom sums up the superiority of reasoned argument as a vehicle of persuasion: "A man convinced against his will is of the same opinion still." Those who accept a position after engaging in a dialogue offering good reasons on both sides will think and act with greater willingness and conviction than those who have been coerced or denied the privilege of participating in the decision.

WHY WRITE?

If we agree that studying argumentation provides important critical tools, one last question remains: Why *write*? Isn't it possible to learn the rules by reading and talking about the qualities of good and bad arguments? Not quite. All writers, both experienced and inexperienced, will probably confess that looking at what they have written, even after long thought, can produce a startled disclaimer: But that isn't what I meant to say! They

---

[3]Wayne C. Booth, "Boring from Within: The Art of the Freshman Essay," adapted from a speech delivered to the Illinois Council of College Teachers of English in May 1963.

know that more analysis and more hard thinking are in order. Writers are also aware that words on paper have an authority and a permanency that invite more than casual deliberation. It is one thing to make an assertion, to express an idea or a strong feeling in conversation, and perhaps even to deny it later; it is quite another to write out an extended defense of your own position or an attack on someone else's that will be read and perhaps criticized by people unsympathetic to your views.

Students are often told that they must become better thinkers if they are to become better writers. It works the other way, too. In the effort to produce a clear and convincing argument, a writer matures as a thinker and a critic. The very process of writing calls for skills that make us better thinkers. Writing argumentative essays tests and enlarges important mental skills—developing and organizing ideas, evaluating evidence, observing logical consistency, expressing ourselves clearly and economically—that we need to exercise all our lives in our various social roles, whether or not we continue to write after college.

THE TERMS OF ARGUMENT

One definition of argument, emphasizing audience, has been given earlier: "Argumentation is the art of influencing others, through the medium of reasoned discourse, to believe or act as we wish them to believe or act." A distinction is sometimes made between argument and persuasion. Argument, according to most authorities, gives primary importance to logical appeals. Persuasion introduces the element of ethical and emotional appeals. The difference is one of emphasis. In real-life arguments about social policy, the distinction is hard to measure. In this book we use the term *argument* to represent forms of discourse that attempt to persuade readers or listeners to accept a claim, whether acceptance is based on logical or on emotional appeals or, as is usually the case, on both. The following brief definition includes other elements: *An argument is a statement or statements offering support for a claim.*

An argument is composed of at least three parts: the claim, the support, and the warrant.[4]

■ The Claim

The claim (also called a *proposition*) answers the question "What are you trying to prove?" It may appear as the thesis statement of your essay,

---

[4]Some of the terms and analyses used in this text are adapted from Stephen Toulmin's *The Uses of Argument* (Cambridge: Cambridge University Press, 1958).

although in some arguments it may not be stated directly. There are three principal kinds of claim (discussed more fully in Chapter 4): claims of fact, of value, and of policy. (The three dialogues at the beginning of this chapter represent these three kinds of claim respectively.) *Claims of fact* assert that a condition has existed, exists, or will exist and are based on facts or data that the audience will accept as being objectively verifiable:

> The present cocaine epidemic is not unique. From 1885 to the 1920s, cocaine was as widely used as it is today.
>
> Horse racing is the most dangerous sport.
>
> California will experience colder, stormier weather for the next ten years.

All these claims must be supported by data. Although the last example is an inference or an educated guess about the future, a reader will probably find the prediction credible if the data seem authoritative.

Claims of value attempt to prove that some things are more or less desirable than others. They express approval or disapproval of standards of taste and morality. Advertisements and reviews of cultural events are one common source of value claims, but such claims emerge whenever people argue about what is good or bad, beautiful or ugly.

> The opera *Tannhäuser* provides a splendid viewing as well as listening experience.
>
> Football is one of the most dehumanizing experiences a person can face. —Dave Meggyesy
>
> Ending a patient's life intentionally is absolutely forbidden on moral grounds. —Presidential Commission on Medical Ethics, 1983

Claims of policy assert that specific policies should be instituted as solutions to problems. The expression *should, must,* or *ought to* usually appears in the statement.

> Prisons should be abolished because they are crime-manufacturing concerns.
>
> Our first step must be to immediately establish and advertise drastic policies designed to bring our own population under control. —Paul Ehrlich, biologist
>
> The New York City Board of Education should make sure that qualified women appear on any new list of candidates for Chancellor of Education.

Policy claims call for analysis of both fact and value. (A full discussion of claims follows in Chapter 4.)

■ The Support

Support consists of the materials used by the arguer to convince an audience that his or her claim is sound. These materials include *evidence* and *motivational appeals.* The evidence or data consist of facts, statistics, and testimony from experts. The motivational appeals are the ones that the arguer makes to the values and attitudes of the audience to win support for the claim. The word *motivational* points out that these appeals are the reasons that move an audience to accept a belief or adopt a course of action. For example, in his argument advocating population control, the claim of which is presented above, Paul Ehrlich first offered statistical evidence to prove the magnitude of the population explosion. But he also made a strong appeal to the generosity of his audience to persuade them to sacrifice their own immediate interests to those of future generations. (See Chapter 5 for detailed discussion of support.)

■ The Warrant

Certain assumptions underlie all the claims we make. In argument, the term *warrant* is used for such an assumption, a belief or principle that is taken for granted. It may be stated or unstated. If the arguer believes that the audience shares his assumption, he may feel it unnecessary to express it. But if he thinks that the audience is doubtful or hostile, he may decide to state the assumption to emphasize its importance or argue for its validity. The warrant, stated or not, allows the reader to make the same connection between the support and the claim that the author does.

This is how the warrant works. In the dialogue beginning this chapter, one speaker made the claim that vegetarianism was more healthful than a diet containing meat. As support he offered the evidence that the authors of a book he had read recommended vegetarianism for greater health and longer life. He did not state his warrant—that the authors of the book were trustworthy guides to theories of healthful diet. In outline form the argument looks like this:

CLAIM: Adoption of a vegetarian diet leads to healthier and longer life.

SUPPORT: The authors of *Becoming a Vegetarian Family* say so.

WARRANT: The authors of *Becoming a Vegetarian Family* are reliable sources of information on diet.

A writer or speaker may also need to offer support for the warrant. In the case cited above, the second speaker is reluctant to accept the unstated warrant, suggesting that the authors may be quacks. The first speaker will need to provide support for the assumption that the authors are trustworthy, perhaps by introducing proof of their credentials in science and medicine. Notice that although the second speaker accepts the evidence, he cannot agree that the claim has been proved unless he also accepts the warrant. If he fails to accept the warrant—that is, if he refuses to believe that the authors are credible sources of information about diet—then the evidence cannot support the claim.

The following example demonstrates how a different kind of warrant, based on values, can also lead an audience to accept a claim.

CLAIM: Laws making marijuana illegal should be repealed.

SUPPORT: People should have the right to use any substance they wish.

WARRANT: No laws should prevent citizens from exercising their rights.

Support for repeal of the marijuana laws often consists of medical evidence that marijuana is harmless. Here, however, the arguer contends that an important ethical principle is at work: Nothing should prevent people from exercising their rights, including the right to use any substance, no matter how harmful. Let us suppose that the reader agrees with the supporting statement, that individuals should have the right to use any substance. But to accept the claim, the reader must also agree with the principle expressed in the warrant—that government should not interfere with the individual's right. He or she can then agree that laws making marijuana illegal should be repealed. Notice that this warrant, like all warrants, certifies that the relationship between the support and the claim is sound.

One more important characteristic of the warrant deserves mention. In many cases, the warrant is a more general statement of belief than the claim. It can, therefore, support many claims, not only the one in a particular argument. For example, the warrant you have just read—"No laws should prevent citizens from exercising their rights"—is a broad assumption or belief that we take for granted and that can underlie claims about many other practices in American society. (For more on warrants, see Chapter 6.)

THE AUDIENCE

All arguments are composed with an audience in mind. We have already pointed out that an argument is an implicit dialogue or exchange. Often the writer of an argument about a public issue is responding to another writer or speaker who has made a claim that needs to be supported or opposed. In writing your own arguments, you should assume that there is a reader who may not agree with you. Throughout this book, we will continue to refer to ways of reaching such a reader.

Speechmakers are usually better informed than writers about their audience. Some writers, however, are familiar with the specific persons or groups who will read their arguments; advertising copywriters are a conspicuous example. They discover their audiences through sophisticated polling and marketing techniques and direct their messages to a well-targeted group of prospective buyers. Other professionals may be required to submit reports to persuade a specific and clearly defined audience of certain beliefs or courses of action: An engineer may be asked by an environmental interest group to defend his plans for the building of a sewage treatment plant; or a town planner may be called on to tell the town council why she believes that rent control may not work; or a sales manager may find it necessary to explain to his superior why a new product should be launched in the Midwest rather than the South.

In such cases the writer asks some or all of the following questions about the audience:

Why has this audience requested this report? What do they want to get out of it?

How much do they already know about the subject?

Are they divided or agreed on the subject?

What is their emotional involvement with the issues?

Providing abundant evidence and making logical connections between the parts of an argument may not be enough to win agreement from an audience. In fact, success in convincing an audience is almost always inseparable from the writer's credibility or the audience's belief in the writer's trustworthiness. Aristotle, the Greek philosopher who wrote a treatise on argument that has influenced its study and practice for more than two thousand years, considered credibility—what he called *ethos*—the most important element in the arguer's ability to persuade the audience to accept his or her claim.

Aristotle named "intelligence, character, and goodwill" as the attributes that produce credibility. Today we might describe these qualities somewhat differently, but the criteria for judging a writer's credibility remain essentially the same. First, the writer must convince the audience that he is knowledgeable, that he is as well informed as possible about the subject. Second, he must persuade his audience that he is not only truthful in the presentation of his evidence but also morally upright and dependable. Third, he must show that, as an arguer with good intentions, he has considered the interests and needs of others as well as his own.

As an example in which the credibility of the arguer is at stake, consider a wealthy Sierra Club member who lives on ten acres of a magnificent oceanside estate and who appears before a community planning board to argue against future development of the area. His claim is that more building will destroy the delicate ecological balance of the area. The board, acting in the interests of all the citizens of the community, will ask

themselves: Has the arguer proved that his information about environmental impact is complete and accurate? Has he demonstrated that he
sincerely desires to preserve the wilderness, not merely his own privacy
and space? And has he also made clear that he has considered the needs
and desires of those who might want to live in a housing development by
the ocean? If the answers to all these questions are yes, then the board
will hear the arguer with respect, and the arguer will have begun to establish his credibility.

A reputation for intelligence, character, and goodwill is not often
won overnight. And it can be lost more quickly than it is won. Once a
writer or speaker has betrayed an audience's belief in her character or
judgment, she may find it difficult to persuade an audience to accept subsequent claims, no matter how sound her data and reasoning are. "We
give no credit to a liar," said Roman statesman Cicero, "even when he
speaks the truth."

Political life is full of examples of lost and squandered credibility.
After it was discovered that President Lyndon Johnson had deceived the
American public about U.S. conduct in the Vietnam War, he could not regain his popularity. After President Gerald Ford pardoned former President Richard Nixon for his complicity in the cover up of the bugging and
burglary of the Democratic National Committee headquarters at the Wa-
tergate office complex, Ford was no longer a serious candidate for reelec-
tion. After proof that President Clinton had lied to a grand jury and the
public about his sexual relationship with a young White House intern,
public approval of his political record remained high, but approval of his
moral character declined and threatened to diminish his influence.

We can see the practical consequences when an audience realizes that
an arguer has been guilty of a deception — misusing facts and authority,
suppressing evidence, distorting statistics, violating the rules of logic. But
suppose the arguer is successful in concealing his or her manipulation of
the data and can persuade an uninformed audience to take the action or
adopt the idea that he or she recommends. Even supposing that the argument promotes a "good" cause, is the arguer justified in using evasive
or misleading tactics?

The answer is no. To encourage another person to make a decision on
the basis of incomplete or dishonestly used data is profoundly unethical.
It indicates lack of respect for the rights of others — their right to know at
least as much as you do about the subject, to be allowed to judge and
compare, to disagree with you if they challenge your own interests. If the
moral implications are still not clear, try to imagine yourself not as the
perpetrator of the lie but as the victim.

There is also a danger in measuring success wholly by the degree to
which audiences accept our arguments. Both as writers and readers, we
must be able to respect the claim, or proposition, and what it tries to
demonstrate. The English philosopher Stephen Toulmin has said: "To
conclude that a proposition is true, it is not enough to know that this

[person] or that finds it 'credible': the proposition itself must be *worthy* of credence."[5]

No matter what the subject, there are certain basic steps that a writer can take to insure that not only the proposition, or claim, but the whole argument, is worthy of credence. You are not yet an expert in many of the subjects you will deal with in assignments, although you are knowledgeable about many other things, including your cultural and social activities. But there are several ways in which you can develop confidence by your discussion of topics derived from academic disciplines, such as political science, psychology, economics, sociology, and art, on which most assignments will be based. The following steps that every writer of argumentative texts should follow will be the basis for Chapters 3 to 8.

■ Defining Key Terms (Chapter 3)

Many of the controversial questions you will read or write about are primarily arguments of definition. Such terms as *abortion, pornography, racism, poverty, freedom of speech,* and *terrorism* must be defined before useful solutions to the problems they represent can be formulated. Even if the primary purpose of your essay is not definition, you can successfully communicate with an audience only if that audience understands how you are using key terms.

■ Choosing an Appropriate Claim (Chapter 4)

It must be clear to the individual or group that constitutes your audience what change in thought or what action you hope to achieve by presenting your case. If you are seeking a change in your audience's thinking on a subject, you will have a much greater chance of accomplishing your goal if you consider the audience's current thinking on the subject and are realistic about the extent to which you might hope to change that thinking. If there is something you want your audience to do, that action must be realistically within the power of that audience.

■ Choosing and Documenting Appropriate Sources (Chapter 5)

You must submit evidence of careful research, demonstrating that you have been conscientious in finding the best authorities, giving credit, and attempting to arrive at the truth.

---

[5] *An Examination of the Place of Reason in Ethics* (Cambridge: Cambridge University Press, 1964), p. 71.

■ Analyzing Assumptions (Chapter 6)

You must consider the warrant or assumption on which your argument is based. A warrant need not be expressed if it is so widely accepted that you can assume any reasonable audience will not need proof of its validity. You must be prepared to defend any other warrant.

■ Avoiding Logical Errors (Chapter 7)

Understanding the ways in which inductive and deductive reasoning processes work can help you to determine the truth and validity of your arguments, as well as other arguments, and to identify and correct faulty reasoning.

■ Editing for Appropriate Language (Chapter 8)

Another important resource is the careful use of language, not only to define terms and express personal style but also to reflect clarity of thought, to avoid the clichés and outworn slogans that frequently substitute for fresh ideas, and to avoid word choices that would make your audience unwilling to consider your ideas.

Now let us turn to one of the most famous arguments in American history and examine its elements.

SAMPLE ANALYSIS

The Declaration of Independence

THOMAS JEFFERSON

When in the course of human events, it becomes necessary for one people to dissolve the political bands which have connected them with another, and to assume among the Powers of the earth, the separate and equal station to which the Laws of Nature and Nature's God entitle them, a decent respect to the opinions of mankind requires that they should declare the causes which impel them to the separation.

We hold these truths to be self-evident, that all men are created equal, that they are endowed by their Creator with certain unalienable Rights, that among these are Life, Liberty and the pursuit of Happiness.

That to secure these rights, Governments are instituted among Men, deriving their just powers from the consent of the governed.

Thomas Jefferson (1743–1826) served as governor of Virginia, minister to France, secretary of state, vice president under John Adams, and president from 1801 to 1809.

That whenever any Form of Government becomes destructive of these ends, it is the Right of the People to alter or to abolish it, and to institute a new Government laying its foundation on such principles and organizing its powers in such form, as to them shall seem most likely to effect their Safety and Happiness. Prudence, indeed, will dictate that Governments long established should not be changed for light and transient causes; and accordingly all experience hath shown that mankind are more disposed to suffer, while evils are sufferable, than to right themselves by abolishing the forms to which they are accustomed. But when a long train of abuses and usurpations pursuing invariably the same Object evinces a design to reduce them under absolute Despotism, it is their right, it is their duty, to throw off such government, and to provide new Guards for their future security.

Such has been the patient sufferance of these Colonies; and such is   5
now the necessity which constrains them to alter their former Systems of Government. The history of the present King of Great Britain is a history of repeated injuries and usurpations, all having in direct object the establishment of an absolute Tyranny over these States. To prove this, let Facts be submitted to a candid world.

He has refused his Assent to Laws, the most wholesome and necessary for the public good.

He has forbidden his Governors to pass Laws of immediate and pressing importance, unless suspended in their operation till his Assent should be obtained; and when so suspended, he has utterly neglected to attend to them.

He has refused to pass other Laws for the accommodation of large districts of people, unless those people would relinquish the right of Representation in the Legislature, a right inestimable to them and formidable to tyrants only.

He has called together legislative bodies at places unusual, uncomfortable, and distant from the depository of their Public Records, for the sole purpose of fatiguing them into compliance with his measures.

He has dissolved Representative Houses repeatedly, for opposing with 10
manly firmness his invasions on the rights of the people.

He has refused for a long time, after such dissolutions, to cause others to be elected; whereby the Legislative Powers, incapable of Annihilation, have returned to the People at large for their exercise; the State remaining in the mean time exposed to all the danger of invasion from without, and convulsions within.

He has endeavored to prevent the population of these States; for that purpose obstructing the Laws of Naturalization of Foreigners; refusing to pass others to encourage their migration hither, and raising the conditions of new Appropriations of Lands.

He has obstructed the Administration of Justice, by refusing his Assent to Laws for establishing Judiciary Powers.

He has made Judges dependent on his Will alone, for the tenure of their offices, and the amount and payment of their salaries.

He has erected a multitude of New Offices, and sent hither swarms of 15 Officers to harass our People, and eat out their substance.

He has kept among us, in time of peace, Standing Armies without the consent of our Legislature.

He has affected to render the Military independent of and superior to the Civil Power.

He has combined with others to subject us to jurisdictions foreign to our constitution, and unacknowledged by our laws; giving his Assent to their acts of pretended Legislation:

For quartering large bodies of armed troops among us:

For protecting them, by a mock Trial, from Punishment for any Mur- 20 ders which they should commit on the Inhabitants of these States:

For cutting off our Trade with all parts of the world:

For imposing Taxes on us without our Consent:

For depriving us in many cases, of the benefits of Trial by Jury:

For transporting us beyond Seas to be tried for pretended offenses:

For abolishing the free System of English Laws in a Neighbouring 25 Province, establishing therein an Arbitrary government, and enlarging its boundaries so as to render it at once an example and fit instrument for introducing the same absolute rule into these Colonies:

For taking away our Charters, abolishing our most valuable Laws, and altering fundamentally the Forms of our Governments:

For suspending our own legislatures, and declaring themselves in-vested with Power to legislate for us in all cases whatsoever.

He has abdicated Government here, by declaring us out of his Pro-tection and waging War against us.

He has plundered our seas, ravaged our Coasts, burnt our towns and destroyed the Lives of our people.

He is at this time transporting large Armies of foreign Mercenaries to 30 compleat the works of death, desolation and tyranny, already begun with circumstances of Cruelty & perfidy scarcely paralleled in the most bar-barous ages, and totally unworthy the Head of a civilized nation.

He has constrained our fellow Citizens taken Captive on the high Seas to bear Arms against their Country, to become the executioners of their friends and Brethren, or to fall themselves by their Hands.

He has excited domestic insurrections amongst us, and has endeav-ored to bring on the inhabitants of our frontiers, the merciless Indian Sav-ages, whose known rule of warfare is an undistinguished destruction of all ages, sexes, and conditions.

In every stage of these Oppressions We Have Petitioned for Redress in the most humble terms. Our repeated petitions have been answered only by repeated injury. A Prince, whose character is thus marked by every act which may define a Tyrant, is unfit to be the ruler of a free People.

Not have We been wanting in attention to our British brethren. We have warned them from time to time of attempts by their legislature to extend an unwarrantable jurisdiction over us. We have reminded them of the circumstances of our emigration and settlement here. We have appealed to their native justice and magnanimity and we have conjured them by the ties of our common kindred to disavow these usurpations, which would inevitably interrupt our connections and correspondence. They too have been deaf to the voice of justice and of consanguinity. We must, therefore, acquiesce in the necessity, which denounces our Separation, and hold them, as we hold the rest of mankind, Enemies in War, in Peace Friends.

We, therefore, the Representatives of the United States of America, in   35 General Congress, Assembled, appealing to the Supreme Judge of the world for the rectitude of our intentions, do, in the Name, and by Authority of the good People of these Colonies, solemnly publish and declare, That these United Colonies are, and of Right ought to be, Free and Independent States; that they are Absolved from all Allegiance to the British Crown, and that all political connection between them and the State of Great Britain, is and ought to be totally dissolved; and that as Free and Independent States, they have full power to levy War, conclude Peace, contract Alliances, establish Commerce, and to do all other Acts and Things which Independent States may of right do. And for the support of this Declaration, with a firm reliance on the protection of Divine Providence, we mutually pledge to each other our lives, our Fortunes and our sacred Honor.

■ Analysis

The Declaration of Independence is addressed to several audiences: to the American colonists; to the British people; to the British Parliament; to the British king, George III; and to humanity or a universal audience. Not all the American colonists were convinced by Jefferson's argument. Large numbers remained loyal to the king and for various reasons opposed an independent nation. In the next-to-the-last paragraph, Jefferson refers to previous addresses to the British people. Not surprisingly, most of the British citizenry as well as the king also rejected the claims of the Declaration. But the universal audience, the decent opinion of humanity, found Jefferson's argument overwhelmingly persuasive. Many of the liberal reform movements of the eighteenth and nineteenth centuries were inspired by the Declaration. In basing his claim on universal principles of justice and equality, Jefferson was certainly aware that he was addressing future generations.

Definition: Several significant terms are not defined. Modern readers will ask for further definition of "all men are created equal," "Life, Liberty and the pursuit of Happiness," "Laws of Nature and Nature's God," among others. We must assume that the failure to explain these terms more strictly was deliberate, in part because Jefferson thought that his readers would understand the references—for example, to the eighteenth-century belief in freedom as the birthright of all human beings—and in part because he wished the terms to be understood as universal principles of justice, applicable in all struggles, not merely those of the colonies against the king of England. But a failure to narrow the terms of argument can have unpredictable consequences. In later years the Declaration of Independence would be used to justify other rebellions, including the secession of the South from the Union in 1861.

Claim: What is Jefferson trying to prove? *The American colonies are justified in declaring their independence from British rule.* Jefferson and his fellow signers might have issued a simple statement such as appears in the last paragraph, announcing the freedom and independence of these United Colonies. Instead, however, they chose to justify their right to do so.

Support: What does Jefferson have to go on? The Declaration of Independence bases its claim on two kinds of support: *factual evidence* and *motivational appeals* or appeals to the values of the audience.

FACTUAL EVIDENCE: Jefferson presents a long list of specific acts of tyranny by George III, beginning with "He has refused his Assent to Laws, the most wholesome and necessary for the public good." This list constitutes more than half the text. Notice how Jefferson introduces these grievances: "The history of the present King of Great Britain is a history of repeated injuries and usurpations, all having in direct object the establishment of an absolute Tyranny over these States. *To prove this, let Facts be submitted to a candid world*" (italics for emphasis added). Jefferson hopes that a recital of these specific acts will convince an honest audience that the United Colonies have indeed been the victims of an intolerable tyranny.

APPEAL TO VALUES: Jefferson also invokes the moral values underlying the formation of a democratic state. These values are referred to throughout. In the second and third paragraphs he speaks of equality, "Life, Liberty and the pursuit of Happiness," "just powers," "consent of the governed," and in the fourth paragraph, safety. In the last paragraph he refers to freedom and independence. Jefferson believes that the people who read his appeal will, or should, share these fundamental values. Audience acceptance of these values constitutes the most important part of the support. Some historians have called the specific acts of oppression cited by Jefferson trivial, inconsequential, or distorted. Clearly, however, Jefferson felt that the list of specific grievances was vital to definition of the abstract terms in which values are always expressed.

Warrant: How does Jefferson get from support to claim? *People have a right to revolution to free themselves from oppression.* This warrant is explicit:

"But when a long train of abuses and usurpations pursuing invariably the same Object evinces a design to reduce them under absolute Despotism, it is their right, it is their duty, to throw off such government, and to provide new Guards for their future security." Some members of Jefferson's audience, especially those whom he accuses of oppressive acts, will reject the principle that any subject people have earned the right to revolt. But Jefferson believes that the decent opinion of mankind will accept this assumption. Many of his readers will also be aware that the warrant is supported by seventeenth-century political philosophy, which defines government as a social compact between the government and the governed.

If Jefferson's readers do, in fact, accept the warrant and if they also believe in the accuracy of the factual evidence and share his moral values, then they will conclude that his claim has been proved—that Jefferson has justified the right of the colonies to separate themselves from Great Britain.

Logic: As a logical pattern of argument, the Declaration of Independence is largely *deductive*. Deduction usually consists of certain broad general statements which we know or believe to be true and which lead us to other statements that follow from the ones already laid down. The Declaration begins with such general statements, summarizing a philosophy of government based on the equality of men, the inalienable rights derived from the Creator, and the powers of the governed. These statements are held to be "self-evident"—that is, not needing proof—and if we accept them, then it follows that a revolution is necessary to remove the oppressors and secure the safety and happiness to which the governed are entitled. The particular grievances against the king are proof that the king has oppressed the colonies, but they are not the basis for revolution.

The fact that Jefferson emphasized the universal principles underlying the right of revolution meant that the Declaration of Independence could appeal to all people everywhere, whether or not they had suffered the particular grievances in Jefferson's list.

Language: Although some stylistic conventions of eighteenth-century writing would not be observed today, Jefferson's clear, elegant, formal prose—"a surprising mixture of simplicity and majesty," in the words of one writer—remains a masterpiece of English prose and persuades us that we are reading an important document. Several devices are worth noting:

1. *Parallelism,* or balance of sentence construction, gives both emphasis and rhythm to the statements in the introduction (first four paragraphs) and the list of grievances.
2. *Diction* (choice of words) supports and underlines the meaning: nouns that have positive connotations—*safety, happiness, prudence, right, duty, Supreme Judge, justice;* verbs and verbals that suggest

Writer's Guide: Learning the Key Terms

Claim — the proposition that the author or writer is trying to prove. The claim may appear as the thesis statement of an essay but may be implied rather than stated directly.

- *Claims of fact* assert that a condition has existed, exists, or will exist and are based on facts or data that the audience will accept as being objectively verifiable.

- *Claims of value* attempt to prove that some things are more or less desirable than others; they express approval or disapproval of standards of taste and morality.

- *Claims of policy* assert that specific plans or courses of action should be instituted as solutions to problems.

Support — the materials used by the arguer to convince an audience that his or her claim is sound; those materials include evidence and motivational appeals.

Warrant — an inference or assumption; a belief or principle that is taken for granted in an argument.

negative actions (taken by the king) — *refused, forbidden, dissolved, obstructed, plundered, depriving, abolishing.*

3. The *tone* suggests reason and patience on the part of the author or authors (especially paras. 5, 33, and 34).

ASSIGNMENTS FOR UNDERSTANDING ARGUMENT

1. Classify each of the following as a claim of fact, value, or policy.
   a. Congress should endorse the right-to-life amendment.
   b. Solar power can supply 20 percent of the energy needs now satisfied by fossil and nuclear power.
   c. Homosexuals should have the same job rights as heterosexuals.
   d. Rapists should be treated as mentally ill rather than depraved.
   e. Whale hunting should be banned by international law.
   f. Violence on television produces violent behavior in children who watch more than four hours a day.
   g. Both creationism and evolutionary theory should be taught in the public schools.
   h. Mentally defective men and women should be sterilized or otherwise prevented from producing children.

    i. History will pronounce Reggie Jackson a greater all-around baseball player than Joe DiMaggio.

    j. Bilingual instruction should not be permitted in the public schools.

    k. Some forms of cancer are caused by a virus.

    l. Dogs are smarter than horses.

    m. Curfews for teenagers will reduce the abuse of alcohol and drugs.

    n. The federal government should impose a drinking age of twenty-one.

    o. The United States should proceed with unilateral disarmament.

    p. Security precautions at airports are out of proportion to the dangers of terrorism.

    q. Bodybuilding cannot be defined as a sport; it is a form of exhibitionism.

2. Choose one of the more controversial claims in the previous list and explain the reasons it is controversial. Would it be difficult or impossible to support? Are the warrants unacceptable to many people? Try to go as deeply as you can, exploring, if possible, systems of belief, traditions, societal customs. You may confine your discussion to personal experience with the problem in your community or group. If there has been a change over the years in the public attitude toward the claim, offer what you think may be an explanation for the change.

3. Report on an argument you have heard recently. Identify the parts of that argument—claim, support, warrant—as they are defined in this chapter. What were the strengths and weaknesses in the argument you heard?

4. Discuss an occasion when a controversy arose that the opponents could not settle. Describe the problem, and tell why you think the disagreement was not settled.

5. In the following excerpt a student expresses his feelings about standard grading—that is, grading by letter or number on a scale that applies to a whole group.

> You go to school to learn, not to earn grades. To be educated, that's what they tell you. "He's educated, he graduated magna cum laude." What makes a magna cum laude man so much better than a man that graduates with a C? They are both still educated, aren't they? No one has a right to call someone less educated because they got a C instead of an A. Let's take both men and put them in front of a car. Each car has something wrong with it. Each man must fix his broken car. Our C man goes right to work while our magna cum laude man hasn't got the slightest idea where to begin. Who's more educated now?

Compare the preceding passage to the following one, written on the same subject by a student. Analyze the two pieces using the terminology introduced in this chapter and applied above to the Declaration of Independence.

> Grades are the play money in a university Monopoly game. As long as the tokens are offered, the temptation will be largely irresistible to play for them. Students are so busy taking notes, doing tests, and

getting tokens that they have forgotten to ask: Of what worth is all this? Or perhaps they ask and the grade is their answer.

One certainly learns something in the passive lecture-note-read-note-test process: how to do it all more efficiently next time (in the hope of eventually owning Boardwalk and Park Place). As Marshall McLuhan has said, we learn what we do. In this process most students come to view learning as studying and remembering what other people have learned. They assume that knowledge is logically and for practical reasons divided up into discrete pieces called "disciplines" and that the highest knowledge is achieved by specializing in a discipline. By getting good grades in a lot of disciplines they conclude they have learned a lot. They have indeed, and it is too bad.[6]

[6]Roy E. Terry in "Does Standard Grading Encourage Excessive Competitiveness?" *Change*, September 1974, p. 45.

CHAPTER 2

Responding to Argument

Most of us learn how to read, to listen, to write—and, with the increased use of computer technology, to view—arguments by attending critically to the arguments of those who have already mastered the important elements as well as those who have not. As we acquire skill in analyzing arguments, we learn to uncover the clues that reveal meaning and to become sensitive to the kinds of claims and support, language and visuals that experienced writers use in persuading their audiences. Listening, too, is a skill often underrated but increasingly important in an era when the spoken voice can be transmitted worldwide with astonishing speed. In becoming more expert listeners, we can engage in discussions with a wide and varied audience and gain proficiency in distinguishing between responsible and irresponsible speech. In becoming more expert users and viewers of electronic texts, we become part of a worldwide conversation that would have been inconceivable until recently.

A full response to any argument means more than understanding the message. It also means evaluating, deciding whether the message is successful and then determining *how* it succeeds or fails in persuading us. In making these judgments about the written, oral, and visual arguments of others, we learn how to deliver our own. We try to avoid what we perceive to be flaws in another's arguments, and we adapt the strategies that produce clear, honest, forceful arguments.

RESPONDING AS A CRITICAL READER

Critical reading is essential for mastery of most college subjects, but its importance for reading and writing about argument, where meaning is often complex and multilayered, cannot be overestimated. Reading arguments critically requires you to at least temporarily suspend notions of absolute "right" and "wrong" and to intellectually inhabit grey areas that do not allow for simple "yes" and "no" answers. Of course, even in these areas, significant decisions about such things as ethics, values, politics, and the law must be made, and in studying argument you shouldn't fall into the trap of simple relativism: the idea that all answers to a given problem are equally correct at all times. We must make decisions about arguments with the understanding that reasonable people can disagree on the validity of ideas. Read or listen to others' arguments carefully and consider how their ideas can contribute to or complicate your own. Also recognize that what appears to be a final solution will always be open to further negotiation as new participants, new historical circumstances, and new ideologies become involved in the debate.

The ability to read arguments critically is essential to advanced academic work—even in science and math—since it requires the debate of multifaceted issues rather than the memorization of facts. Just as important, learning to read arguments critically helps you develop the ability to *write* effective arguments, a process valued at the university, in the professional world, and in public life.

■ Critical Reading Strategies

The first step in the critical reading process is comprehension—understanding what an author is trying to prove. Comprehending academic arguments can be difficult, because they are often complex and often challenge accepted notions. Academic writing also sometimes assumes that readers already have a great deal of knowledge about a subject, and can require further research for comprehension.

Reading a text on its own terms means reading rhetorically. Imagine the initial context the author was writing in, the problem the author was trying to deal with, the author's ideal audience: Who would respond most favorably to the author's words and why? What values and ideals are shared by the author and the audience most likely to agree with the argument? How do these values and ideals help make sense of the content?

GENERAL READING STRATEGIES

Whether reading to comprehend or to evaluate any text, do the following:

1. Take prereading activities seriously. Clearly, the more information you have about an author and subject, the easier and more productive your reading

will be. However, you should learn to read in a way that allows you to discover not just meaning in the text itself but information about the author's point of view and background, the audience the author is writing for, and the author's motives and ideology. Such understanding comes from close analysis of texts, background reading on the author or the subject (a task made significantly easier by the Internet), and discussion with your classmates and instructors on the material.

2. Work hard to understand the kind of text you are reading. Was it published recently? Was it written for a specific or a general audience? Is it a textbook and therefore likely to cover the basic points of an issue but not to take a strong stance on anything? Does it come from a journal that publishes primarily conservative or liberal writers?

3. When reading an Internet site, carefully read the Web address or URL. This can provide clues about the author of the site (is it an individual or an organization?) and about the purpose of the Web site (for example, the domain suffix *.com* represents a business site, while *.edu* represents academic institutions). In addition, most Web material is not checked for factual accuracy, so you must learn to distinguish between Web writing that represents a free-for-all of ideas and Web writing that has certain standards of reliability, especially when dealing with new information (see the sections on Sample Analysis of a Web Site (p. 52) and Evaluating Web Sources (p. 407) for more information).

SAMPLE ANNOTATED ESSAY

The Pursuit of Whining: Affirmative Action circa 1776

JOHN PATRICK DIGGINS

Usually means that a second glance will show the opposite

Means it's not what it seems

So he's against aff. action because it violates the D of I?

At first glance, affirmative action appears to be consistent with America's commitment to egalitarianism, which derives from the Declaration of Independence and its ringing pronouncement that "all men are created equal" and are "endowed by their creator with certain unalienable rights." Actually affirmative action, as carried out, has little to do with equality and is so dependent on biology, ancestry, and history that it subverts the individualist spirit of the Declaration.

John Patrick Diggins teaches history at the Graduate Center of the City University of New York. This column appeared in the *New York Times* on September 25, 1995.

Seems to be his thesis; is group opportunity bad?

But the second part of the Declaration, which no one remembers, may affirm affirmative action as the politics of group opportunity.

The Declaration held rights to be equal and unalienable because in the state of nature, before social conventions had been formed, "Nature and Nature's God" (Jefferson's phrase) gave no person or class the authority to dominate over others.

Reason for the Revolution

Aristocracy became such a class, and the idea of equality was not so much an accurate description of the human species as it was a protest against artificial privilege and hereditary right.

Interesting point — today's affirmative action is like yesterday's aristocracy (both claim privileges of birth).

Today we have a new identity politics of entitlement, and who one is depends on ethnic categories and descriptions based on either ancestry or sex. This return to a pseudo-aristocratic politics of privilege based on inherited rights by reason of birth means that equality has been replaced by diversity as the criteri[on] of governmental decisions.

The founding fathers were against inherited privileges.

Jefferson loved diversity, but he and Thomas   5
Paine trusted the many and suspected the few who saw themselves entitled to preferential treatment as an accident of birth. Paine was unsparing in his critique of aristocracy as a parasitic "no-ability." Speaking for the colonists, many of whom had worked their way out of conditions of indentured servitude, he insisted that hereditary privilege was "as absurd as an hereditary mathematician, or an hereditary wise man; and as ridiculous as an hereditary poet-laureate."

So far, he's proved that first part of D of I argues against affirmative action.

But the second part, listing grievances, is consistent with it.

But if America's egalitarian critique of aristocratic privilege could be in conflict with affirmative action, the second part of the Declaration may be perfectly consistent with it. Here begins the art of protest as the Declaration turns to the colonists' grievances, and we are asked to listen to a long tale of woe. Instead of admitting that they simply had no desire to cough up taxes, even to pay for a war that drove the French out of North America and thus made possible a situation where settlers were now secure enough to demand self-government, the colonists blamed King George for every outrage conceivable.

Thinks the colonists are crybabies!

Strong language

Even Jefferson gets a few lumps!

Help! I can't find it in the D of I! (Look it up?)

Wow!

Were any of their complaints justified?

"Paranoia" seems a bit much.
He's talking about blacks and women. Is he saying, "no justification for complaints against whites and males?" No way!

Explain a bit further
Our choices

An ending that's all questions. I like it. But they're fake questions. He knows the answers and wants us to agree with him.

"He has erected . . . swarms of offices to harass our people and eat out their substance." Because the King, in response to the colonists' refusal to pay for the cost of protection, withdrew such protection, he is charged with abdicating "his allegiance and protection: he has plundered our seas, ravaged our coasts, burnt our towns, destroyed the lives of our people." Even Edmund Burke, the British parliamentarian and orator who supported the colonists, saw them as almost paranoid, "protestants" who protest so much that they would "snuff the approach of tyranny in every tainted breeze."

The ultimate hypocrisy comes when Jefferson accuses the King of once tolerating the slave trade, only "he is now exciting those very people to rise up in arms among us, and to purchase their liberty of which he has deprived them, by murdering the people upon whom he has obtruded them." The notion that slavery was forced upon the innocent colonists, who in turn only sought to be free of "tyranny," suggests the extent to which the sentiment of the Revolution grumbles with spurious charges.

The Declaration voiced America's first proclamation of victimology. Whatever the theoretical complexities embedded in the doctrine of equality, the Declaration demonstrated that any politics that has its own interests uppermost is best put forward in the language of victimization and paranoia.

The very vocabulary of the document ("harass," "oppress," and so on) is consistent with affirmative action, where white racists and male chauvinists have replaced King George as the specter of complaint.   10

Seeing themselves as sufferers to whom awful things happen, the colonists blamed their alleged oppressors and never acknowledged that they had any responsibility for the situation in which they found themselves.

What then is America's core value? Is it equality and civic virtue? Or is it the struggle for power that legitimizes itself in the more successful, and least demanding, shameless politics of whining?

COMPREHENDING ARGUMENTS

Readers sometimes fail to comprehend a text they disagree with or that is new to them, especially in dealing with essays or books making controversial, value-laden arguments. Some research even shows that readers will sometimes remember only those parts of texts that match their points of view.[1] The study of argument does not require you to accept points of view you find morally or otherwise reprehensible, but to engage with these views, no matter how strange or repugnant they might seem, on your own terms.

To comprehend difficult texts you should understand that reading and writing are linked processes, and use writing to help your reading. This can mean writing comments in the margins of the book or essay itself or in a separate notebook; highlighting passages in the text that seem particularly important; or freewriting about the author's essential ideas after you finish reading. For complex arguments, write down the methods the author uses to make the argument: Did the text make use of historical evidence or rely on the voice of experts? Were emotional appeals made to try to convince readers, or did the text rely on scientific or logical forms of evidence? Did the author use analogies or comparisons to help readers understand the argument? Was some combination of these or other strategies used? Writing down the author's methods for argumentation can make even the most complex arguments understandable.

STRATEGIES FOR COMPREHENDING ARGUMENTS

1. Skim the article or book for the main idea and overall structure. At this stage, avoid concentrating on details. As part of your prereading activities, try some or all of the following:

   a. Pay attention to the title, as it may state the purpose of the argument in specific terms, as in "Single-Sex Education Benefits Men Too" (p. 181). The title of the previous article, "The Pursuit of Whining" (p. 27), brings to mind the famous "pursuit of Happiness" phrase from the Declaration of Independence. The subtitle clinches the connection: "Affirmative Action circa 1776." Titles can also express the author's attitude toward the subject, and in the case of "The Pursuit of Whining," we realize that "whining," because it has negative connotations, will probably be attacked as a means of achieving happiness.

---

[1]See, for example, Patrick J. Slattery, "The Argumentative, Multiple-Source Paper: College Students Reading, Thinking, and Writing about Multiple Points of View," *Journal of Teaching Writing* 10, Fall/Winter 1991, 181–99.

b. Make a skeleton outline of the text in your mind or on paper. From this outline and the text itself, consider the relationship between the beginning, middle, and end of the argument. How has the author divided these sections? Are there subheadings in the body of the text? If you are reading a book, how are the chapters broken up? What appears to be the logic of the author's organization?

c. From your overview, what is the central claim or argument of the essay? What is the main argument against the author's central claim and how would the author respond to it?

2. Remember that the central argument — also known as the thesis statement or claim — is usually in one of the first two or three paragraphs (if it is an essay) or in the first chapter (if it is a book). The beginning of an argument can have other purposes, however; it may describe the position that the author will oppose, or provide background for the whole argument.

3. Pay attention to topic sentences. The topic sentence is usually but not always the first sentence of a paragraph. It is the general statement that controls the details and examples in the paragraph.

4. Don't overlook language signposts, especially transitional words and phrases that tell you whether the writer will change direction or offer support for a previous point — words and phrases like *but, however, nevertheless, yet, moreover, for example, at first glance, more important, the first reason,* and so on.

5. When it comes to vocabulary, you can either guess the meaning of an unfamiliar word from the context and go on, or look it up immediately. The first method makes for more rapid reading and is sometimes recommended by teachers, but guessing can be risky. Keep a good dictionary handy. If a word you don't understand seems crucial to meaning, look it up before going on.

6. If you use a colored marker to highlight main points, use it sparingly. Marking passages in color is meant to direct you to the major ideas and reduce the necessity for rereading the whole passage when you review. Look over the marked passages after reading and do a five-minute freewrite to sum up the central parts of the argument.

7. Once you are done reading, think again about the original context the text was written in: Why did the author write it and for whom? Why might an editor have published it in a book or journal and why did your instructor assign it for you to read?

EVALUATING ARGUMENTS

The second step in the critical reading of arguments involves evaluation — careful judgment of the extent to which the author has succeeded in making a point — which can be difficult because some readers who do not thoroughly engage with an author's point of view may immediately label an argument they disagree with as "wrong," and some readers believe they are incapable of evaluating the work of a published, "expert" author because they do not feel expert enough to make such judgments.

Evaluating arguments means moving beyond comprehending the context the author was writing within and starting to question it. One way to do this is to envision audiences the text was probably *not* written for, by considering, for example, whether an essay written for an academic audience takes into account the world outside the university. In addition, why is the problem significant to the author? For whom would it not be significant, and why?

When you evaluate an argument, imagine at least two kinds of audience for the text. Decide whose views would conflict most with the author's, and why. What ideology or values underlie the point of view most diametrically opposed to the author's argument? Then imagine yourself as a friend of the writer who simply wants him or her to succeed in clarifying and developing the argument. You could ask what additional methods the author should use to make the argument more effective or how the writer could more fully address opposing points of view. Are there any significant questions or issues the author has left unaddressed? How could he or she build on the strengths of the argument and downplay the weaknesses?

At this point, consider how you personally respond to the argument presented in the text, and your own response in light of the questions you've asked. Critically evaluating an argument means not simply reading a text and agreeing or disagreeing with it, but doing serious analytical work that addresses multiple viewpoints before deciding on the effectiveness of an argument.

STRATEGIES FOR EVALUATING ARGUMENTS

1. As you read the argument, don't be timid about asking questions of the text. No author is infallible, and some are not always clear. Disagree with the author if you feel confident of the support for your view, but first read the whole argument to see if your questions have been answered. If not, this may be a signal to read the article again. Be cautious about concluding that the author hasn't proved his or her point.

2. Reading an assigned work is usually a solitary activity, but what follows a reading should be shared. Talk about the material with classmates or others who have read it, especially those who have responded to the text differently than yourself. Consider their points of view. You probably know that discussion of a book or a movie strengthens both your memory of details and your understanding of the whole. And defending or modifying your evaluation will mean going back to the text and finding clues that you may have overlooked. Not least, it can be fun to discuss even something you didn't enjoy.

3. Consider the strengths of the argument, and examine the useful methods of argumentation, the points that are successfully made, (and those which help the reader to better understand the argument), and what makes sense about the author's argument.

4. Consider the weaknesses of the argument, and locate instances of faulty reasoning, unsupported statements, and the limitations of the author's assumptions about the world (the warrants that underlie the argument).

5. Consider how effective the title of the reading is, and whether it accurately sums up a critical point of the essay. Come up with an alternative title that would suit the reading better, and be prepared to defend this alternative title.

6. Evaluate the organizational structure of the essay. The author should lead you from idea to idea in a logical progression, and each section should relate to the ones before it and after it and to the central argument in significant ways. Determine whether the writer could have organized things more clearly, logically, or efficiently.

7. Look at how the author follows through on the main claim, or thesis, of the argument. The author should stick with this thesis, and not waver throughout the text. If the thesis does waver, there could be a reason for the shift in the argument or perhaps the author is being inconsistent. The conclusion should drive home the central argument.

8. Evaluate the vocabulary and style the author uses. Is it too simple or too complicated? The vocabulary and sentence structure the author uses could relate to the audience the author was initially writing for.

SAMPLE ANALYSIS

The Gettysburg Address

ABRAHAM LINCOLN

Four score and seven years ago our fathers brought forth on this continent, a new nation, conceived in Liberty, and dedicated to the proposition that all men are created equal.

Now we are engaged in a great civil war, testing whether that nation, or any nation so conceived and so dedicated, can long endure. We are met on a great battle-field of that war. We have come to dedicate a portion of that field, as a final resting place for those who here gave their lives that that nation might live. It is altogether fitting and proper that we should do this.

Abraham Lincoln (1809–1865), the sixteenth president of the United States, delivered this speech at Gettysburg, Pennsylvania, on November 19, 1863.

But, in a larger sense, we can not dedicate—we can not consecrate—we can not hallow—this ground. The brave men, living and dead, who struggled here, have consecrated it, far above our poor power to add or detract. The world will little note, nor long remember what we say here, but it can never forget what they did here. It is for us the living, rather, to be dedicated here to the unfinished work which they who fought here have thus far so nobly advanced. It is rather for us to be here dedicated to the great task remaining before us—that from these honored dead we take increased devotion to that cause for which they gave the last full measure of devotion—that we here highly resolve that these dead shall not have died in vain—that this nation, under God, shall have a new birth of freedom—and that government of the people, by the people, for the people, shall not perish from the earth.

The following evaluation is by Charles Adams, whose stand on the Civil War is clear from the title of the book from which the excerpt is taken: *When in the Course of Human Events: Arguing the Case for Southern Secession* (2000). Lincoln made his famous short speech in 1863 as a memorial to the thousands who had died at Gettysburg, but in doing so, he was also making an argument. The text in quotation marks is from the address itself. The rest is Adams's evaluation of it. As you read, consider what argument Lincoln is making but also whether or not you agree with Adams's evaluation.

Lincoln's Logic

CHARLES ADAMS

> Lincoln has become one of our national deities and a realistic examination of him is thus no longer possible.   —H. L. Mencken, 1931

At the Gettysburg Cemetery

L incoln's mental processes and his logic have fascinated me ever since my university days. In a class in logic, we studied his Gettysburg Address. The analysis showed that this famous speech didn't fit the real world. It was good poetry, perhaps, but was it good thinking? It's chiseled

Charles Adams, a leading scholar on the history of taxation, is the author of *Fight, Flight, Fraud* (1982); *Those Dirty Rotten Taxes* (1998); and *For Good and Evil* (1999). His essay comes from *When in the Course of Human Events: Arguing the Case for Southern Secession* (2000).

in stone in the Lincoln Memorial in Washington, and it ranks in the minds of most Americans with the Declaration of Independence and the Constitution. This oration was given to dedicate the cemetery at Gettysburg, where tens of thousands of young men died in a battle that was probably the turning point of the war. The address is reminiscent of the funeral oration of Pericles of Athens in the fifth century b.c. But Pericles's oration seemed to fit the real world of his day and the virtues of Athenian democracy. Lincoln's address did not fit the world of his day. It reflected his logic, which was based on a number of errors and falsehoods. That it has survived with such reverence is one of the most bizarre aspects of the war.

"Four Score and Seven Years Ago"

By simple arithmetic that would be 1776, when the Revolutionary War started and the Declaration of Independence was signed. That declaration was written with "decent respect for the opinions of mankind," to explain the reasons for the separation of the thirteen colonies from Great Britain. It contained no endowment of governmental power and created no government. The government came later in 1781 with the Articles of Confederation. The articles stated that this confederation was established by "sovereign states," like many of the leagues of states throughout history. To be accurate, Lincoln should have said "four score and two years ago," or better still, "three score and fourteen years ago." Even the Northern newspapers winced. The *New York World* sharply criticized this historical folly. "*This* United States" was not created by the Declaration of Independence but "the result of the ratification of a compact known as the Constitution," a compact that said nothing about equality. Others accused Lincoln of "gross ignorance or willful misstatement." Yet today, that gross ignorance is chiseled in stone as if it were some great truth like scripture, instead of a willful misstatement.

"Our Fathers Brought Forth on This Continent, a New Nation"

The federal compact among the former thirteen colonies, the new "sovereign states," as expressed in the Articles of Confederation in 1781, was not a nation as that term was then and is normally used. That was recently explained by Carl N. Degler, professor of American history at Stanford University, in a memorial lecture given at Gettysburg College in 1990: "The Civil War, in short, was not a struggle to save a failed union, but to create a nation that until then had not come into being."

Thus Lincoln's "new nation" really came into being by force of arms in the war between the states. Lincoln, according to Professor Degler, had a lot in common with Germany's Otto von Bismarck, who built a united Germany in the nineteenth century and believed that "blood and iron" were the main force for national policy. When it came to blood, Lincoln surpassed them all. The slaughter of Confederate men only matched, on a proportionate basis, the losses incurred by the Russians and the Germans in World War II.

In Lincoln's first inaugural address he used the word "Union" twenty 5
times but "nation" not at all. But once the South seceded, the term began
to disappear, and by the time of the Gettysburg Address, it was the American "nation" that was used, and the word "Union" had disappeared completely.

Thus the call from Northern peace Democrats — "the constitution as
it is; the Union as it was" — seems to make sense, but as Lincoln took over
control of the federal government, he soon wanted no part of it. Although he tried to trace the "new nation" back to 1776, he had to ignore
history and the intention and words of the Founders, and create a new
"gospel according to Lincoln" on the American commonwealth. Lincoln's new nation had no constitutional basis — no peaceful legal process.
It was created by war, by "blood and iron," like Bismarck's Germany, and
has survived to this day. In a sense, Lincoln did more to create America
than did the Founding Fathers. It is Lincoln who is the father of our present country, not George Washington. Lincoln's Gettysburg reference to
the Founders creating a new nation was not true. Just as Julius Caesar created an imperial order out of a republic, so Lincoln created a nation out
of a compact among states, and both used their military forces to do so.

"Conceived in Liberty"

A leading man of letters in Britain during the American Revolution,
Samuel Johnson, replied to the Americans' claims of tyranny in his book
Taxation Not Tyranny (1775). He said, "How is it that we hear the loudest
yelps for liberty among the drivers of negroes?"

The British are still chiding us for the absurdity of the Declaration of
Independence. Some years ago, while I was living in a British colony, we
Americans got together on the Fourth of July for a barbecue. One of my
older English friends asked me what the celebration was all about. I took
the bait and told him it was to celebrate the signing of the Declaration of
Independence. He replied, "Wasn't that document kind of a farce? All
that verbiage about equality of all men and liberty when over a million
black people were in bondage for life, and their children and children's
children?" Of course I had no answer, for the term "all men" meant all
white men. And to make matters worse, it really meant "white guys," as
white women weren't much better off. What is not known is that when
Lincoln issued his Emancipation Proclamation, many of the early
women's rights groups asked, How about us too? Thus the declaration
that Lincoln refers to in his address, of four score and seven years ago, was
not conceived in liberty *nor* was it dedicated to the proposition that all
men were created equal. So much for logic and reality.

Lincoln's logic at Gettysburg, as elsewhere, reveals a trial lawyer with
a tool of his craft — using the best logic he can muster to support his
client's (the North's) case, however bad that case may be. It is also, of
course, the craft of a politician, which may explain why so many politicians are lawyers.

"Today We Are Engaged in a Great Civil War"

Actually, it wasn't a civil war as that term was then, and is now, defined. 10
A civil war is a war that breaks out in a nation between opposing groups
for control of the state, for example, in Russia in 1917 with the Red
against the Whites or in China in the 1940s.

The War of Rebellion, as the war was called in the North, was really a
war for Southern independence. The Southern states had withdrawn from
the Union by democratic process—the same process they had followed to
join the Union initially. The Northern federation went to war to prevent
their secession from the Union just as Britain went to war in 1776 to prevent the colonies from seceding from the British nation. It was the fundamentals of the Revolutionary War, eighty-five years before. It was, if
you get down to the nuts and bolts of it, a war of conquest by the North
to destroy the Confederacy and to establish a new political leadership
over the conquered territories. Illiterate slaves were given the vote, and
the rest of the Southern society, the ruling groups, were not permitted to
vote. The poor, illiterate blacks were then told by Northern occupation
forces to vote as directed, and they did so, infuriating the conquered
people and creating a zeal for white supremacy that is only in our time
losing its grip on Southern society.

"Testing Whether That Nation . . . Can Long Endure"

That comment seems to presuppose that the South was out to conquer
the Northern federation. That is as absurd as saying that the revolting
colonies in 1776 were out to destroy the British nation. The thirteen
colonies' withdrawal from the British Empire in 1776 was the same as the
attempt of the Southern states to withdraw in 1861 from the 1789 federation. In reality, the 1789 federation was not in any danger. It would have
endured with secession. Unlike Grant, Lee was not out to conquer the
North. In reality, this logic was as absurd as the rest of Lincoln's funeral
oration.

"A Final Resting Place for Those Who Here Gave Their Lives That That Nation Might Live"

Again, "that nation" was not in danger of dying—that was not Southern
Confederate policy and Lincoln knew it. But again, he was only being a
good lawyer, arguing his client's case as best he could, and with no rebuttal he was an easy winner.

"And That Government of the People, by the People and for the People Shall Not Perish from the Earth"

Why did Lincoln even suggest that secession by the Southern states
would mean that democracy would perish from the earth—in America or
elsewhere? That was perfect nonsense, and Lincoln knew it, but again,
there was no one to rebut his argument.

Lincoln's repeated assertion that secession would amount to a 15
failure of the American experiment with democracy and liberty "just
is plain nonsense," wrote Professor Hummel in his refreshing book
on the Civil War, *Emancipating Slaves, Enslaving Free Men*.[2] The
London *Times* seems to have best understood what was going on in
America with the Northern invasion to prevent secession: "If North-
erners . . . had peaceably allowed the seceders to depart, the result
might fairly have been quoted as illustrating the advantages of Democracy, but when Republicans put empire above liberty, and resorted
to political oppression and war . . . It was clear that nature at Washington was precisely the same as nature at St. Petersburg. . . . Democracy
broke down. . . . when it was upheld, like any other Empire, by force of
arms."[3]

By 1860 democracy was strongly entrenched throughout Western civilization, and certainly in the American states. The democratic process
had emerged decades before in Europe—in Britain, France, the Netherlands, Switzerland, and so on. The war in America for Southern independence was in no way a danger to the concept of government "of the
people." Strange as it may seem, as it turned out, it was Lincoln who was
out to destroy governments of the people in the eleven Southern states.
The declaration's assertion that governments derive their "just powers
from the consent of the governed" was not an acceptable idea in Lincoln's mind so far as the South was concerned. Like a good lawyer he ignored it.

What makes Lincoln's ending so outrageous is that he didn't believe
in the self-determination of peoples, as British writers noted in 1861 and
a hundred years later in 1961.

Ordinances of secession had been adopted in the Southern states,
often with huge majorities. Their right to govern by consent was not acceptable to Lincoln's thinking—that would undermine his client's case.
Yet it was Lincoln who ended up destroying the Union as it was and substituting an all-powerful national government in which the states were
relegated to not much more than county status. There emerged the "imperial presidency" that is with us to this day, in which presidents can go
to war, without congressional approval, spend money without congressional approval; in fact, they can rule by decree like the consuls of Rome.
In other Western democracies, this is not so. Their chief executive must
have the permission and approval of their legislature to do such things.
Thus Lincoln did more to destroy the Union than preserve it. Is not this
irony at its best?

---

[2]Jeffrey Hummel, *Emancipating Slaves, Enslaving Free Men* (Chicago: Open Court
1997), p. 352.

[3]*Times* editorial, September 13, 1862, p. 8, cited in *Emancipating Slaves*, p. 352.

RESPONDING AS A WRITER

Notice the difference between the annotations a student made in response to the following essay and those another student made earlier in response to "The Pursuit of Whining" (p. 27). In the earlier example, the student was making marginal notes primarily on the ideas presented in the essay. Here the annotations focus on how the essay is written. In other words, the student is looking at the piece from a writer's perspective.

The essay is a claim of value in which, as the title suggests, the author claims that competitive sports are destructive. In arguments about values, the author may or may not suggest a solution to the problem caused by the belief or behavior. If so, the solution will be implicit—that is, unexpressed, or undeveloped—as is the case here, and the emphasis will remain on support for the claim.

Keep in mind that an essay of this length can never do justice to a complicated and highly debatable subject. It will probably lack sufficient evidence, as this one does, to answer all the questions and objections of readers who enjoy and approve of competitive games. What it can do is provoke thought and initiate an intelligent discussion.

SAMPLE ANNOTATED ESSAY

No-Win Situations

ALFIE KOHN

Intro: personal experience

I learned my first game at a birthday party. You remember it: X players scramble for X-minus-one chairs each time the music stops. In every round a child is eliminated until at the end only one is left triumphantly seated while everyone else is standing on the sidelines, excluded from play, unhappy . . . losers.

This is how we learn to have a good time in America.

This article by Alfie Kohn, author of *No Contest: The Case against Competition* (1986) and *The Case against Standardized Testing* (2000), appeared in *Women's Sports and Fitness Magazine* (July–August 1990).

Competition

Warrant

Several years ago I wrote a book called *No Contest*, which, based on the findings of several hundred studies, argued that competition undermines self-esteem, poisons relationships, and holds us back from doing our best. I was mostly interested in the win/lose arrangement that defines our workplaces and classrooms, but I found myself nagged by the following question: If competition is so destructive and counterproductive during the week, why do we take for granted that it suddenly becomes benign and even desirable on the weekend?

This is a particularly unsettling line of inquiry for athletes or parents. Most of us, after all, assume that competitive sports teach all sorts of useful lessons and, indeed, that games by definition must produce a winner and a loser. But I've come to believe that recreation at its best does not require people to try to triumph over others. Quite to the contrary.

Claim or thesis statement

Terry Orlick, a sports psychologist at the University of Ottawa, took a look at musical chairs and proposed that we keep the basic format of removing chairs but change the goal; the point becomes to fit everyone on a diminishing number of seats. At the end, a group of giggling children tries to figure out how to squish onto a single chair. Everybody plays to the end; everybody has a good time.

Support: expert opinion, alternatives to competitive games

Orlick and others have devised or collected hundreds of such games for children and adults alike. The underlying theory is simple: All games involve achieving a goal despite the presence of an obstacle, but nowhere is it written that the obstacle has to be someone else. The idea can be for each person on the field to make a specified contribution to the goal, or for all the players to reach a certain score, or for everyone to work with her partners against a time limit.

Refuting the opposing view

Note the significance of an "opponent" becoming a "partner." The entire dynamic of the game shifts, and one's attitude toward the other players changes with it. Even the friendliest game of tennis can't help but be affected by the game's inherent structure, which demands that each per-

5

son try to hit the ball where the other can't get to it. You may not be a malicious person, but to play tennis means that you try to make the other person fail.

No advantages in competition

I've become convinced that not a single one of the advantages attributed to sports actually requires competition. Running, climbing, biking, swimming, aerobics — all offer a fine workout without any need to try to outdo someone else.

1) Some people point to the camaraderie that results from teamwork, but that's precisely the benefit of cooperative activity, whose very essence is that *everyone* on the field is working together for a common goal. By contrast, the distinguishing feature of team competition is that a given player works with and is encouraged to feel warmly toward only half of those present. Worse, a we-versus-they dynamic is set up, which George Orwell once called "war minus the shooting."

2) The dependence on sports to provide a sense of accomplishment or to test one's wits is similarly misplaced. One can aim instead at an objective standard (How far did I throw? How many miles did we cover?) or attempt to do better than last week. Such individual and group striving — like cooperative games — provides satisfaction and challenge without competition.

If large numbers of people insist that we can't 10 do without win/lose activities, the first question to ask is whether they've ever tasted the alternative. When Orlick taught a group of children noncompetitive games, two-thirds of the boys and all of the girls preferred them to the kind that require opponents. If our culture's idea of fun requires beating someone else, it may just be because we don't know any other way.

3) It may also be because we overlook the psychological costs of competition. Most people lose in most competitive encounters, and it's obvious why that causes self-doubt. But even winning doesn't build character. It just lets us gloat temporarily. Studies have shown that feelings of self-worth become dependent on external sources of evaluation as a result of competition. Your value is defined by what you've done and who you've beaten. The whole affair soon becomes a

vicious circle: The more you compete, the more you *need* to compete to feel good about yourself. It's like drinking salt water when you're thirsty. This process is bad enough for us; it's a disaster for our children.

4) While this is going on, competition is having an equally toxic effect on our relationships. By definition, not everyone can win a contest. That means that each child inevitably comes to regard others as obstacles to his or her own success. Competition leads children to envy winners, to dismiss losers (there's no nastier epithet in our language than "loser!"), and to be suspicious of just about everyone. Competition makes it difficult to regard others as potential friends or collaborators; even if you're not my rival today, you could be tomorrow.

This is not to say that competitors will always detest one another. But trying to outdo someone is not conducive to trust — indeed it would be irrational to trust a person who gains from your failure. At best, competition leads one to look at others through narrowed eyes; at worst, it invites outright aggression.

Changing the Structure of Sports

Conclusion

But no matter how many bad feelings erupt during competition, we have a marvelous talent for blaming the individuals rather than focusing on the structure of the game itself, a structure that makes my success depend on your failure. Cheating may just represent the logical conclusion of this arrangement rather than an aberration. And sportsmanship is nothing more than an artificial way to try to limit the damage of competition. If we weren't set against each other on the court or the track, we wouldn't need to keep urging people to be good sports; they might well be working *with* each other in the first place.

New idea that confirms his claim

As radical or surprising as it may sound, the problem isn't just that we compete the wrong way or that we push winning on our children too early. The problem is competition itself. What we need to be teaching our daughters and sons is that it's possible to have a good time — a better time — without turning the playing field into a battlefield.

15

■ Analysis

The pattern of organization in this essay is primarily a *defense of the main idea*—that competitive sports are psychologically unhealthy. But because the author knows that competitive sports are hugely popular, not only in the United States but in many other parts of the world, he must also try to *refute the opposing view*—that competition is rewarding and enjoyable. In doing so, Kohn fails to make clear distinctions between competitive sports for children, who may find it difficult to accept defeat, and for adults, who understand the consequences of any competitive game and are psychologically equipped to deal with them. Readers may therefore share Kohn's misgivings about competition for children but doubt that his criteria apply equally to adults.

The *claim,* expressed as the *thesis statement* of the essay, appears at the end of paragraph 4: "recreation at its best does not require people to try to triumph over others. Quite to the contrary." The three-paragraph introduction recounts a relevant personal experience as well as the reasons that prompted Kohn to write his essay. Because we are all interested in stories, the recital of a personal experience is a popular device for introducing almost any subject (see "The Childswap Society," p. 343).

The rest of the essay, until the last two paragraphs, is devoted to summarizing the benefits of cooperative play and the disadvantages of competitive sport. The emphasis is overwhelmingly on the disadvantages as stated in the third paragraph: "competition undermines self-esteem, poisons relationships, and holds us back from doing our best." This is the *warrant,* the assumption that underlies the claim. In fact, here Kohn is referring to a larger study that he wrote about competition in workplaces and classrooms. We must accept this broad generalization, which applies to many human activities, before we can agree that the claim about competition in sports is valid.

Kohn relies for support on examples from common experience and on the work of Terry Orlick, a sports psychologist. The examples from experience are ones that most of us will recognize. Here we are in a position to judge for ourselves, without the mediation of an expert, whether the influence of competition in sports is as hurtful as Kohn insists. Orlick's research suggests a solution—adaptations of familiar games that will provide enjoyment but avoid competition. On the other hand, the results from studies by one psychologist whose work we aren't able to verify and the mention of "studies" in paragraph 3 without further attribution are probably not enough to answer all the arguments in favor of competition. Critics may also ask if Kohn has offered support for one of his contentions—that competition "holds us back from doing our best" (para. 3). (Support for this may appear in one of Kohn's books.)

The last two paragraphs sum up his argument that "The problem is competition itself" (para. 15)—the structure of the game rather than the people who play. Notice that this summary does not merely repeat the main idea. Like many thoughtful summaries, it also offers a new idea about good sportsmanship that confirms his conclusion.

The language is clear and direct. Kohn's article, which appeared in a women's sports magazine, is meant for the educated general reader, not the expert. This is also the audience for whom most student papers are written. But the written essay need not be unduly formal. Kohn uses contractions and the personal pronouns "I" and "you" to establish a conversational context. One of the particular strengths of his style is the skillful use of transitional expressions, words like "this" and "also" and clauses like "This is not to say that" and "Note the significance of" to make connections between paragraphs and new ideas.

The tone is temperate despite the author's strong feelings about the subject. Other authors, supporting the same argument, have used language that borders on the abusive about coaches and trainers of children's games. But a less inflammatory voice is far more effective with an audience that may be neutral or antagonistic.

You will find it helpful to look back over the essay to see how the examples we've cited and others work to fulfill the writer's purpose.

RESPONDING AS A CRITICAL LISTENER

Of course, not all public arguments are written. Oral arguments on radio and television now enjoy widespread popularity and influence. In fact, their proliferation means that we listen far more than we talk, read, or write. Today the art of listening has become an indispensable tool for learning about the world we live in. One informed critic predicts that the dissemination of information and opinions through the electronic media will "enable more and more Americans to participate directly in making the laws and policies by which they are governed."[4]

Because we are interested primarily in arguments about public issues—those that involve democratic decision making—we will not be concerned with the afternoon television talk shows that are largely devoted to personal problems. (Occasionally, however, *Oprah* introduces topics of broad social significance.) More relevant to the kinds of written arguments you will read and write about in this course are the television and radio shows that also examine social and political problems. The most intelligent and responsible programs usually consist of a panel of experts—politicians, journalists, scholars—led by a neutral moderator (or one who, at least, allows guests to express their views). Some of these programs are decades old; others are more recent—*Meet the Press, Face the*

[4]Lawrence K. Grossman, *The Electronic Republic: Reshaping Democracy in the Information Age* (New York: Viking, 1995).

Nation, Firing Line, The McLaughlin Group, The NewsHour with Jim Lehrer. An outstanding radio show, *Talk of the Nation* on National Public Radio, invites listeners, who are generally informed and articulate, to call in and ask questions of, or comment on remarks made by, experts on the topic of the day.

Several enormously popular radio talk shows are hosted by people with strong, sometimes extreme ideological positions. They may use offensive language and insult their listeners in a crude form of theater. Among the most influential shows are those of Don Imus and Howard Stern. In addition, elections and political crises bring speeches and debates on radio and television by representatives of a variety of views. Some are long and formal, written texts that are simply read aloud, but others are short and impromptu.

Whatever the merits or shortcomings of individual programs, significant general differences exist between arguments on radio and television and arguments in the print media. These differences include the degree of organization and development and the risk of personal attacks.

First (excluding for the moment the long, prepared speeches), contributions to a panel discussion must be delivered in fragments, usually no longer than a single paragraph, weakened by time constraints, interruptions, overlapping speech, memory gaps, and real or feigned displays of derision, impatience, and disbelief by critical panelists. Even on the best programs, the result is a lack of both coherence — or connections between ideas — and solid evidence that requires development. Too often we are treated to conclusions with little indication of how they were arrived at.

The following brief passage appeared in a newspaper review of "Resolved: The flat tax is better than the income tax," a debate on *Firing Line* by an impressive array of experts. It illustrates some of the difficulties that accompany programs attempting to capture the truth of a complicated issue on television or radio.

> "It is absolutely true," says a proponent. "It is factually untrue," counters an opponent. "It's factually correct," responds a proponent. "I did my math right," says a proponent. "You didn't do your math right," says an opponent. At one point in a discussion of interest income, one of the experts says, "Oh, excuse me, I think I got it backward."

No wonder the television critic called the exchange "disjointed and at times perplexing."[5]

In the sensational talk shows the participants rely on personal experience and vivid anecdotes, which may not be sufficiently typical to prove anything.

Second, listeners and viewers of all spoken arguments are in danger of evaluating them according to criteria that are largely absent from

[5]Walter Goodman, "The Joys of the Flat Tax, Excluding the Equations," *New York Times*, December 21, 1995, sec. C, p. 14.

GUIDELINES TO CRITICAL LISTENING

Listening is hearing with attention, a natural and immensely important human activity, which, unfortunately, many people don't do very well. The good news is that listening is a skill that can be learned and, unlike some other skills, practiced every day without big investments of money and effort.

Here are some of the characteristics of critical listening most appropriate to understanding arguments.

1. Above all, listening to arguments requires concentration. If you are distracted, you cannot go back as you do with the written word to clarify a point or recover a connection. Devices such as flow sheets and outlines can be useful aids to concentration. In following a debate, for example, judges and other listeners often use flow sheets — distant cousins of baseball scorecards — to record the major points on each side and their rebuttals. For roundtable discussions or debates you can make your own simple flow chart to fill out as you listen, with columns for claims, different kinds of support, and warrants. Leave spaces in the margin for your questions and comments about the soundness of the proof. An outline is more useful for longer presentations, such as lectures. As you listen, try to avoid being distracted by facts alone. Look for the overall pattern of the speech.

2. Listeners often concentrate on the wrong things in the spoken argument. We have already noted the distractions of appearance and delivery. Research shows that listeners are likely to give greater attention to the dramatic elements of speeches than to the logical ones. But you can enjoy the sound, the appearance, and the drama of a spoken argument without allowing these elements to overwhelm what is essential to the development of a claim.

3. Good listeners try not to allow their prejudices to prevent careful evaluation of the argument. This doesn't mean accepting everything or even most of what you hear. It means trying to avoid premature judgments about what is actually said. This precaution is especially relevant when the speakers and their views are well known and the listener has already formed an opinion about them, favorable or unfavorable.

evaluation of written texts. It is true that writers may adopt a persona or a literary disguise, which the tone of the essay will reflect. But many readers will not be able to identify it or recognize their own response to it. Listeners and viewers, however, can hardly avoid being affected by characteristics that are clearly definable: a speaker's voice, delivery, bodily mannerisms, dress, and physical appearance. In addition, listeners may be adversely influenced by clumsy speech containing more slang, colloquialisms, and grammar and usage errors than written texts that have had the benefit of revision.

But if listeners allow consideration of physical attributes to influence their judgment of what the speaker is trying to prove, they are guilty of an ad hominem fallacy—that is, an evaluation of the speaker rather than the argument. This is true whether the evaluation is favorable or unfavorable. (See p. 289 for a discussion of this fallacy.)

Talk shows may indeed be disjointed and perplexing, but millions of us find them both instructive and entertaining. Over time we are exposed to an astonishing variety of opinions from every corner of American life, and we also acquire information from experts who might not otherwise be available to us. Then there is the appeal of hearing the voices, seeing the faces of people engaged in earnest, sometimes passionate, discourse — a short, unrehearsed drama in which we also play a part as active listeners in a far-flung audience.

RESPONDING TO A VISUAL ARGUMENT

Man has been communicating by pictures longer than he has been using words. With the development of photography in this century we are using pictures as a means of communication to such an extent that in some areas they overshadow verbal language.[6]

You've probably seen some of the powerful images in photographic journalism to which the author refers: soldiers in battle, destruction by weather disasters, beautiful natural landscapes, inhuman living conditions, the great mushroom cloud of early atomic explosions. These photographs and thousands of others encapsulate arguments of fact, value, and policy. We don't need to read their captions to understand what they tell us: *The tornado devastated the town. The Grand Canyon is our most stupendous national monument. We must not allow human beings to live like this.* The pictures stay with us long after we have forgotten the words that accompanied them.

Photographs, of course, function everywhere as instruments of persuasion. Animal-rights groups show pictures of brutally mistreated dogs and cats; children's rights advocates publish pictures of sick and starving children in desolate refugee camps. On a very different scale, alluring photographs from advertisers — travel agencies, restaurants, sporting goods manufacturers, clothiers, jewelers, movie studios — promise to fulfill our dreams of pleasure.

But photographs are not the only visual images we respond to. We are also susceptible to other kinds of illustrations and to signs and symbols which over the years have acquired connotations, or suggestive significance. The flag or bald eagle, the shamrock, the crown, the cross, the hammer and sickle, and the swastika can all rouse strong feelings for or against the ideas they represent. These symbols may be defined as

---

[6] Paul Wendt, "The Language of Pictures," in S. I. Hayakawa, ed., *The Use and Misuse of Language* (Greenwich, Conn.: Fawcett, 1962), p. 175.

abbreviated claims of value. They summarize the moral, religious, and political principles by which groups of people live and often die. In commercial advertisements we recognize symbols that aren't likely to enlist our deepest loyalties but, nevertheless, have impact on our daily lives: the apple with a bite in it, the golden arches, the Prudential rock, the Nike swoosh, and a thousand others.

In fact, a closer look at commercial and political advertising, which is heavily dependent on visual argument and is something we are all familiar with, provides a useful introduction to this complex subject. We know that advertisements, with or without pictures, are short arguments, often lacking fully developed support, whose claims of policy urge us to take an action: Buy this product or service; vote for this candidate or issue. The claim may not be directly expressed, but it will be clearly implicit. In print, on television, or on the Internet, the visual representation of objects, carefully chosen to appeal to a particular audience, can be as important as, if not more important than, any verbal text.

In a political advertisement, for example, we often see a picture of the candidate surrounded by a smiling family. The visual image is by now a cliché, suggesting traditional values—love and security, the importance of home and children. Even if we know little or nothing about his or her platform, we are expected to make a sympathetic connection with the candidate.

In a commercial advertisement the image may be a picture of a real or fictitious person to whom we will react favorably. Consider the picture on a jar of spaghetti sauce. As a famous designer remarked, "When you think about it, sauce is mostly sauce. It's the label that makes the difference."[7] And what, according to the designer, does the cheerful face of Paul Newman on jars of his spaghetti sauce suggest to the prospective buyer? "Paul Newman. Paul Newman. Paul Newman. Blue eyes. All the money goes to charity. It's humanitarian, funny, and sexy. Selling this is like falling off a log." Not a word about the quality of the sauce.

Even colleges, which are also selling a product, must think of appropriate images to attract their prospective customers—students. Today the fact that more women than men are enrolled in college has caused some schools to rethink their images. One college official explained:

> We're having our recruiting literature redesigned, and we've been thinking about what's a feminine look and what's a masculine look. We have a picture of a library with a lot of stained glass, and people said that was kind of a feminine cover. Now we're using a picture of the quadrangle.[8]

In addition to the emblem itself, the designer pays careful attention to a number of other elements in the ad: colors, light and shadow, fore-

[7] Tibor Kalman, "Message: Sweet-Talking Spaghetti Sauce," *New York Times Magazine,* December 13, 1998, p. 81.

[8] *New York Times,* December 6, 1998, p. 38.

ground and background, relative sizes of pictures and text, and placement of objects on the page or screen. Each of these contributes to the total effect, although we may be unaware of how the effect has been achieved. (In the ad that follows, you will be able to examine some of the psychological and aesthetic devices at work.)

When there is no verbal text, visual images are less subject to analysis and interpretation. For one thing, if we are familiar with the objects in the picture, we see the whole image at once, and it registers immediately. The verbal message is linear and takes far longer to be absorbed. Pictures, therefore, appear to need less translation. Advertisers and other arguers depend on this characteristic to provide quick and friendly acceptance of their claims, although the image may, in fact, be deceptive.

This expectation of easy understanding poses a danger with another visual ally of the arguer—the graph or chart. Graphics give us factual information at a glance. In addition to the relative ease with which they can be read, they are "at their best . . . instruments for reasoning about quantitative information. . . . Of all methods for analyzing and communicating statistical information, well-designed data graphics are usually the simplest and at the same time the most powerful."[9]

Nevertheless, they may mislead the quick reader. Graphics can lie. "The lies are told about the major issues of public policy—the government budget, medical care, prices, and fuel economy standards, for example. The lies are systematic and quite predictable, nearly always exaggerating the rate of recent change."[10]

Visual images, then, for all their apparent immediacy and directness, need to be read with at least the same attention we give to the verbal message if we are to understand the arguments they represent.

Consider these questions as you analyze images:

1. What does the arguer want me to do or believe? How important is the visual image in persuading me to comply?

2. Has the visual image been accompanied by sufficient text to answer questions I may have about the claim?

3. Are the visual elements more prominent than the text? If so, why?

4. Is the visual image representative of a large group, or is it an exception that cannot support the claim?

5. Does the arrangement of elements in the message tell me what the arguer considers most important? If so, what is the significance of this choice?

6. Can the validity of this chart or graph be verified?

[9]Edward R. Tufte, *The Visual Display of Quantitative Information* (Cheshire, Conn.: Graphics Press, 1983), introduction.
[10]Tufte, *The Visual Display,* p. 76.

7. Does the visual image lead me to entertain unrealistic expectations? (Can using this shampoo make hair look like that shining cascade on the television screen? Does the picture of the candidate for governor, shown answering questions in a classroom of eager, smiling youngsters, mean that he has a viable plan for educational reform?)

■ Sample Analysis of an Advertisement

We have pointed out that a commercial advertisement is a short argument that makes an obvious policy claim, which may or may not be explicit: *You should buy this product.* Depending on the medium — television, print, radio, or Internet — an ad may convey its message through language, picture, or sound.

Here is how one analyst of advertising sums up the goals of the advertiser: (1) attract attention, (2) arouse interest, (3) stimulate desire, (4) create conviction, and (5) get action.[11] Needless to say, not every ad successfully fulfills all these objectives. If you examine the ad reproduced on page 51, you can see how the advertiser brings language and visual image together in an attempt to support the claim.

The image in the ad appeals to our common knowledge as Americans. We have probably all heard the story of how George Washington, as a boy, chopped down a cherry tree. The clothes that the young boy in the ad is wearing — particularly the tricorner hat — along with the architecture, suggest a colonial setting. The hatchet hidden behind the boy's back combined with the exclamation "Oops!" calls to mind the specific story about Washington. Upon hearing the story, you may have envisioned a much smaller tree and less substantial damage, but it is critical to the ad's effect that in this rendering of the story of our first president's youth, the tree has fallen on someone's house, possibly the Washingtons'. The ad appears to have been reproduced on parchment, another detail that helps to place the incident historically, and each corner is subtly decorated with a cherry.

What has made the cherry tree story a classic for teaching morals is what the young Washington is said to have done after he chopped down the tree. All of us are familiar with the words "I can not tell a lie," Washington's response when questioned about what he had done. It was a fitting reply for a man who would later be chosen to lead the new nation. The largest text on the page — and the text most likely therefore to catch the attention of a reader casually flipping through *Newsweek* — is a play on this famous quote that changes *I* to *we*. The identification with Washington and his famous words is particularly critical for a company whose name may not be a household word. The designers of the ad, having captured the attention of the reader with the image and the quote, go on in the smaller text to build on the foundation they have established.

[11]J. V. Lund, *Newspaper Advertising* (New York: Prentice-Hall, 1947), p. 83.

Like most ads, this one is a claim of policy asking the audience to buy a product. In this case the product is Encompass Insurance. One of the frustrations of dealing with an insurance company is that not every possible type of loss is covered by the standard policy. Unfortunately, the homeowner often does not find this out until the damage has already been done. The ad is designed to sell the company's *Elite* policy, which "covers many of life's unexpected perils," unlike most insurance companies, which "only cover things that are specifically listed in your policy."

The text continues, "It covers pretty much everything that befalls your household, even if something like 'damage caused by child chopping down cherry tree' isn't specifically listed." Two examples of the sorts of damage that the company might cover are Worker's Compensation for an employee in your household and the recovery of lost computer data.

The support for the claim is not specific. The writer carefully avoided absolute statements, using instead such qualifiers as *many, pretty much,* and *most everything.* The last two are colloquial expressions that are designed to suggest that those who work for Encompass are simple folks with whom the average reader could identify. And if you want any more specifics about what the policy actually says—after all, the legal document that is an insurance policy can hardly use such qualifiers—you can call toll-free or visit the company's Web site.

The underlying warrant is that it is better to buy an insurance policy that covers you against damages that are not specifically listed on the policy than one that does not. A person in the market for insurance would certainly want to read the fine print and know the cost of the insurance compared to that offered by other companies before accepting the warrant and thus the claim.

The colloquial language and even the name of the policy—The Encompass Universal Security Policy—Elite—are designed to appeal to the reader's need to feel secure. The word choice also adds a subtle humor, from the cartoon-like "Oops!" to the final echo of the Pledge of Allegiance: "Liberty, Justice, and Really Good Insurance."

■ Sample Analysis of a Web Site

The Internet provides an important forum for individuals and organizations to make arguments. Through the Internet, anyone with access to a networked computer can potentially publish his or her ideas. While this ease of publication is exciting, it also means writers hoping to obtain reliable information from the Web need to read Web sites critically (see Critical Reading Strategies on page 26 for further insight into this issue).

With new genres being created daily, some researchers[12] have noted five major types of Web pages:

1. *Advocacy Web Pages:* Advocacy pages are typically created by not-for-profit organizations wishing to influence public opinion, and the URL for the site is likely to contain the domain suffix *.org* (organization).

2. *Business/Marketing Web Pages:* The majority of businesses in the United States have a Web presence today, and most business pages are either advertising or provide online opportunities to purchase

[12]See, for example, the Widener University Wolfgram Memorial Library Web site at http://www2.widener.edu/Wolfgram-Memorial-Library/webevaluation/webeval.htm.

goods and services. The addresses for such sites typically contain the domain suffix *.com* (for commercial).

3. *News Web Pages:* News pages provide current information on local, national, and international events. The addresses for news sites also contain the abbreviation *.com,* reflecting the fact that the news industry is also a business.

4. *Informational Web Pages:* Informational pages provide data such as that found in dictionaries or atlases. The addresses for these sites sometimes include *.edu* (university), *.k12* (primary or secondary school), or *.gov* (government) because they are often sponsored by academic institutions or government agencies.

5. *Personal Web Pages:* Personal pages are created by individuals, and can be intimate, entertaining, informative, bizarre, or some combination of these things. While the addresses for personal sites can end in *.com, .edu, .k12, .org,* or *.gov,* the presence of a tilde (~) in the address suggests that the page represents an individual.

On page 54 is a copy of the home page for *The Hunger Site* (a home page introduces and often provides a guide or table of contents for an entire site, which can consist of many pages). At first glance, *The Hunger Site* appears to be a combination informational page (because it contains facts about world hunger) and business/marketing page (because it advertises a variety of products). It is in fact both these things as well as a site for philanthropy (since advertisers' money pays for the food).

The significance of charitable giving to the site's mission is suggested by several things. Maybe most directly, a viewer's eye is immediately drawn to a gold icon reading "GIVE FREE FOOD: Click Here." This icon appears in the center of the home page and draws the eye immediately with its color and placement. It also presents an appealing prospect to readers: that they can be generous by supporting a significant cause and do so without spending money (the food is "free"). When you click on the icon, *The Hunger Site* donates two cups of food (or the financial equivalent) to the hungry.

The emphasis on giving is furthered by a link on the right side of the page that reads "Register Today & Give Up to 8 Extra Cups." As this suggests, readers can register as a member of *The Hunger Site* and donate additional food to hungry people. Directly underneath this is the announcement reading "More Ways To Help: Each purchase made gives up to 50 cups of food." Clicking here offers more opportunities to provide food for others, opportunities linked to purchases made from sponsoring companies.

It is this connection that links *The Hunger Site* to business interests, interests highlighted by the *.com* in the site's URL. Though donations can be given without spending money, the site also links consumer needs and desires to philanthropy by providing visitors the opportunity to support

The Hunger Site Home Page

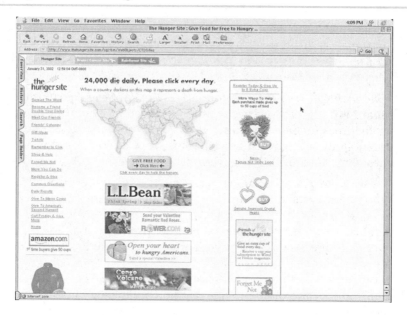

the hungry by purchasing a wide variety of goods—from clothing to flowers to seasonal gifts and decorations. Consumer givers, then, can feel good that the money they are spending is contributing to a valuable cause. In return, site sponsors, companies such as L.L. Bean who help subsidize the donations made to the hungry, receive advertising and gain new customers. In this way, viewers feel inspired to shop more, meaning that *The Hunger Site* has the potential to bind together corporate interests, consumer interests, and international benevolence.

In many ways, then, *The Hunger Site* reads like a traditional advertisement. It appeals to customers because it represents an easy way to do something socially responsible. To develop customer loyalty, businesses and organizations strive for "brand recognition," and *The Hunger Site* is no exception. It uses a golden strand of wheat as its logo. Gold, symbolizing both wheat and true value, is the color of the central icon that allows browsers to contribute food with a single click.

However, while *The Hunger Site* incorporates many traditional methods in appealing to its readers, it also makes use of Web technology. Directly above the "GIVE FREE FOOD" icon is a map that reflects deaths from hunger under the headline "24,000 die daily. Please click every day," and every few seconds a different country on the map darkens to represent a death from hunger. The print statistic that "24,000 die daily" is supplemented by this graphic reminder, of what it means for so many thousands to die every day. Viewers cannot help noticing the slow and steady stream of blackening countries, which make an abstract number more real.

The Hunger Site Thank You Page

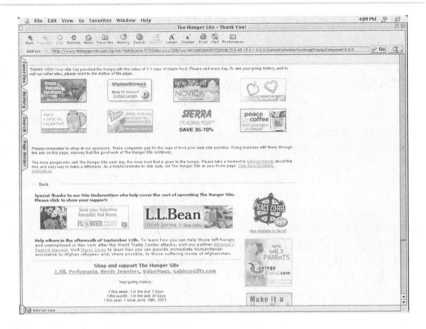

Interactivity is further displayed in the way the site acknowledges its readers' influence and importance. For example, the menu on the left-hand side of the home page begins with four links that directly involve visitor participation. The first, which reads "Spread the Word," opens onto a page that gives viewers the opportunity to e-mail friends an electronic form letter with prewritten statistics and information provided by *The Hunger Site*. However, viewers are also encouraged to personalize the e-mail with their own thoughts and ideas about the significance of *The Hunger Site*. In this way, viewers become coauthors of a letter with the authors of the site. Other icons acknowledge and celebrate "friends" of *The Hunger Site*. Becoming a friend of the site can be accomplished virtually instantaneously, and friends are then able to enter the "Friends' Gateway," which offers unique opportunities for both purchasing and giving. The value of this option is also made more real because it involves an actual locking out of those who have not attained the status of friends.

The emphasis on the immediacy of this interaction between reader and text can also be seen in the features that allow readers of the site to keep track of their giving by clicking on the link that reads "See your giving history at the bottom of our Thank You page." This displays up-to-the-minute statistics regarding the number of clicks the viewer has made, making the visitor feel like a carefully accounted for participant in the fight against hunger. In addition, the "Remember to Click" and "Forget Me Not" features bind viewers to the site. If viewers sign up for the

"Remember to Click" option, an e-mail reminder regularly reminds them to visit the site and click to give food. The "Forget Me Not" option reminds the computer user whenever he or she begins to shop online to shop through *The Hunger Site*. Visitors can choose these options, and they can always be dismantled once they are chosen, giving individuals control over how they are marketed to and connected to the Web site.

Distinguishing *The Hunger Site* from traditional print text is its embeddedness in a "web" of other pages. *The Hunger Site* links directly to pages that provide additional information about the site as well as sales and charitable giving opportunities. Some pages are official parts of *The Hunger Site;* others such as *Second Harvest,* which receives donations from *The Hunger Site,* are separate sites.

One aim of a comprehensive Web site is to provide answers to questions about the site. Unlike a print advertisement, *The Hunger Site* has enough space to provide, for example, information about the site owners and answers to frequently asked questions (FAQ) about the site. Readers interested in more information on *The Hunger Site* can do a general search of the Web to determine the legitimacy of the site.

Although it consists of multiple pages, *The Hunger Site* is also different from printed articles and books because it does not follow any traditional sense of order. Readers typically start on the site's home page, but from there they can go in multiple directions, each one equally logical. The authors of *The Hunger Site* have not determined a set path for readers to follow: Viewers can find information about world hunger, about hunger in the United States, about the owners of the site, about ways of providing food to the hungry, and about bargains at L.L. Bean or Patagonia. The reader is in control of the direction to be taken in the text, and the possible directions are numerous and cater to multiple needs.

RESPONDING ONLINE

You have learned that writers need the responses of readers and other writers to improve their writing. As the influence of computers permeates our society and more people rely on the Internet to send e-mail, it has become ever easier for writers to distribute their writing and for readers to respond to it. Only a decade ago, if you wanted feedback for your writing, you had to either read it aloud to others or copy and distribute it by hand or postal mail. Both methods were cumbersome and time-consuming, even expensive. Electronic networks now allow your writing to be distributed almost instantaneously to dozens or even thousands of readers with virtually no copying or mailing costs. Readers can respond to you just as quickly and cheaply. Even though there can be pitfalls and problems with communicating online, the overall ease of use encourages writers to seek, and readers to provide, editorial feedback.

■ Guidelines for Responding Online

You know that in face-to-face conversation the words themselves constitute only a part of your message. Much of what you say is communicated through your body language and tone of voice. Written words provide a much narrower channel of communication, which is why you must be more careful when you write to others than when you speak directly to them. Electronic writing, however, especially through e-mail, fosters a casualness and immediacy that often fools writers into assuming they are talking privately rather than writing publicly. Online you may find yourself writing quickly, carelessly, and intimately; without the help of your tone and body language, you may end up being seriously misunderstood. Words written hastily are often read much differently than intended; this is especially true when the writer attempts an ironic or sarcastic tone. For example, if a classmate walks up to you with a critical comment about one of your sentences and you respond by saying "I didn't realize you were so smart," the words, if unaccompanied by a placating smile and a pleasant, jocular tone, may come across as sarcastic or hostile. In e-writing, the same words appear without the mitigating body language and may be perceived as harsh, possibly insulting. You must keep this danger in mind as you respond online or risk alienating your reader.

Keep in mind, too, that e-mail may be read not only by your addressee but also by anyone with whom the addressee chooses to share your message. An intemperate or indiscreet message may be forwarded to other classmates or your instructor, or, depending on the limits of the system, to many other readers whom you do not know.

Experienced online communicators advocate a set of network etiquette guidelines called *Netiquette*. Here are some generally accepted Netiquette rules:

- Keep your sentences short and uncomplicated.

- Separate blocks of text—which should be no more than four or five lines long—by blank lines. For those rare occasions when a comment requires more than ten or fifteen consecutive lines of text, use subheadings on separate lines to guide your reader.

- Refer specifically to the text to which you are responding. You may want to quote directly from it, cutting and pasting phrases or sentences from the document to help show exactly what you are responding to.

- Greet the person(s) to whom you are writing politely and by name.

- Be wary about attempting to be funny. Humor, as just explained, often requires a context, tone of voice, and body language to emphasize that it is not to be taken seriously. Writing witty comments that are sure to be taken humorously calls for skill and care, and e-mail messages usually are written too quickly for either.

- Avoid profanity or invective, and be wary of brusque or abrupt statements. Consider how you would feel if someone wrote to you that way.

- Avoid discussion of politics or religion unless that is the specific topic of your message.

- Do not ridicule public figures. Your reader may not share your opinions of, say, Senator Edward Kennedy or radio talk show host Rush Limbaugh.

- Frame all comments in a helpful, not critical, tone. For instance, rather than beginning a critique with "I found a number of problems in your text," you may want to start out more like this: "You have some good ideas in this paper, and with a few changes I think it will do well."

DOCUMENTING YOUR SOURCES

Chapter 10 will explain in detail how to use both the Modern Language Association (MLA) and the American Psychological Association (APA) systems for citing publications. In the meantime, if you need to refer in your writing to one or more works that you have read, here is an overview of the basics.

Writer's Guide: Documenting Use of Summary, Paraphrase, and Quotation

1. The single most important thing to remember is why you need to inform your reader about your use of sources. Once it is clear from your writing that an idea or some language came from a source and thus is not your own original thought or language, full documentation provides the reader with a means of identifying and, if necessary, locating your source. If you do not indicate your source, your reader will naturally assume that the ideas and the language are yours. It is careless to forget to give credit to your sources. It is dishonest to intentionally take credit for what is not your own intellectual property.

2. One of the most common mistakes that student writers make is to think that material needs to be documented only if they use another author's own words. In fact, you must give credit for any *ideas* you get from others, not only for wording you get from them.

3. You must identify the author and the location of ideas that you summarize. A *summary* is the condensing of a longer passage into a shorter

one using your own words. You will use summary often in your academic writing when you want to report briefly on an idea covered at greater length in your source.

4. You must identify the author and the location of ideas that you paraphrase. A *paraphrase* is a rewording of another author's idea into your own words. A paraphrased passage is roughly the same length as the original.

5. You must identify the author and the location of the ideas that you quote. A *quotation* is the copying of the exact wording of your source and is placed in quotation marks. Remember that *exact* means just that. You cannot change anything inside quotation marks with these exceptions: (1) If there is a portion of the quotation that is not relevant to the point that you are trying to make and that can be omitted without distorting the author's meaning, you may indicate an omission of a portion of the quote with an ellipsis (. . .). If there is a sentence break within the portion you are omitting, you add a fourth period to the ellipsis to so indicate. (2) If you need to make a very slight change in the quote to make the quote fit grammatically into your own text or to avoid confusion and if the change does not distort the author's meaning, you may make that slight change and place the changed portion in brackets ([ ]). This method is used primarily to change the tense of a quoted passage to match that of your text or to identify a person identified in the quotation only by a pronoun.

6. Both the MLA and the APA system make use of in-text or parenthetical documentation. That means that while a complete bibliographical listing for each work summarized, paraphrased, or quoted in your text is included in a works cited list at the end of your paper, each is also identified exactly at the point in the text where you use the source. If you are using the MLA system of documentation, the system most commonly used in the humanities, immediately following the sentence in which you use material from a source you need to add in parentheses the author's name and the page number on which the material you are using appeared in the original source. However, since the credibility of your sources is critical in argumentative writing, it is even better to name the source in your own sentence and to identify the position or experience that makes that person a reliable source for the subject being discussed. In that case, you do not need to repeat the author's name in the parentheses. In fact, any time the author's name is clear from the context, you do not need to repeat it in the parentheses.

Acceptable: The mall has been called "a common experience for the majority of American youth" (Kowinski 117).

Better: According to William Severini Kowinski, author of *The Malling of America,* "The mall is a common experience for the majority of American youth" (Kowinski 117).

In the APA system, the system most commonly used in the social sciences, in-text or parenthetical documentation is handled a bit differently because the citation includes the year of publication. The most basic forms are these:

The mall has been called "a common experience for the majority of American youth" (Kowinski, 1985, p. 117).

Kowinski (1985) writes, "The mall is a common experience for the majority of American youth" (p. 117).

7. Remember that these examples show only the most basic form for documenting your sources. Some works will have more than one author. Sometimes you will be using more than one work by the same author. Usually Web sites do not have page numbers. Long quotations need to be handled differently from short ones. For all questions about documenting your use of sources not covered here, see Chapter 10.

Note: If you are writing about an essay in this book, you have a slightly more complicated situation than if you were looking at the essay in its original place of publication. Unless your instructor indicates otherwise, use the page numbers on which the essay appears in this textbook when summarizing, paraphrasing, or quoting from it instead of going back to the page numbers of the original. Also, unless your instructor indicates otherwise, use this model for listing in your works cited page an essay reprinted here:

Kowinski, William Severini. "Kids in the Mall: Growing Up Controlled." *The Malling of America: An Inside Look at the Great Consumer Paradise.* New York: Morrow, 1985. Rpt. in *Elements of Argument: A Text and Reader.* Annette T. Rottenberg and Donna Haisty Winchell. 8th ed. Boston: Bedford, 2006. 116–21.

ASSIGNMENTS FOR RESPONDING TO ARGUMENT

1. Choose an editorial of at least two paragraphs from your school paper or another newspaper on a controversial subject that interests you. The title will probably reveal the subject. Annotate the editorial as you read, questioning, agreeing, objecting, offering additional ideas. (The annotation of "The Pursuit of Whining," p. 27, will suggest ways of doing this, although your personal responses are what make the annotation useful.) Then read the editorial again. You should discover that annotating the article caused you to read more carefully, more critically, with greater comprehension and a more focused response.

2. Summarize the claim of the editorial in one sentence. Omit the supporting data and concentrate on the thesis. Then explain briefly your reaction to it. Has the author proved his or her point? Your annotation will show

you where you expressed doubt or approval. If you already know a good deal about the subject, perhaps you will be reasonably confident of your judgment. If not, you may find that your response is tentative and that you need to read further for more information about the subject and to consult guidelines for making evaluations about the elements of argument.

3. Summarize in one or two paragraphs one of the Classic Arguments. Include and document correctly at least one direct quotation from the reading. Remember to remain objective and not to interject your opinion into the summary.

4. People sometimes object to lectures as an educational tool. Think about some of the specific lectures you have listened to recently, and analyze the reasons that you liked or disliked them (or liked some aspects and disliked others). Do you think that you learned everything that the lecturer intended you to learn? If the results were doubtful, how much did your listening skills, good or bad, contribute to the result? Should the lecturer have done something differently to improve your response?

5. Watch (and *listen* to) one of the afternoon talk shows like *Oprah Winfrey* in which audiences discuss a controversial social problem. (The *TV Guide* and daily newspapers often list the subject. Past topics on *Oprah* include when parents abduct their children and when children kill children.) Write a critical review of the discussion, mentioning as completely as you can the major claims, the most important evidence, and the declared or hidden warrants. (Unspoken warrants or assumptions may be easier to identify in arguments on talk shows where visual and auditory clues can reveal what participants try to hide.) How much did the oral format contribute to success or failure of the argument(s)?

6. Listen to one of the television talk shows that feature invited experts. Write a review, telling how much you learned about the subject(s) of discussion. Be specific about the elements of the show that were either helpful or unhelpful to your understanding.

7. Listen with a friend or friends to a talk show discussion. Take notes as you listen. Then compare notes to discover if you agree on the outstanding points, the degree to which claims have been supported, and the part that seeing or hearing the discussion played in your evaluation. If there is disagreement about any of the elements, how do you account for it?

8. With three or four of your classmates select an argumentative essay in this book that all of you agree to read. Each of you should draft a response to the essay, either agreeing or disagreeing with the author's position, citing evidence to support your position. Then each of you prepare a letter soliciting a response to your draft from the members of your group. For example, you may want to state what your objective was, suggest what you think are the strengths and weaknesses of the draft, and ask what sort of revisions seem appropriate. E-mail the letter and the draft to each of your peer responders. Based on their comments, which should either be e-mailed to you or handwritten on a printed copy of your draft, revise your draft.

CHAPTER 3

Definition

Before we examine the other elements of argument, we need to consider definition, a component you may have to deal with early in writing an essay. Definition may be used in two ways: to clarify the meanings of vague or ambiguous terms or as a method of development for the whole essay. In some arguments your claims will contain words that need explanation before you can proceed with any discussion. But you may also want to devote an entire essay to the elaboration of a broad concept or experience that cannot be adequately defined in a shorter space.

The Roman statesman Cicero said, "Every rational discussion of anything whatsoever should begin with a definition in order to make clear what is the subject of dispute." You have probably already discovered the importance of definition in argument. If you have ever had a disagreement with your parents about using the car or drinking or dyeing your hair or going away for a weekend or staying out till three in the morning, you know that you were really arguing about the meaning of the term *adolescent freedom*.

Arguments often revolve around definitions of crucial terms. For example, how does one define *democracy*? Does a democracy guarantee freedom of the press, freedom of worship, freedom of assembly, and freedom of movement? In the United States, we would argue that such freedoms are essential to any definition of *democracy*. But countries in which these freedoms are nonexistent also represent themselves as democracies or governments of the people. In the words of Senator Daniel P. Moynihan, "For years now the most brutal totalitarian regimes have called themselves 'people's' or 'democratic' republics." Rulers in such governments are aware that defining their regimes as democratic may win the approval of people who would otherwise condemn them. In his formidable attack on totalitarianism, *1984*, George Orwell coined the slogans "War Is Peace" and "Slavery Is Freedom," phrases that represent the corrupt use of definition to distort reality.

But even where there is no intention to deceive, the snares of definition are difficult to avoid. How do you define *abortion*? Is it "termination of pregnancy"? Or is it "murder of an unborn child"? During a celebrated trial in 1975 of a physician who performed an abortion and was accused of manslaughter, the prosecution often used the word *baby* to refer to the fetus, but the defense referred to "the products of conception." These definitions of *fetus* reflected the differing judgments of those on opposite sides. Not only do judgments create definitions; definitions influence judgments. In the abortion trial, the definitions of *fetus* used by both sides were meant to promote either approval or disapproval of the doctor's action.

Definitions can indeed change the nature of an event or a "fact." How many farms are there in the state of New York? The answer to the question depends on the definition of *farm*. In 1979 the *New York Times* reported:

> Because of a change in the official definition of the word "farm," New York lost 20 percent of its farms on January 1, with numbers dropping from 56,000 to 45,000. . . .
> Before the change, a farm was defined as "any place from which $250 or more of agricultural products is sold" yearly or "any place of 10 acres or more from which $50 or more of agricultural products is sold" yearly. Now a farm is "any place from which $1,000 or more of agricultural products is sold" in a year.[1]

A change in the definition of *poverty* can have similar results. An article in the *New York Times*, whose headline reads, "A Revised Definition of Poverty May Raise Number of U.S. Poor," makes this clear.

> The official definition of *poverty* used by the Federal Government for three decades is based simply on cash income before taxes. But in a report to be issued on Wednesday, a panel of experts convened by the [National] Academy of Sciences three years ago at the behest of Congress says the Government should move toward a concept of poverty based on disposable income, the amount left after a family pays taxes and essential expenses.[2]

[1] *New York Times*, March 4, 1979, sec. 1, p. 40.
[2] *New York Times*, April 10, 1995, sec. A, p. 1.

The differences are wholly a matter of definition. But such differences can have serious consequences for those being defined, most of all in the disposition of billions of federal dollars in aid of various kinds. In 1992 the Census Bureau classified 14.5 percent of Americans as poor. Under the new guidelines, at least 15 or 16 percent would be poor, and, under some measures recommended by a government panel, 18 percent would be so defined.

In fact, local and federal courts almost every day redefine traditional concepts that can have a direct impact on our everyday lives. The definition of *family*, for example, has undergone significant changes that acknowledge the existence of new relationships. In January 1990 the New Jersey Supreme Court ruled that a family may be defined as "one or more persons occupying a dwelling unit as a single nonprofit housekeeping unit, who are living together as a stable and permanent living unit, being a traditional family unit or the *functional equivalent* thereof" (italics for emphasis added). This meant that ten Glassboro State College students, unrelated by blood, could continue to occupy a single-family house despite the objection of the borough of Glassboro.[3] Even the legal definition of maternity has shifted. Who is the mother—the woman who contributes the egg or the woman (the surrogate) who bears the child? Several states, acknowledging the changes brought by medical technology, now recognize a difference between the birth mother and the legal mother.

DEFINING THE TERMS IN YOUR ARGUMENT

In some of your arguments you will introduce terms that require definition. We've pointed out that a definition of *poverty* is crucial to any debate on the existence of poverty in the United States. The same may be true in a debate about the legality of euthanasia, or mercy killing. Are the arguers referring to passive euthanasia (the withdrawal of life-support systems) or to active euthanasia (the direct administration of drugs to hasten death)?

It is not uncommon, in fact, for arguments about controversial questions to turn into arguments about the definition of terms. If, for example, you wanted to argue in favor of the regulation of religious cults, you would first have to define *cult*. In so doing, you might discover that it is not easy to distinguish clearly between conventional religions and cults. Then you would have to define *regulation*, spelling out the legal restrictions you favored so as to make them apply only to cults, not to established religions. An argument on the subject might end almost before it began if writer and reader could not agree on definitions of these terms. While clear definitions do not guarantee agreement, they do ensure that all parties understand the nature of the argument.

[3] *New York Times*, February 1, 1990, sec. B, p. 5.

■ Defining Vague and Ambiguous Terms

You will need to define other terms in addition to those in your claim. If you use words and phrases that have two or more meanings, they may appear vague and ambiguous to your reader. In arguments of value and policy abstract terms such as *freedom, justice, patriotism,* and *equality* require clarification. Despite their vagueness, however, they are among the most important in the language because they represent the ideals that shape our laws. When conflicts arise, the courts must define these terms to establish the legality of certain practices. Is the Ku Klux Klan permitted to make disparaging public statements about ethnic and racial groups? That depends on the court's definition of *free speech.* Can execution for some crimes be considered cruel and unusual punishment? That, too, depends on the court's definition of *cruel and unusual punishment.* In addition, such terms as *happiness, mental health, success,* and *creativity* often defy precise definition because they reflect the differing values within a society or a culture.

The definition of *success,* for example, varies not only among social groups but also among individuals within the group. One scientist has postulated five signs by which to measure success: wealth (including health), security (confidence in retaining the wealth), reputation, performance, and contentment.[4] Consider whether all of these are necessary to your own definition of *success.* If not, which may be omitted? Do you think others should be added? Notice that one of the signs—reputation—is defined by the community; another—contentment—can be measured only by the individual. The assessment of performance probably owes something to both the group and the individual.

Christopher Atkins, an actor, gave an interviewer an example of an externalized definition of success—that is, a definition based on the standards imposed by other people:

> Success to me is judged through the eyes of others. I mean, if you're walking around saying, "I own a green Porsche," you might meet somebody who says, "Hey, that's no big deal. I own a green Porsche and a house." So all of a sudden, you don't feel so successful. Really, it's in the eyes of others.[5]

So difficult is the formulation of a universally accepted measure for success that some scholars regard the concept as meaningless. Nevertheless, we continue to use the word as if it represented a definable concept because the idea of success, however defined, is important for the identity and development of the individual and the group. It is clear, however, that when crossing subcultural boundaries, even within a small group, we need to be aware of differences in the use of the word. If contentment—that is, the satisfaction of achieving a small personal goal—is enough,

---

[4] Gwynn Nettler, *Social Concerns* (New York: McGraw-Hill, 1976), pp. 196–97.
[5] *New York Times,* August 6, 1982, sec. 3, p. 8.

then a person lying under a palm tree subsisting on handouts from pic-
nickers may be a success. But you should not expect all your readers to
agree that these criteria are enough to define *success.*

In arguing about aesthetic matters, whose vocabulary is almost always abstract, the criteria for judgment must be revealed, either directly
or indirectly, and then the abstract terms that represent the criteria must
be defined. If you want to say that a film is distinguished by great acting,
have you made clear what you mean by *great?* That we do not always understand or agree on the definition of *great* is apparent, say, on the morning after the Oscar winners have been announced.

Even subjects that you feel sure you can identify may offer surprising
insights when you rethink them for an extended definition. One critic,
defining *rock music,* argued that the distinguishing characteristic of rock
music was noise — not beat, not harmonies, not lyrics, not vocal style, but
noise, "nasty, discordant, irritating noise — or, to its practitioners, unfettered, liberating, expressive noise."[6] In producing this definition, the author had to give a number of examples to prove that he was justified in
rejecting the most familiar criteria.

Consider the definition of *race,* around which so much of American
history has revolved, often with tragic consequences. Until recently, the
only categories listed in the census were white, black, Asian-Pacific, and
Native American, "with the Hispanic population straddling them all." But
rapidly increasing intermarriage and ethnic identity caused a number of
political and ethnic groups to demand changes in the classifications of
the Census Bureau. Some Arab Americans, for example, prefer to be
counted as "Middle Eastern" rather than white. Children of black-white
unions are defined as black 60 percent of the time, while children of
Asian-white unions are described as Asian 42 percent of the time. Research is now being conducted to discover how people feel about the
terms being used to define them. As one anthropologist pointed out, "Socially and politically assigned attributes have a lot to do with access to
economic resources."[7]

METHODS FOR DEFINING TERMS

The following strategies for defining terms in an argument are by no
means mutually exclusive. You may use all of them in a single argumentative essay.

---

[6]Jon Pareles, "Noise Evokes Modern Chaos for a Band," *New York Times,* March 9,
1986, sec. H, p. 26.

[7] *Wall Street Journal,* September 9, 1995, sec. B, p. 1.

■ Dictionary Definition

Giving a dictionary definition is the simplest and most obvious way to define a term. An unabridged dictionary is the best source because it usually gives examples of the way a word can be used in a sentence; that is, it furnishes the proper context.

In many cases, the dictionary definition alone is not sufficient. It may be too broad or too narrow for your purpose. Suppose, in an argument about pornography, you wanted to define the word *obscene*. *Webster's New International Dictionary* (third edition, unabridged) gives the definition of *obscene* as "offensive to taste; foul; loathsome; disgusting." But these synonyms do not tell you what qualities make an object or an event or an action "foul," "loathsome," and "disgusting." In 1973 the Supreme Court, attempting to narrow the definition of *obscenity*, ruled that obscenity was to be determined by the community in accordance with local standards. One person's obscenity, as numerous cases have demonstrated, may be another person's art. The celebrated trials in the early twentieth century about the distribution of novels regarded as pornographic—D. H. Lawrence's *Lady Chatterley's Lover* and James Joyce's *Ulysses*—emphasized the problems of defining obscenity.

Another dictionary definition may strike you as too narrow. *Patriotism,* for example, is defined in one dictionary as "love and loyal or zealous support of one's country, especially in all matters involving other countries." Some readers may want to include an unwillingness to support government policies they consider wrong.

■ Stipulation

In stipulating the meaning of a term, the writer asks the reader to accept a definition that may be different from the conventional one. He or she does this to limit or control the argument. Someone has said, "Part of the task of keeping definitions in our civilization clear and pure is to keep a firm democratic rein on those with the power, or craving the power, to stipulate meaning." Perhaps this writer was thinking of a term like *national security,* which can be defined by a nation's leaders in such a way as to sanction persecution of citizens and reckless military adventures. Likewise, a term such as *liberation* can be appropriated by terrorist groups whose activities often lead to oppression rather than liberation.

Religion is usually defined as a belief in a supernatural power to be obeyed and worshiped. But in an article entitled "Civil Religion in America," a sociologist offers a different meaning.

> While some have argued that Christianity is the national faith, and others that church and synagogue celebrate only the generalized religion of "the American way of life," few have realized that there actually exists alongside of and rather clearly differentiated from the churches an elaborate and well-institutionalized civil religion in America. This

article argues not only that there is such a thing, but also that this religion . . . has its own seriousness and integrity and requires the same care in understanding that any other religion does.[8]

When the author adds, "This religion—there seems no other word for it—was neither sectarian nor in any specific sense Christian," he emphasizes that he is distinguishing his definition of religion from definitions that associate religion and church.

Even the word *violence,* which the dictionary defines as "physical force used so as to injure or damage" and whose meaning seems so clear and uncompromising, can be manipulated to produce a definition different from the one normally understood by most people. Some pacifists refer to conditions in which "people are deprived of choices in a systematic way" as "institutionalized quiet violence." Even where no physical force is employed, this lack of choice in schools, in the workplace, in the black ghettos is defined as violence.[9]

In *Through the Looking-Glass* Alice asked Humpty Dumpty "whether you can make words mean so many different things."

> "When *I* use a word," Humpty Dumpty said scornfully, "it means just what I choose it to mean—neither more nor less."[10]

A writer, however, is not free to invent definitions that no one will recognize or that create rather than solve problems between writer and reader.

■ Negation

To avoid confusion it is sometimes helpful to tell the reader what a term is *not.* In discussing euthanasia, a writer might say, "By euthanasia I do not mean active intervention to hasten the death of the patient."

A negative definition may be more extensive, depending on the complexity of the term and the writer's ingenuity. The critic of rock music quoted earlier in this chapter arrived at his definition of *noise* by rejecting attributes that seemed misleading. The former Communist party member Whittaker Chambers, in a foreword to a book on the spy trial of Alger Hiss, defined *communism* this way:

> First, let me try to say what Communism is not. It is not simply a vicious plot hatched by wicked men in a subcellar. It is not just the writings of Marx and Lenin, dialectical materialism, the Politburo, the labor theory of value, the theory of the general strike, the Red Army

---

[8] Robert N. Bellah, "Civil Religion in America," *Daedalus*, Winter 1967, p. 1.
[9] Newton Garver, "What Violence Is," in James Rachels, ed., *Moral Choices* (New York: Harper and Row, 1971), pp. 248–49.
[10] Lewis Carroll, *Alice in Wonderland and Through the Looking-Glass* (New York: Grosset and Dunlap, 1948), p. 238.

secret police, labor camps, underground conspiracy, the dictatorship of the proletariat, the technique of the coup d'état. It is not even those chanting, bannered millions that stream periodically, like disorganized armies, through the heart of the world's capitals: Moscow, New York, Tokyo, Paris, Rome. These are expressions, but they are not what Communism is about.[11]

This, of course, is only part of the definition. Any writer beginning a definition in the negative must go on to define what the term *is*.

■ Examples

One of the most effective ways of defining terms in an argument is to use examples. Both real and hypothetical examples can bring life to abstract and ambiguous terms. The writer in the following passage defines *preferred categories* (classes of people who are meant to benefit from affirmative action policies) by invoking specific cases:

> The absence of definitions points up one of the problems with preferred categories. . . . These preferred categories take no account of family wealth or educational advantages. A black whose father is a judge or physician deserves preferential treatment over any nonminority applicant. The latter might have fought his way out of the grinding poverty of Appalachia, or might be the first member of an Italian American or a Polish American family to complete high school. But no matter.[12]

Insanity is a word that has been used and misused to describe a variety of conditions. Even psychiatrists are in dispute about its meaning. In the following anecdote, examples narrow and refine the definition.

> Dr. Zilboorg says that present-day psychiatry does not possess any satisfactory definition of mental illness or neurosis. To illustrate, he told a story: A psychiatrist was recently asked for a definition of a "well-adjusted person" (not even slightly peculiar). The definition: "A person who feels in harmony with himself and who is not in conflict with his environment." It sounded fine, but up popped a heckler. "Would you then consider an anti-Nazi working in the underground against Hitler a maladjusted person?" "Well," the psychiatrist hemmed, "I withdraw the latter part of my definition." Dr. Zilboorg withdrew the first half for him. Many persons in perfect harmony with themselves, he pointed out, are in "distinctly pathological states."[13]

■ Extended Definition

When we speak of an extended definition, we usually refer not only to length but also to the variety of methods for developing the definition.

---

[11]*Witness* (New York: Random House, 1952), p. 8.
[12]Anthony Lombardo, "Quotas Work Both Ways," *U.S. Catholic*, February 1974, p. 39.
[13]Quoted in *The Art of Making Sense*, p. 48.

Let's take the word *materialism*. A dictionary entry offers the following sentence fragments as definitions: "1. the doctrine that comfort, pleasure, and wealth are the only or highest goals or values. 2. the tendency to be more concerned with material than the spiritual goals or values." But the term *materialism* has acquired so many additional meanings, especially emotional ones, that an extended definition serves a useful purpose in clarifying the many different ideas surrounding our understanding of the term.

Below is a much longer definition of *materialism*, which appears at the beginning of an essay entitled "People and Things: Reflections on Materialism."[14]

> There are two contemporary usages of the term *materialism*, and it is important to distinguish between them. On the one hand we can talk about *instrumental materialism*, or the use of material objects to make life longer, safer, more enjoyable. By instrumental, we mean that objects act as essential means for discovering and furthering personal values and goals of life, so that the objects are instruments used to realize and further those goals. There is little negative connotation attached to this meaning of the word, since one would think that it is perfectly sensible to use things for such purposes. While it is true that the United States is the epitome of materialism in this sense, it is also true that most people in every society aspire to reach our level of instrumental materialism.
>
> On the other hand the term has a more negative connotation, which might be conveyed by the phrase terminal materialism. This is the sense critics use when they apply the term to Americans. What they mean is that we not only use our material resources as instruments to make life more manageable, but that we reduce our ultimate goals to the posses- sion of things. They believe that we don't just use our cars to get from place to place, but that we consider the ownership of expensive cars one of the central values in life. Terminal materialism means that the object is valued only because it indicates an end in itself, a possession. In instrumental materialism there is a sense of directionality, in which a person's goals may be furthered through the interactions with the ob- ject. A book, for example, can reveal new possibilities or widen a person's view of the world, or an old photograph can be cherished be- cause it embodies a relationship. But in terminal materialism, there is no sense of reciprocal interaction in the relation between the object and the end. The end is valued as final, not as itself a means to further ends. And quite often it is only the status label or image associated with the object that is valued, rather than the actual object.

In the essay from which this passage is taken, the authors distinguish be- tween two kinds of materialism and provide an extended explanation, using contrast and examples as methods of development. They are aware that the common perception of materialism—the love of things for their

---

[14]Mihaly Csikszentmihalyi and Eugene Rochberg-Halton, "People and Things: Reflections on Materialism," *University of Chicago Magazine*, Spring 1978, pp. 7–8.

own sake—is a negative one. But this view, according to the authors, doesn't fully account for the attitudes of many Americans toward the things they own. There is, in fact, another more positive meaning that the authors call *instrumental materialism*. You will recognize that the authors are *stipulating* a meaning with which their readers might not be familiar. In their essay they distinguish between *terminal materialism*, in which "the object is valued only because it indicates an end in itself," and *instrumental materialism*, "the use of material objects to make life longer, safer, more enjoyable." Since *instrumental materialism* is the less familiar definition, the essay provides a great number of examples that show how people of three different generations value photographs, furniture, musical instruments, plants, and other objects for their memories and personal associations rather than as proof of the owners' ability to acquire the objects or win the approval of others.

THE DEFINITION ESSAY

The argumentative essay can take the form of an extended definition. An example of such an essay is the one from which we've just quoted, as well as the essays at the end of this chapter. The definition essay is appropriate when the idea under consideration is so controversial or so heavy with historical connotations that even a paragraph or two cannot make clear exactly what the arguer wants his or her readers to understand. For example, if you were preparing a definition of *patriotism*, you would probably use a number of methods to develop your definition: personal narrative, examples, stipulation, comparison and contrast, and cause-and-effect analysis.

Writer's Guide: Writing a Definition Essay

The following important steps should be taken when you write an essay of definition.

1. Choose a term that needs definition because it is controversial or ambiguous, or because you want to offer a personal definition that differs from the accepted interpretation. Explain why an extended definition is necessary. Or choose an experience that lends itself to treatment in an extended definition. One student defined *culture shock* as she had experienced it while studying abroad in Hawaii among students of a different ethnic background.

2. Decide on the thesis — the point of view you wish to develop about the term you are defining. If you want to define *heroism*, for example, you

may choose to develop the idea that this quality depends on motivation and awareness of danger rather than on the specific act performed by the hero.

3. Begin by consulting the dictionary for the conventional definition. Make clear whether you want to elaborate on the dictionary definition or take issue with it because you think it is misleading or inadequate.

4. Distinguish wherever possible between the term you are defining and other terms with which it might be confused. If you are defining *love*, can you make a clear distinction between the different kinds of emotional attachments contained in the word?

5. Try to think of several methods of developing the definition — using examples, comparison and contrast, analogy, cause-and-effect analysis. However, you may discover that one method alone — say, use of examples — will suffice to narrow and refine your definition. See the sample essay "The Nature of Prejudice" on page 80 for an example of such a development.

6. Arrange your supporting material in an order that gives emphasis to the most important ideas.

SAMPLE ANNOTATED ESSAY

Cloning Misperceptions

LEE M. SILVER

Why do four out of five Americans think that human cloning is "against God's will" or "morally wrong"? Why are people so frightened by this technology? One important reason is that many people have a muddled sense of what cloning is. They confuse the popular meaning of the word *clone* and the specific meaning it takes on in the context of biology.

Part of the confusion about cloning is confusion about definitions

Reason #1 for fear

In its popular usage, *clone* refers to something that is a duplicate, or cheaper imitation, of a brand-name person, place, or thing. The British

Lee M. Silver is a professor of molecular biology at Princeton University. This essay is from *Remaking Eden: Cloning and Beyond in a Brave New World* (1997).

The popular image of cloning

"Actual cloning technology"

Different definitions of "life" are also a source of confusion

Reason #2 for fear

politician Tony Blair has been called a clone of Bill Clinton, and an IBM PC clone is not only built like an IBM PC, it *behaves* like an IBM PC. It is this popular meaning of the word that caused many people to believe that human cloning would copy not just a person's body but a person's consciousness as well. This concept of cloning was at the center of the movie *Multiplicity*, which was released just months before the Dolly announcement. In it, a geneticist makes a clone of the star character played by Michael Keaton and explains that the clone will have "all of his feelings, all of his quirks, all of his memories, right up to the moment of cloning." The clone himself says to the original character, "You are me, I am you." It is this image that Jeremy Rifkin probably had in mind when he criticized the possible application of the sheep cloning technology to humans by saying, "It's a horrendous crime to make a Xerox (copy) of someone."

But this popular image bears absolutely no resemblance to actual cloning technology, in either process or outcome. Scientists cannot make full-grown adult copies of any animal, let alone humans. All they can do is start the process of development over again, using genetic material obtained from an adult. Real biological cloning can only take place at the level of the cell — life *in the general sense*. It is only long after the cloning event is completed that a unique — and independent — life *in the special sense* could emerge in the developing fetus. Once again, it is the inability of many people to appreciate the difference between the two meanings of "life" that is the cause of confusion.

A second reason people fear cloning is based on the notion that a clone is an imperfect imitation of the real thing. This causes some people to think that — far from having the same soul as someone else — a clone would have no soul at all. Among the earliest popular movies to explore this idea was *Blade Runner*, in which synthetic people were produced that were just like humans in all respects but one — they had no empathy. (Coincidentally, *Blade Runner* was based on a 1968 book by Philip K. Dick entitled *Do Androids Dream of*

*Examples of popular
images of cloning*

Electric Sheep?) And the same general idea of im-perfection is explored in *Multiplicity* when a clone of the Michael Keaton character has himself cloned. The clone of the clone is a dimwitted clown because, as the original clone says, "Some-times you make a copy of a copy and it's not as sharp as the original."

The Irvine, California, rabbi Bernard King was 5 seriously frightened by this idea when he asked, "Can the cloning create a soul? Can scientists cre-ate the soul that would make a being ethical, moral, caring, loving, all the things we attribute humanity to?" The Catholic priest Father Saun-ders suggested that "cloning would only produce humanoids or androids—soulless replicas of human beings that could be used as slaves." And Brent Staples, a member of the *New York Times* editorial board, warned that "synthetic hu-mans would be easy prey for humanity's worst instincts."

Yet there is nothing synthetic about the cells used in cloning. They are alive before the cloning process, and they are alive after fusion has taken place. The newly created embryo can only de-velop inside the womb of a woman in the same way that all embryos and fetuses develop. Cloned children will be full-fledged human beings, indis-tinguishable in biological terms from all other members of the species. Thus, the notion of a soulless clone has no basis in reality.

*Attempt to dispel fear
that clones would not
have souls*

*His definition of a
clone*

When the misperceptions are tossed aside, it becomes clear what a cloned child will be. She, or he, will simply be a later-born identical twin—nothing more and nothing less. And while she may go through life looking similar to the way her progenitor-parent looked at a past point in time, she will be a unique human being, with a completely unique consciousness and a unique set of memories that she will build from scratch.

To many people, the mere word *clone* seems ominous, conjuring up images from movies like *The Boys from Brazil* with evil Nazis intent on rul-ing the world. How likely is it that governments or organized groups will use cloning as a tool to build future societies with citizens bred to fulfill a particular need?

A key question

The *Brave New World* Scenario

Quotation from
Huxley's novel Brave
New World

"Bokanovsky's Process," repeated the director. . . . One egg, one embryo, one adult—normality. But a bokanovskified egg will bud, will proliferate, will divide. From eight to ninety-six buds, and every bud will grow into a perfectly formed embryo, and every embryo into a full-sized adult. Making ninety-six human beings grow where only one grew before. Progress. . . . Identical twins—but not in piddling twos and threes as in the old viviparous days, when an egg would sometimes accidentally divide; actually by dozens, by scores at a time. . . . "But, alas," the Director shook his head, "we can't bokanovskify indefinitely." Ninety-six seemed to be the limit; seventy-two a good average.

Thus did Aldous Huxley present one of the technological underpinnings of his brave new world where cloning would be used "as one of the major instruments of social stability." With cloning, it was possible to obtain "standard men and women; in uniform batches. The whole of a factory staffed with the products of a single bokanovskified egg."

Brave New World evoked powerful feelings 10 within people not only because they could see inklings of the rigid conformity of the brave new world society within their own, but because the science was presented in a hyperrealistic manner. Even the most minor technical details were carefully described.

Huxley, for one, was convinced that political forces would evolve in the direction he described. In the foreword to the 1946 edition, he wrote: "It is probable that all the world's governments will be more or less completely totalitarian even before the harnessing of atomic energy; that they will be totalitarian during and after the harnessing seems almost certain." It was the *science* that he was less certain of.

Yet, like so many other twentieth-century intellectuals, Huxley underestimated the power of technology to turn yesterday's fantasy into today's reality. Only sixty-four years after he speculated on the possibility of human cloning, it is on the verge of happening. But now that one aspect of science has caught up to *Brave New World,* what can we say about the politics? Will there be governments that choose to clone?

Definitely not in a democratic society for a very simple reason. Cloned children cannot appear out of the air. Each one will have to develop within the womb of a woman (for the time being). And in a free society, the state cannot control women's bodies and minds in a way that would be necessary to build an army of clones.

But what about a totalitarian government that wanted to produce clones to serve its own social needs: "Standard men and women; in uniform batches. The whole of a factory staffed with the products of a single bokanovskified egg."

This scenario is highly improbable. First, only 15 an extremely controlling totalitarian state would have the ability to enslave women en masse to act as surrogate mothers for babies that would be forcibly removed and raised by the state. Ruling governments this extreme are rare at the end of the twentieth century. But even if one did emerge, it is hard to imagine why it would want to clone people.

Would it be to produce an army of powerful soldiers? Any government that could clone would certainly get more fighting power out of high-tech weapons of destruction than even the most muscular and obedient soldier clones.

Would it be to produce docile factory workers? Cloning is not necessary for this objective, which has already been reached throughout many societies. And mind control could be achieved much more effectively with New Age drugs targeted at particular behaviors and emotions (another prediction made by Huxley).

Would it be to produce people with great minds? It is not clear how a government would choose a progenitor for such clones, or what it would do during the twenty years or so that it took for clones to mature into adults. After all that time, a new set of leaders might decide that the wrong characteristics had been chosen for cloning. A better approach would be to simply build a superior system of public education that allowed the brightest children to rise to the top, no matter where on society's ladder they began their lives.

In the end, one is hard-pressed to come up with a single strategic advantage that any government might get from breeding clones rather than allowing a population to regenerate itself naturally. Thus, the Huxleyan use of cloning as a means for building a stable society seems very unlikely. But there is an obvious exception—one that could occur in a state or society controlled by a single egomaniacal dictator with substantial financial and scientific resources.

Example of an exception

The example that comes to mind is that of the 20 Japanese cult leader Shoko Asahara. Asahara's group, Aum Shinrikyo, included well-educated chemists who produced nerve gas for the purpose of holding the Japanese government hostage. The group was exposed, and their leader was arrested and put on trial after a lethal gas attack on the Tokyo subway system in March 1995. Based on what we have learned about the group, it is possible that it might have had both the financial and technical resources required to put together the facility and equipment needed for cloning, as well as the power of persuasion required to convince skilled personnel to carry it out. And the aura that Asahara projected was such that he might well have succeeded in convincing women to become pregnant with his clones. Finally, Asahara himself seems to have been exactly the kind of egomaniac who would have preferred child clones over naturally conceived sons.

I doubt that we could stop people like Shoko Asahara from cloning themselves. But would it make any difference? Let us imagine that Asahara had cloned himself into a dozen children. It seems extremely unlikely that these children would have any greater effect on society, twenty years down the road, than sons conceived the old-fashioned way. It's not only that they wouldn't grow up in the same adverse environment that played an important role in turning Asahara into the cult leader that he became. It's also that they would grow up among different people who would be unlikely to respond to them

Another extreme example

in exactly the same way that people responded to Asahara. The same could be said for modern-day clones of Adolf Hitler. In both cases, the original men were catapulted into positions of leadership through chance personal or historical events that will never repeat themselves. An adult alive today with Adolf Hitler's mind, personality, and behavior would be more likely to find himself barricaded in a militia outpost or in jail than in the White House or the German Bundesrat.

Unstated claim of fact: It is highly unlikely that governments will ever make use of cloning to control the breeding of their citizens.

While Hitler's Third Reich and Asahara's Aum Shinrikyo were both short-lived phenomena, there are still examples of royal families—albeit with little real power today—that have handed down the crown from parent to child over hundreds of years. If after ascending to the throne, Prince Charles of Great Britain decided to place his clone—rather than his eldest son—next in line, would that upset the world order? On the contrary, I doubt if anyone would care.

■ Analysis

Although Silver is a professor of molecular biology, this essay is from a book published in 1997 with a lay audience rather than his fellow specialists in mind. The title of the book, *Remaking Eden: Cloning and Beyond in a Brave New World*, includes at the same time a reference to the Garden of Eden of Biblical fame and a reference to the 1932 novel *Brave New World* by Aldous Huxley. Silver later refers to Huxley's novel in a section heading and quotes from it. Readers familiar with that novel know that it is about a world gone awry due to man's tinkering with the natural human reproductive process. When a character named John the Savage, one of the few human beings allowed to develop naturally, without scientific intervention, cries out the quotation from Shakespeare "O brave new world, that has such people in it!" he is being ironic because he has had a glimpse of a world that no longer even knows that Shakespeare ever existed—a world supposedly without pain and suffering, but one that he loathes because it is also a world without feelings. On the other hand, the main title, *Remaking Eden*, suggests the possibility of rediscovering the idyllic life lived by the first man and woman before they disobeyed God's command and ate of the fruit of the Tree of the Knowledge of Good and Evil. There seems to be the suggestion that if humanity erred by wanting to know too much, it may yet be possible to attain once more—or remake—what was lost. The title of the essay, "Cloning Misperceptions," alerts Silver's readers to the fact that he feels that cloning is misunderstood. His goal in the essay is to correct some of the misperceptions to which the title refers. In his first sentence he acknowledges that 80 percent of his audience are likely to see cloning as wrong.

As any good arguer does, Silver makes clear how is he using his key term *clone*. In fact, he begins the essay by pointing out that many of the misperceptions about cloning come about because of the confusion between the popular meaning of the term and the more specialized one used by biologists. He also points out at the end of the third paragraph that people are often confused by two different meanings of the word *life*. To explain that cloning is not the same as Xeroxing a person, he writes, "Real biological cloning can only take place at the level of the cell—life *in the general sense*. It is only long after the cloning event is complete that a unique—and independent—life *in the special sense* could emerge in the developing fetus" [his italics].

In the opening paragraph of his extended definition, Silver is making use of a technique often used in definition: He is telling his readers what cloning is *not*. He is taking issue not with the dictionary definition of the term but with the popular notion of cloning. He makes use of examples from movies to show how the fictionalized images of cloning in them differ from the reality. What all of the examples have in common is that they show cloning in some way gone wrong.

The first section of Silver's extended definition is clearly organized around the two reasons he feels people fear cloning. Near the end of that section, he most clearly states his definition of a cloned child: "She, or he, will simply be a later-born identical twin—nothing more and nothing less." He ends that first section with a question which he attempts to answer in the next section, the one headed "The *Brave New World* Scenario": "How likely is it that governments or organized groups will use cloning as a tool to build future societies with citizens bred to fulfill a particular need?"

If Huxley believed that governments would use cloning to control citizens, Silver does not. If Huxley perhaps overestimated the willingness of governments to use cloning, he underestimated the ability of science to make such cloning possible. Silver's answer to the question whether there will be governments that choose to clone, however, is, "Definitely not in a democratic society." He is appealing to his readers' need to feel secure in their ability to maintain control of their own bodies when he points out that a cloned fetus cannot yet develop outside the body of the human female. (In Huxley's novel, it can.)

Much of the rest of Silver's essay is organized around a series of questions and answers. Here he is appealing to his readers' reason as he questions what advantage there could be for even the most totalitarian state in producing masses of identical clones. He concludes with the rare examples of two extreme individuals who might have been egomaniacal enough to try. He once again appeals to his readers' need for security when he points out how unlikely it would be for the conditions to be right for such extreme individuals to make their plan work.

Silver's unstated claim is a claim of fact: It is highly unlikely that governments will ever make use of cloning to control the breeding of their citizens.

READINGS FOR ANALYSIS

The Nature of Prejudice

GORDON ALLPORT

Before I attempt to define *prejudice*, let us have in mind four instances that I think we all would agree are prejudice.

The first is the case of the Cambridge University student who said, "I despise all Americans. But," he added, a bit puzzled, "I've never met one that I didn't like."

The second is the case of another Englishman, who said to an American, "I think you're awfully unfair in your treatment to Negroes. How *do* Americans feel about Negroes?" The American replied, "Well, I suppose some Americans feel about Negroes just the way you feel about the Irish." The Englishman said, "Oh, come now. The Negroes are human beings."

Then there's the incident that occasionally takes place in various parts of the world (in the West Indies, for example, I'm told). When an American walks down the street the natives conspicuously hold their noses till the American goes by. The case of odor is always interesting. Odor gets mixed up with prejudice because odor has great associative power. We know that some Chinese deplore the odor of Americans. Some white people think Negroes have a distinctive smell and vice versa. An intrepid psychologist recently did an experiment; it went as follows. He brought to a gymnasium an equal number of white and colored students and had them take shower baths. When they were nice and clean he had them exercise vigorously for fifteen minutes. Then he brought his judges in, and each went to the sheeted figures and sniffed. They were to say "white" or "black," guessing at the identity of the subject. The experiment seemed to prove that when we are sweaty we all smell the same way. It's good to have experimental demonstration of the fact.

Gordon Allport (1897–1967) was a psychologist who taught at Harvard University from 1924 until his death. He was the author of numerous books, among them *Personality: A Psychological Interpretation* (1937). Allport delivered "The Nature of Prejudice" at the Seventeenth Claremont Reading Conference in 1952. The speech was published as a paper in 1952 in the Seventeenth Claremont Reading Conference Yearbook.

The fourth example I'd like to bring before you is a piece of writing 5
that I quote. Please ask yourselves who, in your judgment, wrote it. It's a
passage about the Jews.

> The synagogue is worse than a brothel. It's a den of scoundrels. It's a
> criminal assembly of Jews, a place of meeting for the assassins of Christ,
> a den of thieves, a house of ill fame, a dwelling of iniquity. Whatever
> name more horrible to be found, it could never be worse than the syna-
> gogue deserves.
>   I would say the same things about their souls. Debauchery and
> drunkenness have brought them to the level of lusty goat and pig. They
> know only one thing: to satisfy their stomachs and get drunk, kill, and
> beat each other up. Why should we salute them? We should not even
> have the slightest converse with them. They are lustful, rapacious,
> greedy, perfidious robbers.

Now who wrote that? Perhaps you say Hitler, or Goebbels, or one of
our local anti-Semites? No, it was written by Saint John Chrysostom, in
the fourth century A.D. Saint John Chrysostom, as you know, gave us the
first liturgy in the Christian church, still used in the Orthodox churches
today. From it all services of the Holy Communion derive. Episcopalians
will recognize him also as the author of that exalted prayer that closes the
offices of both matins and evensong in the *Book of Common Prayer.* I include this incident to show how complex the problem is. Religious people
are by no means necessarily free from prejudice. In this regard be patient
even with our saints.

What do these four instances have in common? You notice that all of
them indicate that somebody is "down" on somebody else—a feeling of
rejection, or hostility. But also, in all these four instances, there is indication that the person is not "up" on his subject—not really informed
about Americans, Irish, Jews, or bodily odors.

So I would offer, first a slang definition of prejudice: *Prejudice is being
down on somebody you're not up on.* If you dislike slang, let me offer the
same thought in the style of St. Thomas Aquinas. Thomists have defined
prejudice as *thinking ill of others without sufficient warrant.*

You notice that both definitions, as well as the examples I gave, specify two ingredients of prejudice. First there is some sort of faulty generalization in thinking about a group. I'll call this the process of
categorization. Then there is the negative, rejective, or hostile ingredient,
a *feeling* tone. "Being down on something" is the hostile ingredient; "that
you're not up on" is the categorization ingredient; "thinking ill of others"
is the hostile ingredient; "without sufficient warrant" is the faulty categorization.

Parenthetically I should say that of course there is such a thing as *pos-* 10
itive prejudice. We can be just as prejudiced *in favor of* as we are *against.*
We can be biased in favor of our children, our neighborhood, or our college. Spinoza makes the distinction neatly. He says that *love prejudice* is

"thinking well of others, through love, more than is right." *Hate prejudice,* he says, is "thinking ill of others, through hate, more than is right."

READING AND DISCUSSION QUESTIONS

1. This was a speech, obviously not delivered extemporaneously but read to the audience. What characteristics suggest an oral presentation? If you were to revise this essay into a paper, what changes would you make? Why?

2. Allport has arranged his anecdotes carefully. What principle of organization has he used?

3. Allport says that "'thinking ill of others' is the hostile ingredient; 'without sufficient warrant' is the faulty categorization" (para. 9). How would you define the word *warrant* in this part of Allport's definition? How is it related to the definition given on page 11?

4. This essay was written in 1952. Are there any references or examples that seem dated? Why or why not?

WRITING SUGGESTIONS

5. Some media critics claim that negative prejudice exists in the treatment of certain groups in movies and television: If you agree, select a group that seems to you to be the object of prejudice in these media, and offer evidence of the prejudice and the probable reasons for it. Or disagree with the media critics, and provide evidence that certain groups are *not* the object of prejudice.

6. Can you think of examples of what Allport calls *positive prejudice*? Perhaps you can find instances that are less obvious than the ones Allport mentions. Explain in what way these prejudices represent a love that is "more than is right" (para. 10).

Race by the Numbers

ORLANDO PATTERSON

In recent weeks, reporting and commentary that misinterpret early census results have been persistently misinforming the nation about its ethnic and racial composition. The misinformation is dangerous, since it fuels fears of decline and displacement among some whites, anxieties that are not only divisive but groundless. The Center for Immigration Studies, for example, a think tank in Washington, recently warned that by the middle of the century non-Hispanic whites will cease to be a majority and

Orlando Patterson is a professor of sociology at Harvard and the author of *Rituals of Blood*, the second volume of a trilogy on race relations.

that "each group in the new minority-majority country has longstanding grievances against whites."

Many articles have echoed the view that whites are fast becoming a minority in many areas of the country, largely because of the growth of the Hispanic population. The *New York Times* reported that seventy-one of the top 100 cities had lost white residents and made clear only in the third paragraph of the article that it is really "non-Hispanic whites" who are now a minority in these cities. Similarly, the *Miami Herald* reported that 20 cities and unincorporated communities in Miami-Dade county "went from majority to minority white, non-Hispanic." Left without commentary was the fact that the total white population—including Hispanic whites—of Miami, for example, is actually a shade under 70 percent.

These articles and too many others have failed to take account of the fact that nearly half of the Hispanic population is white in every social sense of this term; 48 percent of so-called Hispanics classified themselves as solely white, giving only one race to the census taker. Although all re-ports routinely note that "Hispanics can be of any race," they almost al-ways go on to neglect this critical fact, treating Hispanics as if they were, in fact, a sociological race comparable to "whites" and "blacks."

In any case, the suggestion that the white population of America is fast on the way to becoming a minority is a gross distortion. Even if we view only the non-Hispanic white population, whites remain a robust 69.1 percent of the total population of the nation. If we include Hispanic whites, as we should, whites constitute 75.14 percent of the total popula-tion, down by only 5 percent from the 1990 census. And this does not take account of the 6.8 million people who identified in the census with "two or more races," 80 percent of whom listed white as one of these races.

Even with the most liberal of assumptions, there is no possibility that whites will become a minority in this nation in this century. The most re-cent census projections indicate that whites will constitute 74.8 percent of the total population in 2050, and that non-Hispanic whites will still be 52.8 percent of the total. And when we make certain realistic sociological assumptions about which groups the future progeny of Hispanic whites, mixed couples, and descendants of people now acknowledging two or more races are likely to identify with, there is every reason to believe that the non-Hispanic white population will remain a substantial majority— and possibly even grow as a portion of the population.

Recent studies indicate that second-generation Hispanic whites are intermarrying and assimilating mainstream language and cultural pat-terns at a faster rate than second-generation European migrants of the late nineteenth and early twentieth centuries.

The misleading reports of white proportional decline are likely not only to sustain the racist fears of white supremacist groups but also to affect the views of ordinary white, nonextremist Americans. A false

assumption that whites are becoming a minority in the nation their ancestors conquered and developed may be adding to the deep resentment
of poor or struggling whites toward affirmative action and other policies
aimed at righting the wrongs of discrimination.

How do we account for this persistent pattern of misinformation?
Apart from the intellectually lazy journalistic tendency to overemphasize
race, two influences are playing into the discussion.

One is the policy of the Census Bureau itself. Though on the one
hand, the census has taken the progressive step of allowing citizens to
classify themselves in as many racial ways as they wish, breaking up the
traditional notion of races as immutable categories, on the other hand it
is up to its age-old mischief of making and unmaking racial groups. As it
makes a new social category out of the sociologically meaningless collection of peoples from Latin America and Spain, it is quietly abetting the
process of demoting and removing white Hispanics from the "true" white
race — native-born non-Hispanic whites.

There is a long history of such reclassification by federal agencies. In the 10
early decades of the twentieth century, the Irish, Italians, and Jews were
classified as separate races by the federal immigration office, and the practice was discontinued only after long and vehement protests from Jewish
leaders. In 1930 Mexicans were classified as a separate race by the Census
Bureau — which reclassified them as white in 1940, after protests. Between then and the 1960s, people from Latin America were routinely classified as whites; then, when vast numbers of poor immigrants began
coming from Latin America, the Hispanic category emerged.

The first stage of racial classification, now nearly successfully completed for Hispanics, is naming and nailing them all together while disingenuously admitting that they can be "of any race." Next, the repeated
naming and sociological classification of different groups under a single
category inevitably leads to the gradual perception and reconstruction of
the group as another race. Much the same process of racialization is
taking place with that other enormous sociological nongroup, Asian
Americans.

The other influence on perceptions of who is "white" originates
among the so-called Hispanics. For political and economic reasons, including the benefits of affirmative action programs, the leadership of
many Hispanic groups pursues a liberal, coalition-based agenda with
African Americans and presses hard for a separate, unified Latino classification. This strategy is highly influential even though nearly half of Hispanics consider themselves white.

For African Americans, the nation's major disadvantaged minority,
these tendencies are problematic, although African American leaders are
too shortsighted to notice. Latino coalition strategies, by vastly increasing
the number of people entitled to affirmative action, have been a major
factor in the loss of political support for it. And any fear of a "white"

group that it might lose status tends to reinforce stigmatization of those Americans who will never be "white."

In this volatile transitional situation, where the best and worst are equally possible in our racial relations and attitudes, the very worst thing that journalists, analysts and commentators can do is to misinform the white majority that it is losing its majority status—something that recent surveys indicate it is already all too inclined to believe. We should stop obsessing on race in interpreting the census results. But if we must compulsively racialize the data, let's at least keep the facts straight and the interpretations honest.

READING AND DISCUSSION QUESTIONS

1. Where does Patterson state his claim?
2. What subtitles can you provide for the different parts of his argument? The topic sentences in several paragraphs offer clues to the organization.
3. According to Patterson, how is the matter of definition relevant to statistics about race?
4. Patterson's claim is strongly supported by statistics, history, and political analysis. Do you think these different kinds of support are equally persuasive? Which one is most susceptible to challenge? Why?
5. What is Patterson's objection to the definitions of *Hispanic* and *non-Hispanic* that are published by the Census Bureau and other agencies?

WRITING SUGGESTIONS

6. Narrate an experience you have had in which you felt you were either aided or hindered by the fact that you were defined as a member of a specific group. It could be a group such as those defined by gender, race, religious affiliation, or membership on a team or in a club.
7. Would adoption at the state level of a policy prohibiting classifying people by race, color, ethnicity, or national origin be beneficial or pernicious for the individual and for society? In other words, what is good or bad about classifying people?
8. Find a subject in which definition is critical to how statistics are interpreted and which can be argued successfully in a 750- to 1,000-word paper. Your essay should provide proof for a claim. (Patterson uses numbers to prove that whites need not fear that their numbers are declining.) Other subjects that depend on statistical support can be found throughout this book.

Family a Symbol of Love and Life, but Not Politics

ERIC ZORN

*F*amily is one of our loveliest words. It speaks of a warm, enveloping, comforting, inspiring connection—a love relationship, a commitment, a safe harbor, a common enterprise.

Sometimes, sure, it's a messy and maddening entanglement. But even when it's imperfect, family is the foundation of identity and the cornerstone of success.

To many people—people of all faiths, orientations, and political beliefs—"family" is the word that expresses that which they hold most dear.

Not money. Not possessions. Not fame. Not career. Not country. Not friendship. Not romance. Not even freedom.

Family.   5

So it's time we took it back.

Sorry, Family PAC and Illinois Family Institute.

You, too, Focus on the Family, Family Research Council, Family Foundation, Pro-Family Network, American Family Association, and Culture and Family Institute.

Set that word down and back away slowly. It belongs to all of us.

You and other conservative organizations have monopolized it for 10 too long, turned it into shorthand for a social and political outlook that excludes rather than includes, and hectors those who don't, can't, or won't conform to your notions of morality.

"Family values" has come to mean the promotion of abstinence-only sex education, religion in the public sphere, education vouchers, traditional gender roles, and censorship. It's come to mean opposition to abortion rights and, particularly these days, resistance to the extension of full civil rights to gays and lesbians.

In covering the landmark beginning of legal gay marriages in Massachusetts last week, virtually every news organization featured the fulminations of officials from the Massachusetts Family Institute ("The piece of paper that says 'marriage' has been redefined and devalued!"), while Peter LaBarbera, executive director of the Illinois Family Institute ("A man marrying another man is a far cry from Rosa Parks!"), has become the go-to guy for local journalists seeking quotes from opponents of gay marriage.

The irony is that gay weddings mark an endorsement of family—of the power of that formal and lasting bond.

Eric Zorn is a columnist for the *Chicago Tribune,* where this essay was first published on May 23, 2004, and coauthor of *Murder of Innocence* (1990).

When two people get married, they are saying to society, "Yes! We believe in the fundamental importance of this institution in building and maintaining family ties. We want to join it and affirm that belief to the world."

And when a culture expands its definition of marriage to include the 15
expressions of lifelong commitment between two people of the same sex, it strengthens families by advancing the acceptance and tolerance of gay people.

Not every parent is as accepting of his gay child as Chicago Alderman Richard Mell, whose personal and political support for his daughter, who is a lesbian, has become a local legend. But the more our society loses its judgmental attitude about who loves whom and what sorts of unions are most normal, the closer we get to the day when extended families no longer are ripped apart by homosexuality.

I could argue that strengthening families is why we need to provide quality day care for working parents, why we need to work hard to maintain strict government neutrality in matters of faith, and why we should offer nonideological sex education to children and reproductive choice to women.

I could make the case that it reflects good family values to shift more of the tax burden to the rich, to support stem cell medical research and universal health care, to devote our energies to boosting public education, and to protect our natural environment against industrial polluters.

I could, but I won't.

"Family" is too important to too many of us to drag its name through 20
the muck of our bitter sociopolitical debates, let alone to yield it to one side or the other in the culture wars.

No one owns it. The left doesn't own peace and compassion, the right doesn't own the flag or the family.

The word "family" resonates profoundly in all of us—married, single, gay, straight, adopted, "biological," living alone or in crowded households bursting with the exuberant chaos of children. To have family, to be family with others, is to be fully human.

Mom always taught me to share. So, shall we?

READING AND DISCUSSION QUESTIONS

1. Where does Zorn most directly define the term *family*?
2. What does he mean when he says that we need to take family back? From whom?
3. How has the definition of the word *family* been politicized?
4. How do gay marriages expand the definition of family, according to Zorn?
5. What strategy is Zorn using when he tells his readers what he could argue, but won't?
6. What claim is Zorn supporting in the essay?

WRITING SUGGESTIONS

7. Even if you do not support same-sex marriage, do you believe that the definition of marriage is changing? Explain.

8. Explain whether or not you agree with this statement by Zorn: "And when a culture expands its definition of marriage to include the expressions of lifelong commitment between two people of the same sex, it strengthens families by advancing the acceptance and tolerance of gay people."

Don't Torture English to Soft-Pedal Abuse

GEOFFREY NUNBERG

"Torture is torture is torture," Secretary of State Colin Powell said this week in an interview on *Fox News Sunday* with Chris Wallace.

That depends on what papers you read. The media in France, Italy, and Germany have been routinely using the word "torture" in the headings of their stories on the abuses in the Abu Ghraib prison. And so have the British papers, not just the left-wing *Guardian* ("Torture at Abu Ghraib") but the right-wing *Express* ("Outrage at U.S. Torture of Prisoners") and Rupert Murdoch's *Times* ("Inside Baghdad's Torture Jail").

But the American press has been more circumspect, sticking with vaguer terms such as "abuse" and "mistreatment." In that, they may have been taking a cue from Defense Secretary Donald Rumsfeld. Asked about torture in the prison, he said, "What has been charged so far is abuse, which is different from torture. I'm not going to address the 'torture' word."

Some on the right have depicted the abuses even more mildly than that. In an opinion piece in the Los Angeles *Times*, Midge Decter called the treatment of detainees a "nasty hazing." Rush Limbaugh said it was "no different than what happens at the Skull and Bones initiation." On a San Francisco radio station, shock jocks were describing the prison as "Abu Grab-Ass" and talking about the treatment in a ribald way that made it sound like *Animal House III—Bluto Bonks Baghdad.*

Some American media have avoided "the 'torture' word" because   5 they want to play down the abuse of prisoners. Others are nervous about provoking attacks from the moral equivalence police: "Are you suggesting we're as bad as they are?"

Geoffrey Nunberg is a consulting professor in Stanford University's Department of Linguistics, the author of the book *Going Nucular* (2004), and a featured radio commentator. This essay was adapted from a piece he did on NPR's *Fresh Air*, that appeared in *Newsday* in May 2004.

But to a lot of Americans, *torture* and *torturer* don't seem quite the right words for the scenes in those photos. Torture may be familiar in the modern world, but it's also remote; we only see it up close in the movies. *Torture* suggests an aestheticized ritual. It doesn't seem odd that the torture scenes in *Battle of Algiers* should have a Bach chorale in the background.

In the movies, the torturer's cruelty is ironically counterpoised by a cosmopolitan and often effete manner—Laurence Olivier in *Marathon Man*, Gert Frobe in *Goldfinger*, or the Mohammed Khan character in *Lives of a Bengal Lancer* telling Gary Cooper, "We have ways of making men talk."

There are no middle-class middle-American torturers in our gallery, much less torturers with the pudding faces of those GIs who could have been working at McDonald's a year ago. And the humiliations they were inflicting didn't seem to have much in common with the rituals of pain and submission that *torture* brings to mind. The GIs went down another road, even if it fell off just as sharply.

That's what creates the sense of incongruity we feel when we see those photos. Those may have been far from Delta House high jinks, but you wouldn't know it from the clowning poses the GIs were striking.

True, "hazing" is a shamefully dishonest name for this. Leaving aside   10 the severity of the abuses, the prisoners weren't in a position to resign from the club, nor were they about to be given membership pins when pledge week was over. You may as well say that the Los Angeles police were hazing Rodney King.

But what went on in Abu Ghraib has at least this in common with

By Gary Varvel, *The Indianapolis Star,* Creators Syndicate

hazing: It's the sort of thing that any adolescent with a normal libido might be capable of—or worse, if the circumstances permit. As the Stanford psychologist Phil Zimbardo showed in a famous experiment more than thirty years ago, it doesn't take a lot to transform a group of well-mannered college students into sadistic prison guards, provided someone in authority seems to be giving them the nod.

Granted, what the Americans did in Abu Ghraib isn't remotely comparable to what went on there during Saddam Hussein's regime.

But it was torture, not just by the definitions of the Geneva Conventions, but by any ordinary standards of decency. Torture is torture is torture, as Secretary Powell put it—it isn't a place to be drawing fine semantic distinctions.

And it would be a good thing to acknowledge that "torture" is not quite as exotic an activity as the movies make it out to be. Looking at the unsettlingly familiar faces of the American soldiers in the Abu Ghraib photos, you realize that what can be most disturbing isn't the brutality that is inhuman so much as the brutality that is all too.

READING AND DISCUSSION QUESTIONS

1. Nunberg argues that the media control, to a certain extent at least, how the public perceive events. Besides the treatment of prisoners at Abu Ghraib prison in Iraq, how have the media exerted control over public perceptions?

2. What is Nunberg referring to when he makes this statement: "Others are nervous about provoking attacks from the moral equivalence police: 'Are you suggesting we're as bad as they are?'"

3. What is it that creates the sense of incongruity in the pictures from Abu Ghraib to which Nunberg refers?

4. In what sense was what went on at Abu Ghraib similar to hazing, although Nunberg calls hazing "a shamefully dishonest name for this"?

5. Explain what you believe Nunberg means by his last sentence.

WRITING SUGGESTIONS

6. Choose an event other than the Abu Ghraib scandal that was widely publicized and explain to what extent you feel the media controlled public perceptions of the event.

7. Write an essay in which you explain how governments sometimes hide the full truth behind euphemisms and other careful word choices. You may want to compare your ideas about language use with those expressed by George Orwell in his classic 1946 essay "Politics and the English Language."

DISCUSSION QUESTIONS

1. The success of this advertisement depends largely on its play on the word *cool*. Why might the creators of this ad have decided to use that word in a prominent way in the ad? What other types of ads does this one recall?

2. What is the irony of the use of the word *cool* in this context?

3. How are the images in the ad used to make a point? Some of them, for instance, suggest a rugged outdoor lifestyle. Why?

4. How are the words in the smaller text accompanying each of the "prizes" used to reinforce the ad's intent?

5. What is this ad trying to "sell"?

Gay Marriage Shows Why We Need to Separate Church and State

HOWARD MOODY

If members of the church that I served for more than three decades were told I would be writing an article in defense of marriage, they wouldn't believe it. My reputation was that when people came to me for counsel about getting married, I tried to talk them out of it. More about that later.

We are now in the midst of a national debate on the nature of marriage, and it promises to be as emotional and polemical as the issues of abortion and homosexuality have been over the past century. What all these debates have in common is that they involved both the laws of the state and the theology of the church. The purpose of this writing is to suggest that the gay-marriage debate is less about the legitimacy of the loving relationship of a same-sex couple than about the relationship of church and state and how they define marriage.

In Western civilization, the faith and beliefs of Christendom played a major role in shaping the laws regarding social relations and moral behavior. Having been nurtured in the Christian faith from childhood and having served a lifetime as an ordained Baptist minister, I feel obligated first to address the religious controversy concerning the nature of marriage. If we look at the history of religious institutions regarding marriage we will find not much unanimity but amazing diversity—it is really a mixed bag. Those who base their position on "tradition" or "what the Bible says" will find anything but clarity. It depends on which "tradition" in what age reading from whose holy scriptures.

In the early tradition of the Jewish people, there were multiple wives and not all of them equal. Remember the story of Abraham's wives, Sara and Hagar. Sara couldn't get pregnant, so Hagar presented Abraham with a son. When Sara got angry with Hagar, she forced Abraham to send Hagar and her son Ishmael into the wilderness. In case Christians feel superior about their "tradition" of marriage, I would remind them that their scriptural basis is not as clear about marriage as we might hope. We have Saint Paul's conflicting and condescending words about the institution: "It's better not to marry." Karl Barth called this passage the Magna Carta of the single person. (Maybe we should have taken Saint Paul's advice more seriously. It might have prevented an earlier generation of parents from harassing, cajoling, and prodding our young until they were mar-

Reverend Howard Moody is minister emeritus of Judson Memorial Church in New York City. This article was published in July 2004 in the *Nation*.

ried.) In certain religious branches, the church doesn't recognize the licensed legality of marriage but requires that persons meet certain religious qualifications before the marriage is recognized by the church. For members of the Roman Catholic Church, a "legal divorce" and the right to remarry may not be recognized unless the first marriage has been declared null and void by a decree of the church. It is clear that there is no single religious view of marriage and that history has witnessed some monumental changes in the way "husband and wife" are seen in the relationship of marriage.

In my faith-based understanding, if freedom of choice means any-   5
thing to individuals (male or female), it means they have several options. They can be single and celibate without being thought of as strange or psychologically unbalanced. They can be single and sexually active without being labeled loose or immoral. Women can be single with child without being thought of as unfit or inadequate. If these choices had been real options, the divorce rate may never have reached nearly 50 percent.

The other, equally significant choice for people to make is that of lifetime commitment to each other and to seal that desire in the vows of a wedding ceremony. That understanding of marriage came out of my community of faith. In my years of ministry I ran a tight ship in regard to the performance of weddings. It wasn't because I didn't believe in marriage (I've been married for sixty years and have two wonderful offspring) but rather my unease about the way marriage was used to force people to marry so they wouldn't be "living in sin."

The failure of the institution can be seen in divorce statistics. I wanted people to know how challenging the promise of those vows was and not to feel this was something they had to do. My first question in premarital counseling was, "Why do you want to get married and spoil a beautiful friendship?" That question often elicited a thoughtful and emotional answer. Though I was miserly in the number of weddings I performed, I always made exceptions when there were couples who had difficulty finding clergy who would officiate. Their difficulty was because they weren't of the same religion, or they had made marital mistakes, or what they couldn't believe. Most of them were "ecclesiastical outlaws," barred from certain sacraments in the church of their choice.

The church I served had a number of gay and lesbian couples who had been together for many years, but none of them had asked for public weddings or blessings on their relationship. (There was one commitment ceremony for a gay couple at the end of my tenure.) It was as though they didn't need a piece of paper or a ritual to symbolize their lifelong commitment. They knew if they wanted a religious ceremony, their ministers would officiate and our religious community would joyfully witness.

It was my hope that since the institution of marriage had been used to exclude and demean members of the homosexual community, our church, which was open and affirming, would create with gays and lesbians a new kind of ceremony. It would be an occasion that symbolized, between two people of the same gender, a covenant of intimacy of two people to journey together, breaking new ground in human relationships—an alternative to marriage as we have known it.

However, I can understand why homosexuals want "to be married"   10 in the old-fashioned "heterosexual way." After all, most gays and lesbians were born of married parents, raised in a family of siblings; many were nourished in churches and synagogues, taught about a living God before Whom all Her creatures were equally loved. Why wouldn't they conceive their loving relationships in terms of marriage and family and desire that they be confirmed and understood as such? It follows that if these gays and lesbians see their relationship as faith-based, they would want a religious ceremony that seals their intentions to become lifelong partners, lovers and friends, that they would want to be "married."

Even though most religious denominations deny this ceremony to homosexual couples, more and more clergy are, silently and publicly, officiating at religious rituals in which gays and lesbians declare their vows before God and a faith community. One Catholic priest who defied his church's ban said: "We can bless a dog, we can bless a boat, but we can't say a prayer over two people who love each other. You don't have to call it marriage, you can call it a deep and abiding friendship, but you can bless it."

We have the right to engage in "religious disobedience" to the regulations of the judicatory that granted us the privilege to officiate at wedding ceremonies, and suffer the consequences. However, when it comes to civil law, it is my contention that the church and its clergy are on much shakier ground in defying the law.

In order to fully understand the conflict that has arisen in this debate over the nature of marriage, it is important to understand the difference between the religious definition of marriage and the state's secular and civil definition. The government's interest is in a legal definition of marriage—a social and voluntary contract between a man and woman in order to protect money, property, and children. Marriage is a civil union without benefit of clergy or religious definition. The state is not interested in why two people are "tying the knot," whether it's to gain money, secure a dynasty, or raise children. It may be hard for those of us who have a religious or romantic view of marriage to realize that loveless marriages are not that rare. Before the Pill, pregnancy was a frequent motive for getting married. The state doesn't care what the commitment of two people is, whether it's for life or as long as both of you love, whether it's sexually monogamous or an open marriage. There is nothing spiritual, mystical, or romantic about the state's license to marry—it's a legal contract.

Thus, George W. Bush is right when he says that "marriage is a sacred institution" when speaking as a Christian, as a member of his Methodist church. But as president of the United States and leader of all Americans, believers and unbelievers, he is wrong. What will surface in this debate as litigation and court decisions multiply is the history of the conflict between the church and the state in defining the nature of marriage. That history will become significant as we move toward a decision on who may be married.

After Christianity became the state religion of the Roman empire in A.D. 325, the church maintained absolute control over the regulation of marriage for some 1,000 years. Beginning in the sixteenth century, English kings (especially Henry VIII, who found the inability to get rid of a wife extremely oppressive) and other monarchs in Europe began to wrest control from the church over marital regulations. Ever since, kings, presidents, and rulers of all kinds have seen how important the control of marriage is to the regulation of social order. In this nation, the government has always been in charge of marriage.

That is why it was not a San Francisco mayor licensing same-sex couples that really threatened the president's religious understanding of marriage but rather the Supreme Judicial Court of Massachusetts, declaring marriage between same-sex couples a constitutional right, that demanded a call for constitutional amendment. I didn't understand how important that was until I read an op-ed piece in the *Boston Globe* by Peter Gomes, professor of Christian morals and the minister of Memorial Church at Harvard University, that reminds us of a seminal piece of our history:

> The Dutch made civil marriage the law of the land in 1590, and the first marriage in New England, that of Edward Winslow to the widow Susannah White, was performed on May 12, 1621, in Plymouth by Governor William Bradford, in exercise of his office as magistrate.
>
> There would be no clergyman in Plymouth until the arrival of the Reverend Ralph Smith in 1629, but even then marriage would continue to be a civil affair, as these first Puritans opposed the English custom of clerical marriage as unscriptural. Not until 1692, when Plymouth Colony was merged into that of Massachusetts Bay, were the clergy authorized by the new province to solemnize marriages. To this day in the Commonwealth the clergy, including those of the archdiocese, solemnize marriage legally as agents of the Commonwealth and by its civil authority. Chapter 207 of the General Laws of Massachusetts tells us who may perform such ceremonies.

Now even though it is the civil authority of the state that defines the rights and responsibilities of marriage and therefore who can be married, the state is no more infallible than the church in its judgments. It wasn't until the mid-twentieth century that the Supreme Court declared antimiscegenation laws unconstitutional. Even after that decision, many mainline churches, where I started my ministry, unofficially discouraged interracial marriages, and many of my colleagues were forbidden to perform such weddings.

The civil law view of marriage has as much historical diversity as the church's own experience because, in part, the church continued to

15

influence the civil law. Although it was the Bible that made "the husband the head of his wife," it was common law that "turned the married pair legally into one person—the husband," as Nancy Cott documents in her book *Public Vows: A History of Marriage and the Nation* (an indispensable resource for anyone seeking to understand the changing nature of marriage in the nation's history). She suggests that "the legal doctrine of marital unity was called coverture . . . [which] meant that the wife could not use legal avenues such as suits or contracts, own assets, or execute legal documents without her husband's collaboration." This view of the wife would not hold water in any court in the land today.

As a matter of fact, even in the religious understanding of President Bush and his followers, allowing same-sex couples the right to marry seems a logical conclusion. If marriage is "the most fundamental institution of civilization" and a major contributor to the social order in our society, why would anyone want to shut out homosexuals from the "glorious attributes" of this "sacred institution"? Obviously, the only reason one can discern is that the opponents believe that gay and lesbian people are not worthy of the benefits and spiritual blessings of "marriage."

At the heart of the controversy raging over same-sex marriage is the religious and constitutional principle of the separation of church and state. All of us can probably agree that there was never a solid wall of separation, riddled as it is with breaches. The evidence of that is seen in the ambiguity of tax-free religious institutions, "in God we trust" printed on our money and "under God" in the Pledge of Allegiance to our country. All of us clergy, who are granted permission by the state to officiate at legal marriage ceremonies, have already compromised the "solid wall" by signing the license issued by the state. I would like to believe that my authority to perform religious ceremonies does not come from the state but derives from the vows of ordination and my commitment to God. I refuse to repeat the words, "by the authority invested in me by the State of New York, I pronounce you husband and wife," but by signing the license, I've become the state's "handmaiden."

It seems fitting therefore that we religious folk should now seek to sharpen the difference between ecclesiastical law and civil law as we beseech the state to clarify who can be married by civil law. Further evidence that the issue of church and state is part of the gay-marriage controversy is that two Unitarian ministers have been arrested for solemnizing unions between same-sex couples when no state licenses were involved. Ecclesiastical law may punish those clergy who disobey marital regulations, but the state has no right to invade church practices and criminalize clergy under civil law. There should have been a noisy outcry from all churches, synagogues, and mosques at the government's outrageous contravention of the sacred principle of the "free exercise of religion."

I come from a long line of Protestants who believe in a "free church in a free state." In the issue before this nation, the civil law is the determinant of the regulation of marriage, regardless of our religious views, and the Supreme Court will finally decide what the principle of equality means in our Constitution in the third century of our life together as a people. It is likely that the Commonwealth of Massachusetts will probably lead the nation on this matter, as the State of New York led to the Supreme Court decision to allow women reproductive freedom.

So what is marriage? It depends on whom you ask, in what era, in what culture. Like all words or institutions, human definitions, whether religious or secular, change with time and history. When our beloved Constitution was written, blacks, Native Americans, and, to some extent, women were quasi-human beings with no rights or privileges, but today they are recognized as persons with full citizenship rights. The definition of marriage has been changing over the centuries in this nation, and it will change yet again as homosexuals are seen as ordinary human beings.

In time, and I believe that time is now, we Americans will see that all the fears foisted on us by religious zealots were not real. Heterosexual marriage will still flourish with its statistical failures. The only difference will be that some homosexual couples will join them and probably account for about the same number of failed relationships. And we will discover that it did not matter whether the couples were joined in a religious ceremony or a secular and civil occasion for the statement of their intentions.

Will It Be Marriage or Civil Union?

JO ANN CITRON

This fall, while the right was still staggering from the U.S. Supreme Court's decision in *Lawrence v. Texas*, Massachusetts dealt conservatives another body blow when its highest court legalized same-sex marriage. In a 4–3 ruling authored by Chief Justice Margaret Marshall, the Supreme Judicial Court (SJC) held that denying marriage to homosexuals violates the Massachusetts Declaration of Rights, the state constitution. To remedy the violation, the court changed the common-law definition of civil marriage to eliminate its opposite-sex requirement and to compel the issuance of marriage licenses to qualified persons of the same sex. Civil marriage in Massachusetts now means "the voluntary union of two

Jo Ann Citron practices alternate family and civil rights law with the firm Altman & Citron and is a member of the Women's Studies Department at Wellesley College. The article was published in the *Gay and Lesbian Review Worldwide* in March–April 2004.

persons as spouses, to the exclusion of all others." The legislature, which was directed to "take such action as it may deem appropriate in light of this opinion," has been running for cover ever since.[1]

A friend recently asked me how important the Massachusetts decision is in the struggle to achieve marriage equality in the United States. I was struck, first of all, by the terms of the question because "marriage equality" is not the same as "marriage." The issue all along has been whether gays will get marriage or some equivalent formality that will make them equal to their heterosexual counterparts. There are those who say that civil union is marriage equality. It's what Vermont said and what many Massachusetts legislators are saying in their desperate search for an escape route from the SJC ruling. It's also what William Eskridge claimed in his 2002 book, *Equality Practice: Civil Union and the Future of Gay Rights*, where he argues that, while there is no principled basis for withholding marriage from gays and lesbians, the gay community should bow to the political will of the majority and move slowly, accepting the equality of civil union now and pressing for marriage later when it becomes more palatable to the majority. Eskridge views *Baker v. State*, the Vermont civil union decision, as the equivalent of *Brown v. Board of Education*, the 1954 landmark civil rights decision that opened the way to racial integration in this country. Marriage activist Evan Wolfson, on the other hand, views *Baker* as the gay rights version of *Plessy v. Ferguson*, the railway carriage case that authorized "separate but equal" status for disfavored minorities.

This essay is being written during the 180-day waiting period following the issuance of the decision, a period of either genuine confusion or deliberate obfuscation, depending on the degree of cynicism with which you view the political process. It might be useful at this point to summarize what the court said and how the legislature has responded. The court began by reminding everyone that the Massachusetts marriage statute is a licensing law. Because marriage has always been understood to mean the union of a man and a woman, the statute cannot be construed to authorize issuing a license to two people of the same sex. But to bar gay couples from all the benefits, protections, and obligations that accompany marriage violates the Massachusetts constitution, which means that the current marriage licensing law is unconstitutional. The remedy the court fashioned was to change the common law definition of civil marriage to eliminate its opposite-sex requirement, thereby removing the bar that excludes gay couples from obtaining marriage licenses.

Rather than declare that cities and towns must immediately begin to issue marriage licenses to gays, which would have created chaos, the court granted the legislature 180 days to revise state statutes so as to bring them into line with its ruling and to clean up a complicated domestic relations regulatory scheme that refers to husbands and wives. The court reminded the legislature that it retains "broad discretion to regulate marriage." This

---

[1] *Goodridge v. Department of Public Health.*

means that the Legislature can continue to impose certain restrictions upon persons who wish to marry. The legislature may refuse to authorize granting a marriage license to persons under a certain age, or to siblings, or to a parent and child. It may require a blood test or a birth certificate, or that applicants turn around three times and face north, or anything else that would be constitutional. But, as I read the decision, the legislature may not refuse to grant a license to otherwise qualified gay couples.

The SJC was perfectly clear in stating that the remedy for the consti- 5 tutional violation was the reformulation of the definition of civil marriage. Yet many legislators, together with the current attorney general, want to take a different view of the matter. They have seized upon the "protections, benefits, and obligations" language in the opinion in the hope that, by providing the benefits that marriage yields in our society, they can avoid providing marriage itself. The legislature has asked the SJC to render an advisory opinion about a civil union bill, and the SJC has invited interested parties to submit briefs. Meanwhile, the Massachusetts constitutional convention is scheduled to meet on February 11, 2004, to vote on a Defense of Marriage Act or DOMA that, in its present form, would not only prevent gay marriage but would also outlaw domestic partner benefits. If the legislature passes the DOMA in a second convention, the measure would appear on the ballot in November of 2006 and voters could, by a simple majority, amend the state constitution to make gay marriage, civil union, and domestic partnerships illegal. The political reality is that such a DOMA will probably not garner the necessary votes either in the legislature or among voters; however, a simple DOMA limiting itself to marriage is more likely to succeed, especially in the face of the SJC decision, which presents the right with what it would call a "clear and present danger." This means that gay marriage could become legal in Massachusetts on May 18, 2004, via the SJC decision and illegal in Massachusetts on November 14, 2006, via a voter referendum. No one knows what will happen to gay couples who marry in the interim. Let the courts sort through that one!

Massachusetts has a good track record when it comes to gay families: It permits second-parent adoption; it allows two women to appear as "parent" on a child's birth certificate; it protects the relationship between a child and her nonbiological parent. At the very least, *Goodridge* is going to yield "marriage equality" in some form of civil union. The problem, of course, is that there is no such thing as "marriage equality" for anyone who files federal income tax returns, bequeaths an estate, or travels outside of Massachusetts. When it comes to federal benefits or the tax-free transfer of marital property or the ability to have another state recognize your Massachusetts relationship, marriage is the only status that will do. This is why some are downplaying the SJC decision, pointing out that even if people are able to marry in Massachusetts, their status will not be recognized by the federal government or by any other state with a DOMA. In that respect, marriage is indeed no different from civil union.

In fact, it might even be worse for a while. We're beginning to see judges in some states accept the validity of a Vermont civil union. Even in states with a DOMA, it will be possible to find a judge who would give full faith and credit to a civil union because most DOMA laws have nothing to say about civil unions. Not so with marriage. For the time being, a Massachusetts marriage will be even less portable than a Vermont civil union.

But let there be no mistake: Whatever happens in Massachusetts is absolutely critical to how the gay marriage question will be answered in the rest of the United States. What happens here is even more important than what happened in Vermont. Here's why. The next marriage case with a reasonable likelihood of success is working its way through the courts in New Jersey, a state with a history of progressive court decisions. New Jersey will be looking very carefully at the way Vermont and Massachusetts have addressed the marriage question. If the Massachusetts SJC ratifies its decision and mandates the issuance of marriage licenses, New Jersey will look at its predecessor states and see two alternative models, marriage and civil union. New Jersey will choose one or the other. But the SJC could fail to confirm its marriage decision and approve instead some form of civil union. Coupled with the Vermont ruling, this will create a critical mass in favor of civil union, an outcome that will make it far more likely that New Jersey will opt for civil union over marriage. After that, the rest of the states will almost certainly fall into line with civil unions, and that will spell the end of gay marriage, probably forever.

Ironically, it may also mean the end of marriage in its present form, the one that the right is working so hard to preserve. Conservatives Andrew Sullivan and David Brooks have argued that the best way to protect marriage would be to open it to anyone who wants to vow fidelity and is willing to forego an easy exit from a supposedly permanent relationship. Marriage is, after all, a conservative institution, and persons who enter it with the blessing of the state may not leave it without the state's permission. Already, as a result of the marriage cases and their surrounding discourse, the very term "marriage" is being qualified. We now speak of "civil marriage" to distinguish it from the religious ceremonies that are but one of its aspects. Insofar as material benefits are concerned, marriage is a civil institution. Those material benefits can attach just as easily to any civil institution the state cares to identify. This is, after all, the point of wanting to offer gays something called "union" rather than something called "marriage." Nothing but prejudice prevents state and federal governments from offering to partners in a civil union the identical benefits, protections, and obligations that the state now offers to spouses.

William Eskridge is wrong in thinking that civil union is a step on the path towards marriage. Civil union and marriage are not sequential; they are alternatives to one another. There is no reason to think that the country will permit civil union now and confer marriage later. In fact, the reality is likely to be quite the reverse. Because of equal protection considerations, the civil union alternative will have to be available to straights as well as gays. And if my analysis is correct, it will become more widely available to everyone in the coming years. At the moment, there is little incentive for marriage-eligible couples to elect a civil union. But this will change.

It is not difficult to imagine a tacit compromise in which the right is 10 allowed to maintain its stranglehold on marriage in exchange for allowing the material benefits now associated with it to break free and accompany civil union. This is another reason why the Massachusetts decision in favor of marriage is strategically important. As long as even a single state has legalized marriage, civil union becomes more attractive to the right. And the gay community can leverage those few gay marriage licenses into a demand that marriage benefits attach to civil unions.

In my view, this would be a good outcome. I say this as someone who views marriage as a regressive institution that has never been good to women, that insidiously creates insiders and outsiders, and, most importantly, that violates the separation of church and state at the heart of our form of government. The state should not be in the business of attaching material benefits to a religious institution. The right to social security death benefits, the right to favorable tax treatment, the right to take your formalized relationship with you when you travel, should be detached from marriage altogether and should be awarded according to some other equitable system. To the extent that this becomes so, there will eventually be no material difference between the old form of marriage and the new form of civil unions. Traditional marriage will endure as a religious institution. Already there are hundreds of clergy willing to perform marriage ceremonies for gay congregants and thousands of gay couples who have participated in these ceremonies whose benefits are wholly spiritual. Over time, civil union and civil marriage will ultimately come to mean much the same thing. Whether the SJC ratifies its original position or abandons it, *Goodridge* brings us closer to a consensus around civil union. It is time for the gay community to turn its attention to winning for civil union all the rights, benefits, protections, and obligations of marriage. That is the truly revolutionary project.

DISCUSSION QUESTIONS

1. Why is definition a critical element in Moody's argument? Why is it a critical element in Citron's? Do the two of them agree on a definition of marriage?

2. What is Moody's attitude toward same-sex marriage? Why, in his opinion, do more serious problems arise when it comes to the laws of the state than the theology of the church?

3. Why does Moody feel that President Bush was wrong in saying, as president, that "marriage is a sacred institution"? Were you surprised by Moody's explanation of the history of marriage in our country?

4. When Citron published her essay, the nation was awaiting Massachusetts's decision on the legality of same-sex marriages. What was her biggest fear about the future of the legal standing of same-sex relationships?

5. Analyze Citron's analogy between decisions regarding same-sex unions and two Supreme Court decisions regarding racial integration, *Plessy v. Ferguson* and *Brown v. Board of Education.*

6. What is the author's claim in each of the two essays?

TAKING THE DEBATE ONLINE

For these and additional research URLs, see bedfordstmartins.com/rottenberg.

● **www.allianceformarriage.org**

This site is maintained by the Alliance for Marriage (AFM), a nonprofit research and educational organization dedicated to promoting marriage and addressing the epidemic of fatherless families in the United States.

● **www.keepmedia.com/featuredtopics/gaymarriage**

This site keeps updated lists of articles on gay marriage from a variety of publications.

● **www.now.org/issues/lgbi/marr-rep-2.html**

The National Organization for Women's site keeps current on gay and lesbian issues as they impact the lives of women.

● **www.stateline.org/stateline**

Stateline maintains recent information on the status of same-sex marriage, organized by state.

ASSIGNMENTS FOR UNDERSTANDING DEFINITION

1. Contrast the claims made by Jo Ann Citron in "Will It Be Marriage or Civil Union?" and Howard Moody in "Gay Marriage Shows Why We Need to Separate Church and State."

2. Contrast Citron's claim with that supported by Eric Zorn in "Family a Symbol of Love and Life, but Not Politics."

3. Use Orlando Patterson's "Race by the Numbers" as a starting point to discuss to what extent you feel you either are or are not defined by your racial identity.

4. Choose a print ad and analyze how the designer uses text and image to support the ad's claim.

5. Explain how the cartoon on page 89 illustrates how, in politics, the meaning of a term is relative. Or choose another cartoon and explain how different ways of defining a term can be the source of humor.

6. Use one or more cases to illustrate how, in a court of law, guilt or innocence can hinge on the matter of definition.

7. Many recent controversial movements and causes are identified by terms that have come to mean different things to different people. Choose one of the following and define it, explaining both the favorable and unfavorable connotations of the term. Use examples to clarify the meaning.

   a. abortion

   b. Palestinian homeland

   c. affirmative action

   d. assisted suicide

   e. the Patriot Act

8. Choose two words that are sometimes confused, and define them to make their differences clear. *Examples:* authoritarianism and totalitarianism, envy and jealousy, sympathy and pity, cult and established church, justice and equality, liberal and radical, agnostic and atheist.

9. Define *good parent, good teacher,* or *good husband* or *wife.* Try to uncover the assumptions on which your definition is based. (For example, in defining a good teacher, students sometimes mention the ability of the teacher to maintain order. Does this mean that the teacher alone is responsible for classroom order?)

10. Write about an important or widely used term whose meaning has changed since you first learned it. Such terms often come from the slang of particular groups: drug users, rock music fans, musicians, athletes, computer programmers, or software developers.

11. Define the differences between necessities, comforts, and luxuries. Consider how they have changed over time.

CHAPTER 4

Claims

Claims, or propositions, represent answers to the question: "What are you trying to prove?" Although they are the conclusions of your arguments, they often appear as thesis statements. Claims can be classified as *claims of fact, claims of value,* and *claims of policy.*

CLAIMS OF FACT

Claims of fact assert that a condition has existed, exists, or will exist and that their support consists of factual information—information such as statistics, examples, and testimony that most responsible observers assume can be verified.

Many facts are not matters for argument: Our own senses can confirm them, and other observers will agree about them. We can agree that a certain number of students were in the classroom at a particular time, that lions make a louder sound than kittens, and that apples are sweeter than potatoes.

We can also agree about information that most of us can rarely confirm for ourselves—information in reference books, such as atlases, almanacs, and telephone directories; data from scientific resources about the physical world; and happenings reported in the media. We can agree on the reliability of such information because we trust the observers who report it.

However, the factual map is constantly being redrawn by new data in such fields as history and science that cause us to reevaluate our conclusions. For example, the discovery of the Dead Sea Scrolls in 1947 revealed that some books of the Bible—Isaiah, for one—were far older than we had thought. Researchers at New York Hospital–Cornell Medical Center say that many symptoms previously thought inevitable in the aging process are now believed to be treatable and reversible symptoms of depression.[1]

In your conversations with other students you probably generate claims of fact every day, some of which can be verified without much effort, others of which are more difficult to substantiate.

CLAIM: Most of the students in this class come from towns within fifty miles of Boston.

To prove this the arguer would need only to ask the students in the class where they come from.

CLAIM: Students who take their courses pass/fail make lower grades than those who take them for specific grades.

In this case the arguer would need to have access to student records showing the specific grades given by instructors. (In most schools the instructor awards a letter grade, which is then recorded as a pass or a fail if the student has elected this option.)

CLAIM: The Red Sox will win the pennant this year.

This claim is different from the others because it is an opinion about what will happen in the future. But it can be verified (in the future) and is therefore classified as a claim of fact.

More complex factual claims about political and scientific matters remain controversial because proof on which all or most observers will agree is difficult or impossible to obtain.

CLAIM: Bilingual programs are less effective than English-only programs in preparing students for higher education.

CLAIM: The only life in the universe exists on this planet.

Not all claims are so neatly stated or make such unambiguous assertions. Because we recognize that there are exceptions to most generalizations, we often qualify our claims with words such as *generally, usually, probably,* and *as a rule.* It would not be true to state flatly, for example, "College graduates earn more than high school graduates." This statement is generally true, but we know that some high school graduates who are electricians or city bus drivers or sanitation workers earn more than college graduates who are schoolteachers or nurses or social workers. In

[1] *New York Times*, February 20, 1983, sec. 22, p. 4.

making such a claim, therefore, the writer should qualify it with a word that limits the claim.

To support a claim of fact, the writer needs to produce sufficient and appropriate data—that is, examples, statistics, and testimony from reliable sources. Provided this requirement is met, the task of establishing a factual claim would seem to be relatively straightforward. But as you have probably already discovered in ordinary conversation, finding convincing support for factual claims can pose a number of problems. Whenever you try to establish a claim of fact, you will need to ask at least three questions about the material you plan to use: *What are sufficient and appropriate data? Who are the reliable authorities?* and *Have I made clear whether my statements are facts or inferences?*

■ Sufficient and Appropriate Data

The amount and kind of data for a particular argument depend on the importance and complexity of the subject. The more controversial the subject, the more facts and testimony you will need to supply. Consider the claim "The murder rate in New York City is lower this year than last year." If you want to prove the truth of this claim, obviously you will have to provide a larger quantity of data than for a claim that says, "By following three steps, you can train your dog to sit and heel in fifteen minutes." In examining your facts and opinions, an alert reader will want to know if they are accurate, current, and typical of other facts and opinions that you have not mentioned.

The reader will also look for testimony from more than one authority, although there may be cases where only one or two experts who have achieved a unique breakthrough in their field will be sufficient. These cases would probably occur most frequently in the physical sciences. The Nobel Prize winners James Watson and Francis Crick, who first discovered the structure of the DNA molecule, are an example of such experts. However, in the case of the so-called Hitler diaries that surfaced in 1983, at least a dozen experts—journalists, historians, bibliographers who could verify the age of the paper and the ink—were needed to establish that they were forgeries.

■ Reliable Authorities

Not all those who pronounce themselves experts are trustworthy. Your own experience has probably taught you that you cannot always believe the reports of an event by a single witness. The witness may be poorly trained to make accurate observations—about the size of a crowd, the speed of a vehicle, his distance from an object. Or his own physical conditions—illness, intoxication, disability—may prevent him from seeing or hearing or smelling accurately. The circumstances under which he observes the event—darkness, confusion, noise—may also impair his observation. In addition, the witness may be biased for or against the outcome of the event, as in a hotly contested baseball game, where the observer sees the play that he wants to see. You will find the problems associated with the biases of witnesses to be relevant to your work as a reader and writer of argumentative essays.

You will undoubtedly want to quote authors in some of your arguments. In most cases you will not be familiar with the authors. But there are guidelines for determining their reliability: the rank or title of the experts, the acceptance of their publications by other experts, their association with reputable universities, research centers, or think tanks. For example, for a paper on euthanasia, you might decide to quote from an article by Paul R. McHugh, the Henry Phipps Professor of Psychiatry at the Johns Hopkins University School of Medicine and psychiatrist in chief at the Johns Hopkins Hospital in Baltimore. For a paper on crime by youth groups, you might want to use material supplied by Elizabeth Glazer, chief of Crime Control Strategies in the U.S. Attorney's office for the Southern District of New York, where she previously served as chief of both the Organized Crime Unit and Violent Gang Unit. Most readers of your arguments would agree that these authors have impressive credentials in their fields.

What if several respectable sources are in conflict? What if the experts disagree? After a preliminary investigation of a controversial subject, you may decide that you have sufficient material to support your claim. But if you read further, you may discover that other material presented by equally qualified experts contradicts your original claim. In such circumstances you will find it impossible to make a definitive claim. (On pp. 160–73 in the treatment of support of a claim by evidence, you will find a more elaborate discussion of this vexing problem.)

■ Facts or Inferences

We have defined a fact as a statement that can be verified. An inference is "a statement about the unknown on the basis of the known."[2] The difference between facts and inferences is important to you as the writer of an argument because an inference is an *interpretation,* or an opinion reached after informed evaluation of evidence. As you and your classmates wait in your classroom on the first day of the semester, a middle-aged woman wearing a tweed jacket and a corduroy skirt appears and stands in the front of the room. You don't know who this woman is. However, based on what you do know about the appearance of many

---

[2]S. I. Hayakawa, *Language in Thought and Action* (New York: Harcourt, Brace, Jovanovich, 1978), p. 35.

college teachers and the fact that teachers usually stand in front of the classroom, you may *infer* that this woman is your teacher. You will probably be right. But you cannot be certain until you have more information. Perhaps you will find out that this woman has come from the department office to tell you that your teacher is sick and cannot meet the class today.

You have probably come across a statement such as the following in a newspaper or magazine: "Excessive television viewing has caused the steady decline in the reading ability of children and teenagers." Presented this way, the statement is clearly intended to be read as a factual claim that has been or can be proved. But it is an inference. The facts, which can be and have been verified, are (1) the reading ability of children and teenagers has declined and (2) the average child views television for six or more hours a day. (Whether this amount of time is "excessive" is also an opinion.) The cause-and-effect relation between the two facts is an interpretation of the investigator, who has examined both the reading scores and the amount of time spent in front of the television set and *inferred* that one is the cause of the other. The causes of the decline in reading scores are probably more complex than the original statement indicates. Since we can seldom or never create laboratory conditions for testing the influence of television separate from other influences in the family and the community, any statement about the connection between reading scores and television viewing can only be a guess.

By definition, no inference can ever do more than suggest probabilities. Of course, some inferences are much more reliable than others and afford a high degree of probability. Almost all claims in science are based on inferences, interpretations of data on which most scientists agree. Paleontologists find a few ancient bones from which they make inferences about an animal that might have been alive millions of years ago. We can never be absolutely certain that the reconstruction of the dinosaur in the museum is an exact copy of the animal it is supposed to represent, but the probability is fairly high because no other interpretation works so well to explain all the observable data—the existence of the bones in a particular place, their age, their relation to other fossils, and their resemblance to the bones of existing animals with which the paleontologist is familiar.

Inferences are profoundly important, and most arguments could not proceed very far without them. But an inference is not a fact. The writer of an argument must make it clear when he or she offers an inference, an interpretation, or an opinion that it is not a fact.

Writer's Guide: Defending a Claim of Fact

Here are some guidelines that should help you to defend a factual claim. (We'll say more about support of factual claims in Chapter 5.)

1. Be sure that the claim — what you are trying to prove — is clearly stated, preferably at the beginning of your paper.

2. Define terms that may be controversial or ambiguous. For example, in trying to prove that "radicals" had captured the student government, you would have to define "radicals," distinguishing them from "liberals" or members of other ideological groups, so that your readers would understand exactly what you meant.

3. As far as possible, make sure that your evidence — facts and opinions, or interpretations of the facts — fulfills the appropriate criteria. The data should be sufficient, accurate, recent, typical; the authorities should be reliable.

4. Make clear when conclusions about the data are inferences or interpretations, not facts. For example, you might write, "The series of lectures titled Modern Architecture, sponsored by our fraternity, was poorly attended because the students at this college aren't interested in discussions of art." What proof could you offer that this *was* the reason and that your statement was a *fact*? Perhaps there were other reasons that you hadn't considered.

5. Emphasize your most important evidence by placing it at the beginning or the end of your paper (the most emphatic positions in an essay) and devoting more space to it.

SAMPLE ANNOTATED ESSAY: CLAIM OF FACT

A Reassuring Scorecard for Affirmative Action

MICHAEL M. WEINSTEIN

Introduction:
a) Review of the
attack on affirmative
action

Affirmative action—preferential treatment toward women and minority applicants as practiced by employers, university admissions officers, and government contractors—remains under attack thirty-two years after President

---

Michael M. Weinstein, Ph.D., is a senior fellow on the Council on Foreign Relations. He was on the editorial board of the *New York Times* when he wrote this October 17, 2000, article.

Johnson ordered federal contractors to seek female and minority employees. Two states have voted to wipe out the use of race- and gender-based preferences by state agencies. Parents have challenged the race-based admissions policies of public schools. Even Joseph Lieberman, the [2000] Democratic candidate for vice president, once opposed policies "based on group preference instead of individual merit."

b) Specific criticism

Some of affirmative action's critics contend that preferential hiring and admissions are always wrong in principle no matter how attractive the consequences. But other critics focus on affirmative action's alleged failings. According to this argument, the policy creates divisive workplaces, breeds cynicism and corruption, and hurts many of the individuals it is supposed to help. That debate should turn on the facts. Instead it has been fueled almost entirely by anecdotes — until now.

Refutation:
authoritative source
of new data

In the most recent issue of the *Journal of Economic Literature,* a publication of the American Economic Association, two respected economists provide an eighty-five page review of over two hundred serious scientific studies of affirmative action. Harry Holzer of Georgetown University and David Neumark of Michigan State University ferret out every statistic from the studies to measure the effects of affirmative action. Harsh critics of affirmative action will not find much comfort.

Claim: general benefits
for women and
minorities under
affirmative action

The authors concede the evidence is sometimes murky. Yet they find that affirmative action produces tangible benefits for women, for minority entrepreneurs, students, and workers, and for the overall economy. Employers adopting the policy increase the relative number of women and minority employees by an average of between 10 and 15 percent. Affirmative action has helped boost the percentage of blacks attending college by a factor of three and the percentage of blacks enrolled in medical school by a factor of four since the early 1960s. Between 1982 and 1991 the number of federal contracts going to black-owned businesses rose by 125 percent, even though the total number of federal contracts rose by less than 25 percent during the period.

Support: a) Data
about employment,
education, business

To no one's surprise, the two economists rivet   5
on economic performance. Here, the survey is in-

teresting for what it does *not* find. There is, the authors say, little credible evidence that affirmative action appointees perform badly or diminish the overall performance of the economy.

b) Data about credentials

Women hired under affirmative action, they say, largely match their male counterparts in credentials and performance. Blacks and Hispanics hired under affirmative action generally lag behind on credentials, such as education, but usually perform about as well as nonminority employees.

c) Data about worker performance

In a separate study, Mr. Holzer and Mr. Neumark interviewed thousands of supervisors and showed that they ranked most affirmative action hires roughly the same as ordinary hires. The authors find that companies undertaking affirmative action use extensive recruitment and training to bring workers who fall a notch below average on credentials up to the performance level of other workers.

d) Data about student performance

Critics have often pointed to the wide gap between SAT scores of black and white students admitted to selective universities as proof that they are lowering standards for minority students and putting them in settings they cannot handle. But the use of a test gap as a measure of reverse discrimination is misleading. Much of the gap would exist even if admissions were race-blind. Colleges pull applicants from a population that includes many more high-scoring whites than blacks.

A discrimination-free procedure would start by tapping the pool, largely white, of high scorers and then turn to the pool of lower-scoring whites and blacks. The average test scores for whites admitted to the college would thus exceed that of the blacks admitted.

To be sure, some selective universities add to   10 the test gap by giving preference to minority applicants. But, the data shows, black students at elite colleges graduate at greater rates than blacks at less demanding colleges, disproving claims that affirmative action disserves minority students.

e) Data about social benefits

The Holzer-Neumark survey shows that affirmative action in admissions has produced significant social benefits. For example, black doctors choose more often than their white medical school classmates to serve indigent or minority patients in inner cities and rural areas.

Conclusion: Contrary to criticism, evidence justifies affirmative action.

Though favorable, these findings hardly end the debate on affirmative action. The critics who refuse to accept government-sanctioned racial or gender preferences no matter what the benefit will continue to object. Affirmative action can be misused, as when whites running a company create a fiction of black ownership to qualify for credits in seeking government contracts. But the evidence marshaled by the authors largely vindicates affirmative action and should provide the ammunition for rebutting those critics who refuse to take facts into account.

■ Analysis

This article offers evidence that affirmative action provides benefits to women and minorities. A claim of fact often responds to some widely held belief that the author considers to be wrong—in this case, the failure of affirmative action. We need to ask three questions about a claim of fact: Are the data sufficient and appropriate? Are the authorities reliable? Are the distinctions between facts and inferences clear? Within its brief compass, this argument comes close to satisfying these criteria. In addition, its organization is straightforward, with clearly defined introduction, body, and conclusion.

The first three paragraphs constitute the introduction. First, the author reviews some of the claims of the opposition. At the end of the second paragraph, he makes clear his own emphasis: "That debate should turn on the facts." He then cites his source for the facts—a report in a respected professional journal by two university economists, who have examined the data on affirmative action in over two hundred serious scientific studies. This information reassures the reader that the first two criteria for judging a claim of fact will be met.

The body of the essay contains support for the claim, first in a short summary, then in substantial detail. Much of the data is statistical, a specific form of information that most readers find convincing and relatively easy to assimilate. (Of course, readers must regard the source as trustworthy.) The author has offered some interpretations—in paragraph 8, for example—to clarify what he considers a misunderstanding. Notice also the use of "To be sure," an expression that usually indicates that the writer recognizes an exception to his view. But the argument stands firmly on the facts. The ending is one often used by debaters—a modest challenge to the opposing side.

Unlike claims of fact, which attempt to prove that something is true and which can be validated by reference to the data, claims of value make a judgment. They express approval or disapproval. They attempt to prove that some action, belief, or condition is right or wrong, good or bad, beautiful or ugly, worthwhile or undesirable.

CLAIM: Democracy is superior to any other form of government.

CLAIM: Killing animals for sport is wrong.

CLAIM: The Sam Rayburn Building in Washington is an aesthetic failure.

Some claims of value are simply expressions of tastes, likes and dislikes, or preferences and prejudices. The Latin proverb "De gustibus non est disputandum" states that we cannot dispute about tastes. Suppose you express a preference for chocolate over vanilla. If your listener should ask why you prefer this flavor, you cannot refer to an outside authority or produce data or appeal to her moral sense to convince her that your preference is justified.

Many claims of value, however, can be defended or attacked on the basis of standards that measure the worth of an action, a belief, or an object. As far as possible, our personal likes and dislikes should be supported by reference to these standards. Value judgments occur in any area of human experience, but whatever the area, the analysis will be the same. We ask the arguer who is defending a claim of value: *What are the standards or criteria for deciding that this action, this belief, or this object is good or bad, beautiful or ugly, desirable or undesirable? Does the thing you are defending fulfill these criteria?*

There are two general areas in which people often disagree about matters of value: aesthetics and morality. They are also the areas that offer the greatest challenge to the writer. What follows is a discussion of some of the elements of analysis that you should consider in defending a claim of value in these areas.

Aesthetics is the study of beauty and the fine arts. Controversies over works of art—the aesthetic value of books, paintings, sculpture, architecture, dance, drama, and movies—rage fiercely among experts and laypeople alike. They may disagree on the standards for judging or, even if they agree about standards, may disagree about how successfully the art object under discussion has met these standards.

Consider a discussion about popular music. Hearing someone praise the singing of Manu Chao, a hugely popular European singer now playing to American crowds, you might ask why he is highly regarded. You expect Chao's fans to say more than "I like him" or "He's great." You expect them to give reasons to support their claims. They might show you a short review from a respected newspaper that says, "Mr. Chao's gift is simplicity. His music owes a considerable amount to Bob Marley . . . but Mr. Chao has a nasal, regular-guy voice, and instead of the Wailers' brooding, bass-heavy undertow, Mr. Chao's band delivers a lighter bounce. His tunes have the singing directness of nursery rhymes."[3] Chao's fans accept these criteria for judging a singer's appeal.

You may not agree that simplicity, directness, and a regular-guy voice are the most important qualities in a popular singer. But the establishment of standards itself offers material for a discussion or an argument. You may argue about the relevance of the criteria, or you may agree with the criteria but argue about the success of the singer in meeting them. Perhaps you prefer complexity to simplicity. Or even if you choose simplicity, you may not think that Chao has exhibited this quality to good effect.

It is probably not surprising then, that, despite wide differences in taste, professional critics more often than not agree on criteria and whether an art object has met the criteria. For example, almost all movie critics agree that *Citizen Kane* and *Gone with the Wind* are superior films. They also agree that *Plan 9 from Outer Space,* a horror film, is terrible.

Value claims about morality express judgments about the rightness or wrongness of conduct or belief. Here disagreements are as wide and deep as in the arts. The first two examples on page 113 reveal how controversial such claims can be. Although you and your reader may share many values—among them a belief in democracy, a respect for learning, and a desire for peace—you may also disagree, even profoundly, about other values. The subject of divorce, for example, despite its prevalence in our society, can produce a conflict between people who have differing moral standards. Some people may insist on adherence to absolute standards, arguing that the values they hold are based on immutable religious precepts derived from God and biblical scripture. Since marriage is sacred, divorce is always wrong, they say, whether or not the conditions of society change. Other people may argue that values are relative, based on the changing needs of societies in different places and at different times. Since marriage is an institution created by human beings at a particular time in history to serve particular social needs, they may say, it can also be dissolved when other social needs arise. The same conflicts between moral values might occur in discussions of abortion or suicide.

As a writer you cannot always know what system of values your reader holds. Yet it might be possible to find a rule on which almost all readers agree. One such rule was expressed by the eighteenth-century German philosopher Immanuel Kant: "Man and, in general, every rational being exists as an end in itself and not merely as a means to be arbitrarily used by this or that will." Kant's prescription urges us not to subject any creature to a condition that it has not freely chosen. In other words, we cannot use other creatures, as in slavery, for our own purposes.

[3]Jon Pareles, *New York Times,* July 10, 2001, p. B1.

Writer's Guide: Defending a Claim of Value

The following suggestions are a preliminary guide to the defense of a value claim. (We discuss value claims further in Chapter 5.)

1. Try to make clear that the values or principles you are defending are important and relatively more significant than other values. Keep in mind that you and your readers may differ about their relative importance. For example, although your readers may agree with you that brilliant photography is important in a film, they may think that a well-written script is even more crucial to its success. And although they may agree that freedom of the press is a mainstay of democracy, they may regard the right to privacy as even more fundamental.

2. Suggest that adherence to the values you are defending will bring about good results in some specific situation or bad results if respect for the values is ignored. You might argue, for example, that a belief in freedom of the press will make citizens better informed and the country stronger while a failure to protect this freedom will strengthen the forces of authoritarianism.

3. Since value terms are abstract, use examples and illustrations to clarify meanings and make distinctions. Comparisons and contrasts are especially helpful. If you use the term *heroism*, can you provide examples to differentiate between *heroism* and *foolhardiness* or *exhibitionism*?

4. Use testimony of others to prove that knowledgeable or highly regarded people share your values.

(Some philosophers would extend this rule to the treatment of animals by human beings.) This standard of judgment has, in fact, been invoked in recent years against medical experimentation on human beings in prisons and hospitals without their consent and against the sterilization of poor or mentally retarded women without their consent.

Nevertheless, even where people agree about standards for measuring behavior, a majority preference is not enough to confer moral value. If in a certain neighborhood a majority of heterosexual men decide to harass a few gay men and lesbians, that consensus does not make their action right. In formulating value claims, you should be prepared to ask and answer questions about the way in which your value claims and those of others have been arrived at. Lionel Ruby, an American philosopher, sums it up in these words: "The law of rationality tells us that we ought to justify our beliefs by evidence and reasons, instead of asserting them dogmatically."[4]

---

[4] *The Art of Making Sense* (New York: Lippincott, 1968), p. 271.

Of course, you will not always be able to persuade those with whom you argue that your values are superior to theirs and that they should therefore change their attitudes. Nor, on the other hand, would you want to compromise your values or pretend that they were different to win an argument. What you can and should do, however, as Lionel Ruby advises, is give *good reasons* that you think one thing is better than another. If as a child you asked why it was wrong to take your brother's toys, you might have been told by an exasperated parent, "Because I say so." Some adults still give such answers in defending their judgments, but such answers are not arguments and do nothing to win the agreement of others.

SAMPLE ANNOTATED ESSAY: CLAIM OF VALUE

Kids in the Mall:
Growing Up Controlled

WILLIAM SEVERINI KOWINSKI

> Butch heaved himself up and loomed over the group. "Like it was different for me," he piped. "My folks used to drop me off at the shopping mall every morning and leave me all day. It was like a big free baby-sitter, you know? One night they never came back for me. Maybe they moved away. Maybe there's some kind of a Bureau of Missing Parents I could check with."
>
> —Richard Peck,
> *Secrets of the Shopping Mall*,
> a novel for teenagers

Introduction: interesting personal anecdote

From his sister at Swarthmore, I'd heard about a kid in Florida whose mother picked him up after school every day, drove him straight to the mall, and left him there until it closed—all at his insistence. I'd heard about a boy in Washington who, when his family moved from one suburb to another, pedaled his bicycle five miles every day to get back to his old mall, where he once belonged.

William Severini Kowinski is a freelance writer who has been the book review editor and managing arts editor of the *Boston Phoenix*. This excerpt is from his book *The Malling of America: An Inside Look at the Great Consumer Paradise* (1985).

Additional examples of mall experience

These stories aren't unusual. The mall is a common experience for the majority of American youth; they have probably been going there all their lives. Some ran within their first large open space, saw their first fountain, bought their first toy, and read their first book in a mall. They may have smoked their first cigarette or first joint, or turned them down, had their first kiss or lost their virginity in the mall parking lot. Teenagers in America now spend more time in the mall than anywhere else but home and school. Mostly it is their choice, but some of that mall time is put in as the result of two-paycheck and single-parent households, and the lack of other viable alternatives. But are these kids being harmed by the mall?

Reasons for the author's interest

I wondered first of all what difference it makes for adolescents to experience so many important moments in the mall. They are, after all, at play in the fields of its little world and they learn its ways; they adapt to it and make it adapt to them. It's here that these kids get their street sense, only it's mall sense. They are learning the ways of a large-scale, artificial environment; its subtleties and flexibilities, its particular pleasures and resonances, and the attitudes it fosters.

The presence of so many teenagers for so much time was not something mall developers planned on. In fact, it came as a big surprise. But kids became a fact of mall life very easily, and the International Council of Shopping Centers found it necessary to commission a study, which they published along with a guide to mall managers on how to handle the teenage incursion.

Expert opinion

The study found that "teenagers in suburban   5
centers are bored and come to the shopping centers mainly as a place to go. Teenagers in suburban centers spent more time fighting, drinking, littering and walking than did their urban counterparts, but presented fewer overall problems." The report observed that "adolescents congregated in groups of two to four and predominantly at locations selected by them rather than management." This probably had something to do with the decision to install game arcades, which allow management to channel these restless

adolescents into naturally contained areas away from major traffic points of adult shoppers.

The guide concluded that mall management should tolerate and even encourage the teenage presence because, in the words of the report, "The vast majority support the same set of values as does shopping center management." *The same set of values* means simply that mall kids are already preprogrammed to be consumers and that the mall can put the finishing touches to them as hard-core, lifelong shoppers just like everybody else. That, after all, is what the mall is about. So it shouldn't be surprising that in spending a lot of time there, adolescents find little that challenges the assumption that the goal of life is to make money and buy products, or that just about everything else in life is to be used to serve those ends.

Growing up in a high-consumption society already adds inestimable pressure to kids' lives. Clothes consciousness has invaded the grade schools, and popularity is linked with having the best, newest clothes in the currently acceptable styles. Even what they read has been affected. "Miss [Nancy] Drew wasn't obsessed with her wardrobe," noted the *Wall Street Journal*. "But today the mystery in teen fiction for girls is what outfit the heroine will wear next." Shopping has become a survival skill and there is certainly no better place to learn it than the mall, where its importance is powerfully reinforced and certainly never questioned.

The mall as a university of suburban materialism, where Valley Girls and Boys from coast to coast are educated in consumption, has its other lessons in this era of change in family life and sexual mores and their economic and social ramifications. The plethora of products in the mall, plus the pressure on teens to buy them, may contribute to the phenomenon that psychologist David Elkind calls "the hurried child": kids who are exposed to too much of the adult world too quickly and must respond with a sophistication that belies their still-tender emotional development. Certainly the adult products marketed for children—form-fitting designer jeans, sexy tops for preteen girls—add to the social pressure to

Why the malls encourage adolescent presence

Disadvantages:
a) Exposure to high-consumption society

b) Social pressures to buy

look like an adult, along with the home-grown need to understand adult finances (why mothers must work) and adult emotions (when parents divorce).

c) Mall as babysitter

Kids spend so much time at the mall partly because their parents allow it and even encourage it. The mall is safe, doesn't seem to harbor any unsavory activities, and there is adult supervision; it is, after all, a controlled environment. So the temptation, especially for working parents, is to let the mall be their baby-sitter. At least the kids aren't watching TV. But the mall's role as a surrogate mother may be more extensive and more profound.

d) Mall as substitute for home

Karen Lansky, a writer living in Los Angeles, 10 has looked into the subject, and she told me some of her conclusions about the effects on its teenaged denizens of the mall's controlled and controlling environment. "Structure is the dominant idea, since true 'mall rats' lack just that in their home lives," she said, "and adolescents about to make the big leap into growing up crave more structure than our modern society cares to acknowledge." Karen pointed out some of the elements malls supply that kids used to get from their families, like warmth (Strawberry Shortcake dolls and similar cute and cuddly merchandise), old-fashioned mothering ("We do it all for you," the fast-food slogan), and even home cooking (the "homemade" treats at the food court).

e) Encouragement of passivity

The problem in all this, as Karen Lansky sees it, is that while families nurture children by encouraging growth through the assumption of responsibility and then by letting them rest in the bosom of the family from the rigors of growing up, the mall as a structural mother encourages passivity and consumption, as long as the kid doesn't make trouble. Therefore all they learn about becoming adults is how to act and how to consume.

f) Undemanding jobs

Kids are in the mall not only in the passive role of shoppers—they also work there, especially as fast-food outlets infiltrate the mall's enclosure. There they learn how to hold a job and take responsibility, but still within the same value context. When *CBS Reports* went to Oak Park Mall in suburban Kansas City, Kansas, to tape part of their

Example

hour-long consideration of malls, "After the Dream Comes True," they interviewed a teenaged girl who worked in a fast-food outlet there. In a sequence that didn't make the final program, she described the major goal of her present life, which was to perfect the curl on top of the ice-cream cones that were her store's specialty. If she could do that, she would be moved from the lowly soft-drink dispenser to the more prestigious ice-cream division, the curl on top of the status ladder at her restaurant. These are the achievements that are important at the mall.

Details

Other benefits of such jobs may also be over-rated, according to Laurence D. Steinberg of the University of California at Irvine's social ecology department, who did a study on teenage employment. Their jobs, he found, are generally simple, mindlessly repetitive and boring. They don't really learn anything, and the jobs don't lead anywhere. Teenagers also work primarily with other teenagers; even their supervisors are often just a little older than they are. "Kids need to spend time with adults," Steinberg told me. "Although they get benefits from peer relationships, without parents and other adults it's one-side socialization. They hang out with each other, have age-segregated jobs, and watch TV."

Advantages:
a) Time with other
adolescents

Perhaps much of this is not so terrible or even so terribly different. Now that they have so much more to contend with in their lives, adolescents probably need more time to spend with other adolescents without adult impositions, just to sort things out. Though it is more concentrated in the mall (and therefore perhaps a clearer target), the value system there is really the dominant one of the whole society. Attitudes about curiosity, initiative, self-expression, empathy, and disinterested learning aren't necessarily made in the mall; they are mirrored there, perhaps a bit more intensely—as through a glass brightly.

b) Educational
opportunities

Besides, the mall is not without its educational 15 opportunities. There are bookstores, where there is at least a short shelf of classics at great prices, and other books from which it is possible to learn more than how to do sit-ups. There are tools, from hammers to VCRs, and products, from clothes to records, that can help the young find and express themselves. There are older people with stories, and places to be alone or to talk one-on-one with a kindred spirit. And there is always the passing show.

The mall itself may very well be an education about the future. I was struck with the realization, as early as my first forays into Greengate, that the mall is only one of a number of enclosed and controlled environments that are part of the lives of today's young. The mall is just an extension, say, of those large suburban schools—only there's Karmelkorn instead of chem lab, the ice rink instead of the gym: It's high school without the impertinence of classes.

Conclusion and claim of value: mall as a controlled environment that teaches a few valuable lessons

Growing up, moving from home to school to the mall—from enclosure to enclosure, transported in cars—is a curiously continuous process, without much in the way of contrast or contact with unenclosed reality. Places must tend to blur into one another. But whatever differences and dangers there are in this, the skills these adolescents are learning may turn out to be useful in their later lives. For we seem to be moving inexorably into an age of preplanned and regulated environments, and this is the world they will inherit.

Still, it might be better if they had more of a choice. One teenaged girl confessed to *CBS Reports* that she sometimes felt she was missing something by hanging out at the mall so much. "But I'm here," she said, "and this is what I have."

■ Analysis

Kowinski has chosen to evaluate one aspect of an extraordinarily successful economic and cultural phenomenon—the commercial mall. He asks whether the influence of the mall on adolescents is good or bad. The answer seems to be a little of both. The good values may be described as exposure to a variety of experiences, a protective structure for adolescents who often live in unstable environments, and immersion in a world that may well serve as an introduction to adulthood. But the bad values, which Kowinski thinks are more influential (as the title suggests) are those of the shoppers' paradise, a society that believes in acquisition and consumption of goods as ultimate goals, and too much control over the choices available to adolescents. The tone of the judgment, however, is moderate and reflects a balanced, even scholarly, attitude. More than other arguments, the treatment of values requires such a voice, one which respects differences of opinion among readers. But serious doesn't mean heavy. His style is formal but highly readable, brightened by interesting examples and precise details. The opening paragraph is a strikingly effective lead.

Some of his observations are personal, but others are derived from studies by professional researchers, from *CBS Reports* to a well-known writer on childhood. These studies give weight and authority to his conclusions. Here and there we detect an appealing sympathy for adolescents who spend time in their controlled mall environments.

Like any thoughtful social commentator, Kowinski casts a wide net. He sees the mall not only as a hangout for teens but as a good deal more, an institution that offers insights into family life and work, the changing urban culture, the nature of contemporary entertainment, even glimpses of a somewhat forbidding future.

CLAIMS OF POLICY

Claims of policy argue that certain conditions should exist. As the name suggests, they advocate adoption of policies or courses of action because problems have arisen that call for solution. Almost always *should* or *ought to* or *must* is expressed or implied in the claim.

CLAIM: Voluntary prayer should be permitted in public schools.

CLAIM: A dress code should be introduced for all public high schools.

CLAIM: A law should permit sixteen-year-olds and parents to "divorce" each other in cases of extreme incompatibility.

CLAIM: Mandatory jail terms should be imposed for drunk driving violations.

In defending such claims of policy you may find that you must first convince your audience that a problem exists. This will require that, as part of your longer argument, you make a factual claim, offering data to prove that present conditions are unsatisfactory. You may also find it necessary to refer to the values that support your claim. Then you will be ready to introduce your policy, to persuade your audience that the solution you propose will solve the problem.

We will examine a policy claim in which all these parts are at work. The claim can be stated as follows: "The time required for an undergraduate degree should be extended to five years." Immediate agreement with this policy among student readers would certainly not be universal. Some

Writer's Guide: Defending a Claim of Policy

The following steps will help you organize arguments for a claim of policy.

1. Make your proposal clear. The terms in the proposal should be precisely defined.

2. If necessary, establish that there is a need for a change. When changes have been resisted, present reasons that explain this resistance. (It is often wrongly assumed that people cling to cultural practices long after their significance and necessity have eroded. But rational human beings observe practices that serve a purpose. The fact that you and I may see no value or purpose in the activities of another is irrelevant.)

3. Consider the opposing arguments. You may want to state the opposing arguments in a brief paragraph before answering them in the body of your argument.

4. Devote the major part of your essay to proving that your proposal is an answer to the opposing arguments and enumerating its distinct benefits for your readers.

5. Support your proposal with solid data, but don't neglect the moral considerations and the commonsense reasons, which may be even more persuasive.

students would not recognize a problem. They would say, "The college curriculum we have now is fine. There's no need for a change. Besides, we don't want to spend more time in school." First, then, the arguer would have to persuade a skeptical audience that there is a problem — that four years of college are no longer enough because the stock of knowledge in almost all fields of study continues to increase. The arguer would provide data to show that students today have many more choices in history, literature, and science than students had in those fields a generation ago. She would also emphasize the value of greater knowledge and more schooling compared to the value of other goods the audience cherishes, such as earlier independence. Finally, the arguer would offer a plan for implementing her policy. Her plan would have to consider initial psychological resistance, revision of the curriculum, costs of more instruction, and costs of lost production in the workforce. Most important, she would point out the benefits for both individuals and society if this policy were adopted.

In this example, we assumed that the reader would disagree that a problem existed. In many cases, however, the reader may agree that there is a problem but disagree with the arguer about the way to solve it. Most of us, no doubt, agree that we want to reduce or eliminate the following problems: misbehavior and vandalism in schools, drunk driving, crime on the streets, child abuse, pornography, pollution. But how should we go about solving those problems? What public policy will give us well-behaved, diligent students who never destroy school property? Safe streets where no one is ever robbed or assaulted? Loving homes where no child is ever mistreated? Some members of society would choose to introduce rules or laws that punish infractions so severely that wrongdoers would be unwilling or unable to repeat their offenses. Other members of society would prefer policies that attempt to rehabilitate or reeducate offenders through training, therapy, counseling, and new opportunities.

SAMPLE ANNOTATED ESSAY: CLAIM OF POLICY

Dependency or Death?
Oregonians Make a Chilling Choice

WESLEY J. SMITH

Introduction: misinterpretation of information in a new study of assisted suicide

Assisted suicide in Oregon has operated in a shroud of secrecy since the procedure was legalized by a 1997 referendum. But a new study, published in the *New England Journal of Medicine*, purports to shed light on the law's actual workings. Advocates of assisted suicide claim the report proves all is well. But a close reading reveals that many of the worries of assisted-suicide opponents are entirely justified.

Refutation: a) Real reason for suicide

Fifteen people in Oregon, we are told, legally committed suicide with the assistance of their doctors in 1998. According to the report, not one of them was forced into the act by intractable pain or suffering. Rather, those who died had strong personal beliefs in individual autonomy and chose suicide based primarily on fears of future dependence.

That isn't how assisted suicide was supposed to work. For many years, we have been told repeatedly by advocates that assisted suicide is to be a

---

Wesley J. Smith is an attorney and author or coauthor of eight books, including *Culture of Death: The Assault on Medical Ethics in America* (2001). Smith's writing and opinion columns on medical ethics, legal ethics, and public affairs have appeared in publications throughout the country, including *Newsweek,* the *New York Times,* and the *Wall Street Journal,* the source of this February 2, 1999, piece.

"last resort," applied only when nothing else can be done to alleviate "unrelenting and intolerable suffering." Yet pain wasn't a factor in a single one of the Oregon suicides. Thus, rather than being a limited procedure performed out of extreme medical urgency, legalization in Oregon has actually widened the category of conditions for which physician-hastened death is seen as legitimate.

b) Statement of the problem

Disability-rights advocates point out that allowing assisted suicide based upon fear of needing help going to the toilet, bathing, and performing other daily life activities will involve far more disabled and elderly people than terminally ill ones. They also note that dependency is an issue primarily for people who are not actually dependent and that like other difficulties in life dependency is a circumstance to which people adjust with time. To accept the notion that worry about the potential need for living assistance is a legitimate reason for doctors to write lethal prescriptions is to put disabled and elderly people at lethal risk. The dehumanizing message is that society regards such lives as undignified and not worth living. That is why nine national disability-rights organizations have come out strongly against legalizing assisted suicide and none support it.

Support:
a) Fears of the disabled and the elderly

Expression of values

The study also reports that the people who committed assisted suicide had "shorter" relationships with the doctors who prescribed lethally than did a control group of patients who died naturally. The exact time difference is not given, but we do know from earlier media reports that it may be quite short. The first woman to commit assisted suicide in Oregon had a two-and-a-half-week relationship with the doctor who wrote her lethal prescription. Her own doctor had refused to assist her suicide, as had a second doctor who diagnosed her with depression. So she went to an advocacy group, which referred her to a doctor willing to do the deed. Hers was not a unique case. The report states that six of the fifteen people sought lethal prescriptions from two or more doctors.

b) Hasty decisions of doctors

Example

5

Assisted suicide proponents told us this wouldn't happen either. They promised that assisted suicide would only occur after a deep exploration of values between patients and doctors who had long-term relationships. Thanks to the study, we now know that death decisions are being made by doctors the patients barely know. This isn't careful medical practice; it is rampant Kevorkianism.

c) Omission of data from the study

The study is as notable for what it omits as for what it includes. Information about the people who committed assisted suicide came from death-prescribing doctors. Treating doctors who did not participate in their patients' deaths—professionals who could have provided invaluable information about the health of the people who died—were not interviewed. Nor were the doctors who refused to write lethal prescriptions.

Examples

Family members were not contacted either. Significantly, the investigators made no attempt to learn whether the prescribing doctors were affiliated with assisted-suicide advocacy groups, a matter of some importance if we are to judge whether the decisions to prescribe lethally were based on medicine or ideology. Moreover, none of the patients were autopsied to determine whether they were actually terminally ill.

d) Data from the Netherlands of unauthorized euthanasia

Near the end of the report, investigators admit that they do not know whether any unreported assisted suicides occurred. If history is any example, such deaths probably did happen. A recent *Journal of Medical Ethics* study about euthanasia in the Netherlands reveals that the Dutch policy is "beyond effective control" since 59 percent of doctors do not report euthanasia or assisted suicide to authorities as required by law. (In Oregon, there is no punishment for failing to report an assisted suicide.)

Examples

Moreover, killing by doctors in the Netherlands has expanded far beyond the rare case originally contemplated when euthanasia was first permitted in that country more than twenty years ago. Patients who are not terminally ill are routinely assisted in suicide. Depressed people can also be killed upon request even if they have no underlying organic disease. The lives of children born with birth defects are terminated by doctors based primarily on "quality of life" considerations. Most chilling, in one out of five euthanasia cases—nearly 1,000 per year—the patient has not asked to be killed.

Claim of policy: indictment of the present state of affairs, implying that it should be changed

The *New England Journal of Medicine* study is a 10 warning that Oregon has started down the same destructive path. Rather than alleviating concerns, the study reveals that assisted suicide is bad medicine and even worse public policy.

■ Analysis

In this claim of policy, the course of action is suggested in the last paragraph: Assisted suicide must be eliminated because it is "bad medicine and even worse public policy." That is, the law in Oregon that permits assisted suicide must be repealed. In the body of his argument, the author supports this claim with an array of facts and an appeal to deeply felt human values.

He begins, as many arguers do, with a brief reference to the situation he will attack. (It is summarized in the last section of the third paragraph.) The facts he provides come largely from a study in a distinguished professional journal that claims to establish the success of the Oregon law. But Smith interprets the facts of the study—and its omissions—to mean that the program is *not* fulfilling its humanitarian objective. Another study that is cited, from a journal of medical ethics, discusses the state of euthanasia in the Netherlands, where it is legal. This report appears at the end of Smith's article. Its position here emphasizes a disturbing conclusion—the dangerous future that the Oregon law may introduce. (In the Netherlands, says the report, "in one out of five euthanasia cases . . . the patient has not asked to be killed.")

An interesting and effective strategy in this argument is the author's reference to information which has been omitted from the debate on euthanasia. This lack of information is clearly spelled out in two paragraphs of the essay. In any debate, an accusation that the opposite side has failed to supply important data suggests that the data will prove damaging to the opponent's argument.

The most important element of this argument, however, is its appeal, both direct and implied, to the values of compassion and the natural desire to protect the helpless. All the examples are designed to heighten our sensitivity to the plight of those who have been victimized by death-prescribing doctors. But there is also an appeal to fear for readers who can imagine possible threats to their own welfare under such a law.

We don't, of course, expect neutrality from a lawyer for an antieuthanasia organization. Nevertheless, one of the strengths of this argument is its use of sober language, despite the emotionally charged subject matter. There are no vivid descriptions of suffering or maltreatment, and the author does not personalize his account. The absence of the pronoun *I*, in fact, lends his argument the formality of a legal brief. Undecided readers often find such restraint more persuasive than a passionate assault on the opposition.

READINGS FOR ANALYSIS

Happiness Is a Warm Planet

THOMAS GALE MOORE

President Clinton convened a conference on global warming yesterday, as the White House agonizes over its posture at the forthcoming talks in Kyoto, Japan, on a worldwide global warming treaty. Mr. Clinton is eager to please his environmentalist supporters, but industry, labor and members of the Senate have told the administration that this treaty would wreck the economy, cost millions of jobs and provoke a flight of investment to more hospitable climes.

A crucial point gets lost in the debate: Global warming, if it were to occur, would probably *benefit* most Americans.

If mankind had to choose between a warmer or a cooler climate, we would certainly choose the former: Humans, nearly all other animals and most plants would be better off with higher temperatures. The climate models suggest, and so far the record confirms, that under global warming nighttime winter temperatures would rise the most, and daytime summer temperatures the least. Most Americans prefer a warmer climate to a colder one—and that preference is justified. More people die of the cold than of the heat; more die in the winter than the summer. Statistical evidence suggests that the climate predicted for the end of the next century might reduce U.S. deaths by about 40,000 annually.

In addition, less snow and ice would reduce transportation delays and accidents. A warmer winter would cut heating costs, more than offsetting any increase in air conditioning expenses in the summer. Manufacturing, mining and most services would be unaffected. Longer growing seasons, more rainfall and higher concentrations of carbon dioxide would benefit plant growth. Already there is evidence that trees and other plants are growing more vigorously. Although some locales may become too dry, too wet or too warm, on the whole mankind should benefit from an upward tick in the thermometer.

Thomas Gale Moore is a senior fellow at the Hoover Institution. His book *A Politically Incorrect View of Global Warming: Foreign Aid Masquerading as Climate Policy* was published in 1998 by the Cato Institute. This article appeared in the *Wall Street Journal* on October 7, 1997.

What about the economic effects? In the pessimistic view of the In- 5
tergovernmental Panel on Climate Change, the costs of global warming
might be as high as 1.5 percent of the U.S. gross domestic product by the
end of the next century. The cost of reducing carbon dioxide emissions,
however, would be much higher. William Cline of the Institute for International Economics has calculated that the cost of cutting emissions by
one-third from current levels by 2040 would be 3.5 percent of worldwide
GDP. The IPCC also reviewed various estimates of losses from stabilizing
emissions at 1990 levels, a more modest objective, and concluded that
the cost to the U.S. economy would be at least 1.5 percent of GDP by
2050, with the burden continuing to increase thereafter.

The forecast cost of warming is for the end of the next century, not
the middle. Adjusting for the time difference, the cost to the U.S. from a
warmer climate at midcentury, according to the IPCC, would be at most
0.75 percent of GDP, meaning that the costs of holding carbon dioxide to
1990 levels would be twice the gain from preventing any climate change.
But the benefit-cost calculus is even worse. The administration is planning to exempt Third World nations, such as China, India and Brazil,
from the requirements of the treaty. Under such a scheme, Americans
would pay a huge price for virtually no benefit.

And even if the developing countries agreed to return emissions to
1990 levels, greenhouse gas concentrations would not be stabilized. Since
for many decades more carbon dioxide would be added to the atmosphere than removed through natural processes, the buildup would only
slow; consequently temperatures would continue to go up. Instead of saving the full 0.75 percent of GDP by keeping emissions at 1990 levels, we
would be saving much less.

It is true that whatever dangers global warming may pose, they will
be most pronounced in the developing world. It is much easier for rich
countries to adapt to any long-term shift in weather than it is for
poor countries, which tend to be much more dependent on agriculture.
Poor countries lack the resources to aid their flora and fauna in adapting,
and many of their farmers earn too little to survive a shift to new conditions. But the best insurance for these poor countries is an increase in
their wealth, which would diminish their dependence on agriculture and
make it easier for them to adjust to changes in weather, including increases in precipitation and possible flooding or higher sea level. Subjecting Americans to high taxes and onerous regulations will help neither
them—we could buy less from them—nor us.

The optimal way to deal with potential climate change is not to embark on a futile attempt to prevent it, but to promote growth and prosperity so that people will have the resources to deal with the normal set
of natural disasters. Based on the evidence, including historical records,
global warming is likely to be good for most of mankind. The additional
carbon, rain and warmth should promote the plant growth necessary to
sustain an expanding world population. Global change is inevitable;
warmer is better; richer is healthier.

READING AND DISCUSSION QUESTIONS

1. This article is a claim of value in which the author tries to prove that something is good or bad—in this case, that a warmer climate would be better than a cold one. How many different reasons does he give to support his claim?

2. Moore offers a solution for the problems of a warm planet. Does this solution have shortcomings? If so, what are they?

3. Moore, an economist, spends the greater part of his argument on the economic consequences of global warming. Do you think he should have tried to develop other effects? Give examples of data that seem insufficient.

4. How much of the author's evidence comes from experts? If more testimony is needed, what kind should it be?

WRITING SUGGESTIONS

5. To ascertain whether Moore is right about the consequences of global warming, you will have to consult experts who disagree with him. They will not be hard to find. Most of those who have studied climatic changes think we are in trouble. Based on the testimony of other experts, write a paper that refutes some of Moore's claims.

6. Moore says that most of mankind would choose to live in a warm climate (para. 3). If you could choose, would you live in a tropical climate? A subtropical climate? In your answer, try to go beyond the most superficial reasons, like being tan all year long. Provide sufficient detail and personal background to bring to life the various reasons that would govern your choice.

A White Woman of Color

JULIA ÁLVAREZ

Growing up in the Dominican Republic, I experienced racism within my own family—though I didn't think of it as racism. But there was definitely a hierarchy of beauty, which was the main currency in our daughters-only family. It was not until years later, from the vantage point

---

Novelist and poet Julia Álvarez was raised in the Dominican Republic and immigrated to the United States at age ten with her parents. Her work includes the novels *How the García Girls Lost Their Accents* (1991), *In the Time of the Butterflies* (1994), *¡Yo!* (1997), and *In the Name of Salomé* (2000); two books of poems, *Homecoming: New and Collected Poems* (1996) and *The Woman I Kept to Myself* (2004); and a collection of nonfiction essays, *Something to Declare* (1998). She teaches literature and creative writing at Middlebury College. This essay appeared in *Half and Half: Writers on Growing Up Biracial and Bicultural*, edited by Claudine C. O'Hearn (1998).

of this country and this education, that I realized that this hierarchy of beauty was dictated by our coloring. We were a progression of whitening, as if my mother were slowly bleaching the color out of her children.

The oldest sister had the darkest coloring, with very curly hair and "coarse" features. She looked the most like Papi's side of the family and was considered the least pretty. I came next, with "good hair," and skin that back then was a deep olive, for I was a tomboy—another dark mark against me—who would not stay out of the sun. The sister right after me had my skin color, but she was a good girl who stayed indoors, so she was much paler, her hair a golden brown. But the pride and joy of the family was the baby. She was the one who made heads turn and strangers approach asking to feel her silken hair. She was white white, an adjective that was repeated in describing her color as if to deepen the shade of white. Her eyes were brown, but her hair was an unaccountable tow-headed blond. Because of her coloring, my father was teased that there must have been a German milkman in our neighborhood. How could *she* be *his* daughter? It was clear that this youngest child resembled Mami's side of the family.

It was Mami's family who were *really* white. They were white in terms of race, and white also in terms of class. From them came the fine features, the pale skin, the lank hair. Her brothers and uncles went to schools abroad and had important businesses in the country. They also emulated the manners and habits of North Americans. Growing up, I remember arguments at the supper table on whether or not it was proper to tie one's napkin around one's neck, on how much of one's arm one could properly lay on the table, on whether spaghetti could be eaten with the help of a spoon. My mother, of course, insisted on all the protocol of knives and forks and on eating a little portion of everything served; my father, on the other hand, defended our eating whatever we wanted, with our hands if need be, so we could "have fun" with our food. My mother would snap back that we looked like *jibaritas* who should be living out in the country. Of course, that was precisely where my father's family came from.

Not that Papi's family weren't smart and enterprising, all twenty-five brothers and sisters. (The size of the family in and of itself was considered very country by some members of Mami's family.) Many of Papi's brothers had gone to the university and become professionals. But their education was totally island—no fancy degrees from Andover and Cornell and Yale, no summer camps or school songs in another language. Papi's family still lived in the interior versus the capital, in old-fashioned houses without air conditioning, decorated in ways my mother's family would have considered, well, tasteless. I remember antimacassars on the backs of rocking chairs (which were the living-room set), garish paintings of flamboyant trees, ceramic planters with plastic flowers in bloom. They were *criollos*—creoles—rather than cosmopolitans, expansive, proud, colorful. (Some members had a sixth finger on their right—or was it their left hand?) Their features were less aquiline than Mother's family's, the skin darker, the hair coarse and curly. Their money still had the smell of the earth on it and was kept in a wad in their back pockets, whereas my mother's family had money in the Chase Manhattan Bank, most of it with George Washington's picture on it, not Juan Pablo Duarte's.

It was clear to us growing up then that lighter was better, but there was no question of discriminating against someone because he or she was dark-skinned. Everyone's family, even an elite one like Mami's, had darker-skinned members. All Dominicans, as the saying goes, have a little black behind the ears. So, to separate oneself from those who were darker would have been to divide *una familia,* a sacrosanct entity in our culture. Neither was white blood necessarily a sign of moral or intellectual or political superiority. All one has to do is page through a Dominican history book and look at the number of dark-skinned presidents, dictators, generals, and entrepreneurs to see that power has not resided exclusively or even primarily among the whites on the island. The leadership of our country has been historically "colored."

But being black was something else. A black Dominican was referred to as a "dark Indian" (*indio oscuro*) — unless you wanted to come to blows with him, that is. The real blacks were the Haitians who lived next door and who occupied the Dominican Republic for twenty years, from 1822 to 1844, a fact that can still so inflame the Dominican populace you'd think it had happened last year. The denial of the Afro-Dominican part of our culture reached its climax during the dictatorship of Trujillo, whose own maternal grandmother was Haitian. In 1937, to protect Dominican race purity, Trujillo ordered the overnight genocide of thousands (figures range from 4,000 to 20,000) of Haitians by his military, who committed this atrocity using only machetes and knives in order to make this planned extermination look like a "spontaneous" border skirmish. He also had the Dominican Republic declared a white nation despite the evidence of the mulatto senators who were forced to pass this ridiculous measure.

So, black was not so good, kinky hair was not so good, thick lips not so good. But even if you were *indio oscuro con pelo malo y una bemba de aquí a Baní,* you could still sit in the front of the bus and order at the lunch counter — or the equivalent thereof. There was no segregation of races in the halls of power. But in the aesthetic arena — the one to which we girls were relegated as females — lighter was better. Lank hair and pale skin and small, fine features were better. All I had to do was stay out of the sun and behave myself and I could pass as a pretty white girl.

Another aspect of my growing up also greatly influenced my thinking on race. Although I was raised in the heart of a large family, my day-to-day caretakers were the maids. Most of these women were dark-skinned, some of Haitian background. One of them, Misiá, had been spared the machetes of the 1937 massacre when she was taken in and hidden from the prowling *guardias* by the family. We children spent most of the day with these women. They tended to us, nursed us when we were sick, cradled us when we fell down and scraped an elbow or knee (as a tomboy, there was a lot of this scraping for me), and most important, they told us stories of *los santos* and *el barón del cementerio,* of *el cuco* and *las ciguapas,* beautiful dark-skinned creatures who escaped capture because their feet were turned backwards so they left behind a false set of footprints. These women spread the wings of our imaginations and connected us deeply to the land we came from. They were the ones with the stories that had power over us.

We arrived in Nueva York in 1960, before the large waves of Caribbean immigrants created little Habanas, little Santo Domingos, and little San Juans in the boroughs of the city. Here we encountered a whole new kettle of wax—as my malapropping Mami might have said. People of color were treated as if they were inferior, prone to violence, uneducated, untrustworthy, lazy—all the "bad" adjectives we were learning in our new language. Our dark-skinned aunt, Tía Ana, who had lived in New York for several decades and so was the authority in these matters, recounted stories of discrimination on buses and subways. These Americans were so blind! One drop of black and you were black. Everyone back home would have known that Tía Ana was not black: she had "good hair" and her skin color was a light *indio.* All week, she worked in a *factoría* in the Bronx, and when she came to visit us on Saturdays to sew our school clothes, she had to take three trains to our nice neighborhood where the darkest face on the street was usually her own.

We were lucky we were white Dominicans or we would have had a 10 much harder time of it in this country. We would have encountered a lot more prejudice than we already did, for white as we were, we found that our Latino-ness, our accents, our habits and smells, added "color" to our complexion. Had we been darker, we certainly could not have bought our mock Tudor house in Jamaica Estates. In fact, the African American family who moved in across the street several years later needed police protection because of threats. Even so, at the local school, we endured the bullying of classmates. "Go back to where you came from!" they yelled at my sisters and me in the playground. When some of them started throwing stones, my mother made up her mind that we were not safe and began applying to boarding schools where privilege transformed prejudice into patronage.

"So where are you from?" my classmates would ask.

"Jamaica Estates," I'd say, an edge of belligerence to my voice. It was obvious from my accent, if not my looks, that I was not *from* there in the way they meant being from somewhere.

"I mean originally."

And then it would come out, the color, the accent, the cousins with six fingers, the smell of garlic.

By the time I went off to college, a great explosion of American cul- 15 ture was taking place on campuses across the country. The civil rights movement, the Vietnam War and subsequent peace movement, the women's movement, were transforming traditional definitions of American identity. Ethnicity was in: my classmates wore long braids like Native Americans and peasant blouses from Mexico and long, diaphanous skirts and dangly earrings from India. Suddenly, my foreignness was being celebrated. This reversal felt affirming but also disturbing. As huipils, serapes, and embroidered dresses proliferated about me, I had the feeling that my ethnicity had become a commodity. I resented it.

When I began looking for a job after college, I discovered that being a white Latina made me a nonthreatening minority in the eyes of these employers. My color was a question *only* of culture, and if I kept my cultural color to myself, I was "no problem." Each time I was hired for one of my countless "visiting appointments"—they were never permanent "invitations," mind you—the inevitable questionnaire would accompany my contract in which I was to check off my RACE: CAUCASIAN, BLACK, NATIVE AMERICAN, ASIAN, HISPANIC, OTHER. How could a Dominican divide herself in this way? Or was I really a Dominican anymore? And what was a Hispanic? A census creation—there is no such culture—how could it define who I was at all? Given this set of options, the truest answer might have been to check off other.

For that was the way I had begun to think of myself. Adrift from any Latino community in this country, my culture had become an internal homeland, periodically replenished by trips "back home." But as a professional woman on my own, I felt less and less at home on the island. My values, the loss of my Catholic faith, my lifestyle, my wardrobe, my hippy ways, and my feminist ideas separated me from my native culture. I did not subscribe to many of the mores and constraints that seemed to be an intrinsic part of that culture. And since my culture had always been my "color," by rejecting these mores I had become not only Americanized but whiter.

If I could have been a part of a Latino community in the United States, the struggle might have been, if not easier, less private and therefore less isolating. These issues of acculturation and ethnicity would have been struggles to share with others like me. But all my North American life I had lived in shifting academic communities—going to boarding schools, then college, and later teaching wherever I could get those yearly appointments—and these communities reflected the dearth of Latinos in the profession. Except for friends in Spanish departments, who tended to have come from their countries of origin to teach rather than being raised in this country as I was, I had very little daily contact with Latinos.

Where I looked for company was where I had always looked for company since coming to this country: in books. At first the texts that I read and taught were the ones prescribed to me, the canonical works which formed the content of the bread-and-butter courses that as a "visiting instructor" I was hired to teach. These texts were mostly written by white male writers from Britain and the United States, with a few women thrown in and no Latinos. Thank goodness for the occasional creative writing workshop where I could bring in the multicultural authors I wanted. But since I had been formed in this very academy, I was clueless where to start. I began to educate myself by reading, and that is when I discovered that there were others out there like me, hybrids who came in a variety of colors and whose ethnicity and race were an evolving process, not a rigid paradigm or a list of boxes, one of which you checked off.

This discovery of my ethnicity on paper was like a rebirth. I had been 20 going through a pretty bad writer's block: the white page seemed impossible to fill with whatever it was I had in me to say. But listening to authors like Maxine Hong Kingston, Toni Morrison, Gwendolyn Brooks, Langston Hughes, Maya Angelou, June Jordan, and to Lorna Dee Cervantes, Piri Thomas, Rudolfo Anaya, Edward Rivera, Ernesto Galarza (that first wave of Latino writers), I began to hear the language "in color." I began to see that literature could reflect the otherness I was feeling, that the choices in fiction and poetry did not have to be bleached out of their color or simplified into either/or. A story could allow for the competing claims of different parts of ourselves and where we came from.

Ironically, it was through my own stories and poems that I finally made contact with Latino communities in this country. As I published more, I was invited to read at community centers and bilingual programs. Latino students, who began attending colleges in larger numbers in the late seventies and eighties, sought me out as a writer and teacher "of color." After the publication of *How the García Girls Lost Their Accents,* I found that I had become a sort of spokesperson for Dominicans in this country, a role I had neither sought nor accepted. Of course, some Dominicans refused to grant me any status as a "real" Dominican because I was "white." With the color word there was also a suggestion of class. My family had not been among the waves of economic immigrants that left the island in the seventies, a generally darker-skinned, working-class group, who might have been the maids and workers in my mother's family house. We had come in 1960, political refugees, with no money but with "prospects": Papi had a friend who was the doctor at the Waldorf Astoria and who helped him get a job; Mami's family had money in the Chase Manhattan Bank they could lend us. We had changed class in America — from Mami's elite family to middle-class spics — but our background and education and most especially our pale skin had made mobility easier for us here. We had not undergone the same kind of race struggles as other Dominicans; therefore, we could not be "real" Dominicans.

What I came to understand and accept and ultimately fight for with my writing is the reality that ethnicity and race are not fixed constructs or measurable quantities. What constitutes our ethnicity and our race — once there is literally no common ground beneath us to define it — evolves as we seek to define and redefine ourselves in new contexts. My

Latino-ness is not something someone can take away from me or leave me out of with a definition. It is in my blood: it comes from that mixture of biology, culture, native language, and experience that makes me a different American from one whose family comes from Ireland or Poland or Italy. My Latino-ness is also a political choice. I am choosing to hold on to my ethnicity and native language even if I can "pass." I am choosing to color my Americanness with my Dominicanness even if it came in a light shade of skin color.

I hope that as Latinos, coming from so many different countries and continents, we can achieve solidarity in this country as the mix that we are. I hope we won't shoot ourselves in the foot in order to maintain some sort of false "purity" as the glue that holds us together. Such an enterprise is bound to fail. We need each other. We can't afford to reject the darker or lighter varieties, and to do so is to have absorbed a definition of ourselves as exclusively one thing or the other. And haven't we learned to fear that word "exclusive"? This reductiveness is absurd when we are talking about a group whose very definition is that of a mestizo race, a mixture of European, indigenous, African, and much more. Within this vast circle, shades will lighten and darken into overlapping categories. If we cut them off, we diminish our richness and we plant a seed of ethnic cleansing that is the root of the bloodshed we have seen in Bosnia and the West Bank and Rwanda and even our own Los Angeles and Dominican Republic.

As we Latinos redefine ourselves in America, making ourselves up and making ourselves over, we have to be careful, in taking up the promises of America, not to adopt its limiting racial paradigms. Many of us have shed customs and prejudices that oppressed our gender, race, or class on our native islands and in our native countries. We should not replace these with modes of thinking that are divisive and oppressive of our rich diversity. Maybe as a group that embraces many races and differences, we Latinos can provide a positive multicultural, multiracial model to a divided America.

READING AND DISCUSSION QUESTIONS

1. What is the meaning of the title of this essay? Is it an oxymoron?

2. Explain Álvarez's "hierarchy of beauty" (para. 1) in the Dominican Republic. What does she mean by "white in terms of race, and white also in terms of class" (para. 3)?

3. Does such a hierarchy of beauty have parallels in the United States? If it is not skin color, are other physical attributes rated as good or bad? How do you think such preferences arose?

4. Why did Álvarez think of herself as "adrift" (para. 17)? How does Álvarez explain the "discovery of my ethnicity" (para. 20)?

5. Álvarez ends her essay by summarizing what she has learned from her experience as a white woman "of color" (para. 21). How do the last three paragraphs differ in tone and content from the narrative that precedes it? Do you think they are effective? Would the essay have been stronger or weaker if she had ended it before the last three paragraphs?

WRITING SUGGESTIONS

6. Álvarez mentions a number of authors who inspired her with their views of otherness (para. 20). Perhaps you are familiar with their works or the works of other writers who explore ethnicity in America, such as *The Joy Luck Club, I Know Why the Caged Bird Sings, Native Son,* and *Reservation Blues.* Write a review of a book in which the author describes the experience of being different in the United States.

7. If you know any immigrants—in your own family or perhaps on campus—describe their attempts at acculturation. What aspects of American life have been most challenging for them? What aspects have been easiest to understand and accept?

College Life versus My Moral Code

ELISHA DOV HACK

Many people envy my status as a freshman at Yale College. My classmates and I made it through some fierce competition, and we are excited to have been accepted to one of the best academic and extracurricular programs in American higher education. I have an older brother who attended Yale, and I've heard from him what life at Yale is like.

He spent all his college years living at home because our parents are New Haven residents, and Yale's rules then did not require him to live in the dorms. But Yale's new regulations demand that I spend my freshman and sophomore years living in the college dormitories.

I, two other freshmen, and two sophomores have refused to do this because life in the dorms, even on the floors Yale calls "single sex," is contrary to the fundamental principles we have been taught as long as we can remember—the principles of Judaism lived according to the Torah and 3,000-year-old rabbinic teachings. Unless Yale waives its residence requirement, we may have no choice but to sue the university to protect our religious way of life.

Elisha Dov Hack was a member of the Yale College class of 2001. This article appeared on September 9, 1997, in the *New York Times.*

Bingham Hall, on the Yale quadrangle known as the Old Campus, is one of the dorms for incoming students. When I entered it two weeks ago during an orientation tour, I literally saw the handwriting on the wall. A sign titled "Safe Sex" told me where to pick up condoms on campus. Another sign touted 100 ways to make love without having sex, like "take a nap together" and "take a steamy shower together."

That, I am told, is real life in the dorms. The "freshperson" issue of   5 the *Yale Daily News* sent to entering students contained a "Yale lexicon" defining *sexile* as "banishment from your dorm room because your room-mate is having more fun than you." If you live in the dorms, you're ex-pected to be part of the crowd, to accept these standards as the framework for your life.

Can we stand up to classmates whose sexual morality differs from ours? We've had years of rigorous religious teaching, and we've watched and learned from our parents. We can hold our own in the intellectual debate that flows naturally from exchanges during and after class. But I'm upset and hurt by this requirement that I live in the dorms. Why is Yale—an institution that professes to be so tolerant and open-minded—making it particularly hard for students like us to maintain our moral standards through difficult college years?

We are not trying to impose our moral standards on our classmates or on Yale. Our parents tell us that things were very different in college dor-mitories in their day and that in most colleges in the 1950s students who allowed guests of the opposite sex into their dorm rooms were subject to expulsion. We acknowledge that today's morality is not that of the 50s. We are asking only that Yale give us the same permission to live off cam-pus that it gives any lower classman who is married or at least twenty-one years old.

Yale is proud of the fact that it has no "parietal rules" and that sexual morality is a student's own business. Maybe this is what Dean Richard H. Brodhead meant when he said that "Yale's residential colleges carry . . . a moral meaning." That moral meaning is, basically, "Anything goes." This morality is Yale's own residential religion, which it is proselytizing by force of its regulations.

We cannot, in good conscience, live in a place where women are per-mitted to stay overnight in men's rooms, and where visiting men can traipse through the common halls on the women's floors—in various stages of undress—in the middle of the night. The dormitories on Yale's Old Campus have floors designated by gender, but there is easy access through open stairwells from one floor to the next.

The moral message Yale's residences convey today is not one that our   10 religion accepts. Nor is it a moral environment in which the five of us can spend our nights, or a moral surrounding that we can call home.

Yale sent me a glossy brochure when it welcomed me as an entering student. It said, "Yale retains a deep respect for its early history and for the continuity that its history provides—a continuity based on constant reflection and reappraisal." Yale ought to reflect on and reappraise a policy that compels us to compromise our religious principles.

READING AND DISCUSSION QUESTIONS

1. Summarize Hack's "moral code" in a sentence or two. What examples of conduct does he give to make his definition clear?

2. What solution to his problem does the author propose? Why does Yale refuse to accept the solution? Are Yale's rules justified?

3. Hack says that religious students "may have no choice but to sue the university to protect our religious way of life" (para. 3). What support could he offer in a court of law for his claim that these students should be allowed to live off campus? If you can, ask a legal expert for ideas.

4. Many arguments, like this one between religious students and a university, arise out of a conflict not between good and evil but between two goods. Can you propose a compromise that would satisfy both sides in this case?

WRITING SUGGESTIONS

5. How do you think Yale could defend the sexual freedom that prevails on its campus? Write an argument setting out the philosophical principles and cultural values that justify tolerance for the practices Hack rejects.

6. Members of some minority groups on college campuses often insist on living together in separate dorms, taking their meals together, engaging in separate activities, etc. In light of today's emphasis on the multicultural experience, should the university allow such segregation?

Real Marriage, Real Life

E. J. GRAFF

Laughing at marriage, that age-old comedy staple, is trendy once again. *The Bachelor, The Bachelorette, Joe Millionaire,* and the "reality" genre's latest entry, *Married by America*: Watching what fools these mortals be is setting Nielsen records. And why not? Unlike the terrifyingly high-stakes disputes over Iraq, smallpox vaccinations, airport security, and secret detentions, marriage has an easy-to-follow storyline—one we're all sure we understand better than the players do.

But do these programs also reflect a new zeitgeist, a marrying mood? Are millions tuning in merely for distraction from the prospect of

E. J. Graff is a contributing editor to *The American Prospect* and to *Out* magazine, and is a visiting scholar at the Brandeis Women's Studies Research Center. Her book *What Is Marriage For? The Strange Social History of Our Most Intimate Institution* was published in 1999. This essay is from *The American Prospect*.

international thuggery? Or, given our scary times, are they ready to say goodbye to the commitment-free singles on *Seinfeld*, hoping to settle their own uncertain plotlines once and for all? If it's the latter, they'll be disappointed. Once upon a time, marriage could be life's answer. Because of capitalism, that can never be true again.

What's capitalism got to do with it? If you look closely, you'll find two ideas about marriage running through these reality shows. The first: The only moral reason to marry is for love. While that's the American philosophy of marriage today, it's a recent idea historically. The second: Money influences your choice of mate. That thought, currently taboo, is actually quite traditional.

With that in mind, consider *Joe Millionaire*. Twenty women competed to win the affections of a man they thought had inherited $50 million. But as the audience knew (and the women didn't during filming), "Joe" was actually Evan Marriott, a construction worker earning $19,000 a year, a fact he revealed only after choosing his prospective bride. Joe said he liked construction work better than college and would rather be poor than unhappy. In good fairy-tale fashion, our simple hero selected—from the seething pool of aspiring actresses and catty sophisticates hoping never to work again—another simple peasant, er, impoverished substitute teacher doing what she loved. Viewer faith in true love was renewed. But finances are what triumphed: These two are a perfect socioeconomic match.

Or consider *Married by America*, now under way. After having mates   5 chosen for them (first winnowed down by friends and families, final selections by viewer votes), five singles were "engaged" to five strangers on stage. Those couples who do marry after a month's onscreen cohabitation will win a list of consumer prizes, including that American dream, the single-family house—the payoff for making love and war in front of the nation. Here's my bet: Those couples best matched socioeconomically are most likely to win the real estate.

Tying marriage to money may sound crass, but it's more traditional than today's desperation dating. Ketubah, dowry, bride-price, breach-of-contract suits: In most eras and cultures, finances have been negotiated up front. Arranged marriages, in which a person's friends and family selected a prospect of equivalent socioeconomic "worth," worked out just as well as (if not better than) Match.com.

Today we still find love based on compatible finances. You can see it in the *New York Times* wedding pages: Marriages are financial mergers, although today's wealth comes in the form of a CV, a union card, or a string of degrees. What is a college education fund but an updated dowry, an investment in a child's financial future? And when was the last time you knew a corporate lawyer to marry a postal worker or (except in a J. Lo movie) a maid to wed a future U.S. senator?

Here's what's historically new: Few couples today are yoked together in daily labor. Traditionally, husbands and wives were business partners;

one brought in the fish, the other hawked them at the market. Working and sleeping together gave them a good shot at love—and a reason to stay together when love wasn't there.

But capitalism turned us into workers as mobile as cellular phones, able to make a living one by one. There's no FDIC guarantee on today's marital investment; we don't have to stay together to stay alive—even if, in these parlous times, it can seem as if we do.

After the international traumas of the 1930s and '40s, shell-shocked   10 young people raced down the aisle—and then, twenty years later, raced back out again. So far, almost no reality-show pair has made it more than a few minutes after the program's end. That's what makes it comedy. Don't you wish the mistakes in our international reality show could be so easily undone?

READING AND DISCUSSION QUESTIONS

1. What is Graff's strategy in opening with a reference to reality shows? What do those shows suggest about marriage today?

2. What claim is Graff supporting in the essay? Where does she state that claim most directly?

3. What sort of support does she offer? How effective do you find it to be?

4. Graff feels that tying marriage to money is actually a very old concept. What does she find new about today's marriages?

WRITING SUGGESTIONS

5. Like the marriages in the reality shows that Graff refers to, prenuptial agreements are often the target of humor. In all seriousness, do you feel that a prenuptial agreement is a good idea even if neither spouse is extremely wealthy?

6. Use examples from television and/or movies to argue that in the world of fiction, marriages between those of drastically different socioeconomic classes can and do succeed.

7. Attack or defend this statement by Graff: "Marriages are financial mergers, although today's wealth comes in the form of a CV, a union card, or a string of degrees" (para. 7).

Supersize Your Child?

RICHARD HAYES

In the late 1950s, soon after Watson and Crick had discovered DNA's structure, scientists began predicting that someday we'd be able to genetically engineer our children. We'd design them to be healthy, smart, and attractive, with life spans of 200 years, photographic memories, enhanced lung capacity for athletic endurance, and more. Our children would pass these modifications to their own children and add new ones as well. Humanity would take control of its own evolution and kick it into overdrive.

Few people took these speculations very seriously. Could this sort of genetic engineering really be done? Even if it could, would anyone really want to do it? If they did, wouldn't society step in and set limits? In any event, wouldn't it be decades before we'd have to worry about this?

Now it's 2004, and those decades have passed. The era of genetically modified humans is close upon us. Almost every day we read of new breakthroughs: cloning, artificial chromosomes and now high-tech sex selection. Scientists create genetically modified animals on an assembly-line basis. Biotech entrepreneurs discuss the potential market for genetically modified children at investors' conferences. For the most part, society has not stepped in and set limits.

Last year *Science* magazine reported that a variant of the human 5-HTT gene reduces the risk of depression following stressful experiences. Depression can be a devastating condition. Would it be wrong if a couple planning to start a family used in vitro fertilization procedures to have the 5-HTT gene variant inserted into the embryos of their prospective children? Taken as an isolated instance, many people would be hard-pressed to say that it was.

In 1993, University of California at San Francisco biochemist Dr. 5
Cynthia Kenyon discovered a variant of the DAF-2 gene that doubles the two-week life span of nematode worms. The university filed for patents based on knowledge of the metabolic pathway regulated by the human version of the DAF-2 gene. In 1999, Kenyon and others founded Elixir Pharmaceuticals, a biotech firm. In early 2003, Elixir licensed the university's patent rights to Kenyon's discoveries and secured $17 million in private financing. In an earlier interview with *ABC News*, Kenyon said she saw no reason humans might not be able to achieve 200-year life spans.

Richard Hayes is the executive director of the Center for Genetics and Society, a California-based nonprofit organization working for the responsible governance of genetic technologies. This piece was published on the TomPaine.com Web site in February 2004.

"Post-human" Nature

Last June at Yale University, the World Transhumanist Association held its first national conference. The Transhumanists have chapters in more than 20 countries and advocate the breeding of "genetically enriched" forms of "post-human" beings. Other advocates of the new techno-eugenics, such as Princeton University professor Lee Silver, predict that by the end of this century, "All aspects of the economy, the media, the entertainment industry, and the knowledge industry [will be] controlled by members of the GenRich class . . . Naturals [will] work as low-paid service providers or as laborers . . ."

What happens then? Here's Dr. Richard Lynn, emeritus professor at the University of Ulster, who, like Silver, supports human genetic modification: "What is called for here is not genocide, the killing off of the population of incompetent cultures. But we do need to think realistically in terms of the 'phasing out' of such peoples. . . . Evolutionary progress means the extinction of the less competent."

Notice that I've gone, in just four steps, from reducing susceptibility to depression, to extending the human life span, to the creation of a genetic elite, to proposals that genetically inferior people be "phased out."

When first presented with this scenario, people typically respond in one of two ways. Some say, "It's impossible." Others say, "It's inevitable." Notice what these otherwise diametrically different responses have in common: both counsel passivity. If the "post-human future" is impossible, there's no need to try to prevent it. If it's inevitable, such efforts would be in vain.

Will it actually be possible to genetically engineer our children? Most 10 scientists who have studied this question conclude that although the techniques need to be refined, there's no reason to believe it can't be done. Meanwhile, research on stem cells, cloning, artificial chromosomes and more continues to refine those techniques.

Many people believe that to suggest that manipulating genes can affect behavioral and cognitive traits in humans is to indulge discredited ideologies of "genetic determinism." It's true that the crude sociobiology of the 1970s has been discredited, as have simplistic notions that there exist "I.Q. genes" or "gay genes" that determine one's intelligence or sexual orientation. But to say that genes have no influence over traits is equally simplistic. Some genes have minimal influence, others have greater influence. Some have influence in the presence of certain environmental factors but no influence otherwise. Few genes determine anything; most confer propensities.

Deepening Inequality

Suppose scientists found a gene giving male children a 15 percent greater chance of growing one inch taller than they would have grown without that gene, all else equal. If fertility clinics offered to engineer embryos to include this gene, would there be customers? Yes. Couples would say, "In this competitive world, I want to do anything I can that might give my child an edge."

Once we allow children to be designed through embryo modification, where would we stop? If it's acceptable to modify one gene, why not two? If two, why not 20? Or 200? There are some 30,000 genes in the human genome. Each contributes, in smaller or larger proportions, to some propensity. Where would we stop? On what grounds?

Some suggest we allow embryo modification for certified medical conditions and prohibit it for cosmetic or enhancement purposes. It's unlikely that this would succeed. Prozac, Viagra, and Botox were all developed for medical purposes but in the blink of an eye became hugely profitable cosmetic and enhancement consumer products.

Will the use of genetic engineering to redesign our children exacer- 15 bate inequality? Amazingly, the neo-eugenic advocates don't deny that it will. As good libertarians, they celebrate free markets and social Darwinism, and counsel us to accept a rising tide of genetically enhanced inequality as the inevitable result of human ingenuity and desire.

But couldn't this be prevented? Wouldn't society step in? Several years ago, a team of health policy academics examined a range of proposals, including systems of national health insurance making eugenic engineering available to all, or preferentially to the poor, or by lottery. Despite their best efforts, they couldn't identify any realistic set of policies that would prevent the new eugenic technologies, once allowed at all, from generating unprecedented inequality.

And consider the international implications. What happens when some country announces an aggressive program of eugenic engineering explicitly intended to create a new, superior, omni-competent breed of human? What does the rest of the world do then?

We need to take a deep breath and realize what is going on here. The birth of the first genetically modified child would be a watershed moment in human history. It would set off a chain of events that would feed back upon themselves in ways impossible to control.

Unnatural Selection

Everything we experience, everything we know, everything we do is experienced, known and done by a species—homo sapiens—which evolved through natural selection over hundreds of thousands of years. We differ as individuals, but we are a single human species with a shared biology so fundamental to what we are that we are not even conscious of it, or of the manifold ways it unites us. What happens if we begin changing that fundamental shared biology?

Three hundred years ago the scientific and political leaders of that era 20 took as a self-evident fact the division of humanity into "superior" and "inferior" types, designed by Providence respectively as masters and slaves. Human beings were bred, bought and sold, like cattle or dogs.

After three hundred years of struggle and bloodshed we are on the verge—barely—of putting this awful legacy behind us.

Or maybe not. If left uncontrolled, the new human genetic technologies could set us on a trajectory leading to a new Dark Age in which people are once again regarded as little better than cattle or dogs. Here is "bioethicist" Gregory Pence, who has testified in support of human cloning before the U.S. Congress and elsewhere:

> [M]any people love their retrievers and their sunny dispositions around children and adults. Could people be chosen in the same way? Would it be so terrible to allow parents to at least aim for a certain type, in the same way that great breeders . . . try to match a breed of dog to the needs of a family?

The common initial responses to the prospect of the new techno-eugenics—"It's impossible," and "It's inevitable"—are incorrect and unhelpful. The response we need to affirm is at once more realistic and more challenging: The techno-eugenic future certainly is possible, and is certainly not inevitable.

Road to Regulation

In 1997, the Council of Europe negotiated an important international agreement, the Convention on Biomedicine and Human Rights. Thus far, it has been signed by more than two-thirds of the council's 45 member countries. The convention draws the lines on human genetic modification in just the right ways. It allows medical research, including stem cell research, to continue, and does not restrict abortion rights, but it bans genetic modifications that would open the door to high-tech eugenic engineering. Many countries in Asia, Africa, and Latin America have likewise begun to address these issues through legislation.

These efforts are encouraging, but we have a long way to go before such policies are implemented, as they must be, worldwide. In some countries, notably the United States, the politics of the new genetic technologies have become polarized to the point of gridlock. The religious right insists on total bans on nearly all human embryo research, while bio-research interests and the biotech industry insist on nearly total freedom from any meaningful social oversight and accountability.

In other countries, and at the international level, the challenge of a 25 new high-tech, free market eugenics, while worrisome, can seem remote in comparison with the real existing challenges of warfare, hunger, and disease.

What is to be done? More than anything, we need to realize the unprecedented nature of the challenges that the new human genetic technologies present. We need to distinguish benign applications of these technologies from pernicious ones, and support the former while opposing the latter. Concerned organizations and individuals need to engage these challenges and make their voices heard worldwide. National and international leaders in politics, the sciences and the arts need to declare that humanity is not going to let itself be split asunder by human genetic technology. The United Nations and other international bodies need to give these issues the highest attention. The hour is late. There is no greater challenge before us.

READING AND DISCUSSION QUESTIONS

1. Hayes alerts us that he is using the organization of his essay to help make his point. Explain where and how he does that. How does he appeal to his readers' need to feel secure? Why might his readers feel their sense of security being threatened?

2. Is Hayes supporting a claim of fact, value, or policy? Where does he state that claim most directly?

3. What types of support does Hayes offer to back up his opinion? How convincing do you find his support to be?

4. Can you identify the warrant underlying Hayes's argument? In order to accept his claim, what assumption of his must you agree with? Does he state his warrant explicitly anywhere in the essay?

WRITING SUGGESTIONS

5. Write an essay in which you either support or argue against Hayes's claim.

6. Write an essay in which you explain your own position on who should set limits on genetic engineering.

7. Choose an invention or scientific development that people once said was impossible and explain how those skeptics were proved wrong.

8. Choose an invention or scientific development and explain how it is now used, for good or ill, for purposes it was never intended to serve.

DISCUSSION QUESTIONS

1. What does the ad suggest about the intentions that people have when they go on vacation? What does it suggest about the reality of vacations?
2. What claim of policy is the ad supporting? Do you find it effective in supporting that claim? Why or why not?

3. What warrant underlies the ad? What general truth applied beyond this single ad does the ad seem to illustrate?

4. Is the choice of *War and Peace* as the featured book a good one, given that the ad was published in 2004 in *Newsweek*? Think of some different magazines that the ad could appear in. What book would be a better choice for each of the magazines you think of?

5. Since Imodium is the product being advertised, why is the image of the product so small?

DEBATE: Who is responsible for the college cost crisis?

Historical Perspective on College Cost Increases

JOHN A. BOEHNER AND HOWARD P. "BUCK" McKEON

College cost increases have dominated back to school stories in the media this fall, with tuitions jumping as much as 40 percent or more at both public and private colleges and universities across the nation. Although this disturbing trend is regularly blamed on the budget woes of the states facing difficult economic conditions, this analysis overlooks the long-term trends of college costs. America is facing a college cost crisis. This crisis is not the result of a bad economy and a few difficult years for institutions of higher education. The crisis exists because for decades, tuitions have been rising at a rate much more rapid than family income or student aid can keep pace with, and a boiling point has been reached in which students and families are losing out on the opportunity for higher education. Now, as higher education becomes increasingly important in a technologically dominated world, higher education should be more accessible, not less.

According to the College Board, in the 1970s there was little, if any, real growth in college prices. In the early 1980s, however, tuition and fees began to grow much more rapidly than consumer prices—in fact, during the 1980s, the cost of attending college rose over three times as fast as median family income. This trend of rapidly increasing college costs has

John A. Boehner is a Republican congressman from Ohio and chairman of the U.S. House Committee on Education and the Workforce. Howard P. "Buck" McKeon is a Republican congressman from California and chairman of the U.S. House Subcommittee on Twenty-First Century Competitiveness. This article is from their September 4, 2003, report "The College Cost Crisis: A Congressional Analysis of College Costs and Implications for America's Higher Education System."

continued through the 1990s. Over the ten-year period ending in 2002–2003, after adjusting for inflation, average tuition and fees at both public and private four-year colleges and universities rose 38 percent. . . . And according to information gathered from the College Board and the Census Bureau, over the last 22 years (since 1981), the cost of a public four-year college education has increased by 202 percent, while the CPI (Consumer Price Index) has gone up only 80 percent.

This year, average tuition and fees at a public four-year institution is over $4,000, an increase of 9.6 percent over last year. Average tuition and fees at a private college or university is over $18,000, an increase of 5.8 percent over last year's average. These increases exceeded the rise in the Consumer Price Index by 8.4 and 4.7 percent, respectively, and these figures do not include the additional costs associated with higher education, including room and board, books and supplies, lab fees and additional academic costs, transportation, and other personal expenses. Students attending four-year public colleges and universities in all 50 states will feel the squeeze of tuition hikes this fall, with every state in the nation increasing tuition to some degree.

The tuition increases facing students this year are not symptomatic of a single cause such as difficult economic circumstances, but are the culmination of years of disproportionate cost increases caused by a wide variety of influences and factors. . . .

Are Colleges Accountable Enough for Tuition Hikes?

Many observers believe the endlessly increasing tuition rates today's   5
parents and students have been forced to contend with are largely the result of a lack of accountability within the higher education system. Thanks to a combination of factors—including a shortage of easily compared information about tuition increases, and a willingness by government leaders to continue to subsidize higher education regardless of whether institutions make responsible decisions—consumers of higher education (parents and students) are denied the ability to exercise the kind of leverage they would normally expect to have in the marketplace.

A recent *Newsweek* article explores the college cost issue, interviewing a variety of individuals involved with higher education in an effort to identify the root of the problem for parents and students. While state funding cuts are taking a toll, the article notes, colleges are also increasing their expenditures, and they aren't always making the kind of sound economic decisions one might expect them to make in response to consumer unrest.

"Even as budgets are being squeezed, costs are escalating," the *Newsweek* account notes. "To compete in cutting-edge science and technology fields, for instance, universities are shelling out millions for research facilities. But because administrators can be more concerned about raising a college's profile than streamlining operations, says (National

Center for Public Policy and Higher Education president Patrick) Callan, they don't always act the way a private business might—like making all of a campus's divisions negotiate jointly with vendors for lower prices" (Arian Campo-Flores, "Why It Costs So Much; Tough Times Hurt Funding, but Schools Keep Spending," *Newsweek*, September 1, 2003).

Because parents and students keep coming back for more, there is "no market constraint to keep them from raising tuition," *Newsweek* quotes Ronald Ehrenberg, director of the Cornell Higher Education Research Institute, as saying. "People continue to knock on their doors." And, of course, the federal government continues to increase spending for higher education programs. A recent analysis appearing in Forbes suggests dramatic increases in federal spending for higher education programs have only made colleges and universities less accountable to parents and students.

"Over the past three decades the Federal Government has poured three-quarters of a trillion dollars into financial aid for college students," observes writer Ira Carnahan. "So why is college getting less—not more—affordable? One answer seems to be that all those federal dollars have given colleges more room to jack up tuition . . . The more cash the government pumps into parents' pockets, the more the schools siphon from them" ("Back to School: Why Federal College Aid Makes School More Expensive," Ira Carnahan, *Forbes*, September 1, 2003).

Greater competition in higher education, Carnahan's sources suggest,   10 would go a long way toward bringing college costs back down to Earth. Increasing competition among institutions would generate unforeseen savings that "would probably come out of frills like lavish recreational facilities and the salaries and generous perks that are paid to the tenured faculty and senior administrators" at many expensive institutions, Brown University economist Herschel Grossman is quoted as saying by *Forbes*.

"Academia loves Washington's financial aid but seldom feels any obligation to reciprocate," wrote Dr. David Hill in a recent op-ed (Hill, "College Costs become a GOP Issue," *The Hill*, July 30, 2003). But, Hill suggests, the public's tolerance for endless tuition increases may be wearing thin. "[With] even higher tuition rates being proposed, it is evident that widespread public revolt is possible," he observes.

"University officials say they need independence in setting tuition to build better programs, improve efficiencies and hire top rated faculty. But in doing so they must be careful . . . not to price students out of college," warned the *Houston Chronicle* in a July 28, 2003, editorial supporting congressional efforts to address the college cost crisis. "Our state must have more college educated citizens to grow and prosper . . . That will require sensible cost controls over college and university budgets and finding more effective ways to spend higher education dollars."

In the National Commission on the Cost of Higher Education's 1998 report to Congress entitled *Straight Talk about College Costs and Prices*, the Commission reported that, "Institutions of higher education, even to most people in the academy, are financially opaque. Academic institutions have made little effort, either on campus or off, to make themselves more transparent, to explain their finances. As a result, there is no readily available information about college costs and prices nor is there a common national reporting standard for either."

Students and Parents Take a Stand against Skyrocketing Tuition

"I have several friends who said they aren't going to be able to come back or they will have to cut back on their other activities, like clubs and student government, to take on another job." —a State University of New York junior, reacting to a 28 percent increase in tuition for the coming semester, as quoted by the Associated Press (Gormley, "Students, families deal with tuition bills," Associated Press, July 28, 2003).

The college cost crisis is having its most devastating impact on U.S.   15 students, who are most vulnerable to tuition hikes, since many are working their way through school on a shoestring budget.

On July 24, 2003, a group of University of California students filed a class action lawsuit in San Francisco Superior Court in an attempt to block university fee increases, which the student plaintiffs say were made without sufficient advance notice. "I don't know if I'll be able to enroll in school this semester," said Mo Kashmiri, a third-year law student at U.C. Berkeley, noting his bill for this fall will be $2,500 higher than last fall.

A May 1 article in the *Boston Globe* detailed the realities students encounter when faced with tuition increases. "Already working 48 hours a week at a laminating company to pay for his full-time course load at Framingham State College, freshman Brian Avery sighed and shook his head at the prospect of state budget cuts boosting his bill by as much as $1,000 next year. 'It just means more hours, more loans,' he said. 'It puts a damper on the mood around here. A lot of students here pay their own way, which is hard to do. This makes it harder.'" (Schworm, "Rising Costs Worry Students," *Boston Globe*, May 1, 2003).

Similarly, an Associated Press piece described the extreme measures students must undertake to make ends meet when facing tuition hikes. "Students such as (Brandon) Cox, an in-state philosophy major paying his way through college, have been particularly hard-hit. He is taking 20 credit hours per semester and expects his tuition to rise by $800 this year. 'It's almost come to the point of starvation a few times, but I've always managed to find something,' Cox said. 'The plasma center will pay you $20 a pint—if you're willing to bleed for two hours'" (AP, "Tuition Hikes slamming middle-class students," Associated Press, August 25, 2003).

Colleges Caught in Vise

STANLEY FISH

When a parent calls to complain about overcrowded classrooms or a reduction in courses and thinks to cinch the case by saying, "After all, I'm a taxpayer and I pay your salary," I respond by asking a question: What percentage of the university's operating costs do you guess are covered by public funds? Almost always, the answer is something on the order of 75 percent. When I say, no, the figure is just 25 percent and heading downward—and add that in some states the figure has dipped below 10 percent—the reaction is usually equal parts surprise and dismay.

I follow up with another question: What percentage of the cost to educate a student do you guess is covered by tuition? Again, the parent is usually shocked by the answer: If you include not just classroom education but the cost of everything that must be in place for that education to occur—a library, laboratories, computer centers, building maintenance, utilities, safety patrols and more—tuition covers only 26 percent. At this point in the conversation the unhappy parent is beginning to see what public universities are facing these days: "You're telling me that state funds are being withdrawn at the same time expenses are exceeding tuition by a factor of three to one. How can you stay in business?"

That's a good question. It is, however, one that two Republicans on the House education committee, John Boehner and Howard McKeon, do not seem to have spent much time considering. Rather, they have issued a report, "The College Cost Crisis," holding that "institutions of higher learning are not accountable enough to parents, students and taxpayers—the consumers of higher education." This conclusion is not backed by any analysis, except for a couple of references to "wasteful spending." But the message is clear: Universities should operate more like businesses and become more efficient. If they don't, Mr. McKeon has the answer, a bill that would cut federal financing to colleges whose tuition hikes are more than double the rate of inflation or the consumer price index.

But this remedy won't do anything except make the situation worse. If there is a crisis in college costs it has not been caused by price-gouging or bureaucratic incompetence on the part of universities; a better analogy would be the mass circulation magazines of the 1950s like *Collier's* and *Look*, which folded at the very point when they had more readers than ever. The problem was that production costs far outpaced the revenues

---

Stanley Fish is dean emeritus of the College of Liberal Arts and Sciences at the University of Illinois at Chicago. This essay was published in the *New York Times* on September 18, 2003, in response to Boehner and McKeon's September 4, 2003, report "The College Cost Crisis."

from subscriptions and advertisers, and every new reader actually cost them money.

This is just what is happening at many public universities. More people want the product—applications to my university are up 35 percent in the past two years—but as the demand for it rises the government support for delivering it is withdrawn. The result: Each new student we take increases the number on the debit side of the ledger. Moreover, the costs that neither tuition nor public dollars will cover are rising exponentially. Even if states impose salary and hiring freezes, they would be more than offset by increases no state government can control: raises mandated by union contracts, skyrocketing utility and insurance rates, the cost of replacing worn-out equipment, the cost of replacing equipment declared obsolete after three years, the cost of buying equipment that didn't exist 18 months ago, the cost of maintaining a crumbling physical plant, the cost of security measures deemed necessary after 9/11.

And now, on top of this, comes the threat of Mr. McKeon's bill. First of all, it seems curious to find members of the free-market Republican Party advocating price controls. In fact, it is downright unbusinesslike. Because if a business were to find itself with rising costs and falling revenues it would lop off unprofitable lines, close units, downsize the workforce, relax quality control and, of course, raise prices to whatever level the traffic would bear. In university terms, this would mean offering fewer courses, closing departments, sending students elsewhere, skimping on advising, hiring the pedagogical equivalent of migrant workers, eliminating remedial programs, ejecting the students for whom remedial programs are necessary, reducing health and counseling services, admitting fewer students and inventing fees for everything from registration to breathing.

Now, if a university were to offer this list as its plan to be more businesslike, Representatives Boehner and McKeon, the rest of Congress, America's parents and our other "consumers" would scream bloody murder. "That's not what we're paying for," all these aggrieved parties would complain. But, of course, that would be exactly what they were willing to pay for.

If the revenues sustaining your operation are sharply cut and you are prevented by law from raising prices, your only recourse is to offer an inferior product. Those who say, as the state has said to the University of Illinois, "We're taking $200 million from you but we expect you to do the job you were doing and do it even better," are trafficking either in fantasy or hypocrisy. I vote for hypocrisy.

DISCUSSION QUESTIONS

1. What claim are Boehner and McKeon trying to support? How effective do you feel they are in supporting that claim?

2. Fish's article was written in direct response to Boehner and McKeon's report. What weaknesses does he find in their reasoning? What analogy forms the basis for his disagreement with their argument? How effective would his argument be in convincing college students and their parents that higher education is worth the cost?

3. How successful are Boehner and McKeon in supporting the claim of fact that tuition costs have risen faster than family income and federal aid? Are they equally successful in supporting their view of why tuitions costs have risen? Fish refers to Boehner and McKeon's statement that "institutions of higher learning are not accountable enough to parents, students and taxpayers—the consumers of higher education." Is there any validity to Fish's claim that "[t]his conclusion is not backed by any analysis, except for a couple of references to 'wasteful spending'"? Explain.

4. Both articles raise the question of what the term "public" in public education means. Should colleges and universities really be called public institutions when less than 25 percent of their funding comes from public funds or, in some cases, when less than 10 percent does? Some schools whose state funding has been drastically cut have considered going private. What would be some of the advantages and disadvantages of a public institution's going private?

5. How creditable did you find the authors to be? Did you approach the two articles differently knowing that the first was written by two congressmen and the other by a dean at a university? In their formal report, Boehner and McKeon make more extensive use of sources than Fish does in his newspaper article. How reliable, in your opinion, are the sources they cite?

TAKING THE DEBATE ONLINE

For these and additional research URLS, see bedfordstmartins.com/rottenberg.

- *College Cost Central*
  www.house.gov/ed_workforce/issues/108th/education/highereducation/collegecostcentral.htm
  This site, maintained by the Committee on Education and the Workforce of the U.S. House of Representatives, which is chaired by John A. Boehner, is designed as a resource for parents, students, and "taxpayers fed up with the high cost of higher education." A link from this site provides the full report in which "Historical Perspective on College Cost Increases" appears.

- *The Chronicle of Higher Education: The War on Higher Education*
  http://chronicle.com/jobs/2003/11/2003112601c.htm
  This article from Stanley Fish's regular column in the *Chronicle of Higher Education*, is a scathing critique of the College Cost Central site.

- *The Washington Dispatch: Collegiate Hypocrisy*
  www.washingtondispatch.com/printer_7558.shtml

  This article from the *Washington Dispatch*, written by Michael Tremoglie, responds to Fish's critique of the College Cost Central site.

- *American Association of Community Colleges: Costs—the Community College Perspective*
  www.statedirectors.org/Docs/college_costs.html

  This article is the response by the American Association of Community Colleges to what Boehner and McKeon term the "College Cost Crisis."

- *The Student Perspective: FSU Student Testifies to Congress on Tuition Increases*
  www.fsunews.com/vnews/display.v/ART/2003/10/06/3f808c7972c0a ?in_archive=1

  This article is a report from Florida State University's online news service about Jessica Hanson, the only student to testify before the U.S. House Subcommittee on Twenty-First Century Competitiveness in September, 2003, when testimony was heard on the issue of college tuition costs.

- *Cato Institute: The Tuition Aid Trap*
  www.cato.org/cgi-bin/scripts/printtech.cgi/dailys/10-09-03.html

  This article by Neal McCluskey, a policy analyst with the Center for Educational Freedom, argues that colleges and universities will have no incentive to control rising tuition as long as higher education is treated as a federally insured entitlement.

- *Washington Post: When States Pay Less, Guess Who Pays More?*
  http://faculty.wm.edu/dhfeld/washingtonpost_com%20When %20States%20Pay%20Less,%20Guess%20Who%20Pays%20More.htm

  In this article, Robert B. Archibald and David H. Feldman, professors of economics at the College of William and Mary, argue that a decline in political and financial support for affordable education for all is the source of the cost crisis rather than irresponsibility on the part of institutions of higher education.

ASSIGNMENTS FOR UNDERSTANDING CLAIMS

1. "I Like Colonel Sanders" is the title of an article that praises ugly architecture, shopping malls, laundromats, and other symbols of "plastic" America. The author claims that these aspects of the American scene have unique and positive values. Defend or refute his claim by pointing out some of the values of these things and giving reasons for your own assessments.

2. Write an essay in which you explain the function or functions that the mall or another gathering place has served for you and your peers.

3. In professional football and basketball, personality traits sometimes contribute as much to the fans' relationship with individual players as talent

on the field or court. Write an essay developing this idea as it applies to one or both sports and providing adequate evidence for your claim.

4. Write an analysis of the ad for Imodium A-D that appears on page 147. Consider how both text and visuals work to advance the claim.

5. Select a familiar ritual and argue for or against the value it represents. *Examples:* the high school prom, Christmas gift-giving, a fraternity initiation, a wedding, a confirmation or bar mitzvah, a funeral ceremony, a Fourth of July celebration.

8. Choose a recommended policy—from the school newspaper or elsewhere—and argue that it will or will not work to produce beneficial changes. *Examples:* expansion of core curriculum requirements, comprehensive tests as a graduation requirement, reinstitution of a physical education requirement, removal of junk food from vending machines.

9. Have you ever been a member of a group that tried but failed to solve a problem through discussion? Communication theorists talk about *interference*, defined by one writer as "anything that hinders or lessens the efficiency of communication."[5] Some of the elements of interference in the delivery of oral messages are fatigue, anger, inattention, vague language, personality conflict, and political bias. You will probably be able to think of others. Did any of these elements prevent the group from arriving at an agreement? Describe the situation and the kinds of interference that you noticed.

[5] Richard E. Crable, *One to Another* (New York: Harper and Row, 1981), p. 18.

CHAPTER 5

Support

TYPES OF SUPPORT: EVIDENCE AND
APPEALS TO NEEDS AND VALUES

All the claims you make—whether of fact, of value, or of policy—must
be supported. Sometimes you will use your own experience as support for
a claim. At other times you may conduct interviews, field research, lab experiments, or surveys to obtain support for your position. For the majority of your assignments, you will most likely turn primarily to print and
electronic sources. In your written assignments, you may already have
been using the readings from this text to support your ideas. The following, for instance, is the opening paragraph of a response to one of the
writing assignments at the end of Chapter 3. This writer chose to compare
the claims made by Jo Ann Citron and Howard Moody in their essays in
that chapter. To support her own claim, the writer quoted from each of
the authors, documenting by means of the page numbers in parentheses
exactly what page the quoted material came from:

> Although they were both writing during the time in 2004 when Massa-
> chusetts was about to make a critical decision about same-sex marriage
> and both for publications that are considered to be liberal, Jo Ann
> Citron and Howard Moody seem unlikely people to agree on anything.
> Citron is a lawyer writing for *The Gay and Lesbian Review Worldwide*, and
> Moody is a retired minister. They both, however, are compassionate to-
> ward people of the same sex who want to share a commitment to each

other. Surprisingly, Moody agrees with Citron that the definition of marriage is in the hands of the state. In his article "Gay Marriage Shows Why We Need to Separate Church and State," he claims that while both church and state can make mistakes, "it is the civil authority of the state that defines the rights and responsibilities of marriage and therefore who can be married" (95). Citron's claim in her essay is that the courts of Massachusetts should lead the other states in "winning for civil union all the rights, benefits, protections, and obligations of marriage" (101).

You will find that many of the readings included in this book are from newspapers and magazines. It has long been standard form for journalists not to use either footnotes or parenthetical documentation to identify their sources but rather to work their sources, when possible, into the text itself. (Sometimes all that their readers learn is that information is from "a source close to the White House.") In your academic writing, however, you will always be expected to give credit to any sources from which you get ideas or wording. Once you have learned the various types of support, you can find in Chapter 10 a detailed explanation of when and how to give credit to any sources you may use.

Support for a claim represents the answer to the question "What have you got to go on?"[1] There are two basic kinds of support in an argument: evidence and appeals to needs and values.

Evidence, as one dictionary defines it, is "something that tends to prove; ground for belief." When you provide evidence, you use facts, including statistics, and opinions, or interpretations of facts—both your own and those of experts. In the following conversation, the first speaker offers facts and the opinion of an expert to convince the second speaker that robots are exceptional machines.

> *"You know, robots do a lot more than work on assembly lines in factories."*
> *"Like what?"*
> *"They shear sheep, pick citrus fruit, and even assist in neurosurgery. And by the end of the century, every house will have a robot slave."*
> *"No kidding. Who says so?"*
> *"An engineer who's the head of the world's largest manufacturer of industrial robots."*

A writer often appeals to readers' needs (that is, requirements for physical and psychological survival and well-being) and values (or standards for right and wrong, good and bad). In the following conversation, the first speaker makes an appeal to the universal need for self-esteem and to the principle of helping others, a value the second speaker probably shares.

---

[1]Stephen Toulmin, *The Uses of Argument* (Cambridge: Cambridge University Press, 1958), p. 98.

*"I think you ought to come help us at the nursing home. We need an extra
    hand."*
"I'd like to, but I really don't have the time."
*"You could give us an hour a week, couldn't you? Think how good you'd feel
    about helping out, and the old people would be so grateful. Some of them
    are very lonely."*

Although they use the same kinds of support, conversations are less
rigorous than arguments addressed to larger audiences in academic or
public situations. In the debates on public policy that appear in the media
and in the courts, the quality of support can be crucial in settling urgent
matters. The following summary of a well-known court case demonstrates
the critical use of both evidence and value appeals in the support of opposing claims.

On March 30, 1981, President Ronald Reagan and three other men
were shot by John W. Hinckley Jr., a young drifter from a wealthy Colorado family. Hinckley was arrested at the scene of the shooting. In his
trial the factual evidence was presented first: Dozens of reliable witnesses
had seen the shooting at close range. Hinckley's diaries, letters, and
poems revealed that he had planned the shooting to impress actress Jodie
Foster. Opinions, consisting of testimony by experts, were introduced by
both the defense and the prosecution. This evidence was contradictory.
Defense attorneys produced several psychiatrists who defined Hinckley as
insane. If this interpretation of his conduct convinced the jury, then
Hinckley would be confined to a mental hospital rather than a prison.
The prosecution introduced psychiatrists who interpreted Hinckley's motives and actions as those of a man who knew what he was doing and
knew it was wrong. They claimed he was *not* insane by legal definition.
The fact that experts can make differing conclusions about the meaning
of the same information indicates that interpretations are less reliable
than other kinds of support.

Finally, the defense made an appeal to the moral values of the jury.
Under the law, criminals judged to be insane are not to be punished as
harshly as criminals judged to be sane. The laws assume that criminals
who cannot be held responsible for their actions are entitled to more
compassionate treatment, confinement to a mental hospital rather than
prison. The jury accepted the interpretive evidence supporting the claim
of the defense, and Hinckley was pronounced not guilty by reason of insanity. Clearly the moral concern for the rights of the insane proved to be
decisive.

In your arguments you will advance your claims, not unlike a lawyer,
with these same kinds of support. But before you begin, you should ask
two questions: Which kind of support should I use in convincing an audience to accept my claim? and How do I decide that each item of support is valid and worthy of acceptance? This chapter presents the
different types of evidence and appeals you can use to support your claim

and examines the criteria by which you can evaluate the soundness of that support.

EVIDENCE

■ Factual Evidence

In Chapter 4, we defined facts as statements possessing a high degree of public acceptance. In theory, facts can be verified by experience alone. Eating too much will make us sick; we can get from Hopkinton to Boston in a half hour by car; in the Northern Hemisphere it is colder in December than in July. The experience of any individual is limited in both time and space, so we must accept as fact thousands of assertions about the world that we ourselves can never verify. Thus we accept the report that human beings landed on the moon in 1969 because we trust those who can verify it. (Country people in Morocco, however, received the news with disbelief because they had no reason to trust the reporters of the event. They insisted on trusting their senses instead. One man said, "I can see the moon very clearly. If a man were walking around up there, wouldn't I be able to see him?")

Factual evidence appears most frequently as examples and statistics, which are a numerical form of examples.

Examples

Examples are the most familiar kind of factual evidence. In addition to providing support for the truth of a generalization, examples can enliven otherwise dense or monotonous prose.

In the following paragraph the writer supports the claim in the topic sentence by offering a series of specific examples.

> Americans expect the next century to bring some striking political and social changes, but people are discerning. Two-thirds believe gay marriages probably will be legal and over half think that fathers will spend as much time and energy with their kids as mothers. Half of the public also predicts that Social Security will probably die; that view is particularly prevalent among younger Americans. But a majority doubts that cigarette smoking will be illegal or that all racial and gender discrimination will disappear.[2]

Hypothetical examples, which create imaginary situations for the audience and encourage them to visualize what might happen under certain circumstances, can also be effective. The following paragraph illustrates

[2] Elizabeth Crowley, "Putting Faith in Technology for Year 3000." *The Wall Street Journal*, September 15, 2000, A10.

the use of hypothetical examples. (The author is describing megaschools, high schools with more than 2000 students.)

> And in schools that big there is inevitably a critical mass of kids who are neither jocks nor artists nor even nerds, kids who are nothing at all, nonentities in their own lives. . . . The creditable ballplayer who might have made the team in a smaller school is edged out by better athletes. The artist who might have had work hung in a smaller school is supplanted by abler talents. And the disaffected and depressed boy who might have found a niche, or a friend, or a teacher who noticed, falls between the cracks. Sometimes he quietly drops out. Sometimes he quietly passes through. And sometimes he comes to school with a gun.[3]

All claims about vague or abstract terms would be boring or unintelligible without examples to illuminate them. For example, if you claim that a movie contains "unusual sound effects," you will certainly have to describe some of the effects to convince the reader that your generalization can be trusted.

Statistics

Statistics express information in numbers. In the following example statistics have been used to express raw data in numerical form.

> Surveys have shown that almost half of all male high school seniors— and nearly 20 percent of all ninth grade boys—can be called "problem drinkers." . . . Over 5,000 teenagers are killed yearly in auto accidents due to drunken driving.[4]

These grim numbers probably have meaning for you, partly because you already know that alcoholism exists even among young teenagers and partly because your own experience enables you to evaluate the numbers. But if you are unfamiliar with the subject, such numbers may be difficult or impossible to understand. Statistics, therefore, are more effective in comparisons that indicate whether a quantity is relatively large or small and sometimes even whether a reader should interpret the result as gratifying or disappointing. For example, if a novice gambler were told that for every dollar wagered in a state lottery, 50 percent goes back to the players as prizes, would the gambler be able to conclude that the percentage is high or low? Would he be able to choose between playing the state lottery and playing a casino game? Unless he had more information, probably not. But if he were informed that in casino games, the return to the players is over 90 percent and in slot machines and racetracks the return is around 80 percent, the comparison would enable him to evaluate

---

[3] Anna Quindlen, "The Problem of the Megaschool," *Newsweek*, March 26, 2001, p. 68.
[4] "The Kinds of Drugs Kids Are Getting Into" (Spring House, Pa.: McNeil Pharmaceutical, n.d.).

the meaning of the 50 percent return in the state lottery and even to make a decision about where to gamble his money.[5]

Comparative statistics are also useful for measurements over time. A national survey by The Institute for Social Research of the University of Michigan, in which 17,000 of the nation's 2.7 million high school seniors were questioned about their use of drugs, revealed a continuing downward trend.

> 50.9 percent of those questioned in 1989 reported that they had at least tried an illicit drug like marijuana or cocaine, as against 53.9 percent in 1988 and 56.6 percent in 1987.[6]

Diagrams, tables, charts, and graphs can make clear the relations among many sets of numbers. Such charts and diagrams allow readers to grasp the information more easily than if it were presented in paragraph form. The bar graph[7] that is shown on page 163 summarizes the information produced by a poll on gambling habits. A pie chart[8] such as the one on page 164 can also clarify lists of data.

■ Opinions: Interpretations of the Facts

We have seen how opinions of experts influenced the verdict in the trial of John Hinckley. Facts alone were not enough to substantiate the claim that Hinckley was guilty of attempted assassination. Both the defense and the prosecution relied on experts—psychiatrists—to interpret the facts. Opinions or interpretations about the facts are the inferences discussed in Chapter 4. They are an indispensable source of support for your claims.

Suppose a nightclub for teenagers has opened in your town. That is a fact. What is the significance of it? Is the club's existence good or bad? What consequences will it have for the community? Some parents oppose the idea of a nightclub, fearing that it may allow teenagers to escape from parental control and engage in dangerous activities. Other parents approve of a club, hoping that it will serve as a substitute for unsupervised congregation in the streets. The importance of these interpretations is that they, not the fact itself, help people decide what actions they should take. If the community accepts the interpretation that the club is a source of delinquency, they may decide to revoke the owner's license and close it. As one writer puts it, "The interpretation of data becomes a struggle over power."

Opinions or interpretations of facts generally take four forms: (1) They may suggest the cause for a condition or a causal connection between two sets of data; (2) they may offer predictions about the future;

---

[5] Curt Suphee, "Lotto Baloney," *Harper's,* July 1983, p. 201.
[6] *New York Times,* February 14, 1990, sec. A, p. 16.
[7] *New York Times,* May 28, 1989, p. 24.
[8] *Wall Street Journal,* February 2, 1990, sec. B, p. 1.

Bar graph

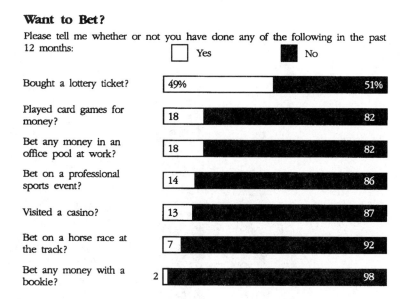

Want to Bet?

Please tell me whether or not you have done any of the following in the past 12 months: ☐ Yes ■ No

Bought a lottery ticket?	49%	51%
Played card games for money?	18	82
Bet any money in an office pool at work?	18	82
Bet on a professional sports event?	14	86
Visited a casino?	13	87
Bet on a horse race at the track?	7	92
Bet any money with a bookie?	2	98

(3) they may suggest solutions to a problem; (4) they may refer to the opinion of experts.

Causal Connection

Anorexia is a serious, sometimes fatal, disease characterized by self-starvation. It is found largely among young women. Physicians, psychologists, and social scientists have speculated about the causes, which remain unclear. A leading researcher in the field, Hilde Bruch, believes that food refusal expresses a desire to postpone sexual development. Another authority, Joan Blumberg, believes that one cause may be biological, a nervous dysfunction of the hypothalamus. Still others infer that the causes are cultural, a response to the admiration of the thin female body.[9]

Predictions about the Future

In the fall and winter of 1989 to 1990 extraordinary events shook Eastern Europe, toppling Communist regimes and raising more popular forms of government. Politicians and scholars offered predictions about future changes in the region. One expert, Zbigniew Brzezinski, former national security adviser under President Carter, concluded that the changes for the Soviet Union might be destructive.

[9]Phyllis Rose, "Hunger Artists," *Harper's,* July 1988, p. 82.

Pie chart

Plastic That Goes to Waste

Components of municipal solid waste,
by volume

Types of plastic in municipal solid waste,
by weight

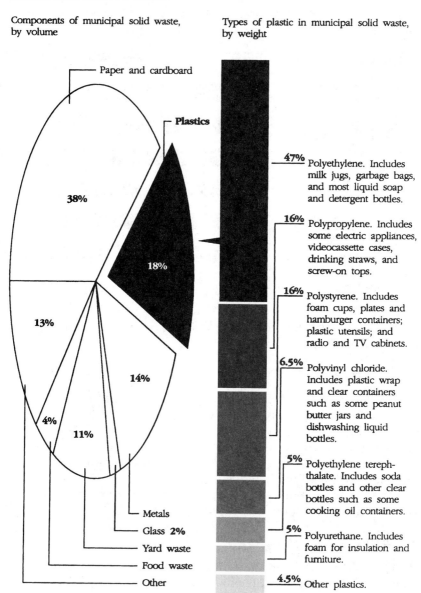

Paper and cardboard

Plastics

38%

18%

13%

14%

4%

11%

Metals

Glass 2%

Yard waste

Food waste

Other

47% Polyethylene. Includes
milk jugs, garbage bags,
and most liquid soap
and detergent bottles.

16% Polypropylene. Includes
some electric appliances,
videocassette cases,
drinking straws, and
screw-on tops.

16% Polystyrene. Includes
foam cups, plates and
hamburger containers;
plastic utensils; and
radio and TV cabinets.

6.5% Polyvinyl chloride.
Includes plastic wrap
and clear containers
such as some peanut
butter jars and
dishwashing liquid
bottles.

5% Polyethylene tereph-
thalate. Includes soda
bottles and other clear
bottles such as some
cooking oil containers.

5% Polyurethane. Includes
foam for insulation and
furniture.

4.5% Other plastics.

Source: Franklin Associates Ltd.

It would be a mistake to see the recent decisions as marking a breakthrough for democracy. Much more likely is a prolonged period of democratizing chaos. One will see the rise in the Soviet Union of increasingly irreconcilable conflicts between varying national political and social aspirations, all united by a shared hatred for the existing Communist nomenklatura. One is also likely to see a flashback of a nationalist type among the Great Russians, fearful of the prospective breakup of the existing Great Russian Empire.[10]

Solutions to Problems

How shall we solve the problems caused by young people in our cities "who commit crimes and create the staggering statistics in teenage pregnancies and the high abortion rate"? The minister emeritus of the Abyssinian Baptist Church in New York City proposes establishment of a national youth academy with fifty campuses on inactive military bases. "It is a 'parenting' institution. . . . It is not a penal institution, not a prep school, not a Job Corps Center, not a Civilian Conservation Camp, but it borrows from them." Although such an institution has not been tried before, the author of the proposal thinks that it would represent an effort "to provide for the academic, moral, and social development of young people, to cause them to become responsible and productive citizens."[11]

Expert Opinion

For many of the subjects you discuss and write about, you will find it necessary to accept and use the opinions of experts. Based on their reading of the facts, experts express opinions on a variety of controversial subjects: whether capital punishment is a deterrent to crime; whether legalization of marijuana will lead to an increase in its use; whether children, if left untaught, will grow up honest and cooperative; whether sex education courses will result in less sexual activity and fewer illegitimate births. The interpretations of the data are often profoundly important because they influence social policy and affect our lives directly and indirectly.

For the problems mentioned above, the opinions of people recognized as authorities are more reliable than those of people who have neither thought about nor done research on the subject. But opinions may also be offered by student writers in areas in which they are knowledgeable. If you were asked, for example, to defend or refute the statement that work has advantages for teenagers, you could call on your own experience and that of your friends to support your claim. You can also draw on your experience to write convincingly about your special interests.

[10] *New York Times*, February 9, 1990, sec. A, p. 13.
[11] Samuel D. Proctor, "To the Rescue: A National Youth Academy," *New York Times*, September 16, 1989, sec. A, p. 27.

One opinion, however, is not as good as another. The value of any opinion depends on the quality of the evidence and the trustworthiness of the person offering it.

EVALUATION OF EVIDENCE

Before you begin to write, you must determine whether the facts and opinions you have chosen to support your claim are sound. Can they convince your readers? A distinction between the evaluation of facts and the evaluation of opinions is somewhat artificial because many facts are verified by expert opinion, but for our analysis we discuss them separately.

■ Evaluation of Factual Evidence

As you evaluate factual evidence, you should keep in mind the following questions:

1. Is the evidence up to date? The importance of up-to-date information depends on the subject. If you are defending the claim that suicide is immoral, you will not need to examine new data. For many of the subjects you write about, recent research and scholarship will be important, even decisive, in proving the soundness of your data. "New" does not always mean "best," but in fields where research is ongoing—education, psychology, technology, medicine, and all the natural and physical sciences—you should be sensitive to the dates of the research.

In writing a paper a few years ago warning about the health hazards of air pollution, you would have used data referring only to outdoor pollution produced by automobile and factory emissions. But writing about air pollution today, you would have to take into account new data about indoor pollution, which has become a serious problem as a result of attempts to conserve energy. Because research studies in indoor pollution are continually being updated, recent evidence will probably be more accurate than past research.

2. Is the evidence sufficient? The amount of evidence you need depends on the complexity of the subject and the length of your paper. Given the relative brevity of most of your assignments, you will need to be selective. For the claim that indoor pollution is a serious problem, one example would obviously not be enough. For a 750- to 1,000-word paper, three or four examples would probably be sufficient. The choice of examples should reflect different aspects of the problem: in this case, different sources of indoor pollution—gas stoves, fireplaces, kerosene heaters, insulation—and the consequences for health.

Indoor pollution is a fairly limited subject for which the evidence is clear. But more complex problems require more evidence. A common fault in argument is generalization based on insufficient evidence. In a 1,000-word paper you could not adequately treat the causes of conflict in the Middle East; you could not develop workable proposals for healthcare reform; you could not predict the development of education in the next century. In choosing a subject for a brief paper, determine whether you can produce sufficient evidence to convince a reader who may not agree with you. If not, the subject may be too large for a brief paper.

3. Is the evidence relevant? All the evidence should, of course, contribute to the development of your argument. Sometimes the arguer loses sight of the subject and introduces examples that are wide of the claim. In defending a national health-care plan, one student offered examples of the success of health maintenance organizations, but such organizations, although subsidized by the federal government, were not the structure favored by sponsors of a national health-care plan. The examples were interesting but irrelevant.

Also keep in mind that not all readers will agree on what is relevant. Is the unsavory private life of a politician relevant to his or her performance in office? If you want to prove that a politician is unfit to serve because of his or her private activities, you may first have to convince some members of the audience that private activities are relevant to public service.

4. Are the examples representative? This question emphasizes your responsibility to choose examples that are typical of all the examples you do not use. Suppose you offered Vermont's experience to support your claim that same-sex marriage should be legal. Is the experience of Vermont typical of what is happening or may happen in other states? Or is Vermont, a small, mostly rural New England state, different enough from other states to make the example unrepresentative?

5. Are the examples consistent with the experience of the audience? The members of your audience use their own experiences to judge the soundness of your evidence. If your examples are unfamiliar or extreme, they will probably reject your conclusion. Consider the following excerpt from Jacob Neusner's hypothetical commencement speech (p. 351), which is meant to represent a faculty member's response to student apathy.

> For years we have created an altogether forgiving world, in which whatever slight effort you gave was all that was demanded. When you did not keep appointments, we made new ones. When your work came in beyond the deadline, we pretended not to care.
> Worse still, when you were boring, we acted as if you were saying something important. When you were garrulous and talked to hear yourself talk, we listened as if it mattered. When you tossed on our desks writing upon which you had not labored, we read it and even

responded, as though you earned a response. When you were dull, we pretended you were smart. When you were predictable, unimaginative, and routine, we listened as if to new and wonderful things. When you demanded free lunch we served it.

If most members of the audience find that such a description doesn't reflect their own attitudes or those of their friends, they will probably question the validity of the claim.

■ Evaluation of Statistics

The questions you must ask about examples also apply to statistics. Are they recent? Are they sufficient? Are they relevant? Are they typical? Are they consistent with the experience of the audience? But there are additional questions directed specifically to evaluation of statistics.

1. Do the statistics come from trustworthy sources? Perhaps you have read newspaper accounts of very old people, some reported to be as old as 135, living in the Caucasus or the Andes, nourished by yogurt and hard work. But these statistics are hearsay; no birth records or other official documents exist to verify them. Now two anthropologists have concluded that the numbers were part of a rural mythology and that the ages of the people were actually within the normal range for human populations elsewhere.[12]

Hearsay statistics should be treated with the same skepticism accorded to gossip or rumor. Sampling a population to gather statistical information is a sophisticated science; you should ask whether the reporter of the statistics is qualified and likely to be free of bias. Among the generally reliable sources are polling organizations such as Gallup, Roper, and Louis Harris and agencies of the U.S. government such as the Census Bureau and the Bureau of Labor Statistics. Other qualified sources are well-known research foundations, university centers, and insurance companies that prepare actuarial tables. Statistics from underdeveloped countries are less reliable for obvious reasons: lack of funds, lack of trained statisticians, lack of communication and transportation facilities to carry out accurate censuses.

2. Are the terms clearly defined? In an example in Chapter 3, the reference to poverty (p. 63) made clear that any statistics would be meaningless unless we knew exactly how *poverty* was defined by the user. *Unemployment* is another term for which statistics will be difficult to read if the definition varies from one user to another. For example, are seasonal workers employed or unemployed during the off-season? Are part-time workers employed? (In Russia they are unemployed.) Are workers on

---

[12] Richard B. Mazess and Sylvia H. Forman, "Longevity and Age Exaggeration in Vilcabamba, Ecuador," *Journal of Gerontology* (1979), pp. 94–98.

government projects employed? (During the 1930s they were considered employed by the Germans and unemployed by the Americans.) The more abstract or controversial the term, the greater the necessity for clear definition.

3. Are the comparisons between comparable things? Folk wisdom warns us that we cannot compare apples and oranges. Population statistics for the world's largest city, for example, should indicate the units being compared. Greater London is defined in one way, greater New York in another, and greater Tokyo in still another. The population numbers will mean little unless you can be sure that the same geographical units are being compared.

4. Has any significant information been omitted? *The Plain Truth,* a magazine published by the World-Wide Church of God, advertises itself as follows:

> *The Plain Truth* has now topped 5,000,000 copies per issue. It is now the fastest-growing magazine in the world and one of the widest circulated mass-circulation magazines on earth. Our circulation is now greater than *Newsweek.* New subscribers are coming in at the rate of around 40,000 per week.

What the magazine neglects to mention is that it is *free.* There is no subscription fee, and the magazine is widely distributed in drugstores, supermarkets, and airports. *Newsweek* is sold on newsstands and by subscription. The comparison therefore omits significant information.

■ Evaluation of Opinions

When you evaluate the reliability of opinions in subjects with which you are not familiar, you will be dealing almost exclusively with opinions of experts. Most of the following questions are directed to an evaluation of authoritative sources. But you can also ask these questions of students or of others with opinions based on their own experience and research. Keep them in mind when doing research on the Web.

1. Is the source of the opinion qualified to give an opinion on the subject? The discussion on credibility in Chapter 1 (pp. 13–15) pointed out that certain achievements by the interpreter of the data — publications, acceptance by colleagues — can tell us something about his or her competence. Although these standards are by no means foolproof (people of outstanding reputations have been known to falsify their data), nevertheless they offer assurance that the source is generally trustworthy. The answers to questions you must ask are not hard to find: Is the source qualified by education? Is the source associated with a reputable institution — a university or a research organization? Is the source credited with having made contributions to the field—books, articles, research studies? Suppose that in writing a paper on organ transplants you came across an article by Peter Medawar. He is identified as follows:

> Sir Peter Medawar, British zoologist, winner of the 1960 Nobel Prize in Physiology or Medicine, for proving that the rejection by the body of foreign organs can be overcome; president of the Royal Society; head of the National Institute for Medical Research in London; a world leader in immunology.

These credentials would suggest to almost any reader that Medawar was a reliable source for information about organ transplants.

If the source is not so clearly identified, you should treat the data with caution. Such advice is especially relevant when you are dealing with popular works about such subjects as miracle diets, formulas for instant wealth, and sightings of monsters and UFOs. Do not use such data until you can verify them from other, more authoritative sources.

In addition, you should question the identity of any source listed as "spokesperson" or "reliable source" or "an unidentified authority." The mass media are especially fond of this type of attribution. Sometimes the sources are people in public life who plant stories anonymously or off the record for purposes they prefer to keep hidden.

Even when the identification is clear and genuine, you should ask if the credentials are relevant to the field in which the authority claims expertise. So specialized are areas of scientific study today that scientists in one field may not be competent to make judgments in another. William Shockley is a distinguished engineer, a Nobel Prize winner for his contribution to the invention of the electronic transistor. But when he made the claim, based on his own research, that blacks are genetically inferior to whites, geneticists accused Shockley of venturing into a field where he was unqualified to make judgments. Similarly, advertisers invite stars from the entertainment world to express opinions about products with which they are probably less familiar than members of their audience. All citizens have the right to express their views, but this does not mean that all views are equally credible or worthy of attention.

2. Is the source biased for or against his or her interpretation? Even authorities who satisfy the criteria for expertise may be guilty of bias. Bias arises as a result of economic reward, religious affiliation, political loyalty, and other interests. The expert may not be aware of the bias; even an expert can fall into the trap of ignoring evidence that contradicts his or her own intellectual preferences. A British psychologist has said:

> The search for meaning in data is bound to involve all of us in distortion to greater or lesser degree. . . . Transgression consists not so much in a clear break with professional ethics, as in an unusually high-

handed, extreme or self-deceptive attempt to promote one particular view of reality at the expense of all others.[13]

Before accepting the interpretation of an expert, you should ask: Is there some reason why I should suspect the motives of this particular source?

Consider, for example, an advertisement claiming that sweetened breakfast cereals are nutritious. The advertisement, placed by the manufacturer of the cereal, provides impeccable references from scientific sources to support its claims. But since you are aware of the economic interest of the company in promoting sales, you may wonder if they have reproduced only facts that favor their claims. Are there other facts that might prove the opposite? As a careful researcher you would certainly want to look further for data about the advantages and disadvantages of sugar in our diets.

It is harder to determine bias in the research done by scientists and university members even when the research is funded by companies interested in a favorable review of their products. If you discover that a respected biologist who advocates the use of sugar in baby food receives a consultant's fee from a sugar company, should you conclude that the research is slanted and that the scientist has ignored contrary evidence? Not necessarily. The truth may be that the scientist arrived at conclusions about the use of sugar legitimately through experiments that no other scientist would question. But it would probably occur to you that a critical reader might ask about the connection between the results of the research and the payment by a company that profits from the research. In this case you would be wise to read further to find confirmation or rejection of the claim by other scientists.

The most difficult evaluations concern ideological bias. Early in our lives we learn to discount the special interest that makes a small child brag, "My mother (or father) is the greatest!" Later we become aware that the claims of people who are avowed Democrats or Republicans or supply-side economists or Yankee fans or zealous San Franciscans or joggers must be examined somewhat more carefully than those of people who have no special commitment to a cause or a place or an activity. This is not to say that all partisan claims lack support. They may, in fact, be based on the best available support. But whenever special interest is apparent, there is always the danger that an argument will reflect this bias.

3. Has the source bolstered the claim with sufficient and appropriate evidence? In an article attacking pornography, one author wrote, "Statistics prove that the recent proliferation of porno is directly related

---

[13]Liam Hudson, *The Cult of the Fact* (New York: Harper and Row, 1972), p. 125.

to the increasing number of rapes and assaults on women."[14] But the author gave no further information—neither statistics nor proof that a cause-effect relation exists between pornography and violence against women. The critical reader will ask, "What are the numbers? Who compiled them?"

Even those who are reputed to be experts in the subjects they discuss must do more than simply allege that a claim is valid or that the data exist. They must provide facts to support their interpretations.

■ When Experts Disagree

Authoritative sources can disagree. Such disagreement is probably most common in the social sciences. They are called the "soft" sciences precisely because a consensus about conclusions in these areas is more difficult to arrive at than in the natural and physical sciences. Consider the controversy over what determines the best interests of the child where both biological and foster parents are engaged in trying to secure custody. Experts are deeply divided on this issue. Dr. Daniel J. Cohen, a child psychologist and director of the Yale Child Study Center, argues that the psychological needs of the child should take precedence. If the child has a stable and loving relationship with foster parents, that is where he should stay. But Bruce Bozer and Bernadine Dohrn of the Children and Family Justice Center at Northwestern University Law School insist that "such a solution may be overly simplistic." The child may suffer in later life when he learns that he has been prevented from returning to biological parents "who fought to get him back."[15]

But even in the natural and physical sciences, where the results of observation and experiment are more conclusive, we encounter heated differences of opinion. A popular argument concerns the extinction of the dinosaurs. Was it the effect of an asteroid striking the earth? Or widespread volcanic activity? Or a cooling of the planet? All these theories have their champions among the experts.

Environmental concerns also produce lively disagreements. Scientists have lined up on both sides of a debate about the importance of protecting the tropical rain forest as a source of biological, especially mammalian, diversity. Dr. Edward O. Wilson, a Harvard biologist, whose books have made us familiar with the term *biodiversity,* says, "The great majority of organisms appears to reach maximum diversity in the rain forest. There is no question that the rain forests are the world's headquarters of diversity." But in the journal *Science* another biologist, Dr. Michael Mares, a professor of zoology at the University of Oklahoma, argues that "if one could choose only a single South American habitat in which to preserve

---

[14] Charlotte Allen, "Exploitation for Profit," *Daily Collegian* [University of Massachusetts], October 5, 1976, p. 2.

[15] *New York Times,* September 4, 1994, sec. E, p. 3.

the greatest mammalian diversity, it would be the dry lands. . . .The dry lands are very likely far more highly threatened than the largely inaccessible rain forests."[16] A debate of more immediate relevance concerns possible dangers in genetically modified foods, as distinguished from foods modified by traditional breeding practices. Dr. Louis Pribyl, a U.S. Food and Drug Administration microbiologist, has accused the agency of claiming "that there are no unintended effects that raise the FDA's level of concern. But . . . there are no data to back up this contention." On the other hand, Dr. James Marjanski, the FDA's biotechnology coordinator, maintains that "as long as developers of these foods follow agency guidelines, genetically engineered foods are as safe as any on the market."[17]

How can you choose between authorities who disagree? If you have applied the tests discussed so far and discovered that one source is less qualified by training and experience or makes claims with little support or appears to be biased in favor of one interpretation, you will have no difficulty in rejecting that person's opinion. If conflicting sources prove to be equally reliable in all respects, then continue reading other authorities to determine whether a greater number of experts support one opinion rather than another. Although numbers alone, even of experts, don't guarantee the truth, nonexperts have little choice but to accept the authority of the greater number until evidence to the contrary is forthcoming. Finally, if you are unable to decide between competing sources of evidence, you may conclude that the argument must remain unsettled. Such an admission is not a failure; after all, such questions are considered controversial because even the experts cannot agree, and such questions are often the most interesting to consider and argue about.

APPEALS TO NEEDS AND VALUES

Good factual evidence is usually enough to convince an audience that your factual claim is sound. Using examples, statistics, and expert opinion, you can prove, for example, that women do not earn as much as men for the same work. But even good evidence may not be enough to convince your audience that unequal pay is wrong or that something should be done about it. In making value and policy claims, an appeal to the needs and values of your audience is absolutely essential to the success of your argument. If you want to persuade the audience to change their minds or adopt a course of action—in this case, to demand legalization of equal pay for equal work—you will have to show that assent to your claim will bring about what they want and care deeply about.

[16]*New York Times,* April 7, 1992, sec. C, p. 4.
[17]*New York Times,* December 1, 1999, A15.

As a writer, you cannot always know who your audience is; it's impossible, for example, to predict exactly who will read a letter you write to a newspaper. Even in the classroom, you have only partial knowledge of your readers. You may not always know or be able to infer what the goals and principles of your audience are. You may not know how they feel about big government, the draft, private school education, feminism, environmental protection, homosexuality, religion, or any of the other subjects you might write about. If the audience concludes that the things you care about are very different from what they care about, if they cannot identify with your goals and principles, they may treat your argument with indifference, even hostility, and finally reject it. But you can hope that decent and reasonable people will share many of the needs and values that underlie your claims.

■ Appeals to Needs

Suppose that you are trying to persuade Joan Doakes, a friend who is still undecided, to attend college. In your reading you have come across a report about the benefits of a college education written by Howard Bowen, a former professor of economics at Claremont (California) Graduate School, former president of Grinnell College, and a specialist in the economics of higher education. Armed with his testimony, you write to Joan. As support for your claim that she should attend college, you offer evidence that (1) college graduates earn more throughout their lifetime than high school graduates; (2) college graduates are more active and exert greater influence in their communities than high school graduates; and (3) college graduates achieve greater success as partners in marriage and as thoughtful and caring parents.[18]

Joan writes back that she is impressed with the evidence you've provided—the statistics, the testimony of economists and psychologists—and announces that she will probably enroll in college instead of accepting a job offer.

How did you succeed with Joan Doakes? If you know your friend pretty well, the answer is not difficult. Joan has needs that can be satisfied by material success; more money will enable her to enjoy the comforts and luxuries that are important to her. She also needs the esteem of her peers and the sense of achievement that political activity and service to others will give her. Finally, she needs the rootedness to be found in close and lasting family connections.

Encouraged by your success with Joan Doakes, you write the same letter to another friend, Fred Fox, who has also declined to apply for admission to college. This time, however, your argument fails. Fred, too, is

---

[18]"The Residue of Academic Learning," *Chronicle of Higher Education,* November 14, 1977, p. 13.

impressed with your research and evidence. But college is not for him, and he repeats that he has decided not to become a student.

Why such a different response? The reason, it turns out, is that you don't know what Fred really wants. Fred Fox dreams of going to Alaska to live alone in the wilderness. Money means little to him, influence in the community is irrelevant to his goals, and at present he feels no desire to become a member of a loving family.

Perhaps if you had known Fred better, you would have offered different evidence to show that you recognized what he needed and wanted. You could have told him that Bowen's study also points out that "college-educated persons are healthier than are others," that "they also have better ability to adjust to changing times and vocations," that "going to college enhances self-discovery" and enlarges mental resources, which encourage college graduates to go on learning for the rest of their lives. This information might have persuaded Fred that college would also satisfy some of his needs.

As this example demonstrates, you have a better chance of persuading your reader to accept your claim if you know what he or she wants and what importance he or she assigns to the needs that we all share. Your reader must, in other words, see some connection between your evidence and his or her needs.

The needs to which you appealed in your letters to Joan and Fred are the requirements for physiological or psychological well-being. The most familiar classification of needs was developed by the psychologist Abraham H. Maslow in 1954.[19] These needs, said Maslow, motivate human thought and action. In satisfying our needs, we attain both long- and short-term goals. Because Maslow believed that some needs are more important than others, he arranged them in hierarchical order from the most urgent biological needs to the psychological needs that are related to our roles as members of a society.

> PHYSIOLOGICAL NEEDS Basic bodily requirements: food and drink; health; sex
>
> SAFETY NEEDS Security; freedom from harm; order and stability
>
> BELONGINGNESS AND LOVE NEEDS Love within a family and among friends; roots within a group or a community
>
> ESTEEM NEEDS Material success; achievement; power, status, and recognition by others
>
> SELF-ACTUALIZATION NEEDS Fulfillment in realizing one's potential

For most of your arguments you won't have to address the audience's basic physiological needs for nourishment or shelter. The desire for health, however, now receives extraordinary attention. Appeals to buy

---

[19] *Motivation and Personality* (New York: Harper and Row, 1954), pp. 80–92.

health foods, vitamin supplements, drugs, exercise and diet courses, and health books are all around us. Many of the claims are supported by little or no evidence, but readers are so eager to satisfy the need for good health that they often overlook the lack of facts or authoritative opinion. The desire for physical well-being, however, is not so simple as it seems; it is strongly related to our need for self-esteem and love.

Appeals to our needs to feel safe from harm, to be assured of order and stability in our lives are also common. Insurance companies, politicians who promise to rid our streets of crime, and companies that offer security services all appeal to this profound and nearly universal need. (We say "nearly" because some people are apparently attracted to risk and danger.) At this writing those who monitor terrorist activity are attempting both to arouse fear for our safety and to suggest ways of reducing the dangers that make us fearful.

The last three needs in Maslow's hierarchy are the ones you will find most challenging to appeal to in your arguments. It is clear that these needs arise out of human relationships and participation in society. Advertisers make much use of appeals to these needs.

BELONGINGNESS AND LOVE NEEDS

"Whether you are young or old, the need for companionship is universal." (ad for dating service)

"Share the Fun of High School with Your Little Girl!" (ad for a Barbie Doll)

ESTEEM NEEDS

"Enrich your home with the distinction of an Oxford library."

"Apply your expertise to more challenges and more opportunities. Here are outstanding opportunities for challenge, achievement, and growth." (Perkin-Elmer Co.)

SELF-ACTUALIZATION NEEDS

"Be all that you can be." (former U.S. Army slogan)

"Are you demanding enough? Somewhere beyond the cortex is a small voice whose mere whisper can silence an army of arguments. It goes by many names: integrity, excellence, standards. And it stands alone in final judgment as to whether we have demanded enough of ourselves and, by that example, have inspired the best in those around us." (*New York Times*)

Of course, it is not only advertisers who use these appeals. We hear them from family and friends, from teachers, from employers, from editorials and letters to the editor, from people in public life.

■ Appeals to Values

Needs give rise to values. If we feel the need to belong to a group, we learn to value commitment, sacrifice, and sharing. And we then respond to arguments that promise to protect our values. It is hardly surprising that values, the principles by which we judge what is good or bad, beautiful or ugly, worthwhile or undesirable, should exercise a profound influence on our behavior. Virtually all claims, even those that seem to be purely factual, contain expressed or unexpressed judgments. When Michael M. Weinstein in Chapter 4 (pp. 109–12) quotes evidence that affirmative action does not promote unqualified candidates, he does so not because he is doing research for academic reasons but because he hopes to persuade people that affirmative action is good social policy.

For our study of argument, we will speak of groups or systems of values because any single value is usually related to others. People and institutions are often defined by such systems of values. We can distinguish, for example, between those who think of themselves as traditional and those who think of themselves as modern by listing their differing values. One writer contrasts such values in this way:

> Among the values of traditionalism are merit, accomplishment, competition, and success; self-restraint, self-discipline, and the postponement of gratification; the stability of the family; and a belief in certain moral universals. The modernist ethos scorns the pursuit of success; is egalitarian and redistributionist in emphasis; tolerates or encourages sensual gratification; values self-expression as against self-restraint; accepts alternative or deviant forms of the family; and emphasizes ethical relativism.[20]

Systems of values are neither so rigid nor so distinct from one another as this list suggests. Some people who are traditional in their advocacy of competition and success may also accept the modernist values of self-expression and alternative family structures. Values, like needs, are arranged in a hierarchy; that is, some are clearly more important than others to the people who hold them. Moreover, the arrangement may shift over time or as a result of new experiences. In 1962, for example, two speech teachers prepared a list of what they called "Relatively Unchanging Values Shared by Most Americans."[21] Included were "puritan and pioneer standards of morality" and "perennial optimism about the future." More than forty years later, an appeal to these values might fall on a number of deaf ears.

You should also be aware of not only changes over time but also different or competing value systems that reflect a multitude of subcultures

---

[20]Joseph Adelson, "What Happened to the Schools," *Commentary,* March 1981, p. 37.
[21]Edward Steele and W. Charles Redding, "The American Value System: Premises for Persuasion," *Western Speech,* 26 (Spring 1962), pp. 83–91.

in our country. Differences in age, sex, race, ethnic background, social environment, religion, even in the personalities and characters of its members define the groups we belong to. Such terms as *honor, loyalty, justice, patriotism, duty, responsibility, equality, freedom,* and *courage* will be interpreted very differently by different groups.

All of us belong to more than one group, and the values of the several groups may be in conflict. If one group to which you belong—say, peers of your own age and class—is generally uninterested in and even scornful of religion, you may nevertheless hold to the values of your family and continue to place a high value on religious belief.

How can a knowledge of your readers' values enable you to make a more effective appeal? Suppose you want to argue in favor of a sex education program in the middle school you attended. The program you support would not only give students information about contraception and venereal disease but also teach them about the pleasures of sex, the importance of small families, and alternatives to heterosexuality. If the readers of your argument are your classmates or your peers, you can be fairly sure that their agreement will be easier to obtain than that of their parents, especially if their parents think of themselves as conservative. Your peers are more likely to value experimentation, tolerance of alternative sexual practices, freedom, and novelty. Their parents are more likely to value restraint, conformity to conventional sexual practices, obedience to family rules, and foresight in planning for the future.

Knowing that your peers share your values and your goals will mean that you need not spell out the values supporting your claim; they are understood by your readers. Convincing their parents, however, who think that freedom, tolerance, and experimentation have been abused by their children, will be a far more challenging task. In one written piece you have little chance of changing their values, a result that might be achieved only over a longer period of time. So you might first attempt to reduce their hostility by suggesting that, even if a community-wide program were adopted, students would need parental permission to enroll. This might convince some parents that you share their values regarding parental authority and primacy of the family. Second, you might look for other values to which the parents subscribe and to which you can make an appeal. Do they prize maturity, self-reliance, responsibility in their children? If so, you could attempt to prove, with authoritative evidence, that the sex education program would promote these qualities in students who took the course.

But familiarity with the value systems of prospective readers may also lead you to conclude that winning assent to your argument will be impossible. It would probably be fruitless to attempt to persuade a group of lifelong pacifists to endorse the use of nuclear weapons. The beliefs, attitudes, and habits that support their value systems are too fundamental to yield to one or two attempts at persuasion.

EVALUATION OF APPEALS TO NEEDS AND VALUES

If your argument is based on an appeal to the needs and values of your audience, the following questions will help you evaluate the soundness of your appeal.

1. Have the values been clearly defined? If you are appealing to the patriotism of your readers, can you be sure that they agree with your definition? Does patriotism mean "Our country, right or wrong!" or does it mean dissent, even violent dissent, if you think your country is wrong? Because value terms are abstractions, you must make their meaning explicit by placing them in context and providing examples.

2. Are the needs and values to which you appeal prominent in the reader's hierarchy at the time you are writing? An affluent community, fearful of further erosion of quiet and open countryside, might resist an appeal to allow establishment of a high-technology firm, even though the firm would bring increased prosperity to the area.

3. Is the evidence in your argument clearly related to the needs and values to which you appeal? Remember that the reader must see some connection between your evidence and his or her goals. Suppose you were writing an argument to persuade a group of people to vote in an upcoming election. You could provide evidence to prove that only 20 percent of the town voted in the last election. But this evidence would not motivate your audience to vote unless you could provide other evidence to show that their needs were not being served by such a low turnout.

Writer's Guide: Using Effective Support

1. In deciding how much support you need for your claim, it is always a good idea to assume that you are addressing an audience that may be at least slightly hostile to that claim. Those who already agree with you do not need convincing.

2. Keep a mental, if not a written, list of the different types of support you use in an essay. Few essays will use all of the different types of support, but being aware of all the possibilities will prevent you from forgetting to draw on one or more types of support that may advance your argument.

3. In that checklist of types of support, don't forget that there are two main categories: evidence and appeals to needs and values. Appeals to needs and values will generally need the reinforcement that comes from more objective forms of evidence, but the two in combination can often

provide the strongest case for your claim. Aristotle explained that in an ideal world, arguers could depend on logic alone, but we live in a world that is far from ideal.

4. Use the following questions about the evaluation of evidence as a checklist to analyze the support you use in your argumentative essays:

Factual evidence:

- Is the evidence up to date?
- Is the evidence sufficient?
- Is the evidence relevant?
- Are the examples representative?
- Are the examples consistent with the experience of the audience?

Statistics:

- Do the statistics come from trustworthy sources?
- Are the terms clearly defined?
- Are the comparisons between comparable things?
- Has any significant information been omitted?

Opinion:

- Is the source of the opinion qualified to give an opinion on the subject?
- Is the source biased for or against his or her interpretation?
- Has the source bolstered the claim with sufficient and appropriate evidence?

5. Also check your essays against the list of questions regarding appeals to needs and values:

- Have the values been clearly defined?
- Are the needs and values to which you appeal prominent in the reader's hierarchy at the time you are writing?
- Is the evidence in your argument clearly related to the needs and values to which you appeal?

Single-Sex Education Benefits Men Too

CLAUDIUS E. WATTS III

Introduction: background of the problem

The values that the author will defend

L ast week Virginia Military Institute, an all-male state college, got the good news from a federal judge that it can continue its single-sex program if it opens a leadership program at Mary Baldwin College, a nearby private women's school. But it is likely that the government will appeal the decision. Meanwhile, the Citadel, another such institution in Charleston, S.C., remains under attack. Unwittingly, so are some fundamental beliefs prevalent in our society: namely, the value of single-sex education, the need for diversity in education, and the freedom of choice in associating with, and not associating with, whomever one chooses.

When Shannon Faulkner received a preliminary injunction to attend day classes with the Citadel's Corps of Cadets, she was depicted as a nineteen-year-old woman fighting for her constitutional rights, while the Citadel was painted as an outdated and chauvinistic Southern school that had to be dragged into the twentieth century.

Claim of policy: to preserve single-sex education for men

But the Citadel is not fighting to keep women out of the Corps of Cadets because there is a grandiose level of nineteenth-century machismo to protect. Rather, we at the Citadel are trying to preserve an educational environment that molds young men into grown men of good character, honor, and integrity. It is part of a single-sex educational system that has proven itself successful throughout history.

Support: expert opinion, appeal to values

The benefits of single-sex education for men are clear: Says Harvard sociologist David Riesman, not only is single-sex education an optimal means of character development, but it also

---

Lieutenant General Claudius E. Watts III, retired from the U.S. Air Force, is a former president of the Citadel in South Carolina. This selection is from the May 3, 1995, edition of the *Wall Street Journal*.

removes the distractions of the "mating-dating" game so prevalent in society and enables institutions to focus students on values and academics.

In short, the value of separate education is, simply, the fact it is separate.   5

In October 1992, a federal appeals court ruled that "single-sex education is pedagogically justifiable." Indeed, a cursory glance at some notable statistics bears that out. For instance, the Citadel has the highest retention rate for minority students of any public college in South Carolina: 67 percent of black students graduate in four years, which is more than 2½ times the national average. Additionally, the Citadel's four-year graduation rate for all students is 70 percent, which compares with 48 percent nationally for all other public institutions and 67 percent nationally for private institutions. Moreover, many of the students come from modest backgrounds. Clearly, the Citadel is not the bastion of male privilege that the U.S. Justice Department, in briefs filed by that agency, would have us all believe.

Support: statistics

While the Justice Department continues to reject the court's ruling affirming the values of single-sex education, others continue to argue that because the federal military academies are coeducational, so should the Citadel be. However, it is not the Citadel's primary mission to train officers for the U.S. armed forces. We currently commission approximately 30 percent of our graduates, but only 18 percent actually pursue military careers. At the Citadel, the military model is a means to an end, not the end itself.

Support: facts, statistics

Today there are eighty-four women's colleges scattered throughout the United States, including two that are public. These colleges defend their programs as necessary to help women overcome intangible barriers in male-dominated professions. This argument has merit; women's colleges produce only 4.5 percent of all female college graduates but have produced one-fourth of all women board members of Fortune 500 companies and one-half of the women in Congress. However, the educational benefits of men's colleges are equally clear; and to allow women alone to benefit from single-sex education seems to per-

Support: facts, statistics

Support: causal connection

petuate the very stereotypes that women—including Ms. Faulkner—are trying to correct.

Warrant: men should enjoy the same freedom of choice

If young women want and need to study and learn in single-sex schools, why is it automatically wrong for young men to want and need the same? Where is the fairness in this assumption?

Support: causal connection

"At what point does the insistence that one individual not be deprived of choice spill over into depriving countless individuals of choice?" asks Emory University's Elizabeth Fox Genovese in an article by Jeffrey Rosen published in the February 14 *New Republic*.   10

Support: appeal to values

Yet so it is at the Citadel. While one student maintains that she is protecting her freedom to associate, we mustn't forget that the Citadel's cadets also have a freedom—the freedom not to associate. While we have read about one female student's rights, what hasn't been addressed are the rights of the 1,900 cadets who chose the Citadel—and the accompanying discipline and drill—because it offered them the single-sex educational experience they wanted. Why do one student's rights supersede all theirs?

Support: predictions about the future

One might be easily tempted to argue on the grounds that Ms. Faulkner is a taxpayer and the Citadel is a tax-supported institution. But if the taxpayer argument holds, the next step is to forbid all public support for institutions that enroll students of only one sex. A draconian measure such as this would surely mean the end of private—as well as public—single-gender colleges.

Backing for warrant: tax-supported education should be equal for men and women

Most private colleges—Columbia and Converse, the two all-female schools in South Carolina, included—could not survive without federal financial aid, tax exemptions, and state tax support in the form of tuition grants. In fact, nearly 900 of Columbia and Converse's female students receive state-funded tuition grants, a student population that is almost half the size of the Corps of Cadets. In essence, South Carolina's two private women's colleges may stand or fall with the Citadel.

Carried to its logical conclusion, then, the effort to coeducate the Citadel might mean the end of all single-sex education—for women as well as men, in private as well as public schools.

■ Analysis: Support

In 1993 Shannon Faulkner, a woman, was rejected for admission to the Citadel, an all-male state-supported military academy in South Carolina. In 1995, after a long court battle, she was admitted but resigned after a week of physical and emotional stress. The Court was asked to decide if an education equal to that of the Citadel could be provided for women at a nearby school.

Claudius Watts III tackles a subject that is no longer controversial in regard to women's colleges: the virtues of single-sex education. But in this essay he argues that colleges for men only deserve the same right as women's colleges to exclude the opposite sex.

The author has taken care in the limited space available to cover all the arguments that have emerged in the case of Shannon Faulkner. At the end of the opening paragraph he lays out the three ideas he will develop—the value of single-sex education, the need for diversity in education, and freedom of choice. In paragraphs 3 through 6 he supports his case for the benefits of separate education by first quoting a prominent sociologist and then offering statistics to prove that the Citadel population is both diverse and successful. In paragraph 7 he refutes a popular analogy—that since the service academies, like West Point and the Naval Academy, admit women, so should the Citadel. The goals of the Citadel, he says, are broader than those of the service academies. But he does more. In paragraph 8 he provides data that women's colleges produce successful graduates. This reinforces his claim that separate education has advantages over coed schooling. Perhaps it also helps to make friends of opponents who might otherwise be hostile to arguments favoring male privileges.

Notice the transition in paragraph 10. This leads the author to the defense of his last point, the far more elusive concept of freedom of choice and the rights of individuals, ideas whose validity cannot be measured in numbers. He introduces this part of his argument by quoting the words of a supporter of single-sex education, a woman professor at Emory University. He makes a strong appeal to the reader's sense of fairness and belief in the rights of the majority, represented here by the male students at the Citadel. There is also an obvious appeal to fear, an implied threat of the danger to women's colleges, in the next-to-last sentence of the essay. Finally, he invokes logic. If single-sex education cannot be defended for males, neither can it be defended for females. He assumes that against logic there can be no real defense.

Some leading advocates for women's rights have, in fact, agreed with General Watts's arguments for that reason. But those who support both Shannon Faulkner's admission to the Citadel and the sanctity of women's colleges will claim that women, as a disadvantaged group, deserve special consideration, while men do not. (One writer even insisted that the

Citadel *needed* women as a civilizing influence.) General Watts's argument, however, should go some distance toward reopening the dialogue.

SAMPLE ANALYSIS

At times, assignments may ask you to analyze or evaluate the evidence and appeals to needs and values offered in support of a claim. At other times, you will have to discover your own support for use in an argument that you are writing. After the following essay about sport utility vehicles and its reading and discussion questions, you will first find an example of an essay of the type you might write if you were asked to evaluate an author's use of support. It is followed by a student essay that illustrates effective use of support.

The True Costs of SUVs

HAL R. VARIAN

Traffic fatalities in the United States fell steadily from 54,600 in 1972 to 34,900 in 1992. But then they started to rise again, and by 2002 there were 38,300 traffic deaths a year.

Our performance compared with other countries has also deteriorated. America's ranking has fallen from first to ninth over the last thirty years, with Australia, Britain, and Canada all having better records.

A big part of the difference between the United States and other countries seems to be the prevalence of sport utility vehicles and pickups on American highways. Sales of light trucks—SUVs, pickups, and minivans—were about a fifth of total automobile sales thirty years ago. Now they account for more than half.

But aren't large vehicles supposed to be safer than small cars? Yes, they are safer for their occupants in collisions, but their design makes them all the more dangerous for anyone they hit.

Michelle White, an economist at the University of California, San 5 Diego, estimates that for each fatality that light-truck drivers avoid for themselves and their passengers, they cause four fatalities involving car occupants, pedestrians, bicyclists, and motorcyclists. "Safety gains for

A professor in the School of Information Management and Systems at the University of California at Berkeley, Hal R. Varian has written economics textbooks as well as columns for the *New York Times*. This piece appeared in the *Times* as the "Economic Scene" article on December 12, 2003.

those driving light trucks," Ms. White said, "come at an extremely high cost to others."

Being larger than ordinary vehicles, SUVs and light trucks cause more damage to upper bodies and heads in collisions. Furthermore, their bumpers do not always align with automobile bumpers, and their body structure is stiffer, transferring more force to other vehicles during impact.

A few weeks ago, the auto industry announced a voluntary plan to deal with some of these design problems. They intend to make side-impact airbags standard to help protect heads and upper bodies better in collisions, and they intend to standardize bumper heights.

These will no doubt be helpful improvements, but do they go far enough?

Recently Ms. White examined the econometrics of traffic accidents in an attempt to measure the benefits and costs of changing the number of light trucks on the road. Professor White's paper can be downloaded from http://econ.ucsd.edu/~miwhite/suv-revision.pdf.

Ms. White notes that changing average vehicle size could, in prin-   10
ciple, increase or decrease the cost of accidents.

The results of an accident in New York involving a sport utility vehicle and a smaller car. Traffic fatalities are on the rise, apparently linked to the increase of SUVs.

G. Paul Burnett/*The New York Times*

Suppose the cost of a small vehicle–large vehicle collision is $50, the cost of a small vehicle–small vehicle collision is $45, and the cost of a large vehicle–large vehicle collision is $40.

If all vehicles are small, and there are 10 accidents a year, the total cost of the accidents is $450. But if 10 percent of the small vehicles are replaced by large ones, the average cost of collisions becomes $458.50, since more collisions will be between large and small vehicles. On the other hand, if 60 percent of the vehicles on the road are large, the average cost of a collision is only $456, since more collisions are between large vehicles.

Think about a safety-conscious soccer mom choosing a vehicle. If there are mostly small cars in her town, she can reduce the risk to her and her family in the event of a collision by buying an SUV.

The unfortunate side effect is that the large SUV would cause significant damage to smaller cars if she was involved in an accident.

The laudable private incentive to choose a safe vehicle could, perversely, reduce overall safety.   15

In addition, Ms. White finds that people involved in single-vehicle crashes are more likely to be killed or seriously injured if they are in SUVs or light trucks rather than cars. This may be a result of the increased likelihood of rollovers.

On the other hand, suppose everybody in town drives an SUV. Then the soccer mom will definitely want to purchase one for herself, since it would both increase her family's safety and reduce the overall costs of collisions.

In this case, private incentives and social incentives are aligned.

The dynamics involved is the same as that of an arms race: If other families buy bigger vehicles, then you will want to as well, if only in self-defense.

To see where we are in this arms race, Ms. White examined crash data   20 maintained by the National Highway Safety Administration at www .nass.nhtsa.dot.gov/nass.

Using this data, Ms. White was able to estimate how the probability of fatalities or serious injury varied with the types of vehicles involved in collisions.

For example, in a two-car accident, the probability of a fatality in the car is 38 percent less than in a car–light truck accident. However, in car–light truck accidents, the probability of fatalities in the light truck is 55 percent less than it would be in a truck–truck accident.

If a light truck hits a pedestrian or a cyclist, the probability of fatalities is about 82 percent greater than if a car is involved.

Ms. White then asked what the impact would be of replacing a million light trucks with cars. She considered two models for driver behavior. In the first, she assumed that the former drivers of light trucks would have the same number of accidents as they did when driving trucks. In the second, she assumed that the former drivers of light trucks would have the same accident probabilities as other car drivers.

Using conventional methods for value-of-life calculations, she finds   25
that each light-truck owner who switches to a car saves about $447 in total expected costs of accidents.

Ms. White examines various policies that might persuade drivers to adopt such changes, including changes in liability rules, traffic rules and insurance rules.

Unfortunately, each of these policies has its problems, so there are no easy solutions.

One interesting way to reduce the arms race problem would be to link automobile liability insurance to gasoline taxes. This means drivers whose cars use more gasoline and those who drive a lot would pay more for their insurance—not unreasonable, since, on average, they impose more costs in accidents.

Aaron Edlin, a professor of economics and law at the University of California, Berkeley, has argued that such "pay at the pump" insurance premiums would have many other benefits (www.bepress.com/aaronedlin/contribution5/). So this type of payment scheme is worth considering for a variety of reasons.

READING AND DISCUSSION QUESTIONS

1. For the purposes of his article, how is Varian defining *light truck*?

2. What relationship does he see between light trucks and number of traffic fatalities?

3. What type of support does Varian use in the three opening paragraphs? Does he use that type of support anywhere else in the essay?

4. What other types of support does Varian make use of in his essay? What types of support do you find most effective in making his argument? What types do you find least effective?

5. What claim is Varian supporting in the essay?

6. How does Varian document his sources? How does he try to establish that his sources are reliable?

The True Confusion about SUV Costs

BETHANY ROYCE

Hal R. Varian entitled his December 18, 2003, *New York Times* piece on sport utility vehicles "The True Costs of SUVs." A more accurate title might have been "The Confusing Costs of SUVs." While Varian turns to the right type of support for his subject—statistics—his use of that support is more confusing than enlightening.

Varian made a wise choice in appealing to his readers' need to feel safe and secure. His statistics are most appealing when he points out that for twenty years the number of traffic fatalities in our country went down and that parents can feel secure knowing that they can make their children safer by buying light trucks (SUVs, pickups, or minivans) instead of cars. In each case, however, there is a negative side. The number of fatalities started rising again between 1992 and 2002, in part because of the increase in the number of sales of light trucks during that time. And Varian tells us that in making their families safer by buying light trucks, they are increasing the risk of doing more harm to others should they be involved in accidents.

For the rest of his support, Varian draws primarily on research done by Michelle White, whom he identifies only "as an economist at the University of California, San Diego" (185). She may have done excellent work, but the way that Varian explains it is confusing and unconvincing. White tries to predict how the cost of accidents would change depending on the size of the vehicles involved. Instead of using realistic cost estimates, however, she arbitrarily assigns the cost of $50 to a small vehicle–large vehicle collision, the cost of $45 to a small vehicle–small vehicle collision, and the cost of $40 to a large vehicle–large vehicle collision. Varian summarizes what this hypothetical scenario reveals:

> If all vehicles are small, and there are 10 accidents a year, the total cost of the accidents is $450. But if 10 percent of the small vehicles are replaced by large ones, the average cost of collisions becomes $458.50, since more collisions will be between large and small vehicles. On the other hand, if 60 percent of the vehicles on the road are large, the average cost of a collision is only $456, since more collisions are between large vehicles. (187)

Average Americans are left wondering what all of this means to them. The hypothetical situation cannot be easily applied to any individual driver and certainly not to any specific accident. How should a reader evaluate the information in attempting to make the decision regarding what size

Bethany Royce teaches business courses and introductory economics at a two-year college in Florida and writes a consumer advice column for a local newspaper.

vehicle to buy? The driver who just paid $3000 in car repairs is going to find any of the numbers Varian cites attractive.

There are a lot of "ifs" in Varian's argument. If you live in a town with lots of SUVs, it is safer to drive one yourself. If you live in a town where there are few SUVs, you should drive a car so that you would not be as likely to hurt someone else in a wreck. If you have a single-vehicle accident in an SUV, you are more likely to be killed. If you hit a pedestrian while driving one, you are more likely to kill that person.

There are also few clear conclusions to be drawn from the support   5 that Varian offers. After Ms. White examines "various policies that might persuade drivers to adopt such changes, including changes in liability rules, traffic rules and insurance rates," the unfortunate conclusion is that "each of these policies has its problems, so there are no easy solutions" (188). The only solution that Varian advances as "worth considering" is one by a colleague of his at the University of California, Berkeley, that would link a vehicle owner's liability insurance to gas taxes (188). Overall the article succeeds more in revealing the complexities involved in the increased use of SUVs than in clarifying any of those complexities.

STUDENT ESSAY

Safer? Tastier? More Nutritious?
The Dubious Merits of Organic Foods

KRISTEN WEINACKER

Organic foods are attractive to some consumers because of the principles behind them and the farming techniques used to produce them. There is a special respect for organic farmers who strive to maintain the ecological balance and harmony that exist among living things. As these farmers work in partnership with nature, some consumers too feel a certain attachment to the earth (Wolf 1–2). They feel happier knowing that these foods are produced without chemical fertilizers, pesticides, and additives to extend their shelf life (Pickerell; Agricultural Extension Service 5). They feel that they have returned to nature by eating organic foods that are advertised as being healthy for maintaining a vigorous lifestyle. Unfortunately, research has not provided statistical evidence that organic foods are more nutritious than conventionally grown ones.

The debate over the nutritional benefits has raged for decades. Defenders of the nutritional value of organic foods have employed excellent

At the time she wrote this essay Kristen Weinacker was an undergraduate at Clemson University.

marketing and sales strategies. First, they freely share the philosophy behind their farming and follow up with detailed descriptions of their management techniques. Second, organic farmers skillfully appeal to our common sense. It seems reasonable to believe that organic foods are more nutritious since they are grown without chemical fertilizers and pesticides. Third, since the soil in which these crops are grown is so rich and healthy, it seems plausible that these crops have absorbed and developed better nutrients. As Lynda Brown asserts in her book *Living Organic*, "Organic farmers believe that growing crops organically provides the best possible way to produce healthy food" (26). Brown provides beautifully illustrated and enlarged microscopic photographs to show the more developed structure of organic foods compared to conventional products to convince the consumer to believe that organic foods are more nutritious (27). Fourth, many consumers view the higher price tags on organic foods and assume that they must be more nutritious. Generalizations permeate the whole world of organic foods. These marketing strategies persuade the consumer that organic foods are healthier than conventional foods without providing any factual comparisons.

In their book *Is Our Food Safe?* Warren Leon and Caroline Smith Dewaal compare organic and conventionally produced foods. They strongly suggest that consumers buy organic foods to help the environment (68). They believe that organic foods are healthier than conventional ones. However, statistics supporting this belief are not provided. The authors even warn consumers that they need to read product labels because some organic foods may be as unhealthy as conventional ones (68–69). An interesting poll involving 1,041 adults was conducted by ABC News asking, "Why do people buy organic?" Analyst Daniel Merkle concluded that 45% of the American public *believes* that organic products are more nutritious than conventionally grown ones. Also, 57% of the population maintains that organic farming is beneficial for the environment. According to the pollsters, the primary reason why people bought organic foods is the belief that they are healthier because they have less pesticide residue. However, there has never been any link established between the nutritional value of organic foods and the residue found on them. Clever marketing strategies have made the need for concrete data really not of prime importance for the consumer to join the bandwagon promoting organic foods.

This pervasive belief among the American public that organic foods are probably healthier than conventionally grown foods was reiterated in my telephone interview with Mr. Joseph Williamson, an agricultural county extension agent working with Clemson University. When asked if organically grown foods are more nutritious than those grown conventionally, he replied that they probably were for two reasons. First, organic crops tend to grow more slowly. Therefore, the nutrients have more time to build up in the plants. Second, organic plants are usually grown locally. The fruits and vegetables are allowed to stay on the plants for a longer period of time. They ripen more than those picked green and transported across miles. He contends that these conditions promote a better nutrient buildup. Unfortunately, the extension agent acknowledges that statistical evidence is not available to support the claim that organic products are more nutritious.

An article entitled "Effects of Agricultural Methods in Nutritional   5
Quality: A Comparison of Organic with Conventional Crops" reports on conclusions drawn by Dr. Virginia Worthington, a certified nutrition specialist. Worthington examines why it is so difficult to ascertain if organic foods are more nutritious. First, "the difference in terms of health effects is not large enough to be readily apparent." There is no concrete evidence that people are healthier eating organic foods or, conversely, that people become more ill eating conventionally grown produce. Second, Dr. Worthington notes that variables such as sunlight, temperature, and amount of rain are so inconsistent that the nutrients in crops vary yearly. Third, she points out that the nutrient value of products can be changed by the way products are stored and shipped. After reviewing at least thirty studies dealing with the question if organic foods are more nutritious than conventionally grown ones, Dr. Worthington concludes that there is too little data available to substantiate the claim of higher nutritional value in organic foods. She also believes that it is an impossible task to make a direct connection between organic foods and the health of those people who consume them.

After being asked for thirty years about organic foods by her readers and associates, Joan Dye Gusson, writer for *Eating Well* magazine, firmly concludes that there is "little hard proof that organically grown produce is reliably more nutritious." Reviewing seventy years' worth of studies on the subject, Gusson has no doubt that organic foods should be healthier because of the way they are produced and cultivated. Gusson brings up an interesting point about chemical and pesticide residue. She believes that the fact that organic foods have been found to have fewer residues does not make them automatically more nutritious and healthier for the consumer. As scientific technologies advance, Gusson predicts that research will someday discover statistical data that will prove that organic foods have a higher nutritional value compared to conventionally grown ones.

In order to provide the public with more information about the nature of organic foods, the well-known and highly regarded magazine *Consumer Reports* decided to take a closer look at organic foods in their January, 1998, magazine, in an article entitled "Organic Foods: Safer? Tastier? More nutritious?" By conducting comparison tests, their researchers discovered that organic foods have less pesticide residue, and that their flavors are just about the same as conventionally grown foods. These scientists came to the conclusion that the "variability within a given crop is greater than the variability between one cropping system and another." *Consumer Reports* contacted Professor Willie Lockeretz from the Tufts University School of Nutrition Science and Policy. He told researchers that "the growing system you use probably does affect nutrition. . . . But it does it in ways so complex you might be studying the problem forever." Keeping in mind these comments made by Dr. Lockeretz, *Consumer Reports* believes it would be an impossible task to compare the nutritional values of organic and conventional foods. Therefore, researchers at *Consumer Reports* decided not to carry out that part of their comparison testing.

Although statistical evidence is not available at this time to support the claim that organic foods are more nutritious than conventionally grown ones, there is a very strong feeling shared by a majority of the general public that they are. We are called back to nature as we observe the love that organic farmers have for the soil and their desire to work in partnership with nature. We are easily lured to the attractive displays of organic foods in the grocery stores. However, we must keep in mind the successful marketing techniques that have been used to convince us that organic foods are more nutritious than conventionally grown ones. Although common sense tells us that organic foods should be more nutritious, research has not provided us with any statistical data to prove this claim.

Works Cited

Agricultural Extension Service. *Organic Vegetable Gardening.* The University of Tennessee. PB 1391.

Brown, Lynda. *Organic Living.* New York: Dorling Kindersley Publishing, Inc., 2000.

Gussow, Joan Dye. "Is Organic Food More Nutritious? *Eating Well* (May/June 1997). 27 March 2003. <http://www.prnac.net/rodmap - nutrition.html>.

"Effect of Agricultural Methods on Nutritional Quality: A Comparison of Organic with Conventional Crops." *Alternative Therapies* 4 (1998): 58–69. 18 Feb. 2003. <http://www.purefood.org/healthier101101.cfm>.

Leon, Warren, and Caroline Smith DeWaal. *Is Our Food Safe?* New York: Three Rivers Press, 2002.

Merkle, Daniel. "Why Do People Buy Organic?" ABCNews.com. 3 Feb. 2000. 27 March 2003.

"Organic Foods: Safer? Tastier? More Nutritious?" *Consumer Reports.* Jan. 1998. 24 Feb. 2003. <http://www.consumerreports.org/main/detailsv2.jsp?content%3%ecnt_id +18959&f>.

Pickrell, John. "Federal Government Launches Organic Standards." *Science News* 162.17 (Nov. 2002). <http://www.sciencenews.org/20021102/food.asp._17_March 2003>.

Williamson, Joseph. Telephone interview. 28 Feb. 2003.

Wolf, Ray, ed. *Organic Farming: Yesterday's and Tomorrow's Agriculture.* Philadelphia: Rodale Press, 1977.

Connecting the Dots . . . to Terrorism

BERNARD GOLDBERG

Most of the time television is nothing more than a diversion—proof, as the old quip goes, that we would rather do anything than talk to each other. We'd also rather watch a bad sitcom than read a good book. Bad sitcoms get millions of viewers; good books get thousands. In an "entertainment culture," even the news is entertainment. Certainly too much local news has been pure fluff for some time now, with their Ken and Barbie anchors who have nothing intelligent to say but look great while they're saying it. And because network news is losing viewers every year, executives and producers are trying to figure out ways to hold on to the ones they still have. They think cosmetics will work, so they change the anchor desk or they change the graphics. They get the anchor to stand instead of sit. They feature more "news you can use." They put Chandra Levy[22] on all over the place, hoping they can concoct a ratings cocktail by mixing one part missing intern with ten parts sex scandal.

And then something genuinely big and really important happens that shakes us to our core, and all those producers who couldn't get enough of Chandra are through with her. Only in the fickle world of television news can someone who has disappeared without a trace disappear a second time.

And it's when that history-making story comes along that Americans—no matter what their politics, religion, age, race, or sex—turn to television, not just for information, but also for comfort and for peace of mind. It doesn't happen often, but when it does, television becomes a lot more than just a diversion.

It happened when John Kennedy was assassinated. We all turned to Walter Cronkite and Huntley and Brinkley, not just for facts, but also for reassurance—that despite the terrible tragedy, America was going to be okay.

It happened when *Challenger* blew up. And it happened again on September 11, 2001, when a band of religious lunatics declared war on the United States of America to punish us for not wanting to dwell in the fourteenth century, where they currently reside, and, of course, to show 5

[22] *Chandra Levy*: A government intern whose disappearance was widely covered in the press in 2001. —EDS.

Bernard Goldberg was a reporter and producer for CBS for more than thirty years. He has won seven Emmy awards and was once rated by *TV Guide* as one of the ten most interesting people on television. This chapter is from his 2002 book *Bias: A CBS Insider Exposes How the Media Distort the News*, written after he left the network.

the world that their intense hatred of Israel—*and of Israel's friends*— knows no bounds. On September 11, they not only killed as many innocent Americans as they could in the most dramatic way they knew how, but, as the *Wall Street Journal* put it, they also "wiped out any remaining illusions that America is safe from mass organized violence."

On that day we all turned to television. We turned to Dan Rather and Peter Jennings and Tom Brokaw and the others. And they did a fine job, as they often do when covering tragedy. They showed empathy. They were fair and accurate, and the information they passed along to us wasn't filtered through the usual liberal political and social sensibilities. They gave us the news on that day the way they should give us the news *all the time*, whether the story is about race or feminism or taxes or gay rights or anything else. *For a change, they gave it to us straight.*

On the night of September 11, 2001, Peter Jennings made a point about how, in times of danger and tragedy, television serves the function that campfires used to serve in the old days when Americans migrated westward in covered wagons. Back then, they would sit around the campfire and get the news from other travelers about what they should look out for down the road. "Some people pulled the wagons around," Peter said, "and discussed what was going on and tried to understand it." But the campfire was more than just a meeting place where families could pick up important information. The campfire also provided a sense of community, a sense that *we're all in this together*. That's what television was on September 11.

As I listened to Peter tell that story, I thought about another American tragedy that shocked us six years earlier, when Timothy McVeigh— another true believer who cared nothing about killing innocent Americans—blew up the federal building in Oklahoma City. I thought about how it took some of the media elites only a few days before they started to play one of their favorite games—connect the dots. What they found back then—or more accurately, what they convinced themselves they found—was a line stretching from Oklahoma City to the Republican Party to conservatives in general and finally to Rush Limbaugh.

Dan Rather said, "Even after Oklahoma City, you can turn on your radio in any city and still dial up hate talk: extremist, racist, and violent from the hosts and those who call in."

Time senior writer Richard Lacayo put it this way: "In a nation that 10 has entertained and appalled itself for years with hot talk on radio and the campaign trail, the inflamed rhetoric of the '90s is suddenly an unindicted coconspirator in the blast."

Nina Easton wrote in the *Los Angeles Times*, "The Oklahoma City attack on federal workers and their children also alters the once-easy dynamic between charismatic talk show host and adoring audience. Hosts who routinely espouse the same antigovernment themes as the militia movement now must walk a fine line between inspiring their audience— and inciting the most radical among them."

On *Face the Nation*, Bob Schieffer asked this question: "Mr. Panetta, there's been a lot of antigovernment rhetoric, it comes over talk radio, it comes from various quarters. Do you think that that somehow has led these people to commit this act, do they feed on that kind of rhetoric, and what impact do you think it had?"

Carl Rowan, the late columnist, was quoted in a *Washington Post* story saying that, "Unless Gingrich and Dole[23] and the Republicans say 'Am I inflaming a bunch of nuts?' you know we're going to have some more events. I am absolutely certain the harsher rhetoric of the Gingriches and the Doles . . . creates a climate of violence in America."

And David Broder had this to say in the *Washington Post*: "The bombing shows how dangerous it really is to inflame twisted minds with statements that suggest political opponents are enemies. For two years, Rush Limbaugh described this nation as 'America held hostage' to the policies of the liberal Democrats, as if the duly elected president and Congress were equivalent to the regime in Tehran. I think there will be less tolerance and fewer cheers for that kind of rhetoric."

The message was clear: Conservative talk radio and conservative   15
politicians created an antigovernment atmosphere in America that spawned Timothy McVeigh and therefore were at least partially to blame for his terrorism. It's true, of course, that the atmosphere in which we live contributes to everything that happens in our culture. Calling people "kikes" or "niggers" makes it easier to see them as less than human and to treat them as something less than human. But to point fingers at talk radio for somehow encouraging Timothy McVeigh strikes me as a stretch at best; more likely it's just another opportunity for liberal journalists to blame conservatives for one more evil. And if this kind of connecting the dots is fair game, then should we also accuse Americans who spoke out loudly and forcefully against the war in Vietnam—including many journalists—of contributing to the 1972 bombing of the Pentagon and to other sometimes deadly terrorism, perpetuated by fanatics on the Left? According to the media elites' rulebook, when liberals rant it's called free speech; when conservatives rant it's called incitement to terrorism.

As I watched the coverage of the attacks on the Pentagon and the World Trade Center, I wondered why I hadn't seen more stories on television news, long before these zealots flew their hijacked planes into American buildings, about the culture of anti-American hate that permeates so much of the Middle East—stories that might help explain how little Arab children can grow up to become fanatical suicide bombers.

If the media found it so important to discuss the malignant atmosphere created by "hot" conservative talk radio, then why didn't they find it important to delve into this malignant atmosphere that seems to have

---

[23] *Gingrich and Dole:* Newt Gingrich (b. 1943) was Speaker of the House of Representatives from 1995 to 1999. Robert Dole (b. 1923) was a Senate majority leader and served in the Senate from 1968 to 1996. —Eds.

bred such maniacal killers? Why would journalists, so interested in connecting the dots when they thought they led to Rush Limbaugh, be so
uninterested in connecting the dots when there might actually be dots to
connect—*from hateful, widely held popular attitudes in much of the Arab
world straight to the cockpits of those hijacked jetliners?*

One of the networks put an American Muslim woman on the news
who said that no one blamed Christianity when McVeigh killed all those
people. Why blame Islam now? The reporter interviewing this woman let
her have her say, never bothering to point out that Timothy McVeigh
didn't kill all those people in the name of Christianity. Suicide airplane
hijackers, on the other hand, are people who actually believe their murderous acts will earn them a one-way ticket to Paradise.

Was what happened on September 11 a subversion of Islam, as pundits and journalists on network and cable TV told us over and over again?
Or was it the result of an *honest* reading of the Koran? It's true, of course,
that if taken too literally by uncritical minds, just about any holy book
can lead to bad things. Still, why are there no Christian suicide bombers,
or Jewish suicide bombers, or Hindu suicide bombers, or Buddhist suicide
bombers, but no apparent shortage of Muslim suicide bombers? If Islam
is "a religion of peace" as so many people from President Bush on down
were telling us (and, for what it's worth, I'm prepared to believe that it is),
then what exactly is it in the Koran that so appeals to these Islamic fanatics? Don't look for that answer on the network news. A Lexis-Nexis
search going back to 1991 linking the words "Koran" and "terrorist" produced absolutely nothing that told us what the Koran actually says which
might encourage a Muslim, no matter how misguided, to commit acts of
terrorism.

I understand that even to ask questions about a possible connection   20
between Islam and violence is to tread into politically incorrect terrain.
But it seems to me that the media need to go there anyway. And any network that can put thousands of stories on the air about sex and murder
should be able to give us a few on the atmosphere that breeds religious
zealotry. It might have helped us see what was coming on September 11.

In fact, I learned much more about the atmosphere that breeds suicide bombers from one short article in *Commentary* magazine than I have
from watching twenty years of network television news. In its September
2001 issue (which came out before the attack on America), there was an
article by Fiamma Nirenstein, an Italian journalist based in Israel, entitled
"How Suicide Bombers Are Made." In it, she tells about a "river of hatred"
that runs through not just the most radical of Arab nations but also much
of what we like to think of as the "moderate" Arab world.

She tells us about a series of articles that ran in the leading
government-sponsored newspaper in Egypt, *Al Ahram*, about how Jews
supposedly use the blood of Christians to make matzah for Passover.

She tells us about a hit song in Cairo, Damascus, and the West Bank
with the catchy title "I Hate Israel."

Why didn't I know this? A computer check soon answered my question. On television, only CNN reported the "I Hate Israel" story. On radio, NPR did a piece. So did the *Christian Science Monitor* and the *Chicago Tribune*. The *Los Angeles Times* ran a short wire service story that said "'I Hate Israel' . . . made an overnight singing sensation of a working-class crooner."

Can you imagine if the big hit song in Israel was "I Hate Palestine" or "I Hate Arabs"? The *New York Times* would have put the story on page one and then run an editorial just to make sure we all got the message—that the song is indecent and contributes to an atmosphere of hate. And since the *Times* sets the agenda for the networks, Dan Rather, Tom Brokaw, and Peter Jennings would have all fallen into line and run big stories on their evening newscasts, too, saying the exact same thing. A week later, Mike Wallace would have landed in Tel Aviv looking absolutely mortified that those Jews would do such a thing.

And that's part of the problem. Despite the liberalism of the media, there is a subtle form of racism at work here. As Fiamma Nirenstein writes, "The Arabs, it is implicitly suggested, are a backward people, not to be held to civilized standards of the West." Of the Israelis, however, the American media expect much more. That is why a song called "I Hate Israel" becomes a big hit, and yet is not a news story. And it is why a series of stories in a government-sponsored newspaper—in a supposedly moderate country—about Jews killing Christians for their blood holds almost no interest for American journalists.

It's true that not long after the twin towers of the World Trade Center came tumbling down, the networks showed us pictures of Palestinians in East Jerusalem honking their horns, firing their guns into the air, and generally having a good old time celebrating the death of so many Americans in New York and Washington. They cheered "God is great" while they handed out candy, which is a tradition in the Arab world when something good happens.

It's not that there's been a total news blackout of anti-American hate in the Middle East—*Nightline* has done some good, intelligent work in this area—it's just that we need more than pictures of happy Palestinians reveling in the death of thousands of Americans. And we need more than what has become a staple of Middle East television news coverage: young children throwing stones at Israeli soldiers—the perfect made-for-television David and Goliath story. What we need are stories that connect the dots, not just back to Afghanistan and its backward and repressive Taliban government, but also between the fanatics in New York and Washington and a cultural environment in the Arab world where even "moderates" hand out candy to celebrate the massacre of Americans.

But here the media—apparently feeling squeamish about stories that put the "underdogs" in a bad light—keep us virtually in the dark. And it's not just little tidbits like "I Hate Israel" and articles about Jews taking Christian blood that I—and almost all Americans—knew nothing about.

Here's a quick rundown of what goes on in much of the Middle East as re-ported by Ms. Nirenstein in *Commentary*—news that is virtually ignored on the big American TV networks:

> In Egypt and Jordan, news sources have repeatedly warned that Israel has distributed drug-laced chewing gum and candy, intended (it is said) to kill children and make women sexually corrupt. . . .
>
> [Palestinian television] recently asserted that, far from being extermi-nation camps, Chelmo, Dachau, and Auschwitz were in fact mere "places of disinfection."
>
> On April 13—observed in Israel as Holocaust Remembrance Day—the official Palestinian newspaper *Al-Hayat al-Jadida* featured a column . . . entitled "The Fable of the Holocaust."
>
> A columnist in Egypt's government-sponsored Al-Akhbar thus ex-pressed his "thanks to Hitler, of blessed memory, who on behalf of the Palestinians took revenge in advance on the most vile criminals on the face of the earth. Still, we do have a complaint against [Hitler], for his revenge on them was not enough."

In addition to these examples, Ms. Nirenstein cites a textbook for Syr-ian tenth graders which teaches them that "the logic of justice obligates the application of the single verdict [on the Jews] from which there is no escape: namely, that their criminal intentions be turned against them and that they be exterminated." And she notes that in June 2001, two weeks after the fatal collapse of a Jewish wedding hall in Jerusalem, Palestinian television broadcast a sermon by a Muslim imam praying that "this op-pressive Knesset [Israel's parliament] will [similarly] collapse over the heads of the Jews."

I did not know any of that because it's simply not the kind of news that we normally get from the Middle East—certainly not from network evening newscasts or from *Dateline, 20/20,* or *48 Hours,* three news mag-azine programs that are usually too busy peddling the trivial and sensa-tional to bother with more significant stories. And besides, that kind of news makes liberal journalists uneasy. After all, these are the same people who bend over backwards to find "moral equivalence" between Palestin-ian terrorists who blow up discos in Tel Aviv filled with teenagers, on the one hand, and Israeli commandos who *preemptively* kill terrorist ringlead-ers *before* they send their suicide bombers into Israel on a mission to kill Jews, on the other.

On September 11, right after the networks showed us the pictures of Palestinians celebrating American deaths, they also showed us Yasser Arafat expressing his condolences and giving blood for the American vic-tims. This, in its way, represented a kind of moral equivalence: while some Palestinians celebrate, the news anchors were suggesting, their leader does not; he is somber and, we're led to believe, absolutely shocked. But we could have done with a little less moral equivalence on the part of the press and a little more tough journalism. Someone should have asked the leader of the Palestinian people if he understood that the cultures that he and other "moderate" Arab leaders preside over "carefully nurture and inculcate resentments and hatreds against America and the non-Arab world," as a *Wall Street Journal* editorial put it. And if that's asking too much of a field reporter covering a seemingly shaken and distraught Arafat in the wake of September 11, then an anchor back in New York should have wondered out loud about that very connection.

But to have asked such a question might have been viewed as anti-Arab (and therefore pro-Israeli), and reporters and anchors would rather be stoned by an angry mob in Ramallah than be seen in that light. So we didn't learn that day if Chairman Arafat quite understood his role in the celebration he so deplored. Nor did we get an explanation on the news about why there were not thousands of other Arabs in the streets—on the West Bank or in Jerusalem or in the "moderate" Arab countries—expressing their *condolences*. Was it because they are afraid to show support for American victims of terrorism? Or was it because they, like the Palestinians we saw with great big smiles, didn't feel that bad about what happened?

If the networks can give us months and months of Chandra and Jon-Benet and Lorena Bobbitt and Joey Buttafuoco, then they can give us more than they do about the river of hatred that breeds suicide bombers.

But this is where journalists—given their liberal tendency to em-   35
pathize with, and sometimes even root for, the "underdog"—run into a big problem: if they start to connect those ideological and religious dots, they may not like what they find.

American journalists who covered the civil rights struggle recognized the pathology of racism and rightly made no allowance for it. They understood that in order for evil to flourish in places throughout the South, all it took was a few fundamentally bad people—while everybody else sat around making believe it wasn't happening, either because they were afraid or because they just didn't want to get involved.

The Middle East, of course, is a place with a long and troubled history. But it should be obvious that a place that turns "I Hate Israel" into a hit, that runs stories in its most important newspaper about Jews killing Christians for their blood, that faults Hitler *only because he did not kill more Jews*, and that celebrates the murder of thousands of innocent Americans is a place populated by many nasty people. Perhaps it has many good people, too, who just don't want to get involved. The point is, a story about all of this is at least as important as a story about Anne Heche and her sex life, even if sex does better in the ratings than disturbing news about raw, ignorant hatred in the world of Islam.

None of this is an argument that the media are intentionally pro-Arab. Rather, like the U.S. State Department, they are pro "moral equivalence." If they connect the dots with stories on the news about hit songs called "I Hate Israel" and all the rest, the Arab world will accuse the "Jewish-controlled" American media of being sympathetic to "Israeli oppression." If journalists—who were so willing to connect the dots when there was a belief that they led to Rush Limbaugh—connected *these* dots, they might find that there are a lot fewer moderates in those moderate places than they keep telling us about.

So they look the other way, which, as Ms. Nirenstein tells us, is not that easy. One has to turn "a determinedly blind eye to this river of hatred . . . [and] to be persuaded that, after all, 'everybody' in the Middle East really wants the same thing."

Obviously, there are legitimate issues about which there are differing 40 viewpoints in the Middle East: Should Israel blow up the houses that belong to the families of terrorists? Should Israel allow the construction of new settlements on the West Bank? These are two that come quickly to mind.

But moral equivalence and the quest for evenhanded journalism should not stop the media from telling us more—much more in my view—about the kind of backwardness and hatred that is alive and well, *not just in places like Kabul and Baghdad,* but in "moderate" cities and villages all over the Arab world. Even if it means going against their liberal sensibilities and reporting that sometimes even the underdog can be evil.

READING AND DISCUSSION QUESTIONS

1. How does Goldberg support his claim that television draws Americans together in times of crisis?

2. How does he feel the news is different during times of crisis from how it usually is?

3. Explain the title that Goldberg chose for this piece. What does he claim the "media elites" have "connected the dots" to find?

4. What does Goldberg feel the news media are *not* telling Americans? What sort of support does he offer for that part of his argument?

5. What type or types of support that Goldberg uses do you find most effective? Why?

WRITING SUGGESTIONS

6. Analyze the types of support that Goldberg makes use of in his essay.

7. Evaluate the effectiveness of the major types of support that he uses in his essay.

8. Attack or defend the claim that Goldberg is advancing in his essay.

9. What is your personal opinion of the media coverage of the tragedies of September 11?

10. Do you feel that your education has exposed you to recent history as well as the more distant past? Explain.

A New Look, an Old Battle

ANNA QUINDLEN

Public personification has always been the struggle on both sides of the abortion battle lines. That is why the people outside clinics on Saturday mornings carry signs with photographs of infants rather than of zygotes, why they wear lapel pins fashioned in the image of tiny feet and shout, "Don't kill your baby," rather than, more accurately, "Don't destroy your embryo." Those who support the legal right to an abortion have always been somewhat at a loss in the face of all this. From time to time women have come forward to speak about their decision to have an abortion, but when they are prominent, it seems a bit like grandstanding, and when they are not, it seems a terrible invasion of privacy when privacy is the point in the first place. Easier to marshal the act of presumptive ventriloquism practiced by the opponents, pretending to speak for those unborn unknown to them by circumstance or story.

But the battle of personification will assume a different and more sympathetic visage in the years to come. Perhaps the change in the weather was best illustrated when conservative Sen. Strom Thurmond invoked his own daughter to explain a position opposed by the anti-abortion forces. The senator's daughter has diabetes. The actor Michael J. Fox has Parkinson's disease. Christopher Reeve is in a wheelchair because of a spinal-cord injury, Ronald Reagan locked in his own devolving mind by Alzheimer's. In the faces of the publicly and personally beloved lies enormous danger for the life-begins-at-conception lobby.

The catalytic issue is research on stem cells. These are versatile building blocks that may be coaxed into becoming any other cell type; they could therefore hold the key to endless mysteries of human biology, as well as someday help provide a cure for ailments as diverse as diabetes, Parkinson's, spinal-cord degeneration, and Alzheimer's. By some estimates, more than 100 million Americans have diseases that scientists suspect could be affected by research on stem cells. Scientists hope that the astonishing potential of this research will persuade the federal government to help fund it and allow the National Institutes of Health to help oversee it. This is not political, researchers insist. It is about science, not abortion.

And they are correct. Stem-cell research is typically done by using frozen embryos left over from in vitro fertilization. If these embryos were placed in the womb, they might eventually implant, become a fetus, then a child. Unused, they are the earliest undifferentiated collection of cells made by the joining of the egg and sperm, no larger than the period at

---

Anna Quindlen is a Pulitzer Prize–winning journalist and best-selling novelist. This piece appeared in the April 9, 2001, issue of *Newsweek* magazine.

the end of this sentence. One of the oft-used slogans of the anti-abortion movement is "abortion stops a beating heart." There is no heart in this preimplantation embryo, but there are stem cells that, in the hands of scientists, might lead to extraordinary work affecting everything from cancer to heart disease.

All of which leaves the anti-abortion movement trying desperately to 5 hold its hard line, and failing. Judie Brown of the American Life League can refer to these embryos as "the tiniest person," and the National Right to Life organization can publish papers that refer to stem-cell research as the "destruction of life." But ordinary people with family members losing their mobility or their grasp on reality will be able to be more thoughtful and reasonable about the issues involved.

The anti-abortion activists know this, because they have already seen the defections. Some senators have abandoned them to support fetal-tissue research, less promising than stem-cell work but still with significant potential for treating various ailments. Elected officials who had voted against abortion rights found themselves able to support procedures that used tissue from aborted fetuses; perhaps they were men who had fathers with heart disease, who had mothers with arthritis and whose hearts resonated with the possibilities for alleviating pain and prolonging life. Senator Thurmond was one, Senator McCain another. Former senator Connie Mack of Florida recently sent a letter to the president, who must decide the future role of the federal government in this area, describing himself "as a conservative pro-life now former member" of Congress, and adding that there "were those of us identified as such who supported embryonic stem-cell research."

When a recent test of fetal tissue in patients with Parkinson's had disastrous side effects, the National Right to Life Web site ran an almost gloating report: "horrific," "rips to shreds," "media cheerleaders," "defy description." The tone is a reflection of fear. It's the fear that the use of fetal tissue to produce cures for debilitating ailments might somehow launder the process of terminating a pregnancy, a positive result from what many people still see as a negative act. And it's the fear that thinking — really thinking — about the use of the earliest embryo for life-saving research might bring a certain long-overdue relativism to discussions of abortion across the board.

The majority of Americans have always been able to apply that relativism to these issues. They are more likely to accept early abortions than later ones. They are more tolerant of a single abortion under exigent circumstances than multiple abortions. Some who disapprove of abortion in theory have discovered that they can accept it in fact if a daughter or a girlfriend is pregnant.

And some who believe that life begins at conception may look into the vacant eyes of an adored parent with Alzheimer's or picture a paralyzed child walking again, and take a closer look at what an embryo really is, at what stem-cell research really does, and then consider the true cost of a cure. That is what Senator Thurmond obviously did when he looked at his daughter and broke ranks with the true believers. It may be an over-simplification to say that real live loved ones trump the imagined unborn, that a cluster of undifferentiated cells due to be discarded anyway is a small price to pay for the health and welfare of millions. Or perhaps it is only a simple commonsensical truth.

READING AND DISCUSSION QUESTIONS

1. Understanding Quindlen's argument requires understanding of the terms she uses. In her introductory paragraph, she refers to "public personification," "grandstanding," and "presumptive ventriloquism." Explain these terms in the context of her argument.

2. Why are anti-abortion activists opposed to the use of stem-cell research? How does Quindlen defend her own position?

3. What does Quindlen mean when she says that stem-cell research "might bring a certain long-overdue relativism to discussions of abortion" (para. 7)? (The meaning of *relativism* is the key.)

4. Although this essay clearly suggests a policy, it is primarily a claim of value: Stem-cell research is vital because it will contribute to the life and health of our loved ones. Point out places in the essay where Quindlen makes an emotional appeal to our compassion.

WRITING SUGGESTIONS

5. The debate about stem-cell research in the Congress, the media, and the medical and scientific professions, expanded after a speech by President Bush on August 9, 2001, in which he agreed to permit limited research on stem cells. Look up some of the news stories, editorials, and letters to the editors that followed his speech, and summarize the opposition to the president's proposal.

6. Quindlen explores the possible influence of stem-cell research on increased acceptance of abortion. Write an essay that argues for or against the right of a woman to an abortion. If you have reservations, make clear what circumstances would govern your judgment.

Marriage-Plus

THEODORA OOMS

The public has been concerned about "family breakdown" for a long time, but it was not until the passage of welfare reform in 1996 that the federal government decided to get into the business of promoting marriage. Although it was little noticed at the time, three of the four purposes of the welfare legislation refer directly or indirectly to marriage and family formation. The law exhorts states to promote "job preparation, work and marriage," to "prevent and reduce the incidence of out-of-wedlock pregnancies," and to "encourage the formation and maintenance of two-parent families."

The Bush administration, as it contemplates this year's extension of welfare legislation, plans to make marriage even more central. The administration's reauthorization proposal, announced February 27, includes $300 million for demonstration grants to focus on promoting healthy marriages and reducing out-of-wedlock births.[24] Meanwhile, Oklahoma Governor Frank Keating has launched a $10 million, multisector marriage initiative, and other smaller-scale government-sponsored initiatives have been enacted in Arizona, Florida, Louisiana, Michigan, and Utah. The federal government is primarily concerned with reducing out-of-wedlock births, which it views as a principal cause of welfare dependency and a host of other social problems. By contrast, state marriage initiatives are most concerned about the effects of high divorce rates and father absence on children.[25]

This new emphasis on marriage as a panacea for social problems is troubling to many liberals. For one thing, it risks being dismissive of children who happen to find themselves in single-parent families. It also can be seen as disparaging single mothers and ignoring the fact that many women have left abusive marriages for good reasons.

That said, it's hard to dismiss an overwhelming consensus of social-science research findings that children tend to be better off, financially and emotionally, when their parents are married to each other. Around 50 percent of all first marriages are expected to end in divorce, and 60 percent of all divorces involve children. One-third of all births are out of

---

[24]See *Working Toward Independence: The President's Plan to Strengthen Welfare Reform*, February 2002. http://www.whitehouse.gov/news/releases/2002/02/welfare-reform-announcement-book.pdf.

[25]Theodora Ooms, "The Role of the Federal Government in Strengthening Marriage," in *Virginia Journal of Social Policy and the Law*, Fall 2002. To be posted on www.clasp.org.

Theodora Ooms is a senior policy analyst at the Center for Law and Social Policy. Her article is an annotated version of one that originally appeared in a special issue of *The American Prospect* on "The Politics of the American Family," April 8, 2002.

wedlock, nearly 40 percent of children do not live with their biological fathers, and too many nonresident fathers neither support nor see their children on a regular basis.

Children living with single mothers are five times as likely to be poor   5
as those in two-parent families. Growing up in a single-parent family also roughly doubles the risk that a child will drop out of school, have difficulty finding a job, or become a teen parent. About half of these effects appear to be attributable to the reduced income available to single parents, but the other half is due to non-economic factors.[26] It's not just the presence of two adults in the home that helps children, as some argue. Children living with cohabiting partners and in stepfamilies generally do less well than those living with both married biological parents.[27]

Marriage also brings benefits to husbands and wives. Married adults are more productive on the job, earn more, save more, have better physical and mental health, and live longer, according to an extensive review of research, conducted by scholar Linda Waite. Although Waite admits that these findings partly reflect the selection of better-adjusted people into marriage, she finds that when people marry, they act in more health promoting and productive ways.[28]

Conservatives are prone to exaggerate these research findings and underplay the importance of economics. If married people are more likely (other things being equal) to produce thriving children, other things are not, in fact, equal. It's not just the case that single mothers find themselves poor because they are unmarried; they find themselves unmarried because they are poor. Successful marriages are more difficult when husbands and wives are poorly educated, lack access to jobs that pay decently, and cannot afford decent child care. Economic hardship and other problems associated with poverty can wreak havoc on couples' relationships.

The controversy mostly isn't about research, however, but about values.[29] Most people regard decisions to marry, divorce, and bear children as intensely private. Any policy proposals that hint at coercing

[26]Sara McLanahan and Julien Teitler, "The Consequences of Father Absence," in *Parenting and Child Development in "Non-Traditional" Families*, ed. Michael E. Lamb (Mahwah, NJ: Lawrence Erlbaum, 1998). Also see Sara McLanahan and Gary Sanderfur, *Growing Up with a Single Parent: What Hurts, What Helps* (Cambridge, MA: Harvard UP, 1994).

[27]See McLanahan and Teitler; Susan L. Brown, "Child Well-Being in Cohabiting Unions" and Wendy D. Manning, "The Implications of Cohabitation for Children's Well-Being," in *Just Living Together: Implications of Cohabitation for Children, Families and Social Policy*, eds. Alan Booth and Ann C. Crouter (Mahwah, NJ: Lawrence Erlbaum, 2002).

[28]Linda J. Waite and Maggie Gallagher, *The Case for Marriage: Why Married People Are Happier, Healthier and Better Off Financially* (New York: Doubleday, 2000).

[29]Theodora Ooms, *Toward More Perfect Unions: Putting Marriage on the Public Agenda* (Washington, DC: Family Impact Seminar, 1998). Available from tooms@clasp.org.

people to marry, reinforcing Victorian conceptions of gender roles, or limiting the right to end bad marriages are viewed as counter to American values of individual autonomy and privacy. Some worry about the existence of hidden agendas that threaten to put women back into the kitchen, ignore domestic violence, and eliminate public assistance for low-income families. Others fear that holding out marriage as the ideal blames single parents, many of whom do a terrific job under difficult circumstances. Use of the term "illegitimate" is especially offensive because it stigmatizes children (and, in fact, is legally inaccurate, as children born outside of marriage now have virtually the same legal rights as those born within marriage).[30] And some worry that the pro-marriage agenda discriminates against ethnic and sexual minorities and their children, particularly gays and lesbians.

There are also more pragmatic concerns. Skeptics of the pro-marriage agenda observe that the decline in marriage is worldwide, a result of overwhelming social and economic forces that cannot be reversed. In their view, attempts to change family formation behavior are largely futile; we should instead just accept and help support the increasing diversity of family forms. For others, the concern is less about the value of promoting marriage and more about whether government, rather than individuals, communities, or faith institutions, should lead the charge.

Finally, marriage per se is too simplistic a solution to the complex 10 problems of the poor. Marrying a low-income, unmarried mother to her child's father will not magically raise the family out of poverty when the parents often have no skills, no jobs, terrible housing, and may be struggling with depression, substance abuse, or domestic violence. Advocates also worry that funds spent on untested marriage-promotion activities will be taken away from programs that provide desperately needed services for single parents, such as child care.

In response to some of these concerns—as well as research showing that serious parental conflict harms children—some marriage advocates respond that marriage per se should not be the goal but rather voluntary, "healthy" marriages.[31] They also agree that protections should be built into programs to guard against domestic violence. But this only raises doubts about how "healthy" will be defined, and by whom, and whether we even know how to help people create better relationships.

There also are some plainly foolish ideas in the marriage movement. West Virginia currently gives married families an extra $100 a month in welfare payments as a "marriage incentive." Robert Rector of the Heritage Foundation has proposed giving a $4,000 government bounty to welfare

---

[30]Ruth-Arlene W. Howe, "Legal Rights and Obligations: An Uneven Evolution," in *Young Unwed Fathers: Changing Roles and Emerging Policies*, eds. Robert I. Lerman and Theodora Ooms (Philadelphia: Temple UP, 1993), pp. 141–69.

[31]See, for example, Robin Toner, "Welfare Chief Is Hoping to Promote Marriage," *New York Times*, February 19, 2002, sec. A, p. 1.

recipients who marry before they have a child and stay married for two years.[32] Charles Murray wants to end public assistance altogether and has proposed eliminating all aid to *unmarried* mothers under 21 in one state to test the idea. This proposal is especially egregious and surely would harm children of single mothers.[33]

Progressives and others thus are placed in a quandary. They don't want to oppose marriage — which most Americans still value highly — but are skeptical of many pro-marriage initiatives. Given that healthy marriage is plainly good for children, however, one can envision a reasonable agenda — one that would gain broad support — that we might call marriage-plus. This approach puts the well-being of children first by helping more of them grow up in married, healthy, two-parent families. However, for many children, the reality is that marriage is not a feasible or even a desirable option for their parents. Thus, a secondary goal is to help these parents — whether unmarried, separated, divorced, or remarried — cooperate better in raising their children. These are not alternative strategies. Children need us to do both.

A marriage-plus agenda does not promote marriage just for marriage's sake. It acknowledges that married and unmarried parents, mothers and fathers, may need both economic resources and non-economic supports to increase the likelihood of stable, healthy marriages and better co-parenting relationships. In addition, a marriage-plus agenda focuses more on the front end — making marriage better to be in — rather than the back end — making marriage more difficult to get out of.

Here are some elements of this agenda.   15

Strengthen "fragile families" at the birth of a child. For many poor families, relationship-education programs may be helpful but not enough. A new national study finds that at the time of their child's birth, one-half of unmarried parents (so-called "fragile families") are living together, and another third are romantically attached but not cohabiting.[34] The majorities of these parents are committed to each other and to their child and have high hopes of eventual marriage and a future together — although these hopes too often are not realized. We should reach out to young parents to help them achieve their desire to remain together as a family. A helpful package of services to offer these young families might include a combination of "soft" services — relationship-skills and

---

[32]Robert Rector, *A Plan to Reduce Illegitimacy*, memorandum handed out at a meeting on Capitol Hill in early 2001.

[33]Charles Murray, "Family Formation," in *The New World of Welfare*, eds. Rebecca M. Blank and Ron Haskins (Washington, DC: Brookings Institution Press, 2001), pp. 137–68).

[34]Sara McLanahan et al., *The Fragile Families and Child Wellbeing Study Baseline Report*, August 2001, http://crcw.princeton.edu/fragilefamilies/nationalreport.pdf; and Sara McLanahan, Irwin Garfinkel, and Ronald B. Mincy, "Fragile Families, Welfare Reform, and Marriage," *Welfare Reform and Beyond Policy Brief*, No. 10, November, 2001. http://www.brookings.edu/dybdocroot/wrb/publications/pb/pb10.htm. For additional papers from the Fragile Families study, see http://crcw.princeton.edu/fragilefamilies/index.htm.

marriage-education workshops, financial-management classes, and peer-support groups—and "hard" services, such as job training and placement, housing, medical coverage, and substance-abuse treatment, if necessary. At present, all we do is get the father to admit paternity and hound him for child support.

Reduce economic stress by reducing poverty. Poverty and unemployment can stress couples' relationships to their breaking point. Results of a welfare-to-work demonstration program in Minnesota suggest that enhancing the income of the working poor can indirectly promote marriage. The Minnesota Family Investment Program (MFIP), which subsidized the earnings of employed welfare families, found that marriage rates increased for both single-parent long-term recipients and two-parent families. Married two-parent families were significantly more likely to remain married. MFIP also reduced the reported incidence of domestic abuse.[35]

Provide better-paying jobs and job assistance for the poor. The inability of low-skilled, unemployed men to provide income to their families is a major reason for their failure to marry the mothers of their children. Better employment opportunities help low-income fathers, and men in general, to become responsible fathers and, perhaps, more attractive and economically stable marriage partners.[36] There is also growing support for making changes in the child-support system to ensure that more support paid by fathers goes to the children (rather than being used to recoup government program costs).[37]

Invest more in proven programs that reduce out-of-wedlock childbearing. Teen pregnancy and birth rates have fallen by over 20 percent since the early 1990s, and there is now strong evidence that a number of prevention programs are effective. A related strategy is enforcement of child support. States that have tough, effective child support systems have been found to have lower nonmarital birth rates, presumably because men are beginning to understand there are serious costs associated with fathering a child.[38]

Institute workplace policies to reduce work/family conflict and stress on 20 *couples.* Stress in the workplace spills over into the home. Persistent

[35]Virginia Knox, Cynthia Miller, and Lisa A. Gennetian, *Reforming Welfare and Rewarding Work: A Summary of the Final Report on the Minnesota Family Investment Program* (New York: Manpower Demonstration Research Corporation, September, 2000).

[36]See Chapter 4, "The Fading Inner-City Family," in William Julius Wilson, *When Work Disappears: The World of the New Urban Poor* (New York: Alfred A. Knopf, 1996), pp. 87–110; Kathy Edin, "Few Good Men: Why Poor Mothers Don't Marry or Remarry," *The American Prospect*, January 3, 2000.

[37]See Vicki Turetsky, Testimony Given to the Social Security and Family Policy Subcommittee of the U.S. Senate Finance Committee, October 11, 2001, and Vick Turetsky, *What If All the Money Came Home?* (Washington, DC: Center for Law and Social Policy, June, 2000). Both available on line at www.clasp.org.

[38]Robert D. Plotnick, Inhoe Ku, Irwin Garfinkel, and Sara S. McLanahan, *The Impact of Child Support Enforcement Policy on Nonmarital Childbearing.* Paper presented at the Association for Public Policy Analysis and Management, Year 2000 Research Conference in Seattle, WA.

overtime, frequent travel, and inflexible leave policies place great strain on couples at all income levels. Employers are increasingly demanding nonstandard work schedules. A recent study found that married couples with children who work night and rotating shifts are at higher risk of separation and divorce.[39] The absence of affordable and reliable child care forces many parents who would prefer a normal workday to working split shifts solely to make sure that a parent is home with children.

Reduce tax penalties and other disincentives to marriage. There has always been strong support for reducing marriage tax penalties for many two-earner families. This is a complicated task because the majority of married couples, in fact, receive tax bonuses rather than penalties.[40] A positive step was taken in 2001 to reduce significantly the marriage penalty affecting low-income working families in the Earned Income Tax Credit program. While there is uncertainty about the extent to which these tax-related marriage penalties affect marital behavior, there is broad general agreement that government has a responsibility to "first do no harm" when it comes to marriage.

Similarly, there is near unanimous agreement that government should not make it harder for eligible two-parent families to receive welfare benefits and assistance. In the past, the old welfare program, Aid to Families with Dependent Children, was much criticized for offering incentives to break up families. At least 33 states already have removed the stricter eligibility rules placed on two-parent families,[41] and the President's welfare reauthorization proposal encourages the other states to do the same. In addition, it proposes to end the higher work participation rate for two-parent families, a federal rule that has been criticized widely by the states. Another needed reform would forgive accumulated child-support debt owed by noncustodial fathers if they marry the mothers of their children. (Currently, such debt is owed to the state if the mothers and children are receiving welfare benefits.)[42]

Educate those who want to marry and stay married about how to have healthy relationships and good marriages. A vast industry is devoted to helping couples plan a successful wedding day — wedding planners, 500-page bridal guides, specialty caterers, the list goes on. But where do young people go to learn about how to sustain good, lifelong marriages? In fact,

---

[39]Harriet B. Presser, "Nonstandard Work Schedules and Marital Instability," *Journal of Marriage and the Family* (February, 2000).

[40]Congressional Budget Office, *For Better or For Worse: Marriage and the Federal Income Tax* (Washington, DC: Congress of the United States, Congressional Budget Office, June, 1997).

[41]Gene Falk and Jill Tauber, *Welfare Reform: TANF Provisions Related to Marriage and Two-Parent Families* (Washington, DC: Congressional Research Service, Library of Congress, October 30, 2001).

[42]Paul Roberts, *An Ounce of Prevention and a Pound of Cure: Developing State Policy on the Payment of Child Support Arrears by Low Income Parents.* (Washington, DC: Center for Law and Social Policy, May, 2001). Available online at www.clasp.org.

we now know a lot about what makes contemporary marriages work. With the transformation of gender roles, there now are fewer fixed rules for couples to follow, meaning they have to negotiate daily about who does what and when. In the absence of the legal and social constraints that used to keep marriages together, there's now a premium on developing effective relationship skills. Building on three decades of research, there are a small but rapidly growing number of programs (both religious and secular) that help people from high school through adulthood understand the benefits of marriage for children and for themselves, develop realistic expectations for healthy relationships, understand the meaning of commitment, and learn the skills and attitudes needed to make marriage succeed.[43] Other programs help married couples survive the inevitable ups and downs that occur in most marriages, and remarried couples with the additional challenges of step-parenting. Oklahoma, Utah, and Michigan have begun using government funds to make these relationship- and marriage-education programs accessible to low-income couples. The Greater Grand Rapids Community Marriage Policy initiative is urging area businesses to include marriage education as an Employee Assistance Program benefit, arguing that it's more cost-effective to prevent marital distress than incur the costs of counseling and lost productivity involved when employees' marriages break up.[44]

A marriage-plus agenda that includes activities such as these is not just the responsibility of government. Some of the strategies proposed here are being implemented by private and religious groups, some by governments, and some by partnerships between these sectors. The approach adopted in Oklahoma, Greater Grand Rapids, and Chattanooga, for example, mobilizes the resources of many sectors of the community—government, education, legal, faith, business, and media—in a comprehensive effort to create a more marriage-supportive culture and to provide new services to promote, support, and strengthen couples and marriage and reduce out-of-wedlock childbearing and divorce. This "saturation model" seems particularly promising because it takes into account the many factors that influence individuals' decisions to marry, to divorce, or to remain unmarried. We should proceed cautiously, trying out and evaluating new ideas before applying them widely.

Ironically, in the midst of this furor about government's role in marriage, it's worth noting that the federal government recently has begun to shirk a basic responsibility: counting the numbers of marriages and divorces in the United States. Since budget cuts in 1995, the government   25

---

[43]See Scott Stanley, "Making a Case for Premarital Education," in *Family Relations* (July 2001). Also see *Directory of Couples and Marriage Education Programs* at www .smartmarriages.com.

[44]Personal communication with Mark Eastburg, Ph.D., director of Pine Rest Family Institute, Grand Rapids, Michigan. See Web site for the Greater Grand Rapids Community Marriage Initiative, www.ggrcmarriagepolicy.org.

has been unable to report on marriage and divorce rates in the states or for the nation as a whole.[45] And, for the first time in the history of the Census, Americans were not asked to give their marital status in the 2000 survey. What kind of pro-marriage message from the government is that?

If liberals and conservatives are serious about strengthening families for the sake of helping children, liberals ought to acknowledge that non-coercive and egalitarian approaches to bolstering marriage are sound policy. Conservatives, meanwhile, should admit that much of what it takes to make marriage work for the benefit of spouses and children is not just moral but economic.

READING AND DISCUSSION QUESTIONS

1. What does Ooms mean when she says in the first paragraph that in 1996 "the federal government decided to get into the business of promoting marriage"?

2. How does Ooms support her belief that children are better off in a two-parent home?

3. What type of support does she use in the sixth paragraph to argue that "[m]arriage also brings benefits to husbands and wives"?

4. What are some of the problems that arise when government gets involved in promoting marriage?

5. What claim is Ooms supporting? How effective is she in supporting that claim? Are some types of support that she uses more effective than others, in your opinion?

6. This essay, unlike the others in the Readings for Analysis, provides a list of works cited. What effect, if any, does that have on the strength of Ooms's argument?

WRITING SUGGESTIONS

7. Write an essay in which you oppose or support Ooms's marriage-plus plan.

8. Analyze the primary types of support that Ooms uses. If you wish, you may go a step further and evaluate the effectiveness of her support.

[45]Stephanie Ventura, "Vital Statistics from the National Center for Health Statistics," in *Data Needs for Measuring Family and Fertility Change after Welfare Reform*, ed. Douglas Besharov (College Park, MD: Maryland School of Public Affairs, Welfare Reform Academy).

one **reason** *barbara whittaker*

GM has purchased more than $44.3 billion in goods and services from minority suppliers over the last 36 years. One reason? Barbara Whittaker. As Executive Director of Machinery & Equipment and Indirect Purchasing, Barbara works directly with GM suppliers from all over the globe, including more than 600 certified minority suppliers like The Bartech Group. Formed under the sponsorship of GM in 1976, The Bartech Group is now a $200 million company, and one of the largest staffing companies in the nation. Which means that they not only help Barbara diversify GM's supplier base, they help to diversify GM's workforce as well.

GM awards more than $7 billion in purchasing and contracts annually to minority firms. Barbara Whittaker is just one reason GM is committed to increasing that number each and every year. For information about GM's Supplier Diversity Program visit www.gmsupplypower.com.

CHEVROLET   SAAB   PONTIAC   GMAC   OLDSMOBILE   SATURN   BUICK   CADILLAC   HUMMER   GMC   gm.com
© 2004 GM Corp. All rights reserved.

DISCUSSION QUESTIONS

1. For what audience does the GM ad seem to have been designed?
2. What claim is the ad supporting?
3. What different types of support are used in the ad? How effective is the support?
4. How does the picture work with the text to advance the argument made by the ad?

Animal Research Saves Human Lives

HELOISA SABIN

That scene in *Forrest Gump* in which young Forrest runs from his schoolmate tormentors so fast that his leg braces fly apart and his strong legs carry him to safety may be the only image of the polio epidemic of the 1950s etched in the minds of those too young to remember the actual devastation the disease caused. Hollywood created a scene of triumph far removed from the reality of the disease.

Some who have benefited directly from polio research, including that of my late husband, Albert, think winning the real war against polio was just as simple. They have embraced a movement that denounces the very process that enables them to look forward to continued good health and promising futures. This "animal rights" ideology—espoused by groups such as People for the Ethical Treatment of Animals, the Humane Society of the United States and the Fund for Animals—rejects the use of laboratory animals in medical research and denies the role such research played in the victory over polio.

The leaders of this movement seem to have forgotten that year after year in the early fifties, the very words *infantile paralysis* and *poliomyelitis* struck great fear in young parents that the disease would snatch their children as they slept. Each summer public beaches, playgrounds, and movie theaters were places to be avoided. Polio epidemics condemned millions of children and young adults to lives in which debilitated lungs could no longer breathe on their own and young limbs were left forever wilted and frail. The disease drafted tiny armies of children on crutches and in wheelchairs who were unable to walk, run, or jump. In the United States, polio struck down nearly 58,000 children in 1952 alone.

Unlike the braces on Forrest Gump's legs, real ones would be replaced only as the children's misshapen legs grew. Other children and young adults were entombed in iron lungs. The only view of the world these patients had was through mirrors over their heads. These memories, however, are no longer part of our collective cultural memory.

Albert was on the front line of polio research. In 1961, thirty years 5 after he began studying polio, his oral vaccine was introduced in the United States and distributed widely. In the nearly forty years since, polio has been eradicated in the Western Hemisphere, the World Health Organization reports, adding that, with a full-scale effort, polio could be eliminated from the rest of the world by the year 2000.

Heloisa Sabin is honorary director of Americans for Medical Progress in Alexandria, Virginia. This essay appeared in the *Wall Street Journal* on October 18, 1995.

Without animal research, polio would still be claiming thousands of lives each year. "There could have been no oral polio vaccine without the use of innumerable animals, a very large number of animals," Albert told a reporter shortly before his death in 1993. Animals are still needed to test every new batch of vaccine that is produced for today's children.

Animal activists claim that vaccines really didn't end the epidemic — that, with improvements in social hygiene, polio was dying out anyway, before the vaccines were developed. This is untrue. In fact, advanced sanitation was responsible in part for the dramatic *rise* in the number of paralytic polio cases in the fifties. Improvements in sanitation practices reduced the rate of infection, and the average age of those infected by the polio virus went up. Older children and young adults were more likely than infants to develop paralysis from their exposure to the polio virus.

Every child who has tasted the sweet sugar cube or received the drops containing the Sabin vaccine over the past four decades knows polio only as a word, or an obscure reference in a popular film. Thank heavens it's not part of their reality.

These polio-free generations have grown up to be doctors, teachers, business leaders, government officials, and parents. They have their own concerns and struggles. Cancer, heart disease, strokes, and AIDS are far more lethal realities to them now than polio. Yet, those who support an "animal rights" agenda that would cripple research and halt medical science in its tracks are slamming the door on the possibilities of new treatments and cures.

My husband was a kind man, but he was impatient with those who 10 refused to acknowledge reality or to seek reasoned answers to the questions of life.

The pioneers of polio research included not only the scientists but also the laboratory animals that played a critical role in bringing about the end of polio and a host of other diseases for which we now have vaccines and cures. Animals will continue to be as vital as the scientists who study them in the battle to eliminate pain, suffering, and disease from our lives.

That is the reality of medical progress.

Why We Don't Need Animal Experimentation

PEGGY CARLSON

The issue of animal experimentation has become so polarized that rational thinking seems to have taken a back seat. Heloisa Sabin's October 18 editorial-page article "Animal Research Saves Lives" serves only to further misinform and polarize. She does a great disservice to science to incorrectly portray the debate about animal experimentation as occurring between "animal rights activists" and scientists. The truth is, the value of animal experimentation is being questioned by many scientists.

Mrs. Sabin uses the example of the polio vaccine developed by her husband to justify animal experimentation. However, in the case of the polio vaccine, misleading animal experiments detoured scientists away from reliable clinical studies thereby, according to Dr. Sabin himself, delaying the initial work on polio prevention. It was also unfortunate that the original polio vaccine was produced using monkey cells instead of available human cells as can be done today. The use of monkey cells resulted in viruses with the potential to cause serious disease being transferred to humans when the polio vaccine was administered.

The polio vaccine example cannot logically be used to justify the current level of animal experimentation—several billion dollars and about 30 million animals yearly. Although most people would prefer to believe that the death and suffering of all these animals is justified, the facts do not support that conclusion.

Nearly everything that medicine has learned about what substances cause human cancer and birth defects has come from human clinical and epidemiological studies because animal experiments do not accurately predict what occurs in humans. Dr. Bross, the former Director of Biostatistics at the Roswell Institute for Cancer Research states, "While conflicting animal results have often delayed and hampered advances in the war on cancer, they have never produced a single substantial advance either in the prevention or treatment of cancer." A 1990 editorial in *Stroke* notes that none of the twenty-five compounds "proven" efficacious for treating stroke in animal experiments over the preceding ten years had been effective for use in humans. From human studies alone we have learned how to lessen the risk of heart attacks. Warnings to the public that smoking cigarettes leads to an increased risk of cancer were delayed as researchers sought, unsuccessfully, to confirm the risk by using animals.

Animal tests for drug safety, cancer-causing potential, and toxicity are 5 unreliable, and science is leading us to more accurate methods that will

---

Peggy Carlson, M.D., was the research director of the Physicians Committee for Responsible Medicine in Washington, D.C., at the time her letter appeared in the *Wall Street Journal* on November 7, 1995.

216

offer greater protection. But if we refuse to acknowledge the inadequacies of animal tests we put a stranglehold on the very progress that will help us. Billions of precious health-care dollars have been spent to fund animal experiments that are repetitious or that have no human relevance.

An uncritical acceptance of the value of animal experiments leads to its overfunding, which, in turn, leads to the underfunding of other more beneficial areas.

DISCUSSION QUESTIONS

1. Sabin uses the vaccine against polio as the principal example in her support of animal research. Does this limit her argument? Should she have been more specific in her references to other diseases?

2. What is the significance of Sabin's repeated references to "reality"?

3. List all the kinds of support that Carlson provides. Which of the supporting materials is most persuasive?

4. Does Carlson refute all the arguments in Sabin's article? Be specific.

5. Sabin makes strong emotional appeals. Describe them, and decide how large a part such appeals play in her argument. Does Carlson appeal to the emotions of her readers?

TAKING THE DEBATE ONLINE

For these and additional research URLs, see bedfordstmartins.com/rottenberg.

- *University of Colorado at Boulder: Frequently Asked Questions*
  www.colorado.edu/Research/animal_resources/faqs.html

  This multilayered site examines animal resources at the university and explores many ethical questions on animal research.

- *National Institutes of Health*
  www.nih.gov/

  This institute investigates America's premier medical research facilities for their treatment of animals.

- *People for the Ethical Treatment of Animals Online*
  www.peta.org

  This association unequivocally condemns animal research.

- *Medical Research Modernization Committee*
  www.mrmcmed.org/Critical_Look.pdf

  The MRMC is a nonprofit health advocacy organization promoting "efficient, reliable, and cost-effective research methods."

- *Scientific American*
  www.sciam.com/

This site contains links to featured stories about animal experimentation in the February 1997 issue of the magazine.

• *Fund for the Replacement of Animals in Medical Experiments*
www.frame.org.uk/

This association promotes the researching of alternatives to animal testing.

ASSIGNMENTS FOR UNDERSTANDING SUPPORT

1. In the summer of 1983, after an alarming rise in the juvenile crime rate, the mayor of Detroit instituted a curfew for young people under the age of eighteen. Explain the pros and cons of using a curfew as a way to cut down on juvenile crime.

2. Write a full-page advertisement to solicit support for a project or cause in which you believe.

3. How do you account for the large and growing interest in fantasy films and books? In addition to their entertainment value, are there other less obvious reasons for their popularity?

4. According to some researchers soap operas are influential in transmitting values, lifestyles, and sexual information to youthful viewers. Do you agree? If so, what values and information are being transmitted? Be specific.

5. Choose one of the following stereotypical ideas and argue that it is true or false or partly both. Discuss the reasons for the existence of the stereotype.

   a. Jocks are stupid.

   b. The country is better than the city for bringing up children.

   c. Television is justly called "the boob tube."

   d. Politicians are dishonest.

   e. Beauty contests are degrading to women.

6. Defend or refute the view that star high school basketball players should be allowed to go directly to the pros.

7. The philosopher Bertrand Russell said, "Most of the work that most people have to do is not in itself interesting, but even such work has certain advantages." Defend or refute this assertion. Use your own experience as support.

8. Choose a product advertised on television by many different makers. (Cars, pain relievers, fast food, cereals, and soft drinks are some of the most popular products.) What kinds of support do the advertisers offer? Why do they choose these particular appeals? Would the support be significantly different in print?

9. From time to time advocates of causes speak on campus. The causes may be broadly based—minority rights, welfare cuts, abortion, foreign aid—or they may be local issues, having to do with harassment policy, course requirements, or tuition increases. Attend a meeting or a rally at which a speaker argues his or her cause. Write an evaluation of the speech, paying particular attention to the kinds of support. Did the speaker provide sufficient and relevant evidence? Did he or she make emotional appeals? What signs, if any, reflected the speaker's awareness of the kind of audience he or she was addressing?

10. Choose one of the Readings for Analysis and write an essay explaining the primary types of support used in it.

11. Choose one of the Readings for Analysis and write an essay evaluating the author's use of support.

12. Write a letter to the editor of your local newspaper encouraging its readers not to buy light trucks. Use information from Varian's essay to support your position. You will not document your letter as you would an academic paper, but in the text of your letter you must make clear that you are drawing on information provided by Varian.

13. Find a subject that might be defended or opposed with the use of statistics but modest enough to be argued successfully in a 750- to 1,000-word essay. Sports, both professional and amateur, for example, offer topics for research: the decline of attendance at big-league baseball games, the high salaries of professional players, injuries and death suffered by high school athletes. Your essay should provide proof for a claim. Other subjects that depend on statistical support can be found throughout this book.

CHAPTER 6

Warrants

We now come to the third element in the structure of the argument—the warrant. Claim and support, the other major elements we have discussed, are more familiar in ordinary discourse, but there is nothing mysterious or unusual about the warrant. All our claims, both formal and informal, are grounded in warrants or assumptions that the audience must share with us if our claims are to prove to be acceptable.

The following exercise provides a good starting point for this chapter. Do the assigned task by yourself or in a small group.

■ Who Should Survive?

Task: A series of environmental catastrophic events has virtually wiped out human life on earth. The only known survivors in your vicinity are the eleven listed below. There are resources to sustain only seven. Choose seven of the following people to survive. List them in the order in which you would choose them and be prepared to explain the reasons for your selection; that is, why you chose these particular persons and why you placed them in this certain order.

- Dr. Dane—thirty-seven, white, no religious affiliation, Ph.D. in history, college professor, in good health (jogs daily), hobby is botany, enjoys politics, married with one child (Bobby).

- Mrs. Dane—thirty-eight, white, Jewish, rather obese, diabetic, MA in psychology, counselor in a mental health clinic, married to Dr. Dane, has one child.

- Bobby Dane—ten, white, Jewish, mentally retarded with IQ of 70, healthy and strong for his age.

- Mrs. Garcia—twenty-three, Spanish American, Catholic, ninth-grade education, cocktail waitress, worked as a prostitute, married at age sixteen, divorced at age eighteen, one son (Juan).

- Juan Garcia—three months old, Spanish American, healthy.

- Mary Evans—eighteen, black, Protestant, trade school education, wears glasses, artistic.

- Mr. Newton—twenty-five, black power advocate, starting last year of medical school, suspected homosexual activity, music as a hobby, physical fitness buff.

- Mrs. Clark—twenty-eight, black, Protestant, daughter of a minister, college graduate, electronics engineer, single now after a brief marriage, member of Zero Population Growth.

- Mr. Blake—fifty-one, white, Mormon, BS in mechanics, married with four children, enjoys outdoors, experienced in construction, quite handy, sympathizes with antiblack views.

- Father Frans—thirty-seven, white, Catholic priest, active in civil rights, former college athlete, farming background, often criticized for liberal views.

- Dr. Gonzales—sixty-six, Spanish American, Catholic, doctor in general practice, two heart attacks in the past five years, loves literature and quotes extensively.

Obviously this is an exercise with no right answer. What it can teach us, however, is to consider the assumptions on which our beliefs are based. There are reasons you might have chosen certain individuals to survive that could be stated as general principles: Those who are in the best physical condition should be allowed to survive. Those with the most useful skills should be allowed to survive. Those who are mentally deficient should not be allowed to survive. Those who are most likely to reproduce should be allowed to survive.

There may have been a great deal of disagreement as to who the survivors should be. If so, different members of your group or your class as a whole were operating under different assumptions or basing their decisions on different warrants. Some of you may have chosen not to let Mrs. Garcia survive because she seemed to have nothing particularly vital to offer to the survival of the group as a whole. Others of you may have felt that she should be allowed to survive along with her son, the infant in the group. Some of you, whether you acknowledge it or not, may have opposed letting Mrs. Garcia survive because she was once a prostitute. Think about the warrant that would underlie the claim that Mrs. Garcia should not be one of the seven allowed to survive. What assumption— what generalized principle—would a person who made that claim be accepting about women who were once prostitutes? What assumption would underlie the claim that Bobby Dane should be allowed to live (or die)?

Fortunately, this is merely an intellectual exercise. Whenever you take a stand in a real-life situation, though, you do so on the basis of certain general principles that guide your choices. Those general principles that you feel most strongly about exist as part of your intellectual and moral being because of what you have experienced in your life thus far. They have been shaped by your observations, your personal experience, and your participation in a culture. But because these observations, experiences, and cultural associations will vary, the audience may not always agree with the warrants or assumptions of the writer.

What does this have to do with argumentation? Any time you support an argumentative claim, you have to analyze the assumptions behind the argument and consider whether the members of your audience share the same assumptions. Some warrants are so widely accepted that you do not need to state them or to offer any proof of their validity. If you argue that every new dorm on campus should have a sprinkler system, you probably do not even need to state your warrant. If you did, it would be something like this: Measures that would increase the likelihood that dorm residents would survive a fire should be implemented in all dorms.

What about claims that are more controversial? Why is it so difficult for those who oppose abortion, for example, to communicate with those who favor it and vice versa? Anyone who believes that abortion is the murder of an unborn child is basing that argument on the warrant that a fetus is a child from conception. Many on the other side of the debate do not accept that warrant and thus do not accept the claim. Obviously disagreements on such emotionally charged issues are very difficult to resolve because the underlying warrants are based on firmly held beliefs that are difficult to change. It is always better to be aware of your opponent's warrants, however, than to simply dismiss them as irrelevant.

The British philosopher Stephen Toulmin, who developed the concept of warrants, dismissed more traditional forms of logical reasoning in favor of a more audience-based, courtroom-derived approach to argumentation. He refers to warrants as "general, hypothetical statements, which can act as bridges" and "entitle one to draw conclusions or make claims."[1] The word *bridges* to denote the action of the warrant is crucial. One dictionary defines warrant as a "guarantee or justification." We use the word *warrant* to emphasize that in an argument it guarantees a connecting link—a

---

[1] Stephen Toulmin, *The Uses of Argument* (Cambridge: Cambridge University Press, 1958), p. 98.

bridge—between the claim and the support. This means that even if a reader agrees that the support is sound, the support cannot prove the validity of the claim unless the reader also agrees with the underlying warrant. Recall the sample argument outlined in Chapter 1 (p. 3):

CLAIM: Adoption of a vegetarian diet leads to healthier and longer life.

SUPPORT: The authors of *Becoming a Vegetarian Family* say so.

WARRANT: The authors of *Becoming a Vegetarian Family* are reliable sources of information on diet.

Notice that the reader must agree with the assumption that the testimony of experts is trustworthy before he or she arrives at the conclusion that a vegetarian diet is healthy. Simply providing evidence that the authors say so is not enough to prove the claim.

The following dialogue offers another example of the relationship between the warrant and the other elements of the argument.

"I don't think that Larry can do the job. He's pretty dumb."
"Really? I thought he was smart. What makes you say he's dumb?"
"Did you know that he's illiterate—can't read above third-grade level? In my book that makes him dumb."

If we put this into outline form, the warrant or assumption in the argument becomes clear.

CLAIM: Larry is pretty dumb.

EVIDENCE: He can't read above third-grade level.

WARRANT: Anybody who can't read above third-grade level must be dumb.

We can also represent the argument in diagram form, which shows the warrant as a bridge between the claim and the support.

Support _____→ *Claim*

Warrant
(Expressed or Unexpressed)

The argument above can then be written like this:

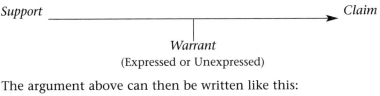

Support ─────────────────→ *Claim*
Larry can't read above   He's pretty dumb.
third-grade level.

Warrant
Anybody who can't read above third-grade
level must be pretty dumb.

Is this warrant valid? We cannot answer this question until we consider the *backing*. Every warrant or assumption rests on something else that gives it authority; this is what we call backing. Backing or authority for the warrant in this example would consist of research data that prove a relationship between stupidity and low reading ability. This particular warrant, we would discover, lacks backing because we know that the failure to learn to read well may be due to a number of things unrelated to intelligence. So if the warrant is unprovable, the claim—that Larry is dumb—is also unprovable, even if the evidence is true. In this case, then, the evidence does not guarantee the soundness of the claim.

Now consider this example of a somewhat more complicated warrant: The beautiful and unspoiled Eastern Shore of Maryland is being discovered by thousands of tourists, vacationers, and developers who will, according to the residents, change the landscape and the way of life, which is now based largely on fishing and farming. In a few years the Eastern Shore may become a noisy, crowded string of resorts. Mrs. Walkup, the Kent County commissioner, says,

> Catering to the wealthy puts property back on the tax rolls, but it's going to make the Eastern Shore look like the rest of the country. Everything that made our way of life so special is being eroded. We are a fragile area. The Eastern Shore is still special, but it is feeling pressure from all directions. Lots of people don't seem to appreciate the fact that God made us to need a little peace and quiet now and then.[2]

In simplified form the argument of those opposed to development would be outlined this way:

CLAIM: Development will bring undesirable changes to the present way of life on the Eastern Shore, a life of farming and fishing, peace and quiet.

SUPPORT: Developers will build express highways, condominiums, casinos, and nightclubs.

WARRANT: A pastoral life of fishing and farming is superior to the way of life brought by expensive, fast-paced modern development.

Notice that the warrant is a broad generalization that can apply to a number of different situations, while the claim is about a specific place and time. It should be added that in other arguments the warrant may not be stated in such general terms. However, even in arguments in which the warrant makes a more specific reference to the claim, the reader can infer an extension of the warrant to other similar arguments. In the vegetarian diet example (p. 3, outlined on p. 11), the warrant mentions a specific book. But it is clear that such warrants can be generalized to apply to

---

[2] Michael Wright, "The Changing Chesapeake," *New York Times Magazine,* July 10, 1983, p. 27.

other arguments in which we accept a claim based on the credibility of the sources.

To be convinced of the validity of Mrs. Walkup's claim, you must first find that the support is true, that the developers plan to introduce drastic changes that will destroy the pastoral life of the Eastern Shore. You may, however, believe that the support is not entirely sound, that the development will be much more modest than residents fear, and that the Eastern Shore will not be seriously altered. Next, you may want to see more justification for the warrant. Is pastoral life superior to the life that will result from large-scale development? Perhaps you have always thought that a life of fishing and farming means poverty and limited opportunities for the majority of the residents. Although the superiority of a way of life is largely a matter of taste and therefore difficult to prove, Mrs. Walkup may need to produce backing for her belief that the present way of life is more desirable than one based on developing the area for new residents and summer visitors. If you find either the support or the warrant unconvincing, you cannot accept the claim.

Remember that a claim is often modified by one or more qualifiers, which limit the claim. Mrs. Walkup might have said, "Development will *probably* destroy *some aspects of* the present way of life on the Eastern Shore." Warrants can also be modified or limited by *reservations*, which remind the reader that there are conditions under which the warrants will not be relevant. Mrs. Walkup might have added, "unless increased prosperity and exposure to the outside world brought by development improve some aspects of our lives."

A diagram of Mrs. Walkup's argument shows the additional elements:

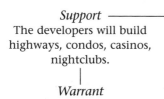

Support —————————————→ *Claim*
The developers will build
highways, condos, casinos,
nightclubs.

Development will bring
undesirable changes to
life on the Eastern Shore.

Warrant
A way of life devoted to farming
and fishing is superior to a way of
life brought by development.

Qualifier
Development will *most likely*
bring undesirable changes.

Backing
We have experienced crowds, traffic,
noise, rich strangers, and high-rises,
and they destroy peace and quiet.

Reservation
But increased development might
improve some aspects of our lives.

Claim and support (or lack of support) are relatively easy to uncover in most arguments. One thing that makes the warrant different is that it is often unexpressed and therefore unexamined by both writer and reader because they take it for granted. In the argument about Larry's intelligence, the warrant was stated. But in the argument about development on the Eastern Shore, Mrs. Walkup did not state her warrant directly, although her meaning is perfectly clear. She probably felt that it was not necessary to be more explicit because her readers would understand and supply the warrant.

We can make the discovery of warrants even clearer by examining another argument, in this case a policy claim. We've looked at a factual claim (that Larry is dumb) and a value claim (that Eastern Shore development is undesirable). Now we examine a policy claim that rests on one expressed and one unexpressed warrant. Policy claims are usually more complicated than other claims because the statement of policy is preceded by an array of facts and values. In addition, such claims may represent chains of reasoning in which one argument is dependent on another. These complicated arguments may be difficult or impossible to summarize in a simple diagram, but careful reading, asking the same kinds of questions that the author may have asked about his claim, can help you to find the warrant or chain of warrants that must be accepted before evidence and claim can be linked.

In a familiar argument that appeared a few years ago,[3] the author argues for a radical reform in college sports—the elimination of subprofessional intermural team sports, as practiced above all in football and basketball. The claim is clear, and evidence for the professional character of college sports not hard to find: the large salaries paid to coaches, the generous perquisites offered to players, the recruitment policies that ignore academic standing, the virtually full-time commitment of the players, the lucrative television contracts. But can this evidence support the author's claim that such sports do not belong on college campuses? Advocates of these sports may ask, Why not? In the conclusion of the article the author states one warrant or assumption underlying his claim.

> Even if the money to pay college athletes could be found, though, a larger question must be answered—namely, why should a system of professional athletics be affiliated with universities at all? For the truth is that the requirements of athletics and academics operate at cross purposes, and the attempt to play both games at once serves only to reduce the level of performance of each.

In other words, the author assumes that the goals of an academic education on the one hand and the goals of big-time college sports on the other hand are incompatible. In the article he develops the ways in which each enterprise harms the other.

[3]D. G. Myers, "Why College Sports?" *Commentary*, December 1990, pp. 49–51.

But the argument clearly rests on another warrant that is not expressed because the author takes for granted that his readers will supply it: The academic goals of the university are primary and should take precedence over all other collegiate activities. This is an argument based on an authority warrant, the authority of those who define the goals of the university—scholars, public officials, university administrators, and others. (Types of warrants are discussed in the following section.)

This warrant makes clear that the evidence of the professional nature of college sports cited above supports the claim that they should be eliminated. If quasiprofessional college sports are harmful to the primary educational function of the college or university, then they must go. In the author's words, "The two are separate enterprises, to be judged by separate criteria. . . . For college sports, the university is not an educational institution at all; it is merely a locus, a means of coordinating the different aspects of the sporting enterprise."

This argument may be summarized in outline form as follows:

CLAIM: Intermural college team sports should be abolished.

SUPPORT: College sports have become subprofessional.

WARRANT: The goals of an academic education and big-time college sports are incompatible.

BACKING FOR THE WARRANT: Academic education is the primary goal of the college and must take precedence over athletic activity.

The next essay, by student writer Stuart Glenn, also examines what activities deserve a place in schools. As you read, consider on what warrant or warrants his argument is based. Remember that a warrant provides a necessary bridge between the support and the claim. Consider how different the essay would have been without the material that Stuart drew from his sources. Stuart's essay makes use of the MLA style of documenting sources.

SAMPLE ESSAY

Musical Reasoning

STUART GLENN

Music has been around for centuries and has functioned mainly as a form of entertainment and artistic expression. It has evolved from simple whistled tunes and percussion to complex arrangements for symphonies and opera. Music has also had various effects on its listeners. Certain types of music calm people while other types generate excitement.

People listen to light jazz, for instance, to relax because that music creates a calm atmosphere for the listener. This could be because light jazz relies heavily on harmony and every note played fits smoothly with others in the tune. Rock, on the other hand, will often evoke excitement in the listener. Rock music has very aggressive musical elements such as dissonant melodic phrasing and the overdriven, distorted tone of the instruments. Some employers use music in training their employees because they have found that music's calming effect can increase productivity (M.D. 1). A person's favorite song can send shivers down the spine, which seems to relate music to the physical nervous system. Studies of this effect suggest that music may trigger nerve responses in a way similar to memories that trigger goose bumps ("Brain Health" 1). Scientists are studying why music is able to achieve all of these diverse effects and have found interesting results. Music is tied to the human brain in some way, and current studies have been investigating what exactly creates the link.

A music study published by Temple Grandin, Matthew Peterson, and Gordon Shaw has given proof that music is somehow able to affect the brain and its ability to perform certain tasks (1). The team investigated how certain types of music can increase the brain's capacity to understand certain concepts. The findings suggest that music can in fact help a person to grasp specific types of concepts. If music has that effect on people, it is reasonable to assume that early and regular music training will have an effect on students. It is widely known that the minds of young children are more susceptible to influence and training than those of older students. Based on the results of music's effect on the brain, it would be beneficial to investigate the implementation of musical training in education ranging from kindergarten through high school.

The results of the study were very interesting and are still being investigated in order to use them to their full potential. The study found a definite link between music and the mind, specifically the area of the brain that can solve tasks known as spatial-temporal tasks. The research team planned a study that would test a control group's performance on spatial-temporal tasks after having listened to a certain type of music for a short amount of time. The team chose Mozart's "Sonata in D major for two pianos" for the control group (Grandin, Peterson, and Shaw 2). The team chose this particular piece because of its complexity and its use of regular patterns and sequences (Reimer 4). Mozart was chosen because he was a child prodigy himself and the team hoped that his music would stimulate some of the same spatial-temporal advances that he had demonstrated in his youth (Grandin, Peterson, and Shaw 2). Mozart's music is filled with patterns and scales. These aspects of music have a strong tie to mathematics in the sense that they are both ordered, repeating sequences. Recent studies have also shown that the mind functions in a manner that can be predicted by math, specifically logarithms ("Can you hum . . ." 2). The brain was mapped by its response to logarithmic sequences, and this map highlights the relationship of the brain to mathematics (Simpson 1). If the brain is related to math and music is related to math as well, then it is reasonable to investigate a relationship between the brain and music. Shaw's research team investigated this by predicting what area of the brain would be affected by Mozart's music and giving tests accordingly. They isolated a group of college students and let them listen to Mozart before taking a spatial-temporal task test (Simpson 1). The effect of the music seemed to last only as long as the study, but the results were very encouraging to the scientists ("Can you hum . . ." 2). These results indicate that music can improve brain function on certain levels. Gordon Shaw of the research team believes that after careful study "specific music could enhance how we think, reason, and create" (Grandin, Peterson, and Shaw 1).

Music training can assist educators in the teaching of spatial-temporal concepts. The current education system does not focus as much on spatial-temporal tasks as it does on language-analytical tasks. Spatial-temporal tasks are those tasks that involve "the transforming and relating of mental images in space and time" (Grandin, Peterson, and Shaw 1). These tasks include many applications that are being taught in schools today. In math, basic patterns and diagrams are examples of spatial-temporal problems. Art and architecture applications also involve spatial-temporal analysis. If music programs are put into place in schools today, the spatial-temporal-based lessons in other subjects will be enhanced. Shaw feels that this would be a much needed improvement since "the current educational system concentrates on developing language-analytical reasoning skills and neglects the complementary spatial-temporal form of reasoning" (Grandin, Peterson, and Shaw 3).

The studies have produced interesting results in how music affects young children. The basis of this research is the fact that infants have shown an understanding of music before they can comprehend language and other stimuli. Music is understood by infants, before language, and could be a way to "train" young minds (Grandin, Peterson, and Shaw 3). This theory prompted further research into the effects of music on pre-school children. These children are still subject to heavy suggestion from educators due to their young age. Their minds are still able to go through easy transformation, and the music training will have a substantial effect (Grandin, Peterson, and Shaw 2). Studies have followed preschool students through different musical training programs. Children who have been through six months of musical training have shown improvement in spatial-temporal tasks (Grandin, Peterson, and Shaw 1). This training could be implemented in school programs. Schools should put basic music theory and keyboarding classes into place for preschool and elementary students. These courses can be made simple enough for preschool age children to understand, but they would also help the children in their other courses. The students in the study showed improvement in reproducing mental images and manipulating them (Grandin, Peterson, and Shaw 3). The benefits of music training will not only be seen in the individual's respect for and greater exposure to the arts, but also in mathematics and higher learning.

The program would also benefit students if it were carried through to graduation. A twelve-year exposure to music education has a good chance of enhancing a student's ability to work spatial-temporal problems in the future. These music programs should not be forced on students, but should be readily available. As a student progresses through high school, the level of difficulty rises sharply in mathematics. Students progress through geometry, trigonometry, and calculus. Each of these mathematics courses requires a strong understanding of spatial-temporal reasoning. Higher mathematics requires students to visualize objects and points without the aid of pen and paper. A student with a background in music education has an advantage in this area, according to the results of the "Mozart" studies. The music education will provide a greater grasp of mental reasoning. The benefits of music will also be helpful in higher learning and in adult life. Higher learning will produce new mathematical challenges in new areas. Students who major in engineering, architecture, programming, or even music will all benefit from an early emphasis on the arts. As these students graduate from college and continue into the work force, they will be valuable to employers that are looking for creative and sharp minds.

The implementation of a music education program in schools will be advantageous to students of all fields of study. The benefits of this program will not end with just school. The students will carry their understanding through to their careers for the rest of their lives. As a bonus, students will also be more exposed to music in general. The benefits of improved spatial-temporal reasoning are enough to justify the implementation of a music program. Yet these students will also grow up with a sense of the history of music as an art form. Music will improve their intelligence while still remaining a form of relaxation and entertainment. Music's use as a tool for increasing reasoning is the next step in its continuing evolution.

Works Cited

"Brain Health: Music and the Mind." *Harvard Health Letter* 27.2 (Dec. 2001): 1–2.

"Can You Hum Your Way to Math Genius?" *Forbes* 163.8 (19 April 1999): 176.

Delahoussaye, Martin. "Requiem for a Trainer." *Training* 39.6 (June 2002): 28.

Grandin, Temple, Matthew Peterson, and Gordon Shaw. "Spatial-Temporal Versus Language-Analytical Reasoning: The Role of Music Training." *Arts Education Policy Review* 99.6 (July–August 1998): 11–14.

Reimer, Bennett. "Facing the Risks of the 'Mozart Effect.'" *Phi Delta Kappan* 81.4 (Dec. 1999: 278.

Simpson, Marion. "Will Listening to Mozart Make You Smarter?" *Student BMJ* (March 2002): 64

Arguers will often neglect to state their warrants for one of two reasons: First, like Mrs. Walkup, they may believe that the warrant is obvious and need not be expressed; second, they may want to conceal the warrant in the hope that the reader will overlook its weakness.

What kinds of warrants are so obvious that they need not be expressed? Here are a few that will probably sound familiar:

Mothers love their children.

The more expensive the product, the more satisfactory it will be.

A good harvest will result in lower prices for produce.

First come, first served.

These statements seem to embody beliefs that most of us would share and that might be unnecessary to make explicit in an argument. The last statement, for example, is taken as axiomatic, an article of faith that we seldom question in ordinary circumstances. Suppose you hear someone make the claim, "I deserve to get the last ticket to the concert." If you ask why he is entitled to a ticket that you also would like to have, he may answer in support of his claim, "Because I was here first." No doubt you accept his claim without further argument because you understand and agree with the warrant that is not expressed: "If you arrive first, you deserve to be served before those who come later." Your acceptance of the warrant probably also takes into account the unexpressed backing that is based on a belief in justice: "It is only fair that those who sacrifice time and comfort to be first in line should be rewarded for their trouble."

In this case it may not be necessary to expose the warrant and examine it. Indeed, as Stephen Toulmin tells us, "If we demanded the credentials of all warrants at sight and never let one pass unchallenged, argument could scarcely begin."[4]

But even those warrants that seem to express universal truths invite analysis if we can think of claims for which these warrants might not, after all, be relevant. "First in line," for example, may justify the claim of a person who wants a concert ticket, but it cannot in itself justify the claim of someone who wants a vital medication that is in short supply. Moreover, offering a rebuttal to a long-held but unexamined warrant can often produce an interesting and original argument. If someone exclaims, "All this buying of gifts! I think people have forgotten that Christmas celebrates the birth of Christ," she need not express the assumption—that the buying of gifts violates what ought to be a religious celebration. It goes unstated by the speaker because it has been uttered so often that she knows the hearer will supply it. But one writer, in an essay titled "God's Gift: A Commercial Christmas," argued that, contrary to popular belief, the purchase of gifts, which means the expenditure of time, money, and thought on others rather than oneself, is not a violation but an affirmation of the Christmas spirit.[5]

---

[4] *The Uses of Argument* (Cambridge: Cambridge University Press, 1958), p. 106.
[5] Robert A. Sirico, *Wall Street Journal*, December 21, 1993, sec. A, p. 12.

The second reason for refusal to state the warrant lies in the arguer's intention to disarm or deceive the reader, although the arguer may not be aware of this. For instance, failure to state the warrant is common in advertising and politics, where the desire to sell a product or an idea may outweigh the responsibility to argue explicitly. The following advertisement is famous not only for what it says but for what it does not say:

> In 1918 Leona Currie scandalized a New Jersey beach with a bathing suit cut above her knees. And to irk the establishment even more, she smoked a cigarette. Leona Currie was promptly arrested.
> Oh, how Leona would smile if she could see you today.
> You've come a long way, baby. *Virginia Slims*. The taste for today's woman.

What is the unstated warrant? The manufacturer of Virginia Slims hopes we will agree that being permitted to smoke cigarettes is a significant sign of female liberation. But many readers would insist that proving "You've come a long way, baby" requires more evidence than women's freedom to smoke (or wear short bathing suits). The shaky warrant weakens the claim.

Politicians, too, conceal warrants that may not survive close scrutiny. In the 1983 mayoral election in Chicago, one candidate revealed that his opponent had undergone psychiatric treatment. He did not have to state the warrant supporting his claim. He knew that many in his audience would assume that anyone who had undergone psychiatric treatment was unfit to hold public office. This same assumption contributed to the withdrawal of a vice-presidential candidate from the 1972 campaign.

TYPES OF WARRANTS

Arguments may be classified according to the types of warrants offered as proof. Because warrants represent the reasoning process by which we establish the relationship between support and claim, analysis of the major types of warrants enables us to see the whole argument as a sum of its parts.

Warrants may be organized into three categories: "*authoritative, substantive*, and *motivational*."[6] We have already given examples of these types of warrants in this chapter and in Chapter 1. The *authoritative warrant* (see p. 223) is based on the credibility or trustworthiness of the source. If we assume that the source of the data is authoritative, then we find that the support justifies the claim. A *substantive warrant* is based on beliefs about reliability of factual evidence. In the example on page 223 the speaker assumes, although mistakenly, that the relationship between

---

[6] D. Ehninger and W. Brockriede, *Decision by Debate* (New York: Dodd, Mead, 1953).

low reading level and stupidity is a verifiable datum, one that can be proved by objective research. A *motivational warrant*, on the other hand, is based on the needs and values of the audience. For example, the warrant on page 12 reflects a preference for individual freedom, a value that would cause a reader who held it to agree that laws against marijuana should be repealed.

Each type of warrant requires a different set of questions for testing its soundness. The following list of questions will help you to decide whether a particular warrant is valid and can justify a particular claim.

1. *Authoritative* (based on the credibility of the sources)

   Is the authority sufficiently respected to make a credible claim?

   Do other equally reputable authorities agree with the authority cited?

   Are there equally reputable authorities who disagree?

2. *Substantive* (based on beliefs about the reliability of factual evidence)

   Are sufficient examples given to convince us that a general statement is justified? That is, are the examples given representative of the whole community?

   If you have argued that one event or condition can bring about another (a cause-and-effect argument), does the cause given seem to account entirely for the effect? Are other possible causes equally important as explanations for the effect?

   If you have used comparisons, are the similarities between the two situations greater than the differences?

   If you have used analogies, does the analogy explain or merely describe? Are there sufficient similarities between the two elements to make the analogy appropriate?

3. *Motivational* (based on the values of the arguer and the audience)

   Are the values ones that the audience will regard as important?

   Are the values relevant to the claim?

The Case for Torture

MICHAEL LEVIN

Introduction: statement of opposing view

It is generally assumed that torture is impermissible, a throwback to a more brutal age. Enlightened societies reject it outright, and regimes suspected of using it risk the wrath of the United States.

Claim of policy: rebuttal of opposing view

I believe this attitude is unwise. There are situations in which torture is not merely permissible but morally mandatory. Moreover, these situations are moving from the realm of imagination to fact.

Support: hypothetical example to test the reader's belief

Suppose a terrorist has hidden an atomic bomb on Manhattan Island which will detonate at noon on July 4 unless . . . (here follow the usual demands for money and release of his friends from jail). Suppose, further, that he is caught at 10 A.M. of the fateful day, but — preferring death to failure — won't disclose where the bomb is. What do we do? If we follow due process — wait for his lawyer, arraign him — millions of people will die. If the only way to save those lives is to subject the terrorist to the most excruciating possible pain, what grounds can there be for not doing so? I suggest there are none. In any case, I ask you to face the question with an open mind.

Torturing the terrorist is unconstitutional? Probably. But millions of lives surely outweigh constitutionality. Torture is barbaric? Mass murder is far more barbaric. Indeed, letting millions of innocents die in deference to one who flaunts his guilt is moral cowardice, an unwillingness to dirty one's hands. If *you* caught the terrorist, could you sleep nights knowing that millions died because you couldn't bring yourself to apply the electrodes?

Once you concede that torture is justified in 5
extreme cases, you have admitted that the deci-

Michael Levin is a professor of philosophy at the City College of New York. This essay is reprinted from the June 7, 1982, issue of *Newsweek*.

sion to use torture is a matter of balancing innocent lives against the means needed to save them. You must now face more realistic cases involving more modest numbers. Someone plants a bomb on a jumbo jet. He alone can disarm it, and his demands cannot be met (or if they can, we refuse to set a precedent by yielding to his threats). Surely we can, we must, do anything to the extortionist to save the passengers. How can we tell 300, or 100, or 10 people who never asked to be put in danger, "I'm sorry, you'll have to die in agony, we just couldn't bring ourselves to . . ."

Here are the results of an informal poll about a third, hypothetical, case. Suppose a terrorist group kidnapped a newborn baby from a hospital. I asked four mothers if they would approve of torturing kidnappers if that were necessary to get their own newborns back. All said yes, the most "liberal" adding that she would administer it herself.

I am not advocating torture as punishment. Punishment is addressed to deeds irrevocably past. Rather, I am advocating torture as an acceptable measure for preventing future evils. So understood, it is far less objectionable than many extant punishments. Opponents of the death penalty, for example, are forever insisting that executing a murderer will not bring back his victim (as if the purpose of capital punishment were supposed to be resurrection, not deterrence or retribution). But torture, in the cases described, is intended not to bring anyone back but to keep innocents from being dispatched. The most powerful argument against using torture as a punishment or to secure confessions is that such practices disregard the rights of the individual. Well, if the individual is all that important—and he is— it is correspondingly important to protect the rights of individuals threatened by terrorists. If life is so valuable that it must never be taken, the lives of the innocents must be saved even at the price of hurting the one who endangers them.

Better precedents for torture are assassination and preemptive attack. No Allied leader would have flinched at assassinating Hitler, had that been possible. (The Allies did assassinate Heydrich.)

Margin notes:

Support: hypothetical example

Support: informal poll

Defense of the claim a) Not punishment but protection of the innocent

Hypothetical examples: b) Analogies with World War II

Americans would be angered to learn that Roosevelt could have had Hitler killed in 1943 — thereby shortening the war and saving millions of lives — but refused on moral grounds. Similarly, if nation A learns that nation B is about to launch an unprovoked attack, A has a right to save itself by destroying B's military capability first. In the same way, if the police can by torture save those who would otherwise die at the hands of kidnappers or terrorists, they must.

c) Denial that
terrorists have rights

There is an important difference between terrorists and their victims that should mute talk of the terrorists' "rights." The terrorist's victims are at risk unintentionally, not having asked to be endangered. But the terrorist knowingly initiated his actions. Unlike his victims, he volunteered for the risks of his deed. By threatening to kill for profit or idealism, he renounces civilized standards, and he can have no complaint if civilization tries to thwart him by whatever means necessary.

Just as torture is justified only to save lives (not   10 extort confessions or recantations), it is justifiably administered only to those *known* to hold innocent lives in their hands. Ah, but how can the authorities ever be sure they have the right malefactor? Isn't there a danger of error and abuse? Won't We turn into Them?

d) Easy identification
of terrorists

Questions like these are disingenuous in a world in which terrorists proclaim themselves and perform for television. The name of their game is public recognition. After all, you can't very well intimidate a government into releasing your freedom fighters unless you announce that it is your group that has seized its embassy. "Clear guilt" is difficult to define, but when 40 million people see a group of masked gunmen seize an airplane on the evening news, there is not much question about who the perpetrators are. There will be hard cases where the situation is murkier. Nonetheless, a line demarcating the legitimate use of torture can be drawn. Torture only the obviously guilty, and only for the sake of saving innocents, and the line between Us and Them will remain clear.

Conclusion warrant:
"Paralysis in the face
of evil is the greater
danger."

There is little danger that the Western democracies will lose their way if they choose to inflict pain as one way of preserving order. Paralysis in the face of evil is the greater danger. Some day soon a terrorist will threaten tens of thousands of lives, and torture will be the only way to save them. We had better start thinking about this.

■ Analysis

Levin's controversial essay attacks a popular assumption that most people have never thought to question — that torture is impermissible under any circumstances. Levin argues that in extreme cases torture is morally justified to bring about a greater good than the rights of the individual who is tortured.

Against the initial resistance that most readers may feel, Levin makes a strong case. Its strength lies in the backing he provides for the warrant that torture is sometimes necessary. This backing consists in the use of two effective argumentative strategies. One is the anticipation of objections. Unprecedented? No. Unconstitutional? No. Barbaric? No. Second, and more important, are the hypothetical examples that compel readers to re-think their positions and possibly arrive at agreement with the author. Levin chooses extreme examples — kidnapping of a newborn child, planting a bomb on a jumbo jet, detonating an atomic bomb in Manhattan — that draw a line between clear and murky cases and make agreement easier. And he bolsters his moral position by insisting that torture is not to be used as punishment or revenge but only to save innocent lives.

To support such an unpopular assumption the writer must convey the impression that he is a reasonable man, and this Levin attempts to do by a searching definition of terms, the careful organization and development of his argument, including references to the opinions of other people, and the expression of compassion for innocent lives.

Another strength of the article is its readability — the use of contractions, informal questions, conversational locutions. This easy, familiar style is disarming; the reader doesn't feel threatened by heavy admonitions from a writer who affects a superior, moral attitude.

Writer's Guide: Recognizing Warrants

1. Locate in your essay the one sentence that best states your claim, or if there is no single sentence that does so, try to express your claim in a single sentence.

2. If you have not already done so, think about for what audience you are writing. How is that audience likely to respond to your claim? The most important question to ask about your audience regarding warrants is this one: What assumption or assumptions must my audience make to be able to accept my claim? The answer to that question will be the warrant or warrants on which your essay is based.

3. The support you offer will make it easier for your audience to accept your claim. Remember that the warrant is the link between claim and support. It may help to use the formula used in this chapter to think systematically through your argument. Ask yourself what the claim is, what support you are offering, and what warrant connects the two. Do that for each major supporting statement that you make.

4. You may not need to state your warrant directly if it is a universally accepted truth that most reasonable readers would agree with it. You should be able to do so, however, in order to check your own logic.

5. If you are asking the members of your audience to accept a warrant that they are not likely to accept, you must offer backing for that warrant or consider restating your claim in a way that does not ask them to agree to an assumption that they will not be willing to agree with.

READINGS FOR ANALYSIS

A Proposal to Abolish Grading

PAUL GOODMAN

Let half a dozen of the prestigious universities — Chicago, Stanford, the Ivy League — abolish grading, and use testing only and entirely for pedagogic purposes as teachers see fit.

Anyone who knows the frantic temper of the present schools will understand the transvaluation of values that would be effected by this modest innovation. For most of the students, the competitive grade has come to be the essence. The naive teacher points to the beauty of the subject and the ingenuity of the research; the shrewd student asks if he is responsible for that on the final exam.

Paul Goodman (1911–1972) was a college professor and writer whose outspoken views were popular with students during the 1960s. This essay is from *Compulsory Miseducation* (1964).

Let me at once dispose of an objection whose unanimity is quite fascinating. I think that the great majority of professors agree that grading hinders teaching and creates a bad spirit, going as far as cheating and plagiarizing. I have before me the collection of essays, *Examining in Harvard College*, and this is the consensus. It is uniformly asserted, however, that the grading is inevitable; for how else will the graduate schools, the foundations, the corporations *know* whom to accept, reward, hire? How will the talent scouts know whom to tap?

By testing the applicants, of course, according to the specific task requirements of the inducting institution, just as applicants for the Civil Service or for licenses in medicine, law, and architecture are tested. Why should Harvard professors do the testing *for* corporations and graduate schools?

The objection is ludicrous. Dean Whitla, of the Harvard Office of 5 Tests, points out that the scholastic-aptitude and achievement tests used for *admission* to Harvard are a superexcellent index for all-around Harvard performance, better than high-school grades or particular Harvard course-grades. Presumably, these college-entrance tests are tailored for what Harvard and similar institutions want. By the same logic, would not an employer do far better to apply his own job-aptitude test rather than to rely on the vagaries of Harvard section-men? Indeed, I doubt that many employers bother to look at such grades; they are more likely to be interested merely in the fact of a Harvard diploma, whatever that connotes to them. The grades have most of their weight with the graduate schools — here, as elsewhere, the system runs mainly for its own sake.

It is really necessary to remind our academics of the ancient history of Examination. In the medieval university, the whole point of the grueling trial of the candidate was whether or not to accept him as a peer. His disputation and lecture for the Master's was just that, a masterpiece to enter the guild. It was not to make comparative evaluations. It was not to weed out and select for an extramural licensor or employer. It was certainly not to pit one young fellow against another in an ugly competition. My philosophic impression is that the medievals thought they knew what a good job of work was and that we are competitive because we do not know. But the more status is achieved by largely irrelevant competitive evaluation, the less will we ever know.

(Of course, our American examinations never did have this purely guild orientation, just as our faculties have rarely had absolute autonomy; the examining was to satisfy Overseers, Elders, distant Regents — and they as paternal superiors have always doted on giving grades, rather than accepting peers. But I submit that this set-up itself makes it impossible for the student to *become* a master, to *have* grown up, and to commence on his own. He will always be making A or B for some overseer. And in the present atmosphere, he will always be climbing on his friend's neck.)

Perhaps the chief objectors to abolishing grading would be the students and their parents. The parents should be simply disregarded; their anxiety has done enough damage already. For the students, it seems to me that a primary duty of the university is to deprive them of their props, their dependence on extrinsic valuation and motivation, and to force them to confront the difficult enterprise itself and finally lose themselves in it.

A miserable effect of grading is to nullify the various uses of testing. Testing, for both student and teacher, is a means of structuring, and also of finding out what is blank or wrong and what has been assimilated and can be taken for granted. Review—including high-pressure review—is a means of bringing together the fragments, so that there are flashes of synoptic insight.

There are several good reasons for testing, and kinds of test. But if the aim is to discover weakness, what is the point of down-grading and punishing it, and thereby inviting the student to conceal his weakness, by faking and bulling, if not cheating? The natural conclusion of synthesis is the insight itself, not a grade for having had it. For the important purpose of placement, if one can establish in the student the belief that one is testing *not* to grade and make invidious comparisons but for his own advantage, the student should normally seek his own level, where he is challenged and yet capable, rather than trying to get by. If the student dares to accept himself as he is, a teacher's grade is a crude instrument compared with a student's self-awareness. But it is rare in our universities that students are encouraged to notice objectively their vast confusion. Unlike Socrates, our teachers rely on power-drives rather than shame and ingenuous idealism.

Many students are lazy, so teachers try to goad or threaten them by grading. In the long run this must do more harm than good. Laziness is a character-defense. It may be a way of avoiding learning, in order to protect the conceit that one is already perfect (deeper, the despair that one *never* can be). It may be a way of avoiding just the risk of failing and being down-graded. Sometimes it is a way of politely saying, "I won't." But since it is the authoritarian grown-up demands that have created such attitudes in the first place, why repeat the trauma? There comes a time when we must treat people as adult, laziness and all. It is one thing courageously to fire a do-nothing out of your class; it is quite another thing to evaluate him with a lordly F.

Most important of all, it is often obvious that balking in doing the work, especially among bright young people who get to great universities, means exactly what it says: The work does not suit me, not this subject, or not at this time, or not in this school, or not in school altogether. The student might not be bookish; he might be school-tired; perhaps his development ought now to take another direction. Yet unfortunately, if such a student is intelligent and is not sure of himself, he *can* be bullied into passing, and this obscures everything. My hunch is that I am describing a common situation. What a grim waste of young life and teacherly effort! Such a student will retain nothing of what he has "passed" in. Sometimes he must get mononucleosis to tell his story and be believed.

And ironically, the converse is also probably commonly true. A student flunks and is mechanically weeded out, who is really ready and eager to learn in a scholastic setting, but he has not quite caught on. A good teacher can recognize the situation, but the computer wreaks its will.

READING AND DISCUSSION QUESTIONS

1. Goodman divides his argument into several parts, each of which develops a different idea. How would you subtitle these parts?

2. Are some parts of the argument stronger than others? Does Goodman indicate what points he wants to emphasize?

3. Why do you think Goodman calls on "half a dozen of the prestigious universities" (para. 1) instead of all universities to abolish grading?

4. Where does the author reveal the purposes of his proposal?

5. Most professors, Goodman argues, think that grading hinders teaching. Why, then, do they continue to give grades? How does Goodman reply to their objections?

6. What does Goodman think the real purpose of testing should be? How does grading "nullify the various uses of testing" (para. 9)?

WRITING SUGGESTIONS

7. Do you agree that grading prevents you from learning? If so, write an essay in which you support Goodman's thesis by reporting what your own experience has been.

8. If you disagree with Goodman, write an essay that outlines the benefits of grading.

9. Is there a better way than grading to evaluate the work of students—a way that would achieve the goals of education Goodman values? Suggest a method, and explain why it would be superior to grading.

An Unjust Sacrifice

ROBERT A. SIRICO

An appeals court in London has made a Solomonic ruling, deciding that eight-week-old twins joined at the pelvis must be separated. In effect, one twin, known as Mary, is to be sacrificed to save the other, known as Jodie, in an operation the babies' parents oppose.

The judges invoked a utilitarian rationale, justified on the basis of medical testimony. The specialists agreed that there is an 80 to 90 percent

Robert A. Sirico, a Roman Catholic priest, is president of the Acton Institute for the Study of Religion and Liberty in Grand Rapids, Michigan. This article appeared in the September 28, 2000, *New York Times.*

chance that the strong and alert Jodie could not survive more than a few months if she continued to support the weak heart and lungs of Mary, whose brain is underdeveloped.

This is a heartbreaking case, and the decision of the court was not arrived at lightly. But even the best of intentions, on the part of the state or the parents, is no substitute for sound moral reasoning. Utilitarian considerations like Mary's quality of life are not the issue. Nor should doctors' expert testimony, which is subject to error, be considered decisive.

Here, as in the case of abortion, one simple principle applies: There is no justification for deliberately destroying innocent life. In this case, the court has turned its back on a tenet that the West has stood by: Life, no matter how limited, should be protected.

While this case is so far unique, there are guidelines that must be fol-   5
lowed. No human being, for instance, can be coerced into donating an organ—even if the individual donating the organ is unlikely to be harmed and the individual receiving the organ could be saved. In principle, no person should ever be forced to volunteer his own body to save another's life, even if that individual is a newborn baby.

To understand the gravity of the court's error, consider the parents' point of view. They are from Gozo, an island in Malta. After being told of their daughters' condition, while the twins were in utero, they went to Manchester, England, seeking out the best possible medical care. Yet, after the birth on August 8, the parents were told that they needed to separate the twins, which would be fatal for Mary.

They protested, telling the court: "We cannot begin to accept or contemplate that one of our children should die to enable the other one to survive. That is not God's will. Everyone has a right to life, so why should we kill one of our daughters to enable the other one to survive?"

And yet, a court in a country in which they sought refuge has overruled their wishes. This is a clear evil: coercion against the parents and coercion against their child, justified in the name of a speculative medical calculus.

The parents' phrase "God's will" is easily caricatured, as if they believed divine revelation were guiding them to ignore science. In fact, they believe in the merit of science, or they would not have gone to Britain for help in the first place.

But utilitarian rationality has overtaken their case. The lawyer ap-   10
pointed by the court to represent Jodie insisted that Mary's was "a futile life." That is a dangerous statement—sending us down a slippery slope where lives can be measured for their supposed value and discarded if deemed not useful enough.

Some might argue that in thinking about the twins, we should apply the philosophical principle known as "double effect," which, in some circumstances, permits the loss of a life when it is an unintended consequence of saving another. But in this case, ending Mary's life would be a deliberate decision, not an unintended effect.

Can we ever take one life in favor of another? No, not even in this case, however fateful the consequences.

READING AND DISCUSSION QUESTIONS

1. Underlying the author's claim that the parents of the twins should not separate them is the warrant—a broad assumption about life, in this case. What sentences express that warrant?

2. If you do not agree with Sirico's argument, point out what you think are flaws in his reasoning, based on your own understanding of moral principles.

3. In the fifth paragraph, Sirico cites another kind of medical dilemma as an analogy to that of the twins. How effective is it in supporting his claim?

4. The author condemns "utilitarianism" (para. 2). This ethical doctrine holds, as one dictionary defines it, "that conduct should be directed toward the greatest happiness of the greatest number of persons." Find statements in this essay that might explain why this philosophy is unacceptable to Sirico.

WRITING SUGGESTIONS

5. The author's conclusion is expressed as an absolute—a rule of behavior for which there are no exceptions. Can you think of any rules of human conduct which ought to be obeyed without exception? Reviewing the Ten Commandments might be a place to start. If so, define the rule, and tell why it must be so observed. If not, explain why some rules of behavior are subject to exception.

6. Peter Singer, a philosopher at Princeton University who subscribes to the utilitarian doctrine, has said that if the parents of a handicapped infant decide to kill him before he is two months old because his death would increase their happiness and decrease the infant's suffering, they have a right to do so. In another case he has argued that instead of spending money to reduce the suffering of a family member, a person should "send the same sum to ease the suffering of ten Sudanese."[7] Write an argument for or against the practice of utilitarianism in one of these cases or any other in which the sacrifice of life is an issue.

[7] George F. Will, "Life and Death at Princeton," *Newsweek*, September 13, 1999, p. 82. This article is critical of Singer's philosophy.

Computers and the Pursuit of Happiness

DAVID GELERNTER

In recent years we have been notified almost continuously that we are living in an "information age." Mankind (it is suggested) has completed a sort of phase shift: the solid agricultural age was replaced two centuries ago by the liquid industrial age, which has now given way to the gaseous (so to speak) age of information. Everyone says so, but is it true? *Has* an old age ended, and are we, thanks to computers and the Internet, living in a new one? A related question: computers have been around for roughly a half-century; have they been good or bad for mankind? And finally: are they likely to do good or bad over the next half-century?

1

We are *not* in an information age, and computers and the Internet are not a revolutionary development in human history.

In the old industrial age (people say) coal, steel, and concrete mattered; in the new age, information counts. Yet it is obvious that coal, steel, and concrete still count just as much as they ever did. We have always needed food, clothing, shelter, possessions, and above all each other. We always *will* need those things, and the "information revolution" will never lessen our needs by half a hair's breadth. So whom are we kidding? What nouveau cyber-billionaire ever used his billions to buy *information?* Who ever worried about poverty because he would be unable to keep his family well-informed?

Not long ago I saw a rented U-Haul trailer with the inevitable Web address in big letters on the side, "uhaul.com"—the information age in nine easy characters. Yes, it is convenient to check a Web site for information about trailers for rent; but the Internet will never (*can* never) change our need for physical stuff, or for trailers to haul it around in. Fifty years from now, it may be possible to download artistically designed experiences and beam them via trick signals into your brain. (To many people this will sound like a junior grade of hell, but some technologists think of it as a Coming Attraction.) The interesting fact remains: virtual gourmet food will make you feel full but will not keep you from starving. Virtual heat will make you feel warm but will not keep you from freezing. Virtual sex will make you feel satisfied in the sense that a pig feels satisfied.

About computers in particular, believers in a new information age 5 make three arguments. They say it is a new age because we now have so-

---

David Gelernter is a professor of computer science at Yale. In addition to the books on computer technology mentioned in this essay, he is the author of the memoir *Drawing Life: Surviving the Unabomber* (1997), and *1939: The Lost World of the Fair* (1996). This essay appeared in the January, 2001 issue of *Commentary*.

phisticated machines to create, store, and deliver information; because computer networks can overcome geography; and because machines (in their own special areas) can act intelligently. All three claims are wrong. Computers have done marvelous deeds—but in each case, their great deeds are in keeping with the long-established patterns of the industrial age. Computation today is a dusting of snow that makes everything look different—on the surface.

Fancy machines to create, move, and store information were a main preoccupation of the whole twentieth century, not just the computerized part of it. Movies, phonographs, color photography and color printing, the electronic transmission of photos, the invention of radio and radio networks and international radio hookups, newsreels, television, transistorized electronics, long-distance phone networks, communication satellites, fax machines, photocopiers, audio and video tapes, compact disks, cell phones, cable TV—and then, with the emergence of PC's and the Internet, suddenly we are in an information age? The twentieth century was one information-gusher after another; information pouring into people's lives through more and more stuck-open faucets.

The defeat of geography? In *Cyberspace and the American Dream* (1994), distributed electronically by the Progress and Freedom Foundation, a distinguished group of authors argued that "we constitute the final generation of an old civilization and, at the very same time, the first generation of a new one." Their claim centered on the idea that, thanks to computer networks, geography had (in effect) been overcome; henceforth, shared interests and not physical proximity would shape community and society.

But using technology to defeat distance has been another goal of the industrial revolution from the start, from railroads through the Panama Canal and onward. Rail networks, telegraph networks, air and phone and highway and radio and TV networks—the Internet is the latest in a long line.

The twentieth century teemed with smart machines, too, long before the computer showed up—simple ones like the thermostat or a car's electrical system (with automatic spark-advance); complex, sophisticated ones like automatic transmissions or the Norden bombsight in World War II. Granted, computers are a huge advance over the machines that came before, but huge advances are the stuff of the industrial age. The Web is a big deal, but flying machines were a pretty big deal, too. Radio and TV changed the nature of American democracy. The electric-power industry turned society inside out.

The cost of not knowing history is not ignorance so much as arro- 10 gance. A popular book about the Internet and the Web begins with this "personal note" from the author:

> The Internet is, by far, the greatest and most significant achievement in the history of mankind. What? Am I saying that the Internet is more impressive than the pyramids? More beautiful than Michelangelo's

David? More important to mankind than the wondrous inventions of the industrial revolution? Yes, yes, and yes.

That sort of statement suggests that technologists are fundamentally unserious. By the way: a useful and interesting book. But the author protests too much. It is hard to picture comparable statements greeting the airplane's or the electric-power industry's emergence; they were too big and too obviously important to need this sort of cheerleading. What the author is really announcing is not a new age of information but a new age of hype, a new age of new ages.

Computers and the Internet *have* made a revolution in science and engineering. Studying computational models of reality can be cheaper and better than studying reality. Sometimes reality is impossible to measure or too steep to scale, and computational models are the only way to get any purchase on it. Those are the *actual* computer revolutions; the others are mostly potential and not real, locked up in awe-inspiring icebergs that just float around eliciting admiration and making trouble. The computer revolution is still frozen, latent, waiting to happen.

As for the information age, it must have begun at least a hundred years ago if it exists at all. *Are* we better informed than we used to be? I doubt it. Is anyone prepared to assert that the U.S. electorate is better informed today than it was at the time of (say) the 1960 presidential election? That our fifth graders are better informed about reading, writing, history, or arithmetic? That our fifth-grade *teachers* are better informed? (Recently my fifth-grade son learned from his English teacher that "incredible" and "incredulous" are synonyms. That's the information age for you.)

2

Have computers been good or bad for mankind since they were invented roughly fifty years ago?

Other things being equal, information is good. Wealth is good. Computers have supplied lots of information, and generated much wealth.

But we are marvelously adaptable. We can take miserable conditions 15 in stride and triumph over them; we can take wonderful conditions in stride and triumph over *them*. Humanity in any given age has a wealth threshold and an information threshold. If you are below either one, living in poverty or ignorance, you need more wealth or information. But once you are over the threshold, only the rate of change matters. Acquire more wealth or information, and presumably you will be happier; then you stabilize at your new, higher level, and chances are you are no happier than before. It is not exactly a deep or novel observation that money doesn't buy happiness. Neither does information.

In this country, the majority—obviously not everyone, but most of us—have been over-threshold in wealth and information for several generations, roughly since the end of World War II. That is a remarkable achievement; it ought to make us proud and thankful. But it follows that increasing our level of wealth or information is unlikely to count terribly much in the larger scheme of things. The increase itself will feel good, but the substance of our new wealth or information won't matter much.

Here is a small case in point. My two boys, who are ten and thirteen, love playing with computers, like most children nowadays. The computer is their favorite toy, and unquestionably it makes them happy. Computer play as it is practiced in real life, at least at our house, is a mindless activity; like many families, we have to limit the time our boys are allowed at it or they would spend all day wrecking pretend Porsches and blowing up enemy airplanes. But mindless activities are fine in reasonable doses. It's good for children to have fun, and I'm glad ours have so much fun with computers.

When my wife and I were children, we didn't have computers to play with. We lacked these wonderful, happiness-generating devices. But—so what? Other things made us happy. We never felt deprived on account of our lack of computer power. It would be crazy to deny that computers are great toys, but it would be equally crazy to argue that they have made children any happier, on the whole, than children used to be. Fifty years from now, the computer-based toys will make today's look pathetic, and children will love all their snazzy new stuff—just as much, probably, as children loved their bats and balls and blocks and trains and jump-ropes and dollhouses in 1900.

What we ordinarily fail to take into account when we are adding up the score is the nature of technological change. Technology is a tool for building social structures. Granted, each new technology is better than the one it replaces. But new technologies engender new social structures, and the important question is not whether the new technology is better but whether the new structure is better. Except in the case of medical technologies, the answer will nearly always be debatable; nearly always *must* be debatable. We can easily show that, with each passing generation, paints have improved. It is much harder to show that art has improved.

Human nature does not change; human needs and wants remain basically the same. Human ingenuity dreams up a new technology, and we put it to use—doing in a new way something we have always done in some other way. In years past, many towns had shared public wells. They were communal gathering places: you met neighbors, heard the news, checked out strangers, sized up the competition, made deals, dates, matches. Plumbing was a great leap forward, which few of us (certainly not me) would be willing to trade in. The old system was a nuisance, especially if *you* were the one carrying the water; but it was neighborly. The new, plumbing-induced social structure was far more convenient, not to say healthier. It was also lonelier. The old and new structures excelled in different ways and cannot be directly compared.

The Web is an improvement much like plumbing, without the health benefits. Fifty years ago, most shopping was face to face. In the Internet age, face-to-face stores will not survive long, any more than communal wells survived the advent of plumbing. To our great-grandchildren, shopping will mean "online," as it meant "face to face" to our great-grandparents. Future generations will look back wistfully but probably not unhappily. On the whole, their happiness and their ancestors' will probably be about the same. To the extent future generations *are* happier or unhappier than we—and "national happiness" does change, it's hard to doubt that America in 1950 was a happier country than America today—we can be fairly sure of one thing. The net change will have nothing to do with technology.

A major new technology remakes society—picks up the shoebox, shakes it hard, puts it back. The new social structures we build almost always incorporate less human labor than the old ones. The old structures (in other words) have a larger "human ingredient," the new ones a larger "machine ingredient." It is nearly always impossible to compare the two directly. And in the meantime the old ones have disappeared. Where technology is concerned, we demolish the past and live in a permanent present.

In the lush technology future, we will be kids in a candy store. The old zero-sum economics of Malthus and his modern disciples has long since been discredited; we will swagger into that Candy Store of the Future with more money all the time, and find more and fancier candy in there every day. Our inventiveness, productivity, and potential wealth are all unlimited. Only our appetite for candy is not.

3

If mankind were somehow prevented from continuing to develop computers and software—that would be a tragedy, and the world would suffer. Nothing comes more naturally to us than building and playing with machines. Inventing technology is the intellectual equivalent of breathing.

Is breathing helpful? Yes. Will it conduce to a better world in 2050? 25 Right again! But only in a certain sense.

In 1991 I published a book called *Mirror Worlds;* in a way, it was a celebration of computing technology (although it was ambivalent about computers in the end). It predicted the emergence of software versions of real-world institutions that you would "tune in" by means of a global network. It claimed that this would be a good development: you would be able to tour the world "without changing out of your pajamas." These mirror worlds would be "the new public square," would "monopolize the energy and attention of thousands . . . broadcast an aesthetic and a world-view to millions, mold behavior and epitomize the age."

Talk about modest claims—although in looking back at the Web boom that began in 1994 they seem, if anything, too modest. In predicting that "the software revolution hasn't begun yet, but it will soon," I was basically right. The industrial age ushered in new categories and possibilities, and computers and software are creating new possibilities, too: new types of structures that are just as unprecedented as the Eiffel Tower.

Consider an online school. Such a school might offer guided nature walks through teeming, chattering, blossoming rain forests of the intellect where your guide knows exactly what you are capable of, can make the path expand or shrink to suit you, can point out the biggest vistas or the tiniest orchid—and the whole structure can be moored in cyberspace, where anyone who likes can climb aboard. Instead of merely reteaching the same class year after year, we could make the path better every year. As a student follows a trail, we could turn that trail into his personal diary, for review or revisiting whenever he likes; he could keep his whole school career in his back pocket. We could plant pictures or maps at the center of lessons if they belonged there, instead of pasting them in as afterthoughts.

And these new software structures could be world-spanning switchboards, connecting the right student to the right teacher. If Mrs. Feinstein is the English teacher for little Kate Smith, then wherever Mrs. Feinstein lives (Auckland, Nome, Passaic), whatever hours she keeps, whatever her formal qualifications, we could patch her into the system.

I would rather put Kate in an actual school where actual teachers 30 could look her in the face when they are trying to teach her something. But American education is in desperate trouble—and under the circumstances, software-based teaching is probably our best hope. In the future we will compare our ubiquitous software schools to the face-to-face education of the pre-1970s the way we compare online shopping to long-ago Main Streets: we will be wistful, as usual, but not wistful enough to do anything about it. On the whole we will be content.

Of course, we are talking about new software *structures*—not mere computers, not mere information. And we are talking about something that *could* happen, but hasn't yet.

Human beings are mainly interested in human beings. If computers do good in the next fifty years, the good they are most likely to do lies in helping mankind know itself better.

A large part of cognitive science is built on a famous analogy, the analogy that did so much for the functionalist school of philosophy in the 1950s and 60s and that many researchers still believe today: mind is to brain as software is to computer. This analogy is fundamentally wrong.

Just the fact that software is portable (it can be moved from one computer to another) and minds are not (they cannot be moved from one brain to another) should have told us at the very start that the analogy was fishy. There is no reason to believe that you will ever be able to offload Joe Schwartz's mind and run it on Melissa Clark's brain. It is not even clear what this would mean in principle, because *part* of Schwartz's mind is the fact that it belongs to Schwartz. "Porting a mind" is not only impossible, but in principle meaningless.

In *The Muse in the Machine* (1994) I argued that you cannot under- 35 stand human thought unless you understand the "cognitive spectrum" that exists in every mind. That spectrum ranges from highly focused, highly aware-of-the-environment "analytic" thought all the way down to "low-focus," oblivious-of-the-environment thought—all the way down, in other words, to the kind of hallucinatory thought that happens routinely when we are asleep and dreaming. We will never get a computer to think until we have figured out how to make one hallucinate. To reproduce thought on a computer, we will need to reproduce the whole cognitive spectrum and not just one narrow slice of it.

For many years, the biggest challenge in cognitive science and philosophy has been to understand how we discover analogies, where we get our amazing capacity to notice that two things—objects, situations, events—that *seem* completely unrelated in fact have deep, hidden similarities. This capacity to draw analogies underlies human creativity and our useful knack of discovering and inventing new things. How does it work?

The evidence suggests, it seems to me, that analogy is driven by emotion. The remarkable thing about human emotion is that two wholly different-*seeming* scenes or memories or circumstances can make us *feel* exactly the same way. Emotion lets us make spectacularly nonobvious connections; in so doing, it lets us discover new analogies, lets us create.

Now, human emotions obviously depend not only on the mind but on the body. You don't think them, you feel them. So we cannot hope to simulate thought on a computer unless we can simulate the discovery of analogies. We cannot hope to do *that* unless we can simulate emotions on a machine. And we cannot hope to do *that* unless we can simulate not merely abstract mental processes but the complex, nuanced physical reality of the human body.

Eventually, this will be done. Certainly not soon (and certainly not by me)—but it will be done. But even at the end of this enormously difficult, complex task, when humanity has achieved the technological marvel of a machine that can accurately fake human emotions and (therefore) can realistically fake human thought, where exactly will we be?

The human body and its brain have the "emergent property"—or 40 "ensemble property"—of consciousness. When you put exactly the right pieces together in exactly the right way . . . consciousness emerges.

There is no reason, in principle, why computers and software could not have this property as well, and thus lead us to a deeper appreciation of what consciousness means and what it represents. It could be that we will wind up with a "thinking machine" that does not merely talk about daffodils, identify them, draw pictures of them; we might in principle end up with a machine that actually knows what a daffodil *is*. That actually experiences fragrance as we do, color as we do, form as we do—or at least experiences fragrance, color, and form in *some* way; or at least experiences *something* in some way. In other words, that is actually conscious.

All this *could* be. But we have no good reason to think it ever will be. It could be that consciousness will emerge from exactly the right combination of electronics and software; it could be that consciousness will emerge from exactly the right combination of mozzarella and tomato sauce, or bricks and mortar, or cardboard and rubber cement. None of these things is (in principle) impossible, but none of them is terribly likely, either.

Machines can move faster than we do; so it cannot be that the important thing (the distinguishing thing) about humans is how fast we are. Cannot be how strong we are. Cannot be how well we do arithmetic. It might easily be that in fifty years, machines will be smarter than we are, too. . . .

But I do not think we will conclude that to be human is no big deal after all. I have heard one of technology's most honored, distinguished men tell a large audience how he wished human beings would stop thinking that they are somehow different from animals; it pained him to hear the old canard about man's "uniqueness." He is offering us an easy out: it is simple to be an animal and complicated (Lord knows) to be a man. Should we stop trying, call it a day, and relocate to the barnyard?

Not yet. Most of us are not quite ready to toss out the scraps of moral- 45 ity and sanctity we have pieced together over the long, hard centuries; they may look shabby but they are the best clothes we own. They might even be as important as the Internet. I think we will decide not that we are merely animals after all but that our uniqueness lies beyond strength, speed *and* intellect.

People have said so for a long time, of course. Jews and Christians have long believed it. Chances are that, fifty years from now—thanks to computers—many more people will believe it. Chances are that, fifty years from now, we will be grateful to computer technology for showing us what marvelously powerful machines we can build—and how little they mean after all.

READING AND DISCUSSION QUESTIONS

1. State the warrant underlying the author's claim that computers cannot guarantee happiness. Look for it in the last part of the essay, although it is not stated directly.

2. Summarize Gelernter's responses to the three questions asked in the first paragraph. Do you find all of his arguments equally persuasive? Explain your answer.

3. Gelernter uses history, psychology, and personal experiences to support his claim. Point out some specific examples of these forms of support. Did any of his evidence surprise you? Does your own experience with computers confirm his insights?

4. The use of language in this essay is worth noting. The author has a highly readable style that encompasses both the formal and the informal. Find places where he speaks directly to the reader, using conversational language—colloquial in both grammar and vocabulary—to reach his audience.

5. The ending of this essay resembles one in a short story (and, in fact, Gelernter writes fiction, too). There is no explicit summing up. The meaning of the ending is indirect: It must be inferred from all that has been said before. (Contrast, for example, the closing statements of "An Unjust Sacrifice.") Why does Gelernter say that computers will not mean much, after all? What is the significance of the reference to Jews and Christians? Do you find the ending inspiring, as the author clearly intends? Or too elusive?

WRITING SUGGESTIONS

6. Write an essay elaborating on some of the ways in which the use of the computer has changed your life, for better or worse. You might want to refute or confirm one or more of the issues raised by Gelernter.

7. A few years ago a student took first prize in an essay contest in which she argued the superiority of printed books over books on the computer. The writer ended her essay this way: "It all boils down to which definition of communication you prefer: interpersonal or technological. A library of empty bookshelves would be a travesty." What is the difference between "interpersonal" and "technological"? Write a response to the student's comment, spelling out some advantages of the electronic book.

DISCUSSION QUESTIONS

1. What is the significance of the name of the product?
2. What assumptions underlie the remaining text in the ad?
3. How do the visual elements reinforce the text?
4. Can you think of other ads that make use of celebrities? What are some of the warrants that underlie the use of celebrities to sell products?

Do We Need the Census Race Question?

NATHAN GLAZER

A FEW years ago, when I was asked to comment on the controversy over how best to handle the demand of so-called multiracial advocacy groups for a "multiracial" category in the census, I made a brash and wildly unrealistic proposal.[1] Before describing my proposal, however, I should explain what concerned me about the existing questions on race, Hispanicity, and ancestry in the census. These questions had evolved by the 1980 and 1990 censuses in a way that was to my mind false to American racial and ethnic reality and incapable of getting coherent responses, to the degree that that is possible and that is normally expected in a census.

The census short form is the piece of official government paper that is probably seen by more Americans than any other, surpassing in the extent of its distribution the income tax forms. It is a message to the American people, and like any message it educates them to some reality: This is what the government needs, this what it wants, this is what it thinks is important. The census tells the American people that the government thinks the most important thing about them is to get them classified by race and ethnicity—ethnicity, that is, only if it qualifies as something called "Hispanic"; otherwise, the government is not interested. The census asks Americans first for the kinds of information that almost any form does, whether for a credit card or a driver's license—name, sex, age, family status—but then it turns out the main thing the government is interested in is their "race," described in the greatest detail, down to distinctions between Samoan and Guamanian and, if the respondent is Hispanic, between Argentinean, Colombian, Dominican, Nicaraguan, and even Spanish.

The government, in this message sent to all of us, apparently considers these matters more important than how educated we are, or whether we are citizens, or whether we are foreign born, or whether we voted in the last election. Scholars and researchers who follow the matter closely know why these questions are there, so prominently, so fully detailed. Do the American people in general know? If they do not—and it is hardly likely they are fully briefed on the legislation and regulations and politics

Nathan Glazer is a professor emeritus at the Graduate School of Education at Harvard University and past professor of sociology at the University of California at Berkeley. He is a former assistant editor for *Commentary* magazine and is a contributing editor of the *New Republic*. His books include *Beyond the Melting Pot* (with Daniel Patrick Moynihan; 1970), *We Are All Multiculturalists Now* (1997), and *The Lonely Crowd* (with David Riesman; rev. ed. 2001). He has served on presidential task forces on education and urban policy and on National Academy of Science committees on urban policy and minority issues.

and the pressures that have made the census form, with respect to race and Hispanicity, what it is today—what are they to conclude?

The census is supposed to give us a portrait of America. Is this what America looks like? Is the matter of race so important that it deserves this prominence and degree of detail?

A further problem is evident: that these questions are trying to im- 5
pose on identities in flux—not all, of course, but many—a categorization scheme that will inevitably confuse many people. It is a scheme in which many cannot place themselves, and one that requires all sorts of manipulations by the census professionals to put the results into a form in which it can be presented to Congress, the press, and the American people. There is bound to be a substantial degree of error in these final figures, which are never rounded to indicate their uncertainty nor presented with any indication of their degree of error—in contrast with public opinion polls. Yet asking about race and ethnicity has many similarities to public opinion polls about attitudes, compared with questions about age, or amount of schooling, or a number of other topics on which respondents are pretty clear.

Finally, there is simply the irrationality of the categories. Why does Hispanicity include people from Argentina and Spain but not those from Brazil or Portugal? Are there really all those races in Asia, where each country seems to consist of a single and different race, compared with simply "white" for all of Europe and the Middle East? Why, indeed, do people of Spanish origin rate special treatment, as against people from Italy, Poland, or Greece?

All this is familiar. And so I made my proposal. I confess that underlying my proposal was an ideological or political position—just as ideological and political positions underlie the present census arrangements. My position was that it is necessary and desirable to recognize and encourage the ongoing assimilation of the many strands that make the American people into a common culture. It is, I realize, a delicate task to draw a line between "recognize"—which is what the census should do—and "encourage," which it should not see as part of its task. Any form of recognition or nonrecognition is also, however, a form of encouragement or dissuasion. One encourages what one recognizes and dissuades what one does not. My proposal also responded to my interest as a social scientist in recording the progress of this change, which has been continuous in American history, affecting all groups in different degree but tragically leaving aside, for most of our history, one major group.

So then, my brash and unrealistic proposal: I proposed reducing the mishmash of race, Hispanicity, and ancestry to basically two questions. One question would determine whether a person considered himself or herself black or African American. That would remain the only race for which the census requested information. A second question or group of questions would ask in which country the respondent was born and in which country his or her parents were born and could be extended to ask where that person's grandparents were born. These questions on the country of birth of parents and grandparents would be filled in by respondents rather than presented in a multiple-choice format with predetermined options.

Why the interest in only one race? The census has counted blacks, slave and free, since the first enumeration of 1790. History alone and the virtues of continuity would make a claim that that determination be continued. There are, of course, far more potent reasons. This is the group that has suffered from prejudice, discrimination, and a lower-caste status since the origins of the Republic. In law, all this is now overcome and does not exist, but African Americans, we know, despite their presence in large numbers from our origins as a group of British colonies on the Atlantic shore, are less integrated in American society than any other large group. They are more segregated residentially. The rate of intermarriage with others outside the group, even if rapidly increasing, is still the lowest for any large group. They have a clear sense of their identity. One can depend on a high degree of reliability in the answers they give to the race question, as census research has shown.

The second question or group of questions replaces the "ancestry" 10 question because of the rapid rate of assimilation of all groups except blacks or African Americans. The limitation of these questions to the parental generation, and possibly the grandparental, is first a response to the reality that by the third generation and certainly by the fourth, the mix of ethnicities is extensive; second, it serves as an indication that the census and the government are not interested in group characteristics in the third generation and beyond.[2] With intermarriage rates in new non-black immigrant groups of 30 percent or thereabouts, we assume that by the third generation assimilation has progressed to the point at which identity is mixed and fluctuating and its ethnic character has become largely symbolic. We leave the question of what that identity consists of to the excellent sociologists, such as Richard Alba and Mary Waters, who have studied the nature of ethnic identification in these later generations. The census thereby gets out of the business of trying to affix an ancestry to each American.

If one thinks that each of the peoples of Asia forms a distinct race, this question will be able to encompass all the immigrants from that country and their children. There are not many yet in the third generation. By the time there is a substantial third generation of the post-1960s wave of immigrants, many will be of mixed ancestry, and the question of their identity will be left to them. Intermarriage statistics suggest the same for Hispanics, the great majority of whom are now immigrants and the children of immigrants. The only distinct group for which the census will try to get statistics on all those identified with it is the black or African American, for historical reasons we all know but also because black or African American identity does not fade after a few generations in this country but maintains itself in a varying but full form generation after generation.

I realize that problems remain regarding American Indians, Alaska Natives, Hawaiians, and part-Hawaiians. All these groups have a legal status, and there are means for determining who does and does not belong to each of these groups. I can see the virtue of specific questions beyond those I have suggested for Hawaii and Alaska, but I do not think 280 million Americans have to be troubled to determine the numbers of these very small groups.

Questions on birthplace and parental birthplace as posed today, as against the same questions during the last great wave of immigration, have one virtue: during that earlier wave, immigrants came from Europe, where many ethnic groups could be found within the boundaries of great multiethnic empires, and thus birthplace said little about ethnicity. In addition, the boundaries of eastern Europe have been radically recast three times in a century, and European immigrants and their children could be properly confused as to the country of their birth. What was the birthplace of a person born in Bukowina? If the census asks, "what country were you born in?" there are at least four reasonable candidates. Most of today's immigrants, in contrast, come from countries whose boundaries have been stable for a century or more, and their birthplaces and those of their parents permit us to make reasonable judgments as to their ethnic group.

This, I argued, was all that was needed in place of the present questions on race, Hispanicity, and ancestry. These two questions would provide less detailed data but more accurate data. They would also be more responsive to what America was like, and what it was becoming.

I knew the proposal was politically naive, but I was not aware of how 15 powerful and steady were the forces that created the present unsatisfactory situation until I went further into the history of the creation of the present categories (Skerry 2000; Nobles 2000; Anderson and Fienberg 1999; Bryant and Dunn 1995; Mitroff, Mason, and Barabba 1983). This research underlines the somewhat utopian character of my proposals today.

The experts seem to agree that when it comes to the census, the political outweighs the scientific, and this is a reality we have to live with. The word "political" can, of course, refer to many things, from the more to the less noble. What we have today in the census is political in all these senses. Some of it is, in part, the result of major civil rights legislation, which, to my mind, falls on the noble side. That legislation had to be interpreted by the courts and by the administrative agencies, however, under the pressure of ethnic groups. As we follow this process further into the details that shaped the form of the census questions, the element of nobility in the political process declines. I am not sure the legislation itself, which was concerned with the right to vote, required what the census has done in its effort to respond to the demand for small-area data on

Hispanics and Asian Americans. One could make a case that questions on birthplace and parental birthplace alone and the language question could give us the data to satisfy the legislation. But it would not give us the data in a form that satisfies proponents of distinct group interests and activists.

There are also the less noble political interventions. The census questions, whatever we think of their incongruity and irrationality, are the direct result of powerful pressures from the ethnic groups concerned, from Congress, and from the Executive Office of the President. These are political, alas, not only in the sense that political actors are involved but also in the narrower and less respectable sense that they are often motivated by narrow partisan political considerations.

Thus, Peter Skerry informs us, the unfortunate "ancestry" question was "criticized by social scientists for being vague and uninformative" in comparison with the question on birthplace of respondent's parents that it replaced. The Census Bureau also opposed it. "So why did the ancestry question end up on the questionnaire?" Skerry asks. "According to former deputy census director Louis Kincannon, who was working at the Statistical Policy Division of OMB when the decision was made, 'the ethnic desk' in the [Carter] White House insisted that the ancestry question go on the census . . . . It is evident that in the period leading up to the 1980 Presidential campaign, politics overrode the objections of both the OMB and the Census Bureau" (Skerry 2000, 37).

Democrats are understandably more responsive than Republicans to ethnic-group pressures, but Skerry tells us that Republican administrations have been no help, either. Concerning the origins of the Hispanic question, he notes that:

> the finalized questionnaires for the 1970 census were already at the printers when a Mexican American member of the U.S. Interagency Committee on Mexican American Affairs demanded that a specific Hispanic-origin question be included. . . . Over the opposition of Census Bureau officials, who argued against inclusion of an untested question so late in the process, Nixon ordered the secretary of commerce and the census director to add the question. . . . So it was hastily added to the long form. As former bureau official Conrad Taeuber recalls, "The order came down that we were to ask a direct question, have the people identify themselves as Hispanic." (Skerry 2000, 37–38)

The pressures initially come from the ethnic groups involved or their 20 leaders. Although there is only an uncertain relation between the numbers and the benefits that members of a group might get from one affirmative action program or another, undoubtedly the notion that one will in some way benefit from being counted as a distinct group plays a role in these pressures. At one time, Asian Indians were divided as to whether they should be "Caucasian" or yet another Asian race. Melissa Nobles reports on the discussion in the 1970s of the Federal Interagency Committee on Education on devising racial and ethnic categories for various federal programs. "The committee debated whether persons from India should be categorized under the 'Asian and Pacific Islander' category or under the 'White/Caucasian' category. . . . In the trial directive, they were classified as Caucasian, but they were reclassified as Asian in the final version (most likely in response to Asian Indian lobbying to ensure racial minority status)" (Nobles 2000, 79).

At the time, many in the Asian Indian community, taking into account their relatively high educational and economic position in the United States, rejected the idea that they should be eligible for benefits. Alas, the possibility of getting preferences for Indians under affirmative action programs for government contracts outweighed other considerations, and Indians—or at least some leadership groups—decided it was best to join the Chinese, Japanese, Koreans, and the rest as an "Asian race." I recall a report in an Indian newspaper that President Ronald Reagan's Small Business Administration (SBA) director had announced to an Indian conference that the SBA had decided to include South Asians among the groups that were considered qualified for preference in bidding for government contracts—this despite the fact that President Reagan was publicly an opponent of affirmative action programs. No doubt the administration hoped to garner a few Indian contributions or votes.

Congressional intervention can go into a level of detail that boggles the mind. Congress intervened in the wording of the 1990 race question when the Census Bureau shortened it to include only seven categories. Representative Robert Matsui introduced legislation "in which the formatting of the . . . race question was spelled out, even to the point of stipulating that 'Taiwanese' be one of the subgroups." Both houses passed it. "It was only President Reagan's pocket veto that blocked this extraordinary degree of congressional involvement in what is ordinarily considered the technical side of questionnaire design" (Skerry 2000, 41).

Social scientists deal with levels of irrationality—irrationality, that is, from the point of view of social science—that cannot be much affected by reasoned argument. Stanley Lieberson describes what happened when he attended a conference preparatory to the 1990 census. "I naively suggested that there was no reason to have a Hispanic question separate from the ethnic ancestry question since the former—as far as I could tell—could be classified as a subpart of the latter. Several participants from prominent Hispanic organizations were furious with such a proposal. They were furious, by the way, not at me (just a naive academic), rather it was in the form of a warning to census personnel of the consequences that would follow were this proposal to be taken seriously" (Lieberson 1993, 30).

So, what else is new? Undoubtedly the degree of political intervention, however we understand the term "political," is now at a peak, and to propose changes in the race, Hispanicity, and ancestry questions is probably an exercise in futility. (I wonder whether Reynolds Farley's excellent suggestion that the three questions be combined into one—

"What is this person's primary identity?"—followed by the five "official" group designations, with write-ins permitted under each, has ever gotten any public discussion.)

In the longer view, we know that politics has always played a signifi- 25 cant role in the census. Melissa Nobles tells us the fascinating history of the use of "mulatto" in the census—a term that was included in censuses from 1850 until 1920 (Nobles 2000). It was originally introduced to support slaveholders' arguments that freedom and intermixture was bad for blacks. The abolition of slavery did not end the use of the category—it could still be used, its proponents believed, to argue that races were best off separated and that intermixture produced an inferior human being. In 1888, a member of Congress from Alabama, having decided that it was necessary to go into more detail on this thesis, introduced legislation— which passed both houses and became law—directing the census to "take such steps as may be necessary to ascertain . . . the birth rate and death rate among pure whites, and among negroes, Chinamen, Indians, and half-breeds or hybrids of any description . . . as well as of mulattoes, quadroons, and octoroons" (quoted in Nobles 2000, 56). Indeed, so directed, the census did have categories for quadroons and octoroons in the 1890 census—however useless may have been the results.

The mulattoes, quadroons, and octoroons are gone. What are the longterm prospects for that astonishing list of races in the census and that equally astonishing list of "Hispanics"? Will the lists get longer in the future, or shorter, and what factors might affect their future?

This is an interesting exercise in forecasting and prediction. It is possible that the pressures that derive from affirmative action and the hope for benefits from it, for example, will decline as affirmative action itself is restricted. It has already been banned, by public referendum, judicial action, or administrative action, in the public colleges and universities of four states. One effect of this ban has been an increase in the number of students giving no racial or ethnic identity to university authorities. There has been a substantial increase in the number of such students at the University of California at Berkeley. Why identify oneself if there is no longer a benefit in doing so? Is there an incipient revolt one can detect against the degree of racial and ethnic categorization that has been institutionalized, a revolt that will reduce further the reliability of these questions?

Much of the institutionalization of these categories in the census can be traced to the Voting Rights Act, and the ill-advised extension of this act in 1975 to "language minorities," persons of Spanish heritage, American Indians, and Asian Americans. I do not know what evidence there was, even in 1975, that these groups were prevented from voting because of lack of knowledge of English. This act requires hundreds of jurisdictions to produce voting materials in various languages—itself an irritation in various parts of the country. I wonder whether there is any evidence this has increased voting among members of these groups.

(I would guess there is not.) These provisions require the census to tabulate and distribute census small-area data on the groups protected in the Voting Rights Act very rapidly after a census has been taken.

There is an inherent contradiction between the assumptions of this act and the requirement that one know English to be naturalized as a citizen. When a large number of Jewish immigrants spoke Yiddish and read only Yiddish-language newspapers, they had no trouble voting in substantial numbers equivalent to their English-speaking neighbors—even electing Socialist legislators. Are matters very different for current immigrants speaking foreign languages? Will these provisions survive, even to the census of 2010? Note that whenever a measure to declare English the "official language" gets on the ballot, as it has in a number of states, it passes. This suggests a popular hostility to these Voting Rights Act provisions. How long would they survive if submitted to a popular vote? The original point of the act was to overcome barriers to voting by blacks in the South, which were indeed great, were enforced by white officials, and had little to do with knowledge of English. The bilingual voting assistance provisions come up for renewal in 2007. Is it possible that some bold member of Congress will suggest that they are no longer needed?

All this suggests that the present distribution of political forces is not 30 eternal, and the time may come when the questions now used for race and Hispanicity will seem as outlandish as the 1890 attempt to count quadroons and octoroons. The powerful assimilatory forces in American life are at work—working more slowly, it is true, for blacks than for other groups but still working to an end that will change how the census asks about race, Hispanicity, and ancestry. I hope that change comes about not because of some xenophobic revolt against this excessive census involvement in racial and ethnic categorization but because the members of the groups so marked out themselves no longer see any reason for the U.S. government to inquire officially into an ever murkier and indeterminate racial and ethnic identity.

Notes

1. My proposal is most easily found in Hartman 1997. It originally appeared in *Poverty and Race*, the newsletter of the Poverty and Race Research Action Council.

2. On the mix of ethnicities, see the impressive demonstration in Perlmann 2000. It is also evident in the analysis of responses to the ancestry question presented in Lieberson and Waters 1998.

References

Anderson, Margo J., & Fienberg, Stephen E. (1999). *Who Counts? The Politics of Census-Taking in Contemporary America*. New York: Russell Sage Foundation.

Bryant, Barbara Everitt, & Dunn, William. (1995). *Moving Power and Money: The Politics of Census Taking*. Ithaca: New Strategist Publications.

Hartman, Chester. (Ed.) (1997). *Double Exposure: Poverty and Race in America*. Armonk: M. E. Sharpe.

Lieberson, Stanley. (1993). "The Enumeration of Ethnic and Racial Groups in the Census: Some Devilish Principles." In *Challenges of Measuring an Ethnic World*. Proceedings of the Joint Canada-United States Conference on the Measurement of Ethnicity. Washington: U.S. Department of Commerce, U.S. Bureau of the Census.

Lieberson, Stanley, & Waters, Mary. (1988). *From Many Strands*. New York: Russell Sage Foundation.

Mitroff, Ian I., Mason, Richard O., & Barabba, Vincent P. (1983). *The 1980 Census: Policymaking Amid Turbulence*. Lexington: Lexington Books.

Nobles, Melissa. (2000). *Shades of Citizenship*. Stanford: Stanford University Press.

Perlmann, Joel. (2000). "Demographic Outcomes of Ethnic Intermarriage in American History: Italian-Americans Through Four Generations." Working Paper 312. Annandale-on-Hudson: Jerome Levy Economics Institute.

Skerry, Peter. (2000). *Counting on the Census: Race, Group Identity, and the Evasion of Politics*. Washington: Brookings Institution.

READING AND DISCUSSION QUESTIONS

1. Glazer is discussing a change in the census form that he suggested "a few years ago." (The article was published in 2002.) What was his proposal?

2. Why does he feel his proposal offers an improvement over the current census form's questions about race and ethnicity?

3. What warrant or warrants underlie his argument?

4. Does his proposal seem to be reasonable? Does it seem to be an improvement on the current form?

5. This article by Glazer appeared on the Web before it was published in print form in a collection of essays. In the online article, Glazer had no documentation. He did have a note, however, that explained that a version with documentation was forthcoming in print. Is there less need for documentation when a piece of writing appears in electronic form? Why add documentation only when the piece moves into print?

WRITING SUGGESTIONS

6. Write an essay in which you either agree or disagree with Glazer's proposed change.

7. Glazer argues that ethnic and racial lines become blurred quickly after a short time in America. Do you feel that is a positive or a negative result of immigration to America?

8. Why do so many forms that we fill out ask for our race or national origin? Are there some situations in which race and national origin are relevant and others in which they are not? Explain. (Can you think of situations in which it is unlawful to ask such a question?)

Absolutely. Government Has No Business Interfering with What You Eat

RADLEY BALKO

Nutrition activists are agitating for a panoply of initiatives that would bring the government between you and your waistline. President Bush earmarked $125 million in his budget for the encouragement of healthy lifestyles. State legislatures and school boards have begun banning snacks and soda from school campuses and vending machines. Several state legislators and Oakland, California, Mayor Jerry Brown, among others, have called for a "fat tax" on high-calorie foods. Congress is considering menu-labeling legislation that would force chain restaurants to list fat, sodium and calories for each item.

That is precisely the wrong way to fight obesity. Instead of intervening in the array of food options available to Americans, our government ought to be working to foster a personal sense of responsibility for our health and well-being.

We're doing just the opposite. For decades, America's health-care system has been migrating toward nationalized medicine. We have a law that requires some Americans to pay for other Americans' medicine, and several states bar health insurers from charging lower premiums to people who stay fit. That removes the financial incentive for making healthy decisions. Worse, socialized health care makes us troublingly tolerant of government trespasses on our personal freedom. If my neighbor's heart attack shows up on my tax bill, I'm more likely to support state regulation of what he eats—restrictions on what grocery stores can put on their shelves, for example, or what McDonald's can put between its sesame-seed buns.

The best way to combat the public-health threat of obesity is to remove obesity from the realm of "public health." It's difficult to think of a matter more private and less public than what we choose to put in our bodies. Give Americans moral, financial and personal responsibility for their own health, and obesity is no longer a public matter but a private one—with all the costs, concerns, and worries of being overweight borne only by those people who are actually overweight.

Let each of us take full responsibility for our diet and lifestyle. We're 5 likely to make better decisions when someone else isn't paying for the consequences.

Radley Balko is a policy analyst with the Cato Institute and a columnist for FoxNews.com. This article first appeared in *Time* on June 7, 2004.

Not If Blaming the Victim Is Just an Excuse to Let Industry Off the Hook

KELLY BROWNELL AND MARION NESTLE

The food industry, like any other, must grow to stay in business. One way it does so is by promoting unhealthy foods, particularly to children. Each year kids see more than 10,000 food ads on TV alone, almost all for items like soft drinks, fast foods and sugared cereals. In the same year that the government spent $2 million on its main nutrition-education program, McDonald's spent $500 million on its We Love to See You Smile campaign. It can be no surprise that teenagers consume nearly twice as much soda as milk (the reverse was true twenty years ago) and that 25 percent of all vegetables eaten in the United States are french fries.

To counter criticism, the food industry and pro-business groups use a public relations script focused on personal responsibility. The script has three elements: (1) if people are overweight, it is their own fault; (2) industry responds to consumer demand but does not create it; and (3) insisting that industry change—say, by not marketing to children or requiring restaurants to reveal calories—is an attack on freedom.

Why quarrel with the personal-responsibility argument?

First, it's wrong. The prevalence of obesity increases year after year. Were people less responsible in 2002 than in 2001? Obesity is a global problem. Is irresponsibility an epidemic around the world?

Second, it ignores biology. Humans are hardwired, as a survival strategy, to like foods high in sugar, fat, and calories.   5

Third, the argument is not helpful. Imploring people to eat better and exercise more has been the default approach to obesity for years. That is a failed experiment.

Fourth, personal responsibility is a trap. The argument is startlingly similar to the tobacco industry's efforts to stave off legislative and regula-

---

Kelly D. Brownell is professor and chair of psychology at Yale University and also serves as professor of epidemiology and public health and as director of the Yale Center for Eating and Weight Disorders. He has written numerous books, and one of his articles, "Understanding and Preventing Relapse," published in the *American Psychologist*, is one of the most frequently cited articles in the field of psychology.

Marion Nestle is Paulette Goddard Professor in the Department of Nutrition, Food Studies, and Public Health at New York University. Her degrees include a Ph.D. in molecular biology and an M.P.H. in public health nutrition, both from the University of California, Berkeley. She is the author of *Food Politics: How the Food Industry Influences Nutrition and Health* (2002) and *Safe Food: Bacteria, Biotechnology, and Bioterrorism* (2003), both from University of California Press.

tory interventions. The nation tolerated personal-responsibility arguments from Big Tobacco for decades, with disastrous results.

Governments collude with industry when they shift attention from conditions promoting poor diets to the individuals who consume them. Government should be doing everything it can to create conditions that lead to healthy eating, support parents in raising healthy children, and make decisions in the interests of public health rather than private profit.

DISCUSSION QUESTIONS

1. In his first paragraph, Balko mentions some specific initiatives that would involve some governmental control over Americans' eating habits. Which of them, if any, do you support?

2. What does Balko favor instead of such initiatives?

3. According to Balko, what mistakes have Americans made in the way they have tried to fight obesity?

4. Why do Brownell and Nestle feel that the government must bear some of the blame for obesity?

5. What does the food industry offer in its defense?

6. How did the practice of making health the personal responsibility of the consumer work when it came to smoking?

7. Whose argument do you find more convincing and why?

TAKING THE DEBATE ONLINE

For these and additional research URLs, see bedfordstmartins.com/rottenberg.

- *American Obesity Association*
  www.obesity.org

  The "leading organization for advocacy and education on obesity" presents "the most comprehensive site on obesity" on the Internet.

- *National Association to Advance Fat Acceptance*
  www.naafa.org

  This is the Web site where "fat is not a four-letter word."

- *Understanding Adult Obesity*
  www.niddk.nih.gov/health/nutrit/pubs/unders.htm

  This site, from the National Institute of Diabetes & Digestive & Kidney Diseases, considers the causes and consequences of obesity.

- *Action to Help Fight Obesity*
  http://banzhaf.net/obesitylinks

  This site, maintained by John F. Banzhaf III, Professor of Public Interest Law at George Washington University Law School, contains links to the latest developments in using the court system to fight obesity.

- *National Restaurant Association*
  http://restaurant.org

  This site is devoted to "representing, educating, and promoting the restaurant/hospitality industry"; its position on obesity is that "the emphasis should be on education, personal responsibility, moderation, and healthier lifestyles," not on holding restaurants responsible.

ASSIGNMENTS FOR UNDERSTANDING WARRANTS

1. What are some of the assumptions underlying the preference for *natural* foods and medicines? Can *natural* be clearly defined? Is this preference part of a broader philosophy? Try to evaluate the validity of the assumption.

2. Is plagiarism wrong? What assumptions about education are relevant to the issue of plagiarism? (Some students defend it. What kinds of arguments do they provide?)

3. Choose an advertisement, and examine the warrants on which the advertiser's claim is based.

4. "Religious beliefs are (or are not) necessary to a satisfactory life." Explain the warrants underlying your claim. Define any ambiguous terms.

5. Should students be given a direct voice in the hiring of faculty members? On what warrants about education do you base your answer?

6. Discuss the validity of the warrant in this statement from *The Watch Tower* (a publication of the Jehovah's Witnesses) about genital herpes: "The sexually loose are indeed 'receiving in themselves the full recompense, which was due for their error' (Romans 1:27)."

7. Read the following passage about suicide by the Greek philosopher Aristotle (adapted from his *Ethics*). Then defend or attack his argument, being careful to make clear both Aristotle's and your own warrants.

   Just as a murderer does not have the right to take a mother from her family or a child from her parents and simultaneously to deny society the use of a productive citizen, so the suicide, even though he or she freely chooses to be his or her own victim, does not possess the right to thus diminish the welfare of so many others.

8. In view of increasing interest in health in general, and nutrition and exercise in particular, do you think that universities and colleges should impose physical education requirements? If so, what form should they take? If not, why not? Defend your reasons.

9. Both state and federal governments have been embroiled in controversies concerning the rights of citizens to engage in harmful practices. In Massachusetts, for example, a mandatory seat-belt law was repealed by rebellious voters who considered the law an infringement of their freedom. What principles do you think ought to guide government regulation of dangerous practices?

10. The author of the following passage, Katherine Butler Hathaway, became a hunchback as a result of a childhood illness. Here she writes about the relationship between love and beauty from the point of view of someone who is deformed. Discuss the warrants on which the author bases her conclusion.

> I could secretly pretend that I had a lover . . . but I could never risk showing that I thought such a thing was possible for me . . . with any man. Because of my repeated encounters with the mirror and my irrepressible tendency to forget what I had seen, I had begun to force myself to believe and to remember, and especially to remember, that I would never be chosen for what I imagined to be the supreme and most intimate of all experience. I thought of sexual love as an honor that was too great and too beautiful for the body in which I was doomed to live.

11. People often complain that they aren't listened to. Children complain about parents, patients about doctors, wives about husbands, citizens about government. Are the complaints to be taken literally? Or are they based on unexpressed warrants or assumptions about communication? Choose a specific familiar situation, and explain the meaning of the complaint.

12. Barbara Ehrenreich, in a *Time* essay, defends "talk shows of the *Sally Jessy Raphael* variety" as highly moralistic. Listen to a couple of these shows— *Ricki Lake, Jerry Springer*—and determine what moral assumptions about personal relationships and behavior underlie the advice given to the participants by the host and the audience. Do you think Ehrenreich is correct?

13. Explain which argument you find more convincing, Balko's or Brownell and Nestle's.

CHAPTER 7

Induction, Deduction, and Logical Fallacies

Throughout the book we have pointed out the weaknesses that cause arguments to break down. In the vast majority of cases these weaknesses represent breakdowns in logic or the reasoning process. We call such weaknesses *fallacies*, a term derived from the Latin. Sometimes these false or erroneous arguments are deliberate; in fact, the Latin word *fallere* means "to deceive." But more often these arguments are either carelessly or unintentionally constructed. Thoughtful readers learn to recognize them; thoughtful writers learn to avoid them.

The reasoning process was first given formal expression by Aristotle, the Greek philosopher, almost 2,500 years ago. In his famous treatises, he described the way we try to discover the truth—observing the world, selecting impressions, making inferences, generalizing. In this process Aristotle identified two forms of reasoning: *induction* and *deduction*. Both forms, he realized, are subject to error. Our observations may be incorrect or insufficient, and our conclusions may be faulty because they have violated the rules governing the relationship between statements. The terms we've introduced may be unfamiliar, but the processes of reasoning, as well as the fallacies that violate these processes, are not. Induction and deduction are not reserved only for formal arguments about important problems; they also represent our everyday thinking about the most ordinary matters. As for the fallacies, they, too, unfortunately, may crop up anywhere, whenever we are careless in our use of the reasoning process.

In this chapter we examine some of the most common fallacies. First, however, a closer look at induction and deduction will make clear what happens when fallacies occur.

INDUCTION

Induction is the form of reasoning in which we come to conclusions about the whole on the basis of observations of particular instances. If you notice that prices on the four items you bought in the campus bookstore are higher than similar items in the bookstore in town, you may come to the conclusion that the campus store is a more expensive place to shop. If you also noticed that all three of the instructors you saw on the first day of school were wearing faded jeans and running shoes, you might say that your teachers are generally informal in their dress. In both cases you have made an *inductive leap*, reasoning from what you have learned about a few examples to what you think is true of a whole class of things.

How safe are you in coming to these conclusions? As we've noticed in discussing data and generalization warrants, the reliability of your conclusion depends on the quantity and quality of your observations. Were four items out of the thousands available in the campus store a sufficiently large sample? Would you come to the same conclusion if you chose fifty items? Might another selection have produced a different conclusion? As for the casually dressed instructors, perhaps further investigation would disclose that the teachers wearing jeans were all teaching assistants and that associate and full professors usually wore business clothes. Or the difference might lie in the academic discipline; anthropology teachers might turn out to dress less formally than business school teachers.

In these two situations, you could come closer to verifying your conclusions by further observation and experience—that is, by buying more items at both stores over a longer period of time and by coming into contact with a greater number of professors during a whole semester. Even without pricing every item in both stores or encountering every instructor on campus, you would be more confident of your generalization as the quality and quantity of your samples increased.

In some cases you can observe all the instances in a particular situation. For example, by acquiring information about the religious beliefs of all the residents of the dormitory, you can arrive at an accurate assessment of the number of Buddhists. But since our ability to make definitive observations about everything is limited, we must also make an inductive leap about categories of things that we ourselves can never encounter in their entirety. For some generalizations, as we have learned about evidence, we rely on the testimony of reliable witnesses who report that they have experienced or observed many more instances of the phenomenon. A television documentary may give us information about unwed teenage mothers in a city neighborhood; four girls are interviewed and followed for several days by the reporter. Are these girls typical of thousands of others? A sociologist on the program assures us that, in fact, they are. She herself has consulted with hundreds of other young mothers and can vouch for the fact that a conclusion about them, based on our observation of the four, will be sound. Obviously, though, our conclusion can only be probable, not certain. The sociologist's sample is large, but she can account only for hundreds, not thousands, and there may be unexamined cases that will seriously weaken our conclusions.

In other cases, we may rely on a principle known in science as "the uniformity of nature." We assume that certain conclusions about oak trees in the temperate zone of North America, for example, will also be true for oak trees growing elsewhere under similar climatic conditions. We also use this principle in attempting to explain the causes of behavior in human beings. If we discover that institutionalization of some children from infancy results in severe emotional retardation, we think it safe to conclude that under the same circumstances all children would suffer the same consequences. As in the previous example, we are aware that certainty about every case of institutionalization is impossible. With rare exceptions, the process of induction can offer only probability, not certain truth.

SAMPLE ESSAY: AN INDUCTIVE ARGUMENT

True or False: Schools Fail Immigrants

RICHARD ROTHSTEIN

A common indictment of public schools is that they no longer offer upward mobility to most immigrants. It is said that in the first half of the twentieth century, children learned English, went to college, and joined the middle class but that many of today's immigrants are more likely to drop out, take dead-end jobs, or end up in prison.

Many true accounts reinforce these beliefs. But less noticed are equally valid anecdotes pointing to an opposite claim.

Policy by anecdote is flawed because too often we notice only what confirms our preconceptions. California's recent experience with Mexican immigrants provides ample material for stories about school failure. But on a day to celebrate the American promise, we might also turn to anecdotes of another kind.

Richard Rothstein is a research associate of the Economic Policy Institute, a senior correspondent of the *American Prospect*, and the national education columnist of the *New York Times*, where this article appeared on July 4, 2001. He is the author of *The Way We Were: Myths and Realities of America's Student Achievement* (1997).

Recent college commencements across California featured many immigrants from impoverished families whose first language was Spanish, who came through much-maligned bilingual education programs, learned English, and now head for graduate schools or professions.

At California State University at Fresno, for example, about 700 of   5
4,000 graduates this spring were Latino, typically the first in their families to attend college. Top-ranked were Pedro Nava and Maria Rocio Magaña, Mexican-born children of farm laborers and cannery workers.

Mr. Nava did not settle in the United States until the third grade. Before that, he lived in migrant labor camps during harvests and in Mexico the rest of the year. His California schooling was in Spanish until the fifth grade, when he was moved to English instruction. Now, with a college degree, he has enrolled in management and teacher training courses.

Ms. Magaña did not place into English classes until the second half of the eleventh grade. Now fluent in both academic and conversational English, she will soon begin a Ph.D. program in anthropology at the University of Chicago.

Their achievements are not unique. Both credit success to their mothers' emphasis on education. Both mothers enrolled in English and high school equivalency courses at the local community college.

Across California, these two-year institutions play an especially important role for immigrants.

Lourdes Andrade just finished her junior year at Brown University,   10
having transferred there after getting associate of arts degrees in history and liberal arts at Oxnard Community College, about forty miles northwest of Los Angeles.

Ms. Andrade arrived here at the age of four and all through elementary school worked with her mother making beds and cleaning bathrooms in hotels. Ms. Andrade, too, attributes her success to her mother's strong academic pressure and also to mentoring she received in a federally financed program to give extra academic support to migrant children.

The program's director, Lorenzo Moraza, also grew up speaking only Spanish. Now a school principal, Mr. Moraza estimates that about 30 percent of the immigrant children he has worked with acquired public school records that led them to college. Those who receive bachelor's degrees are many fewer, but Mr. Moraza says he thinks most drop out of college for economic reasons, not academic ones.

At the Fresno campus, nearly two-thirds of the immigrants and children of immigrants who enter as freshmen eventually graduate. The university operates special support services to help them do so.

You cannot spend time in California without noticing an extensive middle class of Latino schoolteachers, doctors, lawyers, and small-business people. Not all are recent immigrants, but many are. Some attended Catholic schools, but most are products of the public system.

Many had bilingual education in the 1970s, 80s, and 90s. California has now banned such instruction, assuming it failed.

There are plenty of anecdotes to support a claim that schools fail im- 15 migrant children or an equally persuasive claim that schools serve them well. Getting better statistics should be a priority. Government numbers do not distinguish between students who are immigrants (or whose parents immigrated) from Hispanics with American roots for several generations.

To help interpret California's experience, the best federal data tell only that in 1996, there were 100,000 college students nationwide who were American citizens born in Mexico. This is less than 1 percent of all college students. But uncounted are even larger numbers of those born here to recent migrants.

Even a balanced collection of anecdotes that include successes as well as failures cannot determine whether California schools are less effective than we should expect, and whether wholesale change is needed to move more immigrants to the middle class. But the answer is certainly more complex than the stereotypes of systematic failure that pervade most accounts.

■ Analysis

An inductive argument proceeds by examining particulars and arriving at a generalization that represents a probable truth. The author of this article arrives at the truth he will defend—that public schools have been more successful than is often acknowledged in moving many immigrants into the middle class—by offering statistical data and a number of stories about immigrants from poor families who have entered graduate school or one of the professions.

Rothstein begins, as many arguers do, with a brief summary of the popular position with which he disagrees. At the end of the third paragraph, he announces that he will provide examples that point to a different conclusion.

The reader should ask three questions of an inductive argument: Is the evidence sufficient? Is it representative? Is it up-to-date? The evidence that Rothstein assembles consists of a series of anecdotes and statistical data about the performance of immigrant students. The success stories of five real persons are impressive, despite limitations imposed by the brevity of the essay, in part because they offer vivid examples of struggle that appeal to our emotions and bring to life an issue with which some of us may not be familiar. But five stories are hardly enough to prove a case; perhaps they are not representative. Rothstein, therefore, adds other data about the rate at which immigrant students graduate and the growing number of Latino professionals and businesspeople.

The reader has some reason to believe that the facts are up-to-date. First, Rothstein writes a regular column for a prestigious daily newspaper whose readers will be quick to find errors in arguments of which they're critical. Second, he refers to "recent college commencements," a graduation "this spring," bilingual education in the 1990s, and "the best federal data for California in 1996." At the same time, he does not claim that his argument is beyond debate, since the data are incomplete. Even the title suggests that the issue is still unsettled. Modesty in the arguer is always welcome and disposes the reader to view the argument more favorably.

DEDUCTION

While induction attempts to arrive at the truth, deduction guarantees sound relationships between statements. If each of a series of statements, called *premises*, is true, deductive logic tells us that the conclusion must also be true. Unlike the conclusions from induction, which are only probable, the conclusions from deduction are certain. The simplest deductive argument consists of two premises and a conclusion. In outline such an argument looks like this:

MAJOR PREMISE: All students with 3.5 averages and above for three years are invited to become members of Kappa Gamma Pi, the honor society.

MINOR PREMISE: George has had a 3.8 average for over three years.

CONCLUSION: Therefore, he will be invited to join Kappa Gamma Pi.

This deductive conclusion is *valid* or logically consistent because it follows necessarily from the premises. No other conclusion is possible. Validity, however, refers only to the form of the argument. The argument itself may not be satisfactory if the premises are not true—if Kappa Gamma Pi has imposed other conditions or if George has only a 3.4 average. The difference between truth and validity is important because it alerts us to the necessity for examining the truth of the premises before we decide that the conclusion is sound.

One way of discovering how the deductive process works is to look at the methods used by Sherlock Holmes, that most famous of literary detectives, in solving his mysteries. His reasoning process follows a familiar pattern. Through the inductive process—that is, observing the particulars of the world—he came to certain conclusions about those particulars. Then he applied deductive reasoning to come to a conclusion about a particular person or event.

On one occasion Holmes observed that a man sitting opposite him on a train had chalk dust on his fingers. From this observation Holmes deduced that the man was a schoolteacher. If his thinking were outlined, it would take the form of the syllogism, the classic form of deductive reasoning:

MAJOR PREMISE: All men with chalk dust on their fingers are schoolteachers.

MINOR PREMISE: This man has chalk dust on his fingers.

CONCLUSION: Therefore, this man is a schoolteacher.

One dictionary defines *syllogism* as "a formula of argument consisting of three propositions." The first proposition is called the major premise and offers a generalization about a large group or class. This generalization has been arrived at through inductive reasoning or observation of particulars. The second proposition is called the minor premise, and it makes a statement about a member of that group or class. The third proposition is the conclusion, which links the other two propositions, in much the same way that the warrant links the support and the claim.

If we look back at the syllogism that summarizes Holmes's thinking, we see how it represents the deductive process. The major premise, the first statement, is an inductive generalization, a statement arrived at after observation of a number of men with chalk on their fingers. The minor premise, the second statement, assigns a particular member, the man on the train, to the general class of those who have dust on their fingers.

But although the argument may be logical, it is faulty. The deductive argument is only as strong as its premises. As Lionel Ruby pointed out, Sherlock Holmes was often wrong.[1] Holmes once deduced from the size of a large hat found in the street that the owner was intelligent. He obviously believed that a large head meant a large brain and that a large brain indicated intelligence. Had he lived one hundred years later, new information about the relationship of brain size to intelligence would have enabled him to come to a different and better conclusion.

In this case, we might first object to the major premise, the generalization that all men with chalk dust on their fingers are schoolteachers. Is it true? Perhaps all the men with dusty fingers whom Holmes had so far observed had turned out to be schoolteachers, but was his sample sufficiently large to allow him to conclude that all dust-fingered men, even those with whom he might never have contact, were teachers? Were there no other vocations or situations that might require the use of chalk? Draftsmen or carpenters or tailors or artists might have fingers just as white as those of schoolteachers. In other words, Holmes may have ascertained that all schoolteachers have chalk dust on their fingers, but he

---

[1] *The Art of Making Sense* (Philadelphia: Lippincott, 1954), ch. 17.

had not determined that *only* schoolteachers can be thus identified. Sometimes it is helpful to draw circles representing the various groups in their relation to the whole.

If a large circle (see the figure below) represents all those who have chalk dust on their fingers, we see that several different groups may be contained in this universe. To be safe, Holmes should have deduced that the man on the train *might* have been a schoolteacher; he was not safe in deducing more than that. Obviously, if the inductive generalization or major premise is false, the conclusion of the particular argument is also false or invalid.

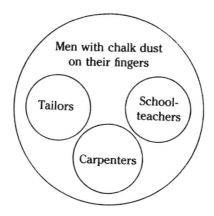

The deductive argument may also go wrong elsewhere. What if the minor premise is untrue? Could Holmes have mistaken the source of the white powder on the man's fingers? Suppose it was not chalk dust but flour or confectioner's sugar or talcum or heroin? Any of these possibilities would weaken or invalidate his conclusion.

Another example, closer to the kinds of arguments you will examine, reveals the flaw in the deductive process.

MAJOR PREMISE: All Communists oppose organized religion.

MINOR PREMISE: Robert Roe opposes organized religion.

CONCLUSION: Therefore, Robert Roe is a Communist.

The common name for this fallacy is "guilt by association." The fact that two things share an attribute does not mean that they are the same thing. The following diagram makes clear that Robert Roe and Communists do not necessarily share all attributes. Remembering that Holmes may have misinterpreted the signs of chalk on the traveler's fingers, we may also want to question whether Robert Roe's opposition to organized religion has been misinterpreted.

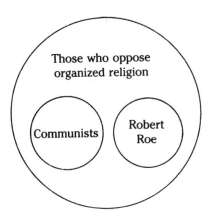

An example from history shows us how such an argument may be used. In a campaign speech during the summer of 1952, Senator Joseph McCarthy, who had made a reputation as a tireless enemy of communism, said, "I do not tell you that Schlesinger, Stevenson's number one man, number one braintrust, I don't tell you he's a Communist. I have no information on that point. But I do know that if he were a Communist he would also ridicule religion as Schlesinger has done."[2] This is an argument based on a sign warrant. Clearly the sign referred to by Senator McCarthy, ridicule of religion, would not be sufficient to characterize someone as a Communist.

Some deductive arguments give trouble because one of the premises, usually the major premise, is omitted. As in the warrants we examined in Chapter 6, a failure to evaluate the truth of the unexpressed premise may lead to an invalid conclusion. When only two parts of the syllogism appear, we call the resulting form an *enthymeme*. Suppose we overhear the following snatch of conversation:

> *"Did you hear about Jean's father? He had a heart attack last week."*
> *"That's too bad. But I'm not surprised. I know he always refused to go for his annual physical checkups."*

The second speaker has used an unexpressed major premise, the cause-and-effect warrant "If you have annual physical checkups, you can avoid heart attacks." He does not express it because he assumes that it is unnecessary to do so. The first speaker recognizes the unspoken warrant and may agree with it. Or the first speaker may produce evidence from reputable sources that such a generalization is by no means universally true, in which case the conclusion of the second speaker is suspect.

---

[2]Joseph R. McCarthy, "The Red-Tinted Washington Crowd," speech delivered to a Republican campaign meeting at Appleton, Wisconsin, November 3, 1952.

A knowledge of the deductive process can help guide you toward an evaluation of the soundness of your reasoning in an argument you are constructing. The syllogism is often clearer than an outline in establishing the relations between the different parts of an argument.

Suppose you wanted to argue that your former high school should introduce a dress code. You might begin by asking these questions: What would be the purpose of such a regulation? How would a dress code fulfill that purpose? What reasons could you provide to support your claim?

Then you might set down part of your argument like this:

Dressing in different styles makes students more aware of social differences among themselves.

The students in this school dress in many different styles.

Therefore, they are more aware of differences in social status among the student body.

As you diagram this first part of the argument, you should ask two sets of questions:

1. Is the major premise true? Do differences in dress cause awareness of differences in social status? Has my experience confirmed this?

2. Is the minor premise true? Has my observation confirmed this?

The conclusion, of course, represents something that you don't have to observe. You can deduce with certainty that it is true if both the major and minor premises are true.

So far the testing of your argument has been relatively easy because you have been concerned with the testing of observation and experience. Now you must examine something that does not appear in the syllogism. You have determined certain facts about perceptions of social status, but you have not arrived at the policy you want to recommend: that a dress code should be mandated. Notice that the dress code argument is based on acceptance of a moral value.

Reducing awareness of social differences is a desirable goal for the school.

A uniform dress code would help to achieve that goal.

Therefore, students should be required to dress uniformly.

The major premise in this syllogism is clearly different from the previous one. While the premise in the previous syllogism can be tested by examining sufficient examples to determine probability, this statement, about the desirability of the goal, is a value judgment and cannot be proved by counting examples. Whether equality of social status is a desirable goal depends on an appeal to other, more basic values.

Setting down your own or someone else's argument in this form will not necessarily give you the answers to questions about how to support your claim, but it should clearly indicate what your claims are and, above all, what logical connections exist between your statements.

SAMPLE ANNOTATED ESSAY:
A DEDUCTIVE ARGUMENT

Divorce and Our National Values

PETER D. KRAMER

Introduction: The problem: a marital crisis caused by opposing views of marriage

How shall we resolve a marital crisis? Consider an example from the advice column of Ann Landers. An "Iowa Wife" wrote to ask what she should do about her husband's habit, after thirty years of marriage, of reading magazines at table when the couple dined out. Ann Landers advised the wife to engage her husband by studying subjects of interest to him.

Examples of opposing views

Readers from around the country protested. A "Fourteen-Year-Old Girl in Pennsylvania" crystallized the objections: "You told the wife to read up on sports or business, whatever he was interested in, even though it might be boring to her. Doesn't that defeat the basic idea of being your own self?" Chastened, Ann Landers changed course, updated her stance: Reading at table is a hostile act, perhaps even grounds for divorce.

When it comes to marriage, Ann Landers seems a reasonable barometer of our values. In practical terms, reading the sports pages might work for some Iowa wife — but we do not believe that is how spouses ought to behave. Only the second response, consider divorce, expresses our overriding respect for autonomy, for the unique and separate self.

Claim of fact or thesis statement: Divorce expresses respect for the separate self.
A proposed solution to the problem: "covenant marriage"

Look south now from Iowa and Pennsylvania to Louisiana, where a new law allows couples to opt for a "covenant marriage" — terminable only

Peter D. Kramer, a clinical professor of psychiatry at Brown University, is the author of *Listening to Prozac* (1993), *Should You Leave?* (1997), and the novel *Spectacular Happiness* (2001). This article appeared on the op-ed page of the *New York Times* on August 29, 1997.

after a lengthy separation or because of adultery, abandonment, abuse, or imprisonment. The law has been praised by many as an expedient against the epidemic of divorce and an incarnation of our "traditional values."

Whether the law will lower the divorce rate is   5 an empirical question to be decided in the future, but it is not too soon to ask: Does covenant marriage express the values we live by?

History seems to say no. American literature's one great self-help book is *Walden,* a paean to self-reliance and an homage to Henry David Thoreau's favorite preacher, Ralph Waldo Emerson, who declaimed: "Say to them, O father, O mother, O wife, O brother, O friend, I have lived with you after appearances hitherto. Henceforward, I am the truth's. . . . I must be myself. I cannot break my self any longer for you, or you."

The economic philosophy we proudly export, fundamentalist capitalism, says that society functions best when members act in a self-interested manner. The nation's founding document is a bill of divorcement. Autonomy is the characteristic American virtue.

As a psychiatrist, I see this value embedded in our psychotherapy, the craft that both shapes and expresses the prevailing common sense. In the early 1970s, Carl Rogers, known as the "Psychologist of America," encapsulated the post–World War II version of our ideals: A successful marriage is one that increases the "self-actualization" of each member. Of a failed union, he wrote: "If Jennifer had from the first insisted on being her true self, the marriage would have had much more strife and much more hope."

Rogers was expressing the predominant viewpoint; for most of the past fifty years, enhanced autonomy has been a goal of psychotherapy. Erik Erikson began the trend by boldly proclaiming that the search for identity had become as important in his time as the study of sexuality was in Freud's. Later, Murray Bowen, a founder of family therapy, invoked a scale of maturity whose measure is a person's ability to maintain his or her beliefs in the face of family pressures. The useful response to crises within couples, Bowen suggested, is to hold fast to your values and challenge your partner to rise to meet your level of maturity.

But autonomy was a value for men only, and 10 largely it was pseudoautonomy, the successful man propped up by the indentured wife and overburdened mother. (No doubt Thoreau sent his clothes home for laundering.)

*(3) autonomy
extended to women*

The self-help movement, beginning in the 1970s, extended this American ideal to women. Once both partners are allowed to be autonomous, the continuation of marriage becomes more truly voluntary. In this sense, an increase in divorce signals social progress.

It signals social progress, except that divorce is itself destructive. So it seems to me the question is whether any other compelling value counterbalances the siren song of self-improvement.

*Another opposing
view: mutuality as a
preferable value*

Turning again to psychotherapy, we do hear arguments for a different type of American value. Answering Erikson's call for individual identity, Helen Merrell Lynd, a sociologist at Sarah Lawrence College, wrote, "Nor must complete finding of oneself . . . precede finding oneself in and through other persons."

Her belief entered psychiatry through the writings of her pupil, Jean Baker Miller. A professor of psychiatry at Boston University, Dr. Miller faults most psychotherapy for elevating autonomy at the expense of qualities important to women, such as mutuality. To feel connected (when there is genuine give-and-take) is to feel worth. Miller wants a transformed culture in which mutuality "is valued as highly as, or more highly than, self-enhancement."

*Refutation (the
warrant): Americans
do not value mutuality.*

Mutuality is an ideal the culture believes it 15 should honor but does not quite. Ours is a society that does a half-hearted job of inculcating compromise, which is to say that we still teach these skills mainly to women. Much of psychotherapy addresses the troubles of those who make great efforts at compromise only to be taken advantage of by selfish partners.

Often the more vulnerable spouse requires rescue through the sort of move Ann Landers recommends, vigorous self-assertion, and even divorce.

Backing for the warrant: Self-assertion in school, office, and marketplace

Mutuality is a worthy ideal, one that might serve as a fit complement and counterbalance to our celebration of the self. But if we do not reward it elsewhere — if in the school and office and marketplace, we celebrate self-assertion — it seems worrisome to ask the institution of marriage to play by different rules.

What is insidious about Louisiana's covenant marriage is that, contrary to claims on its behalf, it is out of touch with our traditional values: self-expression, self-fulfillment, self-reliance.

The Louisiana law invites couples to lash themselves to a morality the broader culture does not support, an arrangement that creates a potential for terrible tensions.

Conclusion: restatement of the claim: Divorce reflects our national values.

Though we profess abhorrence of divorce, I 20 suspect that the divorce rate reflects our national values with great exactness, and that conventional modern marriage — an eternal commitment with loopholes galore — expresses precisely the degree of loss of autonomy that we are able to tolerate.

■ Analysis

A deductive argument proceeds from a general statement that the writer assumes to be true to a conclusion that is more specific. Deductive reasoning is commonplace, although seldom so pure as the definition suggests. In Kramer's article the conclusion appears at the end of paragraph 3: "the second response, consider divorce, expresses our overriding respect for autonomy, for the unique and separate self." The major premise or general statement may be summed up as "Self-actualization is an important American value," and the minor premise as "Divorce is an expression of self-actualization."

Kramer's defense of the major premise is admirable. Despite its brevity, the article brims with significant quotations and instructive examples from literature, psychiatry, and social and economic history that began, as he reminds us, with a "bill of divorcement" (para. 7) from England in 1776.

Finding support for the minor premise is a more difficult exercise because the reader here confronts a *specific* consequence of self-fulfillment — divorce. In all arguments, details and examples test the strength of our generalizations, and while self-actualization is suitably vague, divorce is not. We know that it does not always represent liberation for both partners. Kramer is aware of the problem. In the same paragraph he has insisted both that divorce "signals social progress" and that it is "destructive" (para. 12). He knows that his critics will call on him to reconcile this contradiction.

So far Kramer's argument has been largely factual, proof of the existence of the American ideal. Now he advances onto shakier ground in an examination of values: "the question is whether any other compelling value counterbalances the siren song of self-improvement" (para. 12).

Kramer then responds to those therapists who value a different ideal — that of mutuality, cooperation, and compromise rather than self-assertion. He admires such virtues but finds them unlikely to prevail against the ideal of self-fulfillment that pervades all areas of American life. Divorce, he believes, is simply one expression of that ideal, and he rejects the proposition that we should "ask the institution of marriage to play by different rules" (para. 17).

In deductive argument the conclusion must be true. Questions of social behavior, however, are not so easily proved. We accept the conclusions in such cases if they are plausible — well supported and consistent with experience. Within the limits of this brief essay, Kramer's findings are convincing.

One other element is worth noting: Kramer's objectivity, his role as observer rather than advocate. For the most part, he has excluded himself from the argument. We suspect that, as a psychiatrist, he supports values of self-expression, but in this article he is describing not his own views but those of most Americans. He does not explicitly defend divorce; he explains it. On the whole, this is an effective strategy. We do not need to agree on the morality of self-fulfillment to accept his conclusion.

A NOTE ON THE SYLLOGISM AND THE TOULMIN MODEL

In examining the classical deductive syllogism, you may have noticed the resemblance of its three-part outline to the three-part structure of claim, support, and warrant that we have used throughout the text to illustrate the elements of argument. We mentioned that the syllogism was articulated over two thousand years ago by the Greek philosopher Aristotle. By contrast, the claim-support-warrant structure is based on the model of argument proposed by the modern British philosopher Stephen Toulmin.

Now, there is every reason to think that all models of argument will share some similarities. Nevertheless, the differences between the formal syllogism and the informal Toulmin model suggest that the latter is a more effective instrument for writers who want to know which questions to ask, both before they begin and during the process of developing their arguments.

The syllogism is useful for laying out the basic elements of an argument, as we have seen in several examples. It lends itself more readily to simple arguments. The following syllogism summarizes a familiar argument.

MAJOR PREMISE: Advertising of things harmful to our health should be legally banned.

MINOR PREMISE: Cigarettes are harmful to our health.

CONCLUSION: Therefore, advertising of cigarettes should be legally banned.

Cast in the form of a Toulmin outline, the argument looks like this:

CLAIM: Advertising of cigarettes should be legally banned.

SUPPORT (EVIDENCE):   Cigarettes are harmful to our health.

WARRANT: Advertising of things harmful to our health should be legally banned.

or in diagram form:

> *Support* ——————————————▶ *Claim*
> Cigarettes are harmful   Advertising of cigarettes
> to our health.   should be legally banned.
>
> *Warrant*
> Advertising of things harmful to our
> health should be legally banned.

In both the syllogism and the Toulmin model the principal elements of the argument are expressed in three statements. You can see that the claim in the Toulmin model is the conclusion in the syllogism—that is, the proposition that you are trying to prove. The evidence (support) in the Toulmin model corresponds to the minor premise in the syllogism. And the warrant in the Toulmin model resembles the major premise of the syllogism.

But the differences are significant. One difference is the use of language. The syllogism represents an argument "in which the validity of the assumption underlying the inference 'leap' is uncontested."[3] That is, the words "major premise" seem to suggest that the assumption has been proved. They do not emphasize that an analysis of the premise—"Advertising of things harmful to our health should be legally banned"—is nec-

---

[3] Wayne E. Brockenreide and Douglas Ehninger, "Toulmin on Argument: An Interpretation and Application," *Contemporary Theories of Rhetoric: Selected Readings*, ed. Richard L. Johannesen (New York: Harper and Row, 1971), p. 245. This comparative analysis is indebted to Brockenreide and Ehninger's influential article.

essary before we can decide that the conclusion is acceptable. Of course, a careful arguer will try to establish the truth and validity of all parts of the syllogism, but the terms in which the syllogism is framed do not encourage him or her to examine the real relationship among the three elements. Sometimes the enthymeme (see p. 277), which uses only two elements in the argument and suppresses the third, makes analyzing the relationship even more difficult.

In the Toulmin model, the use of the term *warrant* indicates that the validity of the proposition must be established to *guarantee* the claim or make the crossing from support to claim. It makes clear that the arguer must ask *why* such advertising must be banned.

Nor is the term *minor premise* as useful to the arguer as "support." The word *support* instructs the arguer that he or she must take steps to provide the claim with factual evidence or an appeal to values.

A second difference is that while the syllogism is essentially static, with all three parts logically locked into place, the Toulmin model suggests that an argument is a *movement* from support to claim by way of the warrant, which acts as a bridge. Toulmin introduced the concept of warrant by asking "How do you get there?" (His first two questions, introducing the claim and support, were, "What are you trying to prove?" and "What have you got to go on?")

Lastly, recall that in addition to the three basic elements, the Toulmin model offers supplementary elements of argument. The *qualifier,* in the form of words like "probably" or "more likely," shows that the claim is not absolute. The *backing* offers support for the validity of the warrant. The *reservation* suggests that the validity of the warrant may be limited. These additional elements, which refine and expand the argument itself, reflect the real flexibility and complexity of the argumentative process.

COMMON FALLACIES

In this necessarily brief review it would be impossible to discuss all the fallacies listed by logicians, but we can examine the ones most likely to be found in the arguments you will read and write. Fallacies are difficult to classify, first, because there are literally dozens of systems for classifying, and second, because under any system there is always a good deal of overlap. Our discussion of the reasoning process, however, tells us where faulty reasoning occurs.

Inductive fallacies, as we know, result from the wrong use of evidence: That is, the arguer leaps to a conclusion on the basis of an insufficient sample, ignoring evidence that might have altered his or her conclusion. Deductive fallacies, on the other hand, result from a failure to follow the logic of a series of statements. Here the arguer neglects to make a clear connection between the parts of his or her argument. One of the commonest strategies is the introduction of an irrelevant issue, one that has little or no direct bearing on the development of the claim and serves only to distract the reader.

It's helpful to remember that, even if you cannot name the particular fallacy, you can learn to recognize it and not only refute it in the arguments of others but avoid it in your own as well.

■ 1. Hasty Generalization

In Chapter 5 (see pp. 166–67) we discussed the dangers in drawing conclusions on the basis of insufficient evidence. Many of our prejudices are a result of hasty generalization. A prejudice is literally a judgment made before the facts are in. On the basis of experience with two or three members of an ethnic group, for example, we may form the prejudice that all members of the group share the characteristics that we have attributed to the two or three in our experience. (See Gordon Allport, "The Nature of Prejudice," on p. 80.)

Superstitions are also based in part on hasty generalization. As a result of a very small number of experiences with black cats, broken mirrors, Friday the thirteenth, or spilled salt, some people will assume a cause-and-effect relation between these signs and misfortunes. *Superstition* has been defined as "a notion maintained despite evidence to the contrary." The evidence would certainly show that, contrary to the superstitious belief, in a lifetime hundreds of such "unlucky" signs are not followed by unfortunate events. To generalize about a connection is therefore unjustified.

■ 2. Faulty Use of Authority

Faulty use of authority—the attempt to bolster claims by citing the opinions of experts—was discussed in Chapter 5. Both writers and readers need to be especially aware of the testimony of authorities who may disagree with those cited. In circumstances where experts disagree, you are encouraged to undertake a careful evaluation and comparison of credentials.

■ 3. Post Hoc or Doubtful Cause

The entire Latin term for this fallacy is *post hoc, ergo propter hoc,* meaning, "After this, therefore because of this." The arguer infers that because one event follows another event, the first event must be the cause of the second. But proximity of events or conditions does not guarantee a causal relation. The rooster crows every morning at 5:00 and, seeing the sun rise immediately after, decides that his crowing has caused the sun to rise. A month after A-bomb tests are concluded, tornadoes damage the area where the tests were held, and residents decide that the tests caused the tornadoes. After the school principal suspends daily prayers in the classroom, acts of vandalism increase, and some parents are convinced that failure to conduct prayer is responsible for the rise in vandalism. In each of these cases, the fact that one event follows another does not prove a causal connection. The two events may be coincidental, or the first event may be only one, and an insignificant one, of many causes that have produced the second event. The reader or writer of causal arguments must determine whether another more plausible explanation exists and whether several causes have combined to produce the effect. Perhaps the suspension of prayer was only one of a number of related causes: a decline in disciplinary action, a relaxation of academic standards, a change in school administration, and changes in family structure in the school community.

In the previous section we saw that superstitions are the result not only of hasty generalization but also of the willingness to find a cause-and-effect connection in the juxtaposition of two events. A belief in astrological signs also derives from erroneous inferences about cause and effect. Only a very few of the millions of people who consult the astrology charts every day in newspapers and magazines have submitted the predictions to statistical analysis. A curious reader might try this strategy: Save the columns, usually at the beginning or end of the year, in which astrologers and clairvoyants make predictions for events in the coming year, allegedly based on their reading of the stars and other signs. At the end of the year evaluate the percentage of predictions that were fulfilled. The number will be very small. But even if some of the predictions prove true, there may be other less fanciful explanations for their accuracy.

In defending simple explanations against complex ones, philosophers and scientists often refer to a maxim called *Occam's razor,* a principle formulated by the medieval philosopher and theologian William of Occam. A modern science writer says this principle "urges a preference for the simplest hypothesis that does all we want it to do."[4] Bertrand Russell, the twentieth-century British philosopher, explained it this way:

> It is vain to do with more what can be done with fewer. That is to say, if everything in some science can be interpreted without assuming this or that hypothetical entity, there is no ground for assuming it. I have myself found this a most fruitful principle in logical analysis.[5]

In other words, choose the simpler, more credible explanation wherever possible.

We all share the belief that scientific experimentation and research can answer questions about a wide range of natural and social phenomena: evolutionary development, hurricanes, disease, crime, poverty. It is

---

[4]Martin Gardner, *The Whys of a Philosophical Scrivener* (New York: Quill, 1983), p. 174.

[5]*Dictionary of Mind, Matter and Morals* (New York: Philosophical Library, 1952), p. 166.

true that repeated experiments in controlled situations can establish what seem to be solid relations suggesting cause and effect. But even scientists prefer to talk not about cause but about an extremely high probability that under controlled conditions one event will follow another.

In the social sciences cause-and-effect relations are especially susceptible to challenge. Human experiences can seldom be subjected to laboratory conditions. In addition, the complexity of the social environment makes it difficult, even impossible, to extract one cause from among the many that influence human behavior.

■ 4. False Analogy

Many analogies are merely descriptive and offer no proof of the connection between the two things being compared. In recent years a debate has emerged between weight-loss professionals about the wisdom of urging overweight people to lose weight for health reasons. Susan Wooley, director of the eating disorders clinic at the University of Cincinnati and a professor of psychiatry, offered the following analogy in defense of her view that dieting is dangerous.

> We know that overweight people have a higher mortality rate than thin people. We also know that black people have a higher mortality rate than white people. Do we subject black people to torturous treatments to bleach their skin? Of course not. We have enough sense to know skin-bleaching will not eliminate sickle-cell anemia. So why do we have blind faith that weight loss will cure the diseases associated with obesity?"[6]

But it is clear that the false analogy between black skin and excessive weight does not work. The color of one's skin does not cause sickle-cell anemia, but there is an abundance of proof that excess weight influences mortality.

Historians are fond of using analogical arguments to demonstrate that particular circumstances prevailing in the past are being reproduced in the present. They therefore feel safe in predicting that the present course of history will follow that of the past. British historian Arnold Toynbee argues by analogy that humans' tenure on earth may be limited.

> On the evidence of the past history of life on this planet, even the extinction of the human race is not entirely unlikely. After all, the reign of man on the Earth, if we are right in thinking that man established his present ascendancy in the middle paleolithic age, is so far only about 100,000 years old, and what is that compared to the 500 million or 900 million years during which life has been in existence on the surface of this planet? In the past, other forms of life have enjoyed reigns

[6] *New York Times*, April 12, 1992, sec. C, p. 43.

which have lasted for almost inconceivably longer periods—and which yet at last have come to an end.[7]

Toynbee finds similarities between the limited reigns of other animal species and the possible disappearance of the human race. For this analogy, however, we need to ask whether the conditions of the past, so far as we know them, at all resemble the conditions under which human existence on earth might be terminated. Is the fact that human beings are also members of the animal kingdom sufficient support for this comparison?

■ 5. Ad Hominem

The Latin term *ad hominem* means "against the man" and refers to an attack on the person rather than on the argument or the issue. The assumption in such a fallacy is that if the speaker proves to be unacceptable in some way, his or her statements must also be judged unacceptable. Attacking the author of the statement is a strategy of diversion that prevents the reader from giving attention where it is due—to the issue under discussion.

You might hear someone complain, "What can the priest tell us about marriage? He's never been married himself." This ad hominem accusation ignores the validity of the advice the priest might offer. In the same way an overweight patient might reject the advice on diet by an overweight physician. In politics it is not uncommon for antagonists to attack each other for personal characteristics that may not be relevant to the tasks they will be elected to perform. They may be accused of infidelity to their partners, homosexuality, atheism, or a flamboyant social life. Even if certain accusations should be proved true, voters should not ignore the substance of what politicians do and say in their public offices.

This confusion of private life with professional record also exists in literature and the other arts. According to their biographers, the American writers Thomas Wolfe, Robert Frost, and William Saroyan—to name only a few—and numbers of film stars, including Charlie Chaplin, Joan Crawford, and Bing Crosby, made life miserable for those closest to them. Having read about their unpleasant personal characteristics, some people find it hard to separate the artist from his or her creation, although the personality and character of the artist are often irrelevant to the content of the work.

Ad hominem accusations against the person do *not* constitute a fallacy if the characteristics under attack are relevant to the argument. If the politician is irresponsible and dishonest in the conduct of his or her personal life, we may be justified in thinking that the person will also behave irresponsibly and dishonestly in public office.

---

[7]*Civilization on Trial* (New York: Oxford University Press, 1948), pp. 162–63.

■ 6. False Dilemma

As the name tells us, the false dilemma, sometimes called the *black-white fallacy,* poses an either-or situation. The arguer suggests that only two alternatives exist, although there may be other explanations of or solutions to the problem under discussion. The false dilemma reflects the simplification of a complex problem. Sometimes it is offered out of ignorance or laziness, sometimes to divert attention from the real explanation or solution that the arguer rejects for doubtful reasons.

You may encounter the either-or situation in dilemmas about personal choices. "At the University of Georgia," says one writer, "the measure of a man was football. You either played it or worshiped those who did, and there was no middle ground."[8] Clearly this dilemma—"Love football or you're not a man"—ignores other measures of manhood.

Politics and government offer a wealth of examples. In an interview with the *New York Times* in 1975, the Shah of Iran was asked why he could not introduce into his authoritarian regime greater freedom for his subjects. His reply was, "What's wrong with authority? Is anarchy better?" Apparently he considered that only two paths were open to him—authoritarianism or anarchy. Of course, democracy was also an option, which, perhaps fatally, he declined to consider.

■ 7. Slippery Slope

If an arguer predicts that taking a first step will lead inevitably to a second, usually undesirable step, he or she must provide evidence that this will happen. Otherwise, the arguer is guilty of a slippery slope fallacy.

Asked by an inquiring photographer on the street how he felt about censorship of a pornographic magazine, a man replied, "I don't think any publication should be banned. It's a slippery slope when you start making decisions on what people should be permitted to read. . . . It's a dangerous precedent." Perhaps. But if questioned further, the man should have offered evidence that a ban on some things leads inevitably to a ban on everything.

Predictions based on the danger inherent in taking the first step are commonplace:

> Legalization of abortion will lead to murder of the old and the physically and mentally handicapped.
>
> The Connecticut law allowing sixteen-year-olds and their parents to divorce each other will mean the death of the family.
>
> If we ban handguns, we will end up banning rifles and other hunting weapons.

[8]Phil Gailey, "A Nonsports Fan," *New York Times Magazine,* December 18, 1983, sec. 6, p. 96.

Distinguishing between probable and improbable predictions—that is, recognizing the slippery-slope fallacy—poses special problems because only future developments can verify or refute predictions. For example, in 1941 the imposition of military conscription aroused some opponents to predict that the draft was a precursor of fascism in this country. Only after the war, when 10 million draftees were demobilized, did it become clear that the draft had been an insufficient sign for a prediction of fascism. In this case the slippery-slope prediction of fascism might have been avoided if closer attention had been paid to other influences pointing to the strength of democracy.

More recently, the debate about cloning has raised fears of creation of genetic copies of adults. The *New York Times* reported that

> Many lawmakers today warned that if therapeutic cloning went forward, scientists would step onto a slippery slope that would inevitably lead to cloning people.[9]

Most scientists, however, reject this possibility for the foreseeable future.

Slippery slope predictions are simplistic. They ignore not only the dissimilarities between first and last steps but also the complexity of the developments in any long chain of events.

■ 8. Begging the Question

If the writer makes a statement that assumes that the very question being argued has already been proved, the writer is guilty of begging the question. In a letter to the editor of a college newspaper protesting the failure of the majority of students to meet the writing requirement because they had failed an exemption test, the writer said, "Not exempting all students who honestly qualify for exemption is an insult." But whether the students are honestly qualified is precisely the question that the exemption test was supposed to resolve. The writer has not proved that the students who failed the writing test were qualified for exemption. She has only made an assertion *as if* she had already proved it.

In an effort to raise standards of teaching, some politicians and educators have urged that master teachers be awarded higher salaries. Opponents have argued that such a proposal begs the question because it assumes that the term *master teachers* can be or has already been defined.

Circular reasoning is an extreme example of begging the question: "Women should not be permitted to join men's clubs because the clubs are for men only." The question to be resolved first, of course, is whether clubs for men only should continue to exist.

[9] August 1, 2001, p. A11.

■ 9. Straw Man

The straw-man fallacy consists of an attack on a view similar to but not the same as the one your opponent holds. It is a familiar diversionary tactic. The name probably derives from an old game in which a straw man was set up to divert attention from the real target that a contestant was supposed to knock down.

One of the outstanding examples of the straw-man fallacy occurred in the famous Checkers speech of Senator Richard Nixon. In 1952 during his vice-presidential campaign, Nixon was accused of having appropriated $18,000 in campaign funds for his personal use. At one point in the radio and television speech in which he defended his reputation, he said:

> One other thing I probably should tell you, because if I don't they will probably be saying this about me, too. We did get something, a gift, after the election.
>
> A man down in Texas heard Pat on the radio mention the fact that our two youngsters would like to have a dog, and, believe it or not, the day before we left on this campaign trip we got a message from Union Station in Baltimore saying they had a package for us. We went down to get it. You know what it was?
>
> It was a little cocker spaniel dog, in a crate that he had sent all the way from Texas, black and white, spotted, and our little girl, Tricia, the six-year-old, named it Checkers.
>
> And, you know, the kids, like all kids, loved the dog, and I just want to say this, right now, that regardless of what they say about it, we are going to keep it.[10]

Of course, Nixon knew that the issue was the alleged misappropriation of funds, not the ownership of the dog, which no one had asked him to return.

■ 10. Two Wrongs Make a Right

The two-wrongs-make-a-right fallacy is another example of the way in which attention may be diverted from the question at issue.

After President Jimmy Carter in March 1977 attacked the human rights record of the Soviet Union, Russian officials responded:

> As for the present state of human rights in the United States, it is characterized by the following facts: millions of unemployed, racial discrimination, social inequality of women, infringement of citizens' personal freedom, the growth of crime, and so on.[11]

---

[10]Radio and television address of Senator Nixon from Los Angeles on September 23, 1952.

[11]*New York Times,* March 3, 1977, p. 1.

The Russians made no attempt to deny the failure of *their* human rights record; instead they attacked by pointing out that the Americans are not blameless either.

■ 11. Non Sequitur

The Latin term *non sequitur,* which means "it does not follow," is another fallacy of irrelevance. An advertisement for a book, *Worlds in Collision,* whose theories about the origin of the earth and evolutionary development have been challenged by almost all reputable scientists, states:

> Once rejected as "preposterous"! Critics called it an outrage! It aroused incredible antagonism in scientific and literary circles. Yet half a million copies were sold and for twenty-seven years it remained an outstanding bestseller.

We know, of course, that the popularity of a book does not bestow scientific respectability. The number of sales, therefore, is irrelevant to proof of the book's theoretical soundness—a non sequitur.

Other examples sometimes appear in the comments of political candidates. Donald Trump, the wealthy real-estate developer, in considering a run for president of the United States in 2000, told an interviewer:

> My entire life, I've watched politicians bragging about how poor they are, how they came from nothing, how poor their parents and grandparents were. And I said to myself, if they can stay so poor for so many generations, maybe this isn't the kind of person we want to be electing to higher office. How smart can they be? They're morons. . . . Do you want someone who gets to be president and that's literally the highest paying job he's ever had?[12]

As a brief glance at U.S. history shows, it does not follow that men of small success in the world of commerce are unfit to make sound decisions about matters of state.

■ 12. Ad Populum

Arguers guilty of the *ad populum* fallacy make an appeal to the prejudices of the people (*populum* in Latin). They assume that their claim can be adequately defended without further support if they emphasize a belief or attitude that the audience shares with them. One common form of ad populum is an appeal to patriotism, which may allow arguers to omit evidence that the audience needs for proper evaluation of the claim. In the following advertisement the makers of Zippo lighters made such an appeal in urging readers to buy their product.

[12]*New York Times,* November 28, 1999, p. 11.

It's a grand old lighter. Zippo—the grand old lighter that's made right here in the good old U.S.A.

We truly make an all-American product. The raw materials used in making a Zippo lighter are all right from this great land of ours.

Zippo windproof lighters are proud to be Americans.

■ 13. Appeal to Tradition

In making an appeal to tradition, the arguer assumes that what has existed for a long time and has therefore become a tradition should continue to exist *because* it is a tradition. If the arguer avoids telling his or her reader *why* the tradition should be preserved, he or she may be accused of failing to meet the real issue.

The following statement appeared in a letter defending the membership policy of the Century Club, an all-male club established in New York City in 1847 that was under pressure to admit women. The writer was a Presbyterian minister who opposed the admission of women.

> I am totally opposed to a proposal which would radically change the nature of the Century. . . . A club creates an ethos of its own over the years, and I would deeply deplore a step that would inevitably create an entirely different kind of place.
>
> A club like the Century should surely be unaffected by fashionable whims. . . .[13]

■ 14. Faulty Emotional Appeals

In some discussions of fallacies, appeals to the emotions of the audience are treated as illegitimate or "counterfeit proofs." All such appeals, however, are *not* illegitimate. As we saw in Chapter 5 on support, appeals to the values and emotions of an audience are an appropriate form of persuasion. You can recognize fallacious emotional appeals if (1) they are irrelevant to the argument or draw attention from the issues being argued or (2) they appear to conceal another purpose. Here we treat two of the most popular appeals—to pity and to fear.

Appeals to pity, compassion, and natural willingness to help the unfortunate are particularly hard to resist. The requests for aid by most charitable organizations—for hungry children, victims of disaster, stray animals—offer examples of legitimate appeals. But these appeals to our sympathetic feelings should not divert us from considering other issues in a particular case. It would be wrong, for example, to allow a multiple murderer to escape punishment because he or she had experienced a wretched childhood. Likewise, if you are asked to contribute to a charitable cause, you should try to learn how many unfortunate people or animals are being helped and what percentage of the contribution will be

---

[13] David H. C. Read, letter to the *New York Times,* January 13, 1983, p. 14.

allocated to maintaining the organization and its officers. In some cases the financial records are closed to public review, and only a small share of the contribution will reach the alleged beneficiaries.

Appeals to fear are likely to be even more effective. But they must be based on evidence that fear is an appropriate response to the issues and that it can move an audience toward a solution to the problem. (Fear can also have the adverse effect of preventing people from taking a necessary action.) Insurance companies, for example, make appeals to our fears of destitution for ourselves and our families as a result of injury, unemployment, sickness, and death. These appeals are justified if the possibilities of such destitution are real and if the insurance will provide relief. It would also be legitimate to arouse fear of the consequences of drunk driving, provided, again, that the descriptions were accurate. On the other hand, it would be wrong to induce fear that fluoridation of public water supplies causes cancer without presenting sound evidence of the probability. It would also be wrong to instill a fear of school integration unless convincing proof were offered of undesirable social consequences.

An emotional response by itself is not always the soundest basis for making decisions. Your own experience has probably taught you that in the grip of a strong emotion like love or hate or anger you often overlook good reasons for making different and better choices. Like you, your readers want to be given the opportunity to consider all the available kinds of support for an argument.

Writer's Guide: Avoiding Logical Fallacies

1. If you are making use of induction, that is, drawing a conclusion based on a number of individual examples, do you have enough examples with variety to justify the conclusion? In other words, will your readers be able to make the inductive leap from examples to the conclusion you are asking them to make?

2. If you are making use of deduction, is your conclusion a logical one based on the premises underlying it? To be sure, write out your argument in the form of a syllogism. Also avoid wording your thesis in absolute terms like *all*, *every*, *everyone*, *everybody*, and *always*.

3. It is relatively easy — and sometimes humorous — to notice other writers' logical fallacies. It is harder to notice your own. Use the list of fallacies in this chapter as a checklist as you read the draft of each of your essays with a critical eye, looking for any breakdown in logic. It may be useful to read your essay aloud to someone because if that listener cannot follow your logic, you may need to clarify your points.

On Nation and Race

ADOLF HITLER

There are some truths which are so obvious that for this very reason they are not seen or at least not recognized by ordinary people. They sometimes pass by such truisms as though blind and are most astonished when someone suddenly discovers what everyone really ought to know. Columbus's eggs lie around by the hundreds of thousands, but Columbuses are met with less frequency.

Thus men without exception wander about in the garden of Nature; they imagine that they know practically everything and yet with few exceptions pass blindly by one of the most patent principles of Nature's rule: the inner segregation of the species of all living beings on this earth.

Even the most superficial observation shows that Nature's restricted form of propagation and increase is an almost rigid basic law of all the innumerable forms of expression of her vital urge. Every animal mates only with a member of the same species. The titmouse seeks the titmouse, the finch the finch, the stork the stork, the field mouse the field mouse, the dormouse the dormouse, the wolf the she-wolf, etc.

Only unusual circumstances can change this, primarily the compulsion of captivity or any other cause that makes it impossible to mate within the same species. But then Nature begins to resist this with all possible means, and her most visible protest consists either in refusing further capacity for propagation to bastards or in limiting the fertility of later offspring; in most cases, however, she takes away the power of resistance to disease or hostile attacks.

This is only too natural.   5

Any crossing of two beings not at exactly the same level produces a medium between the level of the two parents. This means: The offspring will probably stand higher than the racially lower parent, but not as high as the higher one. Consequently, it will later succumb in the struggle against the higher level. Such mating is contrary to the will of Nature for a higher breeding of all life. The precondition for this does not lie in associating superior and inferior, but in the total victory of the former. The stronger must dominate and not blend with the weaker, thus sacrificing his own greatness. Only the born weakling can view this as cruel, but he after all is only a weak and limited man; for if this law did not prevail, any conceivable higher development of organic living beings would be unthinkable.

Adolf Hitler (1889–1945) became the Nazi dictator of Germany in the mid-1930s. "On Nation and Race" (editor's title) begins Chapter 11 of *Mein Kampf* (*My Struggle*), vol. 1, published in 1925.

The consequence of this racial purity, universally valid in Nature, is not only the sharp outward delimitation of the various races, but their uniform character in themselves. The fox is always a fox, the goose a goose, the tiger a tiger, etc., and the difference can lie at most in the varying measure of force, strength, intelligence, dexterity, endurance, etc., of the individual specimens. But you will never find a fox who in his inner attitude might, for example, show humanitarian tendencies toward geese, as similarly there is no cat with a friendly inclination toward mice.

Therefore, here, too, the struggle among themselves arises less from inner aversion than from hunger and love. In both cases, Nature looks on calmly, with satisfaction, in fact. In the struggle for daily bread all those who are weak and sickly or less determined succumb, while the struggle of the males for the female grants the right or opportunity to propagate only to the healthiest. And struggle is always a means for improving a species' health and power of resistance and, therefore, a cause of its higher development.

If the process were different, all further and higher development would cease and the opposite would occur. For, since the inferior always predominates numerically over the best, if both had the same possibility of preserving life and propagating, the inferior would multiply so much more rapidly that in the end the best would inevitably be driven into the background, unless a correction of this state of affairs were undertaken. Nature does just this by subjecting the weaker part to such severe living conditions that by them alone the number is limited, and by not permitting the remainder to increase promiscuously, but making a new and ruthless choice according to strength and health.

No more than Nature desires the mating of weaker with stronger in- 10 dividuals, even less does she desire the blending of a higher with a lower race, since, if she did, her whole work of higher breeding, over perhaps hundreds of thousands of years, might be ruined with one blow.

Historical experience offers countless proofs of this. It shows with terrifying clarity that in every mingling of Aryan blood with that of lower peoples the result was the end of the cultured people. North America, whose population consists in by far the largest part of Germanic elements who mixed but little with the lower colored peoples, shows a different humanity and culture from Central and South America, where the predominantly Latin immigrants often mixed with the aborigines on a large scale. By this one example, we can clearly and distinctly recognize the effect of racial mixture. The Germanic inhabitant of the American continent, who has remained racially pure and unmixed, rose to be master of the continent; he will remain the master as long as he does not fall a victim to defilement of the blood.

The result of all racial crossing is therefore in brief always the following:

(a) Lowering of the level of the higher race;

(b) Physical and intellectual regression and hence the beginning of a slowly but surely progressing sickness.

To bring about such a development is, then, nothing else but to sin 15 against the will of the eternal creator.

And as a sin this act is rewarded.

When man attempts to rebel against the iron logic of Nature, he comes into struggle with the principles to which he himself owes his existence as a man. And this attack must lead to his own doom.

Here, of course, we encounter the objection of the modern pacifist, as truly Jewish in its effrontery as it is stupid! "Man's role is to overcome Nature!"

Millions thoughtlessly parrot this Jewish nonsense and end up by really imagining that they themselves represent a kind of conqueror of Nature; though in this they dispose of no other weapon than an idea, and at that such a miserable one, that if it were true no world at all would be conceivable.

But quite aside from the fact that man has never yet conquered Na- 20 ture in anything, but at most has caught hold of and tried to lift one or another corner of her immense gigantic veil of eternal riddles and secrets, that in reality he invents nothing but only discovers everything, that he does not dominate Nature, but has only risen on the basis of his knowledge of various laws and secrets of Nature to be lord over those other living creatures who lack this knowledge — quite aside from all this, an idea cannot overcome the preconditions for the development and being of humanity, since the idea itself depends only on man. Without human beings there is no human idea in this world; therefore, the idea as such is always conditioned by the presence of human beings and hence of all the laws which created the precondition for their existence.

And not only that! Certain ideas are even tied up with certain men. This applies most of all to those ideas whose content originates, not in an exact scientific truth, but in the world of emotion, or, as it is so beautifully and clearly expressed today, reflects an "inner experience." All these ideas, which have nothing to do with cold logic as such, but represent only pure expressions of feeling, ethical conceptions, etc., are chained to the existence of men, to whose intellectual imagination and creative power they owe their existence. Precisely in this case the preservation of these definite races and men is the precondition for the existence of these ideas. Anyone, for example, who really desired the victory of the pacifistic idea in this world with all his heart would have to fight with all the means at his disposal for the conquest of the world by the Germans; for, if the opposite should occur, the last pacifist would die out with the last German, since the rest of the world has never fallen so deeply as our own people, unfortunately, has for this nonsense so contrary to Nature and reason. Then, if we were serious, whether we liked it or not, we would have to wage wars in order to arrive at pacifism. This and nothing else was what Wilson, the American world savior, intended, or so at least our German visionaries believed — and thereby his purpose was fulfilled.

In actual fact the pacifistic-humane idea is perfectly all right perhaps when the highest type of man has previously conquered and subjected the world to an extent that makes him the sole ruler of this earth. Then this idea lacks the power of producing evil effects in exact proportion as its practical application becomes rare and finally impossible. Therefore, first struggle and then we shall see what can be done. Otherwise mankind has passed the high point of its development and the end is not the domination of any ethical idea but barbarism and consequently chaos. At this point someone or other may laugh, but this planet once moved through the ether for millions of years without human beings and it can do so again some day if men forget that they owe their higher existence, not to the ideas of a few crazy ideologists, but to the knowledge and ruthless application of Nature's stern and rigid laws.

Everything we admire on this earth today—science and art, technology and inventions—is only the creative product of a few peoples and originally perhaps of *one* race. On them depends the existence of this whole culture. If they perish, the beauty of this earth will sink into the grave with them.

However much the soil, for example, can influence men, the result of the influence will always be different depending on the races in question. The low fertility of a living space may spur the one race to the highest achievements; in others it will only be the cause of bitterest poverty and final undernourishment with all its consequences. The inner nature of peoples is always determining for the manner in which outward influences will be effective. What leads the one to starvation trains the other to hard work.

All great cultures of the past perished only because the originally cre- 25 ative race died out from blood poisoning.

The ultimate cause of such a decline was their forgetting that all culture depends on men and conversely; hence that to preserve a certain culture the man who creates it must be preserved. This preservation is bound up with the rigid law of necessity and the right to victory of the best and stronger in this world.

Those who want to live, let them fight, and those who do not want to fight in this world of eternal struggle do not deserve to live.

Even if this were hard—that is how it is! Assuredly, however, by far the harder fate is that which strikes the man who thinks he can overcome Nature, but in the last analysis only mocks her. Distress, misfortune, and diseases are her answer.

The man who misjudges and disregards the racial laws actually forfeits the happiness that seems destined to be his. He thwarts the triumphal march of the best race and hence also the precondition for all human progress, and remains, in consequence, burdened with all the sensibility of man, in the animal realm of helpless misery.

It is idle to argue which race or races were the original representative of 30 human culture and hence the real founders of all that we sum up under the word *humanity.* It is simpler to raise the question with regard to the present, and here an easy, clear answer results. All the human culture, all the results of art, science, and technology that we see before us today, are almost exclusively the creative product of the Aryan. This very fact admits of the not unfounded inference that he alone was the founder of all higher humanity, therefore representing the prototype of all that we understand by the word *man*. He is the Prometheus of mankind from whose bright forehead the divine spark of genius has sprung at all times, forever kindling anew that fire of knowledge which illumined the night of silent mysteries and thus caused man to climb the path to mastery over the other beings of this earth. Exclude him—and perhaps after a few thousand years darkness will again descend on the earth, human culture will pass, and the world turn to a desert.

READING AND DISCUSSION QUESTIONS

1. Find places in the essay where Hitler attempts to emphasize the scientific objectivity of his theories.

2. Are some passages difficult to understand? (See, for example, para. 11.) How do you explain the difficulty?

3. In explaining his ideology, how does Hitler misinterpret the statement that "Every animal mates only with a member of the same species" (para. 3)? How would you characterize this fallacy?

4. Hitler uses the theory of evolution and his interpretation of the "survival of the fittest" to justify his racial philosophy. Find the places in the text where Hitler reveals that he misunderstands the theory in its application to human beings.

5. What false evidence about race does Hitler use in his assessment of the racial experience in North America? Examine carefully the last sentence of paragraph 11: "The Germanic inhabitant of the American continent, who has remained racially pure and unmixed, rose to be master of the continent; he will remain the master as long as he does not fall a victim to defilement of the blood."

6. What criticism of Jews does Hitler offer? How does this criticism help to explain Hitler's pathological hatred of Jews?

7. Hitler believes that pacifism is a violation of "Nature and reason" (para. 21). Would modern scientists agree that the laws of nature require unremitting struggle and conflict between human beings—until the master race conquers?

WRITING SUGGESTION

8. Use your responses to the Reading and Discussion Questions as the basis of an essay evaluating Hitler's logic in "On Nation and Race."

9. Do some research in early human history to discover the degree of truth in this statement: "All the human culture, all the results of art, science, and technology that we see before us today, are almost exclusively the creative product of the Aryan" (para. 30). You may want to limit your discussion to one area of human culture.

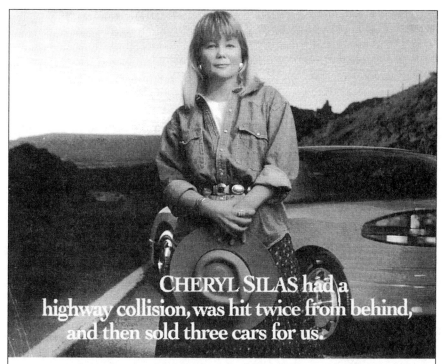

CHERYL SILAS had a highway collision, was hit twice from behind, and then sold three cars for us.

When Cheryl unbuckled her shoulder harness and lap belt, it took her a moment to realize her Saturn coupe was really a mess. And that, remarkably, she wasn't. That's when she decided to get another SC.

Several other people arrived at similar conclusions. A policeman at the accident scene came in soon after and ordered himself a sedan. As did a buddy of his, also on the force. Then Cheryl's brother, glad he still had a sister, bought yet another Saturn in Illinois.

Now, good referrals are important to any product. And we're always glad to have them. But we'd be more than happy if our customers found less dramatic ways to help spread the word.

A DIFFERENT KIND _of_ COMPANY. A DIFFERENT KIND _of_ CAR.

DISCUSSION QUESTIONS

1. What example of inductive reasoning does the advertiser use? How would you evaluate the probability of the conclusion?

2. To what extent does the use of an alleged real person in a narrative contribute to the effectiveness of the advertiser's pitch? Should the ad have contained more factual information?

Show Biz Encourages Looser Teen Sex Habits

SHERYL McCARTHY

As the high school prom season winds down, we are learning more than we ever wanted to know about the social and sexual mores of today's teenagers.

Such as how they're avoiding "dating," opting instead to attend the prom with groups of friends. Everybody has a blast without suffering the angst of waiting for some guy to ask you to be his date, or worrying that the girl you ask will reject you.

This seems a lot healthier than it was when I went to my high school prom. I was lucky enough to have a great date and a wonderful prom night. But I've heard countless women complain thirty years later about missing their prom because nobody invited them. Going as a group takes the power to decide who gets to go out of the boys' hands, and takes the pressure of having to find a date off everybody.

Some of the other recent trends aren't so hot. A newspaper reporter who attended several local proms this year was shocked by the highly sexualized dancing that went on. When I was in school, the occasional guy put you in a back-breaking full-body lock that lasted the duration of a song. But now, virtually all the males and females engage in "freaking" and "backing up" — which amounts to simulating sex on the dance floor.

And there's the growing phenomenon of "hooking up." Having 5 steady boyfriends or girlfriends has been replaced by kids who travel in packs, breaking away to have casual sexual encounters with friends or mere acquaintances. These encounters range from kissing to petting, masturbating each other to oral sex — all without emotional strings. And they say they like it that way.

I find this retreat from intimacy rather depressing. My classmates weren't into sex, by and large. But there was something nice about the boyfriend-girlfriend thing. In endless phone calls or Sunday night sofa-sitting, we achieved a certain emotional intimacy, along with our sexual gropings. The guys may have been thinking mostly about sex, but there was at least an idealized notion of what it meant to be a couple.

The current teenage social scene strikes me as rather aimless. Those who work with teenagers attribute the surge in dirty dancing to the music videos in which young musical stars like Britney Spears, Christina Aguilera, and Beyonce Knowles provocatively shake their scantily-clad booties, and legions of gorgeous females swarming over ordinary-looking

Sheryl McCarthy is on the faculty of the Graduate School of Journalism of Columbia University. She has been a reporter for the *Boston Globe*, the *Baltimore Evening Sun*, and the New York *Daily News* and a national correspondent for ABC News. She is now a columnist for *Newsday*, where this article appeared on June 24, 2004.

men seem to define what relations between males and females are supposed to be.

Tamar Rothenberg, editor of *New Youth Connections*, a newspaper put out by New York City high school students, says she worries about the message the videos give to teenagers trying to figure out what they're supposed to be doing in relationships.

"Hooking-up" apparently results from teenagers wanting to avoid being tied down in relationships that can cause pain and disappointment. Teenage girls may also be rebelling against the old sexual double standard and wanting to have the same freedom as boys. But the girls are often on the giving end of the casual sex, and teens often don't realize that they can catch diseases from oral sex.

The moguls of MTV and BET and the video producers and the titans 10 of hip-hop deserve a lot of the blame for this, and deserve to be booed off any stage where they are hypocritical enough to lament the high rate of teen pregnancy and the social fallout from irresponsible male sexual behavior.

But so do the spineless politicians and educators and the squeamish parents who are far more obsessed with keeping teenagers chaste than with helping them to have responsible relationships.

That's why I applaud groups like Planned Parenthood and *New Youth Connections* that treat teenagers like the semi-adults they are, and try to be helpful instead of self-righteous.

"I'm cool with kids having sex if they're being careful," says Rothenberg. "But they have to understand the possible emotional consequences and the health consequences."

Yeah, it was nice having prom dates who made no sexual demands, and having boyfriends instead of sexual hookups. But times have changed, and, to be helpful to teens living in a more sexualized world, the adults have to change too.

READING AND DISCUSSION QUESTIONS

1. Did McCarthy choose to use an inductive or a deductive approach to her subject?

2. Do you find the conclusions that McCarthy has drawn about today's teens convincing? Are they discredited by your own observations of teens?

3. Do you feel that there are any logical fallacies in McCarthy's argument? If so, what type of fallacies are they?

WRITING SUGGESTIONS

4. Examine how teen dating and/or sex habits are characterized on at least one current television show.

5. How do you respond to McCarthy's indictment of teens' sexual mores?

Food for Thought (and for Credit)

JENNIFER GROSSMAN

Want to combat the epidemic of obesity? Bring back home economics. Before you choke on your 300-calorie, trans-fat-laden Krispy Kreme, consider: Teaching basic nutrition and food preparation is a far less radical remedy than gastric bypass surgery or fast-food lawsuits. And probably far more effective. Obesity tends to invite such drastic solutions because it is so frustratingly difficult to treat. This intractability, coupled with the sad fact that obese children commonly grow up to be obese adults, argues for a preventative approach. As the new school year begins, we need to equip kids with the skills and practical knowledge to take control of their dietary destinies.

Despite its bad rep as Wife Ed 101, home economics has progressive roots. At the turn of the century it "helped transform domesticity into a vehicle to expand women's political power," according to Sarah Stage in *Rethinking Home Economics: Women and the History of a Profession.* In time, focus shifted from social reform to the practical priorities of sanitation and electrification, and then again to an emphasis on homemaking after World War II — giving ammunition to later critics like Betty Friedan who charged home ec with having helped foster the "feminine mystique."

Banished by feminists, Becky Home-ecky was left to wander backwater school districts. For a while it seemed that mandating male participation might salvage the discipline while satisfying political correctness. By the late 1970s one-third of male high school graduates had some home-ec training, whereas they comprised a mere 3.5 percent of home-ec students in 1962. Since then, "home economics has moved from the mainstream to the margins of American high school," according to the United States Department of Education, with even female participation — near universal in the 1950s — plummeting by 67 percent.

What has happened since? Ronald McDonald and Colonel Sanders stepped in as the new mascots of American food culture, while the number of meals consumed outside the home has doubled — from a quarter in 1970 to nearly half today. As a result, market economics has increasingly determined ingredients, nutrient content, and portion size. Agricultural surpluses and technological breakthroughs supplied the

---

Jennifer Grossman is director of the Dole Nutrition Institute, which distributes health information to the public through lectures and publications. Formerly, she was director of Education Policy at the Cato Institute and a speechwriter for President George H. W. Bush. She appears frequently as a commentator on shows such as *Larry King Live*, the *O'Reilly Factor*, the *Today Show*, and *Politically Incorrect*. She has written editorials for the *New York Times*, where this column appeared on September 2, 2003; the *Wall Street Journal*; the *Los Angeles Times*; the *New York Post*; the *Weekly Standard*; the *National Review*; and the *Women's Quarterly*.

cheap sweeteners and hydrogenated oils necessary for food to survive indefinitely on store shelves or under fast-food heat lamps.

Unsurprisingly, the caloric density of such foods soared relative to 5 those consumed at home. Good value no longer meant taste, presentation, and proper nutrition—but merely more-for-less. Thus, the serving of McDonald's French fries that contained 200 calories in 1960 contains 610 today. The lure of large was not limited to fast-food, inflating everything from snack foods to cereal boxes.

But the hunger for home economics didn't die with its academic exile. Martha Stewart made millions filling the void, vexing home-ec haters like Erica Jong for having "earned her freedom by glorifying the slavery of home." Home and Garden TV, the Food Network, and countless publications thrive on topics once taught by home ec.

All of which begs the question: If the free market has done such a good job of picking up the slack, why bring home ec back? Because much of the D.I.Y. (do-it-yourself) culture is divorced from the exigencies of everyday life. It's more like home rec: catering to pampered chefs with maids to clean up the kitchen.

The new home economics should be both pragmatic and egalitarian. Traditional topics—food and nutrition, family studies, home management—should be retooled for the twenty-first century. Children should be able to decipher headlines about the dangers of dioxin or the benefits of antioxidants. Subjects like home finance might include domestic problem-solving: How would you spend $100 to feed a family of four, including a diabetic, a nursing mother, and infant, for one week?

While this kind of training might most benefit those low-income minority children at highest risk of obesity, all children will be better equipped to make smart choices in the face of the more than $33 billion that food companies spend annually to promote their products. And consumer education is just part of the larger purpose: to teach kids to think, make, fix, and generally fend for themselves.

Some detractors will doubtless smell a plot to turn women back into 10 stitching, stirring Stepford Wives. Others will argue that schools should focus on the basics. But what could be more basic than life, food, home and hearth? A generation has grown up since we swept home ec into the dust heap of history and hung up our brooms. It's time to reevaluate the domestic discipline, and recapture lost skills.

READING AND DISCUSSION QUESTIONS

1. How would the students at the high school you attended have responded to a course such as the one Grossman describes?

2. Do you think that offering such a course would be a good idea? Why or why not?

3. How convincing is Grossman's argument that there is a need for consumer education? How convincing is her argument that it should be offered in school?

4. Do you feel there are any logical fallacies in her argument? If so, what type of fallacies are they?

WRITING SUGGESTIONS

5. Write a claim of policy essay arguing that the sort of course Grossman describes should be required of high school students.

6. Write an essay refuting what Grossman suggests.

7. Write an essay in which you argue that the majority of teenagers are responsible consumers or that they are not.

DEBATE: Should the federal government fund embryonic stem-cell research?

Use the Body's "Repair Kit": We Must Pursue Research on Embryonic Stem Cells

CHRISTOPHER REEVE

With the life expectancy of average Americans heading as high as 75 to 80 years, it is our responsibility to do everything possible to protect the quality of life of the present and future generations. A critical factor will be what we do with human embryonic stem cells. These cells have the potential to cure diseases and conditions ranging from Parkinson's and multiple sclerosis to diabetes and heart disease, Alzheimer's, Lou Gehrig's disease, even spinal-cord injuries like my own. They have been called the body's self-repair kit.

Their extraordinary potential is a recent discovery. And much basic research needs to be done before they can be sent to the front lines in the battle against disease. But no obstacle should stand in the way of responsible investigation of their possibilities. To that end, the work should be funded and supervised by the federal government through the National Institutes of Health. That will avoid abuses by for-profit corporations, avoid secrecy and destructive competition between laboratories, and en-

---

Christopher Reeve was a well-established actor when in 1995 he was paralyzed from the shoulders down in a riding accident. From that time until his death in 2004, he served as an outspoken and respected advocate for the sort of stem-cell research he believed would eventually help him and others like him. Through his personal example and his books *Still Me* (1999) and *Nothing Is Impossible: Reflections on a New Life* (2002), he offered hope and inspiration to the disabled and others. This article is from the May 1, 2000, edition of *Time*.

sure the widest possible dissemination of scientific breakthroughs. Human trials should be conducted either on the NIH campus or in carefully monitored clinical facilities.

Fortunately, stem cells are readily available and easily harvested. In fertility clinics, women are given a choice of what to do with unused fertilized embryos: they can be discarded, donated to research, or frozen for future use. Under NIH supervision, scientists should be allowed to take cells only from women who freely consent to their use for research. This process would not be open ended; within one to two years a sufficient number could be gathered and made available to investigators. For those reasons, the ban on federally funded human embryonic stem-cell research should be lifted as quickly as possible.

But why has the use of discarded embryos for research suddenly become such an issue? Is it more ethical for a woman to donate unused embryos that will never become human beings, or to let them be tossed away as so much garbage when they could help save thousands of lives?

Treatment with stem cells has already begun. They have been taken   5 from umbilical cords and become healthy red cells used as a potential cure for sickle-cell anemia. Stem-cell therapy is also being used against certain types of cancer. But those are cells that have significantly differentiated; that is, they are no longer pluripotent, or capable of transforming into other cell types. For the true biological miracles that researchers have only begun to foresee, medical science must turn to undifferentiated stem cells. We need to clear the path for them as rapidly as possible.

Controversy over the treatment of certain diseases is nothing new in this country: witness the overwhelming opposition to government funding of AIDS research in the early '80s. For years the issue was a political football—until a massive grass-roots effort forced legislators to respond. Today, the NIH is authorized to spend approximately $1.8 billion annually on new protocols, and the virus is largely under control in the United States.

While we prolong the stem-cell debate, millions continue to suffer. It is time to harness the power of government and go forward.

The Misleading Debate on Stem-Cell Research

MONA CHAREN

Addressing the Democratic National Convention, Ron Reagan told the delegates that in the debate over funding research on embryonic stem cells, we face a choice between "the future and the past; between reason and ignorance; between true compassion and mere ideology." Not satisfied with that contrast, he elaborated that "a few of these folks (who oppose funding this research) are just grinding a political axe, and they should be ashamed of themselves."

It is Reagan who ought to be ashamed. As the mother of a ten-year-old with juvenile diabetes, I yearn more than most for breakthroughs in scientific research. My son takes between four and six shots of insulin daily and must test his blood sugar by pricking his finger the same number of times. This disease affects every major organ system in the body and places him in the high-risk category for more problems than I care to name. When he settles down to sleep at night, I can never be entirely sure that he won't slip into a coma from a sudden low blood sugar. How happily I would take the disease upon myself if I could only spare him! So please don't lecture me about grinding a political axe.

But like millions of others, I am troubled by the idea of embryonic stem-cell research. It crosses a moral line that this society should be loath to cross—even for the best of motives. Taking the stem cells from human embryos kills them. Before turning to the arguments of the pro-research side, permit a word about the pro-life position. Too many pro-life activists, it seems to me, have argued this case on the wrong grounds. My inbox is full of missives about the scientific misfires that stem-cell research has led to, as well as breathless announcements that adult stem cells actually hold more promise.

This is neither an honest nor a productive line of argument. The reason pro-lifers oppose embryonic stem-cell research is because they hold life sacred at all stages of development. They ought not to deny this or dress it up in a lab coat to give it greater palatability. The moral case is an honorable one. Leave it at that.

Proponents of embryonic stem-cell research point out that some of 5 the embryos currently sitting in freezers in fertility clinics around the world are going to be washed down the drain anyway—which surely kills them, and without any benefit to mankind. This is true. There are several

Mona Charen is a syndicated columnist whose column appears in over two-hundred newspapers nationwide and a political analyst who for six years was a regular on CNN's *Capital Gang* and *Capital Gang Sunday*. From 1984 to 1986, she worked at the White House as a speechwriter for Nancy Reagan and in the Public Affairs Office. This article appeared on townhall.com in August 2004.

answers to this. The first is that a society that truly honored each human life would take a different approach. Fertility clinics and the couples who use them would understand the moral obligation not to create more embryos than they can reasonably expect to transfer to the mother's uterus. In cases where this was impossible, the embryos could be placed for adoption with other infertile couples (this is already a widespread practice).

Once you begin to pull apart a human embryo and use its parts, you have thoroughly dehumanized it. You have justified taking one life to (speculatively) save another. Despite the rosy future painted by Ron Reagan and others, those of us who follow the field with avid interest have been disappointed by avenues of research that have failed, thus far, to pan out. Still, opponents of stem-cell research should not argue that the research is going to be fruitless. No one knows. The problem is that this kind of research is morally problematic. Germany, Italy, Portugal, Luxembourg, and Austria ban it. (The United States does not. We simply withhold federal funding.)

There is something else, as well. While the idea of growing spare parts — say, spinal nerves for a paraplegic — in a Petri dish seems wonderful, it may not be possible to do so from embryonic stem cells. As the *Wall Street Journal* reported on August 12 [2004], scientists have been frustrated by their inability to get stem cells to grow into endoderm (the cells that make up the liver, stomach, and pancreas), whereas they can coax them to become heart and nerve tissue.

"Scientists speculate," the *Journal* explained, "that might be because the embryo early on needs blood and nerve tissue to grow, while endoderm-based organs aren't needed until later." If we can use the stem cells of normal human embryos for research, by what logic would we shrink from allowing an embryo to reach a later stage of development in order to study better how endoderm forms?

These are treacherous moral waters we're setting sail in, and those who hesitate ought not to be scorned as ignorant, uncompassionate, or blinkered.

DISCUSSION QUESTIONS

1. Do both of these authors use both evidence and appeal to needs and values? Explain. How is your reading of each piece affected by the author's personal circumstances?

2. What is the effect of Reeve's choosing to call stem cells "the body's self-repair kit"? Give other examples of how his word choice either helps or hurts his argument.

3. Is the language that Reeve uses in discussing the embryos different from that used by Charen? How and why?

4. In what other ways does Charen's choice of words affect her argument?

5. Where does each author most directly state the claim of their piece?

TAKING THE DEBATE ONLINE

For these and additional research URLs, see bedfordstmartins.com/rottenberg.

- *NIH Stem Cell Information*
  http://stemcells.nih.gov/index.asp
  The official National Institutes of Health resource for stem-cell research.

- *Remarks by the President on Stem Cell Research*
  www.whitehouse.gov/news/releases/2001/08/20010809-2.html
  A transcript of a radio address given by President George W. Bush on August 9, 2001.

- *Stem Cell Research Foundation*
  www.stemcellresearchfoundation.org/
  The mission of the Stem Cell Research Foundation is to support research into the development of cell therapies to help find treatments and cures for a wide variety of diseases.

- *DoNoHarm: The Coalition of Americans for Research Ethics*
  www.stemcellresearch.org/
  The mission of DoNoHarm is to promote treatments that "do not require the destruction of human life, including the human embryo" and to "support continuation of federal laws prohibiting the federal funding of research that requires the destruction of human life, including the human embryo."

- *The International Society for Stem Cell Research*
  www.isscr.org/mission/index.htm
  The ISSSCR is an independent, nonprofit organization established to promote and foster the exchange and dissemination of information and ideas relating to stem cells.

ASSIGNMENTS FOR UNDERSTANDING INDUCTION, DEDUCTION, AND LOGICAL FALLACIES

1. For practice, decide whether the reasoning in the following examples is faulty. Explain your answers.

   1. The presiding judge of a revolutionary tribunal, on being asked why people were being executed without trial: "Why should we put them on trial when we know that they're guilty?"
   2. Since good nutrition is essential to the health of its citizens, the government should punish people who eat junk food.

3. Children who watch game shows rather than situation comedies receive higher grades in school. So it must be true that game shows are more educational than situation comedies.

4. The meteorologist predicted the wrong amount of rain for May. Obviously the meteorologist is unreliable.

5. Women ought to be permitted to serve in combat. Why should men be the only ones to face death and danger?

6. If Cher uses Equal, it must taste better than Sweet 'n Low.

7. People will gamble anyway, so why not legalize gambling in this state?

8. Because so much money was spent on public education in the last decade while educational achievement declined, more money to improve education can't be the answer to reversing the decline.

9. He's a columnist for the campus newspaper, so he must be a pretty good writer.

10. We tend to exaggerate the need for standard English. You don't need much standard English for most jobs in this country.

11. It's discriminatory to mandate that police officers must conform to a certain height and weight.

12. A doctor can consult books to make a diagnosis, so a medical student should be able to consult books when being tested.

13. Because this soft drink contains so many chemicals, it must be unsafe.

14. Core requirements should be eliminated. After all, students are paying for their education, so they should be able to earn a diploma by choosing the courses they want.

15. We should encourage a return to arranged marriages in this country since marriages based on romantic love haven't been very successful.

16. I know three redheads who have terrible tempers, and since Annabel has red hair, I'll bet she has a terrible temper, too.

17. Supreme Court Justice Byron White was an All-American football player while at college, so how can you say that athletes are dumb?

18. Benjamin H. Sasway, a student at Humboldt State University in California, was indicted for failure to register for possible conscription. Barry Lynn, president of Draft Action, an antidraft group, said, "It is disgraceful that this administration is embarking on an effort to fill the prisons with men of conscience and moral commitment."

19. James A. Harris, former president of the National Education Association: "Twenty-three percent of schoolchildren are failing to graduate, and another large segment graduate as functional illiterates. If 23 percent of anything else failed—23 percent of automobiles didn't run, 23 percent of the buildings fell down, 23 percent of stuffed ham spoiled—we'd look at the producer."

20. A professor at Rutgers University: "The arrest rate for women is rising three times as fast as that of men. Women, inflamed by the doctrines of feminism, are pursuing criminal careers with the same zeal as business and the professions."

21. Physical education should be required because physical activity is healthful.

22. George Meany, former president of the AFL-CIO, in 1968: "To these people who constantly say you have got to listen to these younger people, they have got something to say, I just don't buy that at all. They smoke more pot than we do and if the younger generation are the hundred thousand kids that lay around a field up in Woodstock, New York, I am not going to trust the destiny of the country to that group."

23. That candidate was poor as a child, so he will certainly be sympathetic to the poor if he's elected.

24. When the federal government sent troops into Little Rock, Arkansas, to enforce integration of the public school system, the governor of Arkansas attacked the action, saying that it was as brutal an act of intervention as Russia's sending troops into Hungary to squelch the Hungarians' rebellion. In both cases, the governor said, the rights of a freedom-loving, independent people were being violated.

25. Governor Jones was elected two years ago. Since that time constant examples of corruption and subversion have been unearthed. It is time to get rid of the man responsible for this kind of corrupt government.

26. Are we going to vote a pay increase for our teachers, or are we going to allow our schools to deteriorate into substandard custodial institutions?

27. You see, the priests were right. After we threw those virgins into the volcano, it quit erupting.

28. The people of Rome lost their vitality and desire for freedom when their emperors decided that the way to keep them happy was to provide them with bread and circuses. What can we expect of our own country now that the government gives people free food and there is a constant round of entertainment provided by television?

29. From Mark Clifton, "The Dread Tomato Affliction" (proving that eating tomatoes is dangerous and even deadly): "Ninety-two point four percent of juvenile delinquents have eaten tomatoes. Fifty-seven point one percent of the adult criminals in penitentiaries throughout the United States have eaten tomatoes. Eighty-four percent of all people killed in automobile accidents during the year have eaten tomatoes."

30. From Galileo, *Dialogues Concerning Two New Sciences*: "But can you doubt that air has weight when you have the clear testimony of Aristotle affirming that all elements have weight, including air, and excepting only fire?"

31. Robert Brustein, artistic director of the American Repertory Theatre, commenting on a threat by Congress in 1989 to withhold funding from an offensive art show: "Once we allow lawmakers to become art critics, we take the first step into the world of Ayatollah Khomeini, whose murderous review of *The Satanic Verses* still chills the heart of

everyone committed to free expression." (The Ayatollah Khomeini called for the death of the author, Salman Rushdie, because he had allegedly committed blasphemy against Islam in his novel.)

2. Find the printed text of a major political speech such as a state of the Union address, a major political convention speech, or an inaugural address and analyze its logic. Does it use an inductive approach, a deductive approach, or a combination? What types of support are used? Do you detect any logical fallacies? Write an essay about the speech that supports either a claim of fact or a claim of value.

3. Compare the argument made to Congress by President Roosevelt on the day after the attack on Pearl Harbor in 1941 and the one made by President Bush after the attacks on the World Trade Center and the Pentagon in 2001.

4. Write an essay explaining the logical fallacies in one of the essays from the Readings for Analysis portion of this chapter.

5. Explain in an essay whether you find Paige's or Weaver's argument more convincing and discuss why.

CHAPTER 8

Language and Thought

Words play such a critical role in argument that they deserve special treatment. An important part of successful writers' equipment is a large and active vocabulary, but no single chapter in a book can give this to you; only reading and study can widen your range of word choices. Even in a brief chapter, however, we can point out how words influence the feelings and attitudes of an audience, both favorably and unfavorably.

One kind of language responsible for shaping attitudes and feelings is *emotive language,* language that expresses and arouses emotions. Understanding it and using it effectively are indispensable to the arguer who wants to move an audience to accept a point of view or undertake an action.

Long before you thought about writing your first argument, you learned that words had the power to affect you. Endearments and affectionate and flattering nicknames evoked good feelings about the speaker and yourself. Insulting nicknames and slurs produced dislike for the speaker and bad feelings about yourself. Perhaps you were told, "Sticks and stones may break your bones, but words will never hurt you." But even to a small child it is clear that ugly words are as painful as sticks and stones and that the injuries are sometimes more lasting.

Nowhere is the power of words more obvious and more familiar than in advertising, where the success of a product may depend on the feelings that certain words produce in the prospective buyer. Even the names of products may have emotive significance. In recent years a new industry, composed of consultants who supply names for products, has emerged. Although most manufacturers agree that a good name won't save a poor product, they also recognize that the right name can catch the attention of the public and persuade people to buy a product at least once. According to an article in the *Wall Street Journal,* a product name not only should be memorable but also should "remind people of emotional or physical experiences." One consultant created the name Magnum for a malt liquor from Miller Brewing Company: "The product is aimed at students, minorities, and lower-income customers." The president of the consulting firm says that Magnum "implies strength, masculinity, and more bang for your buck."[1] This naming of products has been called the "Rumpelstiltskin effect," a phrase coined by a linguist. "The whole point," he said, "is that when you have the right name for a thing, you have control over it."[2]

Even scientists recognize the power of words to attract the attention of other scientists and the public to discoveries and theories that might otherwise remain obscure. A good name can even enable the scientist to visualize a new concept. One scientist says that "a good name," such as "quark," "black hole," "big bang," "chaos," or "great attractor," "helps in communicating a theory and can have substantial impact on financing."

It is not hard to see the connection between the use of words in conversation and advertising and the use of emotive language in the more formal arguments you will be writing. Emotive language reveals your approval or disapproval, assigns praise or blame—in other words, makes a judgment about the subject. Keep in mind that unless you are writing purely factual statements, such as scientists write, you will find it hard to avoid expressing judgments. Neutrality does not come easily, even where it may be desirable, as in news stories or reports of historical events. For this reason you need to attend carefully to the statements in your argument, making sure that you have not disguised judgments as statements of fact. Of course, in attempting to prove a claim, you will not be neutral. You will be revealing your judgment about the subject, first in the selection of facts and opinions and the emphasis you give to them and second in the selection of words.

Like the choice of facts and opinions, the choice of words can be effective or ineffective in advancing your argument, moral or immoral in the honesty with which you exercise it. The following discussions offer some insights into recognizing and evaluating the use of emotive language in the arguments you read, as well as into using such language in your own arguments where it is appropriate and avoiding it where it is not.

[1] *Wall Street Journal,* August 5, 1982, p. 19.
[2] *Harvard Magazine,* July–August 1995, p. 18.

CONNOTATION

The connotations of a word are the meanings we attach to it apart from its explicit definition. Because these added meanings derive from our feelings, connotations are one form of emotive language. For example, the word *rat* denotes or points to a kind of rodent, but the attached meanings of "selfish person," "evil-doer," "betrayer," and "traitor" reflect the feelings that have accumulated around the word.

In Chapter 3 we observed that definitions of controversial terms, such as *poverty* and *unemployment,* may vary so widely that writer and reader cannot always be sure that they are thinking of the same thing. A similar problem arises when a writer assumes that the reader shares his or her emotional response to a word. Emotive meanings originate partly in personal experience. The word *home,* defined merely as "a family's place of residence," may suggest love, warmth, and security to one person; it may suggest friction, violence, and alienation to another. The values of the groups to which we belong also influence meaning. Writers and speakers count on cultural associations when they refer to our country, our flag, and heroes and enemies we have never seen. The arguer must also be aware that some apparently neutral words trigger different responses from different groups—words such as *cult, revolution, police, beauty contest,* and *corporation.*

Various reform movements have recognized that words with unfavorable connotations have the power not only to reflect but also to shape our perceptions of things. The words *Negro* and *colored* were rejected by the civil rights movement in the 1960s because they bore painful associations with slavery and discrimination. Instead, the word *black,* which was free from such associations, became the accepted designation; more recently, the Reverend Jesse Jackson suggested another term, *African American,* to reflect ethnic origins. People of "Spanish/Hispanic/Latino" origin (as they are designated on the 2000 census) are now engaged in a debate about the appropriate term for a diverse population of more than 22 million American residents from Mexico, Puerto Rico, Cuba, and more than a dozen Central and South American countries. To some, the word *Hispanic* is unacceptable because it is an anglicization and recalls the colonization of America by Spain and Portugal.

The women's liberation movement also insisted on changes that would bring about improved attitudes toward women. The movement condemned the use of *girl* for a female over the age of eighteen and the use in news stories of descriptive adjectives that emphasized the physical appearance of women. And the homosexual community succeeded in reintroducing the word *gay,* a word current centuries ago, as a substitute for words they considered offensive. Now *queer,* a word long regarded as offensive, has been adopted as a substitute for *gay* by a new generation of gays and lesbians, although it is still considered unacceptable by many members of the homosexual community.

Members of certain occupations have invented terms to confer greater respectability on their work. The work does not change, but the workers hope that public perceptions will change if janitors are called custodians, if garbage collectors are called sanitation engineers, if undertakers are called morticians, if people who sell makeup are called cosmetologists. Events considered unpleasant or unmentionable are sometimes disguised by polite terms, called *euphemisms*. During the 1992 to 1993 recession new terms emerged that disguised, or tried to, the grim fact that thousands of people were being dismissed from their jobs: *skill-mix adjustment, workforce-imbalance correction, redundancy elimination, downsizing, indefinite idling,* even a daring *career-change opportunity*. Many people refuse to use the word *died* and choose *passed away* instead. Some psychologists and physicians use the phrase *negative patient care outcome* for what most of us would call *death*. Even when referring to their pets, some people cannot bring themselves to say *put to death* but substitute *put to sleep* or *put down*. In place of a term to describe an act of sexual intercourse, some people use *slept together* or *went to bed together* or *had an affair*.

Polite words are not always so harmless. If a euphemism disguises a shameful event or condition, it is morally irresponsible to use it to mislead the reader into believing that the shameful condition does not exist. In his powerful essay "Politics and the English Language" George Orwell pointed out that politicians and reporters have sometimes used terms like "pacification" or "rectification of frontiers" to conceal acts that result in torture and death for millions of people. An example of such usage was cited by a member of Amnesty International, a group monitoring human rights violations throughout the world. He objected to a news report describing camps in which the Chinese were promoting "reeducation through labor." This term, he wrote, "makes these institutions seem like a cross between Police Athletic League and Civilian Conservation Corps camps." On the contrary, he went on, the reality of "reeducation through labor" was that the victims were confined to "rather unpleasant prison camps." The details he offered about the conditions under which people lived and worked gave substance to his claim.[3] More recently, when news organizations referred to the expulsion of Romanian gypsies from Germany as part of a "deportation treaty," an official of Germany's press agency objected to the use of the word *deportation*. "You must know that by using words such as *deportation* you are causing great sadness. . . . We prefer that you use the term *readmission* or *retransfer*."[4]

Some of the most interesting changes in language usage occur in modern Bible translations. The vocabulary and syntax of earlier versions have been greatly simplified to make the Bible more accessible to that half of the American public who cannot read above eighth-grade level. Another change responds to arguments by feminists, environmentalists, and

---

[3] Letter to the *New York Times,* August 30, 1982, p. 25.
[4] *International Herald Tribune,* November 5, 1992.

multiculturalists for more "inclusive language." God is no longer the *Father,* human beings no longer have *dominion* over creation, and even the word *blindness* as a metaphor for sin or evil has been replaced by other metaphors.

Perhaps the most striking examples of the way that connotations influence our perceptions of reality occur when people are asked to respond to questions of poll-takers. Sociologists and students of poll-taking know that the phrasing of a question, or the choice of words, can affect the answers and even undermine the validity of the poll. In one case poll-takers first asked a selected group of people if they favored continuing the welfare system. The majority answered no. But when the poll-takers asked if they favored government aid to the poor, the majority answered yes. Although the terms *welfare* and *government aid to the poor* refer to essentially the same forms of government assistance, *welfare* has acquired for many people negative connotations of corruption and shiftless recipients.

In a *New York Times*/CBS poll conducted in January 1998, "a representative sample of Americans were asked which statement came nearer to their opinion: 'Is abortion the same thing as murdering a child, or is abortion not murder because the fetus really isn't a child?'" Thirty-eight percent chose "the fetus really isn't a child." But 58 percent, including a third of those who chose "abortion is the same thing as murdering a child," agreed that abortion "was sometimes the best course in a bad situation." The author of the report suggests an explanation of the fact that a majority of those polled seemed to have chosen "murder" as an acceptable solution to an unwanted pregnancy:

> These replies reveal, at least, a considerable moral confusion.
>
> Or maybe only verbal confusion? Should the question have asked whether abortion came closer, in the respondent's view, to "killing" rather than "murdering" a child? That would leave room for the explanation that Americans, while valuing life, are ultimately not pacifists: killing, they hold, may be justified in certain circumstances (self-defense, warfare, capital punishment).
>
> So one can challenge the wording of the question. Indeed, one can almost always challenge the wording of poll questions. . . . Poll takers themselves acknowledge the difficulty of wording questions and warn against relying too much on any single finding.[5]

This is also true in polls concerning rape, another highly charged subject. Dr. Neil Malamuth, a psychologist at the University of California at Los Angeles, says, "When men are asked if there is any likelihood they would force a woman to have sex against her will if they could get away with it, about half say they would. But if you ask them if they would rape a woman if they knew they could get away with it, only about 15 percent

---

[5] Peter Steinfels, "Beliefs," *New York Times,* January 24, 1998, sec. A, p. 15.

say they would." The men who change their answers aren't aware that "the only difference is in the words used to describe the same act."[6]

The wording of an argument is crucial. Because readers may interpret the words you use on the basis of feelings different from your own, you must support your word choices with definitions and with evidence that allows readers to determine how and why you made them.

SLANTING

Slanting, says one dictionary, is "interpreting or presenting in line with a special interest." The term is almost always used in a negative sense. It means that the arguer has selected facts and words with favorable or unfavorable connotations to create the impression that no alternative view exists or can be defended. For some questions it is true that no alternative view is worthy of presentation, and emotionally charged language to defend or attack a position that is clearly right or wrong would be entirely appropriate. We aren't neutral, nor should we be, about the tragic abuse of human rights anywhere in the world or even about less serious infractions of the law, such as drunk driving or vandalism, and we should use strong language to express our disapproval of these practices.

Most of your arguments, however, will concern controversial questions about which people of goodwill can argue on both sides. In such cases, your own judgments should be restrained. Slanting will suggest a prejudice — that is, a judgment made without regard to all the facts. Unfortunately, you may not always be aware of your bias or special interest; you may believe that your position is the only correct one. You may also feel the need to communicate a passionate belief about a serious problem. But if you are interested in persuading a reader to accept your belief and to act on it, you must also ask: If the reader is not sympathetic, how will he or she respond? Will he or she perceive my words as "loaded" — one-sided and prejudicial — and my view as slanted?

R. D. Laing, a Scottish psychiatrist, defined *prayer* in this way: "Someone is gibbering away on his knees, talking to someone who is not there."[7] This description probably reflects a sincerely held belief. Laing also clearly intended it for an audience that already agreed with him. But the phrases "gibbering away" and "someone who is not there" would be offensive to people for whom prayer is sacred.

The following remarks by one writer attacking another appeared in *Salon,* an online magazine:

---

[6]*New York Times,* August 29, 1989, sec. C, p. 1.

[7]"The Obvious," in David Cooper, ed. *The Dialectics of Liberation* (Penguin Books, 1968), p. 17.

Urging the hyperbolic *Salon* columnist David Horowitz to calm down and cite facts instead of spewing insults seems as pointless as asking a dog not to defecate on the sidewalk. In either instance, the result is always and predictably the same: Somebody has to clean up a stinking pile.[8]

An audience, whether friendly or unfriendly, interested in a discussion of the issues, would probably be both embarrassed and repelled by this use of language in a serious argument.

In the mid-1980s an English environmental group, London Greenpeace, began to distribute leaflets accusing the McDonald's restaurants of a wide assortment of crimes. The leaflets said in part:

> McDollars, McGreedy, McCancer, McMurder, McDisease, McProfits, McDeadly, McHunger, McRipoff, McTorture, McWasteful, McGarbage.
>
> This leaflet is asking you to think for a moment about what lies behind McDonald's clean, bright image. It's got a lot to hide. . . .
>
> McDonald's and Burger King are two of the many U.S. corporations using lethal poisons to destroy vast areas of Central American rain forest to create grazing pastures for cattle to be sent back to the States as burgers and pet food. . . .
>
> What they don't make clear is that a diet high in fat, sugar, animal products and salt . . . and low in fiber, vitamins and minerals—which describes an average McDonald's meal—is linked with cancers of the breast and bowel, and heart disease. . . .[9]

Even readers who share the belief that McDonald's is not a reliable source of good nutrition might feel that London Greenpeace has gone too far, and that the name-calling, loaded words, and exaggeration have damaged the credibility of the attackers more than the reputation of McDonald's.

[8] July 6, 2000.

[9] *New York Times,* August 6, 1995, sec. E, p. 7. In 1990 McDonald's sued the group for libel. In June 1997, after the longest libel trial in British history, the judge ruled in favor of the plaintiff, awarding McDonald's £60,000. In March 1999 an appeal partially overturned the verdict, and reduced the damages awarded to McDonald's by approximately one-third.

Selection, Slanting, and Charged Learning

NEWMAN P. BIRK AND GENEVIEVE B. BIRK

A. THE PRINCIPLE OF SELCTION

Before it is expressed in words, our knowledge, both inside and outside, is influenced by the principle of selection. What we know or observe depends on what we notice; that is, what we select, consciously or unconsciously, as worthy of notice or attention. As we observe, the principle of selection determines which facts we take in.

Suppose, for example, that three people, a lumberjack, an artist, and a tree surgeon, are examining a large tree in the forest. Since the tree itself is a complicated object, the number of particulars or facts about it that one could observe would be very great indeed. Which of these facts a particular observer will notice will be a matter of selection, a selection that is determined by his interests and purposes. A lumberjack might be interested in the best way to cut the tree down, cut it up and transport it to the lumber mill. His interest would then determine his principle of selection in observing and thinking about the tree. The artist might consider painting a picture of the tree, and his purpose would furnish his principle of selection. The tree surgeon's professional interest in the physical health of the tree might establish a principle of selection for him. If each man were now required to write an exhaustive, detailed report on every thing he observed about the tree, the facts supplied by each would differ, for each would report those facts that his particular principle of selection led him to notice. . . .[1]

The principle of selection then serves as a kind of sieve or screen through which our knowledge passes before it becomes our knowledge. Since we can't notice everything about a complicated object or situation or action or state of our own consciousness, what we do notice is determined by whatever principle of selection is operating for us at the time we gain the knowledge. . . .

This selection first appeared in *Understanding and Using English* (1972). Together, the Birks also wrote *A Handbook of Grammar, Rhetoric, Mechanics, and Usage* (1976).

[1]Of course, all three observers would probalby report a good many facts in common— the height of the tree, for example, and the size of the trunk. The point we wish to make is that each observer would give us a different impression of the tree because of the different principle of selection that guided his observation. [All notes are the authors.]

B. THE PRINCIPLE OF SLANTING

When we put our knowledge into words, a second process of selection, the process of slanting, takes place. Just as there is something, a rather mysterious principle of selection, which chooses for us what we will notice, and what will then become our knowledge, there is also a principle which operates, with or without our awareness, to select certain facts and feelings from our store of knowledge, and to choose the words and emphasis that we shall use to communicate our meaning.[2] Slanting my be defined as the porcess of selecting (1) knowledge—factual and attitudinal; (2) words; and (3) emphasis, to achieve the intention of the communicator. Slanting is present in some degree in all communication: one may *slant for* (Favorable slanting), *slant against* (unfavorable slanting), or *slant both ways* (balanced shifting). . . .

C. SLANTING BY USE OF EMPHASIS

Slanting by use of the devices of emphasis is unavoidable,[3] for emphasis is simply the giving of stress to subject matter, and so indicating what is important and what is less important. In speech, for example, if we say that Socrates was a wise old man, we can give several slightly different meanings, one by stressing wise, another by stressing old, another by giving equal stress to wise and old, and still another by giving chief stress to man. Each different stress gives a different slant (favorable or unfavorable or balanced) to the statement because it conveys a different attitude toward Socrates or a different judgement of him. Connectives and word order also slant by the emphasis they give: Consider the difference in slanting or emphasis produced *by old but wise, old and wise, wise but old.* In writing, we cannot indicate subtle stresses on words as clearly as in speech, but we can achieve our emphasis and so can slant by the use of more complex patterns of word order, by marks of punctuation that indicate short or long pauses and so give light or heavy emphasis. Question marks, quotation marks, and exclamation points can also contribute to slanting.[4] It is impossible either in speech or in writing to put two facts about a man, his awkwardness and his strength, we subtly slant those facts favorably or unfavorably in whatever way we may choose to join them.

[2] Notice that the "principle of selection" is at work as *we take in* knowledge, and that slanting occurs *as we express* our knowledge in words.

[3] When emphasis is present—and we can think of no instance in the use of language in which it is not—it necessarily influences the meaning by playing a part in the favorable, unfavorable, or balanced slant of the communicator. We are likely to emphasize by voice stress, even when we answer *yes* or *no* to simple questions.

[4] Consider the slanting achieved by punctuation in the following sentences: He called the Senator an honest man? *He* called the Senator an honest man? He called the Senator an honest man! He said one more such "honest" senator would corrupt the state.

More Favorable Slanting	*Less Favorable Slanting*
He is awkward and strong.	He is strong and awkward.
He is awkward but strong.	He is strong but awkward.
Although he is somewhat awkward, he is very strong.	He may be strong, but he's very awkward.

With more facts and in longer passages it is possible to maintain a delicate balance by alternating favorable emphasis and so producing a balanced effect

All communication, then, is in some degree slanted by the *emphasis* of the communicator.

D. SLANTING BY SELECTION OF FACTS

To illustrate the technique of slanting by selection of facts, we shall examine three passages of informative writing which achieve different effects simply by the selection and emphasis of material. Each passage is made up of true statements or facts about a dog, yet the reader is given three different impressions. The first passage is an example of objective writing or balanced slanting, the second is slanted unfavorably, and the third is slanted favorably.

1. Balanced Presentation

Our dog, Toddy, sold to us as a cocker, produces various reactions in various people. Those who come to the back door she usually growls and barks at (a milkman has said that he is afraid of her); those who come to the front door, she whines at and paws; also she tries to lick people's faces unless we have forestalled her by putting a newspaper in her mouth. (Some of our friends encourage these actions; others discourage them. Mrs. Firmly, one friend, slaps the dog with a newspaper and says, "I know how hard dogs are to train.") Toddy knows and responds to a number of words and phrases, and guests sometimes remark that she is a "very intelligent dog." She has fleas in the summer, and she sheds, at times copiously, the year round. Her blonde hairs are conspicuous when they are on people's clothing or on rugs or furniture. Her color and her large brown eyes frequently produce favorable comment. An expert on cockers would say that her ears are too short and set too high and that she is at least six ounds too heavy.

The passage above is made up of facts, verifiable facts,[5] deliberately selected and emphasized to produce a *balanced* impression. Of course not

---

[5] *Verifiable* facts are facts that can be checked and agreed upon and proved to be true by people who wish to verify them. That a particular theme received a failing grade is a verifiable fact; one needs merely to see the theme with the grade on it. That the instructor should have failed the theme or not, strictly speaking, a verifiable fact, but a matter of opinion. That women on the average live longer than men is a verifiable fact; that they live better is a matter of opinion, *a value judgement.*

all the facts about the dog have been given—to supply *all* the facts on any subject, even such a comparatively simple one, would be an almost impossible task. Both favorable and unfavorable facts are used, however, and an effort has been made to alternate favorable and unfavorable details so that neither will receive greater emphasis by position, proportion, or grammatical structure.

2. Facts Slanted Against

That dog put her paws on my white dress as soon as I came in the door, and she made so much noise that it was two minutes before she had quieted down enough for us to talk and hear each other. Then the gas man came and she did a great deal of barking. And her hairs are on the rug and on the furniture. If you wear a dark dress they stick to it like lint. When Mrs. Firmly came in, she actually hit the dog with a newspaper to make it stay down, and she made some remark about training dogs. I wish the Birks would take the hint or get rid of that noisy, shorteared, overweight "cocker" of theirs.

This unfavorably slanted version is based on the same facts, but now these facts have been selected and given a new emphasis. The speaker, using her selected facts to give her impression of the dog, is quite possibly unaware of her negative slanting.

Now for a favorably slanted version:

3. Facts Slanted For

What a lively and responsible dog! When I walked in the door, there she was with a newspaper in her mouth, whining and standing on her hind legs and wagging her tail all at the same time. And what an intelligent dog. If you suggest going for a walk, she will get her collar from the kitchen and hand it to you, and she brings Mrs. Birk's slippers whenever Mrs. Birk says she is "tired" or mentions slippers. At a command she catches balls, rolls over, "speaks," or stands on her hind feet and twirls around. She sits up and balances a piece of bread on her nose until she is told to take it; then she tosses it up and catches it. If you are eating something, she sits up in front of you and "begs" with those big dark brown eyes set in that light, buff-colored face of hers. When I got up to go and told her I was leaving, she rolled her eyes at me and sat up like a squirrel. She certainly is a lively and intelligent dog.

Speaker 3, like Speaker 2, is selecting from the "facts" summarized in balance version 1, and is emphasizing his facts to communicate his impression.

All three passages are examples of *reporting* (i.e., consist only of verifiable facts), yet they give three very different impressions of the same dog because of the different ways the speakers slanted the facts. Some people say that figures don't lie, and many people believe that if they have the "facts," they have the "truth," Yet if we carefully examine the ways of thought and language, we see that any knowledge that comes to us through words has been subjected to the double screening of the principle of selection and the slanting of language. . . .

Wise listeners and readers realize that the double screening that is produced by the principle of selection and by slanting takes place even when people honestly try to report the facts as they know them. (Speakers 2 and 3, for instance, probably thought of themselves as simply giving information about a dog and were not deliberately trying to mislead.) Wise listeners and readers know too that deliberate manipulators of language, by mere selection and emphasis, can make the slanted facts appear to support almost any cause.

In arriving at opinions and values we cannot always be sure that the facts that sift into our minds through language are representative and relevant and true. We need to remember that much of our information about politics, governmental activities, business conditions, and foreign affairs comes to us selected and slanted. More than we realize, our opinions on these matters may depend on what newspaper we read or what news commentator we listen to. Worthwhile opinions call for knowledge of reliable facts and reasonable arguments for and against—and such opinions include beliefs about morality and truth and religion as well as about public affairs. Because complex subjects involve knowing and dealing with many facts on both sides, reliable judgements are at best difficult to arrive at. If we want to be fairminded, we must be willing to subject our opinions to continual testing by new knowledge, and must realize that after all they *are* opinions, more or less trustworthy. Their trustworthiness will depend on the representativeness of our facts, on the quality of our reasoning, and on the standard of values that we choose to apply.

We shall not give here a passage illustrating the unscrupulous slanting of facts. Such a passage would also include irrelevant facts and false statements presented as facts, along with various subtle distortions of fact. Yet to the uninformed reader the passage would be indistinguisable from a passage intended to give a fair account. If two passages (2 and 3) of casual and unintentional slanting of facts about a dog can give such contradictory impressions of a simple subject, the reader can imagine what a skilled and designing manipulation of facts and statistics could do to mislead an uninformed reader about a really complex subject. An example of such manipulation might be the account of the United States that Soviet propaganda has supplied to the average Russian. Such propaganda, however, would go beyond the mere slanting of the facts: It would clothe the selected facts in charged words and would make use of the many other devices of slanting that appear in charged language.

E. SLANTING BY USE OF CHARGED WORDS

In the passages describing the dog Toddy, we were illustrating the tech- 15
nique of slanting by the selection and emphasis of facts. Though the facts
selected had to be expressed in words, the words chosen were as factual
as possible, and it was the selection and emphasis of facts and not of
words that was mainly responsible for the two distinctly different impressions of the dog. In the passages below we are demonstrating another
way of slanting—by the use of charged words. This time the accounts are
very similiar in the facts they contain; the different impressions of the
subject, Corlyn, are produced not by different facts but by the subtle selection of charged words.

The passages were written by a clever student who was told to choose
as his subject a person in action, and to write two descriptions, each using
the "same facts." The instructions required that one description be
slanted positively and the other negatively, so that the first would make
the reader favorably inclined toward the person and the action, and the
second would make him unfavorably inclined.

Here is the favorably charged description. Read it carefully and form
your opinion of the person before you go on to read the second description.

Corlyn

Corlyn paused at the entrance to the room and glanced about. A well-
cut black dress draped subtly about her slender form. Her long blonde
hair gave her chiseled features the simple frame they required. She
smiled an engaging smile as she accepted a cigarette from her escort. As
he lit it for her she looked over the flame and into his eyes. Coryln had
that rare talent of making every male feel that he was the only man in
the world.

She took his arm and they descended the steps into the room. She
walked with an effortless grace and spoke with equal ease. They each took
a cup of coffee and joined a group of friends near the fire. The flickering
light danced across her face and lent an ethereal quality to her beauty.
The good conversation, the crackling logs, and the stimulating coffee
gave her a feeling of internal warmth. Her eyes danced with each leap of
the flames.

Taken by itself this passage might seem just a description of an attractive girl. The favorable slanting by use of charged words has been
done so skillfully that it is inconspicuous. Now we turn to the unfavorable slanted description of the "same" girl in the "same" actions:

Corlyn

Corlyn halted at the entrance to the room and looked around. A plain black dress hung on her thin frame. Her stringy bleached hair accentuated her harsh features. She smiled an inane smile as she took a cigarette from her escort. As he lit it for her she stared over the lighter and into his eyes. Corlyn had a habit of making every male feel that he was the last man on earth.

She grasped his arm and they walked down the steps and into the room. Her pace was fast and ungainly, as was her speed. They each reached for some coffee and broke into a group of acquaintances near the fire. The flickering light played across her face and revealed every flaw. The loud talk, the fire, and the coffee she had gulped down made her feel hot. Her eyes grew more red with each leap of the flames.

When the reader compares these two descriptions, he can see how charged words influence the reader's attitude. One needs to read the two descriptions several times to appreciate all the subtle differences between them. Words, some rather heavily charged, others innocent-looking but lightly charged, work together to carry to the reader a judgement of a person and a situation. If the reader had seen only the first description of Corlyn, he might well have thought that he had formed his "own judgement on the basis of the facts." And the examples just given only begin to suggest the techniques that may be used in heavily charged language. For one thing, the two descriptions of Corlyn contain no really good example of the use of charged abstraction; for another, the writer was obligated by the assignment to use the same set of facts and so could not slant by selecting his material.

F. SLANTING AND CHARGED LANGUAGE

. . . When slanting the facts, or words, or emphasis, or any combination of the three *significantly influences* feelings toward, or judgements about, a subject, the language used is charged language. . . . 20

Of course communications vary in the amount of charge they carry and in their effort on different people; what is very favorably charged for one person may have little or no charge, or may even be adversely charged, for others. It is sometimes hard to distinguish between charged and uncharged expression. But it is safe to say that whenever we wish to convey any kind of inner knowledge—feelings, attitudes, judgements, values—we are obliged to convey that attitudinal meaning through the medium of charged language; and when we wish to understand the inside knowledge of others, we have to interpret the charged language that they choose, or are obliged to use. Charged language, then, is the natural and necessary medium for the communication of charged or attitudinal meaning. At times we have difficulty in living with it, but we should have even greater difficulty in living without it.

Some of the difficulties in living with charged language are caused by its use in dishonest propaganda, in some editorials, in many political speeches, in most advertising, in certain kinds of effusive salesmanship, and in blatantly insincere, or exaggerated, or sentimental expressions of emotion. Other difficulties are caused by the misunderstandings and misinterpretations that charged language produces. A charged phrase misinterpreted in a love letter; a charged word spoken in haste or in anger; an acrimonious argument about religion or politics or athletics or fraternities; the frustating uncertainty produced by the effort to understand the complex attitudinal meaning in a poem or play or a short story—these troubles, all growing out of the use of charged language, may give us the feeling that Robert Louis Stevenson expressed when he said, "The battle goes sore against us to the going down of the sun. . . ."

READING AND DISCUSSION QUESTIONS

1. How do the Birks distinguish between the process of selection and the process of slanting?
2. Explain the three types of slanting described by the Birks and illustrate each with examples from your own experience.
3. According to the Birks, why is charged language unavoidable— and ultimately desirable?

WRITING SUGGESTIONS

4. Choose a printed ad and analyze the use of language, applying the Birks' terminology.
5. Choose one or more editorials or letters to the editor and show how word choice reveals a writer's attitude toward a subject.

We find slanting everywhere, not only in advertising and propaganda, where we expect to find it, but in news stories, which should be strictly neutral in their recounting of events, and in textbooks. In the field of history, for example, it is often difficult for scholars to remain impartial about significant events. Like the rest of us, they may approve or disapprove, and their choice of words will reflect their judgments.

The following passage by a distinguished Catholic historian describes the events surrounding the momentous decision by Henry VIII, king of England, to break with the Roman Catholic Church in 1534, in part because of the Pope's refusal to grant him a divorce from the Catholic princess Catherine of Aragon so that he could marry Anne Boleyn.

The *protracted* delay in receiving an annulment was very *irritating* to the *impulsive* English king. . . . Gradually Henry's former *effusive* loyalty to Rome gave way to a settled conviction of the tyranny of the papal power, and there *rushed* to his mind the recollections of efforts of earlier English rulers to restrict that power. A few *salutary* enactments against the Church might *compel* a favorable decision from the Pope.

Henry seriously opened his campaign against the Roman Church in 1531, when he *frightened* the clergy into paying a fine of over half a million dollars for violating an *obsolete* statute . . . and in the same year he *forced* the clergy to recognize himself as supreme head of the Church. . . .

His *subservient* Parliament then empowered him to stop the payments of annates to the Pope and to appoint bishops in England without recourse to the papacy. *Without waiting longer* for the decision from Rome, he had Cranmer, *one of his own creatures,* whom he had just named Archbishop of Canterbury, declare his marriage null and void. . . .

Yet Henry VIII encountered considerable *opposition* from the *higher clergy,* from the monks, and from many *intellectual leaders.* . . . A *popular uprising*—the Pilgrimage of Grace—was *sternly* suppressed, and such men as the *brilliant* Sir Thomas More and John Fisher, the *aged* and *saintly* bishop of Rochester, were beheaded because they retained their former belief in papal supremacy.[10] [Italics added]

In the first paragraph the italicized words help make the following points: that Henry was rash, impulsive, and insincere and that he was intent on punishing the church (the word *salutary* means healthful or beneficial and is used sarcastically). In the second paragraph the choice of words stresses Henry's use of force and the cowardly submission of his followers. In the third paragraph the adjectives describing the opposition to Henry's campaign and those who were executed emphasize Henry's cruelty and despotism. Within the limits of this brief passage the author has offered support for his strong indictment of Henry VIII's actions, both in defining the statute as obsolete and in describing the popular opposition. In a longer exposition you would expect to find a more elaborate justification with facts and authoritative opinion from other sources.

The advocate of a position in an argument, unlike the reporter or the historian, must express a judgment, but the preceding examples demonstrate how the arguer should use language to avoid or minimize slanting and to persuade readers that he or she has come to a conclusion after careful analysis. The careful arguer must not conceal his or her judgments by presenting them as if they were statements of fact, but must offer convincing support for his or her choice of words and respect the audience's feelings and attitudes by using temperate language.

---

[10]Carlton J. H. Hayes, *A Political and Cultural History of Modern Europe,* vol. 1 (New York: Macmillan, 1933), pp. 172–73.

Depending on the circumstances, *exaggeration* can be defined, in the words of one writer, as "a form of lying." An essay in *Time* magazine, "Watching Out for Loaded Words," points to the danger for the arguer in relying on exaggerated language as an essential part of the argument.

> The trouble with loaded words is they tend to short-circuit thought. While they may describe something, they simultaneously try to seduce the mind into accepting a prefabricated opinion about the something described.[11]

PICTURESQUE LANGUAGE

Picturesque language consists of words that produce images in the mind of the reader. Students sometimes assume that vivid picture-making language is the exclusive instrument of novelists and poets, but writers of arguments can also avail themselves of such devices to heighten the impact of their messages.

Picturesque language can do more than render a scene. It shares with other kinds of emotive language the power to express and arouse deep feelings. Like a fine painting or photograph, it can draw readers into the picture where they partake of the writer's experience as if they were also present. Such power may be used to delight, to instruct, or to horrify. In 1741 the Puritan preacher Jonathan Edwards delivered his sermon "Sinners in the Hands of an Angry God," in which people were likened to repulsive spiders hanging over the flames of Hell to be dropped into the fire whenever a wrathful God was pleased to release them. The congregation's reaction to Edwards's picture of the everlasting horrors to be suffered in the netherworld included panic, fainting, hysteria, and convulsions. Subsequently Edwards lost his pulpit in Massachusetts, in part as a consequence of his success at provoking such uncontrollable terror among his congregation.

Language as intense and vivid as Edwards's emerges from very strong emotion about a deeply felt cause. In an argument against abortion, a surgeon recounts a horrifying experience as if it were a scene in a movie.

> You walk toward the bus stop. . . . It is all so familiar. All at once you step on something soft. You feel it with your foot. Even through your shoe you may have the sense of something unusual, something marked by a special "give." It is a foreignness upon the pavement. Instinct pulls your foot away in an awkward little movement. You look down, and you see . . . a tiny naked body, its arms and legs flung apart, its head thrown back, its mouth agape, its face serious. A bird, you think, fallen from the nest. But there is no nest here on 73rd Street, no bird so big. It

---

[11] *Time,* May 24, 1982, p. 86.

is rubber, then. A model, a . . . a joke. And you bend to see. Because you must. And it is no joke. Such a gray softness can be but one thing. It is a baby, and dead. You cover your mouth, your eyes. You are fixed. Horror has found its chink and crawled in, and you will never be the same as you were. Years later you will step from a sidewalk to a lawn, and you will start at its softness and think of that upon which you have just trod.[12]

Here the use of the pronoun *you* serves to draw readers into the scene and intensify their experience.

The rules governing the use of picturesque language are the same as those governing other kinds of emotive language. Is the language appropriate? Is it too strong, too colorful for the purpose of the message? Does it result in slanting or distortion? What will its impact be on a hostile or indifferent audience? Will they be angered, repelled? Will they cease to read or listen if the imagery is too disturbing?

We expect strong language in arguments about life and death. For subjects about which your feelings are not so passionate, your choice of words will be more moderate. The excerpt below, from an article arguing against repeal of Sunday closing laws, creates a sympathetic picture of a market-free Sunday. Most readers, even those who oppose Sunday closing laws, would enjoy the picture and perhaps react more favorably to the argument.

Think of waking in the city on Sunday. Although most people no longer worship in the morning, the city itself has a reverential air. It comes to life slowly, even reluctantly, as traffic lights blink their orders to empty streets. Next, joggers venture forth, people out to get the paper, families going to church or grandma's. Soon the city is its Sunday self: People cavort with their children, discuss, make repairs, go to museums, gambol. Few people go to work, and any shopping is incidental. The city on Sunday is a place outside the market. Play dominates, not the economy.[13]

CONCRETE AND ABSTRACT LANGUAGE

Writers of argument need to be aware of another use of language—the distinction between concrete and abstract. Concrete words point to real objects and real experiences. Abstract words express qualities apart from particular things and events. *Beautiful roses* is concrete; we can see, touch, and smell them. *Beauty* in the eye of the beholder is abstract; we can

---

[12] Richard Selzer, *Mortal Lessons: Notes on the Art of Surgery* (New York: Simon and Schuster, 1974), pp. 153–54.

[13] Robert K. Manoff, "New York City, It Is Argued, Faces 'Sunday Imperialism,'" *New York Times,* January 2, 1977, sec. 4, p. 13.

speak of the quality of beauty without reference to a particular object or event. *Returning money found in the street to the owner, although no one has seen the discovery* is concrete. *Honesty* is abstract. In abstracting we separate a quality shared by a number of objects or events, however different from each other the individual objects or events may be.

Writing that describes or tells a story leans heavily on concrete language. Although arguments also rely on the vividness of concrete language, they use abstract terms far more extensively than other kinds of writing. Using abstractions effectively, especially in arguments of value and policy, is important for two reasons: (1) Abstractions represent the qualities, characteristics, and values that the writer is explaining, defending, or attacking; and (2) they enable the writer to make generalizations about his or her data. Equally important is knowing when to avoid abstractions that obscure the message.

In some textbook discussions of language, abstractions are treated as inferior to concrete and specific words, but such a distinction is misleading. Abstractions allow us to make sense of our experience, to come to conclusions about the meaning of the bewildering variety of emotions and events we confront throughout a lifetime. One writer summarized his early history as follows: "My elementary school had the effect of *destroying any intellectual motivation*, of *stifling* all *creativity*, of *inhibiting personal relationships* with either my teachers or my peers" (emphasis added). Writing in the humanities and in some social and physical sciences would be impossible without recourse to abstractions that express qualities, values, and conditions.

You should not, however, expect abstract terms alone to carry the emotional content of your message. The effect of even the most suggestive words can be enhanced by details, examples, and anecdotes. One mode of expression is not superior to the other; both abstractions and concrete detail work together to produce clear, persuasive argument. This is especially true when the meanings assigned to abstract terms vary from reader to reader.

In establishing claims based on the support of values, for example, you may use such abstract terms as *religion, duty, freedom, peace, progress, justice, equality, democracy,* and *pursuit of happiness.* You can assume that some of these words are associated with the same ideas and emotions for almost all readers; others require further explanation. Suppose you write, "We have made great progress in the last fifty years." One dictionary defines *progress* as "a gradual betterment," another abstraction. How will you define "gradual betterment" for your readers? Can you be sure that they have in mind the same references for progress that you do? If not, misunderstandings are inevitable. You may offer examples: supersonic planes, computers, shopping malls, nuclear energy. Many of your readers will react favorably to the mention of these innovations, which to them represent progress; others, for whom these inventions represent change but not progress, will react unfavorably. You may not be able to convince all of your readers that "we have made great progress," but all of them will now understand what you mean by "progress." And intelligent disagreement is preferable to misunderstanding.

Abstractions tell us what conclusions we have arrived at; details tell us how we got there. But there are dangers in either too many details or too many abstractions. For example, a writer may present only concrete data without telling readers what conclusions are to be drawn from them. Suppose you read the following:

> To Chinese road-users, traffic police are part of the grass . . . and neither they nor the rules they're supposed to enforce are paid the least attention. . . . Ignoring traffic-lights is only one peculiarity of Chinese traffic. It's normal for a pedestrian to walk straight out into a stream of cars without so much as lifting his head; and goodness knows how many Chinese cyclists I've almost killed as they have shot blindly in front of me across busy main roads.[14]

These details would constitute no more than interesting gossip until we read, "It's not so much a sign of ignorance or recklessness . . . but of fatalism." The details of specific behavior have now acquired a significance expressed in the abstraction *fatalism*.

A more common problem, however, in using abstractions is omission of details. Either the writer is not a skilled observer and cannot provide the details, or he or she feels that such details are too small and quiet compared to the grand sounds made by abstract terms. These grand sounds, unfortunately, cannot compensate for the lack of clarity and liveliness. Lacking detailed support, abstract words may be misinterpreted. They may also represent ideas that are so vague as to be meaningless. Sometimes they function illegitimately as short cuts (discussed on pp. 335–42), arousing emotions but unaccompanied by good reasons for their use. The following paragraph exhibits some of these common faults. How would you translate it into clear English?

> We respectively petition, request, and entreat that due and adequate provision be made, this day and the date hereinafter subscribed, for the satisfying of these petitioners' nutritional requirements and for the organizing of such methods of allocation and distribution as may be deemed necessary and proper to assure the reception by and for said petitioners of such quantities of baked cereal products as shall, in the judgment of the aforesaid petitioners, constitute a sufficient supply thereof.[15]

If you had trouble decoding this, it was because there were almost no concrete references — the homely words *baked* and *cereal* leap out of the paragraph like English signposts in a foreign country — and too many

14 Philip Short, "The Chinese and the Russians," *The Listener,* April 8, 1982, p. 6.
15 *New York Times,* May 10, 1977, p. 35.

long words or words of Latin origin when simple words would do: *requirements* instead of *needs, petition* instead of *ask.* An absence of concrete references and an excess of long Latinate words can have a depressing effect on both writer and reader. The writer may be in danger of losing the thread of the argument, the reader at a loss to discover the message.

The paragraph above, according to James B. Minor, a lawyer who teaches courses in legal drafting, is "how a federal regulation writer would probably write, 'Give us this day our daily bread.'" This brief sentence with its short, familiar words and its origin in the Lord's Prayer has a deep emotional effect. The paragraph composed by Minor deadens any emotional impact because of its preponderance of abstract terms and its lack of connection with the world of our senses.

That passage was invented to educate writers in the government bureaucracy to avoid inflated prose. But writing of this kind is not uncommon among professional writers, including academics. If the subject matter is unfamiliar and the writer an acknowledged expert, you may have to expend a special effort in penetrating the language. But you may also rightly wonder if the writer is making unreasonable demands on you.

> The human race is now entering upon a new phase of evolutionary consciousness and progress, a phase in which, impelled by the forces of evolution itself, it must converge upon itself and convert itself into one single human organism infused by a reconciliation of knowing and being in their inner unity and destined to make a qualitative leap into a higher form of consciousness as we know it, or otherwise destroy itself. For the entire universe is one vast field, potential for incarnation, and achieving incandescence here and there of reason and spirit. And in the whole world of *quality* with which by the nature of our minds we necessarily make contact, we here and there apprehend preeminent value. This can be achieved only if we recognize that we are unable to focus our attention on the particulars of the whole, without diminishing our comprehension of the whole, and of course, conversely, we can focus on the whole only by diminishing our comprehension of the particulars which constitute the whole.[16]

You probably found this paragraph even more baffling than the previous example. Although there is some glimmer of meaning here—that mankind must attain a higher level of consciousness, or perish—you should ask whether the extraordinary overload of abstract terms is justified. In fact, most readers would be disinclined to sit still for an argument with so little reference to the real world. One critic of social science prose maintains that if preeminent thinkers like Bertrand Russell can make themselves clear but social scientists continue to be obscure, "then you can justifiably suspect that it might all be nonsense."[17]

---

[16] Ruth Nanda Anshen, "Credo Perspectives," introduction to James Bryant Conant, *Two Modes of Thought* (New York: Simon and Schuster, 1964), p. x.

[17] Stanislav Andreski, *Social Sciences as Sorcery* (New York: St. Martin's Press, 1972), p. 86.

Finally, there are the moral implications of using abstractions that conceal a disagreeable reality. George Orwell pointed them out more than forty years ago in "Politics and the English Language." Another essayist, Joseph Wood Krutch, in criticizing the attitude that cheating "doesn't really hurt anybody," observed, "'It really doesn't hurt anybody' means it doesn't do that abstraction called society any harm." The following news story reports a proposal with which Orwell and Krutch might have agreed. His intention, says the author, is to "slow the hand of any President who might be tempted to unleash a nuclear attack."

> It has long been feared that a President could be making his fateful decision while at a "psychological distance" from the victims of a nuclear barrage; that he would be in a clean, air-conditioned room, surrounded by well-scrubbed aides, all talking in abstract terms about appropriate military responses in an international crisis, and that he might well push to the back of his mind the realization that hundreds of millions of people would be exterminated.
>
> So Roger Fisher, professor of law at Harvard University, offers a simple suggestion to make the stakes more real. He would put the codes needed to fire nuclear weapons in a little capsule, and implant the capsule next to the heart of a volunteer, who would carry a big butcher knife as he accompanied the President everywhere. If the President ever wanted to fire nuclear weapons, he would first have to kill, with his own hands, that human being.
>
> He has to look at someone and realize what death is—what an innocent death is. "It's reality brought home," says Professor Fisher.[18]

The moral lesson is clear: It is much easier to do harm if we convince ourselves that the object of the injury is only an abstraction.

SHORT CUTS

Short cuts are arguments that depend on readers' responses to words. Short cuts, like other devices we have discussed so far, are a common use of emotive language but are often mistaken for valid argument.

Although they have power to move us, these abbreviated substitutes for argument avoid the hard work necessary to provide facts, expert opinion, and analysis of warrants. Even experts, however, can be guilty of using short cuts, and the writer who consults an authority should be alert to that authority's use of language. Two of the most common uses of short cuts are clichés and slogans.

---

[18] *New York Times,* September 7, 1982, sec. C, p. 1.

■ Clichés

"I'm against sloppy, emotional thinking. I'm against fashionable thinking. I'm against the whole cliché of the moment."[19] This statement by the late Herman Kahn, the founder of the Hudson Institute, a famous think tank, serves as the text for this section. A cliché is an expression or idea grown stale through overuse. Clichés in language are tired expressions that have faded like old photographs; readers no longer see anything when clichés are placed before them. Clichés include phrases like "cradle of civilization," "few and far between," "rude awakening," "follow in the footsteps of," "fly in the ointment."

But more important to recognize and avoid are clichés of thought. A cliché of thought may be likened to a formula, which one dictionary defines as "any conventional rule or method for doing something, especially when used, applied, or repeated without thought." Clichés of thought represent ready-made answers to questions, stereotyped solutions to problems, "knee-jerk" reactions. Two writers who call these forms of expression "mass language" describe it this way: "Mass language is language which presents the reader with a response he is expected to make without giving him adequate reason for having this response."[20] These "clichés of the moment" are often expressed in single words or phrases. For example, the term "Generation Y" has been repeated so often that it has come to represent an undisputed truth about a huge age group from 12 to 18 who are supposed to share the same primitive tastes in entertainment. But, in fact, moviemakers attempting to capitalize on their alleged preferences for horror and teen romance have discovered that "There is no way to program them." One of the teenagers says, "Our generation is very diverse."[21]

Certain cultural attitudes encourage the use of clichés. The liberal American tradition has been governed by hopeful assumptions about our ability to solve problems. A professor of communications says that "we tell our students that for every problem there must be a solution."[22] But real solutions are hard to come by. In our haste to provide them, to prove that we can be decisive, we may be tempted to produce familiar responses that resemble solutions.

History teaches us that a solution to an old and serious problem is almost always accompanied by unexpected drawbacks. As the writer quoted in the previous paragraph warns us, "Life is not that simple. There is no

---

[19] *New York Times,* July 8, 1983, sec. B, p. 1.

[20] Richard E. Hughes and P. Albert Duhamel, *Rhetoric: Principles and Usage* (Englewood Cliffs, N.J.: Prentice-Hall, 1962), p. 161.

[21] Bruce Orwall, "It's Hollywood's Turn to Scream," *Wall Street Journal,* August 10, 2001, Bi.

[22] Malcolm O. Sillars, "The New Conservatism and the Teacher of Speech," *Southern Speech Journal* 21 (1956), p. 240.

one answer to a given problem. There are multiple solutions, all with advantages and disadvantages." By solving one problem, we often create another. Automobiles, advanced medical techniques, industrialization, and liberal divorce laws have all contributed to the solution of age-old problems: lack of mobility, disease, poverty, domestic unhappiness. We now see that these solutions bring with them new problems that we nevertheless elect to live with because the advantages seem greater than the disadvantages. A well-known economist puts it this way: "I don't look for solutions; I look for trade-offs. I think the person who asks, 'What is the solution to this problem?' has a fundamental misconception of the way the world works. We have trade-offs, and that's all we have."[23]

This means that we should be skeptical of solutions promising everything and ignoring limitations and criticism. Such solutions have probably gone around many times. Having heard them so often, we are inclined to believe that they have been tried and proven. Thus they escape serious analysis.

Some of these problems and their solutions represent the fashionable thinking to which Kahn objected. They confront us everywhere, like the public personalities who gaze at us week after week from the covers of magazines and tabloid newspapers at the checkout counter in the supermarket. Alarms about the failures of public education, about drug addiction or danger to the environment or teenage pregnancy are sounded throughout the media continuously. The same solutions are advocated again and again: "Back to basics"; "Impose harsher sentences"; "Offer sex education." Their popularity, however, should not prevent us from asking: Are the problems as urgent as their prominence in the media suggests? Are the solutions workable? Does sufficient evidence exist to justify their adoption?

Your arguments will not always propose solutions. They will sometimes provide interpretations of or reasons for social phenomena, especially for recurrent problems. Some explanations have acquired the status of folk wisdom, like proverbs, and careless arguers will offer them as if they needed no further support. One object of stereotyped responses is the problem of juvenile delinquency, which liberals attribute to poverty, lack of community services, meaningless education, and violence on television. Conservatives blame parental permissiveness, decline in religious influence, lack of individual responsibility, lenient courts. Notice that the interpretations of the causes of juvenile delinquency are related to an ideology, to a particular view of the world that may prevent the arguer from recognizing any other way of examining the problem. Other stereotyped explanations for a range of social problems include inequality, competition, self-indulgence, alienation, discrimination, technology, lack of patriotism, excessive governmental regulation, and lack of sufficient

[23]Thomas Sowell, "Manhattan Report" (edited transcript of *Meet the Press*) (New York: International Center for Economic Policy Studies, 1981), p. 10.

governmental regulation. All of these explanations are worthy of consideration, but they must be defined and supported if they are to be used in a thoughtful, well-constructed argument.

Although formulas change with the times, some are unexpectedly hardy and survive long after critics have revealed their weaknesses. Overpopulation is often cited as the cause of poverty, disease, and war. It can be found in the writing of the ancient Greeks 2,500 years ago. "That perspective," says the editor of *Food Monitor,* a journal published by World Hunger Year, Inc., "is so pervasive that most Americans have simply stopped thinking about population and resort to inane clucking of tongues."[24] If the writer offering overpopulation as an explanation for poverty were to look further, he or she would discover that the explanation rested on shaky data. Singapore, the most densely populated country in the world (11,574 persons per square mile) is also one of the richest ($16,500 per capita income per year). Chad, one of the most sparsely populated (11 persons per square mile) is also one of the poorest ($190 per capita income per year).[25] Strictly defined, overpopulation may serve to explain some instances of poverty; obviously it cannot serve as a blanket to cover all or even most instances. "By repeating stock phrases," one columnist reminds us, "we lose the ability, finally, to hear what we are saying."

■ Slogans

I have always been rather impressed by those people who wear badges stating where they stand on certain issues. The badges have to be small, and therefore the message has to be small, concise, and without elaboration. So it comes out as "I hate something" or "I love something," or ban this or ban that. There isn't space for argument, and I therefore envy the badge-wearer who is so clear-cut about his or her opinions.[26]

The word *slogan* has a picturesque origin. A slogan was the war cry or rallying cry of a Scottish or Irish clan. From that early use it has come to mean a "catchword or rallying motto distinctly associated with a political party or other group" as well as a "catch phrase used to advertise a product."

Slogans, like clichés, are short, undeveloped arguments. They represent abbreviated responses to often complex questions. As a reader you need to be aware that slogans merely call attention to a problem; they cannot offer persuasive proof for a claim in a dozen words or less. As a writer you should avoid the use of slogans that evoke an emotional re-

---

[24] Letter to the *New York Times,* October 4, 1982, sec. A, p. 18.

[25] *World Almanac and Book of Facts,* 1995 (New York: World Almanac, 1995), pp. 754, 818.

[26] Anthony Smith, "Nuclear Power—Why Not?" *The Listener,* October 22, 1981, p. 463.

sponse "without giving [the reader] adequate reason for having this response."

Advertising slogans are the most familiar. Some of them are probably better known than nursery rhymes: "Got milk?" "L'Oréal, because I'm worth it," "Nike, just do it." Advertisements may, of course, rely for their effectiveness on more than slogans. They may also give us interesting and valuable information about products, but most advertisements give us slogans that ignore proof—short cuts substituting for argument.

The persuasive appeal of advertising slogans heavily depends on the connotations associated with products. In Chapter 5 (see p. 173, under "Appeals to Needs and Values"), we discussed the way in which advertisements promise to satisfy our needs and protect our values. Wherever evidence is scarce or nonexistent, the advertiser must persuade us through skillful choice of words and phrases (as well as pictures), especially those that produce pleasurable feelings. "Let it inspire you" is the slogan of a popular liqueur. It suggests a desirable state of being but remains suitably vague about the nature of the inspiration. Another familiar slogan—"Noxzema, clean makeup"—also emphasizes a quality that we approve of, but what is "clean" makeup? Since the advertisers are silent, we are left with warm feelings about the word and not much more.

Advertising slogans are persuasive because their witty phrasing and punchy rhythms produce an automatic yes response. We react to them as we might react to the lyrics of popular songs, and we treat them far less critically than we treat more straightforward and elaborate arguments. Still, the consequences of failing to analyze the slogans of advertisers are usually not serious. You may be tempted to buy a product because you were fascinated by a brilliant slogan, but if the product doesn't satisfy, you can abandon it without much loss. However, ignoring ideological slogans coined by political parties or special-interest groups may carry an enormous price, and the results are not so easily undone.

Ideological slogans, like advertising slogans, depend on the power of connotation, the emotional associations aroused by a word or phrase. In the 1960s and 1970s, a period of well-advertised social change, slogans flourished; they appeared by the hundreds of thousands on buttons, T-shirts, and bumper stickers. One of them read, "Student Power!" To some readers of the slogan, distrustful of young people and worried about student unrest on campuses and in the streets, the suggestion was frightening. To others, mostly students, the idea of power, however undefined, was intoxicating. Notice that "Student Power!" is not an argument; it is only a claim. (It might also represent a warrant.) As a claim, for example, it might take this form: Students at this school should have the power to select the faculty. Of course, the arguer would need to provide the kinds of proof that support his or her claim, something the slogan by itself cannot do. Many people, whether they accepted or rejected the claim, supplied the rest of the argument without knowing exactly what the issues were and how a developed argument would proceed. They were accepting or rejecting the slogan largely on the basis of emotional reaction to words.

American political history is, in fact, a repository of slogans. Leaf through a history of the United States and you will come across "Tippecanoe and Tyler, too," "manifest destiny," "fifty-four forty or fight," "make the world safe for democracy," "the silent majority," "the domino theory," "the missile gap," "the window of vulnerability." Each administration tries to capture the attention and allegiance of the public by coining catchy phrases. Roosevelt's New Deal in 1932 was followed by the Square Deal and the New Frontier. Today, slogans must be carefully selected to avoid offending groups that are sensitive to the ways in which words affect their interests. In 1983 Senator John Glenn, announcing his candidacy for president, talked about bringing "old values and new horizons" to the White House. "New horizons" apparently carried positive connotations. His staff, however, worried that "old values" might suggest racism and sexism to minorities and women.

A professor of politics and international affairs at Princeton University explains why public officials use slogans, despite their obvious shortcomings:

> Officials long have tried to capture complicated events and to dominate public discussion of foreign policy by using simple phrases and slogans. They engage in phrase-making in order to reach wide audiences. . . .
>
> Slogans and metaphors often express the tendencies of officials and academics who have a common wish to be at once sweeping, unequivocal, easily understood, and persuasive. The desire to capture complicated phenomena through slogans stems also from impatience with the particular and unwillingness or inability to master interrelationships.[27]

Over a period of time slogans, like clichés, can acquire a life of their own and, if they are repeated often enough, come to represent an unchanging truth we no longer need to examine. "Dangerously," says the writer quoted above, "policy makers become prisoners of the slogans they popularize."

Following are two examples. The first is part of the second inaugural address of George C. Wallace, governor of Alabama, in 1971. The second is taken from an article in the *Militia News,* the organ of a group that believed the United States government was engaged in a "satanic conspiracy" to disarm the American people and then enslave them. Timothy McVeigh, who blew up the Oklahoma City federal building in 1995, was influenced by the group.

> The people of the South and those who think like the South, represent the majority viewpoint within our constitutional democracy, but they are not organized and do not speak with a loud voice. Until the day ar-

---

[27] Henry Bienen, "Slogans Aren't the World," *New York Times,* January 16, 1983, sec. 4, p. 19.

rives when the voice of the people of the South and those who think like us is, within the law, thrust into the face of the bureaucrats, only then can the "people's power" express itself legally and ethically and get results. . . . Too long, oh, too long, has the voice of the people been silenced by their own disruptive government—by governmental bribery in quasi-governmental handouts such as H.E.W. and others that exist in America today! An aroused people can save this nation from those evil forces who seek our destruction. The choice is yours. The hour is growing late![28]

Every gun owner who is the least bit informed knows that those who are behind this conspiracy—who now have their people well placed in political office, in the courts, in the media, and in the schools, are working for the total disarming of the American people and the surrender of our nation and our sovereignty. . . . The time is at hand when men and women must decide whether they are on the side of freedom and justice, the American republic, and Almighty God, or if they are on the side of tyranny and oppression, the New World Order, and Satan.[29]

Whatever power these recommendations might have if their proposals were more clearly formulated, as they stand they are collections of slogans and loaded words. (Even the language falters: Can the voice of the people be thrust into the face of the bureaucrats?) We can visualize some of the slogans as brightly colored banners: "Dislodge Big Money!" "Power to the People!" "Save This Nation from Evil Forces!" "The Choice Is Yours!" Do all the groups mentioned share identical interests? If so, what are they? Given the vagueness of the terms, it is not surprising that arguers on opposite sides of the political spectrum—loosely characterized as liberal and conservative—sometimes resort to the same clichés and slogans: the language of populism, or a belief in conspiracies against God-fearing people, in these examples.

Slogans have numerous shortcomings as substitutes for the development of an argument. First, their brevity presents serious disadvantages. Slogans necessarily ignore exceptions or negative instances that might qualify a claim. They usually speak in absolute terms without describing the circumstances in which a principle or idea might not work. Their claims therefore seem shrill and exaggerated. In addition, brevity prevents the sloganeer from revealing how he or she arrived at conclusions.

Second, slogans may conceal unexamined warrants. When Japanese cars were beginning to compete with American cars, the slogan "Made in America by Americans" appeared on the bumpers of thousands of American-made cars. A thoughtful reader would have discovered in this slogan several implied warrants: American cars are better than Japanese cars; the American economy will improve if we buy American; patriotism

[28] Second Inaugural Address as governor of Alabama, January 18, 1971.
[29] Chip Berlet and Matthew N. Lyons, *Right-Wing Populism in America* (New York: Guildford Press, 2000), p. 301.

can be expressed by buying American goods. If the reader were to ask a few probing questions, he or she might find these warrants unconvincing.

Silent warrants that express values hide in other popular and influential slogans. "Pro-life," the slogan of those who oppose abortion, assumes that the fetus is a living being entitled to the same rights as individuals already born. "Pro-choice," the slogan of those who favor abortion, suggests that the freedom of the pregnant woman to choose is the foremost or only consideration. The words *life* and *choice* have been carefully selected to reflect desirable qualities, but the words are only the beginning of the argument.

Third, although slogans may express admirable sentiments, they often fail to tell us how to achieve their objectives. They address us in the imperative mode, ordering us to take an action or refrain from it. But the means of achieving the objectives may be nonexistent or very costly. If the sloganeer cannot offer workable means for implementing his or her goals, he or she risks alienating the audience.

Sloganeering is one of the recognizable attributes of propaganda. Propaganda for both good and bad purposes is a form of slanting, of selecting language and facts to persuade an audience to take a certain action. Even a good cause may be weakened by an unsatisfactory slogan. The slogans of some organizations devoted to fundraising for people with physical handicaps have come under attack for depicting those with handicaps as helpless. According to one critic, the popular slogan "Jerry's kids" promotes the idea that Jerry Lewis is the sole support of children with muscular dystrophy. Perhaps increased sensitivity to the needs of people with disabilities will produce new words and new slogans. If you assume that your audience is sophisticated and alert, you will probably write your strongest arguments, devoid of clichés and slogans.

The Childswap Society

SANDRA FELDMAN

Introduction: reference to a sci-fi story that suggests her subject

The subject: the problem of child neglect

Development: the plot of the sci-fi story

Many years ago, when I was a teenager, I read a science fiction story that I've never been able to forget. It came back to me with special force this holiday season because I was thinking about this country's national shame—a child poverty rate of 25 percent—and about our lack of urgency in dealing with the problems this poverty creates.

The story described a society with a national child lottery which was held every four years. Every child's name was put into it—there were no exceptions—and children were randomly redistributed to new parents, who raised them for the next four years.

Babies were not part of this lottery. Parents got to keep their newborn children until the next lottery, but then they became part of the national childswap. The cycle was broken every third swap and kids were sent back to their original parents until the next lottery. So by the time you were considered an adult, at age twenty-six, the most time you could have spent with your birth parents was ten years. The other sixteen were simply a matter of chance.

The Luck of the Draw

Maybe one of your new parents would be the head of a gigantic multinational company and the most powerful person in the country or the president of a famous university. Or you might find yourself the child of a family living in a public housing project or migrant labor camp.

The whole idea sounded horrible to me, but 5 people in the childswap society took the lottery for granted. They didn't try to hide their children

---

Sandra Feldman is a former president of the American Federation of Teachers. This essay appeared in the *New York Times* on January 4, 1998, as part of an ongoing "Where We Stand" advertising campaign for the American Federation of Teachers.

343

or send them away to other countries; childswapping was simply part of their culture. And one thing the lottery did was to make the whole society very conscientious about how things were arranged for kids. After all, you never knew where your own child would end up after the next lottery, so in a very real sense everyone's child was — or could be — yours. As a result, children growing up under this system got everything they needed to thrive, both physically and intellectually, and the society itself was harmonious.

Virtues of the childswap society

What if someone wrote a story about what American society in the late twentieth century takes for granted in the arrangements for its children? We might not want to admit it, but don't we take for granted that some kids are going to have much better lives than others? Of course. We take for granted that some will get the best medical treatment and others will be able to get little or none. We take for granted that some kids will go to beautiful, well-cared-for schools with top-notch curriculums, excellent libraries, and computers for every child and others will go to schools where there are not enough desks and textbooks to go around — wretched places where even the toilets don't work.

Further development and support: contrast of the childswap society with American society

(Implicit warrant: All children are entitled to decent lives.)

We take for granted that teachers in wealthy suburban schools will be better paid and better trained than those in poor inner-city or rural schools. We take for granted, in so many ways, that the children whom the lottery of birth has made the most needy will get the least. "After all," we say to ourselves, "it's up to each family to look after its own. If some parents can't give their children what they need to thrive, that's *their* problem."

What Would Happen?

Transition to conclusion

Obviously I'm not suggesting that the United States adopt a childswap system. The idea makes me cringe, and, anyway, it's just a fable. But I like to imagine what would happen if we did.

Conclusion: claim of policy

We'd start with political figures and their children and grandchildren, with governors and mayors and other leaders. What do you suppose

We should treat all children as if they were our own.

would happen when they saw that their children would have the same chance as the sons and daughters of poor people—no more and no less? What would happen to our schools and health-care system—and our shameful national indifference to children who are not ours?

I bet we'd quickly find a way to set things 10 straight and make sure *all* children had an equal chance to thrive.

■ Analysis

This essay concerns a serious educational challenge—equalizing opportunities for all children in this country, whatever their social or economic status. This subject might appear in a State of the Union address or another formal public-policy pronouncement before a large audience. In this essay the author has chosen to treat the subject as if she were engaged in a dialogue with the reader, speaking in familiar language that is neither technical, scholarly, nor literary. But despite its informality, it retains the patterns and grammar of written, not spoken, discourse.

Feldman begins with a kind of introduction that you've already encountered in other essays, an anecdote recounting a personal experience. Because this anecdote consumes a third of the essay, we know that the author considers it a crucial element in her appeal. Although no single personal experience unaccompanied by other evidence provides enough support to change public policy, it can gain our attention and arouse suspense. It can be effective in arguments about policies where personal feelings are relevant and where scientific research has little or no influence on the conclusion. And the use of the personal pronoun throughout ("I," "you," and "we")—even if the subject of the essay is not the author, as in this case—can often make a broad generalization seem more immediate.

Other stylistic devices contribute to the informality of the language. Feldman uses contractions such as "didn't," "can't," and "I've" to maintain the closeness to ordinary speech. In addition, she introduces expressions like "I bet" and the word "kids" for children and homely examples, like "even the toilets don't work." She also inserts rhetorical questions—to which she knows the answers—as a way of provoking thought about the issues. Even using "and" and "but" to begin sentences, a practice frowned on in technical and scientific papers, emphasizes the conversational style of the argument.

In a technical or scientific paper expression of the author's personality and feelings might divert attention from the objective research on which a sound conclusion rests. Feldman's language is appropriate for an article on the op-ed page of a newspaper or a column like "My Turn" in *Newsweek*. In an essay on the future of children or, for that matter, on any

---

Writer's Guide: Choosing Your Words Carefully

1. Be sure you have avoided language with connotations that might produce a negative reaction in your audience that would weaken your argument.
2. If you have used slanted language, consider whether it will advance your argument instead of weakening it.
3. Use picturesque language where appropriate for your purposes.
4. Replace abstract language with concrete language to be more effective.
5. Edit out any clichés or slogans from your early drafts.
6. Achieve a voice that is appropriate for your subject and audience.

---

subject about human welfare that stirs compassion, the language of personal concern can go far in persuading the reader to sympathize with the arguer and her claim.

READINGS FOR ANALYSIS

Americans Entitled to Cheap Gas — Right?

JOAN RYAN

Over the years, Americans have taken a lot of vicious abuse for being selfish and irresponsible. We are often portrayed as a nation that wants to have its cake and eat it too, which, as any American knows, is patently untrue. We also want our ice cream and maybe some Cool Whip.

I bring this up because, once again, we are the targets of international ridicule, this time for our anger over rising gas prices. Gas is up now to about $2 a gallon around the nation. It is averaging $2.31 in California. These prices are outrageous, as indicated by the newspaper and TV-news stories quoting motorists as saying, "These prices are outrageous."

The rest of the world, however, is not sympathetic. They think that because gas is $5.22 a gallon in England, $4.24 a gallon in Tokyo, and $4.92 a gallon in France, we are being piggy for complaining about per-gallon gas prices that, even with the recent spike, are still cheaper than a Starbucks Frappuccino.

Joan Ryan is a columnist for the *San Francisco Chronicle*, where this column appeared on May 20, 2004.

Apparently the rest of the world doesn't understand the underlying sociological reasons we react as we do to increases in gas prices. Unlike them, we drive cars the size of Paris apartments. They obviously don't realize how much gas cars like these consume! It apparently has come as something of a surprise to many of us, too.

When asked to rank the importance of 56 characteristics they considered when buying a new car, Americans ranked fuel economy 44th. This explains why sport utility vehicles, minivans, and light trucks accounted for 54 percent of all new cars bought last year.   5

"It's still more important to have the right number of cup holders than high fuel economy," said Art Spinella, director of CNW Marketing Research, which conducted the survey.

Peter Rennert sells cars at John Irish Jeep in San Rafael. He showed a gray Grand Cherokee to a woman one morning earlier this week. She took the slow stroll around the vehicle, opened the doors, checked out the cargo space, took it for a test drive.

"What kind of gas mileage does it get?" she asked Rennert. He showed her the manufacturer's sticker on the window: 17 to 21 miles per gallon highway.

"That was the last I ever heard about it," Rennert said. "People bring it up mostly because they believe they're supposed to." (The woman loved the car and said she'd be back soon with her husband to hammer out a deal.)

To understand Americans, it is essential for the rest of the world to remember that, underneath it all, we are socially responsible beings just like they are, except we like big things and lots of them. In the United States, there are now 204 million cars and 191 million drivers, more cars than we have people to operate them. Blueberry muffins here are the size of our heads. Soda cups are big enough to harbor small children. We build houses designed on the well-known scientific practice of multiplying the number of family members by pi to reach the appropriate number of bathrooms.   10

If the rest of the world wants to understand us better, I recommend they see the new movie, *Supersize Me!* It's a documentary about a guy who eats nothing but McDonald's food for a month. The movie reinforces what we Americans already know and have known for years: Fast food makes us fat and unhealthy. The movies shows, too, that this knowledge makes no difference whatsoever in our behavior. We still pull up to the golden arches, breathe in that great deep-fry aroma, and order a sack of cholesterol to go.

Why? For the same reasons we buy big cars despite our heartfelt concerns about saving the environment and weaning ourselves from Middle East oil: because it makes us feel good, and because everybody else is doing it.

Across the bay in Richmond, at the ARCO station on Cutting Boulevard and Harbor Way, Sandra Currier filled up her 1998 Chevy Blazer for

$42 the other day. "This is the most I've ever paid," she said of the $2.29 regular unleaded. "It's got to come down."

She is a mobile notary public from Castro Valley who sometimes has to travel as much as 200 miles in a day. She is considering charging more for her services to cover the rising price of gas, but gas is not yet expensive enough to consider trading in her Blazer for something smaller and more fuel-efficient. Maybe when it hits $2.75 a gallon, she said.

"I feel my daughter is safer in the SUV," Currier said. "I don't want to   15
be lower (than everybody else on the road), looking up and getting crunched."

In other words, if everybody else downsized, she would, too. Until then, she's not going to put herself in harm's way by being the poodle on a freeway of water buffalo.

How can the rest of the world blame her? They would do the same under the same circumstances, according to another CNW survey. In Western Europe, respondents said if gas prices were low enough, they would buy SUVs and big sedans, just like the Americans.

"It is kind of amusing," Spinella said. "When we do an international wish list, it's remarkable how similar people are in the kinds of things they would like to get their hands on."

See? There it is. We could be as responsible as the rest of the world if we had the benefit they do of high gas prices. The low price of gas in the United States enables our SUV indulgences. To put this complex social dynamic in the parlance of the latest psychological research: It is not our fault.

Therefore, since this situation is not of our own making, we should   20
not have to pay higher gas prices and give up the big-car life to which we have become accustomed. That would not be right.

And if there is one thing Americans believe in, it is doing what's right.

READING AND DISCUSSION QUESTIONS

1. In the first paragraph, how does Ryan reveal her attitude toward Americans' spending habits?
2. Does Ryan offer any support for her opinion other than her own emotional response to the values of other Americans?
3. How does Ryan's choice of language help her to make her point?
4. Is Ryan's use of sarcasm and exaggeration effective?

WRITING SUGGESTIONS

5. Rewrite Ryan's article using objective language.
6. Choose another one of America's "passions" and write an essay poking gentle fun at it. (Consider, for example, Americans' consumption of fast food.)
7. Compare Ryan's use of language in this piece with that used by Varian in "The True Cost of SUVs" in Chapter 5.

$hotgun Weddings

KATHA POLLITT

What would the government have to do to convince you to get married when you otherwise wouldn't? More than pay you $80 a month, I'll bet, the amount Wisconsin's much-ballyhooed "Bridefare" pilot program offered unwed teen welfare mothers beginning in the early nineties, which is perhaps why then-Governor Tommy Thompson, now Health and Human Services Secretary,[1] was uninterested in having it properly evaluated and why you don't hear much about Bridefare today. OK, how about $100 a month? That's what West Virginia is currently offering to add to a couple's welfare benefits if they wed. But even though the state has simultaneously cut by 25 percent the checks of recipients living with adults to whom they are not married (including, in some cases, their own grown children, if you can believe that!), results have been modest: Only around 1,600 couples have applied for the bonus and presumably some of these would have married anyway. With the state's welfare budget expected to show a $90 million shortfall by 2003, the marriage bonus is likely to be quietly abolished.

Although welfare reform was sold to the public as promoting work, the Personal Responsibility and Work Opportunity Reconciliation Act of 1996 actually opens with the declaration that "marriage is the foundation of a successful society." According to Charles Murray, Robert Rector, and other right-wing ideologues, welfare enabled poor women to rely on the state instead of husbands; forcing them off the dole and into the rigors of low-wage employment would push them into marriage, restore "the family," and lift children out of poverty. That was always a silly idea. For one thing, as any single woman could have told them, it wrongly assumed that whether a woman married was only up to her; for another, it has been well documented that the men available to poor women are also poor and often (like the women) have other problems as well: In one study, 30 percent of poor single fathers were unemployed in the week before the survey and almost 40 percent had been incarcerated; drugs, drink, violence, poor health, and bad attitudes were not uncommon. Would Murray want *his* daughter to marry a guy with even one of those strikes against him? Not surprisingly, there has been no upsurge of marriage among former welfare recipients since 1996. Of all births, the proportion that are to unwed mothers has stayed roughly where it was, at 33 percent.

---

[1]Thompson resigned on December 3, 2004.

Katha Pollitt has written about controversial moral and political issues for *The Nation*, *The New Yorker*, and the *New York Times*. This selection originally appeared in the February 4, 2002, edition of *The Nation*.

Since the stick of work and the carrot of cash have both proved ineffective in herding women to the altar, family values conservatives are calling for more lectures. Marriage promotion will be a hot item when welfare reform comes up for reauthorization later this year. At the federal level conservatives are calling for 10 percent of all TANF [Temporary Assistance for Needy Families] money to be set aside for promoting marriage; Utah, Arizona, and Oklahoma have already raided TANF to fund such ventures as a "healthy marriage" handbook for couples seeking a marriage license. And it's not just Republicans: Senator Joe Lieberman and Representative Ben Cardin, the ranking Democrat on the House Ways and Means Committee, are also interested in funding "family formation." In place of cash bonuses to individuals, which at least put money in the pockets of poor people, look for massive funding of faith-based marriage preparation courses (and never you mind that pesky separation of church and state), for fatherhood intervention programs, classes to instruct poor single moms in the benefits of marriage (as if they didn't know!), for self-help groups like Marriage Savers, abstinence education for kids and grownups alike and, of course, ingenious pilot projects by the dozen. There's even been a proposal to endow pro-marriage professorships at state universities—and don't forget millions of dollars for evaluation, follow-up, filing and forgetting.

There's nothing wrong with programs that aim to raise people's marital IQ—I love that journalistic evergreen about the engaged couple who take a quiz in order to qualify for a church wedding and call it off when they discover he wants seven kids and she wants to live in a tree. But remember when it was conservatives who argued against social engineering and micromanaging people's private lives and "throwing money at the problem"?

Domestic violence experts have warned that poor women may find   5
themselves pushed into marrying their abusers and staying with them—in a disturbing bit of Senate testimony, Mike McManus of Marriage Savers said domestic violence could usually be overcome with faith-based help. Is that the message women in danger should be getting? But there are even larger issues: Marriage is a deeply personal, intimate matter, involving our most private, barely articulated selves. Why should the government try to maneuver reluctant women into dubious choices just because they are poor? Even as a meal ticket wedlock is no panacea—that marriage is a cure for poverty is only true if you marry someone who isn't poor, who will share his income with you and your children, who won't divorce you later and leave you worse off than ever. The relation between poverty and marriage is virtually the opposite of what pro-marriage ideologues claim: It isn't that getting married gives feckless poor people middle-class values and stability; it's that stable middle-class people are the ones who can "afford" to be married. However marriage functioned a half-century ago, today it is a class marker. Instead of marketing marriage as a poverty program, how much better to invest in poor women—and

poor men — as human beings in their own right: with education, training for high-paying jobs, housing, mental health services, really good child-care for their kids. Every TANF dollar spent on marital propaganda means a dollar less for programs that really help people.

The very fact that welfare reformers are reduced to bribing, cajoling, and guilt-tripping people into marriage should tell us something. Or have they just not hit on the right incentive? As a divorced single mother, I've given some thought to what it would take for me to marry against my own inclination in order to make America great again. Here's my offer: If the government brings Otis Redding back to life and books him to sing at my wedding, I will marry the Devil himself. And if the Devil is unavail-able, my ex-husband says he's ready.

READING AND DISCUSSION QUESTIONS

1. What claim is Pollitt supporting in the essay?
2. What does Pollitt reveal about the history of welfare reform as it relates to marriage? Where does Pollitt say the money for welfare reform is going? Where should it go?
3. Where does Pollitt's word choice reveal her bias? Does her own opinion keep her from being fair?

WRITING SUGGESTIONS

4. Write an essay in which you either support or refute Pollitt's claim.
5. If a monetary marriage bonus is not enough to entice many unwed Amer-icans to get married, what might be enough?

The Speech the Graduates Didn't Hear

JACOB NEUSNER

We the faculty take no pride in our educational achievements with you. We have prepared you for a world that does not exist, indeed, that cannot exist. You have spent four years supposing that failure leaves no record. You have learned at Brown that when your work goes poorly, the painless solution is to drop out. But starting now, in the world to which you go, failure marks you. Confronting difficulty by quitting leaves you changed. Outside Brown, quitters are no heroes.

Jacob Neusner, formerly university professor at Brown University and distinguished professor of religious studies at the University of South Florida in Tampa, is now a re-search professor of religion and theology at Bard College. His speech appeared in Brown's *Daily Herald* on June 12, 1983.

With us you could argue about why your errors were not errors, why mediocre work really was excellent, why you could take pride in routine and slipshod presentation. Most of you, after all, can look back on honor grades for most of what you have done. So, here grades can have meant little in distinguishing the excellent from the ordinary. But tomorrow, in the world to which you go, you had best not defend errors but learn from them. You will be ill-advised to demand praise for what does not deserve it, and abuse those who do not give it.

For four years we created an altogether forgiving world, in which whatever slight effort you gave was all that was demanded. When you did not keep appointments, we made new ones. When your work came in beyond the deadline, we pretended not to care.

Worse still, when you were boring, we acted as if you were saying something important. When you were garrulous and talked to hear yourself talk, we listened as if it mattered. When you tossed on our desks writing upon which you had not labored, we read it and even responded, as though you earned a response. When you were dull, we pretended you were smart. When you were predictable, unimaginative, and routine, we listened as if to new and wonderful things. When you demanded free lunch, we served it. And all this why?

Despite your fantasies, it was not even that we wanted to be liked by   5 you. It was that we did not want to be bothered, and the easy way out was pretense: smiles and easy Bs.

It is conventional to quote in addresses such as these. Let me quote someone you've never heard of: Professor Carter A. Daniel, Rutgers University (*Chronicle of Higher Education,* May 7, 1979):

> College has spoiled you by reading papers that don't deserve to be read, listening to comments that don't deserve a hearing, paying attention even to the lazy, ill-informed, and rude. We had to do it, for the sake of education. But nobody will ever do it again. College has deprived you of adequate preparation for the last fifty years. It has failed you by being easy, free, forgiving, attentive, comfortable, interesting, unchallenging fun. Good luck tomorrow.

That is why, on this commencement day, we have nothing in which to take much pride.

Oh, yes, there is one more thing. Try not to act toward your co-workers and bosses as you have acted toward us. I mean, when they give you what you want but have not earned, don't abuse them, insult them, act out with them your parlous relationships with your parents. This too we have tolerated. It was, as I said, not to be liked. Few professors actually care whether or not they are liked by peer-paralyzed adolescents, fools so shallow as to imagine professors care not about education but about popularity. It was, again, to be rid of you. So go, unlearn the lies we taught you. To Life!

READING AND DISCUSSION QUESTIONS

1. Neusner condemns students for various shortcomings. But what is he saying, both directly and indirectly, about teachers? Find places where he reveals his attitude toward them, perhaps inadvertently.

2. Pick out some of the language devices—connectives, parallel structures, sentence variety—that the author uses effectively.

3. Pick out some of the words and phrases—especially adjectives and verbs—used by Neusner to characterize both students and teachers. Do you think these terms are loaded? Explain.

4. Has the author chosen "facts" to slant his article? If so, point out where slanting occurs. If not, point out where the article seems to be truthful.

5. As a student you will probably object to Neusner's accusations. How would you defend your behavior as a student in answer to his specific charges?

WRITING SUGGESTIONS

6. Rewrite Neusner's article with the same "facts"—or others from your experience—using temperate language and a tone of sadness rather than anger.

7. Write a letter to Neusner responding to his attack. Support or attack his argument by providing evidence from your own experience.

8. Write your own short commencement address. Do some things need to be said that commencement speakers seldom or never express?

9. Write an essay using the same kind of strong language as Neusner uses about some aspect of your education of which you disapprove. Or write a letter to a teacher using the same form as "The Speech the Graduates Didn't Hear."

Tightening the Nuts and Bolts of Death by Electric Chair

A. C. SOUD JR., WITH TOM KUNTZ

No one doubts that things went wrong at the execution of Pedro Medina in Florida last March: as thousands of volts of electricity coursed through the murderer's body, flames burst from his face mask, startling the assembled witnesses and prompting a public outcry. But does this unsettling episode mean that execution in Florida's electric chair is cruel and unusual punishment?

A. C. Soud Jr. is a circuit court judge in Jacksonville, Florida. Tom Kuntz writes for the *New York Times*, where this article appeared on August 3, 1997.

*No, a Florida circuit court judge ruled last month. In rejecting a death-row in-
mate's constitutional challenge, Judge A. C. Soud Jr. provided many details of
the mechanics and procedures of electrocution in Florida, along with the reasoning behind his decision. Excerpts follow.*

—Tom Kuntz

*The judge upheld Florida's execution procedures, attributing the malfunction at
the Medina execution to "unintentional human error" that caused a sponge used
to conduct electricity to the inmate's head to ignite inside his headgear. A similar problem was blamed in the fiery execution of Jesse Tafero in 1990. The judge
gave details of execution procedures since then:*

Findings of Fact

1. . . . There were sixteen executions carried out between the execution of Tafero and the most recent execution of Pedro Medina. There were
no changes made in the design to or the material used in the electric chair
apparatus during that period of time. No malfunction of the electric chair
occurred during the sixteen executions. . . .

2. The procedures used for testing the electric chair and its apparatus   5
have been consistently the same, through the Medina execution, for all
seventeen executions since Tafero's execution. The testing procedures included the testing of the electrical equipment, the meters, the switches,
the voltage output, and the amount of amperage created. Testing occurred three times before an execution: when the [death] warrant was
signed, a week before the scheduled execution, and the day before an
execution. . . .

The judge paid particular attention to the preparation of sponges:

3. The procedures for the preparation of the sponges used in an execution have been employed consistently since the Tafero execution. . . .
The preparation consisted of soaking one large and two smaller natural
sea sponges in a container of water having a 9 percent saline content [salt-
water]. The sponges were placed in the saline solution the night before
the day of a scheduled execution. The large wet sponge is placed around
the inmate's shaved right leg and the leg electrode is then placed on the
inmate's right calf. The leg electrode is three-and-a-half inches high and
eight inches long shaped in a semicircular fashion. The leg electrode was
made of lead. The head piece is principally made of leather. The inside
crown of the head piece consists of a brass screen secured by a nut to a
high voltage wire, which enters the head piece from the outside. The
brass screen is round and measures four inches in diameter. A dry natural
sea sponge was laced into the bottom of the brass screen electrode. This
component served as the head electrode. The head piece is turned over
and one of the two smaller wet sponges is placed on top of the dry sponge
in the head piece. The head piece is then turned back to an upright posi-

tion and placed on top of the inmate's head (the brass head electrode was, therefore, separated from the inmate's head by a dry sponge and a wet sponge, in that descending order). The second smaller soaked sponge is left in the soaking solution as a spare.

4. Preparation of inmate Medina was performed in all respects as was performed on the previous sixteen inmates who were executed since the execution of Tafero in 1990, and consisted of the shaving of Medina's head and the application of the normal amount of electroconductive gel to Medina's scalp. The gel is used to further reduce the normal amount of postmortem burning that occurs to the inmate's scalp during the electrocution process. . . .

5. Consistent with the previous sixteen executions, Medina was placed in the electric chair and straps were placed around Medina's chest, abdomen, arms, and legs. Medina's head was firmly secured to the back of the chair using a mouth and chin strap. A large wet (saline soaked) sponge was placed around Medina's right leg and the leg electrode was then strapped to his leg. The head piece, as previously described, was then placed over Medina's head.

6. Pursuant to the standard procedure used by the death chamber 10 team, death was brought on by activating the electrical system, which automatically—by a programmed controlled circuitry—administered three cycles of electricity in the following amounts and durations without interruption:

First Cycle: High Voltage—2,200 to 2,350 volts—for eight seconds;

Second Cycle: Low Voltage—750 to 1,000 volts—for twenty-two seconds;

Third Cycle: High Voltage—2,200 to 2,350 volts—for eight seconds.

As with the sixteen previous executions, and according to the normal procedures used, the third cycle was manually shut down four seconds into the third cycle.

The switch at the panel box was activated at 7:04 A.M. Electricity was administered to Medina at 7:04.50 A.M. and cut off at 7:05.25 A.M. Electricity was administered continually for 35 seconds. Medina was pronounced dead at 7:10 A.M.

The judge then turned to what went wrong:

7. When Pedro Medina was executed on March 25, 1997, the following events occurred. When the electrical current was activated, within seconds, a little smoke emanated from under the right side of Medina's head piece, followed by a four- to five-inch yellow-orange flame, which lasted four to five seconds and then disappeared. After the flame went out, more smoke emanated from under the head piece to the extent that

the death chamber was filled with smoke—but the smoke was not dense enough to impair visibility. . . .

Although several witnesses to the execution tried to describe the odor 15 of the smoke, only one witness, Florida State prison Superintendent Ronald McAndrews, described the odor as burnt sponge. Mr. McAndrews was the only witness who was subsequently in attendance on April 8, 1997, when two experts appointed by the Governor [Lawton Chiles] were conducting tests on the electric chair apparatus and similarly ignited a dry sponge, resulting in smoke. Mr. McAndrews described both odors as being the same. This court finds that the odor smelled was burnt sponge, not burnt flesh. . . .

There was a further unsettling moment when a physician examined Mr. Medina just after the current was turned off.

Medina's chest was seen to move two or three times in a two- to four-minute period. A couple of witnesses thought Medina was trying to breathe. . . . A neurologist testified that this movement could be caused by the last vestiges of survival in the brain stem after the brain itself has died. . . .

The malfunction was widely reported (journalists are always included among the witnesses in an observation room), and the state ordered an autopsy of Mr. Medina's body:

[The pathologists] concluded in their testimony that Medina's death was instantaneous due to massive depolarization of Medina's brain and brain stem when the initial surge of 2,200 to 2,350 volts of electricity entered Medina's head. [One doctor] described it as "like turning the lights off." . . . Cause of death was further exacerbated by a dramatic rise in the brain's temperature to between 138 degrees Fahrenheit to 148 degrees Fahrenheit. . . .

But other expert witnesses called to testify on behalf of the death-row inmate 20 seeking to avoid the chair theorized that Mr. Medina might have suffered an agonizing death. The appellant was Leo Alexander Jones, sentenced to death by Judge Soud for the 1981 slaying of a police officer. The judge rejected the alternate theories:

He suffered no conscious pain. This can be said for all inmates who will be executed in Florida's electric chair hereafter. . . . The Florida electric chair—its apparatus, equipment, and electrical circuitry—is in excellent condition. Testimony in this regard is unrefuted. . . .

But the judge did recommend improvements:

1. The fire and smoke during the Medina execution was the result of the dry sponge laced onto the brass electrode in the head piece catching fire and burning almost completely due to a lack of saline solution in that sponge. The lack of saline solution in the dry sponge caused the dry

sponge to act as a resistor. The resistance produced heat which ignited and consumed the dry sponge.

2. Any future executions should be performed using only one wet sponge in the head piece. . . . The sponge should be thoroughly soaked in a saturated saline solution and not a 9 percent saline solution . . . [to] further reduce any possibility of a reoccurrence of a burning sponge. . . .

[In addition,] although the lead leg electrode was not defective . . . it 25 should be changed from lead to brass, as brass is a better conductor of electricity than lead. . . .

READING AND DISCUSSION QUESTIONS

1. What is your reaction to this objective description of an electrocution? Notice that this description appeared in a ruling by a judge that electrocution was not a violation of the Eighth Amendment's prohibition of cruel and unusual punishment. Does the description's lack of emotional language make the act itself seem less terrible? Explain the reason for your response.

2. Find the places in the report where specific language has been used to depersonalize the act of electrocution and remove emotional connotations. Is this strategy successful in distancing the reader from the actual event?

3. Why do you think the newspaper published this report?

4. If you were revolted by this description, do you think it would make any difference to know the details of the crime(s) that the murderer has committed? Theodore Kaczinski, the Unabomber, wrote in his diary about a secretary who opened a package containing a bomb he had mailed to her boss: "The bomb drove fragments of wood into her flesh. But no indication that she was permanently disabled. Frustrating that I can't seem to make a lethal bomb." Does such a specific reference make you more inclined to favor a death sentence for the bomber, or not?

WRITING SUGGESTIONS

5. Look up "A Hanging" by George Orwell (from *Shooting an Elephant and Other Essays*), a powerful description of an execution Orwell witnessed as an officer in the Indian Imperial Police in Burma. Compare Orwell's treatment of an execution with Soud's treatment in the report you have just read. Choose a claim that establishes the main difference between the two descriptions, and develop two or three points of difference in the language as support for your claim.

6. Write an essay about some incident in your life that taught you an important lesson. You might begin with a statement that summarizes what you learned. Use the language of description and emotion—rich vocabulary, details, metaphors—to make the experience vivid to the reader.

A gun in the home is much more likely to
kill a family member than to kill an intruder.

CEASE FIRE

Think about your family before you think about getting a handgun.

Cease Fire, Inc. P.O. Box 33424, Washington, D.C. 20033-0424.

DISCUSSION QUESTIONS

1. Would this claim of policy be just as successful if the note were excluded? Would additional facts about guns contribute to its effectiveness?

2. Why is the gun so much larger than the printed message?

3. What is the basis of the emotional appeal? Is there more than one? Does the note go too far in exploiting our emotions?

The Right to Bear Arms

WARREN E. BURGER

Our metropolitan centers, and some suburban communities of America, are setting new records for homicides by handguns. Many of our large centers have up to ten times the murder rate of all of Western Europe. In 1988, there were 9,000 handgun murders in America. Last year, Washington, D.C., alone had more than 400 homicides—setting a new record for our capital.

The Constitution of the United States, in its Second Amendment, guarantees a "right of the people to keep and bear arms." However, the meaning of this clause cannot be understood except by looking to the purpose, the setting, and the objectives of the draftsmen. The first ten amendments—the Bill of Rights—were not drafted at Philadelphia in 1787; that document came two years later than the Constitution. Most of the states already had bills of rights, but the Constitution might not have been ratified in 1788 if the states had not had assurances that a national Bill of Rights would soon be added.

People of that day were apprehensive about the new "monster" national government presented to them, and this helps explain the language and purpose of the Second Amendment. A few lines after the First Amendment's guarantees—against "establishment of religion," "free exercise" of religion, free speech and free press—came a guarantee that grew out of the deep-seated fear of a "national" or "standing" army. The same First Congress that approved the right to keep and bear arms also limited the national army to 840 men; Congress in the Second Amendment then provided:

> A well regulated Militia, being necessary to the security of a free State, the right of the people to keep and bear Arms, shall not be infringed.

In the 1789 debate in Congress on James Madison's proposed Bill of Rights, Elbridge Gerry argued that a state militia was necessary:

> to prevent the establishment of a standing army, the bane of liberty. . . . Whenever governments mean to invade the rights and liberties of the people, they always attempt to destroy the militia in order to raise an army upon their ruins.

We see that the need for a state militia was the predicate of the 5 "right" guaranteed; in short, it was declared "necessary" in order to have

---

Warren E. Burger (1907–1995) was chief justice of the United States from 1969 to 1986. This article is from the January 14, 1990, issue of *Parade* magazine.

a state military force to protect the security of the state. That Second Amendment clause must be read as though the word "because" was the opening word of the guarantee. Today, of course, the "state militia" serves a very different purpose. A huge national defense establishment has taken over the role of the militia of 200 years ago.

Some have exploited these ancient concerns, blurring sporting guns—rifles, shotguns, and even machine pistols—with all firearms, including what are now called "Saturday night specials." There is, of course, a great difference between sporting guns and handguns. Some regulation of handguns has long been accepted as imperative; laws relating to "concealed weapons" are common. That we may be "overregulated" in some areas of life has never held us back from more regulation of automobiles, airplanes, motorboats, and "concealed weapons."

Let's look at the history.

First, many of the 3.5 million people living in the thirteen original Colonies depended on wild game for food, and a good many of them required firearms for their defense from marauding Indians—and later from the French and English. Underlying all these needs was an important concept that each able-bodied man in each of the thirteen independent states had to help or defend his state.

The early opposition to the idea of national or standing armies was maintained under the Articles of Confederation; that confederation had no standing army and wanted none. The state militia—essentially a part-time citizen army, as in Switzerland today—was the only kind of "army" they wanted. From the time of the Declaration of Independence through the victory at Yorktown in 1781, George Washington, as the commander in chief of these volunteer-militia armies, had to depend upon the states to send those volunteers.

When a company of New Jersey militia volunteers reported for duty 10 to Washington at Valley Forge, the men initially declined to take an oath to "the United States," maintaining, "Our country is New Jersey." Massachusetts Bay men, Virginians, and others felt the same way. To the American of the eighteenth century, his state was his country, and his freedom was defended by his militia.

The victory at Yorktown—and the ratification of the Bill of Rights a decade later—did not change people's attitudes about a national army. They had lived for years under the notion that each state would maintain its own military establishment, and the seaboard states had their own navies as well. These people, and their fathers and grandfathers before them, remembered how monarchs had used standing armies to oppress their ancestors in Europe. Americans wanted no part of this. A state militia, like a rifle and powder horn, was as much a part of life as the automobile is today; pistols were largely for officers, aristocrats—and dueling.

Against this background, it was not surprising that the provision concerning firearms emerged in very simple terms with the significant predicate—basing the right on the *necessity* for a "well regulated militia," a state army.

In the two centuries since then—with two world wars and some lesser ones—it has become clear, sadly, that we have no choice but to maintain a standing national army while still maintaining a "militia" by way of the National Guard, which can be swiftly integrated into the national defense forces.

Americans also have a right to defend their homes, and we need not challenge that. Nor does anyone seriously question that the Constitution protects the right of hunters to own and keep sporting guns for hunting game any more than anyone would challenge the right to own and keep fishing rods and other equipment for fishing—or to own automobiles. To "keep and bear arms" for hunting today is essentially a recreational activity and not an imperative of survival, as it was 200 years ago; "Saturday night specials" and machine guns are not recreational weapons and surely are as much in need of regulation as motor vehicles.

Americans should ask themselves a few questions. The Constitution 15 does not mention automobiles or motorboats, but the right to keep and own an automobile is beyond question; equally beyond question is the power of the state to regulate the purchase or the transfer of such vehicle and the right to license the vehicle and the driver with reasonable standards. In some places, even a bicycle must be registered, as must some household dogs.

If we are to stop this mindless homicidal carnage, is it unreasonable:

1. to provide that, to acquire a firearm, an application be made reciting age, residence, employment, and any prior criminal convictions?

2. to require that this application lie on the table for ten days (absent a showing for urgent need) before the license would be issued?

3. that the transfer of a firearm be made essentially as that of a motor vehicle?

4. to have a "ballistic fingerprint" of the firearm made by the manufacturer and filed with the license record so that, if a bullet is found in a victim's body, law enforcement might be helped in finding the culprit?

These are the kinds of questions the American people must answer if we are to preserve the "domestic tranquility" promised in the Constitution.

A God-Given Natural Right

ROGER D. McGRATH

I do not believe in unilateral disarmament: not for the nation; not for our citizens. Neither did the Founding Fathers. They were students of history, especially of classical antiquity. They knew the history of the Greek city-states and Rome as well as they knew the history of the American colonies. This led them to conclude that an armed citizenry is essential to the preservation of freedom and democracy. Once disarmed, populations either submit meekly to tyrants or fight in vain.

The ancient Greeks knew this. The Greek city-state of Laconia had a population that was five percent Spartan (the warrior aristocracy), one percent *perioeci* (small merchants and craftsmen), and 94 percent *helots* (serfs bound to the soil). It is no mystery how five percent of the population kept 94 percent of the people enslaved. The *helots* were kept disarmed and, if found in possession of a weapon, were put to death.

Meanwhile, most of the Greek city-states were bastions of democracy because they had developed strong middle classes of armed citizens known as *hoplites*. Supplying their own weapons and equipment, the *hoplites* went into battle not out of fear of punishment or in hopes of plunder and booty, as did subject peoples of the Oriental empires, but to defend their liberties and to protect hearth and home. They fought side by side with neighbors, brothers, fathers, sons, uncles, and cousins. They did their utmost to demonstrate courage, side by side with their comrades in arms. If they lost a battle to the armies of an Oriental despot, they stood to lose everything—property, freedom, democracy. A defeat for subject peoples usually meant nothing more than a change of rulers.

The ancient Romans also knew this. When Tarquin, the Etruscan king of Rome, issued an order—for the public good, for safety and security—that the Romans be disarmed, they rose in rebellion. Tarquin was driven from the city, and the early Roman Republic was established. For several hundred years, Rome was defended not by a professional army of mercenaries or subject peoples but by armed citizen-soldiers who left the farm from time to time to serve the republic. Once the system broke down, the Roman Republic was transformed into an empire similar to the despotic regimes of the East.

For fifteen years, Roger McGrath taught courses in the history of the American West, California, and the United States at UCLA. He now teaches at California State University, Northridge, and is a captain in the Naval Detachment of the California State Military Reserve. His articles have appeared in the *Wall Street Journal, American Guardian, Chronicles,* the *New York Times,* and *Harper's,* among others, and he appears extensively in documentaries about the West and has served as a consultant for television and movies. He is the author of *Gunfighters, Highwaymen, and Vigilantes* (1984) and coauthor of *Violence in America* (1989). This article appeared in the October 2003 issue of *Chronicles.*

Death and destruction commonly followed disarmament. England   5
did it to the Gaels—the Irish and Scots—and the consequences beggar
description. England had been fighting in Ireland for hundreds of years
by the time the English got Irish leader Patrick Sarsfield to sign the Treaty
of Limerick in 1691. The treaty guaranteed all Irish full civil, religious,
and property rights. In return, it required that Sarsfield and more than
20,000 of his soldiers leave Ireland for the Continent.

With the armed defenders of Ireland overseas, England began to ab-
rogate the rights supposedly guaranteed by the treaty. Beginning in 1709,
England passed the statutes that collectively became known as the Penal
Laws. One of the first of these laws declared that, for public safety, no
Irish Catholic could keep and bear arms. Then the Irish Catholic was denied the right to an education, to enter a profession, to hold public office,
to engage in trade or commerce, to own a horse of greater value than five
pounds, to purchase or lease land, to vote, to attend the worship of his
choice, to send his children abroad to receive an education. By the time
the last of the Penal Laws was enacted, the Irish, although they were not
chattel property, in many ways had fewer rights than black slaves in
America. The Irish were kept on a near starvation diet, and their life expectancy was the lowest in the Western world.

Things were not much better in the Highlands of Scotland. England
had subdued the Lowlands by the fourteenth century, but the Highlands,
the truly Gaelic portion of Scotland, continued to be troublesome well
into the eighteenth century. A major rebellion erupted in 1715; another,
in 1745. The end for the Highlanders came at the Battle of Culloden in
1746. Following the battle, the English built a series of forts across the
Highlands and passed laws for the Highlanders—who were originally
Irish, of course—similar to the Penal Laws. England made it a crime for
the Highlanders to wear kilts, play bagpipes, and keep and bear arms. A
Highlander found with a claymore or any other kind of sword or arm was
put to death. The English army, understanding that it is easier to starve a
fierce enemy into submission than to fight him, eagerly slaughtered the
cattle herds of the Highlands, precipitating a great starvation. Thousands
of Highlanders died or fled. The English later engaged in the infamous
"clearances" in which thousands more were driven from the land. Without arms, the Highlanders were helpless.

What the English did to the Irish and Scots was not lost on our
Founding Fathers or on the colonists in general. More than a quarter of
the colonists were Irish or Scottish or Scotch-Irish. When England tried to
disarm the American colonists, all under the guise of preserving public
order and peace, the colonists reacted violently. While it is rarely taught
in schools today, the reason the British army marched to Lexington and
Concord was to confiscate the arms caches of the local citizenry.

It is not by accident, then, that the Framers of the Constitution ensured that the government could not infringe on "the right of the people
to keep and bear arms." It is important to understand that the Second

Amendment grants no right to the people to keep and bear arms. This is a point misunderstood by most Americans today, even by most of those who are interested in keeping their guns.

The Second Amendment, like the First, recognizes a God-given, natural right of the people and guarantees that the government not interfere with the exercise of that right. Note the wording of the amendment. Nowhere does it say, "This Constitution grants the people the right to . . ." Instead, it says "the right of the people . . . shall not be infringed." The right to keep and bear arms, like that of freedom of speech, is known, constitutionally, as an inherent right. By contrast, the Sixth Amendment right to be represented by an attorney in a criminal case is a derivative right—a right that comes from the Constitution.

To understand this is critical to all arguments about guns, or about freedom of speech, or religion, or the press. These freedoms were not given to us by the Founding Fathers. They were recognized by the Founding Fathers as God-given, natural rights that existed long before the establishment of our republic. These rights are not granted to men by a benevolent government but given to man by God. They are not to be destroyed, suppressed, or even compromised. When they are, it is the duty of the citizens to rise in revolt, overthrow the government, and establish a government that will protect these unalienable rights. Sound familiar? It should. This was the philosophy of our Founding Fathers.

The most basic of the natural rights of man is the right to self-preservation, the right to self-defense. No one would deny that we have such a right. In debates at universities and at other public forums, in debates on radio, in debates on television, I have never seen anyone deny that man has a natural right to self-defense. It follows that, if man has a natural right to self-defense, then he has a right to the arms necessary for that self-defense. The right to be armed is a logical and inescapable corollary of the right to self-defense. We cannot have one without the other.

If we do not have the right to the arms necessary for self-defense, then the right of self-defense is purely theoretical—something like having freedom of the press but not being allowed access to a printing press. Can you imagine the National Rifle Association telling the *New York Times* that it has freedom of the press but it may not have printing presses, or that the *Times* can purchase only one printing press per month, or that its writers must undergo background checks by the government, or that it cannot buy ink for the presses in New York City, or that its presses have limits on their speed and capacity, or that its presses must meet certain design requirements? If any of this were suggested, the *Times* would squeal like a stuck pig, and well it should.

Some people, presumably well intentioned, argue that the right to arms (and, thus, the right to self-defense) should be compromised—compromised further than it already has been—in an effort to make society safer. Such a position is ironic on two counts.

First, many of the same people who make gun-restriction arguments, 15
such as the ACLU, would be apoplectic if it were suggested that freedom
of speech be curtailed to ensure greater public safety. For example, we
could have a two-week waiting period on expressing an opinion after the
opinion was duly registered with a government agency. That way, the
government could screen the opinion to ensure that it was politically
correct.

The compromise-your-rights-for-safety argument is also ironic because the thousands of gun laws on the books — municipal, county, state,
and federal — have done nothing to stop crime. In fact, they have done
the opposite. The laws, for the most part, have disarmed, or made access
to guns more difficult for, the law-abiding, peaceable citizen. Criminals
do not turn in their guns. Murderers, rapists, and robbers do not obey gun
laws. However, they do calculate the risks involved in committing crime.
If they can assume that potential victims are unarmed, they are emboldened and are more likely to attack.

John Lott, in *More Guns Less Crime*, an exhaustive county-by-county
study of rates of gun ownership and crime, concludes that the counties
with the highest rates of gun ownership have the least crime and that
those with the lowest rates of gun ownership have the most crime. For
years, this has been obvious when looking at cities. Washington, D.C.,
and New York City, for example, with the most restrictive gun laws in the
nation, have, for a generation, been cesspools of crime. Criminals there
know that they can count on their victims being unarmed.

I suspect that even deeply disturbed killers, such as the teenage boys
in Littleton, Colorado, understood that they could kill with impunity in
the disarmed environment of the high school. The presence of a highly
trained, armed security guard, with a reputation as an expert marksman,
may have deterred them. If not, then the guard might have granted them
their suicidal wish before they were able to commit mass murder. One or
two key teachers, trained and armed, might also have made a difference.
Certainly, gun laws did nothing to stop the killers. The two boys violated
more than a dozen different gun laws, including one of the oldest on the
books — possession of a sawed-off shotgun. Gun laws promise much and
deliver little, because they affect only the law abiding, something like
sheep passing resolutions requiring vegetarianism while wolves circle the
flock.

I grew up in Los Angeles when gun laws were few and crime was low.
Nearly everyone I knew had a 30.06, a couple of .22s, a shotgun, and a re-
volver or two sitting around their house. We could buy guns mail-order
and pick up our ammunition at the local grocery store. A gun was a common companion to the road maps in the glove compartment of the car.
Did this cause crime? In 1952, there were 81 murders in Los Angeles. In
1992, 40 years and many gun laws later, there were 1,092 murders. If the
increase in murder had kept pace with the increase in population, there

would have been 142 murders, a 75 percent increase. Instead, murder increased 1,350 percent. Other crimes had similar increases: robbery, 1,540 percent; auto theft, 1,100 percent.

The Los Angeles Police Department used to solve more than 90 per-   20
cent of the murders committed in the city. Today, the figure is 60 percent. Detectives complain that the caseload is too great to conduct the kind of thorough investigations that were common in the '40s and '50s. It is far worse for lesser crimes. Merchants complain that customers brazenly walk out of their stores without paying for merchandise because they know that the police will not respond (at least in a timely fashion) to a call reporting shoplifting. Cars are stolen so often, some 200 per day, that the LAPD does nothing more than list the vehicle on a "hot sheet" and wish the victim good luck.

In the '50s, if your bicycle were stolen, the police would come out to your house and take a report. Try calling the LAPD today and telling them that your bike has been stolen! The police are simply overwhelmed by the sheer volume of crime and are kept fully occupied by murder, armed robbery, and rape—occupied, that is, by the aftermath of murder, armed robbery, and rape. When police arrive at the scene of a crime, the crime has already taken place—the victim has already been murdered, robbed, or raped.

"Carjacking" has become quite common in Los Angeles, because the carjackers know that California drivers cannot legally carry loaded firearms and will nearly always be unarmed. Occasionally, carjackers make poor choices. Three such carjackers followed my friend's son, Justin, as he drove home in his new car late one night. Little did they know that Justin was a reserve police officer. They did not know that he was well armed and an expert marksman.

When Justin pulled into the family driveway and got out of his car, one of the carjackers jumped out of his own vehicle and yelled at Justin, whose back was turned, "Freeze, motherf---er!" It was exactly what Justin had expected. Justin spun about and emptied the contents of his .45 into the carjacker. The carjacker's partners sped away as fast as their car would take them, leaving their good buddy very dead on my friend's front lawn.

Not long after Justin had sent the carjacker to the great salvage yard in the sky, I read of an off-duty police officer who had a similar encounter. On his way home and wearing plainclothes, he stopped to make a phone call. While he stood talking to his wife on an outdoor public phone, two muggers rushed up to him. One of them brandished a gun and said: "Your wallet!" Instead of pulling out his wallet, the cop drew a gun and sent the mugger to the morgue.

The *Los Angeles Times* noted that the mugger certainly picked on the   25
wrong person. This is the same *Los Angeles Times* that regularly editorializes against an armed citizenry and has never seen a gun law that it did not like. Somehow, the newspaper thinks that disarming peaceable, lawabiding citizens will affect criminal behavior for the better. Disarming

peaceable, law-abiding citizens *will* affect criminal behavior—but for the worse. Criminals will be emboldened because their chances of picking on the wrong person will be dramatically reduced. Shouldn't the opposite be the case? Shouldn't every person be the wrong person or, at least, potentially the wrong person?

Grandstanding politicians love to rail against the gun. Inanimate objects are good targets to beat up on. That way, politicians do not have to address the real problems in our society. We pay a price for this craven misdirection, though, in thousands of murders, muggings, rapes, robberies, and burglaries.

Yet that is not the greatest danger we face. The Founding Fathers knew that *governments* could turn criminal. That is the principal reason they wanted every man armed: An armed citizenry militates against the development of tyranny. The Founding Fathers did not want every man armed in order to shoot a burglar, although they had nothing against doing so. The Founding Fathers did not want every man armed in order to shoot Bambi or Thumper, although they had nothing against doing so. The Founding Fathers wanted every man armed in order to shoot soldiers or police of tyrannical regimes who suppress the rights of free men.

When governments become criminal, they disarm the populace. Then the numbers of deaths reach the tens of thousands, the hundreds of thousands, the millions. Can't happen? Ask the Irish and the Scots, or the Armenians, the Ukrainians, the Jews, the Chinese, the Cambodians.

In the Marine Corps, I was trained never to surrender my weapon. It was good advice then, and it is good advice now. I shall put my faith not in the goodwill of governments but in an armed citizenry—a band of brothers—steeped in the ideology of the Founding Fathers and the spirit of Patrick Henry, who said: "Is life so dear or peace so sweet as to be purchased at the price of slavery and chains? I know not what course others may take, but as for me, give me liberty or give me death."

DISCUSSION QUESTIONS

1. What does Burger understand the intent of the Second Amendment to have been, in context? How has history changed the way it should now be read?

2. What analogy does Burger make between guns and automobiles? Is his point a good one?

3. What questions does Burger feel Americans should be answering if we are to stop what he calls "this mindless homicidal carnage" (para. 15)?

4. Does McGrath make use of history in the same way and for the same purpose as Burger does? Explain.

5. What does McGrath mean when he says, "It is important to understand that the Second Amendment grants no right to the people to keep and bear arms" (para. 9)?

6. What is the warrant underlying Burger's essay? McGrath's?

7. What is McGrath's response to the claim that restrictions on guns would lead to a safer society?

8. Do you detect any logical fallacies in either essay?

9. Compare the authors' use of language. Do the authors use slanted or emotive language? Short cuts? Where in McGrath's essay is there a shift in the type of language used and why?

TAKING THE DEBATE ONLINE

For these and additional research URLs, see bedfordstmartins.com/rottenberg.

- *Handgun Control*
  www.handguncontrol.org/

  Handgun Control is "a non-partisan, not-for-profit organization that lobbies in favor of common-sense gun regulations at both a state and national level."

- *National Rifle Association of America*
  www.nra.org

  The objective of the National Rifle Association is to protect the right to bear arms. Click here to learn about the NRA's lobbying and legislative activities, youth programs and publications, relevant news articles, and firearms laws.

- *After Columbine*
  www.salon.com/news/special/littleton/

  Salon is an online magazine full of cultural criticism, book and film reviews, and political punditry. Click here for dozens of articles on gun control, the Columbine and Littleton shootings, and the culture of violence in America.

- *GunCite: Gun Control and Second Amendment Issues*
  www.guncite.com/

  GunCite has links to articles arguing against gun control.

- *The Bureau of Alcohol, Tobacco, and Firearms*
  www.atf.treas.gov/

  The Bureau of Alcohol, Tobacco, and Firearms (ATF) is a law enforcement organization within the United States Department of Treasury. Their Web site offers information about the use of firearms in violence, gangs, and youth crime.

1. Select one or two related bumper stickers visible in your town or city. Examine the hidden warrants on which they are based, and assess their validity.

2. For a slogan found on a bumper sticker or elsewhere, supply the evidence to support the claim in the slogan. Or find evidence that disproves the claim.

3. Examine a few periodicals from fifty or more years ago. Select either an advertising or a political slogan in one of them, and relate it to beliefs or events of the period. Or tell why the slogan is no longer relevant.

4. Discuss the origin of a cliché or slogan. Describe, as far as possible, the backgrounds and motives of its users.

5. Make up your own slogan for a cause that you support. Explain and defend your slogan.

6. Discuss the appeal to needs and values of some popular advertising or political slogan.

7. Choose a cliché, and find evidence to support or refute it. *Examples:* People were much happier in the past. Mother knows best. Life used to be simpler. Money can't buy happiness.

8. Choose one of the statements in Assignment 7 or another statement, and write a paper telling why you think such a statement remains in use.

9. Select a passage, perhaps from a textbook, written largely in abstractions, and rewrite it using simpler and more concrete language.

10. In watching television dramas about law, medicine, or criminal or medical investigation, do you find that the professional language, some of which you may not fully understand, plays a positive or negative role in your enjoyment of the show? Explain your answer.

11. Listen to a radio or television report of a sports event. Do the announcers use a kind of language, especially jargon, that would not be used in print reports? One critic thinks that sports broadcasting has had a "destructive effect . . . on ordinary American English." Is he right or wrong?

12. Whose argument about the right to bear arms do you find more convincing, Burger's or McGrath's? Explain.

Writing,
Researching,
and Presenting
Arguments

CHAPTER 9

Writing an Argumentative Paper

The person who understands how arguments are constructed has an important advantage in today's world. Television commercials, political speeches, newspaper editorials, and magazine advertisements, as well as many communications between individuals, all draw on the principles we have examined in the preceding chapters. By now you should be fairly adept at picking out claims, support, and warrants (explicit or unstated) in these presentations. The next step is to apply your skills to writing an argument of your own. The process of using what you have learned will enhance your ability to analyze critically the marketing efforts with which we are all bombarded every day. Mastering the writing of arguments also gives you a valuable tool for communicating with other people in school, on the job, and even at home.

In this chapter we move through the various stages involved in creating an argumentative paper: choosing a topic, defining the issues, organizing the material, writing the essay, and revising. We also consider the more general question of how to use the principles already discussed in order to convince a real audience. The more carefully you follow the guidelines set out here and the more thought you give to your work at each point, the better you will be able to utilize the art of argument when this course is over.

FINDING AN APPROPRIATE TOPIC

An old British recipe for jugged hare is said to begin, "First, catch your hare." To write an argumentative paper, you first must choose your topic. This is a relatively easy task for someone writing an argument as part of his or her job—a lawyer defending a client, for example, or an advertising executive presenting a campaign. For a student, however, it can be daunting. Which of the many ideas in the world worth debating would make a good subject?

Several guidelines can help you evaluate the possibilities. Perhaps your assignment limits your choices. If you have been asked to write a research paper, you obviously must find a topic on which research is available. If your assignment is more open-ended, you need a topic that is worth the time and effort you expect to invest in it. In either case, your subject should be one that interests you. Don't feel you have to write about what you know—very often finding out what you don't know will turn out to be more satisfying. You should, however, choose a subject that is familiar enough for you to argue about without fearing you're in over your head.

■ Invention Strategies

As a starting point, think of conversations you've had in the past few days or weeks that have involved defending a position. Is there some current political issue you're concerned about? Some dispute with friends that would make a valid paper topic? One of the best sources is controversies in the media. Keep your project in mind as you watch TV, read, or listen to the radio. You may even run into a potential subject in your course reading assignments or classroom discussions. Fortunately for the would-be writer, nearly every human activity includes its share of disagreement.

As you consider possible topics, write them down. One that looks unlikely at first glance may suggest others or may have more appeal when you come back to it later. Further, simply putting words on paper has a way of stimulating the thought processes involved in writing. Even if your ideas are tentative, the act of converting them into phrases or sentences can often help in developing them.

■ Evaluating Possible Topics

Besides interesting you, your topic must interest your audience. Who is the audience? For a lawyer it is usually a judge or jury; for a columnist, anyone who reads the newspaper in which his or her column appears. For the student writer, the audience is to some extent hypothetical. You should assume that your paper is directed at readers who are reasonably intelligent and well informed, but who have no specific knowledge of the subject. It may be useful to imagine you are writing for a local or school publication—this may be the case if your paper turns out well.

Be sure, too, that you choose a topic with two sides. The purpose of an argument is to defend or refute a thesis, which means the thesis must be debatable. In evaluating a subject that looks promising, ask yourself:

Can a case be made for the opposing view? If not, you have no workable ground for building your own case.

Finally, check the scope of your thesis. Consider how long your paper will be, and whether you can do justice to your topic in that amount of space. For example, suppose you want to argue in favor of worldwide nuclear disarmament. Is this a thesis you can support persuasively in a short paper? One way to find out is by listing the potential issues or points about which arguers might disagree. Consider the thesis: "The future of the world is in danger as long as nuclear weapons exist." Obviously this statement is too general. You would have to specify what you mean by the future of the world (the continuation of human life? of all life? of the earth itself?) and exactly how nuclear weapons endanger it before the claim would hold up. You could narrow it down: "Human beings are error-prone; therefore as long as nuclear weapons exist there is the chance that a large number of people will be killed accidentally." Though this statement is more specific and includes an important warrant, it still depends on other unstated warrants: that one human being (or a small group) is in the position to discharge a nuclear weapon capable of killing a large number of people; that such a weapon could, in fact, be discharged by mistake, given current safety systems. Can you expect to show sufficient evidence for these assumptions in the space available to you?

By now it should be apparent that arguing in favor of nuclear disarmament is too broad an undertaking. A more workable approach might be to defend or refute one of the disarmament proposals under consideration by the U.S. Congress, or to show that nuclear weapons pose some specific danger (such as long-term water pollution) that is sufficient reason to strive for disarmament.

Can a thesis be too narrow? Certainly. If this is true of the one you have chosen, you probably realized it when you asked yourself whether the topic was debatable. If you can prove your point convincingly in a paragraph, or even a page, you need a broader thesis.

At this preliminary stage, don't worry if you don't know exactly how to word your thesis. It's useful to write down a few possible phrasings to be sure your topic is one you can work with, but you need not be precise. The information you unearth as you do research will help you to formulate your ideas. Also, stating a thesis in final terms is premature until you know the organization and tone of your paper.

■ To This Point

Let's assume you have surveyed a range of possible topics and chosen one that provides you with a suitable thesis for your paper. Before you go on, check your thesis against the following questions:

1. Is this topic one that will interest both me and my audience?

2. Is the topic debatable?

3. Is my thesis appropriate in scope for a paper of this length?

4. Do I know enough about my thesis to have a rough idea of what ideas to use in supporting it and how to go about finding evidence to back up these ideas?

DEFINING THE ISSUES

■ Preparing an Initial Outline

An outline, like an accounting system or a computer program, is a practical device for organizing information. Nearly every elementary and high school student learns how to make an outline. What will you gain if you outline your argument? Time and an overview of your subject. The minutes you spend organizing your subject at the outset generally save at least double the time later, when you have few minutes to spare. An outline also enables you to see the whole argument at a glance.

Your preliminary outline establishes an order of priority for your argument. Which supporting points are issues to be defended, which are warrants, and which are evidence? Which supporting points are most persuasive? By constructing a map of your territory, you can identify the research routes that are likely to be most productive. You can also pinpoint any gaps in your reasoning.

List each issue as a main heading in your outline. Next, write below it any relevant support (or sources of support) that you are aware of. Then reexamine the list and consider which issues appear likely to offer the strongest support for your argument. You should number these in order of importance.

■ Computers in the Outlining Process

Word-processing software can make outlining simpler by providing an automatic outlining function. If you begin an outline with the roman numeral *I* followed by a period, many word-processing systems automatically supply *II* when you hit the enter key and move to the next line. If you have subtopics (marked by *A*s or *1*s), the outlining function will also automatically supply the next letters or numbers when you hit "Enter." This function is a simple but useful tool that can help you create hierarchies of ideas and skeletal texts.

Even more useful is the cut-and-paste function that is a part of all word-processing software because outlines are typically revised as writers discover new information and ideas or new connections between information and ideas. Revising outlines—experimenting with the order of ideas or with whether an idea should be a major or subpoint, for example—is easier with a computer, and the speed of cutting and pasting makes the revision process central to every part of the writing process, including outlining.

Finally, word-processing software also makes outlining done after a draft is completed much simpler. One way to see how a draft of a paper is working, for example, is to take the first (or topic) sentence of each paragraph and to put them in a list. Seeing how these individual sentences build from each other and connect to each other can help you see how the paper as a whole is working. If done with a pen, such a process can be time-consuming, but cutting and pasting by computer makes this helpful strategy easy.

■ Case Study: School Uniforms

To see how we raise and evaluate issues in a specific context, let's look at a controversy that has surfaced recently in many of our nation's public schools. Some schools are considering requiring school uniforms, but that proposal has not been met with unanimous support from students or their parents.

In one particular school district, those in favor of school uniforms raised these issues:

1. Other schools that initiated a uniform requirement experienced an improvement in discipline.
2. Buying uniforms is economical for parents.
3. Wearing uniforms takes away undesirable distinctions based on social and economic class.
4. Students who wear uniforms are not distracted by what they or others are wearing.
5. A uniform requirement does away with the need for increasingly detailed dress codes.

On the other side, those who opposed school uniforms introduced the following issues:

1. Requiring uniforms does not guarantee improved discipline.
2. A uniform requirement prevents parents from buying inexpensive clothing alternatives.
3. Students have the right to express themselves through their choice of clothing.
4. A dress code can eliminate fashions that are distracting to other students without taking away the student's choice of clothing completely.
5. Some students' weight, body shape, etc., may make them uncomfortable and self-conscious in the style of uniform chosen.

Now let's analyze these issues, comparing their strengths and weaknesses.

1. It is clear that not all the issues in this dispute were equally important. The arguers decided, therefore, to give greater emphasis to the issues most likely to be persuasive to their audiences and less attention to those difficult to prove or narrower in their appeal. At this time in some of the communities in the district, massive layoffs had forced parents out of work. Therefore, the cost of switching to uniforms was a major concern. If parents did not have to spend money on uniforms, they could shop for the most economic alternatives or let their younger children wear clothes their older children had outgrown. Within the district, there had been few problems with fashions that were extreme enough to be a distraction to other students, and those few could be addressed with minor additions to the dress code, certainly an easy accommodation to make. To those opposed to the uniform requirement, the economic concerns seemed to outweigh the use of uniforms as a means of establishing discipline, a goal they felt could be accomplished by other means.

2. It was also clear that, as in several of the other cases we have examined, the support on both sides consisted of both factual data and appeals to values. With regard to the factual data, each side reported evidence to prove that:

   a. the wearing of uniforms leads or does not lead to a reduced number of discipline problems.

   b. uniforms are or are not an economical alternative.

   c. the majority of students favored or opposed wearing uniforms.

   d. the majority of parents favored or opposed the uniform requirement.

The factual data were important. If opponents could prove that uniforms would place an increased financial burden on families already hurt by layoffs, the argument in favor of uniforms would be weakened. It would be weakened further if factual data from other similar districts showed no improvement in discipline.

Let us assume that the factual claims either were settled or remained in abeyance. We now turn our attention to a second set of issues, a contest over the values to be served.

3. Both sides in the dispute were concerned about the well-being of the students. Related to that, of course, was the well-being of their families. Improved discipline in the schools would benefit all students because the focus could be on education, not on policing student behavior. Beyond both of these concerns, however, were the issues of students' rights and their need to express themselves. If the majority of the students opposed uniforms, was that a strong enough concern to override the financial burden on their families? What about the minority who favored

uniforms and perhaps had felt stigmatized by being unable to afford the clothes in style among their peers? In such a situation, should a vote by the students play a major role in policy decisions? Students are not allowed to hire their own teachers or to choose their manner of instruction, their courses of study, their grades, or the rules of admission. In the school community, administrators argued, the experienced are required to lead and instruct the inexperienced.

In making our way through this debate, we have summarized a procedure for tackling the issues in any controversial problem.

1. Raise the relevant issues and arrange them in order of importance. Plan to devote more time and space to issues you regard as crucial.

2. Produce the strongest evidence you can to support your factual claims, knowing that the opposing side or critical readers may try to produce conflicting evidence.

3. Defend your value claims by finding support in the fundamental principles with which most people in your audience would agree.

4. Argue with yourself. Try to foresee what kinds of refutation are possible. Try to anticipate and meet the opposing arguments.

ORGANIZING THE MATERIAL

Once you are satisfied that you have identified all the issues that will appear in your paper, you should begin to determine what kind of organization will be most effective for your argument. Now is the time to organize the results of your thinking into a logical and persuasive form. If you have read about your topic, answered questions, and acquired some evidence, you may already have decided on ways to approach your subject. If not, you should look closely at your outline now, recalling your purposes when you began your investigation, and develop a strategy for using the information you have gathered to achieve those purposes.

The first point to establish is what type of thesis you plan to present. Is your intention to make readers aware of some problem? To offer a solution to the problem? To defend a position? To refute a position held by others? The way you organize your material will depend to a great extent on your goal. With that goal in mind, look over your outline and reevaluate the relative importance of your issues. Which ones are most convincing? Which are backed up by the strongest support? Which ones relate to facts, and which concern values?

With these points in mind, let us look at various ways of organizing an argumentative paper. It would be foolish to decide in advance how many paragraphs a paper ought to have; however, you can and should choose a general strategy before you begin writing. If your thesis presents an opinion or recommends some course of action, you may choose simply to state your main idea and then defend it. If your thesis argues against an opposing view, you probably will want to mention that view and then refute it. Both these organizations introduce the thesis in the first or second paragraph (called the *thesis paragraph*). You may decide that two or more differing positions have merit and that you want to offer a compromise between or among positions. A fourth possibility is to start establishing that a problem exists and then introduce your thesis as the solution; this method is called *presenting the stock issues*. Although these four approaches sometimes overlap in practice, examining each one individually can help you structure your paper. Let's take a look at each arrangement.

■ Defending the Main Idea

All forms of organization will require you to defend your main idea, but one way of doing this is simple and direct. Early in the paper state the main idea that you will defend throughout your argument. You can also indicate here the two or three points you intend to develop in support of your claim; or you can raise these later as they come up. Suppose your thesis is that widespread vegetarianism would solve a number of problems. You could phrase it this way: "If the majority of people in this country adopted a vegetarian diet, we would see improvements in the economy, in the health of our people, and in moral sensitivity." You would then develop each of the claims in your list with appropriate data and warrants. Notice that the thesis statement in the first (thesis) paragraph has already outlined your organizational pattern.

Defending the main idea is effective for factual claims as well as policy claims, in which you urge the adoption of a certain policy and give the reasons for its adoption. It is most appropriate when your thesis is straightforward and can be readily supported by direct statements.

■ Refuting the Opposing View

Refuting an opposing view means to attack it in order to weaken, invalidate, or make it less credible to a reader. Since all arguments are dialogues or debates—even when the opponent is only imaginary—refutation of the other point of view is always implicit in your arguments. As you write, keep in mind the issues that an opponent may raise. You will be looking at your own argument as an unsympathetic reader may look at it, asking yourself the same kinds of critical questions and trying to find its weaknesses in order to correct them. In this way every argument you write becomes a form of refutation.

How do you plan a refutation? Here are some general guidelines.

1. If you want to refute the argument in a specific essay or article, read the argument carefully, noting all the points with which you disagree. This advice may seem obvious, but it cannot be too strongly emphasized. If your refutation does not indicate scrupulous familiarity with your opponent's argument, he or she has the right to say, and often does, "You haven't really read what I wrote. You haven't really answered my argument."

2. If you think that your readers are sympathetic to the opposing view or are not familiar with it, summarize it at the beginning of your paper, providing enough information to give readers an understanding of exactly what you plan to refute. When you summarize, it's important to be respectful of the opposition's views. You don't want to alienate readers who might not agree with you at first.

3. If your argument is long and complex, choose only the most important points to refute. Otherwise the reader who does not have the original argument on hand may find a detailed refutation hard to follow. If the argument is short and relatively simple — a claim supported by only two or three points — you may decide to refute all of them, devoting more space to the most important ones.

4. Attack the principal elements in the argument of your opponent.

   a. Question the evidence. (See pp. 166–73 in the text.) Question whether your opponent has proved that a problem exists.

   b. Attack the warrants or assumptions that underlie the claim. (See pp. 232–33 in the text.)

   c. Attack the logic or reasoning of the opposing view. (Refer to the discussion of fallacious reasoning on pp. 285–95 in the text.)

   d. Attack the proposed solution to a problem, pointing out that it will not work.

5. Be prepared to do more than attack the opposing view. Supply evidence and good reasons in support of your own claim.

■ Finding the Middle Ground

Although an argument, by definition, assumes a difference of opinion, we know that opposing sides frequently find accommodation somewhere in the middle. As you mount your own argument about a controversial issue, you need not confine yourself to support of any of the differing positions. You may want to acknowledge that there is some justice on all sides and that you understand the difficulty of resolving the issue.

Consider these guidelines for an argument that offers a compromise between competing positions:

1. Early in your essay explain the opposing positions. Make clear the major differences separating the two (or more) sides.

2. Point out, whenever possible, that the opposing sides already agree to some exceptions to their stated positions. Such evidence may prove that the opposing sides are not so extreme as their advocates insist. Several commentators, writing about the budget conflict between Democrats and Republicans in late 1998, adopted this strategy, suggesting that compromise was possible because the differences were narrower than the public believed.

3. Make clear your own moderation and sympathy, your own willingness to negotiate. An example of this attitude appears in an essay on abortion in which the author infers how Abraham Lincoln might have treated the question of abortion rights.

> In this debate I have made my own position clear. It is a pro-life position (though it may not please all pro-lifers), and its model is Lincoln's position on slavery from 1854 until well into the Civil War: tolerate, restrict, discourage. Like Lincoln's, its touchstone is the common good of the nation, not the sovereign self. Like Lincoln's position, it accepts the legality but not the moral legitimacy of the institution that it seeks to contain. It invites argument and negotiation; it is a gambit, not a gauntlet.[1]

4. If you favor one side of the controversy, acknowledge that opposing views deserve to be considered. For example, in another essay on abortion, the author, who supports abortion rights, says,

> Those of us who are pro-choice must come to terms with those thoughtful pro-lifers who believe that in elevating the right to privacy above all other values, the most helpless form of humanity is left unprotected and is, in fact, defined away. They deserve to have their views addressed with sympathy and moral clarity.[2]

5. Provide evidence that accepting a middle ground can offer marked advantages for the whole society. Wherever possible, show that continued polarization can result in violence, injustice, and suffering.

6. In offering a solution that finds a common ground, be as specific as possible, emphasizing the part that you are willing to play in reaching a settlement. In an essay titled "Pro-Life and Pro-Choice? Yes!" the author concludes with this:

> Must those of us who abhor abortion, then, reconcile ourselves to seeing it spread unchecked? By no means. We can refuse to practice it ourselves—or, if we are male, beseech the women who carry our children to let them be born, and promise to sup-

[1] George McKenna, "On Abortion: A Lincolnian Position," *The Atlantic Monthly,* September 1995, p. 68. (A gauntlet or glove is flung down in order to challenge an opponent to combat; a gambit is the opening move in a chess game, or in the words of one dictionary, "a concession that invites discussion."—Eds.)

[2] Benjamin C. Schwarz, "Judge Ginsburg's Moral Myopia," *New York Times,* July 30, 1993, sec. A, p. 27.

port them, and mean it and do it. We can counsel and preach to others; those of us who are religious can pray. . . . What we must not do is ask the state to impose our views on those who disagree.[3]

On a different subject, a debate on pornography, the author, who is opposed to free distribution of obscene material, nevertheless refuses to endorse censorship.

I think that, by enlarging the First Amendment to protect, in effect, freedom of expression, rather than freedom of speech and of the press, the courts made a mistake. The courts have made other mistakes, but I do not know a better way of defining the interests of the community than through legislation and through the courts. So I am willing to put up with things I think are wrong in the hope that they will be corrected. I know of no alternative that would always make the right decisions.[4]

■ Presenting the Stock Issues

Presenting the stock issues, or stating the problem before the solution, is a type of organization borrowed from traditional debate format. It works for policy claims when an audience must be convinced that a need exists for changing the status quo (present conditions) and for introducing plans to solve the problem. You begin by establishing that a problem exists (need). You then propose a solution (plan), which is your thesis. Finally, you show reasons for adopting the plan (advantages). These three elements—need, plan, and advantages—are called the stock issues.

For example, suppose you wanted to argue that measures for reducing acid rain should be introduced at once. You would first have to establish a need for such measures by defining the problem and providing evidence of damage. Then you would produce your thesis, a means for improving conditions. Finally you would suggest the benefits that would follow from implementation of your plan. Notice that in this organization your thesis paragraph usually appears toward the middle of your paper, although it may also appear at the beginning.

■ Ordering Material for Emphasis

Whichever way you choose to work, you should revise your outline to reflect the order in which you intend to present your thesis and supporting ideas. Not only the placement of your thesis paragraph but also the wording and arrangement of your ideas will determine what points in your paper receive the most emphasis.

---

[3] George Church, *Time*, March 6, 1995, p. 108.
[4] Ernest van den Haag, *Smashing Liberal Icons: A Collection of Debates* (Washington, D.C.: Heritage Foundation, 1981), p. 101.

Suppose your purpose is to convince the reader that cigarette smoking is a bad habit. You might decide to concentrate on three unpleasant attributes of cigarette smoking: (1) it is unhealthy; (2) it is dirty; (3) it is expensive. Obviously, these are not equally important as possible deterrents. You would no doubt consider the first reason the most compelling, accompanied by evidence to prove the relationship between cigarette smoking and cancer, heart disease, emphysema, and other diseases. This issue, therefore, should be given greater emphasis than the others.

There are several ways to achieve emphasis. One is to make the explicit statement that you consider a certain issue the most important.

> Finally, and *most importantly,* human culture is often able to neutralize or reverse what might otherwise be genetically advantageous consequences of selfish behavior.[5]

This quotation also reveals a second way — placing the material to be emphasized in an emphatic position, either first or last in the paper. The end position, however, is generally more emphatic.

A third way to achieve emphasis is to elaborate on the material to be emphasized, treating it at greater length, offering more data and reasons for it than you give for the other issues.

■ Considering Scope and Audience

With a working outline in hand that indicates the order of your thesis and claims, you are almost ready to begin turning your notes into prose. First, however, it is useful to review the limits on your paper to be sure your writing time will be used to the best possible advantage.

The first limit involves scope. As mentioned earlier, your thesis should introduce a claim that can be adequately supported in the space available to you. If your research has opened up more aspects than you anticipated, you may want to narrow your thesis to one major subtopic. Or you could emphasize only the most persuasive arguments for your position (assuming these are sufficient to make your case) and omit the others. In a brief paper (three or four pages), three issues are probably all you have room to develop. On the other hand, if you suspect your thesis can be proved in one or two pages, look for ways to expand it. What additional issues might be brought in to bolster your argument? Alternatively, is there a larger issue for which your thesis could become a supporting idea?

Other limits on your paper are imposed by the need to make your points in a way that will be persuasive to an audience. The style and tone you choose depend not only on the nature of the subject but also on how you can best convince readers that you are a credible source. *Style* in this

[5] Peter Singer, *The Expanding Circle* (New York: New American Library, 1982), p. 171.

context refers to the elements of your prose—simple versus complex sentences, active versus passive verbs, metaphors, analogies, and other literary devices. *Tone* is the approach you take to your topic—solemn or humorous, detached or sympathetic. Style and tone together compose your voice as a writer.

Many students assume that every writer has only one voice. In fact, a writer typically adapts his or her voice to the material and the audience. Perhaps the easiest way to appreciate this is to think of two or three works by the same author that are written in different voices. Or compare the speeches of two different characters in the same story, novel, or film. Every writer has individual talents and inclinations that appear in most or all of his or her work. A good writer, however, is able to amplify some stylistic elements and diminish others, as well as to change tone, by choice.

It is usually appropriate in a short paper to choose an *expository* style, which emphasizes the elements of your argument rather than your personality. You may want to appeal to your readers' emotions as well as their intellects, but keep in mind that sympathy is most effectively gained when it is supported by believable evidence. If you press your point stridently, your audience is likely to be suspicious rather than receptive. If you sprinkle your prose with jokes or metaphors, you may diminish your credibility by detracting from the substance of your case. Both humor and analogy can be useful tools, but they should be used with discretion.

You can discover some helpful pointers on essay style by reading the editorials in newspapers such as the *New York Times,* the *Washington Post,* or the *Wall Street Journal.* The authors are typically addressing a mixed audience comparable to the hypothetical readers of your own paper. Though their approaches vary, each writer is attempting to portray himself or herself as an objective analyst whose argument deserves careful attention.

Again, remember your goals. You are trying to convince your audience of something; an argument is, by its nature, directed at people who may not initially agree with its thesis. Therefore, your voice as well as the claims you make must be convincing.

■ To This Point

The organizing steps that come between preparation and writing are often neglected. Careful planning at this stage, however, can save much time and effort later. As you prepare to start writing, you should be able to answer the following questions:

1. Is the purpose of my paper to persuade readers to accept a potentially controversial idea, to refute someone else's position, to find middle ground, or to propose a solution to a problem?

2. Can or should my solution also incorporate elements of compromise and negotiation?

3. Have I decided on an organization that is likely to accomplish this purpose?

4. Does my outline arrange my thesis and issues in an appropriate order to emphasize the most important issues?

5. Does my outline show an argument whose scope suits the needs of this paper?

6. What questions of style and tone do I need to keep in mind as I write to ensure that my argument will be persuasive?

WRITING

■ Beginning the Paper

Having found a claim you can defend and the voice you will adopt toward your audience, you must now think about how to begin. An introduction to your subject should consist of more than just the first paragraph of your paper. It should invite the reader to give attention to what you have to say. It should also point you in the direction you will take in developing your argument. You may want to begin the actual writing of your paper with the thesis paragraph. It is useful to consider the whole paragraph rather than simply the thesis statement for two reasons. First, not all theses are effectively expressed in a single sentence. Second, the rest of the paragraph will be closely related to your statement of the main idea. You may show why you have chosen this topic or why your audience will benefit from reading your paper. You may introduce your warrant, qualify your claim, and in other ways prepare for the body of your argument. Because readers will perceive the whole paragraph as a unit, it makes sense to approach it that way.

Consider first the kind of argument you intend to present. Does your paper make a factual claim? Does it address values? Does it recommend a policy or action? Is it a rebuttal of some current policy or belief? The answers to those questions will influence the way you introduce the subject.

If your thesis makes a factual claim, you may be able to summarize it in one or two opening sentences. "Whether we like it or not, money is obsolete. The currency of today is not paper or coin, but plastic." Refutations are easy to introduce in a brief statement: "Contrary to popular views on the subject, the institution of marriage is as sound today as it was a generation ago."

A thesis that defends a value is usually best preceded by an explanatory introduction. "Some wars are morally defensible" is a thesis that can be stated as a simple declarative opening sentence. However, readers who disagree may not read any further than the first line. Someone defending this claim is likely to be more persuasive if he or she first gives an example of a situation in which war is or was preferable to peace or presents the thesis less directly.

One way to keep such a thesis from alienating the audience is to phrase it as a question. "Are all wars morally indefensible?" Still better would be to prepare for the question:

> Few if any of us favor war as a solution to international problems. We are too vividly aware of the human suffering imposed by armed conflict, as well as the political and financial turmoil that inevitably result. Yet can we honestly agree that no war is ever morally defensible?

Notice that this paragraph gains appeal from use of the first person *we*. The author implies that he or she shares the readers' feelings but has good reasons for believing those feelings are not sufficient grounds for condemning all wars. Even if readers are skeptical, the conciliatory phrasing of the thesis should encourage them to continue reading.

For any subject that is highly controversial or emotionally charged, especially one that strongly condemns an existing situation or belief, you may sometimes want to express your indignation directly. Of course, you must be sure that your indignation can be justified. The author of the following introduction, a physician and writer, openly admits that he is about to make a case that may offend readers.

> Is there any polite way to introduce today's subject? I'm afraid not. It must be said plainly that the media have done about as sorry and dishonest a job of covering health news as is humanly possible, and that when the media do not fail from bias and mendacity, they fail from ignorance and laziness.[6]

If your thesis advocates a policy or makes a recommendation, it may be a good idea, as in a value claim, to provide a short background. The following paragraph introduces an argument favoring relaxation of controls in high schools.

> "Free the New York City 275,000" read a button worn by many young New Yorkers some years ago. The number was roughly the total of students enrolled in the City's high schools.
>
> The condition of un-freedom which is described was not, however, unique to the schools of one city. According to the Carnegie Commission's comprehensive study of American public education, *Crisis in the Classroom,* public schools across the country share a common characteristic, namely, "preoccupation with order and control." The result is that students find themselves the victims of "oppressive and petty rules which give their schools a repressive, almost prison-like atmosphere."[7]

---

[6]Michael Halberstam, "TV's Unhealthy Approach to Health News," *TV Guide,* September 20–26, 1980, p. 24.

[7]Alan Levine and Eve Carey, *The Rights of Students* (New York: Avon Books, 1977), p. 11.

There are also other ways to introduce your subject. One is to begin with an appropriate quotation.

> "Reading makes a full man, conversation makes a ready man, and writing makes an exact man." So Francis Bacon told us around 1600. Recently I have been wondering how Bacon's formula might apply to present-day college students.[8]

Or you may begin with an anecdote. In the following introduction to an article about the relation between cancer and mental attitude, the author recounts a personal experience.

> Shortly after I moved to California, a new acquaintance sat in my San Francisco living room drinking rose-hip tea and chainsmoking. Like so many residents of the Golden West, Cecil was "into" all things healthy, from jogging to *shiatsu* massage to kelp. Tobacco didn't seem to fit, but he told me confidently that there was no contradiction. "It all has to do with energy," he said. "Unless you have a lot of negative energy about smoking cigarettes, there's no way they can hurt you; you won't get cancer."[9]

Finally, you may introduce yourself as the author of the claim.

> I wish to argue an unpopular cause: the cause of the old, free elective system in the academic world, or the untrammeled right of the undergraduate to make his own mistakes.[10]

> My subject is the world of Hamlet. I do not of course mean Denmark, except as Denmark is given a body by the play; and I do not mean Elizabethan England, though this is necessarily close behind the scenes. I mean simply the imaginative environment that the play asks us to enter when we read it or go to see it.[11]

You should, however, use such introductions with care. They suggest an authority about the subject that you shouldn't attempt to assume unless you can demonstrate that you are entitled to it.

■ Guidelines for Good Writing

In general, the writer of an argument follows the same rules that govern any form of expository writing. Your style should be clear and readable, your organization logical, your ideas connected by transitional phrases

[8] William Aiken, "The Conversation on Campus Today Is, Uh . . . ," *Wall Street Journal,* May 4, 1982, p. 18.

[9] Joel Guerin, "Cancer and the Mind," *Harvard Magazine,* November–December 1978, p. 11.

[10] Howard Mumford Jones, "Undergraduates on Apron Strings," *Atlantic Monthly,* October 1955, p. 45.

[11] Maynard Mack, "The World of Hamlet," *Yale Review,* June 1952, p. 502.

and sentences, your paragraphs coherent. The main difference between an argument and expository writing, as noted earlier, is the need to persuade an audience to adopt a belief or take an action. You should assume your readers will be critical rather than neutral or sympathetic. Therefore, you must be equally critical of your own work. Any apparent gap in reasoning or ambiguity in presentation is likely to weaken the argument.

As you read the essays in this book and elsewhere, you will discover that good style in argumentative writing shares several characteristics:

- Variety in sentence structure: a mixture of both long and short sentences, different sentence beginnings

- Rich but standard vocabulary: avoidance of specialized terms unless they are fully explained, word choice appropriate to a thoughtful argument

- Use of details and examples to illustrate and clarify abstract terms, principles, and generalizations

You should take care to avoid the following:

- Unnecessary repetition: making the same point without new data or interpretation

- Exaggeration or stridency, which can create suspicion of your fairness and powers of observation

- Short paragraphs of one or two sentences, which are common in advertising and newspaper writing to get the reader's attention but are inappropriate in a thoughtful essay

In addition to these stylistic principles, seven general points are worth keeping in mind:

1. Although *you,* like *I,* should be used judiciously, it can be found even in the treatment of weighty subjects. Here is an example from an essay by the distinguished British mathematician and philosopher, Bertrand Russell.

> Suppose you are a scientific pioneer and you make some discovery of great scientific importance and suppose you say to yourself, "I am afraid this discovery will do harm": you know that other people are likely to make the same discovery if they are allowed suitable opportunities for research; you must therefore, if you do not wish the discovery to become public, either discourage your sort of research or control publication by a board of censors.[12]

Don't be afraid to use *you* or *I* when it is useful to emphasize the presence of the person making the argument.

---

[12]"Science and Human Life," in *What Is Science?* edited by James R. Newman (New York: Simon and Schuster, 1955), p. 12.

2. Don't pad. This point should be obvious; the word *pad* suggests the addition of unnecessary material. Many writers find it tempting, however, to enlarge a discussion even when they have little more to say. It is never wise to introduce more words into a paper that has already made its point. If the paper turns out to be shorter than you had hoped, it may mean that you have not sufficiently developed the subject or that the subject was less substantial than you thought when you selected it. Padding, which is easy to detect in its repetition and sentences empty of content, weakens the writer's credibility.

3. For any absolute generalization—a statement containing words such as *all* or *every*—consider the possibility that there may be at least one example that will weaken the generalization. Such a precaution means that you won't have to backtrack and admit that your generalization is not, after all, universal. A student who was arguing against capital punishment for the reason that all killing was wrong suddenly paused in her presentation and added, "On the other hand, if given the chance, I'd probably have been willing to kill Hitler." This admission meant that she recognized important exceptions to her rule and that she would have to qualify her generalization in some significant way.

4. When offering an explanation, especially one that is complicated or extraordinary, look first for a cause that is easier to accept, one that doesn't strain credibility. (In Chapter 8, we called attention to this principle. See pp. 286–88.) For example, years ago a great many people were bemused by reports about the mysterious Bermuda Triangle, which had apparently swallowed up ships and planes since the mid-nineteenth century. The forces at work were variously described as space-time warps, UFOs that transported earthlings to other planets, and sea monsters seeking revenge. But a careful investigation revealed familiar, natural causes. A reasonable person interested in the truth would have searched for more conventional explanations before accepting the bizarre stories of extraterrestrial creatures. He or she would also exercise caution when confronted by conspiracy theories that try to account for controversial political events, such as the assassination of John F. Kennedy.

5. Check carefully for questionable warrants. Your outline should specify your warrants. When necessary, these should be included in your paper to link claims with support. Many an argument has failed because it depended on an unstated warrant with which the reader did not agree. If you were arguing for a physical education requirement at your school, you might make a good case for all the physical and psychological benefits of such a requirement. But you would certainly need to introduce and develop the warrant on which your claim was based—that it is the proper function of a college or university to provide the benefits of a physical education. Many readers would agree that physical education is valuable, but they might question the assumption that an academic institution should introduce a nonintellectual enterprise into the curriculum. At any

point where you draw a controversial or tenuous conclusion, be sure your reasoning is clear and logical.

6. Avoid conclusions that are merely summaries. Summaries may be needed in long technical papers, but in brief arguments they create endings that are without force or interest. In the closing paragraph you should find a new idea that emerges naturally from the development of the whole argument.

7. Strive for a paper that is unified, coherent, and emphatic where appropriate. A *unified* paper stays focused on its goal and directs each claim, warrant, and piece of evidence toward that goal. Extraneous information or unsupported claims impair unity. *Coherence* means that all ideas are fully explained and adequately connected by transitions. To ensure coherence, give especially close attention to the beginnings and ends of your paragraphs: Is each new concept introduced in a way that shows it following naturally from the one that preceded it? *Emphasis,* as we have mentioned, is a function partly of structure and partly of language. Your most important claims should be placed where they are certain of receiving the reader's attention: key sentences at the beginning or end of a paragraph, key paragraphs at the beginning or end of your paper. Sentence structure can also be used for emphasis. If you have used several long, complex sentences, you can emphasize a significant point by stating it briefly and simply. You can also create emphasis with verbal flags, such as "The primary issue to consider . . ." or "Finally, we cannot ignore. . . ."

All clear expository prose will exhibit the qualities of unity, coherence, and emphasis. But the success of an argumentative paper is especially dependent on these qualities because the reader may have to follow a line of reasoning that is both complicated and unfamiliar. Moreover, a paper that is unified, coherent, and properly emphatic will be more readable, the first requisite of an effective argument.

REVISING

The final stage in writing an argumentative paper is revising. The first step is to read through what you have written for mistakes. Next, check your work against the guidelines listed under "Organizing the Material" and "Writing." Have you omitted any of the issues, warrants, or supporting evidence on your outline? Is each paragraph coherent in itself? Do your paragraphs work together to create a coherent paper? All the elements of the argument—the issues raised, the underlying assumptions, and the supporting material—should contribute to the development of the claim in your thesis statement. Any material that is interesting but irrelevant to that claim should be cut. Finally, does your paper reach a clear conclusion that reinforces your thesis?

Be sure, too, that the style and tone of your paper are appropriate for the topic and the audience. Remember that people choose to read an argument because they want the answer to a troubling question or the solution to a recurrent problem. Besides stating your thesis in a way that invites the reader to join you in your investigation, you must retain your audience's interest through a discussion that may be unfamiliar or contrary to their convictions. The outstanding qualities of argumentative prose style, therefore, are clarity and readability.

Style is obviously harder to evaluate in your own writing than organization. Your outline provides a map against which to check the structure of your paper. Clarity and readability, by comparison, are somewhat abstract qualities. Two procedures may be helpful. The first is to read two or three (or more) essays by authors whose style you admire and then turn back to your own writing. Awkward spots in your prose are sometimes easier to see if you get away from it and respond to someone else's perspective than if you simply keep rereading your own writing.

The second method is to read aloud. If you have never tried it, you are likely to be surprised at how valuable this can be. Again, start with someone else's work that you feel is clearly written, and practice until you achieve a smooth rhythmic delivery that satisfies you. And listen to what you are reading. Your objective is to absorb the patterns of English structure that characterize the clearest, most readable prose. Then read your paper aloud, and listen to the construction of your sentences. Are they also clear and readable? Do they say what you want them to say? How would they sound to a reader? According to one theory, you can learn the rhythm and phrasing of a language as you learn the rhythm and phrasing of a melody. And you will often *hear* a mistake or a clumsy construction in your writing that has escaped your eye in proofreading.

PREPARING THE MANUSCRIPT

Print your typed essay on one side of 8½-by-11-inch white computer paper, double-spacing throughout. Leave margins of 1 to 1½ inches on all sides, and indent each paragraph one-half inch or five spaces. Unless a formal outline is part of the paper, a separate title page is unnecessary. Instead, beginning about one inch from the top of the first page and flush with the left margin, type your name, the instructor's name, the course title, and the date, each on a separate line; then double-space and type the title, capitalizing the first letter of the words of the title except for articles, prepositions, and conjunctions. Double-space and type the body of the paper.

Writer's Guide: Checklist for Argumentative Papers

1. Present a thesis that interests both you and the audience, is debatable, and can be defended in the amount of space available.

2. Back up each statement offered in support of the thesis with enough evidence to give it credibility. Cite data from a variety of sources. Fully document all quotations and direct references to primary or secondary sources.

3. The warrants linking claims to support must be either specified or implicit in your data and line of reasoning. No claim should depend on an unstated warrant with which skeptical readers might disagree.

4. Present the thesis clearly and adequately introduce it in a thesis paragraph, indicating the purpose of the paper.

5. Organize supporting statements and data in a way that builds the argument, emphasizes your main ideas, and justifies the paper's conclusions.

6. Anticipate all possible opposing arguments and either refute or accommodate them.

7. Write in a style and tone appropriate for the topic and the intended audience. Your prose should be clear and readable.

8. Make sure your manuscript is clean, carefully proofed, and typed in an acceptable format.

Number all pages at the top right corner, typing your last name before each page number in case pages are mislaid. If an outline is included, number its pages with lowercase roman numerals.

Use the spell-check and grammar-check functions of your word-processing program, but keep in mind that correctness depends on context. A spell-check program will not flag a real word that is used incorrectly, such as the word *it's* used where the word *its* is needed. Also, a grammar-check function lacks the sophistication to interpret the meaning of a sentence and may flag as incorrect a group of words that is indeed correct while missing actual errors. It is ultimately up to you to proofread the paper carefully for other mistakes. Correct the errors, and reprint the pages in question.

CHAPTER 10

Researching an Argumentative Paper

The success of any argument, short or long, depends in large part on the quantity and quality of the support behind it. Research, therefore, can be crucial for any argument outside your own experience. Most papers will benefit from research in the library and elsewhere because development of the claim requires facts, examples, statistics, and informed opinions that are available only from primary and secondary research sources. This chapter offers information and advice to help you work through the steps of writing a research paper, from getting started to preparing the finished product.

GETTING STARTED

The following guidelines will help you keep your research on track:

1. Focus your investigation on building your argument, not merely on collecting information about the topic. Do follow any promising leads that turn up from the sources you consult, but don't be diverted into general reading that has no direct bearing on your thesis.

2. Look for at least two pieces of evidence to support each point you make. If you cannot find sufficient evidence, you may need to revise or abandon the point.

3. Use a variety of sources. Seek evidence from different kinds of sources (books, magazines, Web sites, government reports, even personal interviews with experts) and from different fields.

Writer's Guide: Why Use Sources?

1. You cannot be an authority on every subject. That means that you must turn to those who are authorities on subjects you know little about.

2. Because you may not yet have a name or credentials that are recognized for their authority, you may need to use those who are considered experts as sources of information and prestige.

3. The use of sources shows that you have taken the time do so some research on the subject at hand, including researching positions other than your own.

4. As in a court of law, the more evidence you can provide for your position, the stronger your case will be.

4. Be sure your sources are authoritative. We have already pointed out elsewhere the necessity for examining the credentials of sources. Although it may be difficult or impossible for those outside the field to conclude that one authority is more trustworthy than another, some guidelines are available. Articles and essays in scholarly journals are probably more authoritative than articles in college newspapers. Authors whose credentials include many publications and years of study at reputable institutions are probably more reliable than newspaper columnists and the so-called man in the street. However, we can judge reliability much more easily if we are dealing with facts and inferences than with values and emotions.

5. Don't let your sources' opinions outweigh your own. Your paper should demonstrate that the thesis and ideas you present are yours, arrived at after careful reflection and supported by research. The thesis need not be original, but your paper should be more than a collection of quotations or a report of the facts and opinions you have been reading. It should be clear to the reader that the quotations and other materials support *your* claim and that *you* have been responsible for finding and emphasizing the important issues, examining the data, and choosing between strong and weak opinions.

6. Prepare for research by identifying potential resources and learning how they work. Make sure you know how to use the library's catalog and other databases available either in the library or through the campus network. For each database that looks useful, explore how to execute a subject search, how to refine a search, and how to print out or download results. Make sure you know how to find books, relevant reference materials, and journals. Find out whether interlibrary loan is an option and how long it takes. If you plan to use government publications, find out if your library is a depository for federal documents. Identify relevant organizations using the *Encyclopedia of Associations* and visit their Web sites.

Finally, discuss your topic with a librarian at the reference desk to make sure you haven't overlooked anything.

MAPPING RESEARCH: A SAMPLE OUTLINE

To explore a range of research activities, let's suppose that you are preparing a research paper, six to ten pages long. You have chosen to defend the following thesis: *Conventional zoos should be abolished because they are cruel to animals and cannot provide the benefits to the public that they promise.* To keep your material under control and give direction to your reading, you would sketch a preliminary outline, which might look like this:

Why We Don't Need Zoos

I. Moral Objection: Animals have fundamental right to liberty
   A. Must prove animals are negatively affected by captivity
      1. research?
      2. research?
   B. Must refute claims that captivity is not detrimental to animals
      1. Brownlee's description of dolphin: "seeming stupor"; eating "half-heartedly"; not behaving like wild dolphins
      2. Personal experience: watching leopards running in circles in cages for hours

II. Practical Objection: Zoos can't accomplish what they claim to be their goals
   A. "Educational benefits" zoo provides are inaccurate at best: Public is not learning about wild animals at all but about domesticated descendants of same (support with research from [I.A] above)
   B. Conservation programs at zoos are ineffective
      1. It's difficult to breed animals in zoos
      2. Resultant offspring, when there is any, is victim of inbreeding. Leads to inferior stock that will eventually die out (research?)

Now you need to begin the search for the materials that will support your argument. There are two principal ways of gathering the materials — primary research and secondary research. Most writers will not want to limit themselves to one kind of research, but one method may work better than another for a particular project.

USING SOURCES: PRIMARY RESEARCH

Primary research involves looking for firsthand information. By *firsthand* we mean information taken directly from the original source, including field research (interviews, surveys, personal observations, or experiments). If your topic relates to a local issue involving your school or community, or if it focuses on a story that has never been reported by others, field research may be more valuable than anything available in the library. However, the library can be a source of firsthand information. Memoirs and letters written by witnesses to past events, photographs, contemporary news reports of historical events, or expert testimony presented at congressional hearings are all primary sources that may be available in your library. The Internet, too, can be a source of primary data. A discussion list, newsgroup, or chat room focused on your topic may give you a means to converse with activists and contact experts. Web sites of certain organizations provide documentation of their views, unfiltered by others' opinions. The text of laws, court opinions, bills, debates in Congress, environmental impact statements, and even selected declassified FBI files can be found through government-sponsored Web sites. Other sites present statistical data or the text of historical or political documents.

One of the rewards of primary research is that it often generates new information, which in turn produces new interpretations of familiar conditions. It is a favored method for anthropologists and sociologists, and most physical and natural scientists use observation and experiment at some point as essential tools in their research.

Consider the sample thesis that *zoos should be abolished*. Remember that you need to prove that *zoos are cruel to animals* and that *they cannot provide the benefits to the public that they promise*. It is possible to go directly to primary sources without consulting books or journals. For example:

- Phone the local area chapter of any animal rights group and ask to interview members on their opinions concerning zoos.

- Talk to the veterinarian on call at your local zoo and ask about animal injuries, illnesses, neuroses, and so forth.

- Search the World Wide Web for sites sponsored and developed by the groups associated with the animal rights movement. Many such informational sites will provide the text of current or proposed laws concerning this issue.

- Locate Internet newsgroups or discussion lists devoted to animal rights and identify experts in the field such as animal scientists who would be willing to provide authoritative opinions for your paper.

The information gleaned from primary research can be used directly to support your claim, or can provide a starting point for secondary research at the library.

USING SOURCES: SECONDARY RESEARCH

Secondary research involves locating commentary and analysis of your topic. In addition to raw evidence found through primary research, secondary sources provide a sense of how others are examining the issues and can provide useful information and analysis. Secondary sources may be written for a popular audience, ranging from news coverage, to popular explanations of research findings, to social analysis, to opinion pieces. Or they may be scholarly publications—experts presenting their research and theories to other researchers. These sources might also come in the form of analytical reports written to untangle possible courses of action, such as a report written by staff members for a congressional committee or an analysis of an issue by a think tank that wants to use the evidence it has gathered to influence public opinion.

Whatever form it may take, be sure when you use a secondary source that you consider the author's purpose and the validity of the material presented to ensure that it is useful evidence for your argument. An opinion piece published in a small-town paper, for example, may be a less impressive source for your argument than an analysis written by a former cabinet member. A description of a scientific discovery published in a magazine will carry less weight as evidence than the article written by the scientists making the discovery, presenting their research findings in a scientific journal.

The nature of your topic will determine which route you follow to find good sources. If the topic is current, you may find it more important to use articles than books and might bypass the library catalog altogether. If the topic has to do with social policy or politics, government publications may be particularly useful, though they would be unhelpful for a literary paper. If the topic relates to popular culture, the Internet may provide more information than more traditional publications. Consider what kinds of sources will be most useful as you choose your strategy. If you aren't certain which approaches fit your topic best, consult with a librarian at the reference desk.

■ Selecting and Searching Databases

You will most likely use one or more *databases* (online catalogs of reference materials) to locate books and articles on your topic. The library catalog is a database of books and other materials owned by the library; other databases may cover articles in popular or specialized journals and may even provide the full text of articles. Some databases may be available only in the library; others may be accessible all over campus. Here are some common features that appear in many databases.

Keyword or Subject Searching. You might have the option of searching a database by *keyword*—using the words that you think are most relevant to your search—or by subject. Typically, a keyword search will search for any occurrence of your search term in titles, notes, or the descriptive headings provided by database catalogers or indexers. The advantage to keyword searching is that you can use terms that come naturally to you to cast your net as widely as possible. The disadvantage is that there may be more than one way to express your topic and you may not capture all the relevant materials unless you use the right keywords.

With *subject searching,* you use search terms from a list of subject headings (sometimes called *descriptors*) established by the creators of the database. To make searching as efficient as possible, they choose one word or phrase to express a subject. Every time a new source is entered into the database, the indexers describe it using words from the list of subject headings: When you use the list to search the database, you retrieve every relevant source. You might find that a database lists these subject headings through a thesaurus feature. The sophisticated researcher will always pay attention to the subject headings or descriptors generally listed at the bottom of a record for clues to terms that might work best and for related terms that might be worth trying.

Searching for More Than One Concept. Most database searches allow you to combine terms using the connectors *and, or,* and *not.* These connectors (also known as *Boolean operators*) group search terms in different ways. If you search for zoos *and* animal rights, for example, the resulting list of sources will include only those that deal with both zoos and animal rights, leaving out any that deal with only one subject and not the other. If you connect terms with *or,* your list will contain sources that deal with either concept: A search for dogs *or* cats will create a list of sources that cover either animal. *Not* excludes concepts from a search. A search for animal rights *not* furs will search for the concept animal rights and then cut out any sources that deal with furs.

Limiting a Search. Most databases have some options for limiting a search by a number of variables, such as publication date, language, or format. If you find a large number of sources in a database search, you might limit your search to sources published in English in the past three years. If you need a visual aid for a presentation, you might limit a search of the library's catalog to videos, and so on.

Truncating Search Terms with Wild Cards. At times you will search for a word that has many possible endings. A wild card is a symbol that, placed at the end of a word root, allows for any possible ending for a word. For example, *animal** will allow a search for *animal* or *animals.*

Options for Saving Records. You may have the opportunity to print, download to a disk, or e-mail to yourself the citations you find in a database. Many databases have a feature for marking just the records you want so you save only those of interest.

Help Screens. Most databases offer some kind of online help that explains how to use the database effectively. If you invest five minutes getting familiar with the basics of a database, it may save you twenty minutes later.

■ Types of Databases

The Library Catalog. If you want to search for books, videos, or periodical publications, the library catalog is the database to search. Most libraries now have computerized catalogs, but some still have a card catalog. In either case, the type of information provided is the same. Every book in the library has an entry in the catalog that gives its author, title, publisher, date, length, and subject headings and perhaps some notes about its contents. It also gives the call number or location on the shelf and often some indication as to whether it is currently available. You can search the catalog for an author, title, subject, or keyword. Most online catalogs have ways of combining and limiting searches and for printing results. Remember when searching the catalog, though, that entries are created for whole books and not for specific parts of them. If you use too narrow search terms, you may not find a book that has a chapter that includes exactly what you are looking for. Use broad search terms, and check the subject headings for search terms that will work best. Plan to browse the shelves and examine the tables of contents of the books that you find through the catalog to see which, in fact, are most helpful for your topic.

General Periodical Databases. If you want to search for articles, you can find a number of options at your library. Most libraries have a generalized database of periodical articles that may include citations, citations with abstracts (brief summaries), or the entire text of articles. *EBSCOhost, Infotrac, Searchbank, Readers' Guide Abstracts,* and *ProQuest* are all online indexes of this type. Ask a librarian what is available in your library. These are particularly good for finding current information in fairly nonspecialized sources, though they may include some scholarly journals. If you are looking for articles published before the 1980s—say, for news accounts published when the atomic bomb was dropped on Hiroshima—you would most likely need to use a print index such as the *Readers' Guide to Periodical Literature,* which began publication in 1900.

Specialized Databases. In addition to these general databases, you may find you need to delve deeper into a particular subject area. Every academic discipline has some sort of in-depth index to its research, and though the materials they cover tend to be highly specialized, they can provide more substantial support for your claims because they tend to cover sources written by experts in their fields. These resources may be available in electronic or print form:

Sample Online Catalog Record

You searched for the TITLE—animal rights movement

```
CALL #       Z7164.C45 M38 1994.
AUTHOR       Manzo, Bettina, 1943-
TITLE        The animal rights movement in the United States, 1975-
             1990 : an annotated bibliography / by Bettina Manzo.
IMPRINT      Metuchen, N.J. : Scarecrow Press, 1994.
PHYS DESCR   xi, 296 p. ; 23 cm.
NOTE         Includes indexes.
CONTENTS     Animal rights movement -- Activists and organizations --
             Philosophy, ethics, and religion -- Law and legislation
             -- Factory farming and vegetarianism -- Trapping and
             fur industry -- Companion animals -- Wildlife --
             Circuses, zoos, rodeos, dog
SUBJECT      Animal rights movement --United States --Bibliography.
             Animal rights --United States --Bibliography.
             Animal experimentation --United States --Bibliography.
OCLC #       30671149.
ISBN/ISSN    GB95-17241.
```

Art Index

Biological Abstracts (the online version is known as *Biosis*)

Business Periodicals Index

ERIC (focused on education research)

Index Medicus (*Medline* or *PubMed* online)

Modern Languages Association International Bibliography (*MLA Bibliography* online)

Psychological Abstracts (*PsychInfo* or *PsychLit* online)

Sociological Abstracts (*Sociofile* online)

Check with a librarian to find out which specialized databases or indexes that relate to your topic are available in your library.

Database Services. In addition to individual databases, many libraries subscribe to database services that provide access to a number of databases from one search screen. *FirstSearch,* for example, provides access to a variety of subject-specific databases as well as *WorldCat,* a massive database of library catalogs. *Lexis/Nexis* is a collection of databases to over a billion texts, most of them available in full text; it is a strong source for news coverage, legal research, and business information. These may be available to you through the Web anywhere on campus. Again, a visit with a librarian will help you quickly identify what your library has available.

■ Encyclopedias

General and specialized encyclopedias offer quick overviews of topics and easy access to factual information. They also tend to have excellent selective bibliographies, pointing you toward useful sources. You will find a wide variety of encyclopedias in your library's reference collection; you may also have an online encyclopedia, such as *Britannica Online*, available through the Web anywhere on campus. Some specialized encyclopedias include the following:

> *Encyclopedia of African American History and Culture*
>
> *Encyclopedia of American Social History*
>
> *Encyclopedia of Bioethics*
>
> *Encyclopedia of Educational Research*
>
> *Encyclopedia of Hispanic Culture in the United States*
>
> *Encyclopedia of International Relations*
>
> *Encyclopedia of Philosophy*
>
> *Encyclopedia of Sociology*
>
> *Encyclopedia of the United States in the Twentieth Century*
>
> *Encyclopedia of World Cultures*
>
> *International Encyclopedia of Communications*
>
> *McGraw-Hill Encyclopedia of Science and Technology*
>
> *Political Handbook of the World*

■ Statistical Resources

Often statistics are used as evidence in an argument. If your argument depends on establishing that one category is bigger than another, that the majority of people hold a certain opinion, or that one group is more affected by something than another group, statistics can provide the evidence you need. Of course, as with any other source, you need to be sure that your statistics are as reliable as possible and that you are reporting them responsibly.

It isn't always easy to find things counted the way you want. If you embark on a search for numbers to support your argument, be prepared to spend some time locating and interpreting data. Always read the fine print that explains how and when the data were gathered. Some sources for statistics include these:

U.S. Bureau of the Census. This government agency produces a wealth of statistical data, much of it available on CD-ROM or through the Web at <www.census.gov>. A handy compilation of their most useful tables is found in the one-volume annual handbook, *Statistical Abstract of the United States,* which also includes statistics from other government sources.

Other Federal Agencies. Numerous federal agencies gather statistical data. Among these are the National Center for Education Statistics, the National Center for Health Statistics, the National Bureau of Labor Statistics, and the Federal Bureau of Investigation, which annually compiles national crime statistics. One handy place to find a wide variety of federal statistics is a Web site called *FedStats* at <www.fedstats.gov>.

United Nations. Compilations of international data published by the United Nations include the *Demographic Yearbook* and *Statistical Yearbook.* Some statistics are also published by U.N. agencies such as the Food and Health Organization. Some are available from the U.N. Web site at <www.un.org>.

Opinion Polls. Several companies conduct opinion polls, and some of these are available in libraries. One such compilation is the Gallup Poll series, which summarizes public opinion polling from 1935 to the present. Other poll results are reported by the press. Search a database that covers news publications by using your topic and *polls* as keywords to help you locate some summaries of results.

■ Government Publications

Beyond statistics, government agencies compile and publish a wealth of information. For topics that concern public welfare, health, education, politics, foreign relations, earth sciences, the environment, or the economy, government documents may provide just the information you need.

The U.S. federal government is the largest publisher in the world. Its publications are distributed free to libraries designated as document depositories across the country. If your library is not a depository, chances are there is a regional depository somewhere nearby. Local, state, and foreign governments are also potential sources of information.

Federal documents distributed to depository libraries are indexed in *The Monthly Catalog of U.S. Government Documents,* available in many libraries as an electronic database. These include congressional documents such as hearings and committee reports, presidential papers, studies conducted by the Education Department or the Centers for Disease Control, and so on. Many government documents are available through the Internet. If you learn about a government publication through the news media, chances are you will be able to obtain a copy at the Web site of the sponsoring agency or congressional body. In fact, government publications are among the most valuable of resources available on the Web because they are rigorously controlled for content. You know you are looking at a U.S. federal government site when you see the domain suffix *.gov* in the URL.

■ Searching the Web

The World Wide Web is becoming an increasingly important resource for researchers. It is particularly helpful if you are looking for information about organizations, current events, political debates, popular culture, or government-sponsored research and activities. It is not an especially good place to look for literary criticism, historical analysis, or scholarly research articles, which are still more likely to be published in traditional ways. Biologists reporting on an important experiment, for example, are more likely to submit an article about it to a prestigious journal in the field than simply post their results on the Web.

Because anyone can publish whatever they like on the Web, searching for good information can be frustrating. Search engines operate by means of automated programs that gather information about sites and match search terms to whatever is out there, regardless of quality. A search engine may locate thousands of Web documents on a topic, but most are of little relevance and dubious quality. The key is to know in advance what information you need and who might have produced it. For example, if your topic has to do with some aspect of free speech and you know that the American Civil Liberties Union is involved in the issue, a trip to the ACLU home page may provide you with a wealth of information, albeit from a particular perspective. If your state's pollution control agency just issued a report on water quality in the area, you may find the report published at their Web site or the e-mail address of someone who could send it to you. The more you know about your topic before you sit down to surf, the more likely you will use your time productively.

If you have a fairly broad topic and no specific clues about where it might be covered, you may want to start your search using a selective guide to good sites. For example, the University of Texas maintains an excellent directory to sites relating to Latin America. Subject guides that selectively list valuable sites can be found at the *Argus Clearinghouse* at <www.clearinghouse.net>, the University of California's *Infomine* at <http://infomine.ucr.edu>, and the *World Wide Web Virtual Library* project at <www.vlib.org/Home.html>. Reference librarians will also be able to point you to quality sites that relate to your topic.

If you have a fairly specific topic in mind or are looking for a particular organization or document on the Web, a search engine can help you find it. *Google* is one of the best. No matter what search engine you choose, find out how it works, how it ranks results, and how deeply it indexes Web pages. Some search engines will retrieve more results than others simply because of the way the program gathers information from sites. As with databases, there are usually ways to refine a search and improve your results. Many search engines offer an advanced search option that may provide some useful options for refining and limiting a search.

It is important to know what will not be retrieved by a search engine. Because publishing and transmitting texts on the Web is relatively easy, it is becoming more common for libraries to subscribe to databases and electronic journals that are accessed through a Web browser. You may have *Britannica Online* and *Lexis/Nexis* as options on your library's home page. However, the contents of those subscriptions will be available only to your campus community and will not be searched by general Web search engines.

EVALUATING SOURCES

When you begin studying your sources, read first to acquire general familiarity with your subject. Make sure that you are covering both sides of the question—in this case arguments both for and against the existence of zoos—as well as facts and opinions from a variety of sources. In investigating this subject, you will encounter data from biologists, ecologists, zoo directors, anthropologists, animal-rights activists, and ethical philosophers; their varied points of view will contribute to the strength of your claim.

As you read, look for what seem to be the major issues. They will probably be represented in all or most of your sources. For the claim about zoos the major issues may be summarized as follows: (1) the fundamental right wild animals have to liberty; (2) the harm done to animals who are denied this right and kept in captivity. On the other side, these issues will emerge: (1) the lack of concrete evidence that animals suffer or are harmed by being in zoos; (2) the benefits, in terms of entertainment, education, and conservation efforts that the public derives from zoos. The latter two, of course, are the issues you will have to refute. Your note taking should emphasize these important issues.

Record questions as they occur to you in your reading. Why do zoos exist? What are their major goals, and how well do they meet them? What happens to animals who are removed from the wild and placed in zoos? What happens to animals born and reared in captivity? How do these groups compare with their wild counterparts, who are free to live in their natural habitats? Do animals really have a right to liberty? What are the consequences of denying them this right? Are there consequences to humanity?

■ Evaluating Print Sources

The sources you find provide useful information that you need for your paper and help you support your claims. One key to supporting claims effectively is to make sure you have the best evidence available. It is tempting when searching a database or the Web to take the first sources that look good, print them or copy them, and not give them another thought until you are sitting down to compose your argument—only to discover that the sources aren't as valuable as they could be. Sources that looked pretty good at the beginning of your research may turn out to be less useful once you have learned more about the topic. And a source that seems interesting at first glance may turn out to be a rehash or digest of a much more valuable source, something you realize only when you sit down and look at it carefully.

To find the right stuff, be a critical thinker from the start of your research process. Scan and evaluate the references you encounter throughout your search. As you examine options in a database, choose sources that use relevant terms in their titles, seem directed to an appropriate audience, and are published in places that will look good in your Works Cited list. For example, a Senate Foreign Relations Committee report will be more impressive as a source than a comparable article in *Good Housekeeping.* An article from the scholarly journal *Foreign Affairs* will carry more clout than an article from *Reader's Digest,* even if they are on the same subject.

Skim and quickly evaluate each source that looks valuable.

- Is it relevant to your topic?
- Does it provide information you haven't found elsewhere?
- Can you learn anything about the author, and does what you learn inspire confidence?

As you begin to learn more about your topic and develop an outline, you can use sources to help direct your search. If a source mentions an organization, for example, you may use that clue to run a search on the Web for that organization's home page. If a newspaper story refers to a study published in a scientific journal, you may want to seek out that study to see the results of the research firsthand. And if you have a source that includes references to other publications, scan through them, and see which might also prove helpful to you. When you first started your research, chances are you weren't quite sure what you were looking for. Once you are familiar with your topic, you need to concentrate on finding sources that will best support the claims you want to make, and your increasing familiarity with the issue will make it easier to identify the best sources. That may mean a return trip to the library.

Once you have selected some useful sources to support your claims, make a more in-depth evaluation to be sure you have the best evidence available.

- Is it current enough? Have circumstances changed since this text was published?

- Is the author someone I want to call on as an expert witness? Does the author have the experience or credentials to make a solid argument that carries weight with my readers?

- Is it reliable information for my purposes? It may be highly opinionated, but are the basic facts it presents confirmed in other sources? Is the evidence presented in the text convincing?

These questions are not always easy to answer. In some cases, articles will include some information about the author, such as where he or she works. In other cases, no information or even an author's name is given. In that case, it may help to evaluate the publication and its reputation. If you aren't familiar with a publication and don't feel confident making your own judgment, see if it is described in Katz's *Magazines for Libraries*, which evaluates the reputation and quality of periodicals.

■ Evaluating Web Sources

Web sites pose challenges and offer unique opportunities for researchers, for one reason because they are part of a developing genre of writing. When evaluating a Web site, first examine what kind of site you are reading. Is the Web page selling or advertising goods or services (a business site)? Is it advocating a point of view (an advocacy site) or providing relatively neutral information, such as that found in the yellow pages (an informative or educational site)? Is the Web site addressing the interests of people in a particular organization or with common interests (an information-sharing site)? Is it reporting up-to-the-minute news (a news site) or appealing to some aspect of an individual's life and interests (a personal site)? Useful information for a research paper may be obtained from any of these kinds of Web pages, but it is helpful to know what the main purpose of the site is—and who its primary audience is—when determining how productive it will be for your research.

As you weigh the main purpose of the site, evaluate its original context. Does the site originate in a traditional medium, such as a print journal or an encyclopedia? Is the site part of an online journal, in which case its material had to go through a screening process? Or is the site the product of one individual's or organization's desire to create a Web page, which means the work may not have been screened or evaluated by any outside agency? In that case, the information may still be valuable, but you must be even more careful when evaluating it.

Answering preliminary questions like these help you before you begin a more specific evaluation of the site's content. To find answers to many of these questions, make a brief overview of the site itself, by looking, for example, at the clues contained in the Web address. That is, *.com* in the address means a business or commercial site; *.edu,* a site sponsored by a university or college; *.k12* is a site associated with a primary or secondary school; *.gov* indicates that the federal government sponsored the site; and *.org* suggests that the site is part of a nonprofit or noncommercial group. Sites originating outside the United States have URLs that end with a two-letter country abbreviation, such as *.uk* for United Kingdom. Although these address clues can reveal a great deal about the origins and purposes of a Web site, remember that personal Web sites may also contain some of these abbreviations. Institutions such as schools and businesses sometimes sponsor individuals' personal Web sites (which are often unscreened by the institution) as well as official institutional sites. One possible key to determining whether a Web site is a personal page, however, is to look for a tilde (~) plus a name or part of a name in the address. Finally, if you are unsure of the sponsoring organization of a page, try erasing all the information in the URL after the first slash (/) and pressing the "Enter" key. Doing so often brings you to the main page of the organization sponsoring the Web site.

Most Web sites include a way to contact the author or sponsoring organization of the site, usually through e-mail. This is often a quick and easy way to get answers to the preliminary questions. If the site contains an address or phone number as part of its contact information, this means the organization or individual is available and probably willing to stand behind the site's content. If you can't find contact information the site may not be suitable to use as a primary resource. The information is not necessarily invalid, but such clues should alert you that information found on that page needs to be verified.

For the next step—that of more closely evaluating the contents of any Web site—Web researchers generally agree on the importance of five criteria: the authority, accuracy, objectivity, currency, and coverage of the site.[1] These criteria are just as important in evaluating traditional print texts, but electronic texts require special care. To understand how these criteria work, let's look at a specific example.

■ Evaluating a Web Page: One Example

Your latest assignment for a course in argumentation is to research and write on a topic of significance to you and your future. You are a woman thinking about a career in technology, and you want to know how women fare in such careers. You remember hearing that many women

---

[1] Wolfram Memorial Library Web site.

GirlTECH Home Page

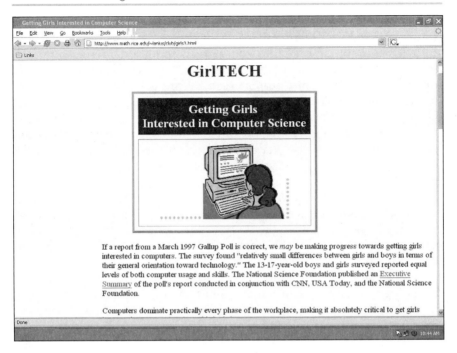

GirlTECH

Getting Girls
Interested in Computer Science

If a report from a March 1997 Gallup Poll is correct, we *may* be making progress towards getting girls interested in computers. The survey found "relatively small differences between girls and boys in terms of their general orientation toward technology." The 13-17-year-old boys and girls surveyed reported equal levels of both computer usage and skills. The National Science Foundation published an Executive Summary of the poll's report conducted in conjunction with CNN, USA Today, and the National Science Foundation.

Computers dominate practically every phase of the workplace, making it absolutely critical to get girls

don't choose technology as a career path, despite the opportunities for personal and financial enrichment. You decide to research the subject so that you can write an argument that addresses this issue, maybe one that encourages women to enter computer science. Ultimately, though, your argument will depend on what facts, statistics, and debates you unearth about the broader issue of women following careers in technology. As you research, then, you have at least two competing goals in mind: first, to learn as much as you can about a topic that you find interesting and may affect your professional aspirations, and second, to gather data for a tentative argument you want to make, in this case counteracting the apparent tendency of women to avoid careers in technology.

You begin by using the databases of academic and nonacademic articles typically located through your college's or university's library Web page. These databases direct you to both academic and less formal articles stored in journals that are kept either online or as print materials in your library. You also check the library's catalog for books on the subject. These texts likely will result in a range of sources for your search, and comparing a number of them will give you an idea of what the existing published research about women in technology covers. These kinds of sources—published online or in print—also can provide in-depth coverage of your topic, something that your average Web page found through *Yahoo!* or

Google does not. The different issues covered also will make you realize how important it will be to narrow your topic about women and technology so that you can write an argument on a manageable piece of a complex subject.

After your initial foray into your library's traditional research materials, you want to explore World Wide Web resources. Can women find support on the Web in any online organizations for their choice of a technological career? What resources about this topic are available to someone who may have access to a computer but not to a research library?

You begin searching for answers through at least two of the standard search engines (*Lycos, Ask Jeeves,* or *Yahoo!,* for example). Because each search engine has different strengths and weaknesses, you are likely to find different sources on each. Searches on "Women and Technology" and "Women and Computers" lead to a site titled "Getting Girls Interested in Computer Science" (the home page of which is reproduced here). When the page first comes up, you notice the title underneath the linked name *Cynthia Lanius* in the upper left corner and the heading "Girl-TECH."

Scrolling down, you notice a few paragraphs of text about women in technology (not an in-depth analysis but some potentially useful statistics and resources). You also can see at a glance that Lanius is making use

Cynthia Lanius's Personal Web Page

of a documentation style that is possible only in electronic texts. She acknowledges her sources by means of linking directly to electronic versions of them rather than using the more traditional endnotes or parenthetical documentation. Readers who are interested can delve further into the subject by clicking on the links. They can also recognize Lanius as the author of the text on the home page of the site through her use of first person. Hers is the e-mail address they are invited to send comments to, and her linked name is the first thing that viewers see at the top left of the page.

Before you closely examine the page to evaluate its content, pay attention to the site's URL <http://math.rice.edu/~lanius/club/girls3.html>. The *.edu* means that an educational institution sponsors the site, that the institution is Rice University, and even more specifically, that the mathematics department of Rice University sponsors the site. All of this information is determined by erasing the information after *.edu* in the URL. It is also important to note *~lanius* in the URL because it signifies a personal Web page representing the ideas of Cynthia Lanius rather than those of Rice University as an institution. That in itself doesn't disqualify the site as a source of useful information, but it does remind careful readers to examine Cynthia Lanius's credentials and why she created the site. Her exact affiliation with Rice University cannot be told from this opening page and requires further investigation.

A quick review of the whole page shows no sign that it originates from existing publication or is part of an online journal. This, then, is another reason for the reader to take care in evaluating this site's content. Such a review also reveals that the page is concerned with advocacy as well as with education.

After this preliminary work is completed, you can apply the five criteria for evaluating Web sites: authority, accuracy, objectivity, currency, and coverage.

Authority

You have already begun to wonder about the authority of the author Cynthia Lanius. (The word *author* is the root for *authority*. Think about how these words became connected and how that connection is sometimes abused; not all authors are authorities.) Click on the link Lanius provides at the top of the page, which leads to her home page. This page shows the logo for Rice University, affiliating Lanius with this reputable institution, and also includes a variety of links, including sample math lessons that Lanius created for girls and a variety of reference sources. Most important for an evaluation of her authority, however, is the information about her work experience and the lists of publications, presentations, and awards Lanius provides in her biography. Before her years at Rice University, she taught high school math, at Rice she was Executive Director of the Center for Excellence and Equity in Education, and she is now Technology Integration Specialist for a school district in Texas. The link to some of her presentations shows that Lanius has given numerous speeches on girls, science, math, technology, and education. Clearly, serious organizations and individuals value her ideas and research, which suggests that Lanius's site is potentially useful and that she carries authority as an expert on women and technology.

Lanius's biography also lists the committees she is a member of, with each committee title serving as a link to the group's site. Her site links as well to organizations from which Lanius has received rewards and institutions at which she has worked. This sort of linking makes it possible to verify much of Lanius's information. Obviously you will not be able to verify every detail from every source, but the Web can help you check an authority's credentials and background.

Accuracy

Lanius's GirlTECH Web site includes many different kinds of information: statistics regarding the number of women who received computer science degrees in U.S. universities from 1985 to 1995, statistics that suggest a serious gap between the number of men studying computer science and the number of women pursuing this field, and statistics about the number of boys and girls in high schools taking advanced placement classes and

Lanius's Biography Page

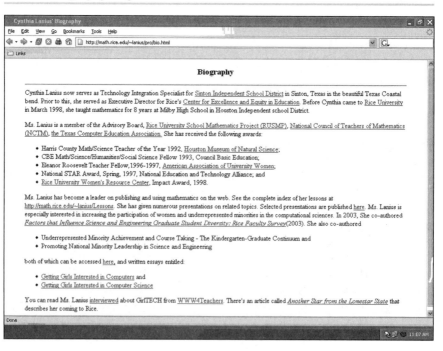

exams in science and math. Since Lanius's Web site—and much of her career—is based on combating statistics such as these, finding out more about these numbers is critical. Statistics come from many sources and are presented (and manipulated) in many ways; understanding their sources and how they compare to other statistics on the same or related issues is imperative. On the GirlTECH home page, Lanius provides links to the National Science Foundation and the College Board, two reliable resources that can help confirm the numbers. As you continue researching, be on the lookout for further statistics and compare them with Lanius's. What larger story about women and technology can you create based on statistical studies and reports?

In the text on the GirlTECH home page, Lanius moves from statistics to her experience working with female high school students. She ends the opening essay with a quote from two of her colleagues at Rice that explains their love of computer science. Such personal testimony cannot be evaluated for accuracy in the same way as can statistics. To evaluate its effectiveness, a thoughtful reader should put himself or herself into the role of a student who feels shut out of technology classes or careers and consider whether the strategy Lanius offers would help alleviate insecurities or difficulties. A reader could also compare Lanius's ideas with those in literature on education and marginalized groups. Most important, though, a reader should recognize that anecdotal information (which may be supported by research but does not represent universal fact) is different from statistical information and must be evaluated using different strategies. Go to the GirlTECH Web site and read through more of its content and the content of some of the links provided. How many kinds of knowledge (facts, opinions, arguments, etc.) are represented? What kinds of strategies will be needed to determine their accuracy?

Objectivity

Objectivity is an especially important and difficult factor to determine for a Web site such as "Getting Girls Interested in Computer Science." The site is concerned both with education and advocacy and is making an argument for a specific issue. The question, then, is not whether the site has any biases; it admits to a clear bias: that of greater inclusion of girls and women in the world of technology. In fact, all sites, even the most neutral ones, have biases; it is not possible to create a perfectly inclusive, objective, value-free text.

For most sites, then, the job of the research writer is to determine the nature of the biases and the degree to which they interfere with the information provided. This process involves analyzing the assumptions, or *warrants,* underlying the argument of a Web page and determining the basis for these warrants.

Lanius's site takes at least three things for granted, that is, it operates from three basic warrants. First, Lanius's site assumes that the number of women in technology-related fields is too low. Second, the site assumes that this low number represents a problem and not simply a difference between the genders that we should accept. Third, the site assumes that early intervention through education can change this trend and help girls see technological fields as options.

The first warrant is easy to analyze. By looking at several studies of women in technological fields (including some of the sites Lanius links to), we can determine that, indeed, the number of women in technological careers is significantly lower than we might expect based on the number of women in the workforce. More difficult is evaluating the objectivity of the second warrant: that this underrepresentation is a problem all educators and, in fact, all people should be concerned about. Such an assumption will provoke a variety of interpretations. Some readers, for example, may believe the low number of women in technological fields to be a reflection of where women's interests lie. Others may view professional career choices as a matter of individual choice and not something that schools or educators should address directly. Still others may assume that any discussion about inclusion of underrepresented groups automatically means quotas or reverse discrimination. It is important for the discriminating reader to understand why Lanius and Rice University would conclude that the low number of women in technological fields is a problem. Similarly, in evaluating the objectivity of Lanius's third warrant, it is important to ask why she believes education is a key to changing this situation.

Only when readers carefully examine issues such as these, while trying to put themselves into Lanius's shoes, can they determine whether an unfair bias makes the information, opinions, and suggestions that Lanius offers tainted or suspect. Such work can be done only when Lanius's work is compared with other research on girls, women, technology, and education, which she, helpfully, has provided access to on her Web site.

Currency

Currency is critical when evaluating Web sites. When a site was first created and when it was last updated influence the way you read the site and how you assess the other four criteria. Take the first criteria of authority, for example.

If you go to the Rice University math department page, you may be surprised to find that Lanius is not listed among the faculty. If you look further, though, you will find her listed under "Resources and Projects." She explains in her biography that while she was formerly on the faculty at Rice, she now works for a public school district. Because GirlTECH is an ongoing project begun at Rice, its site continues to be maintained through the university's site. It is clear from the dates on her publications and presentations that Lanius maintained the site at least through 2003.

Currency plays an equally important role in the second criterion, accuracy. Statistics, for example, change rapidly, and what were cutting-

edge numbers a few years ago might now be completely different (for example, the number of Internet users has changed dramatically over the
past decade and even in the last few years). It is always useful to analyze
how current the statistics and arguments being offered on a Web site may
be and to compare the dates of statistics such as the ones Lanius offers to
the dates of other studies you encounter. Close analysis helps assure that
you can present the most accurate research in your argument and are able
to counter arguments based on less current information.

Coverage

Finally, readers of a Web site must evaluate the site's coverage, another
difficult issue since no one text or Web site can cover a topic as large and
complex as girls and women in technology. One way to gauge the coverage of a Web site is to look carefully at its primary topic and to examine
other positions and opinions not represented by the site. Search for these
perspectives in other forms of research, both Web-based and print, and
think about why the author of the Web site chose not to include them in
the text. Are they not of primary importance to the author's ideas? Is it
possible that he or she may not be familiar with these alternative perspectives? Is it possible that they are not very reliable? How do you think
the author would respond to such perspectives?

Analyzing the variety, quality, and number of links a Web site provides is also important. "Getting Girls Interested in Computer Science" is
a successful Web site because it offers a long list of resources and links to
other academic centers and professional organizations that promote technological fields for girls and women. It also includes links to online articles describing women in technology and sites that have been
specifically created for girls. You may still want to pursue other research
that takes the contrary view that the small number of women in technological professions is not the problem that Lanius sees. Nevertheless, this
site does provide an excellent, well-rounded coverage of girls, women,
and technology.

Conclusion

Evaluating Web sites as sources of information — indeed, evaluating any
research text — is a difficult process. The five criteria we've used to evaluate Cynthia Lanius's "Getting Girls Interested in Computer Science" overlap. Starting with any one of the five criteria almost inevitably leads to
the others: The accuracy of the information, for example, is clearly related
to the authority of the Web site's author, to the biases present in the site,
and to the coverage of the information offered. For some sites, one of
these criteria will be most important; for others you may have to address
all five in detail. You will not be able to analyze every Web site the way
we have, but do subject the most important Web sites you encounter to
this analysis before you tap them for information central to your work.

WORKING WITH SOURCES

■ Taking Notes

While everyone has methods of taking notes, here are a few suggestions that should be useful to research writers who need to read materials quickly, comprehend and evaluate the sources, use them as part of a research paper assignment, and manage their time carefully.

When taking notes from a source, summarize instead of quoting long passages. Summarizing as you read saves time. If you feel that a direct quote is more effective than anything you could write and provides crucial support for your argument, copy the material word for word. Leave all punctuation exactly as it appears and insert ellipsis points ("...") if you delete material. Enclose all quotations in quotation marks and copy complete information about your source, including the author's name, the title of the book or article, the journal name if appropriate, page numbers, and publishing information. If you quote an article that appears in an anthology, record complete information about the book itself.

Note Card with Quotation

> *Hediger*   **25**
>
> *"The wild animal, with its marked tendency to escape, is notorious for the fact that it is never completely released from that all-important activity, avoiding enemies, even during sleep, but is constantly on alert."*

Note Card with Summary

> *Hediger*   **25**
>
> *Animals who live in the wild have to be on the watch for predators constantly.*

If you aren't sure whether you will use a piece of information later, don't copy the whole passage. Instead, make a note of its bibliographic information so that you can find it again if you need it. Taking too many notes, however, is preferable to taking too few, a problem that will force you to go back to the library for missing information.

Record complete bibliographical information for each source that you intend to use in your paper (as well as for those sources you may use). This ensures that you will have all the information necessary to document your paper. Some researchers keep two sets of note cards: one set for the bibliographical information and one set for the notes themselves. Each source then appears on a card by itself, ready to be arranged in alphabetical order for the Works Cited or References page of the paper.

Use the note-taking process as a prewriting activity. Often when you summarize an author's ideas or write down direct quotes, you see or understand the material in new ways. Freewrite about the importance of these quotes, paraphrases, or summaries, or at least about those that seem especially important. If nothing else, take a minute to justify in writing why you chose to record the notes. Doing so will help you clarify and develop your thoughts about your argument.

Note Card with Statistics	*Reiger* **32** *By end of decade, worldwide extinction rate will be one species per hour.* *Other statistics, too, in Reiger, "The Wages of Growth," Field and Stream, July 1981:32.*
Bibliography Note Card	*Hediger, Heini. The Psychology and Behavior of Animals in Zoos and Circuses. Trans. Geoffrey Sircom. New York: Dover, 1968.*

Taking this prewriting step seriously will help you analyze the ideas you record from outside sources. You will then be better prepared for the more formal (and inevitable) work of summarizing, paraphrasing, and composing involved in thinking critically about your topic and writing a research paper. Maybe most important, such work will help with that moment all writers face when they realize they "know what they want to say but can't find the words to say it." Overcoming such moments does not depend on finding inspiration while writing the final draft of a paper. Instead, successfully working through this common form of writer's block depends more on the amount of prewriting and thoughtful consideration of the notes done early in the research process.

As you take notes, also remember to refer to your outline to ensure that you are acquiring sufficient data to support all the points you intend to raise. Of course, you will be revising your outline during the course of your research as issues are clarified and new ideas emerge, but the outline will serve as a rough guide throughout the writing process. Keeping close track of your outline will also prevent you from recording material that is interesting but not relevant.

Relying on the knowledge of others is an important part of doing research; expert opinions and eloquent arguments help support your claims when your own expertise is limited. But remember, this is *your* paper. Your ideas and insights into other people's ideas are just as important as the information you uncover at the library. When writing an argument, do not simply regurgitate the words and thoughts of others in your essay. Work to achieve a balance between providing solid information from expert sources and offering your own interpretation of the argument and the evidence that supports it.

Using word-processing software can invigorate the process of note taking and of outlining (see p. 376). Taking notes using a computer gives you more flexibility than using pen and paper alone. For example, you can save your computer-generated notes and your comments on them in numerous places (at home, school, or work, or on a disk); you can cut and paste the text into various documents; you can add to the notes or modify them and still revert to the originals with ease. (Be sure not to delete or save over your original files, by always using the Save As function when modifying your original files.)

If your computer allows access to the World Wide Web, you can link notes to background material that may be useful once you begin writing drafts of your paper. For example, you could create links to an author's Web page or to any of his or her other works published on the Web. You could create a link to a study or an additional source cited in your notes, or you could link to the work of other researchers who support or argue against the information you recorded.

Because you can record information in any number of ways on your computer, your notes act as tools in the writing process. One of the best ways to start is to open a file for each source; enter the bibliographic information; directly type into the file a series of potentially useful quotations, paraphrases, and summaries; and add your initial ideas about the source. (For each entry, note the correct page references as you go along and indicate clearly whether you are quoting, paraphrasing, or summarizing.) You can then use the capabilities of your computer to aid you in the later stages of the writing process. For example, you can collect all your research notes into one large file in which you group like sources, evaluate whether you have too much information about one issue or one side of an argument, or examine sources that conflict with one another. You can imagine various organizational schemes for your paper based on the central themes and issues of the notes you have taken, and you can more clearly determine which quotes and summaries are essential to your paper and which may not be needed.

When you're ready to begin your first draft, the computer allows you to readily integrate material from your source notes into your research paper by cutting and pasting, thus eliminating the need to retype and reducing the chance of error. You can also combine all the bibliographic materials you have saved in separate files and then use the computer to alphabetize your sources for your final draft.

Although word processors do not dramatically change the research process, they do highlight the fact that taking notes, prewriting, drafting a paper, and creating bibliographies are integrated activities that should build from one another. When you take notes from a journal, book, or Web site, you develop your note-taking abilities so that they help with the entire writing process.

■ Quoting

You may want to quote passages or phrases from your sources if they express an idea in words more effective than your own. In this particular project, you might come across a statement that provides succinct, irrefutable evidence for an issue you wish to support. If the author of this statement is a professional in his or her field, someone with a great deal of authority on the subject, it would be appropriate to quote that author. Suppose, during the course of your research for the zoo paper, you find that many sources agree that zoos don't have the money or space necessary to maintain large enough animal populations to ensure successful captive breeding programs. But so far you only have opinions to that effect. You have been unable to find any concrete documentation of this fact until you come across Ulysses S. Seal's address to the National Zoological Park Symposia for the Public, September 1982. Here is how you could use Seal's words in your paper (using reference citation style of the American Psychological Association):

> Bear in mind that "none of these [zoo] budgets is allocated specifically for species preservation. Zoos have been established primarily as recreational

> institutions and are only secondarily developing programs in conservation, education and research" (Seal, 1982, p. 74).

Notice the use of brackets (not parentheses) in the first sentence, which enclose material that did not appear in the original source but is necessary for clarification. Brackets must be used to indicate any such changes in quoted material. Equally important, however, is that you introduce the author of the quote in such a way as to establish that person's authority on the subject under discussion. This is even more important in argumentation than in other types of writing. In the example above, it is unlikely that anyone except zoo employees—and probably not even those individuals—would know who Seal is simply from seeing his name mentioned in parentheses. Your argument will have more power if you establish the authority of each author from whose work you quote, paraphrase, or summarize. To establish authority, you may refer to the person's position, institutional affiliation, publications, or some other similar "claim to fame."

> According to the late Ulysses S. Seal III (1982), founder of the Conservation Breeding Specialist Group and of a "computer dating service" for mateless animals, "None of these [zoo] budgets is allocated specifically for species preservation. Zoos have been established primarily as recreational institutions and are only secondarily developing programs in conservation, education, and research" (p. 74).

Notice that once the name of the author being cited is mentioned in the writer's own text, it does not have to be repeated in the parentheses. This particular example uses APA style. Later in the chapter, you will see more examples of both APA and MLA styles of documentation.

Writer's Guide: Incorporating Quotations into Your Text

1. The most effective way to lead into the first quotation from a source is to use the author's full name and his or her claim to authority — a few words identifying the person by title, institutional affiliation, or publications. Remember that for nonspecialists, the name of an author you are quoting may have little meaning, and relegating the last name to parentheses at the end of the quotation does not use that author's authority to strengthen your argument. Once you have used the full name once, any future references may use only the last name of the author. If the author's name, full or last only, is used in your lead-in to the quote, you do not have to repeat it in the parentheses that complete the documentation. One additional advantage of mentioning the author or authors is that a reader can tell where your ideas leave off and those from your source begin.

2. There are three primary means of linking a supporting quotation to your own text. Remember that in each case, the full citation for the source will be listed alphabetically by the author's name in the list of works cited at the end of the paper, or by title if no author is given. The number in parentheses is the page of that source on which the quotation appears. The details of what appears in parentheses will be covered later in the discussion of MLA (Modern Language Association) and APA (American Psychological Association) documentation styles.

• You may choose to make a brief quotation a grammatical part of your own sentence. In that case, you do not separate the quotation from your sentence with a comma, unless there is another reason for the comma, and you do not capitalize the first word of the quotation, unless there is another reason for doing so. In this sort of situation, there may be times when you have to change the tense of a verb, in brackets, to make the quote fit smoothly into your text or when you need to make other small changes, always in brackets.

EXAMPLES

APA style

James Rachels (1976), University Professor of Philosophy at the University of Alabama at Birmingham and author of several books on moral philosophy, explains that animals' right to liberty derives from "a more basic right not to have one's interests needlessly harmed" (p. 210).

MLA style

James Rachels, University Professor of Philosophy at the University of Alabama at Birmingham and author of several books on moral philosophy, explains that animals' right to liberty derives from "a more basic right not to have one's interests needlessly harmed" (210).

• You may use a traditional speech tag such as "he says" or "she writes." This is the most common way of introducing a quote. Be sure to put a comma after the tag and begin the quotation with a capital letter. At the end of the quotation, close the quote, add the page number and any other necessary information in parentheses, and then add the period.

EXAMPLES

APA style

James Rachels (1976), University Professor of Philosophy at the University of Alabama at Birmingham and author of several books on moral philosophy, writes, "The right to liberty — the right to be free of external constraints on one's actions — may then be seen as derived from a more basic right not to have one's interests needlessly harmed" (p. 210).

MLA style

James Rachels, University Professor of Philosophy at the University of Alabama at Birmingham and author of several books on moral philosophy, writes, "The right to liberty — the right to be free of external constraints on one's actions — may then be seen as derived from a more basic right not to have one's interests needlessly harmed" (210).

Students are sometimes at a loss as to what sorts of verbs to use in these tag statements. Try using different terms from this list or others like them. Remember that in writing about a printed or electronic text, it is customary to write in present tense unless there is a compelling reason to use past tense.

argues	declares	replies
asks	explains	responds
asserts	implores	states
concludes	insists	suggests
continues	proclaims	
counters	questions	

- You may vary the way you introduce quotations by using a colon to separate the quotation from a *complete sentence* that introduces it.

EXAMPLES

APA style

For example, the Zurich Zoo's Dr. Heini Hediger (1985) protests that it is absurd to attribute human qualities to animals at all, but he nevertheless resorts to a human analogy: "Wild animals in the zoo rather resemble estate owners. Far from desiring to escape and regain their freedom, they are only bent on defending the space they inhabit and keeping it safe from invasion" (p. 9).

MLA style

The late Ulysses S. Seal III, founder of the Conservation Breeding Specialist Group and of a "computer dating service" for mateless animals, acknowledges the subordinate position species preservation plays in budgeting decisions: "Zoos have been established primarily as recreational institutions and are only secondarily developing programs in conservation, education, and research" (74).

3. Long quotations are handled differently from shorter ones. In MLA style, a quotation of more than four lines and in APA style, a quotation of more than forty words are set off as a block quotation. That means that the writer must double-space before and after the quotation — as well as double-spacing the quotation itself — and indent the whole quotation ten additional spaces (MLA) or five spaces (APA) from the left margin. The passage is not placed in quotation marks because the placement on the page indicates that it is a quotation. With block quotations, the parentheses used to provide documentation at the end of the passage are placed after, rather than before, the period. Block quotations should be used even more sparingly than shorter ones.

4. Avoid "floating" quotations. That is, do not jump from a sentence of your own text into a quotation with no connection between the two. Introduce every direct quotation.

5. Avoid back-to-back quotations. There should always be some of your own ideas to justify including a quotation, so some of your own text should always intervene between quoted passages. Quotations should be introduced logically and gracefully in your text. Make sure that the quoted material either supports or illustrates the point you have just made or the point you are about to make and that your writing remains grammatically correct once the quotation is introduced.

Quotations should be introduced logically and gracefully in your text. Make sure that the quoted material either supports or illustrates the point you have just made or the point you are about to make and that your writing remains grammatically correct once the quotation is introduced.

Quotations are an important tool for establishing your claims, but it is important not to overuse them. If you cannot say most of what you want to say in your own words, you probably haven't thought hard enough about what it is you want to say.

■ Paraphrasing

Paraphrasing involves restating the content of an original source in your own words. It is most useful when the material from your source is too long for your paper, can be made clearer to the reader by rephrasing, or is written in a style markedly different from your own.

A paraphrase should be as true to the original source as you can make it: Do not change the tone or the ideas, or even the order in which the ideas are presented. Take care not to allow your own opinions to creep into your paraphrase of someone else's argument. Your readers should always be aware of which arguments belong to you and which belong to outside sources.

Like a quotation, a paraphrase must *always* include documentation, or you will be guilty of plagiarism. Even though you are using your own words, the ideas in a paraphrase belong to someone else, and that person deserves credit for them. One final caveat: When putting a long passage into your own words, beware of picking up certain expressions and turns of phrase from your source. If you do end up using your source's exact words, make sure to enclose them in quotation marks.

Below is a passage from Shannon Brownlee's "First It Was 'Save the Whales,' Now It's 'Free the Dolphins'" (*Discover*, December 1986, pp. 70–72), along with a good paraphrase of the passage and two unacceptable paraphrases. Following APA style, the author's last name and the date of publication are provided in parentheses in the original because they are not mentioned in the text.

ORIGINAL PASSAGE

But are we being good caretakers by holding a dolphin or a sea lion in a tank? Yes, if two conditions are met: that they're given the best treatment possible and, no less important, that they're displayed in a way that educates and informs us. Captive animals must be allowed to serve as ambassadors for their species (Brownlee, 1986, p. 72).

A PARAPHRASE THAT PLAGIARIZES

In "First It Was 'Save the Whales,' Now It's 'Free the Dolphins,'" Shannon Brownlee (1986) argues that it's all right for people to hold animals in captivity as long as (1) the animals are treated as well as possible, and (2) the animals are displayed in a way that educates the public. Brownlee insists that animals be allowed to serve as "ambassadors for their species" (p. 72).

A PARAPHRASE THAT ALTERS THE MEANING OF THE ORIGINAL PASSAGE

According to Shannon Brownlee (1986), a captive animal is being treated fairly as long as it's kept alive and its captivity gives people pleasure. In her essay, "First It Was 'Save the Whales,' Now It's 'Free the Dolphins,'" she argues that people who keep animals in cages are responsible to the animals in only two ways: (1) they should treat their captives as well as possible (even if a small tank is all that can be provided), and (2) they should make sure that the spectators enjoy watching them (p. 72).

A GOOD PARAPHRASE

Shannon Brownlee (1986) holds that two criteria are necessary in order for the captivity of wild animals to be considered worthwhile. First, the animals should be treated as well as possible. Second, their captivity should have educational value for the people who come to look at them. "Captive animals," Brownlee claims, "must be allowed to serve as ambassadors for their species" (p. 72).

■ Summarizing

A summary, like a paraphrase, involves shortening the original passage as well as putting it in your own words. It gives the gist of the passage, including the important points while leaving out details. What makes summarizing difficult is that it requires you to capture often long and complex texts in just a few lines or a short paragraph. To do such work, you must be able to comprehend a variety of materials (see page 26 on "Responding as a Critical Reader" and specifically the section on "Comprehending Arguments" for further advice on this issue). To summarize well, you need to imagine yourself as the author of the piece you are summarizing and be true to the ideas that the author is expressing, even when those ideas conflict with your point of view. You must then move smoothly from being a careful reader to being a writer who, in your own words, recreates another's thoughts.

We summarize for many reasons: to let our boss know the basics of what we have been doing or to tell a friend why she should or should not see a movie. In your classes you are often asked to summarize articles or books, and even when this is not an explicit part of an assignment, the ability to summarize is usually expected. That is, when you are instructed to analyze an essay or to compare and contrast two novels, central to this work is the ability to carefully comprehend and recreate authors' ideas. Summarizing is the cornerstone on which all other critical reading and writing tasks are built.

When writing a research paper, the ability to summarize effectively is especially critical, because sources, though useful for your argument, will simply be too long to include in your text. It is up to you, then, to summarize those points and ideas that are most critical for your argument either because they support that argument or because they represent a counter point of view.

For instance, in the paper at the end of this chapter, "Why Zoos Should Be Eliminated," the statement "It is generally acknowledged that it is difficult to breed zoo animals" is not a direct quotation. The idea comes from Jon Luoma's article in *Audubon* magazine (the writer of this essay acknowledges that this idea comes from Luoma). Returning to the original source makes it clear that neither quoting nor fully paraphrasing would have been suitable choices because the writer was able to reduce the following passage from Luoma's article to one sentence.

> But the successful propagation of entire captive species poses awesome management problems. . . . Sanford Friedman, the Minnesota Zoo's director of biological programs, had explained to me that long-term maintenance of a species in captivity demands solutions to these fundamental problems. "First, we have to learn *how* to breed them. Second, we have to decide *who* to breed. And third, we have to figure out *what* to do with them and their offspring once we've bred them."

This passage is far too long to include in a brief research paper but is easily summarized without losing any of its effectiveness.

When summarizing long or difficult texts, try some of the following strategies to help you comprehend the essential points of the text.

1. Before you summarize, analyze the text following the strategies given in the section on "Responding as a Critical Reader" (p. 26). For example, you should always utilize prereading strategies by looking over the text as a whole before you read it carefully. Such work will often yield clues about the central ideas of the text from the title, the subheadings, and the introduction. Also, use your pen once you begin to read the text so that you link the acts of reading and writing. Underline important ideas, ask questions in the margins about difficult or significant ideas, and highlight

topic sentences. Take a few minutes after reading the essay to jot down the essential ideas and any questions you have about the reading.

2. Reread the introduction and conclusion after you have read the essay once or twice. These two sections should complement each other and offer clues to the most significant issues of the text. An introduction or conclusion is often more than one paragraph; therefore, it is important that you read the first and last few paragraphs of an essay to understand what the author is trying to impress upon the reader. If you are summarizing a book, look especially at the preface, the first and last chapters, and any reviewers' comments. These sections will not tell you everything you need to know to summarize an entire book, but they will help you decide which points matter.

3. For a difficult essay, you may want to list all the subheadings (if they are used) or the topic sentence of each paragraph. These significant guideposts will map the piece as a whole: What do they tell you about the central ideas and the main argument the author is making? After reviewing the subheads or topic sentences, can you reread the essay and engage more easily with its finer points? For a book, you can do the same thing with chapter headings to break down the essential ideas. Remember that when you summarize, you must put another's words into your own (and cite the original text as well), so do not simply let a list of the subheadings or chapter titles stand in for your summary. They likely won't make sense when put together in paragraph form, but they will provide you with valuable ideas regarding the central points of the text.

4. Remember that summarizing requires attention to overall meaning and not to specific details. Therefore, avoid including many specific examples or concrete details from the text you are summarizing and try to let your reader know what these examples and details add up to. Some of the specificity and excitement of the original text will be lost, but when summarizing, the goal is not to recreate all that is interesting about the original text. Rather, the writer's goal is to let the reader know the essential meaning of the original text in a clear, straightforward way.

■ Avoiding Plagiarism

Plagiarism is the use of someone else's words or ideas without adequate acknowledgment—that is, presenting such words or ideas as your own. Putting something in your own words is not in itself a defense against plagiarism; the source of the ideas must be identified as well. Giving credit to the sources you use serves three important purposes: (1) it reflects your own honesty and seriousness as a researcher; (2) it enables the reader to find the source of the reference and read further, sometimes to verify that the source has been correctly used; and (3) it adds the authority of experts to your argument. Deliberate plagiarism is nothing less than cheating and theft, and it is an offense that deserves serious punishment.

Accidental plagiarism can be avoided if you take a little care when researching and writing your papers.

The writer of the zoo paper, for instance, uses and correctly introduces the following direct quotation by James Rachels (para. 4):

> As James Rachels (1976) writes:
>
> > Humans have a right to liberty because they have various other interests that will suffer if their freedom is unduly restricted. The right to liberty -- the right to be free of external constraints on one's actions -- may then be seen as derived from a more basic right not to have one's interests needlessly harmed. (p. 210)

If the writer of the zoo paper had chosen to state this idea more briefly, in her own words, the result might have been something like this: "Human beings believe in their fundamental right to liberty because they all agree that they would suffer without it. The right to liberty, then, stems from the right not to suffer unnecessarily." Although the wording has been significantly altered, if this statement appeared as is, undocumented, the author of the paper would be guilty of plagiarism because the ideas are not original. To avoid plagiarism, the author needs to include a reference to James Rachels at the beginning of the summary and a citation of the page number at the end. Taking care to document sources is an obvious way to avoid plagiarism. You should also be careful in taking notes and, when writing your paper, indicating where your ideas end and someone else's ideas begin.

When taking notes, make sure either to quote word-for-word *or* to paraphrase: one or the other, not a little bit of both. If you quote, enclose any language that you borrow from other sources in quotation marks. That way, when you look back at your note cards weeks later, you won't mistakenly assume that the language is your own. If you know that you aren't going to use a particular writer's exact words in your paper, then take the time to summarize that person's ideas right away. That will save you time and trouble later.

When using someone else's ideas in your paper, always let the reader know where that person's ideas begin and end. Here is an example from the zoo paper (para. 11):

> When zoo animals do mate successfully, the offspring is often weakened by inbreeding. According to geneticists, this is because a population of 150 breeder animals is necessary in order to "assure the more or less permanent survival of a species in captivity" (Ehrlich & Ehrlich, 1981, p. 211).

The phrase "according to geneticists" indicates that the material to follow comes from another source, cited parenthetically at the end of the borrowed material. If the student had not included the phrase "according to geneticists," it might look as if she only borrowed the passage in quotation marks, and not the information that precedes that passage.

Material that is considered common knowledge—that is, familiar or at least accessible to the general public—does not have to be documented. The author of *Hamlet,* the date the Declaration of Independence was signed, or the definition of *misfeasance,* while open to dispute (some scholars, for example, claim that William Shakespeare did not write *Hamlet*) are indisputably considered to be common knowledge in our culture. Unfortunately, it is not always clear whether a particular fact *is* common knowledge. Although too much documentation can clutter a paper and distract the reader, it's still better to cite too many sources than to cite too few and risk being accused of dishonesty. In general, if you are unsure whether or not to give your source credit, you should document the material.

■ Including Visuals in Your Paper

In this world of instantaneous Internet access to millions of documents and sites, it is easy to perceive knowledge as free for our use. The fact that information is easy to access does not relieve you of the responsibility of giving credit to those who originated the ideas expressed there. In fact, the ease with which material can be posted to the Internet makes it even more difficult to separate valid information from that which is questionable at best.

Since the Internet is a world of images as well as words, it may give you ideas for livening up your own work with all sorts of visuals. Don't forget, though, that you are obligated to give credit to the source of your visuals along with the ideas and words that you use. A graph or chart may provide just the sort of statistical support that will make a key point in your argument, and it can be easily cut and pasted or scanned into your electronic text, but you must document that graph or chart just as you would text. You should acknowledge the location where you found the visual and as much information as is provided about who produced it. If you use copyrighted graphs or charts in work that you publish either in print or electronic form, you should seek permission for their use. The same is true for photographs and other illustrations, although some books and Web sites offer images that you can use free of charge. You may be surprised to find that something as common as your school's logo is copyrighted and cannot be used on your Web page, for example, without permission.

■ Keeping Research under Control

Your preliminary outline provides guideposts for your research. You will need to revise it as you go along to make room for new ideas and evidence and for the questions that come up as you read. Rather than try to fit each new piece of information into your outline, you can use the numbering or lettering system in your outline to cross-reference your notebooks or file cards.

As much as possible, keep all materials related to the same point in the same place. You might do this by making a separate pile of file cards for each point and its support and questions or by reserving several pages in your notebook for information bearing on each point.

How do you know when you have done enough research? If you have kept your outline updated, you have a visual record of your progress. Check this against the guidelines on pages 394–96. Is each point backed by at least two pieces of support? Do your sources represent a range of authors and of types of data? If a large proportion of your support comes from one book, or if most of your references are to newspaper articles, you probably need to keep working. On the other hand, if your notes cite five different authorities making essentially the same point, you may have collected more data than you need. It can be useful to point out that more than one authority holds a given view and to make notes of examples that are notably different from one another. But it is not necessary to take down all the passages or examples expressing the same idea.

■ To This Point

Before you leave the library or your primary sources and start writing, check to make sure your research is complete.

1. Does your working outline show any gaps in your argument?

2. Have you found adequate data to support your claim?

3. Have you identified the warrants linking your claim with data and ensured that these warrants too are adequately documented?

4. If you intend to quote or paraphrase sources in your paper, do your notes include exact copies of all statements you may want to use and complete references?

5. Have you answered all the relevant questions that have come up during your research?

6. Do you have enough information about your sources to document your paper?

Writer's Guide: Checklist for Research Papers

1. If your assignment required a certain number of sources, have you *used* at least that many and not simply listed that many in your Works Cited page? (Remember that you list only the works you actually quote from, paraphrase, or summarize in your paper.)

2. Have you introduced each direct quotation, identifying the source by name and claim to authority?

3. Have you provided parenthetical documentation for any material that you quoted, paraphrased, or summarized, according to the style that you are using (MLA or APA)?

4. If the author is clearly identified in your sentence, have you omitted the name from the parentheses?

5. If a reader looks for that author's name in the Works Cited page, will he or she find it in proper alphabetical order?

6. If a reader looks for the information cited on the page you give in parentheses, will he or she find it on that page?

7. If there is more than one author, have you acknowledged all of the authors instead of only the first one?

8. If you have a quotation long enough to be handled as a block quote, have you indented it properly; provided the proper documentation, properly punctuated; and left off the quotation marks (except for any that were in the original)?

9. Is any wording in quotation marks *exactly* as it was in the original except for any wording in brackets or any omissions indicated by ellipses?

10. Have you avoided any back-to-back quotations that have none of your text in between?

11. Have you double-spaced the paper throughout, including any block quotations and the entries in the Works Cited page?

12. Have you checked for accuracy every entry on your Works Cited page, using the examples in this book as models?

13. Are the second and following lines in a Work Cited entry indented five spaces more than the first line?

14. Have you edited for any errors in grammar and mechanics?

COMPILING AN ANNOTATED BIBLIOGRAPHY

An annotated bibliography is a list of sources that includes the usual bibliographic information followed by a paragraph describing and evaluating each source. Its purpose is to provide information about each source in a bibliography so that the reader has an overview of the resources related to a given topic.

For each source in an annotated bibliography, the same bibliographic information included in a Works Cited or References list is provided, alphabetized by author. Each reference also has a short paragraph that describes the work, its main focus, and, if appropriate, the methodology used in or the style of the work. An annotation might note special features such as tables or illustrations. Usually an annotation evaluates the source by analyzing its usefulness, reliability, and overall significance for understanding the topic. An annotation might include some information on the credentials of the author or the organization that produced it.

A SAMPLE ANNOTATION USING THE MLA CITATION STYLE

Warner, Marina. "Pity the Stepmother." New York Times. 12 May 1991, late
    ed.: D17. Lexis/Nexis Universe 12 Dec. 1998 <http://web.lexis-nexis
    .com/universe/form/academic/univ_gennews.html>.

The author asserts that many fairy tales feature absent or cruel mothers,
transformed by romantic editors such as the Grimm brothers into stepmothers because the idea of a wicked mother desecrated an ideal. She
argues that figures in fairy tales should be viewed in their historical context and that social conditions often affected the way that motherhood
figured in fairy tales. Warner, a novelist and author of books on the images of Joan of Arc and the Virgin Mary, writes persuasively about the
social roots of a fairy-tale archetype.

A SAMPLE ANNOTATION USING THE APA CITATION STYLE

"Don't Zoos Contribute to the Saving of Species from Extinction?" Animal
    Rights Resource Site. Envirolink Network. 14 Dec. 1998 <http://arrs
    .envirolink.org/Faqs+Ref/ar-faq/Q68.html>.

This Web site provides arguments against the idea that zoos save species
from extinction. Breeding in captivity doesn't always work, and the limited gene pool creates problems. Habitat restoration is difficult, and
until the problems of poaching and pollution are solved, the habitat
will be dangerous for reintroduced species. Meanwhile, the individual
animals living in zoos lose their freedom because of an abstract and
possibly faulty concept. This Web site, part of the Animal Rights Resource Site sponsored by the Envirolink organization, is brief but
outlines the major arguments against zoos' role in preserving species.

MLA SYSTEM FOR CITING PUBLICATIONS

One of the simplest methods of crediting sources is the Modern Language
Association (MLA) in-text system, which is used in the research paper on
fairy tales in this chapter. In the text of your paper, immediately after any
quotation, paraphrase, or anything else you wish to document, simply insert a parenthetical mention of the author's last name and the page number on which the material appeared. You don't need a comma after the
author's name or an abbreviation of the word "page" or "p." For example,
the following sentence appears in the fairy tale paper:

> Famines in the seventeenth century often reduced the peasantry to a diet
> of "bad black bread, acorns, and roots" (Weber 96).

The parenthetical reference tells the reader that the information in this
sentence came from page 96 of the book or article by Eugen Weber that

appears in the Works Cited, at the end of the paper. The complete reference on the Works Cited page provides all the information readers need to locate the original source in the library:

Weber, Eugen. "Fairies and Hard Facts: The Reality of Folktales." Journal of the
    History of Ideas 42 (1981): 93-113.

If the author's name is mentioned in the same sentence, it is also acceptable to place only the page numbers in parentheses; it is not necessary to repeat the author's name. For example,

> Bettelheim sees symbolic meaning in every motif and element in the story,
> and assumes that children interpret these symbolically as well (159-66).

If you are using more than one work by the same author, you will need to provide in the parentheses the title or a recognizable shortened form of the title of the particular work being cited. If the author's name is not mentioned in the sentence, you should include in parentheses the author's last name, the title, and the page number, with a comma between the author's name and the title. If both the author's name and the title of any work being cited are mentioned in the sentence, the parentheses will include only the page number.

Some sources do not name an author. To cite a work with an unknown author, give the title, or a recognizable shortened form, in the text of your paper. If the work does not have numbered pages, often the case in Web pages or nonprint sources, do not include page numbers. For example,

> In some cases Sephardic Jews, "converted" under duress, practiced Chris-
> tianity openly and Judaism in secret until recently ("Search for the Buried
> Past").

The list of works cited includes all material you have used to write your research paper. This list appears at the end of your paper and always starts on a new page. Center the title Works Cited, double-space between the title and the first entry, and begin your list, which should be arranged alphabetically by author. Each entry should start at the left margin; indent all subsequent lines of the entry five spaces. Number each page, and double-space throughout.

Another method of documenting sources is to use notes, either footnotes (at the foot of the page) or endnotes (on a separate page at the end of the paper). The note method is not as commonly used today as the in-text system because reference notes repeat almost all the information already given on the Works Cited page. If footnotes or endnotes are used, most word-processing programs have functions that make the insertion of these notes convenient.

Nevertheless, it is a valid method, so we illustrate it here. Superscript numbers go at the end of the sentence or phrase being referenced:

Roman authors admit to borrowing frequently from earlier Greek writers for their jokes, although no joke books in the original Greek survive today.[1]

The reference note for this citation would be

[1]Alexander Humez and Nicholas Humez, Alpha to Omega (Boston: Godine, 1981) 79.

On the Works Cited page this reference would be:

Humez, Alexander, and Nicholas Humez. Alpha to Omega. Boston: Godine, 1981.

Notice that the page number for a book citation is given in the note but not the reference and that the punctuation differs. Otherwise the information is the same. Number the notes consecutively throughout your paper.

One more point: *Content notes*, which provide additional information not readily worked into a research paper, are also indicated by superscript numbers. Susan Middleton's paper on fairy tales features four such notes, included on a Notes page before the list of Works Cited.

Following are examples of the citation forms you are most likely to need as you document your research. In general, for both books and magazines, information should appear in the following order: author, title, and publication information. Each item should be followed by a period. When using as a source an essay that appears in this book, follow the citation model for "Material reprinted from another source," unless your instructor indicates otherwise. Consult the *MLA Handbook for Writers of Research Papers*, Fifth Edition, by Joseph Gibaldi (New York: Modern Language Association of America, 1999) for other documentation models and a list of acceptable shortened forms of publishers.

■ Print Sources

A BOOK BY A SINGLE AUTHOR

Gubar, Susan. Racechanges: White Skin, Black Face in American Culture. New York: Oxford UP, 1997.

AN ANTHOLOGY OR COMPILATION

Dark, Larry, ed. Prize Stories 1997: The O. Henry Awards. New York: Anchor, 1997.

A BOOK BY TWO AUTHORS

Alderman, Ellen, and Caroline Kennedy. The Right to Privacy. New York: Vintage, 1995.

Note: This form is followed even for two authors with the same last name.

Ehrlich, Paul, and Anne Ehrlich. <u>Extinction: The Causes and Consequences of the Disappearance of Species</u>. New York: Random, 1981.

A BOOK BY TWO OR MORE AUTHORS

Heffernan, William A., Mark Johnston, and Frank Hodgins. <u>Literature: Art and Artifact</u>. San Diego: Harcourt, 1987.

If there are more than three authors, name only the first and add "et al." (and others).

A BOOK BY A CORPORATE AUTHOR

Poets & Writers, Inc. <u>The Writing Business: A Poets & Writers Handbook</u>. New York: Poets & Writers, 1985.

A WORK IN AN ANTHOLOGY

Head, Bessie. "Woman from America." <u>Wild Women: Contemporary Short Stories by Women Celebrating Women</u>. Ed. Sue Thomas. Woodstock: Overlook, 1994. 45-51.

AN INTRODUCTION, PREFACE, FOREWORD, OR AFTERWORD

Callahan, John F. Introduction. <u>Flying Home and Other Stories</u>. By Ralph Ellison. Ed. John F. Callahan. New York: Vintage, 1996. 1-9.

MATERIAL REPRINTED FROM ANOTHER SOURCE

Diffie, Whitfield, and Susan Landau. "Privacy: Protections and Threats." <u>Privacy on the Line: The Politics of Wiretapping and Encryption</u>. Cambridge, MA: MIT P, 1998. Rpt. in <u>Elements of Argument: A Text and Reader</u>. Annette T. Rottenberg. 7th ed. Boston: Bedford/St. Martin's, 2003. 554.

A MULTIVOLUME WORK

Skotheim, Robert Allen, and Michael McGiffert, eds. <u>Since the Civil War</u>. Vol. 2 of <u>American Social Thought: Sources and Interpretations</u>. 2 vols. Reading: Addison, 1972.

AN EDITION OTHER THAN THE FIRST

Charters, Ann, ed. <u>The Story and Its Writer: An Introduction to Short Fiction</u>, 5th ed. Boston: Bedford/St. Martin's, 1999.

A TRANSLATION

Allende, Isabel. <u>The House of the Spirits</u>. Trans. Magda Bogin. New York: Knopf, 1985.

A REPUBLISHED BOOK

Weesner, Theodore. The Car Thief. 1972. New York: Vintage-Random, 1987.

Note: The only information about original publication you need to provide is the publication date, which appears immediately after the title.

A BOOK IN A SERIES

Eady, Cornelius. Victims of the Latest Dance Craze. Omnation Press Dialogues on Dance Series 5. Chicago: Omnation, 1985.

AN ARTICLE FROM A DAILY NEWSPAPER

Doctorow, E. L. "Quick Cuts: The Novel Follows Film into a World of Fewer Words." New York Times 15 Mar. 1999, sec. B: 1+.

AN ARTICLE FROM A PERIODICAL

Schulhofer, Stephen. "Unwanted Sex." Atlantic Monthly Oct. 1998: 55-66.

AN UNSIGNED EDITORIAL

"Medium, Message." Editorial. Nation 28 Mar. 1987: 383-84.

ANONYMOUS WORKS

"The March Almanac." Atlantic Mar. 1995: 20.

Citation World Atlas. Maplewood: Hammond, 1987.

AN ARTICLE FROM A JOURNAL WITH SEPARATE PAGINATION FOR EACH ISSUE

Brewer, Derek. "The Battleground of Home: Versions of Fairy Tales." Encounter 54.4 (1980): 52–61.

AN ARTICLE IN A JOURNAL WITH CONTINUOUS PAGINATION THROUGHOUT THE VOLUME

McCafferty, Janey. "The Shadders Go Away." New England Review and Bread Loaf Quarterly 9 (1987): 332–42.

Note that the issue number is not mentioned here; because the volume has continuous pagination throughout the year, only the volume number 9 is needed.

A REVIEW

Walker, David. Rev. of A Wave, by John Ashbery. Field 32 (1985): 63-71.

AN ARTICLE IN A REFERENCE WORK

"Bylina." The Princeton Encyclopedia of Poetry and Poetics. Ed. Alex Preminger. Enlarged ed. Princeton: Princeton UP, 1974.

A GOVERNMENT DOCUMENT

United States. National Endowment for the Arts. <u>1989 Annual Report</u>. Washington: Office of Public Affairs, 1990.

Frequently the Government Printing Office (GPO) is the publisher of federal government documents.

REPORTS

Gura, Mark. <u>The Gorgeous Mosaic Project: A Work of Art by the Schoolchildren of the World</u>. Teacher's packet. East Brunswick: Children's Atelier, 1990. ERIC ED 347 257.

Kassebaum, Peter. Cultural Awareness Training Manual and Study Guide. ERIC, 1992. ED 347 289.

The ERIC number at the end of the entry indicates that this source is available through ERIC (Educational Resource Information Center); some libraries have these available on microfiche. The number indicates which report to look for. Some ERIC documents were published elsewhere, as in the first example. If no other publishing information is given, treat ERIC (with no city given) as the publisher, as shown in the second entry. Reports are also published by NTIS (National Technical Information Service), state geological surveys, organizations, institutes within universities, and so on and may be called "technical reports," or "occasional papers." Be sure to include the source and the unique report number, if given.

AN UNPUBLISHED MANUSCRIPT

Leahy, Ellen. "An Investigation of the Computerization of Information Systems in a Family Planning Program." Unpublished master's degree project. Div. of Public Health, U of Massachusetts, Amherst, 1990.

A LETTER TO THE EDITOR

Flannery, James W. Letter. <u>New York Times Book Review</u> 28 Feb. 1993: 34.

PERSONAL CORRESPONDENCE

Bennett, David. Letter to the author. 3 Mar. 1993.

A CARTOON

Henley, Marian. "Maxine." Cartoon. <u>Valley Advocate</u> 25 Feb. 1993: 39.

■ **Electronic Sources**

A WEB SITE

<u>Fairy Tales: Origins and Evolution</u>. Ed. Christine Daaé. 12 Dec. 1998 <http://www.darkgoddess.com/fairy>.

Include the title if available; the author's name if available or, if not, a generic description such as "Home page"; the sponsoring organization or institution except in the case of commercial sponsorship; date of access; and URL in angle brackets.

A PAGE WITHIN A WEB SITE

"Don't Zoos Contribute to the Saving of Species from Extinction?" Animal Rights
    Resource Site. Envirolink Network. 14 Dec. 1998 <http://arrs.envirolink
    .org/faqs+Ref/ar-faq/Q68.html>.

A BOOK AVAILABLE ON THE WEB

Kramer, Heinrich, and James Sprenger. The Malleus Maleficarum. Trans.
    Montague Summers. New York: Dover, 1971. 14 Dec. 1998 <http://www
    .geocities.com/Athens/2962/witchcraze/malleus_2_ii_html>.

In this case the book had been previously published, and information about its original publication was included at the site.

AN ARTICLE FROM AN ELECTRONIC JOURNAL

Minow, Mary. "Filters and the Public Library: A Legal and Policy Analysis."
    First Monday 2.12 (1 Dec. 1997). 28 Nov. 1998 <http:www
    .firstmonday.dk/issues/issue2_12/minow/index.html>.

MATERIAL ACCESSED THROUGH A COMPUTER SERVICE

Boynton, Robert S. "The New Intellectuals." Atlantic Monthly Mar. 1995.
    Atlantic Unbound. America Online. 3 Mar. 1995. Keyword: Atlantic.

A CD-ROM

Corcoran, Mary B. "Fairy Tale." Grolier Multimedia Encyclopedia. CD-ROM. Dan-
    bury: Grolier, 1995.

AN ARTICLE FROM A FULL-TEXT DATABASE AVAILABLE THROUGH THE WEB

Warner, Marina. "Pity the Stepmother." New York Times. 12 May 1991, late ed.:
    D17. Lexis/Nexis Universe 12 Dec. 1998. <http://web.lexis-nexis.com/
    universe/form/academic/univ_gennews.html>.

Include the original source information and the name of the database, access date, and URL.

AN ARTICLE FROM A CD-ROM FULL-TEXT DATABASE

"Tribal/DNC Donations." News from Indian Country. (Dec. 1997). Ethnic
    Newswatch. CD-ROM. Softline. 12 Oct. 1998.

Include the original source information and the name of the database, the designation *CD-ROM,* the publisher of the CD-ROM, and the electronic publication data, if available.

AN ARTICLE FROM AN ELECTRONIC REFERENCE WORK

"Folk Arts." Britannica Online. <u>Encyclopaedia Britannica</u>. 14 Dec. 2002.
   <http://www.eb.com:180>.

A PERSONAL E-MAIL COMMUNICATION

Franz, Kenneth. "Re: Species Reintroduction." E-mail to the author. 12 Oct.
   2001.

AN E-MAIL COMMUNICATION POSTED TO A DISCUSSION LIST

Lee, Constance. "Re: Mothers and Stepmothers." Online posting. 10 Sept. 2002.
   Folklore Discussion List <mglazer@panam.edu>.

If the address of the discussion list archives is known, include that information in angle brackets; if not, place the moderator's e-mail address in
angle brackets.

A POSTING TO A WEB FORUM

DeYoung, Chris. Online posting. 12 Dec. 1998. Issues: Gay Rights. 14 Dec. 1998
   <http://community.cnn.com/cgi-bin/WebX?14@52.7bmLaPoSc49^0@
   .ee7239c/12479>.

Include the author, header (if any) in quotation marks, the designation
Online posting, the date of the posting, the name of the forum, the date of
access, and the URL.

A NEWSGROUP POSTING

Vining, Philip. "Zoos and Infotainment." Online posting. 16 Oct. 2002. 12 Dec.
   2002. <news:alt.animals.ethics.vegetarian>.

Include the author, header in quotation marks, the designation *Online
posting*, the date of posting, the date of access, and the name of the newsgroup.

A SYNCHRONOUS COMMUNICATION

Krishnamurthi, Ashok. Online discussion of cyberlaw and the media. "Reinvent-
   ing Copyright in a Digital Environment." 25 Oct. 2002. MediaMOO. 25 Oct.
   2002 <telnet://purple-crayon.media.mit.edu:8888>.

To cite a synchronous communication from a MUD or a MOO, include
the name of the speaker, a description of the event, the date, the forum,
the date of access, and the electronic address.

▓ Other Sources

A LECTURE

Calvino, Italo. "Right and Wrong Political Uses of Literature." Symposium on European Politics. Amherst College, Amherst. 25 Feb. 1976.

A FILM

The Voice of the Khalam. Prod. Loretta Pauker. Perf. Leopold Senghor, Okara, Birago Diop, Rubadiri, and Francis Parkes. Contemporary Films/McGraw-Hill, 1971. 16 mm, 29 min.

Other pertinent information to give in film references, if available, is the writer and director (see model for radio/television program for style).

A TELEVISION OR RADIO PROGRAM

The Shakers: Hands to Work, Hearts to God. Narr. David McCullough. Dir. Ken Burns and Amy Stechler Burns. Writ. Amy Stechler Burns, Wendy Tilghman, and Tom Lewis. PBS. WGBY, Springfield. 28 Dec. 1992.

A VIDEOTAPE

Style Wars! Videotape. Prod. Tony Silver and Henry Chalfont. New Day Films, 1985. 69 min.

DVD

Harry Potter and the Sorcerer's Stone. DVD. Prod. Chris Columbus. Warner Bros., 2001. 152 min.

A PERFORMANCE

Quilters: A Musical Celebration. By Molly Newman and Barbara Damashek. Dir. Joyce Devlin. Musical dir. Faith Fung. Mt. Holyoke Laboratory Theatre, South Hadley, MA. 26 Apr. 1991. Based on The Quilters: Women and Domestic Art by Patricia Cooper and Norma Bradley Allen.

AN INTERVIEW

Hines, Gregory. Interview. With D. C. Denison. Boston Globe Magazine 29 Mar. 1987: 2.

Note: An interview conducted by the author of the paper would be documented as follows:

Hines, Gregory. Personal interview. 29 Mar. 1987.

SAMPLE RESEARCH PAPER (MLA STYLE)

The following paper, prepared in the MLA style, was written for an advanced composition course. Told to compose a research paper on a literary topic, Susan Middleton chose to write on fairy tales—a subject literary enough to satisfy her instructor, yet general enough to encompass her own interest in developmental psychology. But as she explored the subject, she found herself reading in a surprising array of disciplines, including folklore, anthropology, and history. Although she initially expected to report on the psychological importance of fairy tales, Middleton at last wrote an argument about the importance of their historical and cultural roots. Her paper, as is typical for literary papers, anchors its argument in the events and details of its chosen text, "Hansel and Gretel." But it also makes effective use of sources to help readers understand that there is more to the tale than a story that sends children happily off to sleep.

When a Fairy Tale Is Not Just a Fairy Tale

By
Susan Middleton

Professor Herrington
English 2A
October 2004

Include a title page if an outline is part of the paper. If no outline is required, include name, instructor's name, course name, and date at the upper left corner of page 1.

Middleton ii

Outline

I. Introduction:

  A. Dictionary definition of "fairy tale"

  B. Thesis: "Hansel and Gretel" has historical roots

II. Origin and distribution of tale

III. Historical basis of motifs

  A. Physical and economic hardship

    1. Fear of the forest

    2. Poverty and starvation

    3. Child abandonment

    4. Fantasies of finding treasure

  B. Cruel stepmother

  C. Wicked witch

    1. Eating meat associated with cannibalism and upper classes

    2. Elderly caretaker for unwanted children

    3. Witches in community

    4. Witchcraft as remnant of ancient fertility religion

IV. Rebuttals to historical approach

  A. Motivation for telling realistic tales

  B. Psychological interpretations

    1. Fairy tales dreamlike, not literal

    2. Freudian interpretation

V. Conclusion

Middleton 1

When a Fairy Tale Is Not Just a Fairy Tale

"Hansel and Gretel" is a well-known fairy tale, beloved of
many children in both Europe and North America.[1] Although
it has no fairies in it, it conforms to the definition of "fairy
tale" given in <u>Merriam-Webster's Collegiate Dictionary</u>, Tenth
Edition: "a story (as for children) involving fantastic forces
and beings (as fairies, wizards, and goblins)." As anyone familiar with this tale will remember, Hansel and Gretel are two
children on an adventure in the woods, where they encounter
a wicked witch in a gingerbread house, who plans to fatten
and eat them. Through their ingenuity they outsmart her,
burn her up in her own oven, and return home triumphantly
with a hoard of riches found in her house.

We think of fairy tales as being lighthearted fantasies
that entertain but don't have much relevance to daily life. We
often borrow the word to describe a movie with an unlikely
plot, or a person not quite grounded in reality: "Oh, he's living in a fairy tale world; he hasn't got his head on his shoulders." In fact, the second definition of "fairy tale" in
<u>Webster's</u> is "a made-up story usually designed to mislead."

So what is the meaning of "Hansel and Gretel"? Is it simply a story of make-believe, or something more? Fairy tales
are told, read, and heard in the context of a time and place.
Today we are exposed to them through illustrated storybooks,
cartoons, and film. But in Europe, before technologies in
printing made mass publishing possible, folktales were passed
on orally. Women were the primary tellers of folktales, though
they were later gathered and published by male writers such
as Charles Perrault and the Grimm Brothers ("Tales"). They
were told by adults mostly for adult audiences, although
people often first heard them as children. They served to entertain and to relieve the boredom of repetitive work in the
fields during the day and in the home in the evening (Weber
93, 113). In peasant and aboriginal communities, that is
often still the case (Taggart 437).

I believe that "Hansel and Gretel" has historical
meaning. Embedded in this simple narrative is a record of the

---

Title centered

*Raised, super-
script number
refers to notes
giving infor-
mation at the
end of the
paper.*

*Writer briefly
summarizes
tale to orient
readers.*

*In-text citation
of author and
pages; citation
appears at the
end of the sen-
tence before
the period.*

*Thesis with
claim of fact
that the writer
must support*

Middleton 2

experiences and events once common in the lives of the people who first told and listened to it.

Where did "Hansel and Gretel" come from? We do not know for certain. In oral form this tale shows wide distribution. Different versions have been recorded all over Europe, India, Japan, Africa, the Caribbean, Pacific Islands, and among native North and South Americans ("Hansel and Gretel"). As with all folktales, there is no agreement among folklorists[2] about whether all these versions migrated from one place to another, sprang up independently, or derive from some combination of the two ("Hansel and Gretel"). Most oral versions of it have been recorded in Europe (Aarne 117). This does not prove that the tale originated there -- it may simply reflect the eagerness of people in Europe during the nineteenth and twentieth centuries to record their own folk history -- but it is the best guideline for now.

The tale may be very ancient, since folktales can be passed on faithfully from one generation to another without change. (The origins of "Cinderella," for example, can be traced back to China in the ninth century [Thompson, Folktale 126].) But we can't know that for sure. So, even though "Hansel and Gretel" may have originated hundreds or even thousands of years ago, it probably is only safe to compare a tale with the historical period when the tale was first recorded. For "Hansel and Gretel" this means Europe in the seventeenth to nineteenth centuries.[3]

Eugen Weber is one historian who sees direct parallels between the characters and motifs in "Hansel and Gretel" (and other Grimms' fairy tales) and the social and economic conditions in Europe during this period. One of the central themes in the tale is poverty and abandonment. Recall how the tale begins: Hansel and Gretel live with their parents near a huge forest; their father is a woodcutter. The family is facing starvation because there is a famine. Twice their parents abandon them in the woods to save themselves. The first time the children are able to find their way home, but the second time they get lost.

Reference to dictionary article — page number not necessary

Square brackets used to represent parentheses within parentheses

Specific support from the tale cited

Middleton 3

As Weber points out, until the middle of the nineteenth century, the forest, especially for northern Europeans, carried the real potential for encountering danger in the form of robbers, wild animals, and getting lost (96-97). Moreover, conditions of poverty, starvation, early death, and danger from unknown adults were common throughout Europe for peasants and the working class (96). The majority of Europeans at the beginning of the eighteenth century were farmers, and the average life expectancy was about twenty-five years (Treasure 660, 667). Famines in the seventeenth century often reduced the peasantry to a diet of "bad black bread, acorns, and roots" (Weber 96). Hansel and Gretel are treated by the witch to a dinner of pancakes and sugar, milk, nuts, and apples (101). This may not sound particularly nourishing to our ears because we assume a healthy dinner must have vegetables and/or meat. But when you're starving, anything is likely to taste good; this would have been a sumptuous meal for Hansel and Gretel.

Childhood was thought of differently then than today. "Valued as an extra pair of hands or deplored as an extra mouth to feed, the child belonged to no privileged realm of play and protection from life's responsibilities" (Treasure 664). Social historian John Boswell estimates that anywhere from 10 to 40 percent of children in towns and cities were abandoned during the eighteenth century. Parental motivation included removing the stigma of illegitimate or physically deformed children, being unable to support their children and hoping to give them a better life with strangers, desiring to promote one child's inheritance over another's, or simply lacking interest in raising the child (48, 428).

Weber points out that peasants had very little cash and didn't use banks. Hiding and finding treasure -- gold, silver, and jewelry -- was a much more common occurrence two centuries ago than it is today (101), a kind of lottery for the poor. In this light, the riches the children find in the witch's house could reflect the common person's fantasy of striking it rich.

Consecutive references immediately following an identified source ("Weber") cite only the pages within the source without repeating the source.

Narrative details linked to historical facts

Source cited after direct quotation

Writer's interpretation of one aspect of the story

Middleton 4

A central motif in the story is the stepmother who wants to abandon the children to keep herself and her husband from starving. (The father, at first reluctant, eventually gives in to his wife's plan.) As Weber and others have noted, stepmothers were not unusual in history. The death rate among childbearing women was much higher in past centuries than it is today. When women died in childbirth, there was strong economic motivation for fathers to remarry. In the seventeenth and eighteenth centuries, 20 to 80 percent of widowers remarried within the year of their wife's death. By the mid-nineteenth century, after life expectancy rose, only 15 percent of widowers did so (94, 112).

Reference to a newspaper

What accounts for the stereotype of the heartless stepmother? Warner argues that mothers, not stepmothers, actually appeared in many of the tales in their original forms, until romantic editors, like the Grimm brothers, "rebelled against this desecration of motherhood and changed mothers into wicked stepmothers" (D17). Weber suggests that stepmothers were assigned the role of doing evil to children for economic reasons: The family would risk losing its good name and perhaps its land if a biological parent killed a child (107). There is also the issue of inheritance from the stepmother's point of view: If her husband dies, her husband's children, not she, would inherit the land and property. Literary and legal evidence of stepmothers plotting to eliminate stepchildren, especially stepsons, shows up in European literature as far back as two millennia ago (Boswell 128).

Transition to new topic: witches

Another major theme in "Hansel and Gretel" is the wicked witch, which also shows up in lots of other fairy tales. One of the common beliefs about witches was that they ate children. According to the words of a purported witch in the Malleus Maleficarum, a treatise on witchcraft published originally around 1486, "[we] cook them in a cauldron until the whole flesh comes away from the bones to make a soup that may be easily drunk" (Kramer and Sprenger, ch. 2, para. 12). The authors of this work were alarmists, describing in sometimes improbable terms the evil behavior of witches, but the question remains: Were there witches in European history, and if so, where did the reputation for eating children come from?

Middleton 5

Weber notes that in fairy tales only evil figures eat meat of any kind, whether animal or human flesh. Before the middle of the nineteenth century the peasantry rarely ate meat, but the aristocracy and bourgeoisie did. This discrepancy may be the origin of the motif in some fairy tales of evil figures of upper-class background wanting to eat children (112, 101). Weber seems to imply that child-eating witches symbolized to the peasantry either resentment of or paranoia about the aristocracy.

Although the witch's cottage in "Hansel and Gretel" is not described as grand or large, there are other allusions to wealth and comfort. The witch puts the two children to bed between clean sheets, a luxury for much of the peasantry, who slept on straw and for whom bed lice were a common reality (Treasure 661-62). And of course there is the hoard of coin money and jewelry the children later discover there. Perhaps more significantly, the witch herself has a lot of power, just as the aristocracy was perceived to have, including the power to deceive and take away life.

David Bakan suggests that the historical basis for the witch is the unmarried elderly woman in the community who took in unwanted, illegitimate children and was often paid to do this (66-67). There is also evidence that witchcraft, ranging from white magic to sorcery (black magic), was practiced by both individual women and men among the peasantry during this time. For example, "the 'cunning folk' were at least as numerous in sixteenth-century England as the parish clergy. Moreover, in their divinatory, medical, and religious functions they were far more important in peasant society than were the official clergy" (Horsley 697). Witches were called on to influence the weather, provide love potions, find lost objects, midwife, identify thieves, and heal illnesses (698). Some services performed by witches were ambiguous: "Apparently some peasants would conjure the storms or weather spirits to avoid striking their own fields -- but to strike someone else's instead," but for the most part the wisewomen and sorcerers were different people (698).

The idea that an organized witch cult, as portrayed by the Catholic Church during the Middle Ages, actually existed is dismissed today by most social historians. Jesse Nash thinks we should reconsider the possibility that some of the behavior witches were accused of, including ritual cannibalism and sexual orgies in the woods, actually occurred in some form (12). He sees witchcraft as "a surviving remnant of a religion which was concerned with the fertility of crops, animals, humans, and with the alteration of seasons and with the identification of humans with animals" (13). These practices date back to a matriarchal goddess religion which flourished in Europe 5,000 to 7,000 years ago, before invasion of the patriarchal cultures from India (Marija Gimbutas in Nash 12). This religion included human sacrifice and was based on the concept of maintaining balance in the universe: The goddess of life was at the same time the goddess of death. Woodwives and fairies, who lived in the forest, "were mediators of sacred knowledge to their communities" (16).

Source within a source cited

Nash suggests that in Europe, although Christianity became the official way of thinking about the world, it did not replace the old beliefs entirely, despite strong attempts by the Church to eliminate them. Religious beliefs and practices can persist hidden for generations if need be.[4] The peasants were able to live with and practice both Christianity and paganism in combination for centuries (25).

So we have seen there is validity to the claim that many of the motifs of "Hansel and Gretel" have historical roots. However, one might well ask why people would want to hear stories so close to their own experiences. If oral tales during this time were meant as entertainment mostly for adults, wouldn't they want something to take their minds off their troubles? Weber suggests a couple of motivations for telling fairy tales. One was to experience "the delights of fear" (97). Fairy tales were told along with ghost stories, gossip, jokes, and fables. I suspect it was similar to the thrill some people get today watching scary movies with happy endings.

Having supported her major claim, the writer continues by anticipating and addressing possible rebuttals.

Second, fairy tales helped to explain how the world worked. To most people not able to read, the world of cause and effect was mysterious and could only be explained through symbolism and analogy. Folktales had been used in

Middleton 7

church sermons since the fourteenth century (Weber 110, Zipes 22).

Two sources cited at once

But the industrial age ushered in the scientific revolution, and with it came the concept of explaining the unknown by breaking it down into working parts (Weber 113). Reading became available to large numbers of people. By this time fairy tales were no longer meaningful ways to explain the world for ordinary adults, so they became the province of children's entertainment (113).

Folklorist Alan Dundes thinks it is naive to assume fairy tales have literal meaning. In recent years he and a number of other people have looked to psychology to explain the origin of fairy tales. "Fairy tales are like dreams -- can you find the historic origin of dreams?" (Dundes). In their structure and characters fairy tales do have a number of dreamlike aspects: They rarely state the feelings of the hero directly, and all inner experiences of the hero are projected outward into objects in nature and other people (Tatar 91). The other characters seem not to have separate lives of their own; all their actions and intentions relate to the hero (Brewer 55). Also, magical things happen: Elements of nature speak, granting favors to the hero or threatening success or even life. In one version of "Hansel and Gretel," for example, a white duck talks to the children and carries them across a lake on their way home.

Competing theories presented

Telephone interview — no page numbers

The symbolic nature of fairy tales, however, doesn't deny the validity of examining them for historical origins. As anyone who has recorded their own dreams knows, people and objects from mundane, daily life show up regularly in them. Sometimes these elements are disguised as symbols, but other times they are transparently realistic. Similarly, the talking duck and the gingerbread house in "Hansel and Gretel" may be unreal, but other themes have more literal counterparts in history.

One of the most quoted interpreters of fairy tales is psychologist Bruno Bettelheim, whose The Uses of Enchantment analyzes fairy tales in Freudian terms. In his view, "Hansel and Gretel" represents the task each of us as children must

Middleton 8

face in coming to terms with anxiety -- not the anxiety of facing starvation and being literally abandoned in the woods,
but the ordinary fear of separating from our parents (especially mother) in the process of growing up to become independent adults. Bettelheim sees symbolic meaning in every
motif and element in the story, and assumes that children
interpret these symbolically as well (159-66).

Partial validity of competing theories acknowledged

Undeniably, there are themes in "Hansel and Gretel" -- as
in many of our most common fairy tales -- that strike deep
psychological chords with both children and adults. The
wicked stepmother is a good example: Children often fantasize
they are really stepchildren or adopted as a way to account
for feeling victimized and abused by their parents. "In real
life this fantasy occurs among children with a very high frequency" (Bakan 76).

Having quali-fied her major claim in light of other theo-ries, student goes on to reiterate the support of her major claim in her conclusion.

These themes help to explain the enduring popularity of
fairy tales among middle-class children over the last two centuries. But we cannot treat fairy tales as if they spring full-
blown from the unconscious and tell us nothing about the
past. For the people who told and heard "Hansel and Gretel"
in the seventeenth to nineteenth centuries in Europe, the tale
was describing events and phenomena that happened, if not
to them, then to someone they knew. Everyone in rural communities was likely to have been exposed, whether in person
or by hearsay, to some elderly woman claiming powers to alter
weather patterns, heal the sick, cast spells, midwife, or take
in illegitimate babies. Stepmothers were common, poverty and
famine ongoing, and abandonment and child abuse very real.
In addition to providing entertainment, tales like "Hansel and
Gretel" reassured teller and listener alike that the ordinary
physical hardships, which for most of us today are fictions,
were possible to overcome.

Middleton 9

Notes

Content notes appear at the end of the paper, before Works Cited.

[1] We in the United States know it primarily in printed form, as it has come to us from Germany. Between 1812 and 1857, the Grimm brothers, Jacob and Wilhelm, published several editions of <u>Kinder und Hausmarchen</u> (<u>Children's and Household Tales</u>) (Zipes 6, 41, 79). In addition to "Hansel and Gretel," this book included over 200 other folktales (though not all of them were fairy tales). The anthology increased in popularity until by the turn of the twentieth century it outsold all other books in Germany except the Bible (Zipes 15). To date it has been translated into some seventy languages (Denecke).

[2] Folklorists collect folktales from around the world and analyze them. Tales are categorized according to <u>type</u> (basic plot line) and <u>motifs</u> (elements within the tale). Two widely used references for folklorists are Antti Aarne's <u>Types of the Folklore</u> and Stith Thompson's <u>Motif-index</u>. "Hansel and Gretel" is type 327A in the Aarne classification.

Space included between superscript number and beginning of note

[3] The Grimms were the first to record tale type 327A in 1812 (see note 1). A related tale about Tom Thumb (tale type 327B) was first recorded by Charles Perrault from France in 1697 (Thompson, <u>Folktale</u> 37, 182).

Indent five spaces to superscript number; rest of note is flush left.

[4] Consider the example of Sephardic Jews who "converted" to Christianity under duress in Spain in the fifteenth century. Some of them moved to North America, and their descendants continued to practice Christianity openly and Judaism in secret until recently ("Search for the Buried Past").

Middleton 10

Sources arranged alphabetically by author's last name or by title

First line flush left in citation, rest indented five spaces

Works Cited

Aarne, Antti. The Types of the Folktale: Classification and
    Bibliography. Trans. and ed. Stith Thompson. 2nd rev.
    ed. FF Communications 184. Helsinki: Suomalainen
    Tiedeakatemia, 1964.

Bakan, David. Slaughter of the Innocents. Toronto: Canadian
    Broadcasting System, 1971.

Bettelheim, Bruno. The Uses of Enchantment: The Meaning
    and Importance of Fairy Tales. 1976. New York: Vintage,
    1977.

Book

Boswell, John. The Kindness of Strangers: The Abandonment
    of Children in Western Europe from Late Antiquity to the
    Renaissance. New York: Pantheon, 1988.

Periodical

Brewer, Derek. "The Battleground of Home: Versions of Fairy
    Tales." Encounter 54.4 (1980): 52–61.

Encyclopedia article

Denecke, Ludwig. "Grimm, Jacob Ludwig Carl and Wilhelm
    Carl." Encyclopaedia Britannica: Macropaedia. 1992 ed.

Interview

Dundes, Alan. Telephone interview. 10 Feb. 1993.

"Fairy tale." Merriam-Webster's Collegiate Dictionary. 10th ed.
    1993.

"Hansel and Gretel." Funk & Wagnalls Standard Dictionary of
    Folklore, Mythology, and Legend. Ed. Maria Leach. New
    York: Funk & Wagnalls, 1949.

Horsley, Richard A. "Who Were the Witches? The Social Roles
    of the Accused in the European Witch Trials." Journal of
    Interdisciplinary History 9 (1979): 689-715.

An online book

Kramer, Heinrich, and James Sprenger. The Malleus Malefi-
    carum. Trans. Montague Summers. New York: Dover,
    1971. 14 Dec. 1998. <http://www.geocities.com/Athens/
    2962/witchcraze/malleus_2_ii_html>.

Nash, Jesse. "European Witchcraft: The Hidden Tradition."
    Human Mosaic 21.1-2 (1987): 10-30.

"Search for the Buried Past." The Hidden Jews of New

Radio broadcast

    Mexico. Prod. Nan Rubin. WFCR, Amherst, MA.
    13 Sept. 1992.

Taggart, James M. " 'Hansel and Gretel' in Spain and Mexico."
    Journal of American Folklore 99 (1986): 435-60.

Middleton 11

"The Tales and Their Tellers." Ed. Christine Daaé. <u>Fairy Tales:</u> <u>Origins and Evolution</u>. 12 Dec. 1998. <http://www .darkgoddess.com/fairy/tellers.htm>. *A page within a Web site*

Tatar, Maria. "Folkloristic Phantasies: Grimm's Fairy Tales and Freud's Family Romance." <u>Fairy Tales as Ways of Knowing: Essays on Marchen in Psychology, Society and Literature</u>. Ed. Michael M. Metzger and Katharina Mommsen. <u>Germanic Studies in America</u> 41. Berne: Lang, 1981. 75-98. *Article in an edited anthology*

Thompson, Stith. <u>The Folktale</u>. New York: Holt, 1946. *Two consecutive works by the same author*

---. <u>Motif-index of Folk-literature: A Classification of Narrative Elements in Folktales, Ballads, Myths, Fables, Mediaeval Romances, Exempla, Fabliaux, Jest-books, and Local Legends</u>. Rev. ed. 6 vols. plus index. Bloomington: Indiana UP, 1957. *Volume in a multivolume revised edition*

Treasure, Geoffrey R. R. "European History and Culture: The Emergence of Modern Europe, 1500-1648." <u>Encyclopaedia Britannica: Macropaedia</u>. 1992 ed. 657-83.

Warner, Marina. "Pity the Stepmother." <u>New York Times</u>. 12 May 1991, late ed.: D17. <u>Lexis/Nexis Universe</u> 12 Dec. 1998. <http://web.lexis-nexis.com/universe/form/ academic/univ_gennews.html>. *Newspaper online from a computer service*

Weber, Eugen. "Fairies and Hard Facts: The Reality of Folktales." <u>Journal of the History of Ideas</u> 42 (1981): 93-113.

Zipes, Jack. <u>The Brothers Grimm: From Enchanted Forests to the Modern World</u>. New York: Routledge, 1988.

APA SYSTEM FOR CITING PUBLICATIONS

Instructors in the social sciences might prefer the citation system of the American Psychological Association (APA). Like the MLA system, the APA system calls for a parenthetical citation in the text of the paper. Unlike the MLA system, the APA system includes the year of publication in the parenthetical reference. Here is an example:

Even though many South American countries rely on the drug trade for their economic survival, the majority of South Americans disapprove of drug use (Gorriti, 1989, p. 72).

The complete publication information for Gorriti's article will appear at the end of your paper, on a page titled "References." (Sample citations for the "References" page follow.)

If your list of references includes more than one work written by the same author in the same year, cite the first work as *a* and the second as *b*. For example, Gorriti's second article of 1989 would be cited in your paper as (Gorriti, 1989b).

Following are examples of the citation forms you are most likely to use. If you need the format for a type of publication not listed here, consult the *Publication Manual of the American Psychological Association*, Fifth Edition (2001).

■ Print Sources

A BOOK BY A SINGLE AUTHOR

Briggs, J. (1988). *Fire in the crucible: The alchemy of creative genius*. New York: St. Martin's Press.

MULTIPLE WORKS BY THE SAME AUTHOR IN THE SAME YEAR

Gardner, H. (1982a). *Art, mind, and brain: A cognitive approach to creativity*. New York: Basic.

Gardner, H. (1982b). *Developmental psychology: An introduction* (2nd ed.). Boston: Little, Brown.

AN ANTHOLOGY OR COMPILATION

Gioseffi, D. (Ed.). (1988). *Women on war*. New York: Simon & Schuster.

A BOOK BY TWO OR MORE AUTHORS OR EDITORS

Atwan, R., & Roberts, J. (Eds.). (1996). *Left, right, and center: Voices from across the political spectrum*. Boston: Bedford Books.

Note: List the names of *all* the authors or editors, no matter how many.

A BOOK BY A CORPORATE AUTHOR

International Advertising Association. (1977). *Controversy advertising: How advertisers present points of view on public affairs*. New York: Hastings House.

A WORK IN AN ANTHOLOGY

Mukherjee, B. (1988). The colonization of the mind. In Gioseffi, D. (Ed.) *Women on war* (pp. 140-142). New York: Simon & Schuster.

AN INTRODUCTION, PREFACE, FOREWORD, OR AFTERWORD

Hemenway, R. (1984). Introduction. In Z. N. Hurston, *Dust tracks on a road*. Urbana: University of Illinois Press, ix-xxxix.

AN EDITION OTHER THAN THE FIRST

Gumpert, G., & Cathcart, R. (Eds.). (1986). *Inter/media: Interpersonal communication in a media world* (3rd ed.). New York: Oxford University Press.

A TRANSLATION

Sartre, J. P. (1962). *Literature and existentialism*. (B. Frechtman, Trans.). New York: Citadel Press. (Original work published 1949.)

A REPUBLISHED BOOK

James, W. (1969). *The varieties of religious experience: A study in human nature*. London: Collier Books. (Original work published 1902.)

A BOOK IN A SERIES

Berthrong, D. J. (1976). *The Cheyenne and Arapaho ordeal: Reservation and agency life in the Indian territory, 1875-1907. Vol. 136. The civilization of the American Indian series*. Norman: University of Oklahoma Press.

A MULTIVOLUME WORK

Mussen, P. H. (Ed.). (1983). *Handbook of child psychology* (4th ed., Vols. 1–4). New York: Wiley.

AN ARTICLE FROM A DAILY NEWSPAPER

Hottelet, R. C. (1990, March 15). Germany: Why it can't happen again. *Christian Science Monitor,* p. 19.

AN ARTICLE FROM A PERIODICAL

Gorriti, G. A. (1989, July). How to fight the drug war. *Atlantic Monthly,* 70-76.

AN ARTICLE IN A JOURNAL WITH CONTINUOUS PAGINATION THROUGHOUT THE VOLUME

Cockburn, A. (1989). British justice, Irish victims. *The Nation, 249,* 554-555.

AN ARTICLE FROM A JOURNAL WITH SEPARATE PAGINATION FOR EACH ISSUE

Mukerji, C. Visual language in science and the exercise of power: The case of cartography in early modern Europe. *Studies in Visual Communication,* 10(3), 30–45.

AN ARTICLE IN A REFERENCE WORK

Frisby, J. P. (1990). Direct perception. In M. W. Eysenck (Ed.), *Blackwell dictionary of cognitive psychology* (pp. 95-100). Oxford: Basil Blackwell.

A GOVERNMENT PUBLICATION

United States Dept. of Health, Education, and Welfare. (1973). *Current ethical issues in mental health.* Washington, DC: U.S. Government Printing Office.

AN ABSTRACT

Fritz, M. (1990/1991). A comparison of social interactions using a friendship awareness activity. *Education and Training in Mental Retardation,* *25,* 352-359. (From *Psychological Abstracts,* 1991, 78, Abstract No. 11474)

When the dates of the original publication and of the abstract differ, give both dates separated by a slash.

AN ANONYMOUS WORK

The status of women: Different but the same. (1992-1993). *Zontian, 73*(3), 5.

If the primary contributors to developing the program are known, begin the reference with those as the author(s) instead of the corporate author. If you are citing a documentation manual rather than the program itself, add the word "manual" before the closing bracket. If there is additional information needed for retrieving the program (such as report and/or acquisition numbers), add this at the end of the entry, in parentheses after the last period.

A REVIEW

Harris, I. M. (1991). [Review of the book *Rediscovering masculinity: Reason, language, and sexuality*]. *Gender and Society,* 5, 259-261.

Give the author of the review, not the author of the book being reviewed. Use this form for a film review also. If the review has a title, place it before the bracketed material, and treat it like an article title.

A LETTER TO THE EDITOR

Pritchett, J. T., & Kellner, C. H. (1993). Comment on spontaneous seizure activity [Letter to the editor]. *Journal of Nervous and Mental Disease, 181,*
138-139.

PERSONAL CORRESPONDENCE

B. Ehrenreich (personal communication, August 7, 1992).

(B. Ehrenreich, personal communication, August 7, 1992.)

Cite all personal communications to you (such as letters, memos, e-mails,
and telephone conversations) in text only, *without* listing them among
the references. The phrasing of your sentences will determine which of
the two above forms to use.

AN UNPUBLISHED MANUSCRIPT

McIntosh, P. (1988). *White privilege and male privilege: A personal account of
coming to see correspondences through work in women's studies.* Working
Paper 189. Unpublished manuscript, Wellesley College, Center for Research
on Women, Wellesley, MA.

PROCEEDINGS OF A MEETING, PUBLISHED

Guerrero, R. (1972/1973). Possible effects of the periodic abstinence method. In
W. A. Uricchio & M. K. Williams (Eds.), *Proceedings of a Research Conference
on Natural Family Planning* (pp. 96-105). Washington, DC: Human Life
Foundation.

If the date of the symposium or conference is different from the date of
publication, give both, separated by a slash. If the proceedings are published annually, treat the reference like a periodical article.

■ Electronic Sources

AN ARTICLE FROM AN ONLINE PERIODICAL

Palya, W., Walter, D., Kessel, R., & Lucke, R. (2001). Linear modeling of steady-
state behavioral dynamics [Electronic version]. *Journal of the Experimental
Analysis of Behavior, 77,* 3-27.

If the article duplicates the version which appeared in a print periodical,
use the same basic primary journal reference. See "An Article from a Periodical." If you have viewed the article only in its electronic form, add in
brackets [Electronic version].

Riordan, V. (2001, January 1). Verbal-performance IQ discrepancies in children
attending a child and adolescent psychiatry clinic. *Child and Adolescent*

Psychiatry On-Line. Retrieved August 9, 2002, from http://www.priory.com/
psych/iq.htm

If the article does not have a corresponding print version, include the
date of access and the URL.

A NONPERIODICAL WEB DOCUMENT

Munro, K. (2001, February). *Changing your body image.* Retrieved February 5,
2002, from http://www.kalimunro.com/article_changing_body
_image.html

In general, follow this format: author's name, the date of publication (if
no publication date is available, use "n.d."), the title of the document in
italics, date of access, and the source's URL.

A CHAPTER OR SECTION IN A WEB DOCUMENT

National Council of Welfare, Canada. (1998). Other issues related to poverty
lines. In *A new poverty line: Yes, no or maybe?* (chap. 5). Retrieved July 9,
2002, from http://www.ncwcnbes.net/htmdocument/reportnewpovline/
chap5.htm

AN E-MAIL

Do not include personal communications such as e-mails in your list of
references. See "Personal Correspondence."

A MESSAGE POSTED TO A NEWSGROUP

Isaacs, K. (2002, January 20). Philosophical roots of psychology [Msg 1]. Message posted to news://sci.psychology.psychotherapy.moderated

Include an online posting in your reference list only if the posting is
archived and is retrievable. Otherwise, cite an online posting as a personal
communication and do not include it in the list of references. Care
should be taken when citing electronic discussions. In general, they are
not scholarly sources.

AN ARTICLE FROM A DATABASE

Lopez, F. G., Melendez, M. C., Sauer, E. M., Berger, E., & Wyssmann, J. (1998).
Internal working models, self-reported problems, and help-seeking attitudes
among college students. *Journal of Counseling Psychology, 45,* 79-83. Retrieved April 1, 2002, from PsycARTICLES database.

To cite material retrieved from a database, follow the format appropriate
to the work retrieved and add the date of retrieval and the name of the
database.

■ Other Sources

A FILM

Wachowski, A., & Wachowski, L. (Writers/Directors). Silver, J. (Producer). (1999). *The matrix.* [Motion picture]. United States: Warner Bros.

Include the name and the function of the originator or primary contributor (director or producer). Identify the work as a motion picture. Include the country of origin and the studio. If the motion picture is of limited circulation, provide the name and address of the distributor in parentheses at the end of the reference.

A TELEVISION SERIES

Jones, R. (Producer). (1990). *Exploring consciousness.* [Television series]. Boston: WGBH.

SAMPLE RESEARCH PAPER (APA STYLE)

The following paper urges a change in our attitude toward zoos. Arguing the value claim that it is morally wrong for humans to exploit animals for entertainment, the student combines expert opinion gathered from research with her own interpretations of evidence. She is always careful to anticipate and represent the claims of the opposition before going on to refute them.

The student uses the APA style, modified to suit the preferences of her writing instructor. APA style requires a title page with a centered title, author, affiliation, and a short title that can be used as a "running head" on each page. An abstract page follows the title page and includes a one-paragraph abstract or summary of the article. Amanda Repp was told she could omit the title page and abstract recommended by the APA. A full description of APA publication conventions can be found in the *Publication Manual of the American Psychological Association,* Fifth Edition (2001).

Amanda Repp   Zoos   1

English 102-G

Mr. Kennedy

Fall 2004

Short title and page number, per APA style. Some instructors may prefer the student's name instead of the short title as a running head.

Why Zoos Should Be Eliminated

Zoos have come a long way from their grim beginnings. Once full of tiny cement-block steel cages, the larger zoos now boast simulated jungles, veldts, steppes, and rain forests, all in an attempt to replicate the natural habitats of the incarcerated animals. The attempt, however admirable, is misguided. It is morally wrong to keep wild animals in captivity, and no amount of replication, no matter how realistic, can compensate for the freedom these creatures are denied.

First paragraph ends with the thesis.

Peter Batten (1976) argues that a wild animal's life "is spent in finding food, avoiding enemies, sleeping, and in mating or other family activities. . . . Deprivation of any of these fundamentals results in irreparable damage to the individual" (p. 1). The fact that humans may be stronger or smarter than beasts does not give them the right to ambush and exploit animals for the purposes of entertainment.

Citation includes author, year of publication, and page number. Ellipses (. . .) indicate omitted words; a period after ellipses indicates that the omission included the end of a sentence.

We humans take our own liberty quite seriously. Indeed, we consider liberty to be one of our inalienable rights. But too many of us apparently feel no obligation to grant the same right to animals, who, because they cannot defend themselves against our sophisticated methods of capture and because they do not speak our language, cannot claim it for themselves.

But the right to liberty is not based on the ability to claim it, or even on the ability to understand what it is. As James Rachels (1976) writes:

Set long quotations of more than 40 words as block quotations. Indent all lines five spaces, double-space throughout, and put the page number of the quotations in parentheses after the final punctuation.

> Humans have a right to liberty because they have various other interests that will suffer if their freedom is unduly restricted. The right to liberty -- the right to be free of external constraints on one's actions -- may then be seen as derived from a more basic right not to have one's interests needlessly harmed. (p. 210)

Animals, like people, have interests that are harmed if they are kept in captivity: They are separated from their families and prevented from behaving according to their natural instincts by being removed from the lives they know, which are the lives they were meant to lead.

Some argue that animals' interests are not being harmed when they are kept in zoos or aquariums -- that no damage is being done to the individual -- but their claims are highly disputable. For example, the Zurich Zoo's Dr. Heini Hediger (1985) protests that it is absurd to attribute human qualities to animals at all, but he nevertheless resorts to a human analogy: "Wild animals in the zoo rather resemble estate owners. Far from desiring to escape and regain their freedom, they are only bent on defending the space they inhabit and keeping it safe from invasion" (p. 9). How can Dr. Hediger explain the actions of the leopards and cheetahs I have seen executing figure eights off the walls and floors of their cages for hours on end? I have watched, spellbound by their grace but also horrified; it is impossible to believe that these animals do not want their freedom. An estate owner would not spend his time running frantically around the perimeters of his property. These cats know they are not lords of any estate. The senseless repetition of their actions suggests that the cats know that they are caged and that there is nothing to defend against, no "estate" to protect.

Shannon Brownlee (1986) also believes that there is no concrete evidence that incarcerated animals are suffering or unhappy, but she weakens her own case in her description of Jackie, a dolphin in captivity who "spends the day in a seeming stupor" and "chews on the mackerel half-heartedly" at feeding time (p. 70). Clearly there *is* something wrong with Jackie; this becomes apparent when Brownlee contrasts Jackie's lethargic behavior with that of wild dolphins cavorting in the bay. Brownlee points out that Jackie has never tried to escape through a hole in his enclosure, although he knows it is there. But this fact does not necessarily mean that Jackie enjoys captivity. Instead, it may mean that Jackie's spirit has been broken and that he no longer remembers or cares what his earlier days were like. Granted we have no way of knowing what Jackie is really feeling, but does that give us the right to *assume* that he is not feeling anything?

Summary of an opposing argument

Argument flaw

Refutation of opposing argument based on evidence from personal experience

Summary of a second opposing argument; argument flaw

Challenge to an unstated warrant in the argument

Zoos   3

To be fair, Brownlee does not go that far. She does allow Jackie one emotional state, attributing his malaise to boredom. But perhaps if the author were removed from members of her family, as well as all other members of her species, and prevented from engaging in activities that most mattered to her, she would recognize Jackie's problems as something more than boredom. In any case, why should we inflict boredom on Jackie, or any other animal, just because we happen to have the means to do so?

The writer shifts to the second half of her argument.

Having registered these basic objections to zoos -- that keeping any creature in captivity is a fundamental infringement on that creature's right to liberty and dignity -- I want to take a closer look at the zoo as an institution, in order to assess fairly its goals and how it tries to meet them. Most zoo professionals today maintain that zoos exist for two main reasons: to educate humans and to conserve animal species.

Clarifying word in square brackets

These are both admirable goals, certainly, but as Seal (1985) notes, "none of these [zoo] budgets is allocated specifically for species preservation. Zoos have been established primarily as recreational institutions and are only secondarily developing programs in conservation, education, and research" (p. 74). The fact is most zoos do not have the money, space, or equipment required to make significant contributions in this area. The bulk of their money goes to the upkeep of the

Another opposing argument, with refutation

animals and exhibits -- that is, to put it crudely, to the displays.

On behalf of the education a zoo provides, a common argument is that there is nothing like seeing the real thing. But what you see in the zoo is not a real thing at all. According to a statement from the Animal Rights Resource Site, "The conditions under which animals are kept in zoos typically distorts their behavior significantly" (How will people see). Many zoo and aquarium animals, like Jackie the dolphin, have been domesticated to the point of lethargy, in part because they are being exhibited alone or with only one other member of

Summary of two expert opinions that zoos do not help endangered species

their species, when what they are used to is traveling in groups and finding their own food, instead of being fed. Anyone who wants to see the real thing would be better off watching some of the excellent programming about nature and wildlife that appears on public television.

As for conservation, it is clearly a worthwhile effort, but zoos are not effective agents of species preservation. It is generally acknowledged that it is difficult to breed zoo animals (Luoma, 1982, p. 104). Animals often do not reproduce at all -- quite possibly because of the artificial, and consequently unsettling, circumstances in which they live. When zoo animals do mate successfully, the offspring is often weakened by inbreeding. According to geneticists, this is because a population of 150 breeder animals is necessary in order to "assure the more or less permanent survival of a species in captivity" (Ehrlich & Ehrlich, 1981, p. 211). Few zoos have the resources to maintain populations that size. When zoos rely on smaller populations for breeding (as many do), the species' gene pool becomes more and more limited, "vigor and fecundity tend to decline" (Ehrlich & Ehrlich, 1981, p. 212), and this can eventually lead to extinction. In other words, we are not doing these animals any favors by trying to conserve them in zoos. Indeed, Wilson (1995) writes that "all the zoos in the world today can sustain a maximum of only 2,000 species of mammals, birds, reptiles, and amphibians, out of about 24,000 known to exist" (p. 57). Reserves and preservations, which have room for the larger populations necessary for successful conservation efforts and which can concentrate on breeding animals rather than on displaying them, are much more suitable for these purposes.

For what purposes, then, are zoos suitable? Are they even necessary? At present, they must house the many generations of animals that have been bred there, since these animals have no place else to go. Most animals in captivity cannot go back to the wild for one of two reasons. The first is that the creatures would be unable to survive there, since their instincts for finding their own food and protecting themselves from predators, or even the weather, have been greatly diminished during their time spent in captivity (Morton, 1985, p. 155). Perhaps this is why Jackie the dolphin chooses to remain in his enclosure.

Author, date, page cited parenthetically

Source with two authors cited parenthetically

Paraphrase with source cited parenthetically

Zoos 5

The other reason animals cannot return to the wild is an even sadder one: In many cases, their natural habitats no longer exist. Thanks to deforesting and clearing of land for homes, highways, factories, and shopping malls--which are continually being built with no regard for the plant and animal life around them--ecosystems are destroyed constantly, driving increasing numbers of species from their homes. Air and water pollution and toxic waste, results of the ever-increasing urbanization and industrialization throughout the world, are just some of the agents of this change. It is a problem I wish to address in closing.

The writer closes by proposing a solution of her own.

If zoos were to leave breeding programs to more appropriate organizations and to stop collecting animals, the zoo as an institution would eventually be phased out. Animals would cease to be exhibits and could resume being animals, and the money previously used to run zoos could be put to much better use. Ideally it could be used to investigate why endangered species are endangered, and why so many of the original habitats of these species have disappeared. Most important, it could be used to explore how we can change our habits and reorient our behavior, attitudes, and priorities, so we can begin to address these issues.

The problem of endangered species does not exist in a vacuum; it is a symptom of a much greater predicament. Humankind is responsible for this predicament, and it is up to us to recognize this before it is too late. Saving a selected species here and there will do none of us any good if those species can exist only in isolated, artificial environments, where they will eventually breed themselves into extinction. The money that has been concentrated on such efforts should be devoted instead to educating the public about the endangered planet--not just its animals--or, like the animals, none of us will have any place to go.

Zoos   6

References

Batten, P. (1976). *Living trophies.* New York: Crowell.

Brownlee, S. (1986, December). First it was "save the whales,"
now it's "free the dolphins." *Discover,* 70-72.

Ehrlich, P., & Ehrlich, A. (1981). *Extinction: The causes and
consequences of the disappearance of species.* New York:
Random House.

Hediger, H. (1985). From cage to territory. In R. Kirchschofer
(Ed.), *The world of zoos: A survey and gazetteer* (pp.
9-20). New York: Viking.

How will people see wild animals and learn about them without zoos? (n.d.). In *Animal Rights Resource Site.* Retrieved December 14, 1998, from http://arrs.envirolink
.org/faqs+Ref/ar-faq/Q70.html

Luoma, J. (1982, November). Prison or ark? *Audubon,*
102-109.

Morton, E. S. (1985). The realities of reintroducing species to
the wild. In J. R. Hoage (Ed.), *Animal extinctions: What
everyone should know* (pp. 147-158). National Zoological
Park Symposia for the Public series. Washington, DC:
Smithsonian Institution.

Rachels, J. (1976). Do animals have a right to liberty? In
T. Regan & P. Singer (Eds.), *Animal rights and human ob-
ligations* (pp. 205-223). Englewood Cliffs, NJ: Prentice-
Hall.

Seal, U. S. (1985). The realities of preserving species in captivity. In J. R. Hoage (Ed.), *Animal extinctions: What
everyone should know* (pp. 147-158). National Zoological
Park Symposia for the Public series. Washington, DC:
Smithsonian Institution.

Wilson, E. (1995, October 30). Wildlife: Legions of the
doomed. *Time,* 57-62. Retrieved December 12, 1999, from
Lexis/Nexis Universe.

*References
start a new
page.*

*A book with
two authors*

*A work in an
anthology*

*An article from
a periodical*

*For each refer-
ence, flush left
on first line,
and indent five
spaces on sub-
sequent lines.*

*An article on-
line from a
database*

CHAPTER 11

Presenting an Argument Orally

Speech is the basic skill overlooked by many who urge a return to the Three R's. The ability to speak clearly and persuasively, and to think on one's feet can be as vital to success as reading and writing. Beginning with the job interview, speech classifies a person.[1]

You already know a good deal about the power of persuasive speech. You've not only listened to it from parents, teachers, preachers, coaches, friends, and enemies; you've practiced it yourself with varying degrees of success.

A classics scholar points out that the oratorical techniques we use today were "invented in antiquity and have been used to great effect ever since."[2] But history is not our only guide to the principles of public speaking. Much of what we know about the power of persuasive speech is knowledge based on lifelong experience—things we learn in everyday discourse with different kinds of people who respond to different appeals. Early in life you learned that you did not use the same language or the same approach to argue with your mother or your teacher as you used with your sibling or your friend. You learned, or tried to learn, how to convince people to listen to you and to trust you because you were truthful and knew what you were talking about. And perhaps equally important, if you won the argument, you wanted to make it clear that your victory would not mean hardship for the loser (no obvious gloating).

---

[1] Fred M. Hechinger, "About Education," *New York Times*, May 11, 1988, sec. B, p. 7.
[2] Mary Lefkowitz, "Classic Oratory," *New York Times*, January 24, 1999, sec. W, p. 15.

Although speeches to a larger, less familiar audience will require much more preparation, many of the rules of argument that guided you in your personal encounters can be made to work for you in more public arenas.

You will often be asked to make oral presentations in your college classes. Many jobs, both professional and nonprofessional, will call for speeches to groups of fellow employees or prospective customers, to community groups, and even government officials. Wherever you live, there will be controversies and public meetings about schooling and political candidates, about budgets for libraries and road repairs and pet control. The ability to rise and make your case before an audience is one that you will want to cultivate as a citizen of a democracy. Great oratory is probably no longer the most powerful influence in our society, and computer networks have usurped the role of oral communication in many areas of public life. But whether it's in person or on television there is still a significant role for a live presenter, a real human being to be seen and heard.

Some of your objectives as a writer will also be relevant to you as a speaker: making the appropriate appeal to an audience, establishing your credibility, finding adequate support for your claim. But other elements of argument will be different: language, organization, and the use of visual and other aids.

Before you begin a brief examination of these elements, keep in mind the larger objectives of the speechmaker. A good introduction to the process of influencing an audience is *the motivated sequence*.[3] This outline, created by a professor of speech communication, lists the five steps that must be taken in order to motivate an audience to adopt a policy, an action, or a belief.

1. Getting attention (attention step)
2. Showing the need: describing the problem (need step)
3. Satisfying the need: presenting the solution (satisfaction step)
4. Visualizing the results (visualization step)
5. Requesting action or approval (action step)

Perhaps you noticed that these steps resemble the steps taken by advertisers. (That list appears in the sample analysis of an ad in Chapter 2.) The resemblance is not accidental. According to the author of the motivated sequence, this is a description of the way "people systematically think their way through to a decision."

As you read the following discussions of audience, credibility, language, organization, support, and visual and aural aids, try to think of occasions in your own experience when you were aware of these elements in spoken argument, formal or informal.

---

[3] Alan H. Monroe and Douglas Ehninger, *Principles of Speech Communication* (Glenview, Ill.: Scott, Foresman, 1969), p. 261.

THE AUDIENCE

Most speakers who confront a live audience already know something about the members of that audience. They may know why the audience is assembled to hear the particular speaker, their vocations, their level of education, and their familiarity with the subject. They may know whether the audience is friendly, hostile, or neutral to the views that the speaker will express. Analyzing the audience is an essential part of speech preparation. If speakers neglect it, both audience and speaker will suffer. At some time all of us have been trapped as members of an audience, forced to listen to a lecture, a sermon, an appeal for action when it was clear that the speaker had little or no idea what we were interested in or capable of understanding. In such situations the speaker who seems indifferent to the needs of the audience will also suffer because the audience will either cease to listen or reject his claim outright.

In college classes students who make assigned speeches on controversial topics are often encouraged to first survey the class. Questionnaires and interviews can give the speaker important clues to the things he should emphasize or avoid: They will tell him whether he should give both sides of a debatable question, introduce humor, use simpler language, and bring in visual or other aids.

But even where such specific information is not immediately available, speakers are well advised to find out as much as they can about the beliefs and attitudes of their audience from other sources. They will then be better equipped to make the kinds of appeals—to reason and to emotion—that the audience is most responsive to. For example, two young evangelists for a religious group (not students at the university) were invited to visit a speech class and present an argument for joining their group. The visitors knew that the class was learning the principles of persuasive speaking; they had no other information about the listeners. After the speech, the students in the class asked questions about some practices of the religious group which had received unfavorable media attention, but the speakers turned aside all questions, saying they did not engage in argument but were instructed only to describe the rewards of joining their group. Before some other audience, such a strategy might have been emotionally satisfying and ultimately persuasive. For this class, however, which was prepared to look for hard evidence, logic, and valid assumptions, the refusal to answer questions suggested evasion and indifference to the interests of their audience. Class evaluations of the speech revealed, to no one's surprise, that the visitors had failed to motivate their listeners.

If you know something about your audience, ask yourself what impression your clothing, gestures and bodily movements, voice, and general demeanor might convey. It might be worth pointing out here that the visitors cited above arrived dressed in three-piece suits and sporting crew cuts to confront an audience in tee shirts, torn jeans, and long hair. The fact that both speakers and listeners were the same age was not quite enough to overcome an impression of real differences. Make sure, too, that you understand the nature of the occasion—is it too solemn for humor? too formal for personal anecdotes?— and the purpose of the meeting, which can influence your choice of language and the most effective appeal.

CREDIBILITY

The evaluation of audience and the presentation of your own credibility are closely related. In other words, what can you do to persuade this particular audience that you are a reliable exponent of the views you are expressing? Credibility, as you learned in Chapter 1, is another name for *ethos* (the Greek word from which the English word *ethics* is derived) and refers to the honesty, moral character, and intellectual competence of the speaker.

Public figures, whose speeches and actions are reported in the media, can acquire (or fail to acquire) reputations for being endowed with those characteristics. And there is little doubt that a reputation for competence and honesty can incline an audience to accept an argument that would be rejected if offered by a speaker who lacks such a reputation. One study, among many that report similar results, has shown that the same speech will be rated highly by an audience that thinks the Surgeon General of the United States has delivered it but treated with much less regard if they hear it delivered by a college sophomore.

How, then, does a speaker who is unknown to the audience or who boasts only modest credentials convince his listeners that he is a responsible advocate? From the moment the speaker appears before them, members of the audience begin to make an evaluation, based on external signs, such as clothing and mannerisms. But the most significant impression of the speaker's credibility will be based on what the speaker says and how he says it. Does the speaker give evidence that he knows the subject? Does he seem to be aware of the needs and values of the audience? Especially if he is arguing an unpopular claim, does he seem modest and conciliatory?

An unknown speaker is often advised to establish his credentials in the introduction to his speech, to summarize his background and experience as proof of his right to argue the subject he has chosen. A prizewinning and widely reprinted speech by a student begins with these words:

> When you look at me, it is easy to see several similarities between us. I
> have two arms, two legs, a brain, and a heart just like you. These are my

hands, and they are just like yours. Like you, I also have wants and desires; I am capable of love and hate. I can laugh and I can cry. Yes, I'm just like you, except for one very important fact—I am an ex-con.[4]

This is a possibly risky beginning—not everybody in the audience will be friendly to an ex-con—but it signifies that the speaker brings some authority to his subject, which is prison reform. It also attests to the speaker's honesty and may rouse sympathy among certain listeners. (To some in the audience, the speaker's allusions to his own humanity will recall another moving defense, the famous speech by Shylock, the Jewish moneylender, in Shakespeare's *The Merchant of Venice*.)

The speaker will often use an admission of modesty as proof of an honest and unassuming character. He presents himself not as an expert but as one well aware of his limitations. Such an appeal can generate sympathy in the audience (if they believe him) and a sense of identification with the speaker.

The professor of classics quoted earlier has analyzed the speech of a former senator who defended President Clinton at his impeachment trial. She found that the speaker "made sure his audience understood that he was one of them, a friend, on their level, not above them. He denied he was a great speaker and spoke of his friendship with Mr. Clinton." As the writer points out, this confession brings to mind the speech by Mark Antony in *Julius Caesar:*

> I am no orator, as Brutus is,
> But (as you know me all) a plain blunt man
> That loves my friend; (3.2.226–28)

The similarity of these attempts at credibility, separated by almost four hundred years (to say nothing of the fact that Aristotle wrote about *ethos* 2,500 years ago) tells us a good deal about the enduring influence of *ethos* or character on the speaker's message.

ORGANIZATION

Look at the student speech at the end of this chapter. The organization of this short speech—the usual length of speeches delivered in the classroom—is easily mastered and works for all kinds of claims.

At the end of the first paragraph the speaker states what he will try to prove, that a vegetarian diet contributes to prevention of chronic diseases. In the third paragraph the speaker gives the four points that he will

---

[4]Richard M. Duesterbeck, "Man's Other Society," in Wil Linkugel, R. R. Allen, and Richard Johannesen, eds., *Contemporary American Speeches* (Belmont, Calif.: Wadsworth, 1965), p. 264.

develop in his argument for vegetarianism. Following the development of these four topics, the conclusion urges the audience to take action, in this case, to stop eating meat.

This basic method of organizing a short speech has several virtues. First, the claim or thesis statement that appears early in a short speech, if the subject is well chosen, can engage the interest of the audience at once. Second, the list of topics guides the speaker in planning and developing his speech. Moreover, it tells the audience what to listen for as they follow the argument.

A well-planned speech has a clearly defined beginning, middle, and end. The beginning, which offers the introduction, can take a number of forms, depending on the kind of speech and its subject. Above all, the introduction must win the attention of the audience, especially if they have been required to attend, and encourage them to look forward to the rest of the speech. The authors of the motivated sequence suggest seven basic attention-getters: (1) referring to the subject or occasion, (2) using a personal reference, (3) asking a rhetorical question, (4) making a startling statement of fact or opinion, (5) using a quotation, (6) telling a humorous anecdote, (7) using an illustration.[5]

The speeches by the ex-con and the vegetarian provide examples of two of the attention-getters cited above—using a personal reference and asking a rhetorical question. In another kind of argument, a claim of fact, the student speaker uses a combination of devices to introduce her claim that culturally deprived children are capable of learning:

> In Charles Schulz's popular cartoon depiction of happiness, one of his definitions has special significance for the American school system. The drawing shows Linus, with his eyes closed in a state of supreme bliss, a broad smile across two-thirds of his face and holding a report card upon which is a big bold "A." The caption reads: "Happiness is finding out you're not so dumb after all." For once, happiness is not defined as a function of material possessions, yet even this happiness is practically unattainable for the "unteachables" of the city slums. Are these children intellectually inferior? Are they unable to learn? Are they not worth the time and the effort to teach? Unfortunately, too many people have answered "yes" to these questions and promptly dismissed the issue.[6]

The middle or body of the speech is, of course, the longest part. It will be devoted to development of the claim that appeared at the beginning. The length of the speech and the complexity of the subject will determine how much support you provide. Some points will be more important than others and should therefore receive more extended treatment. Unless the order is chronological, it makes sense for the speaker to arrange

[5]Monroe and Ehninger, p. 206.
[6]Carolyn Kay Geiman, "Are They Really 'Unteachables'?" in Linkugel, Allen, and Johannesen, p. 123.

the supporting points in emphatic order, that is, the most important at the end because this may be the one that listeners will remember.

The conclusion should be brief; some rhetoricians suggest that the ending should constitute 5 percent of the total length of the speech. For speeches that contain several main points with supporting data, you may need to summarize. Or you may return to one of the attention-getters mentioned earlier. One writer recommends this as "the most obvious method" of concluding speeches, "particularly appropriate when the introduction has included a quotation, an interesting anecdote, a reference to an occasion or a place, an appeal to the self-interest of the audience, or a reference to a recent incident."[7]

An example of such an ending appears in a speech given by Bruce Babbitt, Secretary of the Interior, in 1996. Speaking to an audience of scientists and theologians, the Secretary defended laws that protected the environment. This is how the speech began:

> A wolf's green eyes, a sacred blue mountain, the words from Genesis, and the answers of children all reveal the religious values manifest in the 1977 Endangered Species Act.

(The children Babbitt refers to had written answers to a question posed at an "eco-expo" fair, "Why Save the Environment?")

And this is the ending of the speech:

> I conclude here tonight by affirming that those religious values remain at the heart of the Endangered Species Act, that they make themselves manifest through the green eyes of the grey wolf, through the call of the whooping crane, through the splash of the Pacific salmon, through the voices of America's children.
>
> We are living between the flood and the rainbow: between the threats to creation on the one side and God's covenant to protect life on the other.
>
> Why should we save endangered species?
>
> Let us answer this question with one voice, the voice of the child at that expo, who scrawled her answer at the very bottom of the sheet: "Because we can."[8]

The speaker must also ensure the smooth flow of his argument throughout. Coherence, or the orderly connections between ideas, is even more important in speech than in writing because the listener cannot go back to uncover these connections. The audience listens for expressions that serve as guideposts — words, phrases, and sentences to indicate which direction the argument will take. The student speech on vegetarianism uses these words among others: *next, then, finally, here, first*

---

[7]James C. McCroskey, *An Introduction to Rhetorical Communication* (Englewood Cliffs, N.J.: Prentice-Hall, 1968), p. 204.

[8]Calvin McLeod Logue and Jean DeHart, eds., *Representative American Speeches, 1995–1996* (New York: Wilson, 1996), p. 70ff.

of all, whereas, in addition, secondly, in fact, now, in conclusion. Other expressions can also help the listener to follow the development. Each of the following examples from real speeches makes a bridge from a previous idea to a new one: "Valid factual proof, right? No, wrong!" "Consider an illustration of this misinformation." "But there is another way." "Up to this point, I've spoken only of therapy." "And so we face this new challenge." "How do we make this clear?" "Now, why is this so important?"

LANGUAGE

It should be observed that each kind of rhetoric has its own appropriate style. That of written prose is not the same as that of spoken oratory.

— Aristotle

In the end, your speech depends on the language. No matter how accurate your analysis of the audience, how appealing your presentation of self, how deep your grasp of the material, if the language does not clearly and emphatically convey your argument, the speech will probably fail. Fortunately, the effectiveness of language does not depend on long words or complex sentence structure; quite the contrary. Most speeches, especially those given by beginners to small audiences, are distinguished by an oral style that respects the rhythms of ordinary speech and sounds spontaneous.

The vocabulary you choose, like the other elements of spoken discourse we have discussed, is influenced by the kind of audience you confront. A student audience may be entertained or moved to identification with you and your message if you use the slang of your generation; an assembly of elderly church members at a funeral may not be so generous. Use words that both you and your listeners are familiar with, language that convinces the audience you are sharing your knowledge and opinions, neither speaking down to them nor over their heads. As one writer puts it, "You never want to use language that makes the audience appear ignorant or stupid."

Make sure, too, that the words you use will not be considered offensive by some members of your audience. Today we are all sensitive, sometimes hypersensitive, to terms we once used freely if not wisely. One word, improperly used, can cause some listeners to reject the whole speech.

The short speeches you give will probably not be devoted to elaborating grand abstractions, but it is not only abstract terms that need definition. When you know your subject very well, you forget that others can be ignorant of it. Think whether the subject is one that the particular audience you are addressing is not likely to be familiar with. If this is the case, then explain even the basic terms. In one class a student who had chosen to discuss a subject about which he was extremely knowl-edgeable, betting on horse races, neglected to define clearly the words *exacta, subfecta, trifecta, parimutuel,* and others, leaving his audience fairly befuddled.

Wherever it is appropriate, use concrete language with details and ex-amples that create images and cause the listener to feel as well as think. One student speaker used strong words to good effect in providing some unappetizing facts about hot dogs: "In fact, the hot dog is so adulterated with chemicals, so contaminated with bacteria, so puffy with gristle, fat, water, and lacking in protein, that it is nutritionally worthless."[9]

Another speech on a far more serious subject offered a personal ex-perience with vivid details. The student speaker was a hemophiliac mak-ing a plea for blood donations.

> I remember the three long years when I couldn't even walk because re-peated hemorrhages had twisted my ankles and knees to pretzel-like forms. I remember being pulled to school in a wagon while other boys rode their bikes and pushed to my table. I remember sitting in the dark empty classroom by myself during recess while the others went out in the sun to run and play. And I remember the first terrible day at the big high school when I came on crutches and built-up shoes carrying my books in a sack around my neck.[10]

As a rule, the oral style demands simpler sentences. That is because the listener must grasp the grammatical construction without the visual clues of punctuation available on the printed page. Simpler means shorter and more direct. Use subject-verb constructions without a string of phrases or clauses preceding the subject or interrupting the natural flow of the sentence. Use the active voice frequently. In addition to assuring clarity for the audience, such sentences are easier for the speaker to re-member and to say. (The sentences in the paragraph above are long, but notice that the sentence elements of subject, verb, and subordinate clause are arranged in the order dictated by natural speech.)

Simpler, however, does not mean less impressive. A speech before any audience may be simply expressed without loss of emotional or intellec-tual power. "The Nature of Prejudice" in Chapter 3 is a noteworthy example. First delivered as a speech to an audience of experts, it never-theless reflects the characteristics of conversation. One of the most elo-quent short speeches ever delivered in this country is the surrender speech in 1877 by Chief Joseph of the Nez Percé Tribe, which clearly demonstrates the power of simple words and sentences.

> I am tired of fighting. Our chiefs are killed. Looking Glass is dead. Toohulsote is dead. The old men are all dead. It is the young men who

---

[9] Donovan Ochs and Anthony Winkler, *A Brief Introduction to Speech* (New York: Har-court, Brace, Jovanovich, 1979), p. 74.

[10] Ralph Zimmerman, "Mingled Blood," in Linkugel, Allen, and Johannesen, p. 200.

say no and yes. He who led the young men is dead. It is cold and we have no blankets. The little children are freezing to death. My people, some of them, have run away to the hills and have no blankets, no food. No one knows where they are—perhaps they are freezing to death. I want to have time to look for my children and see how many of them I can find. Maybe I shall find them among the dead. Hear me, my chiefs. I am tired. My heart is sad and sick. From where the sun now stands I will fight no more forever.[11]

If you are in doubt about the kind of language in which you should express yourself, you might follow Lincoln's advice: "Speak so that the most lowly can understand you, and the rest will have no difficulty."

A popular stylistic device—repetition and balance or parallel structure—can emphasize and enrich parts of your message. Look back to the balanced sentences of the passage from the student speaker on hemophilia, sentences beginning with "I remember." Almost all inspirational speeches, including religious exhortation and political oratory, take advantage of such constructions, whose rhythms evoke an immediate emotional response. It is one of the strengths of Martin Luther King Jr.'s "I Have a Dream." Keep in mind that the ideas in parallel structures must be similar and that, for maximum effectiveness, they should be used sparingly in a short speech. Not least, the subject should be weighty enough to carry this imposing construction.

SUPPORT

The support for a claim is essentially the same for both spoken and written arguments. Factual evidence, including statistics, and expert opinion, as well as appeals to needs and values, are equally important in oral presentations. But time constraints will make a difference. In a speech the amount of support that you provide will be limited to the capacity of listeners to digest and remember information that they cannot review. This means that you must choose subjects that can be supported adequately in the time allotted. The speech by Secretary Babbitt, for example, on saving the environmental protection laws, developed material on animals, national lands, water, his own history, religious tradition, and the history of environmental legislation, to name only the most important. It would have been impossible to defend his proposition in a half-hour speech. Although his subject was far more limited, the author of the argument for vegetarianism could not do full justice to his claim for lack of time. Meat-eaters would find that some of their questions remain unanswered, and

---

[11]M. Gidley, *Kopet: A Documentary Narrative of Chief Joseph's Last Years.* (Chicago: Contemporary Books, 1981), p. 31.

even those listeners friendly to the author's claim might ask for more evidence from authoritative sources.

While both speakers and writers use logical, ethical, and emotional appeals in support of their arguments, the forms of presentation can make a significant difference. The reasoning process demanded of listeners must be relatively brief and straightforward, and the supporting evidence readily assimilated. The ethical appeal or credibility of the speaker is affected not only by what he says but by his appearance, bodily movements, and vocal expressions. And the appeal to the sympathy of the audience can be greatly enhanced by the presence of the speaker. Take the excerpt from the speech of the hemophiliac. The written descriptions of pain and heartbreak are very moving, but place yourself in the audience, looking at the victim and imagining the suffering experienced by the human body standing in front of you. No doubt the effect would be deep and long-lasting, perhaps more memorable even than the written word.

Because the human instrument is so powerful, it must be used with care. You have probably listened to speakers who used gestures and voice inflections that had been dutifully rehearsed but were obviously contrived and worked, unfortunately, to undermine rather than support the speaker's message and credibility. If you are not a gifted actor, avoid gestures, body language, and vocal expressions that are not truly felt.

Some speech theorists treat support or proofs as *nonartistic* and *artistic*. The nonartistic support—factual data, expert opinion, examples—is considered objective and verifiable. Its acceptability should not depend on the character and personality of the speaker. It is plainly different from the artistic proof, which is subjective, based on the values and attitudes of the listener, and therefore more difficult for the speaker to control. This form of support is called artistic because it includes creative strategies within the power of the speaker to manipulate. In earlier parts of this chapter we have discussed the artistic proofs, ways of establishing credibility, and recognizing the values of the audience.

PRESENTATION AIDS

■ Charts, Graphs, Handouts

Some speeches, though not all, will be enhanced by visual and other aids: charts, graphs, maps, models, objects, handouts, recordings, and computer technology. These aids, however, no matter how visually or aurally exciting, should not overwhelm your own oral presentation. The objects are not the stars of the show. They exist to make your spoken argument more persuasive.

Charts and graphs, large enough and clear enough to be seen and understood, can illuminate speeches that contain numbers of any kind, especially statistical comparisons. You can make a simple chart yourself, on paper for use with an easel or a transparency for use with a slide projector. Enlarged illustrations or a model of a complicated machine—say, the space shuttle—would help a speaker to explain its function. You already know that photographs or videos are powerful instruments of persuasion, above all in support of appeals for humanitarian aid, for both people and animals.

Court cases have been won or lost on the basis of diagrams or charts that purport to prove the innocence or guilt of a defendant. Such aids do not always speak for themselves. No matter how clear they are to the designer, they may be misinterpreted or misunderstood by a viewer. Some critics have argued that the jury in the O. J. Simpson case failed to understand the graphs of DNA relationships that experts for the prosecution displayed during the trial. Before you show any diagrams or charts of any complexity to your audience, ask friends if they find them easy to understand.

The use of a handout also requires planning. It's probably unwise to put your speech on hold while the audience reads or studies a handout that requires time and concentration. Confine the subject matter of handouts to material that can be easily grasped as you discuss or explain it.

■ Audio

Audio aids may also enliven a speech or even be indispensable to its success. One student played a recording of a scene from *Romeo and Juliet*, spoken by a cast of professional actors, to make a point about the relationship between the two lovers. Another student chose to define several types of popular music, including rap, goth, heavy metal, and techno. But he used only words, and the lack of any musical demonstration meant that the distinctions remained unclear.

■ Video

With sight, sound, and movement, a video can illustrate or reinforce the main points of a speech. A speech warning people not to drink and drive will have a much greater effect if enhanced by a video showing the tragic and often gruesome outcome of car accidents caused by drunk driving. Schools that teach driver's education frequently rely on these bone-chilling videos to show their students that getting behind the wheel is a serious responsibility, not a game. If you want to use video, check to make sure that a VCR and television are available to you. Most schools have an audio-visual department that manages the delivery, setup, and return of all equipment.

■ Multimedia

Multimedia presentation software programs enable you to combine several different media such as text, charts, sound, and still or moving pictures into one unit. In the business world, multimedia presentations are commonly used in situations where you have a limited amount of time to persuade or teach a fairly large audience. For instance, the promotion director of a leading teen magazine is trying to persuade skeptical executives that a magazine Web site would increase sales and advertising revenue. Since the magazine is sold through newsstand and subscription, some executives question whether the cost of creating and maintaining a Web site outweighs the benefits. Using multimedia presentation software, the promotion director can integrate: demographic charts and graphs showing that steadily increasing numbers of teenagers surf the Web, a segment from a television news program reporting that many teens shop online (an attraction for advertisers), and downloaded pages from a competitor's Web site to demonstrate that others are already reaping the benefits of the Internet. With several studies reporting that people today are increasingly "visual" in their learning styles, multimedia software may be the most effective aid for an important presentation.

Though effective when done well, technically complicated presentations require large amounts of time and careful planning. First you must ensure that your computer is powerful enough to adeptly handle presentation software such as Microsoft PowerPoint, Lotus Freelance, Harvard Graphics, Adobe Persuasion, Cintel Charisma, and Asymetrix Compel. Then you need to familiarize yourself with the program. Most presentation software programs come equipped with helpful tutorials. If the task of creating your own presentation from scratch seems overwhelming, you can use one of the many preformatted presentation templates: You will simply need to customize the content. Robert Stephens, the founder of the Geek Squad, a Minneapolis-based business that provides on-site emergency response to computer problems, gives the following tips for multimedia presentations:

1. In case of equipment failure, always bring two of everything.

2. Back up your presentation not only on floppy disk, but on CD-ROM, or a Zip drive.

3. Avoid live visits to the Internet. Because connections can fail or be painfully slow, and sites can move or disappear, if you must visit the Internet in your presentation, download the appropriate pages onto your hard drive ahead of time. It will still look like a live visit.

4. In the end, technology cannot replace creativity. Make sure that you are using multimedia to reinforce not replace your main points.[12]

---

[12] Robert Stephens as paraphrased in "When Your Presentation Crashes . . . Who You Gonna Call?" by Eric Matson, *Fast Company*, February/March 1997, p. 130.

Make sure that any necessary apparatus will be available at the right time. If you have never used the devices you need for your presentation, practice using them before the speech. Few things are more disconcerting for the speechmaker and the audience than a speaker who is fumbling with his materials, unable to find the right picture or to make a machine work.

SAMPLE PERSUASIVE SPEECH

The following speech was delivered by C. Renzi Stone to his public speaking class at the University of Oklahoma. Told to prepare a persuasive speech, Stone chose to speak about the health benefits of vegetarianism. Note his attention-grabbing introduction.

Live Longer and Healthier: Stop Eating Meat!

C. RENZI STONE

What do Steve Martin, Dustin Hoffman, Albert Einstein, Jerry Garcia, Michael Stipe, Eddie Vedder, Martina Navratilova, Carl Lewis, and 12 million other Americans all have in common? All of these well-known people were or are vegetarians. What do they know that we don't? Consuming a regimen of high-fat, high-protein flesh foods is a sure-fire prescription for disaster, like running diesel fuel through your car's gasoline engine. In the book *Why Do Vegetarians Eat Like That?* David Gabbe asserts that millions of people today are afflicted with chronic diseases that can be directly linked to the consumption of meat. Eating a vegetarian diet can help prevent many of those diseases.

In 1996, 12 million Americans identified themselves as vegetarians. That number is twice as many as in the decade before. According to a recent National Restaurant Association poll found in *Health* magazine, one in five diners say they now go out of their way to choose restaurants that serve at least a few meatless entrees. Obviously, the traditionally American trait of a meat-dominated society has subsided in recent years.

In discussing vegetarianism today, first I will tell how vegetarians are perceived in society. Next, I will introduce several studies validating my claim that a meatless diet is extraordinarily healthy. I will then show how a veggie diet can strengthen the immune system and make the meatless body a shield from unwanted diseases such as cancer and heart disease. Maintaining a strict vegetarian diet can also lead to a longer life. Finally, I will put an image into the audience's mind of a meatless society that relies on vegetables for the main course at breakfast, lunch, and dinner.

Moving to my first point, society generally holds two major misperceptions about vegetarians. First of all, society often perceives vegetarians as a radical group of people with extreme principles. In this view, vegetarians are seen as a monolithic group of people who choose to eat vegetables because they are opposed to the killing of animals for food. The second major misconception is that because vegetarians do not eat meat, they do not get the proper amounts of essential vitamins and minerals often found in meat.

Here is my response to these misconceived notions. First of all, vege- 5 tarians are not a homogeneous group of radicals. Whereas many vegetarians in the past did join the movement on the principle that killing animals is wrong, many join the movement today mainly for its health benefits. In addition, there are many different levels of vegetarianism. Some vegetarians eat nothing but vegetables. Others don't eat red meat but do occasionally eat chicken and fish.

Secondly, contrary to popular opinion, vegetarians get more than enough vitamins and minerals in their diet and generally receive healthier nourishment than meat eaters. In fact, in an article for *Health* magazine, Peter Jaret states that vegetarians actually get larger amounts of amino acids due to the elimination of saturated fats which are often found in meat products. Studies show that the health benefits of a veggie lifestyle contribute to increased life expectancy and overall productivity.

Hopefully you now see that society's perceptions of vegetarians are outdated and just plain wrong. You are familiar with many of the problems associated with a meat-based diet, and you have heard many of the benefits of a vegetarian diet. Now try to imagine how you personally can improve your life by becoming a vegetarian.

Can you imagine a world where people retire at age eighty and lead productive lives into their early 100s? Close your eyes and think about celebrating your seventieth wedding anniversary, seeing your great-grandchildren get married, and witnessing 100 years of world events and technological innovations. David Gabbe's book refers to studies that have shown a vegetarian diet can increase your life expectancy up to fifteen years. A longer life is within your reach, and the diet you eat has a direct impact on your health and how you age.

In conclusion, vegetarianism is a healthy life choice, not a radical cult. By eliminating meat from their diet, vegetarians reap the benefits of a vegetable-based diet that helps prevent disease and increase life expectancy. People, take heed of my advice. There are many more sources of information available for those who want to take a few hours to research the benefits of the veggie lifestyle. If you don't believe my comments, discover the whole truth for yourself.

Twelve million Americans know the health benefits that come with 10 being a vegetarian. Changing your eating habits can be just as easy as making your bed in the morning. Sure, it takes a few extra minutes and some thought, but your body will thank you in the long run.

You only live once. Why not make it a long stay?

Part Three

Multiple Viewpoints

The following section contains a variety of viewpoints on eight controversial questions. These questions generate conflict among experts and laypeople alike for two principal reasons. First, even when the facts are not in dispute, they may be interpreted differently by opposing sides. Second, and certainly more difficult to resolve, equally worthwhile values may be in conflict.

Multiple Viewpoints lends itself to classroom debates, both formal and informal. It can also serve as a useful source of informed opinions, which can lead to further research. First, read all the articles in one chapter of a Multiple Viewpoints section. You may wish to begin further research by choosing material to support your claim from two or three articles in the text or by exploring recommended sources on the Web (see Taking the Debate Online at the end of each chapter).

Ask the following questions about each controversy:

1. Are there two — or more — different points of view on the subject? Do all sides make clear what they are trying to prove? Summarize their claims.
2. Do all sides share the same goals? If not, how are they different?
3. How important is definition of key terms? Do all sides agree on the definitions? If so, what are they? If not, how do they differ? Does definition become a significant issue in the controversy?
4. How important is evidence in support of the claims? Does the support fulfill the appropriate criteria? If not, what are its weaknesses? Do the authorities have convincing credentials?
5. Do the arguers base any part of their arguments on needs and values that their readers are expected to share? What are they? Do the arguers provide examples of the ways these values function? Is there a conflict of values? If so, which seem more important?
6. What warrants or assumptions underlie the claims? Are they implicit or explicit? Do the arguers examine them for the reader? Are the warrants acceptable? If not, point out their weaknesses.
7. What are the main issues? Is there a genuine debate — that is, does each side try to respond to arguments on the other side?
8. Do the arguers propose solutions to a problem? Are the advantages of their proposals clear? Are there obvious disadvantages?
9. Does each argument follow a clear and orderly organization, one that lends itself to a good outline? If not, what are the weaknesses?
10. Does language play a part in the argument? Are there any examples of misuse of language — slanted or loaded words, clichés, slogans?
11. Do the arguers show an awareness of audience? How would you describe the audience(s) for whom the various arguments are presented?
12. Do you think that one side won the argument? Can you find examples of negotiation and compromise, of attempts to establish a common ground? Explain your answer in detail.

CHAPTER 12

How Far Will We Go to Change Our Body Image?

We live in a society where appearance matters. How much it matters is clear from magazines, television shows, movies, and advertisements. It is clear from the number of diets hyped on talk shows and in bookstores. It is clear from the alarming number of young women with anorexia and bulimia, from the celebrities that our youth, male and female, choose to idolize and emulate, and from the drastic increase in recent years in the amount of plastic surgery being performed. We exercise, count our carbs, and are acutely aware of the face that stares back at us in the mirror.

Cosmetic surgery has changed countless lives by correcting birth defects and other abnormalities. It does not save lives, although at times cosmetic surgery may be closely linked to corrective surgery, as when a cleft lip is corrected in conjunction with correcting a cleft palate or when plastic surgery repairs the ravages of severe burns once the burns themselves are no longer life threatening. A cleft palate interferes with one's health. A cleft lip is repaired primarily for aesthetic reasons. The scars left on a burn victim may require plastic surgery to help heal the psychological damage left after the body has healed.

Having a nose job or a breast enlargement purely for aesthetic reasons was once the sort of thing only movie stars and the extremely wealthy would have considered. Today many average citizens are enhancing or reshaping their bodies. In fact, the quest for the perfect body has become such a popular concept that television networks are cashing in on it with shows that chronicle the transformation of ugly ducklings into swans. Individuals dissatisfied with their bodies are willing to undergo surgery and endure the experience on a television show seen by millions in hopes of remaking themselves into the image that exists in their fantasies. Thousands more seek transformation more quietly in the privacy of their doctors' offices to the point that, for some, changing each imperfection becomes an obsession. Women are generally accused of being the most conscious of body image. The steroids that men take, though, improve physique as well as athletic performance—and increase the chances of lasting damage to the body.

The dangers associated with the use of drugs, diets, and plastic surgery to enhance body image are the frequent focus of argumentative speech or writing. The psychological dangers may be as grave as the physical ones. We must question why so many are willing to tamper with their physical appearance and wonder how they feel once the changes are made. To whose model of physical perfection are we aspiring? Is it right, for example, to seek to remove physical signs of ethnicity? Some regard such changes as a betrayal of the race. In changing what makes each of us distinct, are we giving in, as one author included here suggests, to "the tyranny of the normal"? How much are we willing to spend—how much money and how much pain or discomfort—to look good?

Putting Your Best Face Forward

CARL ELLIOTT

BEFORE READING: What does the popularity of cosmetic surgery suggest about Americans' values? How is it related to social and economic class?

If a team of alien anthropologists were looking for clues to understand the habits and sensibilities of twenty-first century Americans, it could start with the new Fox reality show, *The Swan*. Like *Extreme Makeover*, its predecessor on ABC, *The Swan* invites guests to undergo dramatic self-transformations with the help of fitness trainers, hair stylists, makeup consultants, and cosmetic surgeons. Unlike the guests on *Extreme Makeover*, however, contestants on *The Swan* will be prevented from seeing how their cosmetic surgery has turned out until the season finale. In that episode, called "The Ultimate Swan Pageant," eighteen surgically al-

Carl Elliott is associate professor of pediatrics and director of graduate studies of the Center for Bioethics at the University of Minnesota. He holds both an M.D. from the Medical University of South Carolina and a Ph.D. in philosophy from Glasgow University in Scotland. He has written on the ethics of enhancement technologies and the philosophy of psychiatry. His most recent book is *Better Than Well: American Medicine Meets the American Dream* (2003). This article appeared in the May/June 2004 issue of *Psychology Today*.

tered finalists will compete against one another in a televised, two-hour beauty contest. For the anthropologist, here is an artifact that promises to combine some of the most significant aspects of contemporary American life: grueling competition, the possibility of extreme social humiliation, and plenty of women in bathing suits.

The fact that so many people eagerly undergo such dramatic procedures (and that millions of people watch them do it) suggests that something deeper is at work here. In fact, the desire for self-transformation has been a part of American life since the earliest days of the republic. How many other countries can count a best-selling self-help author such as Benjamin Franklin among their founding fathers? Cosmetic surgery, once a slightly shameful activity, is now performed at elite medical institutions such as the Mayo Clinic and Johns Hopkins University. According to the American Society of Aesthetic Plastic Surgery, Americans underwent 8.3 million cosmetic medical procedures in 2003. That figure represents a 20 percent increase from the previous year and a 293 percent increase since 1997.

At the beginning of the twentieth century, sociologist Charles Cooley described the American identity as a "looking-glass self." Our sense of ourselves, wrote Cooley, is formed by our imagination of the way we appear in the eyes of others. Other people are a looking glass in which we see not merely our own reflection but a judgment about the value of that reflection. ("Each to each a looking glass/Reflects the other that doth pass," he wrote.) If we are lucky, we feel pride in that imagined self; if not, we feel mortification.

The metaphor of the looking glass suggests Narcissus, bewitched by his own image, but Cooley did not think that we are entirely self-centered. As he pointed out, we are often keenly aware of the characteristics of the people in whose minds we imagine ourselves. We are more self-conscious about our looks in the presence of people who are exceptionally beautiful, and more ashamed of being cowardly in the presence of the brave. But in the end, when we gaze into the looking glass, we are interested in the reflections mainly because they are ours. "Enough about me," as the old joke goes. "What do *you* think about me?"

In fact, there is a sense in which Cooley's looking-glass self is built right   5
into our moral system. The moral ideal at work here is "recognition." As the philosopher Charles Taylor has written, today we feel that it is crucially important to be recognized and respected for who we are. This has not always been the case. The desire for recognition is not as important in times or places in which identity is considered immutable and predetermined—where it is part of the natural order, for example, or part of a social hierarchy. We find recognition so important today precisely because so many aspects of our identities are neither immutable nor predetermined. We are not simply born into a caste or social role. We are expected to build an individual identity for ourselves by virtue of how we

live and the way we present ourselves to others. Manners, accent, clothes, hair, job, home, even personality: All are now seen as objects of individual control that express something important about who we are.

But building a successful identity cannot be done in isolation. It depends on the recognition of others. And that recognition can be withheld. (You can insist you are a woman, for example, while others insist you are really a man.) Sometimes recognition can be given, yet given in a way that demeans the person being recognized. It's no surprise that from its inception, cosmetic surgery has been enthusiastically employed to efface markers of ethnicity, such as the "Jewish nose" or "Asian eyes." Recognition is necessary for self-respect, and if it is denied, as W. E. B. Du Bois famously put it, one is placed in the position of "measuring one's soul by the tape of a world that looks on in amused contempt and pity." Many Americans have given up on changing the world and have decided to change themselves instead.

Some people will see shows such as *Extreme Makeover* and *The Swan* as a kind of institutionalized cruelty. After all, they search for contestants whose special psychological vulnerability is an abiding shame about their physical appearance, and then offer them the chance for redemption only if they agree to appear on national television in their underwear. (A Fox vice president, sounding eerily like Nurse Ratched from *One Flew Over the Cuckoo's Nest*, adds that contestants will be put through "rigorous emotional and physical reconditioning.")

Yet there is something weirdly appropriate about cosmetic surgery winding up on television. This may be the logical end point of the looking-glass self. It is not just that people on television are on average much better-looking than the rest of us, though that is certainly true. It is also that the average American spends four hours a day watching television. It would be surprising if all that viewing time did not make us more self-conscious. As the novelist David Foster Wallace puts it, four hours a day spent watching television means four hours a day of unconscious reinforcement that genuine human worth dwells in the phenomenon of being watched. No wonder we can't turn away.

Absolutely the Pitts: MTV's and Fox's Plastic-Surgery Shows Mess with Faces—and Heads

MARC PEYSER

BEFORE READING: Why has there been a surge of interest in recent years in reality shows about "remaking" people by means of plastic surgery?

Remember the good old days when TV networks copied each other without even trying to be creative? Now every ripoff comes with a twist, as in "How about *Survivor* where all the challenges make you sick?" or "Let's do *The Bachelor* with little people!" But none of those copycats are as shameless as the imitators spawned by *Extreme Makeover*, a feel-good show that follows people before, during, and after plastic surgery. In fact, MTV's *I Want a Famous Face* and Fox's *The Swan* may be two of the ugliest reality shows yet.

I Want a Famous Face is disgusting in so many ways, it's hard to know where to begin. The show is exactly what it sounds like—a look at people who not only don't like their appearance, they want to assume the identity of their favorite celebrity. A plus-size woman gets tucked, lifted, and lipoed in hopes of looking like Kate Winslet. A professional Britney Spears impersonator goes in for Britney-size breasts. Most freakish of all, identical twins *both* want to look like Brad Pitt. Do any of these wanna-bes end up looking like their idols? Occasionally. But that's not the point. *Famous Face* sends horrendous messages about self-esteem and celebrity worship, not to mention potentially demoralizing young viewers who can't afford this kind of plastic happiness. MTV, which doesn't pay for the medical work, argues it's just monitoring a social phenomenon—it calls *Famous Face* a documentary, not a reality show. But every time a doctor comes on screen, the producers play music that chimes "ta-da!" like an angel has entered the room. That's hardly the work of a serious documentary.

MTV is clearly nervous about how *Famous Face* might affect its impressionable audience. The show goes out of its way to include gruesome footage of the procedures, apparently to convince viewers that plastic surgery is no picnic. To underline that warning, many episodes include a short segment called "Another Story," where various patients soberly ex-

---

Marc Peyser is a senior writer for *Newsweek*'s Arts and Entertainment section, covering television. He earlier served as a general editor of the arts portion of the magazine's Nation section. He has a background in English and journalism and early in his career was a newspaper reporter in New Jersey. This article appeared in the April 12, 2004, issue of *Newsweek*.

plain how their surgery was botched. But all the blood and pain are largely forgotten by the end of the show, when the medically induced celebrities return and proclaim themselves thrilled. "Now when I go out, I know I'm looking good," says one "Pitt" twin, who required chin implants, jaw implants, cheek implants, a nose job, and tooth veneers to achieve the desired effect. "It's good to have that confidence." The message is clear, unbeautiful people. Brads do have more fun.

Review tapes of *The Swan* haven't been circulated yet—that's not unusual for reality shows—but the concept is creepy even for Fox. Each week two self-described "ugly" women get plastic surgery. At the end of each episode, judges decide which one is most improved. Nasty? It gets worse. The winners go on to compete in a beauty pageant, where they'll suffer the same shallow and judgmental treatment that drove them to plastic surgery in the first place. One of them, of course, will win. Everyone else goes back to being a loser.

All to Be Tall

JOE KITA

BEFORE READING: Should any restrictions be placed on unnecessary plastic surgery? Where would you draw the line?

Vertically challenged men are paying up to $80,000 to have their legs broken, caged, and then lengthened.

The gain: 3 inches.

The pain: extraordinary.

The cages surround Jim Conran's legs like little scaffolds. Each has eleven metal pins that screw into his broken bones. Every six hours, he must turn these pins ever so slightly in order to tighten wires that pull the bones apart and align them correctly. He has been doing this now for sixty-eight days. And all the time, the pain has been intensifying.

"It's like tuning a violin," he explains. "With each turn of the knobs,   5 the ligaments and muscles and skin come under more tension. Each day

Joe Kita is a writer and editor at *Men's Health*. His book *GuyQ* (2003) is a compilation of the 1,305 best tips on men's health and fitness published in the fifteen years of the magazine's existence. When at forty he hit a mid-life crisis, he looked back at his biggest regrets and decided to do something about them. The result was the humorous *Another Shot: How I Relived My Life in Less Than a Year* (2001). Another year was devoted to systematically confronting each of his fears. Those experiences are recounted in *Accidental Courage: Finding Out I'm a Bit Brave After All* (2002). This article appeared in the January/February 2004 issue of *Men's Health*.

everything gets tighter. It's incredibly painful." So much so that Conran[1] won't allow himself to sleep for longer than three hours. "I'm frightened I'll miss a dose of medication, and the pain will get ahead of me," he says. Recently, he was given morphine, and that's helped somewhat. But he's still confined to a wheelchair and can stagger only short distances around his Manhattan apartment.

Before you start pitying Conran, you should know that he was not in a horrible accident that shattered his legs, nor does he suffer from a birth defect that's finally being corrected. No, he is an otherwise healthy, forty-five-year-old, single attorney who is paying $70,000 for this voluntary procedure. In fact, he's been looking forward to this for much of his life. Despite how it seems, he is living his dream.

You see, Jim Conran is $5'5\frac{3}{4}''$ tall. Or rather, he was $5'5\frac{3}{4}''$ tall. In the past few months, he has "grown" 1 millimeter per day (about $\frac{1}{25}''$) by turning his 22 pins ever so precisely. And as he's done so, new bone has been steadily forming in the gaps where the segments of tibia and fibula are being pulled apart. When he last checked—and he checks daily—he was $5'8\frac{1}{4}''$. When he (hopefully) reaches his goal height of $5'9''$ and this violin tuning ends, he's confident his life will finally be in harmony.

Short. It's a five-letter word that carries four-letter connotations for men below the national average of $5'9''$. Unless you're one of them, you don't know how much it hurts to be called that.

Imagine this scenario. You've been accepted at Harvard, West Point, and Annapolis. You're an A student. You've won seven varsity letters, and you nearly qualified for the Olympics. Yet to get into West Point (your first choice), you must meet a height requirement of $5'6''$. You're slightly below that. So the night before your admittance physical, you have your father repeatedly whack you on top of the head with a textbook in order to raise a bump. Next day, you officially measure in at $5'6\frac{1}{16}''$. You go on to graduate with honors, serve your country overseas, and eventually end up as an aide to the president of the United States. And you know, your whole life long, that you might have missed all of this—by a quarter inch.

"From a very early age, you start getting clear, institutionalized mes-   10 sages that you're less desirable," says George Holdt, the soldier in question, who, like Conran, is now undergoing limb lengthening. "From the violence you experience in school to the behavior you encounter throughout your social and professional life, the discrimination is always there."

Today, height requirements in any workplace are largely a thing of the past (the military's cutoff is now 5'). But it's an example of the frustration that is the legacy of the diminutive man. And no, it isn't his imagination. Numerous scientific studies have verified the advantages of height. For example, taller men . . .

---

[1] The name has been changed for privacy. —Eds.

. . . Are more likely to be hired. When recruiters in one study from Eastern Michigan University were asked to choose between two equally qualified candidates who differed in height, 72 percent chose the taller applicant.

. . . Make more money. Graduating seniors at the University of Pittsburgh who were 6'2" or taller enjoyed starting salaries $4,000 higher than counterparts 5'5" or under. Economists at the University of Pennsylvania even estimate that added height is worth nearly 2 percent in additional income per inch per annum.

. . . Are chosen as leaders. Nancy Etcoff, Ph.D., a professor of psychology at Harvard Medical School, points out in her book *Survival of the Prettiest*, "the easiest way to predict the winner in a United States election is to bet on the taller man." Of 43 American presidents, only five have been significantly below average height. What's more, Etcoff cites a study of *Fortune* 500 CEOs that found that more than half were taller than 6 feet, and just 3 percent were shorter than 5'7".

. . . Make better first impressions. Surveys by Henry Biller, Ph.D., a 15 professor of psychology at the University of Rhode Island and coauthor of *Stature and Stigma*, show that compared with shorter men, guys of average and above-average height are seen as "more mature, uninhibited, positive, secure, masculine, active, complete, successful, optimistic, dominant, capable, confident, and outgoing."

While all of this pisses off short guys, what really bothers them is how they're viewed by women. Walter W. Windisch, Ph.D., is a psychologist in Towson, Maryland, who evaluates short men who are considering limb lengthening. "The average patient," he notes, "is 28 years old, male, college educated, professional, of some financial means, the product of parents who expressed concern about height, and, in every case, single."

Indeed, if you read the personals section of your local newspaper or log onto any online dating service, you'll find lots of ads from women listing height preferences. Why are they so particular, especially when they're paying by the letter? Certainly a portion of it stems from the statistics cited earlier — that taller men earn more and enjoy a higher social status. Some of it also comes from Hollywood, where leading ladies routinely look up into the eyes of the tall, dark, and handsome man. It's the romantic ideal. But a good chunk is also based on an almost primitive assessment. Is he a good provider, a worthy protector, a gifted procreator? And on some anthropological level, it's as if she ultimately decides the short man is not. Less than one-half of 1 percent of women marry men who are shorter than they are, according to Etcoff.

"Someone once asked Sigmund Freud, 'What is the goal of life?' and his answer was, 'To love and to work,'" says Windisch. "That's a fairly good summary of what's bugging these guys. They're looking to love and be loved, to work and be valued. It's just that their stature, something totally beyond their control, is keeping them from it."

About 2,500 kilometers east of Moscow, at the western edge of Siberia, is the Ilizarov Scientific Center for Restorative Traumatology and Orthopedics. Located in the Russian city of Kurgan, in the shadow of the Ural Mountains, it was founded in 1971 by Professor Gavriil Abramovich Ilizarov. Decades earlier, faced with treating a large number of World War II veterans with complicated limb fractures, he began experimenting with "circular external fixators" to keep bones aligned and to speed heal ing. Their use as limb-lengthening tools, however, was discovered by accident. While Ilizarov was on vacation, a nurse adjusted a fixator in the wrong direction. When he returned and examined the patient's X-ray, he noticed new bone forming in the gap. This set the stage for a variety of new applications, including the correction of leg-length deformities, bow legs, anchondroplasia (dwarfism), and, lately, short stature. More than a half century later, the Ilizarov method — as it's come to be known — is still being used in a surprisingly unevolved form throughout the world.

Here's how it works: After taking a series of X-rays to map out the pre- 20 cise dimensions of the bones, the surgeon orders a regional anesthetic and makes two half-inch-long incisions in each leg (usually below the knee). Using a surgical chisel, he then cracks the tibias and fibulas, being careful to disrupt as little of the surrounding tissue as possible. (Note: When a doctor breaks your legs, it's called an "osteotomy.") Next, he attaches the circular aluminum frames. This requires piercing each leg with eleven arrow-sharp carbide pins and pushing them in until they bottom out against bone. The pins are of varying lengths and diameters, with the thicker ones being positioned closer to the breaks for added stability. Once the pins are in position, the surgeon slowly screws them into the hard calcium-and-collagen shell that surrounds the marrow. The rest is comparatively straightforward: Affix the adjustment wires to the pins, sew the two osteotomy incisions shut, treat and bandage the pin wounds. For all that's involved, the entire operation takes just $2\frac{1}{2}$ hours. Patients typically remain in the hospital for two to three days, after which they can take a dozen or so steps.

But this is the easy part. The frames usually stay on for three to six months, during which time the bones are gradually separated. This is called the "distraction phase." All but one of the men we spoke with said that, even with heavy doses of narcotics, such as Vicodin, the resulting pain was just on the edge of bearable.

"It will reduce the toughest man to a crying little girl in a matter of weeks," says Jack Turner, a 39-year-old salesman who "grew" $2\frac{1}{2}$ inches as a result of this surgery.

"It's an act of aggression against your own body," adds Conran.

Just as difficult is the helplessness that results. Patients are dependent on wheelchairs, walkers, and the supportive arms of friends and relatives to get around. Most are bedridden except for periodic doctor visits and daily physical therapy. Work is out of the question. This is true not only during the distraction phase but also for three months or more after the frames come off and the new bone is hardening. "You need somebody to take care of you virtually all the time," says Rick Morgan, another patient. "Sometimes you can't even reach the bathroom."

Although some doctors make lofty promises, most legs won't tolerate 25 being stretched past three inches. It's not the bones that balk but rather the muscles and tendons that surround them. Overall, there's a 25 percent complication rate from this surgery, with the most frequent problem being pin-site infection. That's why patients are given a prescription for oral antibiotics, which they're told to begin taking at the first sign of redness, tenderness, or discolored drainage at the pin entry points. If an infection goes unnoticed, it will spread into the deep leg tissue and then the bone.

A less common but still serious complication is nerve damage. In one study review of 814 limb lengthenings, approximately 10 percent of patients had experienced some form of temporary nerve damage, characterized by chronic pain or impaired motor skills.

But the most catastrophic possibility doesn't present itself until the frames are removed. Even though the doctor will have taken X-rays to gauge structural integrity (the whiter the area, the stronger the bone), there's still a chance that what took months of agonizing pain and tens of thousands of dollars to build will, at the moment of truth, snap. Or the new bone will hold, only to buckle and break weeks later. Either way, doctors call this a refracture; there's a one-in-twelve chance of its happening.

If you're a short man seeking salvation through surgery, you've probably heard of the International Center for Limb Lengthening, in Baltimore. An affiliate of Sinai Hospital, the ICLL was the first facility of its kind in North America and remains the largest—half of all the limb lengthenings for height are performed here. The bulk of its business, however, deals with correcting functional deformities. "I'm very strict when it comes to doing this surgery on otherwise healthy people," says fortyseven-year-old chief surgeon Dror Paley, M.D., himself 6'. "In fact, I try to discourage it. The magnitude of what you have to go through is so large, it's not in the realm of having your nose done or your tummy tucked."

Dr. Paley generally will not operate on men over 5'6" (or women over 5'2"), and he requires that all prospective patients first undergo an intensive, ten-hour psychological exam by Windisch. Only about 10 percent go on to have the operation. "You must be careful," says Dr. Paley. "I've had some real nutcases—people who were willing to sell their houses, steal their wives' money, do unbelievable things for a few extra inches."

Depending on the facility and the specifics of the case, those inches 30 typically run between $50,000 and $80,000. When limb lengthening is done on a healthy person, medical insurance won't pay for it. However, if done to correct a leg-length discrepancy, bow legs, or any other limb deformity, it is usually covered.

Some of those people who can't raise the necessary funds or who don't pass the screening process go elsewhere—like Jack Turner, who ended up in Italy after being "dumped," as he calls it, by Dr. Paley. "The cost turned out to be one-eighth what it was in America," he explains, "and I felt I got better care."

And yet, even though it's been almost three years since Turner had his operation, he says he's still at only 80 percent of his former physical ability. "I don't think anyone can break both legs and come back 100 percent," he says. "For instance, I can't run as fast, and I have pain when the weather is damp."

The long-term effects are unknown. Although some doctors insist that dwarves who were lengthened as much as a foot decades ago show no traces of bone weakening or arthritis, other experts remain skeptical. "There's an enormous risk," says Michael Ain, M.D., a 4'3" orthopedic surgeon at Johns Hopkins Hospital in Baltimore. "Nobody really knows what's going to happen to people getting this surgery."

Neither the American Society for Aesthetic Plastic Surgery nor the American Academy of Orthopedic Surgeons (AAOS) endorses cosmetic limb lengthening. Others condemn it outright. "I'm appalled that our society has become so imbued with self-image that patients are willing to put their necks on the line like this. There are just too many risks," says William Tipton, M.D., director of medical affairs for the AAOS. "And the surgeons who are doing these operations on otherwise healthy people should remember this: *Primum non nocere.* That's Latin for 'First, no injury.'"

One of those surgeons is S. Robert Rozbruch, M.D., director of the In-   35 stitute for Limb Lengthening and Reconstruction at the Hospital for Special Surgery, in New York City. He counters: "Seeing the profound impact this surgery can have on someone has convinced me that, for a very select group of people, it should be brought out of the closet and done more freely."

Paul Steven Miller, for one, thinks limb lengthening is unnecessary. Miller is an attorney and the commissioner of the U.S. Equal Employment Opportunity Commission. He also happens to be a 4'5" dwarf, who has experienced height discrimination firsthand. "One law firm told me they feared their clients would think they were running a circus freak show if they hired me," he recounts. Nonetheless, Miller says cosmetic limb lengthening is "silly." "I have a hard time believing it really makes a difference in these people's lives."

With predicted advances in limb lengthening, combined with the recent FDA approval of growth-hormone therapy for short children, will Diminutive Man soon take his place next to Cro-Magnon in the Museum of Natural History? Are we entering an era of stature cleansing?

"The way we need to judge this," says David Sandberg, Ph.D., an associate professor of psychiatry at the University of Buffalo's School of Medicine, "is not by what's happening physically to these patients. Rather, what must be demonstrated is that increased height is actually translating into a better quality of life."

And only the patients themselves can assess that. Among the men we spoke with, sentiments are mixed. "It's kind of like the old P. T. Barnum thing," says Turner, "where you pay a quarter to go look at something that isn't very good. But when you come out, you have to basically say it was great. Not getting 3+ inches was disappointing, but on the other hand, I'm much more comfortable being 5'7" than 5'4+". I can only surmise that it's making subtle differences in my life. Overall, I think it's a great way for men with a height issue to increase their rank in the pecking order, but you're not going to suddenly be dating supermodels."

"Before I had this surgery, I was depressed and very self-conscious," 40 says Mark Pace, DO, an osteopath in South Florida who was 4'11". "I was afraid to walk into a roomful of children because they would make fun of me, and I could barely talk to women. I had zero confidence. Now, I'm just under 5'3", and the difference is unbelievable. I'm seeing eye-to-eye with people, and I'm actually dating."

"I've gained about $2\frac{1}{2}$ inches," says Conran, "and it feels great. In fact, I'm reluctant to let the thrill wear off. I'm almost 5'9". Now, I sure don't consider that tall, but it's not short. It's average, and that's all I ever wanted to be. I wanted to be accepted on my own merits without having my height held against me."

"I can't wait to walk down the streets of New York City, visit my old neighborhood, and see things from a slightly different perspective," adds Jose Rodriguez, who recently got his frames removed and is $2\frac{3}{4}$ inches taller. "Those extra inches make you a little more confident, a little more happy, and the day a little brighter."

If you're still skeptical, Rodriguez suggests an experiment. "Take a few books, set them on the floor, and stand on top of them," he says. "You don't think a couple of inches can make a difference, but it's amazing."

Smooth Operations

ALLISON SAMUELS

> BEFORE READING: Why do you think few African Americans elected to have cosmetic surgery until quite recently?

Long before Janet Jackson revealed a little too much of her body, Tanisha Rollins was obsessed with having one just like it. After watching the singer strut in a 1993 video, Rollins embarked on a quest for

---

Allison Samuels is a correspondent in *Newsweek*'s Los Angeles bureau, covering sports and entertainment. Earlier she worked as a researcher at Quincy Jones Entertainment and as a reporter for the *Los Angeles Times*. She is on the UCLA Black Studies Department Board of Directors. This article is from the July 5, 2004, issue of *Newsweek*.

washboard abs. For the next decade she stuck to a rigorous regimen. But her abs pretty much stayed the same. Then a friend skipped all the hard work and got a tummy tuck. "I was just like, 'What magazines have you been reading?!'" says Rollins, twenty-nine, an administrative assistant in Dayton, Ohio. She thought nipping and tucking was only for "rich white people and Michael Jackson," not African American women like her, making $30,000 a year.

Last year Rollins shelled out $5,000 for a tummy tuck of her own, joining the small but growing ranks of African Americans opting for cosmetic surgery. The number of blacks seeking facial or reconstructive surgery more than tripled between 1997 and 2002, reflecting both the growing affluence of African Americans and the subtle easing of some long-held cultural taboos against such procedures. Except for the Jacksons (or perhaps because of them), even black celebrities, whose looks are essential to their livelihood, have been loath to go under the knife. "I was just so worried about looking crazy or looking like Jennifer Grey, who no one recognized after she had her nose job," says one forty-year-old black actress, who decided last year to have her nose and breasts done after being inspired by singer Patti LaBelle. (Though LaBelle, sixty, talks about her nose job, the actress requested anonymity.)

In an age when plastic surgeons advertise their services on the subway, it may come as a surprise that cosmetic surgery is frowned upon in the black community. "People want to look good," says Dr. Karen Low, who is African American and a plastic surgeon in Greensboro, North Carolina, "but they also want to avoid any criticism that might come from the community, which has for years supported larger frames, wider noses, and not-so-perfect features. Changing those things is sometimes seen as an insult to our ancestors and to the culture." Rollins experienced that backlash when she told her family she was having a tummy tuck. Not only did they think it was risky and expensive, they couldn't understand why she wanted to tinker with "God's work." "It's hard telling your mother that you don't want to look like her when you're fifty," Rollins says. "I think my mother resented that and felt hurt, but I had to be honest."

There's a lot more at work here than simple vanity. "I think African American women have finally just decided that it's time to love ourselves," says *Essence* magazine beauty editor Miki Taylor. African Americans have become the biggest consumers of beauty products in the United States, spending at least $20 billion a year, as companies like L'Oreal, which opened its Institute for Ethnic Hair and Skin Research in 2003, are well aware. The increase in plastic surgery is in many ways an extension of that trend.

Blacks accounted for nearly 5 percent of the 8.7 million cosmetic-surgery procedures done last year. As the numbers have grown, doctors have had to adapt to their clientele. For starters, black women and white women tend to want to tune up different areas of their bodies. While the   5 nose is Job No. 1 for whites, black women's top request is the tummy tuck. Breast enhancement? More black women want reductions. "Let's be clear that I did it for my health," says rapper-actress Queen Latifah, who went from a double-E bra cup to a D. Facelifts are not as popular as they are among white women, a testament, perhaps, to a long-held belief in the African American community: "Black don't crack."

But black skin does scar, much more easily than white skin, and that has been a big deterrent to African Americans considering elective surgery. Doctors try to be as minimally invasive as possible, using lasers and making smaller incisions, hiding scars in inconspicuous places, and using electron-beam radiation to diminish the appearance of scars. Dermatologist Marcia Glenn, who opened Odyssey Medispa in Marina del Rey, California, with an eye toward African American women like herself, encourages patients to try less-invasive procedures like Botox before choosing surgery.

Like many women who have cosmetic surgery, Patti LaBelle was hoping to cut away at her insecurities in the process. Looking at childhood pictures, "I realized I wasn't a very good-looking girl," says the singer, who was teased mercilessly about her broad nose. "I didn't like the way that made me feel." As middle age sank in, she hoped surgery would make her feel better about herself. Rather than go for a button nose, LaBelle was sensitive about keeping her features looking African American. "Nothing drastic, just enough to make me feel and look as good as I could," she says. "If, in a few years, I want to get some more work done on my chin or my neck, I will."

How Men Really Feel about Their Bodies

TED SPIKER

BEFORE READING: Are men and women equally concerned about body image? Explain.

Dressed only in my underwear, I'm eight years old and sitting on the pediatrician's exam table, waiting for my checkup. My mother points to the two mounds of fatty flesh between my chest and belly. She asks the doctor, "Could they be tumors?"

"No," he says, "it's just fat."

Since that day, my fat has absorbed more darts than the back wall of a bar.

When I turned fourteen, my new doctor asked me, "Do you get embarrassed on the beach because of your femininely shaped hips and chest?" . . . In high school, locker-room jokesters composed a song about my love handles. And in college, a friend analyzed my body shape by explaining that I have "a low center of gravity and those childbearing hips."

At 6′2″ and 215 pounds, I'm not huge. I just carry my weight where women do—in my hips, butt, and thighs. And I hate it. I hate the way clothes fit. I hate that friends say I use the "big-butt defense" in basketball. 5

But I'm not the only man who wishes his body looked more like Michael Jordan's and less like a vat of pudding. A recent survey showed that only 18 percent of men are happy enough with their physiques that they wouldn't change them. "Men used to see their bodies as functional objects—to lift things, to play sports, to do something," says Roberto Olivardia, Ph.D., a clinical psychologist at Harvard Medical School and coauthor of *The Adonis Complex*. "Over the past 20 years, the tide has changed. The idea of men's bodies as sexual objects has intensified."

So while women got there first, they don't have a monopoly on stressing over looks. Here, eight fundamental truths about men:

1. We have more body angst than you realize, but we'll never have a serious conversation with you about it.

Look at the standards we have to measure up to: If we're fat, we're labeled as beer-guzzling couch potatoes. Too thin, and we're deemed wimpy. Too short, and we're ruled out for a date. We can have too little hair on our heads or too much on our backs. And maybe worst of all, we can be too big in the backside of our pants yet too small in the front.

Ted Spiker, an assistant professor of journalism at the University of Florida, is a contributing editor to *Men's Health* and collaborated with Ted Zinczenko on *The Abs Diet: The Six-Week Plan to Flatten Your Stomach and Keep You Lean for Life* (2004). This article appeared in the August 2003 *O: The Oprah Magazine*.

Now add the fact that our mental struggle has two layers. "A man 10 thinks, Not only does it bother me that I'm fat and my hair is thinning. It bothers me that it bothers me, because I'm not supposed to feel this way," says Thomas Cash, Ph.D., a professor of psychology at Old Dominion University in Norfolk, Virginia. "The thinking is that it's like a woman to worry about looks."

So we won't talk to you about our insecurities. Nor will you ever catch us asking a friend for advice: "Hey Bill, do these pants slim my beer gut? Do I need to trim my chest hair? Which accentuates my triceps, the blue shirt or the red?"

2. Instead, we'll joke about our bodies.

When a friend recently saw the size of the pizza I was about to eat, he said, "Ted, that pizza should have its own zip code." I responded, "So should my ass." We make fun of ourselves to cover up what we're really feeling—frustration, embarrassment, and anger that we're not perfect.

But other people's jokes sting. Mark Meador, thirty-seven, of Westerville, Ohio, returned from a trip to Disney World with photos of himself. "Man, you look like Big Pun," Meador's friend said, referring to the obese rapper who died of a heart attack. Meador laughed off the comment, not letting on that it hurt. That same weekend, his daughter said, "Dad, you look like you're having a baby." Fortunately for Meador, the gentle pokes inspired him to change. He dropped junk food, started Tae Bo, and lost more than forty pounds.

3. We're worried about our bodies because we're competing for 15 you—and against you.

With more people both marrying later and getting divorced, it's a competitive environment for finding mates. And since this generation of women can support themselves, they're freer to pick a man for his cute butt. Lynne Luciano, Ph.D., who has researched body-image issues at California State University at Dominguez Hills, says women are tired of being objectified and have turned the tables on men. "They don't like a man to be overly vain," she says. "He shouldn't care too much about the way he looks, but on the other hand, he should look good."

At the same time, men are also shaping up because they're seeing that people who are fit are more successful at work. "Women are very good at using their looks for competition," Cash says. "So men think, I'd better clean up my act."

4. We're not just checking you out.

We're a visual gender. We like the way you look. A lot. But that doesn't mean we don't compare ourselves to other men the way women compare themselves to other women. I notice the way men look on the beach, at work, or simply walking by. Maybe it's male competitiveness or primal instincts, but we don't just want to have better bodies to attract you. We want better bodies to improve our position among ourselves. A scary thought that proves the point: When Luciano interviewed doctors who perform penis enlargements, they reported that the main reason

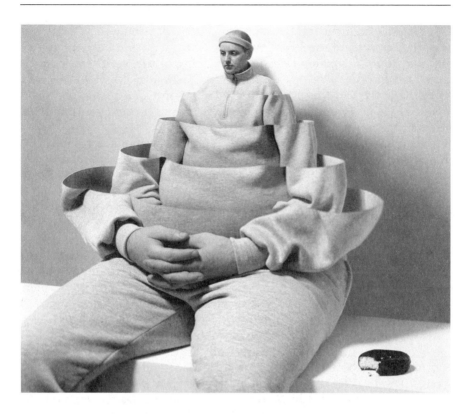

men undergo the surgery isn't to improve their relationships but to be more impressive in the locker room.

5. We want to look like we're twenty-five.   20

It used to be that our mythical heroes had wisdom, experience, and maturity. Think Harrison Ford as Indiana Jones. Now our heroes are baby faced with six-pack abs. Think Tobey Maguire as Spider-Man. "The youth movement has been cruel to men," says Luciano. "The Cary Grants have fallen though the cracks. Today's ideal is younger, buffer, more muscular. A lot of men in their 40s and 50s have trouble trying to emulate that." So men, like women, are swimming against the age current. That might explain why from 1997 to 2001, the number of men who had cosmetic surgery increased 256 percent. (Last year more than 800,000 men — and north of six million women — went under the knife.)

Fear of aging also explains why going bald is so painful. We can try to stop it (Rogaine, Propecia), hide it (hats, comb-overs), or live with it (doing nothing, shaving our heads), but hair loss signifies a loss of vitality and control. "If a man's not in a relationship, if he hasn't fallen in love, he figures that's it, that's the end of romance," Cash says. "He thinks no one will ever want to be with him."

6. Desperation makes us do desperate things. Delusion makes us do nothing.

I can't remember the last pair of pants that fit me well. If I buy size 38s, they fit around the waist but suffocate my hips and butt. If I go to a 40, they're roomy where I need it but gaping in the waist. Several years ago, I tried on my wife's post-pregnancy size-20 jeans to see if they were cut differently. Did I just admit that? Trying on women's jeans—this is about as low as it gets, I thought. Then I realized it could get lower: The jeans fit me perfectly.

I wore those jeans for six months, and I felt leaner every day I wore them. My wife asked me why I didn't just buy a big pair of men's jeans and have a tailor alter them. My answer: Why pay for alterations when I know that tomorrow I'm going to start an exercise routine that will change my body shape forever? It's been my mantra for two decades. 25

7. Men's body-image problems can be just as dangerous as women's.

For some men, poor body image can lead to anger, anxiety, depression, sexual dysfunction, and steroid abuse. Doctors may fail to recognize eating disorders or muscle dysmorphia (the need to constantly bulk up), even though it's estimated that eating disorders affect one million men. Olivardia, the Harvard psychologist, says secrecy reinforces the patients' sense of shame. "I've treated men who would tell people they were alcoholics, but they'd never admit they were bulimic," he says.

Cody Swann, a twenty-one-year-old graduate student from Stuart, Florida, was so obsessed with being thin that he measured himself on a body-fat scale every day. "I remember how happy I was when I stood on the thing and it came back 'error' because I didn't have enough body fat for it to read," he says. "It wouldn't read below 2 percent, which is what I was. Woohoo, can't do much better than that." It took Swann one year to realize he was anorexic. At six feet tall, Swann is now a muscular 205 pounds and feels he has overcome the disorder. But he still obsesses about his appearance. He exercises three to four hours every day and has eaten in a restaurant only twice in the past two years. If he can't weigh his food, he won't eat it. Swann watches every last morsel. "My rule is that I have to chew a piece of gum for thirty minutes so I burn off the calories in it."

8. We don't blame anyone (except maybe Tiger Woods and Taco Bell). But we'll be grateful to anyone who makes us feel good about shaping up.

We know what it's like to be bombarded with images of perfect bodies. We see the men in commercials and on magazine covers, the bigger-stronger-better mentality that dominates our culture. "Look at Tiger Woods. The best golfer in the world has an outstanding physique. Golfers used to be everyday men," says J. Kevin Thompson, Ph.D., professor of psychology at the University of South Florida. "Basketball players used to be skinny. They're all muscular now." Hell, even our president runs sub-seven-minute miles. 30

As much as I'd like to, I won't blame my shape on genetics or the media. I'd love to blame stress or lack of time. But the real culprit is my elephantine appetite and a four-times-a-week Taco Bell habit.

Nine years ago, though, I'd had enough. I took a 150-mile charity bike ride and gained weight rather than lost it because of all the cookies I ate at the pit stops. That was my epiphany. Four months later, I dropped from my all-time high of 231 pounds to 191. My wife dubbed me "Little" as I started to lose weight. That encouragement kept me on my program. But now I'm back around 215 and want desperately to drop to 180—for my health, for my looks, for my confidence, for the quest to find a perfect-fitting pair of pants.

It's not that I can't change my body; it's just that I haven't. All I do know is that I'll never stop trying to shrink my hips, tighten my gut, and deflate my rear tire. Because if there's one thing I believe in, it's that every love-handle story should have a happy ending.

Not Too Rich or Too Thin

LISA TAKEUCHI CULLEN

> BEFORE READING: There is an old saying that "you can never be too rich or too thin." Do you tend to associate images of slender bodies with the wealthy? Why or why not?

One of the first things that strike foreigners visiting the United States is that the rich tend to be skinny and the poor fat. Studies bear this out. The less money you have in America, the likelier you are to be overweight. One in 4 adults below the poverty level is obese, compared with 1 in 6 in households with an income of $67,000 or more. For minorities, poverty has an even heavier effect: Obesity strikes one in three poor African Americans.

On the surface, this makes little sense. If the poor must struggle to buy groceries, how can they pack away enough to gain all that weight? The assumption used to be that the poor were making bad food and lifestyle choices—Krispy Kremes instead of crispy greens. But now researchers have begun to suspect that the blame lies elsewhere.

The cost of food—quality food—is perhaps the best place to start. Calorically speaking, the best bang for the buck tends to be packed with sugar, fat, and refined grains (think cookies and candy bars). In general, processed foods hog ever larger portions of all Americans' diets—one reason we spend just a tenth of our incomes on food today, compared with a fifth in 1950. But a pound of lean steak costs a lot more than a pound of hot dogs. "The stomach is a dumb organ," says J. Larry Brown,

Lisa Takeuchi Cullen writes for *Time* magazine. This article appeared in the June 7, 2004, issue.

director of the Center on Hunger and Poverty in Waltham, Massachusetts. "It doesn't know anything about quality. It knows only when it's full."

Processed foods aren't just cheap, tasty, and filling. They're also more accessible. One study found that 28 percent of Americans live in what nutritionists call "food deserts," places where big supermarkets are at least ten miles, or a twenty-minute drive, away. People who live in these places wind up buying much of their daily groceries from convenience stores or gas stations, where they can find Chef Boyardee but not baby carrots. Some communities are trying to remedy this. Philadelphia, for instance, recently announced a $100 million effort to open ten supermarkets in urban neighborhoods. But for much of the country, says Troy Blanchard, a sociology professor at Mississippi State University who studies this issue, "you have people who are literally distanced out of healthy diets."

Children of the poor face especially steep odds in fighting obesity.   5
The cash-strapped schools many of them attend are more likely than others to cut physical-education classes and strike franchise deals with snack-food and beverage makers. After school, working parents would rather their kids stay inside watching TV than play outside in unsafe streets. Those hours in front of the tube, meanwhile, feed them a diet of ads heavy on sugary cereals and greasy burgers. No wonder obese adolescents are twice as likely to come from low-income families.

Though the ballooning obesity problem among the poor is finally getting the attention of academics and the government, nobody has yet come up with an easy fix. "Our remedies are very middle class," says Adam Drewnowski, director of the Center for Public Health Nutrition at the University of Washington. "They tell you, Seek a healthy diet and exercise. Well, if you're working two jobs and living in a trailer, you're in no mood to get home and make a salad." In the end, fitness may have less to do with genetics than with tax brackets.

*"Now that we're old and covered with wrinkles,
they come out with the camera phone."*

The Tyranny of the Normal

LESLIE FIEDLER

BEFORE READING: How do you define the term normal as it applies to physical appearance? Is the ability to be physically "normal" related to social class?

I am not a doctor or a nurse or a social worker, confronted in my daily rounds with the problem of physical disability; not even a lawyer, philosopher, or theologian trained to deal with its moral and legal

Leslie Fiedler (1917–2003) was best known as a literary critic and theorist. Until his death, he for many years was on the American literature faculty at the State University of New York at Buffalo. His interest in variations on the "normal" was spurred by research and interviews he did for his book *Freaks: Myths and Images of the Secret Self* (1978). This essay is from his book of the same title: *The Tyranny of the Normal* (1996).

implications. I am only a poet, novelist, critic—more at home in the world of words and metaphor than fact, which is to say, an expert, if at all, in reality once removed. Yet despite this, I have been asked on numerous occasions to address groups of health-care professionals about this subject—no doubt because I once published a book called *Freaks: Myths and Images of the Secret Self.* In that book, I was primarily interested in exploring (as the subtitle declares) the fascination of "normals" with the sort of congenital malformations traditionally displayed at Fairs and Sideshows, and especially the way in which such freaks are simultaneously understood as symbols of the absolute Other and the essential Self. Yet in the long and difficult process of putting that study together (it took almost six years of my life and led me into dark places in my own psyche I was reluctant to enter), I stumbled inadvertently into dealing also with the subject of "the care of imperiled newborns."

How difficult and dangerous a topic this was I did not realize, however, until just before my book was due to appear. I was at a party celebrating the imminent event when I mentioned offhand to one of my fellow-celebrants, a young man who turned out to be an M.D., one of the discoveries I had made in the course of my research: that in all probability more "abnormal" babies were being allowed to die (in effect, being killed) in modern hospitals than had been in the Bad Old Days when they were exposed and left to perish by their fathers. And I went on to declare that in my opinion, at least, this was not good; at which point, my interlocutor screamed at me (rather contradictorily, I thought) that what I asserted was simply not true—and that, in any case, it was perfectly all right to do so. Then he hurled his Martini glass at the wall behind me and stalked out of the room.

He did not stay long enough for me to explain that our disagreement was more than merely personal, based on more than the traditional mutual distrust of the scientist and the humanist. Both of our attitudes, I wanted to tell him, had deep primordial roots: sources far below the level of our fully conscious values and the facile rationalizations by which we customarily defend them. It is, therefore, to certain ancient myths and legends that we must turn—and here my literary expertise stands me in good stead—to understand the roots of our deep ambivalence toward fellow creatures who are perceived at any given moment as disturbingly deviant, outside currently acceptable physiological norms. That ambivalence has traditionally impelled us toward two quite different responses to the "monsters" we beget. On the one hand, we have throughout the course of history killed them—ritually at the beginning, as befits divinely sent omens of disaster, portents of doom. On the other hand, we have sometimes worshiped them as if they were themselves divine, though never without overtones of fear and repulsion. In either case, what prompted our response was a sense of wonder and awe: a feeling that such "unnatural" products of the natural process by which we continue the species are mysterious, uncanny, finally "taboo."

Though it may not be immediately evident, the most cursory analysis reveals that not only have that primitive wonder and awe persisted into our "scientific," secular age, but so also have the two most archaic ways of expressing it. In the first place, we continue to kill, or at least allow to die, monstrously malformed neonates. We euphemize the procedure, however, disguise the superstitious horror at its roots, by calling what we do "the removal of life supports from nonviable *terata*" (*terata* being Greek for "monster"). Moreover, thanks to advanced medical techniques, we can do better these days than merely fail to give malformed preemies a fair chance to prove whether or not they are really "viable." We can detect and destroy before birth, babies likely to be born deformed; even abort them wholesale when the occasion arises, as in the infamous case of the Thalidomide babies of the sixties. That was a particularly unsavory episode (which we in this country were spared), since the phocomelic infants,[1] carried by mothers dosed with an antidote prescribed for morning sickness, were in the full sense of the word "iatrogenic[2] freaks." And the doctors who urged their wholesale abortion (aware that less than half of them would prove to be deformed, but why take chances?) were in many cases the very ones who had actually prescribed the medication.

To be sure, those responsible for such pre-infanticide did not   5
confess—were not even aware, though any poet could have told them—that they were motivated by vestigial primitive fears of abnormality, exacerbated by their guilt at having caused it. They sought only, they assured themselves and the rest of the world, to spare years of suffering to the doomed children and their parents; as well as to alleviate the financial burden on those parents and the larger community, which would have to support them through what promised to be a nonproductive lifetime. We do, however, have at this point records of the subsequent lives of some of the Thalidomide babies whose parents insisted on sparing them (a wide-ranging study was made some years later in Canada), which turned out to have been, from their own point of view, at least, neither notably nonproductive, nor especially miserable. None of them, at any rate, were willing to confess that they would have wished themselves dead.

But such disconcerting facts do not faze apologists for such drastic procedures. Nor does the even more dismaying fact that the most wholehearted, full-scale attempt at teratacide occurred in Hitler's Germany, with the collaboration, by the way, of not a few quite respectable doctors and teratologists, most notably a certain Etienne Wolff of the University of Strasbourg. Not only were dwarfs and other "useless people" sent to Nazi extermination camps and parents adjudged "likely" to beget anomalous children sterilized; but other unfortunate human beings

---

[1]*Phocomelic infants:* children born with extremely short limbs. [All notes are the editors'.]

[2]*Iatrogenic:* A condition inadvertently caused by a doctor or by medical treatment.

regarded—at that time and in that society—as undesirable deviations from the Norm were also destroyed: Jews and Gypsies first of all, with Blacks, Slavs, and Mediterraneans presumably next in line. It is a development which should make us aware of just how dangerous enforced physiological normality is when the definition of its parameters falls into the hands of politicians and bureaucrats. And into what other hands can we reasonably expect it to fall in any society we know or can imagine in the foreseeable future?

Similarly, even as the responsibility for the ritual slaughter of Freaks was passing from the family to the State, the terrified adoration of Freaks was passing from the realm of worship to that of entertainment and art. To be sure, the adoration of Freaks in the Western world was never a recognized religion but at best an underground Cult. Think, for instance, of the scene in Fellini's *Satyricon*,[3] in which a Hermaphrodite is ritually displayed to a group of awestricken onlookers, who regard him as more than a curiosity, though not quite a god: after all, the two reigning myth-systems of our culture, the Hellenic and the Judaeo-Christian, both disavowed the portrayal of the divine in freakish guise, regarding as barbarous or pagan the presentation of theriomorphic, two-headed, or multilimbed divinities.

Yet there would seem always to have been a hunger in all of us, a need to behold in quasi-religious wonder our mysteriously anomalous brothers and sisters. For a long time, this need was satisfied in Courts for the privileged few, at fairs and sideshows for the general populace, by collecting and exhibiting Giants, Dwarfs, Intersexes, Joined Twins, Fat Ladies, and Living Skeletons. Consequently, even in a world that grew ever more secular and rational, we could still continue to be baffled, horrified, and moved by Freaks, as we were able to be by fewer and fewer other things once considered most sacred and terrifying. Finally though, the Sideshow began to die, even as the rulers of the world learned to be ashamed of their taste for human "curiosities." By then, however, their images had been preserved in works of art, in which their implicit meanings are made manifest.

Walk through the picture galleries of any museum in the western world and you will find side by side with the portraits of Kings and Courtesans depictions of the Freaks they once kept to amuse them, by painters as distinguished as Goya and Velasquez. Nor has the practice died out in more recent times, carried on by artists as different as Currier and Ives (who immortalized such stars of P. T. Barnum's sideshow as General Tom Thumb) and Pablo Picasso (who once spent more than a year painting over and over in ever shifting perspectives the dwarfs who first appeared in Velasquez's *Las Meninas*). Nor did other popular forms of representa-

---

[3] *Fellini's* Satyricon: Federico Fellini (1920–1993) was an Italian film director known for bizarre and colorful films, including *Satyricon* (1969).

tion abandon that intriguing subject. Not only have photographers captured on film the freaks of their time, but after a while they were portrayed in fiction as well. No sooner, in fact, had the novel been invented, than it too began to portray the monstrous and malformed as objects of pity and fear and — however secularized — wonder, always wonder. Some authors of the nineteenth century, indeed, seem so freak-haunted that remembering them, we remember first of all the monsters they created. We can scarcely think of Victor Hugo, for instance, without recalling his grotesque Hunchback of Notre Dame, any more than we can recall Charles Dickens without thinking of his monstrous dwarf, Quilp, or our own Mark Twain without remembering "Those Incredible Twins." And the tradition has been continued by postmodernists like John Barth and Donald Barthelme and Vladimir Nabakov, who, turning their backs on almost all the other trappings of the conventional novel, still reflect its obsession with Freaks.

In the twentieth century, the images of congenital malformations are, 10 as we might expect, chiefly preserved in the artform it invented, the cinema: on the one hand, in Art Films intended for a select audience of connoisseurs, like the surreal fantasies of Fellini and Ingmar Bergman; and on the other, in a series of popular movies from Todd Browning's thirties' masterpiece, *Freaks*, to the more recent *Elephant Man*, in its various versions. Browning's extraordinary film was by no means an immediate success; in fact, it horrified its earliest audience and first critics, who drove it from the screen and its director into early retirement. But it was revived in the sixties and has since continued to be replayed all over the world, particularly in colleges and universities. And this seems especially appropriate, since in the course of filming his fable of the Freaks' revenge on their "normal" exploiters, Browning gathered together the largest collection of showfreaks ever assembled in a single place: an immortal Super-Sideshow, memorializing a popular artform on the verge of disappearing along with certain congenital malformations it once "starred" (but that are now routinely "repaired"), like Siamese Twins.

For this reason, perhaps, we are these days particularly freak-obsessed, as attested also by the recent success of *The Elephant Man* on stage and TV and at the neighborhood movie theatre. The central fable of that parabolic tale, in which a Doctor, a Showman, the Press, and the Public contend for the soul of a freak, though the events on which it is based happened in Victorian times, seems especially apposite to our present ambivalent response to human abnormality, reminding us of what we now otherwise find it difficult to confess except in our REM sleep: that those wretched caricatures of our idealized body image, which at first appear to represent the absolutely "Other" (thus reassuring us who come to gape that we are "normal") are really a revelation of what in our deepest psyches we recognize as the Secret Self. After all, not only do we know that each of us is a freak to someone else; but in the depths of our unconscious (where the insecurities of childhood and adolescence never die) we seem forever freaks to ourselves.

Perhaps it is especially important for us to realize that *there are no normals*, at a moment when we are striving desperately to eliminate freaks, to normalize the world. This misguided impulse represents a third, an utterly new response to the mystery of human anomalies—made possible for the first time by modern medical technology and sophisticated laboratory techniques. Oddly enough (and to me terrifyingly), it proved possible for such experimental scientists to produce monsters long before they learned to prevent or cure them. To my mind, therefore, the whole therapeutic enterprise is haunted by the ghosts of those two-headed, three-legged, one-eyed chicks and piglets that the first scientific teratologists of the eighteenth century created and destroyed in their laboratories.

Nonetheless, I do not consider those first experimenters with genetic mutation my enemies, for all their deliberate profanation of a mystery dear to the hearts of the artists with whom I identify. Nor would I be presumptuous, heartless enough to argue—on esthetic or even moral grounds—that congenital malformations under no circumstances be "repaired," or if need be, denied birth, to spare suffering to themselves or others. I am, however, deeply ambivalent on this score for various reasons, some of which I have already made clear, and others of which I will now try to elucidate. I simply do not assume (indeed, the burden of evidence indicates the contrary) that being born a freak is per se an unendurable fate. As I learned reading scores of biographies of such creatures in the course of writing my book about them, the most grotesque among them have managed to live lives neither notably worse nor better than that of most humans. They have managed to support themselves at work which they enjoyed (including displaying themselves to the public); they have loved and been loved, married and begot children—sometimes in their own images, sometimes not.

More often than not, they have survived and coped; sometimes, indeed, with special pride and satisfaction because of their presumed "handicaps," which not a few of them have resisted attempts to "cure." Dwarfs in particular have joined together to fight for their "rights," one of which they consider to be *not* having their size brought up by chemotherapy and endocrine injections to a height we others call "normal," but that they refer to, less honorifically, as "average." And I must say I sympathize with their stand, insofar as the war against "abnormality" implies a dangerous kind of politics, which beginning with a fear of difference, eventuates in a tyranny of the Normal. That tyranny, moreover, is sustained by creating in those outside the Norm shame and self-hatred—particularly if they happen to suffer from those "deformities" (which are still the vast majority) that we cannot prevent or cure.

Reflecting on these matters, I cannot help remembering not only 15 the plight of the Jews and Blacks under Hitler but the situation of the same ethnic groups—more pathetic-comic than tragic, but deplorable all the same—here in supposedly non-totalitarian America merely a generation or two ago. At that point, many Blacks went scurrying off to their corner pharmacy in quest of skin bleaches and hair straighteners; and Jewish women with proud semitic beaks turned to cosmetic surgeons for nose jobs. To be sure, as the example of Barbra Streisand makes clear, we have begun to deliver ourselves from the tyranny of such ethnocentric Norms in the last decades of the twentieth century; so that looking Niggerish or Kike-ish no longer seems as freakish as it once did, and the children of "lesser breeds" no longer eat their hearts out because they do not look like Dick and Jane, the WASP-lets portrayed in their Primers.

But the Cult of Slimness, that aberration of Anglo-Saxon taste (no African or Slav or Mediterranean ever believed in his homeland that "no one can be too rich or too thin") still prevails. And joined with the Cult of Eternal Youth, it has driven a population growing ever older and fatter to absurd excesses of jogging, dieting, and popping amphetamines—or removing with the aid of plastic surgery those stigmata of time and experience once considered worthy of reverence. Nor do things stop there; since the skills of the surgeon are now capable of recreating our bodies in whatever shape whim and fashion may decree as esthetically or sexually desirable: large breasts and buttocks at one moment, meagre ones at another. By why *not*, after all? If in the not-so-distant future, the grosser physiological abnormalities that have for so long haunted us disappear forever—prevented, repaired, aborted, or permitted to die at birth—those of us allowed to survive by the official enforcers of the Norm will be free to become ever more homogeneously, monotonously beautiful; which is to say, supernormal, however that ideal may be defined. And who except some nostalgic poet, in love with difference for its own sake, would yearn for a world where ugliness is still possible? Is it not better to envision and work for one where all humans are at last *really* equal—physiologically as well as socially and politically?

But, alas (and this is what finally gives me pause), it is impossible for all of us to achieve this dubious democratic goal—certainly not in the context of our society as it is now and promises to remain in the foreseeable future: a place in which supernormality is to be had not for the asking but only for the buying (cosmetic surgery, after all, is not included in Medicare). What seems probable, therefore, as a score of science-fiction novels have already prophesied, is that we are approaching with alarming speed a future in which the rich and privileged will have as one more, ultimate privilege the hope of a surgically, chemically, hormonally induced and preserved normality—with the promise of immortality by organ transplant just over the horizon. And the poor (who, we are assured on good authority, we always have with us) will be our sole remaining Freaks.

THINKING AND WRITING ABOUT BODY IMAGE

QUESTIONS FOR DISCUSSION AND WRITING

1. Elliott ends his essay with a paraphrase of novelist David Foster Wallace: "Four hours a day spent watching television means four hours a day of unconscious reinforcement that genuine human worth dwells in the phenomenon of being watched." Do you agree or disagree with this idea? Explain.

2. Elliott also quotes Charles Cooley's term "looking-glass self" and paraphrases him: "Our sense of ourselves . . . is formed by our imagination of the way we appear in the eyes of others. Other people are a looking glass in which we see not merely our own reflection but a judgment about the value of that reflection" (para. 3). Use your own experience, your research, or a combination of both to agree or disagree.

3. Do you find the ad focusing on the class reunion, (p. 487) effective and, if so, why? What is the warrant that underlies it?

4. Jot down some of the conclusions about cosmetic surgery that you have reached after having read some or all of the selections in this unit. Use those conclusions to write one example of a claim of fact, one of a claim of value, and one of a claim of policy about cosmetic surgery. Develop one of those claims as the thesis for an essay, using one or more of the readings to support it.

5. Do the research necessary to find out what percentage of those having cosmetic surgery are men, what percentage are women, and what types of surgery are most frequent for each gender. Present the results of your research in an essay based on a claim of fact.

6. Which of the essays in this unit do you feel makes most effective use of support? Explain.

7. Write an essay in which you explain what point Fiedler is making when he uses the term "the tyranny of the normal" and discuss whether you agree with him or not.

TOPICS FOR RESEARCH

"Make-over" reality shows

How gender affects frequency and types of cosmetic surgery

The search for the perfect body: an addiction?

The costs of cosmetic surgery

Medical malpractice and cosmetic surgery

TAKING THE DEBATE ONLINE

For these and additional research URLs, see bedfordstmartins.com/rottenberg.

- *International Eating Disorder Referral Organization: Body Image*
  www.edreferral.com/body_image.htm

  This site contains information on body image perception, a body image questionnaire, and several bibliographies for further research.

- *BodyPositive*
  www.bodypositive.com

  BodyPositive's mission is to look at ways we can feel good in the bodies we have.

- *National Women's Health Information Center*
  www.4woman.gov/BodyImage

  This site on body image and health is sponsored by the Department of Health and Human Services. It provides a gateway to an array of federal women's health sites and other information resources.

- *Enhancing Male Body Image*
  www.korrnet.org/katfed/male2.html

  Tips for men on thinking about their body image.

- *How Botox Works*
  http://health.howstuffworks.com/botox.htm

  In this article, you'll find out what Botox is, how and why it's used, and how it is connected to botulism.

CHAPTER 13

How Has Terrorism Affected the American Idea of Justice?

September 11, 2001, has been called a day that changed America. Some of the changes were immediate, horrifying, and painful. Thousands of families mourned the loss of loved ones. Thousands more mourned the loss of friends and coworkers. Almost all mourned the loss of a sense of security that our nation may never experience again.

The changes in America that followed the attacks of September 11 are felt in small ways like having to go through increased security at airports. We have our backpacks and purses searched to enter football games, museums, and even those national monuments that are still open to the public. And the changes that followed those attacks are felt in large ways like losing hundreds of soldiers in Iraq or wondering if it could be one of our schools next that is taken over by armed foreigners.

Just as the aftermath of September 11 has threatened the American way of life, it has also threatened the American system of justice. Abuse at a prison in Iraq brought before us vivid and startling pictures of Americans caught in the act at the very site where Saddam Hussein became notorious for the mistreatment and torture of his people. Americans were supposed to offer something better to a nation we had gone to war to help. Newspapers worldwide carried front-page stories that questioned whether America was any longer in a position to boast about justice.

As accusations about who was responsible for what happened at Abu Ghraib worked their way up the chain of command, it became increasingly clear that questions had earlier been passed up along the same chain of command about how far interrogators could go in their attempt to elicit from prisoners information that might foil future terrorist attacks.

There were also hard-to-answer questions about how terrorists should be tried in our country. Our court system is designed to give the accused the greatest possible protection under the law. But what if the accused is suspected of having plotted the bombing of the World Trade Center and the Pentagon? What if the accused just doesn't look "American" enough? Ironically, those who participated in the atrocities at Abu Ghraib looked surprisingly like the kids next door.

The USA PATRIOT Act: Preserving Life and Liberty

WWW.LIFEANDLIBERTY.GOV

> BEFORE READING: In what ways, large or small, has your life been affected by the increased security that followed the terrorist attacks of September 11, 2001?

Congress enacted the Patriot Act by overwhelming, bipartisan margins, arming law enforcement with new tools to detect and prevent terrorism: The USA Patriot Act was passed nearly unanimously by the Senate 98–1, and 357–66 in the House, with the support of members from across the political spectrum.

The Act Improves Our Counterterrorism Efforts in Several Significant Ways:

1. The Patriot Act allows investigators to use the tools that were already available to investigate organized crime and drug trafficking. Many of the tools the act provides to law enforcement to fight terrorism have been used for decades to fight organized crime and drug dealers, and have been reviewed and approved by the courts. As Senator Joseph Biden (D-Delaware) explained during the floor debate about the act, "the FBI could get a wiretap to investigate the Mafia, but they could not get one to investigate terrorists. To put it bluntly, that was crazy! What's good for the mob should be good for terrorists." (*Congressional Record,* 10/25/01)

- *Allows law enforcement to use surveillance against more crimes of terror.* Before the Patriot Act, courts could permit law enforcement to conduct electronic surveillance to investigate many ordinary, nonterrorism crimes, such as drug crimes, mail fraud, and passport

---

This explanation of the effects of the USA Patriot Act (Uniting and Strengthening America by Providing Appropriate Tools Required to Intercept and Obstruct Terrorism) is found on the Department of Justice Web site at www.lifeandliberty.gov.

fraud. Agents also could obtain wiretaps to investigate some, but not all, of the crimes that terrorists often commit. The act enabled investigators to gather information when looking into the full range of terrorism-related crimes, including chemical-weapons offenses, the use of weapons of mass destruction, killing Americans abroad, and terrorism financing.

- *Allows federal agents to follow sophisticated terrorists trained to evade detection.* For years, law enforcement has been able to use "roving wiretaps" to investigate ordinary crimes, including drug offenses and racketeering. A roving wiretap can be authorized by a federal judge to apply to a particular suspect rather than a particular phone or communications device. Because international terrorists are sophisticated and trained to thwart surveillance by rapidly changing locations and communication devices such as cell phones, the act authorized agents to seek court permission to use the same techniques in national security investigations to track terrorists.

- *Allows law enforcement to conduct investigations without tipping off terrorists.* In some cases if criminals are tipped off too early to an investigation, they might flee, destroy evidence, intimidate or kill witnesses, cut off contact with associates, or take other action to evade arrest. Therefore, federal courts in narrow circumstances long have allowed law enforcement to delay for a limited time when the subject is told that a judicially approved search warrant has been executed. Notice is always provided, but the reasonable delay gives law enforcement time to identify the criminal's associates, eliminate immediate threats to our communities, and coordinate the arrests of multiple individuals without tipping them off beforehand. These delayed notification search warrants have been used for decades, have proven crucial in drug and organized crime cases, and have been upheld by courts as fully constitutional.

- *Allows federal agents to ask a court for an order to obtain business records in national security terrorism cases.* Examining business records often provides the key that investigators are looking for to solve a wide range of crimes. Investigators might seek select records from hardware stores or chemical plants, for example, to find out who bought materials to make a bomb, or bank records to see who's sending money to terrorists. Law enforcement authorities have always been able to obtain business records in criminal cases through grand jury subpoenas and continue to do so in national security cases where appropriate. These records were sought in criminal cases such as the investigation of the Zodiac gunman, where police suspected the gunman was inspired by a Scottish occult poet and wanted to learn who had checked the poet's books out of the library. In national security cases where use of the grand jury process was not appropriate, investigators previously had limited tools at their disposal to obtain certain business records. Under the Patriot Act, the government can now ask a federal court (the Foreign Intelligence Surveillance Court), if needed to aid an investigation, to order production of the same type of records available through grand jury subpoenas. This federal court, however, can issue these orders only after the government demonstrates the records concerned are sought for an authorized investigation to obtain foreign intelligence information not concerning a U.S. person or to protect against international terrorism or clandestine intelligence activities, provided that such investigation of a U.S. person is not conducted solely on the basis of activities protected by the First Amendment.

2. The Patriot Act facilitated information sharing and cooperation among government agencies so that they can better "connect the dots." The act removed the major legal barriers that prevented the law enforcement, intelligence, and national defense communities from talking and coordinating their work to protect the American people and our national security. The government's prevention efforts should not be restricted by boxes on an organizational chart. Now police officers, FBI agents, federal prosecutors, and intelligence officials can protect our communities by "connecting the dots" to uncover terrorist plots before they are completed. As Senator John Edwards (D–North Carolina) said about the Patriot Act, "we simply cannot prevail in the battle against terrorism if the right hand of our government has no idea what the left hand is doing." (Press release, 10/26/01)

- Prosecutors can now share evidence obtained through grand juries with intelligence officials — and intelligence information can now be shared more easily with federal prosecutors. Such sharing of information leads to concrete results. For example, a federal grand jury recently indicted an individual in Florida, Sami al-Arian, for allegedly being the U.S. leader of the Palestinian Islamic Jihad, one of the world's most violent terrorist outfits. Palestinian Islamic Jihad is responsible for murdering more than one hundred innocent people, including a young American named Alisa Flatow who was killed in a tragic bus bombing in Gaza. The Patriot Act assisted us in obtaining the indictment by enabling the full sharing of information and advice about the case among prosecutors and investigators. Alisa's father, Steven Flatow, has said, "When you know the resources of your government are committed to right the wrongs committed against your daughter, that instills you with a sense of awe. As a father, you can't ask for anything more."

3. The Patriot Act updated the law to reflect new technologies and new threats. The act brought the law up to date with current technology, so we no longer have to fight a digital-age battle with antique weapons — legal authorities left over from the era of rotary telephones. When investigating the murder of *Wall Street Journal* reporter Daniel Pearl, for example, law enforcement used one of the act's new authorities to use high-tech means to identify and locate some of the killers.

- *Allows law enforcement officials to obtain a search warrant anywhere a terrorist-related activity occurred.* Before the Patriot Act, law enforcement personnel were required to obtain a search warrant in the district where they intended to conduct a search. However, modern terrorism investigations often span a number of districts, and officers therefore had to obtain multiple warrants in multiple jurisdictions, creating unnecessary delays. The act provides that warrants can be obtained in any district in which terrorism-related activities occurred, regardless of where they will be executed. This provision does not change the standards governing the availability of a search warrant but streamlines the search-warrant process.

- *Allows victims of computer hacking to request law enforcement assistance in monitoring the "trespassers" on their computers.* This change made the law technology-neutral; it placed electronic trespassers on the same footing as physical trespassers. Now, hacking victims can seek law enforcement assistance to combat hackers, just as burglary victims have been able to invite officers into their homes to catch burglars.

4. The Patriot Act increased the penalties for those who commit terrorist crimes. Americans are threatened as much by the terrorist who pays for a bomb as by the one who pushes the button. That's why the Patriot Act imposed tough new penalties on those who commit and support terrorist operations, both at home and abroad. In particular, the act:

- *Prohibits the harboring of terrorists.* The act created a new offense that prohibits knowingly harboring persons who have committed or are about to commit a variety of terrorist offenses, such as destruction of aircraft; use of nuclear, chemical, or biological weapons; use of weapons of mass destruction; bombing of government property; sabotage of nuclear facilities; and aircraft piracy.

- *Enhanced the inadequate maximum penalties for various crimes likely to be committed by terrorists,* including arson, destruction of energy facilities, material support to terrorists and terrorist organizations, and destruction of national-defense materials.

- *Enhanced a number of conspiracy penalties,* including for arson, killings in federal facilities, attacking communications systems, material support to terrorists, sabotage of nuclear facilities, and interference with flight crew members. Under previous law, many terrorism statutes did not specifically prohibit engaging in conspiracies to commit the underlying offenses. In such cases, the government could only bring prosecutions under the general federal conspiracy provision, which carries a maximum penalty of only five years in prison.

- *Punishes terrorist attacks on mass transit systems.*

- *Punishes bioterrorists.*

- *Eliminates the statutes of limitations for certain terrorism crimes and lengthens them for other terrorist crimes.*

The government's success in preventing another catastrophic attack on the American homeland since September 11, 2001, would have been much more difficult, if not impossible, without the USA Patriot Act. The authorities Congress provided have substantially enhanced our ability to prevent, investigate, and prosecute acts of terror.

Surveillance under the USA PATRIOT Act

AMERICAN CIVIL LIBERTIES UNION

BEFORE READING: Do you ever feel that our nation has too many laws designed to protect the rights of those accused of wrongdoing? Explain.

What Is the USA PATRIOT Act?

Just six weeks after the September 11 attacks, a panicked Congress passed the "USA Patriot Act," an overnight revision of the nation's surveillance laws that vastly expanded the government's authority to spy on its own citizens, while simultaneously reducing checks and balances on those powers like judicial oversight, public accountability, and the ability to challenge government searches in court.

Why Congress Passed the Patriot Act

Most of the changes to surveillance law made by the Patriot Act were part of a long-standing law enforcement wish list that had been previously rejected by Congress, in some cases repeatedly. Congress reversed course because it was bullied into it by the Bush administration in the frightening weeks after the September 11 attack.

The Senate version of the Patriot Act, which closely resembled the legislation requested by Attorney General John Ashcroft, was sent straight to the floor with no discussion, debate, or hearings. Many senators complained that they had little chance to read it, much less analyze it, before

---

This article is from the Web site of the American Civil Liberties Union and the ACLU Foundation, www.aclu.org.

having to vote. In the House, hearings were held, and a carefully constructed compromise bill emerged from the Judiciary Committee. But then, with no debate or consultation with rank-and-file members, the House leadership threw out the compromise bill and replaced it with legislation that mirrored the Senate version. Neither discussion nor amendments were permitted, and once again members barely had time to read the thick bill before they were forced to cast an up-or-down vote on it. The Bush administration implied that members who voted against it would be blamed for any further attacks—a powerful threat at a time when the nation was expecting a second attack to come any moment and when reports of new anthrax letters were appearing daily.

Congress and the administration acted without any careful or systematic effort to determine whether weaknesses in our surveillance laws had contributed to the attacks, or whether the changes they were making would help prevent further attacks. Indeed, many of the act's provisions have nothing at all to do with terrorism.

The Patriot Act increases the government's surveillance powers in   5
four areas:

1. Records searches. It expands the government's ability to look at records on an individual's activity being held by third parties. (Section 215)

2. Secret searches. It expands the government's ability to search private property without notice to the owner. (Section 213)

3. Intelligence searches. It expands a narrow exception to the Fourth Amendment that had been created for the collection of foreign intelligence information (Section 218).

4. "Trap and trace" searches. It expands another Fourth Amendment exception for spying that collects "addressing" information about the origin and destination of communications, as opposed to the content (Section 214).

1. Expanded Access to Personal Records Held by Third Parties

One of the most significant provisions of the Patriot Act makes it far easier for the authorities to gain access to records of citizens' activities being held by a third party. At a time when computerization is leading to the creation of more and more such records, Section 215 of the Patriot Act allows the FBI to force anyone at all—including doctors, libraries, bookstores, universities, and Internet service providers—to turn over records on their clients or customers.

The result is unchecked government power to rifle through individuals' financial records, medical histories, Internet usage, bookstore purchases, library usage, travel patterns, or any other activity that leaves a record. Making matters worse:

- The government no longer has to show evidence that the subjects of search orders are an "agent of a foreign power," a requirement that previously protected Americans against abuse of this authority.

- The FBI does not even have to show a reasonable suspicion that the records are related to criminal activity, much less the requirement for "probable cause" that is listed in the Fourth Amendment to the Constitution. All the government needs to do is make the broad assertion that the request is related to an ongoing terrorism or foreign intelligence investigation.

- Judicial oversight of these new powers is essentially nonexistent. The government must only certify to a judge—with no need for evidence or proof—that such a search meets the statute's broad criteria, and the judge does not even have the authority to reject the application.

- Surveillance orders can be based in part on a person's First Amendment activities, such as the books they read, the Web sites they visit, or a letter to the editor they have written.

- A person or organization forced to turn over records is prohibited from disclosing the search to anyone. As a result of this gag order, the subjects of surveillance never even find out that their personal records have been examined by the government. That undercuts an important check and balance on this power: the ability of individuals to challenge illegitimate searches.

Section 215 of the Patriot Act violates the Constitution in several ways. It:

- Violates the Fourth Amendment, which says the government cannot conduct a search without obtaining a warrant and showing probable cause to believe that the person has committed or will commit a crime.

- Violates the First Amendment's guarantee of free speech by prohibiting the recipients of search orders from telling others about those orders, even where there is no real need for secrecy.

- Violates the First Amendment by effectively authorizing the FBI to launch investigations of American citizens in part for exercising their freedom of speech.

- Violates the Fourth Amendment by failing to provide notice—even after the fact—to persons whose privacy has been compromised. Notice is also a key element of due process, which is guaranteed by the Fifth Amendment.

2. More Secret Searches

For centuries, common law has required that the government can't go into your property without telling you, and must therefore give you notice before it executes a search. That "knock and announce" principle has long been recognized as a part of the Fourth Amendment to the Constitution.

The Patriot Act, however, unconstitutionally amends the Federal 10 Rules of Criminal Procedure to allow the government to conduct searches without notifying the subjects, at least until long after the search has been executed. This means that the government can enter a house, apartment, or office with a search warrant when the occupants are away, search through their property, take photographs, and in some cases even seize property—and not tell them until later.

Notice is a crucial check on the government's power because it forces the authorities to operate in the open, and allows the subjects of searches to protect their Fourth Amendment rights. For example, it allows them to point out irregularities in a warrant, such as the fact that the police are at the wrong address, or that the scope of the warrant is being exceeded (for example, by rifling through dresser drawers in a search for a stolen car). Search warrants often contain limits on what may be searched, but when the searching officers have complete and unsupervised discretion over a search, a property owner cannot defend his or her rights.

Finally, this new "sneak and peek" power can be applied as part of normal criminal investigations; it has nothing to do with fighting terrorism or collecting foreign intelligence.

3. Expansion of the Intelligence Exception in Wiretap Law

Under the Patriot Act, the FBI can secretly conduct a physical search or wiretap on American citizens to obtain evidence of crime without proving probable cause, as the Fourth Amendment explicitly requires.

A 1978 law called the Foreign Intelligence Surveillance Act (FISA) created an exception to the Fourth Amendment's requirement for probable cause when the purpose of a wiretap or search was to gather foreign intelligence. The rationale was that since the search was not conducted for the purpose of gathering evidence to put someone on trial, the standards could be loosened. In a stark demonstration of why it can be dangerous to create exceptions to fundamental rights, however, the Patriot Act expanded this once-narrow exception to cover wiretaps and searches that DO collect evidence for regular domestic criminal cases. FISA previously allowed searches only if the primary purpose was to gather foreign intelligence. But the Patriot Act changes the law to allow searches when "a significant purpose" is intelligence. That lets the government circumvent the Constitution's probable cause requirement even when its main goal is ordinary law enforcement.

The eagerness of many in law enforcement to dispense with the re- 15 quirements of the Fourth Amendment was revealed in August 2002 by the secret court that oversees domestic intelligence spying (the "FISA Court"). Making public one of its opinions for the first time in history, the court revealed that it had rejected an attempt by the Bush administration to allow criminal prosecutors to use intelligence warrants to evade the Fourth Amendment entirely. The court also noted that agents applying for warrants had regularly filed false and misleading information. That opinion is now on appeal.

4. Expansion of the "Pen Register" Exception in Wiretap Law

Another exception to the normal requirement for probable cause in wiretap law is also expanded by the Patriot Act. Years ago, when the law governing telephone wiretaps was written, a distinction was created between two types of surveillance. The first allows surveillance of the content or meaning of a communication, and the second only allows monitoring of the transactional or addressing information attached to a communication. It is like the difference between reading the address printed on the outside of a letter, and reading the letter inside, or listening to a phone conversation and merely recording the phone numbers dialed and received.

Wiretaps limited to transactional or addressing information are known as "Pen register/trap and trace" searches (for the devices that were used on telephones to collect telephone numbers). The requirements for getting a PR/TT warrant are essentially nonexistent: the FBI need not show probable cause or even reasonable suspicion of criminal activity. It must only certify to a judge—without having to prove it—that such a warrant would be "relevant" to an ongoing criminal investigation. And the judge does not even have the authority to reject the application.

The Patriot Act broadens the pen register exception in two ways:

"Nationwide" pen register warrants. Under the Patriot Act PR/TT orders issued by a judge are no longer valid only in that judge's jurisdiction but can be made valid anywhere in the United States. This "nationwide service" further marginalizes the role of the judiciary because a judge cannot meaningfully monitor the extent to which his or her order is being used. In addition, this provision authorizes the equivalent of a blank warrant: The court issues the order, and the law enforcement agent fills in the places to be searched. That is a direct violation of the Fourth Amendment's explicit requirement that warrants be written "particularly describing the place to be searched."

Pen register searches applied to the Internet. The Patriot Act applies the distinction between transactional and content-oriented wiretaps to the Internet. The problem is that it takes the weak standards for access to transactional data and applies them to communications that are far more than addresses. On an e-mail message, for example, law enforcement has interpreted the "header" of a message to be transactional information accessible with a PR/TT warrant. But in addition to routing information, e-mail headers include the subject line, which is part of the substance of a communication — on a letter, for example, it would clearly be inside the envelope.

The government also argues that the transactional data for Web surfing is a list of the URLs or Web site addresses that a person visits. For example, it might record the fact that they visited <www.aclu.org> at 1:15 in the afternoon and then skipped over to <www.fbi.gov> at 1:30. This claim that URLs are just addressing data breaks down in two different ways:

- Web addresses are rich and revealing content. The URLs or "addresses" of the Web pages we read are not really addresses, they are the titles of documents that we download from the Internet. When we "visit" a Web page, what we are really doing is downloading that page from the Internet onto our computer, where it is displayed. Therefore, the list of URLs that we visit during a Web session is really a list of the documents we have downloaded — no different from a list of electronic books we might have purchased online. That is much richer information than a simple list of the people we have communicated with; it is intimate information that reveals who we are and what we are thinking about — much more like the content of a phone call than the number dialed. After all, it is often said that reading is a "conversation" with the author.

- Web addresses contain communications sent by a surfer. URLs themselves often have content embedded within them. A search on the Google search engine, for example, creates a page with a custom-generated URL that contains material that is clearly private content, such as <www.google.com/search?hl=en&lr=&ie=UTF-8&oe=UTF-8&q=sexual+orientation>.

Similarly, if I fill out an online form — to purchase goods or register my preferences, for example — those products and preferences will often be identified in the resulting URL.

The Erosion of Accountability

Attempts to find out how the new surveillance powers created by the Patriot Act were implemented during their first year were in vain. In June 2002 the House Judiciary Committee demanded that the Department of Justice answer questions about how it was using its new authority. The Bush/Ashcroft Justice Department essentially refused to describe how it was implementing the law; it left numerous substantial questions unanswered and classified others without justification. In short, not only has the Bush administration undermined judicial oversight of government spying on citizens by pushing the Patriot Act into law, but it is also undermining another crucial check and balance on surveillance powers: accountability to Congress and the public.

Nonsurveillance Provisions

Although this fact sheet focuses on the direct surveillance provisions of the Patriot Act, citizens should be aware that the act also contains a number of other provisions. The act:

- Puts CIA back in the business of spying on Americans. The Patriot Act gives the director of Central Intelligence the power to identify domestic intelligence requirements. That opens the door to the same abuses that took place in the 1970s and before, when the CIA engaged in widespread spying on protest groups and other Americans.

- Creates a new crime of "domestic terrorism." The Patriot Act transforms protesters into terrorists if they engage in conduct that "involves acts dangerous to human life" to "influence the policy of a government by intimidation or coercion." How long will it be before an ambitious or politically motivated prosecutor uses the statute to charge members of controversial activist groups like Operation Rescue or Greenpeace with terrorism? Under the Patriot Act, providing lodging or assistance to such "terrorists" exposes a person to surveillance or prosecution. Furthermore, the law gives the attorney general and the secretary of state the power to detain or deport any noncitizen who belongs to or donates money to one of these broadly defined "domestic terrorist" groups.

- Allows for the indefinite detention of noncitizens. The Patriot Act gives the attorney general unprecedented new power to determine the fate of immigrants. The attorney general can order detention based on a certification that he or she has "reasonable grounds to believe" a noncitizen endangers national security. Worse, if the foreigner does not have a country that will accept them, they can be detained indefinitely without trial.

From the USA PATRIOT Act:
H.R. 3162, Sections 213 and 215

BEFORE READING: How would you differentiate between acts of terrorism and any other illegal activity?

Sec. 213. Authority for Delaying Notice of the Execution of a Warrant.

Section 3103a of title 18, United States Code, is amended—

1. by inserting "a. IN GENERAL—" before "In addition"; and

2. by adding at the end the following:

"b. DELAY—With respect to the issuance of any warrant or court order under this section, or any other rule of law, to search for and seize any property or material that constitutes evidence of a criminal offense in violation of the laws of the United States, any notice required, or that may be required, to be given may be delayed if—

"1. the court finds reasonable cause to believe that providing immediate notification of the execution of the warrant may have an adverse result (as defined in section 2705);

"2. the warrant prohibits the seizure of any tangible property, any wire or electronic communication (as defined in section 2510), or, except as expressly provided in chapter 121, any stored wire or electronic information, except where the court finds reasonable necessity for the seizure; and

"3. the warrant provides for the giving of such notice within a reasonable period of its execution, which period may thereafter be extended by the court for good cause shown."

Sec. 215. Access to Records and Other Items under the Foreign Intelligence Surveillance Act.

Title V of the Foreign Intelligence Surveillance Act of 1978 (50 U.S.C. 1861 et seq.) is amended by striking sections 501 through 503 and inserting the following:

"Sec. 501. Access to Certain Business Records for Foreign Intelligence and International Terrorism Investigations.

"a.1. The Director of the Federal Bureau of Investigation or a designee of the Director (whose rank shall be no lower than Assistant Special Agent in Charge) may make an application for an order requiring the production of any tangible things (including books, records, papers, documents, and other items) for an investigation to protect against international terrorism or clandestine intelligence activities, provided that such investigation of a United States person is not conducted solely upon the basis of activities protected by the first amendment to the Constitution.

"a.2. An investigation conducted under the section shall—

"A. be conducted under guidelines approved by the Attorney General under Executive Order 12333 (or a successor order); and

"B. not be conducted of a United States person solely upon the basis of activities protected by the first amendment to the Constitution of the United States.

"b. each application under this section—
"b.1. shall be made to—

"A. a judge of the court established by section 103(a); or

"B. a United States Magistrate Judge under chapter 43 of title 28, United States Code, who is publicly designated by the Chief Justice of the United States to have the power to hear applications and grant orders for the production of tangible things under this section on behalf of a judge of that court; and

"b.2. shall specify that the records concerned are sought for an authorized investigation conducted in accordance with subsection a.2. to protect against international terrorism or clandestine intelligence activities.

"c.1. Upon an application made pursuant to this section, the judge shall enter an ex parte order as requested, or as modified, approving the release of records if the judge finds that the application meets the requirements of this section.

"c.2. An order under this subsection shall not disclose that it is issued for purposes of an investigation described in subsection a.

"d. No person shall disclose to any other person (other than those persons necessary to produce the tangible things under this section) that the Federal Bureau of Investigation has sought or obtained tangible things under this section.

"e. A person who, in good faith, produces tangible things under an order pursuant to this section shall not be liable to any other person for such production. Such production shall not be deemed to constitute a waiver of any privilege in any other proceeding or context.

"Sec. 502. Congressional Oversight.

"a. On a semiannual basis, the Attorney General shall fully inform the Permanent Select Committee on Intelligence of the House of Representatives and the Select Committee on Intelligence of the Senate concerning all requests for the production of tangible things under section 402.

"b. On a semiannual basis, the Attorney General shall provide to the Committees on the Judiciary of the House of Representatives and the Senate a report setting forth with respect to the preceding six-month period—

"1. the total number of applications made for orders approving requests for the production of tangible things under section 402; and

"2. the total number of such orders either granted, modified, or denied."

The Patriot Act and You

JENNIFER HAHN AND WASIM SALFITI

BEFORE READING: How could the USA Patriot Act pose a threat to your personal privacy?

The Patriot Act and You

George W. Bush calls it "vital legislation" that protects us from the threat of terrorism; John Kerry says "there are good parts to it and bad parts to it"; the ACLU claims it threatens "the very rights and freedoms that we are struggling to protect." The Patriot Act has been condemned by librarians and by city councils from Los Angeles to Philadelphia. But how does the law affect you? Below, a visual survey of how a (particularly unlucky) U.S. citizen might run afoul of the "Uniting and Strengthening America by Providing Appropriate Tools Required to Intercept and Obstruct Terrorism (USA PATRIOT) Act of 2001."

SECTION 213: Changes standards for search warrants to allow "sneak and peek" searches in any investigation. Instead of serving the warrant in person, a federal agent can now snoop first and let you know later—often much later. SECTION 218: Expands an exception to the Fourth Amendment, allowing secret U.S. courts to authorize secret searches if the government can allege a foreign-intelligence rationale. Any evidence discovered can now be used in court.

SECTION 206: Permits "roving wiretaps," which allow the government to tap all phones or computers a suspect *might* use—including, say, those at a neighborhood pool hall or Internet café. Unconnected third parties can easily be swept into this wider net. Along with SECTION 220, it curtails judicial oversight of such wiretaps.

SECTION 214: By claiming relevance to a terrorism investigation, the government can track your incoming and outgoing calls without a warrant or probable cause.

SECTION 215: Without demonstrating probable cause, the FBI can obtain a subpoena to search your personal records held by a library, bookstore, church, bank, video store, etc. The subpoena cannot be challenged in court, and it includes a "gag order" to keep you from ever knowing it was served. SECTION 505: Just like 215, but there's no judge required. Anyone from John Ashcroft down to an FBI field officer can demand the same kinds of records simply by issuing a "national security letter." The agent has only to satisfy himself that the information might be "relevant" to an ongoing terror investigation.

SECTION 216: Allows, with a judge's approval, Internet wiretaps to be used in any criminal investigation. Authorities are supposed to be limited to collecting address information, not "content." But privacy advocates note that web addresses provide a direct path to content.

SECTION 802: Defines the new crime of "domestic terrorism" as illegal acts "dangerous to human life" that "appear to be intended" to influence government policy by "intimidation or coercion." The vague wording has activists ranging from environmentalists to anti-abortionists worried that their civil disobedience might be reclassified as terror. SECTION 806: Allows the Justice Department—without a hearing—to seize the assets of alleged domestic terrorists and their supporters.

Declared Unconstitutional:
SECTION 805(a)(2)(B): Banned giving "expert advice or assistance" to government-designated "foreign terrorist organizations." A federal judge tossed out this provision, noting that its "impermissibly vague" language could encompass "pure speech and advocacy protected by the First Amendment."

Research by Jennifer Hahn and Wasim Salfiti.

Name Withheld: Harsh Justice for a September 11 Detainee

ELIZABETH AMON

BEFORE READING: Do you recall witnessing, reading about, or hearing about any change in Americans' attitude toward those of other nationalities living in this country in the aftermath of September 11?

In its investigation of the September 11 attacks, the U.S. government rounded up hundreds of Middle Eastern, South Asian, and Muslim immigrants. The precise number is unknown. In November 2001, the Department of Justice reported that 1,182 people had been arrested, but it has refused to supply a total since then. This June, a report from its Office of the Inspector General (OIG) chronicled the detention of 762 of the arrestees for violating immigration laws—typically, for over-staying visas. Almost all the September 11 detainees were men, and most remained in custody for months. Many were eventually deported, while others, like M., the man who is interviewed in this document, were released but are too anxious about their immigration status to talk openly to the press. The government has refused to give out the names of the detainees, whom it has labeled "special-interest." In fact, there was little more reason to arrest them than to arrest any of the eight million other out-of-status immigrants living on U.S. soil. Neither M. nor any of the other detainees was shown to have had any connection to terrorism.

M. lives in a brick home in a neat, middle-class subdivision. When I visited him this spring, a half-melted snowman, complete with carrot nose and coal eyes, was sinking into his front yard. A soft-spoken, middle-aged man with a slight accent, M. is cautious in conversation, and his anger at what has happened to him is apparent only occasionally in his words and never in his manner. In November 2001, he was at home with his young son and his wife, who suffers from lupus, when an FBI agent and multiple INS agents appeared at the door. A coworker at the medical clinic where M. worked had called the FBI; M., she contended, wore a surgical mask "more than necessary." The INS brought M. to their headquarters for further questioning. Despite the fact that his immigration papers, which had been pending at the time of his arrest, were approved six weeks later, M. spent the next five months in a New Jersey jail.

Beginning in December 2001, lawyers from the American Civil Liberties Union visited several of the New York–area facilities where the detainees were being held. Despite Attorney General John Ashcroft's assurances to the Senate that "all persons being detained have the right to contact their lawyers and families," the attorneys at first had tremendous difficulty gaining access. In some cases, the prisons claimed that they were unable to "prepare" the men for questioning; in others, they were told that the INS had not given approval for the visit. When the lawyers were able to meet with the detained, they wrote up a brief report on each. The notes from M.'s interview, portions of which the ACLU released and all of which was approved for release by M., are at right.

Elizabeth Amon writes for *The National Law Journal* and was a 2003 Soros Justice Media Fellow. This article appeared in the August 2003 issue of *Harper's Magazine*.

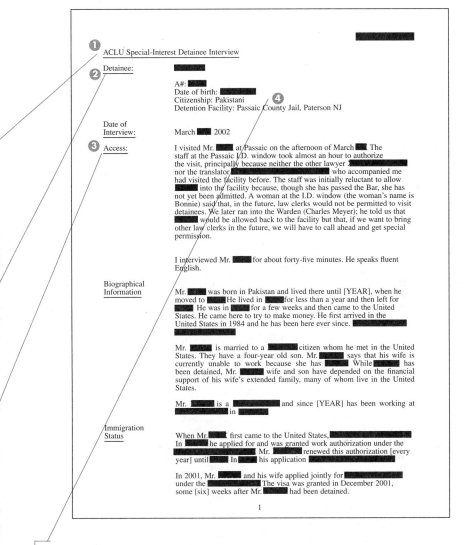

① ACLU Special-Interest Detainee Interview

② Detainee: ▮▮▮▮▮

A#: ▮▮▮
Date of birth: ▮▮▮▮▮
Citizenship: Pakistani **④**
Detention Facility: Passaic County Jail, Paterson NJ

Date of
Interview: March ▮▮ 2002

③ Access: I visited Mr. ▮▮▮ at Passaic on the afternoon of March ▮▮ The staff at the Passaic I.D. window took almost an hour to authorize the visit, principally because neither the other lawyer ▮▮▮▮▮▮▮▮ nor the translator ▮▮▮▮▮▮▮▮▮▮▮ who accompanied me had visited the facility before. The staff was initially reluctant to allow ▮▮▮ into the facility because, though she has passed the Bar, she has not yet been admitted. A woman at the I.D. window (the woman's name is Bonnie) said that, in the future, law clerks would not be permitted to visit detainees. We later ran into the Warden (Charles Meyer); he told us that ▮▮▮ would be allowed back to the facility but that, if we want to bring other law clerks in the future, we will have to call ahead and get special permission.

I interviewed Mr. ▮▮▮ for about forty-five minutes. He speaks fluent English.

Biographical
Information Mr. ▮▮▮ was born in Pakistan and lived there until [YEAR], when he moved to ▮▮▮ He lived in ▮▮▮▮ for less than a year and then left for ▮▮▮ He was in ▮▮▮ for a few weeks and then came to the United States. He came here to try to make money. He first arrived in the United States in 1984 and he has been here ever since. ▮▮▮▮▮▮▮▮▮ ▮▮▮▮▮

Mr. ▮▮▮▮ is married to a ▮▮▮▮ citizen whom he met in the United States. They have a four-year old son. Mr. ▮▮▮ says that his wife is currently unable to work because she has ▮▮▮ While ▮▮▮ has been detained, Mr. ▮▮▮ wife and son have depended on the financial support of his wife's extended family, many of whom live in the United States.

Mr. ▮▮▮▮ is a ▮▮▮▮▮▮ and since [YEAR] has been working at ▮▮▮▮▮▮ in ▮▮▮▮▮▮

Immigration
Status When Mr. ▮▮▮ first came to the United States, ▮▮▮▮▮▮▮▮▮▮▮ In ▮▮▮▮ he applied for and was granted work authorization under the ▮▮▮▮▮▮▮▮▮▮ Mr. ▮▮▮▮ renewed this authorization [every year] until ▮▮▮ In ▮▮▮ his application ▮▮▮▮▮▮▮▮

In 2001, Mr. ▮▮▮ and his wife applied jointly for ▮▮▮▮▮▮▮ under the ▮▮▮▮▮▮▮▮ The visa was granted in December 2001, some [six] weeks after Mr. ▮▮▮ had been detained.

1

④ A third of the detainees were, like M., from Pakistan, by far the most common country of origin; the next most common were Egypt, Turkey, Jordan, and Yemen. All the detainees were immigrants, and after September 11, at the attorney general's request, the chief U.S. immigration judge allowed their hearings to be closed to the public and even to family members. At least 611 of the detainees were subjected to secret hearings, a practice that the Supreme Court this May allowed to stand as constitutional. The Department of Justice has argued that releasing even the detainees' names would compromise its terrorism investigations, despite the fact that the names of other terrorism suspects—e.g., Ernest James Ujaama in Seattle, Jeffrey Leon Battle in Portland, Sahim Alwan and Yahya Goba in Buffalo—have been trumpeted in the press by Ashcroft himself.

Of the 762 detainees covered by the OIG report, more than 80 percent were in custody by the end of November 2001. At the time, Ashcroft seemed to consider the numbers good P.R., and whenever speaking of the detainees he would take care to invoke "terrorism" once or, better yet, twice. (A typical statement, from October 2001: "Our anti-terrorism offensive has arrested or detained nearly 1,000 individuals as part of the September 11 terrorism investigation.") To this day Ashcroft, in his public statements, continues to imply a link between the detainees and terrorism. But the director of the Center for National Security Studies, which filed a lawsuit to obtain information about the detainees, says that in court papers, government officials never connect the detainees to terrorism. A General Accounting Office report from January 2003 found that nearly half of the DOJ's "terrorism" convictions had been misclassified as such. In New Jersey, 60 of the 62 terrorism indictments touted by the U.S. Attorney's Office involved foreign students who had hired others to take English proficiency tests on their behalf.

At 3:30 A.M. on the morning after his arrest, M. was taken to the Passaic jail and charged with having overstayed his visa—a civil, not a criminal, offense. On September 17, 2001, the INS changed its long-standing policy on immigrant detention, extending the time period that an immigrant could be held without charges from 24 to 48 hours and adding that, in "extraordinary circumstances," arrestees could be held uncharged for "an additional reasonable period of time." The DOJ's definition of "reasonable" has proved quite spacious. Of the special-interest detainees, 317 are known to have been held for more than 48 hours without charges, 36 for four weeks or more, 13 for more than 40 days, and nine for more than 50. Such arbitrary practices of detention contradict even the USA Patriot Act, which required that detainees be charged within seven days.

In December 2001, M.'s work permit and residency application were approved by the INS, and yet he was not released. The following month, the FBI cleared him of having any connection to terrorism, and yet still he was not released. Many detainees spent months in jail after they had been cleared; some had even received orders of deportation, or had volunteered to leave the country. Others were deported so quickly after September 11 that they weren't able to pursue any legal strategies for remaining. In many cases, men were sent to home countries where they had not lived or even visited for decades. The INS deported one Pakistani man, detained for having missed an immigration hearing more than five years earlier, without informing his American-born wife. The man was deposited, penniless, in Islamabad, even though his family lived in Karachi, more than 1,000 miles away.

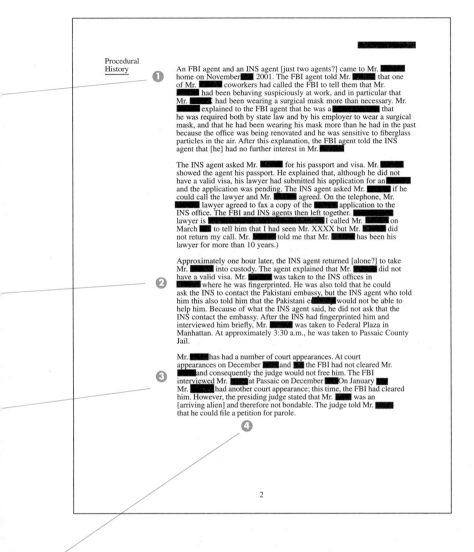

Procedural
History

① An FBI agent and an INS agent [just two agents?] came to Mr. ▮▮▮▮ home on November▮▮ 2001. The FBI agent told Mr. ▮▮▮▮ that one of Mr. ▮▮▮▮ coworkers had called the FBI to tell them that Mr. ▮▮▮▮ had been behaving suspiciously at work, and in particular that Mr. ▮▮▮▮ had been wearing a surgical mask more than necessary. Mr. ▮▮▮▮ explained to the FBI agent that he was a ▮▮▮▮▮▮▮ that he was required both by state law and by his employer to wear a surgical mask, and that he had been wearing his mask more than he had in the past because the office was being renovated and he was sensitive to fiberglass particles in the air. After this explanation, the FBI agent told the INS agent that [he] had no further interest in Mr. ▮▮▮▮

The INS agent asked Mr. ▮▮▮▮ for his passport and visa. Mr. ▮▮▮▮ showed the agent his passport. He explained that, although he did not have a valid visa, his lawyer had submitted his application for an ▮▮▮▮ and the application was pending. The INS agent asked Mr. ▮▮▮▮ if he could call the lawyer and Mr. ▮▮▮▮ agreed. On the telephone, Mr. ▮▮▮▮ lawyer agreed to fax a copy of the ▮▮▮▮ application to the INS office. The FBI and INS agents then left together. ▮▮▮▮ lawyer is ▮▮▮▮▮▮▮▮ I called Mr. ▮▮▮▮ on March ▮▮ to tell him that I had seen Mr. XXXX but Mr. ▮▮▮▮ did not return my call. Mr. ▮▮▮▮ told me that Mr. ▮▮▮▮ has been his lawyer for more than 10 years.)

② Approximately one hour later, the INS agent returned [alone?] to take Mr. ▮▮▮▮ into custody. The agent explained that Mr. ▮▮▮▮ did not have a valid visa. Mr. ▮▮▮▮ was taken to the INS offices in ▮▮▮▮ where he was fingerprinted. He was also told that he could ask the INS to contact the Pakistani embassy, but the INS agent who told him this also told him that the Pakistani e▮▮▮▮would not be able to help him. Because of what the INS agent said, he did not ask that the INS contact the embassy. After the INS had fingerprinted him and interviewed him briefly, Mr. ▮▮▮▮ was taken to Federal Plaza in Manhattan. At approximately 3:30 a.m., he was taken to Passaic County Jail.

③ Mr. ▮▮▮▮has had a number of court appearances. At court appearances on December ▮▮▮and ▮▮ the FBI had not cleared Mr. ▮▮▮▮and consequently the judge would not free him. The FBI interviewed Mr. ▮▮▮at Passaic on December ▮▮On January ▮▮ Mr. ▮▮▮▮ had another court appearance; this time, the FBI had cleared him. However, the presiding judge stated that Mr. ▮▮▮▮ was an [arriving alien] and therefore not bondable. The judge told Mr. ▮▮▮▮ that he could file a petition for parole.

④

2

④ Requests by M.'s lawyer to have him released on bond were repeatedly rebuffed, even after he had been cleared by the FBI. Most people detained on minor immigration violations, such as M.'s, have traditionally been released on bond until their court hearings. But, as revealed in the OIG report, the Department of Justice in September 2001 ordered a "no bond" policy for all the special-interest detainees, even in cases in which there was no evidence that bond should be denied. Soon thereafter, a new regulation allowed the immigration service to overrule an immigration judge about whether *any* detainee is released on bond, even if he is not suspected of a crime or of terrorist activity. Thus the government trial attorney, who essentially is the prosecutor in an immigration proceeding, is allowed to take on a crucial judicial role as well.

In general, only one detained immigrant in five obtains a lawyer, even though doing so greatly increases the chance of success—in asylum cases, for example, by four times or more. Because immigration proceedings are considered civil actions, the immigrant does not have a right to an appointed attorney. M. was fortunate to have worked with the same attorney for sixteen years, and to have been able to contact him during his detention. Many of the detainees had no attorney, and the lists of free attorneys at the jails were invariably outdated or incorrect. At the Brooklyn MDC, not a single number on the list was a working number for an attorney willing to take on cases. Prisoners there were not always offered their allotted call per week, and when guards did offer it they employed a cryptic shorthand, asking, "Are you okay?" A call to an inaccurate number on the jail's list was counted as the weekly call. According to the OIG's report, the director of the federal prison bureau was told she should "not be in a hurry" to allow the detainees their telephone calls.

In late April 2002, M.'s request for parole was finally granted; he was released on a $5,000 bond, and had to get himself home by taking a bus to a train and then walking two miles in the rain. Both M. and his wife say they often are unable to sleep as a result of his experience, but they worry more about the impact on their five-year-old son (who sometimes asks, when M. leaves the house for work, "Is Daddy coming home?"). Moreover, M.'s five months of incarceration left his family $30,000 in debt. Despite these emotional and fiscal scars, M. is fortunate in how his case was resolved. Other of the detainees have not come home at all: An Egyptian man was deported and forced to leave behind his American-citizen wife and two American-born children; a Canadian man, originally from Syria, was deported to Syria—in violation of international law—where he disappeared for weeks. For others, detention was literally a physical trial. Two detainees contracted tuberculosis in the Brooklyn MDC. Another detainee there had a broken hand and was refused treatment.

Perhaps the most frightening aspect of the September 11 arrests was, in the end, how arbitrary they were. As a result, millions of other U.S. Muslims and Arabs— many of whom came here, as have immigrants for four centuries, in search of asylum from repression or hardship overseas—now see themselves as potential targets. Most of the detainees did violate U.S. immigration law, and for many Americans this fact seems to have absolved the government for its harsh and capricious justice. But in undermining the presumption of innocence, as well as the constitutional rights to due process, to counsel, and to a speedy and public trial, the Bush administration has weakened these protections for all, citizens and aliens alike. In the process, it has tarnished American democracy, even as it hopes to export this democracy to the very nations from which these men arrived.

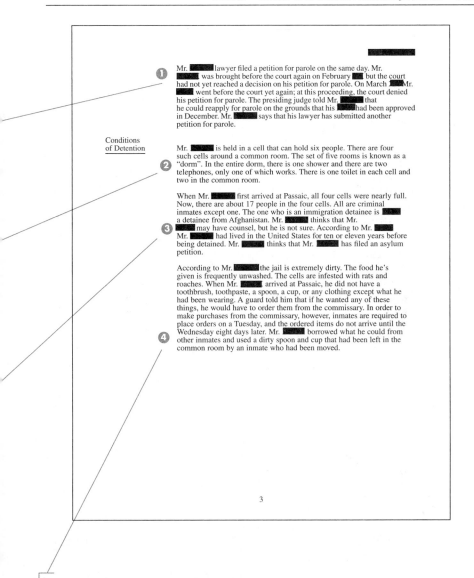

Mr. ▓▓▓ lawyer filed a petition for parole on the same day. Mr. ▓▓▓ was brought before the court again on February ▓▓ but the court had not yet reached a decision on his petition for parole. On March ▓▓Mr. ▓▓▓ went before the court yet again; at this proceeding, the court denied his petition for parole. The presiding judge told Mr. ▓▓▓ that he could reapply for parole on the grounds that his ▓▓▓had been approved in December. Mr. ▓▓▓ says that his lawyer has submitted another petition for parole.

Conditions of Detention

Mr. ▓▓▓ is held in a cell that can hold six people. There are four such cells around a common room. The set of five rooms is known as a "dorm". In the entire dorm, there is one shower and there are two telephones, only one of which works. There is one toilet in each cell and two in the common room.

When Mr. ▓▓▓ first arrived at Passaic, all four cells were nearly full. Now, there are about 17 people in the four cells. All are criminal inmates except one. The one who is an immigration detainee is ▓▓▓ a detainee from Afghanistan. Mr. ▓▓▓ thinks that Mr. ▓▓▓ may have counsel, but he is not sure. According to Mr. ▓▓▓ Mr. ▓▓▓ had lived in the United States for ten or eleven years before being detained. Mr. ▓▓▓ thinks that Mr. ▓▓▓ has filed an asylum petition.

According to Mr. ▓▓▓the jail is extremely dirty. The food he's given is frequently unwashed. The cells are infested with rats and roaches. When Mr. ▓▓▓ arrived at Passaic, he did not have a toothbrush, toothpaste, a spoon, a cup, or any clothing except what he had been wearing. A guard told him that if he wanted any of these things, he would have to order them from the commissary. In order to make purchases from the commissary, however, inmates are required to place orders on a Tuesday, and the ordered items do not arrive until the Wednesday eight days later. Mr. ▓▓▓ borrowed what he could from other inmates and used a dirty spoon and cup that had been left in the common room by an inmate who had been moved.

3

"My wife laughs at me," says M., "because I don't like my shoelace to touch the ground." The dirtiness of jail was an ordeal for M., who saw rats and roaches in his cell every day. More disturbing, the detainees—few of whom were guilty of anything more than having overstayed a visa—were forced to share cells with violent criminals. At the Metropolitan Detention Center (MDC) in Brooklyn, where many of the other detainees were held, conditions were even more brutal. The men were locked down for 23 hours a day and imprisoned in perpetual light. Ostensibly the lights were for videotaping—to ensure that the prisoners were not abused—but when the OIG tried to examine the tapes for evidence of abuse it found that those more than 30 days old had been destroyed. Prisoners at the MDC were routinely slammed against walls by guards and were allegedly taunted with anti-Arab slurs. The OIG's report notes that supervisors had told the facility's staff that the detainees were "suspected terrorists."

Justice for Terrorists

J. ANDREW KENT

BEFORE READING: What are the pros and cons of trying accused international terrorists in our traditional American criminal justice system?

No aspect of the Bush administration's policies since 9/11 has presented a more enduring source of controversy than its treatment of accused terrorists in its custody. The President's first response, in the immediate wake of the attacks, was to authorize the creation of military tribunals to try those captured in the campaign in Afghanistan against al Qaeda and the Taliban regime. After more than two-and-a-half years, however, the administration has yet to use these tribunals, and has slated just six detainees for trial before them, only two of whom have been formally charged.

Instead, in the dozens of terrorism-related indictments that the Justice Department has brought over this period, the administration has turned to civilian courts, often asking judges to relax the ordinary rules of procedure in light of the intelligence and national-security concerns at stake. But at every turn, whether with the military tribunals or in civilian courts, the Bush administration's efforts to restrict the usual workings of legal due process have prompted howls of outrage from both the Left and the libertarian Right.

The charges made by these critics are serious indeed. Such legal shortcuts, they argue, defy not just the best traditions of the United States but the actual guarantees imposed by federal law and the Constitution. In their view, compromising these longstanding protections puts the liberties of all Americans at risk. Moreover, they insist, whatever one's interpretation of the relevant laws, riding roughshod over the rights of accused terrorists only serves to advance their cause, reducing the standing of the United States in the world and putting the lie to our claims of openness and freedom.

For the most vociferous opponents of these policies, the Bush administration's basic mistake is conceptual. Heinous as our captured enemies may be, their deeds (it is said) are not acts of war but crimes, and should be handled as such, with the full force—and ordinary safeguards—of criminal law. The refrain of these critics is simple: give the courts a chance.

Since 9/11, the case of *United States* v. *Zacarias Moussaoui* is undoubtedly 5 the best known example of using civilian courts to try an accused terror-

---

J. Andrew Kent is a lawyer in private practice in New York. This article originally appeared in *Commentary* in June 2004.

ist. A French national of Moroccan descent, Moussaoui was picked up on immigration charges in Minnesota prior to 9/11 and was indicted in late 2001. He was charged with conspiracy to commit international terrorism, to hijack an aircraft, to use the aircraft as a weapon of mass destruction, to kill U.S. government employees, and to destroy U.S. property—in short, with being a member of al Qaeda and intending to act as the twentieth hijacker on 9/11.

For the prosecution, the case has been difficult from the outset. Part of the problem is Moussaoui himself, who appears mentally unbalanced and has insisted at times on acting as his own lawyer, deluging the court with lengthy, ranting pleadings and demands. Moussaoui has confessed in court to membership in al Qaeda and to owing his allegiance to Osama bin Laden—but he has vehemently denied any involvement in the attacks of 9/11.

More vexing to prosecutors than the spectacle of the defendant himself, however, has been the burden placed on their case by the standard rules of disclosure, rules dictated by various federal statutes and Supreme Court rulings. In civilian trials, the government must make available to the defense a great deal of information—not just documents but also witnesses who are in custody. In Moussaoui's case, prosecutors have reluctantly complied with this obligation by providing his lawyers with written reports describing in great detail the interrogations of captured al-Qaeda operatives, including (as we can guess from various sources) such key figures as Khalid Sheikh Mohammed, Ramzi bin al-Shibh, and Abu Zubaydah. What the prosecutors have repeatedly rejected is Moussaoui's demand to question al-Qaeda detainees. Indeed, the proceedings in the case have been stopped and started several times by sharp disputes between the government and the judge about whether Moussaoui's lawyers, in the interest of bolstering his defense, should be allowed this privilege.

In an ordinary criminal trial, none of this would be an issue; both the defendant and his lawyers would have access to all relevant documents and witnesses. Cumbersome as this requirement may be at times, it is the cornerstone of any fair system of criminal justice. Here, however, it is essential to keep in mind the peculiar character of the case. The men whose testimony Moussaoui has sought are not petty criminals or mobsters. Khalid Sheikh Mohammed is thought to have been the master strategist of the 9/11 attack, Ramzi bin al-Shibh the operational planner. In the middle of a vicious, unfinished war with al Qaeda, it is problematic, to say the least, to make known the details of their lengthy interrogations.

The rules governing such disclosures in federal courts are extremely broad. They require prosecutors to share any evidence that is "favorable to the accused" or "exculpatory," or that is even "material" to the defense. Prosecutors and law-enforcement agents working on a case are also required to take the additional step of searching their files for *any* information (not just evidence, in the strict sense) that might meet these criteria; such materials must be turned over to the defense as well. Nor is that all. According to various court rulings on these matters, any government agency that becomes "aligned" or "actively involved" with the prosecutors, or functions in some way as part of the "prosecution team," must similarly search its files and, upon request, disclose information to the defense.

In law-enforcement lingo, this issue is referred to simply as "align- 10 ment." Over the years, courts have found alignment—and hence a duty to search for and disclose information—between federal prosecutors and such far-flung agencies as the United States Postal Service, the Internal Revenue Service, the Food and Drug Administration, a state environmental testing laboratory, and even foreign governments. In terrorism cases, the demands for transparency point to all those parts of the government holding our most sensitive secrets, including the Central Intelligence Agency, the National Security Agency, and the Defense Intelligence Agency.

Under these rules, indeed, the disclosure of reams of information gathered by the military and intelligence communities has become a routine part of terrorism prosecutions. A February 2001 decision in the case of Wadih el-Hage—Osama bin Laden's personal secretary, who helped co-ordinate the 1998 embassy bombings in Africa—ordered the government to hand over a virtual encyclopedia of antiterrorist intelligence: materials "relating to the alleged al-Qaeda terrorist training camps in the Sudan"; "information that led the government to believe that . . . associates of Mr. bin Laden visited [the defendant's] former residence in Nairobi"; "items which indicate that al Qaeda operated under a 'cell' structure in which participants were informed of plans and activities only on a 'need-to-know' basis"; and any documents containing "information that impeaches statements that the government intends to use that were uttered by . . . Osama bin Laden" and other al-Qaeda members. As Andrew C. McCarthy, a former prosecutor who tried Islamist terrorists in federal court during the 1990's, recently noted in these pages, such disclosures "illuminate not only what the government knows about terrorist organizations but the intelligence agencies' methods and sources for obtaining that information."[1]

Enter, here, an additional complication, and one paradoxically engendered by the intelligence reforms instituted since 9/11. These altogether necessary and long-overdue reforms have, in themselves, significantly increased the risk that our antiterrorism efforts will be compromised by disclosures in court.

As various commissions and commentators have concluded, legal "walls" erected in the past between law-enforcement and intelligence

[1] "The Intelligence Mess: How It Happened, What to Do About It," *Commentary*, April 2004.

agencies prevented the sharing of crucial information that might have averted the attacks. Fortunately, the most prominent of these barriers have already come down. The USA Patriot Act, for instance, undid rules limiting the dissemination of grand-jury materials and the fruits of law-enforcement wiretaps. And a November 2002 decision by the special federal appeals court that handles foreign-intelligence surveillance over-turned a lower-court decision that had limited the sharing of information between, on the one hand, those prosecutors and FBI agents working on intelligence and, on the other hand, those conducting law-enforcement investigations.

Combined with other changes in process even before 9/11, all this has helped break down the institutional and cultural divides between in-telligence and law enforcement, especially in the realms of information technology and personnel. Though much remains to be done, there is more cooperation now than ever before between these crucial and com-plementary agencies of the federal government.

And that is the problem. To a defense lawyer with a client who is an accused terrorist, these reforms represent a giant neon billboard flashing the word "alignment." In the future, defense counsel will be able to argue that the files of our intelligence agencies should be subject to ever more extensive search and disclosure obligations, for the simple reason that the agencies themselves will be acting ever more cooperatively. Significant parts of the federal intelligence apparatus, it can be claimed plausibly, will now be the "prosecution team."

The pernicious effects of such courtroom disclosure are likely to extend well beyond tipping the government's hand to our enemies. *Foreign* in-telligence services, as well as freelance sources in the field, are already leery of working with the United States for fear that their secrets—and their identities—will show up in congressional hearings or press leaks; heightened concern about exposure in court can only make matters worse. The same is true of cooperation within the federal government, es-pecially in light of longstanding fears at the CIA that joint ventures with the FBI will draw the agency into potentially damaging legal proceedings.

There is also the very real possibility that revelations in court will in-creasingly interfere with ongoing intelligence operations. As R. James Woolsey, the former Director of Central Intelligence, has observed about the gathering of national-security information, the "only way you will know in the future something that you may need to know is if you can stay with an asset for a long time." Law enforcement, by contrast, de-mands a faster timetable, pushed along by statutes of limitation and the requirement for a "speedy trial." To the extent that the two functions are further combined, the needs of intelligence-gathering are likely to suffer.

Worse, the record-keeping practices that are needed to comply with—and limit the damage caused by—the disclosure standards set by courts tend to inhibit the wide-ranging analysis and prediction of national-security threats. The FBI's information-management system has come under harsh criticism for segregating—"stovepiping," in current Washington parlance—information and preventing the salutary "connecting of dots." According to U.S. Senator Richard Shelby, a frequent critic of our intelligence efforts, the FBI still suffers from a "tyranny of the case-file" because it stores and reviews information with an eye to proving "elements of crimes against specific potential defendants in a court of law." Rather than rectifying this problem, we risk generalizing it across *all* of our intelligence agencies, making it more likely that we will repeat the errors of oversight leading up to the attacks of 9/11.

A related difficulty is that intelligence agencies are far more likely than their counterparts in law enforcement to generate information that is arguably "exculpatory," and therefore subject to disclosure in court. As Stewart Baker, former general counsel of the National Security Agency, observed some years ago in *Foreign Policy* magazine, law-enforcement agencies "have learned to live with" these rules by assuming that any internal document "will be read by a defense attorney at the end of the day." Intelligence agencies operate very differently. Their uses of information "are more diverse," Baker noted, "the process more fluid"; much of the information they collect consists of "casual speculation or fragments of data." But the unreliability of this raw intelligence has no bearing in court. Because it might be useful to the defense, it may well have to be searched and disclosed.

So how can we render justice to someone like Zacarias Moussaoui while at the same time prosecuting the war on terror and protecting vital intelligence operations? How can fair adjudication be combined with a due regard for secrecy? Officials in all three branches of government have struggled with this question for years, and no one has come up with a wholly satisfactory answer. 20

Some protections for sensitive information are already in place. The Justice Department, for example, has long had rules to limit and monitor contacts between prosecutors and intelligence agencies like the CIA, so as to avoid pretexts for dragging agents and analysts into court. Judges have the discretion to rule that certain information will be disclosed only to defense lawyers who have security clearances, and not to their clients. (This is what has occurred in the Moussaoui case.) And the Classified Information Procedures Act (CIPA, passed in 1980) allows prosecutors to request the disclosure of a nonclassified version of sensitive information.

But these safeguards go only so far. In a civilian trial, any limitation on disclosure must be guided, according to the congressional report accompanying CIPA, by a "presumption that the defendant should not stand in a worse position, because of the fact that classified information is involved." As the Court of Appeals for the Fourth Circuit stated in its recent decision in the Moussaoui case, the prosecution's "interest in protecting classified information does not overcome a defendant's right to present his case." In practice, competent defense counsel can always argue—as they have done in the Moussaoui case—that specific details about the alleged offense, the investigation of it, and the background of the government's witnesses must be disclosed.

Congress could try, of course, to create additional protections. To prevent defense attorneys from going on fishing expeditions in sensitive intelligence files, new laws might define disclosure obligations in such a way as to apply only to the specific files at "aligned" intelligence agencies that are directly involved with a given case. Or Congress could simply grant a broad exemption to intelligence agencies, making their files off-limits except in certain very narrow circumstances. But the problem with such measures, especially the last, is that they almost certainly would be struck down in court. Though some of the existing disclosure requirements are purely statutory, others spring from Supreme Court cases, especially the landmark ruling in *Brady* v. *Maryland* (1963). "*Brady* obligations" (as they are commonly called) are now a deeply entrenched part of American legal culture, and there is no reason to think the Supreme Court would accept any effort to curtail them.

Despite the hue and cry of libertarian critics, the least objectionable solution to these dilemmas is the one with which the Bush administration started: military tribunals. Civilian courts are simply not equipped—nor should they be equipped—to deal with the likes of Zacarias Moussaoui. Terrorism and terrorist conspiracy demand a different set of rules.

The tribunal procedures announced by the Bush administration in 25 November 2001 may not satisfy the ACLU, but they strike the right balance between due process and due concern for the nation's security. Even under these rules, prosecutors are required to disclose "all information intended for presentation as evidence at trial," especially that which might "exculpate the accused." But these disclosures can be limited in ways that would never be possible in a civilian trial. Any sensitive piece of evidence can be presented in a declassified summary fashion, for example, and the tribunal can close its proceedings to anyone—including the accused and his civilian defense counsel—except the judges, the prosecution team, and a Department of Defense lawyer assigned to represent the accused.

The Bush administration's disinclination to use military tribunals is understandable (though one wonders why the President wasted so much political capital to establish them). No one can be pleased at the idea of denying the fullest possible hearing even to a would-be terrorist like Moussaoui. But, as all Americans have had occasion to learn in recent years, our elected officials have duties that are even more urgent than ensuring perfectly fair trials, especially when the country is faced with threats that no mere criminal could ever pose.

From *The Geneva Convention Relative to the Treatment of Prisoners of War*

THE DIPLOMATIC CONFERENCE FOR THE ESTABLISHMENT OF INTERNATIONAL CONVENTIONS FOR THE PROTECTION OF VICTIMS OF WAR

BEFORE READING: Brainstorm anything you know about the Geneva Convention. In what context or contexts have you heard that term?

Part II. General Protection of Prisoners of War

A rticle 12. Prisoners of war are in the hands of the enemy Power, but not of the individuals or military units who have captured them. Irrespective of the individual responsibilities that may exist, the Detaining Power is responsible for the treatment given them.

Prisoners of war may only be transferred by the Detaining Power to a Power which is a party to the Convention and after the Detaining Power has satisfied itself of the willingness and ability of such transferee Power to apply the Convention. When prisoners of war are transferred under such circumstances, responsibility for the application of the Convention rests on the Power accepting them while they are in its custody.

Nevertheless if that Power fails to carry out the provisions of the Convention in any important respect, the Power by whom the prisoners of war were transferred shall, upon being notified by the Protecting Power, take effective measures to correct the situation or shall request the return of the prisoners of war. Such requests must be complied with.

Article 13. Prisoners of war must at all times be humanely treated. Any unlawful act or omission by the Detaining Power causing death or seriously endangering the health of a prisoner of war in its custody is prohibited, and will be regarded as a serious breach of the present Convention. In particular, no prisoner of war may be subjected to physical mutilation or to medical or scientific experiments of any kind which are not justified by the medical, dental, or hospital treatment of the prisoner concerned and carried out in his interest.

Likewise, prisoners of war must at all times be protected, particularly   5
against acts of violence or intimidation and against insults and public curiosity.

This agreement was the revision of one signed at Geneva, Switzerland, in 1864 establishing a code for the treatment of the sick and wounded, those killed in battle, and prisoners of war. It was also the code that provided for the protection of buildings and vehicles having the emblem of the Red Cross. It was adopted on August 12, 1949.

Measures of reprisal against prisoners of war are prohibited.

Article 14. Prisoners of war are entitled in all circumstances to respect for their persons and their honour. Women shall be treated with all the regard due to their sex and shall in all cases benefit by treatment as favourable as that granted to men. Prisoners of war shall retain the full civil capacity which they enjoyed at the time of their capture. The Detaining Power may not restrict the exercise, either within or without its own territory, of the rights such capacity confers except in so far as the captivity requires.

Article 15. The Power detaining prisoners of war shall be bound to provide free of charge for their maintenance and for the medical attention required by their state of health.

Article 16. Taking into consideration the provisions of the present Convention relating to rank and sex, and subject to any privileged treatment which may be accorded to them by reason of their state of health, age, or professional qualifications, all prisoners of war shall be treated alike by the Detaining Power, without any adverse distinction based on race, nationality, religious belief, or political opinions, or any other distinction founded on similar criteria.

A Tortured Debate

MICHAEL HIRSH, JOHN BARRY, AND DANIEL KLAIDMAN

BEFORE READING: Considering the post-9/11 threat of terrorist attacks, how far should our government go in trying to elicit from prisoners information that might prevent future attacks? How far can we go and still maintain our integrity as a nation of law? Who decides?

Ibn al-Shaykh al-Libi was America's first big trophy in the war on terror: a senior Qaeda operative captured amid the fighting in Afghanistan. What is less known is that al-Libi, who ran Qaeda training camps, quickly became the subject of a bitter feud between the FBI and the CIA over how to interrogate terror suspects. At the time of al-Libi's capture on November 11, 2001, the questioning of detainees was still the FBI's province. For years the bureau's "bin Laden team" had sought to win suspects over with a carrots-and-no-sticks approach: favors in exchange for cooperation.

This article appeared in *Newsweek* on June 21, 2003. It was prepared by the senior editor of the magazine's Washington bureau, Michael Hirsh; the bureau's national security correspondent, John Barry; and its bureau chief, Daniel Klaidman, with contributions by Michael Isikoff, Mark Hosenball, and Tamara Lipper.

One terrorist, in return for talking, even wangled a heart transplant for his child.

With al-Libi, too, the initial approach was to read him his rights like any arrestee, one former member of the FBI team told *Newsweek*. "He was basically cooperating with us." But this was post-9/11; President Bush had declared war on Al Qaeda, and in a series of covert directives, he had authorized the CIA to set up secret interrogation facilities and to use new, harsher methods. The CIA, says the FBI source, was "fighting with us tooth and nail."

The handling of al-Libi touched off a long-running battle over interrogation tactics inside the administration. It is a struggle that continued right up until the Abu Ghraib scandal broke in April—and it extended into the White House, with Condoleezza Rice's National Security Council pitted against lawyers for the White House counsel and the vice president. Indeed, one reason the prison abuse scandal won't go away—two months after gruesome photos were published worldwide—is that a long paper trail of memos and directives from inside the administration has emerged, often leaked by those who disagreed with rougher means of questioning.

Last week the White House dismissed news accounts of one such memo, an explosive August 2002 brief from the Justice Department's Office of Legal Counsel disclosed by the *Washington Post*. The memo, drafted by former OLC lawyer John Yoo, has been widely criticized for seeming to flout conventions against torture. It defends most interrogation methods short of severe, intentionally inflicted pain and permanent damage. White House officials told reporters that such abstract legal reasoning was insignificant and did not reflect the president's orders. But *Newsweek* has learned that Yoo's August 2002 memo was prompted by CIA questions about what to do with a top Qaeda captive, Abu Zubaydah, who had turned uncooperative. And it was drafted after White House meetings convened by George W. Bush's chief counsel, Alberto Gonzales, along with Defense Department general counsel William Haynes and David Addington, Vice President Dick Cheney's counsel, who discussed specific interrogation techniques, says a source familiar with the discussions. Among the methods they found acceptable: "water-boarding," or dripping water into a wet cloth over a suspect's face, which can feel like drowning; and threatening to bring in more brutal interrogators from other nations.

Al-Libi's capture, some sources say, was an early turning point in the government's internal debates over interrogation methods. FBI officials brought their plea to retain control over al-Libi's interrogation up to FBI Director Robert Mueller. The CIA station chief in Afghanistan, meanwhile, appealed to the agency's hawkish counterterrorism chief, Cofer Black. He in turn called CIA Director George Tenet, who went to the White House. Al-Libi was handed over to the CIA. "They duct-taped his mouth, cinched him up, and sent him to Cairo" for more-fearsome Egyptian interrogations, says the ex-FBI official. "At the airport the CIA case officer goes up to him and says, 'You're going to Cairo, you know. Before you get there I'm going to find your mother and I'm going to f--- her.' So we lost that fight." (A CIA official said he had no comment.)

The FBI, with its "law enforcement" mind-set, found itself more and more marginalized. The struggle extended to the Guantanamo Bay detention center in early 2002, as "high value" suspects were shipped there for interrogation. Frustrated FBI officials, along with military interrogators like those from the Naval Criminal Investigation Service, found themselves "like kids with their noses pressed up against the glass," says a source involved in the early days at Gitmo. "Law enforcement had a long history of interrogating people. The intelligence community did not. Back in the cold war, they'd debriefed defectors. But that was all. So the intelligence community, once it got the mission, was searching for effective techniques of interrogation—and in their inexperience were floundering for a while."

Even within the CIA and the Defense Intelligence Agency, the debates never ceased. CIA officials remembered all too well how the agency was blamed in the 1970s human-rights backlash over covert plots. The agency, say senior intelligence officials, made sure it had explicit, written authorization from lawyers and senior policymakers before using new interrogation techniques. At the same time the agency felt intense pressure to extract information from suspects. So it began experimenting with methods like water-boarding and open-handed slapping. The CIA also asked to use "mock burial," in which a top Qaeda captive would be led to believe he was going to be buried alive. Administration officials declined to say whether the proposal was ever adopted. "My overwhelming impression is that everyone was focused on trying to avoid torture, staying within the line, while doing everything possible to save American lives," Tim Flanigan, formerly Bush's deputy White House counsel, told *Newsweek*.

As with al-Libi, the internal debates usually turned on what to do with a specific Qaeda detainee. That's what happened in the summer of 2002 after the capture of Abu Zubaydah, who refused to cooperate after an initial spate of talkativeness. Frustrated CIA officials went to OLC lawyer Yoo for an opinion on bolder methods.

Another high-value Qaeda suspect captured toward the end of 2002, Mohamed al Qatani, provoked a major change of approach at Guantanamo Bay. "There was a spike in a lot of intel that we were picking up in terms of more attacks" on America, said General James Hill, chief of the U.S. Southern Command. "We weren't getting anything out of him" using standard techniques outlined in Army Field Manual 34-52. So CIA and military-intel interrogators came up with new tactics based on the sorts of methods that U.S. Special Forces are specifically trained to resist, a Defense source says. The Special Forces' Survival, Evasion, Resistance, and Escape course culminates in interrogations that include some physical roughing up; sensory, food, and sleep deprivation; and a "water pit" in which detainees have to stand on tip-toe to keep from drowning.

Some inside the military criminal-investigation units at Gitmo, espe- 10 cially Navy personnel, approached Navy Secretary Alberto Mora with their concerns about violations of the Geneva Conventions. Perturbed, Mora in January 2003 went to see the Defense Department's Haynes and argued that the DOD was getting into unethical territory, and he warned of unhappiness among the uniformed military on this issue. Haynes concurred. On January 15, 2003, according to a chronology supplied by Pentagon officials, Defense Secretary Donald Rumsfeld suspended use of the heightened techniques. Haynes, on Rumsfeld's orders, then set up an Interrogation Working Group that issued a March 6, 2003, memo on accepted practices, which in turn was based on the reasoning of Yoo's August 2002 Justice Department brief.

It's still not clear whether these first decisions made in the war on terror eventually led to the abuses at Abu Ghraib. What does seem clear is that despite early efforts to vet interrogation techniques, the administration grew less and less careful as pressure built to get good intelligence. White House officials last week insisted that President Bush had made clear in an early-2002 policy directive that torture would not be used during the interrogation of Qaeda detainees. "The instructions went out to our people to adhere to the law," Bush himself told reporters. But the law according to whom? Bush originally said this was a war in which the old rules did not apply. But he may be learning now that they do.

Abu Ghraib and Beyond

JOHN BARRY, MARK HOSENBALL, AND BABAK DEHGHANPISHEH

BEFORE READING: Reflect on what you recall about the Abu Ghraib scandal when it was first publicized. What was your reaction?

A bu Ghraib Prison sits in the middle of one of Iraq's nastiest patches. Ever since "major combat" ended a year ago, snipers hidden in the palm groves that surround the vast prison compound have routinely fired on U.S. patrols. The guardrails on the highway in front of the prison are mangled for miles from the large number of IEDs (improvised explosive devices). Helicopters constantly buzz around. At night, soldiers in the

John Barry is the national security correspondent for *Newsweek*, Mark Hosenball is an investigative correspondent for the magazine, and Babak Dehghanpisheh is one of its Baghdad correspondents. This article appeared in the May 17, 2004, issue.

guard towers get drawn into raging gun battles. And mortars rain on the prison like a lethal hailstorm. "I can't even count how many mortar attacks we've had," Staff Sergeant Joseph Lane, an operating-room technician in the prison hospital, told *Newsweek* last week. "Sometimes there are two or three in a day." And all this while military police must process thousands of Iraqis each month, never knowing who among them is a "bad guy" trying to kill them.

It's hard to imagine a more high-pressure job. And late in the blazing-hot summer of 2003, military-intelligence officers working at Abu Ghraib were taking flak from their superiors inside as well as the insurgents outside. A series of bombings in August had leveled the Jordanian Embassy and the main United Nations office in Baghdad and killed a pro-U.S. ayatollah. At the Pentagon and in the field, military commanders began to mutter that too many intelligence personnel were engaged in the seemingly fruitless search for WMD [weapons of mass destruction] and too few assets were assigned to find out who was killing American troops. The word came down from Washington: we need better intelligence. "There was extraordinary pressure being put on MI [military intelligence] from every angle to get better info," says Brigadier General Janis Karpinski, the former 800th MP Brigade commander, who at the time was responsible for Abu Ghraib and other Iraqi prisons. "Where is Saddam? Find Saddam. And we want the weapons of mass destruction."

So Lieutenant General Ricardo Sanchez, the Coalition commander in Iraq, and his top intel officer Major General Barbara Fast, asked for a fixer. They got one in Major General Geoffrey Miller, the commandant at Guantanamo Bay, Cuba, where the U.S. military had held more than 600 detainees for more than two years without charges. A Texan with a jutting jaw and thinning hair, Miller was nothing if not self-assured, much like his ultimate superior, Defense Secretary Donald Rumsfeld. According to a subsequent inquiry by Major General Antonio Taguba, Miller's task was "to review current Iraqi Theater ability to rapidly exploit internees for actionable intelligence." Translated into English, that meant to beef up interrogation techniques so as to break prisoners more quickly. Or as Karpinski puts it, Miller's plan was to "Gitmo-ize" the place, to teach the soldiers manning Abu Ghraib his best psychological and physical techniques for squeezing information out of detainees. That included using Karpinski's MPs to "enhance the intelligence effort." At a meeting of top military-intelligence and MP commanders last September, Miller bluntly told Karpinski: "You're going to see. We have control, and [the prisoners] know it."

Miller delivered another message to Karpinski. After touring all sixteen prisons under the control of Karpinski's MP brigade, he declared that Abu Ghraib was the best choice for his interrogation purposes and that military intelligence was going to take it over. Karpinski said she responded: "Sir, Abu Ghraib is not mine to give you." She noted it was formally under the control of Iraq's Coalition Provisional Authority and that she and her military team ran it (like all other facilities) for the CPA. General Miller was in no mood for dissent, according to Karpinski's account. "I don't care. Rick Sanchez said I could have whatever I want. And I want Abu Ghraib," Miller said. He even cleared the room, Karpinski relates, saying, "Everybody out. I want to talk with the general." Miller then told Karpinski: "Look, we can do this my way or we can do it the hard way. We are going to take Abu Ghraib."

Exactly what Miller wanted with Abu Ghraib, and what duties he intended for Karpinski's MPs to perform there, remains unclear. Miller says that the recommendations he gave were "in keeping" with the Geneva Conventions, and that he asked only that MPs be involved in "passive intelligence collection"—observing and listening to prisoners. But what happened next no one can dispute, least of all an administration that once unambiguously touted U.S. power as a force for good but that is now asking the world's forgiveness. Gitmo's aggressive interrogation techniques and underlying philosophy of secrecy may have morphed into something terrible in the heat of a brutal guerrilla war. In the dead of night, Iraqi prisoners were brutalized and photographed in obscene and degrading poses. Karpinski's MPs, seven of whom are now charged, maintain that they were simply following new orders, which were, they say, to "soften up" prisoners for interrogation.

Last week Rumsfeld and his top brass desperately sought to minimize the damage—and to preempt further fallout from what Rumsfeld called "disgusting" new photos and videos from Abu Ghraib (and, sources tell *Newsweek*, other detention centers). In hearings on Capitol Hill, Rumsfeld and Joint Chiefs Chairman General Richard Myers apologized for what they and top brass repeatedly called "the actions of a few" rogue MPs and the military-intelligence personnel who egged them on (also named was Colonel Thomas Pappas, commander of the 205th MI Brigade). Above all, Rumsfeld and his brass tried to cut off the blame at Karpinski, who had been asked to resign at full pay. Despite his role in having brought Miller in, General Sanchez came away unscathed. General Fast has since been promoted and is slated to head the Fort Huachuca school in Arizona where most of the military interrogators train.

Perhaps most amazingly, the commander who last month was sent in to clean up Abu Ghraib turns out to be none other than the man who Karpinski claims had ordered her to hand it over to military-intel officers back in 2003, General Miller. Today, Miller says, detainees are no longer subjected to sleep-deprivation techniques, nor forced into "stress positions," nor blinded with hoods—unless such methods are specifically approved by a general. And he seems as self-assured as ever while denying that his orders to Karpinski were in any way related to the abuses there. "I will personally guarantee this will not happen again," Miller told *Newsweek* last week.

But it may be too late for such promises. There is evidence that the 372nd MP Company at Abu Ghraib had some bad apples in it, and that

Karpinski failed as a commander. There is also evidence of a possible Pentagon cover-up. According to Taguba's report, which was first revealed in *The New Yorker*, a previous Army investigator, Major General Donald Ryder, somehow failed to note last fall that MPs were being asked to facilitate interrogation. In addition, a mounting body of other evidence around the world suggests that abuses did not stop there or even in Iraq, that the Geneva Conventions protecting prisoners of war from beatings and humiliation were being routinely flouted in an environment where, as at Gitmo and Abu Ghraib, almost anything can happen because almost no one is held accountable. In Afghanistan, the abuse of prisoners seems to have led to at least three deaths at U.S. interrogation facilities. According to U.S. military pathologists, two Afghan detainees died of "blunt force injuries" to "the lower extremities" and "legs" at Baghram in December 2002 and another Afghan prisoner died at a U.S. military camp in Kunar province in June 2003. Yet eighteen months after the first deaths, a military investigation is still incomplete, and no broad inquiry like the Taguba probe has been launched into conditions at Baghram, according to a military spokesman in Kabul.

Rumsfeld insisted last week that the U.S. military has observed the Geneva Conventions regarding POWs and civilians in Iraq. But in his public statements (at least until last week), Rumsfeld has also declared that Geneva Conventions rules do not necessarily mean that all detainees—especially so-called unlawful combatants—will get all the rights and privileges normally accorded prisoners of war. And in recent months, *Newsweek* has learned, some senior members of Congress have been given highly classified briefings, indicating, in the words of one official, that U.S. interrogators were not necessarily "going to stick with the Geneva Convention." More stressful techniques were going to be used, the briefers indicated, apparently including some measure of physical discomfort.

Many critics say the Bush administration routinely uses the global 10 war on terrorism as a blanket justification for all sorts of human-rights violations. "The United States is running a gulag, a series of detention centers around the world where international legal standards are not having sway," says Carroll Bogert of Human Rights Watch. "They opened the door to a little bit of torture, and a whole lot of torture walked through." Nigel Rodley, who was the U.N. special rapporteur on torture and has written an authoritative book, *The Treatment of Prisoners Under International Law*, dismisses Rumsfeld's claims that the Geneva Conventions have been observed. Rodley says that even some interrogation practices the Pentagon acknowledges using are "clearly violations both of international human-rights law and international humanitarian law as codified in the Geneva Conventions." He adds that the problem "goes back to the whole process of essentially creating legal black holes where people are held in the dark and secret reaches of state power. When that happens it breeds a sense of impunity and people do things that they shouldn't do."

One American intelligence officer admitted as much, telling *Newsweek:* "The U.S. government and military capitalizes on the dubious status [as sovereign states] of Afghanistan, Diego Garcia, Guantanamo Bay, Iraq, and aircraft carriers, to avoid certain legal questions about rough interrogations. Whatever humanitarian pronouncements a state such as ours may make about torture, states don't perform interrogations, individual people do. What's going to stop an impatient soldier, in a supralegal location, from whacking one nameless, dehumanized shopkeeper among many?"

Sources say these mysterious prisons include some undeclared facilities set up by the CIA and other "black"-program operatives. The so-called ghost facilities, whose existence has never been publicly acknowledged by the Bush administration, are believed to be where top Qaeda leaders like Khalid Shaikh Mohammed and Abu Zubaida are held and questioned. One such detention center, where the Indonesian terrorist Hambali and the 9/11 co-conspirator Ramzi bin al-Shibh were believed to have been questioned, reportedly is located in Thailand. Another, according to a knowledgeable source, is located somewhere in the North-West Frontier province of Pakistan.

Even many stalwart Republicans are appalled by what's happened— and what may yet come out. "This is not a few bad apples. This is a system failure, a massive failure," said Senate Armed Services Committee member Lindsay Graham, a conservative Republican who once helped to prosecute the impeached Bill Clinton. Graham told *Newsweek* he believes that more allegations of murder and rape of detainees are likely to surface. Senator John McCain, whose arms were broken by North Vietnamese torturers, could barely suppress his rage during last week's hearings. Questioning Rumsfeld, the Arizona Republican reduced the normally self-assured Pentagon chief to a helpless sputter when McCain repeatedly demanded, "Who was in charge of the interrogations?" Rumsfeld did not give him a straight answer.

The Pentagon's effort at containment was undermined not just by the accounts of Karpinski and some of her soldiers, but by the conclusions of Rumsfeld's own lead investigator, General Taguba. Last week Army Chief of Staff Peter Schoomaker acknowledged that Army regulations forbid military police from participating in "military-intelligence-supervised interrogation sessions." Deputy CENTCOM commander Lieutenant General Lance Smith insisted that Miller's changes at Abu Ghraib in 2003 "didn't have anything to do with the methods of interrogating." But Taguba's report clearly outlines Miller's attempt to turn Abu Ghraib guards into "enablers" for interrogation. Taguba cites as evidence the testimony of Sergeant Javal Davis of the 372nd and others, who related that military intel was telling them to "loosen this guy up for us," to "make sure this guy has a bad night" and to "give him the treatment." Taguba describes how military-intel officials even complimented one of the charged MPs, Specialist Charles Graner Jr., on his handling of prisoners with statements like, "Good job, they're breaking down real fast."

Just what was "the treatment" given to Iraqis? The answer to that 15
question could ultimately decide Rumsfeld's fate. According to the Red
Cross, interrogation methods at the U.S. military's "high-value detention" facility in Iraq, Camp Cropper, located near Baghdad International
Airport, include "hooding a detainee in a bag, sometimes in conjunction
with beatings, thus increasing anxiety as to when blows would come";
handcuffs so tight they broke the skin; beatings with rifles and pistols;
threats against family members; and stripping detainees naked for several
days in solitary confinement in a completely dark cell.

General Miller, in a press briefing, tried to show how he was now
cleaning up interrogation procedures at Abu Ghraib. "We have approximately fifty approved interrogation techniques. They come from Army
Field Manual 34-52," Miller said. Asked to explain what Miller meant,
U.S. Army Intelligence Center spokesperson Tanja Linton said she would
go away and inquire. She came back to report: "They have no idea what
he is talking about." But a senior Defense Department official, speaking
on background, confirms that there is a secret list of what he called "categories" of interrogation techniques—which, he says, can be used only
with the case-by-case approval of Defense Secretary Rumsfeld.

No one knows exactly what went wrong at Abu Ghraib. But Miller's
"Gitmo rules" were being introduced into a much more uncontrolled environment in Iraq. Gitmo has no "hot" war outside its walls and only
600–800 detainees, all of them pre-screened as terrorist suspects and controlled by 800 guards. Abu Ghraib has had as many as 7,000 detainees—
and about 700 guards, which is shockingly low. (Karpinski has pointed
out that a civilian U.S. prison would have double that prisoner-to-guard
ratio.) Many soldiers say they are just as horrified and saddened as the
U.S. public by the photos. Sergeant Stacy Renee Ferguson of Factoryville,
Pennsylvania, was with the 320th Military Police Battalion when it
shifted out of Abu Ghraib and the 372nd MP unit shifted in. Last week
she recalled that the 372nd was full of bad attitudes because they had
been jerked around—idling forever in Kuwait, told they were shipping
back to the United States, eventually detailed to Abu Ghraib. "They obviously didn't want to be there."

Still, some question how seriously Rumsfeld is taking the allegations
even now. At hearings last week, he was not shy about admitting mistakes. But he reserved most of his self-flagellation not for moral offenses
but for, as he put it, "not understanding and knowing" there were hundreds of photos "that could eventually end up in the public and do the
damage they've done." The role and culpability of the military-
intelligence hierarchy remained carefully shrouded. And before the
photos came out, noted Senator Jack Reed sardonically, none of the senior officers in the affair had suffered worse than a reprimand. "Is that because a trial, and due process, would bring this out?" Reed asked. We are
now likely to discover just that.

What Abu Ghraib Taught Me

BARBARA EHRENREICH

BEFORE READING: What is your position on women's role in combat? Has America's war in Iraq changed your position? Explain.

E ven those people we might have thought were impervious to shame, like the Secretary of Defense, admit that the photos of abuse in Iraq's Abu Ghraib prison turned their stomachs.

The photos did something else to me, as a feminist: They broke my heart. I had no illusions about the U.S. mission in Iraq—whatever exactly it is—but it turns out that I did have some illusions about women.

Of the seven U.S. soldiers now charged with sickening forms of abuse in Abu Ghraib, three are women: Specialist Megan Ambuhl, Private First Class Lynndie England, and Specialist Sabrina Harman.

It was Harman we saw smiling an impish little smile and giving the thumbs-up sign from behind a pile of hooded, naked Iraqi men—as if to say, "Hi Mom, here I am in Abu Ghraib!" It was England we saw with a naked Iraqi man on a leash. If you were doing PR for Al Qaeda, you couldn't have staged a better picture to galvanize misogynist Islamic fundamentalists around the world.

Here, in these photos from Abu Ghraib, you have everything that the 5 Islamic fundamentalists believe characterizes Western culture, all nicely arranged in one hideous image—imperial arrogance, sexual depravity . . . and gender equality.

Maybe I shouldn't have been so shocked. We know that good people can do terrible things under the right circumstances. This is what psychologist Stanley Milgram found in his famous experiments in the 1960s. In all likelihood, Ambuhl, England, and Harman are not congenitally evil people. They are working-class women who wanted an education and knew that the military could be a stepping-stone in that direction. Once they had joined, they wanted to fit in.

And I also shouldn't be surprised because I never believed that women were innately gentler and less aggressive than men. Like most feminists, I have supported full opportunity for women within the military—(1) because I knew women could fight, and (2) because the military is one of the few options around for low-income young people.

Although I opposed the 1991 Persian Gulf War, I was proud of our servicewomen and delighted that their presence irked their Saudi hosts. Secretly, I hoped that the presence of women would over time change the

Barbara Ehrenreich is the author of *Nickel and Dimed: On (Not) Getting By in America* (2001). This article was first published in the Sunday Opinion section of the *Los Angeles Times*, on July 24, 2004.

military, making it more respectful of other people and cultures, more capable of genuine peacekeeping. That's what I thought, but I don't think that anymore.

A certain kind of feminism, or perhaps I should say a certain kind of feminist naiveté, died in Abu Ghraib. It was a feminism that saw men as the perpetual perpetrators, women as the perpetual victims, and male sexual violence against women as the root of all injustice. Rape has repeatedly been an instrument of war and, to some feminists, it was beginning to look as if war was an extension of rape. There seemed to be at least some evidence that male sexual sadism was connected to our species' tragic propensity for violence. That was before we had seen female sexual sadism in action.

But it's not just the theory of this naive feminism that was wrong. So 10 was its strategy and vision for change. That strategy and vision rested on the assumption, implicit or stated outright, that women were morally superior to men. We had a lot of debates over whether it was biology or conditioning that gave women the moral edge—or simply the experience of being a woman in a sexist culture. But the assumption of superiority, or at least a lesser inclination toward cruelty and violence, was more or less beyond debate. After all, women do most of the caring work in our culture, and in polls are consistently less inclined toward war than men.

I'm not the only one wrestling with that assumption today. Mary Jo Melone, a columnist for the *St. Petersburg* (Florida) *Times*, wrote on May 7: "I can't get that picture of England [pointing at a hooded Iraqi man's genitals] out of my head because this is not how women are expected to behave. Feminism taught me thirty years ago that not only had women gotten a raw deal from men, we were morally superior to them."

If that assumption had been accurate, then all we would have had to do to make the world a better place—kinder, less violent, more just— would have been to assimilate into what had been, for so many centuries, the world of men. We would fight so that women could become the generals, CEOs, senators, professors, and opinion-makers —and that was really the only fight we had to undertake. Because once they gained power and authority, once they had achieved a critical mass within the institutions of society, women would naturally work for change. That's what we thought, even if we thought it unconsciously—and it's just not true. Women can do the unthinkable.

You can't even argue, in the case of Abu Ghraib, that the problem was that there just weren't enough women in the military hierarchy to stop the abuses. The prison was directed by a woman, General Janis Karpinski. The top U.S. intelligence officer in Iraq, who also was responsible for reviewing the status of detainees before their release, was Major General Barbara Fast. And the U.S. official ultimately responsible for managing the occupation of Iraq since October was Condoleezza Rice. Like Donald H. Rumsfeld, she ignored repeated reports of abuse and torture until the undeniable photographic evidence emerged.

What we have learned from Abu Ghraib, once and for all, is that a uterus is not a substitute for a conscience. This doesn't mean gender equality isn't worth fighting for for its own sake. It is. If we believe in democracy, then we believe in a woman's right to do and achieve whatever men can do and achieve, even the bad things. It's just that gender equality cannot, all alone, bring about a just and peaceful world.

In fact, we have to realize, in all humility, that the kind of feminism   15 based on an assumption of female moral superiority is not only naive; it also is a lazy and self-indulgent form of feminism. Self-indulgent because it assumes that a victory for a woman — a promotion, a college degree, the right to serve alongside men in the military — is by its very nature a victory for all of humanity. And lazy because it assumes that we have only one struggle — the struggle for gender equality — when in fact we have many more.

The struggles for peace and social justice and against imperialist and racist arrogance, cannot, I am truly sorry to say, be folded into the struggle for gender equality.

What we need is a tough new kind of feminism with no illusions. Women do not change institutions simply by assimilating into them, only by consciously deciding to fight for change. We need a feminism that teaches a woman to say no — not just to the date rapist or overly insistent boyfriend but, when necessary, to the military or corporate hierarchy within which she finds herself.

In short, we need a kind of feminism that aims not just to assimilate into the institutions that men have created over the centuries but to infiltrate and subvert them.

To cite an old, and far from naive, feminist saying: "If you think equality is the goal, your standards are too low." It is not enough to be equal to men, when the men are acting like beasts. It is not enough to assimilate. We need to create a world worth assimilating into.

THINKING AND WRITING ABOUT THE EFFECT OF TERRORISM ON THE AMERICAN IDEA OF JUSTICE

QUESTIONS FOR DISCUSSION AND WRITING

1. Look at the essay "The Case for Torture" in Chapter 6. Does Levin's argument seem more relevant after the attacks of September 11? Why or why not?

2. Do you feel that the use of torture is ever justified? Explain.

3. Do you feel that your rights have in any way been threatened by the increased security since September 11? Refer to at least one of the readings in this chapter in your response.

4. What do you consider to be the greatest threat to Americans' rights posed by the USA Patriot Act?

5. One group opposed to the Patriot Act have been librarians. Why would this group be concerned about this piece of legislation? Are their concerns justified?

6. Do you ever feel that our nation has too many laws designed to protect the rights of those accused of wrongdoing? Could the Patriot Act help change that, even in cases where the suspected crime is not terrorism?

7. "Name Withheld" tells the story of one unidentified man held for four months largely because his nationality made him suspect. Are such cases the unavoidable price we pay for national security? Explain. (Had the man referred to as "M." done anything wrong?)

8. Having read Kent's "Justice for Terrorists," do you feel that military tribunals are a logical alternative to trying suspected terrorists in our civilian court system?

9. Do you feel that those accused of prisoner abuse at Abu Ghraib were justified in arguing that they were simply following orders? Explain.

10. Should American women who want to serve in combat be allowed to do so? Explain why or why not.

TOPICS FOR RESEARCH

The effect the Patriot Act has had on libraries

Military tribunals

The internment of Japanese Americans during World War II

The outcome of the Abu Ghraib trials

TAKING THE DEBATE ONLINE

For these and additional research URLs, see bedfordstmartins.com/rottenberg.

- *American Civil Liberties Union*
  www.aclu.org/

  The ACLU says, "Our job is to conserve America's original civic values — the Constitution and the Bill of Rights."

- *United States Department of Justice*
  www.usdoj.gov/

  This site contains documents, publications, and policy statements by the department charged with administering justice at the federal level.

- *International Responsibilities Task Force of the American Library Association's Social Responsibilities Round Table*
  www.pitt.edu/~ttwiss/irtf/Alternative.html

This site's stated intention is "to provide information and advocate socially responsible positions on issues of international concern"; the site contains links to various "alternative resources on the U.S. 'War on Terrorism.'"

- *Social Criticism Review*
  www.socialcritic.org/terror.htm

  This page contains dozens of links to selected readings on the "War on Terrorism" in America.

- *Preserving Life and Liberty*
  www.lifeandliberty.gov/

  This site was created by the Department of Justice to "educate Americans about how we are preserving life and liberty by using the USA Patriot Act." It contains the full text of the act in addition to numerous speeches and articles related to it.

CHAPTER 14

What Is the Future of the Family?

The traditional family is still alive but growing weaker. As depicted in Norman Rockwell paintings and the movies and TV series of more than a generation ago, this idyllic family lived in a white house with a picket fence and consisted of a breadwinner father, a homemaker mother, two or three lively but dutiful children, and a friendly dog. In 1998 a research group found that only 26 percent of American households consisted of married couples with children. The director of the survey observed that Americans seem to be accepting of "the modern family," and to be more tolerant of separation and divorce, whether or not there are children.

Some of the socioeconomic forces behind these changes are not hard to find: a wider endorsement of the values of individualism and personal freedom, a relaxation of divorce laws, vastly increased numbers of women in the workforce, even the movement of young people to colleges away from home. Perhaps it is not surprising that the importance of biological kinship itself has come under attack. The legal correspondent of the *New York Times* wrote that a court case in 2000 "opened the door to a profound debate over the definition of family."[1] Can someone not related to a child be given visiting rights if the family court concludes that "visitation would be in the best interests of the child"? A gay rights organization argued that "the quality and security of the relationship between individual children and adults rather than blood ties or labels" should govern legal decisions.

---

[1]Linda Greenhouse, "Case on Visitation Rights Hinges on Defining Family," *New York Times,* January 4, 2001, sec. A, p. 11.

In fact, it is not only the legal definition of family that is a source of controversy. We have always debated the influence of family in shaping our lives. One of the reasons for a range of opinions is that everyone is a member of a family, and each member may experience the family differently. An expert on family law asks:

> Are families havens of love, care, attention, and affection? Or are they hells of manipulation, guilt, and oppression? Are families natural preserves, where social and legal rules follow biology and passion? Or are they social institutions created and regulated by government to serve specific public purposes?[2]

We know, of course, that traditional families are not necessarily happy and fulfilled. Often they are bound only by marriage and blood—what the poet Stephen Spender called "loveless intimacy." The family of the past sometimes remained intact because release was difficult or impossible.

But freedom from family does not come without a price. A prominent psychoanalyst has warned that the tradeoff for freedom from the commitments and responsibilities of family may be loneliness and insecurity. And the emotional and economic consequences for broken families, especially for women and children, are often devastating. Folk wisdom has it that "the past is prologue," but it's not clear how much the history of the family so far can tell us about the direction the family will take in an American society that keeps changing. (See also "Divorce and Our National Values" by Peter D. Kramer, p. 279.)

Family Is One of the Few Certainties We Will Take with Us Far into the Future

CAROL SHIELDS

> BEFORE READING: If unrelated people live, work, and play together, can they be defined as a family? Why, or why not?

Six-year-old Christopher spotted something from the rear window of his grandparents' car. Three great radio towers stood close together in a field, one of them immensely tall, one slightly shorter, and one just half

---

[2]Martha Minow, *Family Matters* (New York: New Press, 1993), p. 1.

Carol Shields (1935–2003), a novelist, won the 1995 Pulitzer Prize for her novel *The Stone Diaries*. Her other works include *Dressing Up for the Carnival* (2002), *Unless* (2002), and *Dropped Threads: More of What We Aren't Told* (2003). This article comes from the *Wall Street Journal*, January 1, 2000.

the size of the second. "A family," Christopher mumbled nonchalantly against the glass.

Father, mother, and child—the iconography offered by these three steel structures was clear, even to a boy of six. Here they stood, shoulder to shoulder, breaking the line of the horizon and suggesting, with their bold, leggy presence, human creatures, nakedly acknowledging their spatial relationship.

My husband and I smiled, as we often do when Christopher comes up with one of his poetic stretches. This symbolic configuration of the family must live at the very front of his brain, an image so simplified, stylized, and accessible he can express it without a hint of self-consciousness or of misunderstanding. A family, yes. Or at least an archetypal representation. Its resolute triangularity has entered his primary imagination where it holds authority over wider society, whose circles of power and permanence he only dimly perceives.

By the year 2050, given good health, reasonable luck, and a peaceful society, Christopher will be a man in his mid-fifties. Chances are reasonably good that he will be a father by that time and perhaps even a grandfather. Almost certainly, though, he will be embedded in some form of family, traditional or otherwise. Human beings are social creatures, interdependent economically, linked to each other by emotional need, sexual desire, and the drive to perpetuate their species. This Darwinian truth may seem reductive, but it isn't so easily set aside.

Even now, this sometimes willful and stubbornly independent child 5 sitting in the back seat must sense he isn't yet able to stand outside the family rubric. He would perish. His existence would be without meaning.

Belonging to Someone

This weekend, the world passes an imaginary divide. Our clocks and calendars declare their own importance, adjuring us to pay attention, to celebrate or grieve or at the very least meditate upon our human arrangements and how they have served or failed us.

The condition of family is one of the few certainties we will take with us into the next thousand years; each of us is, and will continue to be, someone's son or daughter. The most wretchedly isolated street person occupies a twig on a branch of a family tree, however invisible. The solitarily inclined, the viciously misanthropic—these, too, share gene structures with a chain of forebears, known or unknown. St. Jerome clinging to his rocky isle is remembered as that extraordinarily rare individual who needed no one other than God. (God the father? It seems even our deities are arranged in familial groupings.) St. Jerome aside, the rest of us, whatever our considered choices, belong to others.

Evolution is a slow-grinding process, and millions of years would be required to redesign our basic regenerative mechanics, transforming us, in fact, into another species altogether. Men bearing offspring or communes of women reproducing by parthenogenesis will probably remain, for the time being, inhabitants of science fiction.

The specter of cloning, introduced in the last decade of our own century, may, on the other hand, offer serious alternatives and stir what has already become one of the prime philosophical arguments of our time. Yet even the specter of genetic manipulation will come down in the end to a specific mother's egg specifically stimulated.

But the family has proved particularly difficult to decode. It is, has al- 10 ways been, a walking, talking irony. We speak about the family being the bosom of love and comfort, romantic language that adheres to the word *family* without the least embarrassment. *Family* also is another word for *tyranny*. James Joyce called the family a snare, the ultimate and damaging intimacy of enemies, which must be confronted once the simple demands of infancy are satisfied.

Families imply care, expectation, control, or, on the other side of the wallpaper, neglect, and abuse. Almost no one is tutored in family courtesy, no one is given a list of rules. And very few are afforded a second chance to repair the lives with which they collide. Jane Austen wrote six splendid novels, each of which concludes with the ceremony of marriage and the implied continuation of family, and yet the happiness of all her families is deformed by sibling rivalry, parental ignorance, insensitivity, embarrassment, and economic expediency. Interestingly, she didn't marry or have a child, remaining with her blood family to the end.

It might be argued that all art is ultimately about family, the creation of structures—music, sculpture, poetry, dance—that reflect our immediate circle, what families do to us and how they can be reimagined or transcended. What is a novel but a story about the fate of a child? What is a play—think of Shakespeare, Ibsen, Shaw, Pinter, and Stoppard—but the interaction of those who are randomly thrown together, the testimony of the most (or least) reliable witnesses we are afforded: our families?

Less Fruitful

The family of the future will carry on its shoulders many of the changes we have seen in our own lifetime. We understand more and more about the ways in which poverty and family intersect. The relative ease of divorce has fractured our assumptions about the two-parent family.

Families are smaller now that we have the means to prevent conception, at least in modern industrial countries. Once, a large number of children was considered an economic benefit, but that is no longer the case. Concern about overpopulation, too, has limited procreation, so that social norms about family size have shifted. Child care has become a critical issue since the women's movement led to a reduction in the number of stay-at-home mothers.

And in the Western world we complain that we never have enough 15 time; yet the nurturing of children is the one thing that cannot be compressed. The speed of milk flowing from a mother's nipple into the baby's mouth is fixed. The reading aloud of, say, *The Wind in the Willows*, even when summarized or excerpted, is dependent on narrative comprehension, which follows neurological laws—which demand sequencing, not multitasking.

There is no turning back from this knowledge. The notion of quality time has been exposed as a sham or else a fantasy—one of the many hopeful fantasies entertained about family and family life.

Diverse Forms

What is certain is that families will continue to exist in diverse forms, just as they always have. Sometimes this surprises us; sometimes we find it a relief from the various shades of guilt that attach to family membership.

The stereotypical family—malevolent or wholesome—has existed only as a diversion or a type of shorthand; each actual family gestures toward an infinite number of variations.

Medieval craftsmen living under the same roof with their apprentices formed ad hoc families, with, perhaps, subtly gauged degrees of intimacy or distance. Those large, bustling, prosperous Victorian families—almost certainly closer to being a fiction than a reality—came in their own variations, though usually dependent on servants who had their own very different, often concealed, family models. The so-called Boston marriage—two women living together, sexually connected or not—represents another experiment in family.

Of course, there always have been de facto families: gay families, 20 monastic families, gatherings of friends or acquaintances who have agreed to share a roof, a kitchen, a bed. Couples who consider themselves a family must be resentful when asked whether they have "any family." But can a single person constitute a "family"? I wouldn't dismiss the notion.

We can't really talk about abstract families; family studies may be the darling of sociologists, psychologists and Freudians, statistical extrapolations, and conclusions, but there is no such thing as *the* family. Geography, class, culture, historical time, perception—all these interfere with an overall notion of what the family is.

It may be true, after all, that Ozzie and Harriet invented the standard modern family, something that scarcely existed outside of radio land: two cheerful, committed parents, bumbling but well-intentioned, and a couple of healthy kids who test them and sometimes teach them new pieties. The fact is, families are more protected than almost any other institution by a veil of secrecy, their domestic moments hidden from view. And it may well be that the questions posed within families are as cloaked as those that come from outside, and the answers as subversive or evasive or pointless.

The best we can do is look into our individual histories and hope we can back far enough away, squinting, peering, in order to get a little perspective—even though we know that distancing ourselves from family is a challenging, and perhaps impossible, assignment.

The "Normal" Family

Oak Park, Illinois, where I was born, seemed intent in the 1940s and 1950s on projecting an image of homogeneity. This was where the "taverns leave off and church steeples begin." It was assumed that this safe and prosperous and progressive community (they called themselves a village, even though the population exceeded 70,000) operated from a secure nexus of white families: each household provided with a mother (at home), a father (with an office job in downtown Chicago), and children (healthy, intelligent, enrolled in one of the excellent public schools, each named after an American poet, Hawthorne, Longfellow, Whittier).

I believed this narrative, even though everything I saw belied it.   25

Next door to us on Emerson Avenue lived the Ollershaws with their four children, all of whom attended the local Catholic school where, we were told, the teachers were brides of Jesus. Mr. Ollershaw was intermittently unemployed, and the second child, Patsy, went into frequent and dramatic epileptic seizures, even while we played hopscotch, jump rope, or kick-the-can in the early evening.

On the other side of us was Mrs. Anderson, a widow, a witch, or so we believed, able to cast spells. Next to her was the Shavaughan family with their two children, the oldest of whom was, for some mysterious reason, unable to ride a bicycle. What was the matter with Bobby Shavaughan?

Mrs. Dastas, next to the Shavaughans, lived with her husband, dyed her hair, grew dahlias, and spoke to no one. Next to her was a house split into apartments. The first floor was occupied by an elderly man and his young son, Teddy Woolhouse. There was no mother, no woman in this family. How did they manage? We couldn't imagine. Upstairs, alone, lived Miss Spokie, who drew fashion illustrations for the *Chicago Tribune*. We never saw her, in fact, not even once. She must have come and gone after dark.

The Wiggens family further down the block had recently lost their head of household. It was said that he collapsed and died on the train platform, falling directly into the path of a commuter train. Years later the truth occurred to me: He jumped—of course, he jumped. The Worthingtons had a daughter in an upstairs bedroom who had been asleep for nine years. A coma, it was called. The Tomeks spoke with a foreign accent and ate pancakes for supper instead of breakfast. Mary Louise Fulton's mother stayed in bed all day while Mary Louise was at school. She was a beautiful woman, everyone said, as though her beauty might, after all, have sustained and heartened her.

Perhaps we—my mother, father, brother, sister, and I—were the only   30 true family in our little American neighborhood, healthy, thriving, "normal." But I didn't think that, growing up. I felt, as perhaps all children do, that we were the ones who were different. I longed to enter the wholly untroubled world of Dick and Jane: Dick who never picked on little kids, Jane with her clean white socks, sunny Sally, even the cheerful, housebroken Spot.

What I've come to understand, and with surprising relief, is that we existed as a part of that enormous diversity we call the family, not "normal" at all, but fragile, self-created, provisional, and eager to avoid concerning ourselves with the arrangements of others.

Diversity is both our reality and our hope. There is a sense in which the creation of families is the ultimate opportunity for freedom (although the Chinese experiment with the one-child family seems a denial of this truth).

Gender option in our own society may tighten the pattern of openness, but we will, one hopes, remain aware in the next century, perhaps the next millennium, of our essential dependence on the knit of family structure, caught up in the surprise of love we feel for those who surround us, their randomness, their uniqueness, their ability to give definition to us—their family.

Why Do We Marry?

JANE SMILEY

> BEFORE READING: Reflect on the families of friends and relatives in which the parents have divorced. Did some family members gain and others lose as the result of the divorce?

My guinea-pig child, now twenty-one, was home from her senior year in college for Christmas vacation. This child was not by temperament suited to be the unbuffered firstborn of a literary, free-thinking mother and an anxiety-prone father, the child of divorce, joint custody, and stepparenting. Her whole life, she has been a girl who liked things steady and predictable. Thus it came as a surprise to me when she disclosed her ideal family, the one she aims to have when she is the matriarch. The word she used was *welcoming*. Should you want to be in her family, whoever you are, well, she is going to be happy to have you. Her house will have plenty of beds and plenty of dishes and plenty of congenial people sitting around discussing issues like women's health care and the third wave of feminism. I liked it. It sounded quite like the home she has grown up in, of which I have been the matriarch.

The last night before my daughter went back to college, we had another one of those family dinners—you know, me, my boyfriend, his daughter and son by his second wife, my daughters by my second

Jane Smiley is the author of numerous novels, among them *A Thousand Acres,* which won a Pulitzer Prize in 1992. Her most recent is *Good Faith* (2003). Her essay is reprinted from the *Utne Reader* for September/October 2000.

husband, and my seven-year-old son by my third husband. The topic of conversation was how my son came to walk home from school—more than a mile up a steep, winding road on a very warm day. "What did you do when cars went by?" I asked.

"I stepped to the side of the road!" he answered. He was laughing at the success of his exploit. Not only had he been a very bold boy who had accomplished something he had been wanting to do; he had been impressively disobedient. We all laughed, and my boyfriend and I squeezed each other's hands, pleased and seduced by that happy-family idea, everyone safe and well-fed, getting along, taken care of.

But we are not married, and we have no plans to blend our families. I come to the theory and practice of marriage at the start of the new millennium with a decidedly checkered past and an outsider's view. But, I admit, I'm still paying attention, implicated, at least, by the fact that my children assume they will get married. I see the breakdown of the traditional family not as a dark and fearsome eventuality but rather as something interesting to observe, something that I have endured, survived, and actually benefited from, something that will certainly be part of the material from which my children build their lives.

High-Tech Parenting

AMITAI ETZIONI

BEFORE READING: How much have technical innovations affected your family? Do you regard some changes as undesirable?

The parental crisis is over. Salvation has arrived in the form of technology that opens up a whole new world of Remote Parenting. One pioneer of the movement is attorney Mary Croft. Too busy to talk with her twelve-year-old daughter about the happenings of a school day, boy-and-girl things, or permission to stop over at a friend's house, Ms. Croft purchased a pair of beepers so the child could cue her mom "talk needed" as the mother-attorney raced around taking care of her clients. Alas, the beepers didn't prove efficient enough. The elder Croft often found that when her daughter needed a response, the phone booths on street corners or in airport stalls were occupied. So a pair of cellular phones were added to the mother-daughter relationship.

Amitai Etzioni is university professor at George Washington University. He is the author of twenty-four books, including *My Brother's Keeper: A Memoir and a Message* (2003) and *From Empire to Community: A New Approach to International Relations* (2004). His essay appeared in the January/February 1998 issue of *The American Enterprise*.

Parents are not to worry that beep-and-ring relations are less affectionate than old-fashioned talks-and-hugs on the way to Little League or while stacking dishes in the washer. Reassuring experts ranging from professors to electronic device-makers insist that "teleparenting"—or, more advanced yet, "virtual parenting"—is the wave of the future. For long-distance parenting to succeed, psychologists promise, children need only have clear routines. Once those are in place, parents can click in to check that the TV has been turned off as scheduled and homework turned on; that the wholesome tuna sandwich has been prepared; and that the dog (who does not get the beep-and-ring thing yet) has been let out. Those who fear that children will learn to game the system—turning off the idiot box when the phone rings, claiming to be home on the third beep while they are actually in a friend's liquor cabinet—need not panic. Surely the industry is hard at work designing cellular picture phones armed with place-identifiers, using satellites to verify the exact location of the speaker.

"Quality time" has long since replaced quantity time in many high-powered homes. The notion that a child opens up to parental guidance at unpredictable times—during a long walk, a prolonged conversation—is discounted by careerist parents. Many now seem to believe that they and their children can "relate" on demand, during times set aside for that purpose. Today's new twist is that even the truncated face-to-face "quality time" is being replaced—by quality phone calls. Tax accountant Jane Maddow says cellular phones are an indispensable part of her parenting. Almost every day, even at the busy peak of tax season, she will push other things aside so that she can talk for as long as *five minutes,* to each of her two boys when they return home from school.

Computer scientists at Rice University are working on something called the cyborg blanket, with the aim of freeing parents from the heavy responsibility of tending infants. The "blanket" will play soothing music or prerecorded warm words from mother or father when an infant engages in "low-intensity" crying. High-intensity crying will lead to a beep being broadcast to parents.

Parents had better keep these marvelous gizmos in good repair, be-   5 cause family get-togethers may soon be replaced by conference calls. Expect a beep and a ring at future wedding anniversaries or other big days. Cost will be no problem, because the children have been well trained to keep phone calls short, constantly reminded by the clicks of call-waiting that others compete with them for their parents' time. And as parents grow old and find themselves installed in a nursing home, they had better take a modem with them; e-mails from their children are sure to follow. As time allows.

*"Before we begin this family meeting, how about we go around
and say our names and a little something about ourselves."*

The Sting of Divorce

WILLIAM S. POLLACK with TODD SHUSTER

BEFORE READING: How has divorce affected some of the young people you know?

I don't know why they got divorced. They were a happy couple.

—Garcia, twelve, from a city in the Northeast

I felt like someone had put a hundred daggers in my heart. I never before knew what divorce really meant or what went with it. . . . My dad moved out less than a month later.

—Bruce, fourteen, from a suburb in northern New England

Not Simple by Any Means: Chip, fifteen, from a Small Town in New England

There are some things in life that we just don't want to deal with, accept, or even acknowledge as existing.

Almost a month ago—and it seems like a lot less—I found out that my parents would be getting a divorce. That sounds simple, sounds common, sounds like something that would be accepted and possibly even expected, as one-half of all marriages end in divorce.

It doesn't matter what it sounds like! If it sounds simple, then believe me when I tell you that it is not. If it sounds common, then believe me that I have never had anything remotely close to this happen in my family. If it sounds like something acceptable, then, by God, believe me when I say it is not. As for being expected, there was no hint, no warning, no smoke before everything went up in flames. It was sudden, harsh, cold, and impersonal; and worst of all, it was my family that it was happening to.

The divorce process is not simple by any means. Trust me, I've done my homework, I've done research, and I've found out everything that is supposed to happen. I've been blessed with a very caring girlfriend who went through the same process when she was five. Although her circumstances were vastly different from mine, she has helped me tremendously by telling me what is supposed to happen, and what I'm going to feel like as it is happening. That's the worst part of a divorce, by the way—it's the *not knowing,* the feeling that you're being left behind, that the divorce is not a subject to be discussed, that it's just something which is supposed to happen on its own. It's a feeling of indescribable loneliness.

William S. Pollack, a clinical psychologist, is assistant clinical professor of psychology at Harvard Medical School and director of the Center for Men at McLean Hospital in Belmont, Massachusetts. Todd Shuster is a journalist. This selection is taken from *Real Boys' Voices* (2000).

It's such an emptiness, such a hole in your very soul which can't be 5
filled; at times you will be doing some routine mechanical thing, like
homework, and you'll think, "Oh, I don't know how to do this, I'll just
ask my dad . . ." and things trail off as you realize that you don't have a
dad who will be coming home that evening. You have a dad who lives
down the street, or in the next town, or around the world; it doesn't matter. The important thing is that you have a dad who doesn't live at home.
This is the hardest part, recognizing the change in the normal routine.
Recognizing and realizing that from now on you will be split between two
parents, or will not see one except on weekends, or will not see one again.
I don't know which of these things is worse.

Although statistically half of all marriages end in divorce, that doesn't
mean anything. Saying that is like saying, "You have a one in five thousand chance of having a fatal accident while driving." That means that
one of those other five thousand people driving home *will* have a wreck,
not you. Numbers, statistics, percentages, while they never lie, make
lousy condolences and even worse reminders. I never thought at all, ever,
not once, that something like this would happen in my family.

There is no history of divorce on either side of my family, and I've
checked. Both sets of grandparents have very detailed genealogy records
dating back literally hundreds of years, and nowhere in either one will
you find a dashed line, which represents a divorce. This is something
completely new, completely wrong that is happening to my family. This
was never supposed to happen to the little kid with the funny mom and
the really tall dad. This was not supposed to happen!

As for this being acceptable, allow me to quote with great emphasis
that bald guy from *Apollo 13:* "Failure is not, *ever,* an option!" This is giving up, this is quitting, and this is failure on the grandest scale. That is divorce, simply and bluntly. Quitting. What a disgusting, dishonorable, and
altogether deplorable act.

Talking or thinking about or even feeling all that the word *divorce* encompasses is difficult. In fact, this is the most difficult thing that has ever
happened in my fifteen years of life. I have overcome many obstacles in
my hopes of one day walking on the ocean floor, once diving deeper than
all the safe limits to save a friend. I have jumped off cliffs with nothing
but a thin rope dangling in the air to hold me to this earth. I have done
things that other men only imagine. Yet dealing with my parents' divorce
is more difficult, more challenging, and more taxing on me mentally and
physically than all of these feats combined.

The only advice I can offer to anyone else going through this is the 10
advice which my girlfriend gave me: "Hang in there, baby. Hang in
there."

" THESE STRAIGHT LITTLE, BIBLE-BELT, DISNEY-RAISED, GIRL-NEXT-DOOR TYPES ARE MAKING A MOCKERY OF THE INSTITUTION OF MARRIAGE!"

Great Expectations

POLLY SHULMAN

BEFORE READING: Do you believe that there is one person somewhere who is your true soul mate?

Marriage is dead! The twin vises of church and law have relaxed their grip on matrimony. We've been liberated from the grim obligation to stay in a poisonous or abusive marriage for the sake of the kids or for appearances. The divorce rate has stayed constant at nearly 50 percent for the last two decades. The ease with which we enter and dissolve unions makes marriage seem like a prime-time spectator sport, whether it's Britney Spears in Vegas or bimbos chasing after the Bachelor.

Long live the new marriage! We once prized the institution for the practical pairing of a cash-producing father and a home-building mother. Now we want it all—a partner who reflects our taste and status, who sees us for who we are, who loves us for all the "right" reasons, who helps us become the person we want to be. We've done away with a rigid social order, adopting instead an even more onerous obligation: the mandate to find a perfect match. Anything short of this ideal prompts us to ask: Is

Polly Shulman is a freelance writer in New York City. This article appeared in the March/April 2004 issue of *Psychology Today*.

this all there is? Am I as happy as I should be? Could there be somebody out there who's better for me? As often as not, we answer yes to that last question and fall victim to our own great expectations.

That somebody is, of course, our soul mate, the man or woman who will counter our weaknesses, amplify our strengths, and provide the unflagging support and respect that is the essence of a contemporary relationship. The reality is that few marriages or partnerships consistently live up to this ideal. The result is a commitment limbo, in which we care deeply for our partner but keep one stealthy foot out the door of our hearts. In so doing, we subject the relationship to constant review: Would I be happier, smarter, a *better person* with someone else? It's a painful modern quandary. "Nothing has produced more unhappiness than the concept of the soul mate," says Atlanta psychiatrist Frank Pittman.

Consider Jeremy, a social worker who married a businesswoman in his early twenties. He met another woman, a psychologist, at age twenty-nine, and after two agonizing years, left his wife for her. But it didn't work out—after four years of cohabitation, and her escalating pleas to marry, he walked out on her as well. Jeremy now realizes that the relationship with his wife was solid and workable but thinks he couldn't have seen that ten years ago, when he left her. "There was always someone better around the corner—and the safety and security of marriage morphed into boredom and stasis. The allure of willing and exciting females was too hard to resist," he admits. Now forty-two and still single, Jeremy acknowledges, "I hurt others and I hurt myself."

Like Jeremy, many of us either dodge the decision to commit or   5 commit without fully relinquishing the right to keep looking—opting for an arrangement psychotherapist Terrence Real terms "stable ambiguity."

"You park on the border of the relationship, so you're in it but not of it," he says. There are a million ways to do that: You can be in a relationship but not be sure it's really the right one, have an eye open for a better deal or something on the side, choose someone impossible or far away.

Yet commitment and marriage offer real physical and financial rewards. Touting the benefits of marriage may sound like conservative policy rhetoric, but nonpartisan sociological research backs it up: Committed partners have it all over singles, at least on average. Married people are more financially stable, according to Linda Waite, a sociologist at the University of Chicago and a coauthor of *The Case for Marriage: Why Married People Are Happier, Healthier, and Better Off.* Both married men and married women have more assets on average than singles; for women, the differential is huge.

The benefits go beyond the piggy bank. Married people, particularly men, tend to live longer than people who aren't married. Couples also live better: When people expect to stay together, says Waite, they pool their resources, increasing their individual standard of living. They also pool their expertise—in cooking, say, or financial management. In general, women improve men's health by putting a stop to stupid bachelor tricks and bugging their husbands to exercise and eat their vegetables. Plus, people who aren't comparing their partners to someone else in bed have less trouble performing and are more emotionally satisfied with sex. The relationship doesn't have to be wonderful for life to get better, says Waite: The statistics hold true for mediocre marriages as well as for passionate ones.

The pragmatic benefits of partnership used to be foremost in our minds. The idea of marriage as a vehicle for self-fulfillment and happiness is relatively new, says Paul Amato, professor of sociology, demography, and family studies at Penn State University. Surveys of high school and college students fifty or sixty years ago found that most wanted to get married in order to have children or own a home. Now, most report that they plan to get married for love. This increased emphasis on emotional fulfillment within marriage leaves couples ill-prepared for the realities they will probably face.

Because the early phase of a relationship is marked by excitement and 10 idealization, "many romantic, passionate couples expect to have that excitement forever," says Barry McCarthy, a clinical psychologist and coauthor—with his wife, Emily McCarthy—of *Getting It Right the First Time: How to Build a Healthy Marriage.* Longing for the charged energy of the early days, people look elsewhere or split up.

Flagging passion is often interpreted as the death knell of a relationship. You begin to wonder whether you're really right for each other after all. You're comfortable together, but you don't really connect the way you used to. Wouldn't it be more honest—and braver—to just admit that it's not working and call it off? "People are made to feel that remaining in a marriage that doesn't make you blissfully happy is an act of existential cowardice," says Joshua Coleman, a San Francisco psychologist.

Coleman says that the constant cultural pressure to have it all—a great sex life, a wonderful family—has made people ashamed of their less-than-perfect relationships and question whether such unions are worth hanging on to. Feelings of dissatisfaction or disappointment are natural, but they can seem intolerable when standards are sky-high. "It's a recent historical event that people expect to get so much from individual partners," says Coleman, author of *Imperfect Harmony*, in which he advises couples in lackluster marriages to stick it out—especially if they have kids. "There's an enormous amount of pressure on marriages to live up to an unrealistic ideal."

Michaela, twenty-eight, was drawn to Bernardo, thirty, in part because of their differences: She'd grown up in European boarding schools, he fought his way out of a New York City ghetto. "Our backgrounds made us more interesting to each other," says Michaela. "I was a spoiled brat, and he'd been supporting himself from the age of fourteen, which I admired." Their first two years of marriage were rewarding, but their fights took a toll. "I felt that because he hadn't grown up in a normal family, he didn't grasp basic issues of courtesy and accountability," says Michaela. They were temperamental opposites: He was a screamer, and she was a sulker. She recalls, "After we fought, I needed to be drawn out of my corner, but he took that to mean that I was a cold bitch." Michaela reluctantly concluded that the two were incompatible.

In fact, argue psychologists and marital advocates, there's no such thing as true compatibility.

"Marriage is a disagreement machine," says Diane Sollee, founder of   15
the Coalition for Marriage, Family, and Couples Education. "All couples disagree about all the same things. We have a highly romanticized notion that if we were with the right person, we wouldn't fight." Discord springs eternal over money, kids, sex, and leisure time, but psychologist John Gottman has shown that long-term, happily married couples disagree about these things just as much as couples who divorce.

"There is a mythology of 'the wrong person,'" agrees Pittman. "All marriages are incompatible. All marriages are between people from different families, people who have a different view of things. The magic is to develop binocular vision, to see life through your partner's eyes as well as through your own."

The realization that we're not going to get everything we want from a partner is not just sobering, it's downright miserable. But it is also a necessary step in building a mature relationship, according to Real, who has written about the subject in *How Can I Get Through to You: Closing the Intimacy Gap Between Men and Women.* "The paradox of intimacy is that our ability to stay close rests on our ability to tolerate solitude inside a relationship," he says. "A central aspect of grown-up love is grief. All of us long for—and think we deserve—perfection."

We can hardly be blamed for striving for bliss and self-fulfillment in our romantic lives—our inalienable right to the pursuit of happiness is guaranteed in the first blueprint of American society.

This same respect for our own needs spurred the divorce-law reforms of the 1960s and 1970s. During that era, "The culture shifted to emphasize individual satisfaction, and marriage was part of that," explains Paul Amato, who has followed more than 2,000 families for twenty years in a long-term study of marriage and divorce. Amato says that this shift did some good by freeing people from abusive and intolerable marriages. But it had an unintended side effect: encouraging people to abandon relationships that may be worth salvaging.

In a society hell-bent on individual achievement and autonomy,   20
working on a difficult relationship may get short shrift, says psychiatrist Peter Kramer, author of *Should You Leave?*

"So much of what we learn has to do with the self, the ego, rather than giving over the self to things like a relationship," Kramer says. In our competitive world, we're rewarded for our individual achievements rather than for how we help others. We value independence over cooperation,

and sacrifices for values like loyalty and continuity seem foolish. "I think we get the divorce rate that we deserve as a culture."

The steadfast focus on our *own* potential may turn a partner into an accessory in the quest for self-actualization, says Maggie Robbins, a therapist in New York City. "We think that this person should reflect the beauty and perfection that is the inner me—or, more often, that this person should compensate for the yuckiness and mess that is the inner me," says Robbins. "This is what makes you tell your wife, 'Lose some weight—you're making me look bad,' not 'Lose some weight, you're at risk for diabetes.'"

Michaela was consistently embarrassed by Bernardo's behavior when they were among friends. "He'd become sullen and withdrawn—he had a shifty way of looking off to the side when he didn't want to talk. I felt like it reflected badly on me," she admits. Michaela left him and is now dating a wealthy entrepreneur. "I just thought there had to be someone else out there for me."

The urge to find a soul mate is not fueled just by notions of romantic manifest destiny. Trends in the workforce and in the media create a sense of limitless romantic possibility. According to Scott South, a demographer at the State University of New York at Albany, proximity to potential partners has a powerful effect on relationships. South and his colleagues found higher divorce rates among people living in communities or working in professions where they encounter lots of potential partners—people who match them in age, race, and education level. "These results hold true not just for unhappy marriages but also for happy ones," says South.

The temptations aren't always living, breathing people. According to 25 research by psychologists Sara Gutierres and Douglas Kenrick, both of Arizona State University, we find reasonably attractive people less appealing when we've just seen a hunk or a hottie—and we're bombarded daily by images of gorgeous models and actors. When we watch *Lord of the Rings*, Viggo Mortensen's kingly mien and Liv Tyler's elfin charm can make our husbands and wives look all too schlumpy.

Kramer sees a similar pull in the narratives that surround us. "The number of stories that tell us about other lives we could lead—in magazine articles, television shows, books—has increased enormously. We have an enormous reservoir of possibilities," says Kramer.

And these possibilities can drive us to despair. Too many choices have been shown to stymie consumers . . . and an array of alternative mates is no exception. In an era when marriages were difficult to dissolve, couples rated their marriages as more satisfying than do today's couples, for whom divorce is a clear option, according to the National Opinion Research Center at the University of Chicago.

While we expect marriage to be "happily ever after," the truth is that for most people, neither marriage nor divorce seem to have a decisive impact on happiness. Although Waite's research shows that married people are happier than their single counterparts, other studies have found that after a couple years of marriage, people are just about as happy (or unhappy) as they were before settling down. And assuming that marriage will automatically provide contentment is itself a surefire recipe for misery.

"Marriage is not supposed to make you happy. It is supposed to make you married," says Pittman. "When you are all the way in your marriage, you are free to do useful things, become a better person." A committed relationship allows you to drop pretenses and seductions, expose your weaknesses, be yourself—and know that you will be loved, warts and all. "A real relationship is the collision of my humanity and yours, in all its joy and limitations," says Real. "How partners handle that collision is what determines the quality of their relationship."

Such a down-to-earth view of marriage is hardly romantic, but that 30 doesn't mean it's not profound: An authentic relationship with another person, says Pittman, is "one of the first steps toward connecting with the human condition—which is necessary if you're going to become fulfilled as a human being." If we accept these humble terms, the quest for a soul mate might just be a noble pursuit after all.

Nostalgia as Ideology

STEPHANIE COONTZ

BEFORE READING: In what ways is family life in the United States changing? Is the definition of the word *family* changing?

The more I listen to debates over whether we should promote marriage, the more I am reminded of one of my father's favorite sayings: "If wishes were horses, then beggars would ride." Yes, kids raised by married parents do better, on average, than kids raised in divorced or single-parent homes. Yes, the long-term commitment of marriage confers economic, emotional, and even health benefits on adults as well. Certainly, we should remove marriage disincentives from government programs—sixteen states, for instance, still discriminate against married couples in welfare policy. We should expand health coverage to include "couples counseling" for all who wish it. With better support systems, we may be able to save more potentially healthy marriages and further reduce rates of unwed childbearing among teenagers.

But there is no way to reestablish marriage as the main site of child rearing, dependent care, income pooling, or interpersonal commitments

Stephanie Coontz is on the history and family studies faculty of Evergreen State College in Olympia, Washington. She is the national co-chair of the Council on Contemporary Families and the author of *The Way We Never Were: American Families and the Nostalgia Trap* (2000) and *The Way We Really Are: Coming to Terms with America's Changing Families* (1997).

in the modern world. Any movement that sets this as a goal misunderstands how irreversibly family life and marriage have changed, and it will inevitably be dominated by powerful "allies" who are not interested in supporting the full range of families that exist today and are likely to in the future.

For more than a thousand years, marriage was the main way that society transferred property, forged political alliances, raised capital, organized children's rights, redistributed resources to dependents, and coordinated the division of labor by age and gender. Precisely because marriage served so many political, social, and economic functions, not everyone had access to it. Those who did almost never had free choice regarding partners and rarely could afford to hold high expectations of their relationships.

During the last two hundred years, the growth of bureaucracies, banks, schools, hospitals, unemployment insurance, Social Security, and pension plans slowly but surely eroded the political and economic roles that marriage traditionally had played. It increasingly became an individual decision that could be made independently of family and community pressures. By the early 1900s, love and companionship had become not just the wistful hope of a husband or wife but the legitimate goal of marriage in the eyes of society. But this meant that people began expecting more of married life than ever before in history—at the exact time that older methods of organizing and stabilizing marriages were ceasing to work. The very things that made marriage more satisfying, and increasingly more fair to women, are the same things that have made marriage less stable.

The outlines of the problem were clear by the early twentieth century.   5
The more that people saw marriage as their main source of intimacy and commitment, the less they were prepared to enter or stay in a marriage they found unsatisfying. Divorce rates shot up so quickly that by the 1920s many observers feared that marriage was headed for extinction. Books warned of "the marriage crisis." Magazines asked, "Is Marriage on the Skids?"

During the 1930s and 1940s, these fears took a backseat to more immediate survival issues, but abandonment rates rose during the Great Depression, out-of-wedlock sex shot up during the war, and by 1946 one in three marriages was ending in divorce. At the end of the 1940s, politicians and other concerned Americans began a campaign to reverse these trends. For a while it looked as if they would succeed. During the 1950s, the divorce rate dipped, the age at which people initially married plummeted, and fertility rates soared. But most historians agree that this decade was an aberration stimulated by the most massive government subsidization of young families in American history. And below the surface, the underpinnings of traditional marital stability continued to erode. Rates of unwed motherhood tripled between 1940 and 1948. The number of working mothers grew by 400 percent in the 1950s.

By the late 1960s, divorce rates were rising again, and the age of first marriage began to rise, too. The divorce rate peaked in the late 1970s and early 1980s, and has fallen by 26 percent since then. But the marriage rate has dropped at the same time, while the incidence of unmarried couples cohabiting, singles living alone, delayed marriage, and same-sex partnerships continued to increase throughout the 1990s.

Though welfare-state policies diverge, these trends are occurring in every industrial country in the world. Where divorce remains hard to get and out-of-wedlock birth is stigmatized, as in Italy and Japan, rates of marriage have plunged, suggesting that the historical trends undermining the universality of marriage will, if blocked in one area, simply spill over into another.

There is no way to reverse this trend short of a repressiveness that would not long be tolerated even in today's patriotic climate (and that would soon wipe out many of the benefits people now gain from marriage). Divorced families, stepfamilies, single parents, gay and lesbian families, lone householders, and unmarried cohabiting couples will never again become such a minor part of the family terrain that we can afford to count on marriage as our main institution for allocating income or caring for dependents.

I don't believe that marriage is on the verge of extinction — nor that 10 it should become extinct. Most cohabiting couples eventually do get married, either to each other or to someone else. Gay men and lesbians are now demanding access to marriage — a demand that many marriage advocates perversely interpret as an attack on the institution. And marriage continues to be an effective foundation for interpersonal commitments and economic stability. Of course we must find ways to make marriage more possible for couples who want it and to strengthen the marriages they contract. But there's a big difference between supporting concrete measures to help marriages succeed and supporting an organized marriage movement.

Despite the benefits associated with marriage for most couples, unhappily married individuals are more distressed than people who are not married. Women in bad marriages lose their self-confidence, become depressed, develop lowered immune functions, and are more likely to abuse alcohol than women who get out of such marriages. A recent study of marriages where one spouse had mild hypertension found that in happy couples, time spent together lowered the blood pressure of the at-risk spouse. In unhappily married couples, however, even small amounts of extra togetherness led to increases in blood pressure for the at-risk spouse.

For children, living with two cooperating parents is better than living with a single parent. But high conflict in a marriage, or even silent withdrawal coupled with contempt, is often more damaging to children than divorce or growing up in a single-parent family. According to the National Center on Addiction and Substance Abuse at Columbia University, teens who live in two-parent households are less likely, on average, to abuse drugs and alcohol than teens in one-parent families; but teens in two-parent families who have a fair to poor relationship with their father are more likely to do so than teens who live with a single mother.

The most constructive way to support modern marriages is to improve work-life policies so that couples can spend more time with each other and their kids, to increase social-support systems for children, and to provide counseling for all couples who seek it. But many in the center-right marriage movement resist such reforms, complaining that single parents and unmarried couples—whether heterosexual or of the same sex—could "take advantage" of them. If we grant other relationships the same benefits as marriage, they argue, we weaken people's incentives to get married.

But that is a bullet we simply have to bite. I am in favor of making it easier for couples to marry and to sustain that commitment. But that cannot substitute for a more far-reaching, inclusive program to support the full range of relationships in which our children are raised and our dependents cared for.

THINKING AND WRITING ABOUT THE FUTURE OF THE FAMILY

QUESTIONS FOR DISCUSSION AND WRITING

1. What is Shields's definition of a family? Do you think her definition is too broad? (Notice that the word *normal* is in quotation marks in paragraph 30.) Explain your answer.

2. Why does Smiley welcome the breakdown of the traditional family? Does her family arrangement seem attractive or unsettling?

3. What aspects of family life is Etzioni satirizing? His article was published in 1998. As you read this a number of years later, have some of the author's predictions become facts of family life? If so, are the changes good or bad?

4. What are the sources of Chip's suffering in the wake of his parents' divorce in "The Sting of Divorce"? Do any of the other authors have arguments that might console him?

5. Is Shulman expecting too little out of marriage? Explain.

6. Who presents a more convincing argument about marriage and family, Shields or Coontz? Explain.

TOPICS FOR RESEARCH

The family on TV

Welfare: good or bad for the family?

The case for or against having children

The legacy of divorce

Unconventional families

TAKING THE DEBATE ONLINE

For these and additional research URLs, see bedfordstmartins.com/rottenberg.

- *The American Family Association*
  www.afa.net

  The American Family Association defends traditional family values, particularly against what it sees as assaults in the entertainment media.

- *Facts for Families*
  www.aacap.org/info_families/index.htm

  Presented by the American Academy of Child and Adolescent Psychiatry, the Facts for Families Web site includes fifty-one fact sheets covering many of the issues faced by families today. Among the topics covered in the collection are children and divorce, eating disorders, TV violence, learning disabilities, sexual abuse, AIDS, lead exposure, and anxiety.

- *Gay and Lesbian Family Values*
  www.angelfire.com/co/GayFamilyValues

  This site defines the family as "a unit of love, with one or more consenting adults regardless of gender, creed, or color."

- *Research Forum on Children, Families, and the New Federalism*
  www.researchforum.org

  The Research Forum offers a comprehensive database of research projects that explore welfare reform, child well-being, and links to other important research and advocacy groups.

- *U.S. Census Bureau American Fact Finder*
  http://factfinder.census.gov/java_prod/dads.ui.homePage.HomePage

  The Census Bureau's Fact Finder provides authoritative maps, tables, and statistics on who lives together in the United States, including information on race, gender, and income.

CHAPTER 15

Are Limits on Freedom of Speech Ever Justified?

The First Amendment to the Constitution of the United States reads, "Congress shall make no laws respecting an establishment of religion, or prohibiting the free expression thereof; or abridging the freedom of speech, or of the press; or the right of the people peaceably to assemble, and to petition the Government for a redress of grievances." (The first ten amendments were ratified on December 15, 1791, and form what is known as the Bill of Rights.) The arguments in this section will consider primarily the issue of "abridging the freedom of speech."

The limits of free speech in the United States are constantly being adjusted as social values change and new cases testing those limits emerge. Several prominent areas of controversy are emphasized in the following selection of essays.

In 1969, the U.S. Supreme Court ruled that neither students nor teachers "shed their constitutional right to freedom of speech or expression at the schoolhouse gate" (*Tinker v. Des Moines Independent School District*). High schools, colleges, and universities are places where the exchange of ideas is generally welcome. The controversy arises over whether or not there are some ideas—some language, some symbols—that are not welcome. The First Amendment has been at the heart of court cases over everything from racist and sexist speech to the words or symbols printed on a T-shirt.

Those same students and teachers step outside the "schoolhouse gate" to confront a world in which many feel even the news is not fit for children, let alone prime-time television or even many movies rated G or PG, which one parent claims now stands for "profanity guaranteed." Rap music enrages those who find its attitude toward women and its call to violence offensive while others defend it as art protected by the First Amendment. The Federal Communications Commission has tightened its enforcement of rules against language or actions that go against the "public interest," but many consumers argue that it has not done enough. One of the authors included here even argues that the very existence of the FCC is unconstitutional.

Times of crisis resurrect old concerns about freedom of speech in times of crisis. Do American citizens have the right to speak out against a war in which Americans are fighting and dying? Should they? In some of these selections you will hear a sincere expression of concern that even in our patriotism we must not sacrifice our First Amendment right to freedom of speech.

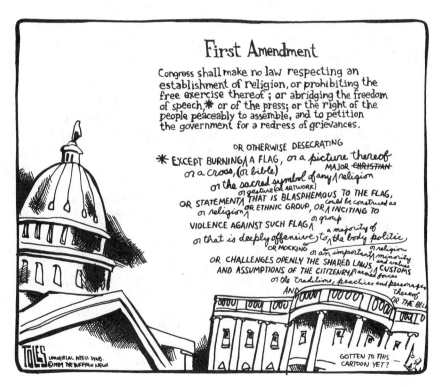

TOLES © 1986 The Buffalo News. Reprinted with permission of UNIVERSAL PRESS SYNDICATE. All rights reserved.

Student Sues School District for Banning Anti-War T-Shirt

ALANA KEYNES

BEFORE READING: What restrictions, if any, did your high school have on what words, pictures, or symbols could be displayed on students' clothing? How did you feel about that policy? Was it necessary, in your opinion? Why or why not?

A case addressing students' right to protest the Iraqi war in school has landed in the courts, with the American Civil Liberties Union (ACLU) suing a Michigan school district on behalf of a student sent home for wearing a T-shirt calling President Bush an "International Terrorist."

The suit, filed March 27 at the U.S. Eastern District Court of Michigan, alleges that Dearborn, Michigan, school officials violated the free-speech rights of Bretton Barber, a junior at Dearborn High School, since there was no evidence the T-shirt caused any disruption at school.

"There are strong indications in this case that the reaction of Dearborn High School officials to Barber's T-shirt was prompted by their disagreement with the message," the complaint states. "The only rationale given when Barber pressed for one was that the shirt would promote terrorism, which plainly could not have been a serious contention."

School administrators' claim that the shirt was disruptive is a "ludicrous charge," said Wendy Wagenheim, spokeswoman for the ACLU of Michigan. "They don't want to rock the boat in any way." There have been no instances of students causing problems by fighting with each other or teachers over the message conveyed in the T-shirt, she said. The complaint cites *Castorina v. Madison County School Board* (246 F.2d 536), the 6th Circuit Court of Appeals' decision that school officials could not ban two Kentucky students from wearing T-shirts with a picture of the Confederate flag to school (*ED*, March 12, 2001). Michigan is one of four states governed by the 6th Circuit.

Administrators also did not have a right to send Barber home, according to the complaint, because legal precedent only permits schools to discipline students who are violating a written rule, and the Dearborn district does not have a policy banning political speech.   5

But the 11th Circuit Court of Appeals ruled last month that a Florida school district could suspend students who brought Confederate flags to school, though there was no written policy prohibiting them on campus (*ED*, March 26).

Alana Keynes is on the editorial staff at both *Education Daily*, where this article appeared on April 4, 2003, and *Federal Grants and Contracts Weekly*.

Wagenheim said she is not concerned that the 11th Circuit ruling will affect the ACLU's case, since federal appellate courts often issue conflicting rulings.

A spokesman from the Dearborn school district refused to comment on the suit. The district's superintendent issued a statement saying "this is now an issue for the courts to decide. The school district has no further remarks at this time."

Students' and teachers' right to express their views about the war has become a major issue in schools nationwide, as administrators continue to grapple with the appropriate limits of free speech in school (*ED*, March 21).

This is the first case the ACLU has taken on students' free-speech 10 rights in response to the Iraqi war, Wagenheim said, but many of its offices nationwide have received calls from students inquiring about their right to demonstrate against the war during school hours.

"Those inquiries are common occurrences at this point," she said.

Bethel School District No. 403 v. Fraser

SUPREME COURT OF THE UNITED STATES

BEFORE READING: Should school officials censor in any way a speech delivered by a student at a school assembly? Give reasons why or why not.

C hief Justice Burger delivered the opinion of the Court.
We granted certiorari to decide whether the First Amendment prevents a school district from disciplining a high school student for giving a lewd speech at a school assembly.

I:A

On April 26, 1983, respondent Matthew N. Fraser, a student at Bethel High School in Pierce County, Washington, delivered a speech nominating a fellow student for student elective office. Approximately 600 high school students, many of whom were fourteen-year-olds, attended the assembly. Students were required to attend the assembly or to report to the study hall. The assembly was part of a school-sponsored educational program in self-government. . . . During the entire speech, Fraser referred to his candidate in terms of an elaborate, graphic, and explicit sexual metaphor.

This selection comes from Jamin B. Raskin's 2000 book *We the Students*. Raskin is professor of constitutional law at American University Washington College of Law.

Two of Fraser's teachers, with whom he discussed the contents of his speech in advance, informed him that the speech was "inappropriate and that he probably should not deliver it" and that his delivery of the speech might have "severe consequences."

During Fraser's delivery of the speech, a school counselor observed   5 the reaction of students to the speech. Some students hooted and yelled; some by gestures graphically simulated the sexual activities pointedly alluded to in respondent's speech. Other students appeared to be bewildered and embarrassed by the speech. One teacher reported that on the day following the speech, she found it necessary to forgo a portion of the scheduled class lesson in order to discuss the speech with the class.

A Bethel High School disciplinary rule prohibiting the use of obscene language in the school provides:

> Conduct which materially and substantially interferes with the educational process is prohibited, including the use of obscene, profane language or gestures.

The morning after the assembly, the Assistant Principal called Fraser into her office and notified him that the school considered his speech to have been a violation of this rule. Fraser was presented with copies of five letters submitted by teachers, describing his conduct at the assembly; he was given a chance to explain his conduct, and he admitted to having given the speech described and that he deliberately used sexual innuendo in the speech. Fraser was then informed that he would be suspended for three days and that his name would be removed from the list of candidates for graduation speaker at the school's commencement exercises.

Fraser sought review of this disciplinary action through the School District's grievance procedures. The hearing officer determined that the speech given by respondent was "indecent, lewd, and offensive to the modesty and decency of many of the students and faculty in attendance at the assembly." The examiner determined that the speech fell within the ordinary meaning of "obscene," as used in the disruptive-conduct rule, and affirmed the discipline in its entirety. Fraser served two days of his suspension and was allowed to return to school on the third day.

I:B

. . . [Fraser] alleged a violation of his First Amendment right to freedom of speech and sought both injunctive relief and monetary damages. . . . The District Court held that the school's sanctions violated respondent's right to freedom of speech under the First Amendment to the United States Constitution, that the school's disruptive-conduct rule is unconstitutionally vague and overbroad, and that the removal of respondent's name from the graduation speaker's list violated the Due Process Clause of the Fourteenth Amendment because the disciplinary rule makes no mention of such removal as a possible sanction. The District Court awarded [Fraser] $278 in damages, $12,750 in litigation costs and attorney's fees, and enjoined the School District from preventing [him] from speaking at the commencement ceremonies. [Fraser], who had been elected graduation speaker by a write-in vote of his classmates, delivered a speech at the commencement ceremonies on June 8, 1983.

The Court of Appeals for the Ninth Circuit affirmed the judgment of 10 the District Court, holding that [Fraser's] speech was indistinguishable from the protest armband in *Tinker v. Des Moines Independent Community School District.* . . .[1]

We granted certiorari. We reverse. . . .

III

[Following is the decision of the U.S. Supreme Court overturning the decision of the State Court of Appeals.]

. . . The undoubted freedom to advocate unpopular and controversial views in schools and classrooms must be balanced against the society's countervailing interest in teaching students the boundaries of socially appropriate behavior. Even the most heated political discourse in a democratic society requires consideration for the personal sensibilities of the other participants and audiences.

In our Nation's legislative halls, where some of the most vigorous political debates in our society are carried on, there are rules prohibiting the use of expressions offensive to other participants in the debate. Senators have been censured for abusive language directed at other Senators. . . . Can it be that what is proscribed in the halls of Congress is beyond the reach of school officials to regulate?

The First Amendment guarantees wide freedom in matters of adult 15 public discourse. A sharply divided Court upheld the right to express an antidraft viewpoint in a public place, albeit in terms highly offensive to most citizens. It does not follow, however, that simply because the use of an offensive form of expression may not be prohibited to adults making what the speaker considers a political point, the same latitude must be permitted to children in a public school. . . .

Surely it is a highly appropriate function of public school education to prohibit the use of vulgar and offensive terms in public discourse. . . . The determination of what manner of speech in the classroom or in school assembly is inappropriate properly rests with the school board. . . .

The pervasive sexual innuendo in Fraser's speech was plainly offensive to both teachers and students—indeed to any mature person. By glorifying male sexuality, and in its verbal content, the speech was acutely insulting to teenage girl students. The speech could well be seriously damaging to its less mature audience, many of whom were only fourteen years old and on the threshold of awareness of human sexuality. Some students

[1]The high school students in the *Tinker* case wore black armbands to protest American involvement in the Vietnam War. — Eds.

were reported as bewildered by the speech and the reaction of mimicry it provoked. . . .

We hold that petitioner School district acted entirely within its permissible authority in imposing sanctions upon Fraser in response to his offensively lewd and indecent speech. Unlike the sanctions imposed on the students wearing armbands in *Tinker,* the penalties imposed in this case were unrelated to any political viewpoint. The First Amendment does not prevent the school officials from determining that to permit a vulgar and lewd speech such as respondent's would undermine the school's basic educational mission. A high school assembly or classroom is no place for a sexually explicit monologue directed towards an unsuspecting audience of teenage students. Accordingly, it was perfectly appropriate for the school to disassociate itself to make the point to the pupils that vulgar speech and lewd conduct is wholly inconsistent with the "fundamental values" of public school education. . . .

Reversed.

Justice Marshall, dissenting. 20

. . . I dissent from the Court's decision . . . because in my view the School District failed to demonstrate that respondent's remarks were indeed disruptive. The District Court and Court of Appeals conscientiously applied *Tinker v. Des Moines Independent Community School District* and concluded that the School District had not demonstrated any disruption of the educational process. I recognize that the school administration must be given wide latitude to determine what forms of conduct are inconsistent with the school's educational mission; nevertheless, where speech is involved, we may not unquestioningly accept a teacher's or administrator's assertion that certain pure speech interfered with education.

Ice-T: The Issue Is Creative Freedom

BARBARA EHRENREICH

> BEFORE READING: To what extent are fantasies of violence — killing, torture, sexual assault — dangerous either to the individual or to society?

I ce-T's song "Cop Killer" is as bad as they come. This is black anger — raw, rude, and cruel — and one reason the song's so shocking is that in postliberal America, black anger is virtually taboo. You won't find it on

Barbara Ehrenreich, honorary chair of Democratic Socialists of America, is the author of numerous books, including *Blood Rites: Origins and History of the Passions of War* (1997) and *Nickel and Dimed: On (Not) Getting by in America* (2001). This article is from the July 20, 1992, issue of *Time.*

TV, not on the *McLaughlin Group* or *Crossfire,* and certainly not in the placid features of Arsenio Hall or Bernard Shaw. It's been beaten back into the outlaw subcultures of rap and rock, where, precisely because it is taboo, it sells. And the nastier it is, the faster it moves off the shelves. As Ice-T asks in another song on the same album, "Goddamn what a brotha gotta do / To get a message through / To the red, white, and blue?"

But there's a gross overreaction going on, building to a veritable paroxysm of white denial. A national boycott has been called, not just of the song or Ice-T, but of all Time Warner products. The president himself has denounced Time Warner as "wrong" and Ice-T as "sick." Ollie North's Freedom Alliance has started a petition drive aimed at bringing Time Warner executives to trial for "sedition and anarchy."

Much of this is posturing and requires no more courage than it takes to stand up in a VFW hall and condemn communism or crack. Yes, "Cop Killer" is irresponsible and vile. But Ice-T is as right about some things as he is righteous about the rest. And ultimately, he's not even dangerous — least of all to the white power structure his songs condemn.

The "danger" implicit in all the uproar is of empty-headed, suggestible black kids, crouching by their boom boxes, waiting for the word. But what Ice-T's fans know and his detractors obviously don't is that "Cop Killer" is just one more entry in pop music's long history of macho hyperbole and violent boast. Flip to the classic-rock station, and you might catch the Rolling Stones announcing "the time is right for violent revoloo-shun!" from their 1968 hit "Street Fighting Man." And where were the defenders of our law-enforcement officers when a white British group, the Clash, taunted its fans with the lyrics: "When they kick open your front door / How you gonna come / With your hands on your head / Or on the trigger of your gun?"

"Die, Die, Die Pig" is strong speech, but the Constitution protects   5
strong speech, and it's doing so this year more aggressively than ever. The Supreme Court has just downgraded cross burnings to the level of bonfires and ruled that it's no crime to throw around verbal grenades like "nigger" and "kike." Where are the defenders of decorum and social stability when prime-time demagogues like Howard Stern deride African Americans as "spear chuckers"?

More to the point, young African Americans are not so naive and suggestible that they have to depend on a compact disc for their sociology lessons. To paraphrase another song from another era, you don't need a rap song to tell which way the wind is blowing. Black youths know that the police are likely to see them through a filter of stereotypes as miscreants and potential "cop killers." They are aware that a black youth is seven times as likely to be charged with a felony as a white youth who has committed the same offense, and is much more likely to be imprisoned.

They know, too, that in a shameful number of cases, it is the police themselves who indulge in "anarchy" and violence. The U.S. Justice

Department has received 47,000 complaints of police brutality in the past six years, and Amnesty International has just issued a report on police brutality in Los Angeles, documenting forty cases of "torture or cruel, inhuman, or degrading treatment."

Menacing as it sounds, the fantasy in "Cop Killer" is the fantasy of the powerless and beaten down—the black man who's been hassled once too often ("A pig stopped me for nothin'!"), spread-eagled against a police car, pushed around. It's not a "responsible" fantasy (fantasies seldom are). It's not even a very creative one. In fact, the sad thing about "Cop Killer" is that it falls for the cheapest, most conventional image of rebellion that our culture offers: the lone gunman spraying fire from his AK-47. This is not "sedition"; it's the familiar, all-American, Hollywood-style pornography of violence.

Which is why Ice-T is right to say he's no more dangerous than George Bush's pal Arnold Schwarzenegger, who wasted an army of cops in *Terminator 2.* Images of extraordinary cruelty and violence are marketed every day, many of far less artistic merit than "Cop Killer." This is our free market of ideas and images, and it shouldn't be any less free for a black man than for other purveyors of "irresponsible" sentiments, from David Duke to Andrew Dice Clay.[1]

Just, please, don't dignify Ice-T's contribution with the word *sedition.*   10 The past masters of sedition—men like George Washington, Toussaint L'Ouverture, Fidel Castro, or Mao Zedong, all of whom led and won armed insurrections—would be unimpressed by "Cop Killer" and probably saddened. They would shake their heads and mutter words like "infantile" and "adventurism." They might point out that the cops are hardly a noble target, being, for the most part, honest working stiffs who've got stuck with the job of patrolling ghettos ravaged by economic decline and official neglect.

There is a difference, the true seditionist would argue, between a revolution and a gesture of macho defiance. Gestures are cheap. They feel good, they blow off some rage. But revolutions, violent or otherwise, are made by people who have learned how to count very slowly to ten.

---

[1] David Duke, an advocate of white supremacy, was defeated in his bid for governor of Louisiana in 1991. Andrew Dice Clay is a stand-up comedian known for his use of offensive language against women and minorities.

Why We Need to Abolish the FCC

ROBERT GARMONG

BEFORE READING: The Federal Communications Commission regulates what can be said on the air. Do you feel that the FCC is too restrictive, not restrictive enough, or generally right on target in deciding what should be allowed on the broadcast media?

Since the infamous "wardrobe malfunction" at the Super Bowl, there have been strident demands for a crackdown by a tougher, stricter Federal Communications Commission. The FCC's various commissioners now call for the power to regulate cable TV in addition to broadcast media.

In June, Congress voted to increase the maximum fine the FCC can impose tenfold, from $27,500 to $275,000. Commissioner Michael Copps has vowed that he will not be satisfied until "I see us send one or two . . . cases for license revocation."

In this headlong rush to expand the government's authority over the media, no one has paused to consider whether the government should have such authority in the first place. No one has noticed that the very existence of the FCC is a flagrant violation of the right to free speech.

Central Premise of the United States

Throughout history, the norm was tyranny over the mind. Men were allowed to speak only by government imprimatur, until America's First Amendment established freedom of speech as a central premise of our nation.

The First Amendment declares that "Congress shall pass no law . . . abridging the freedom of speech, or of the press." This language could not be clearer, or more absolute: no matter who disagrees with you or considers your speech offensive, the government may not abridge your right to say it.

Free speech is the protection of the rational mind and its literary, intellectual, and scientific products. It means the absolute right to express one's views, so long as one does not violate the rights of others.

Free speech means no American should fear the fate of Galileo, persecuted for daring to assert scientific truths that contradicted the official Church's doctrines, nor that of Socrates, put to death for offending the state.

Yet the FCC exists to dictate what can be said on-air. Each year since the early days of radio, every broadcast station must apply to the FCC for

---

Robert Garmong holds a Ph.D. in philosophy and is a writer for the Ayn Rand Institute in Irvine, California. This article originally appeared in the *San Diego Business Journal* on August 9, 2004.

permission to use the airwaves. In exchange for their licenses, broadcasters must promise to serve the "public interest." Stations that the FCC regards as having failed to do so can be fined, or even shut down, at the FCC's sole discretion.

The putative justification for the FCC's regulation of broadcasters is that the airwaves are public property. But just as the government does not own—and so has no legitimate control over—the presses of the *New York Times*, so it has no business regulating what may be broadcast over airwaves.

The airwaves, which would be useless without the transmission net- 10 works created by radio and TV stations, belong to the individuals and companies that developed them. Broadcasters should not have to plead to the authorities for annual licenses, any more than a homeowner should have to beg for an annual license to use the patch of land he has developed.

No other media in America is subjected to such persecution. If the *New York Times* or Barnes & Noble publishes and distributes content some members of the public disapprove of, the government cannot threaten them with fines or penalties. But let Howard Stern offend a listener, and Clear Channel is hammered with more than a million dollars in fines.

"Indecency" Crackdown

So far, only "indecency" has been targeted by the FCC's crackdown—but politicians on both sides of the aisle have begun whispering demands to censor PBS or the Fox News Channel on the grounds that their alleged biases violate the "public interest."

Both the liberals, with their political correctness, and the conservatives, with their puritanical religious ethic, claim to speak for the "public interest." Can it be long before the two sides begin the battle over which ideas and values Americans are allowed to see and hear on-air?

As the FCC wields its club ever more fiercely, broadcasters are running scared. Clear Channel has canceled its "shock-jock" programs. Skittish station managers have bleeped out words such as "urinate," "damn," and "orgy" from the Rush Limbaugh program. Most ominous, the National Association of Broadcasters convened a "Summit on Responsible Programming" to define industrywide standards of self-censorship.

America was founded on the freedom of speech—on the right and re- 15 sponsibility of the individual to decide what to say, and what to listen to. Yet in the name of protecting ourselves from being offended—and almost without noticing it—we are well on the way to surrendering that crucial right to the control of the omnipotent state.

Freedom of Speech and My Right to Silence at Bath Time

PATTI WALDMEIR

BEFORE READING: What is your opinion of the do-not-call registry designed to keep citizens from receiving calls from telemarketers? Are there two sides to the argument?

It is funny how the U.S. Constitution intrudes into one's daily life in America. Some countries do not even have one; ours dictates the smallest details of mundane life — such as whether I can bathe my children in peace or catch a catnap on a Sunday without an invasion of the telemarketers.

Today a federal appeals court in Oklahoma will address the pressing national question of whether I have a constitutional right to silence at bath time.

The case before the court tests the constitutionality of the federal do-not-call registry, which allows Americans to assert their right to silence by banning commercial telemarketing calls. The registry is wildly popular — the single most popular thing the federal government has done in years. But that does not make it constitutional; and the fate of do-not-call efforts could well foretell the future of do-not-spam.

Either way, it is a question of commercial free speech: advertisers have a right to broadcast their wares, but consumers have a right to refuse to listen. This case will test the role of government in helping consumers block their ears. It could have big implications, not just for junk calls and junk e-mail but also for the future of corporate free speech in America.

Eventually, one of the new generation of do-not-advertise cases will probably end up before the U.S. Supreme Court, but that may take a while. Until then, proponents of a crackdown can brandish powerful quotes from former Supreme Court justices that appear to condemn the invasion of the advertisers: Justice Louis Brandeis said the right to be let alone was "the right most valued by civilized men"; Justice William O. Douglas said it was "the beginning of all freedoms." They were not talking about telemarketing. But their views are a powerful rhetorical tool for those who think a man's home should be more than a spam receptacle.

So what happens when a man's right to preserve the privacy of his castle collides with the free speech rights of advertisers? That is the issue before the 10th circuit court of appeals in Tulsa today: Can the government help consumers place a gag order on telemarketers by enforcing a

Patti Waldmeir writes a column about law and society for the *Financial Times* in London. Before her move to London, she was the U.S. editor for the *Financial Times*, based in Washington, D.C.

national do-not-call list? Or does the first amendment to the U.S. Constitution prohibit the registry as a free speech violation?

Judge Edward Nottingham became one of the most despised men in America when he struck down the registry as unconstitutional in September. And the grounds for his ruling made it seem all the more absurd: He objected because the registry would block only commercial calls and not charitable solicitations. Judge Nottingham argued that the government had no right to discriminate between a sales pitch from AT&T and one from the Policemen's Benevolent Association. Ironically, he struck down the registry not because it banned too much speech but because it banned too little.

But although his decision enraged the 50 million American households that had already signed up for the registry, that does not make it wrong. Judge Nottingham insisted the government had failed to show why the registry should apply to one kind of call and not the other. Charitable calls disrupt my nap and bother my bath time just as surely as any other solicitation. In fact, I find charity calls from the police even more upsetting than offers of double-glazing and cheap credit. I do not feel threatened by window salesmen; but when policemen ask me for funds, I feel I have been hit for protection money. Both kinds of call are annoying and upsetting. Should one be allowed and not the other?

There is no satisfactory answer to that question, says Stuart Banner of UCLA law school, who argues that every do-not-advertise effort will encounter first amendment problems. If government enforces a ban against all solicitation, commercial and noncommercial, it may be restricting speech that is essentially political and that enjoys the highest form of first amendment protection. Commercial speech gets less protection; but the government still needs a good reason to hinder it unless it is fraudulent. So there is no way, he argues, to write a do-not-call or do-not-spam rule that does not end up in the courts.

Still, he predicts most such efforts will survive because most judges 10 are pragmatic rather than purist: "Judges don't usually pursue constitutional doctrines to their logical end if doing so would require dashing the hopes of tens of millions of Americans (especially if some of those Americans are judges, as I imagine they are)," he wrote recently in the *Washington Post*. In a world where judges get spam too, do-not-spam efforts probably have a guaranteed future.

As Michael Powell, chairman of the Federal Communications Commission, said when the FCC do-not-call registry was first challenged: "I refuse to believe that the Constitution of the United States shuts down the ability of consumers to protect the sanctity of their homes." He is probably right, which is good news for the sanctity of bath time. But it could be seriously bad news for commercial speech in the United States: Telemarketers have rights too. We all share the same constitution; somehow, it must protect us all.

Dare Call It Treason

ERIC FONER

BEFORE READING: Do you feel that Americans should be able to speak out against a war their country is involved in? Brainstorm what you know about the history of such dissent in the United States.

Few traditions are more American than freedom of speech and the right to dissent. But an equally powerful American tradition has been the effort by government and private "patriots" to suppress free expression in times of crisis. During the fighting in Iraq, former military leaders who criticized planning for the war were denounced for endangering troops in the field and warned to remain silent. A number of scholars, including myself, were branded "Traitor Professors" on a television talk show. If criticism of a war while it is in progress makes one a traitor, that category will have to include Abraham Lincoln, who denounced the Mexican War while serving in Congress in 1847; Mark Twain, who vehemently attacked government policy in the Spanish-American and Philippine wars at the turn of the last century; and Martin Luther King Jr., who eloquently called for an end to the war in Vietnam.

With the exception of World War II, every significant war in American history has inspired vigorous dissent. Many colonists remained loyal to Britain during the American Revolution. Most New Englanders opposed the War of 1812. Numerous Americans considered the Mexican War an effort to extend the territory of slavery. Both North and South were internally divided during the Civil War. World War I and Vietnam produced massive antiwar movements. This is part of our democratic tradition.

Equally persistent, however, have been efforts to suppress wartime dissent. The Alien and Sedition Acts during the "quasi-war" with France in 1798 allowed the president to deport aliens and made it illegal to criticize the government. Both Union and Confederate governments suppressed opposition newspapers and jailed critics. World War I witnessed a massive repression of freedom of speech, with critics of the war, socialists, and labor leaders jailed or deported; those suspected of disloyalty

---

Eric Foner is the DeWitt Clinton Professor of History at Columbia University and has also taught at Oxford, Cambridge, and Moscow State universities. He is an elected fellow of the American Academy of Arts and Sciences and the British Academy and has served as president of both the Organization of American Historians and the American Historical Association. Foner has written a number of books about American history, including the 2004 textbook *Give Me Liberty! An American History*. He was invited to revise the presentation of American history at the Hall of Presidents at Disney World and Meet Mr. Lincoln at Disneyland and has served as consultant to several National Parks Service historical sites and historical museums.

rounded up by private vigilantes; and the speaking of German banned in some places. Universities, including my own, fired professors who opposed American involvement.

Self-proclaimed patriots not only seek to determine the boundaries of acceptable speech about the present but rewrite history to create a more politically useful past. During World War I, the Committee on Public Information, a government propaganda agency, published pamphlets demonstrating the "common principles" of Oliver Cromwell, Jean-Jacques Rousseau, and Thomas Jefferson in order to create a historical lineage for the Anglo-French-American military alliance. Today, statements about history that in normal times would seem uncontroversial have been labeled treasonous. Daniel Pipes said in his syndicated newspaper column that I "hate America" because I noted that Japan invoked the idea of preemptive war to justify its attack on Pearl Harbor (a point also made by that well-known anti-American, Arthur Schlesinger Jr.). My comment to a reporter that the United States has frequently embarked on military ventures without being attacked, as in Haiti, the Dominican Republic, and Vietnam, prompted accusations of treason in the media.

In the aftermath of the Civil War, a far greater crisis than the war on   5
Iraq, the Supreme Court in the *Milligan* case invalidated the use of military tribunals to try civilians. The Court proclaimed that the Constitution is not suspended in wartime: "It is a law for rulers and people, equally in war and in peace." Alas, we have not always lived up to this ideal. The history of civil liberties in the United States is not a straight-line trajectory toward ever-greater freedom. It is a complex story in which victories can prove temporary and regression can follow progress.

Our civil liberties are neither self-enforcing nor self-correcting. Historians today view past suppressions of free speech as shameful episodes. But we are now living through another moment when many commentators, both in and out of government, seem to view freedom of expression as at best an inconvenience and at worst unpatriotic. The incessant attacks on dissenters as traitors are intended to create an atmosphere of shock and awe within the United States, so that those tempted to speak their mind become too intimidated to do so.

George W. Bush has claimed that America's enemies wish to destroy our freedoms. If we surrender freedom of speech in the hope that this will bring swifter victory on current and future battlefields, who then will have won the war?

A Case the Scouts Had to Win

STEFFEN N. JOHNSON

BEFORE READING: Should college fraternities and sororities be permitted to limit their membership to certain races and religions? Are these practices an example of free association guaranteed by the First Amendment?

To the dismay of gay rights groups and some civil libertarians, the Supreme Court ruled on Wednesday that it is unconstitutional for the state to require a Boy Scout troop to admit a gay scoutmaster. The court's decision, however, goes to the heart of the First Amendment's guarantee of free association. It may be a civil right to have access to employment, or to transportation, or to hotels and restaurants. But it is not a civil right to assist in raising other people's children.

In the past, the court had understandably ruled that society's interest in ensuring access to certain opportunities like jobs, school, and other basic necessities must sometimes override the right to associate with whomever one pleases. Everyone needs to make a living. Everyone needs an education. Thus, the court ruled that businesses or commercial gatherings like the Rotary Club cannot exclude women from their ranks.

But serving as a role model for young children whose parents share common values is not the same sort of privilege as a job or an education. It is a service, and one entrusted to few people.

To extend the reach of anti-discrimination laws to private groups whose purpose is not to make a profit but to bring together people with similar values, would destroy the nation's diverse tradition of voluntary collaboration for common causes. And a world in which the government could declare which causes and which moral positions benefit society, and which do not, could only be described as Orwellian.

The case arose when the Scouts informed James Dale that he could 5 not serve as a leader of a troop in Monmouth County, New Jersey. Mr. Dale sued, claiming that the Scouts had unlawfully discriminated against him because he was gay, and the New Jersey courts agreed. But the Supreme Court, in a five to four ruling, said that forcing a group to accept certain members may impair its ability to "express those views, and only those views, that it intends to express."

Exercising the right to exclude others may seem intolerant, but such a right is indispensable to private groups seeking to define themselves, to chart their own moral course, and to work together for common ends. If the Boy Scouts were required to admit leaders who advocated a position contrary to its own, then men could assert the right to lead the Girl

---

Steffen N. Johnson is a lawyer and a lecturer at the University of Chicago Law School. His article was published in the June 30, 2000, edition of the *New York Times*.

Scouts, gentiles could assert the right to head Jewish groups, and heterosexuals could assert the right to lead gay groups.

Mr. Dale's supporters said that the case was about status-based discrimination and that enforcing anti-discrimination laws against voluntary groups like the Scouts was valid because antigay beliefs are not what brought the Scouts together. But a group should not need to have an antigay agenda to hold the view that homosexual behavior is wrong. Many churches, for example, teach that homosexual activity is immoral while affirming that gay people should be treated with equal dignity and respect. That does not mean that they have given up their right not to appoint homosexuals to leadership.

Like many Americans, the Boy Scouts attempt to walk the line between tolerance of everyone and disapproval of certain types of conduct. That they wish to express their view by example or by quiet persuasion, rather than an outspoken campaign, does not diminish their right to take a position on moral issues.

As the court's majority understood, people's rights to hold moral positions, to associate with others who share the same views, and to instill those views in their children without threat of outside interference are liberties that belong as much to gay men and lesbians as to the Boy Scouts, as much to those who advocate alternative lifestyles as to those who advocate traditional morality.

THINKING AND WRITING ABOUT THE LIMITS ON FREEDOM OF SPEECH

QUESTIONS FOR DISCUSSION AND WRITING

1. In *Bethel School District No. 403 v. Fraser,* the U.S. Supreme Court ruled that children in a public school — in this case, high school students — do not have the same rights as adults to use sexual speech in a public forum. What reasons did the Court give for making a distinction? What reason did Justice Marshall give for his dissent? This case was argued in 1986. Do you think that the lewd speech at a school graduation would be treated in the same way today?

2. Do you find the cases discussed in *"Bethel School District No. 403 v. Fraser"* and in "Student Sues District for Banning Anti-War T-Shirt" similar, or are there significant differences between the two cases? Explain.

3. How do you feel the court should decide in the case of the student who wore the anti-war T-shirt?

4. Can you think of circumstances in which creative freedom should bow to social responsibility? What evidence does Ehrenreich use to prove that "Cop Killer" is not dangerous? Is it convincing?

5. Explain your position on how much control there should be on what is broadcast over the air waves — and who should control it.

6. Although the majority of Americans seem to celebrate the do-not-call registry, Waldmeir explains that there are two sides to the controversy. Write an essay in which you make clear why this is not a clear-cut case of one group being right and the other wrong.

7. Do you feel there should be any restrictions on Americans' right to speak out against a war they feel is wrong? Explain.

8. What distinction does Johnson make between the right to a job or an education and the right to associate with particular people? Explain why Johnson believes that the Scouts are protected by the First Amendment.

TOPICS FOR RESEARCH

Lyrics in rock music: How dangerous are they?

Codes of speech conduct at some colleges and universities: goals and effects

Religious displays on public land

Freedom of speech on the Internet

Prayer in public schools

Free speech issues in school newspapers

TAKING THE DEBATE ONLINE

For these and additional research URLs, see bedfordstmartins.com/rottenberg.

- *American Civil Liberties Union*
  www.aclu.org/issues/freespeech/hmfs.html
  The ACLU's site condemns censorship in cinema, literature, and life.

- *Massachusetts Music Industry Coalition*
  www.massmic.com
  This site condemns the censorship of musical expression.

- *Internet Free Expression Alliance*
  www.ifea.net/mission.html
  The mission of this organization is to ensure the continuation of the Internet as a forum for open, diverse, and unimpeded expression and to oppose any governmental effort to promote, coerce, or mandate the rating or filtering of online content.

- *Scouting for All*
  www.scoutingforall.org
  This group advocates allowing the Boy Scouts of America to accept gay and atheist scouts.

CHAPTER 16

What Threats to Privacy Exist in the Information Age?

Although the word *privacy* is nowhere mentioned in the Constitution, the right to privacy has been inferred from the intent of several Amendments: the First, the Third, the Ninth, and the Fourteenth. Needless to say, the makers of that document could not have foreseen the worldwide dissemination of information, private as well as public, which the development of technology would make possible at the end of the twentieth century. Today the courts, wrestling with charges that the right to privacy is being violated, must try to strike a balance between the right to privacy and the right to know and to speak freely.

Electronic purveyors of information can make our financial records, our medical history, our buying habits, and other data available to those who are interested. Television talk shows encourage people to divulge intimate secrets to millions of viewers. Employers test their employees for drug use and demand information about personal habits and life choices. On computer Web sites strangers are invited to enter our homes and share our lives. Even in the open air we are being watched. In an effort to control crime, more than two thousand surveillance cameras have been mounted in the streets and parks of Manhattan to monitor public activity.

One disturbing result of this information explosion has been the exposure of children to adult knowledge. Neil Postman, author of *The Disappearance of Childhood,* says,

> With the new technologies, television being at the forefront, there are fewer and fewer secrets, medical secrets, sexual secrets, political secrets.

Adults used to reveal secrets to you, the child, in stages, in school, in books. When you knew all the secrets, you became an adult. But now all of that is available on the Internet or TV.[1]

But the capacity of machines to provide information would not be enough to make us vulnerable to public scrutiny. Changes in the social and moral climate of the last four decades have removed many of our defenses. "Letting it all hang out" strikes millions of people as an acceptable guide to behavior. It may be hard to believe that in the not-so-distant past extramarital pregnancy, homosexuality, even a diagnosis of cancer were deeply held secrets. Now we express ourselves far more freely in our language, both in everyday speech and in literature, in our clothing, and in our sexual relationships. Births have been televised; so has a death.

Some observers, however, think that today's absence of privacy is no more serious than that experienced by earlier generations who lived in small towns and villages where everybody's activities were a matter of common knowledge. In the city people can and often do remain anonymous. Even the decline of the extended family, in which personal behavior was closely watched and evaluated by an army of relatives, has contributed to a greater sense of privacy.

Nevertheless, the questions surrounding this issue will multiply as public and private places become increasingly interchangeable. If people value the convenience of having wide access to information, services, and entertainment, as well as the right to express themselves freely, are they justified in thinking that they will also be able to guard their privacy? Do they perhaps regard the loss of privacy as a price they are willing to pay for admission to the global village? If not, how can their privacy be protected?

---

[1] Anthony Ramirez, "Lolitas Don't Shock Anymore, but *Lolita* Still Does," *New York Times*, August 2, 1998, p. Wk 5.

Privacy: Protections and Threats

WHITFIELD DIFFIE AND SUSAN LANDAU

BEFORE READING: Have the terrorist attacks on September 11, 2001, changed American beliefs about privacy? Explain.

Protecting the national security and enforcing the laws are basic societal values. Often they stand in competition with another basic societal value: privacy. The competition is hardly an equal contest. National security and law enforcement not only have political constituencies, they are represented by major societal organizations. Privacy has no such muscle behind it. As a result, although an attachment to privacy endures and at times grows, privacy is often violated.

The Dimensions of Privacy

Two hundred years ago, if you chose to speak to a colleague about private matters, you had to do it in person. Others might have seen the two of you walk off together, but to overhear your conversation an eavesdropper would have had to follow closely and would likely have been observed. Today, the very communication links that have made it possible to converse at a distance have the potential to destroy the privacy such conversations previously enjoyed.

From video cameras that record our entries into shops and buildings to supermarket checkout tapes that list every container of milk and package of cigarettes we buy, privacy is elusive in modern society. There are records of what we do, with whom we associate, where we go. Insurance companies know who our spouses are, how many children we have, how often we have our teeth cleaned. The increasing amount of transactional information—the electronic record of when you left the parking lot, the supermarket's record of your purchase—leaves a very large public footprint and presents a far more detailed portrait of the individual than those recorded at any time in the past. Furthermore, information about individuals is no longer under the control of the person to whom the information pertains; such loss of control is loss of privacy.

Privacy as a Fundamental Human Right

Privacy is at the very soul of being human. Legal rights to privacy appeared two thousand years ago in Jewish laws such as this: "[If one man

---

Whitfield Diffie is the inventor of public-key cryptography, which allows the use of a public key to create a document in codes to be decoded by the recipient with a private key. Susan Landau is a former professor of computer science at the University of Massachusetts, Amherst. Both work at Sun Microsystems. Excerpted here is a chapter from their book *Privacy on the Line: The Politics of Wiretapping and Encryption* (1998). The original notes have been omitted, and bibliographic footnotes inserted.

builds a wall opposite his fellow's] windows, whether it is higher or lower than them . . . it may not be within four cubits [If higher, it must be four cubits higher, for privacy's sake]."[1] The Talmud explains that a person's neighbor "should not peer and look into his house."

Privacy is the right to autonomy, and it includes the right to be let alone. Privacy encompasses the right to control information about ourselves, including the right to limit access to that information. The right to privacy embraces the right to keep confidences confidential and to share them in private conversation. Most important, the right to privacy means the right to enjoy solitude, intimacy, and anonymity.[2]   5

Not all these rights can be attained in modern society. Some losses occur out of choice. (In the United States, for example, candidates for office make public much personal information, such as tax and medical records, that private citizens are allowed to keep private.) Some losses are matters of convenience. (Almost no one pays bills in cash anymore.) But the maintenance of some seclusion is fundamental to the human soul. Accordingly, privacy is recognized by the international community as a basic human right. Article 12 of the 1948 Universal Declaration of Human Rights states:

> No one shall be subjected to arbitrary interference with his privacy, family, home or correspondence, nor to attacks upon his honour and reputation. Everyone has the right to the protection of the law against such interference or attacks.[3]

The 1967 International Covenant on Human Rights makes the same point.

The Soviet Union, East Germany, and other totalitarian states rarely respected the rights of individuals, and this includes the right to privacy. Those societies were permeated by informants, telephones were assumed to be tapped and hotel rooms to be bugged: life was defined by police surveillance. Democratic societies are supposed to function differently.

Privacy in American Society

Privacy is essential to political discourse. The fact is not immediately obvious because the most familiar political discourse is public. History records political speeches, broadsides, pamphlets, and manifestos, not the quiet conversations among those who wrote them. Without the opportunity to discuss politics in private, however, the finished positions that appear in public might never be formulated.

---

[1] Herbert Danby, *The Mishnah* (Oxford: Oxford UP, 1933), p. 367.

[2] David Flaherty, *Protecting Privacy in Surveillance Societies: The Federal Republic of Germany, Sweden, France, Canada, and the United States* (Chapel Hill: U of North Carolina P, 1989), p. 8.

[3] Academy on Human Rights, *Handbook of Human Rights* (1993), p. 3.

Democracy requires a free press, confidential lawyer-client relations, and the right to a fair trial. The foundations of democracy rest upon privacy, but in various democratic societies the protection of privacy is interpreted in varying ways. Britain, for example, has much looser laws regarding wiretaps than the United States. A number of European nations extend more protection to individuals' data records than the United States does.

Privacy is culture dependent. Citizens of crowded countries such as   10
India and the Netherlands hold very different views of what constitutes privacy than citizens of the United States. The American concept developed in a land with a bountiful amount of physical space and in a culture woven from many disparate nationalities.

In the 1970s, as rapid computerization brought fear of a surveillance society, some nations sought to protect individuals from the misuse of personal data. Sweden, Germany, Canada, and France established data-protection boards to protect the privacy and the integrity of records on individual citizens. When the U.S. congress passed a Privacy Act with a similar goal, President Gerald Ford objected to the creation of another federal bureaucracy, and no U.S. data-protection commission was ever established.[4] Ten states have data-protection laws, and California includes a right to privacy in its state constitution. New York is the only state that attempts any oversight (ibid.). It would, however, be a mistake to view the lack of a major regulatory apparatus in the United States as a lack of legal protection of privacy.

Privacy Protection in the United States

Most Americans believe that privacy is a basic right guaranteed by the Constitution. The belief has some truth to it, but not nearly as much as some believe. Nowhere is the word privacy mentioned in the Constitution, nor is a right to privacy explicit in any amendment. Privacy is nonetheless implicit to the Constitution.

The First Amendment protects the individual's freedoms of expression, religion, and association. The Third Amendment protects the private citizen against the state's harboring an army in his home, the Fourth against unreasonable search or seizure. The Fifth Amendment ensures that an individual cannot be compelled to provide testimony against himself. The Ninth Amendment reserves to "the people" those rights that are not enumerated in the Constitution. And "the Fourteenth Amendment's guarantee that no person can be deprived of life, liberty or property without due process of law, provides an additional bulwark against governmental interference with individual privacy."[5] . . .

---

[4]Flaherty, p. 305.

[5]United States Senate, Committee on the Judiciary, Subcommittee on Constitutional Rights, *Federal Data Banks and Constitutional Rights*, Vol. I (Washington, D.C.: U.S. Government Printing Office, Ninety-Third Congress, Second Session, 1974), p. ix.

Why Privacy?

Despite strictures to prevent abuses, the U.S. government has invaded citizens' privacy many times over the last fifty years, in many different political situations, targeting individuals and political groups. Politicians have been wiretapped, and lawyers' confidential conversations with clients have been eavesdropped upon by FBI investigators.

Sometimes invasion of privacy has been government policy; some- 15 times a breach has occurred because an individual within the government misappropriated collected information. The history of the last five decades shows that attacks on privacy are not an anomaly. When government has the power to invade privacy, abuses occur.

Conflict between protecting the security of the state and the privacy of its individuals is not new, but technology has given the state much more access to private information about individuals than it once had. As Justice Louis Brandeis so presciently observed in his dissenting opinion in *Olsmstead,*

> "in the application of a constitution, our contemplation cannot be only of what has been but of what may be." The progress of science in furnishing the government with means of espionage is not likely to stop with wiretapping. Ways may some day be developed by which the Government, without removing papers from secret drawers, can reproduce them in court, and by which it will be enabled to expose to a jury the most intimate occurrences of the home. Advances in the psychic and related sciences may bring means of exploring unexpressed beliefs, thoughts and emotions. . . . Can it be that the Constitution affords no protection against such invasions of individual security?[6]

Preservation of privacy is critical to a democratic political process. Change often begins most tentatively, and political discussion often starts in private. Journalists need to operate in private when cultivating sources. Attorneys cannot properly defend their clients if their communications are not privileged. As the Church Committee observed:

> Personal privacy is protected because it is essential to liberty and the pursuit of happiness. Our Constitution checks the power of Government for the purpose of protecting the rights of individuals, in order that all our citizens may live in a free and decent society. Unlike totalitarian states, we do not believe that any government has a monopoly on truth.
>
> When Government infringes those rights of nurturing and protecting them, the injury spreads far beyond the particular citizens targeted to untold numbers of other Americans who may be intimidated.
>
> Persons most intimidated may well not be those at the extremes of the political spectrum, but rather those nearer the middle. Yet voices of

---

[6]Louis Brandeis, Dissenting opinion in *Olmstead* v. *United States* (277 U.S. 438, 1928), p. 474.

moderation are vital to balance public debate and avoid polarization of our society.[7]

What type of society does the United States seek to be? The incarceration of Japanese Americans during World War II began with an invasion of privacy and ended in the tyrannical disruption of many individual lives. Could the roundup of Japanese Americans have occurred so easily if the Census Bureau's illegal cooperation had not made the process so efficient? The purpose of the Bill of Rights is to protect the rights of the people against the power of the government. In an era when technology makes the government ever more efficient, protection of these rights becomes ever more important.

Citizens of the former Eastern Bloc countries attest to the corruption of society that occurs when no thought or utterance is private. No one suggests that people living in the United States face imminent governmental infringements of this type, but in 1972 congressional staffers wrote that "what separates military intelligence in the United States from its counterparts in totalitarian states, then, is not its capabilities, but its intentions."[8] Electing officials we believe to be honest, trusting them to appoint officials who will be fair, and insulating the civil service from political abuse, we hope to fill the government with people of integrity. Recent history is replete with examples of abuse of power. Relying solely on intentions is dangerous for any society, and the Founding Fathers were careful to avoid it.

The right to be let alone is not realistic in modern society. But in a world that daily intrudes upon our personal space, privacy and confidentiality in discourse remain important to the human psyche. Thoughts and values still develop in the age-old traditions of talk, reflection, and argument, and trust and privacy are essential. Our conversations may be with people who are at a distance, and electronic media may transmit discussions that once might have occurred over a kitchen table or on a walk to work. But confidentiality—and the perception of confidentiality—are as necessary for the soul of mankind as bread is for the body. 20

[7]United States Senate, Senate Select Committee to Study Governmental Operations with Respect to Intelligence Activities, *Intelligence Activities and the Rights of Americans, Final Report, Book II*, Report 94–755 (Ninety-Fourth Congress, Second Session, April 23, 1976), pp. 290–91.

[8]United States Senate, Committee on the Judiciary, Staff of the Subcommittee on Constitutional Rights, *Army Surveillance of Civilians: A Documentary Analysis* (Ninety-Second Congress, Second Session, 1972), p. 96.

Remote Control

AVRAHAM BALABAN

BEFORE READING: Do you prefer conversation by e-mail or telephone? Explain your preference.

Recently I needed to call a friend and colleague to find out the deadline for proposals for a comparative-literature conference that we both planned to attend. A moment before calling, I hesitated: isn't a telephone call an intrusion? An imposition? Isn't it more appropriate to send her an e-mail, so that she can answer when it's convenient?

In the good old days, in nice weather people sat on their front porches. If you wanted to talk to them or spend a leisurely hour in their company, all you had to do was walk down the street, exchange pleasantries, and be invited for tea or coffee.

Once air-conditioning closed people off in their homes, porch life disappeared, and the idea that people could simply stop by unannounced vanished. The order of the day changed. We now call ahead and set up an appointment before visiting. The idea that once upon a time people would show up uninvited is hard to imagine. "What do you mean the Goldmans are here? Why didn't they call ahead?"

In 1984, I was a visiting scholar at Harvard, coming all the way from Tel Aviv. A week or so after we moved into our house, I saw my new neighbor over the fence. We introduced ourselves, and he invited my wife and me to stop by sometime. So we did. The rest of the year he was careful to stay clear of these newcomers who were not familiar with the local code.

The telephone used to be how Americans communicated while maintaining their privacy and controlling whom they wanted to see. The advent of e-mail has added a new dimension to the game. You send an e-mail to your friend, your colleague, or your dean, who replies when he or she has an answer or has a minute between other urgent e-mails. Your correspondent has the luxury of finding the right information before responding but also has control over the length of the answer and the length of the communicative act itself.

Next to e-mail, the telephone suddenly feels like an invasion. Can I simply call my colleague and ask her for the deadline for our proposals? Maybe it's not a good time for her. Maybe she's racing to an appointment or brushing her teeth. Maybe she doesn't like to answer on the spot,

---

Avraham Balaban is chair of the Department of African and Asian Languages and Literature of the University of Florida. "Remote Control" was printed in the *New York Times* on March 22, 1999.

doesn't like to be cornered. E-mail would be so much neater, more considerate, more respectful of privacy.

Yes, e-mail gives us the cocoon we have always dreamed of; now we can be as alienated as we want to be.

Can Anything Be Done to Protect Your Privacy in Cyberspace?

MARK MAREMONT

> BEFORE READING: Have you ever suffered as a result of an invasion of your privacy? Did the experience change your behavior in any way?

It's 2005, and within hours of booking a flight to Las Vegas online, your e-mail inbox is spilling over with messages from hotels offering room specials. Knowing you subscribe to an online newsletter for heart-bypass patients, one hotel trumpets its in-room defibrillators. A nearby casino, tipped off that you recently have surfed pornography Web sites, touts its lap dancing. The car-rental company you attempted to book rejects you after a database reveals you've had a recent accident.

So much for a private getaway.

The digital age has brought people instant access to information, given consumers more choices, and helped speed communications. But for most people, the era of near-ubiquitous computers is also eroding privacy. Vast amounts of electronic information are being collected each day from credit cards, e-mail, Web surfing, and even highway toll passes. Technically, the Las Vegas scenario would require nothing more than tying several databases together.

And that's just the beginning. With access to your genetic profile, insurance companies could predict your likelihood of contracting certain diseases. Potential employers could examine the political opinions you expressed online years earlier. Ubiquitous surveillance cameras matched with pattern-recognition technology could track your movements almost anywhere.

"The technological capacity to reduce privacy to a nonexistent level 5 is already there," says Reg Whitaker, a political scientist at York University in Toronto and author of a recent book on the subject.

It's the leading source of future dread in America. For all the obvious benefits conferred by the unimpeded flow of information, Americans

Mark Maremont is a staff reporter in the *Wall Street Journal*'s Boston bureau. This article appeared in that newspaper on January 1, 2000.

cited loss of personal privacy as their number 1 concern about the twenty-first century, ahead of overpopulation, terrorism, and global warming, in a *Wall Street Journal*/NBC poll.

But don't mourn for privacy just yet.

Already, some of the same technologies that threaten privacy are being used to defend it, and the arms race has only begun. There's also a growing sense among privacy gurus that individuals will not just complain about invasive technologies but will rebel against them, exhibiting biologically encoded human yearning for privacy.

"A Deep Drive"

"People have a deep drive to develop their privacy and their space," says Harvard University sociobiologist Edward O. Wilson, who likens the human desire for privacy to the territorial instinct of all animals. Even in primitive societies where people live in close quarters, he says, individuals always insist on a minimum distance from others. Dr. Wilson believes highly personal information such as financial and medical records have become part of our individual space, something we instinctively defend.

Individual companies perceived to be violating privacy rights have 10 come in for a barrage of criticism. Consider the recent case of Image Data LLC, a Nashua, New Hampshire, outfit that collected digitized driver's license photos from three states for a commercial database. Public outrage over the plan, intended to combat check and credit-card fraud, forced the states to cancel the arrangement.

Marc Rotenberg, executive director of the Electronic Privacy Information Center, Washington, sees parallels with the environmental movement. Initially, many companies argued they could never abandon certain practices, such as toxic dumping. Yet most such outfits have changed those practices under pressure of public opinion and new legal standards.

The popular perception, fueled by George Orwell's classic *1984*, is that technological advancement automatically causes the loss of privacy. But technology itself is already playing a strong role in the defense of privacy.

Just as junk e-mail, or digital spam, became a problem, technologies emerged to block it from e-mail inboxes. Powerful encryption programs have made it easier for people to surf the Internet anonymously, and digital cash helps mask buyers' profiles. Alan F. Westin, an emeritus professor of law at Columbia University who has studied privacy issues for decades, believes that technology advances will continue to aid privacy.

Unwanted solicitations could be halted with filtering software that permits consumers to specify what types of solicitations they want, he says. The filtering tools could be equipped with a "privacy preference" feature, which would screen out transmissions from senders that don't comply with certain privacy standards, while the standards would be monitored by independent agencies.

Privacy Seal

The Council of Better Business Bureaus, Arlington, Virginia, earlier this 15 year took a first step in this direction by announcing an online-privacy "seal" program, in which participating companies agree to adhere to a code of privacy practices. Among other things, the code requires a site to disclose how it intends to use the information being collected, mandates that consumers be allowed to opt out of data collection, and requires site operators to obtain parental permission to collect data on children. More than 100 companies have signed up already.

Dr. Westin believes that managing our privacy will become an every-day activity in the twenty-first century and beyond, requiring as much energy and thought as managing finances has in the twentieth century. "My grandchildren will be absolutely conscious of privacy management," he adds, including knowing their privacy rights and what their personal information is worth to a marketer.

Sensing a market opportunity, a host of small companies are devel-oping privacy-enhancement tools and services. One, Zero Knowledge Sys-tems of Montreal, is testing software that encrypts outgoing Internet traffic, including e-mail, and sends it through a series of electronic de-tours to conceal its origins. The software also makes it easier for users to employ pseudonyms to conduct disparate activities on the Web, for, say, political activities or job searching.

Another theoretically popular concept, still in infancy, is the so-called infomediary, a vendor that defends privacy by acting as a middle-man be-tween consumers and marketers. A consumer shopping for a new car, for example, might supply the infomediary with buying specifications, such as features and price range. The infomediary would release selected infor-mation to car dealers, which would in turn communicate with the mid-dleman and not the consumer.

But the infomediary model is fraught with challenges. Funneling transactions through third parties or electronic aliases may add time and hassle. Many people may not bother because of the inconvenience or cost. Cell phones, for example, are vastly less private than land lines, yet millions use them without thinking twice.

Some technologists also believe that privacy will be impossible to de- 20 fend against a determined and well-funded intrusion. "Privacy will be a technology race, and the winner will be the side with more money," says Bruce Schneier, a cryptography expert and chief technology officer of Counterpane Internet Security Inc., San Jose, California. He says technol-ogy is likely to give people some protection against their fellow citizens but not against big government agencies or anybody really intent on dig-ging out private information.

Some types of information might not be protectable at all. Arthur Caplan, director of the Center for Bioethics at the University of Pennsylvania, predicts that a person's genetic information will be easily extracted from a Kleenex or urinal or even through a rapid body scan that could be undetectable to the subject. "Biological information will be so readily available to so many people, personal privacy will go right out the window," he says.

Information All Around?

The prospect that laws and technology might not be enough to preserve any real measure of privacy has led David Brin, a physicist and science-fiction author, to propose a radical solution: complete transparency. In a recent book, he argues that it will be impossible to keep any information truly private. Instead, he proposes to open nearly all information to everyone. This, he argues, would help ensure that information is not misused.

If a corporate boss can monitor the keystrokes of telemarketing employees, Mr. Brin suggests, then those employees ought to have the legal right to watch what the boss does, perhaps with video cameras following him everywhere. This will make the boss think twice about how much information he really needs on the employees, he says.

As peculiar as Mr. Brin's proposition may seem, it addresses an unassailable truth: For all the power of public outrage and for all the technology power marshaled by individuals, we will never be as private in the future as we are now, just as we're not as private now as we were a century ago. The question is not whether we can retain privacy, but what we can do to keep it from disappearing entirely.

"A crisis point for privacy is facing us now," says Austin Hill, president of Zero Knowledge. "If we don't make sure privacy is really around, it will be gone, and the next thousand years will be very scary."   25

Too Much Privacy Is a Health Hazard

THOMAS LEE

BEFORE READING: Is there anything in your life that you would prefer not to tell your doctor? Suppose the secret posed a danger to your health.

Most patients like what they see on the computer monitor on my desk. There are lists of their medications and medical problems, laboratory results, and reminders to do mammograms. They are impressed that all the doctors at our hospital work with the same information about them. They are amused that I can check their test results from a laptop computer on an airplane. But more than a few people find cause to worry in this cutting-edge system. Could their diagnosis of diabetes leak to employers? Insurers? Companies making products for diabetics? A few years from now, will their genetic codes be flying around the Internet?

These are not paranoid fantasies. Threats to our medical privacy are proliferating as technology speeds the flow of information—and people are fighting back. Patients are increasingly reluctant to release their health records, and states are passing laws to restrict access to them. Unfortunately, these efforts can backfire. In Maine lawmakers tried earlier this year to bar the release of any information without a patient's written consent. The law seemed reasonable at first, but the result was chaos. Doctors caring for the same patient couldn't compare notes without first seeking permission. Clinical labs had to stop giving patients their results over the phone. You couldn't even call a local hospital to find out if a loved one had been admitted. Confidentiality is a vital component of the trust between patients and physicians, and protecting it is worth some inconvenience. But information is the lifeblood of good health care. In short, privacy can be hazardous to your health.

Consider what happens when a doctor writes you a prescription. If that doctor doesn't know about every other drug you're using, the results can be disastrous. Patients have died because one doctor prescribed Viagra for impotence and another ordered nitroglycerin for angina—a combination that causes dangerous drops in blood pressure. Fatal reactions have also occurred when patients on Prozac or Zoloft were given monoamine oxidase inhibitors (another type of antidepressant). Most deaths from drug interactions could be prevented by databases that show every prescription written for a particular patient. But insurers usually withhold that information, for fear of offending subscribers. The result is that physicians have to rely on what patients remember or choose to disclose.

Thomas Lee is the medical director of Partners Community HealthCare, Inc., in Boston. His article was published in *Newsweek* on August 16, 1999.

611

Drug interactions are not the only potential hazard. Suppose a person whose records are on file at one hospital shows up in the emergency room of another. Even if the records can be transferred, state law may bar the release of information about mental illness or HIV status, forcing the ER physician to fly halfblind. A laceration on a patient with a history of severe depression may warrant more than sutures — it may have been a suicide gesture. Likewise, pneumonia in a patient with HIV requires different tests and treatments than it would in someone else.

Even when privacy advocates concede that doctors need unfettered   5
access to patients' records, most favor shielding them from HMO administrators. But a responsible health plan can put clinical information to good use. As part of a "disease management" program, an HMO may use computer software to determine whether patients with a chronic condition, such as asthma or hypertension, are filling their prescriptions and showing up for appointments. Those who fall behind may get a reminder by mail or phone. These programs can measurably improve people's health, but patients often miss out on them by refusing to authorize access to their records. Some plans hesitate even to launch such programs. One Massachusetts HMO is now debating whether to send flu-shot reminders to members with HIV. The program would almost surely save lives, but it would just as surely draw criticism as a breach of confidentiality.

Privacy advocates are especially wary of electronic data. If we can't keep tabs on nuclear secrets at Los Alamos, they ask, how likely are we to keep computerized medical records out of hostile hands? But electronic record keeping may actually reduce the risk, even while making information more accessible. No one can tell who has looked at a paper chart, but anyone who opens a secure electronic record leaves a computerized fingerprint. A psychiatrist at a New England teaching hospital was recently fined for peeking at an acquaintance's medical records seven times. The bad news is that it was so easy for the psychiatrist to gain access. The good news is that she was so easily caught.

The real challenge is not just to detect such breaches but to prevent them. The doctors in my network will soon have to answer a series of questions before opening a patient's computerized record. We'll have to explain how we're involved in the patient's care, and how long our need for access will continue. And logging on to our system requires not only a password but also a smart card that generates new access codes every thirty seconds. Anyone who stole my smart card would also need my password, and vice versa. These safeguards cost money and time, and doctors will grumble about the extra keystrokes. But with a little creativity and common sense, we'll find a way to protect privacy while ensuring that doctors have the information they need to take good care of people.

What Privacy Rights?

BOB HERBERT

BEFORE READING: If you drafted a law to protect the right to privacy, what personal information would the law make it illegal to distribute? Think of all the places where information about you is on file.

A recent report out of Washington tells a story about Dr. Louis Hafken, a psychiatrist in Providence, Rhode Island, who received a letter from a company that reviews prescription drug benefits for insurers and employers.

The letter contained what should have been confidential information about one of Dr. Hafken's patients, including a printout of her prescription records. It noted that she was taking Ativan, an antianxiety drug. The company wanted to know why. Was the patient depressed, or suffering from panic disorder, or experiencing alcohol withdrawal? Did the doctor plan to continue giving her Ativan?

The doctor did not provide the requested information. "Frankly," he was quoted as saying, "it's none of their business."

The patient was naturally upset to learn that her employer had examined the records of her psychiatric treatment. The implications of such snooping are obvious. Dr. Hafken said many of his patients "are afraid to be completely honest in therapy" because they fear that people other than their doctors will learn of matters that were supposed to have remained secret.

They have reason to be worried. We are very close to the day 5 when strangers will know, or will be able to know, anything they want about you.

Your financial profile and buying habits have long since been catalogued and traded like baseball cards. Your medical records, supposedly secure, are not. Your boss may well be monitoring your telephone conversations and e-mail. Hidden video cameras have been installed—sometimes legally and sometimes not—in dressing rooms and public bathrooms. Thieves armed with your social security number can actually hijack your identity.

"Nothing Sacred: The Politics of Privacy" is a report released last month by the Center for Public Integrity, a highly regarded nonpartisan research organization. The report warned that the privacy of Americans "is being compromised and invaded from many angles" and asserted that Congress has not done nearly enough to slow the assault.

Bob Herbert is a columnist for the *New York Times*. This article appeared in his In America column on September 27, 1998.

"Time and again," said Charles Lewis, director of the center, "Congress has put the economic interests of various privacy invaders ahead of the privacy interests of the American public."

According to the report, Congress first heard testimony that there were problems keeping medical records confidential in 1971. But it still has not passed legislation designed to curb the abuses.

So you still get cases like that of Mark Hudson, a former insurance   10
company employee who told the *Times* in 1996 that he was shocked to find during his computer training that he could call up the records of any of the company's subscribers, including information about his own psychiatric treatment and the antidepressant medication he was taking.

"I can tell you unequivocally that patient confidentiality is not eroding," he said. "It can't erode because it's simply nonexistent."

The right to privacy in the workplace is virtually nonexistent as well.

"Most people assume that Federal laws protect Americans from being spied upon in the workplace," said the report. "To the contrary, over the years Congress has rejected legislation spelling out basic privacy protections for employees."

In addition to the possible monitoring of telephone conversations and e-mail, workers are frequently subjected to the scrutiny of hidden video cameras, can be required to type at computers that monitor the number of errors they make and the number of breaks they take, and often are compelled to provide urine samples and submit to psychological exams.

For some jobs, the scrutiny is reasonable. For others, it is not. In all   15
cases it should be properly regulated, and the guidelines should be clear. That is not what is happening. As the center's report noted, Congress has gone out of its way to preserve the right of employers to eavesdrop and otherwise spy upon and collect personal data on their employees.

For decades, privacy advocates have called for legislation that would spell out and guarantee a citizen's basic right to privacy. But tremendous amounts of money are being made from the rampant transfer of the most personal types of information. The huge corporate interests and others that benefit from that gold mine do not want it sealed.

Talk Show Telling versus Authentic Telling: The Effects of the Popular Media on Secrecy and Openness

EVAN IMBER-BLACK

BEFORE READING: Are you surprised that people are so willing to disclose their secrets on TV talk shows? Is such a development good or bad?

> Well, my guests today say that they can't bear to keep their secrets locked inside of them any longer. And they've invited their spouse or lover to come on national television to let them hear the secrets for the first time. — Montel Williams

The young woman entered my therapy room slowly, with the usual hesitation of a new client. I settled her in a chair, expecting to begin the low-key question-and-answer conversation that usually takes the entire first session. Almost before she could pronounce my name, she began telling me a deeply personal and shameful secret. In an effort to slow her down and start to build a relationship that might be strong enough to hold her enormous pain, I gently asked her what made her think it was all right to tell me things so quickly. "I see people doing it on *Oprah* all the time," she replied.

Throughout history human beings have been fascinated by other people's secrets. In great literature, theater, and films we view how people create and inhabit secrets and cope with the consequences of planned or unplanned revelation. Life-changing secrets are central to such ancient dramas such as *Oedipus* or Shakespeare's *Macbeth* as well as to twentieth-century classics such as Ibsen's *A Doll's House*, Eugene O'Neill's *Long Day's Journey into Night*, Arthur Miller's *Death of a Salesman* and *All My Sons*, or Lorraine Hansberry's *A Raisin in the Sun*. Like me, you may remember the poignancy of the sweet secrets in the O. Henry tale "Gift of the Magi," where a wife secretly cuts and sells her hair to buy her husband a watch chain for Christmas, while he, unbeknownst to her, sells his watch in order to buy silver combs for her hair. Contemporary popular films, such as *Ordinary People*, *The Prince of Tides*, or *The Wedding Banquet*, also illustrate the complexity of secrets and their impact on every member of a family. Literary and dramatic portrayals of perplexing secrets and their often

Evan Imber-Black, Ph.D., is director of the Center for Families and Health at the Ackerman Institute for the Family in New York City and a professor of psychiatry at the Albert Einstein College of Medicine. Her published work includes *Rituals for Our Times* (with Janine Roberts, Ed.D., 1992) and *Secrets in Families and Family Therapy* (1993). Printed here is an excerpt from her book *The Secret Life of Families: Truth-Telling, Privacy, and Reconciliation in a Tell-All Society* (1998).

complicated and messy resolutions help us to remember that keeping and opening secrets is not simple. Perhaps most important, they help us appreciate our own deep human connection to the dilemmas of others.

Since the advent of television, however, we have begun to learn about other people's secrets and, by implication, how to think about our own secrets in a very different way. Exploiting our hunger for missing community, both afternoon talk shows and evening magazine shows have challenged all of our previously held notions about secrecy, privacy, and openness. While such shows have been around for nearly thirty years, in the 1980s something new began to appear: celebrities began to open the secrets in their lives on national television.[1] As we heard about Jane Fonda's bulimia, Elizabeth Taylor's drug addiction, or Dick Van Dyke's alcoholism—formerly shameful secrets spoken about with aplomb—centuries of stigma seemed to be lifting. Other revelations enabled us to see the pervasiveness of wife battering and incest. The unquestioned shame and secrecy formerly attached to cancer, adoption, homosexuality, mental illness, or out-of-wedlock birth began to fall away.

This atmosphere of greater openness brought with it many benefits. In my therapy practice I experienced an important shift as the people I worked with displayed a greater ease in raising what might never have been spoken about a decade earlier. Frightening secrets lost some of their power to perpetuate intimidation. Those who had been silenced began to find their voices and stake their claim as authorities on their own lives.

But as the arena of the unmentionable became smaller and smaller, a   5
more dangerous cultural shift was also taking place: the growth of the simplistic belief that telling a secret, regardless of context, is automatically beneficial. This belief, promulgated by television talk shows and media exposés, has ripped secrecy and openness away from their necessary moorings in connected and empathic relationships. Painful personal revelations have become public entertainment, used to sell dish soap and to manufacture celebrity.

If cultural norms once made shameful secrets out of too many happenings in human life, we are now struggling with the reverse assumption: that opening secrets—no matter how, when, or to whom—is morally superior and automatically healing. The daily spectacle of strangers opening secrets in our living rooms teaches us that no distinctions need be drawn, no care need be taken, no thought given to consequences.

Talk Show Telling

From a Sally Jessy Raphael show in 1994, we hear and see the following conversation:

---

[1] For a complete discussion of the history of talk television and the wider context in which it is embedded, see J. A. Heaton and N. L. Wilson, *Tuning In Trouble: Talk TV's Destructive Impact on Mental Health* (San Francisco: Jossey-Bass, 1995).

Sally: Let's meet David and Kelly. They're newlyweds. They got married in December. . . . As newlyweds, what would happen if he cheated on you? What would you do?

Kelly: I don't know.

[Before David begins to speak, the print at the bottom of the screen reads, "Telling Kelly for the first time that he's cheating on her," thus informing the audience of the content of the secret before Kelly is told.]

David: I called Sally and told the producer of the show that I was living a double life. . . . I had a few affairs on her.

Sally (to Kelly): Did you know about that?

[Camera zooms in on Kelly's shocked and pained expression; she is speechless and in tears, and she shakes her head while members of the audience chuckle.]

Sally: Kelly, how do you feel? On the one hand, listen to how awful and bad this is. On the other hand, he could have just not ever told you. He loves you so much that he wanted to come and get this out. . . .

In the late 1960s the *Phil Donahue Show* began a new media format for sharing interesting information and airing issues. This shifted in the late 1970s and 1980s to celebrity confessions and the destruction of taboos. In the 1990s talk TV brings us the deliberate opening of secrets that one person in a couple or a family has never heard before. In a cynical grab for ratings and profits, the format of such shows has changed rapidly from one where guests were told ahead of time that they were going to hear a secret "for the first time on national television" to one where guests are invited to the show under some other ruse. These programs are referred to as "ambush" shows.

According to former talk show host Jane Whitney, "Practically anyone willing to 'confront' someone—her husband's mistress, his wife's lover, their promiscuous best friend—in a televised emotional ambush could snare a free ticket to national notoriety. *Those who promised to reveal some intimate secret to an unsuspecting loved one got star treatment*" (italics added).[2] Presently there are over thirty talk shows on every weekday. Forty million Americans watch these shows, and they are syndicated in many other countries.[3] Even if you have never watched a talk show, you live in an environment where assumptions about secrets have been affected by talk show telling.

Opening painful secrets on talk TV shows promotes a distorted sense 10 of values and beliefs about secrecy and openness. While viewers are drawn into the sensational content of whatever secret is being revealed, the impact on relationships after the talk show is over is ignored. Indeed,

---

[2]J. Whitney, "Why I Simply Had to Shut Up," *New York Daily News*, June 11, 1995, p. 6.

[3]Talk television is extremely profitable. A typical show costs about $200,000 a week to produce, compared to an average $1 million a week for a drama. In 1992, for instance, Oprah Winfrey's show earned $157 million, Phil Donahue's show $90 million, and Sally Jessy Raphael's show $60 million (Heaton and Wilson, *Tuning In Trouble*).

when there has been severe relationship fallout, or even tragedy following the opening of a secret, talk show hosts and producers claim they
have no responsibility, intensifying the belief that secrets can be reck-
lessly opened without any obligation to be concerned about the aftermath. Consider the following:

- In one notorious incident in 1995, a young man named Jonathon
  Schmitz murdered an acquaintance, Scott Amedure, following an
  unwelcome revelation on the *Jenny Jones* show.[4] Schmitz had been
  told that he was coming on the show to meet a "secret admirer." He
  was *not* told that the show was about "men who have secret crushes
  on men."[5] When his shock and humiliation resulted in Amedure's
  murder, the host and producers insisted they had no responsibility.

- On the *Montel Williams* show, a woman heard for the first time that
  her sister had been sleeping with her boyfriend for several years. She
  came on the show after being told it was a show about "old
  boyfriends."

- Former talk show host Jane Whitney describes a show she did called
  "Revealing Your Double Life." A mother was invited on who had no
  idea why her son had cut himself off from her for two years.
  Whitney, of course, knew that the son was about to reveal his
  pending sexual reassignment surgery. When she met the mother
  just before the show, the woman implored her, "Do you know
  what's wrong? We were always so close. I don't know what's happened. Is he sick? Does he have AIDS?" Assuring the mother that
  "everything would be all right," Whitney lied and kept the secret in
  order to maximize its revelation on the show.[6]

- Ricki Lake invited on a man who had been keeping his homosexuality a secret from his family. His roommate announced that he had
  taken it upon himself to tell the man's family this secret.[7]

When such actions occur over and over again on talk TV, we lose our
capacity to ask a critical question — namely, under what circumstances do
we have the right to open another person's secret?

On talk television, husbands hear for the first time that their wives
want a divorce; mothers are told the secret of their daughters' sexual

---

[4]*Newsweek*, March 20, 1995, p. 30; *New York Times*, March 12, 1995, p. A22, and
March 14, 1995, pp. A1, A10.

[5]The tragedy attached to this particular show distracts our attention from an important dimension of many of these programs, which is that they commonly pander to
feelings of homophobia, racism, and sexism. See Heaton and Wilson, *Tuning In Trouble*,
for a full discussion of this issue.

[6]Whitney, "Why I Simply Had to Shut Up."

[7]J. A. Heaton, and N. L. Wilson, "Tuning In to Trouble," *Ms.* magazine, September/
October 1995, 6(2), pp. 45–48.

abuse; wives discover that their husbands tell friends about their sexual relationship. And all of this occurs in a context in which the host disingenuously denies any responsibility for what is set in motion in the complex ecology of family relationships.

Talk show telling ignores the importance of committed relationships. Telling can be anonymous and disguised. A studio audience and a viewing audience consisting of strangers hear the previously hidden details of our lives. Commercial breaks cavalierly interrupt the opening and hearing of a painful secret. Eavesdropping stands in for sincere listening. Voyeurism substitutes for witnessing. The host's pseudo-intimate hugs and caresses replace genuine healing.

When secrets are opened on television, several peculiar triangles are created. The relationship between the person telling the secret and the person hearing the secret is immediately invaded by the audience, the host, and the "expert," each with a calculated and repetitious role. These roles are imbued with arrogance: the belief that one knows what is best for other people to do about the secrets in their lives. Talk show telling involves opening secrets to a huge group of uninvolved, faultfinding listeners who have no responsibility for the relationship after the talk show ends.

When a secret is about to be revealed, captions are placed below the 15 image of the person who has not yet heard it. The audience sees such words as "About to hear that his wife just had an abortion" or "Jim is not Ellen's biological father." Thus the audience knows the content of the secret before the person whose life the secret affects. A context of humiliation is constructed. Often the audience laughs or gasps while the camera catches a close-up of the perplexed face of the listener. The recipient of the secret is, in fact, the last to know. This structure reduces empathy and enables the audience to feel separate from and superior to the ambushed guest.

The audience encourages further revelations through applause.[8] As viewers, we get the message over and over that opening a secret, regardless of consequences, gains attention and approval. Loudly applauded, cheered, jeered, and fought over, secrets are in fact trivialized. On talk shows, a secret of sexual abuse equals a secret about family finances equals a secret about being a Nazi equals a secret of paternity.

Once a secret is revealed, both the teller and the recipient are immediately vulnerable to the judgmental advice and criticism of strangers. Blaming and taking sides abound. Not a moment elapses for reflection on the magnitude and gravity of what has occurred. Every secret is instantly reduced to a one-dimensional problem that will yield to simplistic solutions.

---

[8]See R. Cialdini, *Influence: How and Why People Agree to Things* (New York: William Morrow, 1984), for a discussion regarding studies on compliance showing that once people agree to participate in something, they often go along with much more than they originally intended.

Soon after a secret is opened, the host goes into high gear with some variation of the message that opening the secret can have only good results. Sally Jessy Raphael tells the young wife who has just discovered the secret of her husband's affairs in front of millions of unasked-for snoopers, "He loves you so much that he wanted to come and get this out." The message to all is that telling a secret, in and of itself, is curative. There is no place for ambivalence or confusion. Indeed, guests are often scolded for expressing doubt or hesitation about the wisdom of national disclosure of the intimate aspects of their lives.

The host's position as a celebrity can frame the content of a given secret and the process of telling as either normal or abnormal, good or bad. When Oprah Winfrey joins guests who are exposing secrets of sexual abuse or cocaine addiction with revelations of her own, the telling becomes hallowed. No distinctions are drawn between what a famous person with a lot of money and power might be able to speak about without consequences and what an ordinary person who is returning to their family, job, and community after the talk show might be able to express. Conversely, some hosts display initial shock, dismay, and negativity toward a particular secret, its teller, or its recipient. When a guest on the *Jerry Springer Show* who has just discovered that a woman he had a relationship with is a transsexual hides in embarrassment and asks the host what he would do, Springer responds, "Well, I certainly wouldn't be talking about it on national TV!" A context of disgrace is created, only to be transformed at the next commercial break into a context of understanding and forgiveness.

Toward the end of any talk show on which secrets have been revealed, a mental health therapist enters. A pseudo-therapeutic context is created. The real and difficult work that is required after a secret opens disappears in the smoke and mirrors of a fleeting and unaccountable relationship with an "expert" who adopts a position of superiority and assumed knowledge about the lives of people he or she has just met.[9] While we are asked to believe that there are no loose ends when the talk show is over, the duplicitousness of this claim is evident in the fact that many shows now offer "aftercare," or real therapy, to deal with the impact of disclosing a secret on television.[10]

The time needed even to begin to deal adequately with any secret is powerfully misrepresented on talk television. In just under forty minutes

[9]See L. Armstrong, *Rocking the Cradle of Sexual Politics* (New York: Addison-Wesley, 1994), for a thoughtful discussion of the impact of such "experts" on talk television when the topic is incest. According to Armstrong, such a structure diminishes the issue, reducing it from one with crucial political implications to simply a matter of personal opinion.

[10]Jamie Diamond, "Life after Oprah," *Self*, August 1994, pp. 122–125, 162; also see Heaton and Wilson, *Tuning In Trouble*, for a thoughtful critique of the questionable quality of such "aftercare."

on a single *Montel Williams* show, a man told his wife he was in a homosexual relationship; a woman told her husband she was having an affair with his boss; another woman told her boyfriend that she was a transsexual; a wife revealed to her husband that they were $20,000 in debt; and a woman told her boyfriend that she had just aborted their pregnancy. An ethos of "just blurt it out" underpins these shows.

Talk show telling also erases age-appropriate boundaries between parents and children. Children are often in the audience hearing their parents' secrets for the first time. On one show an eight-year-old boy heard his aunt reveal that he had been abandoned by his mother because she "didn't want" him. Children may also be onstage revealing a secret to one parent about the other parent, without a thought given to the guilt children experience when they are disloyal to a parent.[11] The impact on these children, their sense of shame and embarrassment, and what they might encounter when they return to school the next day is never considered.

Ultimately, talk show telling transforms our most private and intimate truths into a commodity. Shows conclude with announcements: "Do you have a secret that you've never told anyone? Call and tell us"; "Have you videotaped someone doing something they shouldn't do? Send us the tape." A juicy secret may get you a free airplane trip, a limousine ride, an overnight stay in a fancy hotel. While no one forces anyone to go on a talk show, the fact that most guests are working-class people who lack the means for such travel makes talk show telling a deal with the devil.

[11] *Sally Jessy Raphael Show*, November 29, 1994, "We Want Mom to Leave Her Cheating Husband"; transcript by Journal Graphics.

"You have the right to remain silent. Anything you say may be used against you in a court of law, newspapers, periodicals, radio, television, all electronic media, and technologies yet to be invented."

Privacy Rights: The New Employee Relations Battlefield

WILLIAM S. HUBBARTT

BEFORE READING: If you were seeking employment, are there some kinds of questions that you would refuse to answer — questions about sexual preference, religion, or use of prescribed drugs, for example — because you doubted their relevance to the job?

Can an employee be dismissed for dating a fellow employee?

Can a manager monitor conversations in his employees' break room?

Does a drug test invade privacy, or is it a reasonable safeguard against accidents on the job?

Is e-mail private correspondence?

These and other questions strike at the heart of the conflict between an employer's concern for managing the safety and security of the workplace and an employee's privacy interest.

The news media are filled with reports of employers who routinely conduct locker searches, monitor telephone calls, mount video cameras that watch employees on the job, and monitor computers and electronic mail systems. Many of these stories emerge when a lawsuit is filed by an outraged employee seeking redress for a perceived violation of his or her privacy.

I say "perceived" because an employee's right to privacy in the private-sector workplace is *not* fundamentally guaranteed by the Constitution or federal laws, even though many employees believe this to be the case. On the other hand, employers do not have carte blanche. Some federal and state laws do afford certain limited privacy protections for employees. But in their desire to control their businesses, some employers clearly cross the boundary between reasonable management practices and outrageous personal violations.

Why are conflicts over privacy increasing?

Companies don't set out to spy on employees or break into desks and 5 lockers. But as companies have watched losses caused by theft and drug abuse soar, they have responded by instituting controls to protect their assets and interests. Such common deterrents as drug testing and workplace surveillance are extremely sensitive and can offend employees if they are not explained adequately and implemented with care.

William S. Hubbartt is the founder and president of Hubbartt and Associates, a human resources consulting firm, and the author of six books, including *The New Battle over Workplace Privacy* (1998), from which this excerpt is taken.

Another "hot spot" is workplace technology. Sophisticated computer and communications technology allows managers to monitor performance by monitoring conversations or counting keystrokes. Again, if such procedures are instituted with little explanation or respect, employees will have strong negative reactions.

Their reactions are understandable. Most of us regard the right to privacy as one of the fundamental freedoms of a democratic society. Our history lessons taught us that the American colonists sought privacy protections and freedom from colonial rule of the English government. Our founding fathers sought to include privacy protections in our Constitution and our government. We grew up believing that individuals should be protected from unwanted prying into their personal lives and activities and that information about one's private life should not be subject to scrutiny by others, by the government, or by one's employer.

With these expectations, it's natural that both employers and employees wonder whether there are laws against employer spying and just what privacy rights employees are entitled to on the job. In truth, there *is* no comprehensive privacy statute. Yes, there is a constitutional provision that limits certain search and seizure actions by the government. And yes, there are laws that limit certain forms of monitoring and specify how an employer can use or release private information. But most of the constitutional protections we enjoy as private citizens vanish when we go to work. While the government, as an employer, is subject to constitutional privacy limitations, laws impose few limitations on the private employer.

Our privacy rights on the job are much more limited than most of us believe. The Constitution affords only limited privacy protections. . . . Local laws vary from state to state and, like federal laws, are subject to judicial interpretation. Many areas of privacy are new and have yet to be legislated. Other laws are so recent that cases that hinge on their interpretation are only now making their way through the court system, so it may be months or years before an employer can see the significance of a ruling. In the meantime, employers and employees find themselves clashing on privacy in a number of areas, as the following summary reveals.

Preemployment Tests

Arlene Kurtz learned that workplace privacy concerns begin at the start of the employment process when she applied for a job as a clerk typist with the city of North Miami, Florida. The city had developed a policy that all job applicants must sign an affidavit stating that they had not used tobacco products for one year before seeking city employment. The city had implemented a no-smoking policy in 1990, claiming that smokers create higher health costs, as much as $4,611 per year more than nonsmokers. When Kurtz refused to sign the affidavit, she was not hired. She then filed suit against the city alleging that the no-smoking rule was an invasion of privacy.

In her suit, Kurtz claimed that the rule interfered with an aspect of her personal life in which she had a legitimate expectation of privacy. She alleged that if the city's ban against the hiring of smokers was permitted, it would allow employers to further regulate personal lives of employees on other matters, such as when to go to bed at night, what to drink on weekends, where to take vacations, or what hobbies to engage in. In evaluating the facts of the case, the courts sided with the city, indicating that the city's concern for protecting employees' health and for controlling health care costs justified the no-smoking rule.[1]

In *Kurtz*, the city was able to justify its preemployment smoking rule. 10 But other kinds of preemployment tests also have been subject to privacy invasion or other legal claims:

Physical exams. Many firms use physical exams in prehire placement and during employment. Improper use of this information can result in a privacy invasion or violate employment laws.

Drug/alcohol screening. Record numbers of firms are conducting drug/alcohol screening tests. The intrusive nature of these tests prompts many privacy invasion claims.

Background checks. Improper handling or disclosure of information gathered from education, credentials, credit, driving, or criminal records can result in privacy claims or other labor law violations.

Reference checks. Résumé fraud and other employee relations problems have led employers to seek verification of employment information provided by job candidates. Careless use of this information can result in privacy or defamation claims.

Testing. Employer use of psychological testing, polygraph testing, and other kinds of paper-and-pencil measuring instruments are subject to legal restrictions. Improper inquiries of handling of test results can lead to privacy invasion claims.

After-Hours Activities

What an employee does off the job is his or her business — or is it? Employer intrusions into personal lives of employees create many questions. Can an employer regulate or prevent employees from taking a second job? Can an employee be fired because he was arrested off the job? What should an employer do if an employee refuses to work because of religious beliefs? Is it lawful for an employer to regulate an employee's drinking or smoking off the job? Is it a privacy invasion when the employer limits dating between employees? These kinds of issues have created many privacy invasion claims.

Consider the case of Robin Joy Brown, who applied to the State of Georgia for a position as a state's attorney.

---

[1] *Kurtz v. City of North Miami,* 11 IER Cases 480, US, No. 95-545 (1996).

Brown had all the prerequisites: a Phi Beta Kappa undergraduate, she had received a law scholarship, edited the law review, received her law degree, and completed law clerk experience. After being offered a job by the Georgia state's attorney's office, she accepted. But prior to starting her employment she advised a deputy state's attorney of her plans for an upcoming wedding and that she would be changing her name from Brown to Shahar. She did not tell the deputy that she planned to marry another woman.

When Georgia Attorney General Bowers learned that the planned wedding was to another woman, he withdrew the job offer stating in a letter that the purported marriage would "jeopardize the proper function of this office." Brown went ahead with her marriage plans, changed her name to Shahar, and filed suit for loss of job. In her suit, Shahar alleged that she was "fired" because of her participation in a private religious ceremony of marriage. The U.S. Court of Appeals ultimately heard the case and found that the employer's action violated the Shahars' constitutional right of intimate association.[2]

Employer involvement in off-the-job conduct usually occurs in one of the following areas:

Criminal and other off-duty misconduct. Some individuals just can't seem to stay out of trouble. Inappropriate collection or release of this information can lead to privacy claims and other liabilities.

Secondary employment. Employees may feel that secondary employment is a private affair, but when it affects the employer's business, the employer may have a say.

Smoking and use of other lawful products off the job. Off-the-job use of lawful products is generally the employee's business. On some issues, an employer may have justification to regulate off-duty conduct, but privacy claims frequently occur when employers try to control this kind of conduct.

Employee dating. Regulation of dating may seem beyond the employer's purview, but sexual harassment claims as well as privacy invasion claims make this a sensitive subject.

Personal beliefs and lifestyles. Employee beliefs and lifestyles may be related to religion, marital status, or sexual preference. These issues are highly personal, and improper handling of them can lead to privacy invasion or other legal claims.

Conclusion

In all aspects of our lives, certain individual freedoms are given up in order to accommodate the greater needs of the public, the government, or an organization such as an employer. Because of terrorism and hijacking, our society readily submits to use of metal detector screens and

---

[2] *Shahar v. Bowers,* 11 IER Cases 521 (1994).

searches of personal belongings when boarding commercial aircraft at the airport. Upon return from overseas trips, travelers customarily accept luggage searches because of the recognized need to control the unauthorized influx of drugs into the country.

Freedom of speech does not protect the calling out of "fire" in a 15 crowded theater. As a society, we tolerate the increased presence of security cameras at banks, retail stores, and other places where cash is handled because we recognize that the use of these devices to deter crime is more important than the loss of certain aspects of our privacy. But privacy rights seem to be diminishing, and employer prying seems to be growing.

THINKING AND WRITING ABOUT THREATS TO PRIVACY IN THE INFORMATION AGE

QUESTIONS FOR DISCUSSION AND WRITING

1. What, according to Diffie and Landau, are the moral and spiritual dimensions of privacy? (Many scholars have noted that three great religions were born in the desert.) Do you feel that you have suffered from a lack of privacy in your life? If so, what were the consequences?

2. Balaban argues that e-mail has made our lives more private—and more distant from the lives of others. Many people would argue the opposite—that e-mail has drawn us closer to each other. Do you think Balaban has proved his claim?

3. In Maremont's article a physicist proposes "complete transparency" (para. 22). Would this solve the problem of preserving privacy or create more problems? (In many schools students are under surveillance in the corridors and rest rooms. Should teachers and administrators also be on camera? Elaborate on the warrant underlying your claim.)

4. Has Lee convinced you that making medical records available to qualified personnel is a good thing? If so, what were the most effective elements of his argument?

5. Herbert wants "legislation that would spell out and guarantee a citizen's basic right of privacy" (para. 16). Does he suggest what legislation he would advise? What feelings do you think Herbert is trying to evoke in his readers?

6. Do you think that talk show telling should be controlled? If so, to what extent should it be controlled and by whom?

7. How far should employers be permitted to go in acquiring information about employees? Summarize Hubbartt's views on the subject. Does the type of work make a difference? Make a list of reasonable and unreasonable requirements. Explain the reasons for your choices.

TOPICS FOR RESEARCH

Privacy in student dormitories

Surveillance in reducing crime

Privacy in Orwell's *1984*

Legal efforts to guarantee electronic privacy

TAKING THE DEBATE ONLINE

For these and additional research URLs, see bedfordstmartins.com/rottenberg.

- *Electronic Privacy Information Center*
  www.epic.org

  EPIC, a public-interest research center in Washington, D.C., includes some of the latest developments in Internet privacy issues, links to many online resources, and policy archives.

- *The Privacy Page*
  www.privacy.org

  This site offers more than two dozen links to privacy-related articles in several online magazines, as well as a resource archive and links to other privacy organizations.

- *Privacy Law in the USA*
  www.rbs2.com/privacy.htm

  Created by attorney Ronald B. Standler, this essay covers the history of privacy law, modern privacy laws, the privacy of businesses, invasions of privacy by journalists, and more.

- *The Privacy Forum*
  www.vortex.com/privacy.html

  The Privacy Forum includes a moderated digest for the discussion and analysis of issues relating to the general topic of privacy in the information age. Topics include a wide range of telecommunications, information, and database collecting and sharing that pertains to the privacy concerns of individuals, groups, businesses, and government.

- *Privacy International*
  www.privacyinternational.org

  Privacy International is a human rights group formed in 1990 as a watchdog on surveillance by governments and corporations. It is based in London and has an office in Washington, D.C. PI has conducted campaigns throughout the world on issues ranging from wiretapping and national security activities, to ID cards, video surveillance, data matching, police information systems, and medical privacy.

- *Online Privacy Alliance*
  www.privacyalliance.org

  The Online Privacy Alliance is a cross-industry coalition of more than eighty global companies and associations committed to promoting the privacy of individuals online.

CHAPTER 17

What Does the Future Hold for Sports?

Success in the world of sports is now measured in hundredths of seconds—and in millions of dollars. Where college once was the proving ground for those hoping to make it big in the pros, in some sports the best athletes are now bypassing college in hopes of earning those millions sooner. Scouting begins before the athletes even reach high school, and now some high school athletes are turning the tables, in a sense, by paying professional services to scout out the best scholarship opportunities and to "sell" their talents to colleges and universities by means of slick publicity packages. Some sports fans, like Robert Glidden, the recently retired president of Ohio University and author of the first of the essays included here, wonder if we have gone too far in letting the sportswriting establishment shape our perspective. Lamenting the fact that money drives sports these days, Glidden concludes, "The real scandal now is how much this issue diverts our attention from things that matter: honest rivalry, real priorities, and true appreciation of college-level athletics." He predicts "some sort of scandal of the sort game shows experienced in the 1950s."

If the payback for those who run the fastest, score the most points, or hit the hardest can be salaries and endorsements in the millions, it is not surprising that the temptation is great to try anything to shave seconds off a run, add points to the scoreboard, or build muscles. The use of drugs in sports, or doping, is hardly new, but it may be more widespread than ever, or at least public awareness of it is. The mid-twentieth century saw Olympic athletes so dosed with hormones that the line between male and female was blurred. Recent Olympics have seen athletes disqualified or stripped of their medals because of the outcome of a drug test. The scandal has even affected baseball, where steroid use is a relatively recent development. Some insiders as well as some fans feel it may be time to let each sport make its own rules about drug use. In the near future, genetic manipulation may make the use of drugs unnecessary anyway.

Just as scientific research has produced drugs that can enhance performance, it has also given us new insights into the mental side of sports. While athletes are seeking the perfect body, the perfect swing, the perfect form, the perfect stride, they are also seeking the perfect mindset that will give them mental control over their game. Golfers have long talked about the mysterious state called "the zone" in which there is the perfect blending of body and mind. Scientists are now studying how to help athletes find their "zone." Their discoveries may help athletes improve their game, but what they gain in championships and earnings will never replace the almost spiritual quality in which for a short time the world seems to stop and an athlete is at one with his or her game.

Championing Intercollegiate Football

ROBERT GLIDDEN

BEFORE READING: What are some of the positive and negative effects of the emphasis placed on collegiate football in America? In your opinion, do the positive effects outweigh the negative or vice versa?

We have just passed the time of year when sportswriters and a few others were concerned that we in the United States might fail to identify a "real collegiate football champion" on the playing field. Because we do not have a championship playoff series, sportswriters (who command too much of our attention anyway) feel betrayed by university presidents and the intercollegiate sports establishment. They find the present system of rankings and bowl games insufficient. Is this really such an important issue? Does it really matter if the coaches think one team is champion and the sportswriters select another, by whatever method? Why not let fans from three or four different universities believe that their team is best in the nation? I think this controversy is driven by the frenzy of the sportswriting establishment.

Robert Glidden retired in 2004 after ten years as president of Ohio University in Athens, Ohio, and eight years of service as founding chair and board member of the Council for Higher Education and Accreditation. One of his first tasks in retirement was to join a team of European rectors and chancellors in the evaluation of the universities in Ireland. This article appeared in the *Journal of College and Character* in 2001.

I am personally undecided about a championship playoff, which means I really don't care that much. There was a time when I was vehemently against it because a playoff promised to extend football into the winter term. I no longer have strong feelings about that because I realize that collegiate football programs of the size and caliber to be competing in a championship series are year-round activities anyway.

I also feared that a playoff would interfere with the bowls, which I believe are a good thing for thousands of players and their fans. Certainly the bowl festivities are good for the communities that host them, as sources of civic pride and tourism dollars. The bowls are a great incentive for players, too—a prize to work toward at the end of the season. If a playoff system would take clever advantage of bowl games to select the final four or eight teams to compete for a championship, I would not be opposed. Nevertheless, the problem would remain a political one. How does the NCAA wrestle away control of the football championship from the commissioners of the major athletics conferences?

It is disappointing to see the effect that the present system, the Bowl Championship Series (BCS), has already had on the prestige of the various bowls—merely by selecting two teams to play for a so-called championship. Where once the Rose Bowl, the Orange Bowl, the Sugar Bowl, the Fiesta Bowl, etc., each had their "place in the sun," now each year only one bowl—the one whose turn it is to host the "championship"—gets most of the attention from the sportswriters. The Rose Bowl, the granddaddy of them all, is now just another game until it takes its turn as the championship game.

It saddens me that college football and men's basketball are now so totally driven by money, and I wonder if it will all come crashing down around us. Perhaps it would be a good thing if it did. University presidents kid themselves into proclaiming that they control college sports. Perhaps we do govern volleyball and track and swimming through the NCAA, but we do not control football or men's basketball. The bowl games and the distribution of revenues from them are decided among the commissioners of the major conferences. Is the sixth place team in the Southeastern Conference really better than the second place team in the Mid-American Conference? I doubt it, but the MAC's second place team never gets the opportunity to prove that. And while I understand and believe in the marketplace as a determiner for most of what we do, the salary competition among the major powers in football and basketball coaches' salaries is becoming obscene.

The culprit, of course, is television and the entertainment dollars it produces. It becomes all the more important for teams in those major sports to win, because winning means dollars for schools and conferences and dollars are desperately needed to pay for the facilities and equipment and salaries of the coaches. Television and the entertainment appeal of college sports are not going to go away, of course; but at some point, in some way, we have to get a grip.

I feel fortunate to be in an institution where our athletics program is viewed by most of our fans and supporters in proper perspective. There are always a few faculty members who resent that sports drain funds from the academic mission of the university, and on the other side there are a few fans who seem to believe that nothing else matters in their lives. But for the most part, we are able to maintain a healthy attitude about the value of sport for the athletes themselves and the value of athletics events for the student and general communities. I wonder what it would take to return that kind of perspective to the sportswriters and major conferences. Alas, in our current media environment, I fear it may be some sort of scandal of the sort game shows experienced in the 1950s. The real scandal now is how much this issue diverts our attention from things that matter: honest rivalry, real priorities, and true appreciation of college-level athletics.

The College Try

KELLEY KING

BEFORE READING: Can you think of examples of athletes who are known as much for their image as for their talent? Is part of the popularity (or notoriety) of an athlete a result of the way he or she is "packaged"? Explain.

Wesley Swafford wasn't the best swimmer on her Cincinnati club team, and she considered herself a long shot to earn a scholarship at her dream school, Penn State. So when her mother, Paula, heard about a company that helps raise the profile of young athletes and attract the interest of college coaches, she quickly signed up her daughter. In November, a year after Paula paid a Cincinnati affiliate of the Birmingham-based National Scouting Report $2,495 to assemble a knockout promotional package — including a brochure, recommendations from NSR scouts, a DVD of Wesley's swimming strokes, and a Web site devoted to her accomplishments — her daughter scored a partial scholarship with the 2002 Big Ten champion Nittany Lions. "She received more attention from more schools than girls who were better than she was," says Paula. "I truly think that NSR helped give her the edge."

Competition for athletic scholarships has become fierce. While the NCAA doesn't keep a record of the number of athletic grants awarded annually by its member schools or the monetary value of those grants, NCAA vice president of championships Judy Sweet says, "There is defi-

---

Kelley King is a writer-reporter covering college football for *Sports Illustrated*, in which this article first appeared on March 17, 2003. King is also a regular contributor to SI.com.

nitely more interest [in receiving aid] than scholarships available." Consequently, the race among entrepreneurs to help athletes gain an edge in the recruiting process is heating up. There are more than fifty services, mostly Internet-based, designed to match student-athletes with schools. NSR, which was founded in 1980 by Robert Rigney, a video-production specialist, is one of the better established, grossing between $2 million and $3 million annually.

Why pay a company to do a job that anyone with a camcorder and a computer could do? NSR assembles slick promotional packages for its clients, ranging from an $895 basic model in which NSR sends out e-mail and paper resumes and includes the player in a monthly promotional mailing, to the $2,495 elite package, which features a DVD and a regularly updated personal Web site. But its calling card is a stable of two hundred scouts in fifty states and several foreign countries. These bird dogs, who include former college coaches and professional athletes, scope the sidelines for talent in all sports. As they drum up business—many of NSR's clients find out about the company when they are approached by a regional rep—the scouts also gather information on athletes for college coaches, who receive reports from NSR free of charge. "We're able to scout when coaches can't," says NSR president Rusty Rigney, Robert's son. He says he receives more than 25,000 queries about athletes from colleges each year. "We've earned the trust of so many coaches who have benefited [from our services]."

The majority of NSR's athletes connect with smaller Division I programs and D-II and D-III schools that cobble together aid packages. Its bread-and-butter customers are low-profile athletes best suited to programs that lack the funding to recruit prospects beyond their region. For example, Makeba Davis, the women's volleyball coach at Quinnipiac (enrollment 4,700) in Hamden, Connecticut, says NSR's comprehensive DVD persuaded him to recruit Kalyn Hundley of Gulf Breeze, Florida, this year. "We have a very limited budget, so I never would have known about Kalyn otherwise," says Davis. "Now I expect her to be one of my top two freshmen next season."

On the other hand, coaches at the biggest programs generally consider NSR and the other scouting services more of a headache than a resource. "Because we feel like we have a good grasp on what players we are interested in, we don't use those companies," says Mike Locksley, an assistant football coach at Maryland. Kelly Graves, the women's basketball coach at Gonzaga, scoffs at what he calls "fancy" player profiles that he regularly receives from NSR. "If you have to spend money to get noticed, we're probably not interested," he says.

The consensus among coaches is that while the slick packaging doesn't hurt, it's the raw material that counts. To Wesley's credit, it turns out that she had a lot more going for her than a cool video. "The kid's an academic achiever with a great personality and athletic potential," says Penn State swimming coach Bill Dorenkott. "The way that was conveyed couldn't have mattered less."

The NBA's Youth Squad

BRIAN HINDO

BEFORE READING: If the National Basketball Association continues to allow high school athletes to move directly into professional basketball, what will be the effects on college basketball? On high school basketball? On the pros?

Chances are you've never heard of Greg Oden. But you can bet that every National Basketball Association scout has. Oden is a specimen—a lithe, 7-foot center, 250 pounds and agile, a deft passer on the low block. He also just finished his sophomore year of high school. Scouts say the sixteen-year-old Indianapolis native could be the first player taken in the 2006 NBA draft—if he wants. For now, Oden says he has other ideas: "I really want to go to college. I want to be a psychologist."

Not many would blame Oden if he puts off college. He would hardly be the first high school prodigy wooed away from it by a guaranteed three-year contract worth more than $10 million—and untold millions more in endorsements. Since 1995, when Kevin Garnett skipped college and was selected fifth in the draft by the Minnesota Timberwolves, twenty-two high schoolers have made the leap. The largest crop ever—as many as ten, led by Atlanta standout Dwight Howard—will enter the league next season after selection at the 2004 draft meeting on June 24.

The influx of teenage millionaires has fundamentally altered the NBA—and may become an issue in labor talks next year. Teams draft on potential, usually investing years of training and millions of dollars in salary before preps develop into stars. Most work out: Of the twenty-two drafted, only three aren't in the league anymore. Some, such as Garnett and Indiana's Jermaine O'Neal, are among the league's elite. Others, such as Washington's Kwame Brown, the No. 1 pick in 2001, are mere role players so far.

More worrisome to NBA Commissioner David Stern have been a couple of disastrous failures. South Carolina hoopster Taj McDavid declared himself eligible for the 1996 draft, thereby forfeiting his college eligibility. He wasn't nearly good enough to be selected and is now out of organized ball (see BusinessWeek Online, 6/24/04, " 'Fantasy' vs. Fact in the NBA").

A handful of others have also made foolhardy draft declarations, only 5 to be passed over. And Leon Smith, a Chicago high school star, attempted suicide shortly after being drafted in 1999 by the Dallas Mavericks. He has since pieced his life together and was recently invited for some tryouts, but he's thought to be a long shot.

Brian Hindo is a writer and staff editor at *BusinessWeek*. This article originally appeared in BusinessWeek Online, www.businessweekonline.com, on June 24, 2003.

The league is eager to avoid any more such cases and to help drafted teens through their often-bumpy first years. It has added three extra sessions for players under twenty to its mandatory, year-long rookie transition course, starting even before Draft Day. Mike Bantom, NBA senior vice-president for player development, has increased his staff of full-timers from six to eleven in the past three years, including a clinical psychologist among the new recruits. "None of these kids is quite prepared for how hard they're expected to work," says Bantom. "And a lot of them feel alone on the road."

His deputy, Chrysa Chin, director of player programs, makes personal visits to each rookie through the year. Trained as a social worker, Chin advises them on matters that eighteen-year-olds usually don't think about, such as how to pay bills. She keeps in constant touch with a two-way pager, a BlackBerry, and a cell phone. "I'm like a mother with newborns," Chin quips.

In addition, twenty-one of the thirty pro teams have created staff positions dedicated to young-player development. Bill Wennington, a retired NBA center, works with youngsters on the Chicago Bulls, a team that bet heavily on high schoolers when it acquired eighteen-year-olds Tyson Chandler and Eddy Curry in 2000. "At times [they have] an inability to focus, but it's amazing how much they want to learn," says Wennington. Among his tasks when the Baby Bulls arrived: getting them to stop playing video games until 5 A.M.

The lessons begin even before young players start wending their way up teams' draft boards. Between games at a four-day June camp hosted by the NBA Players' Association in Richmond, Virginia, Oden and 100 other top high school players attended hour-long classes on SAT prep, "sexual decisions," and burnishing the right image. DeNita Turner, a consultant with Image Builders, based in Laurel, Maryland, drilled the kids about how to leave a proper phone message. One high schooler acted out a scene explaining why his name came up in a police investigation. The lesson: Hanging out with the wrong crowd has consequences.

But Dwight Howard's Class of '04 could be the last to make the prep-to-pros leap. Basketball's collective bargaining agreement expires at the end of next season, and Stern is pushing for a twenty-year-old age limit. Otherwise, "we're going to be faced with a number of kids taking great chances with their futures," the commissioner says.   10

The players, however, won't raise the age limit without a fight because of the oodles of money at stake. Michael McCann, a sports law expert and Harvard Law School visiting scholar, estimates that under the current accord, a player who jumps to the NBA after high school can add as much as $100 million to his career earnings.

And so far, with the NBA's help, the phenoms seem to be handling the pressure. Just look at last year's instant superstars, Cleveland's Lebron James and Denver's Carmelo Anthony. According to McCann, teenagers have had a much higher success rate than foreign and collegiate draftees, mostly because they make up a tiny group who have been scouted since the age of twelve for their athletic talent.

True, as Stern says, "there's more opportunity for rocket scientists and brain surgeons than there is for NBA players." But those jobs sure don't pay as well.

Should Players Be Eligible for the NFL Draft Right Out of High School?

JIM BROWN AND MIKE HAYNES

BEFORE READING: Do you feel that it is best for high school players to go directly into professional sports rather than first playing college sports? Explain.

Yes

Football players should be eligible for the NFL draft as soon as they graduate from high school.

Supporters of the three-year waiting period argue that it's important to encourage players to go to college. I believe in going to college. I'm very glad I graduated from Syracuse University before I played pro football.

But these days, most serious college players are not getting a decent education. Most don't attend classes regularly and many don't graduate.

There's a financial incentive for both colleges and the NFL to require talented players to play on college teams before they turn pro. College football programs, which generate a lot of revenue, act like farm teams for the NFL: They weed out weaker players and groom talented ones, making drafting easier for the pro teams.

A key argument for this rule is that young players are not physically   5 able to take the licks. But we're not talking about teeny-weeny high school students. Phenoms like Maurice Clarett can take the licks.

Pro football is for the exceptionally gifted individual. If you're talking about an ordinary eighteen-year-old, he might have a problem playing in

---

Jim Brown won a spot for himself in the NFL Hall of Fame by playing for the Cleveland Browns from 1957 to 1965. He is now chairman of the Amer-I-Can Foundation, a nonprofit organization promoting social change. Mike Haynes, also a member of the Hall of Fame, played for the New England Patriots and the Los Angeles Raiders from 1976 to 1989 and is now vice president of the National Football League. Their debate appeared in *New York Times Upfront* on December 8, 2003.

the NFL. But if you're talking about an extraordinary eighteen-year-old, he might [not] give you a problem.

The NFL is the only pro league that has this rule. If players don't have the talent, pro teams won't draft them. The current three-year waiting period is unnecessary and has nothing to do with the welfare of young people.

—Jim Brown

No

The NFL requires players to wait three years after they finish high school to be eligible for the draft. Is this policy fair? Absolutely.

I spent fourteen years in the NFL and nothing was more difficult than my rookie season. I spent four years as a student-athlete at Arizona State University, and still the transition to the NFL was the greatest physical, mental, and emotional challenge I have ever undertaken. Because I matured most in my late teens and early twenties, I wouldn't have been prepared without those years in college.

The longer a person is in school, the greater his self-confidence. Jug- 10
gling a practice schedule, a college course load, and a social life is tough, but it prepares you to manage your time efficiently. A typical player's workday at an NFL training camp is fifteen hours long. Clearly, you will be more successful if you can organize your time and set priorities.

Peyton Manning, now a quarterback with the Indianapolis Colts, was a highly regarded college player. Though many experts predicted he would be a first-round draft choice after his junior year, he decided to remain in school. Manning had an outstanding senior season and was the first pick in the draft after his senior season.

Manning let himself mature before entering the NFL. Now he's among the top NFL players in his position and could become among the best ever. The NFL draft eligibility rule benefits college players by giving them a better chance to be successful on and off the football field.

—Mike Haynes

Out of the Park

STEVE SAILER

BEFORE READING: Brainstorm any examples you can recall of athletic events in which the outcome was affected by suspected or confirmed drug use, or of athletes who were suspected or found guilty of drug use. Are there any specific sports that have been affected in significant ways by drug use? Explain.

In the seventeenth year of the world's slowest-moving scandal, baseball's steroid controversy finally picked up momentum as the *San Francisco Chronicle* revealed that federal investigators had implicated superstar sluggers Barry Bonds, Jason Giambi, and Gary Sheffield, among others, in the BALCO doping imbroglio. This followed a State of the Union address in which President George W. Bush used his bully pulpit to call for a crackdown on athletes using chemical muscle-builders, a denunciation that stood in contrast to the Bush dynasty's previous encounters with steroids.

Have you noticed that a lot of steroid cheaters, alleged and admitted, are jerks? So, do jerks take steroids? Or do steroids make jerks? Both are likely true. Good guys don't cheat. And the masculinizing side effects of steroids make many users more volatile, even violent. Baseball's brouhaha illuminates a growing challenge for society in general as the biotechnology-driven masculinity arms race (or, perhaps more precisely, biceps race) expands beyond sports. Politicians, such as Arnold Schwarzenegger and Jesse Ventura, and even pundits, such as Andrew Sullivan, have turbocharged their careers by ingesting the manly molecule. But do we want the most aggressive men to boost their masculinity even further by artificial means? Or is the natural balance best for society as a whole?

A history of baseball's seduction by steroids can now finally be pieced together. First synthesized in central Europe in the 1930s, scientifically savvy athletes, such as Olympic shot-putters, began injecting artificial male hormones in the 1950s. Bodybuilders were close behind. For example, Austrian weightlifters who trained with the teenage Schwarzenegger told the *Los Angeles Times* that the future governor of California started using steroids in 1964 at age seventeen. In the 1970s and 1980s, the manly ladies of East Germany dominated the distaff side of the Olympics because their Communist regime forced steroids upon them.

This trend largely bypassed baseball, however, because ballplayers were among the last athletes (besides golfers) to try honest weightlifting.

Steve Sailer describes himself as "a reporter, movie critic for the *American Conservative*, VDARE.com columnist, and founder of the Human Biodiversity Institute, which runs the invitation-only Human Biodiversity discussion group for top scientists and public intellectuals." This article appeared on April 12, 2004, in the *American Conservative*.

Pumping iron benefits almost all athletes, but the frustrations of reaching maximum natural strength within a few years can encourage some to then move on to steroids.

Baseball has always been, at best, proudly traditional and, at worst, lazily lackadaisical about innovation, especially if it involves hard physical or mental work. Ballplayers justified spending the off-season in the tavern rather than the gym because of the dread fear of becoming "muscle-bound."

There were exceptions. A century ago, Honus Wagner, the slugging shortstop who was probably the greatest National Leaguer before World War II, lifted dumbbells. Similarly, after Babe Ruth's embarrassing 1925 season, most observers thought the hard-living thirty-year-old was permanently washed up. Instead, Ruth hired a personal trainer and worked out in a gym for the next ten winters, in the course of which he broke his own record with sixty homers in 1927. But Wagner and Ruth's stupendous statistics didn't convince lesser players, who refused to lift anything heavier than a beer mug. Mickey Mantle's off-season exercise regimen consisted of going hunting when his hangover wasn't too blinding.

Slowly, conditioning improved. More players cut back on the booze and a few of the most intelligent, such as Tom Seaver, Nolan Ryan, and Brian Downing, started to lift weights.

Baseball's first flagrantly obvious steroid abuser didn't arrive until 1986, when the Oakland A's Jose Canseco won Rookie of the Year. Canseco started out tall and slender in the minor leagues, but eventually bulked up to 240 pounds. Most tellingly, he possessed the juicer's equivalent of the portrait of Dorian Gray: his identical twin Ozzie, who stayed spindly and in the minors for years, before eventually inflating himself too.

"Jose Canseco was the Typhoid Mary of steroids," one baseball agent told me. After Canseco joined a team, some of his new teammates would suddenly beef up. Indeed, Canseco recently told book companies to whom he was peddling his proposal for a tell-all autobiography that he had helped obtain steroids for other players.

In 1988, Canseco won the American League Most Valuable Player award by becoming the first to hit forty homers and steal forty bases in one season. But that made Canseco conspicuous at the wrong time. At the Seoul Olympics that September, Canadian Ben Johnson—the once skinny, shy, and slow sprinter suddenly turned burly, surly, and swift—blasted off like a fuel-injected funny car in the 100 meter dash to beat Carl Lewis and set an astonishing world record. "Benoid's" urine test turned up highly positive, and his gold medal and record were stripped from him. A few days later, during the American League playoffs, Red Sox fans taunted Canseco with chants of "STER-oids!" He responded by posing like a bodybuilder. *Washington Post* sports columnist Tom Boswell publicly accused Canseco of being on the juice.

Following Ben Johnson's disgrace, track became more serious about drug testing. This slowed women runners noticeably. Because women naturally produce only about one-tenth as much testosterone as men, they get more bang for the buck out of a dose of steroids. That's why Warsaw Bloc women dominated women's sprinting, but their menfolk could seldom beat sprinters of West African descent. Tougher testing combined with the collapse of the Communist sports-industrial complexes meant that female medalists ran a striking 0.6 percent slower at the cleaner 1996 Olympics than at the 1988 Festival of Androgens, while men's times continued their steady improvement. Runners still cheat, but can't be as brazen. Most of the absurd women's records set in the 1980s by the communists and by America's late Florence Griffith-Joyner remain untouched.

The National Football League cracked down hard enough that some dopers reportedly had to pump someone else's clean urine up catheters into their bladders. Yet, baseball resolved to remain oblivious to the obvious and didn't test at all. In the subsequent anything-goes years, ballplayers super-sized themselves. Home run totals, fan excitement, and revenue swelled, too.

Worried about schoolboys wishing to emulate their idols, President George H. W. Bush signed a bill making steroids a controlled substance in 1990. Yet he then sent a thoroughly mixed message by appointing movie muscleman Schwarzenegger, the world's most famous role model for steroids, as chairman of the President's Council on Physical Fitness.

The elder Bush was probably naive, but the younger Bush surely knew Canseco's reputation when, as co-managing director of the Texas Rangers, he signed off on a blockbuster trade for the macho man in 1992. (It's important to note that Bush's partners did not allow him much other executive responsibility. Ranger general manager Tom Grieve told PBS, "George was the front man. . . . He was the spokesperson. He dealt with the media, he dealt with the fans, and it was obvious to us right from the start that that's what he was made for." Why a man whose friends didn't consider him qualified to run a ball club is qualified to run the country is a question for another day.)

Canseco's Ranger years are best remembered for the long fly ball that 15 bounced off the outfielder's increasingly block-shaped head and over the fence for a home run. Canseco's abused body became injury-prone and his personality erratic. Last year, the now retired Canseco was jailed when he failed a drug test for steroids, violating the probation stemming from a nightclub brawl he had gotten into alongside his twin Ozzie (who had eventually hulked up to Jose's size).

Other careers began following odd trajectories, too. Journeymen ballplayers would show up at spring training with a radically different shape and crush their career high in homers by almost thirty.

Downsides quickly appeared. Although players drank less, they seemed to get arrested for assault more—what bodybuilders call 'roid rage. Time spent on the disabled list grew 20 percent just between 1997 and 2001, and some injuries were gruesomely unprecedented. A former teammate of Canseco's ruptured his bicep swinging at a pitch. "In all my years of watching sport, I've never seen/heard anything so awful," wrote a fan. "When his muscle ripped, it produced a sharp snap and traveled up his arm and into his shoulder like a scurrying rodent."

In the middle of 1996, both the size and firepower of thirty-three-year-old Ken Caminiti suddenly exploded. He had never hit more than twenty-six homers in a full season but smacked twenty-eight after the All-Star break, winning the MVP award while leading the lowly San Diego Padres to the World Series. Advertisers used the new Caminiti as an icon of masculinity, filming him glowering in black leather on his Harley. As he admitted in 2002, though, the megablasts of anabolic homer-helpers had permanently damaged his health.

Meanwhile, baseball was finally undergoing an intellectual revolution. In the 1970s, a boiler-room attendant named Bill James whiled away the hours by statistically testing baseball's oldest argument over strategy, the one between Ty Cobb's cunning, elegant style of hitting line-drive singles, and Babe Ruth's seemingly vulgar swing-for-the-fences approach. James found that what the Cobb-admiring baseball insiders didn't understand was that Ruth had a second arrow in his offensive quiver. By slamming out of the park strikes thrown down the middle, the Bambino forced pitchers to try to nibble at the edges of the plate. When they missed, he'd accept a walk. Although Cobb's career batting average of .366 was the highest ever, significantly better than Ruth's .342, Ruth's on-base percentage of .474, the less understood but more important number, substantially beat Cobb's .433.

Slowly, the amateur statistician's views on power infiltrated the big 20 leagues, with Oakland A's general managers Sandy Alderson and Billy Beane among the first to get the message. When George Steinbrenner's ultra-rich New York Yankees signed away the A's homers-and-walks king Jason Giambi, Beane still had his underrated little brother Jeremy. Yet, it turned out Jason and Jeremy shared more than genes; they are both implicated in the BALCO scandal.

Bonds, the greatest all-around player of the last decade, may well have been clean until recently. With pumped-up lesser talents like Mark McGwire, who was found with the legal steroid precursor Androstenedione in his locker, becoming folk heroes, Bonds apparently decided to turn himself into the monster that hit 73 home runs in 2001 with the alleged help of steroids and human growth hormone.

That's the real problem: Even guys who want to play fair are under pressure from cheaters to play foul. This arms race is spreading beyond sports. As an opinion journalist, for instance, I have to compete with Androgel Andrew Sullivan, who resurrected his career via prescription testosterone, as he explained in loving detail in the *New York Times* magazine four years ago. On his blog, the enormously energetic Sullivan asked, "Would you rather live till you're eighty-five, gradually sinking into torpor and sexual collapse or have a great time and conk out at sixty-five?"

That is the kind of question that the voluntary lab rats will make all of us confront in the years ahead.

Ever Farther, Ever Faster, Ever Higher?

BEFORE READING: Do you personally feel that the use of drugs to enhance athletic performance is wrong? Does your answer differ from one sport to another or from one level of competition to another? Explain.

The Athens Olympics Will Be a Crucial Battle in Sport's War on Drugs

"Olympism seeks to create a way of life based on the joy found in effort, the educational value of a good example and respect for universal fundamental ethical principles." So said Baron Pierre de Coubertin, the founder of the modern Olympic games. Alas, there is every chance the 28th summer Olympiad, which opens in Athens on August 13th, will make headlines less for the joy of effort—and still less for good example or respect for universal ethics—than for athletes caught cheating with performance-enhancing drugs.

The past year has brought plenty of evidence that "doping" is rife. In June 2003, a syringe containing a hitherto unknown and undetectable steroid, tetrahydrogestrinone (THG), was sent to America's Anti-Doping Agency (USADA), apparently by a disaffected coach. Speedily designed tests, some applied retrospectively to old urine samples, showed that use of THG had been widespread among top athletes. The drug was allegedly made by BALCO (the Bay Area Laboratory Co-operative), in California, as a "nutritional supplement." BALCO's clients included many top sports stars, such as Tim Montgomery, world champion in the 100-meter sprint; his partner, Marion Jones, the reigning women's Olympic 100-meter champion; Shane Mosley, a former boxing world champion; several members of the Oakland Raiders American football team; and Barry Bonds, who holds baseball's record for the most home runs in a season.

Although some of these athletes deny using THG, others have already been banned from their sport for doing so, including Dwain Chambers, a top British sprinter. The USADA is seeking a lifetime ban for Mr. Montgomery. After wide investigations, criminal charges have been brought against several people connected with BALCO—though no athletes, as yet—including its boss, Victor Conte, who has been indicted for allegedly supplying illegal drugs and laundering money. A lawyer for Mr. Conte has hinted that other well-known athletes, due to compete in the Olympics, have yet to be identified as THG users, and that his client may be prepared to name them as part of a plea-bargain.

But the litany of recent illegal drug use stretches far beyond BALCO. Even cricket, the sport of gentlemen, has been tainted. Shane Warne, an

This unsigned article appeared in the August 5, 2004, issue of the *Economist*.

Australian spin bowler, was banned for a year for taking a drug that can be used to mask steroids; on his return, he rivalled the record for the highest number of wickets taken in a Test (a record he shares, ironically, with a Sri Lankan who has been accused of cheating in a more old-fashioned way, by using an illegal bowling action). In soccer, England's top defender, Rio Ferdinand, was banned for eight months for failing to take a mandatory drug test.

Another Briton, Greg Rusedski, escaped a ban this year despite testing positive for nandrolone. The tennis star argued that he had been given the steroid without his knowledge by officials of the sport's governing body, the Association of Tennis Professionals (ATP). In 2003, the ATP let off seven unnamed players who failed drug tests, apparently for the same reason. Drug scandals have erupted in rugby league, ice hockey, orienteering, the triathlon, and so on and on.

Cycling has provided many milestones in the history of doping in sport, including the first sportsman allegedly to die as a result of taking drugs, Arthur Linton, in 1896, and the first drug-related death during a televised event, of Tom Simpson, in the 1967 Tour de France. It continues to be rife with drug-taking. David Millar, a British world champion, has admitted taking steroids. Several top cyclists were recently accused of using a room at the Australian Institute of Sport as a "shooting gallery" in which they injected drugs. Even Lance Armstrong, the American cyclist who (inspirationally) recovered from cancer to become a multiple winner of the Tour de France, entered this year's race—the sixth he has won—embroiled in a court battle with the authors of L.A. Confidential, a book alleging that his achievements were not wholly aboveboard. Mr. Armstrong strenuously denies the allegations, and in 2000 even joked about them in a Nike commercial: "What am I on? I'm on my bike, six hours a day."

Recent drug scandals have led to much rewriting of the record books, as well as the return of unfairly won medals and trophies. Mr. Millar will have to give back his world-champion's rainbow jersey. Michael Johnson, an American runner, may have to return a gold medal because a fellow member of his 4 × 400-meter relay team was found guilty of drug-taking. Tragicomically, Anastasiya Kapachinskaya, a Russian runner, had to give back her world indoor 200-meter gold after failing a drug test, but at the same time was handed the previous year's outdoor 200-meter gold after the woman who beat her, Kelli White, was banned for taking performance-enhancing drugs.

In such a climate, the validity of almost any outstanding sporting achievement is likely to be questioned. And politicians have got interested. George Bush even referred to the problem in this year's State of the Union address, calling on those in charge of sport to "get tough and to get rid of steroids now." Stopping doping is now at the forefront of Mr. Bush's broader war on illegal drugs—not least, cynics say, because it is probably easier to notch up a big success in tackling steroids in sport than to stop cocaine crossing the Mexican border. The BALCO indictments were announced not quietly, by some local prosecutor, but in a blaze of publicity by John Ashcroft, Mr. Bush's attorney general.

Congress has also jumped in. The Senate Commerce, Science, and Transportation Committee—sport being commerce—issued a subpoena to obtain documents from the BALCO investigation, which it then handed over to the USADA. In July, a committee of British MPs produced a report that criticized the inconsistent treatment of drug offenses by the governing bodies of different sports.

Victorian Values

Faced with so much evidence of doping, and with the fact that the dis-   10
covery of THG was a lucky break and not the result of new detection techniques, you might expect the chief crusaders against drugs in sport to be thoroughly depressed. Yet Dick Pound, a Canadian former Olympic swimmer who now runs the World Anti-Doping Agency (WADA), could hardly be more upbeat. He regards the Athens Olympics as a potential turning point in the war against doping and, though he does not proclaim certain victory, he thinks he has the drug cheats on the run.

Mr. Pound is an idealist in the Victorian mold. It was the Victorians who formalized the rules of many of the sports played today, imposing order on what was then anarchy. They saw in sport a way to educate the populace in the importance of the rule of law, and to deepen character by teaching how to play hard but fair: to, as Rudyard Kipling put it, "meet with Triumph and Disaster/And treat those two impostors just the same." De Coubertin's Olympism was the summit of that Victorian idealism.

In a similar spirit, Mr. Pound, as he explains in his new book, *Inside the Olympics* (Wiley), sees sport, and in particular the Olympic movement, as providing young people with the "ethical platform" they need to guide them in a "world that has lost its ethical path." Sport, he says, "can provide an extraordinary value system for today's and tomorrow's youth." But only if it can end the "moral decay" in sport itself, of which doping is a big, though not the only, part: Mr. Pound also headed an investigation into corruption in Olympic bidding after a scandal before the opening of the Salt Lake City Winter Olympics in 2002.

His old-fashioned idealism, and his readiness to criticize those who do not share his enthusiasm for WADA—created by the International Olympic Committee (IOC) and various member governments in 1999, but very much his baby—has made him a controversial figure. Sepp Blatter, head of FIFA, the governing body of soccer, once described WADA as a "kind of monster." The saintly cyclist Mr. Armstrong even criticized Mr. Pound in an open letter in March, after he said that Tour de France cyclists were known to be taking banned substances. "Athletes need to be confident that WADA's programs are run by fair and straightforward people," said Mr. Armstrong.

None of this seems to worry Mr. Pound. WADA today is no longer the six-stone weakling it seemed to be at the 2000 Olympics in Sydney, the first at which the Olympic oath sworn by the athletes included the phrase, "committing ourselves to a sport without doping and without drugs." It has come up with many new tests. For instance, samples collected in Athens are expected to be subject to new tests for human growth hormone, either at the games or later.

More crucially, in order to take part in Athens, the world governing body of each sport in the games has had to sign up to the world anti-doping code, agreed in 2003. This created, among other things, a single list of banned substances, a standard set of sanctions for offenders and a dispute-resolution mechanism through the Court of Arbitration for Sport. All the governing bodies have now signed up, though some have attached caveats that WADA may not agree to at future Olympics. FIFA, for example, has won an exemption from the code's blanket two-year ban for offenders.

Cold War Temptations

Drugs have been part of sport since at least the 1860s, when swimmers in Amsterdam's canal races were doped in various ways, and long before then if alcohol is counted. In the nineteenth century, alcohol and strychnine were commonly used to ease pain during boxing bouts. The technology of doping has clearly advanced in leaps and bounds since then. But Mr. Pound reckons that the failure, at least until now, to tackle the problem owes less to inability to keep pace with science than to lack of will. WADA is the first systematic attempt to test thoroughly for doping, and to punish offenders severely.

Why has it taken so long? One "excusable" factor, says Mr. Pound, was that until the "Olympic economic model" changed, sometime in the 1980s, many sports did not have the money to carry out proper tests. Less excusably, he says, many simply turned a blind eye to the health risks of doping. And during the cold war, many communist countries did not hesitate to dope in order to win. Eastern Germany and, more recently, China at times systematically doped their athletes, often without telling them; who can forget the then-female, now male, East German shot-putter nicknamed "Hormone Heidi"? Western countries, desperate to hold their own, often ignored drug-taking by their own athletes if it brought them success.

Some of that cold-war mentality still persists, says Mr. Pound. Some governments, including America's, have been slow to make promised payments to WADA's budget. Arguably, it took the BALCO scandal to shock America's Olympic Committee into getting serious about doping. This spring Michele Verroken, until this year the head of anti-doping at UK Sport, told a committee of MPs that she may have lost her job because her strong stance on cheating could have damaged Britain's bid to hold the 2012 Olympics in London. Mr. Pound thinks that governments will take the problem far more seriously in future, not least because public anger—combined with governments' full adoption of the WADA code, probably in 2005 in the form of a United Nations convention—will force them to do so.

Public outrage about drug-taking, and the widespread consensus that certain substances must be banned from sport, is unlikely to change. As Mr. Pound points out in his book, the catalyst for the creation of WADA was the public fury that greeted remarks made in 1998 by the then-head of the IOC, Juan Antonio Samaranch. Watching reports of the arrest of cyclists in the Tour de France after police had discovered doping substances, Mr. Samaranch commented to a journalist that prohibited drugs, whether performance-enhancing or not, should be limited to those that are dangerous to health, and that the (then) current list of banned substances was too long. At the emergency meeting of the IOC board soon afterwards, WADA was born, with a philosophy of banning that was a long way from Mr. Samaranch's.

• To be banned by WADA, a drug has to meet at least two of three criteria: It must enhance performance, be harmful to health, and (a very Victorian touch) be against the spirit of sport. Clearly, this would allow a drug to be banned if it had no adverse health effects but was, even so, ruled contrary to whatever is deemed to be the spirit of sport. Mr. Pound, for one, seems to regard any use of a drug to enhance performance as against that spirit: It is, quite simply, cheating.   20

A fierce critic of this approach to drugs in sport is Norman Fost, director of the medical-ethics program at the University of Wisconsin. He calls the claims made about the harmful effects of steroids "incoherent and flat-out wrong." Mostly, they have small, temporary side-effects, he says, not life-threatening ones. Indeed, the risks are much smaller than those routinely taken by athletes. A man who plays American football professionally for three years has a 90 percent chance of suffering a permanent physical injury.

If health is the chief concern, surely certain sports should be banned entirely—and athletes should not be allowed to smoke or drink, activities that do far more harm than taking steroids. As for enhancing performance, that is not seen as cheating if it is done by, say, training at high altitude or in a sealed space that simulates high altitude, says Dr. Fost, though such training would have exactly the same effect—an increase in oxygen-carrying red blood cells—as the banned steroid EPO, which is especially popular with cyclists.

Gary Wadler of the New York University School of Medicine, who is a member of WADA, dismisses such arguments as "university debating points," and notes that athletes may have no idea of the risks they are running when they take drugs. He blames the 1994 legal change that exempted many dietary supplements from approval by America's Food and

Drug Administration, spawning an $18 billion vitamins industry that is now a powerful lobby against re-regulation.

Setting Their Own Rules

In principle, the best way to decide how much performance-enhancement and health risk is acceptable would be by a vote of those who play the particular sport. Yet Mr. Pound directs some of his strongest criticism at so-called "professional sports" (aren't all sports professional nowadays?) that are self-regulated, such as tennis and baseball. WADA currently has no authority over these sports. In major league baseball, with its powerful players' union, the drug-testing regime is part of contract negotiations and is extremely relaxed—last year, 5–7 percent of drug tests showed positive, but offenders were hardly punished.

Arguably, if all the players agree that using performance-enhancers is 25 not cheating, then it isn't really cheating. But Mr. Pound reckons that baseball players are badly led, by people who care more about making money than about the true values of sport. He maintains that baseball's top officials are much more upset by players caught using recreational drugs, such as cannabis, which hurt their brand, than about performance-enhancing drugs, which, after all, may make the game more exciting.

The biggest challenge to WADA is to devise tests to keep up with advances in doping. None will be trickier than the expected emergence of gene therapy, starting with treatments for, say, muscular dystrophy. Hoping to anticipate future doping strategies, WADA held a conference with leading genetic scientists in 2002. Unfortunately, it seems that the likeliest way to detect gene therapy is a muscle biopsy, which, Mr. Pound mercifully concedes, is "too invasive." Instead, WADA is calling for research, to be funded by itself and governments, into how to identify whether gene therapy has been used. Mr. Pound hopes that governments will make creating such a test a condition of winning regulatory approval. Alas, this strategy is rather unlikely to work.

And will the public endorse Mr. Pound's Olympian idealism? Certainly, parents seem to be warming to his message that "children shouldn't have to become chemical stockpiles to succeed in sport, or be cheated by those who are"—though will they still do so when they think that, with a little help, Junior might become the next Barry Bonds? Surveys suggest that 2.5 percent of eighth-graders (thirteen–fourteen-year-olds) have used steroids. UK Sport recently launched "Start Clean," a program to stop sporty twelve–seventeen-year-olds resorting to performance-enhancing drugs. Yet it is hard to see the trend reversing when, outside sport, performance-enhancement seems ever more central to modern life—thanks to Viagra, Prozac, Ritalin, and the rest. And, if doping were defeated, would sports fans really be content with the lack of record-breaking feats?

It would be nice to think so. Yet much of this debate may be academic if WADA fails to create tests to spot the use of gene therapy. Watch out for a surge in world-record breaking in the 2012 Olympics. In the meantime, may the best man or woman win (and we don't mean you, Heidi—sorry, Andreas).

Finding the Zone

JAIME DIAZ

BEFORE READING: Explain why sports take mental discipline as well as physical prowess.

Amid the splendor of the Augusta National's back nine on the most glorious Sunday of his life, Phil Mickelson was in the zone.

There were no brain-wave readings or heart-rhythm monitors to prove it, nor did his body definitively "glow with the First Light," to quote one of Michael Murphy's high-flying attempts to capture the magical state in *Golf in the Kingdom*. The normally voluble Lefty never mentioned the word all week. The closest he came was to allow that before the final round, he had "a different feeling."

But everyone knew it, as surely as people collectively know anything when they see it. It was in his smile, in his stride, in the calm of his eyes, and, most of all, in his performance. Mickelson was indeed different—at peace, in command—his best self. In a near-perfect Masters of hole-outs and clutch play, Phil's felicity was the most perfect thing about it.

"Clearly, Mickelson was in a kind of state—let's call it the zone," says Murphy, now seventy-three, as close an observer of the "transformational tide" as he was when he wrote his underground classic thirty-two years ago. "He surrendered to this grace that was given."

Human beings love the zone. Love to be in it. Love to observe when   5 others are in it. Love to wonder when it will happen again. Centuries before the zone had a name, there was an awareness of an elevated state of performance free of cognitive chatter. "We never do anything well till we

Sports Illustrated senior writer Jaime Diaz has been writing for the Golf Plus section since 1993. Before that he spent seven years covering all sports for *Sports Illustrated* and four years as the golf writer for the *New York Times*. He contributes regularly to CNNSI.com, has won several awards for his work from the Golf Writers Association of America, and has written three books: *Hallowed Ground* (with artist Linda Hartough; 1999), *The Elements of Scoring* (with Raymond Floyd; 2003), and *The World Golf Hall of Fame* (with Tim Rosaforte; 1997). This article appeared in *Golf Digest* in July 2004 as the second in a two-part series on the future of golf.

cease to think about the manner of doing it," wrote the English essayist William Hazlitt. A simple concept, very difficult to follow.

The zone is rare and seemingly random, requiring what is literally a harmonic convergence within the brain's infinitely complex control centers. "Brain cells firing in synchronicity—that's the zone," says Dr. Debbie Crews, a pioneering sport psychologist and researcher at Arizona State who studies brain maps of optimal performance.

Using data gained from a laboratory in which he won nine major championships and some 160 other tournaments worldwide, Gary Player concurs. "The zone is using the utmost of your brain, your entire mental capacity," he says. "When I was in the zone, I was a person made of two extremes. I was walking on air, and yet at the same time I was like a lion in a cage. Jack Nicklaus was that way more than anyone—having that balance of being uptight in terms of concentration, with the ability to relax and let himself perform at just the right time. When a great player unleashes that force within himself, tremendous things are possible."

In those moments, the equation "performance equals potential minus interference" loses its limiting component. The zone results when a skilled actor meticulously first uses the conscious mind to commit lines to memory and inhabit the character, then unleashes the intuitive mind to deliver a performance full of spontaneity, originality, and emotional connection.

Competitive sport is the most public arena in which the human animal tests the limits of body and mind. The search for the zone is why the best play. Tennis great Billie Jean King has said that after playing a brilliant point during which she'd entered the zone, "I wanted to stop the match and grab the microphone and shout, 'That's what it's all about!'"

Even if King had wanted to elaborate, she could not have fully con- 10 veyed the moment. The terms commonly used to describe the zone— *confident, calm, fearless, free, fluid, flow, energized, automatic, peaceful, clear, rapturous, detached*—all carry their fair share of meaning, but even in sum can neither reproduce nor provide entry to the experience. In the zone, action always speaks louder than words.

"That's because the zone has nothing to do with words," says Chuck Hogan, a longtime author and instructor in the psychology of golf. "The zone is the opposite of words."

Adds Al Geiberger, who in 1977 shot the first official 59 in PGA Tour history. "Later on people called it the zone; we didn't even know what to call it. I still don't think anybody really knows how the super-low rounds happen."

No wonder that in this most analyzed of all sports, the zone seems to hover just above its tantalized zealots. In a game where time and a stationary ball seem to give the player the most control—to plan, to rehearse, to adjust—we can easily have the least.

It's the game's cruel joke that the closest the fearful, ego-driven, and brainlocked golfers get to the zone is when, immediately after a poor shot or missed putt, we reflexively drop another ball, and with our mind on nothing else but where the damn thing should have gone in the first place, stripe it down the middle or into the hole.

The zone is quicksilver—the more we grab it, the more it slips away.   15 "The moment you think you're in it, you're out of it," goes the zone conundrum, which seems to extend to those who would profess to understand it. It is *the* mystery of golf.

But lately there's evidence that things are changing. An accelerated collective learning curve has taken over the elite levels of golf. Advances in technique, fitness, and nutrition have been discernible, but the zone has remained elusive.

"It's been the missing piece of the puzzle, and the most important," says Dr. Jim Loehr, a sport psychologist who runs LGE Performance Systems in Orlando.

Just two years ago, a poll revealed that although elite players believed mental skills were half to 80 percent of the game, the majority said they spent less than 10 percent of their practice time on them. At the same time, some 350 players on the PGA, Champions, European, and LPGA tours are wearing a pendant with funny-looking copper wiring called a QLink, which supposedly reduces stress.

Here are four recent factors that have given us a new perspective on the zone:

1. Rejection of Mechanical Thoughts

The rise of the zone has coincided with a growing acceptance that the old   20 Holy Grail—swing mechanics—has fallen victim to the law of diminishing returns.

"What has happened is that the technical side in golf was so prevalent that the mental aspects of getting in the zone have been hidden," says Pia Nilsson, former European team Solheim Cup captain and cofounder of Vision54/Coaching for the Future, the training program named after a hypothetical round of 18 birdies. "People looked at how players like Hogan and Faldo were obsessed with technique, but they didn't realize that those two players hid their equal or even greater commitment to the mental side."

As the ball-striking abilities of the game's best have become more uniform, there is a growing acknowledgment that what separates players most is mental ability.

"The search for the perfect technique will never stop, nor should it," says Joe Parent, the author of *Zen Golf* and Vijay Singh's mental coach. "That's what practice is about. But in competition, the players are beginning to realize that swing thoughts work not as intended—to control the body during the swing with a conscious thought—but more as a security blanket that temporarily produces reduced tension. The trouble is, the more you use a swing thought, the more *thinking* it intrudes on fluidity, until it doesn't work anymore. More of today's players are learning to trust their technique to feelings or images ruled by the intuitive mind rather than engaging the thinking mind with how they intend to do it."

2. The Changing Golf Culture

The Western world has grown increasingly more open to Eastern philosophy, in which disciplines like yoga emphasize the power of the intuitive mind over cognitive thought. In the martial arts, warriors strive to reach the point where they can act with lightning speed against opponents without having to think or reason about the best defensive or offensive moves to make. This is the essence of the zone.

Great golfers through the ages would agree (but not publicly, because 25 of the golf culture's traditional aversion to the touchy-feely). Byron Nelson once told sport psychologist Bob Rotella that in his epic 1945 season he would play rounds so focused on hitting good shots that he never knew how he had scored until after the round. He was in the zone. When Rotella asked why Nelson had never included his mental approach in any of his instruction books, Nelson said, "Aw, people didn't talk about that sort of thing in those days." Today they are less reluctant.

"Western culture is founded on the power of intellect," Parent says. "We conquered the world with intellect—inventing and building and expanding—so we think we can conquer anything with intellect. But intellect doesn't conquer golf, it makes it harder. Finally, we're learning to let go and trust the body to react in the unbelievably precise way it can when it's run by the intuitive mind."

3. Getting "in Flow"

The national best-seller, *Flow: the Psychology of Optimal Experience*, by Mihaly Csikszentmihalyi, brought the desirability and accessibility of the zone state into popular culture. The premise is that flow—the state of being so involved in an activity that nothing else seems to matter—is when people are happiest. In such a state, the quality of the experience becomes more fulfilling than the end result. For people who are thus enlightened, achieving such optimal experiences becomes life's foremost goal.

More than two decades of study showed that flow is most often achieved when a person's body or mind is stretched to its limits in a voluntary effort to accomplish something difficult and worthwhile. The activity itself must be challenging and have defined rules, all the better to promote intense concentration. No wonder golf is so addictive.

The growth that occurs when flow is achieved makes a person more capable and motivated to achieve flow again.

"The pursuit of flow has been very instructive in teaching golfers to 30 play for the right reasons," says Dr. Gio Valiante, a Rollins College psychology professor who works with several tour players, including Chad Campbell. "Someone who plays to impress others or prove something will have too many external thoughts to truly focus. The player who plays to learn, improve and excel is fully involved in the process and its details. That's a player who can get into the zone and be more fulfilled."

4. Tiger and Annika

Because they have entered it so often in their parallel domination of golf, Tiger Woods and Annika Sorenstam have raised curiosity about the zone more than any two golfers in history.

Woods especially has exhibited a fierce yet calm focus as he's consistently harnessed his best golf for the biggest occasions, prompting Davis Love III in 2002 to observe, "Something is going on with him that's not going on with us." Sorenstam's 59 in 2001 and her poise under the extreme scrutiny of playing against the best men last year at Colonial has also made her a mental model.

Though introverted, both can be candid when speaking of the mental side of the game. Woods has said, "My greatest gift is my creative mind." In his most successful year, 2000, he spoke of "almost willing yourself into the zone." Sorenstam is animated when talking about the challenge to improve and "living my dream."

It is surely no accident that both players were nurtured in no-limits learning environments. "More than anything, Tiger is perfectly safe," Chuck Hogan wrote in *Tiger's Bond of Power*. "Psychologically and emotionally, his parents offered him unconditional acceptance. . . . Literally, he cannot know failure."

Sorenstam, meanwhile, honed her ability to visualize and stay in the present. 35

"Annika has given herself permission to be great," says Nilsson. "It shocks some people, being so bold. But it's crucial that you see yourself doing something exceptional, so that when the time comes, you don't bail out. Because you feel you belong there, you stay in the zone."

At the level below the superstars, peak performance is becoming more frequent. Whereas Jack Fleck's 1955 U.S. Open victory was for decades discounted as the unlikeliest kind of fluke by a long-shot journeyman, major-championship victories last year by Ben Curtis and Shaun Micheel only intensified interest in the zone.

"More players are more physically and mentally prepared to play, so more players have a chance for the zone," says Valiante. "The fitness trailer promotes the zone. A clean diet promotes the zone. Being quiet and calm before a round instead of getting fired up promotes the zone. It's reasonable that in a given year, a player will get in the zone four or five times, for an entire round or even an entire tournament. Spread among all the players, that's a lot of exceptional performances."

Searching for the Elusive Final Frontier

It's dangerous, however, to think we might be close to having the zone figured out.

"I would say the experience is less frequent in sports than ever," says 40
Dr. Fran Pirozzolo, a neuropsychologist who works with professional
sports teams and individual athletes. "I look at Sam Snead, an intuitive
genius who played for the intrinsic joy and yet had the discipline to develop his skills. Sam was built to enter the zone, probably quite often. But
our culture today has taken the concept of play out of high-level sports
and replaced it with a photocopy of work. At the same time, there is a
drive in our culture to make things easy. The most important condition
for entering the zone is a high-challenge situation with highly developed
skills to meet the challenge. Without the enjoyment of play, and without
high challenge and high skills, you don't have the zone. And I think we
have less of those things today."

While not as skeptical, Dr. Bob Rotella, the doyen of golf sport psychologists, is leery of claims that the zone has become more accessible.
"Are we getting better at getting players closer to the zone than we were
15 years ago? No question," says Rotella. "Just like the physical game, it's
the quality of your misses. And players are getting better at reducing or
minimizing their mental misses. But we certainly don't have any hard evidence that players are getting into the zone more often. People may be
more fascinated with the zone than ever, and we might understand what
it looks like in a lab more than ever, and that's all very seductive. But that
doesn't make it happen more often."

Rotella worries that unrealistic expectations will end up making the
zone more remote. "The biggest problem players tend to have is thinking
the key to being great is to be in the zone all the time, and they think
they can intentionally make it happen," he says. "Michael Jordan estimated that in his career he was in the zone only 2 percent of the time.
Just like people get lost in trying to hit every shot perfectly, they can also
get lost in criticizing themselves for not being in the zone all the time.
Which is about the surest way to never get in it. The zone happens when
it happens."

Research, meanwhile, focuses on patterns and cause-and-effect.
Debbie Crews measures brain waves and produces brain maps that chart
how the brain works in optimal performance. Crews' findings indicate
that peak performance produces intensity in the body, a fast heart rate,
and high electrical frequencies firing in the brain. The most predominant
characteristic is activity in which the right and left hemispheres of the
brain work together equally. "It's anything but a passive state; it's very
much a heightened state," says Crews. "I think it shows that too many performance coaches are making the mistake of getting people too relaxed."

Most interestingly, Crews has found when subjects can see the real-
time readings from the different areas of the brain and heart on a bar
graph, they can intuitively create changes in the body to produce readings that are closer to the zone's characteristics.

"It's amazing how elite performers can change their numbers," says 45
Crews. "I don't tell them what to feel, I just let them figure it out. It's

nonverbal, which shows the best players know the feeling of the zone. If moving the readings also helps them to remember that feeling later, that could be a breakthrough."

The same principle of self-adjustment applies to a portable device developed by the husband-and-wife sport psychology team of Dr. Deborah Graham and Jon Stabler. The "Mind Meter" is about the size of a cigarette pack. Based on the changing beat-to-beat intervals of the heart, it measures a player's level of "arousal" before, during and after a shot. An optimum level of arousal is determined from the readings of a player's shots (usually between 40 and 60 on a scale of 1–100).

Stabler says that with the device, a player learns that too-high arousal numbers result when thoughts of outcome, swing mechanics, fear or doubt intrude. He says good players quickly become adept at replicating the state of mind that gets a good number.

"It proves to them that arousal control — not swing-fix thoughts — is the key," says Stabler. "They gain trust in their ability to control their arousal in important situations, which builds confidence. We're teaching our clients to get in the zone on demand, or very close to it, on a regular basis, rather than getting there very seldom, and by accident."

Another system, this one devised by HeartMath, focuses on controlling emotions and their negative effects on performance by monitoring the heart and its pathways to the brain and nervous system. HeartMath adherents contend they can synchronize activity in the brain and nervous system through the self-generation of a "coherent" heart rhythm pattern.

The key technique is called Quick Coherence. It begins with a person 50 focusing attention on an area of the heart and pretending to breathe slowly and gently *through* the heart to a count of five or six. While continuing to breathe this way, the subject concentrates on a positive feeling or attitude like compassion or appreciation. The process produces an even and more coherent heart-rate pattern that triggers optimum performance potential in the brain.

Proponents say the technique works anytime or anyplace a person feels nervous or irritated, including the golf course before or after a shot. The effect can be quantified by Freeze-Framer software that provides heart readings with the use of a finger clip.

"I use the techniques in my lessons, and I've seen them bring peacefulness and fluidity back into people's swings," says Laird Small, 2003 PGA Teacher of the Year and director of the Pebble Beach Golf Academy. "It shows people the difference between being in and out of the zone, and they can take it from there."

The Players React

Even with science as a portal to the zone, getting to the destination is the most personal of journeys.

"When I was in college, I read an article about how to get into the zone and did everything exactly," remembers Pia Nilsson. "Nothing happened. To get in the zone, a player has to be intimately aware of their feelings and reactions and experiences. Then when they find the right signal, they have a golden nugget for life."

Just about every top player has his own vision of the zone. Peter 55 Jacobsen says he achieved the zone in winning the Greater Hartford Open last year at age 49. "The key is to create your own reality on the course," Jacobsen says. "Down the stretch at Hartford, I just kept saying to myself, *Be who you are, and the golf shots will be easy.*"

Mickelson went through a similar process in achieving his "different feeling" at the Masters.

"It wasn't anything I worked on with anybody," he says. "I just decided that I had come so close trying to be so focused and so intense, but that's not really the way I am normally. I enjoy having fun, and I wanted to carry that into my play. And that brought out my best game."

It's a story that resonates with Chuck Hogan, who after thirty-five years of pursuing the zone from all angles, has come full circle.

"The zone is all about play," Hogan says. "It's the simplest bypass to all the things we do to screw ourselves up. The whole reason we play is to find that primal joy we once had. We know it's in there, and it becomes its own reward. The way to the zone is your own."

Clearly, golfers are still finding their way. The road ahead will surely 60 include breakthroughs in biofeedback technology that will better define the physiological and psychological conditions of the zone, and help golfers to better control and replicate them. Mental coaches can be expected to refine their messages to more narrowly focus their students on the crucial prerequisites of the zone. And a greater number of increasingly enlightened individuals will be more open to actively seeking heightened states of consciousness.

Though there's a good chance the zone will become more accessible, none of these advances guarantees it won't remain rare and elusive. It's a possibility even the most aggressive seekers placidly accept. Something elemental tells us that the mystery of golf was never meant to be solved.

THINKING AND WRITING ABOUT
THE FUTURE OF SPORTS

QUESTIONS FOR DISCUSSION AND WRITING

1. What is Glidden's claim in "Championship Intercollegiate Football"? Do you agree with that claim?

2. Should athletes ever get special consideration when applying for college admission? Why or why not?

3. What would be the effect on college football if players were allowed to go directly to the pros after graduating from high school?

4. In your opinion, should athletes be allowed to go directly from high school into the professional ranks? Explain.

5. When a college athlete is charged with a criminal offense, should that player be suspended from playing until the case is resolved? Why or why not?

6. When a professional athlete is charged with a criminal offense, should that player be suspended from playing until the case is resolved? Why or why not?

7. What is the unidentified author's claim in "Ever Farther, Ever Faster, Ever Higher"? Do you agree with that claim?

8. How effective is the author's use of support in "Ever Farther, Ever Faster, Ever Higher"?

9. Athletes have long been viewed as role models for our children and youth. What has the increased use of drugs and the increased publicity of that use done to athletes' effectiveness as role models?

10. Have you ever, as an athlete, experienced the sort of state that Diaz calls "the zone"? Do you feel that it is an experience that science can ever teach someone to experience?

11. What sort of changes in sports (or in a particular sport) do you foresee, given the advances being made in medical science? You may want to consider whether you feel those changes would be positive or negative.

TOPICS FOR RESEARCH

Genetic enhancements that will aid athletic performance

The success rate of high school athletes who went directly into professional sports

The prospects of teaching athletes to find their "zone"

The effect of race on athletic performance

Fan attitudes toward athletes' drug use

TAKING THE DEBATE ONLINE

For these and additional research URLs, see bedfordstmartins.com/rottenberg.

• *A Colorful Way to Learn Youth Sports*
  http://youth-sports.com
  This site features several articles on children's sports that discuss topics such as the role of parents and coaches, related health issues, and developing good sportsmanship.

- *ESPN*
  http://espn.com

  This online analog to the popular cable sports station features free online sports news, athlete profiles, and trivia quizzes. The site covers sports ranging from women's college basketball to horse racing.

- *Gender Equity in Sports*
  http://bailiwick.lib.uiowa.edu/ge

  This Web site, maintained at the University of Iowa, offers copious coverage of Title IX and other gender-related sports issues.

- *Minnesota Daily: College Sports Designed to Exploit Student Athletes*
  www.mndaily.com/daily/1999/03/29/editorial_opinions/o0329

  This editorial from the *Minnesota Daily* argues that college sports scholarships are bad for students.

- *Northeastern University: Sport in Society*
  www.sportinsociety.org/index2.html

  Sport in Society seeks to increase awareness of sport and its relation to society and to develop programs that identify problems, offer solutions, and promote the benefits of sport. Programs include AmeriCorps-funded Athletes in Service to America and Urban Youth Sports programs.

- *Title IX Twenty-fifth Anniversary Report*
  www.ed.gov/pubs/TitleIX

  The Department of Education prepared an extensive report on the effects of Title IX to mark the twenty-fifth anniversary of the law's 1972 enactment.

CHAPTER 18

Have We Become Too Reliant on Standardized Testing?

If you attended typical American public schools—and most likely, even if you attended private ones—you arrived at college already something of an expert on standardized testing. The very fact that you are taking a college course suggests that you probably took at least one standardized test for admission. You may also have taken Advanced Placement exams and almost certainly took statewide exams required for you to graduate or for your school to receive funding. Some of you probably started taking preliminary forms of the SAT as early as seventh grade. You may have been placed in or excluded from honors or gifted programs on the basis of a test you took in second grade. As one of the authors represented here reminds us, even some preschools and kindergartens have admissions exams. Whether or not you can use scissors well at the age of three can literally shape your future.

Today more voices than ever before are arguing that our educational system has gone too far in its dependence on standardized testing. Standardized tests are above and beyond any quizzes, tests, or exams that students take in individual courses. One of the primary criticisms of standardized testing is that it ignores all of the grades and other evaluations that students get from the teachers who know them best in favor of a single test that is not necessarily linked in any clear way to a school's curriculum. But because schools depend on state and federal funding, too often the curriculum is reshaped to prepare students for the test. Those on the other side of the debate argue that there is no other way to compare students from different schools since the easy A from one school is not equivalent to the challenging B from another.

The emphasis on standardized testing only increased with the No Child Left Behind Act of 2001, signed into law on January 8, 2002, by President George W. Bush, reauthorizing the Elementary and Secondary Education Act of 1965. The goal is simple: to have every child working at grade level in math and reading by the year 2014. The solution is far from simple, as is the means of proving the "adequate yearly progress" required by the legislation. Educators and parents alike are questioning what schools are giving up in their attempt to satisfy the new requirements.

Even the most firmly established test for college admissions, the SAT, is under fire, with some states threatening to stop using it in admissions decisions at state colleges and universities. The test has long been suspected of bias against minorities, and it has little value as a tool for helping students discover what they might do differently to improve their scores and thus their chances of admission into the college of their choice.

One reason that standardized testing remains a topic ripe for argument is that no one has yet discovered a viable alternative that serves the purpose it now serves.

Why Can't We Let Boys Be Boys?

MARCIA VICKERS

BEFORE READING: What are some of your earliest memories of taking tests? How did you feel about the tests? How did taking them make you feel?

In the fall of 2001, my husband and I were bursting with enthusiasm, anticipating our first-ever parent-teacher conference. We couldn't wait to hear glowing remarks about Christopher, our three-year-old genius. How he could sing the words from almost every Wiggles song and had been reciting the alphabet since he was a year and a half—only leaving out the occasional "t" or "y."

We eagerly walked into his classroom and sat down in midget-size wooden chairs as his two teachers brought out a long manila envelope. Then came the usual "how nice it is to have your son in our class" patter.

Not far into the discussion came the zinger. "Christopher is having a difficult time with stickers," said one teacher, holding up a sheet of green and purple dinosaurs. "What do you mean?" my husband and I asked in unison. "Well, he hasn't figured out that he needs to scratch the edge

---

Marcia Vickers is a writer for *BusinessWeek* magazine, where this article originally appeared on May 26, 2003.

with his fingernail and lift and peel," said the teacher. It turns out, at least according to his teachers, whom we genuinely liked, that he was having trouble with his fine motor skills—grasping and manipulating things with his fingers.

Looking back, the sticker incident was the precise point of liftoff into a world of which I was previously unaware: evaluations with child-development experts, the screening and eventual hiring of occupational and physical therapists (OTs and PTs), and trips to sensory gyms, which supposedly help the brain process sensory information though activities like touching different textures. Like most parents, I wanted to make sure Christopher had every possible advantage to overcome any weakness—however far-fetched it might sound. After all, we're no experts.

But some two years later, I've come to suspect the diagnosis is often 5 flawed. It turns out that it's not uncommon for young boys to have a so-called problem with fine motor skills.

In Manhattan, where we live, this phenomenon has become the status quo. One reason is that four-year-olds must score well on a standardized test to gain acceptance to the city's elite private kindergartens. This test has a section that emphasizes fine motor skills. So multitudes of young boys are in OT or PT. A cottage industry, in fact, has sprung up around it—most private OTs charge upwards of $135 per 45-minute session. There are waiting lists to get kids—mostly boys—into these therapy sessions.

All this for a simple biological fact: Boys typically develop fine motor skills up to six years later than girls. And in the early years, boys tend to be unfairly compared with girls on that score. This can have a devastating effect, say experts. If boys can't draw and color a bunny rabbit or cut simple shapes with scissors, they are subtly made to feel inferior. And a growing number of professionals believe that pressuring boys early only creates a sense of helplessness on their part. That can extend to how they feel about themselves and how they view school for many years.

Educators should be careful not to single out boys as "developmentally delayed" because they can't color in a sunflower as well as a girl. Now that a few experts are focusing on boys' learning gaps, the danger is to address the problem in the wrong way.

Some schools emphasize teaching methods that allow boys to brandish spatial mechanical skills as well as channel their energy. Says Dr. Leonard Sax, executive director of the National Association for Single-Sex Public Education: "Especially in the early years, schools should be playing to boys' strengths, such as playing games, building forts out of blocks, kicking a soccer ball, rather than emphasizing their weaknesses."

Christopher, who will soon turn five, suddenly loves writing his 10 name and drawing things from his incredibly vivid imagination, like space monsters and magic men. Last week, he wrote and illustrated a construction-paper book about a little boy whose hair turns into green beans. I think the therapy he has had has given him more confidence with crayons and scissors. But I'm not convinced he wouldn't have come around on his own.

Recently, he got one of the highest scores possible in vocabulary and general knowledge on that standardized test—though on the part that called for drawing shapes, he fell into the "average" category. Is he still our little genius? More than ever. He has even aced dinosaur stickers. Now, if only he wouldn't put the darned things on the furniture.

Testing Trap: The Single Largest—and Possibly Most Destructive—Federal Intrusion into America's Public Schools

RICHARD F. ELMORE

> BEFORE READING: Do you feel that standardized testing has received too much emphasis in the schools that you have attended? Explain.

Supporters of the reauthorization, last January, of the Elementary and Secondary Education Act hail it for tightening school accountability substantially, for granting more flexibility to states and school districts in the use of federal funds, and for applying sanctions to and providing aid for failing schools. Opponents argue that the bill doesn't go far enough, because congressional supporters of school choice failed to persuade their colleagues and the president's advisers to include vouchers in the bill.

Sadly, from an educational perspective, both sides miss the major issues. This is an "accountability bill" that utterly fails to understand the institutional realities of accountability in states, districts, and schools. And its provisions are considerably at odds with the technical realities of test-based accountability. In the history of federal education policy, the disconnect between policy and practice has never been so evident, nor so dangerous. Ironically, the conservative Republicans who control the White House and the House of Representatives are sponsoring the single largest—and the single most damaging—expansion of federal power over the nation's education system.

Under the new law, the federal government mandates a single test-based accountability system for all states—a system currently operating

Richard F. Elmore is a professor of educational leadership at the Harvard Graduate School of Education and is involved in the study of school accountability. This article was adapted from one entitled "Unwarranted Intrusion" that appeared in the Spring 2002 issue of *Education Next*, published by the Hoover Institution at Stanford University.

in fewer than half the states. It requires annual testing at every grade level, and states must disaggregate their test scores by students' racial and socioeconomic backgrounds—a system currently operating in only a handful of states, and one fraught with technical difficulties. The federal government further mandates a single definition of adequate yearly progress, the amount by which schools must increase their test scores in order to avoid some sort of sanction—an issue that in the past has been decided jointly by states and Washington. Finally, the law sets a single target date by which all students must exceed a state-defined proficiency level—an issue that in the past has been left almost entirely to states and localities.

Thus the federal government is now accelerating the worst trend of the current accountability movement: that performance-based accountability has come to mean testing alone. In the early stages of the current movement, reformers had an expansive view of performance that included, in addition to tests, portfolios and formal exhibitions of students' work, student initiated projects, and teachers' evaluations of their students. The comparative appeal of standardized tests is easy to see: they are relatively inexpensive to administer; can be mandated simply; can be rapidly implemented; and deliver clear, visible results. But relying only on standardized tests dodges the complicated questions of what tests actually measure and of how schools and students react when tests are the sole yardstick of performance.

If this shift in federal policy were based on the accumulated wisdom   5
gained from experiences with accountability in states, districts, and schools, or if it were based on clear design principles that had some basis in practice, it might be worth the risk. In fact, however, it is based on little more than talk among people who know hardly anything about the institutional realities of accountability—and even less about the problems of improving instruction in schools.

The idea of performance-based accountability was introduced in the mid-1980s by the National Governors Association, led by Bill Clinton, then governor of Arkansas. It took the form of what was then called the "horse trade": states would grant schools and districts more flexibility in making decisions about what and how to teach, in return for more accountability for academic performance. This idea became the central theory of today's accountability reforms. It was appealing in principle: governors and state legislators could take credit for improving schools without committing themselves to serious increases in funding. From the beginning, performance-based accountability was an explicitly *political* idea, designed to bring a broad coalition together behind a single vision of reform. As with most such ideas, it was weak on practical details, most of which were left to state and local policymakers and educators.

The movement got a major boost in 1994, when Title I—the flagship federal compensatory education program—was amended to require states to create performance-based accountability systems for schools. The vision behind the 1994 amendments was that Title I would complement and accelerate the trend that began at the state level; the amendments required states to develop academic standards, assessments based on the standards, and progress goals for schools and school districts—all within ambitious timetables. The merger of state and federal accountability policies ("alignment," as it was called) was supposed to occur by 2000. By the end of the decade, it was difficult to find more than one or two states lacking some form of testing program and public release of the results. In all but a few states, however, the basic architecture of accountability remained relatively crude and underdeveloped. In those few states where the idea had been developed most extensively—Texas and Kentucky, for example—the systems worked well enough, according to the testimonials of their sponsors, to legitimate the idea that they were successful in general. But even in these states, there were legitimate criticisms of the accountability system's actual effect on academic performance and drop-out rates.

By the late 1990s, it was abundantly clear that the states had fallen well short of what the crafters of the 1994 Title I amendments had envisioned. It was also clear that the federal government possessed very little leverage with which to force them along. States varied vastly in their administrative capacities to implement performance-based accountability systems. More important, creating accountability systems at the state level is essentially a political act, and Washington's harmless knuckle-rapping was hardly going to overcome the intransigence of a state legislature or governor. The U.S. Department of Education's ability to monitor and enforce compliance was limited; budget cuts whittled away at the Department's Title I staff just as their responsibilities were increasing; and its senior political appointees were reluctant to make life too difficult for governors and chief state school officers, who are among their key political constituencies. So by the target date for full compliance, fewer than half the states had met the requirements. It came as no surprise to learn that by the year 2000, many schools with Title I-eligible students were simply unaware of the program's major policy shift in 1994.

This experience should have signaled to the Bush administration and Congress that complex issues of state and local capacity could not be brushed aside just by tightening the existing law's requirements. If more than half the states were unable or unwilling to comply with the requirements of the previous, less-stringent, more forgiving law, why would one expect all the states to comply with a much more stringent and exacting law?

Even though virtually all the states have joined the accountability 10 bandwagon, doing so was, for many, largely a symbolic act. The designs of the systems are still primitive; state education officials' authority to oversee school districts is still limited in many cases; and the political consequences of imposing large-scale, statewide testing in areas with strong traditions of local control are risky. Moreover, mounting a statewide testing system is beyond the capacity of most state departments of education. Those that have embarked on large-scale testing are stretched to their limits just managing test-development work or monitoring testing contractors. Finally, there are technical issues. Standardized tests inevitably become highly politicized and, in the course of the debate, the limits of testing are subjected to public scrutiny. Many policymakers enter the accountability debate not knowing much about testing, and they often discover, much to their chagrin, that off-the-shelf tests may not validly measure the content specified in state-mandated standards and that norm-referenced tests (tests that deliberately create a normal distribution around a mean) may not be effective in measuring changes in performance.

The working theory behind test-based accountability seems simple—perhaps fatally so. Students take tests that measure their academic performance in various subject areas. The results trigger certain consequences for students and schools—rewards, in the case of high performance, and sanctions for poor performance. Attaching stakes to test scores is supposed to create incentives for students and teachers to work harder and for school and district administrators to do a better job of monitoring their performance. If students, teachers, or schools are chronically low performing, presumably something more must be done: students must be denied diplomas or held back a grade; teachers or principals must be sanctioned or dismissed; and failing schools must be fixed or simply closed. The threat of such measures is supposed to motivate students and schools to ever-higher levels of achievement.

In fact, this is a naive view of what it takes to improve student learning. Fundamentally, *internal* accountability must precede *external* accountability. That is, school personnel must share a coherent, explicit set of norms and expectations about what a good school looks like before they can use signals from the outside to improve student learning. Giving test results to an incoherent, atomized, badly run school doesn't automatically make it a better school. A school's ability to make improvements has to do with the beliefs and practices that people in the organization share, not with the kind of information they receive about their performance. *Low-performing schools aren't coherent enough to respond to external demands for accountability.*

The work of turning a school around entails improving "capacity" (the knowledge and skills of teachers)—changing their command of content and how to teach it—and helping them to understand where their students are in their academic development. Low-performing schools, and the people who work in them, *don't know what to do.* If they did, they would be doing it already. You can't improve a school's performance, or that of any teacher or student in it, without increasing the investment in teachers' knowledge, pedagogical skills, and understanding of students.

Test scores don't tell us much of anything about these important domains; they provide a composite, undifferentiated signal about students' responses to a problem.

Test-based accountability without substantial investments in internal accountability and instructional improvement is unlikely to elicit better performance from low-performing students and schools. Furthermore, the increased pressure of test-based accountability alone is likely to *aggravate* the existing inequalities between low-performing and high-performing schools and students. Most high-performing schools simply reflect the social capital of their students (they are primarily schools with students of high socioeconomic status), rather than the internal capacity of the schools themselves. Most low-performing schools cannot rely on the social capital of students and families and instead must rely on their organizational capacity. With little or no investment in capacity, low-performing schools get worse relative to high-performing schools.

Some changes in the new law provide unrestricted money that states 15 can use to enhance capacity in schools, if they choose to. But neither state nor federal policy addresses the capacity issue with anything like the intensity applied to test-based accountability. The result is an enormous distortion in the relationship between accountability and capacity—a distortion that is being amplified rather than dampened by federal policy.

In today's environment, critics who suggest that there might be problems with the ways tests are used for accountability purposes are branded apologists for a broken system. That the performance of students and schools can be accurately, reliably, measured by test scores is almost an article of faith. As a result, tests are being misused in ways that will eventually undermine the credibility of performance-based accountability systems.

The most serious problem lies in the use of test scores to make decisions about whether students can advance to the next grade or graduate from high school. The American Psychological Association's guidelines for test use (and the consensus of professional judgment in the field of educational testing and measurement) specifically *prohibit* basing any consequential judgment about an individual student on a single test score. Why? Because test scores are associated with a significant margin of error. That margin of error *increases* as the number of cases *decreases*; individual scores are typically much less reliable than aggregates of many individual scores.

The solution is to use multiple measures of a student's performance when making consequential decisions. But this solution is more expensive and it introduces a new level of complexity into the system. Were high-school graduation to be contingent on a composite of grades, test scores, and portfolios of students' work, developing such a composite would be a challenging technical feat. It would also introduce a certain amount of judgment into the system, and policymakers tend to distrust the professionals who make such judgments.

A similar problem arises at the lower-school level. Under Title I, schools are expected to meet their annual yearly progress goals, measured by a school's annual gain in test scores. Title I also requires disaggregating these scores by students' ethnic and economic backgrounds. But such measures are highly unreliable for populations the size of a typical elementary school, and they are particularly unreliable for even smaller sub-groups of students. Schools are often misclassified as low- or high-performing purely because of random variation in their test scores, unrelated to *any* educational factor.

The standards and accountability movement is in danger of being 20 transformed into the testing and accountability movement. States without the human and financial resources to select, administer, and monitor tests are now being forced to begin testing at all grade levels. Instead of creating academic standards that drive the design of an appropriate assessment, low-capacity states will simply select a test based on its expense and ease of administration, making charges of "teaching to the test" increasingly accurate. A test with no external anchor in standards or expectations about student learning becomes a curriculum in itself, trivializing the whole idea of accountability.

The enthusiasm for performance-based accountability plays to the worst weaknesses of the American education system. After World War II, most industrialized countries nationalized their education systems, but not the United States. Because decisions about content and performance were left to states and localities for so long, they never developed the capacity to monitor the quality of teaching and learning in schools, to support the development of teachers' and administrators' knowledge and skill, or to evolve measures of performance that are useful to educators and the public.

The difficult, uneven, and protracted slog toward clearer expectations and supports for learning has barely begun in most states and localities. The history of federal involvement in that long effort is mixed at best. The current law repeats all of the strategic errors of the previous law, but with greater federal intervention. The prognosis is not good.

The best we can hope for is that the capacity problems of states and localities will become more visible as a political issue, triggering responses that will help schools overcome the real obstacles they face in improving the quality and intensity of teaching and learning. Similarly, we can hope that the technical failures of testing will trigger a response that focuses more on broad assessments of student learning.

The worst that can happen is that test-based accountability will widen the gap between schools serving the well-off and those serving the poor, thus confirming the public's suspicion that expecting high levels of learning from all children is unrealistic. Performance-based accountability in education is mutating into a caricature of itself.

Testing Has Raised Students' Expectations, and Progress in Learning Is Evident Nationwide

ROD PAIGE

BEFORE READING: Should standardized test scores be used as a measure to determine how much funding schools receive? Explain.

Testing is a part of life. In fact, testing starts at the beginning stages of life: The moment we are born, neonatologists measure our reflexes and responses and give us what is called an Apgar score on a scale of one to ten. As we grow up, our teachers test us in school and we take other standardized tests that compare us with the rest of the nation's students. We are tested if we want to practice a trade — whether it be to get a cosmetology license, a driver's permit, or pilot training. And often we are retested and retested again to show that our skills remain at peak level.

In short, tests exist for a reason. In the case of a doctor, they certify that he or she is capable of practicing medicine. In the case of a teacher, they show that he or she has the knowledge to help children learn a given subject. And in the case of a student, they demonstrate whether a child has indeed learned and understood the lesson or the subject.

At their core, tests are simply tools — they subjectively measure things. In education, they are particularly important because they pinpoint where students are doing well and where they need help. In fact, testing has been a part of education since the first child sat behind the first desk. Assessments are an important component of educational accountability; in other words, they tell us whether the system is performing as it should. They diagnose, for the teacher, the parent and the student, any problems so that they can be fixed.

Educational accountability is the cornerstone of the No Child Left Behind Act, President George W. Bush's historic initiative that is designed to raise student performance across America. The law embraces a number of commonsense ways to reach that goal: accountability for results, empowering parents with information about school performance and giving them options, more local control, and flexibility to tailor the law to local circumstances.

No Child Left Behind is a revolutionary change, challenging the current educational system and helping it to improve. It aims to challenge 5

Former U.S. Secretary of Education Rod Paige has been a teacher, coach, college dean, schoolboard member, and superintendent of one of the largest school districts in the United States, in Houston. This article first appeared, paired with Reg Weaver's (p. 671), in a symposium titled "Are the tests required by No Child Left Behind making schools more accountable?" in *Insight* magazine, May 11–24, 2004.

the status quo by pushing the educational system into the twenty-first century so that American students leave school better prepared for higher education or the workforce.

Educational accountability is not a new concept—several states have been instituting accountability reforms for years. No Child Left Behind builds on the good work of some of these states that were at the forefront of the reform movement. The truth is that this law has one goal: to get all children reading and doing math at grade level. It's that simple. The law itself is a federal law, but it is nothing more than a framework. Elementary and secondary education are the traditional province of state and local governments, which is why the specific standards, tests and most of the other major tenets of the law are designed and implemented by the state departments of education, because they are in the best position to assess local expectations and parental demands.

The federal role in education also is not a new concept. There is a compelling national interest in education, which is why the federal government is involved and has been for some time. The federal government has stepped in to correct overt unfairness or inequality, starting with measures to enforce civil rights and dismantle segregation in the wake of the *Brown v. Board of Education* case (a Supreme Court decision that is now fifty years old). The federal government's first major legislative involvement in education goes back to 1965 with the Elementary and Secondary Education Act, which marked the first federal aid given to school districts with large percentages of children living in poverty. In 2001 the law was reauthorized as the No Child Left Behind Act (NCLB), which preserves the states' traditional role but asks them to set standards for accountability and teacher quality, thereby improving the quality, inclusivity, fairness, and justice of American education.

NCLB focuses on facts, not just feelings and hunches. It is no longer acceptable simply to believe schools are improving without knowing for certain whether they are. As Robert F. Kennedy asked back in 1965 when this federal education law was first debated, "What happened to the children? [How do we know] whether they can read or not?" With new state-accountability systems—and tests—we will have the full picture.

Let's examine what we do know. According to the nation's report card (the National Assessment of Educational Progress, or NAEP), only one in six African Americans and one in five Hispanics are proficient in reading by the time they are high-school seniors. NAEP math scores are even worse: Only 3 percent of blacks and 4 percent of Hispanics are testing at the proficient level. This is the status quo result of a decades-old education system before the NCLB.

Of the ten fastest-growing occupations in the United States, the top 10 five are computer-related, which are jobs that require high-level skills. High-school dropouts need not apply. We are all concerned about outsourcing jobs overseas, and we should note that the unemployment rate for high-school dropouts is almost twice that of those with high-school diplomas (7.3 percent compared with 4.2 percent) and nearly four times that of college graduates (7.3 percent vs. 2.3 percent). For young black men the unemployment rate is a staggering 26 percent. Even a high-school diploma isn't the cure: A vast majority of employers sadly expect that a high-school graduate will not write clearly or have even fair math skills. No wonder a recent study claimed a high-school diploma has become nothing more than a "certificate of attendance." For millions of children, they were given a seat in the school but not an education of the mind.

It is clear that our system as a whole is not preparing the next generation of workers for the global economy ahead of them. As Federal Reserve Chairman Alan Greenspan noted recently: "We need to be forward looking in order to adapt our educational system to the evolving needs of the economy and the realities of our changing society. . . . It is an effort that should not be postponed." That's why I am so passionate about making these historic reforms and drawing attention to the issue.

The old system—the status quo—is one that we must fight to change. That's why the president and both parties in Congress understood the urgency of the situation and put NCLB into law. They also ensured that the money would be there to get the job done, providing the means to states fully to implement the law; indeed, there's been 41 percent more federal support for education since President Bush took office.

But some defenders of the status quo have aired complaints about the law, saying its requirements are unreasonable and the tests are arbitrary. The bottom line is, these cynics do not believe in the worth of all children—they have written some of them off. You can guess which ones fall into that category. This pessimism relegates these children to failure. The president aptly refers to this phenomenon as the "soft bigotry of low expectations." But NCLB says the excuses must stop—all children must be given a chance.

NCLB helps us zero in on student needs. With little information about individual students' abilities with different skills, most teachers must rely on a "buckshot" approach to teaching their classes, aiming for the middle and hoping to produce a decent average. With an emphasis on scientifically based research techniques and effective use of information, NCLB helps fund programs that teachers can use to identify specific areas of weakness among their students.

For example, the Granite School District in Utah used Title I funds 15 (support for economically disadvantaged students) to procure the "Yearly Progress Pro" computer program. Now a fourth-grade class at Stansbury Elementary School visits the computer lab for a quick 15-minute test each week; the teacher walks out with a printout identifying changes in performance in specific skill areas over the week.

Child by child, the improvements add up. For example, a study by the Council of Great City Schools examined the recent gains in large metropolitan school systems. The Beating the Odds IV report showed that since NCLB has been implemented, public-school students across the country have shown a marked improvement in reading. The report found that the achievement gap in reading and math between African Americans and whites, and Hispanics and whites in large cities, is narrowing for fourth- and eighth-grade students. And it appears, according to the report, that our big-city schools are closing the gap at a faster rate than the statewide rate. Not only are the achievement gaps closing, the report states, but also math and reading achievement are improving.

For a concrete example of how the law is working, look at the Cheltenham School District in Pennsylvania, where leaders are disaggregating data to find the cracks they must fill. Drawing on test results, the district provides schools with specific information about each student's abilities and weaknesses in specific academic areas. Schools receive this data in easily accessible electronic formats in July, before the students arrive, giving them time to plan for the year. Now teachers can account for the effectiveness of their strategies and, if they are not working for some students, adapt to alternatives.

These findings are especially significant because research shows that it is often the students in the large-city schools who need the most help and face the greatest odds. Clearly, this report demonstrates that if you challenge students, they will rise to the occasion. This concept is at the fundamental core of NCLB because we can no longer mask our challenges in the aggregate of our successes. We must make sure that all children, regardless of their skin color and Zip codes, have the opportunity to receive a high-quality education.

While the press focuses on the complaints of the unwilling, whole communities are taking on the challenge of accountability and achieving great results. Perhaps my favorite example is in the Peck School in rural Michigan, where I visited in late March and found that the school culture had embraced the accountability treatment. A huge poster hangs in the hallway of the school emblazoned with No Child Left Behind! Showing creativity and commitment, the school launched a tutoring program, began intervening sooner with low-performing students, and even created a peer-counseling program to address the conflicts that often spill into the classroom and distract from learning. Everyone in the Peck School is taking responsibility for the students' education, truly fostering the character of good citizenship.

It is time to think of the children and to give them what they need. 20 It is time to work to make the law successful. We need to create an American public educational system that matches the vision of this law, where we strive for excellence without exclusion, where our children achieve greatness rather than greatly underachieving, and where 10 or 20 years from now a new generation of adults realize that we gave them a better life because we had courage and conviction now.

NCLB's Excessive Reliance on Testing Is Unrealistic, Arbitrary, and Frequently Unfair

REG WEAVER

BEFORE READING: Should standardized test scores be used as a measure to determine how much funding schools receive? Explain.

A s I travel around the country visiting schools and talking with National Education Association (NEA) members, I sense a growing concern among teachers and parents about the overwhelming emphasis given to standardized testing in America's schools. This concern is heightened when high stakes are attached to the outcomes of such tests. Teachers and parents worry that more and more of the important things that prepare us for life will be pushed off the curriculum plate to make room for test preparation.

According to a recent poll by Public Agenda, 88 percent of teachers say the amount of attention their school pays to standardized test results has increased during the last several years. And 61 percent agreed that teaching to the test "inevitably stifles real teaching and learning."

As any good teacher knows, there is no one-size-fits-all approach to either teaching or learning. In fact, we now have a solid body of research about cognition and learning styles that provides ample confirmation of this. Any good teacher also knows that proper assessment of learning is both complex and multifaceted. Tests—particularly paper and pencil tests that are standardized—are only one type of assessment. Good teachers make judgments about what has been learned on the basis of a variety of assessments. Finally, we know that what constitutes spectacular achievement for a child who suffers serious challenges may not equal the progress of his or her peers, but we honor this progress nonetheless.

The NEA has a proud history of supporting and nurturing our system of public education. When we are critical of the so-called No Child Left Behind (NCLB) Act, our interest is to fix those elements of the law that we see as destructive to public education and, ultimately, to the children we serve.

A consensus is emerging from coast to coast and across the political   5 spectrum that this is a law in need of repair. And the present definition of adequate yearly progress is at the heart of what is wrong with the law.

Reg Weaver is president of the National Education Association. He has thirty years of teaching experience and serves on the executive board of the National Council for the Accreditation of Teacher Education as well as the National Board for Professional Teaching Standards. His article first appeared, in conjunction with Rod Paige's (p. 667), in a symposium titled "Are the tests required by No Child Left Behind making schools more accountable?" in the May 11–24, 2004, issue of *Insight* magazine.

The concept of adequate yearly progress is relatively simple: Set a lofty goal, establish a time frame for accomplishing the goal, establish incremental targets or steps toward achieving the goal, and hold schools accountable for meeting the targets and, ultimately, the goal. The goal is 100 percent proficiency in reading and math, and all schools must meet it by 2014.

Wouldn't life, and particularly parenting and teaching, be simple if progress in learning were linear and time-sensitive? Parents, teachers and cognitive psychologists alike know that learning is anything but linear. And yet we now have a federal law that not only violates what we know to be true about human learning but says that unless schools achieve linear progress, the federal government will punish you.

Do we have a problem with this? You bet we do. Can it be fixed? We think so.

One of our state affiliates, the Connecticut Education Association (CEA), is a leader in recognizing and studying the problems with the federal definition of "adequate yearly progress" (AYP). Shortly after the law was adopted, the CEA had an independent economist develop a scenario based on existing test data in Connecticut in an attempt to visualize the impact of AYP in one of the highest achieving states in the nation. The initial results were shocking; however, because the law had yet to be implemented, the results were still hypothetical. Nonetheless, the prediction became reality last summer when nearly 25 percent of schools in Connecticut were identified as having failed to make AYP. An astonishing 155 elementary and middle schools and 88 high schools were identified as "in need of improvement" under the federal law.

More recently, armed with two years of test data, the CEA asked its 10 economist, Ed Moscovitch of Massachusetts, to update the scenarios. This time the CEA asked what failure rates might look like over the full 12 years of implementation. The new scenario, based on a model that allows for the rate of growth that students actually achieved in the last two years of testing, is very revealing. At the end of 12 years, 744 of 802 elementary and middle schools in Connecticut will have failed to make adequate| yearly progress—that's 93 percent of its elementary and middle schools.

In the first year none of the schools identified had the white non-Hispanic subgroup failing to make AYP. In the final year 585 of the 744 schools will have the white subgroup failing to do so. Even the powerful combination of social capital and great schools in a state that is regarded nationally as a high performer is not adequate to meet the statistical demands of this law.

Only in Lake Wobegon, perhaps, where all the students are above average, is there a chance of meeting the requirements set forth in the so-called No Child Left Behind law.

The current formula for AYP fails to consider the difference between where you start and how quickly you must reach the goal. That is, in my opinion, irresponsible. It is particularly irresponsible as it applies to English-language learners and special-education subgroups. While the Department of Education (DOE) finally has acknowledged that students whose first language is not English may not perform well when given a test in English, it does not go far enough to correct the problem. With respect to special-education students, the DOE has granted some leeway for the small percentage of severely cognitively disabled students, but there are thousands of other students in this subgroup for whom the test is totally inappropriate and emotionally injurious.

What's more, while the department has acknowledged the unfairness of how English-language learners and students with disabilities were tested, it has refused to go back and reconsider schools labeled "in need of improvement" under the old procedures.

Is this all the law of unintended consequences? Or is there, as many 15 believe, an insidious intent to discredit public education, paving the way for a breakup of the current system—an opening of the door to a boutique system with increased privatization and government vouchers?

We believe that for every ideologue who wants to subject public education to market forces, there are scores of policymakers and political officials who supported this law based solely on its stated, laudable intent. Many of them still do not understand the full import of what they supported. So what do we believe needs to be done?

First, we need to ask whether the measurement of AYP is an accurate barometer of a student's progress or a school's effectiveness. We have urged the adoption of multiple indicators. Measuring this year's fourth-graders against next year's fourth-graders tells us little that we need to know about the improvement of individual students. Wouldn't it make more sense to follow the progress of individual children? We have called for this kind of cohort analysis, and recently 14 state superintendents asked for the same change in a meeting with President George W. Bush.

Second, is it fair to have the same starting point for all groups? We need to find a more rational way to acknowledge the dramatic gaps in performance among subgroups. As an example, high-achieving students in Connecticut wait for years for targeted low-achieving subgroups to catch up with their performance, while other groups are asked to fill an unachievable gap in one year just to get to the starting gate. Yet the race begins at the same time and at the same pace for all. For certain subgroups, even dramatic increases in performance relative to their prior performance will only lead to failure. We need to acknowledge and honor progress.

Third, if we really have a goal of improving student achievement, shouldn't we offer tutoring to struggling students first? Right now NCLB adopts an "abandon ship" philosophy of allowing parents to change schools. The focus should be on helping the individual student in the subgroup in need of attention. And by the way, why is it less important to have a highly qualified tutor, or supplemental service provider, than it is to have a highly qualified teacher? Academic tutors should be certified, as well. Current law prohibits states from requiring that tutors be certified.

So in answer to the question "Does AYP increase school accountability?" our answer is no. But it could with serious and thoughtful revision.   20

The NEA and its state affiliates have always supported high standards and accountability. And we believe that no child should be left behind. We believe that every child in a public school should be taught by a highly qualified teacher in an atmosphere that is safe and conducive to learning, and all students should have access to a rich and deep curriculum. We also believe that each child is unique and brings to the classroom a variety of gifts and challenges. We have built a system in the United States that has struggled to honor this notion of gifts and challenges — our doors are open to all — and we have huge systemic challenges in meeting this philosophical ideal. There's much more that the federal government must do to guarantee that No Child Left Behind is more than just an empty promise.

No Child Left Behind: Test-Obsessed Education Won't Move Us Ahead

DAVID MARSHAK

BEFORE READING: What are some of the limitations of standardized testing? What might be some better alternatives for evaluating students and their schools?

But far from being an implement of reform, the intense focus on standardized testing, on which No Child Left Behind relies, tethers schools to the industrial model of education devised during the first two decades of the twentieth century.

As the United States became an industrial power, schools were shaped to fit this same industrial model of efficiency and production. Children were sorted by age. Some were groomed for higher education, but most were deemed best suited for labor and encouraged to drop out and go to work. Competition among students was encouraged, and student/teacher relationships were minimized.

David Marshak teaches in the Graduate School of Education at Seattle University. He is the author of *The Common Vision: Parenting and Educating for Wholeness* (1997). He has also conducted extensive research on multiage elementary classrooms in public and private schools and is the coauthor of *Teaching and Learning in the Intermediate Multiage Classroom* (with Alice Leeds; 2002). This article appeared on February 8, 2003, in the *Seattle Times*.

Now, despite evidence from developmental psychology that children grow and develop at different and variable rates, we still keep age-grading as a key structural element of schooling. Age-grading rewards those who develop more quickly and punishes those who are slower or different, even though they may have great abilities and gifts.

In elementary schools, children move from one teacher to the next every year, trashing the bond built between children and their teacher as well as the teacher's knowledge of the needs and abilities of each student. Each year, we tell every child and teacher to start all over again, even though we know that the teacher's knowledge of and caring for the child is the single most important variable for many children, particularly for children who are most vulnerable, in determining whether or not they will learn and succeed in school.

In secondary schools, students move from one teacher to the next   5
every 50 minutes (or 80 to 100 minutes with block periods). Five or six teachers a day; for many students, new teachers each semester. No wonder that 50 to 70 percent of students pass through their high-school years without developing a single important relationship with an adult in their school. We dump teens into industrially configured high schools, and then we complain that teens are disconnected and alienated from adults.

No Child Left Behind will not change any of this. In its single-minded focus on accountability and testing, it does not address the key issue of moving from an industrial model of school to a post-industrial model that integrates relationships and personalization with academic and personal success for every child. Such a movement requires that _we change the structure and culture of public schools simultaneously._

Two important studies from the late '80s–early '90s, commissioned by the U.S. Department of Labor to connect what students are learning with the needs of employers, acknowledged that basic academic skills, such as reading, writing, and mathematics, were central for student success in school and adult life. But both studies included additional categories of competence and knowledge as being equal in significance to traditional academics: speaking and listening skills, problem-solving skills, creative-thinking skills, knowing-how-to-learn skills, collaboration and organizational effectiveness skills, and personal-management skills.

These reports looked not only at which skills were needed to support the economy, but also considered the wider range of human capacities, including citizenship, personal relationships, creativity, and self-expression. But during the past decade, a string of political leaders (Bill Clinton, Gary Locke and most other governors, and now George W. Bush) have abandoned the needs of the present and future and retreated into the familiar paradigm of the industrial school, only with more testing and more penalties.

Look at Bush's education plan: reading, math, and science. And the only accountability measure that is supposed to matter: standardized tests.

No Child Left Behind puts a standardized test gun to the head of   10
every child, educator, and parent in the nation. It guarantees pain and
suffering for millions of children and teens whose cognitive and learning
styles do not readily fit the narrow structures of standardized testing. It
places huge demands on most states to pay for the development and administration of new tests, monies that states will have to raise either by
taking money away from other state services or by raising taxes.

Finally, it seems likely that the standard for yearly improvement set
by No Child Left Behind will not be met by many schools—certainly
some bad schools but also many schools that serve middle- and upper-
middle-class children that are currently held in high esteem by the parents whose children attend them.

There may eventually be good news to be found in the folly of NCLB,
although it would come at enormous cost to large numbers of children,
teens, and teachers.

Here's what may happen: First, there already is significant hostility toward NCLB in states where its penalties have begun to kick in. Some
school districts have already begun to sue the federal government about
provisions of the act.

But the most significant response, and the rebellion, may come from
middle- and upper-middle-class parents, as they see their children's
schools become increasingly focused on test preparation and test scores,
and the quality and richness of their child's schooling decline. Less attention paid to the arts, social studies, physical education, fewer studies
based on children's interests and curiosities. More drill, more drill, more
test prep. More frustration, more boredom, more anger.

Enough of this and it may take only a few years before parents be-   15
come sufficiently enraged with the standardized-test obsession to demand
an end to it. Perhaps a rebellion against this standardized-testing obsession will open the door to the reshaping of our schools and the implementation of much more sophisticated and effective accountability
measures.

The bulk of our culture is already moving into post-industrial forms
and desperately needs students who can fit into what *Megatrends* author
John Naisbett calls the "high tech, high touch" workplace. We need, as
Naisbett says, to reinvent education by teaching students "how to
think . . . to be creative." That means personalization, small schools, and
relationships between students and teachers developed over several years
(for example, through looping classrooms in which a teacher works with
the same class for two years rather than one, multi-age classroom, and/or
multi-year advisories and tutorials). It also means common learning goals
for all students and individual learning goals for every student, and many
and varied uses of new communication technologies in ways that are intensely student-centered.

Look at how the post-industrial energies take form in the work world:
Effective post-industrial organizations motivate workers by giving them

more responsibility and authority, and by valuing their resourcefulness, knowledge and skills — essentially by treating them as professionals. Contrast that to the way teachers are treated within standardized-testing regimes. Teachers are like assembly-line workers, relying on simplistic rewards and punishments. And students are treated not like unique human beings, but like interchangeable parts.

It's not that standardized testing has no role in the post-industrial school. Indeed, it does have potential value as one of many different assessment tools that can be used to fairly and accurately measure the learning and capabilities of diverse students.

The tragic irony of our times is that we know how to create schools that will prepare responsible, competent citizens and meet the needs of the post-industrial workplace. There are exemplary schools all over the nation that are doing this right now. Not one relies primarily on standardized testing. These schools all have high standards and rigorous accountability, and they respect and value the diversity of their students. And everything that happens in these schools starts with personal, long-term relationships between adults and children.

We also know that the agenda for schooling for the future should in- 20 clude a multidisciplinary curriculum that encourages inventive thinking (problem-solving, synthesis, analysis, creativity) and develops a range of communication, interpersonal and productivity skills.

For example, the Tahoma Public School District in Maple Valley, a district with forward-looking leadership, has the following post-industrial list of desired school outcomes: self-directed learning, collaboration, effective communication, contributors to the community, quality production, and complex thinking. For several years, educators at all grade levels in the district have used these desired outcomes as guides in their curriculum development and in their teaching.

Perhaps the No Child Left Behind Act will be a necessary disaster that will so discredit the industrial paradigm of school that we can finally let it go — and begin to move ahead. Unfortunately a lot of children and teens, and teachers and parents, will get hurt in the process.

The SAT's Greatest Test: Social, Legal, and Demographic Forces Threaten to Dethrone the Most Widely Used College-Entrance Exam

BEN GOSE AND JEFFREY SELINGO

BEFORE READING: How accurately do you feel the SAT (or ACT) predicts a student's success in college? Do you feel it is weighed too heavily in admissions? If so, what other factors should receive more emphasis?

The SAT is to criticism as a halfback is to a football—always on the receiving end.

For most of the past two decades, the College Board, which owns the test, has done a good job holding onto the ball, fending off critics who maintain that the test discriminates against female and minority students.

The board has sponsored several studies that show, for example, that the test usually gives black and Hispanic students a helping hand in the admissions process—it predicts that they will perform *better* in college than they actually do. And the board is scrupulously careful about material that appears on the SAT so that there will be no more embarrassments about questions that would seem to favor students familiar with yachts.

It's hardly surprising, then, that faced with an unprecedented assault from a wholly different quarter, the test's keepers resort to the standard defense.

"This is not a biased test," says Gaston Caperton, the College Board's 5
president, from his office here near Lincoln Center. "What we have is an unequal educational system. It's not the kids. It's not the test."

What Mr. Caperton seems to have missed is that today the battle has shifted drastically, from accusations of bias to questions that undermine the very basis for the test and may, in the end, lead to its demise. Today's critics have opened an assault on the use of what is essentially an IQ test to measure students' ability to learn. The outcome of the debate will affect how colleges with competitive admissions pick students, how racially diverse those students will be, and how high-school students prepare for college.

The College Board has for years tried to distance the SAT from its roots in IQ tests, but the perception remains that the most widely administered college-entrance examination measures intelligence, not a

---

Ben Gose is senior editor and Jeffrey Selingo assistant editor of the Government and Politics section of the *Chronicle of Higher Education*, the section that covers state and federal policies and their effects on colleges, students, and researchers. Their article appeared in the *Chronicle* on October 26, 2001.

mastery of learning. Many education leaders—most notably, Richard C. Atkinson, president of the University of California system—say that legacy creates perverse incentives, as students waste time and money "prepping" for the SAT's idiosyncratic questions, such as the analogies section of the verbal exam.

If college-entrance exams were tied more closely to the curriculum, the critics say, students would have a clear idea of what standards they must meet, and high schools could more easily be held accountable when students fail.

Last February, Mr. Atkinson stunned college leaders by calling on his nine-campus, 170,000-student system to become the first public university with competitive admissions to drop the requirement that applicants take the SAT. The system's size and prominence immediately led to speculation about whether others would dump the SAT; the University of Texas at Austin and North Carolina's public colleges are studying the issue.

Mr. Atkinson's announcement "was by far the most important single   10 anti-SAT effort ever in the history of the test," says Nicholas Lemann, author of *The Big Test: The Secret History of the American Meritocracy* (Farrar, Straus & Giroux), a recent book about the SAT.

In the 1940s, the University of California was the first major public system to require the test. "That was the key to making the SAT the dominant test," says Robert A. Schaeffer, public-education director at the National Center for Fair and Open Testing, also known as Fair Test. "If you follow that historical analogy, you'll find that the key to ending the dominance of the SAT also lies in California."

Other threats also loom. Thirteen top colleges, including Harvard University, the Massachusetts Institute of Technology, and the University of Michigan at Ann Arbor, are participating in a study to determine if state exams already given to high-school students may one day be used in college admissions. And recent court decisions and referendums may lead many colleges seeking a diverse student body to lower the weight they place on the SAT—or to ignore it altogether.

To be sure, the College Board and the Educational Testing Service, which engineers the test, aren't exactly on the ropes. The obsession with identifying—and getting into—the best colleges has been as good for the SAT as it has been for college-guide publishers like *U.S. News & World Report*. Roughly 1.3 million high-school seniors per year take the test, and more than half take it at least twice, yielding an annual revenue stream of more than $200 million. For now, many admissions officers continue to rely on SAT scores to compare students who come from high schools of widely varying quality. Many colleges also feel they must report high average SAT scores to the guidebooks, in order to earn top rankings and keep applications flowing their way.

The SAT also may continue to thrive because the alternatives to the test are embryonic, too expensive, or lacking in political support. Mr.

Lemann champions a national curriculum, with a national exam that matches it, but when the topic comes up on Capitol Hill, "everyone runs and hides," he says. The state-based exams, which for now merely test whether a student has mastered the basic skills needed to graduate from high school, aren't of much use to a college with competitive admissions. Some large state institutions want to de-emphasize the SAT by considering a variety of subjective factors in admissions, such as overcoming adversity, but first they must find money to hire additional people to handle those reviews.

And while much has been made of the correlation between SAT 15 scores and family income—the wealthier you are, the better your score, on average—that connection is even stronger on the standardized subject tests now known as SAT II, formerly called the Achievement Tests, one of Mr. Atkinson's proposed alternatives to the SAT.

"I hear a lot of people criticize the SAT," says Kurt M. Landgraf, president of the Educational Testing Service. "I've yet to hear what should be put in its place."

First administered in 1926, the SAT was designed to measure aptitude, or innate mental ability. It became widely used in the 1940s and 1950s, thanks in large part to James B. Conant, president of Harvard, who believed that subject-based achievement tests favored privileged students, whose families could afford to send them to boarding schools. The SAT, with its multiple-choice questions and systematic scoring, was seen as the great equalizer, a test that would allow the country's future leaders to be tapped based on intelligence rather than family connections. "The new elite's essential quality, the factor that would make its power deserved where the old elite's had been merely inherited, would be brains," Mr. Lemann writes in *The Big Test.*

Today, the enthusiasm for intelligence tests has plummeted, and most colleges claim to put more emphasis on high-school grades than on either the SAT or its primary competitor, the ACT.

Still, the SAT, whose two parts, verbal and mathematics, are each scored on a 200-to-800-point scale, has no shortage of fans. "The test is the one unchanging benchmark that can differentiate between those students who get B's at a tough school and those who coast with A's from an easy school," says John Maguire, an admissions consultant and former admissions director at Boston College.

Enrollment managers also know that recruiting students with high 20 SAT scores is an easy way to improve an institution's reputation. Dan Lundquist, vice president and dean of admissions at New York's Union College, says he uses the SAT as a "scale tipper" with students who are similarly qualified.

But he acknowledges that there's another good reason to do the tipping. "If you get enough [students] with 50 points higher than the rest, you can bring your mean SAT score up," he says.

Mr. Maguire concedes that there's a certain hypocrisy at work. "In public, people will say the SAT's aren't worth a bucket of warm spit," Mr. Maguire says. "Nonetheless, the boards of trustees and the college leadership are looking at [them] as badges similar to the rankings, that indicate that they are improving."

However, critics of the test—and many students who take it—view the SAT as a black box. "When you say someone has 1100, what does that communicate to a high-school student who wants to do better?" asks David T. Conley, an associate professor of education policy at the University of Oregon, who is directing a project on the use of state tests in college admissions. "It doesn't communicate anything but to tell the high-school student to get smarter."

Nor is it clear how to prepare for the exam, which leads many students to Kaplan and Princeton Review, companies seen as possessing "tricks" that help students raise their scores. Even some high-school teachers are taking time away from basic reading and writing instruction to prepare students for the SAT—a practice that Mr. Atkinson criticized.

Bill Wetzel, a freshman at New York University, says the SAT made 25 some courses during his junior and senior years at New Jersey's Red Bank Regional High School downright boring. "I noticed the difference between some classes, where the teachers and the students were trying to get the highest scores possible, and classes that emphasized curiosity and real critical thinking," he says.

Mr. Wetzel, founder of a group called Students Against Testing, notes somewhat sheepishly that his 1420 score helped land him at NYU, although he says that if he had to do it all over again he would attend an SAT-optional college. Now, he hopes to organize creative protests against the SAT and other standardized tests. He cites a recent "testfest" in Colorado in which students read books and played music while their peers took the SAT in a nearby building.

Using state examinations or subject tests would be an improvement, Mr. Wetzel says, but he isn't sure they would solve the core problem. "Both ideas have the potential for high schools to become factories for a different kind of test prep," he says.

Mr. Atkinson believes that his proposal, which would require students to take three SAT II tests (in writing, math, and a subject of each student's choice), would help students better understand the relevance of their high-school courses. There are more than a dozen SAT II exams, each covering a different subject area.

Some educators want to go even further, by using state examinations rather than the SAT. Every state requires its high-school students to undergo some form of statewide assessment, either at the end of their course work in core subjects or as a requirement for graduation. Advocates say the tests could provide a good snapshot of a student's readiness for college.

Last summer, a North Carolina legislator proposed a bill that would   30
make public colleges there drop the SAT requirement in favor of the
state's assessment exam. When college officials balked, saying the tests
don't do a good-enough job of measuring high-level skills, the sides compromised by ordering a study of the issue by college officials. "If we're
going to require students to take state tests, then we should use them for
college entrance," says State Representative Gene G. Arnold, a Republican, who sponsored the bill. "It's unfair to use the SAT when our standard
course of study is not geared toward preparing students for the test."

College officials elsewhere expect similar pressure from lawmakers
who seek a better return on the hundreds of millions of dollars spent annually on the state exams. While those tests were intended to increase the
accountability of public schools, some lawmakers say students have little
at stake, once they realize how easy it is to pass, and thus have failed to
take the tests seriously.

Because admissions officers would need the tests to provide meaningful information, college officials want a role in the development of future state tests. Thirteen research universities are sponsoring a study that
aims to help states design better tests by agreeing on a set of skills needed
by freshmen at their institutions. In addition, the project will create a
database of current state tests, so that colleges can compare scores on tests
in different states if they choose to use them in admissions decisions. The
Association of American Universities, a group of 61 research institutions,
is coordinating the project.

Without such a database, admissions directors say they will face a lo-
gistical nightmare in trying to make sense of scores from different states.
John Katzman, founder and chief executive officer of *Princeton Review* and
a supporter of state tests, says the College Board should take on the role
of comparing state tests, by developing a chart similar to one that provides equivalencies for SAT and ACT scores.

"If the College Board won't do it, because they're too committed to
saving the SAT, then other people will spring up that will, among them
me," says Mr. Katzman, who favors the elimination of the SAT. Already,
100 Princeton Review employees are working on products to prepare students for state tests.

Wayne Camara, the College Board's vice president for research and   35
development, says the group has no intention of assuming that role. He
cites a 1999 study by the National Academy of Sciences that said such efforts were destined to fail. "Comparing the full array of currently administered commercial and state achievement tests to one another, through
the development of a single equivalency or linking scale, is not feasible,"
the study said.

Mr. Camara notes that any effort to correlate the scores would be incredibly complex, because some groups—such as Hispanic students or
women—may score lower on certain state tests than they do on others.

College officials say it may come down to how well the state tests predict freshman grades, which is what the SAT claims to do. In April, the University of Minnesota-Twin Cities released a study, financed by the College Board, that found that the SAT reliably predicts students' academic performance, not only as freshmen but throughout college.

"We may find that the end-of-course tests are great predictors, or we may find that they are consistent with everything else we're doing, in which case why would we have to add yet another measure that schools have to collect and send on to colleges?" asks Gretchen Bataille, senior vice president for academic affairs at the University of North Carolina system.

Mr. Caperton, the College Board president, says that when states learn how much it costs to develop fair questions and ensure security for an admissions test, they will use that money instead for other priorities, like paying teachers more. "Could you turn a statewide test into an admissions test?" he asks rhetorically. "Absolutely. But when you compare what it costs to what you get, nobody is going to spend their money that way."

Mr. Conley, the Oregon researcher who is heading up the Association 40 of American Universities' project on state tests, says the money is worth spending to give students and high schools better measures of where they need to improve.

"The SAT is limited in its ability to provide diagnostic information to schools," Mr. Conley says. "It was never conceived as a means to bring about systemic improvement or to close an achievement gap between groups."

University of California officials agree. They acknowledge that students of different races will probably show the same performance gaps on the SAT II and even state tests. But those exams are better suited to closing the gaps and identifying poor schools, they say. "By having curriculum-based tests, we can relate [students' scores to] the quality of instruction in schools," says Patrick Hayashi, associate president of the University of California system.

The point differential between white and minority students is also leading to a diminished role for the SAT, simply because it lays bare the use of racial preferences in college admissions. In the 2000–2001 academic year, white students scored an average of 1060 on the test, compared with 859 for black students and 925 for Hispanic students.

Asian American students were on top, with an average score of 1095.

Many large public colleges, which generally make admissions deci- 45 sions based on a formula rather than a subjective "reading" of each application, have sought to preserve enrollments of black and Hispanic students by giving them an explicit bonus in the process. But in several high-profile legal decisions—including a ruling by a federal appeals court in August that struck down the admissions process at the University of

Georgia—such mechanical awarding of racial preferences has been successfully challenged as unconstitutional by white students who were denied admission.

As a result, admissions directors say that colleges may be forced to gravitate toward a more holistic set of criteria that recognize a wider range of achievement, such as leadership and overcoming adversity.

"Frankly, even those schools that are not highly selective are going to have to put in place procedures that allow for the reading of all applicants," says Jerome A. Lucido, associate provost and director of admissions at the University of North Carolina at Chapel Hill. "The days of looking solely at students' grades and SAT scores and saying 'they're in' are coming to an end."

Some very selective public institutions, like North Carolina and the University of Virginia, have been reading every admissions folder for decades. Combined, the two universities receive 32,000 applications annually, and both hire temporary staff members to read them all. Officials at both universities admit that taking essays and other written material into consideration is more subjective than using only grades and test scores, but they say that each application is reviewed by two or more readers to ensure consistency.

The Board of Regents at the University of California will vote on whether to establish a similar process, called "comprehensive review," next month. (The board won't decide whether to drop the SAT requirement until next spring.)

The proposed review process would require admissions officers at the university system's nine campuses to evaluate every student on a broad array of criteria, including initiative and hardship.

The super-competitive Berkeley campus has already curtailed the influence of the SAT. In 1998, two years after the state's voters approved a referendum banning affirmative action in public-college admissions, Berkeley officials started reading every application, some 36,000 last year. Before then, the first half of available slots for freshmen, about 4,400 seats, were allocated solely on the basis of SAT scores and high-school grade-point averages.

Now, those coveted first seats are given out based on a much broader and less rigid formula. It still includes an applicant's SAT score and GPA, but adds other academic factors, such as the strength of the curriculum and pattern of grades throughout high school. In the first year that Berkeley relied less on SAT scores, officials found that 25 percent of the admissions decisions were different than if the old procedure had been in place. (The remaining half of the university's freshmen are accepted using the expanded academic criteria and other personal factors.)

Although the changes in the admissions process at Berkeley were aimed in part to capture underrepresented minority students in the wake of the state ban on affirmative action, the number of black and Hispanic students accepted at Berkeley has actually fallen since the new procedures were put in place. University officials say they expected the minority numbers to drop. But "we didn't have the degree of loss that we would have had if we didn't put this extra care and effort into reading every application," says Pamela Burnett, the university's director of undergraduate admissions.

The College Board, which has long urged colleges not to rely too heavily on the SAT, supports the UC system's proposed move to a fuller review—for reasons that are not entirely altruistic. "If UC goes for comprehensive review, there's less pressure to do away with the SAT," says the board's Mr. Camara. The SAT would become just one of many tools in evaluating applicants, he says.

But Robert Laird, a former undergraduate-admissions director at 55 Berkeley, wonders whether the practice of reading every application will become widespread at large public institutions, given the cost involved.

"As state budgets across the country shrink sharply, it's going to be difficult to generate the legislative and institutional financial support to put significantly more money into the undergraduate admissions process," he says.

In the late 1990s, some states facing bans on affirmative action discovered a cheaper way to ensure that their public campuses remained racially diverse. California, Florida, and Texas now automatically admit large numbers of students based solely on class rank, essentially making SAT scores irrelevant. Texas' public colleges began guaranteeing spots for the top 10 percent of the state's high-school classes in 1997, and California and Florida followed in 1999, holding slots for the top 4 percent and 20 percent, respectively. The policies take advantage of the many high schools that are predominantly black or Hispanic.

Now, the University of Texas at Austin is considering whether the SAT is even worth requiring for the half of the freshman class not automatically admitted under the state's 10-percent policy. A faculty committee convened by the university's president, Larry R. Faulkner, started meeting last month to study the fairness of standardized tests in Austin's admissions process.

The trend toward "x-percent plans" and more-subjective admissions policies hasn't escaped the gaze of those who uphold high standards or oppose racial preferences. Michael McIntyre, a professor of organizational and industrial psychology at the University of Tennessee at Knoxville who has studied the SAT, says that if the goal at the University of California is to maintain diversity, officials should be honest about their motives. "A change in policy is very likely to change the demographic mix," Mr. McIntyre says. "If that's the goal of the the change, then let's be upfront about it. Let's admit it if we are trying to achieve some social end, rather than an academic end."

Mr. Lemann, the author, supports affirmative action, but cautions 60 that college officials may be fooling themselves if they think a subjective admissions process will shield them from lawsuits. He says that legal groups leading the fight against racial preferences, like the Center for Individual Rights, would have a more difficult time proving that such policies discriminate against white students, but in some cases would still be able to do so. "The Center for Individual Rights has gone after the low-hanging fruit," Mr. Lemann says, "and there's a lot of it."

The College Board and ETS, meanwhile, occupy a strange position in the affirmative-action debate. Both are firmly within the academic establishment, which strongly defends the use of racial preferences in admissions. The College Board is a membership organization that represents colleges and schools. ETS, meanwhile, lures top researchers, in part, by providing college-like surroundings on its verdant 360-acre campus outside Princeton, New Jersey. Partly because of the scrutiny of affirmative action, both groups have counseled colleges to avoid relying too heavily on test scores.

But now that some colleges are not even considering the SAT in admitting large portions of their students, the traditional alliances may be breaking down. Mr. Landgraf, the ETS president, for example, views the "x-percent plans" as a blow to high standards, even though they are a handy tool for maintaining black and Hispanic enrollments. "Are the interests of the states best served by silencing the debate," Mr. Landgraf asks, "or by doing what's right?"

Mr. Landgraf and nearly everyone else agree that the best way to end the debate would be to eliminate the performance gap between students of different races. Most of those who use the x-percent plans admit privately that they would go back to the SAT in a minute, were it not for those racial gaps. But despite considerable hand-wringing, and efforts at outreach, the gaps between white, black, and Hispanic students have barely budged in more than a decade.

The College Board sponsors a good deal of research aimed at broadening the scope of skills measured by the SAT, and much of that work has the secondary goal of finding measurements upon which black and Hispanic students will score well.

Robert Sternberg, a Yale University psychology professor who believes 65 the SAT should be expanded to measure creative and practical skills, is among the most prominent scholars receiving funds from the board. To measure creativity, Mr. Sternberg suggests showing students a single-frame cartoon and asking them to write a caption for it. To measure practical ability or common sense, he would include a reading about a real-life dilemma that teenagers might face, and ask students to identify the best way to handle the situation.

Mr. Sternberg acknowledges that grading the answers would be more expensive than it is now; particularly on the creative questions, a machine would not be able to do the job. But the College Board could hire readers, as it does to grade essays on Advanced Placement tests. The readers would use examples that would illustrate what types of captions might earn top scores for creativity.

"By measuring a broader range of abilities, you would no longer need affirmative action," Mr. Sternberg says. "Some of the kids who grow up in culturally different environments have to develop creative and practical skills to survive. If you grow up in a white, upper-middle-class environment, you don't need those skills as much."

He and a team of researchers are conducting a study that involves roughly 1,000 college students at 16 sites. "So far, our results are in line with our hypothesis—that we can find better ways of predicting success," he says.

Those sorts of measures generally draw howls of protest from critics of affirmative action, and many of the psychometricians involved in creating the SAT are equally dubious.

"I'd be a little concerned that you could coach someone to pretend to be creative," says Thomas Van Essen, who develops verbal tests at ETS. "Think of those kids you knew in high school who were 'creative'—they all acted the same."

The testing giant's own efforts to narrow the gap in test scores have elicited similar skepticism. In 1999, ETS officials revealed that they were working on a project that would help admissions officers measure disadvantage, by identifying as a "striver" any student who scored more than 200 points above the average score of students from a similar background. The scale took into account 14 variables, such as family income and parents' education, but its developers noted that the only way to achieve "a student body that mirrors the racial composition of the U.S. population" was to use race in the process.

The effort was excoriated by opponents of affirmative action, and quickly condemned by Mr. Caperton. Last month in Princeton, a table of six ETS officials briefly fell silent when the topic was broached.

"We didn't feel there was sufficient technical quality behind it," says Drew H. Gitomer, senior vice president for statistics and research. "While the intent of the study was noble, we didn't feel there was a whole lot there."

Meanwhile, the College Board's efforts to deal with its other problem—the perception that the SAT has no link to the curriculum—can best be described as modest. For years, it reacted mainly with semantics. In 1994, it changed the name "Scholastic Aptitude Test" to "Scholastic Assessment Test," to suggest a measurement of educational accomplishment rather than innate ability. A few years later, it shortened the name to just "SAT."

College Board officials insist that the test has responded to changes in the curriculum over time. They note that they began permitting calculators on the math exam in 1994, to reflect the practice of many schools. The same year, they killed a section of questions on antonyms, to answer critics who suggested that it was encouraging schools to spend too much time on vocabulary devoid of context.

Similar criticisms are now being leveled at the analogies section, and the College Board is studying whether it would be feasible to replace that part with questions on a short, high-level reading passage.

"The notion that this test hasn't changed in 50 years is completely untrue," says Amy Schmidt, the College Board's director of higher-education research and educational evaluation.

Somewhat belatedly, the board is also beginning to help test takers figure out what skills they need to improve to raise their scores. This fall, for the first time, the board is sending score reports to students who have taken the PSAT, which high-school sophomores and juniors take as a warm-up to the SAT.

The reports list specific skills that each student needs to work on — such as understanding the main ideas of a reading passage, or applying the rules of algebra and geometry. There are no immediate plans to provide such reports to students who take the SAT.

"Maybe we could have done a little better job over the years of com-   80
municating what these questions do measure," concedes Mr. Gitomer.

Whether those efforts will be enough to save the SAT remains to be seen. The best hope for the test may be that it's so entrenched in the admissions process.

Mr. Conley, the advocate for state tests, doesn't expect them to be required on college applications anytime soon. "The college-admissions process is a conservative system, and we're talking about a brand-new infrastructure that doesn't exist," he says. "It's like setting a massive ship off in a different direction, and that's never easy or quick."

When a committee studying whether to eliminate the SAT requirement at the University of Texas first met last month, several professors wondered what would replace the test if its use were abolished. They feared that a process without standardized tests would lead to inconsistent admissions decisions.

The SAT is still required at the highly selective public colleges that give every application a thorough read. John A. Blackburn, Virginia's dean of admissions, says the university does not plan to drop the requirement.

"In a major system, where you have to make decisions about a lot of   85
people and where you're responsible to the public, you must have some norm that cuts across high schools," Mr. Blackburn says. "Until we have something better, the SAT is really the only instrument that achieves that."

Are SAT Scores "Worse Than Meaningless"?

BEFORE READING: How does the state in which you attended high school compare with other states when it comes to the perceived quality of education students get in the public schools? Did you feel that you were getting a good education? Did your perception match any published reports about the quality of your state's schools?

Ranking states according to their SAT averages is "worse than meaningless," warn Greg Marchant and Sharon Paulson, education experts at Ball State University, Muncie, Indiana "The state SAT rankings are worthless in determining the quality of the schools in a state, and the potential for basing perceptions and policies on the rankings is even worse," argues Marchant.

Research by Marchant and Paulson determined that the rankings say more about the nature of the students taking the test than about the states' educational systems. Their study examined the characteristics of individuals taking the SAT and compared the ten highest-scoring states with the ten lowest. They found the larger the percentage of students taking the SAT in a state, the lower the average score.

In the ten states with the highest SAT scores, an average of eight percent of their high school students took the SAT, while 69 percent of students took the test in the ten lowest-scoring states. Moreover, the lowest ten states had twice as many high school juniors taking the test and 14 times as many SAT takers overall.

"The states with the highest SAT scores and lowest percentage of SAT takers tend to be testing mostly their best and brightest." Marchant explains. "There is more diversity in the ability of test takers that come from the lower-scoring states. In the top-scoring states, twice as many test takers come from the top 10 percent of their class. Test takers from lower-scoring states represent a far greater range of both class rank and grade-point average." The more a state's education system works to increase college attendance for students who have traditionally not pursued higher education, the lower the state's average SAT scores are likely to be, he points out.

Differences in parent income and parent education of the test takers accounted for 92 percent of the difference among states' average SAT scores. The ten bottom-scoring states had more than 41 times as many test takers from families with incomes less than $10,000. "This is major issue for high school students attempting to be first-generation college students," Marchant notes. Compared to the ten highest-scoring states, the bottom ten states had more than 31 times as many test takers with

---

This unsigned article appeared in the December 1, 2001, issue of *USA Today Magazine*.

parents holding only a high school diploma and more than 60 times as many test takers with parents who did not graduate from high school.

"Policymakers and the general public are likely to be misled about the relative quality of a state's education system," he warns. "They do not understand that the rankings reflect the characteristics of the students taking the test. This confusion can lead to erroneous policy decisions and false perceptions."

THINKING AND WRITING ABOUT STANDARDIZED TESTING

QUESTIONS FOR DISCUSSION AND WRITING

1. Do you agree with Vickers that today's children are pressured too much too early by parents who want them to succeed academically? Is the same true in other areas of the children's lives, such as sports or music?

2. Does your own experience support the claim that Elmore is making in "Testing Trap"? Explain why or why not.

3. Explain how Elmore's language either strengthens or weakens his argument in "Testing Trap."

4. Do you feel that children and teenagers are "pigeonholed" in school because of their performance on standardized tests? Or are there other reasons that some students are assumed, for example, to be "college material" while others are not?

5. Whose argument do you find more convincing, Paige's or Weaver's? Why?

6. Do you feel that schools are guilty of teaching to the test too much? What should be emphasized instead?

7. Argue for or against keeping the SAT as a factor in college admissions. If you favor doing away with the SAT as an admissions tool, what should be used in its place?

8. A part of the accountability movement is the publishing of test results by state, by district, and by school. Does the article from *USA Today* convince you that those published results may not be as straightforward as they seem? Explain.

TOPICS FOR RESEARCH

Bias against minorities in standardized testing

What the SAT really tests

Individual states' success stories with standardized testing

The SAT as a predictor of success in college

What statistics on standardized testing really reveal

TAKING THE DEBATE ONLINE

For these and additional research URLs, see bedfordstmartins.com/rottenberg.

- *On Standardized Testing*
  www.kidsource.com/kidsource/content2/stand.testing.html

  This article presents the case for reducing standardized testing in the primary grade classrooms.

- *FairTest: The National Center for Fair & Open Testing*
  www.fairtest.org/facts/howharm.htm

  The National Center for Fair & Open Testing (FairTest) works to end the misuses and flaws of standardized testing and to ensure that evaluation of students, teachers, and schools is fair, open, valid, and educationally beneficial. This page is a question and answer section on "how standardized testing damages education."

- *Family Education*
  www.familyeducation.com/topic/front/0,1156,1-9028,00.html

  The mission of Family Education Network is to collect "the world's best learning and information resources, personalized to help parents, teachers, and students of all ages take control of their learning and make it part of their everyday lives." This page on the site gathers information on standardized testing.

- *ENC Online Standardized Testing*
  www.enc.org/topics/assessment/testing/?ls=sn

  ENC Online is a K–12 math and science teacher center. It has links to many essays on standardized testing written by educators.

CHAPTER 19

What Is the Role of Sex and Violence in Popular Culture?

The ongoing controversy about explicit sex and violence in movies, television shows, rap music, and computer and video games does not seem likely to subside soon. Depictions of sex and violence become increasingly graphic and increasingly accessible each year. In the essay that opens this unit, Ron Kaufman quotes William F. Baker and George Dessart, who in their book *Down the Tube* (1998) write, "In its simplest terms, the business of television in this country is the buying and selling of eyeballs." The same might be said of the business of making movies or producing computer and video games, and the success of rap music and rap music videos that openly celebrate violence and sexism reinforces the notion that if sex and violence sell, no shortage of entrepreneurs will be ready to cash in.

Are some forms of popular entertainment necessarily dangerous and immoral? How much are viewers affected by continued exposure to depictions of explicit sex and violence? Researchers have argued the point for years, but today a majority believe that long-term viewing does, in fact, alter the behavior of certain audiences. In recent years, what appear to be copycat crimes have followed the release of particularly violent films. Experts also debate the relative effects of fictional and real-life images: Which are more disturbing and potentially more corrupting—the graphic creations in movies or the daily reports of real-life horrors in the news? And do children recognize the difference?

Not surprisingly, even where agreement exists on the nature of the problem, there is disagreement about solutions. However strongly some critics feel about the dangers of exposure, they argue that the dangers of government censorship may, in the long run, be greater. But if government intervention is rejected, can other solutions—a rating system for television shows and music albums, a V-chip in the TV set allowing parents to block undesirable programs, respect by producers for the so-called family hour, and above all, closer monitoring by parents—guarantee that young people will be insulated from exposure to sex and violence in the media? Most Americans are not optimistic.

Of course, popular culture is not the only source of exposure. Movies, television, music, and games reflect the activities, tastes, fantasies, and prejudices of a larger society. Reducing the amount of sex and violence in the media is certainly easier than reforming a whole society. Still, questions remain: Why are some of the most popular forms of entertainment those with the highest body count and the most grisly depiction of carnage and suffering? To what extent can any reform in popular entertainment successfully address the problems of crime and immorality?

Filling Their Minds with Death: TV Violence and Children

RON KAUFMAN

BEFORE READING: Do you feel that television shows and movies have gone too far in the depiction of sex and violence? Is the exposure of such explicit programming to children a legitimate concern?

We do not believe there is anything sexist or violent about the World Wrestling Federation. I think it's unfair of you to insinuate it when there are so many shows and so many different movies, and so many different social problems that really do contribute to violence in this country. —UPN president Dean Valentine in 1999 after a seven-year-old child in Dallas killed his little brother with a "clothesline" maneuver he had seen on a wrestling show.

One fact should not be in dispute: TV is violent! Guns, shootings, murders, hitting, punching, slapping, screaming, kicking, stabbing, explosions, car chases, car smashes, disasters, and death are shown daily throughout TV programming. Most violence is not even in nightly news programs and nearly all of the violence on television is fake. TV presents violent acts through acting—with fake guns and fake blood. For adults,

Ron Kaufman, a journalist and teacher, is the creator of TurnOffYourTV.com, where this article originally appeared. In the online original, he provided links directly to most of his sources.

televised violence is probably not a big deal. When a character is killed off a TV show one week, we know the same actor will reappear the next week on another show on a different network.

A study by the Parents Television Council (PTC) entitled "TV Blood-bath: Violence on Prime Time Broadcast TV" looked at changes in the levels of violence on television from 1998 to 2002. The report notes that on the major noncable broadcast networks, "In 2002, depictions of violence were 41 percent more frequent during the 8:00 P.M. Family Hour, and 134.4 percent more frequent during the 9:00 P.M. hour than in 1998." The study also noted that while CBS was the least violent network, Fox was the most violent, followed closely by UPN and NBC.

The PTC study, though limited, did see increases in certain types of violence such as an increase in blood, guns, deaths, and torture:

8:00–9:00 P.M.	1998 %	2002 %
Fight	44	32
Blood	0	9
Guns and other weapons	29	38
Crashes, explosions, fire	6	5
Threats of violence	7	5
Graphic depictions	10	1
Deaths depicted	4	5
Deaths implied	0	3
Torture	0	2

The Center for Media Literacy presents three common themes with respect to TV violence:

1. Violence Drives the Storyline

Violence is always involved. The fictional programs on television require   5
a crime, murder, or fist-fight to develop plot and story. For example, in January 2004 CBS ran three straight hours of violent shows on Thursday nights starting with *Cold Case:* "Churchgoing People," "Lilly investigates the 1990 murder of a church organist who was found in an alley surrounded by crack vials and racy magazines." This was followed by *CSI:* "Fur and Loathing," "A team explores the world of fetishes after finding a dead man dressed in a raccoon costume; the corpse of a convenience-store employee turns up in an industrial freezer." CBS finished off with *Without a Trace:* "Prodigy," "A fourteen-year-old Russian violinist disappears after a rehearsal for a concert appearance."

Not to be outdone, the Fox network ran *Tru Calling:* "Reunion," "Tru attends her high-school reunion and finds the most popular girl from school dead in a swimming pool." This program was then followed by

Figure 1. Overall Industry Averages: Three-Year Comparisons
(National Television Violence Study, p. 27.)

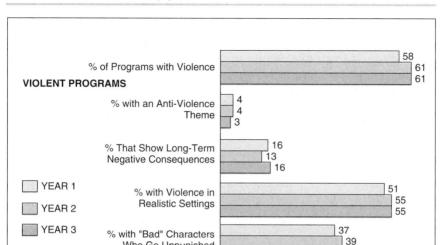

The World's Worst Drivers Caught on Tape 3, "Cameras record motorists creating havoc on the roadways."

The National Cable Television Association's National Television Violence Study (Report 3 released in 1998) states that "across the three years of this study, a steady 60 percent of TV programs contain violence . . . [and] much of the violence is glamorized, sanitized, and trivialized." (see Fig. 1.)

2. Violence Has No Consequences

C'mon now—the hero *always* wins. The hero of TV shows never gets in trouble for his/her violent actions. The hero is always "justified" in one way or another when committing violent acts. "TV rarely shows the consequences of violence. Guardians of law and order whether it's Maxwell Smart, Kojak, or the *Miami Vice* squad emerge from their conflicts with little more than a scrape. Occasionally, unlucky characters (but never the hero!) end up in a nice clean hospital bed," explains the Center for Media Literacy (*Media & Values,* Issue no. 62, Spring 1993, by Barbara Osborn).

Television will never show a main character lose an arm or leg or get killed on screen. In reality, with as much gunplay that appears on TV, main characters should also get shot. The "bad guy" can get shot, killed, burned, or maimed, but never the hero. In fact, the hero can really be as violent has he/she wants.

A study released by the Center for Media and Public Affairs (CMPA) 10 in June 1999 states that though television shows a lot of violence, it rarely shows its outcome. "We found that despite the high volume of televised violence, viewers rarely see it causing adverse effects," states the report. The report found serious acts of violence—murder, rape, kidnapping, and assault with a deadly weapon—occurred once every four minutes on the major TV networks. However, it notes that "no physical harm was shown three quarters (75 percent) of the time violence occurred on broadcast series and over two-thirds (68 percent) of the time it occurred on cable programs. A mere 7 percent of violent acts on broadcast shows and 4 percent on cable resulted in fatalities."

The CMPA report notes that in its study, "serious violence was more likely to have tangible consequences, but a majority of even these more brutal acts had no direct harmful results. Fifty-nine percent of acts of serious violence on broadcast series and 54 percent on cable lacked negative consequences." Only in rare instances, about 10 percent, did violence result in some type of mental distress for the victim or another character. "Thus, fully 90 percent of violent acts on broadcast and 87 percent on cable proved psychologically painless," says the report.

The current trend in TV programs is to permit not only the police to commit justifiable violence but criminals as well. "HBO's *The Sopranos* [is] the beginning of a new trend celebrating what's called the 'criminal protagonist,' in this case a murderous crime boss we can learn to love," says L. Brent Bozell III, president of the Parents Television Council. "Entertainment producers and critics alike love 'moral complexity,' but what they're sowing is moral confusion. They think good and evil, black and

Context of Violence in TV Series (percent)
(Center for Media and Public Affairs: "Merchandising Mayhem: Violence in Popular Entertainment, 1998–1999")

	Broadcast		Cable	
	All	Serious Only	All	Serious Only
Presentation				
Shown	98	82	98	67
Aftermath	2	18	2	33
Physical harm				
None	75	59	68	54
Fatal injury	7	14	4	8
Other injury	11	18	20	32
Property damage	7	8	8	6
Psychological harm				
None	90	84	87	84
Victim	8	8	11	10
Others	2	8	2	6

white, is so old hat. Let's coat everyone and everything with a lovely shade of gray—as the red blood flows."

Bozell's group is not against TV but has serious problems with the amount of violence currently shown on the networks. The PTC has also led many campaigns against advertisers to try and reduce the revenue streams to violent programs. "Imagine my shock—and the shock of millions of others—coming across FX's wicked-cop series *The Shield* . . . the show ended with 'criminal protagonist' Vic Mackey gratuitously shoving a man's face into an electric burner. Watch the melting flesh as Fox counts the advertising dollars."

On TV today, it's not even that "bad" characters go unpunished but that "good" characters are *justified* in being bad. Sure, the cops on *Miami Vice* had to be violent to get the criminals, the *A-Team* was always "wrongly accused," and Buck Rogers didn't ever do a bad thing with a laser gun. The idea of *justifiable violence* is something that should have parents really consider what their children are watching.

3. TV Is a World of Good and Bad

Even though both criminals and cops can commit justifiable violence— television is still a simple medium. TV presents "good guys" and "bad guys." On average, there are fifteen minutes of commercials for every one hour of TV programming, so producers only have a short amount of time in which to establish plot, story, characters, and resolution. Good characters and bad characters must be quickly and simply established.

"Deeper, more realistic, more ambiguous characterizations make it hard for viewers to know who to root for. It also requires more screen time that takes away from on screen action," states the Center for Media Literacy. "As a result, TV and film criminals are reduced to caricatures. They are 100 percent bad. No one could care about them. They have no families. Many of them don't even have full names, only nicknames. They deserve no sympathy and they get what they deserve."

The bad guys, whether they are cops or robbers, have to be 100 percent bad to justify the violence against them. Television violence is the struggle of good versus evil. It's OK to shoot the bad guy—after all, he's the "bad guy."

According to the study by the Center for Media and Public Affairs, the most violent show observed in 1999 was CBS's *Walker, Texas Ranger*. This show "took the top spot for overall violence with a rate of 112 acts per show, over two-thirds of them (82) serious. Almost every episode of this long-running Chuck Norris cop show includes several martial arts fight scenes and some gunplay," says the report. "The fall season's first episode was especially violent. It opened with a combination gun battle/fight scene that ran approximately ten minutes, resulting in several characters being shot and beaten. This episode also featured a montage of violent scenes, including police raids to catch the bad guys as well as another major gun battle."

There have been many studies about the effects of television violence on children. Research shows a number of facts:

1. Children in the United States Watch Many Hours of TV

According to the ACT Against Violence Project, on average, young children spend two to four hours per day watching television. They also spend thirty-five hours per week of screen time with TV or video games. The Kaiser Foundation reports that nearly all children in the United States (99 percent) live in homes with a TV set and one-third have a TV in their bedroom. "The vast majority of children are growing up in homes where television is a near-constant presence," writes the Kaiser Foundation in a report entitled "Zero to Six: Electronic Media in the Lives of Infants, Toddlers, and Preschoolers." (See Fig. 2.) 20

> Two-thirds of zero-to-six-year-olds (65 percent) live in a home where the TV is on at least half the time or more, even if no one is watching and one-third (36 percent) live in "heavy" TV households, where the television is left on "always" or "most of the time."

Figure 2.
(The Henry J. Kaiser Family Foundation, "Zero to Six: Electronic Media in the Lives of Infants, Toddlers, and Preschoolers," Fall 2003, p. 4)

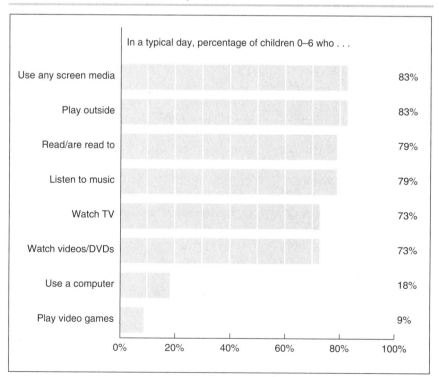

In a typical day, percentage of children 0–6 who . . .

Use any screen media	83%
Play outside	83%
Read/are read to	79%
Listen to music	79%
Watch TV	73%
Watch videos/DVDs	73%
Use a computer	18%
Play video games	9%

2. Violent Behavior Is a Learned Trait

Most psychologists agree that experiences children have during their early years will have a longstanding impact in their lives. "What a child learns about violence, a child learns for life," states ACT Against Violence. The organization breaks down the early years of TV viewing development this way:

INFANTS (0–18 MONTHS)

From birth to 18 months, infants are interested in TV only for brief periods of time because they are attracted to the light and sound.

TODDLERS (18–36 MONTHS)

They pay much more attention to what is on TV and are able to get meaning from programs they watch. They react equally to animated violence and real violence because their link between fantasy and reality is not strong.

PRESCHOOLERS (3–5 YEARS)

Children look forward to shows. They understand what they are viewing but cannot give it a context. They cannot judge reality versus fantasy or commercials versus regular programs. They are attracted to highly vivid scenes, rapid movement, sound, and color. In other words, most children pay the most attention to the most violent scenes on the screen.

ELEMENTARY SCHOOL AGE (6–11 YEARS)

Children believe that TV reflects real life and will become more active and show more aggressive behavior after viewing violent scenes. High viewing levels have been shown to interfere with reading development.

The Kaiser Foundation report states that 81 percent of parents have seen their children imitate either positive (e.g., sharing, helping) or aggressive (e.g., hitting, kicking) behaviors from TV. The report notes that overall, by the time children are six years old, nearly half (47 percent) the parents studied reported that their children imitated aggressive behaviors from TV.

A child's cognitive development during the early years is extremely important. ACT Against Violence explains that "young infants can imitate live models as well as what they see on TV, even without full understanding of their actions; they learn by watching and imitating others." Over the course of a child's first three years, the brain continues to grow and expand at a rapid pace. New nerve connections (called synapses), permit more complex methods of thinking, moving, and talking. Children learn a great deal about the world when they are young and base their future cognitive, motor, and emotional development by "mimicking" adults.

Children exposed to large doses of violent programming will give them violent heroes to imitate (and it doesn't matter if the TV character was *justified* to use violence). It will also show children that violence is the right way to handle conflicts and may also whet their appetite for viewing more violence. Violence usually begets more extreme forms of violence.

The American Psychological Association (APA) notes that research 25 shows that babies as young as twelve months will read and react to actors' emotions on television. The American Association of Pediatrics (AAP) recommends that children under two years old do not watch TV at all. An AAP policy statement asks pediatricians to "encourage more interactive activities [for infants] that will promote proper brain development, such as talking, playing, singing, and reading together."

3. Children Who Watch a Lot of Television Become Aggressive Adults

The most influential research released to date on this subject was published in March 2003. Researchers from the University of Michigan published their findings from a fifteen-year longitudinal study of 329 youths. It showed that men and women who watched violent TV programming as children were more inclined to show violent tendencies as adults.

"Results show that men who were high TV-violence viewers as children were significantly more likely to have pushed, grabbed, or shoved their spouses, to have responded to an insult by shoving a person, to have been convicted of a crime, and to have committed a moving traffic violation. Such men, for example, had been convicted of crimes at over three times the rate of other men," says the study entitled "Longitudinal Relations Between Children's Exposure to TV Violence and Their Aggressive and Violent Behavior in Young Adulthood: 1977–1992."

"Women who were high TV-violence viewers as children were more likely to have thrown something at their spouses, to have responded to someone who made them mad by shoving, punching, beating, or choking the person, to have committed some type of criminal act, and to have committed a moving traffic violation. Such women, for example, reported having punched, beaten, or choked another adult at over four times the rate of other women," says the report.

The report also proves that violent programs that probably have the most detrimental effects on a child's cognitive development are the ones where the hero is *justified* in being violent. "Violent scenes that children are most likely to model their behavior after are ones in which they identify with the perpetrator of the violence, the perpetrator is rewarded for the violence, and in which children perceive the scene as telling about life like it really is," according to the researchers. "Thus, a violent act by someone like Dirty Harry that results in a criminal being eliminated and brings glory to Harry is of more concern than a bloodier murder by a despicable criminal who is brought to justice."

The National Institute of Mental Health has identified three major ef- 30 fects of seeing violence on television:

- Children may become less sensitive to the pain and suffering of others.
- Children may be more fearful of the world around them.
- Children may be more likely to behave in aggressive or harmful ways toward others.

The extent to which these behaviors manifest themselves in a child can depend on other factors—environmental and parental. However, there is a lot of research showing a strong link between televised violence and its effect on children.

The APA notes that children exposed to a large dose of TV violence when they are young will be less aroused by violent scenes as teenagers. In general, the group notes that "they're less bothered by violence in general, and less likely to see anything wrong with it. One example: In several studies, those who watched a violent program instead of a nonviolent one were slower to intervene or to call for help when, a little later, they saw younger children fighting or playing destructively."

"Children who watch the violent shows, even 'just funny' cartoons, were more likely to hit out at their playmates, argue, disobey class rules, and leave tasks unfinished and were less willing to wait for things than those who watched the nonviolent programs," says a researcher commenting on a study done at the University of Pennsylvania.

The question for parents is *not* "Shouldn't entertainment media be less violent?" Whether for good or for bad, violent programming is popular and is here to stay. For adults, TV shows such as *The Sopranos, The Shield, 24,* or *Walker: Texas Ranger* are usually no big deal. Most adults can deal with fake televised violence in a mature manner.

The real question is how the *children* of today's world deal with being bombarded from nearly every entertainment outlet with an array of violent acts, situations, and language? What lessons are children learning about the world? Children are impressionable and look at TV and movies differently than adults. What is TV teaching?

"The amount and influence of violence on television has long been 35 the topic of study and national debate. For close to thirty years, dating from the 1960s to the Surgeon General's report in 1972, the National Institute of Mental Health report in 1982, and the American Psychological Association's report in 1992, more than 1,000 scientific studies have validated the premise that TV violence influences aggressive behavior in some children," writes a doctor from the American Association of Pediatrics.

Because television is our children's No. 1 leisure activity, we should not minimize the ongoing impact of its thousands of visual messages on children, especially those at risk for behavioral problems.

Modern television violence is so much more vivid than a play by William Shakespeare. Families must put limits on the amount of TV young children watch. "Children have fewer checks on primal violent urges than adults. As parents and pediatricians, we hope to contain and rechannel those urges. Unprotected use of media can warp psychological development that allows awareness of human suffering to control violent desires. Knowing media and how they work will allow children to recognize and direct their effects, to use them wisely, and to learn of human suffering through ways that allow them to grow up healthy and safe," says the AAP.

Though cable has its share of violent programming, the CMPA study found that of the 3,381 acts of violence in 284 series episodes it counted during its two week study period, 80 percent of the violence occurred on over-the-air broadcast TV (ABC, CBS, NBC, Fox, UPN, and the WB). "The simple fact . . . is that people watch programs. If the program is something they want to see, they will watch," said William F. Baker and George Dessart in their book *Down the Tube.* "Nothing can make people watch a television program they don't want to see."

Violent programming is obviously popular and commercial television is entirely based on gaining audience. "Commercial television is not in the business of presenting programs; commercial television is not in the business of selling advertising," write Baker and Dessart. "Nor is it in the business of selling time to advertisers. Commercial television is, quite simply, in the business of aggregating and then selling audiences. In its simplest terms, the business of television in this country is the buying and selling of eyeballs."

To a broadcaster, viewers are only numbers. Those numbers are then used to charge a sponsor and adjust advertising revenue. Television watchers, say the authors, only matter in respect to "how much the sponsor is willing to pay to reach any single viewer. Thus, in the marketplace model, programming has only one function: Each program must attract as many viewers as possible." It should go without saying, that television is not about performing a public service. TV networks are only concerned with making money.

The most important task for television networks is the creation and 40 cultivation of viewers. Violent shows are the most popular shows on television. For example, one of the consistently top rated shows on TV is the CBS crime drama *CSI (Crime Scene Investigation).* This program, ranked as the #1 worst show on television for families by the Parents Television Council, almost completely revolves around violence. "*CSI* [provides] graphic depictions of decaying bodies, grisly crime scenes, brutal murders, and themes of incest and sadomasochism," says the PTC. The group notes that during the 2002–2003 season, "episodes of *CSI* have included story lines about cannibalism, S&M sex clubs, and pornographic snuff films. Episodes this season have also contained scenes depicting a man receiving oral sex in an alley, the mutilated victims of a deranged killer, and a man in bed with two women." *CSI* and its spinoff show *CSI: Miami* are two of the top-rated shows on television. They regularly get Nielsen ratings between 13 and 14 which converts to around 15 million households.

Another ultraviolent show on television is NBC's *Kingpin*. Though only on the air for one season, *Kingpin*'s violence was almost unmatched. "*Kingpin* is centered on the criminal protagonist Miguel Cadena, a Mexican drug lord and troubled family man," explains the PTC. "In the six episodes that aired [in 2003], the PTC counted 16 raunchy depictions of sex, 23 murders, 8 depictions of torture, and 16 instances of drug use. In one particularly gruesome episode, a man is shown tossing a human leg to his pet tiger. . . . In yet another episode, a man is brutally beaten and then sodomized by a police officer."

Another popular but extremely violent show is Fox's *24*. Throughout the show's third season (2002–2003), *24* was regularly getting Nielsen ratings of 4.9 (5.1 among adults 18–49) which converts to around 5.3 million households. *New York Daily News* TV critic David Bianculli, who watches a lot of television, was shocked at the brutality on the program. "Kiefer Sutherland's Jack Bauer died at the end of Fox's *24* Tuesday, which may have shocked a lot of people (even though he could be revived). What shocked me was the way he died," explains Bianculli. "He was tortured for most of the show's hour, in some of the most disturbing and graphic depictions of violence I've ever seen on a broadcast network entertainment program. Bauer was hung naked from his wrists, with his mouth forced open by a bit gag. His skin was sliced with a scalpel, he was shocked with electrical current and Tasers, and his flesh was burned until parts of his body emitted smoke." Bianculli also notes that *24* plays on the old "good guys versus bad guys" theme which plagues most TV violence. "Those scenes were so disturbing to me precisely because the characters and the conflicts were credible enough to suck me in. These encounters with evil let us know just how bad the bad guys are in these cases, and how high the stakes can be."

Another TV critic, Matt Feeney, writes that *24* is a show entirely focused on graphic violence. He writes that *24* shows pain in the form of "brute physical agonies of gunshot wounds, heroin withdrawal, and radiation sickness." (In its real-time, single-day format, the show was poised to allow the daylong radiation death of one character to take an entire *24*-show season, but this hideous, closely observed demise was cut short two-thirds of the way through—in an irony of almost comic massiveness—by a nuclear explosion.) Then there is the torture, which occurs with astonishing regularity.

> On *24*, torture is less an unfortunate last resort than an epistemology.
> Whenever an urgent or sticky question of fact arises, someone—bad
> guy or good guy, terrorist or counterterror agent; it doesn't matter—au-
> tomatically sparks up the electrodes or starts filling syringes with seizure
> juice.

Fox scores another violent hit program with *The Shield*. Shown on the FX network, *The Shield* is another program whose entire plot is based on violence. The main character is a TV antihero similar to the Mafia-with-a-heart characters on HBO's *The Sopranos*. *The Shield*'s main character is Vic Mackey, "a crooked, bullying, and bigoted cop who is running his own drug operation within the Los Angeles Police Department," explains *Washington Post* TV critic Tom Shales. "Virtually every episode . . . [includes] scenes of extremely gory, graphic violence. During the opening credits of last week's season premiere, gang members murdered a police informant by putting a gasoline-soaked tire around his neck and lighting it. The screams of agony were chilling, as were shots of the body being consumed by flames," he explains.

> On tonight's show, a cocaine addict vomits blood copiously and, later in the show, the reckless Mackey mercilessly brutalizes a suspected gang leader — first by beating him so furiously that Mackey himself gets splattered in blood, then by forcing the man's face down, repeatedly, on a scalding hot plate.

Though some advertisers have pulled their spots from *The Shield* because of the intense violence, actor Michael Chiklis won an Emmy in 2002 for his work in the principal role.

Shales explains how *justifiable violence* is used in *The Shield* for dramatic effect. "Viewers are likely to find themselves rooting for the 'bad guy,' Mackey, who for all his contemptible traits often seems sympathetic. . . . Chiklis is skillful enough to show a trace of pathos behind the vindictiveness. . . . The good and honest cops, meanwhile, often come off as prudes, stuffed shirts, or spoilsports. CCH Pounder plays a cop who is diligent and tough, but Mackey's slick effectiveness, which includes beating confessions out of suspects, makes humane tactics seem naive or even quaint. Another 'good' cop in the precinct, played by Jay Karnes, comes across as a WASPy dork," writes Shales.

Of course, any discussion of violent TV must include the World Wrestling Federation. The WWF (now called WWE for World Wrestling Entertainment) has been around for decades. It is not a sport — it is not real. WWE wrestling is fake with outrageous acts of physical punishment. The WWE could be called comical or silly or even "mindless television entertainment." However, to say it is *not* violent is quite naive. The WWF is entirely based on physical violence, *machismo,* and blood. As with other violent programming, the WWE gets extremely high ratings: Primetime showings of *WWE Raw* on the Spike Network are some of the highest rated cable programs with around 3.5 million households watching (during the week of April 12, 2004, *WWE Raw Zone* tied for first place in ratings with the George W. Bush presidential news conference concerning the war in Iraq).

The National Institute on Media and the Family quotes a year long study (50 episodes, from 2/12/98 to 2/1/99) by Indiana University's De-

45

partment of Telecommunication of the World Wrestling Federation's *Raw Is War* program. The study recorded instances of sexual and violent interactions:

- crotch grabbing or pointing: 1,658 instances
- garbage cans, chairs, tables, and brooms used in wrestling: 609
- kicks to the groin: 273
- profane descriptions of people: 158
- obscene finger gesture: 157
- simulated sexual activity: 128
- scantily clad women: 70
- urinating (talking about/appearing to): 21

This is really only significant when one considers that 15 percent of the audience for wrestling shows (more than 1 million viewers) is eleven years old or younger.

Overall, only 10 percent of children's viewing time is spent watching TV designed for kids. The other 90 percent of the time is spent watching programs designed for adults (Iowa State University, "Getting Along: Taming the TV," Oct. 1999).

Violent television is popular and high ratings means more advertising revenue. However, a new study actually shows that ad recall is diminished when placed between a program with intense violence or sexual content. In a report called "Violence and Sex Impair Memory for Television Ads," researchers from Iowa State University found that both men and women had problems recalling a particular advertised brand when the content of the TV program showed graphic violence or sex. Their findings were consistent regardless of whether the viewer liked the program or not. "We suggest that sex and violence impair commercial memory because they consume attention and prompt sexual and violent thoughts, thus reducing the likelihood that the commercial message is encoded into long-term memory," says the report.

The study notes that because viewers have a limited amount of at- 50 tention to direct toward TV shows, if they are thinking about violence they are not absorbing commercials. Because violent programs are more engaging and "attention grabbing," advertising will get lost. "The more attentive individuals are toward a TV program, the less attentive capacity they have for the commercials embedded in the program," states the report.

Clearly, the violence shown in TV programs of today is far more graphic and disturbing than in the past. Television of today is gruesome and shocking—gone are the days of *The Lone Ranger, The Untouchables, Gunsmoke, The A-Team* or *Battlestar Galactica.* TV of the past is tame by comparison to today's programs. Part of the reason is that TV networks have been free to become as violent as possible, without any government oversight.

The United States Federal Communications Commission (FCC) is supposed to be the governmental body which holds networks accountable for their programming. The FCC is supposed to enforce the ban on violent programs during the prime time "Family Hour." However, currently there are no laws on the books prohibiting or restricting depictions of violence on television. The only types of broadcasts the FCC chooses to control are those which, in the words of the FCC, display "in a patently offensive way, sexual conduct specifically defined by applicable law." In the eyes of the FCC, breasts, genitalia, or one utterance of the word *fuck* will get maximum fines imposed on a TV network or station. However, murder and torture in a graphic manner can pass over the airwaves without comment.

In the end, however, even if the FCC took a responsible attitude toward televised violence, censorship is not the answer. Censorship is *never* the answer. TurnOffYourTV.com advocates choosing to not watch television — Turn Off *Your* TV and Kill *Your* TV. People should stop watching television because of its effects on the human body and its troubling content. The bottom line is that television is violent, and parents must use discretion to get control over the medium and not allow children to watch inappropriate programming. Only parental involvement, not the government, not a special computer chip, and certainly not the networks themselves will help the situation. The issue of TV violence is a matter of content and parental control.

So for your children . . . Turn Off Your TV!

Cultural Studies and "Forensic Noir"

THOMAS DOHERTY

BEFORE READING: Why are some of the most popular television shows graphic in their portrayal of the victims of crime? Do you personally like to watch the "forensic" dramas that focus on crime scene investigations and autopsies? Why or why not?

"Apparently, people will watch forensics seven nights a week," shrugs David Caruso, star of the hit show *CSI: Miami,* a spinoff of the hit show *CSI: Crime Scene Investigation.* Shilling for the series on Fox's *Pat Sajak Weekend* earlier this year, he cited a CBS survey indicating that autopsy-driven entertainment is the hottest trend in American popular culture. Indeed, avid morgue attendants may also tally up the body count on HBO's *Autopsy,* NBC's *Law & Order: Criminal Intent,* Court TV's *Forensic Files,* A&E's *Cold Case Files,* and, in a more mordant vein, HBO's *Six Feet Under.* As the current season gets under way, CBS also gives us the scientific and forensically flavored *Cold Case* and *Navy NCIS.*

All over television, it seems rigor mortis has become de rigueur.

The purest form of the genre has been dubbed "forensic noir," and already its conventions have hardened like a plaster mold on a femur. A phalanx of experts bearing tweezers and baggies mills around yellow police tape and scours the site for bits of evidence. Back at headquarters, men and women in white lab coats collate data and conduct microscopic analysis on blood, drugs, wood, paint, insects, dirt, metal, and anything else known to the periodic table of elements. The recurring close-ups show investigators sniffing the tips of their white-gloved fingers. Could this be dextromethorphan? Blindsided by science, the culprit is nailed, the case closed.

With such tantalizing roadkill littering the media landscape, one might have expected circling scholars to have already descended for a hermeneutical feast. However, forensic noir is not yet one of the dominant intellectual categories of early twenty-first-century scholarship. In fact, even the last meeting of the ultrahip Society for Cinema and Media Studies failed to devote a panel to the topic (although wait till next year), and the genre is still too new a phenomenon to inspire the title of a university-press book (heads up, Ph.D. students).

Thomas Doherty is an associate professor of film studies at Brandeis University and author of *Cold War, Cool Medium: Television, McCarthyism, and American Culture* (2003); *Pre-Code Hollywood: Sex, Immorality, and Insurrection in American Cinema, 1930–1934* (1999); *Projections of War: Hollywood, American Culture, and World War II* (1993); and *Teenagers & Teenpics: The Juvenilization of American Movies in the 1950s* (1988). This article appeared in the October 24, 2003, issue of *The Chronicle of Higher Education.*

Still, forensic noir has been anticipated and mapped by another kind of CSI   5
team: Cultural-Studies Intellectuals, a dauntless band of scholars committed to digging into the symbolic meanings of the corporeal body. Their
preliminary findings are likely to inform and guide future inquiries into a
genre that has single-handedly revitalized both the flat-lined formula of the
detective series and the flat ratings of prime-time network television.

Of course, the latest academic foray into criminal territory also par-
takes of a rich literary and cinematic tradition. From Victor Hugo to
Mario Puzo, the sordid denizens of the underworld have been rehabili-
tated as merely refracted images of mainstream values, figures whose deviant ways illuminate the greater deviance of a soul-destroying culture:
the Corleone family as the moral equivalents of the Rockefellers, only
with better cuisine. Like the televisual CSI teams, however, the agents of
cultural studies take the corpus delicti for their main text. The criminal
himself is interesting only insofar as he produces the body.

Any examination of the body-as-text within the groves of academe
begins with the high priest of high theory, Michel Foucault, the French
philosopher who died in 1984 but who lives on as the animating footnote
of the field. In his 1975 study *Discipline and Punish: The Birth of the Prison,*
Foucault cast a cold eye on "the power and knowledge relations that invest human bodies and subjugate them by turning them into objects of
knowledge." Brandishing the inevitable pun on the "body politic," he in-
spected bodies docile and tortured, under surveillance and under the
knife. Soon humanities scholars who were once enchanted by the sensu-
ous pulchritude of Renaissance nudes or the chiseled features of Hollywood stars embraced an altogether different body of scholarship. Now
their patients were not just etherized but embalmed upon a table.

Foucault's timing was dead-on for stateside consumption.

Just as his work was being translated and taught in graduate seminars,
a new criminal avatar was stalking the back roads of American culture,
pushing aside drug dealers, gang bangers, and rogue CIA agents as the villain of choice for popular entertainment: the serial killer. Unlike the outlaw of the Old West or the gangster of the urban frontier, the serial killer
struck at random, committed murder for no financial gain, and racked up
a double-digit body count with absolutely no remorse. Yet, as a product
of the mobility and anonymity of late twentieth-century life, he was a pe-
culiarly American figure, cruising the two-lane blacktops of the prairie,
picking up lone hitchhikers, and befriending truck-stop waitresses. No ordinary murderer, he seemed an almost supernatural creature of the night.

Although popular culture understood the new modus operandi im-   10
mediately, the flummoxed forces of law enforcement were slower on the
uptake. A predator who crossed state lines and murdered for reasons of
his own, the serial killer operated under the radar of traditional police
practices. The cops turned to the statistics and science of national data-
banks, criminal profilers, and crime labs with the forensic expertise to
link bodies to each other, and the killer to the bodies.

Using Foucault as a desk reference, an eclectic array of scholarship on pornography, horror, homicide, violent spectacle, and the delights of observing the same also looked anew at those bodies dead or alive. Linda Williams's pioneering *Hard Core: Power, Pleasure, and the "Frenzy of the Visible"* (University of California Press, 1989) and Carol J. Clover's *Men, Women, and Chain Saws: Gender in the Modern Horror Film* (Princeton University Press, 1992) scoped out the scene early; more recent entries include Mark I. Seltzer's *Serial Killers: Death and Life in America's Wound Culture* (Routledge, 1998), Philip L. Simpson's *Psycho Paths: Tracking the Serial Killer Through Contemporary American Film and Fiction* (Southern Illinois University Press, 2000), and Joel Black's *The Reality Effect: Film Culture and the Graphic Imperative* (Routledge, 2002).

By common consent, the famous curtain opener to Foucault's *Discipline and Punish*—an excruciating, play-by-play account of an execution by torture in eighteenth-century France—laid out the preferred method for surgical exegesis. However, it was Williams, a professor of film studies and rhetoric at the University of California at Berkeley, who introduced the elastic term "body genre" into the conversation, detecting an impulse at once voyeuristic and scientific behind cinematic spectatorship. "The desire to see and know more about the human body," she noted, "underlies the very invention of cinema." Although Williams's own lens was focused mainly on gender and pornography, her outlook suggests why the naked exposure of human organs, gushing fluids, and bodily penetration—scenes that comprise what might be called the "money shots" of forensic noir—are so ubiquitous.

This energetic body work is a far better test kit for tracing the tropes of forensic noir than the criticism on what may seem to be the TV fare's parent genre, film noir. Any kinship between the two noirs is only skin-deep. A moody mesh of German expressionism and French existentialism, film noir languishes in a cloud of smoky atmospherics and moral ambiguities, a lush dream world that, for all its dark tone and mean streets, has proved extraordinarily popular, even beloved. To take a classic example: In Robert Siodmak's fluorescent version of Ernest Hemingway's *The Killers* (1946), the investigator is obsessed with the *why* of a mysterious murder, not the how or even the who, when he seeks the motive for a contract hit, and the reason the victim accepted his own execution with such stoic resignation. More a mutant offspring than a direct descendent, forensic noir retains the mystery and murder but rejects the hopeless surrender to the forces of fate that waft through film noir.

Besides, bio-labs and operating rooms require bright lighting, high-tech implements, and smoke-free conditions. Film noir is hard-boiled, resigned, and romantic; forensic noir is air-conditioned, tenacious, and scientific. Film noir is body heat; forensic noir is body stiff. Quoting the film critic André Bazin, Indiana University's James Naremore, in his elegant study *More Than Night: Film Noir and its Contexts* (University of

California Press, 1998), reminds us that, for the French critics who first embraced Hollywood's "black" films—a generation woozy on Sartre, unfiltered Gitanes, and postwar angst—Humphrey Bogart was an existential icon because the alcoholic lines visible on his face revealed "the corpse on reprieve within all of us." The icon of forensic noir gets his philosophy from the *Physician's Desk Reference,* cuts into too many charcoal-filled lungs to think smoking is cool, and succumbs to existential angst only when a rookie cop contaminates the crime scene.

Similarly, though rooted in vintage police procedurals such as Jack   15 Webb's just-the-facts-ma'am *Dragnet* (1951–59, 1967–70) and Quinn Martin's *The F.B.I.* (1965–74), and glimpsed in sanitized form in *Quincy* (1976–83), forensic noir can be readily distinguished from its generic ancestors. It is marked by two obsessions: a superstitious faith in better detecting through chemistry and a ghoulish relish in the rituals of medical dissection. Unlike the hero of the classic police shows, the rule-breaking maverick who played hunches and infuriated the by-the-book captain, the forensic cop is a clinical practitioner of the scientific method, at home amid the sinks, slabs, and scalpels of the morgue. The *locus classicus* for the genre is the scene in *The Silence of the Lambs* (1991), when the FBI profiler Jack Crawford and the trainee Clarice Starling spread Vicks VapoRub under their nostrils to examine a decomposed corpse, the victim of a serial killer. On television, the model was *The X Files* (1993–2002), where another pair of FBI agents—he an excitable agent provocateur, she a level-headed pathologist—spent almost a decade probing and being probed by swarms of extraterrestrial species.

In addition to the usual comforts of serial narrative soothingly resolved in a fixed time frame, forensic noir provides a crash course in the genetic ingenuity of real-life crime fighting, a vocation that is increasingly a matter of fibers, microbes, and DNA. Whether at the FBI or on *CSI,* the emblematic clue is no longer the matchbook cover but saliva or semen, a telltale trace that cracks the case once the results come back from the lab. Significantly, though, the boundless faith in forensic experts is confined to matters after the fact: So resourceful during the crime-scene sweep, the new FBI-*CSI* team has little predictive ability. Quite literally, their skill is all postmortem.

However, once the body is bagged and tagged, forensic noir lives up to its name. Corpses on slabs appear as featured players while body parts and bone fragments serve as set design. The trademark gag shows the coroner digging into his work while munching a slice of pizza. The rookie agent chokes; the home audience smirks. In *The Reality Effect,* Black, a professor of comparative literature at the University of Georgia, finds it unsurprising that a mass-mediated audience awash in spectacles of virtual reality should seek a jolt of flesh-and-blood reality in a "return to art's primitive, ritual originals—to 'regress' from a sublimated aesthetic of ideas and contemplation to an aesthetic of cruelty and sensation."

Innovations in special-effects technology have heightened the impact of the anatomy lessons. CGI (computer-generated imagery) and grisly makeup mock-ups can now render the most grotesque eviscerations with stomach-churning verisimilitude. To enhance the mood, the dissections are accompanied by the buzz of a surgical saw cutting through bone and the whoosh of blood splattering onto a face mask. The camera then zooms in for a traveling shot through the corridors of a human orifice— ears, nose, mouth, you get the picture.

The fixation on the body of the victim represents a telling shift away from the former site of detective work, the mind of the murderer. As with university budget lines, the sure payoffs from the hard sciences have channeled investments away from the uncertain returns of the soft sciences. Preferring pathology to psychology, forensic detectives admit that human motives are beyond their ken.

Where once crime dramas confidently dragged out sociologists and 20 psychologists to offer reassuring explanations for criminal deviance— think of the shrink in the coda to Alfred Hitchcock's *Psycho* (1960)—even liberal Hollywood has given up the quest for a Freudian magic bullet to help comprehend the killer. Unable either to prevent crime, or to understand the criminal, the heroes of forensic noir settle for matching up DNA. They seek closure more than justice; catching the killer is a bonus.

Another even darker cultural impulse may also account for the proliferation of forensic noir. "This knowledge and this mastery constitute what might be called the political technology of the body," declared the chief coroner himself in *Discipline and Punish*. The intrusions of a surveillance society find an apt metaphor in violations of the body conducted by curious technicians. In probing, prying, and cutting into the citizen's no-longer-private parts, the state asserts its ultimate power over the individual, a kind of unanswerable last tag.

How much more can viewers stomach? How much further can television test the limits of forensic noir? In London last year, a doctor conducted a public autopsy for the delectation of a crowd of paying spectators. In the United States, a television producer may already be pitching a high-concept show that will combine the current obsession with a more traditional fixation: *Celebrity Autopsy.*

TV Isn't Violent Enough

MIKE OPPENHEIM

BEFORE READING: Think about some of the violent movies or TV shows you have seen recently. Were you genuinely frightened by their depictions of violence? Did the pictures of the destruction of the World Trade Center towers on September 11, 2001, frighten you in a different way?

Caught in an ambush, there's no way our hero (Matt Dillon, Eliot Ness, Kojak, Hoss Cartwright . . .) can survive. Yet, visibly weakening, he blazes away, and we suspect he'll pull through. Sure enough, he's around for the final clinch wearing the traditional badge of the honorable but harmless wound: a sling.

As a teenager with a budding interest in medicine, I knew this was nonsense and loved to annoy my friends with the facts.

"Aw, the poor guy! He's crippled for life!"

"What do you mean? He's just shot in the shoulder."

"That's the worst place! Vital structures everywhere. There's the blood 5 supply for the arm: axillary artery and vein. One nick and you can bleed to death on the spot."

"So he was lucky."

"OK. If it missed the vessels it hit the brachial plexus: the nerve supply. Paralyzes his arm for life. He's gotta turn in his badge and apply for disability."

"So he's *really* lucky."

"OK. Missed the artery. Missed the vein. Missed the nerves. Just went through the shoulder joint. But joint cartilage doesn't heal so well. A little crease in the bone leaves him with traumatic arthritis. He's in pain the rest of his life—stuffing himself with codeine, spending his money on acupuncture and chiropractors, losing all his friends because he complains all the time. . . . Don't ever get shot in the shoulder. It's the end. . . ."

Today, as a physician, I still sneer at TV violence, though not because 10 of any moral objection. I enjoy a well-done scene of gore and slaughter as well as the next viewer, but "well-done" is something I rarely see on a typical evening in spite of the plethora of shootings, stabbings, muggings, and brawls. Who can believe the stuff they show? Anyone who remembers high-school biology knows the human body can't possibly respond to violent trauma as it's usually portrayed.

On a recent episode, Matt Houston is at a fancy resort, on the trail of a vicious killer who specializes in knifing beautiful women in their hotel

---

When this essay was published in the February 11, 1984, issue of *TV Guide*, Mike Oppenheim was a freelance writer and physician practicing medicine in California.

rooms in broad daylight. The only actual murder sequence was in the best of taste: all the action off screen, the flash of a knife, moans on the sound track.

In two scenes, Matt arrives only minutes too late. The hotel is alerted, but the killer's identity remains a mystery. Absurd! It's impossible to kill someone instantly with a knife thrust—or even render him unconscious. Several minutes of strenuous work are required to cut enough blood vessels so the victim bleeds to death. Tony Perkins in *Psycho* gave an accurate, though abbreviated, demonstration. Furthermore, anyone who has watched an inexperienced farmhand slaughter a pig knows that the resulting mess must be seen to be believed.

If consulted by Matt Houston, I'd have suggested a clue: "Keep your eyes peeled for someone panting with exhaustion and covered with blood. That might be your man."

Many Americans were puzzled at the films of the assassination attempt on President Reagan. Shot in the chest, he did not behave as TV had taught us to expect ("clutch chest, stagger backward, collapse"). Only after he complained of a vague chest pain and was taken to the hospital did he discover his wound. Many viewers assumed Mr. Reagan is some sort of superman. In fact, there was nothing extraordinary about his behavior. A pistol is certainly a deadly weapon, but not predictably so. Unlike a knife wound, one bullet can kill instantly—provided it strikes a small area at the base of the brain. Otherwise, it's no different: a matter of ripping and tearing enough tissue to cause death by bleeding. Professional gangland killers understand the problem. They prefer a shotgun at close range.

The trail of quiet corpses left by TV's good guys, bad guys, and assorted 15 ill-tempered gun owners is ridiculously unreal. Firearms reliably produce pain, bleeding, and permanent, crippling injury (witness Mr. Reagan's press secretary, James Brady: shot directly in the brain but very much alive). For a quick, clean death, they are no match for Luke Skywalker's light saber.

No less unreal is what happens when T. J. Hooker, Magnum, or a Simon brother meets a bad guy in manly combat. Pow! Our hero's fist crashes into the villain's head. Villain reels backward, tipping over chairs and lamps, finally falling to the floor, unconscious. Handshakes all around. . . . Sheer fantasy! After hitting the villain, our hero would shake no one's hand. He'd be too busy waving his own about wildly, screaming with the pain of a shattered fifth metacarpal (the bone behind the fifth knuckle), an injury so predictable it's called the "boxer's fracture." The human fist is far more delicate than the human skull. In any contest between the two, the fist will lose.

The human skull is tougher than TV writers give it credit. Clunked with a blunt object, such as the traditional pistol butt, most victims would not fall conveniently unconscious for a few minutes. More likely, they'd suffer a nasty scalp laceration, be stunned for a second or two, then be extremely upset. I've sewn up many. A real-life, no-nonsense criminal with a blackjack (a piece of iron weighing several pounds) has a much better success rate. The result is a large number of deaths and permanent damage from brain hemorrhage.

Critics of TV violence claim it teaches children sadism and cruelty. I honestly don't know whether or not TV violence is harmful, but if so the critics have it backward. Children can't learn to enjoy cruelty from the neat, sanitized mayhem on the average series. There isn't any! What they learn is far more malignant: that guns or fists are clean, efficient, exciting ways to deal with a difficult situation. Bang!—you're dead! Bop!—you're unconscious (temporarily)!

"Truth-in-advertising" laws eliminated many absurd commercial claims. I often daydream about what would happen if we had "truth in violence"—if every show had to pass scrutiny by a board of doctors who had no power to censor but could insist that any action scene have at least a vague resemblance to medical reality ("Stop the projector! . . . You have your hero waylaid by three Mafia thugs who beat him brutally before he struggles free. The next day he shows up with this cute little Band-aid over his eyebrow. We can't pass that. You'll have to add one eye swollen shut, three missing front teeth, at least twenty stitches over the lips and eyes, and a wired jaw. Got that? Roll 'em . . .").

Seriously, real-life violence is dirty, painful, bloody, disgusting. It 20 causes mutilation and misery, and it doesn't solve problems. It makes them worse. If we're genuinely interested in protecting our children, we should stop campaigning to "clean up" TV violence. It's already too antiseptic. Ironically, the problem with TV violence is: It's not violent enough.

By permission of Mike Luckovich and Creators Syndicate, Inc.

Hollow Claims about Fantasy Violence

RICHARD RHODES

> BEFORE READING: As you grow older, does violence in the media appeal to you
> more — or less? Can you account for your reactions?

The moral entrepreneurs are at it again, pounding the entertainment industry for advertising its Grand Guignolesque[1] confections to children. If exposure to this mock violence contributes to the development of violent behavior, then our political leadership is justified in its indignation at what the Federal Trade Commission has reported about the marketing of violent fare to children. Senators John McCain and Joseph Lieberman have been especially quick to fasten on the FTC report as they make an issue of violent offerings to children.

[1] Grand Guignol, a popular theater founded in Paris in 1897 to present graphic performances of crimes—EDS.

Richard Rhodes is the author of more than two dozen books, including *The Making of the Atomic Bomb* (1986), which won a Pulitzer Prize for nonfiction, and *Why They Kill: The Discoveries of a Maverick Criminologist* (1999). The *New York Times* printed this article on September 17, 2000.

But is there really a link between entertainment and violent behavior?

The American Medical Association, the American Psychological Association, the American Academy of Pediatrics, and the National Institutes of Mental Health all say yes. They base their claims on social science research that has been sharply criticized and disputed within the social science profession, especially outside the United States. In fact, no direct, causal link between exposure to mock violence in the media and subsequent violent behavior has ever been demonstrated, and the few claims of modest correlation have been contradicted by other findings, sometimes in the same studies.

History alone should call such a link into question. Private violence has been declining in the West since the media-barren late Middle Ages, when homicide rates are estimated to have been ten times what they are in Western nations today. Historians attribute the decline to improving social controls over violence—police forces and common access to courts of law—and to a shift away from brutal physical punishment in child-rearing (a practice that still appears as a common factor in the background of violent criminals today).

The American Medical Association has based its endorsement of the media violence theory in major part on the studies of Brandon Centerwall, a psychiatrist in Seattle. Dr. Centerwall compared the murder rates for whites in three countries from 1945 to 1974 with numbers for television set ownership. Until 1975, television broadcasting was banned in South Africa, and "white homicide rates remained stable" there, Dr. Centerwall found, while corresponding rates in Canada and the United States doubled after television was introduced. 5

A spectacular finding, but it is meaningless. As Franklin E. Zimring and Gordon Hawkins of the University of California at Berkeley subsequently pointed out, homicide rates in France, Germany, Italy, and Japan either failed to change with increasing television ownership in the same period or actually declined, and American homicide rates have more recently been sharply declining despite a proliferation of popular media outlets—not only movies and television, but also video games and the Internet.

Other social science that supposedly undergirds the theory, too, is marginal and problematic. Laboratory studies that expose children to selected incidents of televised mock violence and then assess changes in the children's behavior have sometimes found more "aggressive" behavior after the exposure—usually verbal, occasionally physical.

But sometimes the control group, shown incidents judged not to be violent, behaves more aggressively afterward than the test group; sometimes comedy produces the more aggressive behavior; and sometimes there's no change. The only obvious conclusion is that sitting and watching television stimulates subsequent physical activity. Any kid could tell you that.

As to those who claim that entertainment promotes violent behavior by desensitizing people to violence, the British scholar Martin Barker offers this critique: "Their claim is that the materials they judge to be harmful can only influence us by trying to make us be the same as them. So horrible things will make us horrible—not horrified. Terrifying things will make us terrifying—not terrified. To see something aggressive makes us feel aggressive—not aggressed against. This idea is so odd, it is hard to know where to begin in challenging it."

Even more influential on national policy has been a twenty-two year 10 study by two University of Michigan psychologists, Leonard D. Eron and L. Rowell Huesmann, of boys exposed to so-called violent media. The Telecommunications Act of 1996, which mandated the television V-chip, allowing parents to screen out unwanted programming, invoked these findings, asserting, "Studies have shown that children exposed to violent video programming at a young age have a higher tendency for violent and aggressive behavior later in life than children not so exposed."

Well, not exactly. Following 875 children in upstate New York from third grade through high school, the psychologists found a correlation between a preference for violent television at age eight and aggressiveness at age eighteen. The correlation—0.31—would mean television accounted for about 10 percent of the influences that led to this behavior. But the correlation only turned up in one of three measures of aggression: the assessment of students by their peers. It didn't show up in students' reports about themselves or in psychological testing. And for girls, there was no correlation at all.

Despite the lack of evidence, politicians can't resist blaming the media for violence. They can stake out the moral high ground confident that the First Amendment will protect them from having to actually write legislation that would be likely to alienate the entertainment industry. Some use the issue as a smokescreen to avoid having to confront gun control.

But violence isn't learned from mock violence. There is good evidence—causal evidence, not correlational—that it's learned in personal violent encounters, beginning with the brutalization of children by their parents or their peers.

The money spent on all the social science research I've described was diverted from the National Institute of Mental Health budget by reducing support for the construction of community mental health centers. To this day there is no standardized reporting system for emergency-room findings of physical child abuse. Violence is on the decline in America, but if we want to reduce it even further, protecting children from real violence in their real lives—not the pale shadow of mock violence—is the place to begin.

"Bang": Guns, Rap, and Silence

JAY NORDLINGER

BEFORE READING: Do you think music can influence behavior as well as emotion?

A lot of people were interested in the Sean "Puffy" Combs trial: fans of rap music; celebrity-watchers; connoisseurs of popular culture. But one group of people showed no interest whatsoever: gun-control activists. This was rather strange—a dog that didn't bark. The Combs case was awash in guns; so is Combs's world—that of rap, or "hip-hop." But the gun-controllers prefer to ignore this dark corner. Their indifference, or passivity, may be taken to represent a broader failure of liberalism to confront ghetto culture—to look it in the eye and cry, "No!"

Combs—known as "Puff Daddy"—is a major figure in rap, the boss of a record label called "Bad Boy." (Another label is called "Murder, Inc."—one refreshing thing about the rappers is their lack of pretense.) The Combs case dominated New York at the beginning of this year, the trial of a century that is still very young. What happened is this: In December 1999, Combs visited a nightclub with his girlfriend (the pop star Jennifer Lopez), a few "associates," and several of his guns. Someone insulted Combs. Shooting broke out. Three people were injured, two of them badly. Then Combs and his group fled the scene. When the police finally caught up with the getaway car—or rather, the getaway Lincoln Navigator SUV—they found two guns. Combs was subsequently charged with illegal weapons possession and bribery (he had tried to get his driver to accept responsibility for the guns). The rapper's guilt seemed clear, but he denied everything.

In a now-de rigueur move, Combs hired Johnnie Cochran, the O.J. lawyer, who composed a few new rhymes and flashed his smile at the jury. Combs got off. One of those "associates," however, was not so lucky: Jamal "Shyne" Barrow—a rapper described as Combs's protégé—was found guilty of first-degree assault. He now faces twenty-five years in prison.

So, another day, another rap case—this time, no one died. It's easy to look away from rap and its nature. But it should not be so, and it certainly shouldn't be so for gun-controllers. Thug rappers should be their worst nightmare (and a lot of other people's). Yet the antigun activists would rather go after Charlton Heston, rednecks, and other soft targets. It's far more comfortable to torment the NRA, which advocates not only gun rights but gun safety, than to get in the faces of "gangsta" rappers, who

---

Jay Nordlinger is the managing editor of the *National Review*, where this article appeared on April 16, 2001.

glory in guns and gun violence in song after song after song. Most people, by now, are familiar with rap's hideous and constant degradation of women (where are the feminists, incidentally?). They are less familiar with rap's celebration of the gun. Back in 1992, there was a brief furor over a rap called "Cop Killer." The idea of gunning down policemen is certainly an attention-getter. But if rappers are enthusing only about killing one another, that seems to be another matter, something to be swept under the rug.

Liberals have occasionally been interested in this subject. Tipper and 5 Al Gore were, before Hollywood bit their heads off. Usually, though, when you try to interest liberals in the horrors of today's worst music, they roll their eyes and recall how their parents railed against "Elvis's pelvis." Ah, the two magic words: "Elvis's pelvis." Say them, and you shut down any discussion about, for example, rap's effects on the young. And doesn't every generation murmur, with a sigh and a shake of the head, "Kids today . . . ."? But any sensate being can see that "gangsta" rap— with its sanction, even urging, of rape, murder, and other abuse—has nothing at all in common with Elvis Presley's swaying hips. It must be, in part, a fear of uncoolness—of fogeydom—that keeps many people from coming to grips with rap. They are perfectly happy to claim that the sight of Joe Camel causes millions of young'uns to smoke cigarettes; but they are reluctant to consider what rap—poured constantly into young ears— might do.

The Object of Their Affections

Rappers sing of guns with almost lascivious glee. They express close to an erotic feeling about their "pieces": "glocks" (for the Austrian manufacturer), "gats" (short for Gatlings), "nines" or "ninas" (for 9-mm pistols), and so on in a long and chilling lexicon. Bullets and clips are lingered over as eyes and lips might be in love songs. Here's a sample from "Trigga Gots No Heart" by the rapper Spice 1: "Caps [bullets] peel from gangsters in my 'hood. You better use that nina 'cause that deuce-deuce [.22-caliber weapon] ain't no good, and I'm taking up a hobby, maniac murderin', doin' massacre robbery." There is no end of material like this. The rapper Notorious B.I.G., slain by gun in 1997, sang, "Somebody's gotta die. Let the gunshots blow. Somebody's gotta die. Nobody gotta know that I killed yo' a** in the midst, kid." And, "Don't fill them clips too high. Give them bullets room to breathe. Damn, where was I?" Dr. Dre had a hit called "Rat-Tat-Tat-Tat," whose refrain went, "Never hesitate to put a nigga on his back. Rat-tat-tat-tat to the tat like that, and I never hesitate to put a nigga on his back."

During the Combs trial, some thought that Shyne Barrow's lyrics would do the young man no good. They are horrible, but since millions of kids drink them in, their parents might as well know them, too. In "Bad Boyz," Barrow raps, "Now tell me, who wanna f*** with us? Ashes to ashes, dust to dust. I bang—and let your f***in' brains hang. . . . My point is double-fours [a .44 magnum] at your f***in' jaws, pointed hollow point sh** [this is bullet terminology], four point six [?], need I say more? Or do you get the point, b**ch?" In another track — "Bang" — he says, "Niggas wanna bang. We could bang out till the clip's done, or your vital arteries hang out." And: "Got my mind right, like Al Pacino and Nino. I head to Capitol Hill to kidnap Janet Reno. Words droppin' and shockin', guns cockin' and poppin', somebody call Cochran" (that would be the lawyer Johnnie — life imitating art, or is it the other way around?). Barrow continues, "No time to waste, nine in my waist, ready for war, any time, any place. F*** it, just another case."

Are these words meant to be taken seriously, or are they just play — disturbing, maybe, but basically harmless? Shyne Barrow did, indeed, have a "nine in his waist" at that nightclub, and it appears to have been luck that he didn't kill the people he hit. Moral relativism, however, is rife in discussion about rap (such as it is). Barrow's lawyer, Murray Richman, made the following, delicious comment to the *New York Post* last December: "Dostoyevsky wrote about murder — does that implicate him as a murderer?" Or "when Eartha Kitt salaciously sings 'Santa, Baby,' does that mean she really wants to sleep with Santa Claus?" This sort of statement is meant to be a conversation-stopper, like "Elvis's pelvis." You know: Dostoyevsky, Eartha Kitt, Shyne Barrow — artists all, and liable to be misunderstood by the conservative and hung-up. "Kids today . . ." — ha ha.

Now, gun-control groups are concerned — and why shouldn't they be? — with laws and loopholes and gun shows and accidents in homes and Charlton Heston and, of course, school shootings, out of which they make hay. They say nothing about hip-hop culture, and next to nothing about popular culture generally. The groups put out a steady stream of press releases: praising states' "safety initiatives," trying to shame manufacturers, worrying about "children's health." In fact, they seem to burrow into every nook and cranny of American life — but keep mum about the ghetto and its anthems.

Nancy Hwa is spokesman for Handgun Control, Inc. (the Jim and   10
Sarah Brady group). She says that her organization has "called on people in the creative industry not to glamorize guns" but has not dealt with hip-hop in particular. "Other targets have a more direct relationship with getting your hands on guns," she says — for example, "sales at gun shows." And no one group, she sensibly points out, can cover everything. Plus, "when it comes right down to it, you can listen to rap or Marilyn Manson or country music, and, in the end, as long as the young person can't get their hands on a gun, all they're guilty of is questionable taste in music." For Handgun Control, Inc., the issue is "access," plain and simple.

Ted Pascoe speaks for Do It for the Kids!, a gun-control group in Colorado. "We don't address it," he says of the rap issue. "We have enough trouble with the Second Amendment without attacking the First as well."

Meaning? "Well, there is a perception in this country that individuals enjoy the protections conferred by the Second Amendment. But that amendment only confers on states the right to maintain militias. So the individual has no standing in court to make Second Amendment claims. However, Americans tend to believe they *do* have the right to bear arms. So, it's troublesome, because whenever you start talking about passing stronger gun laws, a lot of folks—even if they're not involved in the issue, or vested in it—can invoke the Second Amendment and sometimes effectively take the wind out of your sails." A stance against rap, says Pascoe, would only bring trouble: "The large number of gun-control groups don't want to be seen as attacking every element in the Constitution, or more than one. I think that the First Amendment contains rights that we *do* enjoy—that individuals have First Amendments rights."

The confusion of rights and responsibilities of "what you got a right to do and what is right to do," as the supreme fogey Bill Bennett puts it—is an old one.

Andy Pelosi, who represents New Yorkers against Gun Violence, says that his group "really focuses on legislative issues—we've done a little bit of violence in the media, but not rap." He makes the point that "it would be unfair to look at one genre without looking at the others. You could make a case about heavy metal, alternative rock—you wouldn't want to single out just rap." This would, indeed, be a painful step for most liberals. It would involve a clash of their pieties: gun control—outright demonization of the gun—and a taboo against taking issue with black culture in any of its aspects. The old "No enemies to the left" might mingle with a new slogan: "No enemies among blacks" (with Clarence Thomas and the other Toms excepted, of course).

"Silence Kills"

The country is engaged in a great debate over gun control; but there should be no disagreement about the awfulness—why not go all the way? the evil—of the most violent, dehumanizing, and desensitizing rap. The inner city is bleeding from gun crime. White America should probably think harder about the perpetual Columbines taking place in ghettos. Of course, many excuse rap on grounds that it merely reflects life on the mean streets. And whether this stuff has bloody consequences is an open question. In 1993, a rapper called Masta Ace, talking to the *St. Petersburg Times,* said, "It's like a Schwarzenegger movie—you don't come out wanting to shoot anybody." But he quickly had a second thought: "I think it does shape mentalities and helps develop a callousness to where you could really shoot somebody and not think twice about it."

Sure: There's only so much a gun-control group or conservative 15 alarm-raisers or anyone else can do about (what might be termed) hate rap. But activists, who love to talk—it is their principal activity—might at least talk. A group called the Campus Alliance to End Gun Violence proclaims as its number-one position, "Gun violence disproportionately preys on the young. Silence kills. We must speak." Well, all right: Minus a right-wing militia or two, there is only one class of people—an extremely wealthy and popular class of people—that actually *exalts* gun violence. So . . . ?

Violence Never Solved Anything, but It's Entertaining

HOLMAN W. JENKINS JR.

BEFORE READING: In watching a violent TV show or movie, would your pleasure be reduced if the bad guys won? Why?

The stock market is jittery. Poverty stares us in the face. At least we still have violent programming on TV, but some would take even this solace away from us.

A debatable sociological wisdom crept into the law with the 1996 Telecommunications Act. Children who watch violent television are at risk of becoming aggressive and violent themselves. Adults who steep themselves in the local news develop an exaggerated fear of the world, the so-called mean world syndrome.

As one of the many scholars plying this vein has noted approvingly, "policymakers are taking the position that television programmers should provide warnings to make viewers aware of the risks of watching certain shows." Because we are programmed by TV, we need the V-chip to reprogram our programmer.

Certainly television has wrought changes in the world, but before asking how it has reshaped human nature, how has human nature shaped television?

Since it became popular to denounce the "wasteland" in the early   5 1950s, surprisingly few have asked basic questions about the supply and demand for violent programming. The standard critique assumes supply without demand: The audience is dumbly trapped before the show, which is calculated to lift them to a higher state of "arousal" in order to become more receptive to the messages of advertisers.

Now we have the benefit of an economist looking at all this, James Hamilton of Duke, whose new book is *Channeling Violence: The Economic Market for Violent Television Programming.*

It turns out that broadcasters are neither as dumb nor as smart as the standard critique paints them. Pollsters constantly reiterate that Ameri-

---

Holman W. Jenkins Jr. writes the Business World column for the *Wall Street Journal*. This column appeared on October 28, 1998.

cans find TV "too violent," but combing more finely through the data one finds a substantial minority of dissenters, the people who actually watch violent TV. In Nielsen speak, these are males age eighteen to thirty-four, females age eighteen to thirty-four, and then males age thirty-five to forty-nine. There is demand after all, and it comes from young adults of both sexes.

That broadcasters are prepared to oblige them is no mystery. These viewers are advertisers' most valuable and elusive demographic group. Young adults are out building lives and careers. They are just developing the brand attachments that will last a lifetime but are seldom to be found in front of a TV where marketers can reach them.

Advertisers pay richly to reach youthful consumers. Ted Turner, who can often be heard denouncing television violence from a podium, has given us Saturday Night Nitro on TNT—whole evenings of delicious violence aimed at young adult viewers. Even when competing against *Monday Night Football,* 65 percent of the movies on TNT contained violence. The rest of the year 92 percent contained violence.

Mr. Hamilton says broadcasters don't aim their violence at younger children, and advertisers don't reward broadcasters for young children in the audience. Their viewing is an "externality," like pollution. But someone might have said the same about adult viewers back when the Big Three networks forced everyone to sit through the same programs. 10

Thanks to technology and the proliferation of channels, audiences have been freed to go their separate ways. Cable, especially premium cable, has become the violence medium, while violence has dropped steeply on the major networks.

The action-adventure genre has all but disappeared, with the sorry exceptions of CBS's *Walker, Texas Ranger* and ABC's new *Vengeance Unlimited.* The networks base their survival hopes on compiling the last large audiences in television-land, so they fill up our evenings with news-magazines and sitcoms—shows that attract young people without driving other viewers out of the room.

Why does the younger demographic have a special taste for violent programming? We can at least speculate.

Dolf Zillmann, a psychologist at the University of Alabama, has been one of the few paying attention to the viewer's perspective. Among his several contributions, he has shown that teenagers swarm to horror flicks so the boys can demonstrate their manly unflappability and girls can demonstrate their vulnerable desirability. Boys and girls who fulfill these roles are rated as more sexually desirable by their peers.

Young people, as they set about making room for themselves in the world, are especially full of anxiety about whether good guys or bad guys triumph in the end. Nor are they burdened unduly by a sense of proportionality. Mr. Zillmann points to a program in which a lawyer cheats an old lady out of her savings. The audience's sense of poetic justice is no less fulfilled by "seeing him burn and die in a crash" than seeing him receive a fine and disbarment. 15

Mr. Hamilton, the economist, supplies buttressing evidence when you consider that the young are less discriminating in matters of taste. Unsurprisingly, the more stars *TV Guide* awards a film, the less violent the film is likely to be. Violent shows are often bad shows. A lousy producer working with a bunch of mediocre writers and actors is going to resort to cloddish violence to dramatize what would otherwise have to be rendered by more literary means.

Criminologists have long noted that homicide becomes rarer among elite social groups as those groups make greater use of lawyers. TV seems to be evolving in the same direction. Lawyer shows are proliferating on the networks. Boilerplate courtroom drama may be replacing shoot-em-up as the preferred formula for resolving conflict.

Those who worry about television may sincerely dream of society becoming a nicer, less competitive place. Children do sometimes mow down their school chums, acting out a scene they may have seen on cable. But claiming we have to reprogram the media watched by 99.99 percent of us to influence the behavior of 0.01 percent is to be rendered helpless by a much smaller problem.

Only sick minds are interested in plotless violence. A British censor once explained his methods by saying he made certain cuts "because we were worried about a very few people who might be vulnerable to being influenced by playing one particular scene in that video repeatedly in their home."

These "very few people" surely exist in the audience, but making tele- 20 vision the issue only avoids the question of how we could be doing a better job of identifying the homicidally mentally ill before someone gets hurt.

A Desensitized Society Drenched in Sleaze

JEFF JACOBY

> BEFORE READING: What's the difference between the violence depicted in popular movies and described in the lyrics of some rap songs and the violence portrayed in *Macbeth* or a classic Greek play like *Oedipus Rex*?

I was seventeen years old when I first saw an X-rated movie. It was Thanksgiving in Washington, D.C. My college dorm had all but emptied out for the holiday weekend. With no classes, no tests, and nobody around, I decided to scratch an itch that had long been tormenting me.

I used to see these movies advertised in the old *Washington Star*, and—like any seventeen-year-old boy whose sex life is mostly theoret-

---

Jeff Jacoby is a columnist for the *Boston Globe,* where this essay appeared on June 8, 1995.

ical—I burned with curiosity. I wondered what such films might be like, what awful, thrilling secrets they might expose.

And so that weekend I took myself to see one. Full of anticipation, nervous and embarrassed, I walked to the Casino Royale at 14th Street and New York Avenue. At the top of a long flight of stairs, a cashier sat behind a cage. "Five dollars," he demanded—steep for my budget, especially since a ticket to the movies in the late seventies usually cost $3.50. But I'd come this far and couldn't turn back. I paid, I entered, I watched.

For about twenty minutes. The movie, I still remember, was called *Cry for Cindy,* and what I saw on the screen I'd never seen—I'd never even imagined—before. A man and a woman, oral sex, extreme closeups. The sheer gynecological explicitness of it jolted me. Was *this* the forbidden delight hinted at by those ads? This wasn't arousing, it was repellent. I was shocked. More than that: I was ashamed.

I literally couldn't take it. I bolted the theater and tumbled down the   5 steps. My heart was pounding and my face was burning. I felt dirty. Guilty. I was conscience-stricken.

All that—over a dirty movie.

Well, I was an innocent at seventeen. I was naive and inexperienced, shy with girls, the product of a parochial-school education and a strict upbringing. Explicit sex—in the movies, music, my social life—was foreign to me. Coming from such an environment, who *wouldn't* recoil from *Cry for Cindy* or feel repelled by what it put up on that screen?

But here's the rub: Dirty movies don't have that effect on me anymore. I don't make a practice of seeking out skin flicks or films with explicit nudity, but in the years since I was seventeen, I've certainly seen my share. Today another sex scene is just another sex scene. Not shocking, not appalling, nothing I feel ashamed to look at. Writhing bodies on the screen? Raunchy lyrics in a song? They may entertain me or they may bore me, but one thing they no longer do is make me blush.

I've become jaded. And if a decade and a half of being exposed to this stuff can leave *me* jaded—with my background, my religious schooling, my disciplined origins—what impact does it have on kids and young adults who have never been sheltered from anything? What impact does it have on a generation growing up amid dysfunctional families, broken-down schools, and a culture of values-free secularism?

If sex- and violence-drenched entertainment can desensitize me, it   10 can desensitize anyone. It can desensitize a whole society. It can drag us to the point where nothing is revolting. Where nothing makes us blush.

And what happens to an unblushing society? Why, everything. Central Park joggers get raped and beaten into comas. Sixth-graders sleep around. Los Angeles rioters burn down their neighborhood and murder dozens of their neighbors. The Menendez boys blow off their parents' heads. Lorena Bobbitt mutilates her husband in his sleep. "Artists" sell photographs of crucifixes dunked in urine. Prolife fanatics open fire on abortion clinics. Daytime TV fills up with deviants. The U.S. Naval Academy fills up with cheaters. The teen suicide rate goes through the roof.

And we get used to all of it. We don't blush.

The point isn't that moviegoers walk out of Oliver Stone's latest grotesquerie primed to kill. Or that Geto Boys' sociopathic lyrics ("Leavin' out her house, grabbed the bitch by her mouth / Drug her back in, slam her down on the couch. / Whipped out my knife, said, 'If you scream I'm cutting,' / Open her legs and . . .") cause rape. The point is that when blood and mayhem and sleazy sex drench our popular culture, we get accustomed to blood and mayhem and sleazy sex. We grow jaded. Depravity becomes more and more tolerable because less and less scandalizes us.

Of course, the entertainment industry accepts no responsibility for any of this. Time Warner and Hollywood indignantly reject the criticisms heaped on them in recent days. We don't cause society's ills, they say, we only reflect them. "If an artist wants to deal with violence or sexuality or images of darkness and horror," said film director Clive Barker, "those are legitimate subjects for artists."

They are, true. Artists have dealt with violence and sexuality and   15 horror since time immemorial. But debauchery is not art. There is nothing ennobling about a two-hour paean to bloodlust. To suggest that Snoop Doggy Dogg's barbaric gang-rape fantasies somehow follow in the tradition of Sophocles' tragic drama, Chaucer's romantic poetry, or Solzhenitsyn's moral testimony is to suggest that there is no difference between meaning and meaninglessness.

For Hollywood and Time Warner, perhaps there no longer is. The question before the house is, what about the rest of us?

Rob Rogers reprinted by permission of United Features Syndicate, Inc.

Gore for Sale

EVAN GAHR

BEFORE READING: Did you enjoy violent video games when you were younger? Can you explain why they did or did not appeal to you?

Fresh corpses litter the ground. Blood is everywhere. Victims moan and beg for mercy. Others scream for help.

This may sound like a horrific scene from the Littleton, Colorado, shooting. But players of the computer game Postal just call it fun. They assume the role of Postal Dude, who snaps one day and mows down everyone in sight. For added realism, as the Web site of the developer (Running with Scissors) proudly states: "Corpses stay where they fall for the duration of the game—no mysterious disappearing bodies." But they do not fall right away. First "watch your victims run around on fire."

If you have a perverse fascination with violence, it's no longer necessary to skulk around in search of underground entertainments. Just visit your neighborhood electronics store. At the Wiz on Manhattan's Upper East Side, the notorious game Grand Theft Auto is smack in the middle of a display rack behind the cashier. The game's story line: As either a "gansta" or "psycho bitch" you will be "running over innocent pedestrians, shooting cops, and evading the long arm of the law."

In another game, Duke Nukem (manufactured by GT Interactive), sex and violence combine. Determined to expel from Los Angeles the aliens who are kidnapping scantily clad women, Duke Nukem trolls the seedy quarters of the city and shoots anyone who gets in his way. He even kicks his victims' decapitated heads through goalposts to celebrate.

In Doom, one of the most popular among violent video games and a 5 favorite of one of the Littleton murderers, the player wanders through a maze of rooms, corridors, and halls killing everything in sight. Survive and you make it to the next level. For lethal power you can choose among a pistol, shot gun, rocket launcher, and chainsaw. The aliens and monsters don't go down easily. Bodily fluid spurts all over the walls; aliens are left to lie in pools of blood, their limbs sometimes dangling in the air.

The manufacturer of Doom, id Software, advises that you should "prepare for the most intense mutant-laden, blood-spattered action ever. You don't just play Doom—you live it." You certainly do.

A more advanced version of Doom, called Quake, is an "ultra-violent gorefest," as one online reviewer called it. Players wander through a maze and use every weapon imaginable to slay aliens. (The nail gun is a big hit.)

Evan Gahr is the Washington correspondent for *Jewish World Review* and an adjunct scholar at the Washington-based Center for Equal Opportunity. This article appeared in the *Wall Street Journal* on April 30, 1999.

There's heightened realism because you can view any part of the game from an endless number of angles. For example, it's possible to bounce a grenade off a wall to hit someone around the corner. Lucky you.

What is going on here? Well, for one thing entrepreneurship. Violent computer games are a small but influential part of the $6.2 billion video- and computer-game market. They have proliferated in recent years and are now deeply embedded in youth culture. They are played either on play stations (Nintendo or Sony), PCs, or the Internet, where you battle it out with other players.

With each new release players are promised seemingly endless amounts of blood and gore. The more people you kill and maim the better. It is an entire subculture that uses 3D graphics, spectacular sound effects, and other computer-driven bells and whistles to blur the distinction between reality and fantasy—and to celebrate criminality. The game titles speak for themselves: Blood, Bedlam, Death Rally, and Redneck Rampage.

The idea is not just to kill but to kill with glee. Last year, a new joy- 10 stick system promised: "You get better accuracy and control, but what are you going to do with all the extra bodies? Be the first on your block to make your neighbors say, 'What's that smell?'" Another manufacturer, Interplay Productions, celebrates "the sheer ecstasy of crunching bones against their bumper" in its game Carmageddon. "Drive whatever you want, wherever you want, and over whoever you want. You make the rules. Your motto. Just kill, baby." And watch the blood spatter on the windshield.

Video-game violence is not new. As Eric Rozenman noted in a recent *Washington Times* article, one of the earlier games, Death Race, caused quite a commotion in the mid-1970s: "The game involved an automobile driver running down pedestrians. The latter expired with unconvincing moans, the skilled motorists recording a tally of crucifixes."

Even Space Invaders was considered too violent when it was released in the late 1970s. But the games have become progressively more violent ever since—and vivid. The most remarkable breakthrough came in 1992, when a first-person shooter game called Wolfenstein 3-D hit the market.

Previously, players looked at the screen as if from above. With Wolfenstein 3-D, however, you see the action from the on-screen character's point of view. You become the character. The following year Doom was introduced. A deluge of first-person shooter games followed.

These caught the attention of Senator Joseph Lieberman (Democrat, Connecticut). He and Senator Herb Kohl (Democrat, Wisconsin) held hearings on the games in 1993. Prodded by the senators, the industry adopted a voluntary rating system. Yet the ratings are not even enforced by stores, and incredibly violent games are often rated suitable for kids. More important, parents don't seem to realize what their kids are playing.

Should they be concerned? What message, for example, does Grand 15 Theft Auto send? Jayson Bernstein, spokesman for the manufacturer,

American Softworks Corp., says, "It's just a game." Industry spokesmen also defend their products by contending that there are no studies that conclusively link computer games to violence.

Some academics, too, say the games get a bum rap. The real problem is—big surprise here—social injustice. Henry Jenkins, director of Comparative Media Studies at MIT, recently argued that the focus on video-game violence seems to be the most recent strategy of our culture to shift focus away from the obvious root causes of violence: urban conditions, poverty and the ready availability of guns.

And so on. Luckily, for those who worry about a culture in which these games thrive, a small backlash is evident. In January, the city of Stanton, California, allowed a new arcade to open only after it promised not to use violent or sexually charged games. The Minnesota Legislature is considering banning the sale of violent games to children under eighteen. In Chicago, about fifty people recently demanded that Toys "Я" Us stop selling violent video games and toys. The protesters, from a partnership of several churches, held a mock funeral outside the store. The store ignored them. In the wake of Littleton, how will such protests play?

Like other refuse that litters the cultural landscape, these computer games didn't just magically appear one day. They have flourished in a cultural milieu in which most anything goes. These days, to paraphrase FDR, it sometimes seems that we have nothing left to stigmatize but stigma itself. When parents and community members try to fight such garbage, or even quarantine it, they are derided in certain quarters as intolerant zealots or enemies of the First Amendment.

But if twelve-year-olds wake up one day and discover they no longer have such easy access to Redneck Rampage, free speech will survive. And everyone else might even be a bit safer.

THINKING AND WRITING ABOUT SEX AND VIOLENCE IN POPULAR CULTURE

QUESTIONS FOR DISCUSSION AND WRITING

1. Evaluate the effectiveness of the support that Kaufman offers for his claim. His essay was originally published online at TurnOff Your TV.com. What is the effect of using links to Web sites as one of his primary means of support?

2. Doherty makes this statement: "The fixation on the body of the victim represents a telling shift away from the former site of detective work, the mind of the murderer" (para. 19). Do you agree? Explain.

3. How would you explain the popularity of forensic shows such as *CSI: Crime Scene Investigation*?

4. Although Oppenheim is writing about violence and Jacoby is writing about sex, both their claims are based on a shared assumption. Explain it, and decide whether it is valid.

5. What evidence do you find in these essays that establishes a cause-and-effect relationship between TV violence and actual crimes?

6. Rhodes provides evidence from several studies to prove that TV and movie violence does not influence the behavior of young viewers. How convincing is it?

7. Nordlinger accuses antigun activists of being unwilling to attack rappers who "sing of guns with almost lascivious glee" (para. 6). But antigun groups protest that rappers are protected by the First Amendment. What is Nordlinger's response to that argument? Do you think there might be other reasons for the lack of protest?

8. Why does Jenkins think we should resist trying to "reprogram the media" (para. 18)? Do you agree with his explanation for teenage attraction to violent films? If not, do you have other explanations?

9. Several authors contend that TV or movie violence is not to blame for the high crime rate among young people. What causes do you suggest?

10. You are probably familiar with some of the games Gahr describes or others like them. Do you agree with the manufacturers that they are harmless? How does Gahr answer objections about violations of "freedom of speech"?

TOPICS FOR RESEARCH

Violence in selected TV shows: justified or unjustified?

Sex on TV: what message?

The significance of gangsta rap

Survey of studies on the effect of TV and movie violence

Influence of music videos and sports events on youthful behavior

TAKING THE DEBATE ONLINE

For these and additional research URLs, see bedfordstmartins.com/rottenberg.

- *Media Watch*
  www.mediawatch.com
  Media Watch, an organization whose goal is to challenge abusive stereotypes and other biased images commonly found in the media, provides these links to media-related news stories, videos, and an archive of past content.

- *Federal Communications Commission Consumer Facts: Obscene and Indecent Broadcasts*
  www.fcc.gov/cib/consumerfacts/obscene.html

This page explains what the FCC considers to be obscene broadcasts and explains how standards are enforced.

- *The Free Expression Policy Project*
www.fepproject.org

The Free Expression Policy Project (FEPP) provides research and advocacy on free speech, copyright, and media democracy issues. It is part of the Democracy Program at the NYU School of Law.

- *Popular Culture: Sexuality*
www.wsu.edu/~amerstu/pop/sex.html

The Web site provides resources for the critical analysis of popular culture in the United States, including the impact of that culture beyond national borders.

- *Center for the Study and Prevention of Violence: Fact Sheets and Position Summaries*
www.colorado.edu/cspv/infohouse/factsheets.html

This site, maintained by scholars at the University of Colorado, includes numerous fact sheets on ethnicity, race, class, and adolescent violence; preventing firearm violence; youth handgun violence; and reducing school violence, among others.

- *Hate and Violence: No Simple Answers*
www.discovery.com/stories/history/hateviolence/hateviolence.html

The Discovery Channel and Dateline NBC have collaborated to develop this Web site, which contains information about hate on the Internet, grassroots organizations that are fighting hate and violence around the country, a violence IQ quiz, and important news updates on violence against women, youth violence, and the biological effects of violence.

- *National Institute on Media and the Family*
www.mediaandthefamily.org

The National Institute on Media and the Family studies "the influence of electronic media on early childhood education, child development, academic performance, culture and violence." The group has published reports on the validity of television and video game ratings and on the influence of television violence on children's behavior.

Part Four

Classic
Arguments

From Crito

PLATO

Socrates: . . . Ought a man to do what he admits to be right, or ought he to betray the right?

Crito: He ought to do what he thinks right.

Socrates: But if this is true, what is the application? In leaving the prison against the will of the Athenians, do I wrong any? Or rather do I not wrong those whom I ought least to wrong? Do I not desert the principles which are acknowledged by us to be just—what do you say?

Crito: I cannot tell, Socrates; for I do not know.

Socrates: Then consider the matter in this way:—Imagine that I am 5 about to play truant (you may call the proceeding by any name which you like), and the laws of the government come and interrogate me: "Tell us, Socrates," they say: "what are you about? Are you not going by an act of yours to overturn us—the laws, and the whole state, as far as in you lies? Do you imagine that a state can subsist and not be overthrown, in which the decisions of law have no power, but are set aside and trampled upon by individuals?" What will be our answer, Crito, to these and the like words? Any one, and especially a rhetorician, will have a good deal to say on behalf of the law which requires a sentence to be carried out. He will argue that this law should not be set aside; and shall we reply, "Yes, but the state has injured us and given an unjust sentence." Suppose I say that?

Crito: Very good, Socrates.

Socrates: "And was that our agreement with you?" the law would answer; "or were you to abide by the sentence of the state?" And if I were to express my astonishment at their words, the law would probably add: "Answer, Socrates, instead of opening your eyes—you are in the habit of asking and answering questions. Tell us,—What complaint have you to make against us which justifies you in attempting to destroy us and the state? In the first place did we not bring you into existence? Your father married your mother by our aid and begat you. Say whether you have any objection to urge against those of us who regulate marriage?" None, I should reply. "Or against those of us who after birth regulate the nurture and education of children, in which you also were trained? Were not the laws, which have the charge of education, right in commanding your

---

Plato, who died in 347 B.C., was one of the greatest Greek philosophers. He was a student of the Greek philosopher Socrates, whose teachings he recorded in the form of dialogues between Socrates and his pupils. In this dialogue, Crito visits Socrates—who is in prison, condemned to death for corrupting the youth of Athens—and tries to persuade him to escape. Socrates, however, refuses, basing his decision on his definition of justice and virtue. From Plato's *Crito*, trans. Benjamin Jowett, 3rd ed. (New York: Dial Press, 1982).

father to train you in music and gymnastics?" Right, I should reply. "Well then, since you were brought into the world and nurtured and educated by us, can you deny in the first place that you are our child and slave, as your fathers were before you? And if this is true you are not on equal terms with us; nor can you think that you have a right to do to us what we are doing to you. Would you have any right to strike or revile or do any other evil to your father or your master, if you had one, because you have been struck or reviled by him, or received some other evil at his hands?—you would not say this? And because we think right to destroy you, do you think that you have any right to destroy us in return, and your country as far as in you lies? Will you, O professor of true virtue, pretend that you are justified in this? Has a philosopher like you failed to discover that our country is more to be valued and higher and holier far than mother or father or any ancestor, and more to be regarded in the eyes of the gods and of men of understanding? Also to be soothed, and gently and reverently entreated when angry, even more than a father, and either to be persuaded, or if not persuaded, to be obeyed? And when we are punished by her, whether with imprisonment or stripes, the punishment is to be endured in silence, and if she leads us to wounds or death in battle, thither we follow as is right; neither may any one yield or retreat or leave his rank, but whether in battle or in a court of law, or in any other place, he must do what his city and his country order him; or he must change their view of what is just: and if he may do no violence to his father or mother, much less may he do violence to his country." What answer shall we make to this, Crito? Do the laws speak truly, or do they not?

Crito: I think that they do.

Socrates: Then the laws will say, "Consider, Socrates, if we are speaking truly that in your present attempt you are going to do us an injury. For, having brought you into the world, and nurtured and educated you, and given you and every other citizen a share in every good which we had to give, we further proclaim to any Athenian by the liberty which we allow him, that if he does not like us when he has become of age and has seen the ways of the city, and made our acquaintance, he may go where he pleases and take his goods with him. None of us laws will forbid him or interfere with him. Any one who does not like us and the city, and who wants to emigrate to a colony or to any other city, may go where he likes, retaining his property. But he who has experience of the manner in which we order justice and administer the state, and still remains, has entered into an implied contract that he will do as we command him. And he who disobeys us is, as we maintain, thrice wrong; first, because in disobeying us he is disobeying his parents; secondly, because we are the authors of his education; thirdly, because he has made an agreement with us that he will duly obey our commands; and he neither obeys them nor convinces us that our commands are unjust; and we do not rudely impose them, but give him the alternative of obeying or convincing us; — that is what we offer, and he does neither.

"These are the sort of accusations to which, as we were saying, you, 10 Socrates, will be exposed if you accomplish your intentions; you, above all other Athenians." Suppose now I ask, why I rather than anybody else? They will justly retort upon me that I above all other men have acknowledged the agreement. "There is clear proof," they will say, "Socrates, that we and the city were not displeasing to you. Of all Athenians you have been the most constant resident in the city, which, as you never leave, you may be supposed to love. For you never went out of the city either to see the games, except once when you went to the Isthmus, or to any other place unless when you were on military service; nor did you travel as other men do. Nor had you any curiosity to know other states or their laws: your affections did not go beyond us and our state; we were your special favorites, and you acquiesced in our government of you; and here in this city you begat your children, which is a proof of your satisfaction. Moreover, you might in the course of the trial, if you had liked, have fixed the penalty at banishment; the state which refuses to let you go now would have let you go then. But you pretended that you preferred death to exile, and that you were not unwilling to die. And now you have forgotten these fine sentiments, and pay no respect to us the laws, of whom you are the destroyer; and are doing what only a miserable slave would do, running away and turning your back upon the compacts and agreements which you made as a citizen. And first of all answer this very question: Are we right in saying that you agreed to be governed according to us in deed, and not in word only? Is that true or not?" How shall we answer, Crito? Must we not assent?

Crito: We cannot help it, Socrates.

Socrates: Then will they not say: "You, Socrates, are breaking the covenants and agreements which you made with us at your leisure, not in any haste or under any compulsion or deception, but after you have had seventy years to think of them, during which time you were at liberty to leave the city, if we were not to your mind, or if our covenants appeared to you to be unfair. You had your choice, and might have gone either to Lacedaemon or Crete, both which states are often praised by you for their good government, or to some other Hellenic or foreign state. Whereas you, above all our Athenians, seemed to be so fond of the state, or, in other words, of us her laws (and who would care about a state which has no laws?), that you never stirred out of her; the halt, the blind, the maimed were not more stationary in her than you were. And now you run away and forsake your agreements. Not so, Socrates, if you will take our advice; do not make yourself ridiculous by escaping out of the city.

"For just consider, if you transgress and err in this sort of way, what good will you do either to yourself or to your friends? That your friends will be driven into exile and deprived of citizenship, or will lose their property, is tolerably certain; and you yourself, if you fly to one of the neighboring cities, as, for example, Thebes or Megara, both of which are well governed, will come to them as an enemy, Socrates, and their government will be against you, and all patriotic citizens will cast an evil eye upon you as a subverter of the laws, and you will confirm in the minds of the judges the justice of their own condemnation of you. For he who is a corrupter of the laws is more than likely to be a corrupter of the young and foolish portion of mankind. Will you then flee from well-ordered citizens and virtuous men? And is existence worth having on these terms? Or will you go to them without shame, and talk to them, Socrates? And what will you say to them? What you say here about virtue and justice and institutions and laws being the best things among men? Would that be decent of you? Surely not. But if you go away from well-governed states to Crito's friends in Thessaly, where there is a great disorder and licence, they will be charmed to hear the tale of your escape from prison, set off with ludicrous particulars of the manner in which you were wrapped in a goatskin or some other disguise, and metamorphosed as the manner is of runaways; but will there be no one to remind you that in your old age you were ashamed to violate the most sacred laws from a miserable desire of a little more life? Perhaps not, if you keep them in a good temper; but if they are out of temper you will hear many degrading things; you will live, but how? — as the flatterer of all men, and the servant of all men; and doing what? — eating and drinking in Thessaly, having gone abroad in order that you may get a dinner. And where will be your fine sentiments about justice and virtue? Say that you wish to live for the sake of your children — you want to bring them up and educate them — will you take them into Thessaly and deprive them of Athenian citizenship? Is this the benefit which you will confer upon them? Or are you under the impression that they will be better cared for and educated here if you are still alive, although absent from them; for your friends will take care of them? Do you fancy that if you are an inhabitant of Thessaly they will take care of them, and if you are an inhabitant of the other world that they will not take care of them? Nay: but if they who call themselves friends are good for anything, they will — to be sure they will.

"Listen, then, Socrates, to us who have brought you up. Think not of life and children first, and of justice afterwards, but of justice first, that you may be justified before the princes of the world below. For neither will you nor any that belong to you be happier or holier or juster in this life, or happier in another, if you do as Crito bids. Now you depart in innocence, a sufferer and not a doer of evil; a victim, not of the laws of men. But if you go forth, returning evil for evil, and injury for injury, breaking the covenants and agreements which you have made with us, and wronging those whom you ought least of all to wrong, that is to say, yourself, your friends, your country, and us, we shall be angry with you while you live, and our brethren, the laws in the world below, will receive you as an enemy; for they will know that you have done your best to destroy us. Listen, then, to us and not to Crito."

This, dear Crito, is the voice which I seem to hear murmuring in my 15 ears, like the sound of the flute in the ears of the mystic; that voice, I say, is humming in my ears, and prevents me from hearing any other. And I know that anything more which you may say will be vain. Yet speak, if you have anything to say.

Crito: I have nothing to say, Socrates.

Socrates: Leave me then, Crito, to fulfill the will of God, and to follow whither he leads.

DISCUSSION QUESTIONS

1. What debt to the law and his country does Socrates acknowledge? Mention the specific reasons for which he owes obedience. Is the analogy of the country to parents a plausible one? Why, or why not?

2. Explain the nature of the implied contract that exists between Socrates and the state. According to the state, how has Socrates forfeited his right to object to punishment?

3. What appeal does that state make to Socrates' sense of justice and virtue?

WRITING SUGGESTIONS

4. Socrates bases his refusal to escape the death penalty on his definition of justice and virtue. Basing your own argument on other criteria, make a claim for the right of Socrates to try to escape his punishment. Would some good be served by his escape?

5. The analogy between one's country and one's parents is illustrated at great length in Socrates' argument. In the light of modern ideas about the relationship between the state and the individual in a democracy, write a refutation of the analogy. Perhaps you can think of a different and more fitting one.

A Modest Proposal

JONATHAN SWIFT

It is a melancholy object to those who walk through this great town[1] or travel in the country, when they see the streets, the roads, and cabin doors, crowded with beggars of the female sex, followed by three, four, or six children, all in rags and importuning every passenger for an alms. These mothers, instead of being able to work for their honest livelihood, are forced to employ all their time in strolling to beg sustenance for their helpless infants, who, as they grow up, either turn thieves for want of work, or leave their dear native country to fight for the Pretender in Spain, or sell themselves to the Barbados.[2]

I think it is agreed by all parties that this prodigious number of children in the arms, or on the backs, or at the heels of their mothers, and frequently of their fathers, is in the present deplorable state of the kingdom a very great additional grievance; and therefore whoever could find out a fair, cheap, and easy method of making these children sound, useful members of the commonwealth would deserve so well of the public as to have his statue set up for a preserver of the nation.

But my intention is very far from being confined to provide only for the children of professed beggars; it is of a much greater extent, and shall take in the whole number of infants at a certain age who are born of parents in effect as little able to support them as those who demand our charity in the streets.

As to my own part, having turned my thoughts for many years upon this important subject, and maturely weighed the several schemes of other projectors,[3] I have always found them grossly mistaken in their computation. It is true, a child just dropped from its dam may be supported by her milk for a solar year, with little other nourishment; at most

---

[1] Dublin. — Eds. [All notes are the editors'.]

[2] The Pretender was James Stuart, who was exiled to Spain. Many Irish men had joined an army attempting to return him to the English throne in 1715. Others had become indentured servants, agreeing to work for a set number of years in Barbados or other British colonies in exchange for their transportation out of Ireland.

[3] Planners.

This essay is acknowledged by almost all critics to be the most powerful example of irony in the English language. (*Irony* means saying one thing but meaning another.) In 1729 Jonathan Swift (1667–1745), prolific satirist and dean of St. Patrick's Cathedral in Dublin, was moved to write in protest against the terrible poverty in which the Irish were living under British rule. Notice that the essay is organized according to one of the patterns outlined in Part Two of this book (see Presenting the Stock Issues, Chapter 9, p. 383). First, Swift establishes the need for a change, then he offers his proposal, and finally, he lists its advantages.

not above the value of two shillings, which the mother may certainly get, or the value in scraps, by her lawful occupation of begging; and it is exactly at one year that I propose to provide for them in such a manner as instead of being a charge upon their parents or the parish, or wanting food and raiment for the rest of their lives, they shall on the contrary contribute to the feeding, and partly to the clothing, of many thousands.

There is likewise another great advantage in my scheme, that it will prevent those voluntary abortions, and that horrid practice of women murdering their bastard children, alas, too frequent among us, sacrificing the poor innocent babes, I doubt, more to avoid the expense than the shame, which would move tears and pity in the most savage and inhuman breast.

The number of souls in this kingdom being usually reckoned one million and a half, of these I calculate there may be about two hundred thousand couples whose wives are breeders; from which number I subtract thirty thousand couples who are able to maintain their own children, although I apprehend there cannot be so many under the present distress of the kingdom; but this being granted, there will remain an hundred and seventy thousand breeders. I again subtract fifty thousand for those women who miscarry, or whose children die by accident or disease within the year. There only remain an hundred and twenty thousand children of poor parents annually born. The question therefore is, how this number shall be reared and provided for, which, as I have already said, under the present situation of affairs, is utterly impossible by all the methods hitherto proposed. For we can neither employ them in handicraft or agriculture; we neither build houses (I mean in the country) nor cultivate land. They can very seldom pick up a livelihood by stealing till they arrive at six years old, except where they are of towardly parts;[4] although I confess they learn the rudiments much earlier, during which time they can however be looked upon only as probationers, as I have been informed by a principal gentleman in the county of Cavan, who protested to me that he never knew above one or two instances under the age of six, even in a part of the kingdom so renowned for the quickest proficiency in that art.

I am assured by our merchants that a boy or a girl before twelve years old is no salable commodity; and even when they come to this age they will not yield above three pounds, or three pounds and a half a crown at most on the Exchange; which cannot turn to account either to the parents or the kingdom, the charge of nutriment and rags having been at least four times that value.

I shall now therefore humbly propose my own thoughts, which I hope will not be liable to the least objection.

I have been assured by a very knowing American of my acquaintance in London, that a young healthy child well nursed is at a year old a most

[4] Innate talents.

delicious, nourishing, and wholesome food, whether stewed, roasted, baked, or boiled; and I make no doubt that it will equally serve in a fricassee or a ragout.[5]

I do therefore humbly offer it to public consideration that of the hun- 10
dred and twenty thousand children, already computed, twenty thousand may be reserved for breed, whereof only one fourth part to be males, which is more than we allow to sheep, black cattle, or swine; and my reason is that these children are seldom the fruits of marriage, a circumstance not much regarded by our savages, therefore one male will be sufficient to serve four females. That the remaining hundred thousand may at a year old be offered in sale to the persons of quality and fortune through the kingdom, always advising the mother to let them suck plentifully in the last month, so as to render them plump and fat for a good table. A child will make two dishes at an entertainment for friends; and when the family dines alone, the fore or hind quarter will make a reasonable dish, and seasoned with a little pepper or salt will be very good boiled on the fourth day, especially in winter.

I have reckoned upon a medium that a child just born will weigh twelve pounds, and in a solar year if tolerably nursed increaseth to twenty-eight pounds.

I grant this food will be somewhat dear, and therefore very proper for landlords, who, as they have already devoured most of the parents, seem to have the best title to the children.

Infant's flesh will be in season throughout the year, but more plentiful in March, and a little before and after. For we are told by a grave author, an eminent French physician,[6] that fish being a prolific diet, there are more children born in Roman Catholic countries about nine months after Lent than at any other season; therefore, reckoning a year after Lent, the markets will be more glutted than usual, because the number of popish infants is at least three to one in this kingdom; and therefore it will have one other collateral advantage, by lessening the number of Papists among us.

I have already computed the charge of nursing a beggar's child (in which list I reckon all cottagers, laborers, and four-fifths of the farmers) to be about two shillings per annum, rags included; and I believe no gentleman would repine to give ten shillings for the carcass of a good fat child, which, as I have said, will make four dishes of excellent nutritive meat, when he hath only some particular friend or his own family to dine with him. Thus the squire will learn to be a good landlord, and grow popular among the tenants; the mother will have eight shillings net profit, and be fit for work till she produces another child.

---

[5] Stew.

[6] A reference to Swift's favorite French writer, François Rabelais (1494?–1553), who was actually a broad satirist known for his coarse humor.

Those who are more thrifty (as I must confess the times require) may 15 flay the carcass; the skin of which artificially[7] dressed will make admirable gloves for ladies, and summer boots for fine gentlemen.

As to our city of Dublin, shambles[8] may be appointed for this purpose in the most convenient parts of it, and butchers we may be assured will not be wanting; although I rather recommend buying the children alive, and dressing them hot from the knife as we do roasting pigs.

A very worthy person, a true lover of his country, and whose virtues I highly esteem, was lately pleased in discoursing on this matter to offer a refinement upon my scheme. He said that many gentlemen of his kingdom, having of late destroyed their deer, he conceived that the want of venison might be well supplied by the bodies of young lads and maidens, not exceeding fourteen years of age nor under twelve, so great a number of both sexes in every county being now ready to starve for want of work and service; and these to be disposed of by their parents, if alive, or otherwise by their nearest relations. But with due deference to so excellent a friend and so deserving a patriot, I cannot be altogether in his sentiments; for as to the males, my American acquaintance assured me from frequent experience that their flesh was generally tough and lean, like that of our schoolboys, by continual exercise, and their taste disagreeable; and to fatten them would not answer the charge. Then as to the females, it would, I think with humble submission, be a loss to the public, because they soon would become breeders themselves; and besides, it is not improbable that some scrupulous people might be apt to censure such a practice (although indeed very unjustly) as a little bordering upon cruelty; which, I confess, hath always been with me the strongest objection against any project, how well soever intended.

But in order to justify my friend, he confessed that this expedient was put into his head by the famous Psalmanazar,[9] a native of the island Formosa, who came from thence to London above twenty years ago, and in conversation told my friend that in his country when any young person happened to be put to death, the executioner sold the carcass to persons of quality as a prime dainty; and that in his time the body of a plump girl of fifteen, who was crucified for an attempt to poison the emperor, was sold to his Imperial Majesty's prime minister of state, and other great mandarins of the court, in joints from the gibbet, at four hundred crowns. Neither indeed can I deny that if the same use were made of several plump young girls in this town, who without one single groat to their fortunes cannot stir abroad without a chair, and appear at the playhouse

---

[7] With art or craft.

[8] Butcher shops or slaughterhouses.

[9] Georges Psalmanazar was a Frenchman who pretended to be Japanese and wrote an entirely imaginary *Description of the Isle Formosa*. He had become well known in gullible London society.

and assemblies in foreign fineries which they never will pay for, the kingdom would not be the worse.

Some persons of a desponding spirit are in great concern about that vast number of poor people who are aged, diseased, or maimed, and I have been desired to employ my thoughts what course may be taken to ease the nation of so grievous an encumbrance. But I am not in the least pain upon that matter, because it is very well known that they are every day dying and rotting by cold and famine, and filth and vermin, as fast as can be reasonably expected. And as to the younger laborers, they are now in almost as hopeful a condition. They cannot get work, and consequently pine away for want of nourishment to a degree that if any time they are accidentally hired to common labor, they have not strength to perform it; and thus the country and themselves are happily delivered from the evils to come.

I have too long digressed, and therefore shall return to my subject. I think the advantages by the proposal which I have made are obvious and many, as well as of the highest importance.

For first, as I have already observed, it would greatly lessen the number of Papists, with whom we are yearly overrun, being the principal breeders of the nation as well as our most dangerous enemies; and who stay at home on purpose to deliver the kingdom to the Pretender, hoping to take their advantage by the absence of so many good Protestants, who have chosen rather to leave their country than to stay at home and pay tithes against their conscience to an Episcopal curate.

Secondly, the poorer tenants will have something valuable of their own, which by law may be made liable to distress,[10] and help to pay their landlord's rent, their corn and cattle being already seized and money a thing unknown.

Thirdly, whereas the maintenance of an hundred thousand children, from two years old and upwards, cannot be computed at less than ten shillings a piece per annum, the nation's stock will be thereby increased fifty thousand pounds per annum, besides the profit of a new dish introduced to the tables of all gentlemen of fortune in the kingdom who have any refinement in taste. And the money will circulate among ourselves, the goods being entirely of our own growth and manufacture.

Fourthly, the constant breeders, besides the gain of eight shillings sterling per annum by the sale of their children, will be rid of the charge of maintaining them after the first year.

Fifthly, this food would likewise bring great custom to taverns, where the vintners will certainly be so prudent as to procure the best receipts for dressing it to perfection, and consequently have their houses frequented by all the fine gentlemen, who justly value themselves upon their knowledge in good eating; and a skillful cook, who understands how to oblige his guests, will contrive to make it as expensive as they please.

[10] Subject to possession by lenders.

Sixthly, this would be a great inducement to marriage, which all wise nations have either encouraged by rewards or enforced by laws and penalties. It would increase the care and tenderness of mothers toward their children, when they were sure of a settlement for life to the poor babes, provided in some sort by the public, to their annual profit instead of expense. We should see an honest emulation among the married women, which of them could bring the fattest child to the market. Men would become as fond of their wives during the time of their pregnancy as they are now of their mares in foal, their cows in calf, or sows when they are ready to farrow; nor offer to beat or kick them (as is too frequent a practice) for fear of a miscarriage.

Many other advantages might be enumerated. For instance, the addition of some thousand carcasses in our exportation of barreled beef, the propagation of swine's flesh, and improvements in the art of making good bacon, so much wanted among us by the great destruction of pigs, too frequent at our tables, which are no way comparable in taste or magnificence to a well-grown, fat, yearling child, which roasted whole will make a considerable figure at a lord mayor's feast or any other public entertainment. But this and many others I omit, being studious of brevity.

Supposing that one thousand families in this city would be constant customers for infants' flesh, besides others who might have it at merry meetings, particularly weddings and christenings, I compute that Dublin would take off annually about twenty thousand carcasses, and the rest of the kingdom (where probably they will be sold somewhat cheaper) the remaining eighty thousand.

I can think of no one objection that will possibly be raised against this proposal, unless it should be urged that the number of people will be thereby much lessened in the kingdom. This I freely own, and it was indeed one principal design in offering it to the world. I desire the reader will observe, that I calculate my remedy for this one individual kingdom of Ireland and for no other that ever was, is, or I think ever can be upon earth. Therefore let no man talk to me of other expedients: of taxing our absentees at five shillings a pound: of using neither clothes nor household furniture except what is of our own growth and manufacture: of utterly rejecting the materials and instruments that promote foreign luxury: of curing the expensiveness of pride, vanity, idleness, and gaming in our women: of introducing a vein of parsimony, prudence, and temperance: of learning to love our country, in the want of which we differ even from Laplanders and the inhabitants of Topinamboo:[11] of quitting our animosities and factions, nor acting any longer like the Jews, who were murdering one another at the very moment their city was taken:[12] of being a little cautious not to sell our country and conscience for nothing:

---

[11] District of Brazil.

[12] During the Roman siege of Jerusalem (A.D. 70), prominent Jews were charged with collaborating with the enemy and put to death.

of teaching landlords to have at least one degree of mercy toward their tenants: lastly, of putting a spirit of honesty, industry, and skill into our shopkeepers; who, if a resolution could now be taken to buy only our native goods, would immediately unite to cheat and exact upon us in the price, the measure, and the goodness, nor could ever yet be brought to make one fair proposal of just dealing, though often and earnestly invited to it.

Therefore I repeat, let no man talk to me of these and the like expedients, till he hath at least some glimpse of hope that there will ever be some hearty and sincere attempt to put them in practice. 30

But as to myself, having been wearied out for many years with offering vain, idle, visionary thoughts, and at length utterly despairing of success, I fortunately fell upon this proposal, which, as it is wholly new, so it hath something solid and real, of no expense and little trouble, full in our own power, and whereby we can incur no danger in disobliging England. For this kind of commodity will not bear exportation, the flesh being of too tender a consistence to admit a long continuance in salt, although perhaps I could name a country which would be glad to eat up our whole nation without it.

After all, I am not so violently bent upon my own opinion as to reject any offer proposed by wise men, which shall be found equally innocent, cheap, easy, and effectual. But before something of that kind shall be advanced in contradiction to my scheme, and offering a better, I desire the author or authors will be pleased maturely to consider two points. First, as things now stand, how they will be able to find food and raiment for an hundred thousand useless mouths and backs. And secondly, there being a round million of creatures in human figure throughout this kingdom, whose sole subsistence put into a common stock would leave them in debt two millions of pounds sterling, adding those who are beggars by profession to the bulk of farmers, cottagers, and laborers, with their wives and children who are beggars in effect; I desire those politicians who dislike my overture, and may perhaps be so bold to attempt an answer, that they will first ask the parents of these mortals whether they would not at this day think it a great happiness to have been sold for food at a year old in this manner I prescribe, and thereby have avoided such a perpetual scene of misfortunes as they have since gone through by the oppression of landlords, the impossibility of paying rent without money or trade, the want of common sustenance, with neither house nor clothes to cover them from the inclemencies of the weather, and the most inevitable prospect of entailing the like of greater miseries upon their breed forever.

I profess, in the sincerity of my heart, that I have not the least personal interest in endeavoring to promote this necessary work, having no other motive than the public good of my country, by advancing our trade, providing for infants, relieving the poor, and giving some pleasure to the rich. I have no children by which I can propose to get a single penny; the youngest being nine years old, and my wife past childbearing.

DISCUSSION QUESTIONS

1. What implicit assumption about the treatment of the Irish underlies Swift's proposal? Do expressions such as "just dropped from its dam" (para. 4) and "whose wives are breeders" (para. 6) give the reader a clue?

2. In this essay Swift assumes a persona; that is, for the purposes of the proposal he makes, he pretends to be a different person. Describe the characteristics of that person. Point out the places in the essay that reveal them.

3. In several places, however, Swift reveals himself as the outraged witness of English cruelty and indifference. Note the language that seems to reflect his own feelings.

4. Throughout the essay Swift recites lists of facts, many of them in the form of statistics. How do these facts contribute to the persuasiveness of his argument? How do they affect the reader?

5. What social practices and attitudes of both the Irish and the English does Swift condemn?

6. Does Swift offer any solutions for the problems he attacks? How do you know?

7. When this essay first appeared in 1729, some readers took it seriously and accused Swift of monstrous cruelty. Can you think of reasons that these readers failed to recognize the ironic intent?

WRITING SUGGESTIONS

8. Try an ironical essay of your own. Choose a subject that clearly lends itself to such treatment. As Swift did, use logic and restraint in your language.

9. Choose a problem for which you think you have a solution. Defend your solution by using the stock issues as your pattern of organization.

Civil Disobedience

HENRY DAVID THOREAU

I heartily accept the motto, — "That government is best which governs least"; and I should like to see it acted up to more rapidly and systematically. Carried out, it finally amounts to this, which also I believe, — "That government is best which governs not at all"; and when men are prepared for it, that will be the kind of government which they will have. Government is at best but an expedient; but most governments are usually, and all governments are sometimes, inexpedient. The objections which have been brought against a standing army, and they are many and weighty, and deserve to prevail, may also at last be brought against a standing government. The standing army is only an arm of the standing government. The government itself, which is only the mode which the people have chosen to execute their will, is equally liable to be abused and perverted before the people can act through it. Witness the present Mexican war, the work of comparatively a few individuals using the standing government as their tool; for, in the outset, the people would not have consented to this measure.

This American government, — what is it but a tradition, though a recent one, endeavoring to transmit itself unimpaired to posterity, but each instant losing some of its integrity? It has not the vitality and force of a single living man; for a single man can bend it to his will. It is a sort of wooden gun to the people themselves. But it is not the less necessary for this; for the people must have some complicated machinery or other, and hear its din, to satisfy that idea of government which they have. Governments show thus how successfully men can be imposed on, even impose on themselves, for their own advantage. It is excellent, we must all allow. Yet this government never of itself furthered any enterprise, but by the alacrity with which it got out of its way. *It* does not keep the country free. *It* does not settle the West. *It* does not educate. The character inherent in the American people has done all that has been accomplished; and it would have done somewhat more, if the government had not sometimes got in its way. For government is an expedient by which men would fain succeed in letting one another alone; and, as has been said, when it is most expedient, the governed are most let alone by it. Trade and commerce, if they were not made of India-rubber, would never manage to

---

Henry David Thoreau (1817–1862), philosopher and writer, is best known for *Walden*, an account of his solitary retreat to Walden Pond, near Concord, Massachusetts. Here he remained for more than two years in an effort to "live deliberately, to front only the essential facts of life." "Civil Disobedience" was first given as a lecture in 1848 and published in 1849. It was widely read and influenced both Mahatma Gandhi in the passive-resistance campaign he led against the British in India and Martin Luther King Jr. in the U.S. civil rights movement.

bounce over the obstacles which legislators are continually putting in their way; and, if one were to judge these men wholly by the effects of their actions, and not partly by their intentions, they would deserve to be classed and punished with those mischievous persons who put obstructions on the railroads.

But, to speak practically and as a citizen, unlike those who call themselves no-government men, I ask for, not at once no government, but *at once* a better government. Let every man make known what kind of government would command his respect, and that will be one step toward obtaining it.

After all, the practical reason why, when the power is once in the hands of the people, a majority are permitted, and for a long period continue, to rule, is not because they are most likely to be in the right, nor because this seems fairest to the minority, but because they are physically the strongest. But a government in which the majority rule in all cases cannot be based on justice, even as far as men understand it. Can there not be a government in which majorities do not virtually decide right and wrong, but conscience? — in which majorities decide only those questions to which the rule of expediency is applicable? Must the citizen ever for a moment, or in the least degree, resign his conscience to the legislator? Why has every man a conscience, then? I think that we should be men first, and subjects afterward. It is not desirable to cultivate a respect for the law, so much as for the right. The only obligation which I have a right to assume, is to do at any time what I think right. It is truly enough said, that a corporation has no conscience; but a corporation of conscientious men is a corporation *with* a conscience. Law never made men a whit more just; and, by means of their respect for it, even the well-disposed are daily made the agents of injustice. A common and natural result of an undue respect for law is, that you may see a file of soldiers, colonel, captain, corporal, privates, powder-monkeys, and all, marching in admirable order over hill and dale to the wars, against their wills, aye, against their common sense and consciences, which makes it very steep marching indeed, and produces a palpitation of the heart. They have no doubt that it is a damnable business in which they are concerned; they are all peaceably inclined. Now, what are they? Men at all? or small moveable forts and magazines, at the service of some unscrupulous man in power? Visit the Navy-Yard, and behold a marine, such a man as an American government can make, or such as it can make a man with its black arts, — a mere shadow and reminiscence of humanity, a man laid out alive and standing, and already, as one may say, buried under arms with funeral accompaniments, though it may be, —

> Not a drum was heard, nor a funeral note,
> As his corse to the rampart we hurried;
> Not a soldier discharged his farewell shot
> O'er the grave where our hero we buried.

The mass of men serve the state thus, not as men mainly, but as ma- 5
chines, with their bodies. They are the standing army, and the militia,
jailers, constables, posse comitatus, &c. In most cases there is no free exercise whatever of the judgment or of the moral sense; but they put themselves on a level with wood and earth and stones; and wooden men can
perhaps be manufactured that will serve the purpose as well. Such command no more respect than men of straw, or a lump of dirt. They have
the same sort of worth only as horses and dogs. Yet such as these even are
commonly esteemed good citizens. Others, — as most legislators, politicians, lawyers, ministers, and office-holders, — serve the State chiefly with
their heads; and, as they rarely make any moral distinctions, they are as
likely to serve the Devil, without *intending* it, as God. A very few, as heroes, patriots, martyrs, reformers in the great sense, and *men*, serve the
state with their consciences also, and so necessarily resist it for the most
part, and they are commonly treated as enemies by it. A wise man will
only be useful as a man, and will not submit to be "clay," and "stop a hole
to keep the wind away," but leave that office to his dust at least: —

> I am too high-born to be propertied,
> To be a secondary at control,
> Or useful serving-man and instrument
> To any sovereign state throughout the world.

He who gives himself entirely to his fellow-men appears to them useless and selfish; but he who gives himself partially to them is pronounced
a benefactor and philanthropist.

How does it become a man to behave toward this American government today? I answer that he cannot without disgrace be associated with
it. I cannot for an instant recognize that political organization as *my* government which is the *slave's* government also.

All men recognize the right of revolution; that is, the right to refuse
allegiance to, and to resist, the government, when its tyranny or its inef-
ficiency are great and unendurable. But almost all say that such is not the
case now. But such was the case, they think, in the Revolution of '75. If
one were to tell me that this was a bad government because it taxed certain foreign commodities brought to its ports, it is most probable that I
should not make an ado about it, for I can do without them. All machines
have their friction; and possibly this does enough good to counterbalance
the evil. At any rate, it is a great evil to make a stir about it. But when the
friction comes to have its machine, and oppression and robbery are organized, I say, let us not have such a machine any longer. In other words,
when a sixth of the population of a nation which has undertaken to be
the refuge of liberty are slaves, and a whole country is unjustly overrun
and conquered by a foreign army, and subjected to military law, I think
that it is not too soon for honest men to rebel and revolutionize. What

makes this duty the more urgent is the fact, that the country so overrun is not our own, but ours is the invading army.

Paley, a common authority with many on moral questions, in his chapter on the "Duty of Submission to Civil Government," resolves all civil obligation into expediency; and he proceeds to say, "that so long as the interest of the whole society requires it, that is, so long as the established government cannot be resisted or changed without public inconveniency, it is the will of God that the established government be obeyed, and no longer. . . . This principle being admitted, the justice of every particular case of resistance is reduced to a computation of the quantity of the danger and grievance on the one side, and of the probability and expense of redressing it on the other." Of this, he says, every man shall judge for himself. But Paley appears never to have contemplated those cases to which the rule of expediency does not apply, in which a people, as well as an individual, must do justice, cost what it may. If I have unjustly wrested a plank from a drowning man, I must restore it to him though I drown myself. This, according to Paley, would be inconvenient. But he that would save his life, in such a case, shall lose it. This people must cease to hold slaves, and to make war on Mexico, though it cost them their existence as a people.

In their practice, nations agree with Paley; but does any one think 10 that Massachusetts does exactly what is right at the present crisis?

> A drab of state, a cloth-'o-silver slut,
> To have her train borne up, and her soul trail in the dirt.

Practically speaking, the opponents to a reform in Massachusetts are not a hundred thousand politicians at the South, but a hundred thousand merchants and farmers here, who are more interested in commerce and agriculture than they are in humanity, and are not prepared to do justice to the slave and to Mexico, *cost what it may*. I quarrel not with far-off foes, but with those who, near at home, cooperate with, and do the bidding of, those far away, and without whom the latter would be harmless. We are accustomed to say, that the mass of men are unprepared; but improvement is slow, because the few are not materially wiser or better than the many. It is not so important that many should be as good as you, as that there be some absolute goodness somewhere; for that will leaven the whole lump. There are thousands who are *in opinion* opposed to slavery and to the war, who yet in effect do nothing to put an end to them; who, esteeming themselves children of Washington and Franklin, sit down with their hands in their pockets, and say that they know not what to do, and do nothing; who even postpone the question of freedom to the question of free-trade, and quietly read the prices-current along with the latest advice from Mexico, after dinner, and, it may be, fall asleep over them both. What is the price-current of an honest man and patriot today? They hesitate, and they regret, and sometimes they petition; but they do nothing in earnest and with effect. They will wait, well disposed, for others to remedy the evil, that they may no longer have it to regret. At most, they give only a cheap vote, and a feeble countenance and God-speed, to the right, as it goes by them. There are nine hundred and ninety-nine patrons of virtue to one virtuous man; but it is easier to deal with the real possessor of a thing than with the temporary guardian of it.

All voting is a sort of gaming, like checkers or backgammon, with a slight moral tinge to it, a playing with right and wrong, with moral questions; and betting naturally accompanies it. The character of the voters is not staked. I cast my vote, perchance, as I think right; but I am not vitally concerned that that right should prevail. I am willing to leave it to the majority. Its obligation, therefore, never exceeds that of expediency. Even voting *for the right* is *doing* nothing for it. It is only expressing to men feebly your desire that it should prevail. A wise man will not leave the right to the mercy of chance, nor wish it to prevail through the power of the majority. There is but little virtue in the action of masses of men. When the majority shall at length vote for the abolition of slavery, it will be because they are indifferent to slavery, or because there is but little slavery left to be abolished by their vote. *They* will then be the only slaves. Only *his* vote can hasten the abolition of slavery who asserts his own freedom by his vote.

I hear of a convention to be held at Baltimore, or elsewhere, for the selection of a candidate for the presidency, made up chiefly of editors, and men who are politicians by profession; but I think, what is it to any independent, intelligent, and respectable man what decision they may come to? Shall we not have the advantage of his wisdom and honesty, nevertheless? Can we not count upon some independent votes? Are there not many individuals in the country who do not attend conventions? But no: I find that the respectable man, so called, has immediately drifted from his position, and despairs of his country, when his country has more reason to despair of him. He forthwith adopts one of the candidates thus selected as the only *available* one, thus providing that he is himself *available* for any purposes of the demagogue. His vote is of no more worth than that of any unprincipled foreigner or hireling native, who may have been bought. O for a man who is *a man*, and, as my neighbor says, has a bone in his back which you cannot pass your hand through! Our statistics are at fault: The population has been returned too large. How many *men* are there to a square thousand miles in this country? Hardly one. Does not America offer any inducement for men to settle here? The American has dwindled into an Odd Fellow, — one who may be known by the development of his organ of gregariousness, and a manifest lack of intellect and cheerful self-reliance; whose first and chief concern, on coming into the world, is to see that the Almshouses are in good repair; and, before yet he has lawfully donned the virile garb, to collect a fund for the support of the widows and orphans that may be; who, in short, ventures to live only by the aid of the Mutual Insurance company, which has promised to bury him decently.

It is not a man's duty, as a matter of course, to devote himself to the eradication of any, even the most enormous wrong; he may still properly have other concerns to engage him; but it is his duty, at least, to wash his hands of it, and, if he gives it no thought longer, not to give it practically his support. If I devote myself to other pursuits and contemplations, I must first see, at least, that I do not pursue them sitting upon another man's shoulders. I must get off him first, that he may pursue his contemplations too. See what gross inconsistency is tolerated. I have heard some of my townsmen say, "I should like to have them order me out to help put down an insurrection of the slaves, or to march to Mexico;—see if I would go"; and yet these very men have each, directly by their allegiance, and so indirectly, at least, by their money, furnished a substitute. The soldier is applauded who refuses to serve in an unjust war by those who do not refuse to sustain the unjust government which makes the war; is applauded by those whose own act and authority he disregards and sets at nought; as if the State were penitent to that degree that it hired one to scourge it while it sinned, but not to that degree that it left off sinning for a moment. Thus, under the name of Order and Civil Government, we are all made at last to pay homage to and support our own meanness. After the first blush of sin, comes its indifference; and from immoral it becomes, as it were, *un*moral, and not quite unnecessary to that life which we have made.

The broadest and most prevalent error requires the most disinterested virtue to sustain it. The slight reproach to which the virtue of patriotism is commonly liable, the noble are most likely to incur. Those who, while they disapprove of the character and measures of a government, yield to it their allegiance and support, are undoubtedly its most conscientious supporters, and so frequently the most serious obstacles to reform. Some are petitioning the State to dissolve the Union, to disregard the requisitions of the President. Why do they not dissolve it themselves,—the union between themselves and the State,—and refuse to pay their quota into its treasury? Do not they stand in the same relation to the State, that the State does to the Union? And have not the same reasons prevented the State from resisting the Union which have prevented them from resisting the State?

How can a man be satisfied to entertain an opinion merely, and enjoy 15 *it*? Is there any enjoyment in it, if his opinion is that he is aggrieved? If you are cheated out of a single dollar by your neighbor, you do not rest satisfied with knowing that you are cheated, or with saying that you are cheated, or even with petitioning him to pay you your due; but you take effectual steps at once to obtain the full amount, and see that you are never cheated again. Action from principle, the perception and the performance of right, changes things and relations; it is essentially revolutionary, and does not consist wholly with anything which was. It not only divides states and churches, it divides families; ay, it divides the *individual*, separating the diabolical in him from the divine.

Unjust laws exist: Shall we be content to obey them, or shall we endeavor to amend them, and obey them until we have succeeded, or shall we transgress them at once? Men generally, under such a government as this, think that they ought to wait until they have persuaded the majority to alter them. They think that, if they should resist, the remedy would be worse than the evil. But it is the fault of the government itself that the remedy *is* worse than the evil. *It* makes it worse. Why is it not more apt to anticipate and provide for reform? Why does it not cherish its wise minority? Why does it cry and resist before it is hurt? Why does it not encourage its citizens to be on the alert to point out its faults, and *do* better than it would have them? Why does it always crucify Christ, and excommunicate Copernicus and Luther, and pronounce Washington and Franklin rebels?

One would think, that a deliberate and practical denial of its authority was the only offence never contemplated by government; else, why has it not assigned its definite, its suitable and proportionate penalty? If a man who has no property refuses but once to earn nine shillings for the State, he is put in prison for a period unlimited by any law that I know, and determined only by the discretion of those who placed him there; but if he should steal ninety times nine shillings from the State, he is soon permitted to go at large again.

If the injustice is part of the necessary friction of the machine of government, let it go, let it go: Perchance it will wear smooth, — certainly the machine will wear out. If the injustice has a spring, or a pulley, or a rope, or a crank, exclusively for itself, then perhaps you may consider whether the remedy will not be worse than the evil; but if it is of such a nature that it requires you to be the agent of injustice to another, then, I say, break the law. Let your life be a counter friction to stop the machine. What I have to do is to see, at any rate, that I do not lend myself to the wrong which I condemn.

As for adopting the ways which the State has provided for remedying the evil, I know not of such ways. They take too much time, and a man's life will be gone. I have other affairs to attend to. I came into this world, not chiefly to make this a good place to live in, but to live in it, be it good or bad. A man has not everything to do, but something; and because he cannot do *everything*, it is not necessary that he should do *something* wrong. It is not my business to be petitioning the Governor or the Legislature any more than it is theirs to petition me; and, if they should not hear my petition, what should I do then? But in this case the State has provided no way: Its very Constitution is the evil. This may seem to be harsh and stubborn and unconciliatory; but it is to treat with the utmost kindness and consideration the only spirit that can appreciate or deserves it. So is all change for the better, like birth and death, which convulse the body.

I do not hesitate to say, that those who call themselves Abolitionists 20 should at once effectually withdraw their support, both in person and property, from the government of Massachusetts, and not wait till they constitute a majority of one, before they suffer the right to prevail through them. I think that it is enough if they have God on their side, without waiting for that other one. Moreover, any man more right than his neighbors, constitutes a majority of one already.

I meet this American government, or its representative, the State government, directly, and face to face, once a year — no more — in the person of its tax-gatherer; this is the only mode in which a man situated as I am necessarily meets it; and it then says distinctly, Recognize me; and the simplest, the most effectual, and, in the present posture of affairs, the indispensablest mode of treating with it on this head, of expressing your little satisfaction with and love for it, is to deny it then. My civil neighbor, the tax-gatherer, is the very man I have to deal with, — for it is, after all, with men and not with parchment that I quarrel, — and he has voluntarily chosen to be an agent of the government. How shall he ever know well what he is and does as an officer of the government, or as a man, until he is obliged to consider whether he shall treat me, his neighbor, for whom he has respect, as a neighbor and well-disposed man, or as a maniac and disturber of the peace, and see if he can get over this obstruction to his neighborliness without a ruder and more impetuous thought or speech corresponding with his action? I know this well, that if one thousand, if one hundred, if ten men whom I could name, — if ten *honest* men only, — aye, if *one* HONEST man, in this State of Massachusetts, *ceasing to hold slaves*, were actually to withdraw from this copartnership, and be locked up in the county jail therefor, it would be the abolition of slavery in America. For it matters not how small the beginning may seem to be: What is once well done is done forever. But we love better to talk about it: That we say is our mission. Reform keeps many scores of newspapers in its service, but not one man. If my esteemed neighbor, the State's ambassador, who will devote his days to the settlement of the question of human rights in the Council Chamber, instead of being threatened with the prisons of Carolina, were to sit down the prisoner of Massachusetts, that State which is so anxious to foist the sin of slavery upon her sister, — though at present she can discover only an act of inhospitality to be the ground of a quarrel with her, — the Legislature would not wholly waive the subject the following winter.

Under a government which imprisons any unjustly, the true place for a just man is also a prison. The proper place today, the only place which Massachusetts has provided for her freer and less desponding spirits, is in her prisons, to be put out and locked out of the State by her own act, as they have already put themselves out by their principles. It is there that the fugitive slave, and the Mexican prisoner on parole, and the Indian come to plead the wrongs of his race, should find them; on that separate, but more free and honorable ground, where the State places those who are not *with* her, but *against* her,—the only house in a slave State in which a free man can abide with honor. If any think that their influence would be lost there, and their voices no longer afflict the ear of the State, that they would not be as an enemy within its walls, they do not know by how much truth is stronger than error, nor how much more eloquently and effectively he can combat injustice who has experienced a little in his own person. Cast your whole vote, not a strip of paper merely, but your whole influence. A minority is powerless while it conforms to the majority; it is not even a minority then; but it is irresistible when it clogs by its whole weight. If the alternative is to keep all just men in prison, or give up war and slavery, the State will not hesitate which to choose. If a thousand men were not to pay their tax-bills this year, that would not be a violent and bloody measure, as it would be to pay them, and enable the State to commit violence and shed innocent blood. This is, in fact, the definition of a peaceable revolution, if any such is possible. If the tax-gatherer, or any other public officer, asks me, as one has done, "But what shall I do?" my answer is, "If you really wish to do any thing, resign your office." When the subject has refused allegiance, and the officer has resigned his office, then the revolution is accomplished. But even suppose blood should flow. Is there not a sort of blood shed when the conscience is wounded? Through this wound a man's real manhood and immortality flow out, and he bleeds to an everlasting death. I see this blood flowing now.

I have contemplated the imprisonment of the offender, rather than the seizure of his goods,—though both will serve the same purpose,—because they who assert the purest right, and consequently are most dangerous to a corrupt State, commonly have not spent much time in accumulating property. To such the State renders comparatively small service, and a slight tax is wont to appear exorbitant, particularly if they are obliged to earn it by special labor with their hands. If there were one who lived wholly without the use of money, the State itself would hesitate to demand it of him. But the rich man,—not to make any invidious comparison,—is always sold to the institution which makes him rich. Absolutely speaking, the more money, the less virtue; for money comes between a man and his objects, and obtains them for him; and it was certainly no great virtue to obtain it. It puts to rest many questions which he would otherwise be taxed to answer; while the only new question which it puts is the hard but superfluous one, how to spend it. Thus his moral ground is taken from under his feet. The opportunities of living are diminished in proportion as what are called the "means" are increased. The best thing a man can do for his culture when he is rich is to endeavor to carry out those schemes which he entertained when he was poor. Christ answered the Herodians according to their condition. "Show me the tribute-money," said he;—and one took a penny out of his pocket;—if you use money which has the image of Cæsar on it, and which he has made current and valuable, that is, *if you are men of the State*, and gladly enjoy the advantages of Cæsar's government, then pay him back some of his own when he demands it; "Render therefore to Cæsar that which is Cæsar's, and to God those things which are God's,"—leaving them no wiser than before as to which was which; for they did not wish to know.

When I converse with the freest of my neighbors, I perceive that, whatever they may say about the magnitude and seriousness of the question, and their regard for the public tranquility, the long and the short of the matter is, that they cannot spare the protection of the existing government, and they dread the consequences to their property and families of disobedience to it. For my own part, I should not like to think that I ever rely on the protection of the State. But, if I deny the authority of the State when it presents its tax-bill, it will soon take and waste all my property, and so harass me and my children without end. This is hard. This makes it impossible for a man to live honestly, and at the same time comfortably, in outward respects. It will not be worth the while to accumulate property; that would be sure to go again. You must hire or squat somewhere, and raise but a small crop, and eat that soon. You must live within yourself, and depend upon yourself always tucked up and ready for a start, and not have many affairs. A man may grow rich in Turkey even, if he will be in all respects a good subject of the Turkish government. Confucius said: "If a state is governed by the principles of reason, poverty and misery are subjects of shame; if a state is not governed by the principles of reason, riches and honors are the subjects of shame." No: Until I want the protection of Massachusetts to be extended to me in some distant southern port, where my liberty is endangered, or until I am bent solely on building up an estate at home by peaceful enterprise, I can afford to refuse allegiance to Massachusetts, and her right to my property and life. It costs me less in every sense to incur the penalty of disobedience to the State, than it would to obey. I should feel as if I were worth less in that case.

Some years ago, the State met me in behalf of the Church, and commanded me to pay a certain sum toward the support of a clergyman whose preaching my father attended, but never I myself. "Pay," it said, "or be locked up in the jail." I declined to pay. But, unfortunately, another man saw fit to pay it. I did not see why the schoolmaster should be taxed to support the priest, and not the priest the schoolmaster; for I was not the State's schoolmaster, but I supported myself by voluntary subscription. I did not see why the lyceum should not present its tax-bill, and have the State to back its demand, as well as the Church. However, at the request of the selectmen, I condescended to make some such statement as this in writing:—"Know all men by these presents, that I, Henry Thoreau, do not wish to be regarded as a member of any incorporated society which I have not joined." This I gave to the town clerk; and he has it. The State, having thus learned that I did not wish to be regarded as a member of that church, has never made a like demand on me since; though it said that it must adhere to its original presumption that time. 25

If I had known how to name them, I should then have signed off in detail from all the societies which I never signed on to; but I did not know where to find a complete list.

I have paid no poll-tax for six years. I was put into a jail once on this account, for one night; and, as I stood considering the walls of solid stone, two or three feet thick, the door of wood and iron, a foot thick, and the iron grating which strained the light, I could not help being struck with the foolishness of that institution which treated me as if I were mere flesh and blood and bones, to be locked up. I wondered that it should have concluded at length that this was the best use it could put me to, and had never thought to avail itself of my services in some way. I saw that, if there was a wall of stone between me and my townsmen, there was a still more difficult one to climb or break through, before they could get to be as free as I was. I did not for a moment feel confined, and the walls seemed a great waste of stone and mortar. I felt as if I alone of all my townsmen had paid my tax. They plainly did not know how to treat me, but behaved like persons who are underbred. In every threat and in every compliment there was a blunder; for they thought that my chief desire was to stand the other side of that stone wall. I could not but smile to see how industriously they locked the door on my meditations, which followed them out again without let or hindrance, and *they* were really all that was dangerous. As they could not reach me, they had resolved to punish my body; just as boys, if they cannot come at some person against whom they have a spite, will abuse his dog. I saw that the State was half-witted, and it was timid as a lone woman with her silver spoons, and that it did not know its friends from its foes, and I lost all my remaining respect for it, and pitied it.

Thus the State never intentionally confronts a man's sense, intellectual or moral, but only his body, his senses. It is not armed with superior wit or honesty, but with superior physical strength. I was not born to be forced. I will breathe after my own fashion. Let us see who is the strongest. What force has a multitude? They only can force me who obey a higher law than I. They force me to become like themselves. I do not hear of *men* being *forced* to live this way or that by masses of men. What sort of life were that to live? When I meet a government which says to me, "Your money or your life," why should I be in haste to give it my money? It may be in a great strait, and not know what to do: I cannot help that. It must help itself; do as I do. It is not worth the while to snivel about it. I am not responsible for the successful working of the machinery of society. I am not the son of the engineer. I perceive that, when an acorn and a chestnut fall side by side, the one does not remain inert to make way for the other, but both obey their own laws, and spring and grow and flourish as best they can, till one, perchance, overshadows and destroys the other. If a plant cannot live according to its nature, it dies; and so a man.

The night in prison was novel and interesting enough. The prisoners in their shirt-sleeves were enjoying a chat and the evening air in the doorway, when I entered. But the jailer said, "Come, boys, it is time to lock up"; and so they dispersed, and I heard the sound of their steps returning into the hollow apartments. My roommate was introduced to me by the jailer, as "a first-rate fellow and a clever man." When the door was locked, he showed me where to hang my hat, and how he managed matters there. The rooms were white-washed once a month; and this one, at least, was the whitest, most simply furnished, and probably the neatest apartment in the town. He naturally wanted to know where I came from, and what brought me there; and, when I had told him, I asked him in my turn how he came there, presuming him to be an honest man, of course; and, as the world goes, I believe he was. "Why," said he, "they accuse me of burning a barn; but I never did it." As near as I could discover, he had probably gone to bed in a barn when drunk, and smoked his pipe there; and so a barn was burnt. He had the reputation of being a clever man, had been there some three months waiting for his trial to come on, and would have to wait as much longer; but he was quite domesticated and contented, since he got his board for nothing, and thought that he was well-treated.

He occupied one window, and I the other; and I saw, that if one stayed there long, his principal business would be to look out the window. I had soon read all the tracts that were left there, and examined where former prisoners had broken out, and where a grate had been sawed off, and heard the history of the various occupants of that room; for I found that even here there was a history and a gossip which never circulated beyond the walls of the jail. Probably this is the only house in the town where verses are composed, which are afterward printed in a circular form, but not published. I was shown quite a long list of verses which were composed by some young men who had been detected in an attempt to escape, who avenged themselves by singing them.

I pumped my fellow-prisoner as dry as I could, for fear I should never 30 see him again; but at length he showed me which was my bed, and left me to blow out the lamp.

It was like travelling into a far country, such as I had never expected to behold, to lie there for one night. It seemed to me that I never had heard the town-clock strike before, nor the evening sounds of the village; for we slept with the windows open, which were inside the grating. It was to see my native village in the light of the Middle Ages, and our Concord was turned into a Rhine stream, and visions of knights and castles passed before me. They were the voices of old burghers that I heard in the streets. I was an involuntary spectator and auditor of whatever was done and said in the kitchen of the adjacent village-inn, — a wholly new and rare experience to me. It was a closer view of my native town. I was fairly inside of it. I never had seen its institutions before. This is one of its peculiar institutions; for it is a shire town. I began to comprehend what its inhabitants were about.

In the morning, our breakfasts were put through the hole in the door, in small oblong-square tin pans, made to fit, and holding a pint of chocolate, with brown bread, and an iron spoon. When they called for the vessels again, I was green enough to return what bread I had left; but my comrade seized it, and said that I should lay that up for lunch or dinner. Soon after, he was let out to work at haying in a neighboring field, whither he went every day, and would not be back till noon; so he bade me good-day, saying that he doubted if he should see me again.

When I came out of prison, — for some one interfered, and paid that tax, — I did not perceive that great changes had taken place on the common, such as he observed who went in a youth, and emerged a tottering and gray-headed man; and yet a change had to my eyes come over the scene, — the town, and State, and country, — greater than any that mere time could effect. I saw yet more distinctly the State in which I lived. I saw to what extent the people among whom I lived could be trusted as good neighbors and friends; that their friendship was for summer weather only; that they did not greatly propose to do right; that they were a distinct race from me by their prejudices and superstitions, as the Chinamen and Malays are; that, in their sacrifices to humanity, they ran no risks, not even to their property; that, after all, they were not so noble but they treated the thief as he had treated them, and hoped, by a certain outward observance and a few prayers, and by walking in a particular straight though useless path from time to time, to save their souls. This may be to judge my neighbors harshly; for I believe that many of them are not aware that they have such an institution as the jail in their village.

It was formerly the custom in our village, when a poor debtor came out of jail, for his acquaintances to salute him, looking through their fingers, which were crossed to represent the grating of a jail window, "How do ye do?" My neighbors did not thus salute me, but first looked at me, and then at one another, as if I had returned from a long journey. I was put into jail as I was going to the shoemaker's to get a shoe which was mended. When I was let out the next morning, I proceeded to finish my errand, and having put on my mended shoe, joined a huckleberry party, who were impatient to put themselves under my conduct; and in half an hour, — for the horse was soon tackled, — was in the midst of a huckleberry field, on one of our highest hills, two miles off, and then the State was nowhere to be seen.

This is the whole story of "My Prisons."   35

I have never declined paying the highway tax, because I am as desirous of being a good neighbor as I am of being a bad subject; and, as for supporting schools, I am doing my part to educate my fellow-countrymen now. It is for no particular item in the tax-bill that I refuse to pay it. I simply wish to refuse allegiance to the State, to withdraw and stand aloof from it effectually. I do not care to trace the course of my dollar, if I could, till it buys a man, or a musket to shoot one with, — the dollar is innocent, — but I am concerned to trace the effects of my allegiance. In fact, I quietly declare war with the State, after my fashion, though I will still make what use and get what advantage of her I can, as is usual in such cases.

If others pay the tax which is demanded of me, from a sympathy with the State, they do but what they have already done in their own case, or rather they abet injustice to a greater extent than the State requires. If they pay the tax from a mistaken interest in the individual taxed, to save his property or prevent his going to jail, it is because they have not considered wisely how far they let their private feelings interfere with the public good.

This, then, is my position at present. But one cannot be too much on his guard in such a case, lest his action be biased by obstinacy, or an undue regard for the opinions of men. Let him see that he does only what belongs to himself and to the hour.

I think sometimes, Why, this people mean well; they are only ignorant; they would do better if they knew how: why give your neighbors this pain to treat you as they are inclined to? But I think again, this is no reason why I should do as they do, or permit others to suffer much greater pain of a different kind. Again, I sometimes say to myself, When many millions of men, without heat, without ill will, without personal feelings of any kind, demand of you a few shillings only, without the possibility, such is their constitution, of retracing or altering their present demand, and without the possibility, on your side, of appeal to any other millions, why expose yourself to this overwhelming brute force? You do not resist cold and hunger, the winds and the waves, thus obstinately; you quietly submit to a thousand similar necessities. You do not put your head into the fire. But just in proportion as I regard this as not wholly a brute force, partly a human force, and consider that I have relations to those millions as to so many millions of men, and not of mere brute or inanimate things, I see that appeal is possible, first and instantaneously, from them to the Maker of them, and, secondly, from them to themselves. But, if I put my head deliberately into the fire, there is no appeal to fire or to the Maker of fire, and I have only myself to blame. If I could convince myself that I have any right to be satisfied with men as they are, and to treat them according, and not according, in some respects, to my requisitions and expectations of what they and I ought to be, then, like a good Mussulman and fatalist, I should endeavor to be satisfied with things as they are, and say it is the will of God. And, above all, there is this difference between resisting this and a purely brute or natural force, that I can resist this with some effect; but I cannot expect, like Orpheus, to change the nature of the rocks and trees and beasts.

I do not wish to quarrel with any man or nation. I do not wish to split 40 hairs, to make fine distinctions, or set myself up as better than my neighbors. I seek rather, I may say, even an excuse for conforming to the laws of the land. I am but too ready to conform to them. Indeed, I have reason to suspect myself on this head; and each year, as the tax-gatherer comes round, I find myself disposed to review the acts and position of the general and State governments, and the spirit of the people, to discover a pretext for conformity.

> We must affect our country as our parents;
> And if at any time we alienate
> Our love or industry from doing it honor,
> We must respect effects and teach the soul
> Matter of conscience and religion,
> And not desire of rule or benefit.

I believe that the State will soon be able to take all my work of this sort out of my hands, and then I shall be no better a patriot than my fellow-countrymen. Seen from a lower point of view, the Constitution, with all its faults, is very good; the law and the courts are very respectable; even this State and this American government are, in many respects, very admirable and rare things, to be thankful for, such as a great many have described them; but seen from a point of view a little higher, they are what I have described them; seen from a higher still, and the highest, who shall say what they are, or that they are worth looking at or thinking of at all?

However, the government does not concern me much, and I shall bestow the fewest possible thoughts on it. It is not many moments that I live under a government, even in this world. If a man is thought-free, fancy-free, imagination-free, that which *is not* never for a long time appearing *to be* to him, unwise rulers or reformers cannot fatally interrupt him.

I know that most men think differently from myself; but those whose lives are by profession devoted to the study of these or kindred subjects, content me as little as any. Statesmen and legislators, standing so completely within the institution, never distinctly and nakedly behold it. They speak of moving society, but have no resting-place without it. They may be men of a certain experience and discrimination, and have no doubt invented ingenious and even useful systems, for which we sincerely thank them; but all their wit and usefulness lie within certain not very wide limits. They are wont to forget that the world is not governed by policy and expediency. Webster never goes behind government, and so cannot speak with authority about it. His words are wisdom to those legislators who contemplate no essential reform in the existing government; but for thinkers, and those who legislate for all time, he never once glances at the subject. I know of those whose serene and wise speculations on this theme would soon reveal the limits of his mind's range and hospitality. Yet, compared with the cheap professions of most reformers, and the still cheaper wisdom and eloquence of politicians in general, his are almost the only sensible and valuable words, and we thank Heaven for him. Comparatively, he is always strong, original, and, above all, practical. Still his quality is not wisdom, but prudence. The lawyer's truth is not Truth, but consistency, or a consistent expediency. Truth is always in harmony with herself, and is not concerned chiefly to reveal the justice that may consist with wrong-doing. He well deserves to be called, as he has been called, the Defender of the Constitution. There are really no blows to be given by him but defensive ones. He is not a leader, but a follower. His leaders are the men of '87. "I have never made an effort," he says, "and never propose to make an effort; I have never countenanced an effort, and never mean to countenance an effort, to disturb the arrangement as originally made, by which the various States came into the Union." Still thinking of the sanction which the Constitution gives to slavery, he says, "Because it was a part of the original compact,—let it stand." Notwithstanding his special acuteness and ability, he is unable to take a fact out of its merely political relations, and behold it as it lies absolutely to be disposed of by the intellect,—what, for instance, it behooves a man to do here in America today with regard to slavery, but ventures, or is driven, to make some such desperate answer as the following, while professing to speak absolutely, and as a private man,—from which what new and singular code of social duties might be inferred? "The manner," says he, "in which the governments of those States where slavery exists are to regulate it, is for their own consideration, under their responsibility to their constituents, to the general laws of propriety, humanity, and justice, and to God. Associations formed elsewhere, springing from a feeling of humanity, or any other cause, have nothing whatever to do with it. They have never received any encouragement from me, and they never will."[1]

They who know of no purer sources of truth, who have traced up its stream no higher, stand, and wisely stand, by the Bible and the Constitution, and drink at it there with reverence and humility; but they who behold where it comes trickling into this lake or that pool, gird up their loins once more, and continue their pilgrimage toward its fountainhead.

No man with a genius for legislation has appeared in America. They are rare in the history of the world. There are orators, politicians, and eloquent men, by the thousand; but the speaker has not yet opened his mouth to speak, who is capable of settling the much-vexed questions of the day. We love eloquence for its own sake, and not for any truth which it may utter, or any heroism it may inspire. Our legislators have not yet learned the comparative value of free-trade and of freedom, of union, and of rectitude, to a nation. They have no genius or talent for comparatively humble questions of taxation and finance, commerce and manufactures and agriculture. If we were left solely to the wordy wit of legislators in Congress for our guidance, uncorrected by the seasonable experience and

---

[1] These extracts have been inserted since the Lecture was read.

the effectual complaints of the people, America would not long retain her rank among the nations. For eighteen hundred years, though perchance I have no right to say it, the New Testament has been written; yet where is the legislator who has wisdom and practical talent enough to avail himself of the light which it sheds on the science of legislation?

The authority of government, even such as I am willing to submit 45 to, — for I will cheerfully obey those who know and can do better than I, and in many things even those who neither know nor can do so well, — is still an impure one: To be strictly just, it must have the sanction and consent of the governed. It can have no pure right over my person and property but what I concede to it. The progress from an absolute to a limited monarchy, from a limited monarchy to a democracy, is a progress toward a true respect for the individual. Even the Chinese philosopher was wise enough to regard the individual as the basis of the empire. Is a democracy, such as we know it, the last improvement possible in government? Is it not possible to take a step further towards recognizing and organizing the rights of man? There will never be a really free and enlightened State, until the State comes to recognize the individual as a higher and independent power, from which all its own power and authority are derived, and treats him accordingly. I please myself with imagining a State at last which can afford to be just to all men, and to treat the individual with respect as a neighbor; which even would not think it inconsistent with its own repose, if a few were to live aloof from it, not meddling with it, nor embraced by it, who fulfilled all the duties of neighbors and fellowmen. A State which bore this kind of fruit, and suffered it to drop off as fast as it ripened, would prepare the way for a still more perfect and glorious State, which also I have imagined, but not yet anywhere seen.

DISCUSSION QUESTIONS

1. Summarize briefly Thoreau's reasons for arguing that civil disobedience is sometimes a *duty.*

2. Thoreau, like Martin Luther King Jr. in "Letter from Birmingham Jail" (p. 797), speaks of "unjust laws" (para. 16). Do they agree on the positions that citizens should take in response to these laws? Are Thoreau and King guided by the same principles? In Plato's "Crito" (p. 735), what does Socrates say about obedience to unjust laws?

3. What examples of government policy and action does Thoreau use to prove that civil disobedience is a duty? Explain why they are—or are not—effective.

4. Why do you think Thoreau provides such a detailed account of one day in prison? (Notice that King does not give a description of his confinement.) What observation about the community struck Thoreau when he emerged from jail?

WRITING SUGGESTIONS

5. Argue that civil disobedience to a school policy or action is justified. (Examples might include failure to establish an ethnic studies department, refusal to allow ROTC on campus, refusal to suspend a professor accused of sexual harassment.) Be specific about the injustice of the policy or action and the values that underlie the resistance.

6. Under what circumstances might civil disobedience prove to be dangerous and immoral? Can you think of cases of disobedience when *conscience*, as Thoreau uses the term, did not appear to be the guiding principle? Try to identify what you think is the true motivation for the resistance.

The Crisis

CARRIE CHAPMAN CATT

I have taken for my subject, "The Crisis," because I believe that a crisis has come in our movement which, if recognized and the opportunity seized with vigor, enthusiasm and will, means the final victory of our great cause in the very near future. I am aware that some suffragists do not share this belief; they see no signs nor symptoms today which were not present yesterday; no manifestations in the year 1916 which differ significantly from those in the year 1910. To them, the movement has been a steady, normal growth from the beginning and must so continue until the end. I can only defend my claim with the plea that it is better to *imagine* a crisis where none exists than to fail to recognize one when it comes; for a crisis is a culmination of events which calls for new considerations and new decisions. A failure to answer the call may mean an opportunity lost, a possible victory postponed.

The object of the life of an organized movement is to secure its aim. Necessarily, it must obey the law of evolution and pass through the stages of agitation and education and finally through the stage of realization. As one has put it: "A new idea floats in the air over the heads of the people and for a long, indefinite period evades their understanding but, by and by, when through familiarity, human vision grows clearer, it is caught out of the clouds and crystalized into law." Such a period comes to every movement and is its crisis. In my judgment, that crucial moment, bidding us to renewed consecration and redoubled activity has come to our cause. I believe our victory hangs within our grasp, inviting us to pluck it out of the clouds and establish it among the good things of the world.

If this be true, the time is past when we should say: "Men and women of America, look upon that wonderful idea up there; see, one day it will come down." Instead, the time has come to shout aloud in every city, village and hamlet, and in tones so clear and jubilant that they will reverberate from every mountain peak and echo from shore to shore: "The

---

Carrie Chapman Catt (1859–1947) was an outspoken advocate of women's suffrage and the founder of the League of Women Voters. This speech was given in September 1916 in Atlantic City, New Jersey, at a special convention of the National American Woman Suffrage Association, of which she was president. Her powerful speech is one of the one hundred most important speeches in American history. In it she presents the war in Europe taking place at that time as an opportunity to push for women's right to vote. European women had proven to be such effective "war assets" that it would be hard for them to ever be relegated to the inferior positions they had occupied before the war. American women could hardly be satisfied with less.

Woman's Hour has struck."[1] Suppose suffragists as a whole do not believe a crisis has come and do not extend their hands to grasp the victory, what will happen? Why, we shall all continue to work and our cause will continue to hang, waiting for those who possess a clearer vision and more daring enterprise. On the other hand, suppose we reach out with united earnestness and determination to grasp our victory while it still hangs a bit too high? Has any harm been done? None!

Therefore, fellow suffragists, I invite your attention to the signs which point to a crisis and your consideration of plans for turning the crisis into victory.

First: We are passing through a world crisis. All thinkers of every land 5 tell us so; and that nothing after the great war will be as it was before. Those who profess to know, claim that 100 millions of dollars are being spent on the war every day and that 2 years of war have cost 50 billions of dollars or 10 times more than the total expense of the American Civil War. Our own country has sent 35 millions of dollars abroad for relief expenses.

Were there no other effects to come from the world's war, the transfer of such unthinkably vast sums of money from the usual avenues to those wholly abnormal would give so severe a jolt to organized society that it would vibrate around the world and bring untold changes in its wake.

But three and a half millions of lives have been lost. The number becomes the more impressive when it is remembered that the entire population of the American Colonies was little more than three and one-half millions. These losses have been the lives of men within the age of economic production. They have been taken abruptly from the normal business of the world and every human activity from that of the humblest, unskilled labor to art, science and literature has been weakened by their loss. Millions of other men will go to their homes, blind, crippled and incapacitated to do the work they once performed. The stability of human institutions has never before suffered so tremendous a shock. Great men are trying to think out the consequences but one and all proclaim that no imagination can find color or form bold enough to paint the picture of the world after the war. British and Russian, German and Austrian, French and Italian agree that it will lead to social and political revolution throughout the entire world. Whatever comes, they further agree that the war presages a total change in the status of women.

A simple-minded man in West Virginia, when addressed upon the subject of woman suffrage in that state, replied, "We've been so used to

---

[1] This phrase refers to the frustration of woman's rights activists in the post–Civil War period who were told to defer the demand for woman suffrage because this was "the Negro's hour." [All notes are by Karlyn Kohrs Campbell, the editor of *Man Cannot Speak for Her* (Greenwood, 1989).]

keepin' our women down, 'twould seem queer not to." He expressed what greater men feel but do not say. Had the wife of that man spoken in the same clear-thinking fashion, she would have said, "We women have been so used to being kept down that it would seem strange to get up. Nature intended women for doormats." Had she so expressed herself, these two would have put the entire anti-suffrage argument in a nutshell.

In Europe, from the Polar Circle to the Aegean Sea, women have risen as though to answer that argument. Everywhere they have taken the places made vacant by men and in so doing, they have grown in self-respect and in the esteem of their respective nations. In every land, the people have reverted to the primitive division of labor and while the men have gone to war, women have cultivated the fields in order that the army and nation may be fed. No army can succeed and no nation can endure without food; those who supply it are a war power and a peace power.

Women by the thousands have knocked at the doors of munition fac- 10
tories and, in the name of patriotism, have begged for the right to serve their country there. Their services were accepted with hesitation but the experiment once made, won reluctant but universal praise. An official statement recently issued in Great Britain announced that 660,000 women were engaged in making munitions in that country alone. In a recent convention of munition workers, composed of men and women, a resolution was unanimously passed informing the government that they would forego vacations and holidays until the authorities announced that their munition supplies were sufficient for the needs of the war and Great Britain pronounced the act the highest patriotism. Lord Derby addressed such a meeting and said, "When the history of the war is written, I wonder to whom the greatest credit will be given; to the men who went to fight or to the women who are working in a way that many people hardly believed that it was possible for them to work." Lord Sydenham added his tribute. Said he, "It might fairly be claimed that women have helped to save thousands of lives and to change the entire aspect of the war. Wherever intelligence, care and close attention have been needed, women have distinguished themselves." A writer in the *London Times* of July 18, 1916, said: "But, for women, the armies could not have held the field for a month; the national call to arms could not have been made or sustained; the country would have perished of inanition and disorganization. If, indeed, it be true that the people have been one, it is because the genius of women has been lavishly applied to the task of reinforcing and complementing the genius of men. The qualities of steady industry, adaptability, good judgement and concentration of mind which men do not readily associate with women have been conspicuous features."

On fields of battle, in regular and improvised hospitals, women have given tender and skilled care to the wounded and are credited with the restoration of life to many, many thousands. Their heroism and self-sacrifice have been frankly acknowledged by all the governments; but their endurance, their skill, the practicality of their service, seem for the first time, to have been recognized by governments as "war power." So, thinking in war terms, great men have suddenly discovered that women are "war assets". Indeed, Europe is realizing, as it never did before, that women are holding together the civilization for which men are fighting. A great search-light has been thrown upon the business of nation-building and it has been demonstrated in every European land that it is a partnership with equal, but different responsibilities resting upon the two partners.

It is not, however, in direct war work alone that the latent possibilities of women have been made manifest. In all the belligerent lands, women have found their way to high posts of administration where no women would have been trusted two years ago and the testimony is overwhelming that they have filled their posts with entire satisfaction to the authorities. They have dared to stand in pulpits (once too sacred to be touched by the unholy feet of a woman) and there, without protest, have appealed to the Father of All in behalf of their stricken lands. They have come out of the kitchen where there was too little to cook and have found a way to live by driving cabs, motors and streetcars. Many a woman has turned her hungry children over to a neighbor and has gone forth to find food for both mothers and both families of children and has found it in strange places and occupations. Many a drawing-room has been closed and the maid who swept and dusted it is now cleaning streets that the health of the city may be conserved. Many a woman who never before slept in a bed of her own making, or ate food not prepared by paid labor, is now sole mistress of parlor and kitchen.

In all the warring countries, women are postmen [sic], porters, railway conductors, ticket, switch and signal men. Conspicuous advertisements invite women to attend agricultural, milking and motor-car schools. They are employed as police in Great Britain and women detectives have recently been taken on the government staff. In Berlin, there are over 3,000 women streetcar conductors and 3,500 women are employed on the general railways. In every city and country, women are doing work for which they would have been considered incompetent two years ago.

The war will soon end and the armies will return to their native lands. To many a family, the men will never come back. The husband who returns to many a wife, will eat no bread the rest of his life save of her earning.

What, then, will happen after the war? Will the widows left with families to support cheerfully leave their well-paid posts for those commanding lower wages? Not without protest! Will the wives who now must support crippled husbands give up their skilled work and take up the occupations which were open to them before the war? Will they resignedly say: "The woman who has a healthy husband who can earn for her, has a right to tea and raisin cake, but the woman who earns for herself and a husband who has given his all to his country, must be content with butterless bread"? Not without protest! On the contrary, the economic axiom, denied and evaded for centuries, will be blazoned on every factory, counting house and shop: "Equal pay for equal work"; and common justice will slowly, but surely enforce that law. The European woman has risen. She may not realize it yet, but the woman "doormat" in every land has unconsciously become a "doorjamb"! She will have become accustomed to her new dignity by the time the men come home. She will wonder how she ever could have been content lying across the threshold now that she discovers the upright jamb gives so much broader and more normal a vision of things. The men returning may find the new order a bit queer but everything else will be strangely unfamiliar too, and they will soon grow accustomed to all the changes together. The "jamb" will never descend into a "doormat" again.

The male and female anti-suffragists of all lands will puff and blow at the economic change which will come to the women of Europe. They will declare it to be contrary to Nature and to God's plan and that somebody ought to do something about it. Suffragists will accept the change as the inevitable outcome of an unprecedented world's cataclysm over which no human agency had any control and will trust in God to adjust the altered circumstances to the eternal evolution of human society. They will remember that in the long run, all things work together for good, for progress and for human weal.

The economic change is bound to bring political liberty. From every land, there comes the expressed belief that the war will be followed by a mighty, oncoming wave of democracy for it is now well known that the conflict has been one of governments, of kings and Czars, Kaisers and Emperors; not of peoples. The nations involved have nearly all declared that they are fighting to make an end of wars. New and higher ideals of governments and of the rights of the people under them, have grown enormously during the past two years. Another tide of political liberty, similar to that of 1848, but of a thousandfold greater momentum, is rising from battlefield and hospital, from camp and munitions factory, from home and church which, great men of many lands, tell us, is destined to sweep over the world. On the continent, the women say, "It is certain that the vote will come to men and women after the war, perhaps not immediately but soon. In Great Britain, which was the storm centre of the suffrage movement for some years before the war, hundreds of bitter, active opponents have confessed their conversion on account of the war services of women. Already, three great provinces of Canada, Manitoba, Alberta, and Saskatchawan [sic], have given universal suffrage to their women in sheer generous appreciation of their war work. Even Mr. Asquith, world renouned [sic] for his immovable opposition to the Parliamentary suffrage for British women, has given evidence of a change of view.[2] Some months ago, he announced his amazement at the utterly un-

---

[2] Herbert Henry Asquith (1852–1928), British prime minister (1908–1916) and leader of the Liberal party until 1925, when he was raised to the peerage; he opposed woman suffrage.

expected skill, strength and resource developed by the women and his gratitude for their loyalty and devotion. Later, in reply to Mrs. Henry Fawcett, who asked if woman suffrage would be included in a proposed election bill, he said that when the war should end, such a measure would be considered without prejudice carried over from events prior to the war.[3] A public statement issued by Mr. Asquith in August, was couched in such terms as to be interpreted by many as a pledge to include women in the next election bill.

In Great Britain, a sordid appeal which may prove the last straw to break the opposition to woman suffrage, has been added to the enthusiastic appreciation of woman's patriotism and practical service and to the sudden comprehension that motherhood is a national asset which must be protected at any price. A new voters' list is contemplated. A parliamentary election should be held in September but the voters are scattered far and wide. The whole nation is agitated over the questions involved in making a new register. At the same time, there is a constant anxiety over war funds, as is prudent in a nation spending 50 millions of dollars per day. It has been proposed that a large poll tax be assessed upon the voters of the new lists, whereupon a secondary proposal of great force has been offered and that is, that twice as much money would find its way into the public coffers were women added to the voters' list. What nation, with compliments fresh spoken concerning women's patriotism and efficiency, could resist such an appeal?

So it happens that above the roar of cannon, the scream of shrapnel and the whirr of aeroplanes, one who listens may hear the cracking of the fetters which have long bound the European woman to outworn conventions. It has been a frightful price to pay but the fact remains that a womanhood, well started on the way to final emancipation, is destined to step forth from the war. It will be a bewildered, troubled and grief-stricken womanhood with knotty problems of life to solve, but it will be freer to deal with them than women have ever been before.

"The Woman's Hour has struck." It has struck for the women of Europe and for those of all the world. The significance of the changed status of European women has not been lost upon the men and women of our land; our own people are not so unlearned in history, nor so lacking in National pride that they will allow the Republic to lag long behind the Empire, presided over by the descendant of George the Third. If they possess the patriotism and the sense of nationality which should be the inheritance of an American, they will not wait until the war is ended but will boldly lead in the inevitable march of democracy, our own American specialty. Sisters, let me repeat, the Woman's Hour has struck!

---

[3] Millicent Garrett Fawcett, the leading figure in the National Union of Women's Suffrage Societies, which began in 1867 and stood apart from the more militant suffrage organizations.

Second: As the most adamantine rock gives way under the constant dripping of water, so the opposition to woman suffrage in our own country has slowly disintegrated before the increasing strength of our movement. Turn backward the pages of our history! Behold, brave Abbie Kelley rotten-egged because she, a woman, essayed to speak in public.[4] Behold the Polish Ernestine Rose startled that women of free America drew aside their skirts when she proposed that they should control their own property.[5] Recall the saintly Lucretia Mott and the legal-minded Elizabeth Cady Stanton, turned out of the [W]orld's Temperance Convention in London and conspiring together to free their sex from the world's stupid oppressions.[6] Remember the gentle, sweet-voiced Lucy Stone, egged because she publicly claimed that women had brains capable of education.[7] Think upon Dr. Elizabeth Blackwell, snubbed and boycotted by other women because she proposed to study medicine.[8] Behold Dr. Antoinette Brown Blackwell, standing in sweet serenity before an Assembly of howling clergymen, angry that she, a woman dared to attend a Temperance Convention as a delegate. Revere the intrepid Susan B. Anthony mobbed from Buffalo to Albany because she demanded fair play for women. These are they who builded with others the foundation of political liberty for American women.

Those who came after only laid the stones in place. Yet, what a wearisome task even that has been! Think of the wonderful woman who has wandered from village to village, from city to city, for a generation compelling men and women to listen and to reflect by her matchless eloquence. Where in all the world's history has any movement among men produced so invincible an advocate as our own Dr. Anna Howard Shaw? Those whom she has led to the light are Legion. Think, too, of the con-

---

[4] Abigail ("Abby") Kelley [Foster] (1810–1887), abolitionist and woman's rights lecturer, spoke first in 1838 to a mixed audience in Philadelphia's Pennsylvania Hall. A powerful agitator, she was attacked as a Jezebel and faced angry mobs outraged at a woman speaking effectively to mixed audiences against slavery.

[5] An allusion to the 1836 effort to petition the New York Legislature to amend the Married Woman's Property Act.

[6] Lucretia Coffin Mott and other women were not seated as delegates at the World Anti-Slavery Convention in 1840. Cady Stanton was present but not a delegate.

[7] Lucy Stone (1818–1893), the first Massachusetts woman to take [earn] a college degree (Oberlin, 1847). She became a lecturer for the American Anti-Slavery Society, but also spoke on woman's rights prior to the emergence of a movement, fearlessly facing hostile audiences. Defying convention, she kept her own name after her marriage to Henry Blackwell in 1855. She became the leader of the New England wing of the suffrage movement, a founder of the American Woman Suffrage Association and of the *Woman's Journal* (1870), which after 1872 she and her husband, and later her daughter, Alice Stone Blackwell, edited.

[8] Elizabeth Blackwell (1821–1910), the first woman of modern times to graduate in medicine. She received her degree in 1849 from Geneva College, and founded the New York Infirmary for Women and Children in 1857, and the Woman's Medical College of the New York Infirmary in 1868.

secration, the self-denial, the never-failing constancy of that other noble soul set in a frail but unflinching body,—the heroine we know as Alice Stone Blackwell![9] A woman who never forgets, who detects the slightest flaw in the weapons of her adversary, who knows the most vulnerable spot in his armor, president over the *Woman's Journal* and, like a lamp in lighthouse, the rays of her intelligence, far-sightedness and clear-thinking have enlightened the world concerning our cause. The names of hundreds of other brave souls spring to memory when we pause to review the long struggle.

The hands of many suffrage master-masons have long been stilled; the names of many who laid the stones have been forgotten. That does not matter. The main thing is that the edifice of woman's liberty nears completion. It is strong, indestructible. All honor to the thousands who have helped in the building.

The four Cornerstones of the foundations were laid long years ago. We read upon the first: "We demand for women education, for not a high school or college is open to her"; upon the second, "We demand for women religious liberty for in few churches is she permitted to pray or speak"; upon the third, "We demand for women the right to own property and an opportunity to earn an honest living. Only six, poorly-paid occupations are open to her, and if she is married, the wages she earns are not hers"; upon the fourth, "We demand political freedom and its symbol, the vote."

The stones in the foundation have long been overgrown with the moss and mould of time, and some there are who never knew they were laid. Of late, four capstones at the top have been set to match those in the base, and we read upon the first: "The number of women who are graduated from high schools, colleges and universities is legion"; upon the second, "The Christian Endeavor, that mighty, undenominational church militant, asks the vote for the women and the Methodist Episcopal Church, and many another, joins that appeal"; upon the third, "Billions of dollars worth of property are earned [and] owned by women; more than 8 millions of women are wage-earners. Every occupation is open to them"; upon the fourth: "Women vote in 12 States; they share in the determination of 91 electoral votes."

After the capstones and cornice comes the roof. Across the empty spaces, the roof-tree has been flung and fastened well in place. It is not made of stone but of two *planks*—planks in the platform of the two majority parties, and these are well supported by planks in the platforms of all minority parties.

---

[9]Daughter of Lucy Stone and Henry Blackwell (1857–1950). Following graduation from Boston University in 1881, she bore the main burdens of editing the *Woman's Journal*, the country's leading woman's rights newspaper founded by her parents, for the next thirty-five years.

And we who are the builders of 1916, do we see a crisis? Standing upon these planks which are stretched across the top-most peak of this edifice of woman's liberty, what shall we do? Over our heads, up there in the clouds, but tantalizing [sic] near, hangs the roof of our edifice, — the vote. What is our duty? Shall we spend time in admiring the capstones and cornice? Shall we lament the tragedies which accompanied the laying of the cornerstones? Or, shall we, like the builders of old, chant, "Ho! all hands, all hands, heave to! All hands, heave to!" and while we chant, grasp the overhanging roof and with a long pull, a strong pull and a pull together, fix it in place forevermore?

Is the crisis real or imaginary? If it be real, it calls for action, bold, immediate and decisive.

Let us then take measure of our strength. Our cause has won the endorsement of all political parties. Every candidate for the presidency is a suffragist. It has won the endorsement of most churches; it has won the hearty approval of all great organizations of women. It has won the support of all reform movements; it has won the progressives of every variety. The majority of the press in most States is with us. Great men in every political party, church and movement are with us. The names of the greatest men and women of art, science, literature and philosophy, reform, religion and politics are on our lists.

We have not won the reactionaries of any party, church or society, and   30 we never will. From the beginning of things, there have been Antis. The Antis drove Moses out of Egypt; they crucified Christ who said, "Love thy neighbor as thyself" [Matt. 19:19, 22:39]; they have persecuted Jews in all parts of the world; they poisoned Socrates, the great philosopher; they cruelly persecuted Copernicus[10] and Galileo,[11] the first great scientists; they burned Giordano Bruno at the stake because he believed the world was round;[12] they burned Savonarola who warred upon church corruption;[13]

---

[10]Nicholas Copernicus (1473–1543), Polish astronomer, whose great work, the foundation of modern astronomy, was *De revolutionibus orbium coelestium* (1543), dedicated to Pope Paul III.

[11]Galileo Galilei (1564–1642), Italian astronomer, mathematician, and physicist, who constructed the first complete astronomical telescope, and whose investigations confirmed the Copernican theory of the solar system. In 1616 that theory was denounced as dangerous to faith, but in 1632 Galileo published a work which supported it, and was tried in 1633 by the Inquisition and forced to recant all beliefs and writings holding that the earth and other planets revolved about the sun.

[12]Giordano Bruno (1548–1600), Italian philosopher. His major metaphysical works were *De la causa, principio, et uno* (1584) and *De l'infinito, universo et mondi* (1584). Tried for heresy in Venice in 1591 by the Inquisition, he was imprisoned, then burned to death at Rome.

[13]Girolamo Savonarola (1452–1498), Italian religious reformer, prior of San Marco, the Dominican house in Florence. He was excommunicated by Pope Alexander VI for disobedience after he continued to preach against the scandalously corrupt papal court. Under torture he supposedly confessed to being a false prophet and was hanged for schism and heresy.

they burned Eufame McIlyane [sic] because she used an anaesthetic;[14] they burned Joan d'Arc for a heretic; they have sent great men and women to Siberia to eat their hearts out in isolation; they burned in effigy William Lloyd Garrison; they egged Abbie Kelley and Lucy Stone and mobbed Susan B. Anthony. Yet, in proportion to the enlightenment of their respective ages, these Antis were persons of intelligence and honest purpose. They were merely deaf to the call of Progress and were enraged because the world insisted upon moving on. Antis male and female there still are and will be to the end of time. Give to them a prayer of forgiveness for they know not what they do; and prepare for the forward march.

We have not won the ignorant and illiterate and we never can. They are too undeveloped mentally to understand that the institutions of today are not those of yesterday nor will be those of tomorrow.

We have not won the forces of evil and we never will. Evil has ever been timorous and suspicious of all change. It is an instinctive act of self-preservation which makes it fear and consequently oppose votes for women. As the Hon. Champ Clark said the other day: "Some good and intelligent people are opposed to woman suffrage; but all the ignorant and evil-minded are against it."[15]

These three forces are the enemies of our cause.

Before the vote is won, there must and will be a gigantic final conflict between the forces of progress, righteousness and democracy and the forces of ignorance, evil and reaction. That struggle may be postponed, but it cannot be evaded or avoided. There is no question as to which side will be the victor.

Shall we play the coward, then, and leave the hard knocks for our daughters, or shall we throw ourselves into the fray, bare our own shoulders to the blows, and thus bequeath to them a politically liberated womanhood? We have taken note of our gains and of our resources, and they are all we could wish. Before the final struggle, we must take cognizance of our weaknesses. Are we prepared to grasp the victory? Alas, no! Our movement is like a great Niagara with a vast volume of water tumbling over its ledge but turning no wheel. Our organized machinery is set for the propagandistic stage and not for the seizure of victory. Our supporters are spreading the argument for our cause; they feel no sense of responsibility for the realization of our hopes. Our movement lacks cohesion, organization, unity and consequent momentum.

Behind us, in front of us, everywhere about us are suffragists, — millions of them, but inactive and silent. They have been "agitated and

[14]Euphemia MacCalyean was sentenced to be burned in Scotland on June 15, 1591, for attempting to relieve her pains in giving birth to twins and for other charges related to witchcraft.

[15]James Beauchamp Clark (1850–1921), member U.S. House of Representatives (1893–1895, 1897–1921). He became Democratic leader (1907) and Speaker (1911–1919), and in 1912 was the leading Democratic candidate for the presidency until William Jennings Bryan shifted his support to Woodrow Wilson.

educated" and are with us in belief. There are thousands of women who have at one time or another been members of our organization but they have dropped out because, to them the movement seemed negative and pointless. Many have taken up other work whose results were more immediate. Philanthropy, charity, work for corrective laws of various kinds, temperance, relief for working women and numberless similar public services have called them. Others have turned to the pleasanter avenues of clubwork, art or literature.

There are thousands of other women who have never learned of the earlier struggles of our movement. They found doors of opportunity open to them on every side. They found well-paid posts awaiting the qualified woman and they have availed themselves of all these blessings; almost without exception they believe in the vote but they feel neither gratitude to those who opened the doors through which they have entered to economic liberty nor any sense of obligation to open other doors for those who come after.

There are still others who, timorously looking over their shoulders to see if any listeners be near, will tell us they hope we will win and win soon but they are too frightened of Mother Grundy to help.[16] There are others too occupied with the small things of life to help. They say they could find time to vote but not to work for the vote. There are men, too, millions of them, waiting to be called. These men and women are our reserves. They are largely unorganized and untrained soldiers with little responsibility toward our movement. Yet these reserves must be mobilized. The final struggle needs their numbers and the momentum those numbers will bring. Were never another convert made, there are suffragists enough in this country, if combined, to make so irresistible a driving force that victory might be seized at once.

How can it be done? By a simple change of mental attitude. If we are to seize the victory, that change must take place in this hall, here and now!

The old belief, which has sustained suffragists in many an hour of discouragement, "woman suffrage is bound to come," must give way to the new, "The Woman's Hour has struck." The long drawn out struggle, the cruel hostility which, for years was arrayed against our cause, have accustomed suffragists to the idea of indefinite postponement but eventual victory. The slogan of a movements sets its pace. The old one counseled patience; it said, there is plenty of time; it pardoned sloth and half-hearted effort. It set the pace of an educational campaign. The "Woman's Hour has struck" sets the pace of a crusade which will have its way. It says: "Awake, arise, my sisters, let your hearts be filled with joy,—the time of victory is here. Onward March." 40

If you believe with me that a crisis has come to our movement,—if you believe that the time for final action is now, if you catch the rosy tints of the coming day, what does it mean to you? Does it not give you a thrill

[16]Public opinion personified.

of exaltation; does the blood not course more quickly through your veins; does it not bring a new sense of freedom, of joy and of determination? Is it not true that you who wanted a little time ago to lay down the work because you were weary with long service, now, under the compelling influence of a changed mental attitude, are ready to go on until the vote is won. The change is one of spirit! Aye, and the spiritual effect upon you will come to others. Let me borrow an expression from Hon. John Finlay: What our great movement needs now is a "mobilization of spirit", — the jubilant, glad spirit of victory. Then let us sound a bugle call here and now to the women of the Nation: "The Woman's Hour has struck." Let the bugle sound from the suffrage headquarters of every State at the inauguration of a State campaign. Let the call go forth again and again and yet again. Let it be repeated in every article written, in every speech made, in every conversation held. Let the bugle blow again and yet again. The political emancipation of our sex call[s] you, women of America, arise! Are you content that others shall pay the price of your liberty?

Women in schools and counting house, in shops and on the farm, women in the home with babes at their breasts and women engaged in public careers will hear. The veins of American women are not filled with milk and water. They are neither cowards nor slackers. They will come. They only await the bugle call to learn that the final battle is on.

DISCUSSION QUESTIONS

1. What are the signs Catt sees that suggest America's crisis point in the fight for women's suffrage might turn into victory?
2. In what ways has World War I changed the role of women in Europe?
3. What does Catt predict will happen to women's status in Europe once the war is over?
4. Explain Catt's metaphor of woman as doormat or as doorjamb.
5. Explain the metaphor of the construction of a building that Catt uses to describe the suffrage movement.
6. In what ways does Catt appeal to the emotions of those listening to her speech in 1916?
7. What other effective argumentative strategies does Catt use in the speech?
8. How does she use language effectively to strengthen her speech?

WRITING SUGGESTIONS

9. Argue that Catt's speech is a blend of appeal to the reason and to the emotions of her audience.
10. How does she use her analysis of what is happening in Europe to appeal to an American audience?
11. Explain how Catt's speech, given in 1916, still has relevance in the early twentieth century.

Warfare: An Invention— Not a Biological Necessity

MARGARET MEAD

Is war a biological necessity, a sociological inevitability, or just a bad invention? Those who argue for the first view endow man with such pugnacious instincts that some outlet in aggressive behavior is necessary if man is to reach full human stature. It was this point of view which lay back of William James's famous essay, "The Moral Equivalent of War," in which he tried to retain the warlike virtues and channel them in new directions. A similar point of view has lain back of the Soviet Union's attempt to make competition between groups rather than between individuals. A basic, competitive, aggressive, warring human nature is assumed, and those who wish to outlaw war or outlaw competitiveness merely try to find new and less socially destructive ways in which these biologically given aspects of man's nature can find expression. Then there are those who take the second view: warfare is the inevitable concomitant of the development of the state, the struggle for land and natural resources of class societies springing, not from the nature of man, but from the nature of history. War is nevertheless inevitable unless we change our social system and outlaw classes, the struggle for power, and possessions; and in the event of our success warfare would disappear, as a symptom vanishes when the disease is cured.

One may hold a compromise position between these two extremes; one may claim that all aggression springs from the frustration of man's biologically determined drives and that, since all forms of culture are frustrating, it is certain each new generation will be aggressive and the aggression will find its natural and inevitable expression in race war, class war, nationalistic war, and so on.

All three positions are very popular today among those who think seriously about the problems of war and its possible prevention, but I wish to urge another point of view, less defeatist perhaps than the first and

Margaret Mead (1901–1978) was the first American anthropologist to study childhood, adolescence, and gender. Her work focused primarily on culture rather than biology or race as the primary factor in determining variations in human behavior and personality. As a graduate student, she conducted field research on adolescence and sexuality in Samoa. Her resulting work, the best-selling *Coming of Age in Samoa* (1928), made her a household name in the United States. She went on to publish forty-four books, including *Growing Up in New Guinea* (1930) and *Sex and Temperament* (1935), and hundreds of articles. Her early research in Samoa has been challenged by Derek Freeman, an anthropologist who characterizes Mead's work as being antievolutionary and fundamentally flawed in its portrayal of sexuality in the South Seas. Freeman's accusations, however, have been discredited by many scholars who recognize Mead's important contributions to the field. The following article, in which Mead argues that warfare is a cultural invention and not a biological necessity, was published in *Asia* in 1940.

third, and more accurate than the second: that is, that warfare, by which I mean organized conflict between two groups as *groups,* in which each group puts an army (even if the army is only fifteen Pygmies) into the field to fight and kill, if possible, some of the members of the army of the other group—that warfare of this sort is an invention like any other of the inventions in terms of which we order our lives, such as writing, marriage, cooking our food instead of eating it raw, trial by jury, or burial of the dead, and so on. Some of this list any one will grant are inventions: trial by jury is confined to very limited portions of the globe; we know that there are tribes that do not bury their dead but instead expose or cremate them; and we know that only part of the human race has had a knowledge of writing as its cultural inheritance. But, whenever a way of doing things is found universally, such as the use of fire or the practice of some form of marriage, we tend to think at once that it is not an invention at all but an attribute of humanity itself. And yet even such universals as marriage and the use of fire are inventions like the rest, very basic ones, inventions which were perhaps necessary if human history was to take the turn it has taken, but nevertheless inventions. At some point in his social development man was undoubtedly without the institution of marriage or the knowledge of the use of fire.

The case for warfare is much clearer because there are peoples even today who have no warfare. Of these the Eskimo are perhaps the most conspicuous example, but the Lepchas of Sikkim are an equally good one. Neither of these peoples understands war, not even the defensive warfare. The idea of warfare is lacking, and this lack is as essential to carrying on war as an alphabet or a syllabary is to writing. But whereas the Lepchas are a gentle, unquarrelsome people, and the advocates of other points of view might argue that they are not full human beings or that they had never been frustrated and so had no aggression to expend in warfare, the Eskimo case gives no such possibility of interpretation. The Eskimo are not a mild and meek people; many of them are turbulent and troublesome. Fights, theft of wives, murder, cannibalism occur among them—all outbursts of passionate men goaded by desire or intolerable circumstance. Here are men faced with hunger, men faced with loss of their wives, men faced with the threat of extermination by other men, and here are orphan children, growing up miserably with no one to care for them, mocked and neglected by those about them. The personality necessary for war, the circumstances necessary to goad men to desperation are present, but there is no war. When a traveling Eskimo entered a settlement he might have to fight the strongest man in the settlement to establish his position among them, but this was a test of strength and bravery, not war. The idea of warfare, of one *group* organizing against another *group* to maim and wound and kill them, was absent. And without that idea passions might rage but there was no war.

But, it may be argued, isn't this because the Eskimo have such a low and undeveloped form of social organization? They own no land, they move from place to place, camping, it is true, season after season on the same site, but this is not something to fight for as the modern nations of the world fight for land and raw materials. They have no permanent possessions that can be looted, no towns that can be burned. They have no social classes to produce stress and strains within the society which might force it to go to war outside. Doesn't the absence of war among the Eskimo, while disproving the biological necessity of war, just go to confirm the point that it is the state of development of the society which accounts for war, and nothing else?

We find the answer among the Pygmy peoples of the Andaman Islands in the Bay of Bengal. The Andamans also represent an exceedingly low level of society: they are a hunting and food-gathering people; they live in tiny hordes without any class stratification; their houses are simpler than the snow houses of the Eskimo. But they knew about warfare. The army might contain only fifteen determined Pygmies marching in a straight line, but it was the real thing none the less. Tiny army met tiny army in open battle, blows were exchanged, casualties suffered, and the state of warfare could only be concluded by a peacemaking ceremony.

Similarly, among the Australian aborigines, who built no permanent dwellings but wandered from water hole to water hole over their almost desert country, warfare—and rules of "international law"—were highly developed. The student of social evolution will seek in vain for his obvious causes of war, struggle for lands, struggle for power of one group over another, expansion of population, need to divert the minds of a populace restive under tyranny, or even the ambition of a successful leader to enhance his own prestige. All are absent, but warfare as a practice remained, and men engaged in it and killed one another in the course of a war because killing is what is done in wars.

From instances like these it becomes apparent that an inquiry into the causes of war misses the fundamental point as completely as does an insistence upon the biological necessity of war. If a people have an idea of going to war and the idea that war is the way in which certain situations, defined within their society, are to be handled, they will sometimes go to war. If they are a mild and unaggressive people, like the Pueblo Indians, they may limit themselves to defensive warfare; but they will be forced to think in terms of war because there are peoples near them who have warfare as a pattern, and offensive, raiding, pillaging warfare at that. When the pattern of warfare is known, people like the Pueblo Indians will defend themselves, taking advantage of their natural defenses, the *mesa* village site, and people like the Lepchas, having no natural defenses and no idea of warfare, will merely submit to the invader. But the essential point remains the same. There is a way of behaving which is known to a given people and labeled as an appropriate form of behavior. A bold and warlike people like the Sioux or the Maori may label warfare as desirable as well as possible; a mild people like the Pueblo Indians may label warfare as undesirable; but to the minds of both peoples the possibility of warfare is present. Their thoughts, their hopes, their plans are oriented about this idea, that warfare may be selected as the way to meet some situation.

So simple peoples and civilized peoples, mild peoples and violent, assertive peoples, will all go to war if they have the invention, just as those peoples who have the custom of dueling will have duels and peoples who have the pattern of vendetta will indulge in vendetta. And, conversely, peoples who do not know of dueling will not fight duels, even though their wives are seduced and their daughters ravished; they may on occasion commit murder but they will not fight duels. Cultures which lack the idea of the vendetta will not meet every quarrel in this way. A people can use only the forms it has. So the Balinese have their special way of dealing with a quarrel between two individuals; if the two feel that the causes of quarrel are heavy, they may go and register their quarrel in the temple before the gods, and, making offerings, they may swear never to have anything to do with each other again. Under the Dutch government they registered such mutual "not-speaking" with the Dutch government officials. But in other societies, although individuals might feel as full of animosity and as unwilling to have any further contact as do the Balinese, they cannot register their quarrel with the gods and go on quietly about their business because registering quarrels with the gods is not an invention of which they know.

Yet, if it be granted that warfare is after all an invention, it may nev- 10
ertheless be an invention that lends itself to certain types of personality, to the exigent needs of autocrats, to the expansionist desires of crowded peoples, to the desire for plunder and rape and loot which is engendered by a dull and frustrating life. What, then, can we say of this congruence between warfare and its uses? If it is a form which fits so well, is not this congruence the essential point? But even here the primitive material causes us to wonder, because there are tribes who go to war merely for glory, having no quarrel with the enemy, suffering from no tyrant within their boundaries, anxious neither for land nor loot nor women, but merely anxious to win prestige which within that tribe has been declared obtainable only by war and without which no young man can hope to win his sweetheart's smile of approval. But if, as was the case with the Bush Negroes of Dutch Guiana, it is artistic ability which is necessary to win a girl's approval, the same young man would have to be carving rather than going out on a war party.

In many parts of the world, war is a game in which the individual can win counters — counters which bring him prestige in the eyes of his own sex or of the opposite sex; he plays for these counters as he might, in our society, strive for a tennis championship. Warfare is a frame for such prestige-seeking merely because it calls for the display of certain skills and certain virtues; all of these skills — riding straight, shooting straight, dodging the missiles of the enemy, and sending one's own straight to the mark — can be equally well exercised in some other framework and, equally, the virtues—endurance, bravery, loyalty, steadfastness—can be displayed in other contexts. The tie-up between proving oneself a man and proving this by a success in organized killing is due to a definition which many societies have made of manliness. And often, even in those societies which counted success in warfare a proof of human worth, strange turns were given to the idea, as when the Plains Indians gave their highest awards to the man who touched a live enemy rather than to the man who brought in a scalp—from a dead enemy—because killing a man was less risky. Warfare is just an invention known to the majority of human societies by which they permit their young men either to accumulate prestige or avenge their honor or acquire loot or wives or slaves or sago lands or cattle or appease the blood lust of their gods or the restless souls of the recently dead. It is just an invention, older and more widespread than the jury system, but none the less an invention.

But, once we have said this, have we said anything at all? Despite a few instances, dear to the hearts of controversialists, of the loss of the useful arts, once an invention is made which proves congruent with human needs or social forms, it tends to persist. Grant that war is an invention, that it is not a biological necessity nor the outcome of certain special types of social forms, still, once the invention is made, what are we to do about it? The Indian who had been subsisting on the buffalo for generations because with his primitive weapons he could slaughter only a limited number of buffalo did not return to his primitive weapons when he saw that the white man's more efficient weapons were exterminating the buffalo. A desire for the white man's cloth may mortgage the South Sea Islander to the white man's plantation, but he does not return to making bark cloth, which would have left him free. Once an invention is known and accepted, men do not easily relinquish it. The skilled workers may smash the first steam looms which they feel are to be their undoing, but they accept them in the end, and no movement which has insisted upon the mere abandonment of usable inventions has ever had much success. Warfare is here, as part of our thought; the deeds of warriors are immortalized in the words of our poets; the toys of our children are modeled upon the weapons of the soldier; the frame of reference within which our statesmen and our diplomats work always contains war. If we know that it is not inevitable, that it is due to historical accident that warfare is one of the ways in which we think of behaving, are we given any hope by that? What hope is there of persuading nations to abandon war, nations so thoroughly imbued with the idea that resort to war is, if not actually desirable and noble, at least inevitable whenever certain defined circumstances arise?

In answer to this question I think we might turn to the history of other social inventions, inventions which must once have seemed as firmly entrenched as warfare. Take the methods of trial which preceded the jury system: ordeal and trial by combat. Unfair, capricious, alien as they are to our feeling today, they were once the only methods open to individuals accused of some offense. The invention of trial by jury gradually replaced these methods until only witches, and finally not even witches, had to resort to the ordeal. And for a long time the jury system seemed the one best and finest method of settling legal disputes, but today new inventions, trial before judges only or before commissions, are replacing the jury system. In each case the old method was replaced by a new social invention; the ordeal did not go out because people thought it unjust or wrong, it went out because a method more congruent with the institutions and feelings of the period was invented. And, if we despair over the way in which war seems such an ingrained habit of most of the human race, we can take comfort from the fact that a poor invention will usually give place to a better invention.

For this, two conditions at least are necessary. The people must recognize the defects of the old invention, and some one must make a new one. Propaganda against warfare, documentation of its terrible cost in human suffering and social waste, these prepare the ground by teaching people to feel that warfare is a defective social institution. There is further needed a belief that social invention is possible and the invention of new methods which will render warfare as out-of-date as the tractor is making the plow, or the motor car the horse and buggy. A form of behavior becomes out-of-date only when something else takes its place, and in order to invent forms of behavior which will make war obsolete, it is a first requirement to believe that an invention is possible.

DISCUSSION QUESTIONS

1. Mead uses a common organizational strategy — refuting the opposing view. (See an extended discussion of this on page 380.) In this essay she refutes several theories about the origin of warfare. Summarize these theories. Where does she state her own thesis?

2. Mead supports her argument with examples and analogies. Are they all equally convincing? How can a reader assess the strengths and weaknesses of her examples?

3. In the last part of her essay Mead acknowledges that war is a "usable invention" (para. 12). How does she answer this apparent weakness in her argument?

4. What solution to the problem of warfare does Mead propose? Do you find any flaws in her proposal? Explain your agreement or disagreement with the plausibility of her solution.

WRITING SUGGESTIONS

5. In an article entitled "Where Have All the Young Men Gone? The Perfect Substitute for War," the author marvels at the significance of a gathering in 1998 of more than a million people to celebrate France's victory in the World Cup, a soccer game. "The vast majority of Europeans," he writes, "have found a way to hate one another without hacking one another to

pieces."[1] (In a tragic irony, this article appeared in 1999 during the brutal "ethnic cleansing" of ethnic Albanians in Kosovo and the bombing of Serbia by NATO forces.)

Argue that sporting events do or do not represent a substitute for war. Develop two or three issues—similarities or differences—that support your claim.

6. Pacifism is defined by *Webster's New International Dictionary* as "opposition to war or the use of military force for any purpose." If you consider yourself to be a pacifist, write a defense of your belief, using examples and analogies to make your position clear. But if you believe with Bertrand Russell, the British mathematician and philosopher, that "Absolute pacifism, as a method of gaining your ends, is subject to very severe limitations,"[2] defend your point of view, again using examples, as Mead does.

---

[1] Paul Auster, *New York Times Magazine*, April 4, 1999, p. 144.
[2] *Dictionary of the Mind* (New York: Philosophical Library, 1952), p. 162.

Politics and the English Language

GEORGE ORWELL

Most people who bother with the matter at all would admit that the English language is in a bad way, but it is generally assumed that we cannot by conscious action do anything about it. Our civilization is decadent and our language—so the argument runs—must inevitably share in the general collapse. It follows that any struggle against the abuse of language is a sentimental archaism, like preferring candles to electric light or hansom cabs to aeroplanes. Underneath this lies the half-conscious belief that language is a natural growth and not an instrument which we shape for our own purposes.

Now, it is clear that the decline of a language must ultimately have political and economic causes: It is not due simply to the bad influence of this or that individual writer. But an effect can become a cause, reinforcing the original cause and producing the same effect in an intensified form, and so on indefinitely. A man may take to drink because he feels himself to be a failure, and then fail all the more completely because he drinks. It is rather the same thing that is happening to the English language. It becomes ugly and inaccurate because our thoughts are foolish, but the slovenliness of our language makes it easier for us to have foolish thoughts. The point is that the process is reversible. Modern English, especially written English, is full of bad habits which spread by imitation and which can be avoided if one is willing to take the necessary trouble. If one gets rid of these habits one can think more clearly, and to think clearly is a necessary first step towards political regeneration: So that the fight against bad English is not frivolous and is not the exclusive concern of professional writers. I will come back to this presently, and I hope that by that time the meaning of what I have said here will have become clearer. Meanwhile, here are five specimens of the English language as it is now habitually written.

These five passages have not been picked out because they are especially bad—I could have quoted far worse if I had chosen—but because they illustrate various of the mental vices from which we now suffer. They are a little below the average, but are fairly representative samples. I number them so that I can refer back to them when necessary:

This essay, written shortly after World War II, develops George Orwell's claim that careless and dishonest use of language contributes to careless and dishonest thought and political corruption. Political language, he argues, is "largely the defense of the indefensible." But Orwell (1903–1950), novelist, critic, and political satirist—best known for his books *Animal Farm* (1945) and *1984* (1949)—believes that bad language habits can be reversed, and he lists rules for getting rid of some of the most offensive. This essay first appeared in *Horizon* in April 1946.

(1) I am not, indeed, sure whether it is not true to say that the Milton who once seemed not unlike a seventeenth-century Shelley had not become out of an experience ever more bitter in each year, more alien *[sic]* to the founder of that Jesuit sect which nothing could induce him to tolerate.

Professor Harold Laski (Essay in *Freedom of Expression*)

(2) Above all, we cannot play ducks and drakes with a native battery of idioms which prescribes such egregious collocations of vocables as the Basic *put up with* for *tolerate* or *put at a loss* for *bewilder.*

Professor Lancelot Hogben *(Interglossa)*

(3) On the one side we have the free personality: By definition it is not neurotic, for it has neither conflict nor dream. Its desires, such as they are, are transparent, for they are just what institutional approval keeps in the forefront of consciousness; another institutional pattern would alter their number and intensity; there is little in them that is natural, irreducible, or culturally dangerous. But *on the other side*, the social bond itself is nothing but the mutual reflection of these self-secure integrities. Recall the definition of love. Is not this the very picture of a small academic? Where is there a place in this hall of mirrors for either personality or fraternity?

Essay on psychology in *Politics* (New York)

(4) All the "best people" from the gentlemen's clubs, and all the frantic fascist captains, united in common hatred of Socialism and bestial horror of the rising tide of the mass revolutionary movement, have turned to acts of provocation, to foul incendiarism, to medieval legends of poisoned wells, to legalize their own destruction of proletarian organizations, and rouse the agitated petty-bourgeoisie to chauvinistic fervor on behalf of the fight against the revolutionary way out of the crisis.

Communist pamphlet

(5) If a new spirit *is* to be infused into this old country, there is one thorny and contentious reform which must be tackled, and that is the humanization and galvanization of the BBC. Timidity here will bespeak cancer and atrophy of the soul. The heart of Britain may be sound and of strong beat, for instance, but the British lion's roar at present is like that of Bottom in Shakespeare's *Midsummer Night's Dream* — as gentle as any sucking dove. A virile new Britain cannot continue indefinitely to be traduced in the eyes or rather ears, of the world by the effete languors of Langham Place, brazenly masquerading as "standard English." When the Voice of Britain is heard at nine o'clock, better far and infinitely less ludicrous to hear aitches honestly dropped than the present priggish, inflated, inhibited, school-ma'amish arch braying of blameless bashful mewing maidens!

Letter in *Tribune*

Each of these passages has faults of its own, but, quite apart from avoidable ugliness, two qualities are common to all of them. The first is staleness of imagery: The other is lack of precision. The writer either has a meaning and cannot express it, or he inadvertently says something else, or he is almost indifferent as to whether his words mean anything or not. The mixture of vagueness and sheer incompetence is the most marked characteristic of modern English prose, and especially of any kind of political writing. As soon as certain topics are raised, the concrete melts into the abstract and no one seems to think of turns of speech that are not hackneyed: Prose consists less and less of *words* chosen for the sake of their meaning, and more and more of *phrases* tacked together like the sections of a prefabricated hen-house. I list below, with notes and examples, various of the tricks by means of which the work of prose-construction is habitually dodged:

Dying metaphors.   A newly invented metaphor assists thought by evok-   5
ing a visual image, while on the other hand a metaphor which is technically "dead" (e.g., *iron resolution*) has in effect reverted to being an ordinary word and can generally be used without loss of vividness. But in between these two classes there is a huge dump of worn-out metaphors which have lost all evocative power and are merely used because they save people the trouble of inventing phrases for themselves. Examples are: *ring the changes on, take up the cudgels for, toe the line, ride roughshod over, stand shoulder to shoulder with, play into the hands of, no axe to grind, grist to the mill, fishing in troubled waters, rift within the lute, on the order of the day, Achilles' heel, swan song, hotbed.* Many of these are used without knowledge of their meaning (what is a "rift," for instance?), and incompatible metaphors are frequently mixed, a sure sign that the writer is not interested in what he is saying. Some metaphors now current have been twisted out of their original meaning without those who use them even being aware of the fact. For example, *toe the line* is sometimes written *tow the line.* Another example is *the hammer and the anvil,* now always used with the implication that the anvil gets the worst of it. In real life it is always the anvil that breaks the hammer, never the other way about: A writer who stopped to think what he was saying would be aware of this, and would avoid perverting the original phrase.

Operators or verbal false limbs.   These save the trouble of picking out appropriate verbs and nouns, and at the same time pad each sentence with extra syllables which give it an appearance of symmetry. Characteristic phrases are: *render inoperative, militate against, make contact with, be subjected to, give rise to, give grounds for, have the effect of, play a leading part (role) in, make itself felt, take effect, exhibit a tendency to, serve the purpose of,* etc., etc. The keynote is the elimination of simple verbs. Instead of being a single word, such as *break, stop, spoil, mend, kill,* a verb becomes a *phrase,* made up of a noun or adjective tacked on to some general-purpose verb such as *prove, serve, form, play, render.* In addition, the passive voice is wherever possible used in preference to the active, and noun constructions are used instead of gerunds (*by examination of* instead of *by examining*). The range of verbs is further cut down by means of the *-ize* and *de-* formation, and the banal statements are given an appearance of profundity by means of the *not un-* formation. Simple conjunctions and prepositions are replaced by such phrases as *with respect to, having regard to, the fact that, by dint of, in view of, in the interests of, on the hypothesis that;* and the ends of sentences are saved from anticlimax by such resounding commonplaces as *greatly to be desired, cannot be left out of account, a development to be expected in the near future, deserving of serious consideration, brought to a satisfactory conclusion,* and so on and so forth.

Pretentious diction. Words like *phenomenon, element, individual* (as noun), *objective, categorical, effective, virtual, basic, primary, promote, constitute, exhibit, exploit, utilize, eliminate, liquidate,* are used to dress up simple statements and give an air of scientific impartiality to biased judgments. Adjectives like *epoch-making, epic, historic, unforgettable, triumphant, age-old, inevitable, inexorable, veritable,* are used to dignify the sordid processes of international politics, while writing that aims at glorifying war usually takes on an archaic color, its characteristic words being: *realm, throne, chariot, mailed fist, trident, sword, shield, buckler, banner, jackboot, clarion.* Foreign words and expressions such as *cul de sac, ancien régime, deus ex machina, mutatis mutandis, status quo, gleichshaltung, weltanschauung,* are used to give an air of culture and elegance. Except for the useful abbreviations *i.e., e.g.,* and *etc.,* there is no real need for any of the hundreds of foreign phrases now current in English. Bad writers, and especially scientific, political, and sociological writers, are nearly always haunted by the notion that Latin or Greek words are grander than Saxon ones, and unnecessary words like *expedite, ameliorate, predict, extraneous, deracinated, clandestine, subaqueous,* and hundreds of others constantly gain ground from their Anglo-Saxon opposite numbers.[1] The jargon peculiar to Marxist writing (*hyena, hangman, cannibal, petty bourgeois, these gentry, lackey, flunkey, mad dog, White Guard,* etc.) consists largely of words and phrases translated from Russian, German, or French; but the normal way of coining a new word is to use a Latin or Greek root with the appropriate affix and, where necessary, the *-ize* formation. It is often easier to make up words of this kind (*deregionalize, impermissible, extramarital, nonfragmentatory,* and so forth) than to think up the English words that will cover one's meaning. The result, in general, is an increase in slovenliness and vagueness.

---

[1]An interesting illustration of this is the way in which the English flower names which were in use till very recently are being ousted by Greek ones, *snapdragon* becoming *antirrhinum, forget-me-not* becoming *myosotis,* etc. It is hard to see any practical reason for this change of fashion: It is probably due to an instinctive turning-away from the more homely word and a vague feeling that the Greek word is scientific. [All notes are Orwell's.]

Meaningless words. In certain kinds of writing, particularly in art criticism and literary criticism, it is normal to come across long passages which are almost completely lacking in meaning.[2] Words like *romantic, plastic, values, human, dead, sentimental, natural, vitality,* as used in art criticism, are strictly meaningless in the sense that they not only do not point to any discoverable object, but are hardly ever expected to do so by the reader. When one critic writes, "The outstanding feature of Mr. X's work is its living quality," while another writes, "The immediately striking thing about Mr. X's work is its peculiar deadness," the reader accepts this as a simple difference of opinion. If words like *black* and *white* were involved, instead of the jargon words *dead* and *living,* he would see at once that language was being used in an improper way. Many political words are similarly abused. The word *fascism* has now no meaning except insofar as it signifies "something not desirable." The words *democracy, socialism, freedom, patriotic, realistic, justice,* have each of them several different meanings which cannot be reconciled with one another. In the case of a word like *democracy,* not only is there no agreed definition, but the attempt to make one is resisted from all sides. It is almost universally felt that when we call a country democratic we are praising it: Consequently the defenders of every kind of regime claim that it is a democracy, and fear that they might have to stop using the word if it were tied down to any one meaning. Words of this kind are often used in a consciously dishonest way. That is, the person who uses them has his own private definition, but allows his hearer to think he means something quite different. Statements like *Marshal Pétain was a true patriot, The Soviet Press is the freest in the world, The Catholic Church is opposed to persecution,* are almost always made with intent to deceive. Other words used in variable meanings, in most cases more or less dishonestly, are: *class, totalitarian, science, progressive, reactionary, bourgeois, equality.*

Now that I have made this catalog of swindles and perversions, let me give another example of the kind of writing that they lead to. This time it must of its nature be an imaginary one. I am going to translate a passage of good English into modern English of the worst sort. Here is a well-known verse from Ecclesiastes:

> I returned and saw under the sun, that the race is not to the swift, nor the battle to the strong, neither yet bread to the wise, nor yet riches to men of understanding, nor yet favor to men of skill; but time and chance happeneth to them all.

[2]Example: "Comfort's catholicity of perception and image, strangely Whitmanesque in range, almost the exact opposite in aesthetic compulsion, continues to evoke that trembling atmospheric accumulative hinting at a cruel, an inexorably serene timelessness. . . . Wrey Gardiner scores by aiming at simple bull's-eyes with precision. Only they are not so simple, and through this contended sadness runs more than the surface bittersweet of resignation" (*Poetry Quarterly*).

Here it is in modern English:

> Objective consideration of contemporary phenomena compels the con-
> clusion that success or failure in competitive activities exhibits no
> tendency to be commensurate with innate capacity, but that a consider-
> able element of the unpredictable must invariably be taken into
> account.

This is a parody, but not a very gross one. Exhibit (3), above, for in- 10
stance, contains several patches of the same kind of English. It will be
seen that I have not made a full translation. The beginning and ending of
the sentence follow the original meaning fairly closely, but in the middle
the concrete illustrations—race, battle, bread—dissolve into the vague
phrase "success or failure in competitive activities." This had to be so,
because no modern writer of the kind I am discussing—no one capable
of using phrases like "objective consideration of contemporary phenomena"—would ever tabulate his thoughts in that precise and detailed
way. The whole tendency of modern prose is away from concreteness.
Now analyze these two sentences a little more closely. The first contains
forty-nine words but only sixty syllables, and all its words are those of
everyday life. The second contains thirty-eight words of ninety syllables:
Eighteen of its words are from Latin roots, and one from Greek. The first
sentence contains six vivid images, and only one phrase ("time and
chance") that could be called vague. The second contains not a single
fresh, arresting phrase, and in spite of its ninety syllables it gives only a
shortened version of the meaning contained in the first. Yet without a
doubt it is the second kind of sentence that is gaining ground in modern
English. I do not want to exaggerate. This kind of writing is not yet universal, and outcrops of simplicity will occur here and there in the worst-
written page. Still, if you or I were told to write a few lines on the
uncertainty of human fortunes, we should probably come much nearer to
my imaginary sentence than to the one from Ecclesiastes.

As I have tried to show, modern writing at its worst does not consist
in picking out words for the sake of their meaning and inventing images
in order to make the meaning clearer. It consists in gumming together
long strips of words which have already been set in order by someone
else, and making the results presentable by sheer humbug. The attraction
of this way of writing is that it is easy. It is easier—even quicker once you
have the habit—to say *In my opinion it is a not unjustifiable assumption that*
than to say *I think.* If you use ready-made phrases, you not only don't
have to hunt about for words; you also don't have to bother with the
rhythms of your sentences, since these phrases are generally so arranged
as to be more or less euphonious. When you are composing in a hurry—
when you are dictating to a stenographer, for instance, or making a public speech—it is natural to fall into a pretentious, Latinized style. Tags like
a consideration which we should do well to bear in mind or *a conclusion to
which all of us would readily assent* will save many a sentence from coming

down with a bump. By using stale metaphors, similes, and idioms, you save much mental effort, at the cost of leaving your meaning vague, not only for your reader but for yourself. This is the significance of mixed metaphors. The sole aim of a metaphor is to call up a visual image. When these images clash—as in *The Fascist octopus has sung its swan song, the jackboot is thrown into the melting pot*—it can be taken as certain that the writer is not seeing a mental image of the objects he is naming; in other words he is not really thinking. Look again at the examples I gave at the beginning of this essay. Professor Laski (1) uses five negatives in fifty-three words. One of these is superfluous, making nonsense of the whole passage, and in addition there is the slip *alien* for akin, making further nonsense, and several avoidable pieces of clumsiness which increase the general vagueness. Professor Hogben (2) plays ducks and drakes with a battery which is able to write prescriptions, and, while disapproving of the everyday phrase *put up with*, is unwilling to look *egregious* up in the dictionary and see what it means. (3), if one takes an uncharitable attitude towards it, is simply meaningless: Probably one could work out its intended meaning by reading the whole of the article in which it occurs. In (4), the writer knows more or less what he wants to say, but an accumulation of stale phrases chokes him like tea leaves blocking a sink. In (5), words and meaning have almost parted company. People who write in this manner usually have a general emotional meaning—they dislike one thing and want to express solidarity with another—but they are not interested in the detail of what they are saying. A scrupulous writer, in every sentence that he writes, will ask himself at least four questions, thus: What am I trying to say? What words will express it? What image or idiom will make it clearer? Is this image fresh enough to have an effect? And he will probably ask himself two more: Could I put it more shortly? Have I said anything that is avoidably ugly? But you are not obliged to go to all this trouble. You can shirk it by simply throwing your mind open and letting the ready-made phrases come crowding in. They will construct your sentences for you—even think your thoughts for you, to a certain extent—and at need they will perform the important service of partially concealing your meaning even from yourself. It is at this point that the special connection between politics and the debasement of language becomes clear.

In our time it is broadly true that political writing is bad writing. Where it is not true, it will generally be found that the writer is some kind of rebel, expressing his private opinions and not a "party line." Orthodoxy, of whatever color, seems to demand a lifeless, imitative style. The political dialects to be found in pamphlets, leading articles, manifestos, White Papers, and the speeches of undersecretaries do, of course, vary from party to party, but they are all alike in that one almost never finds in them a fresh, vivid, home-made turn of speech. When one watches some tired hack on the platform mechanically repeating the familiar phrases—*bestial atrocities, iron heel, bloodstained tyranny, free peoples of the world, stand shoulder to shoulder*—one often has a curious feeling that one is not watching a live human being but some kind of dummy; a feeling which suddenly becomes stronger at moments when the light catches the speaker's spectacles and turns them into blank discs which seem to have no eyes behind them. And this is not altogether fanciful. A speaker who uses that kind of phraseology has gone some distance towards turning himself into a machine. The appropriate noises are coming out of his larynx, but his brain is not involved as it would be if he were choosing his words for himself. If the speech he is making is one that he is accustomed to make over and over again, he may be almost unconscious of what he is saying, as one is when one utters the responses in church. And this reduced state of consciousness, if not indispensable, is at any rate favorable to political conformity.

In our time, political speech and writing are largely the defense of the indefensible. Things like the continuance of British rule in India, the Russian purges and deportations, the dropping of the atom bombs on Japan, can indeed be defended, but only by arguments which are too brutal for most people to face, and which do not square with the professed aims of political parties. Thus political language has to consist largely of euphemism, question-begging, and sheer cloudy vagueness. Defenseless villages are bombarded from the air, the inhabitants driven out into the countryside, the cattle machine-gunned, the huts set on fire with incendiary bullets: This is called *pacification*. Millions of peasants are robbed of their farms and sent trudging along the roads with no more than they can carry; this is called *transfer of population* or *rectification of frontiers*. People are imprisoned for years without trial, or shot in the back of the neck, or sent to die of scurvy in Arctic lumber camps: This is called *elimination of unreliable elements*. Such phraseology is needed if one wants to name things without calling up mental pictures of them. Consider for instance some comfortable English professor defending Russian totalitarianism. He cannot say outright, "I believe in killing off your opponents when you can get good results by doing so." Probably, therefore, he will say something like this:

> While freely conceding that the Soviet régime exhibits certain features which the humanitarian may be inclined to deplore, we must, I think, agree that a certain curtailment of the right to political opposition is an unavoidable concomitant of transitional periods, and that the rigors which the Russian people have been called upon to undergo have been amply justified in the sphere of concrete achievement.

The inflated style is itself a kind of euphemism. A mass of Latin words fall upon the facts like soft snow, blurring the outlines and covering up all the details. The great enemy of clear language is insincerity. When there is a gap between one's real and one's declared aims, one turns as it were instinctively to long words and exhausted idioms, like a cuttlefish squirting out ink. In our age there is no such thing as "keeping out of politics." All issues are political issues, and politics itself is a mass of lies, evasions, folly, hatred, and schizophrenia. When the general atmosphere is bad, language must suffer. I should expect to find—this is a guess which I have not sufficient knowledge to verify—that the German, Russian, and Italian languages have all deteriorated in the last ten or fifteen years, as a result of dictatorship.

But if thought corrupts language, language can also corrupt thought. 15 A bad usage can spread by tradition and imitation, even among people who should and do know better. The debased language that I have been discussing is in some ways very convenient. Phrases like *a not unjustifiable assumption, leaves much to be desired, would serve no good purpose, a consideration which we should do well to bear in mind,* are a continuous temptation, a packet of aspirins always at one's elbow. Look back through this essay, and for certain you will find that I have again and again committed the very faults I am protesting against. By this morning's post I have received a pamphlet dealing with conditions in Germany. The author tells me that he "felt impelled" to write it. I open it at random, and here is almost the first sentence that I see: "(The Allies) have an opportunity not only of achieving a radical transformation of Germany's social and political structure in such a way as to avoid a nationalistic reaction in Germany itself, but at the same time of laying the foundations of a cooperative and unified Europe." You see, he "feels impelled" to write—feels, presumably, that he has something new to say—and yet his words, like cavalry horses answering the bugle, group themselves automatically into the familiar dreary pattern. This invasion of one's mind by ready-made phrases *(lay the foundations, achieve a radical transformation)* can only be prevented if one is constantly on guard against them, and every such phrase anesthetizes a portion of one's brain.

I said earlier that the decadence of our language is probably curable. Those who deny this would argue, if they produced an argument at all, that language merely reflects existing social conditions, and that we cannot influence its development by any direct tinkering with words and constructions. So far as the general tone or spirit of a language goes, this may be true, but it is not true in detail. Silly words and expressions have often disappeared, not through any evolutionary process but owing to the conscious action of a minority. Two recent examples were *explore every avenue* and *leave no stone unturned,* which were killed by the jeers of a few journalists. There is a long list of flyblown metaphors which could similarly be got rid of if enough people would interest themselves in the job; and it should also be possible to laugh the *not un-* formation out of existence,[3] to reduce the amount of Latin and Greek in the average sentence, to drive out foreign phrases and strayed scientific words, and, in general, to make pretentiousness unfashionable. But all these are minor points.

---

[3] One can cure oneself of the *not un-* formation by memorizing this sentence: *A not unblack dog was chasing a not unsmall rabbit across a not ungreen field.*

The defense of the English language implies more than this, and perhaps it is best to start by saying what it does *not* imply.

To begin with it has nothing to do with archaism, with the salvaging of obsolete words and turns of speech, or with the setting up of a "standard English" which must never be departed from. On the contrary, it is especially concerned with the scrapping of every word or idiom which has outworn its usefulness. It has nothing to do with correct grammar and syntax, which are of no importance so long as one makes one's meaning clear, or with the avoidance of Americanisms, or with having what is called a "good prose style." On the other hand it is not concerned with fake simplicity and the attempt to make written English colloquial. Nor does it even imply in every case preferring the Saxon word to the Latin one, though it does imply using the fewest and shortest words that will cover one's meaning. What is above all needed is to let the meaning choose the word, and not the other way about. In prose, the worst thing one can do with words is to surrender to them. When you think of a concrete object, you think wordlessly, and then, if you want to describe the thing you have been visualizing you probably hunt about till you find the exact words that seem to fit. When you think of something abstract you are more inclined to use words from the start, and unless you make a conscious effort to prevent it, the existing dialect will come rushing in and do the job for you, at the expense of blurring or even changing your meaning. Probably it is better to put off using words as long as possible and get one's meaning as clear as one can through pictures or sensations. Afterwards one can choose—not simply *accept*—the phrases that will best cover the meaning, and then switch round and decide what impression one's words are likely to make on another person. This last effort of the mind cuts out all stale or mixed images, all prefabricated phrases, needless repetitions, and humbug and vagueness generally. But one can often be in doubt about the effect of a word or a phrase, and one needs rules that one can rely on when instinct fails. I think the following rules will cover most cases:

(i) Never use a metaphor, simile, or other figure of speech which you are used to seeing in print.

(ii) Never use a long word where a short one will do.

(iii) If it is possible to cut a word out, always cut it out.

(iv) Never use the passive where you can use the active.

(v) Never use a foreign phrase, a scientific word, or a jargon word if you can think of an everyday English equivalent.

(vi) Break any of these rules sooner than say anything outright barbarous.

These rules sound elementary, and so they are, but they demand a deep change in attitude in anyone who has grown used to writing in the style now fashionable. One could keep all of them and still write bad English, but one could not write the kind of stuff that I quoted in those five specimens at the beginning of this article.

I have not here been considering the literary use of language, but merely language as an instrument for expressing and not for concealing or preventing thought. Stuart Chase and others have come near to claiming that all abstract words are meaningless, and have used this as a pretext for advocating a kind of political quietism. Since you don't know what Fascism is, how can you struggle against Fascism? One need not swallow such absurdities as this, but one ought to recognize that the present political chaos is connected with the decay of language, and that one can probably bring about some improvement by starting at the verbal end. If you simplify your English, you are freed from the worst follies of orthodoxy. You cannot speak any of the necessary dialects, and when you make a stupid remark its stupidity will be obvious, even to yourself. Political language—and with variations this is true of all political parties, from Conservatives to Anarchists—is designed to make lies sound truthful and murder respectable, and to give an appearance of solidity to pure wind. One cannot change this all in a moment, but one can at least change one's own habits, and from time to time one can even, if one jeers loudly enough, send some worn-out and useless phrase—some *jackboot, Achilles' heel, hotbed, melting pot, acid test, veritable inferno,* or other lump of verbal refuse—into the dustbin where it belongs.

DISCUSSION QUESTIONS

1. Orwell disagrees with a common assumption about language. What is it? Where in the essay does he attack this assumption directly?

2. What faults do his five samples of bad language have in common? Select examples of these faults in each passage.

3. What "tricks" (para. 4) for avoiding good prose does Orwell list? Do you think that some are more dangerous or misleading than others? Explain the reasons for your answer.

4. What different reasons does Orwell suggest for the slovenliness of much political writing and speaking? What examples does he give to support these reasons? Are they persuasive?

5. How does Orwell propose that we get rid of our bad language habits? Do you think his recommendations are realistic? Can the teaching of writing in school assist in the remedy?

6. Why does Orwell urge the reader to "look back through this essay" to find "the very faults I am protesting against" (para. 15)? Can you, in fact, find any?

WRITING SUGGESTIONS

7. Choose a speech or an editorial whose meaning seems to be obscured by pretentious diction, meaningless words, euphemism, or "sheer cloudy

vagueness." Point out the real meaning of the piece. If you think that its purpose is deceptive, expose the unpleasant truth that the author is concealing. Use Orwell's device, giving concrete meaning to any abstractions. (One source of speeches is a publication called *Vital Speeches of the Day.* Another is the *New York Times,* which often prints in full, or excerpts major portions of, speeches by leading figures in public life.)

8. Orwell's essay appeared before the widespread use of television. Do you think that TV makes it harder for politicians to be dishonest? Choose a particular public event—a war, a street riot, a terrorist activity, a campaign stop—and argue either for or against the claim that televised coverage makes it harder for a politician to engage in "sheer cloudy vagueness." Or does it make no difference at all? Be specific in your use of evidence.

Letter from Birmingham Jail

MARTIN LUTHER KING JR.

A Call for Unity: A Letter from Eight White Clergymen

April 12, 1963

We the undersigned clergymen are among those who, in January, issued "An Appeal for Law and Order and Common Sense," in dealing with racial problems in Alabama. We expressed understanding that honest convictions in racial matters could properly be pursued in the courts, but urged that decisions of those courts should in the meantime be peacefully obeyed.

Since that time there had been some evidence of increased forebearance and a willingness to face facts. Responsible citizens have undertaken to work on various problems which cause racial friction and unrest. In Birmingham, recent public events have given indication that we all have opportunity for a new constructive and realistic approach to racial problems.

However, we are now confronted by a series of demonstrations by some of our Negro citizens, directed and led in part by outsiders. We recognize the natural impatience of people who feel that their hopes are slow in being realized. But we are convinced that these demonstrations are unwise and untimely.

We agree rather with certain local Negro leadership which has called for honest and open negotiation of racial issues in our area. And we believe this kind of facing of issues can best be accomplished by citizens of our own metropolitan area, white and Negro, meeting with their knowledge and experience of the local situation. All of us need to face that responsibility and find proper channels for its accomplishment.

Just as we formerly pointed out that "hatred and violence have no 5 sanction in our religious and political traditions," we also point out that such actions as incite to hatred and violence, however technically peaceful those actions may be, have not contributed to the resolution of our local problems. We do not believe that these days of new hope are days when extreme measures are justified in Birmingham.

Martin Luther King Jr. (1929–1968) was a clergyman, author, distinguished civil rights leader, and winner of the Nobel Prize for peace in 1964 for his contributions to racial harmony and his advocacy of nonviolent response to aggression. He was assassinated in 1968. In "Letter from Birmingham Jail," he appears as a historian and philosopher. He wrote the letter from a jail cell on April 16, 1963, after his arrest for participation in a demonstration for civil rights for African Americans. The letter was a reply to eight Alabama clergymen who, in the first letter reprinted here, had condemned demonstrations in the streets. Kings essay is from *A Testament of Hope* (1986).

We commend the community as a whole, and the local news media and law enforcement officials in particular, on the calm manner in which these demonstrations have been handled. We urge the public to continue to show restraint should the demonstrations continue, and the law enforcement officials to remain calm and continue to protect our city from violence.

We further strongly urge our own Negro community to withdraw support from these demonstrations, and to unite locally in working peacefully for a better Birmingham. When rights are consistently denied, a cause should be pressed in the courts and in negotiations among local leaders, and not in the streets. We appeal to both our white and Negro citizenry to observe the principles of law and order and common sense.

> (Signed)
> C.C.J. Carpenter, D.D., L.L.D., Bishop of Alabama; Joseph A. Durick, D.D., Auxiliary Bishop, Diocese of Mobile-Birmingham; Rabbi Milton L. Grafman, Temple Emanu-El, Birmingham, Alabama; Bishop Paul Hardin, Bishop of the Alabama–West Florida Conference of the Methodist Church; Bishop Nolan B. Harmon, Bishop of the North Alabama Conference of the Methodist Church; George M. Murray, D.D., L.L.D., Bishop Coadjutor, Episcopal Diocese of Alabama; Edward V. Ramage, Moderator, Synod of the Alabama Presbyterian Church in the United States; Earl Stallings, Pastor, First Baptist Church, Birmingham.

King's Reply from Birmingham Jail

My dear Fellow Clergymen,

While confined here in the Birmingham city jail, I came across your recent statement calling our present activities "unwise and untimely." Seldom, if ever, do I pause to answer criticism of my work and ideas. If I sought to answer all of the criticisms that cross my desk, my secretaries would be engaged in little else in the course of the day, and I would have no time for constructive work. But since I feel that you are men of genuine good will and your criticisms are sincerely set forth, I would like to answer your statement in what I hope will be patient and reasonable terms.

I think I should give the reason for my being in Birmingham, since you have been influenced by the argument of "outsiders coming in." I have the honor of serving as president of the Southern Christian Leadership Conference, an organization operating in every southern state, with headquarters in Atlanta, Georgia. We have some eighty-five affiliate organizations all across the South—one being the Alabama Christian Movement for Human Rights. Whenever necessary and possible we share staff, educational, and financial resources with our affiliates. Several months ago our local affiliate here in Birmingham invited us to be on call to engage in a nonviolent direct-action program if such were deemed necessary. We readily consented and when the hour came we lived up to our promises. So I am here, along with several members of my staff, because we were invited here. I am here because I have basic organizational ties here.

Beyond this, I am in Birmingham because injustice is here. Just as the eighth-century prophets left their little villages and carried their "thus saith the Lord" far beyond the boundaries of their hometowns; and just as the Apostle Paul left his little village of Tarsus and carried the gospel of Jesus Christ to practically every hamlet and city of the Graeco-Roman world, I too am compelled to carry the gospel of freedom beyond my particular hometown. Like Paul, I must constantly respond to the Macedonian call for aid.

Moreover, I am cognizant of the interrelatedness of all communities and states. I cannot sit idly by in Atlanta and not be concerned about what happens in Birmingham. Injustice anywhere is a threat to justice everywhere. We are caught in an inescapable network of mutuality, tied in a single garment of destiny. Whatever affects one directly affects all indirectly. Never again can we afford to live with the narrow, provincial "outside agitator" idea. Anyone who lives in the United States can never be considered an outsider anywhere in this country.

You deplore the demonstrations that are presently taking place in   5 Birmingham. But I am sorry that your statement did not express a similar concern for the conditions that brought the demonstrations into being. I am sure that each of you would want to go beyond the superficial social analyst who looks merely at effects, and does not grapple with underlying causes. I would not hesitate to say that it is unfortunate that so-called demonstrations are taking place in Birmingham at this time, but I would say in more emphatic terms that it is even more unfortunate that the white power structure of this city left the Negro community with no other alternative.

In any nonviolent campaign there are four basic steps: (1) collection of the facts to determine whether injustices are alive, (2) negotiation, (3) self-purification, and (4) direct action. We have gone through all of these steps in Birmingham. There can be no gainsaying of the fact that racial injustice engulfs this community.

Birmingham is probably the most thoroughly segregated city in the United States. Its ugly record of police brutality is known in every section of this country. Its unjust treatment of Negroes in the courts is a notorious reality. There have been more unsolved bombings of Negro homes and churches in Birmingham than any city in this nation. These are the hard, brutal, and unbelievable facts. On the basis of these conditions Negro leaders sought to negotiate with the city fathers. But the political leaders consistently refused to engage in good faith negotiation.

Then came the opportunity last September to talk with some of the leaders of the economic community. In these negotiating sessions certain promises were made by the merchants—such as the promise to remove the humiliating racial signs from the stores. On the basis of these promises Reverend Shuttlesworth and the leaders of the Alabama Christian Movement for Human Rights agreed to call a moratorium on any type of demonstrations. As the weeks and months unfolded we realized that we were the victims of a broken promise. The signs remained. Like so many experiences of the past we were confronted with blasted hopes, and the dark shadow of a deep disappointment settled upon us. So we had no alternative except that of preparing for direct action, whereby we would present our very bodies as a means of laying our case before the conscience of the local and national community. We were not unmindful of the difficulties involved. So we decided to go through a process of self-purification. We started having workshops on nonviolence and repeatedly asking ourselves the questions, "Are you able to accept blows without retaliating?" "Are you able to endure the ordeals of jail?" We decided to set our direct-action program around the Easter season, realizing that with the exception of Christmas, this was the largest shopping period of the year. Knowing that a strong economic withdrawal program would be the by-product of direct action, we felt that this was the best time to bring pressure on the merchants for the needed changes. Then it occurred to us that the March election was ahead and so we speedily decided to postpone action until after election day. When we discovered that Mr. Connor was in the run-off, we decided again to postpone action so that the demonstrations could not be used to cloud the issues. At this time we agreed to begin our nonviolent witness the day after the run-off.

This reveals that we did not move irresponsibly into direct actions. We too wanted to see Mr. Connor defeated; so we went through postponement after postponement to aid in this community need. After this we felt that direct action could be delayed no longer.

You may well ask, "Why direct action? Why sit-ins, marches, etc.? 10 Isn't negotiation a better path?" You are exactly right in your call for negotiation. Indeed, this is the purpose of direct action. Nonviolent direct action seeks to create such a crisis and establish such creative tension that a community that has constantly refused to negotiate is forced to confront the issue. It seeks so to dramatize the issue that it can no longer be ignored. I just referred to the creation of tension as a part of the work of the nonviolent resister. This may sound rather shocking. But I must confess that I am not afraid of the word tension. I have earnestly worked and preached against violent tension, but there is a type of constructive nonviolent tension that is necessary for growth. Just as Socrates felt that it was necessary to create a tension in the mind so that individuals could rise from the bondage of myths and half-truths to the unfettered realm of creative analysis and objective appraisal, we must see the need of having nonviolent gadflies to create the kind of tension in society that will help men to rise from the dark depths of prejudice and racism to the majestic heights of understanding and brotherhood. So the purpose of the direct action is to create a situation so crisis-packed that it will inevitably open the door to negotiation. We, therefore, concur with you in your call for negotiation. Too long has our beloved Southland been bogged down in the tragic attempt to live in monologue rather than dialogue.

One of the basic points in your statement is that our acts are untimely. Some have asked, "Why didn't you give the new administration time to act?" The only answer that I can give to this inquiry is that the new administration must be prodded about as much as the outgoing one before it acts. We will be sadly mistaken if we feel that the election of Mr. Boutwell will bring the millennium to Birmingham. While Mr. Boutwell is much more articulate and gentle than Mr. Connor, they are both segregationists, dedicated to the task of maintaining the status quo. The hope I see in Mr. Boutwell is that he will be reasonable enough to see the futility of massive resistance to desegregation. But he will not see this without pressure from the devotees of civil rights. My friends, I must say to you that we have not made a single gain in civil rights without determined legal and nonviolent pressure. History is the long and tragic story of the fact that privileged groups seldom give up their privileges voluntarily. Individuals may see the moral light and voluntarily give up their unjust posture; but as Reinhold Niebuhr has reminded us, groups are more immoral than individuals.

We know through painful experience that freedom is never voluntarily given by the oppressor; it must be demanded by the oppressed. Frankly, I have never yet engaged in a direct-action movement that was "well-timed," according to the timetable of those who have not suffered unduly from the disease of segregation. For years now I have heard the words "Wait!" It rings in the ear of every Negro with a piercing familiarity. This "Wait" has almost always meant "Never." It has been a tranquilizing thalidomide, relieving the emotional stress for a moment, only to give birth to an ill-formed infant of frustration. We must come to see with the distinguished jurist of yesterday that "justice too long delayed is justice denied." We have waited for more than 340 years for our constitutional and God-given rights. The nations of Asia and Africa are moving with jetlike speed toward the goal of political independence, and we still creep at horse and buggy pace toward the gaining of a cup of coffee at a lunch counter. I guess it is easy for those who have never felt the stinging darts of segregation to say, "Wait." But when you have seen vicious mobs lynch your mothers and fathers at will and drown your sisters and brothers at whim; when you see hate-filled policemen curse, kick, brutalize, and even kill your black brothers and sisters with impunity; when you see the vast majority of your 20 million Negro brothers smothering in an airtight cage of poverty in the midst of an affluent society; when you suddenly find your tongue twisted and your speech stammering as you seek to explain to your six-year-old daughter why she can't go to the public amusement park that has just been advertised on television, and see tears welling up in her little eyes when she is told that Funtown is closed to colored children, and see the depressing clouds of inferiority begin to form in her little mental sky, and see her begin to distort her little personality by unconsciously developing a bitterness toward white people; when you have to concoct an answer for a five-year-old son asking in agonizing pathos: "Daddy, why do white people treat colored people so mean?"; when you take a cross-country drive and find it necessary to sleep night after night in the uncomfortable corners of your automobile because no motel will accept you; when you are humiliated day in and day out by nagging signs reading "white" and "colored"; when your first name becomes "nigger" and your middle name becomes "boy" (however old you are) and your last name becomes "John," and when your wife and mother are never given the respected title "Mrs."; when you are harried by day and haunted by night by the fact that you are a Negro, living constantly at tiptoe stance never quite knowing what to expect next, and plagued with inner fears and outer resentments; when you are forever fighting a degenerating sense of "nobodiness"; then you will understand why we find it difficult to wait. There comes a time when the cup of endurance runs over, and men are no longer willing to be plunged into an abyss of injustice where they experience the blackness of corroding despair. I hope, sirs, you can understand our legitimate and unavoidable impatience.

You express a great deal of anxiety over our willingness to break laws. This is certainly a legitimate concern. Since we so diligently urge people to obey the Supreme Court's decision of 1954 outlawing segregation in the public schools, it is rather strange and paradoxical to find us consciously breaking laws. One may well ask, "How can you advocate breaking some laws and obeying others?" The answer is found in the fact that there are two types of laws: There are *just* and there are *unjust* laws. I would agree with Saint Augustine that "An unjust law is no law at all."

Now what is the difference between the two? How does one determine when a law is just or unjust? A just law is a man-made code that squares with the moral law or the law of God. An unjust law is a code that is out of harmony with the moral law. To put it in the terms of Saint Thomas Aquinas, an unjust law is a human law that is not rooted in eternal and natural law. Any law that uplifts human personality is just. Any law that degrades human personality is unjust. All segregation statutes are unjust because segregation distorts the soul and damages the personality. It gives the segregator a false sense of superiority, and the segregated a false sense of inferiority. To use the words of Martin Buber, the great Jewish philosopher, segregation substitutes an "I-it" relationship for the "I-thou" relationship, and ends up relegating persons to the status of things. So segregation is not only politically, economically, and sociologically unsound, but it is morally wrong and sinful. Paul Tillich has said that sin is separation. Isn't segregation an existential expression of man's tragic separation, an expression of his awful estrangement, his terrible sinfulness? So I can urge men to disobey segregation ordinances because they are morally wrong.

Let us turn to a more concrete example of just and unjust laws. An 15 unjust law is a code that a majority inflicts on a minority that is not binding on itself. This is difference made legal. On the other hand, a just law is a code that a majority compels a minority to follow that it is willing to follow itself. This is sameness made legal.

Let me give another explanation. An unjust law is a code inflicted upon a minority which that minority had no part in enacting or creating because they did not have the unhampered right to vote. Who can say that the legislature of Alabama which set up the segregation laws was democratically elected? Throughout the state of Alabama all types of conniving methods are used to prevent Negroes from becoming registered voters, and there are some counties without a single Negro registered to vote despite the fact that the Negro constitutes a majority of the population. Can any law set up in such a state be considered democratically structured?

These are just a few examples of unjust and just laws. There are some instances when a law is just on its face and unjust in its application. For instance, I was arrested Friday on a charge of parading without a permit. Now there is nothing wrong with an ordinance which requires a permit for a parade, but when the ordinance is used to preserve segregation and to deny citizens the First Amendment privilege of peaceful assembly and peaceful protest, then it becomes unjust.

I hope you can see the distinction I am trying to point out. In no sense do I advocate evading or defying the law as the rabid segregationist would do. This would lead to anarchy. One who breaks an unjust law must do it *openly, lovingly* (not hatefully as the white mothers did in New Orleans when they were seen on television screaming, "nigger, nigger, nigger"), and with a willingness to accept the penalty. I submit that an individual who breaks a law that conscience tells him is unjust, and willingly accepts the penalty by staying in jail to arouse the conscience of the community over its injustice, is in reality expressing the very highest respect for law.

Of course, there is nothing new about this kind of civil disobedience. It was seen sublimely in the refusal of Shadrach, Meshach, and Abednego to obey the laws of Nebuchadnezzar because a higher moral law was involved. It was practiced superbly by the early Christians who were willing to face hungry lions and the excruciating pain of chopping blocks, before submitting to certain unjust laws of the Roman Empire. To a degree academic freedom is a reality today because Socrates practiced civil disobedience.

We can never forget that everything Hitler did in Germany was 20 "legal" and everything the Hungarian freedom fighters did in Hungary was "illegal." It was "illegal" to aid and comfort a Jew in Hitler's Germany. But I am sure that if I had lived in Germany during that time I would have aided and comforted my Jewish brothers even though it was illegal. If I lived in a Communist country today where certain principles dear to the

Christian faith are suppressed, I believe I would openly advocate disobeying these antireligious laws. I must make two honest confessions to you, my Christian and Jewish brothers. First, I must confess that over the last few years I have been gravely disappointed with the white moderate. I have almost reached the regrettable conclusion that the Negro's great stumbling block in the stride toward freedom is not the White Citizen's Councilor or the Ku Klux Klanner, but the white moderate who is more devoted to "order" than to justice; who prefers a negative peace which is the absence of tension to a positive peace which is the presence of justice; who constantly says, "I agree with you in the goal you seek, but I can't agree with your methods of direct action"; who paternalistically feels that he can set the timetable for another man's freedom; who lives by the myth of time and who constantly advises the Negro to wait until a "more convenient season." Shallow understanding from people of good will is more frustrating than absolute misunderstanding from people of ill will. Lukewarm acceptance is much more bewildering than outright rejection.

I had hoped that the white moderate would understand that law and order exist for the purpose of establishing justice, and that when they fail to do this they become dangerously structured dams that block the flow of social progress. I had hoped that the white moderate would understand that the present tension of the South is merely a necessary phase of the transition from an obnoxious negative peace, where the Negro passively accepted his unjust plight, to a substance-filled positive peace, where all men will respect the dignity and worth of human personality. Actually, we who engage in nonviolent direct action are not the creators of tension. We merely bring to the surface the hidden tension that is already alive. We bring it out in the open where it can be seen and dealt with. Like a boil that can never be cured as long as it is covered up but must be opened with all its pus-flowing ugliness to the natural medicines of air and light, injustice must likewise be exposed, with all of the tension its exposing creates, to the light of human conscience and the air of national opinion before it can be cured.

In your statement you asserted that our actions, even though peaceful, must be condemned because they precipitate violence. But can this assertion be logically made? Isn't this like condemning the robbed man because his possession of money precipitated the evil act of robbery? Isn't this like condemning Socrates because his unswerving commitment to truth and his philosophical delvings precipitated the misguided popular mind to make him drink the hemlock? Isn't this like condemning Jesus because His unique God-consciousness and never-ceasing devotion to His will precipitated the evil act of crucifixion? We must come to see, as federal courts have consistently affirmed, that it is immoral to urge an individual to withdraw his efforts to gain his basic constitutional rights because the quest precipitates violence. Society must protect the robbed and punish the robber.

I had also hoped that the white moderate would reject the myth of time. I received a letter this morning from a white brother in Texas which said: "All Christians know that the colored people will receive equal rights eventually, but it is possible that you are in too great of a religious hurry. It has taken Christianity almost two thousand years to accomplish what it has. The teachings of Christ take time to come to earth." All that is said here grows out of a tragic misconception of time. It is the strangely irrational notion that there is something in the very flow of time that will inevitably cure all ills. Actually time is neutral. It can be used either destructively or constructively. I am coming to feel that the people of ill will have used time much more effectively than the people of good will. We will have to repent in this generation not merely for the vitriolic words and actions of the bad people, but for the appalling silence of the good people. We must come to see that human progress never rolls in on wheels of inevitability. It comes through the tireless efforts and persistent work of men willing to be co-workers with God, and without this hard work time itself becomes an ally of the forces of social stagnation. We must use time creatively, and forever realize that the time is always ripe to do right. Now is the time to make real the promise of democracy, and transform our pending national elegy into a creative psalm of brotherhood. Now is the time to lift our national policy from the quicksand of racial injustice to the solid rock of human dignity.

You spoke of our activity in Birmingham as extreme. At first I was rather disappointed that fellow clergymen would see my nonviolent efforts as those of the extremist. I started thinking about the fact that I stand in the middle of two opposing forces in the Negro community. One is a force of complacency made up of Negroes who, as a result of long years of oppression, have been so completely drained of self-respect and a sense of "somebodiness" that they have adjusted to segregation, and of a few Negroes in the middle class who, because of a degree of academic and economic security, and because at points they profit by segregation, have unconsciously become insensitive to the problems of the masses. The other force is one of bitterness and hatred, and comes perilously close to advocating violence. It is expressed in the various black nationalist groups that are springing up over the nation, the largest and best known being Elijah Muhammad's Muslim movement. This movement is nourished by the contemporary frustration over the continued existence of racial discrimination. It is made up of people who have lost faith in America, who have absolutely repudiated Christianity, and who have concluded that the white man is an incurable "devil." I have tried to stand between these two forces, saying that we need not follow the "donothingism" of the complacent or the hatred and despair of the black nationalist. There is the more excellent way of love and nonviolent protest. I'm grateful to God that, through the Negro church, the dimension of nonviolence entered our struggle. If this philosophy had not emerged, I am convinced that by now many streets of the South would be flowing with floods of blood. And I am further convinced that if our white brothers dismiss us as "rabble-rousers" and "outside agitators" those of us who are working through the channels of nonviolent direct action and refuse to support our nonviolent efforts, millions of Negroes, out of frustration and despair, will seek solace and security in black nationalist ideologies, a development that will lead inevitably to a frightening racial nightmare.

Oppressed people cannot remain oppressed forever. The urge for freedom will eventually come. This is what happened to the American Negro. Something within has reminded him of his birthright of freedom; something without has reminded him that he can gain it. Consciously and unconsciously, he has been swept in by what the Germans call the *Zeitgeist*, and with his black brothers of Africa, and his brown and yellow brothers of Asia, South America, and the Caribbean, he is moving with a sense of cosmic urgency toward the promised land of racial justice. Recognizing this vital urge that has engulfed the Negro community, one should readily understand public demonstrations. The Negro has many pent-up resentments and latent frustrations. He has to get them out. So let him march sometime; let him have his prayer pilgrimages to the city hall; understand why he must have sit-ins and freedom rides. If his repressed emotions do not come out in these nonviolent ways, they will come out in ominous expressions of violence. This is not a threat; it is a fact of history. So I have not said to my people "get rid of your discontent." But I have tried to say that this normal and healthy discontent can be channelized through the creative outlet of nonviolent direct action. Now this approach is being dismissed as extremist. I must admit that I was initially disappointed in being so categorized.

But as I continued to think about the matter I gradually gained a bit of satisfaction from being considered an extremist. Was not Jesus an extremist in love—"Love your enemies, bless them that curse you, pray for them that despitefully use you." Was not Amos an extremist for justice—"Let justice roll down like waters and righteousness like a mighty stream." Was not Paul an extremist for the gospel of Jesus Christ—"I bear in my body the marks of the Lord Jesus." Was not Martin Luther an extremist—"Here I stand; I can do none other so help me God." Was not John Bunyan an extremist—"I will stay in jail to the end of my days before I make a butchery of my conscience." Was not Abraham Lincoln an extremist—"This nation cannot survive half slave and half free." Was not Thomas Jefferson an extremist—"We hold these truths to be self-evident, that all men are created equal." So the question is not whether we will be extremist but what kind of extremist will we be. Will we be extremists for hate or will we be extremists for love? Will we be extremists for the preservation of injustice—or will we be extremists for the cause of justice? In that dramatic scene on Calvary's hill, three men were crucified. We must not forget that all three were crucified for the same crime—the crime of extremism. Two were extremists for immorality, and thusly fell below their environment. The other, Jesus Christ, was an extremist for love, truth, and goodness, and thereby rose above his environment. So, after all, maybe the South, the nation, and the world are in dire need of creative extremists.

I had hoped that the white moderate would see this. Maybe I was too optimistic. Maybe I expected too much. I guess I should have realized that few members of a race that has oppressed another race can understand or appreciate the deep groans and passionate yearnings of those that have been oppressed and still fewer have the vision to see that injustice must be rooted out by strong, persistent, and determined action. I am thankful, however, that some of our white brothers have grasped the meaning of this social revolution and committed themselves to it. They are still all too small in quantity, but they are big in quality. Some like Ralph McGill, Lillian Smith, Harry Golden, and James Dabbs have written about our struggle in eloquent, prophetic, and understanding terms. Others have marched with us down nameless streets of the South. They have languished in filthy roach-infested jails, suffering the abuse and brutality of angry policemen who see them as "dirty nigger-lovers." They, unlike so many of their moderate brothers and sisters, have recognized the urgency of the moment and sensed the need for powerful "action" antidotes to combat the disease of segregation.

Let me rush on to mention my other disappointment. I have been so greatly disappointed with the white church and its leadership. Of course, there are some notable exceptions. I am not unmindful of the fact that each of you has taken some significant stands on this issue. I commend you, Reverend Stallings, for your Christian stance on this past Sunday, in welcoming Negroes to your worship service on a nonsegregated basis. I commend the Catholic leaders of this state for integrating Springhill College several years ago.

But despite these notable exceptions I must honestly reiterate that I have been disappointed with the church. I do not say that as one of the negative critics who can always find something wrong with the church. I say it as a minister of the gospel, who loves the church; who was nurtured in its bosom; who has been sustained by its spiritual blessings, and who will remain true to it as long as the cord of life shall lengthen.

I had the strange feeling when I was suddenly catapulted into the 30 leadership of the bus protest in Montgomery several years ago that we would have the support of the white church. I felt that the white ministers, priests, and rabbis of the South would be some of our strongest allies. Instead, some have been outright opponents, refusing to understand the freedom movement and misrepresenting its leaders; all too many others have been more cautious than courageous and have remained silent behind the anesthetizing security of the stained-glass windows.

In spite of my shattered dreams of the past, I came to Birmingham with the hope that the white religious leadership of this community would see the justice of our cause, and with deep moral concern, serve as the channel through which our just grievances would get to the power structure. I had hoped that each of you would understand. But again I have been disappointed. I have heard numerous religious leaders of the South call upon their worshipers to comply with a desegregation decision because it is the *law*, but I have longed to hear white ministers say, "Follow this decree because integration is morally *right* and the Negro is your brother." In the midst of blatant injustices inflicted upon the Negro, I have watched white churches stand on the sideline and merely mouth pious irrelevancies and sanctimonious trivialities. In the midst of a mighty struggle to rid our nation of racial and economic injustice, I have heard so many ministers say, "Those are social issues with which the gospel has no real concern," and I have watched so many churches commit themselves to a completely otherworldly religion which made a strange distinction between body and soul, the sacred and the secular.

So here we are moving toward the exit of the twentieth century with a religious community largely adjusted to the status quo, standing as a taillight behind other community agencies rather than a headlight leading men to higher levels of justice.

I have traveled the length and breadth of Alabama, Mississippi, and all the other southern states. On sweltering summer days and crisp autumn mornings I have looked at her beautiful churches with their lofty spires pointing heavenward. I have beheld the impressive outlay of her massive religious education buildings. Over and over again I have found myself asking: "What kind of people worship here? Who is their God? Where were their voices when the lips of Governor Barnett dripped with words of interposition and nullification? Where were they when Governor Wallace gave the clarion call for defiance and hatred? Where were their voices of support when tired, bruised, and weary Negro men and women decided to rise from the dark dungeons of complacency to the bright hills of creative protest?"

Yes, these questions are still in my mind. In deep disappointment, I have wept over the laxity of the church. But be assured that my tears have been tears of love. There can be no deep disappointment where there is not deep love. Yes, I love the church; I love her sacred walls. How could I do otherwise? I am in the rather unique position of being the son, the grandson, and the great-grandson of preachers. Yes, I see the church as the body of Christ. But, oh! How we have blemished and scarred that body through social neglect and fear of being nonconformists.

There was a time when the church was very powerful. It was during 35 that period when the early Christians rejoiced when they were deemed worthy to suffer for what they believed. In those days the church was not merely a thermometer that recorded the ideas and principles of popular opinion; it was a thermostat that transformed the mores of society. Wherever the early Christians entered a town the power structure got disturbed and immediately sought to convict them for being "disturbers of the peace" and "outside agitators." But they went on with the conviction that they were "a colony of heaven," and had to obey God rather than man. They were small in number but big in commitment. They were too God-intoxicated to be "astronomically intimidated." They brought an end to such ancient evils as infanticide and gladiatorial contest.

Things are different now. The contemporary church is often a weak, ineffectual voice with an uncertain sound. It is so often the archsupporter of the status quo. Far from being disturbed by the presence of the church, the power structure of the average community is consoled by the church's silent and often vocal sanction of things as they are.

But the judgment of God is upon the church as never before. If the church of today does not recapture the sacrificial spirit of the early church, it will lose its authentic ring, forfeit the loyalty of millions, and be dismissed as an irrelevant social club with no meaning for the twentieth century. I am meeting young people every day whose disappointment with the church has risen to outright disgust.

Maybe again, I have been too optimistic. Is organized religion too inextricably bound to the status quo to save our nation and the world? Maybe I must turn my faith to the inner spiritual church, the church within the church, as the true *ecclesia* and the hope of the world. But again I am thankful to God that some noble souls from the ranks of organized religion have broken loose from the paralyzing chains of conformity and joined us as active partners in the struggle for freedom. They have left their secure congregations and walked the streets of Albany, Georgia, with us. They have gone through the highways of the South on tortuous rides for freedom. Yes, they have gone to jail with us. Some have been kicked out of their churches, and lost support of their bishops and fellow ministers. But they have gone with the faith that right defeated is stronger than evil triumphant. These men have been the leaven in the lump of the race. Their witness has been the spiritual salt that has preserved the true meaning of the gospel in these troubled times. They have carved a tunnel of hope through the dark mountain of disappointment.

I hope the church as a whole will meet the challenge of this decisive hour. But even if the church does not come to the aid of justice, I have no despair about the future. I have no fear about the outcome of our struggle in Birmingham, even if our motives are presently misunderstood. We will reach the goal of freedom in Birmingham and all over the nation, because the goal of America is freedom. Abused and scorned though we may be, our destiny is tied up with the destiny of America. Before the Pilgrims landed at Plymouth we were here. Before the pen of Jefferson etched across the pages of history the majestic words of the Declaration of Independence, we were here. For more than two centuries our foreparents labored in this country without wages; they made cotton king; and they built the homes of their masters in the midst of brutal injustice and shameful humiliation — and yet out of a bottomless vitality they continued to thrive and develop. If the inexpressible cruelties of slavery could not stop us, the opposition we now face will surely fail. We will win our freedom because the sacred heritage of our nation and the eternal will of God are embodied in our echoing demands.

I must close now. But before closing I am impelled to mention one other point in your statement that troubled me profoundly. You warmly commended the Birmingham police force for keeping "order" and "preventing violence." I don't believe you would have so warmly commended the police force if you had seen its angry violent dogs literally biting six unarmed, nonviolent Negroes. I don't believe you would so quickly commend the policemen if you would observe their ugly and inhuman treatment of Negroes here in the city jail; if you would watch them push and curse old Negro women and young Negro girls; if you would see them slap and kick old Negro men and young boys; if you will observe them, as they did on two occasions, refuse to give us food because we wanted to sing our grace together. I'm sorry that I can't join you in your praise for the police department.

It is true that they have been rather disciplined in their public handling of the demonstrators. In this sense they have been rather publicly "nonviolent." But for what purpose? To preserve the evil system of segregation. Over the last few years I have consistently preached that nonviolence demands that the means we use must be as pure as the ends we seek. So I have tried to make it clear that it is wrong to use immoral means to attain moral ends. But now I must affirm that it is just as wrong, or even more so, to use moral means to preserve immoral ends. Maybe Mr. Connor and his policemen have been rather publicly nonviolent, as Chief Pritchett was in Albany, Georgia, but they have used the moral means of nonviolence to maintain the immoral end of flagrant racial injustice. T. S. Eliot has said that there is no greater treason than to do the right deed for the wrong reason.

I wish you had commended the Negro sit-inners and demonstrators of Birmingham for their sublime courage, their willingness to suffer, and their amazing discipline in the midst of the most inhuman provocation. One day the South will recognize its real heroes. They will be the James Merediths, courageously and with a majestic sense of purpose facing jeering and hostile mobs and the agonizing loneliness that characterizes the life of the pioneer. They will be old, oppressed, battered Negro women, symbolized in a seventy-two-year-old woman of Montgomery, Alabama, who rose up with a sense of dignity and with her people decided not to ride the segregated buses, and responded to one who inquired about her tiredness with ungrammatical profundity: "My feet is tired, but my soul is rested." They will be the young high school and college students, young ministers of the gospel, and a host of their elders courageously and nonviolently sitting-in at lunch counters and willingly going to jail for conscience's sake. One day the South will know that when these disinherited children of God sat down at lunch counters they were in reality standing up for the best in the American dream and the most sacred values in our Judeo-Christian heritage, and thusly, carrying our whole nation back to those great wells of democracy which were dug deep by the Founding Fathers in the formulation of the Constitution and the Declaration of Independence.

Never before have I written a letter this long (or should I say a book?). I'm afraid that it is much too long to take your precious time. I can assure you that it would have been much shorter if I had been writing from a comfortable desk, but what else is there to do when you are alone for days in the dull monotony of a narrow jail cell other than write long letters, think strange thoughts, and pray long prayers?

If I have said anything in this letter that is an overstatement of the truth and is indicative of an unreasonable impatience, I beg you to forgive me. If I have said anything in this letter that is an understatement of the truth and is indicative of my having a patience that makes me patient with anything less than brotherhood, I beg God to forgive me.

I hope this letter finds you strong in the faith. I also hope that circumstances will soon make it possible for me to meet each of you, not as an integrationist or a civil rights leader, but as a fellow clergyman and a Christian brother. Let us all hope that the dark clouds of racial prejudice will soon pass away and the deep fog of misunderstanding will be lifted from our fear-drenched communities and in some not too distant tomorrow the radiant stars of love and brotherhood will shine over our great nation with all of their scintillating beauty.

Yours for the cause of Peace and Brotherhood,

Martin Luther King Jr.

DISCUSSION QUESTIONS

1. As in "I Have a Dream" (p. 813), King uses figurative language in his letter. Find some particularly vivid passages, and evaluate their effect in the context of this letter.

2. Explain King's distinction between just and unjust laws. Are there dangers in attempting to make such a distinction?

3. What characteristics of mind and behavior does King exhibit in the letter? Select the specific passages that provide proof.

4. Why does King say that "the white moderate" (para. 27) is a greater threat to African American progress than the outspoken racist? Is his explanation convincing?

5. How does King justify his philosophy of nonviolence in the face of continued aggression against Americans who are of African descent?

WRITING SUGGESTIONS

6. Can you think of a law against which defiance would be justified? Explain why the law is unjust and why refusal to obey is morally defensible.

7. In paragraph 19 King lists the grievances of African Americans in this country. King's catalog is similar to the lists in the Declaration of Independence. Can you think of any other group that might compile a list of grievances? If so, choose a group, and draw up such a list making sure that your list is as clear and specific as those you have read.

I Have a Dream

MARTIN LUTHER KING JR.

Five score years ago, a great American, in whose symbolic shadow we stand, signed the Emancipation Proclamation. This momentous decree came as a great beacon light of hope to millions of Negro slaves who had been seared in the flames of withering injustice. It came as a joyous daybreak to end the long night of captivity.

But one hundred years later, we must face the tragic fact that the Negro is still not free. One hundred years later, the life of the Negro is still sadly crippled by the manacles of segregation and the chains of discrimination. One hundred years later, the Negro lives on a lonely island of poverty in the midst of a vast ocean of material prosperity. One hundred years later, the Negro is still languishing in the corners of American society and finds himself an exile in his own land. So we have come here today to dramatize an appalling condition.

In a sense we have come to our nation's capital to cash a check. When the architects of our republic wrote the magnificent words of the Constitution and the Declaration of Independence, they were signing a promissory note to which every American was to fall heir. This note was a promise that all men would be guaranteed the unalienable rights of life, liberty, and the pursuit of happiness.

It is obvious today that America has defaulted on this promissory note insofar as her citizens of color are concerned. Instead of honoring this sacred obligation, America has given the Negro people a bad check; a check which has come back marked "insufficient funds." But we refuse to believe that the bank of justice is bankrupt. We refuse to believe that there are insufficient funds in the great vaults of opportunity of this nation. So we have come to cash this check—a check that will give us upon demand the riches of freedom and the security of justice. We have also come to this hallowed spot to remind America of the fierce urgency of *now*. This is no time to engage in the luxury of cooling off or to take the tranquilizing drugs of gradualism. *Now* is the time to make real the promises of Democracy. *Now* is the time to rise from the dark and desolate valley of segregation to the sunlit path of racial justice. *Now* is the time to open the doors of opportunity to all of God's children. *Now* is the time to lift our nation from the quicksands of racial injustice to the solid rock of brotherhood.

It would be fatal for the nation to overlook the urgency of the 5 moment and to underestimate the determination of the Negro. This

---

In the widely reprinted "I Have a Dream" speech, Martin Luther King Jr. appears as the charismatic leader of the civil rights movement. This inspirational address was delivered on August 28, 1963, in Washington, D.C., at a demonstration by two hundred thousand people for civil rights for African Americans. From *A Testament of Hope* (1986).

sweltering summer of the Negro's legitimate discontent will not pass until there is an invigorating autumn of freedom and equality. Nineteen sixty-three is not an end, but a beginning. Those who hope that the Negro needed to blow off steam and will now be content will have a rude awakening if the nation returns to business as usual. There will be neither rest nor tranquillity in America until the Negro is granted his citizenship rights. The whirlwinds of revolt will continue to shake the foundations of our nation until the bright day of justice emerges.

But there is something that I must say to my people who stand on the warm threshold which leads into the palace of justice. In the process of gaining our rightful place we must not be guilty of wrongful deeds. Let us not seek to satisfy our thirst for freedom by drinking from the cup of bitterness and hatred. We must forever conduct our struggle on the high plane of dignity and discipline. We must not allow our creative protest to degenerate into physical violence. Again and again we must rise to the majestic heights of meeting physical force with soul force. The marvelous new militancy which has engulfed the Negro community must not lead us to a distrust of all white people, for many of our white brothers, as evidenced by their presence here today, have come to realize that their destiny is tied up with our destiny and their freedom is inextricably bound to our freedom. We cannot walk alone.

And as we walk, we must make the pledge that we shall march ahead. We cannot turn back. There are those who are asking the devotees of civil rights, "When will you be satisfied?" We can never be satisfied as long as the Negro is the victim of the unspeakable horrors of police brutality. We can never be satisfied as long as our bodies, heavy with the fatigue of travel, cannot gain lodging in the motels of the highways and the hotels of the cities. We cannot be satisfied as long as the Negro's basic mobility is from a smaller ghetto to a larger one. We can never be satisfied as long as a Negro in Mississippi cannot vote and a Negro in New York believes he has nothing for which to vote. No, no, we are not satisfied, and we will not be satisfied until justice rolls down like waters and righteousness like a mighty stream.

I am not unmindful that some of you have come here out of great trials and tribulations. Some of you have come fresh from narrow jail cells. Some of you have come from areas where your quest for freedom left you battered by the storms of persecution and staggered by the winds of police brutality. You have been the veterans of creative suffering. Continue to work with the faith that unearned suffering is redemptive.

Go back to Mississippi, go back to Alabama, go back to South Carolina, go back to Georgia, go back to Louisiana, go back to the slums and ghettos of our northern cities, knowing that somehow this situation can and will be changed. Let us not wallow in the valley of despair.

I say to you today, my friends, that in spite of the difficulties and frustrations of the moment I still have a dream. It is a dream deeply rooted in the American dream. 10

I have a dream that one day this nation will rise up and live out the true meaning of its creed: "We hold these truths to be self-evident; that all men are created equal."

I have a dream that one day on the red hills of Georgia the sons of former slaves and the sons of former slaveowners will be able to sit down together at the table of brotherhood.

I have a dream that one day even the state of Mississippi, a desert state sweltering with the heat of injustice and oppression, will be transformed into an oasis of freedom and justice.

I have a dream that my four little children will one day live in a nation where they will not be judged by the color of their skin but by the content of their character.

I have a dream today.   15

I have a dream that one day the state of Alabama, whose governor's lips are presently dripping with the words of interposition and nullification, will be transformed into a situation where little black boys and black girls will be able to join hands with little white boys and white girls and walk together as sisters and brothers.

I have a dream today.

I have a dream that one day every valley shall be exalted, every hill and mountain shall be made low, the rough places will be made plain, and the crooked places will be made straight, and the glory of the Lord shall be revealed, and all flesh shall see it together.

This is our hope. This is the faith with which I return to the South. With this faith we will be able to hew out of the mountain of despair a stone of hope. With this faith we will be able to transform the jangling discords of our nation into a beautiful symphony of brotherhood. With this faith we will be able to work together, to pray together, to struggle together, to go to jail together, to stand up for freedom together, knowing that we will be free one day.

This will be the day when all of God's children will be able to sing 20 with new meaning

My country, 'tis of thee,
Sweet land of liberty,
    Of thee I sing:
Land where my fathers died,
Land of the pilgrims' pride,
From every mountain-side
    Let freedom ring.

And if America is to be a great nation this must become true. So let freedom ring from the prodigious hilltops of New Hampshire. Let freedom ring from the mighty mountains of New York. Let freedom ring from the heightening Alleghenies of Pennsylvania!

Let freedom ring from the snowcapped Rockies of Colorado!

Let freedom ring from the curvaceous peaks of California!

But not only that; let freedom ring from Stone Mountain of Georgia! Let freedom ring from Lookout Mountain of Tennessee!   25

Let freedom ring from every hill and molehill of Mississippi. From every mountainside, let freedom ring.

When we let freedom ring, when we let it ring from every village and every hamlet, from every state and every city, we will be able to speed up that day when all of God's children, black men and white men, Jews and Gentiles, Protestants and Catholics, will be able to join hands and sing in the words of the old Negro spiritual, "Free at last! free at last! thank God almighty, we are free at last!"

DISCUSSION QUESTIONS

1. King's style alternates between the abstract and the concrete, between the grandiloquent and the simple, with abundant use of metaphors. Find examples of these qualities. Are all the stylistic strategies equally effective? Explain your answer.

2. What specific injustices suffered by African Americans does King mention? Why does he interrupt his series of "Let freedom ring" imperatives at the end with the statement, "But not only that" (para. 24)?

3. What values does the speech stress? Would these values be equally appealing to both blacks and whites? Why or why not?

4. Forty years later, how much of King's indictment of conditions remains true? Mention specific changes or lack of changes. If conditions have improved, does that make his speech less meaningful today?

WRITING SUGGESTIONS

5. Using the same material as the original, rewrite this speech for an audience that is not impressed with the inspirational style. Think carefully about the changes in language you would make to convince this audience that, despite your dispassionate treatment, injustices exist and should be rectified.

6. Choose another highly emotional subject—for example, women's rights, child pornography, nuclear power—and write an inspirational speech or advertisement urging your audience to change their views. Be passionate, but try to avoid sentimentality or corniness. (You may want to look at other examples of the inspirational or hortatory style in a collection of speeches, among them speeches made in favor of the abolition of slavery and women's suffrage, declarations of war, and inaugural addresses.)

APPENDIX

Arguing about Literature

Writing a paper about a work of literature—a novel, a short story, a poem, or a play—is not so different from writing about matters of public policy. In both cases you make a claim about something you have read and demonstrate the validity of that claim by providing support. In papers about literature, support consists primarily of evidence from examples and details in the work itself and your own interpretation of the language, the events, and the characters. In addition, you can introduce expert scholarly opinion and history and biography where they are relevant.

First, a note about the differences between imaginative literature and argumentative essays. Although the strategies for writing papers about them may be similar, strategies for reading and understanding the works under review will be different. Suppose you read an essay by a psychologist who wants to prove that lying to children, even with the best intentions, can have tragic consequences. The claim of the essay will be directly stated, perhaps even in the first sentence. But if an author writes a short story or a play about the same subject, he or she will probably not state the central idea directly but will *show* rather than *tell*. The theme will emerge through a narrative of dramatic events, expressions of thoughts and feelings by the characters, a depiction of relationships, descriptions of a specific setting, and other elements of fiction. In other words, you will derive the idea or the theme indirectly. This is one reason that a work of fiction can lend itself to multiple interpretations. But it is also the reason that literature, with its evocation of the mysteries of real life, exerts a perpetual fascination.

Different kinds of literary works emphasize different elements. In the following discussion the elements of fiction, poetry, and drama are briefly summarized. The discussion will suggest ways of reading imaginative literature for both pleasure and critical analysis.

THE ELEMENTS OF FICTION

The basic elements of imaginative prose—a short story, a novel, or a play—are *theme, conflict,* and *character.* Other elements such as language, plot, point of view, and setting also influence the effectiveness of any work, but without a central idea, a struggle between opposing forces, and interesting people, it's unlikely that the work will hold our attention. (On the other hand, literature is full of exceptions, and you will certainly find examples that defy the rules.)

The theme is the central idea. It answers the question, What is the point of this story or play? Does the author give us some insight into a personal dilemma? Does he or she show how social conditions shape human behavior? Do we learn how certain traits of character can influence a human life? The answers to these questions apply not only to the specific situation and invented characters in a particular story. In the most memorable works the theme—the lesson to be drawn, the truth to be learned—embodies an idea that is much larger than the form the story assumes. For example, in "The Use of Force," the short story by William Carlos Williams in this appendix (p. 826), the title refers to the *subject* but not the theme. The author wanted to say something *about* the use of force. His theme is a complicated and unwelcome insight into human nature, with implications for all of us, not just the doctor who is the principal actor in the story.

Conflict is present in some form in almost all imaginative writing. It creates suspense and introduces moral dilemmas. External conflicts occur between individuals and between individuals and natural forces. Internal conflicts take place in the minds and hearts of the characters who must make difficult choices between competing goals and values—between right and wrong, pleasure and duty, freedom and responsibility. These two kinds of conflict are not exclusive of each other. A story of war, for example, may include suspenseful physical encounters between opposing forces, but the characters may also be compelled to make painful choices about their actions. In the best works, conflicts are important, not trivial. They may reveal uncommon virtues or shortcomings in the characters, alter their relationships with other people, and even change the course of their lives.

Conflicts exist only because characters—human beings, or in some satires, animals—engage in them. In contests with forces of nature, as in Hemingway's *The Old Man and the Sea*, it is the courage and persistence of a human being that gives meaning to the story. Memorable fictional characters are not easy to create. As readers we demand that characters be interesting, plausible, consistent, and active, physically and mentally. We must care about them, which is not the same as liking them. To care about characters means retaining enough curiosity about them to keep reading and to regret their departure when the story has come to an end. However different and unfamiliar their activities, we should feel that the characters are real. Even in science fiction we insist that the creatures exhibit human characteristics that we can recognize and identify with. But fictional characters should also be distinguishable from one another. Stereotypes are tiresome and unconvincing.

We learn about characters primarily from their speech and their actions but also from what the author and other characters reveal about them. Remembering that characters often withhold information or conceal their motives, even from themselves, we must often depend on our own knowledge and experience to interpret their behavior and judge their plausibility.

THE ELEMENTS OF DRAMA

Drama shares with fiction the elements we have discussed earlier — theme, conflict, and character. But because a play is meant to be performed, it differs from a written story in significant ways. These differences impose limits on the drama, as opposed to the novel, which can do almost anything.

First, stage action is restricted. Violent action—a war scene, for example—must usually take place offstage, and certain situations—such as the hunt for Moby Dick in Melville's novel—would be hard to reproduce in a theater. This means that a play emphasizes internal rather than external conflict.

Second, the author of a play, unlike the author of a short story or a novel, cannot comment on the action, the characters, or the significance of the setting. (It is true that a narrator sometimes appears on stage as a kind of Greek chorus to offer observation on the action, but this is uncommon.) A much greater burden must therefore rest on what the characters say. They must reveal background, explain offstage events, interpret themselves and others, and move the plot forward largely through speech. If the author of a novel lacks skill in reproducing plausible speech, he can find ways to avoid dialogue, but the playwright has no such privilege. She must have an ear for the rhythms and idioms of language that identify particular characters.

Another element which assumes more importance in a play than in a novel is plot. The dramatist must confine an often complicated and event-filled story to two or three hours on the stage. And, as in any listening experience, the audience must be able to follow the plot without the luxury of going back to review.

As you read a long play, you may find it helpful to keep in mind a simple diagram that explains the development of the plot, whether comedy or tragedy. The Freytag pyramid, created in 1863 by a German critic, shows that almost every three- or five-act play begins in a problem or conflict which sets in motion a series of events, called *the rising action*. At some point there is a *climax*, or turning point, followed by *the falling action*, which reverses the fortunes of the main characters and leads to a conclusion that may be happy or unhappy.

Shakespeare's *Macbeth* is an almost perfect example of the pyramid. The rising action in this tragedy is one of continued success for the main characters. The climax is a crisis on the battlefield, after which the fortunes of Macbeth and Lady Macbeth decline, ending in failure and death. In a comedy, the developments are reversed. The rising action is a series of stumbles and mishaps; then in the climax the hero finds the money or rescues the heroine, and the falling action ushers in a number of welcome surprises that culminate in a happy ending. (Think of a Jim Carrey comedy.) Typically the rising action in any play takes longer and thus creates suspense.

Reading a play is not the same as seeing one on stage. Many playwrights, like novelists, describe their settings and their characters in elaborate detail. In *Long Day's Journey into Night*, Eugene O'Neill's autobiographical play, descriptions of the living-room in which the action occurs and of the mother and father, who appear in the first act, cover more than three pages in small print. When you read, you fill the imaginary stage with your own interpretations of the playwright's descriptions, derived perhaps from places or persons in your own experience. You may forget that the playwright is dependent on directors, set designers, and actors, with other philosophies and approaches to stagecraft, to interpret his or her work. It can come as a surprise to see the stage version of the play you have read and interpreted very differently.

All playwrights want their plays to be performed. Still, the best plays are read far more frequently than they are produced on stage. Fortunately, reading them is a literary experience with its own rewards.

THE ELEMENTS OF POETRY

There are several kinds of poetry, among them epic, dramatic, and lyric. Epic poetry celebrates the heroic adventures of a human or superhuman character in a long, event-filled narrative. Milton's *Paradise Lost* is the preeminent example in English, but you may also be familiar with *The Iliad*, *The Odyssey*, and *The Aeneid*, the epics of ancient Greece and Rome. Dramatic poetry also tells a story, sometimes through monologue, as in Robert Browning's "My Last Duchess," where the Duke recounts the reasons why he murdered his wife; sometimes through dialogue, as in Robert Frost's "The Death of the Hired Man." These stories are often told in blank verse, unrhymed five-beat lines. Playwrights of the past, Shakespeare among others, adopted this poetic form.

Modern poems are much more likely to be lyrics—poetry derived from song. (The term *lyric* comes from the word for an ancient musical instrument, the lyre.) The lyric is most frequently an expression of the poet's feeling rather than an account of events. The characteristics that make poetry harder to read than prose are the very characteristics that define it: compression and metaphor. A lyric poem is highly concentrated. It focuses on what is essential in an experience, the details that illuminate it vividly against the background of our ordinary lives. Metaphor is a form of figurative language, a way of saying one thing to mean something else. It is a simile which omits the "like" or "as": for example, "A mighty fortress is our God." The poet chooses metaphoric images that appeal to our senses in order to reinforce the literal meaning. In a famous poem Thomas Campion compared the beauty of his sweetheart's face to that of a garden.

> There is a garden in her face
> Where roses and white lilies grow,
> A heavenly paradise is that place,
> Wherein all pleasant fruits do flow.

A poem, like an essay, tries to prove something. Like a short story, its message is indirect, expressed in the language of metaphor. It seldom urges a practical course of action. What it tries to prove is that a feeling or a perception—a response to love or death, or the sight of a snowy field on a dark night—is true and real.

The lyric poet's subjects are common ones—love, joy, sorrow, nature, death—but he or she makes uncommon use of words, imagery, and rhythm. These are the elements you examine as evidence of the poet's theme and depth of feeling.

Precisely because the poem will condense her experience, the poet must choose words with immediate impact. For example, in a poem about an encounter with a snake, Emily Dickinson writes,

> But never met this Fellow
> Attended, or alone
> Without a tighter breathing
> And Zero at the bone—

Although we have never seen this use of "zero" before, it strikes us at once as the perfect choice to suggest a kind of chilling fear.

In the best poems images transform the most commonplace experiences. Here is the first quatrain of Shakespeare's sonnet number 73, about loving deeply what will not live forever.

> That time of year thou mayest in me behold
> When yellow leaves or none or few do hang
> Upon those boughs which shake against the cold
> Bare ruined choirs where late the sweet birds sang.

Nowhere does Shakespeare mention that he is growing old. Instead, here and in subsequent stanzas he creates images of dead or dying things—autumn trees, the coming of night, dying fires—that convey feelings of cold and desolation. The final couplet expresses the theme directly:

> Thus thou perceiv'st, which makes thy love more strong,
> To love that well which thou must leave ere long.

It is the imagery, however, that brings the theme to life and enables us to understand and share the poet's feeling.

Rhythm, defined as measured and balanced movement, is almost as important as language. As children, even before we fully understand all the words, we derive pleasure from the sounds of Mother Goose and the Dr. Seuss rhymes. Their sound patterns reflect the musical origin of poetry and the fact that poetry was meant to be chanted rather than read. Listen to the rhythm of these opening lines from Andrew Marvell's "To His Coy Mistress" — "Had we but world enough and time, / This coyness, lady, were no crime" — and hear the lilting four-beat meter that suggests song. If you look through an anthology of poetry written before the twentieth century, you will see even from the appearance of the poems on the page that the cadence or rhythm of most poems creates an orderly pattern. Edgar Allan Poe's "The Raven" is a familiar example of poems in which rhyme and rhythm come together to produce a harmonious design.

Measured movement in poetry is less common today. Free verse breaks with this ancient convention. (The very regularity of "The Raven" is now a subject for parody.) The poet of free verse invents his own rhythms, governed by meaning, free association, and a belief in poetry as a democratic art, one capable of reaching all people. In "Song of Myself," Walt Whitman (1819–1892), one of America's most influential poets, writes in a new voice that resembles the sound of spoken language:

> A child said *What is the grass?* fetching it to me with full hands,
> How could I answer the child? I do not know what it is any more
>   than he.
> I guess it must be the flag of my disposition, out of hopeful green stuff
>   woven.

Notice, however, that the phrase "out of hopeful green stuff woven" is the language of poetry, not prose.

Much twentieth-century poetry dispenses altogether with both rhyme and formal rhythms, but the lyric remains unmistakably alive. Perhaps you have read poems by William Carlos Williams or e. e. cummings, who have used new rhythms to create their own distinctive versions of the lyric.

THE CULTURAL CONTEXT

Even those works that are presumed to be immortal and universal are products of a particular time in history and a particular social and political context. These works may therefore represent points of view with which we are unsympathetic. Today, for example, some women are uncomfortable with Shakespeare's *The Taming of the Shrew*, which finds comic possibilities in the subjugation of a woman to her husband's will. Jews may be offended by the characterization of Shylock in *The Merchant of Venice* as a Jewish money-lender who shows little mercy to his debtor. Some African Americans have resented the portrayal of Jim, the slave in *Huckleberry Finn*. Even *Peter Pan* has provoked criticism for its depiction of American Indians. In your own reading you may find fault with an author's attitude toward his subject; defending your own point of view against that of the author can be a satisfying literary exercise. To bring fresh, perhaps controversial, interpretations into an analysis may, indeed, enliven discussion and even revive interest in older works that no longer move us. But remember that the evidence will be largely external, based on social and political views that will themselves need explanation.

There is, after all, a danger in allowing our ideas about social and political correctness to take over and in imposing our values on those of another time, place, or culture. Literature, like great historical writing, enables us to enter worlds very different from our own. The worlds we read about in novels and plays may be governed by different moral codes, different social conventions, different religious values, many of which we reject or don't understand. Characters in these stories, even those cast as heroes and heroines, sometimes behave in ways we consider ignorant or self-serving. (Russell Baker, the humorist, observed that it was unfortunate that the writers of the past were not so enlightened as we are.) But reading has always offered an experience otherwise unavailable, a ready escape from our own lives into the lives of others, whose ways, however strange, we try to understand, whether or not we approve.

CHOOSING WHAT TO WRITE ABOUT

Your paper can take one of several different approaches. It is worth emphasizing that comedy and tragedy generally share the same literary elements. A tragedy, of course, ends in misfortune or death. A comedy typically ends with a happy resolution of all problems.

1. You may analyze or explain the meaning or theme of a work that is subject to different interpretations. For example, a famous interpretation of *Hamlet* in 1910[1] suggested that Hamlet was unable to avenge his father's murder because of guilt over his own Oedipal love for his mother. Or, having seen a distorted movie version of a familiar book (unfortunately, there are plenty of examples) you can explain what you think is the real theme of the book and how the movie departs from it.

---

[1] Ernest Jones, *Hamlet and Oedipus* (New York: Norton, 1949).

Some stories and plays, although based in reality, seem largely symbolic. "The Lottery," a widely read short story by Shirley Jackson, describes a ritual that hints at other meanings than those usually attributed to lotteries. *Waiting for Godot*, a play by Samuel Beckett, is a work that has inspired a dozen interpretations; the name *Godot*, with the embedded word *God*, suggests several. But exercise caution in writing about symbols. Saul Bellow, the Nobel Prize-winning novelist, has written an essay, "Deep Readers of the World, Beware!" that explains the dangers. He reminds us that "a true symbol is substantial, not accidental. You cannot avoid it, you cannot remove it."

2. You may analyze the conflicts in a story or play. The conflicts that make interesting papers are those that not only challenge our understanding (as with Iago's villainy in *Othello*) but encourage us to reflect on profound moral issues. For example, how does Mark Twain develop the struggle in Huckleberry Finn between his southern prejudices and his respect for Jim's humanity? How does John Proctor, the hero of Arthur Miller's *The Crucible*, resolve the moral dilemmas that lead him to choose death rather than a freedom secured by lies?

3. You may choose to write about an especially vivid or contradictory character, describing his traits in such a way as to make clear why he is worth a detailed examination. The protagonist of *The Stranger* by Albert Camus, for example, is a murderer who, although he tells us little or nothing about himself and is therefore difficult to understand, eventually earns our sympathy.

4. You may concentrate on the setting if it has special significance for the lives of the characters and what they do, as in Joseph Conrad's *Heart of Darkness* and Tennessee Williams's *A Streetcar Named Desire*. Setting may include time or historical period as well as place. Ask if the story or play would have taken shape in quite the same way in another time and place.

5. You may examine the language or style. No analysis of a poem would be complete without attention to the language, but the style of a prose work can also contribute to the impact on the reader. Hemingway's clean, economical style has often been studied, as has Faulkner's dense, complicated prose, equally powerful but very different. But you should probably not attempt an analysis of style unless you are sure you can discuss the uses of diction, grammar, syntax, and rhythm.

GUIDELINES FOR WRITING THE PAPER

1. Decide on a limited topic as the subject for your paper. The most interesting topics, of course, are those that are not so obvious: original interpretations, for example, that arise from a genuine personal response. Don't be afraid to disagree with a conventional reading of the literary work, but be sure you can find sufficient evidence for your point of view.

2. Before you begin to write, make a brief outline of the points that will support your thesis. You may find that you don't have enough evidence to make a good case to a skeptical reader. Or you may find that you have too much for a short paper and that your thesis, therefore, is too broad.

3. The evidence that you provide can be both internal and external. Internal evidence is found in the work itself: an action that reveals motives and consequences, statements by the characters about themselves and others, comments by the author about her characters, and interpretation of the language. External evidence comes from outside the work: a comment by a literary critic, information about the historical period or the geographical location of the work, or data about the author's life and other works he has written.

If possible, use more than one kind of evidence. The most important proof, however, will come from a careful selection of material from the work itself.

4. One temptation to avoid is using quotations from the work or from a critic so abundantly that your paper consists of a string of quotations and little else. Remember that the importance of your paper rests on your interpretations of the evidence. Your own analysis should constitute the major part of the paper. The quotations should be introduced only to support important points.

5. Organize your essay according to the guidelines you have followed for an argumentative essay on a public issue (see Chapter 9, pp. 373–93). Two of the organizational plans that work best are defending the main idea and refuting the opposing view—that is, a literary interpretation with which you disagree. In both cases the simplest method is to state your claim—the thesis you are going to defend—in the first paragraph and then line up evidence point by point in order of importance. If you feel comfortable beginning your paper in a different way, you may start with a paragraph of background: the reasons that you have chosen to explore a particular topic or a description of your personal response to the work—for example, where you first saw a play performed, how a story or poem affected you. (H. L. Mencken, the great American social critic, said discovering *Huckleberry Finn* was "the most stupendous event of my whole life!" What a beginning for an essay!)

It is always useful to look at book or movie reviews in good newspapers and magazines for models of organization and development that suggest a wide range of choices for your own paper.

Read the following short story, and reflect on it for a few moments. Then turn back to the following questions. Were you surprised at the actions of the doctor? What is the author saying about the use of force? Do you agree? What kinds of conflicts has he dramatized? Are some more important than others? How do the characterizations of the people in the story contribute to the theme?

Thinking about the answers to these questions will give you a clearer perspective on the essay written by a student that follows the story. After reading the essay, you may see other elements of fiction that might have been analyzed in a critical paper.

The Use of Force

WILLIAM CARLOS WILLIAMS

They were new patients to me, all I had was the name, Olson. Please come down as soon as you can, my daughter is very sick.

When I arrived I was met by the mother, a big startled looking woman, very clean and apologetic who merely said, Is this the doctor? and let me in. In the back, she added, You must excuse us, doctor, we have her in the kitchen where it is warm. It is very damp here sometimes.

The child was fully dressed and sitting on her father's lap near the kitchen table. He tried to get up, but I motioned for him not to bother, took off my overcoat and started to look things over. I could see that they were all very nervous, eyeing me up and down distrustfully. As often, in such cases, they weren't telling me more than they had to, it was up to me to tell them; that's why they were spending three dollars on me.

The child was fairly eating me up with her cold, steady eyes, and no expression to her face whatever. She did not move and seemed, inwardly, quiet; an unusually attractive little thing, and as strong as a heifer in appearance. But her face was flushed, she was breathing rapidly, and I realized that she had a high fever. She had magnificent blonde hair, in profusion. One of those picture children often reproduced in advertising leaflets and the photogravure sections of the Sunday papers.

She's had a fever for three days, began the father and we don't know 5 what it comes from. My wife has given her things, you know, like people

---

William Carlos Williams (1883–1963) wrote poems, novels, plays, and short stories. A pediatrician in the industrial city of Rutherford, New Jersey, much of his work, including "The Use of Force" (*The Farmers' Daughters*, 1938), depicts the daily hardships of his impoverished patients.

do, but it don't do no good. And there's been a lot of sickness around. So we tho't you'd better look her over and tell us what is the matter.

As doctors often do I took a trial shot at it as a point of departure. Has she had a sore throat?

Both parents answered me together, No . . . No, she says her throat don't hurt her.

Does your throat hurt you? added the mother to the child. But the little girl's expression didn't change nor did she move her eyes from my face.

Have you looked?

I tried to, said the mother, but I couldn't see.   10

As it happens we had been having a number of cases of diphtheria in the school to which this child went during that month and we were all, quite apparently, thinking of that, though no one had as yet spoken of the thing.

Well, I said, suppose we take a look at the throat first. I smiled in my best professional manner and asking for the child's first name I said, come on, Mathilda, open your mouth and let's take a look at your throat.

Nothing doing.

Aw, come on, I coaxed, just open your mouth wide and let me take a look. Look, I said opening both hands wide. I haven't anything in my hands. Just open up and let me see.

Such a nice man, put in the mother. Look how kind he is to you. 15
Come on, do what he tells you to. He won't hurt you.

At that I ground my teeth in disgust. If only they wouldn't use the word "hurt" I might be able to get somewhere. But I did not allow myself to be hurried or disturbed but speaking quietly and slowly I approached the child again.

As I moved my chair a little nearer suddenly with one cat-like movement both her hands clawed instinctively for my eyes and she almost reached them too. In fact she knocked my glasses flying and they fell, though unbroken, several feet away from me on the kitchen floor.

Both the mother and father almost turned themselves inside out in embarrassment and apology. You bad girl, said the mother, taking her and shaking her by one arm. Look what you've done. The nice man . . .

For heaven's sake, I broke in. Don't call me a nice man to her. I'm here to look at her throat on the chance that she might have diphtheria and possibly die of it. But that's nothing to her. Look here, I said to the child, we're going to look at your throat. You're old enough to understand what I'm saying. Will you open it now by yourself or shall we have to open it for you?

Not a move. Even her expression hadn't changed. Her breaths how- 20
ever were coming faster and faster. Then the battle began. I had to do it. I had to have a throat culture for her own protection. But first I told the parents that it was entirely up to them. I explained the danger but said

that I would not insist on a throat examination so long as they would take the responsibility.

If you don't do what the doctor says you'll have to go to the hospital, the mother admonished her severely.

Oh yeah? I had to smile to myself. After all, I had already fallen in love with the savage brat, the parents were contemptible to me. In the ensuing struggle they grew more and more abject, crushed, exhausted while she surely rose to magnificent heights of insane fury of effort bred of her terror of me.

The father tried his best, and he was a big man but the fact that she was his daughter, his shame at her behavior and his dread of hurting her made him release her just at the critical moment several times when I had almost achieved success, till I wanted to kill him. But his dread also that she might have diphtheria made him tell me to go on, go on though he himself was almost fainting, while the mother moved back and forth behind us raising and lowering her hands in an agony of apprehension.

Put her in front of you on your lap, I ordered, and hold both her wrists.

But as soon as he did the child let out a scream. Don't, you're hurt- 25 ing me. Let go of my hands. Let them go I tell you. Then she shrieked terrifyingly, hysterically. Stop it! Stop it! You're killing me!

Do you think she can stand it, doctor! said the mother.

You get out, said the husband to his wife. Do you want her to die of diphtheria?

Come on now, hold her, I said.

Then I grasped the child's head with my left hand and tried to get the wooden tongue depressor between her teeth. She fought, with clenched teeth, desperately! But now I also had grown furious—at a child. I tried to hold myself down but I couldn't. I know how to expose a throat for inspection. And I did my best. When finally I got the wooden spatula behind the last teeth and just the point of it into the mouth cavity, she opened up for an instant, but before I could see anything she came down again and gripping the wooden blade between her molars she reduced it to splinters before I could get it out again.

Aren't you ashamed, the mother yelled at her. Aren't you ashamed to 30 act like that in front of the doctor?

Get me a smooth-handled spoon of some sort, I told the mother. We're going through with this. The child's mouth was already bleeding. Her tongue was cut and she was screaming in wild hysterical shrieks. Perhaps I should have desisted and come back in an hour or more. No doubt it would have been better. But I have seen at least two children lying dead in bed of neglect in such cases, and feeling that I must get a diagnosis now or never I went at it again. But the worst of it was that I too had got beyond reason. I could have torn the child apart in my own fury and enjoyed it. It was a pleasure to attack her. My face was burning with it.

The damned little brat must be protected against her own idiocy, one says to one's self at such times. Others must be protected against her. It is social necessity. And all these things are true. But a blind fury, a feeling of adult shame, bred of a longing for muscular release are the operatives. One goes on to the end.

In a final unreasoning assault I overpowered the child's neck and jaws. I forced the heavy silver spoon back of her teeth and down her throat till she gagged. And there it was—both tonsils covered with membrane. She had fought valiantly to keep me from knowing her secret. She had been hiding that sore throat for three days at least and lying to her parents in order to escape just such an outcome as this.

Now truly she *was* furious. She had been on the defensive before but now she attacked. Tried to get off her father's lap and fly at me while tears of defeat blinded her eyes.

Rampolla 1

Jennifer Rampolla
Professor Harrington
English 102-C
May 2, 2005

Conflicts in "The Use of Force"

"The Use of Force" tells us something about human nature that probably comes as no surprise: The impulse to use violence against a helpless but defiant opponent can be thrilling and irresistible. But the conflict which produces this insight is not a shoot-out between cops and robbers, not a fight for survival against a dangerous enemy, but a struggle between a grown man and a sick child.

In this story two major conflicts are dramatized, one external or physical, the other internal or psychological. The conflicts seem obvious. Even the blunt, unadorned language means to persuade us that nothing is concealed. But below the surface, some motives remain unacknowledged, and we guess at them only because we know how easily people deceive themselves.

The external conflict is vividly depicted, a physical struggle between doctor and child, complete with weapon -- a metal spoon. The outcome is hardly in doubt; the doctor will win. One critic calls this story primarily "an accomplishment (external conflict) story" (Madden 16). But the internal conflict that accompanies a difficult choice is the real heart of the story. The doctor must decide between waiting for a more opportune time to examine the child or exercising brute force to subdue her now. When he decides on brute force, he seems aware of his motives.

> But the worst of it was that I too had got beyond reason. I could have torn the child apart in my own fury and enjoyed it. It was a pleasure to attack her.

This shocking revelation is not, however, the whole story. Why has he got beyond reason? Why does he take pleasure in attacking a child? The answer lies not only in what we know about the antagonists but in what we can assume about their relationship to each other.

Rampolla 2

The child is brilliantly portrayed in a few grim encounters with the doctor. She is strong, stubborn, secretive, and violent. Despite her size and age, she is a match for the doctor, a challenge that at first excites him.

Description of the child

> I had to smile to myself. After all, I had already fallen in love with the savage brat. . . . In the ensuing struggle . . . she surely rose to magnificent heights of insane fury. . . .

Evidence: Quotation

The picture of the doctor is somewhat harder to read. Sixty years ago (when this story was written) the doctor in a working-class community occupied a position of unusual power and authority. He would not be accustomed to challenges at any level. Clearly the differences in social and economic status between the doctor and his clients are another source of conflict that influences his use of force. Like many people in positions of power, the doctor is torn by contradictory emotions toward those below him. On the one hand, he despises those who are deferential to him, in this case the child's parents. On the other hand, it is unthinkable that a child should dare to oppose him, not only in refusing to obey his instructions but in trying, like a desperate small animal, to attack him. It is even more unthinkable that she should prevail in any contest. He confesses to "a feeling of adult shame." If we look for it, there is also a hint of sexual conflict. The child is blond and beautiful; the doctor says he is in love with her. (Would this story have worked in quite the same way if the child had been a boy?) The doctor attempts to rationalize his use of force, but he knows that it is not the child's welfare that finally compels him to overcome her resistance. In the end, reason gives way to pride and vanity.

Description of the doctor

Unexpressed social conflict

Evidence: External, from history

Evidence: Quotation

Perhaps another concealed conflict?

The doctor's real motivation

Most of us respond to this story with a mixture of feelings -- anger at the pleasure the doctor takes in his use of force, confusion and even fear at the realization that doctors may not always behave like gentle and loving helpers, and pity for the little girl with whom it is easy to identify. The author doesn't spell out the moral implications of the doctor's

Conclusion

The reader's mixed reaction

Sympathy for the child

Reaction to the theme

internal conflict. But perhaps it is significant that the author gives the last words to the little girl: "Tears of defeat blinded her eyes." I think he has chosen this ending in order to direct our sympathy to the victim, an unhappy child who struggled hopelessly to protect herself. Although we know that the doctor has performed a necessary and merciful act, we are left to wonder if it matters that he has done it for the wrong reason.

Work Cited

Madden, David. Studies in the Short Story. New York: Holt, 1980.

Trifles

SUSAN GLASPELL

CHARACTERS

> GEORGE HENDERSON, county attorney
> HENRY PETERS, sheriff
> LEWIS HALE, a neighboring farmer
> MRS. PETERS
> MRS. HALE

SCENE: *The kitchen in the now abandoned farmhouse of John Wright, a gloomy kitchen, and left without having been put in order—unwashed pans under the sink, a loaf of bread outside the breadbox, a dish towel on the table—other signs of incompleted work. At the rear the outer door opens and the Sheriff comes in followed by the County Attorney and Hale. The Sheriff and Hale are men in middle life, the County Attorney is a young man; all are much bundled up and go at once to the stove. They are followed by the two women— the Sheriff's wife first; she is a slight wiry woman, a thin nervous face. Mrs. Hale is larger and would ordinarily be called more comfortable looking, but she is disturbed now and looks fearfully about as she enters. The women have come in slowly, and stand close together near the door.*

COUNTY ATTORNEY *(rubbing his hands):* This feels good. Come up to the fire, ladies.

MRS. PETERS *(after taking a step forward):* I'm not—cold.

SHERIFF *(unbuttoning his overcoat and stepping away from the stove as if to mark the beginning of official business):* Now, Mr. Hale, before we move things about, you explain to Mr. Henderson just what you saw when you came here yesterday morning.

COUNTY ATTORNEY: By the way, has anything been moved? Are things just as you left them yesterday?

SHERIFF *(looking about):* It's just about the same. When it dropped below zero last night I thought I'd better send Frank out this morning to make a fire for us—no use getting pneumonia with a big case on, but I told him not to touch anything except the stove—and you know Frank.

Susan Glaspell (1876–1948) was an American playwright and novelist. In 1916 she wrote *Trifles* for the Provincetown Players, a Provincetown, Massachusetts, theater troupe founded by Glaspell and her husband. Based on her recollection of a real murder case that she covered as a journalist in Iowa, *Trifles* was so successful that Glaspell decided to rewrite it as a short story, "A Jury of Her Peers."

COUNTY ATTORNEY: Somebody should have been left here yesterday.

SHERIFF: Oh—yesterday. When I had to send Frank to Morris Center for that man who went crazy—I want you to know I had my hands full yesterday. I knew you could get back from Omaha by today and as long as I went over everything here myself—

COUNTY ATTORNEY: Well, Mr. Hale, tell just what happened when you came here yesterday morning.

HALE: Harry and I had started to town with a load of potatoes. We came along the road from my place and as I got here I said, "I'm going to see if I can't get John Wright to go in with me on a party telephone." I spoke to Wright about it once before and he put me off, saying folks talked too much anyway, and all he asked was peace and quiet—I guess you know about how much he talked himself; but I thought maybe if I went to the house and talked about it before his wife, though I said to Harry that I didn't know as what his wife wanted made much difference to John—

COUNTY ATTORNEY: Let's talk about that later, Mr. Hale. I do want to talk about that, but tell now just what happened when you got to the house.

HALE: I didn't hear or see anything; I knocked at the door, and still it was all quiet inside. I knew they must be up, it was past eight o'clock. So I knocked again, and I thought I heard somebody say, "Come in." I wasn't sure, I'm not sure yet, but I opened the door—this door *(indicating the door by which the two women are still standing)* and there in that rocker—*(pointing to it)* sat Mrs. Wright. *(They all look at the rocker.)*

COUNTY ATTORNEY: What—was she doing?

HALE: She was rockin' back and forth. She had her apron in her hand and was kind of—pleating it.

COUNTY ATTORNEY: And how did she—look?

HALE: Well, she looked queer.

COUNTY ATTORNEY: How do you mean—queer?

HALE: Well, as if she didn't know what she was going to do next. And kind of done up.

COUNTY ATTORNEY: How did she seem to feel about your coming?

HALE: Why, I don't think she minded—one way or other. She didn't pay much attention. I said, "How do, Mrs. Wright, it's cold, ain't it?" And she said, "Is it?"—and went on kind of pleating at her apron. Well, I was surprised; she didn't ask me to come up to the stove, or to set down, but just sat there, not even looking at me, so I said, "I want to see John." And then she—laughed. I guess you would call it a laugh. I thought of Harry and the team outside, so I said a little sharp: "Can't I see John?" "No," she says, kind o' dull like. "Ain't he home?" says I. "Yes," says she, "he's home." "Then why can't I see him?" I asked her, out of patience. "'Cause he's dead," says she. *Dead?* says I. She just nodded her head, not getting a bit excited, but rockin' back and forth. "Why—where is he?" says I, not knowing what to say. She just pointed upstairs—like that *(himself pointing to the room above)*. I started for the stairs, with the idea of going up there. I walked from there to here—then I says, "Why, what did he die of?" "He died of a rope round his neck," says she, and just went on pleatin' at her apron. Well, I went out and called Harry. I thought I might—need help. We went upstairs and there he was lyin'—

COUNTY ATTORNEY: I think I'd rather have you go into that upstairs, where you can point it all out. Just go on now with the rest of the story.

HALE: Well, my first thought was to get that rope off. It looked . . . *(stops; his face twitches)* . . . but Harry, he went up to him, and he said, "No, he's dead all right, and we'd better not touch anything." So we went back downstairs. She was still sitting that same way. "Has anybody been notified?" I asked. "No," says she, unconcerned. "Who did this, Mrs. Wright?" said Harry. He said it businesslike—and she stopped pleatin' of her apron. "I don't know," she says. "You don't *know?*" says Harry. "No," says she. "Weren't you sleepin' in the bed with him?" says Harry. "Yes," says she, "but I was on the inside." "Somebody slipped a rope round his neck and strangled him and you didn't wake up?" says Harry. "I didn't wake up," she said after him. We must 'a' looked as if we didn't see how that could be, for after a minute she said, "I sleep sound." Harry was going to ask her more questions but I said maybe we ought to let her tell her story first to the coroner, or the sheriff, so Harry went fast as he could to Rivers' place, where there's a telephone.

COUNTY ATTORNEY: And what did Mrs. Wright do when she knew that you had gone for the coroner?

HALE: She moved from the rocker to that chair over there *(pointing to a small chair in the corner)* and just sat there with her hands held together and looking down. I got a feeling that I ought to make some conversation, so I said I had come in to see if John wanted to put in a telephone, and at that she started to laugh, and then she stopped and looked at me—scared. *(The County Attorney, who has had his notebook out, makes a note.)* I dunno, maybe it wasn't scared. I wouldn't like to say it was. Soon Harry got back, and then Dr. Lloyd came and you, Mr. Peters, and so I guess that's all I know that you don't.

COUNTY ATTORNEY *(looking around):* I guess we'll go upstairs first—and then out to the barn and around there. *(To the Sheriff.)* You're convinced that there was nothing important here—nothing that would point to any motive?

SHERIFF: Nothing here but kitchen things. *(The County Attorney, after again looking around the kitchen, opens the door of a cupboard closet. He gets up on a chair and looks on a shelf. Pulls his hand away, sticky.)*

COUNTY ATTORNEY: Here's a nice mess. *(The women draw nearer.)*

MRS. PETERS *(to the other woman):* Oh, her fruit; it did freeze. *(To the Lawyer.)* She worried about that when it turned so cold. She said the fire'd go out and her jars would break.

SHERIFF *(rises):* Well, can you beat the woman! Held for murder and worryin' about her preserves.

COUNTY ATTORNEY: I guess before we're through she may have something more serious than preserves to worry about.

HALE: Well, women are used to worrying over trifles. *(The two women move a little closer together.)*

COUNTY ATTORNEY *(with the gallantry of a young politician):* And yet, for all their worries, what would we do without the ladies? *(The women do not unbend. He goes to the sink, takes a dipperful of water from the pail, and pouring it into a basin, washes his hands. Starts to wipe them on the roller towel, turns it for a cleaner place.)* Dirty towels! *(Kicks his foot against the pans under the sink.)* Not much of a housekeeper, would you say, ladies?

MRS. HALE *(stiffly):* There's a great deal of work to be done on a farm.

COUNTY ATTORNEY: To be sure. And yet *(with a little bow to her)* I know there are some Dickson county farmhouses which do not have such roller towels. *(He gives it a pull to expose its full length again.)*

MRS. HALE: Those towels get dirty awful quick. Men's hands aren't always as clean as they might be.

COUNTY ATTORNEY: Ah, loyal to your sex, I see. But you and Mrs. Wright were neighbors. I suppose you were friends, too.

MRS. HALE *(shaking her head):* I've not seen much of her of late years. I've not been in this house—it's more than a year.

COUNTY ATTORNEY: And why was that? You didn't like her?

MRS. HALE: I liked her all well enough. Farmers' wives have their hands full, Mr. Henderson. And then—

COUNTY ATTORNEY: Yes—?

MRS. HALE *(looking about):* It never seemed a very cheerful place.

COUNTY ATTORNEY: No—it's not cheerful. I shouldn't say she had the homemaking instinct.

MRS. HALE: Well, I don't know as Wright had, either.

COUNTY ATTORNEY: You mean that they didn't get on very well?

MRS. HALE: No, I don't mean anything. But I don't think a place'd be any cheerfuller for John Wright's being in it.

COUNTY ATTORNEY: I'd like to talk more of that a little later. I want to get the lay of things upstairs now. *(He goes to the left where three steps lead to a stair door.)*

SHERIFF: I suppose anything Mrs. Peters does'll be all right. She was to take in some clothes for her, you know, and a few little things. We left in such a hurry yesterday.

COUNTY ATTORNEY: Yes, but I would like to see what you take, Mrs. Peters, and keep an eye out for anything that might be of use to us.

MRS. PETERS: Yes, Mr. Henderson. *(The women listen to the men's steps on the stairs, then look about the kitchen.)*

MRS. HALE: I'd hate to have men coming into my kitchen, snooping around and criticizing. *(She arranges the pans under sink which the lawyer had shoved out of place.)*

MRS. PETERS: Of course it's no more than their duty.

MRS. HALE: Duty's all right, but I guess that deputy sheriff that came out to make the fire might have got a little of this on. *(Gives the roller towel a pull.)* Wish I'd thought of that sooner. Seems mean to talk about her for not having things slicked up when she had to come away in such a hurry.

MRS. PETERS *(who has gone to a small table in the left rear corner of the room, and lifted one end of a towel that covers a pan):* She had bread set. *(Stands still.)*

MRS. HALE *(eyes fixed on a loaf of bread beside the breadbox, which is on a low shelf at the other side of the room. Moves slowly toward it.):* She was going to put this in there. *(Picks up loaf, then abruptly drops it. In a manner of returning to familiar things.)* It's a shame about her fruit. I wonder if it's all gone. *(Gets up on the chair and looks.)* I think there's some here that's all right, Mrs. Peters. Yes—here; *(holding it toward the window)* this is cherries, too. *(Looking again.)* I declare I believe that's the only one. *(Gets down, bottle in her hand. Goes to the sink and wipes it off on the outside.)* She'll feel awful bad after all her hard work in the hot weather. I remember the afternoon I put up my cherries last summer. *(She puts the bottle on the big kitchen table, center of the room. With a sigh, is about to sit down in the rocking-chair. Before she is seated realizes what chair it is; with a slow look at it, steps back. The chair which she has touched rocks back and forth.)*

MRS. PETERS: Well, I must get those things from the front room closet. *(She goes to the door at the right, but after looking into the other room, steps back.)* You coming with me, Mrs. Hale? You could help me carry them. *(They go in the other room; reappear, Mrs. Peters carrying a dress and skirt, Mrs. Hale following with a pair of shoes.)* My, it's cold in there. *(She puts the clothes on the big table, and hurries to the stove.)*

MRS. HALE *(examining the skirt):* Wright was close. I think maybe that's why she kept so much to herself. She didn't even belong to the Ladies' Aid. I suppose she felt she couldn't do her part, and then you don't enjoy things when you feel shabby. I heard she used to wear pretty clothes and be lively, when she was Minnie Foster, one of the town girls singing in the choir. But that—oh, that was thirty years ago. This all you want to take in?

MRS. PETERS: She said she wanted an apron. Funny thing to want, for there isn't much to get you dirty in jail, goodness knows. But I suppose just to make her feel more natural. She said they was in the top drawer in this cupboard. Yes, here. And then her little shawl that always hung behind the door. *(Opens stair door and looks.)* Yes, here it is. *(Quickly shuts door leading upstairs.)*

MRS. HALE *(abruptly moving toward her):* Mrs. Peters?

MRS. PETERS: Yes, Mrs. Hale?

MRS. HALE: Do you think she did it?

MRS. PETERS *(in a frightened voice):* Oh, I don't know.

MRS. HALE: Well, I don't think she did. Asking for an apron and her little shawl. Worrying about her fruit.

MRS. PETERS *(starts to speak, glances up, where footsteps are heard in the room above. In a low voice):* Mr. Peters says it looks bad for her. Mr. Henderson is awful sarcastic in a speech and he'll make fun of her sayin' she didn't wake up.

MRS. HALE: Well, I guess John Wright didn't wake when they was slipping that rope under his neck.

MRS. PETERS: No, it's strange. It must have been done awful crafty and still. They say it was such a—funny way to kill a man, rigging it all up like that.

MRS. HALE: That's just what Mr. Hale said. There was a gun in the house. He says that's what he can't understand.

MRS. PETERS: Mr. Henderson said coming out that what was needed for the case was a motive; something to show anger, or—sudden feeling.

MRS. HALE *(who is standing by the table):* Well, I don't see any signs of anger around here. *(She puts her hand on the dish towel which lies on the table, stands looking down at table, one-half of which is clean, the other half messy.)* It's wiped to here. *(Makes a move as if to finish work, then turns and looks at loaf of bread outside the breadbox. Drops towel. In that voice of coming back to familiar things.)* Wonder how they are finding things upstairs. I hope she had it a little more red-up up there. You know, it seems kind of *sneaking.* Locking her up in town and then coming out here and trying to get her own house to turn against her!

MRS. PETERS: But, Mrs. Hale, the law is the law.

MRS. HALE: I s'pose 'tis. *(Unbuttoning her coat.)* Better loosen up your things, Mrs. Peters. You won't feel them when you go out. *(Mrs. Peters takes off her fur tippet, goes to hang it on hook at back of room, stands looking at the under part of the small corner table.)*

MRS. PETERS: She was piecing a quilt. *(She brings the large sewing basket and they look at the bright pieces.)*

MRS. HALE: It's a log cabin pattern. Pretty, isn't it? I wonder if she was goin' to quilt it or just knot it? *(Footsteps have been heard coming down the stairs. The Sheriff enters followed by Hale and the County Attorney.)*

SHERIFF: They wonder if she was going to quilt it or just knot it! *(The men laugh, the women look abashed.)*

COUNTY ATTORNEY *(rubbing his hands over the stove):* Frank's fire didn't do much up there, did it? Well, let's go out to the barn and get that cleared up. *(The men go outside.)*

MRS. HALE *(resentfully):* I don't know as there's anything so strange, our takin' up our time with little things while we're waiting for them to get the evidence. *(She sits down at the big table smoothing out a block with decision.)* I don't see as it's anything to laugh about.

MRS. PETERS *(apologetically):* Of course they've got awful important things on their minds. *(Pulls up a chair and joins Mrs. Hale at the table.)*

MRS. HALE *(examining another block):* Mrs. Peters, look at this one. Here, this is the one she was working on, and look at the sewing! All the rest of it has been so nice and even. And look at this! It's all over the place! Why, it looks as if she didn't know what she was about! *(After she has said this they look at each other, then start to glance back at the door. After an instant Mrs. Hale has pulled at a knot and ripped the sewing.)*

MRS. PETERS: Oh, what are you doing, Mrs. Hale?

MRS. HALE *(mildly):* Just pulling out a stitch or two that's not sewed very good. *(Threading a needle.)* Bad sewing always made me fidgety.

MRS. PETERS *(nervously):* I don't think we ought to touch things.

MRS. HALE: I'll just finish up this end. *(Suddenly stopping and leaning forward.)* Mrs. Peters?

MRS. PETERS: Yes, Mrs. Hale?

MRS. HALE: What do you suppose she was so nervous about?

MRS. PETERS: Oh—I don't know. I don't know as she was nervous. I sometimes sew awful queer when I'm just tired. *(Mrs. Hale starts to say something, looks at Mrs. Peters, then goes on sewing.)* Well, I must get these things wrapped up. They may be through sooner than we think. *(Putting apron and other things together.)* I wonder where I can find a piece of paper, and string. *(Rises.)*

MRS. HALE: In that cupboard, maybe.

MRS. PETERS *(looking in cupboard):* Why, here's a bird-cage. *(Holds it up.)* Did she have a bird, Mrs. Hale?

MRS. HALE: Why, I don't know whether she did or not—I've not been here for so long. There was a man around last year selling canaries cheap, but I don't know as she took one; maybe she did. She used to sing real pretty herself.

MRS. PETERS *(glancing around):* Seems funny to think of a bird here. But she must have had one, or why would she have a cage? I wonder what happened to it?

MRS. HALE: I s'pose maybe the cat got it.

MRS. PETERS: No, she didn't have a cat. She's got that feeling some people have about cats—being afraid of them. My cat got in her room and she was real upset and asked me to take it out.

MRS. HALE: My sister Bessie was like that. Queer, ain't it?

MRS. PETERS (*examining the cage*): Why, look at this door. It's broke. One hinge is pulled apart.

MRS. HALE (*looking too*): Looks as if someone must have been rough with it.

MRS. PETERS: Why, yes. (*She brings the cage forward and puts it on the table.*)

MRS. HALE: I wish if they're going to find any evidence they'd be about it. I don't like this place.

MRS. PETERS: But I'm awful glad you came with me, Mrs. Hale. It would be lonesome for me sitting here alone.

MRS. HALE: It would, wouldn't it? (*Dropping her sewing.*) But I tell you what I do wish, Mrs. Peters. I wish I had come over sometimes when *she* was here. I—(*looking around the room*)—wish I had.

MRS. PETERS: But of course you were awful busy, Mrs. Hale—your house and your children.

MRS. HALE: I could've come. I stayed away because it weren't cheerful—and that's why I ought to have come. I—I've never liked this place. Maybe because it's down in a hollow and you don't see the road. I dunno what it is, but it's a lonesome place and always was. I wish I had come over to see Minnie Foster sometimes. I can see now—(*Shakes her head.*)

MRS. PETERS: Well, you mustn't reproach yourself, Mrs. Hale. Somehow we just don't see how it is with other folks until—something turns up.

MRS. HALE: Not having children makes less work—but it makes a quiet house, and Wright out to work all day, and no company when he did come in. Did you know John Wright, Mrs. Peters?

MRS. PETERS: Not to know him; I've seen him in town. They say he was a good man.

MRS. HALE: Yes—good; he didn't drink, and kept his word as well as most, I guess, and paid his debts. But he was a hard man, Mrs. Peters. Just to pass the time of day with him—(*Shivers.*) Like a raw wind that gets to the bone. (*Pauses, her eye falling on the cage.*) I should think she would 'a' wanted a bird. But what do you suppose went with it?

MRS. PETERS: I don't know, unless it got sick and died. (*She reaches over and swings the broken door, swings it again, both women watch it.*)

MRS. HALE: You weren't raised round here, were you? (*Mrs. Peters shakes her head.*) You didn't know—her?

MRS. PETERS: Not till they brought her yesterday.

MRS. HALE: She—come to think of it, she was kind of like a bird her-self—real sweet and pretty, but kind of timid and—fluttery. How—

she—did—change. *(Silence: then as if struck by a happy thought and relieved to get back to everyday things.)* Tell you what, Mrs. Peters, why don't you take the quilt in with you? It might take up her mind.

MRS. PETERS: Why, I think that's a real nice idea, Mrs. Hale. There couldn't possibly be any objection to it could there? Now, just what would I take? I wonder if her patches are in here—and her things. *(They look in the sewing basket.)*

MRS. HALE: Here's some red. I expect this has got sewing things in it. *(Brings out a fancy box.)* What a pretty box. Looks like something somebody would give you. Maybe her scissors are in here. *(Opens box. Suddenly puts her hand to her nose.)* Why—*(Mrs. Peters bends nearer, then turns her face away.)* There's something wrapped up in this piece of silk.

MRS. PETERS: Why, this isn't her scissors.

MRS. HALE *(lifting the silk)*: Oh, Mrs. Peters—it's—*(Mrs. Peters bends closer.)*

MRS. PETERS: It's the bird.

MRS. HALE *(jumping up)*: But, Mrs. Peters—look at it! Its neck! Look at its neck! It's all—other side *to*.

MRS. PETERS: Somebody—wrung—its—neck. *(Their eyes meet. A look of growing comprehension, of horror. Steps are heard outside. Mrs. Hale slips box under quilt pieces, and sinks into her chair. Enter Sheriff and County Attorney. Mrs. Peters rises.)*

COUNTY ATTORNEY *(as one turning from serious things to little pleasantries)*: Well, ladies, have you decided whether she was going to quilt it or knot it?

MRS. PETERS: We think she was going to—knot it.

COUNTY ATTORNEY: Well, that's interesting, I'm sure. *(Seeing the bird-cage.)* Has the bird flown?

MRS. HALE *(putting more quilt pieces over the box)*: We think the—cat got it.

COUNTY ATTORNEY *(preoccupied)*: Is there a cat? *(Mrs. Hale glances in a quick covert way at Mrs. Peters.)*

MRS. PETERS: Well, not *now*. They're superstitious, you know. They leave.

COUNTY ATTORNEY *(to Sheriff Peters, continuing an interrupted conversation)*: No sign at all of anyone having come from the outside. Their own rope. Now let's go up again and go over it piece by piece. *(They start upstairs.)* It would have to have been someone who knew just the—*(Mrs. Peters sits down. The two women sit there not looking at one another, but as if peering into something and at the same time holding back. When they talk now it is in the manner of feeling their way over strange ground, as if afraid of what they are saying, but as if they cannot help saying it.)*

MRS. HALE: She liked the bird. She was going to bury it in that pretty box.

MRS. PETERS *(in a whisper)*: When I was a girl—my kitten—there was a boy took a hatchet, and before my eyes—and before I could get there—*(Covers her face an instant.)* If they hadn't held me back I would have—*(catches herself, looks upstairs where steps are heard, falters weakly)*—hurt him.

MRS. HALE *(with a slow look around her):* I wonder how it would seem never to have had any children around. *(Pause.)* No, Wright wouldn't like the bird—a thing that sang. She used to sing. He killed that, too.

MRS. PETERS *(moving uneasily):* We don't know who killed the bird.

MRS. HALE: I knew John Wright.

MRS. PETERS: It was an awful thing was done in this house that night, Mrs. Hale. Killing a man while he slept, slipping a rope around his neck that choked the life out of him.

MRS. HALE: His neck. Choked the life out of him. *(Her hand goes out and rests on the bird-cage.)*

MRS. PETERS *(with rising voice):* We don't know who killed him. We don't *know.*

MRS. HALE *(her own feeling not interrupted):* If there'd been years and years of nothing, then a bird to sing to you, it would be awful—still, after the bird was still.

MRS. PETERS *(something within her speaking):* I know what stillness is. When we homesteaded in Dakota, and my first baby died—after he was two years old, and me with no other then—

MRS. HALE *(moving):* How soon do you suppose they'll be through looking for the evidence?

MRS. PETERS: I know what stillness is. *(Pulling herself back.)* The law has got to punish crime, Mrs. Hale.

MRS. HALE *(not as if answering that):* I wish you'd seen Minnie Foster when she wore a white dress with blue ribbons and stood up there in the choir and sang. *(A look around the room.)* Oh, I *wish* I'd come over here once in a while! That was a crime! That was a crime! Who's going to punish that?

MRS. PETERS *(looking upstairs):* We mustn't—take on.

MRS. HALE: I might have known she needed help! I know how things can be—for women. I tell you, it's queer, Mrs. Peters. We live close together and we live far apart. We all go through the same things—it's all just a different kind of the same thing. *(Brushes her eyes, noticing the bottle of fruit, reaches out for it.)* If I was you I wouldn't tell her her fruit was gone. Tell her it *ain't.* Tell her it's all right. Take this in to prove it to her. She—she may never know whether it was broke or not.

MRS. PETERS *(takes the bottle, looks about for something to wrap it in; takes petticoat from the clothes brought from the other room, very nervously begins winding this around the bottle. In a false voice):* My, it's a good thing the men couldn't hear us. Wouldn't they just laugh! Getting all stirred up over a little thing like a—dead canary. As if that could have anything to do with—with—wouldn't they *laugh! (The men are heard coming down stairs.)*

MRS. HALE *(under her breath):* Maybe they would—maybe they wouldn't.

COUNTY ATTORNEY: No, Peters, it's all perfectly clear except a reason for doing it. But you know juries when it comes to women. If there was some definite thing. Something to show—something to make a story about—a thing that would connect up with this strange way of doing it—*(The women's eyes meet for an instant. Enter Hale from outer door.)*

HALE: Well, I've got the team around. Pretty cold out there.

COUNTY ATTORNEY: I'm going to stay here a while by myself. *(To the Sheriff.)* You can send Frank out for me, can't you? I want to go over everything. I'm not satisfied that we can't do better.

SHERIFF: Do you want to see what Mrs. Peters is going to take in? *(The Lawyer goes to the table, picks up the apron, laughs.)*

COUNTY ATTORNEY: Oh, I guess they're not very dangerous things the ladies have picked out. *(Moves a few things about, disturbing the quilt pieces which cover the box. Steps back.)* No, Mrs. Peters doesn't need supervising. For that matter a sheriff's wife is married to the law. Ever think of it that way, Mrs. Peters?

MRS. PETERS: Not—just that way.

SHERIFF *(chuckling):* Married to the law. *(Moves toward the other room.)* I just want you to come in here a minute, George. We ought to take a look at these windows.

COUNTY ATTORNEY *(scoffingly):* Oh, windows!

SHERIFF: We'll be right out, Mr. Hale. *(Hale goes outside. The Sheriff follows the County Attorney into the other room. Then Mrs. Hale rises, hands tight together, looking intensely at Mrs. Peters, whose eyes make a slow turn, finally meeting Mrs. Hale's. A moment Mrs. Hale holds her, then her own eyes point the way to where the box is concealed. Suddenly Mrs. Peters throws back quilt pieces and tries to put the box in the bag she is wearing. It is too big. She opens box, starts to take bird out, cannot touch it, goes to pieces, stands there helpless. Sound of a knob turning in the other room. Mrs. Hale snatches the box and puts it in the pocket of her big coat. Enter County Attorney and Sheriff.)*

COUNTY ATTORNEY *(facetiously):* Well, Henry, at least we found out that she was not going to quilt it. She was going to—what is it you call it, ladies?

MRS. HALE *(her hand against her pocket):* We call it—knot it, Mr. Henderson.

CURTAIN.

To His Coy Mistress

ANDREW MARVELL

Had we but world enough, and time,
This coyness, lady, were no crime.
We would sit down, and think which way
To walk, and pass our long love's day.
Thou by the Indian Ganges' side   5
Should'st rubies find; I by the tide
Of Humber[1] would complain. I would
Love you ten years before the Flood;
And you should, if you please, refuse
Till the conversion of the Jews.   10
My vegetable love should grow
Vaster than empires, and more slow.
An hundred years should go to praise
Thine eyes, and on thy forehead gaze;
Two hundred to adore each breast;   15
But thirty thousand to the rest:
An age at least to every part,
And the last age should show your heart.
For, lady, you deserve this state,
Nor would I love at lower rate.   20
    But at my back I always hear
Time's wingèd chariot hurrying near;
And yonder all before us lie
Deserts of vast eternity.
Thy beauty shall no more be found,   25
Nor in thy marble vault shall sound
My echoing song; then worms shall try
That long-preserved virginity;
And your quaint honor turn to dust,
And into ashes all my lust.   30

---

[1] An estuary in England. — All notes are the editors'.

Andrew Marvell (1621–1678) was a longtime member of the British Parliament and a writer of political satires. Today, however, he is remembered for two splendid poems, "The Garden" and the one that appears here. "To His Coy Mistress" is a noteworthy expression of an idea familiar in the love poems of many languages — *carpe diem*, Latin for "seize the day," the idea that life is fleeting and love and other pleasures should be enjoyed while the lovers are still young and beautiful.

The grave's a fine and private place,
But none, I think, do there embrace.
   Now, therefore, while thy youthful hue
Sits on thy skin like morning dew,
And while thy willing soul transpires   35
At every pore with instant fires,
Now let us sport us while we may;
And now, like amorous birds of prey,
Rather at once our time devour,
Than languish in his slow-chapped[2] power.   40
Let us roll all our strength and all
Our sweetness up into one ball;
And tear our pleasures with rough strife
Thorough[3] the iron gates of life.
Thus, though we cannot make our sun   45
Stand still, yet we will make him run.

[2]Slow-jawed.
[3]Through.

Acknowledgments (continued from page iv)

American Civil Liberties Union. "What Is the USA Patriot Act?" From the *ACLU Online* newsletter, www.aclu.org. Copyright © ACLU. Reprinted by permission of the American Civil Liberties Union.

Elizabeth Amon. "Name Withheld: Harsh Justice for a September 11 Detainee." Copyright © 2003 by *Harper's Magazine*. All rights reserved. Reproduced from the August issue by special permission.

"Back away. Slowly." By permission of Mike Luckovich and Creators Syndicate, Inc.

Avraham Balaban. "Remote Control." From *The New York Times*, March 22, 1999. Copyright © 1999 by The New York Times Company, Inc. Reprinted by permission.

Radley Balko. "Absolutely. Government Has No Business Interfering with What You Eat." Published in *Time* magazine, June 7, 2004. Copyright © 2004 by Radley Balko. Reprinted by permission of the author.

John Barry, Mark Hosenball, and Barry Dehghanpisheh. "Abu Ghraib and Beyond. A *Newsweek* Investigation" From *Newsweek*, May 17, 2004, p. 32. Copyright © 2004 Newsweek, Inc. Reprinted by permission. All rights reserved.

"Before we begin this family meeting." The New Yorker © The New Yorker Collection 2002 Matthew Diffee from cartoonbank .com. All Rights Reserved.

Jim Brown and Mike Haynes. "Should Players Be Eligible for the NFL Draft Right Out of High School?" by Jim Brown and Mike Haynes. Published in *The New York Times Upfront*, December 8, 2003. Copyright © 2003 by Scholastic Inc. Reprinted by permission.

Kelly Brownell and Marion Nestle. "Not If Blaming the Victim Is Just an Excuse to Let Industry Off the Hook." From *Time* magazine, June 7, 2004. Copyright © 2004 by Kelly Brownell and Marion Nestle. Reprinted by permission of the authors.

Warren Burger. "The Right to Bear Arms." Originally published in *Parade*, January 14, 1990. Copyright © 1990 Warren E. Burger. Reprinted with permission from *Parade* and the Estate of Warren Burger. All rights reserved.

"A Call for Unity: A Letter from Eight White Clergymen." Reprinted with permission.

Peggy Carlson. "Why We Don't Need Animal Experimentation." Reprinted with permission by the Physicians Committee for Responsible Medicine (PCRM), 5100 Wisconsin Ave., Suite 400, Washington, DC 20016; www.perm.org.

Carrie Chapman Catt. "The Crisis." From *Man Cannot Speak for Her*, Volume I: *A Critical Study of Early Feminist Rhetoric*, ed. by Karlyn Kohrs Campbell, Greenwood Press. Copyright © 1989 by Karlyn Kohrs Campbell. Reprinted with permission of Greenwood Publishing Group, Inc., Westport, CT.

"Chance of reading on vacation." Imodium ad. Reprinted with permission of McNeil Consumer & Specialty Pharmaceuticals Division of McNeil-PPC, Inc.

Mona Charen. "The Misleading Debate on Stem Cell Research." From *Townhall.com*, August 20, 2004. Copyright © 2004 by News America Syndicate. Reprinted by permission of Mona Charen and Creator's Syndicate, Inc.

Jo Ann Citron. "Will It Be Marriage or Civil Union?" Originally published in *The Gay & Lesbian Review Worldwide*, March/April 2004, v. 11, i2, p. 10(2). Copyright © 2004 The Gay & Lesbian Review Worldwide. Reprinted by permission of the author.

"Cool Gear." The Advertising Archives #30517377.

Stephanie Coontz. "Nostalgia as Ideology." Reprinted with permission from *The American Prospect*, Volume 13, Number 7: April 8, 2002. The American Prospect, 11 Beacon Street, Suite 1120, Boston, MA 02108. All rights reserved.

Lisa Takeuchi Cullen. "Not Too Rich or Too Thin." From *Time* magazine, July 12, 2004. Copyright © 2004 Time, Inc. Reprinted by permission of the publisher.

"Dad . . . is it the entertainment industry's fault that I'm exposed to this?" Cartoon. ROB ROGERS reprinted by permission of United Feature Syndicate, Inc.

Jaime Diaz. "Finding the Zone." Originally published in *Golfdigest.com*, July 2004. Copyright © 2004 by Jaime Diaz. Reprinted by permission.

Whitfield Diffie and Susan Landau. "Privacy: Protections and Threats." From *Privacy on the Line: The Politics of Wiretapping and Encryption* by Whitfield Diffie and Susan Landau. Copyright © 1998 by Whitfield Diffie and Susan Landau. Reprinted by permission of MIT Press.

John Patrick Diggins. "The Pursuit of Whining: Affirmative Action circa 1776." Originally published in *The New York Times*, September 25, 1995. Copyright © 1995 by The New York Times Company. Reprinted by permission.

Thomas Doherty. "Cultural Studies and 'Forensic Noir.'" Originally published in the *Chronicle of Higher Education*, October 24, 2003. Copyright © 2003 by Thomas Doherty. Reprinted with permission of the author.

02108. Reprinted with permission. All rights reserved.

Jennifer Grossman. "Food for Thought (and for Credit)." From *The New York Times*, September 2, 2003, p. 23, col. 1. Copyright © 2003 The New York Times Company. Reprinted with permission.

Elisha Dov Hack. "College Life vs. My Moral Code." Originally published in *The New York Times*, September 9, 1997. Copyright © 1997 by The New York Times Company. Reprinted by permission.

Jennifer Hahn and Wasim Salfiti. "The Patriot Act and You." From www.motherjones.com. Copyright © 2004 the Foundation for National Progress. Reprinted by permission.

Richard Hayes. "Supersize Your Child?" Originally titled "Selective Science." From *Tom Paine.com*. February 12, 2004. Copyright © 2004 Tompaine.com. Reprinted with permission of Institute for America's Future, Inc. www.tompaine.com.

Bob Herbert. "What Privacy Rights?" Originally published in *The New York Times*, September 27, 1998. Copyright © 1998 by The New York Times Company. Reprinted with permission.

Brian Hindo. "The NBA's Youth Squad." From *BusinessWeek Online*, June 24, 2003. www.businessweek.com. Copyright © 2004 The McGraw-Hill Companies, Inc. Reprinted with permission.

Michael Hirsh, John Barry, and Daniel Klaidman. "A Tortured Debate." From *Newsweek*, June 21, 2004. Copyright © 2004 Newsweek, Inc. Reprinted with permission. All rights reserved.

Adolf Hitler. "On Nation and Race." From *Mein Kampf* by Adolf Hitler, translated by Ralph Manheim. Copyright © 1943 and renewed 1971 by Houghton Mifflin Company. Reprinted by permission of Houghton Mifflin Company. All rights reserved. Canadian Rights: Used by permission of The Random House Group Ltd.

William S. Hubbartt. "Privacy Rights: The New Employee Relations Battlefield." Excerpt from *The New Battle Over Workplace Privacy* by William S. Hubbartt. Copyright © 1998. Reprinted by permission of American Management Association/AMACOM in the format Textbook via Copyright Clearance Center.

The Hunger Site home page. Used with permission of CharityUSA.com LLC, owner of The Hunger Site, The Breast Cancer Site, The Rainforest Site, and GreaterGood.com.

Evan Imber-Black. "Talk Show Telling versus Authentic Telling: The Effects of the Popular Media on Secrecy and Openness." From *The Secret Life of Families: Truth-Telling, Privacy, and Reconciliation in a Tell-All Society* by Evan Imber-Black. Copyright © 1998 by Bantam Books. Used by permission of Bantam Books, a division of Random House, Inc.

Jeff Jacoby. "A Desensitized Society Drenched in Sleaze." From *The Boston Globe*, June 8, 1995. Copyright © 1995 by Globe Newspaper Co. (MA) Reproduced with permission of Globe Newspaper Co. (MA) in the format Textbook via Copyright Clearance Center.

Holman W. Jenkins Jr. "Violence Never Solved Anything, but It's Entertaining." From *The Wall Street Journal*, Business World column, October 28, 1998. Copyright © 1998 by Dow Jones & Co., Inc. Reprinted with the permission of Dow Jones & Co., in the format Textbook via Copyright Clearance Center.

"Jihad News" by Gary Varvel cartoon used by permission of Gary Varvel and Creators Syndicate, Inc.

Steffen N. Johnson. "A Case the Scouts Had to Win." Originally published in *The New York Times*, June 30, 2000. Copyright © 2000 by The New York Times Company. Reprinted by permission of the New York Times Syndicate Inc.

Ron Kaufman. "Filling their Minds with Death: TV Violence and Children." From www.turnoffyourtv.com, 2004. Copyright © 2004 by Ron Kaufman. Reprinted with the permission of the author.

J. Andrew Kent. "Justice for Terrorists." Reprinted from *Commentary*, June 2004, by Permission of the author and publisher. All rights reserved.

Alana Keynes. "Student Sues District for Banning Anti-War T-Shirt." From *Education Daily*, April 4, 2003. Copyright © 2003 by LRP Publications. Reprinted by permission.

Kelly King. "The College Try: Some High School Athletes Are Hiring Professional Scouting Services to Help Them Land Scholarships." From *Sports Illustrated*, March 17, 2003, v. 98, i11, p. R10. Copyright © 2003 Time, Inc. Reprinted with permission.

Martin Luther King Jr. "Letter from Birmingham Jail" and "I Have a Dream." Copyright © 1963 by Martin Luther King Jr. Renewed 1991 by Coretta Scott King. Reprinted by arrangement with The Heirs to the Estate of Martin Luther King Jr., c/o Writer's House, Inc., as agent for the proprietor.

Joe Kita. "All to Be Tall." From *Men's Health*, January–February 2004. Copyright © 2004 Rodale Press, Inc. Reprinted with permission.

Alfie Kohn. "No-Win Situations." Reprinted from *Women's Sports and Fitness*, July/August 1990. Copyright © 1990. Reprinted with the author's permission. For more information, please see www.alfiekohn.org.

William Severini Kowinski. "Kids in the Mall: Growing Up Controlled." From *The Malling of America* by William Severini Kowinski (Morrow, 1985). Copyright © 1985 by William Severini Kowinski. Reprinted by permission of the author.

Peter D. Kramer. "Divorce and Our National Values." Originally published in *The New York Times*, August 29, 1997. Copyright © 1997 by The New York Times Company. Reprinted by permission.

Thomas Lee, M.D. "Too Much Privacy Is a Health Hazard." From *Newsweek*, August 16, 1999, pp. 70–71. © 1999 by Newsweek, Inc. All rights reserved. Reprinted by permission.

Michael Levin. "The Case for Torture." Originally published in *Newsweek*, June 7, 1982. Reprinted by permission of the author.

Abraham Lincoln. "The Gettysburg Address." Speech delivered at Gettysburg, Pennsylvania, November 19, 1963. Permission courtesy of the Abraham Lincoln Association.

Mark Maremont. "Can Anything Be Done to Protect Your Privacy in Cyberspace?" From *The Wall Street Journal*, January 1, 2000. © 2000 Dow Jones and Company, Inc. Reprinted by permission of Dow Jones & Company, in Textbook format via Copyright Clearance Center.

David Marshak. "No Child Left Behind: Test-Obsessed Education Won't Move Us Ahead." From *The Seattle Times*, February 8, 2004. Copyright © 2004 The Seattle Times Company. Reprinted by permission.

Sheryl McCarthy. "Show Biz Encourages Looser Teen Sex Habits." Published June 24, 2004. Copyright © 2004 by Newsday. Reprinted with permission of Tribune Media Services.

Roger D. McGrath. "A God-Given Natural Right Shall Not Be Infringed." From *Chronicles*, October 2003. Copyright © 2003. Reprinted by permission of the publisher.

Margaret Mead. "Warfare: An Invention — Not a Biological Necessity." From *Asia*, vol. 40, no. 8, August 1940, pp. 402–405. Copyright © 1940. Reprinted courtesy of The Institute for Intercultural Studies, Inc., New York.

"Metalmoto." Motorola ad. Used by permission.

Howard Moody. "Gay Marriage Shows Why We Need to Separate Church and State." From *The Nation*, July 5, 2004, v. 279, p. 28. Copyright © 2004 The Nation. Reprinted by permission.

Thomas Gale Moore. "Happiness Is a Warm Planet." From *The Wall Street Journal*, October 7, 1998. Reprinted by permission of the author.

Jacob Neusner. "The Speech the Graduates Didn't Hear." From *Brown University Daily Herald*, June 12, 1983. Copyright © 1983 by Jacob Neusner. Reprinted by permission of the author. All rights reserved.

"Newman's Own Grape Juice." The Advertising Archives #30540024.

Jay Nordlinger. "'Bang!': Guns, Rap and Silence." From *National Review*, April 16, 2001, pp. 37–38, 40. © 2001 by National Review, Inc., 215 Lexington Avenue, New York, NY 10016. Reprinted by permission.

"Now that we're old . . ." *Saturday Evening Post.* Cartoon by Earl Engleman.

Geoffrey Nunberg. "Don't Torture English to Soft-Pedal Abuse." From www.newsday.com. Copyright © 2004 by Newsday, Inc. Reprinted by permission of the author.

"One Reason." General Motors Corporation ad. General Motors Corporation.

Theodora Ooms. "Marriage-Plus." Annotated and excerpted from a special issue of *The American Prospect*, April 8, 2002, on "The Politics of the American Family." Copyright © 2002. Reprinted by permission of the American Prospect, 11 Beacon Street, Suite 1120, Boston, MA 02108, and by the Center for Law & Social Policy. All rights reserved.

Mike Oppenheim. "TV Isn't Violent *Enough.*" From *TV Guide*, February 11, 1984. Copyright © 1984 by Mike Oppenheim. Reprinted with permission.

George Orwell. "Politics and the English Language." From *Shooting an Elephant and Other Essays* by George Orwell. Copyright © 1946 by Sonia Brownell Orwell and renewed 1974 by Sonia Orwell. Reprinted by permission of Harcourt, Inc.

Rod Paige. "Yes, Testing Has Raised Students' Expectations, and Progress in Learning Is Evident Nationwide." From *Insight*, May 11–24, 2004. Copyright © 2004 Insight Online. Reprinted by permission of the publisher.

Rod Paige and Reg Weaver. "Are the Tests Required by No Child Left Behind Making Schools More Accountable?" From *Insight*, May 11, 2004. Copyright © 2004 by Insight Online. Reprinted by permission of the publisher.

"The Patriot Act and You." Mother Jones ©2004, Foundation for National Progress.

Orlando Patterson. "Race by the Numbers." Originally published in *The New York Times*, May 8, 2001. Copyright © 2001. Reprinted by permission of the author.

Marc Peyser. "Absolutely the Pitts: MTV's and Fox's Plastic-Surgery Shows Mess with Faces—and Heads." From *Newsweek*, April 12, 2004, p. 62. Copyright © 2004 Newsweek, Inc. Reprinted by permission. All rights reserved.

Hal R. Varian. "Economic Scene: Are Bigger Vehicles Safer? It Depends." From *The New York Times*, December 18, 2003. Copyright © 2003 by The New York Times Company. Reprinted with permission.

Marcia Vickers. "Why Can't We Let Boys Be Boys?" From *BusinessWeek*, May 26, 2003, I 3834, p. 84. Copyright © 2003 The McGraw-Hill Companies, Inc. Reprinted with permission of BusinessWeek.

Patricia Waldmeir. "Freedom of Speech and My Right to Silence at Bath Time." From *Financial Times*, November 10, 2003. Copyright © 2003. Reprinted with permission of the publisher.

Claudius E. Watts III. "Single Education Benefits Men Too." Originally published in *The Wall Street Journal*, May 3, 1995. Reprinted by permission of the author.

Reg Weaver. "No, NCLB's Excessive Reliance on Testing Is Unrealistic, Arbitrary, and Frequently Unfair." From *Insight*, May 11–24, 2004. Copyright © 2004. Reprinted with permission.

"We Can Not Tell A Lie." Encompass Insurance ad. Used by permission.

Michael M. Weinstein. "A Reassuring Scorecard for Affirmative Action." From *The New York Times*, October 17, 2000. Copyright © 2000 by The New York Times Company. Reprinted with permission.

"Who's been trawling through my personal information?" Slane cartoon. Slane, Cartoonists & Writers Syndicate.

William Carlos Williams. "The Use of Force." From *The Collected Stories of William Carlos Williams*. Copyright © 1938 by William Carlos Williams. Reprinted by permission of New Directions Publishing Corp.

"Will I look my age at my class reunion?" LVI ad. Used by permission.

"You have the right to remain silent." The New Yorker © The New Yorker Collection 1999 Arnie Levin from cartoonbank.com. All Rights Reserved.

Eric Zorn. "Family a Symbol of Love and Life, but Not Politics." From the *Chicago Tribune*, May 23, 2004. Copyright © 2004 Chicago Tribune Company. Used with Permission. All rights reserved.

GLOSSARY

Abstract language: language expressing a quality apart from a specific object or event; opposite of *concrete language*

Ad hominem: "against the man"; attacking the arguer rather than the *argument* or issue

Ad populum: "to the people"; playing on the prejudices of the *audience*

Anecdotal evidence: stories or examples used to illustrate a *claim* but that do not prove it with scientific certainty

Appeal to tradition: a proposal that something should continue because it has traditionally existed or been done that way

Argument: a process of reasoning and advancing proof about issues on which conflicting views may be held; also, a statement or statements providing *support* for a *claim*

Audience: those who will hear an *argument;* more generally, those to whom a communication is addressed

Authoritative warrant: a *warrant* based on the credibility or trustworthiness of the source

Backing: the assurances on which a *warrant* or assumption is based

Begging the question: making a statement that assumes that the issue being argued has already been decided

Claim: the conclusion of an argument; what the arguer is trying to prove

Claim of fact: a *claim* that asserts something exists, has existed, or will exist, based on data that the *audience* will accept as objectively verifiable

Claim of policy: a *claim* asserting that specific courses of action should be instituted as solutions to problems

Claim of value: a *claim* that asserts some things are more or less desirable than others

Cliché: a worn-out expression or idea, no longer capable of producing a visual image or provoking thought about a subject

Concrete language: language that describes specific, generally observable, persons, places, or things; in contrast to *abstract language*

Connotation: the overtones that adhere to a word through long usage

Credibility: the audience's belief in the arguer's trustworthiness; see also *ethos*

Data: facts or figures from which a conclusion may be inferred; see *evidence*

Deduction: reasoning by which we establish that a conclusion must be true because the statements on which it is based are true; see also *syllogism*

Definition: an explanation of the meaning of a term, concept, or experience; may be used for clarification, especially of a *claim,* or as a means of developing an *argument*

Definition by negation: defining a thing by saying what it is not

Empirical evidence: *support* verifiable by experience or experiment

Enthymeme: a *syllogism* in which one of the premises is implicit

Ethos: the qualities of character, intelligence, and goodwill in an arguer that contribute to an *audience's* acceptance of the *claim*

Euphemism: a pleasant or flattering expression used in place of one that is less agreeable but possibly more accurate

Evidence: *facts* or opinions that support an issue or *claim;* may consist of *statistics,* reports of personal experience, or views of experts

Extended definition: a *definition* that uses several different methods of development

Fact: something that is believed to have objective reality; a piece of information regarded as verifiable

Factual evidence: *support* consisting of *data* that are considered objectively verifiable by the audience

Fallacy: an error of reasoning based on faulty use of *evidence* or incorrect *inference*

False analogy: assuming without sufficient proof that if objects or processes are similar in some ways, then they are similar in other ways as well

False dilemma: simplifying a complex problem into an either/or dichotomy

Faulty emotional appeals: basing an argument on feelings, especially pity or fear—often to draw attention away from the real issues or conceal another purpose

Faulty use of authority: failing to acknowledge disagreement among experts or otherwise misrepresenting the trustworthiness of sources

Hasty generalization: drawing conclusions from insufficient evidence

Induction: reasoning by which a general statement is reached on the basis of particular examples

Inference: an interpretation of the *facts*

Major premise: see *syllogism*

Minor premise: see *syllogism*

MLA: the Modern Language Association, a professional organization for college teachers of English and foreign languages

Motivational appeal: an attempt to reach an *audience* by recognizing their *needs* and *values* and how these contribute to their decision making

Motivational warrant: a type of *warrant* based on the *needs* and *values* of an *audience*

Need: in the hierarchy of Abraham Maslow, whatever is required, whether psychological, or physiological, for the survival and welfare of a human being

Non sequitur: "it does not follow"; using irrelevant proof to buttress a *claim*

Paraphrase: to restate the content of an original source in your own words

Picturesque language: words that produce images in the minds of the *audience*

Plagiarism: the use of someone else's words or ideas without adequate acknowledgment

Policy: a course of action recommended or taken to solve a problem or guide decisions

Post hoc: mistakenly inferring that because one event follows another they have a causal relation; from *post hoc ergo propter hoc* ("after this, therefore because of this"); also called "doubtful cause"

Proposition: see *claim*

Qualifier: a restriction placed on the *claim* may not always be true as stated

Quote: to repeat exactly words from a printed, electronic, or spoken source

Refutation: an attack on an opposing view to weaken it, invalidate it, or make it less credible

Reservation: a restriction placed on the *warrant* to indicate that unless certain conditions are met, the warrant may not establish a connection between the *support* and the *claim*

Slanting: selecting *facts* or words with *connotations* that favor the arguer's bias and discredit alternatives

Slippery slope: predicting without justification that one step in a process will lead unavoidably to a second, generally undesirable step

Slogan: an attention-getting expression used largely in politics or advertising to promote support of a cause or product

Statistics: information expressed in numerical form

Stipulative definition: a *definition* that makes clear that it will explore a particular area of meaning of a term or issue

Straw man: disputing a view similar to, but not the same as, that of the arguer's opponent

Style: choices in words and sentence structure that make a writer's language distinctive

Substantive warrant: a *warrant* based on beliefs about the reliability of *factual evidence*

Support: any material that serves to prove an issue or *claim;* in addition to *evidence,* it includes appeals to the *needs* and *values* of the *audience*

Syllogism: a formula of deductive *argument* consisting of three propositions: a major premise, a minor premise, and a conclusion

Thesis: the main idea of an essay

Toulmin model: a conceptual system of argument devised by the philosopher Stephen Toulmin; the terms *claim, support, warrant, backing, qualifier,* and *reservation* are adapted from this system

Two wrongs make a right: diverting attention from the issue by introducing a new point, e.g., by responding to an accusation with a counteraccusation that makes no attempt to refute the first accusation

Values: conceptions or ideas that act as standards for judging what is right or wrong, worthwhile or worthless, beautiful or ugly, good or bad

Warrant: a general principle or assumption that establishes a connection between the *support* and the *claim*

INDEX OF SUBJECTS

INDEX OF AUTHORS AND TITLES

Need more help with writing and research?
Visit our Web sites.

We have a wide variety of Web sites designed to help students with their most common writing concerns. You'll find advice from experts, models you can rely on, and exercises that will tell you right away how you're doing. And it's all free and available any hour of the day.

Need help with grammar problems?
Exercise Central   (bedfordstmartins.com/exercisecentral)

Want to see what papers for your other courses look like?
Model Documents Gallery   (bedfordstmartins.com/modeldocs)

Stuck somewhere in the research process? (Maybe at the beginning?)
The Bedford Research Room   (bedfordstmartins.com/researchroom)

Wondering whether a Web site is good enough to use in your paper?
Tutorial for Evaluating Online Sources
(bedfordstmartins.com/onlinesourcetutorial)

Having trouble figuring out how to cite a source?
Research and Documentation Online   (bedfordstmartins.com/resdoc)

Confused about plagiarism?
The St. Martin's Tutorial on Avoiding Plagiarism
(bedfordstmartins.com/plagiarismtutorial)

Want to get more out of your word processor?
Using Your Word Processor   (bedfordstmartins.com/wordprocessor)

Trying to improve the look of your paper?
Using Your Word Processor to Design Documents
(bedfordstmartins.com/docdesigntutorial)

Need to create slides for a presentation?
Preparing Presentation Slides Tutorial
(bedfordstmartins.com/presentationslidetutorial)

Interested in creating a Web site?
Web Design Tutorial   (bedfordstmartins.com/webdesigntutorial)

Resources for Teaching

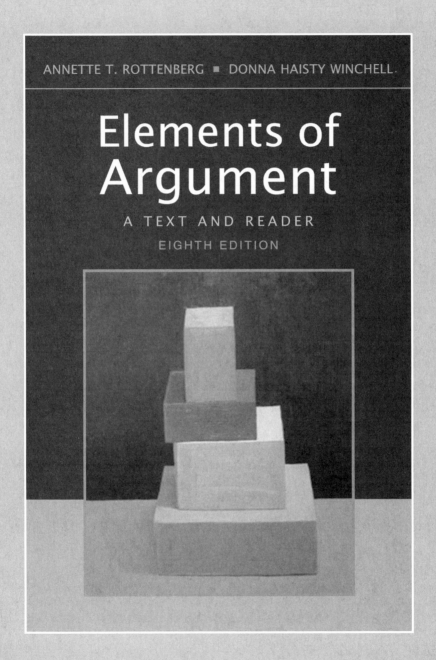

ANNETTE T. ROTTENBERG ■ DONNA HAISTY WINCHELL

Elements of Argument

A TEXT AND READER

EIGHTH EDITION

RESOURCES FOR TEACHING

ELEMENTS OF ARGUMENT

A Text and Reader

EIGHTH EDITION

PREPARED BY

Annette T. Rottenberg

Donna Haisty Winchell

Clemson University

With an essay by
Gail Stygall
University of Washington

BEDFORD/ST. MARTIN'S   BOSTON   ◆   NEW YORK

For information, write: Bedford/St. Martin's
75 Arlington Street, Boston, MA 02116

ISBN: 0–312–43129–5

EAN: 978–0–312–43129–7

Preface

In these notes we have assembled some of the assignments and classroom activities that have proved successful over the years in illuminating the elements of argument and eliciting thoughtful student response. Every teacher will have a collection of favorite devices, and we claim no superiority for ours. If some of the materials are not suitable, they may, however, suggest other kinds that are. Together with the writing suggestions in the text and the "Classic Arguments" they should provide an ample repertory of things to do for every day of the course. Clearly there will be more material than any single class can profitably use.

The text is flexible. Students usually need or want more practice in some areas than others. If the use of support, for example, is one element in which the majority of students are weak, you may want to spend more time on the material in Chapter 5 and omit an extended discussion of language and fallacies. The heart of the text is, of course, Chapters 3, 4, 5, and 6. Chapters 7 and 8 can be handled less intensively.

Part Two treats the writing process itself, analyzing its parts and providing guidelines for organizing, developing, and researching. Chapter 11 focuses on the presentation of oral argument, an increasingly important instrument for both laypeople and professionals. We hope to enable students to become not only more proficient public speakers but more knowledgeable members of an audience.

Part Three, "Multiple Viewpoints," lends itself to formal and informal classroom debate and longer papers that incorporate research. A short unit on debate is included in the *Resources for Teaching*. This chapter-by-chapter section can also be used throughout the course as a reference guide for papers that fulfill different kinds of writing assignments, especially those that call for in-depth analysis of opposing arguments. Part Four, "Classic Arguments," is another source of material for study and reference.

The most ambitious use of "Multiple Viewpoints" is as a source of information and opinion for the research paper. A section on research and use of the library and two documented research papers appear in Chapter 10. Suggestions for research paper subjects appear at the end of each section in "Multiple Viewpoints." For shorter papers students can limit their reading to material in the text. For longer papers they can look for additional material in the library or on the Internet. "Taking the Debate Online" provides students with Web links for the controversial topics in the book. We have included an appendix on Rogerian argument for instructors who would like to introduce the theories of Carl Rogers to their students.

The linear organization of the course should pose no problems. It is true that from the first assignment students will be writing arguments — before they have completed the study of the elements of argument. This practice, however, is the same as that of any other composition course where the process is one of deepening, widening, and enriching a first draft or a series of undeveloped generalizations. Many teachers of composition believe that students should begin to write whole essays from the beginning of the course. Attention to the components of argument follows when students attempt to make their essays stronger by concentrating on the particular areas that need development and revision.

Gail Stygall's essay at the beginning of this manual provides an overview of some of the special concerns and problems instructors should anticipate when teaching a course in argument, as well as practical general suggestions that might be useful in dealing with these concerns and problems.

Finally, teachers and students will find additional resources, including exercises, links, syllabi, assignment ideas, and online debates, at the book's Web site: <bedfordstmartins.com/rottenberg>.

Contents

PART FOUR
Classic Arguments   75

Strategies for
Teaching Argumentation:
An Overview

INTRODUCTION

One of the joys we experience in teaching argumentation is seeing our students take a step into the real world of rhetoric and argument. Instructors who have taught many semesters of introductory freshman composition without including argument notice an immediate difference in the papers they read and evaluate when they do opt for a semester of argumentation. After a semester in the argumentation classroom, students often find they now have a means for articulating the opinions, views, and knowledge that they feel belong in the public discussion. Moreover, the informal logic model, once understood, may be taken into other classrooms as a means for analyzing readings and writing. With the flexibility of *Elements of Argument* and with the dialogue of argument in the classroom, students have access to a practical, everyday logic, so often missing in public discussions of issues.

Although teaching argument is different from teaching the purely expository freshman writing course, it is, in many ways, easier for the instructor. Many freshman composition instructors have struggled to create a real purpose for students when the students have to produce brief explanatory or illustrative essays. Not yet knowledgeable enough to join the essayists who populate their readers, students may not see the point of practicing consistency within forms. Even in the studio classroom, with a peer audience available, students in the expository course may reason that writing is just another form of exercise, not something they might ever need to do in the real world. Argument, on the other hand, diminishes the instructor's struggle to create a real audience. Students may participate immediately, whether the forum is the classroom, campuswide issues, or national elections, and they can see that their writing can make a difference with a real audience.

If you are new to teaching written argumentation, this shift into active argument need not mean you have to reject what you already know. Many of us now teaching English were ourselves taught composition by the modes approach. The various ways in which we articulate arguments make use of those very same patternings — process, cause and effect, classification, comparison, definition. What changes is that we teach our students how to use those structures to serve as support for their arguments.

STUDENTS' EXPERIENCE WITH ARGUMENT

Students arriving in the freshman composition classroom that is focused on argument have rarely been asked to take a stand before in writing contexts. Although many aspects of a process writing curriculum have been developed in the elementary and secondary schools, we still may not take it for granted that our students have had prior practice in argument. A related problem is that students doubt that we really want their opinions; in high school, they probably experienced institutional constraints on their views. Even if they

1

offered their opinions, they may have had those opinions rejected and may now hesitate to trust us. Moreover, prior to college their basic belief systems have probably gone unchallenged. They may offer what appears to them to be the wisdom of a community, but they have not yet had to maintain that wisdom in the face of a decidedly different community, such as the college classroom.

SETTING THE TONE FOR THE CLASSROOM

Because students have often had so little practice in oral or written argument, we must try to maintain a classroom in which open discussion and debate are the standard procedure. Many instructors use intercollegiate debate as a model to set the necessary atmosphere. Instructors may tape sessions of *Washington Week, Meet the Press,* or *The McLaughlin Group* for classroom discussion. Other instructors arrange for their classes to hear a full intercollegiate debate.

Setting the tone, however, goes beyond having students observe impersonal or distanced third-person demonstrations of debate and argumentation. Students need to hear one another assert and defend arguments, and they must have the opportunity to respond to one another face to face. Scheduling discussion time is a useful strategy, following selected reading assignments. Students may be asked to come to class with brief responses to a particular essay, responses that include the students' own arguments about the topic at issue. Arranging for these reaction discussions places tolerance at a premium in the argumentative writing classroom, and the instructor often becomes the immediate arbiter of conflicting views and opinions. You should expect students to ask for your opinion on the various topics, as they invariably will, and prepare your own reactions and responses accordingly.

MAINTAINING THE FORUM: DEBATES ON PAPER

Many instructors continue the open forum by shifting their focus to actual writing assignments, arranging assignments so that one student is graded for responding directly to another student's paper. Argument becomes quite real when a student sees that his or her reasoning does not convince a classmate. Even a skilled writer learns from this assignment that a good argument acknowledges alternative views. Students who quote out of context, don't order their arguments well, or use logical fallacies without understanding what they represent often see during the refutation process what effect these practices have on the audience. Some instructors extend the dialogue even further by requiring a rebuttal paper in response to the refutation paper. For instructors who have been using a process approach to writing, this paper exchange is a means of helping students recognize the value of audience. In a direct exchange of papers, students cannot help being reminded of the dialogic nature of argumentation.

USING PEER RESPONSES

Process approaches can be further adapted for the argumentation classroom through the use of the audience questionnaire, as suggested in Chapter 1 of this manual. Instructors, instead of distributing generic peer-response forms, may ask students to evaluate one another's work in terms of the results of class opinions, requiring students to write briefly about which segments of the class a particular essay will convince, harden, or fail to move. These same peer responders can explore in writing why they think the paper will succeed or fail by pointing to specific parts of the argument and evaluating the strategies informing its delivery. Peer responders may also list and develop counterarguments and offer counterevidence, keeping the focus on the dialogue between writer and reader.

Peer-response exercises can also be used effectively with Part One of *Elements of Argument*. In conjunction with specific chapters, instructors can design peer-response forms for assigned student essays that direct the student responders to the important aspects of argument covered in those chapters. Instructors need to know that students who are inexperienced at focused response may need support in the form of a guided response sheet. Early in the semester, an instructor might ask both the student writer and the peer responder to answer the following questions about the student's essay:

What is the claim being made here? Write several sentences explaining your answer. You may want to quote from the text of the essay.

Is this an argument? Use evidence from Chapter 1 of your text to support your answer.

What type of claim is being made? Explain your answer based on what is said about claims in Chapter 4.

As writer, describe the purpose or the effect you believe your claim will have on the reader.

As reader, describe the actual effect of the claim. Do you agree? Did you agree before you started reading? Did your opinion change? Why, or why not?

Describe the representative person who you believe would be convinced by this essay. Include several characteristics such as age, sex, education, and family background.

Later in the semester, instructors can include further questions that ask students to evaluate the writer's use of definitions or to provide counterdefinitions in response to inadequately developed definitions. Chapter 5 on support and Chapter 6 on warrants also provide opportunities for students to integrate the material of the text with what they are attempting in their own writing.

PROVIDING BACKGROUND INFORMATION TO AID CRITICAL READING

Although peer-response exercises, discussion, and debate can promote critical reading, instructors should expect students to lack knowledge about the issues presented in the readings in the text. Instructors should anticipate that some or all of the students will know little about the issues involved. This cannot be attributed, in our view, to cultural "illiteracy," but rather to reasons of age or development. An issue may simply be one that we do not seek out until it affects us. That is not to say, however, that in an argumentation class we exempt our students from that issue because of their lack of experience. Instead, we simply need to be prepared to support their reading. For example, students may need contextual information to understand Wesley J. Smith's discussion of assisted suicide.

If you have chosen to make "Multiple Viewpoints" the core of your course, you may find it useful before you begin assigning the sections to survey your students on the knowledge they have about the particular issue. Often gaps in knowledge revealed by the survey can be filled with very little discussion. But without the knowledge necessary to evaluate fully the arguments in question, students can have more difficulty than is necessary in discerning even the structure or main points of the essays.

TEACHING WARRANTS AND ASSUMPTIONS

At least partly because our students have had so little practice in argument, they may have problems understanding what we mean by warrants and assumptions. Conflating the terms *warrant* and *assumption* for the purposes of an introductory class, you may want to illustrate the terms by beginning with the exercise "Who Should Survive?" in Chapter 6. A further step in that exercise would be to ask students to rank survivors in order of their correspondence with students' value systems. Invariably, students are unable to reach a consensus, revealing underlying assumptions that they hold about human behavior.

Instructors can also begin teaching warrants by asking students to complete statements beginning with the following leads: All lawyers . . . ; All English teachers . . . ; All students. . . . Such statements allow students to begin to see the kinds of assumptions they use implicitly every day. What they say in a discussion about what all lawyers do often reveals what they believe about the criminal justice system or about the civil recovery system. The beliefs about English teachers are interesting and sometimes disheartening. Students report that they speak more carefully in front of an off-duty English teacher, reveal less about whether they read "popular" fiction, think we value grammar above everything, or believe we are the classic ivory tower type of teacher. Inevitably, students begin to recognize warrants and assumptions. Students realize that they have operating warrants about English teachers; that English teachers are always and on every occasion English teachers; that English teachers read only canonical literature; that grammar is all that counts in an English class; and that English classes have little to do with real life.

These discussions, however time-consuming, are a necessary part of introducing warrants to students. While the terminology may be foreign to students, the process of using warrants is not, and with very little practice students can learn the appropriate questions to ask themselves as they try to discern warrants in their own work and the work of others.

Students can also practice adding a series of "because" clauses to the main points of their papers as a way of clarifying their assumptions. For example, a student writing a paper about how television viewing negatively affects children cited passivity, exposure to violence, and fear as her main points. When in an in-class exercise she was asked to identify her warrants with a "because" clause for each, she wrote, "because interaction, not passivity, is a better learning experience" in response to her first point and "because violence and fear are poor standards for society" to the second and third. Not only did the student gain valuable experience in identifying the warrants behind her claims, she also learned a powerful revision strategy. As her peers pointed out to her, she had grouped two of the points together, with the third being entirely separate. In revising her paper, she concentrated on the last two points, eliminated the first, and turned in a more coherent paper, which included a now-explicit discussion of her warrant.

DIFFERENT WORDINGS OF CLAIMS AND WARRANTS

Students will often propose several versions of claim and warrant for the same essay. Often one group of students will select as claim a very narrow assertion, while another group will select a generalization, perhaps an inference from the text. Likewise, students will show variation in their wording of warrants. As long as students do not go beyond what claims and warrants a particular author might make, some variation in wording not only is acceptable, but also is helpful to students working in an argumentative setting. They will learn that the rhetorical effect of different wording is intrinsic to assessing and addressing their audience.

TEACHING FALLACIES: THE EDITORIAL JOURNAL

Another tool for generating material for argument is the editorial journal. Instructors can require students to maintain a weekly folder containing several examples of what they think are successful and unsuccessful editorials and letters from local or campus newspapers and to record their responses to those editorials and letters in an editorial journal. Students assigned this exercise soon develop a standard against which they judge effective and ineffective arguments. It is then often useful to have students use their developing standard in combination with logical fallacies from Chapter 7. Students can submit for group discussion the most effective and least effective examples they've culled from editorial pages. Asking students to respond to the most troubling and fallacious letters and editorials often bridges the gap between classroom writing and the "real world" of discourse. Many students take the additional step of sending their responses to the local or campus newspaper and sometimes experience the delight of seeing their names in print in those pages.

A variation on this same exercise is an in-class letter-writing task in which students select the most troubling problem on campus and attempt to persuade the appropriate administrator to respond. The instructor may ask different groups to vary their approaches by assigning, for example, one group to argue a claim of fact, another a claim of value. Groups may assess the effectiveness of the arguments of other groups, with the entire class selecting the best letter for the particular audience.

DISTINGUISHING BETWEEN INDUCTION AND DEDUCTION: RESEARCH ASSIGNMENTS

One other aspect of teaching an informal logic model in the writing classroom bears discussion. Many traditional argumentative writing courses have assigned induction and deduction separately. In teaching with an informal Toulmin model, the differences between the traditional and informal approaches often become blurred. Students who have become adept in using the informal model complain vigorously that there is no such thing as a truly inductive paper. Arguing that the Toulmin model requires that warrants be acknowledged, whether the paper is inductive or deductive, students assert that the differences are minimal. For the standard student paper, in which a thesis appears early in the essay, students are indeed correct, and the distinction is difficult to make. A so-called inductive paper with a thesis indicates that the writer has already drawn a conclusion, thus making it less than purely inductive in nature.

If the course you are teaching requires separate inductive and deductive papers, consider making the distinction on the basis of the style of research supporting the paper. For example, assign one essay that focuses on an inductive style of research as a primary research project. These projects, chosen in collaborative groups, may include student-designed surveys of their classmates; observations of behavior on campus, in parking lots, and in shopping malls; and interviews. Essays can be developed from student observations of people's behavior while standing in line, from student interviews with hard-core video game players, and from student surveys addressing the necessity of improving the food available in campus vending machines. Because inferencing and the "inductive leap" are highlighted with this approach, students can more easily see the differences between induction and deduction. For a deductive paper, on the other hand, you can stress a secondary research approach, having students begin from basic assumptions about a subject and then examine a particular instance.

Many philosophers and historians of science have made the same point: that observations are always guided by a particular framework. The informal Toulmin model makes this point quite clear to students. What counts as a fact or as an observation is already warranted before the search for facts and observations begins.

We hope our suggestions will be useful for planning a forum on issues in your writing classroom. It is probable that many of your students will have only the composition classroom in which to engage in written debates on public policy issues. Becoming engaged in the consideration, analysis, and argument of various positions, students truly prepare to take their place in civic discussions. As instructors of written argument, we hold a unique position by virtue of our providing the forum in which this process takes place. Few students leave the argumentation classroom without having experienced a change of some kind, and few teachers can resist that kind of opportunity. By providing a model of analysis of argument useful both inside and outside the classroom and by providing the forum for an exchange of views, we can emphasize the uses of writing in unexpectedly productive ways.

MULTIMEDIA STRATEGIES: I•CLAIM VISUALIZING ARGUMENT CD-ROM

Why i•claim?

Mixed media and everyday arguments can be both more accessible and more challenging for students to examine. These arguments — commercials, comics, speeches, advertisements, and so on — are more recognizable for students, but students are not used to analyzing these types of texts. Nevertheless, a more contemporary, multimedia introduction to argumentation helps students think more critically about the world around them, and the arguments they encounter every day about what to think, what to do, and who to be.

There are also limitations inherent to any textbook's discussion of argument. Arguments use more than words, and exist beyond the printed page. In a book, students can't listen to a speech by Jesse Jackson, watch a presidential campaign commercial, change a greeting card's appeal, or drag and drop images to create their own personal ad. The i•claim CD-ROM offers a new way to visualize argument — because there are things you just can't do in a book.

The i•claim CD-ROM features six tutorials on fundamental qualities good arguments share. Arguments make *claims*. They come from a specific *context*. They are driven by clear *goals*. They need careful *support*. They consider multiple *viewpoints*. And they use *logic*. An illustrated glossary defines 50 key terms from argument theory and classical rhetoric, tying each abstract term to a contemporary visual example. Finally, the arguments section provides direct access to all of the multimedia arguments on the CD-ROM — over 70 in all. This flexible visual index allows you to browse the arguments in multiple ways: by genre and medium (posters, video clips, commercials), by type of appeal (ethos, pathos, logos), and by purpose (definition, evaluation, proposal).

How do I get i•claim?

The i•claim CD-ROM can be packaged for free with *Elements of Argument* and *The Structure of Argument*. To see a sample tutorial, visit <bedfordstmartins .com/iclaim>. For ordering information, contact your local sales representative or e-mail us at sales_support@bfwpub.com.

How does i•claim work?

Launching the i•claim CD-ROM:

Windows

1. Insert the CD-ROM into your CD-ROM drive.

2. Double-click on the "My Computer" icon on your desktop.

3. Double-click on the "i•claim" CD-ROM icon in the "My Computer" window. (For most computers, the CD-ROM drive is designated the "D" drive.)

Macintosh

1. Insert the CD-ROM into the CD-ROM drive.

2. Double-click on the "i•claim" CD-ROM icon that appears on your desktop.

Note: When you use i•claim, the CD-ROM must be in the CD-ROM drive.

Navigating through i•claim

From the main screen, you may start with any of the six tutorials (click on one of the colored circles in the center to select a tutorial), or you may go to the glossary or the arguments index by clicking on the appropriate title. Once you have entered a section of the CD-ROM, you can navigate to any other section by using the top menu bar. If you are within a tutorial, you can go to any other tutorial by clicking on the numbered circles.

Responding to the read and compose assignment questions in the i•claim tutorials:

1. Click on the notebook paper icon in the introductory text for the assignment section of the tutorial.

2. In the pop-up window that appears, click in the desired question's text box. Type in your answer.

3. When you are finished responding to the questions, click on either "Print" to print out your answers or "E-mail" to e-mail your answers. If you choose to e-mail your answers, you will need to fill out the "To" and "From" e-mail address forms.

Note: In order to e-mail your answers to the questions in the assignments, you must be online.

Who can I contact for technical assistance?

For technical support, please contact us at <http://bfwpub.com/techsupport>, tcchsupport@bfwpub.com, or 800-936-6899.

How do I incorporate i•claim into my course?

1. If you follow this book's structure in organizing your course, try directing your students to go through the first tutorial at home after you have introduced the chapter on claims. Similarly, you can assign them the fourth tutorial when you cover the chapter on support; the sixth tutorial when you cover the tutorial on induction, deduction, and logical fallacies; and the fifth tutorial when you cover Part Three on multiple viewpoints.

2. If you have access to a computer classroom, try using the arguments index to present to your students some multimedia examples of different types of arguments as you introduce them in class. Supplement your discussion of the logical fallacies with some of the examples on the CD-ROM, for instance.

3. If your students are having difficulty with the argument terminology you are introducing in class, they can use i•claim's glossary as a handy illustrated reference.

4. If you use the thematically organized chapters in the book, try pairing your discussion of these topics with topically relevant arguments on i•claim:

    How Far Will We Go to Change Our Body Image?

    Sims Online Video Game Trailer (tutorial 03, assignment)

    Details "Gay or L.A." feature (glossary, "definition")

    Cover of *The Low-Carb Baking and Dessert Cookbook* (glossary, "god (and devil) terms")

    How Has Terrorism Affected the American Idea of Justice?

    Gulf Wars Poster (tutorial 02, analysis)

    Kerry Windsurfing Campaign Commercial (tutorial 06, overview)

    Cover of *The Case for Democracy: The Power of Freedom to Overcome Tyranny and Terror* (glossary, "god (and devil) terms")

    Are Limits on Freedom of Speech Ever Justified?

    Adbusters Big Mac TV Spot (tutorial 02, assignment)

    Careless Talk WPA Poster (tutorial 06, overview)

    What Is the Role of Sex and Violence in Popular Culture?

    "Are You Popular" Coronet Instructional Film (tutorial 06, analysis)

    Sims Online Video Game Trailer (tutorial 03, assignment)

Bibliography on the Toulmin Model

Listed below are articles by teachers of composition, rhetoric, speech, and debate that explain and apply the Toulmin model for use in the classroom.

Brockriede, Wayne, and Douglas Ehninger. "Toulmin on Argument: An Interpretation and Application." *The Quarterly Journal of Speech* 46 (1960): 44–53. The authors interpret the Toulmin model as presented in Toulmin's *The Uses of Argument*. They clearly define each element of the model and explain its advantages over traditional systems of logic.

Christenson, Thomas, and Paul R. Nelson. "The Toulmin Model: Asset and Millstone." *Advanced Debate: Readings in Theory, Practice and Teaching.* Ed. David A. Thomas. Skokie, IL: National Textbook, 1975. 228–34. The authors provide a clear summary of Toulmin, distinguishing between the "basic" model — claim, data, and warrant — and the "expanded" model, which introduces the other elements of backing, reservation, and qualifier.

Kaufer, David S., and Christine M. Neuwirth. "Integrating Formal Logic and the New Rhetoric: A Four-Stage Heuristic." *College English* 45 (1983): 380–89. The authors argue that formal logic can be used to supplement insights from the new rhetoric (as put forth by Toulmin and others), believing that an argument should be tested for its deductive certainty as well as for the plausibility of its premises. They provide a four-stage model for teaching students how to integrate logical and probabilistic reasoning in arguments.

Kneupper, Charles W. "Teaching Argument: An Introduction to the Toulmin Model." *College Composition and Communication* 29 (1978): 237–41. Kneupper begins with an attack on the use of logic and fallacies as a means of teaching argumentative composition. He offers a brief summary of Toulmin's model as a superior method, then applies the model to the first paragraph of Thoreau's *Civil Disobedience*, diagramming the argument in simplified form. He emphasizes that for students "how they are arguing will be clearer," and they will be able to see relationships between parts of the argument.

Lunsford, Karen J. "Contextualizing Toulmin's Model in the Writing Classroom: A Case Study." *Written Communication* 19.1 (Jan. 2002): 109–75.

Stratman, James F. "Teaching Written Argument: The Significance of Toulmin's Layout for Sentence-Combining." *College English* 48 (1982): 718–33. The author believes that in using Toulmin's "layout" for argument in sentence-combining, students can learn new syntactic patterns. They can learn "skills appropriate to argument — estimating the relevance of acts, assessing validity, and planning refutations based on premises shared with an opponent." For example, one way of helping students to learn the function and importance of warrants is to have them adapt such warrants explicitly in a sentence-combining exercise. "Toulmin's layout can reveal how syntactic transformations strengthen or weaken the structure implicit in argumentative exercises by revealing changes in the underlying relations between 'claim' and 'evidence' that these transformations may entail." A complicated analysis but thought-provoking.

Trent, Jimmie D. "Toulmin's Model of an Argument: An Examination and Extension." *The Quarterly Journal of Speech* 54 (1968): 252–59. Trent views Toulmin's model as a supplement to syllogistic reasoning. He nevertheless argues that Toulmin presents arguments more clearly and accurately than the classical syllogism.

PART ONE

THE STRUCTURE OF ARGUMENT

CHAPTER 1
Understanding Argument
(text pages 3–24)

1. After discussion of the assignments at the end of the chapter, assign a brief search through newspapers and magazines (beginning perhaps with the school newspaper) for arguments about current affairs. Such a search enables students to arrive at several important conclusions.

   a. The most obvious one is that arguments of the kind they will be reading and writing in class are to be found everywhere and that they are the foundation of the democratic process. Students will also discover that a good deal of the factual reporting about political events is reporting of controversies or arguments.

   b. Without much familiarity with formal arguments, students may at first regard them all as vehicles of reasoned analysis. As they reflect on their examples, they will recognize that passion and ideology are formidable — sometimes the only — components of many arguments.

   c. Many, perhaps most, freshman students believe that hard-core problems in our society remain unsolved because at best we lack the will to solve them, or at worst evil people conspire to frustrate attempts at solution. One other explanation of our failures may not readily occur to them: lack of knowledge. We may ask: What kind of knowledge — that is, data and interpretation of data — do we need in order to solve apparently intractable problems of poverty, war, prejudice, crime, mental illness? When we introduce this question, we may find that some students think that these problems are new and peculiar to American society. Much of the information needed will turn out to be psychological, the kind most difficult to discover or verify. You can use this discussion to encourage a reflective caution when evaluating and advocating solutions.

   d. Not all arguments have two equally valid sides. Some have multiple sides. Others may be said to have only one morally acceptable side. Ask students to suggest subjects that exemplify these conclusions.

2. Students may be asked to keep informal journals that list controversial subjects appearing in newspapers and magazines, on TV and radio, on the campus and in town. For each subject they may set down some of the important facts, values, and general principles underlying the claims. The journal entries can then serve as a source of subjects for assignments or discussion in class and in conferences with the instructor. A worthwhile dividend of such journal keeping is an increase in the practice of reading

and listening, of becoming familiar with the sources and subjects of public controversies.

3.   We suggest leaving discussion and analysis of the three major elements of argument — claim, support, and warrant — to the subsequent chapters. At this point we would require only that students show understanding of the definitions.

4.   In speech classes students sometimes analyze their audience, i.e., their classmates, before making a proposal that might be unpopular. They distribute questionnaires that they themselves have constructed in an effort to discover the social and political preferences of their classmates. The results of the questionnaire help them to choose an argumentative strategy that will persuade this audience to look more favorably on the proposition being argued.

An application of this procedure for a writing class might work as follows: At the beginning of the semester, after having read about audience, a small group of students, perhaps four or five, makes up an informal questionnaire that is filled out by the members of the class. The results of the questionnaire are tabulated and distributed to the class. Later in the semester, for selected papers (for example, arguments of policy) the writers are encouraged to examine the results and add a note describing how and why they have adapted their arguments to the values of this particular audience.

CHAPTER 2
Responding to Argument
(text pages 25–61)

This chapter emphasizes that critical reading, listening, and looking are all essential to the mastery of the elements of argument. Most of us are familiar with the problems encountered by students in reading and responding to a difficult text. The problems are multiple: unfamiliarity with the subject, limited vocabulary, weak sense of metaphor, inability to recognize clues of organization and development. Many of these problems are clearly the result of too little practice — not enough careful attention to hard texts, not enough instruction in the mechanics of reading such material. It's also possible, as Sven Birkerts suggests in *The Gutenberg Elegies* (Faber and Faber, 1994), that reading is becoming more tedious as electronic communication effects a radical change in consciousness and literacy. But so far, there is no real substitute for reading in the print media. (Even Bill Gates and Nicholas Negroponte write books to tell us about computers.) Diagnosing the reading difficulties at the beginning of the course — through short quizzes and discussions — can tell us where to offer help.

If the amount of reading many of us do has declined, the amount of listening has greatly increased. But instruction in listening has not kept pace. Jay Heinrichs, author of "How Harvard Destroyed Rhetoric" (*Harvard Magazine,* July–August 1995) deplores the scarcity of serious academic interest in public speech. Rhetoric at Harvard was once, of course, the study of persuasive oratory. And rhetorical theory, whether or not we use the vocabulary of Aristotle or the Sophists, still animates any study of formal argument. Today the proliferation of "undisciplined argument" has convinced Heinrichs that the study of public speech should be restored. "Too few citizens," he says, "know how to listen critically."

RESPONDING AS A CRITICAL READER

1. Elsewhere in this manual we've suggested calling attention to the vocabulary of an assigned reading *before* students read it. Pointing out the clues that reveal the organization and development of a long, complex argument, again before students read the whole piece, can help them read it more effectively and with greater confidence. Most students find outlining tiresome and unenlightening, partly because they don't do it well, partly because many long articles defy conventional outlining. But early in the course, outlining one or two pieces on the board as students follow the text of an assigned essay can give a sense of what organization means and how it controls the development of the argument. Whether or not they outline their assignments, almost all students will find it useful to write a brief summary of an argument as a means of review.

2. The primary goals of critical reading, of course, are, first, understanding the argument and, then, determining how effectively the arguer supported his or her claim. But there are additional benefits to be derived from careful reading, benefits that can directly affect the student's writing. Critical reading, which often means over-reading, invites an appreciation of language. Winston Churchill spoke of the advantages of having been a relatively slow learner who had to repeat his lessons: "I got into my bones the essential structure of the ordinary British sentence — which is a noble thing."

   This is where annotation pays off for the prospective writer. Students who must respond physically as well as mentally, by writing in the margins, should become more careful readers — more sensitive to diction and to the rhythms of a variety of styles and modes of organization that can be adapted for their own papers.

RESPONDING AS A WRITER

1. If you have asked students to write marginal notes while doing a critical reading of a piece, you may want to ask them to go back to the same piece and annotate it from the perspective of a writer. (It may help if they do so in a different colored ink to see the difference.) This time they will be noticing the writer's techniques more than the ideas, although the two necessarily overlap.

2. It can also be useful to have students do two different types of summaries. You may even want to have them summarize the same essay, with the point of one summary being to summarize the main ideas and the purpose of the other being to summarize the tactics. One summary could start, for instance, "In 'No-Win Situations,' Alfie Kohn argues that just as competition can have destructive effects in the workplace, it can also be destructive when it controls our recreational activities." The other might begin, "In 'No-Win situations,' Alfie Kohn begins with an example of the well-known childhood game of musical chairs to point out the destructive effects of competition in recreational activities."

   Remind students that the summary is not yet the place to express an opinion.

RESPONDING AS A CRITICAL LISTENER

1. Many school libraries have collections of recorded speeches and debates. Tapes allow replay of portions for class analysis. Just as students gloss a written text, they can annotate an oral presentation, expressing approval or disapproval, asking questions when they hear a doubtful statement. The instructor can model critical listening by stopping the tape at relevant intervals and offering a running commentary. She explains the reasons for her judgments and encourages additional response from the class. Students can listen for examples of logical argument and persuasive language. They can also learn to recognize clichés, slogans, short cuts, and other departures from clear thinking. (See Chapter 8.) With relatively little practice, students can become adept at the art of listening.

2. Deborah Tannen, professor of linguistics at Georgetown University, has written several books that interpret the conversational styles of different cultures as well as of men and women, among them *You Just Don't Understand: Women and Men in Conversation* (Ballantine, 1991) and *The Argument Culture: Moving from Debate to Dialogue* (Random House, 1998). Tannen's discussions emphasize the failure to listen attentively and with a will to understand as a major impediment to fruitful communication.

3. Careful listening plays a significant role in jury trials and formal investigations. In some celebrated cases, jurors seemed to have listened selectively. Students may be surprised to learn that jurors are not permitted to take notes during a trial or to ask questions of witnesses. A lawyer who has proposed changes in the jury system says, "Jurors often ignore the instructions or misapply them." We can ask students to be alert to televised trials or congressional committee hearings as sources of exercises in careful listening. Courtrooms, as Toulmin observed, are model venues of argumentation.

4. In learning to listen with attention to the speech of others, students may also improve their ability to hear their own language in writing. Because many students are able to hear errors in grammar and usage that escape the eye, we often ask them to read their papers aloud before submitting them.

Bibliography

Atwan, Robert, Donald McQuade, and John W. Wright. *Edsels, Luckies, and Frigidaires*. New York: Delta, 1979.

"The Content of Television Talk Shows: Topics, Guests, and Interactions." Michigan State U study, 1995. Commissioned by the Henry J. Kaiser Family Foundation.

Corbett, Edward P. J., and Robert J. Connors. *Classical Rhetoric for the Modern Student*. 4th ed. New York: Oxford UP, 1971.

Kurtz, Howard. *Hot Air: All Talk All the Time. An Inside Look at the Performers and the Pundits*. New York: New York Times Book, 1996.

RESPONDING TO A VISUAL ARGUMENT

1. This section examines the visual arguments in commercial advertisements, cartoons, photojournalism, and Web sites. Students are often unaware of the messages that even the simplest landscape or interior is capable of delivering —claims of fact, value, and policy. The great Hungarian photographer André Kertesz, whose reception in New York was less than friendly,

was told, "Your pictures talk too much." And, in fact, his photographs of people reading (*On Reading*, Penguin, 1982) are exquisite examples of value claims.

2. The pictures on TV and in newspapers and magazines that document the damage wrought by terrorist attacks on September 11, 2001, are powerful arguments that seem to need no verbal text. Several publications, including *Newsweek: America Under Attack* (Extra Edition, 2000), *New York Times Magazine* 23 Sept. 2001, and *The Day That Changed America* (American Media, Inc.) offered searing photographs of destruction and suffering. See also "The Expression of Grief and the Power of Art," *New York Times* 13 Sept. 2001: F1, a collection of comments on the subject by art, movie, television, and theatre critics.

3. Students in the class who know something about photography can be asked to explain the way in which composition, color, and other attributes work to convey a point of view. Or a member of the school art department can be invited to speak on the subject of visual argumentation in ads and photojournalism.

4. Explaining the implicit argument in an ad that relies largely on visual imagery is an obvious subject for oral presentation in which visual aids can be used to good effect.

5. Some students may be interested in examining the implied claims in movie posters, such as those they see at the video store. Several critics have suggested interpretations that are not so obvious to the untrained eye. They are entertainingly summarized in *Civilization* Apr./May 1999: 35+.

6. Another accessible subject is fashion advertising, which has come under fire in recent years. Some of the most provocative ads, by Calvin Klein, are directed at young people of college age who will probably recognize the implied claims.

Bibliography

"Defining Moments: How Photography Changed Our World." *U.S. News & World Report* 9–16 July 2001.

RESPONDING ONLINE

Few instructional methods bring home to the student writer the nature of critical reading and revising better than online peer responding. But many teachers have become frustrated when they first attempt to use computer networks for peer responding, sometimes to the extent that they eventually reject online responding altogether, and this in spite of the many exciting successes reported by instructors who use networked computers in writing instruction.

1. The principal rule for instructors who wish to bring their students into the networked writing environment is not to expect too much too soon. Most groups of students respond amazingly well to the requirement to work on-line, but some resist, probably responding more to their own sense of inadequacy with computers than from any inherent antipathy toward technology.

As should happen any time people are introduced to a new environment, especially one as potentially intimidating as networked computers, the instructor should allow considerable time for the students to explore the terrain on their own. There are a number of ways of doing this; perhaps the most straightforward is to have students send each other brief online autobiographies and respond to them uncritically, or exchange online reactions to a local event or important happening.

The instructor should not feel that this acclimatizing is a poor use of time. Most writing done in the industrialized world is done on computers, and an increasing amount of that writing is being done over computer networks. The time may be approaching when "writing" will become synonymous with "writing online"; the writing instructor will more and more come to see the student's ease and dexterity with online writing to be as important as the student's ease and dexterity with language itself.

2. One of the well-documented benefits of online responding is that students write much more than they do in non-networked classrooms, but this benefit can also mean an intimidating increase in the presumed need to evaluate student writing. Instructors experienced in online peer work, however, have developed means by which students can be held accountable for their online assignments and yet the instructor can avoid being overwhelmed by a barrage of electronic text. Although methods vary, the instructor should pay attention to the way student e-mail accounts are assigned, the nature of the text editors the students will be using, the particular characteristics of how a local "mailer" manages e-mail traffic, and the way e-mail client software (such as Eudora or Pegasus) can direct, file, and collate student messages. All of these elements of the online peer environment contribute to managing student work in responsible ways.

3. Using computer networks for peer online responding to student drafts encourages students to develop greater critical reading and revising skills independently of the kind of continual teacher monitoring found in the traditional writing classroom. But occasions arise that require the specific guidance and intervention of the instructor. Generally, there are two kinds of these requirements for intervention: pedagogical and behavioral.

   a. The instructor intervenes pedagogically online when review of the students' drafting or online responding indicates a need for information or advice.

   b. The instructor intervenes for behavioral reasons when students take advantage of the freedoms of online writing to engage in disruptive or illegal behavior. Such behavior may include harassment of various kinds, provocative statements that extend beyond the boundaries of academic discourse, or illegal use of electronic resources. Occasionally (but very rarely) students will engage in "flame wars," or heated verbal exchanges serving no academic purpose.

   In these cases, the instructor sends mail to one or more parties emphasizing that online communication within the classroom context must remain within the terms of the class's policies and that otherwise sanctions may be imposed.

DOCUMENTING YOUR SOURCES

Ideally, students leave high school well versed in documentation skills. The fact that they often do not is no indictment of their high school teachers but more likely an indication that students have not practiced these skills enough — to the point, that is, that they come readily to mind when the students need to incorporate into their writing paragraphed, summarized, or quoted material from sources. It is a good idea to ask your students from the first assignments they do to provide parenthetical citations for any such material. That way, they can move from using as sources one or two works from *Elements of Argument* to using a range of varied outside sources for their independent research papers. In this edition we have provided more guidance to help them do so.

Remind students that source documentation is more than a matter of punctuation and page numbers. It is an important means of establishing the authority of their sources. If they cannot find any identifying information on a source's author, they may want to rethink the value of that source. In our computerized age, it is easy to do a quick search for background information on authors. Finding little or no information on an author may bring into question that person's authority. Information that establishes the author as an expert on the subject under discussion can add strength to the student's argument beyond the words being paraphrased, summarized, or quoted.

CHAPTER 3
Definition
(text pages 62–103)

1. You might want to begin this unit by dividing the class into four or five groups and assigning to each group the definition of a common object — book, bed, chair, cup, shoe. The definitions that emerge from the group are then compared to those in the dictionary. (The definitions by students are often remarkably close.)

    After this exercise, ask students to describe the process of definition they have just engaged in. As the discussion proceeds, students discover, first of all, that in matters of definition we know more than we can tell. (See Michael Polanyi's fascinating examination of this in *The Tacit Dimension,* Routledge & K. Paul, 1967.) Apart from this philosophical dilemma, the attempt to define these familiar objects gives practice in distinguishing the properties that separate similar objects or objects belonging to the same genres. Equally important, students must think of examples if they are to make useful distinctions — between a shoe and a boot, between a chair and a stool, between a book and a magazine. The same necessity to resort to examples will become even clearer when they define abstract terms.

2. You may assign a single vague or ambiguous term, on which there is sure to be disagreement, for an extended discussion by each member of the class: success; the good life; normal sexuality; maturity; heroism; necessities, comforts, and luxuries.

    Some or all of the completed papers may be duplicated and distributed to the whole class. Through a discussion or written assignment the class may examine the criteria governing the different definitions. Can we reach a consensus? Why, or why not? What are the implications of success or failure in reaching consensus about these particular terms?

3. Students can also tackle the definitions of words that have acquired several, sometimes contradictory, meanings. *Example: discrimination.* For most

students, this word carries a negative connotation. You might also offer the following example:

> A young woman who knows nothing about the mechanics of a car finds herself stranded in a parking lot because the engine of her car will not start. Passing near her are two people — a young man and a young woman. The car owner ignores the young woman and turns to the young man, asking him if he can identify and perhaps solve the problem of the stalled car.

Does this action represent *discrimination* in the negative sense? Students must explain their answers in such a way as to make clear how they define the term.

They might also be directed to examine the use of the word in aesthetic criticism. Why has the word taken on negative connotations in other areas of discourse?

4. Students can find examples of implicit definitions even in their popular songs. *Example:* Pink Floyd in "The Wall": "We don't need no education. We don't need no thought control. . . . Teachers, leave us kids alone." How is education defined in this song?

    Stereotype has suffered the same fate as *discrimination.* We've discussed with students a different perception of a word almost always treated nowadays as a reflection of prejudice. From *The Biosexual Factor* by Richard Hagen:

    > Stereotypes are the stuff of prediction. Used correctly, they can save us a great deal of grief. If ignored, they may exact a price. The teenage girl who hitchhikes alone because she doesn't accept stereotypic warnings about male sexual behavior is likely to learn a lot about stereotypes.

5. In recent years the definition of *disability* has received critical attention from the medical and legal professions. The American Psychiatric Association lists more than three hundred illnesses, among them "road rage" and "jury duty disorder." (Week In Review, *New York Times* 28 Sept. 1997.) Students can look up rulings on the Americans with Disabilities Act in *Facts on File* for June 27, 1998. More recent cases include the rights of near-sighted pilots and tournament golfers who cannot walk, among others. See "What Is Golf? What Is a Disability?" *New York Times* 3 June 2001: Wk. 18.

Bibliography

Rosenbaum, Ron. "Degrees of Evil." *The Atlantic Monthly* Feb. 2001: 63–68. "Some thoughts on Hitler, bin Laden, and the hierarchy of wickedness."

DEBATE: IS THE DEFINITION OF MARRIAGE CHANGING?

1. A good starting point for the discussion of the essays by Moody and Citron is to review with students the doctrine of separation of church and state as established in the First Amendment to the Constitution: "Congress shall make no law respecting an establishment of religion, or prohibiting the exercise thereof. . . ." Understanding Moody's argument depends on understanding why he sees the issue of same-sex marriage as a constitutional issue. You might want to give students the assignment of finding

for themselves in the Constitution the wording about separation of church and state (and perhaps the assignment of knowing where to find a copy of the Constitution), since many students draw on this historical document without knowing what it really says (as they do with the proposed Equal Rights Amendment).

2. The topic of same-sex marriage was a logical choice for this chapter because of the heated discussion of the definition of marriage that has arisen with the move to allow same-sex marriage in some states. Citron's essay introduces the possibility that using a term other than *marriage* for a same-sex union might be in the best interests of those who champion gay rights. You might ask your students to consider before they read the two essays how they define *marriage* and on what basis. Who has the right to define the term? Should every state have the right to define the term? What complications are created if the definition varies from state to state?

3. This pair of essays also provides an opportunity to consider the assumptions on which the two authors base their arguments. (If you want to delay that discussion until after studying warrants in more detail in Chapter 6, you can return to these essays later for more practice in identifying warrants.)

Bibliography

Bork, Robert H. "The Necessary Amendment." *First Things: A Monthly Journal of Religion and Public Life* Aug.–Sept. 2004: 17–21.

DeMarco, Donald. "The Abolition of Marriage." *Catholic Insight* Oct. 2004: 24–25.

Detweiler, George. "How to Protect Marriage." *New American* 20.16 (2004): 28–31.

Hope, Melanie. "To Have and to Hold." *Essence* Aug. 2004: 34.

Hudson, Mike. "Marriage Gets Real: Newly Married Same-Sex Couples in Massachusetts Are Fitting In — As Long As They Stay Local and Don't Ask the Feds for Recognition." *Advocate* 12 Oct. 2004: 33–34.

Mohr, Richard D. "Equal Dignity under the Law." *Gay and Lesbian Review Worldwide* Sept.–Oct. 2004: 30–35.

CHAPTER 4
Claims
(text pages 104–56)

CLAIMS OF FACT

1. Students have little difficulty understanding claims of fact. But before giving an assignment, you may want to offer a dozen or more examples of such claims to make clear what kinds of arguments they produce. These are in addition to examples in the book.

2. If students have already elected a major or are about to do so, they can find subjects in their areas of specialization. At this point library research need not be emphasized. Students are often able to find sufficient factual data in their memories or their notes. (Wherever possible, they should, of

course, give credit to their sources, even to a lecturer in an academic course.)

The reports they may be asked to make on the job are often claims of fact, in which they will have to provide proof that a condition exists or that something has been found to be true as a result of research. The claims, or thesis statements of their essays, correspond to the conclusions of their reports, which, like the claims, may appear first. *Example* (in an article about food colorants): "The development of organic chemistry produced a series of compounds that are well suited to coloring food. Today most of the food colorants are chemicals produced by synthesis from simple basic materials." (*A Progress Report,* Massachusetts Agricultural Station, July–Aug. 1974.)

Such straightforward factual reports are not likely to be models of creativity, but they emphasize other important qualities of good writing: adequate support, a direct, unadorned style, and clear transitions between ideas. They offer practice in the kind of clear exposition that all writers are well advised to master before they go further.

3. More challenging are factual claims that are clearly controversial. Some will require only reflection on personal observation as support; others will need objective data. *Examples:* "The students on this campus are increasingly conservative." "Teaching writing on the word processor will not produce better writers." "Children are now judged to be reliable witnesses in child-abuse cases." "Attractive people are regarded by others as more intelligent and sensitive than unattractive people."

Encourage students to stick to the facts and avoid direct expression of value judgments (although, of course, these may be implicit).

4. Another source of assignments may be the materials in Part One's short debates and Part Three's "Multiple Viewpoints." Ask students to choose one of the subjects and, after reading all or most of the selections, derive a limited factual claim. *Example:* "Animal experimentation has provided enormous medical benefits for human beings."

The supporting materials will not be original. This assignment tests the writer's ability to extract relevant data in support of a thesis, express the facts in his or her own language, and organize them logically.

5. In this edition we continue to include advertisements that represent all the elements of argument. In our culture ads are the most prominent examples of abbreviated arguments that often conceal as much as they reveal, and students enjoy uncovering the missing elements. One caution: Although students may have studied ads in high school and can analyze them with some sophistication, they are disposed to treat all advertisement as untruthful. Ads that conceal or distort are usually the most interesting to examine, but try to get students to make careful distinctions between the ads that support their claims, or seem to, and those that don't.

6. Inevitably, controversial claims will move student writers to ascribe causes.

A number of tragic school shootings occurred in 1998 and 1999, both in the United States — Arkansas, Kentucky, Colorado — and abroad, in Scotland and Canada. They occasioned an outpouring of analyses, impassioned attempts to discover the *causes* of such aberrant behavior in children.

Students probably have discussed these events in their high school classes. They have also expressed their opinions about the causes to newspaper and television viewers. The social and psychological conditions that may have contributed to these tragedies are subjects for written assignments. So are suggested solutions as claims of policy.

7. Students must be cautioned to avoid assuming that explanations imply justification. For example, according to psychology professor Erwin Staub, the atrocities that occurred in Kosovo province can be explained: "[E]ven violent leaders often express and even share needs of their people. The needs of the Serbs for a feeling of security and for identity as a people are intense." But, he goes on to say, although these needs help to explain Serb behavior, "they cannot justify it."[1]

8. Affirmative action no longer commands urgent public attention, but the problems it attempts to remedy are still alive. In September 2001 a federal appeals court in Atlanta ruled that an affirmative action policy at the University of Georgia was unconstitutional because "diversity," the intended purpose of the policy, "could not be confined to race." "A white applicant," said the court, "may make a greater contribution than a non-white applicant." Language, in fact, occupies an important place in the debate. Not only *diversity* but other terms such as *racial preferences*, *racially-sensitive policies*, *affirmative access*, and *quotas* are part of the debate vocabulary. Ask students if all these terms refer to the same practices.

Bibliography

Bok, Derek, and William G. Bowen. *The Shape of the River: Long-Term Consequences of Considering Race in College and University Admissions.* Princeton, NJ: Princeton UP, 1998. Evidence that affirmative action has contributed to an emergent middle class.

Chavez, Linda. "Colleges and Quotas." *Wall Street Journal* 22 Feb. 2001: 19. "A new study finds evidence that American universities are guilty of pervasive racial discrimination."

Traub, James. "The Class of Prop. 209." *New York Times Magazine* 2 May 1999: 44+. "In the wake of affirmative action, campuses in California are managing to maintain diversity without racial set-asides. This will satisfy neither liberals nor conservatives, but it's looking a lot like the future."

Classic Arguments

The selections in Part Four, "Classic Arguments," provide more examples of the elements of argument. For comments on the use of these essays, please see the discussions under "Classic Arguments" in these notes.

CLAIMS OF VALUE

1. As they begin to write, students will discover that the line between claims of fact and claims of value is often blurred, but in real-life arguments outside the classroom, these distinctions are not crucial. We make them in the classroom largely because they allow us to examine the elements more

---

[1]*The Campus Chronicle* [University of Massachusetts, Amherst] 23 Apr. 1999: 1.

closely. Before beginning to write a claim of value, students should consult the "Writer's Guide: Defending a Claim of Value," which summarizes the process.

2. Claims of value are more demanding than claims of fact. Facts remain important, but now students must express an attitude toward them. Despite the fact that values are a part of almost every argument — even in claims of fact they may be implicit in the choices of subjects and data — students are sometimes unclear about how to uncover and express them. These approaches may be helpful:

   a. *Ask personal questions.* What do you want out of life? Do you dislike anything about yourself? Do you have religious beliefs? If so, how do they influence your behavior? What are the good things about your family? What are the most valuable things you own? What kind of country do you want the United States to be? And so on. (Of course, for purposes of the exercise the answers need not be true, and it should be clear to students that they are under no obligation to bare their souls. On the other hand, most students, like the rest of us, enjoy talking about themselves.)

   The answers that emerge can be written on the board, listed as positive and negative values. You will probably have to change the language, finding more precise terms than the ones that the students offer. This exercise defines values and value systems in a readily understandable way. Values as a form of support will be discussed more fully in Chapter 5, but this discussion should assist students to find the values that can be defended in their value claims.

   b. *Analyze one or two essays in the text to discover the values of the author.* Look at "From *Crito*," in which Socrates argues against his right to avoid punishment. What character traits does Socrates reveal about himself, both explicitly and implicitly? What traits in the citizen does Socrates admire? What traits does he condemn? How would you define his value system?

   Students can be asked to answer such questions in short, in-class assignments — fifteen minutes — for which they must produce a well-organized paragraph: clear topic sentence and sufficient supporting material. Because they stress economy and directness, such assignments are useful for teaching some elements of style.

3. As with claims of fact, students can draw on campus experience for subjects that lend themselves to class discussion, outlining, and reinforcing the ways in which claims of value differ from claims of fact. *Examples:* "Student evaluations of teachers are worthless." "Funds for Gay Awareness Week are unjustified."

4. In this unit, too, you might want to point out that claims of value are often required on the job in the form of personnel reports or reports that evaluate marketing strategies and campaigns. If students are interested, topics for such papers can be obtained from books on technical writing or from the business departments of the school.

5. A ready-to-use anthology of material for claims of value appears in a special supplement of the *Wall Street Journal* 5 Mar. 1998, called "Divining the American Character." It includes more than a dozen articles on how "the bedrock morals co-exist uneasily with a desire 'to live and let live.'" Needless to say, several of the articles deal with then-President Clinton and public approval/disapproval of his public and private performance.

CLAIMS OF POLICY

1. Since claims of policy assert that something should or should not be done, they presuppose the existence of a problem needing solution. Both facts and values are indispensable to defense of a policy claim, because in many arguments students will first have to establish that a problem exists, then underscore how the desired values will be served by adoption of the proposed solution.

2. As an introduction to this unit, short problems, either real or hypothetical, can test the ability of students to find solutions — that is, to defend claims of policy. The facts are clearly laid out in the summary of the problem. In order to justify the solution, students will need to expose the values that underlie their claims. *Example of a real problem:*

The Plagiarism Problem

John Jones, a senior at U____ M____, was enrolled in a second-semester writing course, *Writing about Film.* A few weeks before the end of the semester he suffered a crisis in his love life. The woman who had been his inseparable companion suddenly informed him that she was no longer interested in continuing their friendship. John lost control of himself for a few weeks; he stayed in his room brooding, drank heavily every night, and stopped going to classes. Three days before the end of the semester, he found out that in order to pass the film course and then to graduate, he had to fulfill a final assignment — attend a film and write a review of it. Frantic, John went to the library, copied out a review of a film by a professional critic, and submitted it to the instructor. The instructor recognized the plagiarism and failed John for the course. The failure meant that John could not graduate despite the fact that he had a job waiting for him in Seattle. He argued with the instructor to no avail. The instructor said that he had made it very clear from the beginning of the semester that any plagiarism would result in a failure for the course. John appealed to the provost, who had the authority to grant a Pass for the course.

Question: Should the provost rule that John need not do anything more to fulfill the writing course and allow him to graduate?

3. We have called attention to this problem in the text, but perhaps it bears repeating. In defending claims of policy, students must guard against offering solutions for enormous problems that have defied solution for decades or even centuries. Their ambitions may be laudable, but nevertheless they should be urged to confine themselves to solutions that can be defended in 750 words.

4. "Multiple Viewpoints" is a collection of problems in search of solutions. Assign readings in any of the subjects and ask students to propose solutions based on their evaluations of the arguments.

   In defending their claims of policy students should try to use the pattern of organization we call *defending the stock issues* — need, plan, and advantage (see Chapter 9, "Writing an Argumentative Paper"). This pattern permits them to be exhaustive without becoming confused by a multitude of details and a variety of possible approaches.

5. Policy claims are, of course, inherent in any business or professional activity. Ask students who have job experience to write out short summaries of specific problems they remember having encountered on the job, either

their own or someone else's. The problems should be substantive, and the facts should be clearly stated. Then ask other students to suggest solutions. Students may also ask for examples of problems from the business departments of the school.

These short writing exercises emphasize clarity, accuracy, and a sensitivity to the audience — the employer, supervisor, or other employees — who will act on the decision.

If the solutions differ, students may discuss the differences and try to uncover the reasons for them. Do the differences derive from lack of sufficient data or from conflicting values? Can the differences be reconciled?

6. Since the imprisonment of Dr. Jack Kevorkian, "the suicide doctor," the press has paid little attention to cases of euthanasia, although it is widely acknowledged that physicians and family members continue to practice "mercy killings." The Netherlands has long tolerated euthanasia, but not many people are aware that only in 2001 did the practice become legal. The legalization aroused intense condemnation in other countries but especially in Germany. Students working toward an evaluation of euthanasia should inform themselves about its use by the Nazis, who put to death about 100,000 "men, women, and children who were physically and mentally handicapped. The aim was to improve what they called the Aryan race by eradicating those who doctors decided had congenital defects." ("Horror Expressed in Germany over Dutch Euthanasia," *New York Times* 11 Apr. 2001: A15.)

   Students may also be interested to know that under Dutch law, when their children reach the ages of sixteen and seventeen, "parents must be informed but no longer have the right to decide." Do students think that doctors and others should be able to assist teenagers to commit suicide? If not, why not? If yes, under what circumstances?

7. Should mentally unstable people be allowed to own guns? A state appeals court in Alaska has ruled that a mentally ill man — who claims that he has a computer chip in his head — need not surrender his gun. "Gun owners argue that state laws safeguard this Second Amendment right."

8. The bibliography on gun-control policy is very large. One item of interest:

   Sullum, Jacob. "Weapon Assault." *Reason* July 1994.

Bibliography

Humphry, Derek. *Let Me Die before I Wake*. Eugene, OR: Hemlock Soc., 1991.

McHugh, Paul R. "Dying Made Easy." *Commentary* Feb. 1999: 13–17.

Miniter, Richard. "The Dutch Way of Death." *Wall Street Journal* 25 Apr. 2001: A20.

DEBATE: WHO IS RESPONSIBLE FOR THE COLLEGE COST CRISIS?

1. College cost is a topic in which all students have some vested interest, depending on factors such as their personal finances and the state in which they attend college. A number of states recently have made drastic cuts in funding for higher education. Others have restructured their

financing of higher education around lottery or scholarship systems. You may want to start this unit by having your students brainstorm, before reading these two essays, on factors affecting the cost of college education. Some questions that they might write about or discuss are these: To what extent was college cost a major factor in your decisions whether to attend college and where to attend? Did you benefit from a statewide lottery or scholarship system, and if so, to what extent did that affect your college choice?

Another question that you might ask students before they read the essays is one that Fish says he asks parents: What percentage of college costs do you think is covered by the tuition that students pay? Students often overestimate the portion of those costs that their tuition provides.

2. Another approach to this pair of essays is to ask students to read and respond to only those sentences in the essay by Boehner and McKeon that are in boldface. Then, after reading both essays, they can return to their responses to the boldfaced sentences to see if they have changed their minds.

3. Ask students to consider the word *crisis*. Do they believe that our nation's colleges are in a state of financial crisis? Does the evidence that Boehner and McKeon provide justify the use of such an emotionally charged word?

Bibliography

Clark, Kim. "Decision Time." *U.S. News & World Report* 19 Apr. 2004: 53.

Finn, Charles E., Jr. "Why Must College Be So Costly?" *Commentary* Apr. 2004: 77.

Lehrer, Eli. "Why College Costs So Much." *American Enterprise* Sept. 2004: 57–58.

Madrick, Jeff. "If Higher Education Is So Important to the Economy, Why Is Its Financing Being Cut More Than That of Other Large Programs?" *New York Times* 5 Aug. 2004: C2.

Orchowski, Peggy. "Congress Questions Sky-High Costs of College Textbooks." *Black Issues in Higher Education* 21.14 (2004): 6–7.

Warren, Elizabeth, and Amelia Warren Tyagi. "Middle Class and Broke." *American Prospect* 15.5 (2004): 42–43.

Winter, Greg. "Public University Tuition Rises Sharply Again for '04." *New York Times* 20 Oct. 2004: A16.

CHAPTER 5

Support

(text pages 157–219)

EVIDENCE

1. Students seem to subscribe to the belief that a knowledge of the facts is sufficient to induce a change in our habits and attitudes, but there is plenty of expert evidence that the plain truth is not enough. Robert Sternberg, a Yale University psychologist, says, "People will go to great lengths to avoid information that contradicts their original stories. There's

a lot of research that shows that people seek to confirm what they think, rather than disconfirm what they think" (*Boston Globe,* 21 Aug. 1993: 7.).

An interesting area for research by students is the relationship between facts about food and the choices people make. Several studies over the years suggest that the facts don't cause most people to alter their eating habits. Students can survey classmates to determine if their behavior confirms the results of these studies.

2. Ask students to create a set of facts, and then request that their classmates derive inferences about the actions or people involved. *Examples:* the contents of a grocery cart in the checkout line; an accident; a crime.

3. Assign reading of the following passage. Ask students to write either a short or a long essay that summarizes some of the inferences we draw from observing what people wear. Since the subject is so large (this excerpt is part of a book about clothing), this exercise gives students practice in narrowing the subject of discussion and choosing a thesis statement or paragraph that can be adequately developed in the number of words assigned.

> For thousands of years human beings have communicated with one another first in the language of dress. Long before I am near enough to talk to you on the street, in a meeting, or at a party, you announce your sex, age, and class to me through what you are wearing — and possibly give me important information (or disinformation) as to your occupation, origin, personality, opinions, tastes, sexual desires, and current mood. I may not be able to put what I observe into words, but I register the information unconsciously, and you simultaneously do the same for me.
>
> By the time we meet and converse we have already spoken to each other in an older and more universal tongue.
>
> — Alison Lurie
> *The Language of Clothes*
> (Random House, 1981)

4. On September 15, 1995, the *New York Times* published a report giving several different versions of an alleged crime: the shooting of a black police officer by a white police officer (p. B1). The white officer argued that he had mistaken the victim for a criminal. The *Times* summarized the disputed accounts in a chart labeled "Sorting It Out." The chart included three different views of the shooting by witnesses and participants and three different opinions of the wound by medical examiners.

A written assignment on this story calls for a clear thesis statement or paragraph, extraction of the most important data, and arrangement of materials, in an orderly and emphatic way. Above all, it calls for an acknowledgment of the distinctions between facts and inferences in the testimony reported in the article and in the students' interpretations of the testimony. Not least, the students find this assignment interesting and provocative.

5. Ask students to look up information by advocates on both sides of the controversies surrounding one of the popular natural mysteries: the Loch Ness monster, the Bermuda Triangle, Findhorn, Bigfoot, or Sasquatch, etc. Then assign a paper, short or long, that reviews the data on both sides and tries to come to a conclusion regarding the validity of the respective claims. Have students justify their conclusions by defending the evidence. If students find that they cannot make up their minds, this is also a conclusion,

but they should be prepared to say why the evidence on both sides proved equally strong or equally weak.

6. From the first paper students have been required to use evidence. Having now read the more elaborate explanations of both factual and opinion evidence in Chapter 5, students can return to their claims of fact, value, and policy and reevaluate the facts and opinions in their essays. Would more data strengthen their claim? If so, what kind? Where can it be found? Would additional expert opinion make their arguments more convincing? If so, whose opinions? Where can they be found?

   If the students show some interest in revising their papers to include more data, encourage them to do so.

7. A popular exercise calls on students to look up the *New York Times* edition that appeared on their birthdays and write a paper that emphasizes straight-forward presentation of data to support their claims. Students must find a thesis around which the information can be organized — about the kinds of films being shown, the nature of women's fashion, advertisements for jobs, scientific discoveries of the day, crimes, etc.

8. Advertisements again. This time students choose ads that offer information about the products. They then evaluate the data. In some cases, of course, they will be unequipped to decide whether the data are accurate or sufficient, but if the ads are directed to a lay audience, readers have a right to ask questions about the sufficiency, relevance, and recency of the data. In other words, if readers think that evidence for the virtues of the product is inadequate, what else would they want to know?

9. Students sometimes approach the subject of information in ads with the preconception that ads do not offer information — only slogans. Students may therefore be asked to contrast two or more ads that offer different amounts and qualities of information. Is information more important in some kinds of ads than others — for example, in automobile advertisements, which are often dense with facts?

10. If there is time for lengthier papers, ask students to examine the evidence in the following cases (or any others that remain controversial):

    a. the Sacco–Vanzetti case, 1921
    b. the kidnapping and murder of the Lindbergh baby, 1932
    c. the assassination of President John F. Kennedy, 1963
    d. the kidnapping of Patty Hearst, 1974
    e. the Bernhard Goetz case, 1987
    f. the Rodney King case, 1991
    g. the O. J. Simpson case, 1994
    h. the Louise Woodward case, 1998
    i. the Scott Peterson case, 2004

11. In leading students to examine the credentials of experts, ask them to consider the authors in the text and the "Multiple Viewpoints" as "experts." It will be easy enough to identify such writers as Gordon Allport, a psychologist, and Marion Nestle, a nutritionist, as authorities in their fields. Even in more problematic disciplines, such as education, we recognize the authority of Paul Goodman, for example, who spent a lifetime studying and writing about the meaning of education and whose opinions are regarded by other experts as authoritative.

But what are we to say of writers who reflect on their personal experience or expound their philosophies? Why do we think Elisha Dov Hack's views are worth reading? After all, he is no more an "expert" on sexual mores than many of his readers. It might come as a small revelation to students, and pertinent to their participation in a writing course, to recognize that the credibility of Hack and other nonprofessional "experts" is based largely on their excellence as writers. They can discover interesting propositions, and organize, develop, and express them in spirited and highly readable prose. They are intelligent, of course, but also curious about most subjects and well informed about many.

12. *The Science of Conjecture* by James Franklin (Johns Hopkins UP, 2001) "provides a history of the rational techniques that mankind has developed to acquire knowledge when certainty is not available — which is most of the time."

13. Students usually need practice in reporting statistics — extracting them from news stories and arranging them in interesting and readable form. Students can research the following subjects and report the information as data that might support a claim. They should, of course, limit the time period for the data. Have them submit their prose summaries to their classmates. Are the data clear and accessible to these readers?

   a.   world population growth
   b.   teenage pregnancies
   c.   women in the labor market
   d.   growth of ethnic populations in the United States
   e.   American marriage patterns
   f.   dimensions of poverty
   g.   voting patterns in the 2004 elections

14. The three books and one article mentioned below are entertaining and informative references for both teachers and students. They are full of useful examples that should help students avoid some of the common pitfalls in interpreting and reporting statistical evidence.

   Campbell, Stephen K., *Flaws and Fallacies in Statistical Thinking.* Englewood Cliffs, NJ: Prentice-Hall, 1974.

   Huff, Darrell. *How to Lie with Statistics.* New York: Norton, 1954.

   Paulos, John Allen. *Innumeracy: Mathematical Illiteracy and Its Con Sequences.* New York: Hill, 1988. Students will discover that six degrees of Kevin Bacon is not so fanciful after all.

   "Fright by the Numbers: Alarming Disease Data Are Frequently Flawed." *Wall Street Journal*, 12 Apr. 1996: B1. Calls attention to the need for caution in reading medical statistics.

   > Most of the numbers are extrapolations or estimates — at best. Yet as the media report them, often uncritically and without context, these conjectures assume the mantle of quantifiable fact.

15. Some students may be interested in and sufficiently informed about polling techniques to evaluate some of the famous polling gaffes: the *Literary Digest* poll of 1936 that predicted that Alfred Landon would defeat Franklin D. Roosevelt or the 1948 Gallup poll that predicted Thomas E. Dewey would defeat Harry S. Truman. Students might want to infer the reasons that such mistakes probably will not recur.

APPEALS TO NEEDS AND VALUES

1. A lively and immediate source of appeals to needs and values is found in
    speeches — students may be directed to *Vital Speeches of the Day*, which
    publishes speeches from a variety of speechmakers.

    In "Classic Arguments," Part Four of this book, Martin Luther King
    Jr.'s "I Have a Dream" is an outstanding example of spoken discourse that
    makes a profoundly emotional appeal. Other famous speeches for the pur-
    poses of this unit include:

    a. Clarence Darrow's "Address to the Prisoners of Cook County Jail" in
        1902
    b. Vice President Richard Nixon's "Checkers" speech in 1952
    c. President John F. Kennedy's Inaugural Address in 1961
    d. Senator Edward Kennedy's TV address explaining to the people of
        Massachusetts his behavior during and after the accident at Chap-
        paquiddick in 1969

    For example, Darrow's speech is remarkable for the inconsistency of
    his argument and its numerous fallacies, both of which have been over-
    looked by textbooks that reprint the address. Edward Kennedy's speech
    makes a personal appeal, arousing sympathy for his suffering and induc-
    ing guilt in the listener for having accused him unjustly.

    Since 1980, the *New York Times* has published "Basic Speeches," deliv-
    ered by the major candidates in presidential campaigns. These appear in
    October of the campaign year. All the speeches contain copious and spe-
    cific references to the values held by the candidates and, presumably, their
    audiences. The inaugural speeches are also revealing of the attention to
    values. In his inaugural speech on January 20, 2001, President George W.
    Bush spoke of America's commitment to "civility, courage, compassion,
    and character." "Our public interest," he said, depends on "private charac-
    ter, on civic duty and family bonds and basic fairness, on uncounted,
    unhonored acts of decency. . . ."

2. Advertisements by large corporations (GE, Microsoft, Wal-Mart) appearing
    frequently in newspapers and magazines comment on political and social
    issues rather than the merits of the companies' products. As short essays
    they can be useful for examination of values based on what is perceived to
    be common consent.

    a. What values do the advertisers assume that we share?
    b. What evidence (examples, facts, statistics) do they offer to convince
        the reader that their proposals will support our values?
    c. What tones are used in the essays (reasonable, generous, angry, sarcas-
        tic, humorous)?

3. Also useful are the ads that promise power, riches, great beauty, etc. Many
    of the most outrageous ones appear in *The National Enquirer* and similar
    publications.

    a. Can you infer to what audience they make a strong appeal?
    b. What fears, needs, desires do they appeal to?
    c. What attempts are made to provide credibility?

4. Quindlen's argument leads to a discussion of problems that depend on
    information unfamiliar to most students. As citizens and voters, however,
    they will be increasingly concerned with questions generated by advances
    in biology. For learners there is plenty of information available. An intro-

duction to the stem-cell debate appears in an issue of *The Science Times* (18 Dec. 2000: sec. D), an eight-page summary of the facts that underlie the controversy. It contains clear definitions, diagrams, photographs, and expert opinion.

5. It is not surprising that the decision of the government to fund stem-cell research, however limited, should have roused some religious organizations to respond. Perhaps some students can speak or write on the positions taken by their churches or temples.

Bibliography

Fox, Cynthia. "Why Stem Cells Will Transform Medicine." *Fortune* 11 June 2001: 159–62.

"The New Animal Farm." *Newsweek* 2 Apr. 2001: 42–45.

DEBATE: IS ANIMAL RESEARCH NECESSARY TO SAVE HUMAN LIVES?

1. Peter Singer, a leading advocate of animal rights, has asked why students are so indifferent to discrimination against animals in campus laboratories. If such laboratories exist in your campus, ask students to interview workers responsible for the experiments and then write an evaluative report that explains the nature of the experiments and the justification for them.

2. One justification for medical use of animals is "self-preservation" of the human species, species preservation being a primary instinct of all members of the animal kingdom. Whether this is a moral defense is something students should be prepared to discuss. Students should be alerted to follow news stories about the harvesting of animal organs for transplant to humans.

3. Students should also be aware of recent developments that might excite moral condemnation: In January 2002 scientists announced that pigs had been cloned for the express purpose of providing organs for human patients.

Bibliography

Coetzee, J. M., Marjorie Garber, Peter Singer, Wendy Doniger, and Barbara Smith. *The Lives of Animals*. Princeton, NJ: Princeton UP, 1999. Fiction and nonfiction in defense of animal rights.

Langley, Gill, ed. *Animal Experimentation: The Consensus Changes*. New York: Chapman, 1989.

Lauerman, John F. "Animal Research." *Harvard Magazine* Jan./Feb. 1999. Explores the "morality and efficacy" of such research.

Linden, Damon. "Rights for Rodents." *Commentary* Apr. 2001: 41–44. An attack on animal rights activists who equate animals with human beings.

Mydans, Seth. "He's Not Hairy, He's My Brother." *New York Times* 12 Aug. 2001: Wk. 5. A debate about rights for apes — "the next step in the development of a moral society."

Rudacille, Deborah. *The Scalpel and the Butterfly: The War between Animal Research and Animal Protection*. New York: Farrar, 2000. Includes an extensive bibliography and names of organizations interested in animal welfare.

CHAPTER 6
Warrants
(text pages 220–68)

1. Although the definition of the warrant in Toulmin's *The Uses of Argument* is more complicated than we have made it appear, for the purposes of a freshman composition course, those of us who have used the Toulmin model with some success believe that the model works best if we define the warrant as synonymous with assumption, a belief we take for granted, or a general principle underlying other beliefs and attitudes. If students raise questions, we can always widen the definition.

   For obvious reasons the concept of the warrant is more difficult for students to assimilate than that of support, in part because they have seldom been required to make their assumptions explicit. Fortunately for teaching purposes, the examples that we can use are so numerous and so varied that we may call attention to the warrant repeatedly without losing student interest.

2. Advertisements offer a rich and accessible source of material. Students may choose their own ads for analysis and write or speak about them to the class. The exercise should emphasize discussion of a controversial warrant. For an oral presentation, an ad that contains more than a paragraph of text can be duplicated for distribution, and the whole class can participate in a discussion of the validity of the warrant.

3. Subjects for examination of warrants appear almost every day in school newspapers. Sometimes the subjects are about education or other matters relevant to the function and management of the school; sometimes they respond to the world outside. Below are some current issues on college campuses today:

   a. A proposal to introduce a core diversity requirement designed to change attitudes on race and sex. (What assumptions about education underlie this proposal?)

   b. A demand that faculty appointments reflect the percentage of women and minorities in the general population. (What assumptions about education and the social and political functions of the university are at work in this affirmative action proposal?)

   c. A demand that Native Americans be allowed to live in a separate dormitory and be given their own student center. (What warrants about ethnic diversity and the goals of an academic institution can be uncovered?)

4. Other sources of analysis of warrants:

   a. *Etiquette books.* An interesting assignment would compare etiquette books of a generation or more ago with contemporary ones. (Judith Martin's books are valuable and amusing sources of comment about present-day manners.) Have there been large changes? Small changes? In what areas? On what assumptions about social relationships and freedom have these changes been based?

      Multicultural Manners: New Rules for a Changing Society by Norine Dresser (Wiley, 1996) gives rules of etiquette that recognize cultural and ethnic differences in this country. One reviewer of the book said, "For all its value, this book can push cultural tolerance to the breaking point."

b. *Advice columns in newspapers and magazines.* What assumptions about marriage, sexual problems, child rearing, religion, etc. underlie the advice of the columnists?

c. *Magazines for teenagers.* Have they changed in the last fifteen or twenty years? On what assumptions about the lives and values of teenagers have the publishers based their changes?

d. *Arguments in magazines and newspapers that make a controversial or unpopular claim.* The views of Peter Singer, a professor of philosophy at Princeton University, are always good for an argument and the unearthing of warrants held by a very small minority. "The Singer Solution to World Poverty" (*New York Times Magazine* 5 Sept. 1999) explores Singer's claim that Americans are obligated to help support the world's poor: "Whatever money you're spending on luxuries, not necessities, should be given away." If students don't agree, they should try to defend the warrants that underlie their claims. And how do students define luxuries and necessities?

5. Go back to the earlier papers of definition and defense of value and policy claims and examine the warrants, expressed or unexpressed. *Example:* In defending his decision never to marry, a student writes that he values his freedom. What does he assume about marriage, love, individuality, commitment, etc.?

ADDITIONAL TYPES OF WARRANTS

In Chapter 6 we discuss three main categories of warrants, derived from Ehninger and Brockriede (1953): *authoritative, substantive,* and *motivational* warrants. If you would like to introduce your students to a more complex range of warrants, all of which are subtypes of the three main categories, we have provided discussions of each of seven types below: *authority, generalization, sign, cause and effect, comparison, analogy,* and *values.* A warrants chart on pages 36–37 shows in schematic form the types of warrants, with examples and critical questions that may help students detect them in arguments. If you do choose to teach these additional types of warrants to your students, you may wish to photocopy and distribute the chart.

Authority

Arguments from authority depend on the credibility of their sources, as in this example.

> [Benjamin] Bloom maintains that most children can learn everything that is taught them with complete competence.[1]

Because Benjamin Bloom was a professor of education at the University of Chicago and a widely respected authority on educational psychology, his statement about the educability of children carried considerable weight. Notice that Professor Bloom has qualified his claim by asserting that "most" children, but not all, can learn everything. The reader might also recognize the limits of the warrant — the authority could be mistaken, or there could be disagreement among authorities.

---

[1]Michael Alper, "All Our Children Can Learn," *University of Chicago Magazine* Summer 1982: 3.

CLAIM:	Most children can learn everything that is taught them with complete competence.
SUPPORT:	Professor Bloom attests that this is so.
WARRANT:	Professor Bloom's testimony is sufficient because he is an accepted authority on educational achievement.
RESERVATIONS:	Unless the data for his studies were inaccurate, unless his criteria for evaluation were flawed, and so on.

Generalization

Arguments from generalization are based on the belief that a general principle can be derived from a series of examples. But these warrants are credible only if the examples are representative of the whole group being described and not too many contradictory examples have been ignored. In the following excerpt the author documents the tragic effects for children born "unnaturally" (outside the mother's womb) or without knowledge of their fathers.

> For years I've collected bits of data about certain unfortunate people in the news: Son of Sam, the Hillside strangler, the Pennsylvania shoemaker who raped and brutalized several women, a Florida man who killed at least thirty-four women, the man sought in connection with the Tylenol scare. All of them grew up not knowing at least one of their natural parents; most knew neither.[2]

In outline the argument takes this form:

CLAIM:	People brought up without a sense of identity with their natural parents will respond to the world with rage and violence.
SUPPORT:	Son of Sam, the Hillside strangler, the Pennsylvania shoemaker, the Florida murderer, the man in the Tylenol scare responded to the world with rage and violence.
WARRANT:	What is true of this sample is true for others in this class.
RESERVATIONS:	Unless this sample is too small or exceptions have been ignored.

Sign

As the name suggests, in arguments based on sign the arguer offers an observable datum as an indicator of a condition. The warrant that a sign is convincing can be accepted only if the sign is appropriate, if it is sufficient, and if other indicators do not dispute it (for example, an argument in which the enjoyment of Virginia Slims is presented as a sign of female liberation). In the following example the warrant is stated:

> There are other signs of a gradual demoting of the professions to the level of ordinary trades and businesses. The right of lawyers and physicians to advertise, so as to reintroduce money competition and break down the "standard practices," is being granted. Architects are being allowed to act as contractors. Teachers have been unionized.[3]

---

[2]Lorraine Dusky, "Brave New Babies?" *Newsweek* 6 Dec. 1982: 30.
[3]Jacques Barzun, "The Professions under Siege," *Harper's* Oct. 1978: 66.

Here, too, a reservation is in order.

CLAIM: Professions are being demoted to the level of ordinary trades and businesses.

SUPPORT: Lawyers and physicians advertise, architects act as contractors, teachers have been unionized.

WARRANT: These business practices are signs of the demotion of the professions.

RESERVATION: Unless these practices are not widespread.

Cause and Effect

Causal reasoning assumes that one event or condition can bring about another. One can reason from the cause to the effect or from the effect to the cause. The following is an example of reasoning from effect (the claim) to cause (the warrant). The quotation is taken from the famous Supreme Court decision of 1954, *Brown v. Board of Education,* which mandated the desegregation of public schools throughout the United States.

Segregation of white and colored children in public schools has a detrimental effect upon the colored children. The impact is greater when it has the sanction of the law; for the policy of separating the races is usually interpreted as denoting the inferiority of the Negro group. A sense of inferiority affects the motivation of a child to learn. Segregation with the sanction of law, therefore, has a tendency to [retard] the educational and mental development of Negro children and to deprive them of some of the benefits they would receive in a racial[ly] integrated school system.[4]

The outline of the argument would take this form:

CLAIM (EFFECT): Colored children have suffered mental and emotional damage in legally segregated schools.

SUPPORT: They suffer from feelings of inferiority, which retard their ability to learn. They are being deprived of important social and educational benefits.

WARRANT (CAUSE): Legal segregation has a tendency to retard the emotional and mental development of Negro children.

In cause-effect arguments the reasoning may be more complicated than an outline suggests. For one thing, events and conditions in the world are not always the result of single causes, nor does a cause necessarily produce a single result. It is probably more realistic to speak of chains of causes as well as chains of effects. A recent headline emphasizes this form of reasoning: "Experts Fear That Unpredictable Chain of Events Could Bring Nuclear War." The article points to the assassination of Archduke Francis Ferdinand of Austria-Hungary in the Bosnian city of Sarajevo in 1914, which "set in motion a series of events that the world's most powerful leaders could not stop" — that is, World War I.

Or, as another example, opinion polls a few years ago indicated Americans' unwillingness to "approve any bellicose activity, unless US interests are seen as truly vital and are clearly defined."[5] The immediate cause of this isolationism is usually attributed to the "Vietnam syndrome," the relic of a

---

[4]*Brown v. Board of Education of Topeka,* 347 U.S. 487–96 (May 17, 1954).
[5]*Public Opinion,* Apr.–May 1982: 16.

bitter experience in an unpopular war. But this single cause, according to some students of the problem, is insufficient to explain the current mood. History, they say, reveals "decades of similar American resistance to foreign involvements." Needless to say, the "Vietnam syndrome" no longer prevails in the wake of the attacks on September 11, 2001, and the very real possibility of further attacks in the future. Some students may want to examine the causes of the furious hatred of the United States that triggered the September 11 attacks and to evaluate the plausibility of those causes.

Causes can also be either *necessary* or *sufficient*. That is, to contract tuberculosis, it is necessary to be exposed to the bacillus, but this exposure in itself may not be sufficient to bring on the disease. However, if the victim's immune system is depressed for some reason, exposure to the bacillus will be sufficient to cause the illness. Or, to make an example from law and politics: To reduce the incidence of drunk driving, it would be necessary to enact legislation that penalized the drunk driver. But that would not be sufficient unless the police and the courts were diligent in making arrests and imposing sentences.

Comparison

In some arguments characteristics and circumstances in two or more cases are compared to prove that what is true in one case ought to be true in another. Unlike the elements in analogies the things being matched in comparison belong to the same class. The following is a familiar argument based on a comparison of similar activities in different countries at different times. On the basis of these apparent similarities the author makes a judgment about America's future.

> Perhaps I'm wrong, but the auguries seem to me threatening. Like the bourgeoisie of pre–World War I in Europe, we are retreating into our well-furnished houses, hoping the storm, when it comes, will strike someone else, preferably the poor. Our narcissistic passion for sports and fitness reminds me of Germany in the twenties and early thirties, when the entire nation turned to hiking, sun-bathing, and the worship of the body beautiful, in part so as not to see what was happening to German politics — not to speak of the family next door. The belief that gold in the garden is more important than government helped to bring France to defeat in 1940 and near civil war in the 1950s. When the middle class stops believing in government or in the future, it's all over, time truly to sew the diamonds in the lining of your coat and make a run for it.[6]

This is the argument in outline form:

CLAIM: The behavior of many middle-class Americans today threatens our future.

SUPPORT: The same kind of behavior by the Germans in the twenties and thirties and by the French in the thirties and forties led to disaster.

WARRANT: Because such behavior brought disaster to Germany and France, it will bring disaster to America.

But is this warrant believable? Are the dissimilarities between the United States now and these European countries in earlier decades greater than the similarities? For example, if the present American passion for sports and fit-

---

[6]Michael Korda, "The New Pessimism," *Newsweek* 14 June 1982: 10.

ness is caused by very different social forces than those that operated in Germany in the twenties and thirties, then the comparison warrant is too weak to support the author's claim.

Analogy

An analogy warrant assumes a resemblance in some characteristics between dissimilar things. Analogies differ in their power to persuade. Some are explanatory; others are merely descriptive. Those that describe are less likely to be useful in a serious argument. In conversation human beings are often likened to other animals — cows, pigs, rats, chickens. Or life and happiness are compared to a variety of objects: "Life is a cabaret," "Life is just a bowl of cherries," "Happiness is a warm puppy." But such metaphorical uses are more colorful than precise. In those examples one quality is abstracted from all the others, leaving us with two objects that remain essentially dissimilar. Descriptive analogies promise immediate access to the reader, as do paintings or photographs. Such short cuts are tempting, but descriptive analogies are seldom enough to support a claim. Consider the following example, which appears in a speech by Malcolm X, the black civil rights leader, criticizing the participation by whites in the march on Washington in 1962 for black rights and employment:

> It's just like when you've got some coffee that's too black, which means it's too strong. What do you do? You integrate it with cream, you make it weak. But if you pour too much cream in it, you won't even know you ever had coffee.[7]

This is the outline of the argument:

CLAIM: Integration of black and white people in the march on Washington weakened the black movement for rights and jobs.

SUPPORT: Putting white cream into black coffee weakens the coffee.

WARRANT: Weakening coffee with cream is analogous to weakening the black rights movement by allowing white people to participate.

The imagery is vivid, but the analogy does not represent convincing proof. The dissimilarities between whitening coffee with cream and integrating a political movement are too great to convince the reader of the damaging effects of integration. Moreover, words like *strong* and *weak* as they apply to a civil rights movement need careful definition. To make a convincing case, the author would have to offer not imagery but facts and authoritative opinion.

The following analogy is more successful because it is explanatory rather than descriptive. The elements on both sides of the analogy are failing or sick human beings and less than productive tests. This excerpt appears in an article by Albert Shanker, late president of the American Federation of Teachers, deploring the low scores of American students in national tests.

> It's not the first time we've heard about the dismal performance of US students in math: NAEP [National Assessment of Educational Progress] has been giving us the same bad news for twenty years. So it should come as no surprise that our kids are nowhere near "first in the world." What can

[7]"Message to the Grass Roots," *Roots of Rebellion,* ed. Richard P. Young (New York: Harper, 1970) 357.

WARRANTS CHART

Type of Warrant	Subtype	Example
Authoritative Warrants are based on the credibility of a source		**Claim:** Cigarette smoking is harmful.
Substantive Warrants are based on beliefs about the reliability of factual evidence	A **Generalization Warrant** is a substantive warrant based on the belief that it is possible to derive a general principle from a series of examples.	**Claim:** Marijuana is a potent medicine for relief of pain in seriously ill patients.
	A **Sign Warrant** is a substantive warrant based on the belief that an observable datum is an indicator of a particular condition.	**Claim:** Press reports and TV news programs deal in lies and deception.
	A **Cause-and-Effect Warrant** is a substantive warrant that assumes that one event or condition can bring about another.	**Claim:** Giving free food to poor countries can be counter-productive.
	A **Comparison Warrant** is a substantive warrant that assumes that what is true in one case ought to be true in another.	**Claim:** The United States should set an annual budget for physician spending, then let doctors do their work.
	An **Analogy Warrant** is a substantive warrant that assumes a resemblance in some characteristics between dissimilar things.	**Claim:** Sports have become the secular religion of America. (Harry Edwards)
Motivational Warrants are based on the values of the arguer and the audience.		**Claim:** People in this country work too hard to enjoy God and family.

SUPPORT: The surgeon general has determined that cigarette smoking is hazardous to your health.	**WARRANT:** The surgeon general is a reliable medical authority.	Could the authority be mistaken in this case? Do other reputable authorities disagree?
SUPPORT: In controlled experiments marijuana has reduced severe side effects and pain of illness and cancer therapy in several patients.	**WARRANT:** What was true for the patients in the experiments will undoubtedly be true for many more.	Are the examples representative of the whole group being described? Have contradictory examples been ignored?
SUPPORT: In 1992, NBC faked exploding gas tanks in an exposé of GM trucks. In the past journalists greatly exaggerated the dangers of dioxin and radon.	**WARRANT:** Such fakery is a sign of the deceptive practices of the media.	Is the sign appropriate? Is the sign sufficient? Do other indicators dispute the sign?
SUPPORT: Poor farmers plant fewer crops if farming becomes unprofitable.	**WARRANT:** People will lack incentive to provide for themselves if others provide for them.	Is the cited cause sufficient to bring about the effect? Have other possible causes been overlooked?
SUPPORT: This practice has enabled Canada to save money without reducing the pay of doctors.	**WARRANT:** Because this practice is successful in Canada, it should be successful in the United States.	Are the dissimilarities between the things being compared greater than the similarities? Have all or only a few of the important characteristics been compared?
SUPPORT: Both sports and religion have gods, saints, houses of worship, and "true believers."	**WARRANT:** The feelings of veneration for the spectacle and values of sports are analogous to the feelings of adherents of formal religion.	Is the analogy explanatory or merely descriptive? Are there sufficient similarities between the two elements to make the analogy appropriate?
SUPPORT: Americans work 20 percent more today than in 1973 and have 32 percent less free time per week.	**WARRANT:** Work should not be an end in itself but a means to enjoyment of "mental culture, moral and social progress, and the Arts of Living." (J. S. Mill)	Might some people disagree with the arguer's values? Is the value relevant to the claim?

we expect now? Only, I'm afraid, that another test will be administered two years from now to see if we're doing any better.

Suppose you were feeling terrible and went to a doctor who tested you, said you had a fever, and asked you to come back in two weeks. And suppose you returned every couple of weeks for a year or so to be tested, and every time, you got the same bad news but still no diagnosis and no advice. Few of us would think much of a doctor who did nothing but test us and give us bad news. But that's what's been going on in education for twenty years.[8]

Shanker's argument may be outlined like this:

CLAIM: Testing students in math year after year without proposing remedies is fruitless.

SUPPORT: Testing a sick person again and again without offering a diagnosis or treatment would be considered unacceptable medical practice.

WARRANT: Math tests which fail to diagnose the problem and propose remedies are analogous to medical tests which offer no diagnosis or treatment for the patient.

This analogy, however, suffers from the weakness of all analogies — dissimilarities between the objects being compared. Many physical illnesses may be easier to diagnose and cure than deficiencies in math. The latter are certainly due to a variety of social, economic, and personal problems that are difficult or impossible for the educational system to treat.

Values

Warrants may also reflect needs and values, and readers accept or reject the claim to the extent that they find the warrants relevant to their own goals and standards. In Chapter 6 Mrs. Walkup and others based their opposition to development of the Eastern Shore on a value warrant: Rural life is superior to the way of life being introduced by developers. Clearly, numbers of outsiders who valued a more sophisticated way of life did not agree.

The persuasive appeal of advertisements, as we know, leans heavily on value warrants, which are often unstated. Sometimes they include almost no printed message except the name of the product accompanied by a picture. The advertisers expect us to assume that if we use their product, we can acquire the desirable characteristics of the attractive people shown using it.

Value warrants are indispensable in arguments on public policy. In the following excerpt from a radio debate, a professor of statistics at Berkeley argues in favor of affirmative action policies to promote the hiring of women faculty. Her claim has been made earlier, but her warrant and any reservations remain unstated. This is her supporting material.

6.9 percent is [a] very tiny proportion of the faculty. You still have to go a long ways to see a woman teaching in this university. Most all of the students go to this university and never, ever have a woman professor, a woman associate professor, even a woman assistant professor teaching them. There's a lack of role models, there's a lack of teaching, and it brings a lack of breadth into the teaching.[9]

[8]"Testing Is Not Enough," *New York Times* 20 Oct. 1991: E7.
[9]Elizabeth Scott, quoted in "Affirmative Action: Not a Black and White Issue," National Public Radio, week of 25 Apr. 1977: 7.

The Berkeley professor's argument may be outlined like this:

CLAIM: The proportion of women on the Berkeley faculty should be increased.

SUPPORT: Because women are only 6.9 percent of the faculty, most students never have a woman teacher.

WARRANT: Exposure of students to women faculty is a desirable educational goal.

RESERVATION: Unless individual women faculty members are significantly less competent than men.

DEBATE: ARE YOU RESPONSIBLE FOR YOUR OWN WEIGHT?

1. A good prewriting question to introduce this topic is whether your students believe there exists an epidemic of obesity in this country. A second question is what has caused a concern about obesity. A third is whether the government could or should take any action to fight that epidemic, if it exists. The two essayists represent the opposite sides in the controversy over the third question.

2. Your students will also be able to follow through on this subject by discussing the ways in which the fast-food industry has responded to charges that their food is contributing to Americans' obesity. How have they justified changing their menus if they do not accept that they have been contributing to the problem? How is their position comparable to — and different from — that of tobacco companies?

3. Now that the students have read a detailed discussion of warrants and practiced identifying them, they should be ready to compare the warrants underlying these two arguments that defend opposite positions in a debate. How do the warrants affect the persuasiveness of each piece?

Bibliography

"Changing the Menu: Convenience Food." *Economist* 22 May 2004: 57.

Devaney, Polly. "Making a Meal of Couch Potatoes and Doughnuts." *Marketing Week* 25 Mar. 2004: 28–29.

"Fast-Food Density in Poor, Black Areas May Contribute to Obesity Epidemic." *Health and Medicine Week* 27 Sept. 2004: 889.

Healy, Melissa. "War on Fat Gets Serious." *Los Angeles Times* 3 Jan. 2004: 1.

Lennon, Robert. "They're Hatin' It." *Corporate Counsel* Apr. 2004: n. pag.

Shreve, Meg. "States Trying to Trim Obesity Litigation." *Business Insurance* 26 July 2004: 4.

"Study Links Fast Food to Overall Poor Nutrition, Obesity Risk." *AScribe Medicine News Service* 5 Jan. 2004: n. pag.

CHAPTER 7

Induction, Deduction, and Logical Fallacies

(text pages 269–313)

1. The teaching of fallacies poses special, though not insuperable, problems. Some fallacious statements by public figures are obvious, like those in the list of exercises in the text. But arguments by professional writers often contain concealed fallacies or fallacies that uninformed students are unable to identify. One example that comes immediately to mind is Ashley Montagu's "Man, the Ignoble Savage?" (from *The Nature of Human Aggression*). This essay, reprinted in several readers, purports to be an attack on the use of examples by others, but Montagu offers only one example in rebuttal, and this example is a scarcely credible rumor that remains unsubstantiated. (An interesting assignment would ask students to look for more convincing research to support Montagu's claim.)

   The rule for all of us — teachers and students alike — is to cultivate fearlessness in our criticism of articles by putative experts. Since freshman students are naturally disinclined to be critical of their mentors (publicly, at least), we may risk overzealousness in uncovering faulty arguments in textbooks, newspapers, and magazines. Advertisers are not the only arguers guilty of concealment or distorted reasoning.

2. Students should be on the alert for dubious arguments in what they read and hear and bring them in for examination by the class. If they are keeping journals, they may record these fallacies or what they interpret as fallacies in their journals. The nomenclature is not important. Some of their entries will turn out to be examples of sound reasoning after all, but no matter. The objective of the exercise is increased alertness. Sensitive discrimination will, we hope, come later.

   In some cases, students will be lucky to find explicit references to fallacies, as in the beginning of this letter (*Wall Street Journal* 15 Nov. 1983): "Your editorial is an illustration of the slippery slope argument." Less explicitly, the writer will say (*Wall Street Journal* 7 Dec. 1983): "Your editorial was critical of Surgeon General C. Everett Koop for 'citing particularly egregious magazine articles and medical cases as proof that the United States could easily slip into some Nazi-like approval of general euthanasia.' I, for one, would not dismiss Dr. Koop's concern quite so readily."

3. Some school newspapers are rife with weak and fallacious arguments in the editorials and letters to the editor. As a source of fallacies, they have two advantages: They are easily available, and students probably feel fewer inhibitions in attacking their peers.

EXERCISES FOR CRITICAL THINKING: ANSWERS

Students generally have no difficulty recognizing and explaining these fallacies even when they cannot find the names for them.

1. *Begging the question.* The judge is assuming the answer to the very question that a trial is supposed to answer.

2. *Non sequitur.* It doesn't follow that because something is good for us the government should enforce compliance.

3. *Post hoc fallacy.* There is no proof that watching these particular TV shows is the cause of high or low school grades. It's more reasonable to suppose that children who do well or poorly in school select one show or the other because of its appeal to their level of intelligence and achievement.

4. *Hasty generalization or small sample.* A faulty prediction for one month is not enough for an accusation of unreliability.

5. *Two wrongs don't make a right.* The writer thinks that death and danger are unacceptable for men in combat, but subjecting women to death and danger doesn't make these "wrongs" more acceptable.

6. *Faulty use of authority.* Taste is a matter of individual preference. It would be hard to prove that Cher, however gifted an actress, is superior to anybody else in her choice of a sweetener. (Of course, we also know that she is only posing for a paid advertisement.)

7. *Two wrongs don't make a right.* The arguer seems to infer that gambling is wrong, but legalizing it won't make it morally right. (This is what Norman Cousins calls "cop-out realism," or "If you can't beat 'em, join 'em.")

8. *Unknown fact or faulty comparison.* What was money spent for in the past? Have conditions changed that may make the expenditure of more money appropriate now?

9. *Non sequitur.* It doesn't follow that campus newspapers select the best or even good writers. They usually have to settle for those who make themselves available.

10. *Begging the question.* The arguer assumes that standard English is necessary only for certain kinds of employment, but that remains to be proved. Standard English has other uses unrelated to employment.

11. *Faulty definition.* In this case discrimination means making judicious choices. It should not be considered pejorative. To perform their duties, which may involve physical exertion, police officers should be required to fulfill certain physical standards.

12. *Faulty comparison or begging the question.* Qualified doctors and medical students are different. By definition a medical student is still being tested, and access to information in books during the testing process may defeat the purposes of testing.

13. *Faulty definition.* Chemicals are the building blocks of nature. Some may be unsafe, but they are not all synonymous with poisons by any means.

14. *Begging the question.* The arguer assumes that the only relevant criterion for choosing courses is payment of tuition. But a student enters into an implicit contract when he or she enrolls in the college or university and accepts the criteria laid down by the institution for the granting of a diploma.

15. *False dilemma.* The writer assumes that there are only two alternatives available to those who want to marry. But there is at least one more — marriages freely chosen that are not based on romantic love. Besides, we have no way of knowing how well arranged marriages worked. Staying married when divorce is difficult or unavailable doesn't prove the success of the marriage.

16. *Hasty generalization or small sample.* Three examples are not sufficient to support a generalization about a population of hundreds of thousands or millions.

17. *Hasty generalization or small sample.* One example of a highly intelligent athlete is not enough to prove the intelligence of a large population.

18. *Unknown fact.* There is insufficient evidence in this quotation to prove the reasons for Sasway's failure to register, which may or may not be based on moral principles.

19. *Faulty analogy.* Harris is making an analogy between inanimate objects — buildings, cars, ham — and animate objects or students. Students, after all, have choices and some control over their education.

20. *Post hoc fallacy.* There is no evidence here that doctrines of feminism have caused women to turn to crime. Anyway, crime is usually the result of many factors that are difficult to separate.

21. *Non sequitur.* It doesn't follow that just because an activity is healthful the university should require it. (There are a number of things that are good for us that a center of academic learning does not choose to introduce into its curriculum.)

22. *Ad hominem.* Meany is attacking the habits of the younger generation, not their views, which remain unknown.

23. *Non sequitur.* It doesn't follow that early poverty makes a candidate sympathetic to the problems of the poor. In fact, the opposite may be true.

24. *Faulty comparison.* In the European cases troops were engaged in crushing freedom; in the Little Rock case they were engaged in extending it.

25. *Post hoc fallacy.* There is no evidence that the election of Governor Jones is the cause of the corruption. His election and government corruption may be coincidental.

26. *False dilemma.* These may not be the only alternatives for the voters. There may be ways to improve education without a pay increase.

27. *Post hoc fallacy.* It would be hard to prove a cause-effect relation.

28. *Faulty comparison.* The dissimilarities between the two states are probably much greater than the similarities.

29. *Post hoc fallacy.* Self-explanatory.

30. *Faulty use of authority.* Even Galileo should have asked for stricter evidence than the great Aristotle could provide on the subject of natural science.

31. *Slippery slope fallacy.* The progression projected by Brustein — from Congress curtailing grants to artists whose work is controversial to Congress ordering the execution of artists whose work is deemed blasphemous — is hardly inevitable.

DEBATE: SHOULD THE FEDERAL GOVERNMENT FUND EMBRYONIC STEM-CELL RESEARCH?

1. Because of the speed with which both scientific advances and public policy are being made in this area, this is a good topic to approach by having the students research the most recent developments in the ongoing debate. This topic works well for instructors who like to have their students do

two or more papers using the same basic research to better understand the different types of claims. Students could be asked to write a claim-of-fact paper on the issue of embryonic stem-cell research and then follow up with a second one supporting a claim of policy regarding such research. The first would be objective and the second, subjective.

2. The Reeve essay will inevitably lead to a discussion of the role that movie stars can or should play in politics. There is no question that Reeve had power as an advocate for stem-cell research in a way the thousands of average Americans who have suffered similar tragic accidents have not had. His loss of mobility was particularly ironic since millions had come to think of him as the Man of Steel. The faith and hope that he openly expressed after his accident revealed a very different type of strength. The emotional appeal of his essay is undeniable. Students can readily think of cases in which the Hollywood factor was not so positive, however. Is a movie star any better qualified than the average citizen to judge who is the better presidential candidate? Is a candidate preferable because of the band that plays at his fund-raiser? And did it really matter that much what Jane Fonda had to say about the Vietnam War or Susan Sarandon about the war in Iraq? (See the related articles in the bibliography below.)

3. Although Charen is not as well known as Reeve was, she is also a public figure. Students can discuss to what extent her essay makes use of emotional appeal. How is her appeal different from that used by Reeve?

Bibliography

"Center for Bioethics and Human Dignity: Ron Reagan Misguided on Embryonic Stem Cell Research, Cloning." *US Newswire* 29 July 2004: n. pag.

"Christian Coalition Commends Mel Gibson for His Strong Stance against Prop. 71 — The $3 Billion Human Embryonic Stem Cell Research Initiative on California Ballot." *US Newswire* 28 Oct. 2004: n. pag.

Daley, George Q. "Missed Opportunities in Embryonic Stem-Cell Research." *New England Journal of Medicine* 351.7 (2004): 627–28.

Friedrich, M. J. "Researchers Make the Case for Human Embryonic Stem Cell Research." *JAMA* 292.7 (2004): 791–92.

"New Study Shows Most Americans Support Embryonic Stem Cell Research." *Stem Cell Week* 8 Nov. 2004: 35.

"Reagan's Son Calls for Support for Embryonic Stem Cell Research." *America's Intelligence Wire* 28 July 2004: n. pag.

"Science Magazine Hosts Discussion of Debate on Embryonic Stem Cell Research." *Gene Therapy Weekly* 4 Nov. 2004: 69.

"'Snowflakes' Bring an Early Winter to Washington, D.C.: Meet the 'Faces' of Embryonic Stem-Cell Research." *US Newswire* 22 Sept. 2004: n. pag.

CHAPTER 8
Language and Thought
(text pages 314–69)

1. Again we turn to advertisements for their use of slogans, clichés, and emotive language. Advertising claims in airline ads, we are told by a national advertising group, "promise great buys and then dissolve into airline jargon filled with restrictions." Ask students to examine some airline ads for jargon and code words that are meaningless or slippery.

    A paperback entitled *I Can Sell You Anything* by Carl P. Wrighter (Ballantine, 1972) offers a popular attack on techniques of advertising. Wrighter supports his claims by offering dozens of examples of "weasel words" in specific commercial advertisements. The claims of each ad are clearly stated. Often the argument is exaggerated, and some of the ads will no longer be familiar to students, but they can use Wrighter's formulas as a model, choosing their own ads and substituting their own weasel words.

    An article in the *New York Times* 26 Nov. 1998, "A Name So Smooth, the Product Glides In," by J. C. Herz, describes in fascinating detail how products are named, that is, how the sounds of letters like *z*, "one of the fastest sounds in the alphabet," can influence the choice of name for the product. "Orwell was dead wrong," says the author. "The language isn't being crushed under the weight of oppression. It is experiencing an algal bloom of new vocabulary." Students need not be linguists to try to uncover — or imagine — the origins of product names which seem to come out of nowhere — Advil, Nuon, Zima.

2. Have students collect literature from various politically active groups on campus. Assign a study of the language based on some of the categories in the text: connotations, euphemisms, clichés, slogans, slanted language, picturesque language.

    a. Is the message persuasive? How much of the persuasive effect is due to the way that language is used?
    b. Identify terms that you consider effective and tell why.
    c. Identify terms that you consider ineffective and tell why.

3. Students can find slogans everywhere. The slogans, of course, will differ from year to year and from place to place, depending on the emergence of new issues. In 2004, an election year, some slogans were generated, though not so many as we might have expected. Ask students to compose their own political slogans and defend them. To whom does the slogan appeal? What short cuts have been taken; that is, what questions about your abbreviated argument might be asked by an unfriendly reader?

4. There are clichés — statements of obvious ideas — everywhere. Students can examine the "Basic Speeches" referred to in assignments for Chapter 5. They might consider answers to the following questions: Can the use of clichés be justified? What would be the effect of substituting unusual ideas, even a surprising and perhaps unpleasant truth?

5. Have students examine some of the classic speeches of the past: Patrick Henry's *Speech before the Virginia Convention of 1775,* Abraham Lincoln's *Gettysburg Address,* Winston Churchill's address to the Congress of the United States of America on December 26, 1941. Students will notice that

all of these speeches contain memorable phrases. Ask whether they think that the language in these speeches differs in any significant way from the language of the "Basic Speeches" of 2004. Have them explain any differences and describe how they contribute to the success or failure of particular speeches.

6. Students might try writing their own high school commencement addresses, avoiding both the congratulatory clichés of most graduation addresses and the bitter invective of Jacob Neusner.

7. We have used an excerpt describing the actions of Henry VIII to demonstrate the use of partisan language by a Catholic historian. Below is a passage from a Protestant historian, G. M. Trevelyan, about the same events of the English Reformation, but exhibiting, through the use of selective language, an entirely different point of view. Students may be asked to pick out the words and phrases that indicate slanting.

> It is often falsely asserted that the [Protestant] Reformation was a plunder of the poor; that it dispossessed them of their heritage in favor of a squirearchy [landed proprietor class]. The fact is that the medieval Church, on its financial side, was a squirearchy richer and more jealous of its possessions than any which had existed since the Reformation. What the revolution did was to transfer enormous wealth from one squirearchy to another; from a squirearchy which, in its very nature, was intensely conservative and seldom let go of anything in its possessions, to another which lived far more among the people, and whose extravagances often led to the division of the land, so that there grew up in Elizabethan and Jacobean times a whole class of small yeoman farmers.
> The medieval Church was, no doubt, more friendly to the poor than any State Institution of those days would have been. But it was far from that Christian fraternity and generous beneficence which is often claimed for it, and which the earliest Christianity had actually displaced. It was deeply feudalized; it was no longer a really democratic institution in any strict sense of the word. Popes were the most absolute sovereigns of their day, and sometimes the most luxurious and most directly responsible for those wars which were chronic in Christendom.

We have tried to encourage students to uncover other examples in their own texts, but they find this difficult to do. The exercise above will at least induce a healthy caution about the objectivity of textbook writers, even distinguished historians.

8. An Internet marketer says that people expect informality on the Web, including "an editorial hook" which catches them right away. "People have it in their minds that a computer is more like a television than a magazine — it's a screen, and that puts them in speed mode." Ask students if they feel that composing essays on their computers is qualitatively different from composing on the typewriter or with pen and pencil. If they have never tried the typewriter or the pen, have them experiment with an assigned essay. Does the computer encourage more informality of language? If so, how do they account for it?

9. Ask students to distinguish between the terms *terrorist* and *freedom fighter*. Their definitions should be based on specific examples that clarify and exclude.

10. The use of computers has clearly influenced language, perhaps in ways that are not so benign. "When the Geeks Get Snide, Computer Slang Scoffs at Wetware (the Humans)" by Michiko Kakutani (*New York Times* 27 June 2000: C1) argues that "geek-speak is flush with disparaging or defensive references to the real world and flesh-and-blood human beings." Students can probably provide examples of her thesis and argue for or against it.

11. One writer yearns for the return of "proper letter-writing" (Tunku Varadarjan, "Spilling Words and Hitting 'Send' — Not Letter-Perfect," *Wall Street Journal* 21 Sept. 2000: A19) as opposed to instantaneous and casual e-mail. Do students feel that the language of e-mail has drawbacks as a mode of communication? Does "proper" letter-writing have a place in their lives?

12. What about names of military operations? We are mostly unaware of the importance that leaders of government attach to the naming of wartime activities. The name first suggested for the war against the Taliban was *Infinite Justice;* then, after criticism, it became *Enduring Freedom.* Churchill said names should not have "an air of despondency, they should not be frivolous and ordinary, and they should not be a target for fun." The decisions about naming offer fascinating excursions into psychology and language. See "Operation Moniker: Military Name Game," *New York Times* 13 Oct. 2001: A15.

DEBATE: DOES THE GOVERNMENT HAVE THE RIGHT TO REGULATE GUNS?

1. This pair of essays can be used to discuss all of the elements of argument, but we chose them for this unit on language because they raise important issues of definition and word choice. Burger does an excellent job of putting the Second Amendment in context. In fact, one of his points is that a portion of the wording of the amendment is often taken out of context. Burger explains the historical context in which the amendment was written and explains how different those circumstances were from the world in which Americans now try to divine the intent of the men who drafted it. McGrath has a different, but interesting, read on the wording of the amendment. One of his main points is that with the reference to the right of the people to keep and bear arms, the members of the First Congress were assuming that such a right existed and did not need to be established through legislation. They were concerned only that a God-given right not be infringed. The significance of the wording of the amendment, in context, is rich subject matter for discussion in a chapter on language and thought.

   You might also ask your students to consider the voice being used in each essay. They might be surprised that a judge could write in language so clear and free of jargon that it can be readily understood by average citizens. Burger lays out his case clearly and objectively. Students can be asked to consider the voice they hear speaking in the McGrath piece. In fact, most students, if pressed, will start to see that there is a shift in voice as the piece progresses. One way of pointing this out is to have them read the first few paragraphs and the last few and consider how the two are different.

2. If you want to go one step farther in the analysis of language in relation to this subject, you can ask your students to look for other essays on the

subject and compare the voices in those essays. Are all of those essayists as reasonable as the two represented in the text? What sorts of warrants underlie some Americans' defense of their right to own guns? What warrants underlie arguments in favor of government regulation of guns? To what extent does emotional appeal enter into the arguments? (The ad that appears immediately before the debate is a good starting point for discussion.)

3. A possible research topic is governmental control (or lack of control) of guns in other countries. How is governmental control related to the homicide rate in this country and elsewhere?

Bibliography

"Add Gun Control to Litany of Misbegotten Government Plans." *Investor's Business Daily* 29 June 2004: A15.

Etzioni, Amitai. "Reasonable Regulation." *National Law Journal* 26.31 (2004): n. pag.

Jacobs, James B., and Kimberly A. Potter. "Keeping Guns Out of the Wrong Hands: The Brady Law and the Limits of Regulation." *Journal of Criminal Law and Criminology* 86.1 (1995): 93–120.

Mondics, Chris. "Outlook for Significant Government Regulations of Guns Clouded." *Knight-Ridder/Tribune News Service* 16 May 1999: K3329.

Stell, Lance K. "The Production of Criminal Violence in America: Is Strict Gun Control the Solution? *Journal of Law, Medicine and Ethics* 32.1 (2004): 38–46.

Zimring, Franklin E. "Firearms, Violence, and the Potential Impact of Firearms Control." *Journal of Law, Medicine and Ethics* 32.1 (2004): 34–37.

PART TWO

WRITING, RESEARCHING, AND PRESENTING ARGUMENTS

INTRODUCTION

Part Two is meant to accompany all writing assignments throughout the semester. It is one thing for students to grasp the concept of a claim of fact, for example, but writing an essay in which they demonstrate their ability to communicate that understanding is quite another. Chapter 9, then, instructs students in the process of preparing a paper from the very beginning: finding a topic, defining the issues, organizing the material, considering the audience, revising, and preparing the manuscript. The discussion of each step is illuminated with examples from good writers.

Chapter 10 presents the research paper as a culmination of a course in argumentative writing. Although students in all their papers so far have been demonstrating their mastery of the elements of argument and the process of composition, the research paper will put their skills to a more demanding test. In this chapter we discuss the purposes of the research paper and the procedures for helping students to produce interesting and authoritative documents: preparing a schedule, conferring with the instructor, using the library, taking notes, organizing the paper, using a style sheet. In this chapter, too, we've provided two student research papers, one in the humanities, "When a Fairy Tale Is Not Just a Fairy Tale," and one in the sciences, "Why Zoos Should Be Eliminated." They have been annotated to show students exactly how the authors proceed in defending a claim of policy and a claim of fact.

Chapter 11 is a unit providing guidelines for oral argument. In a course that emphasizes written discourse, defending a claim before a live audience encourages awareness of the differences between speech and writing. Students must learn to accommodate both language and organization to the differing needs of listeners and readers. They already know the importance of acquiring proficiency in speech, and, despite some initial misgivings, find the speech assignments a useful and enlightening experience.

CHAPTER 9

Writing an Argumentative Paper

(text pages 373–93)

Success in teaching composition, like success in parenting, has its mysteries. Good writers and good children emerge from all kinds of environments — authoritarian, permissive, and unlikely combinations of the two. The sugges-

48

tions that follow have been tested in a wide variety of programs — from some in which an activity and an assignment were designated for each day of the semester to others in which no structure was provided and floundering was a rite of passage.

When we supervise new teaching assistants, we always advise them to teach from their strengths, which might not be the same as ours, and if necessary to adapt any suggestions for assignments and classroom management to ones with which they feel more secure. New teachers who read these ideas will, we hope, be able to make similar adjustments.

ASSIGNMENTS

Three things deserve comment: choosing a topic, preparing students for the assignment, and above all making sure that students understand the *purpose* of the assignment.

1. In helping students to choose a subject, try to mediate between structure and flexibility. Students are constrained by the objectives of the assignment, but they have plenty of choices: the suggestions in the text, new topics I might want to add to those in the text, and still others that the students themselves have chosen, based on their own interests or events that are taking place around them. It's no small dividend for us teachers that papers on many different subjects can make reading them a pleasure rather than a chore.

2. A surprising number of the writing problems students wrestle with are a result of teacher failure to prepare them for the assignment. We cannot assume that reading the material is the same as mastering it. It is worth spending at least fifteen minutes discussing the purposes of the assignment and reviewing the strategies for fulfilling them. For a definition paper, let us say, review with students the suggestions at the end of Chapter 3, making sure that they understand the distinctions between controversial terms, asking for examples of connotations and slang terms that have recently gained popularity.

3. Early in the semester, students should be introduced to the library. See the discussion on the use of the library on page 56 in these notes.

COMPOSITION: STYLE, ORGANIZATION, AND DEVELOPMENT

Not surprisingly, these are the three elements of composition where student arguments are most likely to falter. Weaknesses here can, of course, cripple the most promising ideas. The bad news is that in one semester we can do little to produce polished stylists. The good news, however, is that we *can* teach organization and development.

1. Precision and grace in writing almost always depend on a good ear, long familiarity with good writing, and association with family and friends who know how to use language — conditions over which teachers of college freshmen have little control. We have tried and sometimes seen an improvement in style as a result of sentence-combining exercises, imitation of accessible prose stylists like George Orwell, and rewriting of clumsy passages by the instructor. Our goals should be modest — clarity would be enough — but our successes will also be modest.

One of the obstacles for some students on the way to clear and straight-forward expression is their adoption of an artificial written style that has little resemblance to their own voices. The style is inflated and slightly pompous, but it seems to these writers that a language closer to colloquial speech would be inappropriate and even frivolous. Encourage these students to look closely at the prose of writers who often use one-syllable words and short sentences with strong rhetorical effect. Explain to students that simple prose is not merely an instructor's idiosyncratic preference.

A limited vocabulary, needless to say, is a serious impediment to the reading and writing of arguments. We can encourage use of a full-size desk dictionary; many college students have never consulted anything but a small paperback dictionary and are at a loss to interpret the symbols in a larger one. We can ask questions about the words in the assigned essays and insist that students look them up. We can emphasize words that student writers can usefully introduce into their own essays.

2. Organization for argumentative papers can be taught by formula, to both freshman writers and upperclassmen alike, and we need not apologize for a lack of invention. Invention resides in the choice of topic and the modes of development. Unlike the arrangement of ideas in description, which may be spatial, or in narration, which may be chronological, the arrangement of ideas in argument is logical, and has, therefore, wide application. We can try to make clear to students that the modes of organization outlined in the text are exactly the same as those they will be expected to use in their writing in the workplace or in any activities which call for reports, evaluations, and recommendations.

    If students have trouble arranging the materials of an argument, we can ask them first to establish the nature of their claims, and then to examine essays in the book that exemplify an appropriate organization. Often the first paragraph of an essay serves as an introduction to the kind of organization. Most beginning writers are glad to learn that these forms exist and are ready for use in any argument. As they gain power in using these conventional forms, they will be free to modify them — for example, withholding the main idea until the end.

3. As for development and support, we can stress this throughout the semester in every piece students read and write, pointing out varied strategies that good writers use to convince readers of the soundness of their claims.

    In introducing or summarizing the concepts of organization and development, you may want to use the blackboard. You can write down the claim or thesis statement for an argument suggested by a student — for example, "Schools should remove vending machines of unhealthful snack food" — and then ask students to suggest topic sentences for three paragraphs and the means of supporting the ideas summarized in the topic sentences. You can use this device for the three ways of organizing a claim and can make ample reference to the forms of support that are treated in Chapter 5.

    From time to time you may want to duplicate good student papers, sometimes from a previous semester, for distribution to the class and discuss the successful use of the different ways of organizing and supporting a particular argument. Duplication of less successful papers — without names — can also work if the problems are not severe and the instructor can call attention to some strengths as well.

AVOIDING PLAGIARISM

There is no foolproof way of preventing plagiarism. But a few precautions can reduce the number of incidents.

1. Make sure that students understand the nature of the offense. Many students are genuinely ignorant of the necessity for crediting sources. Review the examples in the text. Some instructors warn students at the beginning of the semester that a finding of plagiarism will result in an F for the course. Urge students to ask questions about citation if they are in doubt.

2. Keep an impromptu paper, one written on the first or second day of class, as a sample of the student's style and thinking. (I assign a short essay in class on a subject that allows students to develop a simple argument.) This paper serves primarily as a test of the skills — or lack of skills — that students bring with them. However, if a subsequent paper exhibits a radical departure in vocabulary, syntax, and development of ideas, the instructor should inquire about the differences. A few judicious questions, starting perhaps with vocabulary, will lead to an acknowledgment of help. This works best, of course, when the source is a professional writer with clearly superior skills.

3. Avoid "free" assignments. Whatever their merits, they may tempt students who have difficulty finding subjects to "borrow" papers from friends or the library.

4. Vary assignments from year to year. It's time-consuming to think of variations on previous assignments, but it should go without saying that if the same assignment is peddled year after year, some student papers will also make the rounds.

5. If your program calls for reviewing several drafts of a paper, you should be able to notice any abrupt changes in the final draft. But be prepared to find that some ambitious plagiarists aren't daunted and will manufacture drafts of another student's essay.

EVALUATION AND GRADING

1. Before assigning the first paper, it is a good idea to discuss with students the criteria for grading. As an introduction, ask them to list in order of importance the elements of composition which ought to enter into an evaluation. In some classes half of the students will head their lists with spelling, punctuation, or grammar. What is probably already obvious to them but what they are afraid to say, knowing how perverse English teachers can be, usually comes as a relief — that nobody reads an essay merely for spelling or punctuation. The criteria ought to be (1) an interesting and important idea; (2) clarity of expression; (3) adequate development; (4) clear organization; (5) correct spelling, grammar, and punctuation. In class discussion you can try to elicit the reasons for this list and the order in which the items appear. Students need to see how these criteria are justified by their claims on the reader. (If the reader of an essay can't understand what the writer is trying to say, a good outline and lots of data will be powerless to save the argument.)

2. Although the emphasis in evaluation rests on the elements of argument, we don't ignore grammar and mechanics in considering the grade. For many students, accuracy will be a hallmark of their professions. In a class of mechanical engineers to whom one of us taught writing, students were told by the engineer who directed the course that sloppy letters of applica-

tion were routinely discarded by most companies. Employers would infer that an engineer who was careless about spelling and punctuation might also be careless about specifications for a machine. In a real sense, then, matters of spelling, grammar, and punctuation are an integral part of the argument, and not only for engineers.

3. What students do read with high interest is the paragraph or two that instructors write in summing up their evaluation of the whole paper. Comments and questions in the margin are helpful but no substitute for this final evaluation, which for students represents part of the ongoing dialogue initiated by their arguments.

As an example, we reproduce here a student paper followed by the sort of evaluation one of us would write. The essay is above average in style, freedom from mechanical errors, organization, and attention to development. But it is weakened by flaws that are typical of many good student arguments. Here is the essay:

The New Drinking Laws: A Sour Taste

All I wanted was an Amaretto sour. To get it, I had to have the little black stamp on the back of my hand that told the bartender I was at least twenty-one. I was only twenty and a half. So there I sat at a North Carolina nightspot with my brother and his girlfriend Debbie, sipping a soda. Six months made the difference between a watery Coke and a taste of liquor.

Debbie had a solution. She led me back to the ladies' room, licked the black stamp on the back of her hand, and pressed it onto my hand. It was light, so I darkened it with black eyeliner.

"It's backwards, but they won't notice," Debbie assured me. "It's dark in here."

Well, the bartender did notice, and I didn't get the Amaretto sour. "This is a fake," he said. "You have to come with me." He walked around to my side of the bar, grabbed my arm, and led me to a small office at the front of the bar. There, he took a bottle of rubbing alcohol out of the desk, wet a piece of cotton with it, and wiped the stamp from my hand. "Now get out of here," he said.

At first, I wanted to cry. But as I walked to the car with Debbie and Grant, I became angry. I was a responsible person, and I had never taken a drink and gotten behind the wheel. I rarely had more than two drinks at a time. Sure, I had skirted the law, but the law was unfair.

Now young people across the country are getting a taste of that unfairness. Under pressure from special-interest groups and a federal government that has threatened to take away their highway funds, every state in the country has raised the legal age for buying and drinking alcohol to twenty-one. I argue that, in raising the drinking age, states have violated the rights of a large group of people. Further, I believe that increasing the age is not the best way to deter drunken driving and reduce traffic fatalities.

Supporters of the current drinking laws question the ability of eighteen-year-olds to drink responsibly. These people need to take a look at the other responsibilities that rest with eighteen-year-olds now. Under United States law, an eighteen-year-old can vote, go to war, get married, and have a family, but cannot legally enjoy a beer. The implication is that people who are under the age of twenty-one are mature enough to assume the responsibilities of adulthood but are not responsible enough to enjoy its pleasures. I find this judgment arbitrary and unfair. Once we have decided what the age of majority should be (and we seem to have decided on the age of eighteen for most activities) we should apply that standard uniformly.

Other supporters of new laws argue that when drinking ages go up, traffic fatalities go down. In fact, studies *have* indicated that in states where the drinking age has been increased, fatalities have dropped by as much as 10 percent. This is good news, but it does not prove that the new drinking laws are entirely responsible for the drop in traffic fatalities. Tougher drunk driving laws and stepped-up efforts to educate the public about the dangers of drinking and driving could also have been major factors in the drop in fatalities.

In the last several years, drunk driving laws and penalties have been made tougher throughout the nation. That is good: Rigorous enforcement of these laws is what we need. Also, education is always a positive force. The better the general public understands the damage that irresponsible drinking can do to individuals and society, the better off everyone will be. There are problem drinkers in all age groups. The law should go after them instead of using an arbitrary age limit that restricts the rights of citizens.

Finally, I do not believe that the higher drinking age will deter people under the age of twenty-one from drinking. Those under the legal age have always found ways to skirt the law and get their hands on alcohol, and they will continue to do so. The quest for the pleasure of intoxication is part of our nature. Restricting the supply of alcohol might make it harder for eighteen-year-olds to get, but it will not make it less desirable.

I wasn't deterred from drinking the night that I got kicked out of that bar in North Carolina. After leaving there, we drove a few miles down the road to another bar, and my brother bought me my Amaretto sour. It might have been more satisfying had it been legal.

The written evaluation would say:

I think this is a hard claim to defend, but you've handled several things very well. The organization is tight, and you make excellent transitions between ideas. I liked the introduction; it's a lively, well-told personal anecdote, and your reference to it at the end makes clear that it was an integral part of your argument. Even more important, in the body of your argument you offer other kinds of support: an appeal to fairness and data about drinking and driving.

But some changes and additions might have made your argument even stronger. (1) You are probably right that the laws alone have not been responsible for the big drop in alcohol-related deaths — among fifteen- to nineteen-year-olds they have plunged from a peak of 6,281 in 1982 to 2,170 in 1988 — but most experts agree that the laws are at least partly responsible. So you would have to argue that the death rate won't rise if the drinking age is lowered. Can you find data and expert opinion to support that view? You say you are a responsible driver — good point — but are you typical? (2) The analogy with other rights granted to eighteen-year-olds is somewhat shaky. Couldn't someone argue that granting those rights to teenagers was a mistake and that we should raise the ages for all the activities you cite? There's nothing special about age eighteen that guarantees maturity. After all, most eighteen-year-olds don't vote, most marriages at eighteen aren't notably successful, and as soldiers in the army, eighteen-year-olds are under strict supervision. (3) Finally, I wonder who your audience is. Are you writing for adults who might be persuaded to change the laws? I'm not sure that your attempts to evade the law would convince them that you are mature and responsible, or that pleading for the "pleasure of intoxication" — at a time when drinking by young people is declining, for good reasons — will be very persuasive. If you like, we can talk more about this in conference, and I can show you the sources of my data.

B

PEER EVALUATION

Peer review is less useful in argumentation courses than in courses that emphasize other modes of discourse. That is because the student reviewer often lacks sufficient knowledge of the subject of the argument to make informed comment. An example: A student writing about prisons had taken all his data from a *Time* magazine article of about fifteen years ago. The paper was well written, but the student reading it had no way of knowing that the data had changed so greatly that the claims were no longer valid. If instructors want to give students practice in evaluating arguments of classmates — a potentially valuable exercise — they are well advised, I think, to limit the areas on which the critic is asked to comment.

It's true, of course, that instructors can also be ignorant of areas of knowledge investigated by a student writer. But most of us have sufficient experience as laborers in various fields of scholarship to know which questions to ask.

CONFERENCES

Some programs mandate a specific number of conferences during the semester. Some even prescribe the amount of time to be spent. One guide for teachers calls for an initial conference of two minutes! Other syllabi leave the number of conferences to the instructor. But why conferences at all?

1. One teacher of composition in a prestigious university says frankly that his function in a conference is to rewrite the student's paper, explaining the point of his revision as he goes. In fact, such an extreme strategy may work in some cases — if the student is alive to nuances of vocabulary and tone and can understand and accept the changes, if he or she learns by imitation, and if he or she has sufficient confidence to take issue with some of the teacher's revisions. Most of us, however, see the conference at its best as a dialogue or a conversation which either the teacher or the student may initiate.

   Arguments, we have told our students, are implicit dialogues, and a conference represents not only our opportunity to respond at greater length to the student's argument but the student's opportunity to respond to *us* —to the written comments, for example — and to talk about the process of composition. As the students articulate their theses, answering our questions and explaining what they tried to do and why they chose to do it this way, some things may become clear that remained opaque when they were engaged in a monologue. Conferences can also function as mini-workshops for two, three, or four students who share a composition problem or have argued the same subject with varying degrees of success.

2. In part, conferences also function as a kinder, gentler substitute for written comments. One instructor wrote, "Think More!" across the top of a student paper. It might be harder to give such peremptory and humiliating advice in person.

Poor writers, although they may come reluctantly to conference, may profit most from these sessions. They may be unwilling to pay the necessary attention to largely negative written comments, but in conference they must confront them, and the comments can be prefaced, softened, and modified to accommodate a vulnerable human presence. These students may also be more articulate in speech than in writing and better able to assist the instructor by giving a clearer sense of what they really wanted to argue.

3. Finally, conferences allow student and teacher to look at mechanical errors and their corrections in a different way. Corrections on the student essay of spelling, grammar, and punctuation errors don't always produce improvement; many students won't — or can't — read them. And a multitude of correction results in a trail of red ink that signifies a disaster. A conference has the virtue of allowing you to ask questions, listen to answers, offer explanations, and, most of all, point out with pencil and finger the things that need change. For such problems a small physical demonstration has an impact that the written correction does not.

CHAPTER 10
Researching an Argumentative Paper
(text pages 394–465)

Unlike many courses in the upper classes, in which the only writing may be an examination and a research paper, our course requires writing from the very first week of class, and students practice research skills at some level throughout the semester. The research paper serves not to introduce but to bring together in a more ambitious exercise the principal elements of argument. But it is only one among many papers.

The purposes of the research paper are twofold: (1) mastering a long paper — perhaps three times longer than any of the weekly writing students have done so far — with its special and more demanding problems of organization; (2) learning how to substantiate more extensive claims of fact, value, and policy that require the data and authoritative opinion the writer cannot supply — in other words, more practice in organization and development.

New teachers who are introducing the research paper for the first time may find suggestions in the following outline that can be adapted to their particular programs.

1. Assign a fast reading of Chapter 10. Take ten or fifteen minutes to turn pages with students, pointing out what they will find and which parts deserve a slightly longer glance. For example, they should read the sample papers with care; for this reading, however, they can skip the MLA and APA style sheets.

   At the next class go over the important parts of the chapter. Concentrate on the tasks that must be accomplished first. Encourage questions. Reassure students that the assignment is not so daunting as they think it is. It might even be fun, and you are ready to help.

2. In class discuss finding a topic. The commonly quoted advice to graduate students about to embark on a dissertation still holds good: Choose some-

thing that really interests you, because you'll have to live with it for a while.

The first and most obvious source of subjects will be in "Multiple Viewpoints," Part Three of the text. Topics are suggested for each chapter, but students may think of others that interest them more. Other subjects may be found in personal experience, at home and at school, and in the neighborhood, in town, or on campus.

3. Work out a schedule for the project. Freshman students need help in managing time, and they are grateful for a structure that defines their responsibilities. We favor making the time available for the research paper no longer than a month. (We've found that allowing more time for research and writing doesn't produce better papers.) Set deadlines for specific stages of the project:

   a. The choice of topic
   b. A briefly annotated list of five sources examined in the first week or ten days. Two of the items may be taken from "Multiple Viewpoints," the other three from other sources. (All of these may not appear in the final bibliography, but they represent a start.)
   c. The final paper

4. Announce the availability of conferences with the instructor at any point during the research and writing. Early in the project we schedule one conference with each student. Later conferences can be based on individual need. Some students will have trouble refining and narrowing the topic. Others will need help finding sources. And still others will encounter problems in organizing and in using the sources appropriately.

5. While students work on their research papers outside of class, you can ask for short papers, sometimes in class, which introduce an idea or present a piece of evidence that is part of the longer paper. Some papers will suggest the need for conference. If not, papers should be returned promptly with comments relevant to the research paper. Needless to say, attention to the ongoing process of the paper should also make plagiarism more difficult.

6. Unless you anticipate and address the problem, some students, drunk with their newly acquired knowledge of the research tool, will produce a series of quotations, sometimes as many as twenty in a six-page paper, tightly strung together like a well-made necklace, with nothing visible between the pearls. This is *not* a research paper. We need to make clear to students that *they* are the authors and that the materials derived from other sources must be used *only* to support their claims. We should emphasize that too much research material can be as fatal as too little. "When a Fairy Tale Is Not Just a Fairy Tale" and "Why Zoos Should Be Eliminated" give students models for the intelligent use of quotations.

USE OF THE LIBRARY

At schools with large libraries it's not uncommon to discover that even by the end of the first semester, freshman students will not have visited the library unless assigned to do so. Big libraries can be intimidating, but a guided tour can reinforce the idea that the library is a friend, not an enemy. *The library tour should take place early in the semester, not at research paper time.* In this course students should begin to use the resources of the library at once, as they tackle the very first paper on defending a claim of fact.

Librarians are usually more than willing to cooperate in helping students to become familiar with library resources, and they can offer helpful experience to new instructors. Try turning to the librarians first and trying to accommodate their recommendations to the purposes of the course. Here are a few suggestions based on trial and error with our own classes.

1. A tour in which twenty students follow the librarian as he or she points out library services seldom works. The students in the back can't hear, and they lose interest. Even those near the speaker will not remember a couple of weeks later exactly what they learned. At most the librarian or the instructor can walk the students through some of the areas where they are likely to be busiest — the card catalog or computerized catalog, the indexes, the major reference works, the microfiche collection.

2. Prepare students for the visit. Go over the material in the book, offering additional information about the sources. Anecdotes about your own experience with research can enliven an apparently lifeless subject.

3. Students will remember much more about the library if they arrive with specific questions. One way to produce questions that will lead to a wide range of answers is to divide the class into three sections: humanities, social sciences, and natural and physical sciences. Each section meets and arrives at a research paper topic in its field; each student in that section then prepares a specific question on the topic. (Some of the questions will be weak, but the librarian can often ask the right questions of the student and elicit a nice rephrasing.) The students assemble with the librarian in a room with a blackboard or a computer where he or she can answer students' questions by writing down or calling up the names of the materials and their locations.

4. Use student resources. Some students in the class will be more proficient than others in unraveling the mysteries of the library, and they are often pleased and proud to be asked to accompany the others and point out how and where to look.

CHAPTER 11
Presenting an Argument Orally
(text pages 466–80)

1. An introduction to speeches by the class might include a student guest speaker whose argument can be evaluated in a class discussion following the speech. Criticism should be based on criteria laid out in Chapter 11. The speaker need not be perfect but should demonstrate abilities against which students in the class can measure their own. An outside speaker allows students to offer a frank evaluation, which they are sometimes reluctant to do openly for a classmate. In many schools with debate clubs and speech or drama departments, instructors can find willing candidates for the role of guest speaker. The instructor should suggest the kind of speech that fulfills the objectives of the speech unit, preferably a claim of policy that will include both facts and values.

2. Students can fill out an evaluation form for each speech, briefly commenting on the main elements. (You can make copies of a simple form with spaces for comment.) Before turning the evaluations over to the speakers,

you can read them to make sure that they are serious and respectful and then remove the names of the critics.

3. When guest speakers appear to address either the whole school or an organization on campus, you can sometimes assign attendance for the class. As with the speeches in their own class, students can fill out evaluation forms. The objectives of any speech unit should, of course, include not only proficiency in delivering a speech, but the critical ability to evaluate an oral argument.

4. "Words Go Right to the Brain, But Can They Stir the Heart?: Some Say Popular Software Debases Public Speaking" discusses the influence of software on oral presentation, especially in business. (*New York Times* 17 Apr. 1999: A17.) Some critics think that PowerPoint and other software presentation aids "contribute to the debasement of rhetoric." A professor of communication asks us to imagine Martin Luther King Jr.'s "I Have a Dream" speech with PowerPoint.

But Stephen Pinker, professor of cognitive science and the author of *The Language Instinct* (Morrow, 1994), argues that human beings are visual creatures. "If anything," he says, "PowerPoint, if used well, would ideally reflect the way we think." Pinker served on a committee at Massachusetts Institute of Technology that "updat[ed] the traditional writing requirement to include both speech and graphic communication."

PART THREE

MULTIPLE VIEWPOINTS

INTRODUCTION (text page 482)

1. The debates, articles, and letters in this section represent the argumentative process in its clearest and most understandable form. If throughout the semester we have emphasized that arguments are dialogues, the selections given here will show students how the dialogues work, that is, how people on opposing sides actually respond to each other, whether well or poorly. Where it is clear that the response is not direct, that there is no clash, the debates can be equally instructive.

2. "Multiple Viewpoints" may be used as a discrete unit or as a source of materials for assignments in the text.

   a. If it is used as a self-contained unit, the introduction and the questions that precede it suggest a number of ways of examining the material and writing about it.

   b. "Multiple Viewpoints" also lends itself to use as a source of data, expert opinion, motivational appeals, warrants, and ethical and unethical use of language. In fulfilling assignments that call for supporting materials, students may find material here, either as a substitute for or in addition to library research. In several places in these notes we have suggested assignments that give students the opportunity to look for support for their claims among the selections in "Multiple Viewpoints."

   c. In addition, as pointed out earlier, "Multiple Viewpoints" can furnish the material for a research paper. Longer papers may require supplementary library research, but there is probably sufficient material in each section for a paper of six to seven pages.

3. Some of these subjects will be more effective than others for a given group of students, depending on their experience with and knowledge of the subject. "Are Limits on Freedom of Speech Ever Justified?," for example, may be more interesting for students in schools where a speech code is being debated or where it has resulted in punishment for infraction.

   When time does not permit using all the subjects, we choose the most provocative ones, those that will produce, as far as we can tell, the liveliest feelings, both for and against.

4. Given the timeliness of these subjects, research to discover whether changes have occurred since the articles and letters in the book were written will be indispensable. Students must be encouraged to read at least one full-coverage daily newspaper, watch TV newscasts and special reports, and listen to radio programs like *Talk of the Nation* (NPR). *Talk of the Nation* has covered every topic in Part Three of this book and a good many other subjects as well. Surveys show that most college students don't read news-

papers or listen to TV newscasts. Some of them do, however, read *Time* or *Newsweek* or *U.S. News & World Report.* These students can be asked to report to the class on the ways in which the same stories are treated in different news magazines.

5. An enormously productive unit may be organized around formal class-room debate. Although debate is almost always an oral exercise, there is plenty of opportunity in a writing class for students to commit their outlines to paper, develop major points that cannot be adequately treated in the five minutes allotted to oral presentation, and make extended critiques of the debates of their classmates.

    Each debate usually requires four people, two on the affirmative side, two on the negative, although the Lincoln–Douglas format — one debater on each side — is also possible. If time does not permit a round of formal debates, the class may choose four or five debate subjects, with each team producing an argument that will be duplicated or read aloud for consideration by the whole class. This organization reduces the arguments to one on each side and eliminates rebuttal time. After reading or hearing the arguments, the class may write evaluations based on answers to the questions on the debate sheet.

    For supporting materials students should confine themselves to the data in this section. Their efforts will involve extracting the relevant issues and organizing them in a succinct and understandable way. They may also, of course, need to do further research for more recent data.

DEBATE

Debate may be considered an extension of the problem-solving analysis. The debaters are considering the merits of a solution to some problem, for example, a plan to restrict government agencies in their investigations of private citizens.

The debate proposition is always a two-sided question; it can be answered yes or no.

The proposition is worded so that the affirmative (yes) side will be arguing for a change in policy, or, in the case of value questions, a new idea. (The argument that violence is justified in civil rights cases is an example of the latter.) Because the affirmative is arguing for a change, they are said to have the *burden of proof,* while the negative has only to defend the status quo.

The affirmative argument usually centers around three *stock issues* that grow out of the problem-solving analysis. The affirmative will argue

1. that there is a need for a change;
2. that their proposal will meet the need;
3. that their proposal is the best solution to the problem. These stock issues are referred to as need, plan, and advantages.

The negative may answer the affirmative case in a number of ways.

1. They may *debate* every issue. "There is no problem, and even if there were, your plan is expensive, inefficient, and undesirable."
2. They may *waive* an issue. "Yes, indeed, we agree there is a serious problem, but your proposed solution is useless."

3. They may propose a *counterplan.* "Things are bad all right, but I have a better idea for improving them than yours." Tournament debaters do not do this too often for strategic reasons: It means the negative must assume part of the burden of proof.

Following are some questions you might consider as you listen to a debate:

1. How important is definition of terms? Does it become an issue in the debate?

2. Does the negative attack the affirmative argument on every point, or does the debate narrow to one or two issues?

3. Do the speakers base their arguments on any generally accepted principles or values, such as justice, individual freedom, constitutional guarantees?

4. Do you find examples of causal argument, argument from example, or argument from analogy?

5. How important is evidence in the debate? Do the speakers question the credibility of each other's sources? To what extent, if any, does the argument center around evidence?

6. What comments would you make on the speakers' oral presentation (delivery)?

7. Which side do you think won, and why?

CHAPTER 12

How Far Will We Go to Change Our Body Image?

(text pages 483–513)

1. One way to begin the discussion of body image is to ask students to bring in advertisements that suggest how our society perceives the human body. How are images of the body used to sell products? What sorts of products? What audiences are the ads appealing to? What do the ads suggest about what our society values?

    One starting point for this discussion is the Metalmoto ad, which uses an image of the muscular body of an African American male to sell a product that has nothing to do with the physical appearance of its user. One question for students to consider is why the designers of this ad chose to hint at our nation's heritage of slavery by presenting this black male torso with jewelry that is reminiscent of chains. Can this ad be linked in any way (or contrasted with) the Samuels essay?

2. Many of your students will know someone who has or may have an eating disorder. Some may have eating disorders themselves. Ask your students to consider the relationships between and among the images of the human body presented in ads, on television, and in the movies and the average human body. There is also recent evidence that your students could find that suggests that more men are developing eating disorders. Kita's and Spiker's essays support the idea that it is not only women who

are concerned about body image. Samuels points out that African Americans are starting to overcome an earlier taboo against plastic surgery that could be seen as an attempt to remove ethnic markers. That notion can be contrasted with the attempt of some of the famous to do exactly that.

3. Students could also look in magazines or online for pictures that support Cullen's claim that it is the poor in America who are overweight because of the unhealthy diet they eat. The evidence students find could be presented in the form of a collage or a PowerPoint presentation.

4. A fascinating topic for research is how advertisements have changed over the years to reflect how body image has been perceived differently in different time periods. (Savacool's article in the bibliography below could be a starting point.) The same is true in the world of fine arts. How have artists defined beauty differently over the centuries?

5. The emphasis in the readings is on *changing* body image through surgery and other means. A rash of television shows in the opening years of the twenty-first century have promised to remake the ugly ducklings of the world. One show's producers even chose to draw on the story of the ugly duckling by calling it *The Swan*. Another interesting topic for research is how those people's lives were changed as a result of their makeovers. A search of a database such as *InfoTrac* or a search engine such as *Google* will lead to articles about their lives after their appearance on these shows. What does a willingness to undergo such change suggest about values?

6. If you are interested in incorporating brief literary pieces on the subject of body image, two excellent choices are "Barbie Doll," a poem by Marge Piercy, and "Barbie-Q," a short story by Sandra Cisneros.

7. With each new advance in the manipulation of human genes, we come closer to the day when parents may be able to predetermine their children's appearance. Possible essay topics on this issue range from a claim-of-fact paper explaining what is now possible and how close scientists are to controlling physical appearance to a claim-of-policy paper on whether such tampering with human development should be allowed.

Bibliography

Kuther, Tara L., and Erin McDonald. "Early Adolescents' Experiences with, and Views of, Barbie." *Adolescence* 39.153 (2004): 39–52.

"Male Eating Disorders Rise amid More Focus on Body Image, Experts Say." *America's Intelligence Wire* 11 May 2004: n. pag.

Pleasant, Lesley. Rev. of *Looking Good: College Women and Body Image, 1875–1930*, by Margaret A. Lowe. *Iris: A Journal About Women* Spring–Summer 2004: 86.

Savacool, Julia. "Women's Ideal Bodies Then and Now." *Marie Claire* Apr. 2004: 102–07.

Wulff, Jennifer. "Pressure To Be Perfect." *People Weekly* 26 July 2004: 72.

CHAPTER 13
How Has Terrorism Affected the American Idea of Justice?
(text pages 514–56)

1. We include in this chapter all or part of two documents that your students almost certainly have heard of but probably have never read: the Geneva Convention and the Patriot Act. Reading the primary sources will aid them in understanding the arguments being made in the essays about the effects that terrorism has had on our justice system and our concept of justice in the broadest sense. The rules for the treatment of prisoners of war that grew out of the Geneva Convention have long been the accepted standard. We like to think that we as Americans are among those who follow the rules, that we are above the sort of atrocities carried out under Adolf Hitler or Saddam Hussein. A small number of the military personnel who represented us in Iraq were clearly not, and the whole Abu Ghraib prisoner abuse scandal brought into question how many others, high up in the chain of command, were willing to consider rewriting the rule book on the treatment of prisoners when those prisoners might be linked to terrorist attacks on American soil.

2. If your students have read Michael Levin's "A Case for Torture" in Chapter 6, they may have already considered whether torture is ever justified as a means of gaining information that could save lives. If not, you might want to link it to this unit. One defense offered by those who abused prisoners at Abu Ghraib was that their superiors encouraged them to do whatever was necessary to get information out of the prisoners.

3. Ehrenreich's essay "What Abu Ghraib Taught Me" expresses a feminist's disappointment that after women fought so hard for the right to serve in the military, some few dishonored other women in uniform. You might ask your students to consider Ehrenreich's piece in conjunction with Part Four's "The Crisis" by Carrie Chapman Catt, which applauds how service in time of war brought out the best in European women in World War I.

4. The pieces related to the Patriot Act are designed to let your students see multiple viewpoints on the issue. One way to begin the unit is by having students read the passage from the act themselves and speculate on what impact it could have on their lives. You might then have them consider the same question again after having read the other three pieces related to the act. By then they might be ready to support a claim of value or claim of policy regarding the potential threat the act poses to the rights of Americans and how that threat compares to the potential threat of terrorism.

5. The pieces by Amon and Kent look at how justice at home in America has been affected by terrorism. Your students could synthesize what they learn from these two essays and perhaps what they learn from other sources that they find to draw some conclusions about how terrorism has affected our American system of justice.

Bibliography

Goldstone, Richard J. "International Law and Justice and America's War on Terrorism." *Social Research* 6.4 (2002): 1045–55.

Ignatieff, Michael. "What Geneva Conventions?" Rev. of *Chain of Command: The Road from 9/11 to Abu Ghraib*, by Seymour M. Hersh. *New York Times Book Review* 17 Oct. 2004: 13.

Neumeister, Larry. "At Close of Prosecution Case in New York Terrorism Trial, References to bin Laden, Sept. 11." *America's Intelligence Wire* 8 Oct. 2004: n. pag.

Slaughter, Anne-Marie. "Terrorism and Justice." *Financial Times* 12 Oct. 2001: 23.

"Terrorism and Justice." *New York Times* 12 Dec. 2001: A30.

CHAPTER 14

What Is the Future of the Family?

(text pages 557–79)

1. Members of the class should be reassured that this examination of family life in America is not a foray into the personal lives of students. Although privacy may no longer be a primary value for many young people, students should be free to exclude autobiography from their analyses or to disguise their roles.

2. A story in the *New York Times* (4 Nov. 2001) makes clear that the events of September 11 had profound effects on families — not only nuclear families but extended families and even families not defined by biology but by relationships in work and leisure. As the nuclear family shrinks, Americans find that family is for millions of them "a network of connections": neighborhood friends, roommates, fraternity brothers, coworkers and clients, after-work pals. Many students can probably identify with the definition of such extended families and describe and analyze them. What are the advantages of these artificial families? Are there any drawbacks to arrangements that substitute for the biological family?

3. Students are surely aware of great differences between the values and behavior of their own generation and those of their grandparents'. What important differences can they uncover? Do they understand the cultural context from which those values emerged? Which of those beliefs and practices are worth preserving?

4. In most classes there will be students whose family values reflect a culture different from that of the country in which they now live. There are plenty of practices and rituals to debate, some of which even have run afoul of American law: dating and sex, marriage outside the cultural family, patriarchical authority, years of schooling, religion. They offer a rich field for informed argument if students are willing to speak or write about them.

Bibliography

"At Last, Good News on the Family (Probably)." *The Economist* 28 July 2001: 29.

Elkind, David. *Ties That Stress: The New Family Inheritance.* Cambridge, MA: Harvard UP, 1994.

Finn, Chester E., Jr. "Can Parents Be Trusted?" *Commentary* Sept. 1999: 49–52. "Self-absorbed and/or workaholic adults . . . try to compensate for their many absences by indulging their children."

Gottlieb, Beatrice. *The Family in the Western World from the Black Death to the Industrial Age.* New York: Oxford UP, 1993.

Waite, Linda J., and Maggie Gallagher. *The Case for Marriage: Why Married People Are Happier, Healthier, and Better Off Financially.* New York: Doubleday, 2000.

Wallerstein, Judith, Julia Lewis, and Sandra Blakeslee. *The Unexpected Legacy of Divorce.* New York: Hyperion, 2000. "Reminds us that it takes a toll on children that adults may not want to acknowledge."

(See also Peter D. Kramer, "Divorce and Our National Values," in Chapter 7.)

CHAPTER 15

Are Limits on Freedom of Speech Ever Justified?

(text pages 580–98)

1. Freedom of speech on campus and on the Internet may be of most relevance to students, especially if there have been incidents of abusive language at their own schools and censorship of material on school-based Web sites. Students ought to examine any policy statements on their own campuses that define *racism, sexism,* or *homophobia* and threaten punishment for their expression. If examples don't exist or are difficult to find, students can be encouraged to supply them. As they do so, they should keep in mind that some schools have been forced to modify their guidelines after courts have ruled that strict speech codes violated the First Amendment.

   Arguers may find themselves walking a narrow line between truth and offense. Students should consider this question: If the truth is offensive to some groups, should it nevertheless be expressed? The issue is complicated by the very nature of the academic purpose, which is usually defined as freedom in the search for truth. And there is another question: Do people have a right to express their feelings even if the expression is morally repugnant? Overtly racist speech or arguments that attempt to prove the superiority of the white race and the inferiority of all others can still be encountered in books and on the Internet. See J. Philippe Rushton, *Race, Evolution, and Behavior: A Life History Perspective* (Port Huron, MI, Charles Darwin Research Institute, 2000). This book, by a professor of psychology at the University of Western Ontario, argues for the superiority of "Orientals" and "whites" in intelligence and other vaguely defined characteristics, such as personality. Ask students to defend or attack the proposition that Rushton, who lectures widely, should be allowed to expound his views at a school assembly.

At the University of Massachusetts a new speech code proposal ensured freedom from harassment based on race, color, national or ethnic origin, gender, sexual orientation, age, religion, marital status, military service status, and disability. The Graduate Employees Organization wanted the policy extended to include citizenship, culture, HIV status, language, parental status, political affiliation or belief, and pregnancy status. A number of faculty members protested the expansion of "protected categories" as a serious impediment to free discussion of social issues in the classroom.

2. Is freedom of speech on campus different from freedom of speech on the street? The president of Emory University argues that free speech doesn't protect "vicious epithets," because universities are places where "the habits and manners of our civil society" are passed on to the next generation. But on the street there may be different rules. In New York State the highest court ruled that abusive speech was protected under federal and state constitutional guarantees of free speech. The case arose when a woman and her son, both mentally retarded, were verbally harassed by a neighbor.

   In February 1998 nine teenagers in a Miami high school went to jail for publishing and circulating a pamphlet, "First Amendment Rights," which included a veiled death threat to the black principal, racist comments, and obscene cartoons. (*New York Times,* 4 March, 1998: A25.) The Miami American Civil Liberties Union defended the students, terming the pamphlet "a satire . . . in terms you hear on late-night stand-up comedy." The deputy superintendent of schools argued that "free speech doesn't give anyone the right to use a word that would inflame."

   The newspaper article points out: "While the US Supreme Court has upheld students' right to political expression, it has also permitted school officials to censor student newspapers and to discipline a student who made suggestive comments in a speech."

   Discuss with the class the limits to free speech in publications written and distributed by students.

   Revisionist history has emerged as a new and troubling issue. It expresses itself not only in denial of the Holocaust but in new interpretations of ancient history. Students, of course, will not find it easy to marshal and examine all the facts in these debates, but they can attempt to assess the advantages and disadvantages of an academic freedom which gives college instructors the right to espouse *any* theory. (This freedom might also encompass the right to teach creationism.) Are there just and reasonable limits to such freedom?

   In January 2001 an appeals court in Pennsylvania ruled that a school district's antiharassment policy violated First Amendment rights of free speech. The policy prohibited "jokes, name-calling, graffiti, innuendo, making fun of a student's clothing, social skills, or surname." The ruling was a response to a lawsuit by two students who feared they would be punished for expressing their religious belief that homosexuality is a sin. If asked to defend or attack the appeals court ruling, how would students define the kind of speech that should be punished?

3. The reference to lyrics in popular music should be of special interest to students. They will almost certainly know some of the offensive lyrics that

have provoked their parents. Is labeling of albums a denial of free speech, a form of censorship? A distinction can be made between censure and censorship, a distinction often ignored in the debate over works of art considered offensive. Students can offer examples that clarify the definitions of these terms.

In the wake of the terrorist attack on September 11, 2001, some radio executives asked program directors not to broadcast certain songs which might be "taken the wrong way," for example, "When You're Falling" by Peter Gabriel. Other executives feared that such action heralded the suppression of free speech in popular music. Is the decision to honor the request a dangerous precedent or a responsible action demanded by a nation at war?

4. In 1996 Congress passed the Communications Decency Act, which forbade distribution of indecent material to minors on the Internet. But in 1999 the ban was ruled unconstitutional by the Supreme Court. Senator John McCain sponsored a bill to require antipornography filters on computers in schools and libraries that might receive federal funds for Internet hookups.

Ask students how they would respond to this kind of censorship. Is it feasible? Is there a better way to control children's access to obscene material on the Internet?

Thousands of underground high school newspapers are now on the Web. To what extent should school authorities be permitted to control or censor them? "Of greater concern," says a newspaper report, "are the Web sites created by students at home to post threats against or mock the teachers." A problem arises, says the deputy chief counsel for the Pennsylvania School Boards Administration, "if students are openly spilling hatred or contemplating violence against the staff." (*New York Times* 7 June 2001: E6.)

5. What about terrorists on the Web? Guerrilla groups now use the Internet to disseminate propaganda and plan attacks. Should they be controlled or censored? Or would this violate their rights to freedom of speech? See "Terrorists on the Web: Electronic 'Safe Haven,'" *U.S. News & World Report* 22 June 1998: 46.

Bibliography

Coles, Robert. "Safety Lessons for the Internet." *New York Times* 11 Oct. 1997: A23. Asks for some legal protection for children from pornography on the Internet.

Hanna, Judith Lynne, "Wrapping Nudity in a Cloak of Law." *New York Times* 29 July 2001: E14.

Hentoff, Nat. *Living the Bill of Rights: How to Be an Authentic American.* New York: HarperCollins, 1998.

Tribe, Laurence H. "The Internet vs. The First Amendment." *New York Times* 28 Apr. 1999: A27. The lessons of Littleton, Colorado: "It would be a mistake to think that good surveillance or control [of the Internet] can play an important role in preventing violent crimes."

CHAPTER 16

What Threats to Privacy Exist in the Information Age?

(text pages 599–628)

1. Students and other adolescents are passionately protective of some private matters and just as passionately dismissive of others — eager, in fact, to share them. Ask students to examine their own hierarchies of privacy: personal health, family conflicts, ambitions, secret loves, wealth, sorrows, etc. We know that many people choose to reveal these things and more to millions of television viewers. How would students characterize the needs and values that determine whether we divulge our secrets?

2. A clinical social worker, author of *Private Matters: In Defense of the Personal Life* (Addison-Wesley, 1997), writes about the expressions of grief in Littleton, Colorado:

   By far the most upsetting current manifestations of television as witness are the news and talk shows that for the past few days have encouraged Columbine students to describe their traumas on the air. What are we to make of these public de-briefings of heart-rending sorrow?

   Ask students to write an analysis of the reasons for the confessions. Should the grief-stricken survivors think of TV as a loving friend? (See Janna Malamud Smith, "Telling Our Terrible Stories to the Tube," *New York Times* 25 Apr. 1999: Wk. 17.)

3. From the *New York Times* 21 Apr. 1999: A20:

   A study by the Federal Trade Commission concluded last June that 89 percent of children's [Web] sites surveyed collected personal information from children and that few of the sites had tried to provide for meaningful parental involvement in the process. The study found that only 23 percent of the sites even tell children to seek parental permission before providing personal information. . . .

   Ask if students have ever responded to such requests. If so, do they feel that some confidence was abused? Should government attempt to regulate these exchanges?

4. One writer thinks that a telephone call has become an intrusion. After all, e-mail, he says, "would be so much neater, more considerate, more respectful of privacy." A question for students that might lead to an evaluative essay: What different purposes are served by different forms of communication, such as the letter, personal contact, the telephone, and e-mail?

5. What about gossip? Is it good or bad? S. T. Karnick thinks gossip is a benign form of social control that helps to enforce proper behavior. "Thus a person who wants to be well-regarded must watch everything he does, lest his friends, relatives, co-workers or neighbors decide to seek other company." ("In Praise of Gossip," *American Outlook* Summer 1998: 2+.) What about gossip on the Internet? Is that different from the way in which information used to travel on the old-fashioned grapevine?

6. Is peer grading an improper release of educational records? Some parents in Oklahoma thought so and sued the school board in 2001 for violating the Buckley Amendment, "a federal education law intended to protect the privacy of students' records." Children in the Oklahoma classrooms had been required to call out the grades for the teacher to enter in a grade book. Ask students to consider the issues before revealing that the US Supreme Court in February 2002 decided that such classroom revelations did not constitute a violation of privacy.

7. Students may be interested in exploring the changing views of privacy in our history and uncovering the ways in which privacy has not only survived but flourished. In "The Re-invention of Privacy" (*The Atlantic Monthly* Mar. 2001: 27+) the author argues that contrary to the opinion that technology is the enemy of privacy, perhaps the opposite is true. He mentions writing, reading, the wristwatch, the mirror, the gummed envelope, the telephone, the automobile, television, and radio as inventions that promoted and protected privacy.

Bibliography

"The End of Privacy." *The Economist* 1 May 1999: 21–23.

Etzioni, Amitai. "Privacy Isn't Dead Yet." *New York Times* 6 Apr. 1999: A27. "We should have laws that protect all personal data, not just some."

O'Rourke, P. J. "The Rights of Digital Man." *The American Spectator* Sept./ Oct. 2001: 38.

Powers, Richard. "Losing Our Souls, Bit by Bit." *New York Times* 15 July 1998: A23.

Rosen, Jeffrey. "A Watchful State." *New York Times Magazine* 7 Oct. 2001: 38–43. The British experience with surveillance. The author decides that "cameras are not consistent with the values of an open society."

Shapiro, Andrew L. "Privacy for Sale: Peddling 'The Internet.'" *The Nation* 23 June 1997.

"The Wired Society." *Harvard Magazine* May/June 1999: 43+. One of the questions explored by a panel of experts in the academic and business worlds is "How will society cope with abuse of the new technologies and the implications for personal privacy?"

CHAPTER 17

What Does the Future Hold for Sports?
(text pages 629–57)

1. Sports may or may not play a major role at your college or university, but it cannot be denied that they play a major role in American society. You may be among those who wonder how the salaries paid star athletes have gotten so out of line with those paid in other professions, and you may feel that college athletes get special consideration that they don't deserve. On the other hand, you may wonder how student athletes can maintain their studies with all of the pressure they feel to perform up to expectations. One of the questions raised by these readings is whether sports receive too much emphasis on our college campuses. Some college athletes argue that they are scrutinized in a way no other students are, that rules

against athletes' receiving special treatment have reached the level of absurdity. Students might investigate what safeguards are in place to try to assure that student athletes do not receive special gifts and services. The other side of the issue would be any evidence your students can find that they do receive such special gifts and services anyway.

2. The new trend of high school basketball players' moving directly to the pros is likely to receive a good deal of attention in the near future, so your students may need to update the information available in the readings. It is still early to judge how this change is going to affect the players and the teams, but there is the potential for widespread effects. Students might investigate how the move has affected individuals who skipped college and went straight to the pros. Another topic to investigate is how college teams will be affected once star players are no longer interested in playing college basketball. A move directly into the professional ranks is not now allowed in football, but your students might investigate changes or proposed changes in policy there.

3. Drug use by athletes remains a hot topic. It is such a large topic that students who choose to do research in this area should be warned to narrow their focus. As is evident from Sailer's article, the history of the use and abuse of drugs within a single sport can be studied at length. Such history, along with specific cases of drug use, can be interesting but may not be appropriate topics for argumentation because they deal with past events. The future of drugs in sports is therefore more fruitful an area of consideration when it comes to research topics. One writer in the chapter even points out that sports would not be as interesting to watch without the benefit of performance-enhancing drugs. What does that suggest about cultural values?

4. Medical advances also raise intriguing questions about what might be possible, aside from using drugs to enhance performance. Diaz's article on golf can be a starting point for a discussion of the extent to which scientists may be able to discover — and perhaps enhance — the root sources of athletic ability.

Bibliography

Adams, Brent. "Biotech Initiative Sees Future in Sports: Partnership to Expand Sports-Medicine Niche." *Indianapolis Business Journal* 25.14 (2004): 19–20.

Bjerklie, David, and Alice Park. "How Doctors Help the Dopers." *Time* 16 Aug. 2004: 58.

Tomatis, David. "Securing the Future of Sports on Television." *Television Week* 15 Sept. 2003: 8.

CHAPTER 18

Have We Become Too Reliant on Standardized Testing?

(text pages 658–91)

1. Standardized testing is a subject that almost all college students have had extensive experience with. Tests most likely helped determine the college they are attending and have been factored in to many other decisions affecting them throughout their education. You might ask your students to do some freewriting on their experiences with standardized testing. What have those experiences been, and how did they feel about them? Some students these days start taking the SAT as early as age twelve. Placement in gifted and talented programs may be made as early as second grade. And as Vickers points out, testing may start influencing children even earlier than that.

2. A major concern is how much the tests affect what goes on in classrooms. As the essays by Paige and Weaver make clear, there is disagreement about whether testing has had a negative effect on education. Sometimes the negative effect may be hard to prove because of the results of the very tests that opponents are fighting against. If test scores look good, the school, the district, and the state look good. Relatively few ever see what goes on in the affected classrooms. Critics point out that there is too much "teaching to the test" and too little room for teachers to make decisions based on what is best for their students. A good topic for research is how teachers feel about the standardized tests that their students are required to take.

3. No Child Left Behind is an initiative of the Bush administration designed to bring all children up to a minimum level of proficiency in reading and math. The number of both supporters and opponents makes this a rich subject for discussion and research. What does this initiative offer the weakest students? What does it offer the best? How have teachers and school districts gone about meeting this mandate? Is what supporters of the bill would like to see happen even possible?

4. The last two essays in the chapter can be a starting point for discussion of and research on the values and the limitations of the SAT.

Bibliography

Boaler, Jo. "When Learning No Longer Matters: Standardized Testing and the Creation of Inequality." *Phi Delta Kappan* 84.7 (2003): 502.

Brady, Marion. "Not-Yet-Answered Questions about Standardized Testing." *Knight Ridder/Tribune Service* 28 Jan. 2003: K1854.

Cardman, Michael. "Study: Human Error Rife in Standardized Testing: Board Outlines Scenarios by Which Faulty Scores Penalized Thousands." *Education Daily* 2 July 2003: 1–2.

Mathews, Jay. "Seeking Alternatives to Standardized Testing." *Washingtonpost.com* 18 Feb. 2004: n. pag.

Winkler, Amber. "Division in the Ranks: Standardized Testing Draws Lines Between New and Veteran Teachers." *Phi Delta Kappan* 84.3 (2002): 219.

CHAPTER 19

What Is the Role of Sex and Violence in Popular Culture?

(text pages 692–731)

1. Students can serve as expert witnesses in cases for or against the censorship of sex and violence. Many of them have been immersed in television culture since early childhood. This doesn't mean, however, that they can be certain of general conclusions based only on personal experience. An analysis of this subject rests on all the important elements of argument.

    a. *Definition.* What constitutes "too much" attention to sex in TV, movies, and music? Can we distinguish "good" and "bad" violence?

    b. *Support.* Students should notice that in many discussions about this subject — including several articles in the text — evidence to support a point of view is *selective.* Students can probably uncover other examples that encourage questions about the strength of an author's conclusions.

    c. *Warrants.* Perhaps the most important issue is the cause-effect relationship between viewing and behavior. Although most experts seem to agree that a relationship exists, one prominent skeptic, Jonathan Freedman of the University of Toronto, continues to argue the weakness of causality: The fact that aggressive children like to watch violent shows hardly proves that the violent shows *cause* aggression. An English study found that it was "the chaos and change that [juvenile offenders] were living in" that promoted violent behavior and that "TV and movies played a relatively small part in their lives."

        It's often been pointed out that Japanese movies, TV programs, and cartoons are at least as violent and pornographic as ours. Yet the rate of crime in Japan is far lower than in the United States. Ask students to find reasons that might account for the difference.

    d. From *The Economist* (13 Aug. 1994: 74):

        > Ron Slaby of Harvard University identifies four ways in which media violence can lay itself out in a child's personality: the aggressor effect, an increase in meanness; the victim effect, an increase in fearfulness and mistrust; the bystander effect, an increase in callousness; and the appetite effect, an increase in the desire to see or commit violence. Simple imitation may also play a part.

2. TV violence has been a target for criticism almost from the inception of television itself. The first congressional hearings on this issue took place in 1954. To date, there have been more than three thousand studies of the effects of TV violence. Students might consult some of these earlier attacks and try to determine first, if the violence on TV has changed, and second, if the nature of the criticism has changed. (A special issue of *TV Guide* on June 14, 1975, was titled "Violence! On TV — Does It Affect Our Society?")

    A high school teacher claims that movies and books that portray violence are different in their effects on the viewer or reader. "While movies can desensitize us to violence, I think reading can make us more sensitive to it. We understand in a much deeper sense, the impact of violence on a victim's life." Do our students think this is true?

3. Biblical stories, fairy tales, even nursery rhymes and lullabies — think of "London Bridge" and "Rockabye Baby" — contain images of cruelty and violence. Students can look for the ways, if any, in which those images are different from the representations in popular culture.

4. Someone has said, only half in jest, that liberals are worried about too much violence, conservatives about too much sex. If students agree that this judgment is true, ask them to examine the cultural assumptions that govern these preferences.

5. Do students agree with the following assessment of sexual content in TV shows and movies?

> The down side is that however much good the entertainment media's sexual liberation has done or may do, it also burdens the audience with additional anxiety by holding up images, over and over, of beauty, nonstop pleasure and excitement that most lives cannot match. (*New York Times* 29 Oct. 1995: H40.)

6. Barbara Ehrenreich's discussion of gangsta rap in Chapter 15, "Ice-T: The Issue Is Creation Freedom," is relevant to this chapter, too.

7. Ann Powers's "The Stresses of Youth, the Strains of Its Music" interprets the massacre in Littleton, Colorado, as an example of "the meanings and effects of youth culture." (*New York Times* 25 Apr. 1999: W18.) The author offers a penetrating analysis, with abundant support, of the violent extremes of music, fashion, and lifestyle which the murderers embraced. "Teachers," she says, "have long showed students how to grasp the nuances of literature and history. But instead of actually exploring youth culture in the company of young people, many adults debate its legality among themselves."

How would students respond to explorations of youth culture in class with their teachers? Would they resent it as an intrusion — or a joke? Could students speak frankly about its appeal? After all, as the author points out, "Popular art aimed at adolescents often trades on alienation."

"The hatemongers have gone global, aided by the Internet and the unmistakable drawing power of white power music." In "High-Decibel Hate" (*New York Times* 20 Aug. 2001: A21), Bob Herbert chronicles the rise of neo-Nazi and skinhead musical groups whose vicious lyrics target blacks, Jews, and gays. It is the music, say observers, that has been instrumental in attracting recruits into a movement that celebrates Hitler and condones violence. Perhaps students who have heard the music and the lyrics can analyze the nature of the appeal. From what youthful population are the recruits drawn?

8. What about comic books and video games? Believe it or not, there is a Comics Code Authority. It was created in 1954 to control the violence content in comic books after Frederick Wertham's celebrated attack on comic and horror books in *Seduction of the Innocent* (Rinehart, 1954). Obviously, the code has relaxed its rules in recent years.

The video games *Doom* and *Quake* were mentioned as favorites of the Littleton killers. Can students find research proving that the influence of violent games and books can also be benign? Has their own experience with such entertainment suggested that there are valuable lessons about life to be learned from those contacts?

Bibliography

Allen, Steve. *Vulgarians at the Gate.* New York: Prometheus, 2001. Skewers Madonna, Howard Stern, Eminem, and *Sex and the City* as purveyors of "moral disorder and tastelessness."

Bok, Sisela. *Mayhem: Violence as Public Entertainment.* Cambridge, MA: Merloyd Lawrence/Perseus, 1998.

Edelstein, David. "Vigilante Vengeance, Hollywood's Response to Primal Fantasies." *New York Times* 10 Feb. 2002: AR15. "Do avengers in films encourage violence in real life? Or do they offer a safe outlet for venting?"

Heins, Marjorie. *Not in Front of the Children: Indecency, Censorship, and the Innocence of Youth.* New York: Hill, 2000. Dismisses the concern that sex and violence in the media can harm children.

Leland, John. "Bring the Noise." *New York Times Magazine* 27 Aug. 2000: 3. "As strident as it may be, the anger in popular music is only a faint reflection of larger forces — isolation, dislocation, fear — and fighting it, instead of them, won't solve much."

Morgenthal, David. "Counterpunch: Time to Rethink This Media Theory?" *Los Angeles Times* 1 Oct. 2001: 3. "Where are the antiviolence talking heads to explain to us why the banning of violent media from Afghani culture didn't lead to a peaceful utopia?"

PART FOUR
CLASSIC ARGUMENTS

INTRODUCTION

"Reading requires more than words." This observation serves as a partial text for the comments that follow on the use of the "Classic Arguments" section. To understand and enjoy the selections in this section, students will need not only the ability to decode the linguistic symbols but also *information*—about historical events and figures and prose forms.

Since each selection in "Classic Arguments" is followed by questions and writing assignments, we offer here only occasional additional questions and suggestions for classroom activities. Instead we have written about the essays as we have discussed them with our students, highlighting both potential difficulties and promising avenues of discussion.

From Crito (p. 735)
PLATO

This selection will enable students to become familiar with the celebrated Socratic dialogue, a teaching strategy in which Socrates arrives at the truth through skillful questioning and prolific use of definitions and examples. Some of your students may have been taught by means of the Socratic method, even though they may not realize it, but the form of this selection, seen in print, may strike them as highly artificial. The dialogues recorded by Plato gave Socrates' listeners little chance to contribute to the dialogue but gave Socrates himself ample opportunity to express his views—in this case, on civil disobedience.

Students usually find Plato's work harder to summarize and paraphrase than more contemporary works. To help with this, point out to them that each long paragraph is itself a dialogue summarized by Socrates. Plato sets up this "dialogue within a dialogue" in paragraph 5. The unlikely speaker questioning Socrates in his imaginative dialogue is "the laws of the government." After pointing out this structure, you might want to begin by having your students summarize in one or two sentences the meaning of each long paragraph before asking them individually or as a class to put those ideas together into a summary of the whole. Once it is extracted, the argument of the dialogue is clear. Socrates, under threat of a death sentence by the state of Athens, refuses to escape because escape would be a violation of the loyalty the state has a right to expect. Having lived under and been protected by the laws of Athens, he asks how he can now refuse to obey them.

In history classes ancient Greece is identified as the cradle of Western democracy. Students therefore believe erroneously that the Greek philosophy of government exalted the individual. Socrates' conviction for introducing new deities and corrupting the youth of Athens and his acquiescence in his punishment remind students of the excesses of totalitarianism. But in *Crito* Socrates interprets his willingness to die as the decision of a good citizen and a just man who is obedient to the laws that the citizens of the state, including him, have enacted. Justice is of all things most dear to him, and he prefers to be remembered as a victim rather than a doer of evil.

Most students will not agree that Socrates should make no attempt to save his own life, especially in view of the questionable nature of his crime. On the other hand, if students think of him as one who died for his faith, will they continue to regard his acceptance of his death as an act of foolishness? Character as well as intellect plays a role in Socrates' decision, and the reader of the defense can find evidence of his dignity, his moderation, his serenity, and his regard for parents, children, and friends.

This is one of the three selections in "Classic Arguments" that deal with civil disobedience. Both King and Thoreau argue that civil disobedience can be justified by recourse to moral laws that supersede the laws of government. This is an argument that students will understand and recognize as integral to the development of American democracy. Socrates and Thoreau stand on opposite sides of the debate over the relationship between the individual and the state. One or two students might want to play devil's advocate and defend Socrates' submission against Thoreau's lofty individualism.

A Modest Proposal (p. 740)
JONATHAN SWIFT

As the note on the first page of the essay points out, in this famous example of irony, Swift is using the pattern called "presenting the stock issues" discussed in Chapter 9. As a means of helping students understand better the structure and thus the argument of the piece, you might ask them to see where the three parts of the pattern are: establishment of the need for change, the proposal, and the advantages of the proposal. Most students can recognize that Swift uses the first nine paragraphs to establish the problems that exist in Ireland because of poverty before presenting his proposal in paragraph 10: that after a certain percentage of the children of the poor are reserved for breeding purposes, "the remaining hundred thousand may at a year old be offered in sale to the persons of quality and fortune through the kingdom . . . plump and fat for a good table." Don't be surprised if some of your students reading the essay for the first time miss the irony and take Swift's proposal literally. Apparently some of his contemporaries in the eighteenth century did.

Swift uses paragraphs 11–16 to elaborate on the specifics of how his plan would work. In paragraphs 17 and 18 he presents and then dismisses the suggestion made by "a very worthy person" that those young people between twelve and fourteen also be included and then concludes in paragraph 19 that there is no need to make plans for ridding the country of the old and disabled poor because they are dying fast enough already.

After acknowledging in paragraph 20 that he has digressed, in paragraph 21 he starts the third part of the pattern, the discussion of the advantages of his plan. Students can discuss the seriousness of his list of advantages. (There are serious undertones.) They should look closely at the list that Swift introduces in paragraph 29 when he begins, "Therefore let no man talk to me of other expedients."

What are the clues that Swift is being ironic? You might ask your students to describe the person ostensibly making the "modest" proposal. The proposer himself calls attention to his characteristics: compassionate but disinterested, thoughtful, reasonable, temperate, well informed. The question is whether such a person—one who is compassionate and reasonable—could make a proposal to breed human infants for food. If students agree that he could not, then why has he done so? If his reasons are not those that he alleges, what can they be?

There are several ways of deciding on the answers. One is to examine the language. Does the voice of the proposer — formal, detached, heavy with statistical data — suggest one who is passionately distressed by the suffering of the Irish? Why does the proposer refer to the Irish in terms descriptive of animals rather than human beings? Is there any place in which the voice and language of the author seem to change, where he offers solutions entirely different in kind from the breeding of children for food? How are we to interpret the difference in these two voices? In the next-to-last paragraph even the voice of the proposer begins to change; to urge that Irish adults would have been fortunate to die within the first year of life is a judgment that can be offered only in bitter irony.

It is not just the language or the disparity between the voices that can give away the ironic stance. There are also the external criteria, including the subject itself. Are there people in Swift's audience, no matter how indifferent to the fate of the Irish, who would enjoy the prospect of eating human infants? Would an Anglican dean be likely to make such a suggestion in the expectation that reasonable people would find it acceptable? Why would an essay outlining a serious proposal to breed children for food survive for more than two hundred years not as a curiosity but as a model of expository prose for readers throughout the English-speaking world? Consideration of these questions ought to lead to a suspicion, even in the most undiscerning reader, that some other interpretation than the literal one must exist.

Civil Disobedience (p. 748)
HENRY DAVID THOREAU

Thoreau's classic defense of civil disobedience is the antithesis of Socrates' defense of the rights of the state. Thoreau believes that that government is best which governs least or not at all. He denies the authority of government to command the allegiance of an individual who does not wish to concede it. Civil disobedience is justified when conscience dictates that a greater harm will result from compliance with the law than from refusal to obey.

Students will need information about the Mexican War of 1846–1848, to which Thoreau makes a number of references. We may assume that students know something about slavery (although a recent study by the National Endowment for the Humanities revealed that 80 percent of college seniors were ignorant of what the Emancipation Proclamation did). They will also need to know that Massachusetts was not a slave state, that Thoreau was objecting to an implicit sanction of slavery for economic reasons.

Thoreau uses the term "unjust laws," but unlike King he fails to define it. Throughout the essay he speaks of "right" and "wrong," "conscience," "a higher law." In the next-to-last paragraph he mentions the New Testament. Students can profitably wrestle with a summary of Thoreau's criteria for judgment. They can uncover clues in his opinions of slavery, the Constitution of the United States, the majority in a democracy, voting, soldiers, imprisonment, Daniel Webster.

Discussing the relevance of Thoreau's ideas and actions to present-day issues — civil rights, racism, US foreign policy, taxation — can test and sharpen student understanding of civil disobedience. What kind of protest would Thoreau engage in today? (His own protest ended after one day in jail when an aunt bailed him out.) What specific issues would be likely to arouse him? If he were a college student today, would he resort to protests against some college rules and activities? Many student protesters who engage in unlawful activities insist on amnesty as a condition of their surrender to the authorities. What would the participants in this civil disobedience symposium — Socrates, Thoreau, and King — have said about the refusal to accept punishment?

What would Thoreau say about the growth of government since his day? Students might speculate on the state of individual rights 150 years after Thoreau. What examples can they offer of restrictions on individual rights? Can these restrictions be justified by taking into account population growth and the increasing complexity of life?

Can the acts of civil disobedience by Thoreau and King be compared or contrasted? Students should take into consideration the causes for which each was jailed and the principles on which each based his defense.

This essay is like a rich cake, studded with unexpected treats. Students may find it indigestible at first, but they can be helped to enjoy it. The claim will be perfectly comprehensible to anyone who is familiar with protests against unjust laws or an unjust government. It is Thoreau's discursive organization and sonorous prose that prevent average or slow readers from appreciating the force of his ideas. Since there is hardly time in one semester to read and discuss a long essay like this one with the thoroughness it deserves, we shall have to settle for an understanding of its major ideas. Fortunately, Thoreau includes homely examples of his most abstract utterances in almost every paragraph. These examples provide the key to decoding the generalizations students may find difficult.

The essay suggests opportunities for short, in-class exercises to increase student comprehension.

Thoreau uses a large number of aphorisms, which stand out like clear-cut jewels in a passage that is so dense with ideas and with complex sentence structures that it is difficult for many contemporary students to read. In fact, there are so many of these aphorisms that sound familiar or impressive that it is hard for students to see the essay as a whole.

If you ask each of your students to note the five sentences that stand out as most important, our experience suggests that students will widely disagree. As a daily assignment, you might want each student to pick one of the five sentences to support in a paragraph. This exercise emphasizes the difference between generalizations and specifics. At times Thoreau is specific, but often he instead offers generalizations.

Another fruitful way of arriving at an understanding of Thoreau's main point is to ask each student to pick out the five sentences that most clearly reveal Thoreau's view of government. You should find a great deal more agreement here. By having students read some of these key sentences aloud and then seek agreement about what claim Thoreau is supporting, you will guide your students to a fuller comprehension of his famous essay.

"Civil Disobedience" is also a good essay to use if you want your students to practice paraphrasing. You can let students pick a paragraph to paraphrase or assign a particular paragraph.

The Crisis (p. 766)
CARRIE CHAPMAN CATT

Reading "The Crisis" provides a good opportunity to discuss the importance of definition. We tend to view the term *crisis* in a negative light, but readers of Catt's essay must understand that she is using it in a much more positive sense. Consider this quote from the second paragraph of this speech, which Catt made in 1916 in Atlantic City, New Jersey:

> As one has put it: "A new idea floats in the air over the heads of the people and for a long, indefinite period evades their understanding but, by and by, when through familiarity, human vision grows clearer, it is caught out of the clouds and crystallized into law." Such a moment comes to every movement and is its crisis. In my judgment, that crucial moment, bidding us to renewed consecration and redoubled activity has come to our cause.

Her cause, of course, was women's suffrage.

Catt may be the least familiar among the authors represented in "Classic Arguments," but her ideas are rich in application to the contemporary world. The opportunity she is referring to came as a result of World War I and the changes that war brought about in the role of women. Wars are obvious times of crisis that can bring out the best as well as the worst in people. You might want to ask your students to apply that idea to the wars that have taken place in their lifetimes and to such moments of crisis as the terrorist attacks of September 11, 2001. Earlier in the same paragraph, Catt writes, "The object of the life of an organized movement is to secure its aim. Necessarily, it must obey the law of evolution and pass through the stages of agitation and education and finally through the stage of realization." Your students may be able to think of examples. There are interesting links, for instance, between the Catt speech and some of the readings in Chapter 13 on terrorism. The essay in that chapter by Barbara Ehrenreich, "What Abu Ghraib Taught Me," works well with Catt's essay because Ehrenreich saw our nation evolve to the point that women gained another right: the right to serve in the armed forces. She was disillusioned when she saw that some of the women finally given the chance to serve their country disgraced it through their abuse of prisoners.

Catt was writing about the contributions European women made to the war effort, but much of what she says applies to American women as well. Students will probably have rather vague notions of how World War II changed women's roles in America. The topic is one that some students might want to research. Once they understand why women took on jobs that traditionally men had filled, they can go on to consider why it was so hard for some women to return to their previous roles once the war was over. Were women's roles changed forever by their stateside participation in World War II? How does that change compare with winning the right to vote? What was *lost* when women joined the workforce?

Bibliography

Hardy, Zoe Tracy. "What Did You Do in the War, Grandma? A Flashback to August, 1945." *Ms.* Aug. 1985: 75–78.

Warfare: An Invention—
Not a Biological Necessity (p. 778)
MARGARET MEAD

In this essay, Mead makes clear that she regards war as a primitive response which, like other early practices, can disappear as man evolves to a higher state. Once students are able to summarize that claim, they can apply it to wars that have occurred since Mead published this essay in 1940, before our nation was involved in World War II. Ask them to consider what they know about how Americans responded to their nation's involvement in that war. What about Vietnam? How was Americans' response to that war different, and why? Susan Sontag's essay "Why Are We in Kosovo?" supports use of our troops in civil war in other parts of the world when the war is a "just war," but is it becoming increasingly difficult to agree on what constitutes a just war? Our involvement in Iraq has been questioned by many who see no direct connection between that nation and the attacks our nation experienced in 2001.

Do these different events suggest an evolution in our view of war? Are we growing past acting on a primitive inclination toward war? Is the reluctance some felt to get involved in Vietnam, in Kosovo, or in Baghdad a sign of increased sophistication—or are we merely less convinced of the political necessity of war when our own soil is not under attack? Note that some reservists who served in Iraq and who were later called up for a second tour of duty simply refused to go. What would have happened to them in earlier wars?

How can the reader verify the accuracy of Mead's examples, especially those of peoples who are likely to be unfamiliar to the general reader? Many arguments are enhanced by, but not necessarily dependent on, examples. In this argument, however, the examples seem to provide indispensable support for a controversial claim. Students should try to decide if they can accept Mead's case as proved if they remain skeptical of the examples.

Students may also find it useful to examine Mead's style, especially her accessible vocabulary, transitions, use of questions, and analogies, in addition to her use of examples. The organization of the essay is also worth comment. Mead rebuts some opposing views before offering her own claim in the fourth paragraph, and then continues throughout the essay to anticipate and refute other objections.

Bibliography

Sankman, Paul. "Margaret Mead, Derek Freeman, and the Issue of Evolution." *The Skeptical Inquirer* Nov./Dec. 1998: 35.

Sontag, Susan. "Why Are We in Kosovo?" *New York Times Magazine* 2 May 1999: 52+.

Politics and the English Language (p. 785)
GEORGE ORWELL

Orwell's language is sometimes an obstacle to students' understanding of this classic piece, but the point that Orwell is making is as relevant now as it was when the piece was originally published in 1946. The essay will have more meaning for today's students if they can find examples in magazines, in newspapers, or elsewhere that illustrate the points that Orwell is making. One possible assignment is to ask them, working individually or in a group, to come up with their own five examples of passages that illustrate Orwell's point that "[o]ur civilization is decadent and our language—so the argument runs—must inevitably share in the general collapse" (para. 1). They must understand that for a language to collapse into decadence does not simply mean an increased use of profanity. Rather, they should look for passages that, to use Orwell's words, "illustrate various of the mental vices from which we now suffer" (para 3). Even before they discuss Orwell, you might ask them to explain what is wrong with the passages they locate. Students often have a sense of what is wrong with language even when they do not know the proper terms to describe the errors.

In order to fully understand Orwell, students must not only understand his terms — *dying metaphors, verbal false limbs, pretentious diction* — but also be able to appreciate the awkwardness and unintelligibility in his examples.

The organization of the essay, fortunately, lends itself to a study of discrete parts without a loss of sense or purpose. As teachers of argument, we should give our greatest attention to those parts that have direct relevance to the way in which bad language can distort an argument. Under "Meaningless Words," for example, Orwell uses selections from politics. But the heart of the essay may fairly be said to begin with paragraph 13. We would therefore concentrate on an understanding of Orwell's claim about the relation between politics and language. For this more examples are crucial (Orwell offers only phrases). There are brief selections in the chapter on language (Ch. 8) to which students may refer. The best long examples will usually be found in the writing and speeches of partisans on the far right and the far left of the political spectrum. You may have to begin by bringing in examples you have found that show what is meant by distortion and deception in political language. Freshman students may not know enough about the history and circumstances surrounding a particular argument to detect its misuse of language. Perhaps some egregious outburst in the school paper will serve.

Letter from Birmingham Jail (p. 797)
MARTIN LUTHER KING JR.

Although students may have a general knowledge of the life and works of Martin Luther King Jr., they may need to know some of the specific background before reading this piece. In 1957 King helped found the Southern Christian Leadership Conference (SCLC), a group of black ministers and churches working to end racial segregation. By the early 1960s, SCLC protests were receiving national attention. One in particular that drew attention occurred in April 1963 when the SCLC joined a local protest in Birmingham, Alabama. The Birmingham police commissioner, Bull Connor, responded violently, ordering his men to use attack dogs and high-pressure water hoses against the protestors, including children and teenagers. Birmingham's city officials obtained a court-ordered injunction barring further protests, which SCLC members violated as an unjust use of the legal process. King was arrested and held at Birmingham jail, where he wrote this letter in response to criticism he had received from local clergy for inciting such violence.

King's letter, which was clearly addressed to a much wider audience than the white Protestant ministers in Birmingham, is a superb example of a long exposition in which students can find skillful use of all the elements of argument. King's use of support deserves special attention.

King's use of *Negro* and *colored* should also be explained. King uses the word *black* only in reference to nationalist groups whose tactics he rejects.

Support

a. He recounts the indignities suffered by Negroes (para. 14). This constitutes a list of grievances like the lists in the Declaration of Independence. The grievances are expressed as personal experiences. (Notice the use of the second person and the reference to his five-year-old son.) Some readers will respond to personal experience when abstractions about law and justice fail to move them.

b. He summarizes the history of attempts to gain civil rights to prove that Negroes have been patient. This is an answer to the accusation that his activities were "untimely."

c. He invokes authorities from ancient Greece, the Bible, Christian and Judaic scholarship, and American statesmen. These authorities support the validity of his protest and his "extremist" approach (para. 31).

d. He refers to the struggles of other oppressed people, struggles with which the white Protestant ministers and his larger audience will sympathize and which they will recognize as analogous to the protests of Negroes.

e. Equally important are his appeals to the values of his two audiences, small and large: a sense of justice, compassion for the oppressed, a love of freedom, admiration and respect for brave, peaceful — and worthy — resistance, and the willingness of the resisters to suffer severe consequences in the service of a noble cause.

Definition

a. Like any classic, King's letter continues to reverberate. However sketchy their knowledge of specific events, students surely know that millions of people throughout the world are actively opposing "unjust" laws, often for the first time in decades and at great risk, and that King's definition of such laws is still highly relevant.

King's definition rests primarily on religious foundations (para. 14). The Declaration of Independence also invokes the Creator as the source of justice and morality. Students can study King's language and try to decide if his definition of just and unjust laws can survive without reference to "the law of God." Some readers may feel that King's definition is too broad, too vague. Is there a danger that we may define any laws that we want to support as the laws of God? (In fact, the laws of slavery were so defined by their supporters.)

Warrant

a. The warrant in "Letter" — oppressed people have the right to protest their oppression — recalls the warrant in the Declaration of Independence. This is one of several similarities between the two documents.

b. The white ministers in Birmingham argued that they disagreed with the *tactics* of the demonstrators. Does King's lengthy response suggest that he believes the ministers might also have disapproved of the *right* to protest?

Tone

a. King's tone reflects dignity, humility, and generosity to the opposition. Throughout the letter he skillfully negotiates a narrow line between criticism of his accusers and the belief that "as men of goodwill" they will understand and accept his argument. This conciliatory tone is very different from the tone adopted by more militant black leaders. Students might find it instructive to compare the two voices.

b. In college newspapers and elsewhere the tone adopted by angry writers is often abusive and self-righteous. Ask students to look for examples and comment on the effect such attitudes have on a neutral or unfriendly reader. If there are differences in the responses, how can we account for them?

Language

King's style is lofty, grave, sermonic. Several of the literary strategies he favors emphasize his role as preacher.

a. King uses rhetorical questions throughout (for example, paras. 22 and 26). What effect might such questions have on a neutral or unfriendly audience?

b. King also uses structural repetition for emphasis (para. 44). "I Have a Dream" is an even more ambitious example of this literary technique, which King employed frequently in all his writing. Some students may recognize parallels to the language of the King James version of the Bible.

Some readers have found King's long, rhythmic sentences and figurative language pretentious and overblown. (See para. 42.) Is this elevated style appropriate in the context? Or would a less decorative style have been more effective?

Students themselves are not so likely to indulge in elaborate metaphorical language when they argue social issues — they usually succumb to this temptation when they write about nature — nor should they be encouraged to do so, but they should be alert to its use in the utterances of public figures and able to evaluate its contribution to the argument.

Organization

This is a long argument with many parts, whose transitions make it seem more closely organized than it really is. The following rough outline indicates how the argument proceeds.

1. background of the march in Birmingham;
   explanation of his imprisonment   pp. 798–801
2. definition of just and unjust laws   802–03
3. disappointment with white moderates   804–05
4. rejection of charge of extremism;
   defense of nonviolent action   805–07
5. disappointment with the white church leadership   807–09
6. optimism about the future   809–10
7. attack on the police use of moral means for immoral ends   810

I Have a Dream (p. 813)

MARTIN LUTHER KING JR.

Someone in the class, whether instructor or student, who can muster a compelling declamatory style, should read part of this speech aloud. If you can obtain a recording of the original speech, so much the better. There is no better way to savor the language and to gain some understanding, however limited, of the impact of this speech on its listeners. Ask students to compare, as far as possible, its effect when read and its effect when listened to. Is there a difference? (There is no doubt that the human voice, with its timbre and its capacity for emotional expression, can indicate values as effectively as words.) Students should also keep in mind that this speech was delivered before a large outdoor crowd. Would this situation influence the kind of argument King needed to make?

Students should be asked to consider this speech as a written argument. What was the purpose of this speech? How specific was King in recommending policy or actions to be undertaken by the audience? Would the speech have been more effective as argument if King had urged the enactment of specific laws and exhorted his audience to work for them?

Finally, students should attend to the language. Does the language enhance the impact of the argument? Or does it sometimes distract? For example, in the fourth paragraph, there is the sustained metaphor of the promissory note. But the succeeding sentences contain figures of speech involving drugs, valleys, sunlit paths, open doors, quicksand, and rocks. Are some metaphors more effective than others? If so, why?

Appendix:
Rogerian Argument

Several instructors have expressed an interest in teaching the theories of Carl Rogers as an adjunct to Toulmin's theory of argument. Since Rogers emphasizes the importance of establishing common ground between two or more parties, his theories can be introduced with discussion of "Finding the Middle Ground" in Chapter 9. In addition to the information for instructors, this appendix includes a brief introduction on Carl Rogers that can be distributed to students as a handout along with an excerpt from his book *A Way of Being* (Houghton Mifflin, 1980).

For the Student

Carl Rogers (1902–1987) was one of the founders of humanistic psychology. Of himself as therapist he wrote: "I enter the relation [with the patient] not as a scientist, not as a physician who can accurately diagnose and cure, but as a person, entering into a personal relationship." He believed that the experience of two people meeting and speaking truly to each other without assuming other roles would have a healing effect.

In later years he became convinced that the same principles of nondirective, nonconfrontational therapy that emphasized attentive listening could work, not only for couples and small groups but also for large groups, even nations, to create more harmonious relationships.

Rogers was not, of course, the only psychologist who thought that a knowledge of psychological principles could offer insight into the causes and resolution of public controversies, even the violent confrontations in war, terrorism, and the taking of hostages. The passage below summarizes another humanistic psychologist's view of the causes of war, a view influenced by Rogers's belief that the failure to understand the "reality" of the enemy was a major cause of war.

> One theory holds that people's misperceptions about their enemies act as hindrances to peace. Possible distortions include an image of the enemy as diabolical, a virile self-image, an overconfident military, lack of empathy for the enemy, selective inattention to facts, and a moral self-image.[1]

Because Rogers was resolutely optimistic about the essential goodness of human nature, a study of Rogerian psychology inevitably provokes the question: Does human nature contain evil? This is the subject of a minidebate between Carl Rogers and Rollo May, a prominent psychoanalyst and author of *Man's Search for Himself* (Norton, 1953). Rollo May answered Yes. Carl Rogers

---

[1]Robert S. Feldman, *Understanding Psychology* (New York: McGraw, 1990) 734. Feldman is summarizing the view of Ralph K. White, editor of a guidebook on the ways that psychology can help to prevent a nuclear disaster.

answered No.[2] The excerpt below emphasizes the warrant on which Rogers based his claim.

Rollo May: Yes

> The culture admittedly has powerful effects upon us. But it could not have these effects were these tendencies not already present. Who makes up the culture except persons like you and me? The culture is evil as well as good because we, the human beings who constitute it, are evil as well as good. . . . We are bundles of both evil and good potentialities. . . . Life, to me, is not a requirement to live out a pre-ordained pattern of goodness, but a challenge coming down through the centuries out of the fact that each of us can throw the lever toward good or toward evil. This seems to me to require the age-old religious truths of mercy and forgiveness, and it leaves no place for self-righteousness.

Carl Rogers: No

> Though I am very well aware of the incredible amount of destructive, cruel, malevolent behavior in today's world — from the threats of war to the senseless violence in the streets — I do not find that this evil is inherent in human nature. In a psychological climate which is nurturant of growth and choice, I have never known an individual to choose the cruel or destructive path. . . . [So] my experience leads me to believe that it is cultural influences which are the major factor in our evil behaviors. . . . I see members of the human species . . . as essentially constructive in their fundamental nature, but damaged by their experience.

In the following passage from one of his books, Rogers reveals his intellectual and emotional journey from contemplation of his own reality to recognition of the realities of others. After reading his argument, you should try to find examples of public controversies — in this book and in the media where they are reported every day — which you think lend themselves to compromise or a middle ground. Try to be specific about the strategies you would suggest for achieving the compromise. Do you think there are controversies in which agreement is not possible or desirable? Be specific here, too, about the basic principles that might limit acceptance of a different point of view. Finally, can you point to a connection between Rogers's views of human nature in the minidebate and the proposals for educational reform that he offers in his book?

From *A Way of Being*
CARL ROGERS

I, and many others, have come to a new realization. It is this: The only reality I can possibly know is the world as *I* perceive and experience it at this moment. The only reality you can possibly know is the world as *you* perceive and experience it at this moment. And the only certainty is that those perceived realities are different. There are as many "real worlds" as there are people! This creates a most burdensome dilemma, one never before experienced in history.

---

[2]David Myers, *Psychology* (New York: Worth, 1989) 428.

From time immemorial, the tribe or the community or the nation or the culture has agreed upon what constitutes the real world. To be sure, different tribes or different cultures might have held sharply different world views, but at least there was a large, relatively unified group which felt assured in its knowledge of the world and the universe, and knew that this perception was *true*. So the community frowned upon, condemned, persecuted, even killed those who did not agree, who perceived reality differently. Copernicus, even though he kept his findings secret for many years, was eventually declared a heretic. Galileo established proof of Copernicus's views, but in his seventies he was forced to recant his teachings. Giordano Bruno was burned at the stake in 1600 for teaching that there were many worlds in our universe.

Individuals who deviated in their perception of religious reality were tortured and killed. In the mid-1800s, Ignaz Semmelweis, an intense young Hungarian physician-scientist, was driven insane by his persecutors because he made the then absurd claim that childbed fever, that dread scourge of the maternity room, was carried from one woman to another by invisible germs on the hands and instruments of the doctors. Obvious nonsense, in terms of the reality of his day. In our own American Colonies, those who were even suspected of having psychic powers were considered witches and were hanged or crushed under great stones. History offers a continuing series of examples of the awful price paid by those who perceive a reality different from the agreed-upon real world. Although society has often come around eventually to agree with its dissidents, as in the instances I have mentioned, there is no doubt that this insistence upon a known and certain universe has been part of the cement that holds a culture together.

Today we face a different situation. The ease and rapidity of worldwide communication means that every one of us is aware of a dozen "realities"; even though we may think some of them absurd (like reincarnation) or dangerous (like communism), we cannot help but be aware of them. No longer can we exist in a secure cocoon, knowing that we all see the world in the same way.

Because of this change, I want to raise a very serious question: Can we today afford the luxury of having "*a*" reality? Can we still preserve the belief that there is a "real world" upon whose definition we all agree? I am convinced that this is a luxury we *cannot* afford, a myth we dare not maintain. Only once in recent history has this been fully and successfully achieved. Millions of people were in complete agreement as to the nature of social and cultural reality — an agreement brought about by the mesmerizing influence of Hitler. This agreement about reality nearly marked the destruction of Western culture. I do not see it as something to be emulated.

In Western culture during this century — especially in the United States — there has also been an agreed-upon reality of values. This gospel can be stated very briefly: "More is better, bigger is better, faster is better, and modern technology will achieve all three of these eminently desirable goals." But now that credo is a crumbling disaster in which few believe. It is dissolving in the smog of pollution, the famine of overpopulation, the Damocles' sword of the nuclear bomb. We have so successfully achieved the goal of "a bigger bang for a buck" that we are in danger of destroying all life on this planet.

Our attempts, then, to live in the "real world" which all perceive in the same way have, in my opinion, led us to the brink of annihilation as a species. I will be so bold as to suggest an alternative.

It appears to me that the way of the future must be to base our lives and our education on the assumption that there are as many realities as there are persons, and that our highest priority is to accept that hypothesis and proceed from there. Proceed where? Proceed, each of us, to explore openmindedly the many, many perceptions of reality that exist. We would, I believe, enrich our own lives in the process. We would also become more able to cope with the reality in which each one of us exists, because we would be aware of many more options. This might well be a life full of perplexity and difficult choices, demanding greater maturity, but it would be an exciting and adventurous life.

The question may well be raised, however, whether we could have a community or a society based on this hypothesis of multiple realities. Might not such a society be a completely individualistic anarchy? That is not my opinion. Suppose my grudging tolerance of your separate world view became a full acceptance of you and your right to have such a view. Suppose that instead of shutting out the realities of others as absurd or dangerous or heretical or stupid, I was willing to explore and learn about those realities? Suppose you were willing to do the same. What would be the social result? I think that our society would be based not on a blind commitment to a cause or creed or view of reality, but on a common commitment to each other as rightfully separate persons, with separate realities. The natural human tendency to care for another would no longer be "I care for you because you are the same as I," but, instead, "I prize and treasure you because you are different from me."

Idealistic, you say? It surely is. How can I be so utterly naive and "unrealistic" as to have any hope that such a drastic change could conceivably come about? I base my hope partly on the view of world history so aptly stated by Charles Beard: "When the skies grow dark, the stars begin to shine." So we may see the emergence of leaders who are moving in this new direction.

I base my hope, even more solidly, on the view enunciated by Lancelot Whyte, the historian of ideas, in his final book before his death. It is his theory, in which he is not alone, that great steps in human history are anticipated, and probably brought about, by changes in the unconscious thinking of thousands and millions of individuals during the period preceding the change. Then, in a relatively short space of time, a new idea, a new perspective, seems to burst upon the world scene, and change occurs. He gives the example that before 1914, patriotism and nationalism were unquestioned virtues. Then began the faint unconscious questioning which built an unconscious tradition reversing a whole pattern of thought. This new perspective burst into the open between 1950 and 1970. "My country, right or wrong" is no longer a belief to live by. Nationalistic wars are out of date and out of favor, and even though they continue, world opinion is deeply opposed. Whyte (1974) points out that "at any moment the *unconscious levels are ahead of the conscious* in the task of unifying emotion, thought and action!" [*The Universe of Experience*, Harper Torchbooks, p. 107.]

For me, this line of thought is entirely congenial. I have stated that we are wiser than our intellects, that our organisms as a whole have a wisdom and purposiveness which goes well beyond our conscious thought. I believe that this idea applies to the concepts I have been presenting in this chapter. I think that men and women, individually and collectively, are inwardly and organismically rejecting the view of one single, culture-approved reality. I believe they are moving inevitably toward the acceptance of millions of separate, challenging, exciting, informative, *individual* perceptions of reality. I regard it as possible that this view — like the sudden and separate discovery of the principles of quantum mechanics by scientists in different countries — may begin to come into effective existence in many parts of the world at once. If so, we will be living in a totally new universe, different from any in history. Is it conceivable that such a change can come about?

Here lies the challenge to educators — probably the most insecure and frightened among any of the professions — battered by public pressures, limited by legislative restrictions, essentially conservative in their reactions. Can they possibly espouse such a view of multiple realities as I have been describing? Can they begin to bring into being the changes in attitudes, behaviors, and values that such a world view would demand? Certainly, by themselves they cannot. But with the underlying change in what Whyte calls "the unconscious tradition," and with the aid of the new person whom I and many others see emerging in our culture, it is just conceivable that they might succeed.

I conclude that if nations follow their past ways, then, because of the speed of world communication of separate views, each society will have to exert more and more coercion to bring about a forced agreement as to what constitutes the real world and its values. Those coerced agreements will differ from nation to nation, from culture to culture. The coercion will destroy individual freedom. We will bring about our own destruction through the clashes caused by differing world views.

But I have suggested an alternative. If we accept as a basic fact of all human life that we live in separate realities; if we can see those differing realities as the most promising resource for learning in all the history of the world; if we can live together in order to learn from one another without fear; if we can do all this, then a new age could be dawning. And perhaps — just perhaps — humankind's deep organic sensings are paving the way for just such a change.

To the Instructor

Most students will respond wholeheartedly to Rogers's summons, since it elicits our most generous impulses and promises a kinder, gentler world for all of us. In addition, his emphasis on education can encourage students to reflect on their own experience with multiculturalism and diversity as they have observed them, or not, at school.

Rogers was not without his critics and his contradictions. However welcome his essentially optimistic view of the human capacity for change and growth, his theories can also invite a lively dialogue. Before considering Rogers's policy recommendations, students should be familiar with the history on which Rogers bases his conclusions. They should be prepared to discuss the values that underlie his claims. (See the reference to Rogers in Chapter 7's "Divorce and Our National Values.") And, of course, they should be encouraged to ask hard questions.

We would begin by asking students to consider answers to these questions: Can you think of other examples of separate realities? Do you think that all realities are equally deserving of respect and accommodation? (Be specific.) Does Rogers try to prove that they are? Does recent history — since the publication of *A Way of Being* in 1980 — confirm or deny Rogers's hopes and convictions? Do you think Rogers and King in "I Have a Dream" agree about the shape of a future world?

Some students may want to know whether the analogy between private and public reconciliations can hold. Not everyone agrees that the therapies which are successful in solving problems between individuals can be called on to resolve the profound differences in the public arena. "In the context of a marriage, say, it does seem plausible that a husband and wife may have common goals. But is this also true in public life? [I]n many cases we don't share first principles at all — just think of the fights over abortion." (Larissa MacFarquhar, "Thank You for Not Fighting," rev. of *The Argument Culture*, by Deborah Tannen, *New York Times Book Review* 5 Apr. 1998: 38.)

Students may want to consult Tannen's book, which offers a Rogerian perspective. From the review quoted above, "Tannen's is a communitarian view of the world, in which we share enough first principles that we should in theory be able to agree on the right thing to do."